TWENTIETH EDITION

Economics Today

Roger LeRoy Miller

Research Professor of Economics,
University of Texas–Arlington

Dedication

For Jay Hagenbuch,

You are the best expert at putting economics
to work in the real world.

Thanks for letting me be a small part of your vision.

R.L.M.

Please contact https://support.pearson.com/getsupport/s/contactsupport with any queries on this content.

Cataloging-in-Publication Data is available on file at the Library of Congress.

1 2020

ISBN 10:   0-13-585730-9
ISBN 13: 978-0-13-585730-4

BRIEF CONTENTS

CONTENTS

PART 2 Introduction to Macroeconomics and Economic Growth

PART 3   Real GDP Determination and Fiscal Policy

10   Real GDP and the Price Level in the Long Run   203

11   Classical and Keynesian Macro Analyses   222

12   Consumption, Real GDP, and the Multiplier   243

13   Fiscal Policy   270

PART 6 Market Structure, Resource Allocation, and Regulation

PART 7 Labor Resources and the Environment

PREFACE

I have modified the learning and teaching package for this 20th edition of *Economics Today* to make learning more efficient for your students. At the same time, the hallmark of each previous edition has been maintained—teaching and learning through examples.

Solving Learning and Teaching Challenges

Improving Student Success Through Videos and Animation

Depending on which version you choose for your students, there are available:

- Concept videos with voiceovers
- Concept videos with on-screen live instructor presence
- Improved animated graphs, often with live instructor presence

In addition, for those of you who require that your students access an online version of the text, all of the **Self Check** exercises have easily viewable click-on answers available. These *Self Checks* are numbered for easy reference by you.

Learning Economic Skills That Are Practical

An increasing number of beginning economics students want concrete examples about economics that can help them today and tomorrow in their real life. To this end, I have done the following in this new edition:

- I have added short paragraphs throughout the text, which relate previously discussed theory with practical applications.
- I have also added *Real Application* questions throughout. These questions relate to careers, managerial decision making, future household behavior, and voting choices, to list just a few.
- Each chapter ends with a feature called ***Economics in Your Life***, plus an additional *Real Application* question.
- Each chapter-ending ***Issue and Application*** ends with a *Real Application* question.

What's New to This Edition

Explaining Artificial Intelligence (AI) Applications in the Real World

New to this edition, I have added a feature entitled ***AI—Decision-Making Through Data***. There are almost three dozen of these, including:

- The Global Tourism Industry (Chapter 3)
- Contemplating Big Data as a Public Good (Chapter 5)
- Preserving National Tax Bases (Chapter 6)

Other New Features

Already mentioned are the chapter-ending features called *Economics in Your Life*. Another new feature is ***What Happens When*** . . . . This new feature will help students apply previously discussed theory. Some examples are:

- What Happens When . . . people's actual reactions to incentives differ from how they claim they would respond in answers to survey questions? (Chapter 1)

- What Happens When . . . *both* buyers *and* sellers anticipate that the price of an item will increase in the future? (Chapter 3)

- What Happens When . . . the New York City government effectively raises the legal minimum price of cigarettes within the city's boundaries to almost twice the average U.S. price? (Chapter 4)

All Other Features That Are New to This Edition

Economics Today has always been known to provide the latest high-interest features. To this end, I have replaced every feature in the text, including:

- All chapter-opening ***Did You Know That*** . . . features
- All ***Examples, Policy Examples***, and ***International Examples***
- All ***Behavioral Economics Examples***
- All ***Issues and Applications***

ABOUT THE AUTHOR

Roger LeRoy Miller studied at the University of California at Berkeley where he earned a B.S. in economics while garnering the Departmental Prize. He graduated Phi Beta Kappa and Summa Cum Laude and was the recipient of numerous fellowships, including a National Science Foundation Fellowship. He chose to become a Lilly Honor Fellow at the University of Chicago and received his Ph.D. in a record 2½ years.

He has taught at the University of Washington and the University of Miami, where he also co-founded The Law and Economics Center. He is currently Research Professor of Economics at the University of Texas, Arlington. In addition to writing *Economics Today*, he has authored or co-authored dozens of textbooks, including *Applied Econometrics, Intermediate Microeconomics, Intermediate Macroeconomics, Money and Banking*, and *The Economics of Public Issues*.

He continues to be a passionate athlete, regularly entering sanctioned triathlons, cross-country ski races, and road-bike time trials.

ACKNOWLEDGMENTS

As always, I receive a continuing set of suggestions from those professors who use my text. And as always, I try to satisfy every criticism and comment. In addition, a number of professors have been asked by the publisher to review the 19th edition. To all of you listed below, please accept my sincere appreciation for the great work that you have done.

Thomas Elliot, *Columbia College*
Maria Giuili, *Diablo Valley College*
Sanja Grubacic, *Southern Connecticut State University*
Ronald Halcrow, *Antelope Valley College*
Timothy Hamilton, *Columbia College*
Samuel Imarhiagbe, *Collin College*
Ninos Malek, *San Jose State University and De Anza College*

Margaret McDaniel, *Community College of Allegheny County*
Kevin McWoodson, *Moraine Valley Community College*
Alex Obiya, *San Diego City College*
Jeff Salavitabar, *Delaware County Community College*
James Sondgeroth, *Austin Community College*
Alan Traverse, *Columbia College*
Ricardo Vicente, *BYU-Hawaii*

I also thank the reviewers of previous editions:

Rebecca Abraham, Cinda J. Adams, Esmond Adams, John Adams, Bill Adamson, Carlos Aguilar, John R. Aidem, Mohammed Akacem, Ercument Aksoy, M. C. Alderfer, John Allen, Ann Al-Yasiri, Charles Anderson, Leslie J. Anderson, Fatma W. Antar, Len Anyanwu, Kenneth Ardon, Rebecca Arnold, Mohammad Ashraf, Ali A. Ataiifar, Aliakbar Ataiifar, Leonard Atencio, John Atkins, Glen W. Atkinson, Thomas R. Atkinson, James Q. Aylesworth, John Baffoe-Bonnie, Kevin Baird, Maurice B. Ballabon, Charley Ballard, G. Jeffrey Barbour, Robin L. Barlett, Daniel Barszcz, Kari Battaglia, Robert Becker, Kevin Beckwith, Charles Beem, Glen Beeson, Bruce W. Bellner, Daniel K. Benjamin, Emil Berendt, Charles Berry, Abraham Bertisch, John Bethune, Barbara Blake Gonzalez, R. A. Blewett, Scott Bloom, John Bockino, M. L. Bodnar, Mary Bone, Theologos Homer Bonitsis, Karl Bonnhi, Thomas W. Bonsor, John M. Booth, Wesley F. Booth, Thomas Borcherding, Melvin Borland, Tom Boston, Barry Boyer, Austin Boyle, Walter Boyle, Maryanna Boynton, Ronald Brandolini, Fenton L. Broadhead, Elba Brown, William Brown, James Buck, Michael Bull, William Burrows, Maureen Burton, Conrad P. Caligaris, Steven Capolarello, Kevin Carey, James Carlson, Robert Carlsson, Joel Caron, Dancy R. Carr, Scott Carson, Doris Cash, Thomas H. Cate, Richard J. Cebula, Catherine Chambers, K. Merry Chambers, Richard Chapman, Xudong Chen, Ronald Cherry, David Ching, Young Back Choi, Marc Chopin, Carol Cies, Joy L. Clark, Curtis Clarke, Gary Clayton, Marsha Clayton, Dale O. Cloninger, Warren L. Coats, Ed Coen, Pat Conroy, James Cox, Stephen R. Cox, Eleanor D. Craig, Peggy Crane, Jerry Crawford, Patrick M. Crowley, Richard Croxdale, Joanna Cruse, John P. Cullity, Will Cummings, Thomas Curtis, Joel Dalafave, Margaret M. Dalton, Andrew J. Dane, Mahmoud Davoudi, Diana Denison, Edward Dennis, Julia G. Derrick, Sowjanya Dharmasankar, Carol Dimamro, William Dougherty, Stephen Downing, Tanya Downing, Brad Duerson, Barry Duman, Diane Dumont, Floyd Durham, G. B. Duwaji, James A. Dyal, Ishita Edwards, Robert P. Edwards, Alan E. Ellis, Miuke Ellis, Steffany Ellis, Frank Emerson, Carl Enomoto, Zaki Eusufzai, Patricia Euzent, Sandy Evans, John L. Ewing-Smith, Jamie Falcon, Frank Falero, Frank Fato, Elizabeth Faunce, Maurita Fawls, Abdollah Ferdowsi, Grant Ferguson, Victoria L. Figiel, Mitchell Fisher, David Fletcher, James Foley, John Foreman, Diana Fortier, Ralph G. Fowler, Julia Frankland, Deborah Frazier, Arthur Friedberg, Peter Frost, Timothy S. Fuerst, Tom Fullerton, E. Gabriel, James Gale, Hamilton Galloway, Byron Gangnes, Frank Garland, Peter C. Garlick, Steve Garner, Neil Garston, Alexander Garvin, Joe Garwood, Doug Gehrke, Robert Gentenaar, J. P. Gilbert, Otis Gilley, Frank Glesber, Jack Goddard, George Goerner, Michael G. Goode, Allen C. Goodman, Richard J. Gosselin, Paul Graf, Anthony J. Greco, Edward Greenberg, Gary Greene, Peter A. Groothuis, Philip J. Grossman, Nicholas Grunt, William Gunther, Kwabena Gyimah-Brempong, Demos Hadjiyanis, Reza G. Hamzaee, Martin D. Haney, Mehdi Haririan, Ray Harvey, Michael J. Haupert, E. L. Hazlett, Dennis Heiner, Sanford B. Helman, William Henderson, Robert Herman, Gus W. Herring, Aref Hervani, Charles Hill, John M. Hill, Morton Hirsch, Benjamin Hitchner, Charles W. Hockert, Stella Hofrenning, R. Bradley Hoppes, James Horner, Grover Howard, Nancy Howe-Ford, Cedric Howie, Calvin Hoy, Yu-Mong Hsiao, Yu Hsing,

Peng Huang, James Hubert, George Hughes, Joseph W. Hunt Jr., Scott Hunt, John Ifediora, R. Jack Inch, Christopher Inya, Tomotaka Ishimine, E. E. Jarvis, Ricot Jean, Parvis Jenab, Allan Jenkins, John Jensel, Mark Jensen, S. D. Jevremovic, J. Paul Jewell, Nancy Jianakoplos, Frederick Johnson, David Jones, Lamar B. Jones, Paul A. Joray, Daniel A. Joseph, Craig Justice, M. James Kahiga, Septimus Kaikai, Michael Kaluya, Lillian Kamal, Mohammad Kasraian, Devajyoti Kataky, Timothy R. Keely, Ziad Keilany, Norman F. Keiser, Michele Kegley, Sukanya Kemp, Brian Kench, Randall G. Kesselring, Alan Kessler, E. D. Key, Saleem Khan, M. Barbara Killen, Bruce Kimzey, Terrence Kinal, Philip G. King, E. R. Kittrell, David Klingman, Charles Knapp, Jerry Knarr, Tori Knight, Faik Koray, Janet Koscianski, Dennis Lee Kovach, Marie Kratochvil, Richard W. Kreissle, Peter Kressler, Paul J. Kubik, Michael Kupilik, Margaret Landman, Richard LaNear, Larry Landrum, Keith Langford, Theresa Laughlin, James M. Leaman, Anthony T. Lee, Jim Lee, Loren Lee, Bozena Leven, Donald Lien, George Lieu, Stephen E. Lile, Jane Lopus, Lawrence W. Lovick, Marty Ludlum, William Kent Lutz, Brian Lynch, Brian Macfie, Michael Machiorlatti, Laura Maghoney, G. Dirk Mateer, John McArthur, Robert McAuliffe, James C. McBrearty, Howard J. McBride, Bruce McClung, Jeremy McCracken, John McDowell, E. S. McKuskey, James J. McLain, Kevin McWoodson, John L. Madden, Mary Lou Madden, John Marangos, Dan Marburger, Glen Marston, John M. Martin, Paul J. Mascotti, James D. Mason, Paul M. Mason, Tom Mathew, Warren Matthews, Akbar Marvasti, Pete Mavrokordatos, Fred May, G. Hartley Mellish, Mike Melvin, Diego Mendez-Carbajo, Dan C. Messerschmidt, Michael Metzger, Charles Meyrick, Herbert C. Milikien, Joel C. Millonzi, Glenn Milner, Ida Mirzaie, Daniel Mizak, Khan Mohabbat, Thomas Molloy, William H. Moon, Margaret D. Moore, William E. Morgan, Stephen Morrell, Irving Morrissett, James W. Moser, Thaddeaus Mounkurai, Kevin Murphy, Martin F. Murray, Densel L. Myers, George L. Nagy, Solomon Namala, Ronald M. Nate, Jerome Neadly, James E. Needham, Claron Nelson, Douglas Nettleton, William Nook, Gerald T. O'Boyle, Greg Okoro, Dr. Larry Olanrewaju, Richard E. O'Neill, Lucian T. Orlowski, Diane S. Osborne, Joan Osborne, Melissa A. Osborne, James O'Toole, Tomi Ovaska, Lawrence Overlan, Benny E. Overton, Jan Palmer, Zuohong Pan, Gerald Parker, Ginger Parker, Randall E. Parker, Mohammed Partapurwala, Kenneth Parzych, Elizabeth Patch, Joseph Patton, Norm Paul, Teddi Paulson, Wesley Payne, Raymond A. Pepin, Martin M. Perline, Timothy Perri, Jerry Petr, Maurice Pfannesteil, Van Thi Hong Pham, Chris Phillips, James Phillips, Raymond J. Phillips, I. James Pickl, Bruce Pietrykowski, Dennis Placone, Mannie Poen, William L. Polvent, Robert Posatko, Greg Pratt, Leila J. Pratt, Steven Pressman, Rick Pretzsch, Reneé Prim, Robert E. Pulsinelli, Rod D. Raehsler, Kambriz Raffiee, Sandra Rahman, Jaishankar Raman, John Rapp, Richard Rawlins, Gautam Raychaudhuri, Kenneth Rebeck, Ron Reddall, Mitchell Redlo, Annette Redmon, Charles Reichhelu, Robert S. Rippey, Charles Roberts, Ray C. Roberts, Leila Angelica Rodemann, Richard Romano, Judy Roobian-Mohr, Duane Rosa, Richard Rosenberg, Larry Ross, Barbara Ross-Pfeiffer, Marina Rosser, Philip Rothman, John Roufagalas, Stephen Rubb, Henry Ryder, Lewis Sage, Basel Saleh, Patricia Sanderson, Thomas N. Schaap, William A. Schaeffer, William Schamoe, David Schauer, A. C. Schlenker, David Schlow, Paul Schoofs, Scott J. Schroeder, Bill Schweizer, William Scott, Dan Segebarth, Paul Seidenstat, Swapan Sen, Augustus Shackelford, Richard Sherman Jr., Liang-rong Shiau, Gail Shields, Jeff Shmidl, David Shorow, Vishwa Shukla, R. J. Sidwell, Jonathan Silberman, David E. Sisk, Alden Smith, Garvin Smith, Howard F. Smith, Lynn A. Smith, Phil Smith, William Doyle Smith, Brian Sommer, Lee Spector, George Spiva, Richard L. Sprinkle, Alan Stafford, Amanda Stallings-Wood, Herbert F. Steeper, Diane L. Stehman, Columbus Stephens, William Stine, Allen D. Stone, Daniel Strang, Jialu Streeter, Osman Suliman, J. M. Sullivan, Rebecca Summary, Terry Sutton, Joseph L. Swaffar, Thomas Swanke, Manjuri Talukdar, Frank D. Taylor, Ian Taylor, Daniel Teferra, Lea Templer, Gary Theige, Dave Thiessen, Robert P. Thomas, Deborah Thorsen, Richard Trieff, George Troxler, William T. Trulove, William N. Trumbull, Patricia Turco, Arianne K. Turner, Kay Unger, Anthony Uremovic, Ezgi Uzel, John Vahaly, Jim Van Beek, David Van Hoose, Lee J. Van Scyoc, Roy Van Til, Reuben Veliz, Sharmila Vishwasrao, Craig Walker, Robert F. Wallace, Henry C. Wallich, Jacqueline Ward, Milledge Weathers, Ethel C. Weeks, Roger E. Wehr, Don Weimer, Robert G. Welch, Terence West, James Wetzel, Wylie Whalthall, James H. Wheeler, Everett E. White, Michael D. White, Oxana Wieland, Mark A. Wilkening, Raburn M. Williams, James Willis, George Wilson, Travis Wilson, Mark Wohar, Ken Woodward, Tim Wulf, Peter R. Wyman, Whitney Yamamura, Donald Yankovic, Alex Yguado, Paul Young, Shik Young, Michael Youngblood, Mohammed Zaheer, Ed Zajicek, Charles Zalonka, Sourushe Zandvakili, Paul Zarembka, Erik Zemljic, George K. Zestos, William J. Zimmer, Jr.

For this 20th edition of *Economics Today*, I was fortunate to again have production management masterfully managed by Kathy Smith, working for SPi Global. She remains at the top of her field by making sure that every correction is made, every graph is perfect, and every table remains error free. I'm also thankful for the impact of the following: Shweta Jain, content producer; Chris DeJohn, content strategy manager; Thomas Hayward, content strategy analyst; Samantha Lewis, product manager; and Adrienne D'Ambrosio, director of product management. I'd also like to thank Ashley DePace and Nayke Heine on their work on the marketing plans.

To my faithful, long-standing, and amazingly accurate "super reviewer," Professor Dan Benjamin, a heartfelt thank you from me. I am sure that those of you reading this text will recognize how error-free it is, and Professor Benjamin is largely responsible for that level of detail. To my assistant, Sue Jasin, who was responsible for the many drafts of all of the updated revisions, thank you for "burning the midnight oil."

I welcome ideas and criticisms from both professors and students alike.

R.L.M.

1

The Nature of Economics

LEARNING OBJECTIVES

After reading this chapter, you should be able to:

1.1 Define economics and discuss the difference between microeconomics and macroeconomics

1.2 Identify the three basic economic questions and the two opposing sets of answers

1.3 Evaluate the role that rational self-interest plays in economic analysis

1.4 Explain why economics is a science

1.5 Distinguish between positive and normative economics

In 1950, the typical woman who married did so at age 20. Now, however, she is waiting until age 27. Furthermore, a larger number of women are choosing not to marry at all. Contributing to delayed marriages and nonmarriages is the fact that fewer women are agreeing to marry non-college-educated men employed by or seeking to work in manufacturing industries. In this chapter, you will learn that diminished prospects for male employment by manufacturing firms and decreased male earnings at these companies have provided women with *economic incentives* that reduce their willingness to marry these men. Indeed, you will learn that such incentives play significant roles in most decisions made by all individuals, including choices about when and whether to marry.

more than one out of every four vehicles on Russian roads is equipped with a dashboard camera? Russian residents likely are no more tech savvy than residents of many other nations, but they have stronger incentives to document auto accidents that may occur while they are driving. Russia's Arctic winter conditions and poor maintenance of many of its roads contribute to large numbers of accidents that drivers might wish to document in case their insurers question whether they or other drivers were at fault. In addition, Russian Highway Patrol officers commonly stop drivers who have committed no driving offenses and threaten them with tickets unless they pay bribes. Furthermore, criminal organizations commonly stage accidents or provide damaged vehicles as evidence for filing insurance claims against motorists. Taken together, the prevalence of icy roads, police corruption, and faked accident claims gives drivers in Russia particularly strong incentives to install dashboard cameras and compile video documentation of every second their vehicles spend on the road.

In this chapter, you will learn why contemplating the nature of self-interested responses to **incentives** is the starting point for analyzing choices people make in all walks of life. After all, how much time you devote to studying economics in this introductory course depends in part on the incentives established by your instructor's grading system. As you will see, self-interest and incentives are the underpinnings for all the decisions you and others around you make each day.

Incentives
Rewards or penalties for engaging in a particular activity.

1.1 Define economics and discuss the difference between microeconomics and macroeconomics

The Power of Economic Analysis

Simply knowing that self-interest and incentives are central to any decision-making process is not sufficient for predicting the choices that people will actually make. You also have to develop a framework that will allow you to analyze solutions to each economic problem. You must do so whether you are trying to decide how much to study, which courses to take, or to finish school, or whether you are evaluating if the U.S. government should provide more grants to universities or raise taxes. The framework that you will learn in this text is the *economic way of thinking*.

This framework gives you power—the power to reach informed judgments about what is happening in the world. You can, of course, live your life without the power of economic analysis as part of your analytical framework. Indeed, most people do. Economists believe, though, that economic analysis can help you make better decisions concerning your career, your education, financing your home, and other important matters.

In the business world, the power of economic analysis can help increase your competitive edge as an employee or as the owner of a business. As a voter, for the rest of your life you will be asked to make judgments about policies that are advocated by political parties. Many of these policies will deal with questions related to international economics, such as whether the U.S. government should encourage or discourage immigration or restrict other countries from selling their goods here.

Defining Economics

Economics is part of the social sciences and, as such, seeks explanations of real events. All social sciences analyze human behavior, as opposed to the physical sciences, which generally analyze the behavior of electrons, atoms, and other nonhuman phenomena.

Economics
The study of how people allocate their limited resources to satisfy their unlimited wants.

> *Economics is the study of how people allocate their limited resources in an attempt to satisfy their unlimited wants. As such, economics is the study of how people make choices.*

To understand this definition fully, two other words need explaining: *resources* and *wants*. **Resources** are things that have value and, more specifically, are used to produce goods and services that satisfy people's wants. **Wants** are all of the items that people would purchase if they had unlimited income.

Resources
Things used to produce goods and services to satisfy people's wants.

Wants
What people would buy if their incomes were unlimited.

Whenever an individual, a business, or a nation faces alternatives, a choice must be made, and economics helps us study how those choices are made. For example, you have to choose how to spend your limited income. You also have to choose how to spend your limited time. You may have to choose how many of your company's limited resources to allocate to advertising and how many to allocate to new-product research. In economics, we examine situations in which individuals choose how to do things, when to do things, and with whom to do them. Ultimately, the purpose of economics is to explain choices.

Microeconomics versus Macroeconomics

Economics is typically divided into two types of analysis: **microeconomics** and **macroeconomics**.

> *Microeconomics is the part of economic analysis that studies decision making undertaken by individuals (or households) and by firms. It is like looking through a microscope to focus on the small parts of our economy.*

> *Macroeconomics is the part of economic analysis that studies the behavior of the economy as a whole. It deals with economywide phenomena such as changes in unemployment, in the general price level, and in national income.*

Microeconomic analysis, for example, is concerned with the effects of changes in the price of gasoline relative to that of other energy sources. It examines the effects of new taxes on a specific product or industry. If the government establishes new health care regulations, how individual firms and consumers will react to those regulations would be in the realm of microeconomics. The effects of higher wages brought about by an effective union strike would also be analyzed using the tools of microeconomics.

In contrast, issues such as the rate of inflation, the amount of economywide unemployment, and the yearly growth in the output of goods and services in the nation all fall into the realm of macroeconomic analysis. In other words, macroeconomics deals with **aggregates**, or totals—such as total output in an economy.

Be aware, however, of the blending of microeconomics and macroeconomics in modern economic theory. Modern economists are increasingly using microeconomic analysis—the study of decision making by individuals and by firms—as the basis of macroeconomic analysis. They do this because even though macroeconomic analysis focuses on aggregates, those aggregates are the result of choices made by individuals and firms.

Recent technological developments have contributed further to the theoretical blending of microeconomics and macroeconomics. Increasingly, businesses, governments, and even individuals are turning to **artificial intelligence (AI) technologies**, which are digital-app-based or -assisted tools utilized in making and implementing decisions. AI technologies often implement sophisticated and typically automated *data-analytics methods* for working with very substantial volumes of information, commonly known as *big data*, to reveal previously hidden relationships. In the past, people applied their skills in using basic statistical techniques to examine and learn from large sets of data. To a growing extent, however, people now have adopted *machine learning*, or the application of simple or sophisticated AI-guided programming of digital devices, to search through massive bodies of data that human minds might struggle to comprehend. Increasingly, AI technologies also entail the use of *virtual-reality techniques*, which allow people to view or perceive fully artificial environments, or *augmented-reality methods*, which enable individuals to observe virtual overlays of information alongside real images. With such AI technologies, businesses, governments, and consumers can make more informed decisions. Furthermore, a growing number of economists also are employing AI technologies to examine people's decision making and choices.

Why does the application of big data analytics potentially have microeconomic *and* macroeconomic implications?

Microeconomics
The study of decision making undertaken by individuals (or households) and by firms.

Macroeconomics
The study of the behavior of the economy as a whole, including such economywide phenomena as changes in unemployment, the general price level, and national income.

Aggregates
Total amounts or quantities. Aggregate demand, for example, is total planned expenditures throughout a nation.

Artificial intelligence (AI) technologies
The development and implementation of methods of utilizing automated data-analytics techniques, machine learning, or virtual- or augmented-reality techniques to examine and evaluate information in an effort to help consumers, businesses, and governments to make decisions.

AI DECISION MAKING THROUGH DATA

Microeconomic and Macroeconomic Applications

AI technologies can be applied to both microeconomic and macroeconomic issues. At the level of a company, for instance, data-analytics techniques can be applied to vast amounts of information on prices of products, quality features, numbers of units, amounts purchased, and so on. For example, U.S. companies, such as Amazon, Apple, and Google, currently are spending tens of billions of dollars per year on digital equipment used to conduct automated data analytics. Information about prices, characteristics, and quantities purchased can be subjected to a variety of automated data-analytics techniques. Even though substantial volumes of individual bits of information may be contained in such a large set of data, the scope of such an evaluation would be *micro* economic.

In contrast, practitioners of big data analytics use the techniques to contemplate large sets of data involving economic aggregates. For example, central banks interested in coordinating their policies must evaluate considerable information encompassing annual price levels, total outputs of goods and services, levels of employment of workers, and so on for many of the world's economies over a lengthy interval. The nature of analyzing such very large sets of data via automated data-analytics techniques is *macro* economic.

In spite of the differences in microeconomic and macroeconomic scopes of various large sets of data, the methods of big data analytics used to study the datasets are similar. This fact helps to explain why the advent of AI technologies has tended to increase the blending of microeconomics and macroeconomics.

FOR CRITICAL THINKING

Why do you suppose that economists might sometimes disagree about whether to classify as a microeconomic or macroeconomic endeavor the application of big data analytics to massive volumes of information encompassing virtually all of a nation's industries and interactions among those industries?

Sources are listed at the end of this chapter.

1.2 Identify the three basic economic questions and the two opposing sets of answers

Economic system
A society's institutional mechanism for determining the way scarce resources are used to satisfy human desires.

ECONOMICS IN YOUR LIFE
To contemplate a recent example from U.S. housing finance regarding choosing among answers to the three basic economic questions, take a look at **Government Involvement Enables a Private U.S. Housing Finance Company to Provide "Cheap" Loans** on page 12.

The Three Basic Economic Questions and Two Opposing Sets of Answers

In every nation, three fundamental questions must be addressed irrespective of the form of its government or who heads that government, how rich or how poor the nation may be, or what type of **economic system**—the institutional mechanism through which resources are utilized to satisfy human wants—has been chosen.

The Three Basic Questions

The three fundamental questions of economics concern the problem of how to allocate society's scarce resources:

1. *What and how much will be produced?* Some mechanism must exist for determining which items will be produced while others remain inventors' pipe dreams or individuals' unfulfilled desires.

2. *How will items be produced?* There are many ways to produce a desired item. It is possible to use more labor and fewer machines, or vice versa. It is possible, for instance, to produce an item with an aim to maximize the number of people employed. Alternatively, an item may be produced with an aim to minimize the total expenses that members of society incur. Somehow, a decision must be made about the mix of resources used in production, the way in which they are organized, and how they are brought together at a particular location.

3. *For whom will items be produced?* Once an item is produced, who should be able to obtain it? People use scarce resources to produce any item, so typically people value access to that item. Thus, determining a mechanism for distributing produced items is a crucial issue for any society.

Now that you know the questions an economic system must answer, how do current systems actually answer them?

Two Opposing Sets of Answers

At any point in time, every nation has its own economic system. How a nation's residents go about answering the three basic economic questions depends on that nation's economic system.

Centralized Command and Control

Throughout history, one common type of economic system has been *command and control* (also called *central planning*). Such a system is operated by a centralized authority, such as a king or queen, a dictator, a central government, or some other type of authority. Such an entity assumes responsibility for addressing fundamental economic issues. Under command and control, this authority decides what items to produce and how many, determines how the scarce resources will be organized in the items' production, and identifies who will be able to obtain the items.

For instance, in a command-and-control economic system, a government might decide that particular types of automobiles ought to be produced in certain numbers. The government might issue specific rules for how to manage the production of these vehicles, or it might even establish ownership over those resources so that it can make all such resource allocation decisions directly. Finally, the government may then decide who will be authorized to purchase or otherwise utilize the vehicles.

The Price System

The alternative to command and control is the *price system* (also called a *market system*), which is a shorthand term describing an economic system that answers the three basic economic questions via decentralized decision making. Under a pure price system, individuals and families own all of the scarce resources used in production. Consequently, choices about what and how many items to produce are left to private parties to determine on their own initiative, as are decisions about how to go about producing those items. Furthermore, individuals and families choose how to allocate their own incomes to obtain the produced items at prices established via privately organized mechanisms.

In the price system, which you will learn about in considerable detail in later chapters, prices define the terms under which people agree to make exchanges. Prices signal to everyone within a price system which resources are relatively scarce and which are relatively abundant. This *signaling* aspect of the price system provides information to individual buyers and sellers about what and how many items should be produced, how production of items should be organized, and who will choose to buy the produced items.

Thus, in a price system, individuals and families own the facilities used to produce automobiles. They decide which types of automobiles to produce, how many of them to produce, and how to bring labor and machines together within their facilities to generate the desired production. Other individuals and families decide how much of their earnings they wish to spend on automobiles.

Mixed Economic Systems

By and large, the economic systems of the world's nations are mixed economic systems that incorporate aspects of both centralized command and control and a decentralized price system. At any given time, some nations lean toward centralized mechanisms of command and control and allow relatively little scope for decentralized decision making. At the same time, other nations limit the extent to which a central authority dictates answers to the three basic economic questions, leaving people mostly free to utilize a decentralized price system to generate their own answers.

A given country may reach different decisions at different times about how much to rely on command and control versus a price system to answer its three basic economic questions. Until 2008, for instance, U.S. residents preferred to rely mainly on a decentralized price system to decide which and how many financial services to produce and how to produce them. During some years since then, the U.S. government has owned substantial fractions of financial firms and hence has exerted considerable command-and-control authority over production of financial services.

1.3 Evaluate the role that rational self-interest plays in economic analysis

The Economic Approach: Systematic Decisions

Economists assume that individuals act *as if* they systematically pursue self-motivated interests and respond predictably to perceived opportunities to attain those interests. This central insight of economics was first clearly articulated by Adam Smith in 1776. Smith wrote in his most famous book, *An Inquiry into the Nature and Causes of the Wealth of Nations*, that "it is not from the benevolence [good will] of the butcher, the brewer, or the baker that we expect our dinner, but from their regard to their own interest." Thus, the typical person about whom economists make behavioral predictions is assumed to act *as though* he or she systematically pursues self-motivated interest.

The Rationality Assumption

Rationality assumption
The assumption that people do not intentionally make decisions that would leave them worse off.

The **rationality assumption** of economics, simply stated, is as follows:

> *We assume that individuals do not intentionally make decisions that would leave them worse off.*

The distinction here is between what people may think—the realm of psychology and psychiatry and perhaps sociology—and what they do. Economics does *not* involve itself in analyzing individual or group thought processes. Economics looks at what people actually do in life with their limited resources. It does little good to criticize the rationality assumption by stating, "Nobody thinks that way" or "I never think that way" or "How unrealistic! That's as irrational as anyone can get!" In a world in which people can be atypical in countless ways, economists find it useful to concentrate on discovering the baseline. Knowing what happens on average is a good place to start. In this way, we avoid building our thinking on exceptions rather than on reality.

Take the example of driving. When you consider passing another car on a two-lane highway with oncoming traffic, you have to make very quick decisions: You must estimate the speed of the car that you are going to pass, the speed of the oncoming cars, the distance between your car and the oncoming cars, and your car's potential rate of acceleration. If we were to apply a model to your behavior, we would use the rules of calculus. In actual fact, you and most other drivers in such a situation do not actually think of using the rules of calculus, but to predict your behavior, we could make the prediction *as if* you understood those rules.

Responding to Incentives

If it can be assumed that individuals never intentionally make decisions that would leave them worse off, then they will respond to changes in incentives. Indeed, much of human behavior can be explained in terms of how individuals respond to changing incentives over time.

Schoolchildren are motivated to do better by a variety of incentive systems, ranging from gold stars and certificates of achievement when they are young, to better grades with accompanying promises of a "better life" as they get older. Of course, negative incentives affect our behavior, too. Penalties, punishments, and other forms of negative incentives can raise the total cost of engaging in various activities.

How have earnings-based and tuition-expense-related incentives of pursuing a college degree changed in recent years?

EXAMPLE

The Altered Incentives Confronting Prospective College Students

In 1975, an individual considering enrolling in a college and successfully completing about four years of coursework required for a bachelor's degree could anticipate an inflation-adjusted annual payoff of about $20,000 every year following graduation. By 2000, this inflation-adjusted annual earnings incentive to earn a college degree had increased to about $33,000. This substantial jump in average annual income helps to explain why the percentage of U.S. adults holding college degrees steadily increased from 13 percent in 1975 to 33 percent today.

Since 2000, however, the average inflation-adjusted annual earnings gain from obtaining a college degree has dropped to about $29,500 per year. Accompanying this 11 percent decrease in the anticipated earnings payoff from a college degree has been an inflation-adjusted increase in average tuition and fees of 75 percent over the same interval. Thus, today's dollars-and-cents incentives to pursue a college degree are much weaker than was true a generation ago.

REAL APPLICATION

Sometimes adults tell young people to "get all the education you can get." Does that mean you should necessarily obtain an advanced degree?

Sources are listed at the end of this chapter.

Defining Self-Interest

Self-interest does not always mean increasing one's wealth measured in dollars and cents. We assume that individuals seek many goals, not just increased wealth measured in monetary terms. Thus, the self-interest part of our economic-person assumption includes goals relating to prestige, friendship, love, power, helping others, creating works of art, and many other matters. We can also think in terms of enlightened self-interest, whereby individuals, in the pursuit of what makes them better off, also achieve the betterment of others around them. In brief, individuals are assumed to want the ability to further their goals by making decisions about how items around them are used. The head of a charitable organization usually will not turn down an additional contribution, because accepting the funds yields control over how they are used, even though their use is for other people's benefit.

Does the fact that many people donate to charity necessarily imply that the donors only wish to help others?

BEHAVIORAL EXAMPLE

Assessing Whether Charitable Donations Reflect Caring for Others or for Oneself

When contemplating making a charitable donation, people often consider two motivations. The first is a desire to help others. The second is the possibility of benefiting from incentives that governments provide to those who make donations, such as certain tax deductions granted to charitable donors by tax authorities.

Three behavioral economists—Eiji Yamamura of Seinan Gakuin University, Yoshiro Tsutsui of Konan University, and Fumio Ohtake of Osaka University—have studied how these motivations interacted in Japan during the years following an unusually damaging earthquake in the eastern part of the country. Under Japan's tax laws, people were allowed to respond to the earthquake by directing portions of their local tax payments, potentially supplemented with extra donations, to municipalities that suffered most from the quake. At the same time, however, municipal governments in Japan could compete for directed tax payments and donations by offering donors reciprocal gifts, including gift cards, digital devices, home appliances, jewelry, and even gold or silver.

The researchers find evidence that Japan's taxpayers definitely responded to the earthquake in a caring manner by directing more taxes and additional donations to earthquake-stricken municipalities. Yet directed taxes and donations to regions whose governments offered gifts were more than six times larger than those that taxpayers directed to areas in which governments offered no gifts. The researchers conclude that allowing governments unaffected by the earthquake to offer reciprocal gifts reduced directed taxes and donations to governments of regions damaged by the quake. Thus, in the absence of governmental reciprocal gifts to donors, even more funds would have reached parts of Japan that suffered the greatest harm from the earthquake.

FOR CRITICAL THINKING

How might the fact that the U.S. government allows larger tax deductions for some charitable donations than for others affect U.S. taxpayers' incentives about how much to donate and to whom they direct their donations?

Sources are listed at the end of this chapter.

1.4 Explain why economics is a science

Models, or theories
Simplified representations of the real world used as the basis for predictions or explanations.

Variables
Choices that people make or other human outcomes that are subject to change.

Economics as a Science

Economics is a social science that employs the same kinds of methods used in other sciences, such as biology, physics, and chemistry. Like these other sciences, economics uses models, or theories. Economic **models, or theories,** are simplified representations of the real world that we use to help us understand, explain, and predict economic phenomena in the real world. There are, of course, differences between sciences. Social scientists, including economists, tend to make less use of laboratory experiments in which changes in **variables**—human choices or outcomes subject to change—are studied under controlled conditions. Social scientists often test their models, or theories, by examining what has already happened in the real world.

Models and Realism

At the outset it must be emphasized that no model in *any* science, and therefore no economic model, is complete in the sense that it captures *every* detail or interrelationship that exists. Indeed, a model, by definition, is an abstraction from reality. It is conceptually impossible to construct a perfectly complete realistic model. For example, in physics we cannot account for every molecule and its position and certainly not for every atom and subatomic particle. Not only is such a model unreasonably expensive to build, but working with it would be impossibly complex.

The nature of scientific model building is that the model should capture only the *essential* relationships that are sufficient to analyze the particular problem or answer the particular question with which we are concerned. *An economic model cannot be faulted as unrealistic simply because it does not represent every detail of the real world.* A map of a city that shows only major streets is not faulty if, in fact, all you wish to know is how to pass through the city using major streets. As long as a model is able to shed light on the *central* issue at hand or forces at work, it may be useful.

A map is the quintessential model. It is *always* a simplified representation. It is *always* unrealistic. It is, however, also useful in making predictions about the world. If the model—the map—predicts that when you take Campus Avenue to the north, you always run into the campus, that is a prediction. If a simple model can explain observed behavior in repeated settings just as well as a complex model, the simple model has some value and is probably easier to use.

Assumptions

Every model, or theory, must be based on a set of assumptions. Assumptions define the array of circumstances in which our model is most likely to be applicable. When some people predicted that sailing ships would fall off the edge of the earth, they used the *assumption* that the earth was flat. Columbus did not accept the implications of such a model because he did not accept its assumptions. He assumed that the world was round. The real-world test of his own model refuted the flat-earth model. Indirectly, then, it was a test of the assumption of the flat-earth model.

Is it possible to use our knowledge about assumptions to understand why driving directions sometimes contain very few details?

EXAMPLE

Getting Directions

Assumptions are a shorthand for reality. Imagine that you have decided to drive from your home in San Diego to downtown San Francisco. Because you have never driven this route, you decide to use a travel-planner device such as global-positioning-system equipment.

When you ask for directions, the electronic travel planner could give you a set of detailed maps that shows each city through which you will travel—Oceanside, San Clemente, Irvine, Anaheim, Los Angeles, Bakersfield, Modesto, and so on—with the individual maps showing you exactly how the freeway threads through each of these cities. You would get a nearly complete description of reality because the GPS travel planner will not have used many simplifying assumptions. It is more likely, however, that the travel planner will simply say, "Get on Interstate 5 going north. Stay on it for about 500 miles. Follow the signs for San Francisco. After crossing the toll bridge, take any exit marked 'Downtown.'" By omitting all of the trivial details, the travel planner has told you all that you really need and want to know. The models you will be using in this text are similar to the simplified directions on how to drive from San Diego to San Francisco—they focus on what is relevant to the problem at hand and omit what is not.

FOR CRITICAL THINKING

In what way do small talk and gossip represent the use of simplifying assumptions?

The *Ceteris Paribus* Assumption: All Other Things Being Equal Everything in the world seems to relate in some way to everything else in the world. It would be impossible to isolate the effects of changes in one variable on another variable if we always had to worry about the many other variables that might also enter the analysis. Similar to other sciences, economics uses the ***ceteris paribus*** assumption. *Ceteris paribus* means "other things constant" or "other things equal."

Consider an example taken from economics. One of the most important determinants of how much of a particular product a family buys is how expensive that product is relative to other products. We know that in addition to relative prices, other factors influence decisions about making purchases. Some of them have to do with income, others with tastes, and yet others with custom and religious beliefs. Whatever these other factors are, we hold them constant when we look at the relationship between changes in prices and changes in how much of a given product people will purchase.

Ceteris paribus [KAY-ter-us PEAR-uh-bus] assumption
The assumption that nothing changes except the factor or factors being studied.

Deciding on the Usefulness of a Model

We generally do not attempt to determine the usefulness, or "goodness," of a model by evaluating how realistic its assumptions are. Rather, we consider a model "good" if it yields usable predictions that are supported by real-world observations. In other words, can we use the model to predict what will happen in the world around us? Does the model provide useful implications about how things happen in our world?

Once we have determined that the model may be useful in predicting real-world phenomena, the scientific approach to the analysis of the world around us requires that we consider evidence. Evidence is used to test the usefulness of a model. This is why we call economics an **empirical** science. *Empirical* means that evidence (data) is looked at to see whether we are right. Economists are often engaged in empirically testing their models.

Empirical
Relying on real-world data in evaluating the usefulness of a model.

Models of Behavior, *Not* Thought Processes

Take special note of the fact that economists' models do not relate to the way people *think*. Economic models predict how people *act* and what they do in life with their limited resources. The economist does not attempt to predict how people will think about a particular topic, such as a higher price of oil products, accelerated inflation, or higher taxes. Rather, the task at hand is to predict how people will behave, which may be quite different from what they *say* they will do (much to the consternation of poll takers and market researchers). Thus, people's *declared* preferences are generally of little use in testing economic theories, which aim to explain and predict people's *revealed* preferences. The people involved in examining thought processes are psychologists and psychiatrists, not typically economists.

WHAT HAPPENS WHEN...

people's actual reactions to incentives differ from how they claim they would respond in answers to survey questions?

When businesses contemplate actions, such as price increases, that alter people's incentives to consume a product, the firms sometimes conduct surveys to try to gauge how purchases might be affected. For instance, large banks often hire public-opinion firms to survey people about how they think they would respond to a new fee on banking services previously provided at no charge. A common response people give to such questions is that they would halt entirely their consumption of such services. In fact, however, what typically occurs is that, although the total quantity of banking services purchased declines after a fee is imposed, many people pay the new fee and continue to utilize the services. Hence, the *declared* preferences of consumers do not necessarily accord with their true preferences.

Behavioral Economics and Bounded Rationality

In recent years, some economists have proposed paying more attention to psychologists and psychiatrists. They have suggested an alternative approach to economic analysis. Their approach, known as **behavioral economics**, examines consumer behavior in the face of psychological limitations and complications that may interfere with rational decision making.

Bounded Rationality Proponents of behavioral economics suggest that traditional economic models assume that people exhibit three "unrealistic" characteristics:

1. *Unbounded selfishness.* People are interested only in their own satisfaction.
2. *Unbounded willpower.* Their choices are always consistent with their long-term goals.
3. *Unbounded rationality.* They are able to consider every relevant choice.

As an alternative, advocates of behavioral economics have proposed replacing the rationality assumption with the assumption of **bounded rationality,** which assumes that people cannot examine and think through every possible choice they confront. As a consequence, behavioral economists suggest, individuals cannot always pursue, on their own, their best long-term personal interests. They sometimes require help.

Rules of Thumb A key behavioral implication of the bounded rationality assumption is that people should use so-called *rules of thumb:* Because every possible choice cannot be considered, an individual will tend to fall back on methods of making decisions that are simpler than trying to sort through every possibility.

A problem confronting advocates of behavioral economics is that people who *appear* to use rules of thumb may in fact behave *as if* they are fully rational. For instance, if a person faces persistently predictable ranges of choices for a while, the individual may rationally settle into repetitive behaviors that an outside observer might conclude to be consistent with a rule of thumb. According to the bounded rationality assumption, the person will continue to rely on a rule of thumb even if there is a major change in the environment that the individual faces. Time and time again, however, economists find that people respond to altered circumstances by fundamentally changing their behaviors. Economists also generally observe that people make decisions that are consistent with their own self-interest and long-term objectives.

Behavioral Economics Goes Mainstream The bulk of economic analysis continues to rely on the rationality assumption as the basis for constructing economic models. In most contexts, economists view the rationality assumption as a reasonable foundation for constructing models intended to predict human decision making.

Nevertheless, a growing number of economists are exploring ways in which psychological elements might improve analysis of decision making by individual consumers, firm owners and managers, and government officials. These economists are applying the bounded rationality assumption to study effects of limitations on people's capabilities to pursue self-interest, to assess how choices relate to long-term goals, or to consider all available choices. As you will learn in later chapters, behavioral theories and methods are being applied to the study of both microeconomic and macroeconomic issues.

Behavioral economics
An approach to the study of consumer behavior that emphasizes psychological limitations and complications that potentially interfere with rational decision making.

Bounded rationality
The hypothesis that people are *nearly,* but not fully, rational, so that they cannot examine every possible choice available to them but instead use simple rules of thumb to sort among the alternatives that happen to occur to them.

1.5 Distinguish between positive and normative economics

Positive versus Normative Economics

Economics uses *positive analysis*, a value-free approach to inquiry. No subjective or moral judgments enter into the analysis. Positive analysis relates to statements such as "If A, then B." For example, "If the price of gasoline goes up relative to all other prices, then the amount of it that people buy will fall." That is a positive economic statement. It is a statement of *what is*. It is not a statement of anyone's value judgment or subjective feelings.

Distinguishing between Positive and Normative Economics

For many problems analyzed in the "hard" sciences such as physics and chemistry, the analyses are considered to be virtually value-free. After all, how can someone's values enter into a theory of molecular behavior? Economists, however, face a different problem. They deal with the behavior of individuals, not molecules. That makes it more difficult to stick to what we consider to be value-free or **positive economics** without reference to our feelings.

When our values are interjected into the analysis, we enter the realm of **normative economics,** involving *normative analysis.* A positive economic statement is "If the price of gas rises, people will buy less." If we add to that analysis the statement "so we should not allow the price to go up," we have entered the realm of normative economics— we have expressed a value judgment. In fact, any time you see the word *should,* you will know that values are entering into the discussion. Just remember that positive statements are concerned with *what is,* whereas normative statements are concerned with *what ought to be.*

Each of us has a desire for different things. That means we have different values. When we express a value judgment, we are simply saying what we prefer, like, or desire. Because individual values are diverse, we expect—and indeed observe—that people express widely varying value judgments about how the world ought to be.

Positive economics
Analysis that is *strictly* limited to making either purely descriptive statements or scientific predictions. For example, "If A, then B." A statement of *what is.*

Normative economics
Analysis involving value judgments about economic policies; relates to whether outcomes are good or bad. A statement of *what ought to be.*

A Warning: Recognize Normative Analysis

It is easy to define positive economics. It is quite another matter to catch all unlabeled normative statements in a textbook, even though an author goes over the manuscript many times before it is printed or electronically created. Therefore, do not get the impression that a textbook author will be able to keep all personal values out of the book. They will slip through. In fact, the very choice of which topics to include in an introductory textbook involves normative economics. There is no value-free way to decide which topics to use in her or his textbook. The author's values ultimately make a difference when choices have to be made. From your own standpoint, though, you might want to be able to recognize when you are engaging in normative as opposed to positive economic analysis. Reading this text will help equip you for that task.

ECONOMICS AS IT APPLIES TO YOUR EVERYDAY LIFE AND YOUR FUTURE

Throughout this new edition, you will find numerous examples of how to apply economics to your everyday life and to decision making with respect to your career, your family, and even how you analyze political statements. In other words, *you will learn economic skills that are practical.*

In many of the examples and other features throughout the text, you will find a ***Real Application*** question. These questions relate to:

- Career choices

- Managerial choices if you decide to go into business

- Future behavior in your household

- Voting choices

The next-to-last chapter-ending feature, called *Economics in Your Life,* always ends with a *Real Application* question.

The last feature in each chapter, called *Issues & Applications,* will also always end with a *Real Application* question.

ECONOMICS IN YOUR LIFE

Government Involvement Enables a Private U.S. Housing Finance Company to Provide "Cheap" Loans

David Brickman, an executive vice president of a government-sponsored financial company called the Federal Home Loan Mortgage Corporation—FHLMC or "Freddie Mac"—has announced a new program to provide real-estate owners with loans at interest rates lower than those available from the private price system. Recipients of this special loan must agree not to raise rents on tenants during the full ten-year term of the loan.

"There's nothing about our typical loan that prevents someone from raising rents," even though, "[t]he supply of workforce housing is rapidly declining," says Brickman. "There's an urgent need to pre-serve [current housing] and find ways that you can effectively create more." For these reasons, he explains, Freddie Mac has created its low-interest loan to induce landlords who receive the funds to agree to maintain fixed rents for a decade.

FOR CRITICAL THINKING

Overall, does it appear that the affordable-housing loans offered by Freddie Mac arise from the application of centralized command and control, the price system, or a mix of the two? Explain your reasoning.

REAL APPLICATION

Assume that you and two friends decide to buy an apartment building next to a college. Renters are primarily full-time students. Should you take advantage of the low-interest-rate loan? What calculations do you have to make?

Sources are listed at the end of this chapter.

ISSUES & APPLICATIONS

Why Fewer Men in Manufacturing Jobs Helps to Explain Why Fewer Women Are Married

Shutterstock

CONCEPTS APPLIED

➤ Self-Interest

➤ Rationality Assumption

➤ Incentives

Naturally, whether to marry is a personal decision for any woman who contemplates the possibility. It is also a self-interested decision that involves assessing tangible valuations of the economic contributions that a man has to offer to a combined household. Considerable evidence indicates that during recent years, women have begun placing lower valuations on the potential economic contributions of non-college-educated men who are employed or regularly seek employment in manufacturing industries. The result has been a reduction in the number of women who have decided to marry these men. This fact helps to explain why the prevalence of marriage has decreased.

The Choice Faced by a Woman Considering Marriage to a Man Working or Seeking Work in Manufacturing

In years past, inflation-adjusted hourly earnings of male manufacturing workers were among the highest available to men not receiving education beyond high school. In 2000, more than 16 million men had these higher-paying manufacturing jobs, but in the years since, the number of men working in manufacturing industries has declined by about 25 percent.

If a woman's behavior is consistent with the rationality assumption, she will recognize that fewer non-college-educated men are now finding manufacturing employment and earning the higher incomes associated with such jobs. This fact reduces the tangible valuation placed on marriage to such a man. Her response to this incentive could be either to postpone marriage until her valuation of such a man's likely economic contribution to a marriage rises or to perhaps not marry at all.

Male Employment and Earnings Losses in Manufacturing and a Decrease in the Number of Married Women

In fact, the prevalence of marriage on the part of women, which has declined steadily over the past several decades, has dropped even further in recent years. More women are marrying at a later age or opting not to marry. Researchers have found evidence that a disproportionate number of women choosing to postpone matrimony or deciding not to marry are among those who otherwise likely would have married men with jobs or seeking jobs in manufacturing.

FOR CRITICAL THINKING

Why do you think that the prevalence of marriages by women to higher-income-earning men has remained relatively steady in recent years? (*Hint:* More higher-income-earning men have completed more years of education and have more stable employment prospects than men who work for manufacturing firms.)

REAL APPLICATION

Currently, a larger percentage of women are obtaining advanced degrees than are men. What are some of the real-world implications of this trend with respect to marriage?

Sources are listed at the end of this chapter.

What You Should Know

Here is what you should know after reading this chapter.

LEARNING OBJECTIVES

1.1 Define economics and discuss the difference between microeconomics and macroeconomics *Economics is the study of how individuals make choices to satisfy wants. Microeconomics is the study of decision making by individual households and firms, and macroeconomics is the study of nationwide phenomena such as inflation and unemployment.*

1.2 Identify the three basic economic questions and the two opposing sets of answers *The three basic economic questions ask what and how much will be produced, how items will be produced, and for whom items will be produced. The two opposing answers to these questions are provided by the type of economic system: either centralized command and control or the price system.*

1.3 Evaluate the role that rational self-interest plays in economic analysis *Rational self-interest is the assumption that people never intentionally make decisions that would leave them worse off. Instead, they are motivated mainly by their self-interest, which can relate to monetary and nonmonetary goals, such as love, prestige, and helping others.*

1.4 Explain why economics is a science *Economic models, or theories, are simplified representations of the real world. Economic models are never completely realistic because by definition they are simplifications using assumptions that are not directly testable. Nevertheless, economists can subject the predictions of economic theories to empirical tests in which real-world data are used to decide whether or not to reject the predictions.*

KEY TERMS

incentives, 2
economics, 2
resources, 2
wants, 2
microeconomics, 3
macroeconomics, 3
aggregates, 3
artificial intelligence (AI)
   technologies, 3

economic system, 4

rationality assumption, 6

models, or theories, 8
variables, 8
ceteris paribus assumption, 9
empirical, 9
behavioral economics, 10
bounded rationality, 10

LEARNING OBJECTIVES

1.5 **Distinguish between positive and normative economics** *Positive economics deals with what is, whereas normative economics deals with what ought to be. Positive economic statements are of the "if... then" variety. They are descriptive and predictive. In contrast, statements embodying values are within the realm of normative economics, or how people think things ought to be.*

KEY TERMS

positive economics, 11
normative economics, 11

PROBLEMS

1-1. Define economics. Explain briefly how the economic way of thinking—in terms of rational, self-interested people responding to incentives—is involved in each of the following situations.

    a. A student deciding whether to purchase a textbook for a particular class

    b. Government officials seeking more funding for mass transit through higher taxes

    c. A municipality taxing hotel guests to obtain funding for a new sports stadium

1-2. Some people claim that the "economic way of thinking" does not apply to issues such as health care. Explain how economics does apply to this issue by developing a "model" of an individual's choices.

1-3. Does the phrase "unlimited wants and limited resources" apply to both a low-income household and a middle-income household? Can the same phrase be applied to a very high-income household?

1-4. In a single sentence, contrast microeconomics and macroeconomics. Next, categorize each of the following issues as a microeconomic issue, a macroeconomic issue, or not an economic issue.

    a. The national unemployment rate

    b. The decision of a worker to work overtime or not

    c. A family's choice to have a baby

    d. The rate of growth of the money supply

    e. The national government's budget deficit

    f. A student's allocation of study time across two subjects

1-5. One of your classmates, Sally, is a hardworking student, serious about her classes, and conscientious about her grades. Sally is also involved, however, in volunteer activities and an extracurricular sport. Could Sally be displaying rational behavior? Based on what you read in this chapter, construct an argument supporting the conclusion that she is.

1-6. Recently, a bank was trying to decide what fee to charge for "expedited payments"—payments the bank would transmit with extra speed so that customers could avoid late fees on cable TV bills, electric bills, and the like. To try to determine what fee customers were willing to pay for expedited payments, the bank conducted a survey. It was able to determine that many of the people surveyed already paid fees for expedited payment services that *exceeded* the maximum fees they said they were willing to pay. How does the bank's finding relate to economists' traditional focus on what people do, rather than what they *say* they will do?

1-7. Explain, in your own words, the rationality assumption, and contrast it with the assumption of bounded rationality proposed by adherents of behavioral economics.

1-8. Why does the assumption of bounded rationality suggest that people might use rules of thumb to guide their decision making instead of considering every possible choice available to them?

1-9. Under what circumstances might people appear to use rules of thumb, as suggested by the assumption of bounded rationality, even though they really are behaving in a manner suggested by the rationality assumption?

1-10. For each of the following approaches that an economist might follow in examining a decision-making process, identify whether the approach relies on the rationality assumption or on the assumption of bounded rationality.

    a. To make predictions about how many apps a person will download onto her tablet device, an economist presumes that the individual faces limitations that make it impossible for her to examine every possible choice among relevant apps.

b. In evaluating the price that an individual will be willing to pay for a given quantity of a particular type of health care service, a researcher assumes that the person considers all relevant health care options in pursuit of his own long-term satisfaction with resulting health outcomes.

c. To determine the amount of time that a person will decide to devote to watching online videos each week, an economist makes the assumption that the individual will feel overwhelmed by the sheer volume of videos available online and will respond by using a rule of thumb.

1-11. For each of the following approaches that an economist might follow in examining a decision-making process, identify whether the approach relies on the rationality assumption or on the assumption of bounded rationality.

a. An economic study of the number of online searches that individuals conduct before selecting a particular item to purchase online presumes that people are interested only in their own satisfaction, pursue their ultimate objectives, and consider every relevant option.

b. An economist seeking to predict the effect that an increase in a state's sales tax rate will have on consumers' purchases of goods and services presumes that people are limited in their ability to process information about how the sales-tax-rate increase will influence the after-tax prices those consumers will pay.

c. To evaluate the impact of an increase in the range of choices that an individual confronts when deciding among devices for accessing the Internet, an economic researcher makes the assumption that the individual is unable to take into account every new Internet-access option available to her.

1-12. Which of the following predictions appear(s) to follow from a model based on the assumption that rational, self-interested individuals respond to incentives?

a. For every ten exam points Myrna must earn in order to pass her economics course and meet her graduation requirements, she will study one additional hour for her economics test next week.

b. A coin toss will best predict Leonardo's decision about whether to purchase an expensive business suit or an inexpensive casual outfit to wear next week when he interviews for a high-paying job he is seeking.

c. Celeste, who uses earnings from her regularly scheduled hours of part-time work to pay for her room and board at college, will decide to purchase and download a newly released video this week only if she is able to work two additional hours.

1-13. Write a sentence contrasting positive and normative economic analysis.

1-14. Based on your answer to Problem 1-13, categorize each of the following conclusions as resulting from positive analysis or normative analysis.

a. A higher minimum wage will reduce employment opportunities for minimum wage workers.

b. Increasing the earnings of minimum wage employees is desirable, and raising the minimum wage is the best way to accomplish this.

c. Everyone should enjoy open access to health care at no explicit charge.

d. Health care subsidies will increase the consumption of health care.

1-15. Consider the following statements, based on a positive economic analysis that assumes all other things remain constant. For each, list one other thing that could independently change in a way that offsets the outcome stated.

a. Increased demand for digital devices will drive up their price.

b. Falling gasoline prices will result in additional vacation travel.

c. A reduction of income tax rates will result in more people working.

1-16. Suppose that the U.S. federal government has borrowed $500 billion to expand its total spending on goods and services across the entire economy in an effort to boost by $500 billion the aggregate production by the nation's firms. Would we apply microeconomic or macroeconomic analysis to analyze this policy action?

1-17. Suppose that the government has raised by $10 a per-carat tax rate it imposes on diamonds in an effort to influence production of this particular good by each of the firms that produce it and purchases by individual consumers. Would we apply microeconomic or macroeconomic analysis to analyze this policy action?

1-18. Centralized command and control prevails throughout a certain nation's economy. What three key economic questions have been addressed in this nation, and what has been the common element of the nation's answers to those questions?

1-19. During her years of college, Dominique discovered that her three favorite subjects were astronomy, chemistry, and political science. She chose to major in astronomy because she had seen data indicating that science majors earn higher-than-average wages and because she liked astronomy better than both chemistry and political science. Upon graduation, however, she learned that average wages in chemistry fields were 20 percent higher than average wages earned by astronomers. Did Dominique's behavior violate the rationality assumption?

1-20. Sebastian is a financial analyst who is convinced that his clients do not always make choices that are consistent with their long-term objectives. He has also determined that his clients do not consider every relevant choice and often fail to act in their own self-interest. Does Sebastian perceive that his clients' behavior necessarily accords with the rationality assumption or the assumption of bounded rationality?

1-21. Maneesha has completed an analysis of the market for a prescription medication. She concludes that the policymaker should act to prevent an increase in the price of this drug on the grounds that the mainly older consumers of the medication already have spent their lives paying too much for pharmaceuticals. They ought not to have to pay higher prices, Maneesha has concluded, so the government should act to halt any further price increases in this market. Has Maneesha applied positive or normative economic analysis?

REFERENCES

AI—DECISION MAKING THROUGH DATA: Microeconomic And Macroeconomic Applications

"Big Data in the Modern Economy," American Economic Association Annual Meeting, Atlanta, January 5, 2019 (https://www.aeaweb.org/conference/2019/preliminary).

Vic Bageria, "New Age of Retailing and Big Data Analytics," *WWD*, April 6, 2018.

Emma Glass, "Big Data in Central Banks," *Central Banking*, August 2, 2018.

EXAMPLE: The Altered Incentives Confronting Prospective College Students

"Trends in Higher Education: Average Rates of Growth of Published Charges by Decade," College Board (https://trends.collegeboard.org/college-pricing/figures-tables/average-rates-growth-published-charges-decade), 2019.

"Why Governments Have Overestimated the Economic Returns of Higher Education," *Economist*, February 27, 2018.

Gail MarksJarvis, "College Payoff Seems Elusive for Many U.S. Young People," CNBC, June 7, 2018.

BEHAVIORAL EXAMPLE: Assessing Whether Charitable Donations Reflect Caring for Others or for Oneself

"Government Adopts Bill to Limit Value of Gifts in Japan Hometown Tax Donation System," *Japan Times* (https://www.japantimes.co.jp/news/2019/02/08/national/government-adopts-bill-limit-value-gifts-japan-hometown-tax-donation-system/#.XG6CuS3MzJw), February 8, 2019.

"Expanding Hometown Tax Donation Program Shows New Value in Times of Disaster," Nippon.com (https://www.nippon.com/en/features/h00246/), July 25, 2018.

Eiji Yamamura, Yoshiro Tsutsui, and Fumio Ohtake, "Altruistic and Selfish Motivations for Charitable Giving: Case of the Hometown Tax Donation System in Japan," MPRA Paper 86181, Munich, Germany, 2018.

ECONOMICS IN YOUR LIFE: Government Involvement Enables a Private U.S. Housing Finance Company to Provide "Cheap" Loans

"Freddie Mac 'Duty to Serve' Underserved Markets Plan, 2018–2020," Federal Home Loan Mortgage Corporation (http://www.freddiemac.com/singlefamily/duty-to-serve/docs/Freddie-Mac-AffordableHousingPreservation-Underserved-Markets-Plan.pdf), 2019.

Alistair Gray, "U.S. Housing: How Fannie Mae and Freddie Mac Became Rental Powerhouses," *Financial Times*, April 25, 2018.

Laura Kusisto, "Freddie Mac Offers Cheap Loans to Affordable-Housing Landlords," *Wall Street Journal*, May 3, 2018.

ISSUES & APPLICATIONS: Why Fewer Men in Manufacturing Jobs Helps to Explain Why Fewer Women Are Married

James Rogers, "Puzzling NBER Reports on Blue-Collar Men, Marriage, and Manufacturing," *Law and Liberty*, February 1, 2019.

David Autor, David Dorn, and Gordon Hanson, "When Work Disappears: Manufacturing Decline and the Falling Marriage-Market Value of Men," Massachusetts Institute of Technology, University of Zurich, and University of California at San Diego, April 2018.

Drake Bear, "Why American Men Are Getting Less Marriageable," *Business Insider*, January 20, 2018.

Reading and Working with Graphs

A graph is a visual representation of the relationship between variables. In this appendix, we'll deal with just two variables: an **independent variable,** which can change in value freely, and a **dependent variable,** which changes as a result of changes in the value of the independent variable. For example, even if nothing else is changing in your life, your weight depends on your intake of calories. The independent variable is caloric intake, and the dependent variable is weight.

A table is a list of numerical values showing the relationship between two (or more) variables. Any table can be converted into a graph, which is a visual representation of that list. Once you understand how a table can be converted to a graph, you will understand what graphs are and how to construct and use them.

Consider a practical example. A conservationist may try to convince you that driving at lower highway speeds will help you conserve gas. Table A-1 shows the relationship between speed—the independent variable—and the distance you can go on a gallon of gas at that speed—the dependent variable. This table does show a pattern. As the data in the first column get larger in value, the data in the second column get smaller.

Now let's take a look at the different ways in which variables can be related.

Direct and Inverse Relationships

Two variables can be related in different ways, some simple, others more complex. For example, a person's weight and height are often related. If we measured the height and weight of thousands of people, we would surely find that taller people tend to weigh more than shorter people. That is, we would discover there is a **direct relationship** between height and weight. By this we simply mean that an *increase* in one variable is usually associated with an *increase* in the related variable. This can easily be seen in panel (a) of Figure A-1.

Independent variable

A variable whose value is determined independently of, or outside, the equation under study.

Dependent variable

A variable whose value changes according to changes in the value of one or more independent variables.

TABLE A-1

Gas Mileage as a Function of Driving Speed

Miles per Hour	Miles per Gallon
45	25
50	24
55	23
60	21
65	19
70	16
75	13

FIGURE A-1

Direct and Inverse Relationships

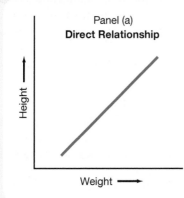

Panel (a)
Direct Relationship

Height / Weight ⟶

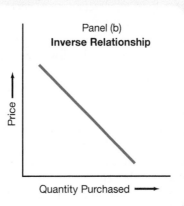

Panel (b)
Inverse Relationship

Price / Quantity Purchased ⟶

Direct relationship

A relationship between two variables that is positive, meaning that an increase in one variable is associated with an increase in the other and a decrease in one variable is associated with a decrease in the other.

Horizontal Number Line

-20 -10 0 10 20 30 40

Inverse relationship
A relationship between two variables that is negative, meaning that an increase in one variable is associated with a decrease in the other and a decrease in one variable is associated with an increase in the other.

Number line
A line that can be divided into segments of equal length, each associated with a number.

Let's look at another simple way in which two variables can be related. Much evidence indicates that as the price of a specific commodity rises, the amount purchased decreases—there is an **inverse relationship** between the variable's price per unit and quantity purchased. Such a relationship indicates that for higher and higher prices, smaller and smaller quantities will be purchased. We see this relationship in panel (b) of Figure A-1.

Constructing a Graph

Let us now examine how to construct a graph to illustrate a relationship between two variables.

A Number Line

The first step is to become familiar with what is called a **number line.** One is shown in Figure A-2. You should know two things about it:

1. The points on the line divide the line into equal segments.

2. The numbers associated with the points on the line increase in value from left to right. Saying it the other way around, the numbers decrease in value from right to left. However you say it, what you're describing is formally called an *ordered set of points*.

On the number line, we have shown the line segments—that is, the distance from 0 to 10 or the distance between 30 and 40. They all appear to be equal and, indeed, are each equal to $\frac{1}{2}$ inch. When we use a distance to represent a quantity, such as barrels of oil, graphically, we are *scaling* the number line. In the example shown, the distance between 0 and 10 might represent 10 barrels of oil, or the distance from 0 to 40 might represent 40 barrels. Of course, the scale may differ on different number lines. For example, a distance of 1 inch could represent 10 units on one number line but 5,000 units on another. Notice that on our number line, points to the left of 0 correspond to negative numbers and points to the right of 0 correspond to positive numbers.

Of course, we can also construct a vertical number line. Consider the one in Figure A-3 alongside. As we move up this vertical number line, the numbers increase in value. Conversely, as we descend, they decrease in value. Below 0 the numbers are negative, and above 0 the numbers are positive. As on the horizontal number line, all the line segments are equal. This line is divided into segments such that the distance between −2 and −1 is the same as the distance between 0 and 1.

Vertical Number Line

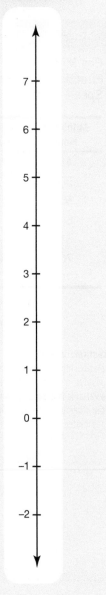

Combining Vertical and Horizontal Number Lines

By drawing the horizontal and vertical lines on the same sheet of paper, we are able to express the relationships between variables graphically. We do this in Figure A-4. We draw them (1) so that they intersect at each other's 0 point and (2) so that they are perpendicular to each other. The result is a set of coordinate axes, where each line is called an *axis*. When we have two axes, they span a *plane*.

For one number line, you need only one number to specify any point on the line. Equivalently, when you see a point on the line, you know that it represents one number or one value. With a coordinate value system, you need two numbers to specify a

FIGURE A-4

A Set of Coordinate Axes

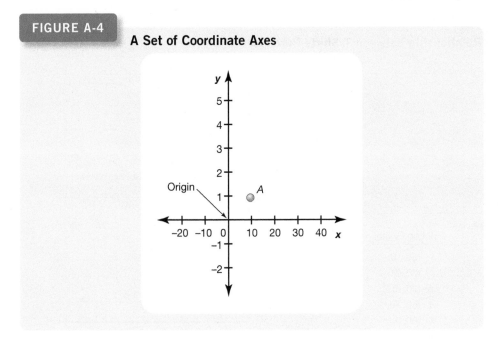

single point in the plane. When you see a single point on a graph, you know that it represents two numbers or two values.

The basic things that you should know about a coordinate number system are that the vertical number line is referred to as the **y axis**, the horizontal number line is referred to as the **x axis**, and the point of intersection of the two lines is referred to as the **origin**.

Any point such as A in Figure A-4 represents two numbers—a value of x and a value of y. We know more than that, though: We also know that point A represents a positive value of y because it is above the x axis, and we know that it represents a positive value of x because it is to the right of the y axis.

Point A represents a "paired observation" of the variables x and y. In particular, in Figure A-4, A represents an observation of the pair of values $x = 10$ and $y = 1$. Every point in the coordinate system corresponds to a paired observation of x and y, which can be simply written (x, y)—the x value is always specified first and then the y value. When we give the values associated with the position of point A in the coordinate number system, we are in effect giving the coordinates of that point. A's coordinates are $x = 10$, $y = 1$, or $(10, 1)$.

y axis
The vertical axis in a graph.

x axis
The horizontal axis in a graph.

Origin
The intersection of the y axis and the x axis in a graph.

Graphing Numbers in a Table

Consider Table A-2. Column 1 shows different prices for T-shirts, and column 2 gives the number of T-shirts purchased per week at these prices. Notice the pattern of these numbers. As the price of T-shirts falls, the number of T-shirts purchased per week increases. Therefore, an inverse relationship exists between these two variables, and as soon as we represent it on a graph, you will be able to see the relationship. We can graph this relationship using a coordinate number system—a vertical and horizontal number line for each of these two variables. Such a graph is shown in panel (b) of Figure A-5.

In economics, it is conventional to put dollar values on the y axis and quantities on the horizontal axis. We therefore construct a vertical number line for price and a horizontal number line, the x axis, for quantity of T-shirts purchased per week. The resulting coordinate system allows the plotting of each of the paired observation points. In panel (a), we repeat Table A-2, with a column added expressing these points in paired-data (x, y) form. For example, point J is the paired observation $(30, 9)$. It indicates that when the price of a T-shirt is $9, 30 will be purchased per week.

TABLE A-2

T-Shirts Purchased

(1) Price of T-Shirts	(2) Number of T-Shirts Purchased per Week
$10	20
9	30
8	40
7	50
6	60
5	70

Graphing the Relationship between T-Shirts Purchased and Price

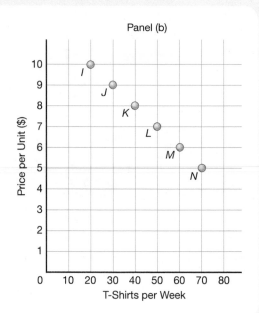

Panel (b)

Panel (a)

Price per T-Shirt	T-Shirts Purchased per Week	Point on Graph
$10	20	I (20, 10)
9	30	J (30, 9)
8	40	K (40, 8)
7	50	L (50, 7)
6	60	M (60, 6)
5	70	N (70, 5)

If it were possible to sell parts of a T-shirt ($\frac{1}{2}$ or $\frac{1}{20}$th of a shirt), we would have observations at every possible price. That is, we would be able to connect our paired observations, represented as lettered points. Let's assume that we can make T-shirts perfectly divisible so that the linear relationship shown in Figure A-5 also holds for fractions of dollars and T-shirts. We would then have a line that connects these points, as shown in the graph in Figure A-6.

Connecting the Observation Points

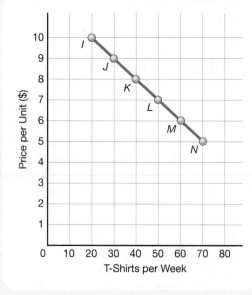

FIGURE A-7

A Positively Sloped Curve

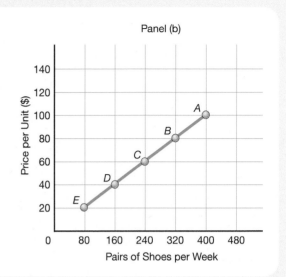

Panel (b)

Panel (a)

Price per Pair	Pairs of Shoes Offered per Week	Point on Graph
$100	400	A (400, 100)
80	320	B (320, 80)
60	240	C (240, 60)
40	160	D (160, 40)
20	80	E (80, 20)

In short, we have now represented the data from the table in the form of a graph. Note that an inverse relationship between two variables shows up on a graph as a line or curve that slopes *downward* from left to right. (You might as well get used to the idea that economists call a straight line a "curve" even though it may not curve at all. Economists' data frequently turn out to be curves, so they refer to everything represented graphically, even straight lines, as curves.)

The Slope of a Line (A Linear Curve)

An important property of a curve represented on a graph is its *slope*. Consider Figure A-7, which represents the quantities of shoes per week that a seller is willing to offer at different prices. Note that in panel (a) of Figure A-7, as in Figure A-5, we have expressed the coordinates of the points in parentheses in paired-data form. Let's consider how to measure slope between points along linear, or straight-line, curves.

Slopes of Linear (Straight-Line) Curves

The **slope** of a line is defined as the change in the *y* values divided by the corresponding change in the *x* values as we move along the line. Let's move from point *E* to point *D* in panel (b) of Figure A-7. As we move, we note that the change in the *y* values, which is the change in price, is +20, because we have moved from a price of $20 to a price of $40 per pair. As we move from *E* to *D*, the change in the *x* values is +80. The number of pairs of shoes willingly offered per week rises from 80 to 160 pairs. The slope, calculated as a change in the *y* values divided by the change in the *x* values, is therefore

$$\frac{20}{80} = \frac{1}{4}$$

It may be helpful for you to think of slope as a "rise" (movement in the vertical direction) over a "run" (movement in the horizontal direction). We show this abstractly in Figure A-8. The slope is the amount of rise divided by the amount of run. In the example in Figure A-8, and of course in Figure A-7, the amount of rise is positive and so is the amount of run. That's because it's a direct relationship. We show an inverse

Slope
The change in the *y* value divided by the corresponding change in the *x* value of a curve; the "incline" of the curve.

FIGURE A-8

Figuring Positive Slope

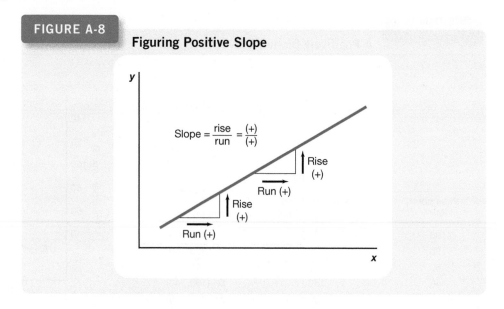

$$\text{Slope} = \frac{\text{rise}}{\text{run}} = \frac{(+)}{(+)}$$

Rise (+)

Run (+)

Rise (+)

Run (+)

relationship in Figure A-9. The slope is still equal to the rise divided by the run, but in this case the rise and the run have opposite signs because the curve slopes downward. This fact means that the slope is negative and that we are dealing with an inverse relationship.

Now let's calculate the slope for a different part of the curve in panel (b) of Figure A-7. We will find the slope as we move from point B to point A. Again, we note that the slope, or rise over run, from B to A equals

$$\frac{20}{80} = \frac{1}{4}$$

A specific property of a straight line is that its slope is the same between any two points. In other words, the slope is constant at all points on a straight line in a graph.

We conclude that for our example in Figure A-7, the relationship between the price of a pair of shoes and the number of pairs of shoes willingly offered per week is *linear*, which simply means "in a straight line," and our calculations indicate a constant slope. Moreover, we calculate a direct relationship between these two variables, which turns out to be an upward-sloping (from left to right) curve. Upward-sloping curves have positive slopes—in this case, the slope is $+\frac{1}{4}$.

FIGURE A-9

Figuring Negative Slope

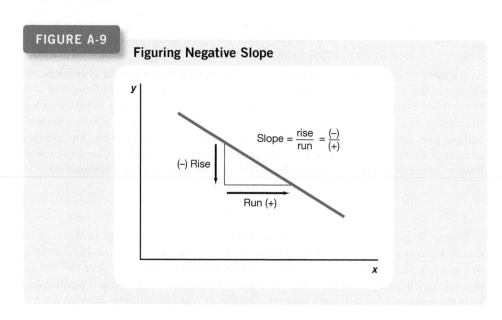

$$\text{Slope} = \frac{\text{rise}}{\text{run}} = \frac{(-)}{(+)}$$

(−) Rise

Run (+)

The Slope of a Nonlinear Curve

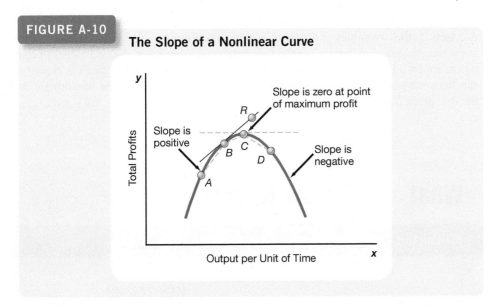

We know that an inverse relationship between two variables is a downward-sloping curve—rise over run will be negative because the rise and run have opposite signs, as shown in Figure A-9. When we see a negative slope, we know that increases in one variable are associated with decreases in the other. Therefore, we say that downward-sloping curves have negative slopes. Can you verify that the slope of the graph representing the relationship between T-shirt prices and the quantity of T-shirts purchased per week in Figure A-6 is $-\frac{1}{10}$?

Slopes of Nonlinear Curves

The graph presented in Figure A-10 indicates a *nonlinear* relationship between two variables, total profits and output per unit of time. Inspection of this graph indicates that, at first, increases in output lead to increases in total profits. That is, total profits rise as output increases. Beyond some output level, though, further increases in output cause decreases in total profits.

Slope Varies along a Nonlinear Curve Can you see how the curve in Figure A-10 rises at first, reaches a peak at point *C*, and then falls? This curve relating total profits to output levels appears mountain-shaped.

Considering that this curve is nonlinear (it is obviously not a straight line), should we expect a constant slope when we compute changes in *y* divided by corresponding changes in *x* in moving from one point to another? A quick inspection, even without specific numbers, should lead us to conclude that the slopes of lines joining different points in this curve, such as between *A* and *B*, *B* and *C*, or *C* and *D*, will *not* be the same. The curve slopes upward (in a positive direction) for some values and downward (in a negative direction) for other values. In fact, the slope of the line between any two points on this curve will be different from the slope of the line between any two other points. Each slope will be different as we move along the curve.

Measuring Slope at a Point along a Nonlinear Curve Instead of using a line between two points to discuss slope, mathematicians and economists prefer to discuss the slope *at a particular point*. The slope at a point on the curve, such as point *B* in the graph in Figure A-10, is the slope of a line tangent to that point. A tangent line is a straight line that touches a curve at only one point. For example, it might be helpful to think of the tangent at *B* as the straight line that just "kisses" the curve at point *B*.

To calculate the slope of a tangent line, you need to have some additional information besides the two values of the point of tangency. For example, in Figure A-10, if we knew that the point *R* also lay on the tangent line and we knew the two values of that point, we could calculate the slope of the tangent line. We could calculate rise over run between points *B* and *R*, and the result would be the slope of the line tangent to the one point *B* on the curve.

What You Should Know

Here is what you should know after reading this appendix.

LEARNING OBJECTIVES

Direct and Inverse Relationships *In a direct relationship, a dependent variable changes in the same direction as the change in the independent variable. In an inverse relationship, the dependent variable changes in the opposite direction of the change in the independent variable.*

Constructing a Graph *When we draw a graph showing the relationship between two economic variables, we are holding all other things constant (the Latin term for which is* ceteris paribus*).*

Graphing Numbers *We obtain a set of coordinates by putting vertical and horizontal number lines together. The vertical line is called the y axis; the horizontal line, the x axis.*

The Slopes of Linear and Nonlinear Curves *The slope of any linear (straight-line) curve is the change in the y values divided by the corresponding change in the x values as we move along the line. Otherwise stated, the slope is calculated as the amount of rise over the amount of run, where rise is movement in the vertical direction and run is movement in the horizontal direction. The slope of a nonlinear curve changes. The slope is positive when the curve is rising and negative when the curve is falling. At a maximum or minimum point, the slope of the nonlinear curve is zero.*

KEY TERMS

independent variable, 17
dependent variable, 17
direct relationship, 17
inverse relationship, 18

number line, 18
y axis, 19
x axis, 19
origin, 19

slope, 21
Key Figures
Figure A-8, 22
Figure A-9, 22
Figure A-10, 23

PROBLEMS

A-1. Explain which is the independent variable and which is the dependent variable for each of the following examples.

  a. Once you determine the price of a flash drive at the college bookstore, you will decide how many flash drives to buy.

  b. You will decide how many credit hours to register for this semester once the university tells you how many work-study hours you will be assigned.

  c. You anticipate earning a higher grade on your next economics exam because you studied more hours in the weeks preceding the exam.

A-2. For each of the following items, state whether a direct or an inverse relationship is likely to exist.

  a. The number of hours you study for an exam and your exam score

  b. The price of pizza and the quantity purchased

  c. The number of games the university basketball team won last year and the number of season tickets sold this year

A-3. Review Figure A-4, plot the points on coordinate axes, and then state whether each of the following paired observations is on, above, or below the x axis and on, to the left of, or to the right of the y axis.

  a. $(-10, 4)$

  b. $(20, -2)$

  c. $(10, 0)$

A-4. State whether each of the following functions specifies a direct or an inverse relationship.

  a. $y = 5x$

  b. $y = 10 - 2x$

  c. $y = 3 + x$

  d. $y = -3x$

A-5. Given the function $y = 5x$, complete the following schedule and plot the curve.

y	x
	−4
	−2
	0
	2
	4

A-6. Given the function $y = 8 - 2x$, complete the following schedule and plot the curve.

y	x
	−4
	−2
	0
	2
	4

A-7. Calculate the slope of the function you graphed in Problem A-5.

A-8. Calculate the slope of the function you graphed in Problem A-6.

2 Scarcity and the World of Trade-Offs

LEARNING OBJECTIVES

After reading this chapter, you should be able to:

2.1 Evaluate why everyone, whether poor or affluent, faces the problem of scarcity

2.2 Explain why the scarcity problem causes people to consider opportunity costs and trade-offs among choices

2.3 Discuss why obtaining increasing increments of any particular good typically entails giving up more and more units of other goods

2.4 Explain why the economy faces a trade-off between consumption goods and capital goods

2.5 Distinguish between absolute and comparative advantage

An average automobile is in motion only 5 percent of the time. During the remaining time, the automobile either occupies space in which it has been parked or is immobilized in congested traffic, which can be slowed by people searching for parking spots. Land that is allocated to parking spaces for automobiles could have been utilized for a different purpose, such as housing a family or a business. The time that people devote to finding locations to park could otherwise have been allocated to an alternative use, such as working for pay or engaging in a leisure activity. In this chapter, you will learn how to assess the fundamental costs of decisions to allocate land to automobile parking and to devote part of one's available time to searching for parking spots.

the typical U.S. resident sleeps almost 9 hours per day? This amount of time spent slumbering is more than a quarter of an hour longer than persons usually slept five years ago. Economists have found that a large portion of this quarter of an hour devoted to sleep is time that people previously devoted to income-earning work. More people have found in recent years that they do not have the opportunity to be employed as much time in earning income. Consequently, people now sacrifice less income, on average, when they sleep a few more minutes each day. As you will learn in this chapter, the next-highest-valued alternative to sleeping 15 more minutes is the *opportunity cost* of that 15 minutes of extra slumber. Before you consider this idea, however, you must first learn about another important concept, known as *scarcity*.

Scarcity

Whenever individuals or communities cannot obtain everything they desire simultaneously, they must make choices. Choices occur because of *scarcity*. **Scarcity** is the most basic concept in all of economics. Scarcity means that we do not ever have enough of everything, including time, to satisfy our *every* desire. Scarcity exists because human wants always exceed what can be produced with the limited resources and time that nature makes available.

What Scarcity Is Not

Scarcity is not a shortage. After a hurricane hits and cuts off supplies to a community, TV newscasts often show people standing in line to get minimum amounts of cooking fuel and food. A news commentator might say that the line is caused by the "scarcity" of these products. Cooking fuel and food, however, are always scarce—we cannot obtain all that we want at a zero price. Therefore, do not confuse the concept of scarcity, which is general and all-encompassing, with the concept of shortages, as evidenced by people waiting in line to obtain a particular product.

Scarcity is not the same thing as poverty. Scarcity occurs among the poor and among the rich. Even the richest person on earth faces scarcity. For instance, even the world's richest person has only limited time available. Low income levels do not create more scarcity. High income levels do not create less scarcity.

Scarcity is a fact of life, like gravity. And just as physicists did not invent gravity, economists did not invent scarcity—it existed well before the first economist ever lived. It has existed at all times in the past and will exist at all times in the future.

Scarcity and Resources

Scarcity exists because resources are insufficient to satisfy our every desire. Resources are the inputs used in the production of the things that we want. **Production** can be defined as virtually any activity that results in the conversion of resources into products that can be used in consumption. Production includes delivering items from one part of the country to another. It includes taking ice from an ice tray to put it in your soft-drink glass. The resources used in production are called *factors of production*, and some economists use the terms *resources* and *factors of production* interchangeably. The total quantity of all resources that an economy has at any one time determines what that economy can produce.

Factors of production can be classified in many ways. Here is one such classification:

1. **Land** encompasses all the nonhuman gifts of nature, including timber, water, fish, minerals, and the original fertility of land. It is often called the *natural resource*.

2. **Labor** is the *human resource*, which includes productive contributions made by individuals who work, such as Web page designers, iPad applications creators, and professional football players.

2.1 Evaluate why everyone, whether poor or affluent, faces the problem of scarcity

Scarcity
A situation in which the ingredients for producing the things that people desire are insufficient to satisfy all wants at a zero price.

Production
Any activity that results in the conversion of resources into products that can be used in consumption.

Land
The natural resources that are available from nature. Land as a resource includes location, original fertility and mineral deposits, topography, climate, water, and vegetation.

Labor
Productive contributions of humans who work.

Physical capital
All manufactured resources, including buildings, equipment, machines, and improvements to land that are used for production.

Human capital
The accumulated training and education of workers.

Entrepreneurship
The component of human resources that performs the functions of raising capital; organizing, managing, and assembling other factors of production; making basic business policy decisions; and taking risks.

Goods
All things from which individuals derive satisfaction or happiness.

Economic goods
Goods that are scarce, for which the quantity demanded exceeds the quantity supplied at a zero price.

Services
Mental or physical labor or assistance purchased by consumers. Examples are the assistance of physicians, lawyers, dentists, repair personnel, housecleaners, educators, retailers, and wholesalers; items purchased or used by consumers that do not have physical characteristics.

3. **Physical capital** consists of the factories and equipment used in production. It also includes improvements to natural resources, such as irrigation ditches. The acquisition of physical capital involves financial investments, and owners of capital must be compensated for use of this resource via payments of interest.

4. **Human capital** is the economic characterization of the education and training of workers. How much the nation produces depends not only on how many hours people work but also on how productive they are, and that in turn depends in part on education and training. To become more educated, individuals have to devote time and resources, just as a business has to devote resources if it wants to increase its physical capital. Whenever a worker's skills increase, human capital has been improved.

5. **Entrepreneurship** (actually a subdivision of labor) is the component of human resources that performs the functions of organizing, managing, and assembling the other factors of production to create and operate business ventures. Entrepreneurship also encompasses taking risks that involve the possibility of losing large sums of wealth. It includes new methods of engaging in common activities and generally experimenting with any type of new thinking that could lead to making more income. Without entrepreneurship, hardly any business organizations could continue to operate.

Goods versus Economic Goods

Goods are defined as all things from which individuals derive satisfaction or happiness. Goods therefore include air to breathe and the beauty of a sunset as well as food, cars, and iPhones.

Economic goods are a subset of all goods—they are scarce goods, about which we must constantly make decisions regarding their best use. By definition, the desired quantity of an economic good exceeds the amount that is available at a zero price. Almost every example we use in economics concerns economic goods—cars, tablet devices, smartphones, socks, baseball bats, and corn. Weeds are a good example of *bads*—goods for which the desired quantity is much *less* than what nature provides at a zero price.

Sometimes you will see references to "goods and services." **Services** are tasks that are performed by individuals, often for someone else, such as laundry, Internet access, hospital care, restaurant meal preparation, car polishing, psychological counseling, and teaching. One way of looking at services is to think of them as *intangible goods*.

Wants and Needs

Wants are not the same as needs. Indeed, from the economist's point of view, the term *needs* is objectively undefinable. When someone says, "I need some new clothes," there is no way to know whether that person is stating a vague wish, a want, or a life-saving requirement. If the individual making the statement were dying of exposure in a northern country during the winter, we might conclude that indeed the person does need clothes—perhaps not new ones, but at least some articles of warm clothing. Typically, however, the term *need* is used very casually in conversation. What people mean, usually, is that they desire something that they do not currently have.

Humans have unlimited wants. Just imagine that every single material want that you might have was satisfied. You could have all of the clothes, cars, houses, downloadable movies, yachts, and other items that you want. Does that mean that nothing else could add to your total level of happiness? Undoubtedly, you might continue to think of new goods and services that you could obtain, particularly as they came to market. You would also still be lacking in fulfilling all of your wants for compassion, friendship, love, affection, helping others, musical abilities, sports abilities, and the like.

In reality, every individual has competing wants but cannot satisfy all of them, given limited resources. This is the reality of scarcity. Each person must therefore make choices. Whenever a choice is made to produce or buy something, something else that is also desired is not produced or not purchased. In other words, in a world of scarcity, every want that ends up being satisfied causes one or more other wants to remain unsatisfied or to be forfeited.

Opportunity Cost, Trade-Offs, and Choices

The natural fact of scarcity implies that we must make choices. One of the most important results of this fact is that every choice made means that some opportunity must be sacrificed. Every choice involves giving up an opportunity to produce or consume something else.

2.2 Explain why the scarcity problem causes people to consider opportunity costs and trade-offs among choices

Valuing Forgone Alternatives

Consider a practical example. Every choice you make to study economics for one more hour requires that you give up the opportunity to choose to engage in an hour of any one of the following activities: study more of another subject, watch streaming video series, sleep, update your Facebook page, send tweets, or access a friend's Instagram account. The most highly valued of these opportunities is forgone if you choose to study economics an additional hour.

Because there were so many alternatives from which to choose, how could you determine the value of what you gave up to engage in that extra hour of studying economics? First of all, no one else can tell you the answer because only *you* can put a value on the alternatives forgone. Only you know the value of another hour of sleep or of an hour looking for the latest digital music downloads—whatever one activity *you* would have chosen if you had not opted to study economics for that hour. This means that only you can determine the highest-valued, next-best alternative that you had to sacrifice in order to study economics one more hour.

Opportunity Cost

The value of the next-best alternative is called **opportunity cost.** The opportunity cost of any action is the value of what is given up—the next-highest-ranked alternative—because a choice was made. What is important is the choice that you would have made if you hadn't studied one more hour. Your opportunity cost is the *next-highest-ranked* alternative, not *all* alternatives.

Opportunity cost
The highest-valued, next-best alternative that must be sacrificed to obtain something or to satisfy a want.

In economics, cost is always a forgone opportunity.

One way to think about opportunity cost is to understand that when you choose to do something, you lose something else. What you lose is being able to engage in your next-highest-valued alternative. The cost of your chosen alternative is what you lose, which is by definition your next-highest-valued alternative. This is your opportunity cost.

Why do people with the highest hourly incomes typically allocate just as much time to leisure as everyone else, even though the opportunity cost of the time they allocate to such activities is greater?

ECONOMICS IN YOUR LIFE

To contemplate the role that opportunity cost has played in making New Zealand a prime location from which to fire rockets into space, read **Extreme Specialization Leads One Person to Pursue Small-Rocket Launches** on page 41.

BEHAVIORAL EXAMPLE

Why People with the Highest Hourly Opportunity Cost Allocate as Much Time to Leisure as Everyone Else

Studies consistently reveal that people who earn the highest hourly incomes allocate about as much time each week to leisure as do people who earn lower hourly incomes. How can this finding be true, given that the opportunity cost of hours devoted to leisure—that is, foregone income earnings—is so much greater than that incurred by people who earn lower hourly incomes?

Behavioral research indicates that those who earn the highest incomes engage in particularly "active" forms of leisure, such as

(Continued)

exercising and volunteering to spend time on charity projects. In contrast, people who earn lower incomes tend to allocate leisure time to more "passive" types of leisure, such as watching television or relaxing. Consistent with such evidence, behavioral economists have found that people derive more enjoyment from active forms of leisure than from passive leisure pursuits. Available evidence indicates that the highest-income individuals engage in higher-quality activities during the time they allocate to leisure. Thus, people who earn the highest incomes devote as much time to leisure because their leisure activities yield greater levels of enjoyment.

The World of Trade-Offs and Your Future Expected Income

Whenever you engage in any activity using any resource, even time, you are *trading off* the use of that resource for one or more alternative uses. The extent of the trade-off is represented by the opportunity cost. The opportunity cost of studying economics has already been mentioned—it is the value of the next-best alternative. When you think of *any* alternative, you are thinking of trade-offs.

In college, you decide what major to take. Normally, the major you choose means that there are many other majors you do not choose—a trade-off occurs. If you choose a relatively "soft" major, that means you have not chosen one in, say, science or engineering. You can predict, at least based on historical averages, that you will earn less income by opting for a "soft" major than if you had decided on a science or engineering major.

Let's consider a hypothetical example of a trade-off between the results of spending time studying economics and mathematics. For the sake of this argument, we will assume that additional time studying either economics or mathematics will lead to a higher grade in the subject to which additional study time is allocated. One of the best ways to examine this trade-off is with a graph. (If you would like a refresher on graphical techniques, study Appendix A at the end of Chapter 1 before going on.)

Graphical Analysis

In Figure 2-1, the expected grade in mathematics is measured on the vertical axis of the graph, and the expected grade in economics is measured on the horizontal axis. We simplify the world and assume that you have a maximum of 6 hours per week to spend studying these two subjects and that if you spend all 6 hours on economics, you will get an A in the course. You will, however, fail mathematics. Conversely, if you spend all of your 6 hours studying mathematics, you will get an A in that subject, but you will flunk economics. Here the trade-off is a special case: one to one.

FIGURE 2-1

Production Possibilities Curve for Grades in Mathematics and Economics (Trade-Offs)

We assume that only 6 hours can be spent per week on studying. If the student is at point *x*, equal time (3 hours a week) is spent on both courses, and equal grades of C will be received. If a higher grade in economics is desired, the student may go to point *y*, thereby receiving a B in economics but a D in mathematics. At point *y*, 2 hours are spent on mathematics and 4 hours on economics.

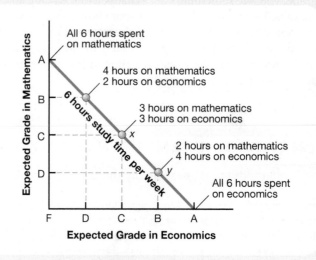

A one-to-one trade-off means that the opportunity cost of receiving one grade higher in economics (for example, improving from a C to a B) is one grade lower in mathematics (falling from a C to a D).

The Production Possibilities Curve (PPC)

The graph in Figure 2-1 illustrates the relationship between the possible results that can be produced in each of two activities, depending on how much time you choose to devote to each activity. This graph shows a representation of a **production possibilities curve (PPC)**.

Production Possibilities for Course Grades
Consider that you are producing a grade in economics when you study economics and a grade in mathematics when you study mathematics. Then the line that goes from A on one axis to A on the other axis therefore becomes a production possibilities curve. This line defines the maximum quantity of one good or service that can be produced, given that a specific quantity of another is produced. It is a curve that shows the possibilities available for increasing the output of one good or service by reducing the amount of another. In the example in Figure 2-1, your time for studying was limited to 6 hours per week. The two possible outputs were your grade in mathematics and your grade in economics.

The particular production possibilities curve presented in Figure 2-1 is a graphical representation of the opportunity cost of studying one more hour in one subject. It is a *straight-line production possibilities curve*, which is a special case. (The more general case will be discussed next.)

Measuring Trade-Offs Along a Production Possibilities Curve
If you decide to be at point *x* in Figure 2-1, you will devote 3 hours of study time to mathematics and 3 hours to economics. The expected grade in each course will be a C. If you are more interested in getting a B in economics, you will go to point *y* on the production possibilities curve, spending only 2 hours on mathematics but 4 hours on economics. Your expected grade in mathematics will then drop from a C to a D.

Note that these trade-offs between expected grades in mathematics and economics are the result of *holding constant* total study time as well as all other factors that might influence your ability to learn, such as online study aids. Quite clearly, if you were able to spend more total time studying, it would be possible to have higher grades in both economics and mathematics. In that case, however, we would no longer be on the specific production possibilities curve illustrated in Figure 2-1. We would have to draw a new curve, farther to the right, to show the greater total study time and a different set of possible trade-offs.

Why are many new passenger airplanes going into service fitted out with smaller restrooms?

Production possibilities curve (PPC)
A curve representing all possible combinations of maximum outputs that could be produced, assuming a fixed amount of productive resources of a given quality.

EXAMPLE

The Economic Explanation for Shrinking Airline Restrooms

For a number of years, in a typical coach-class restroom on a passenger airplane, the distance from the mirror on one side to a wall on the other measured about 33 inches. On newly produced jetliners now going into service, the restroom width is closer to 26 inches—a reduction of more than 20 percent.

The reason for the decrease is that the previously more "spacious" restrooms required airline companies to incur a significant opportunity cost. Reducing the widths of the forward and rear restrooms by 7 inches each gains half the distance required to add an extra row of seats on a typical jetliner. Airline companies can obtain the additional space for an extra row of seats by removing closets, shrinking galleys, and placing all other rows of seats a little closer together. By adding a row of seats, an airline company gains millions of dollars of additional revenue over the lifetime of a typical plane. This fact explains why these companies came to view the opportunity cost of the larger restrooms of the past as too high to continue to incur.

FOR CRITICAL THINKING

Why do you suppose that some airlines have simply removed a restroom or two from each of their passenger planes?

Sources are listed at the end of this chapter.

2.3 Discuss why obtaining increasing increments of any particular good typically entails giving up more and more units of other goods

The Economic Choices a Nation's People Face

The straight-line production possibilities curve presented in Figure 2-1 can be generalized to demonstrate the related concepts of scarcity, choice, and trade-offs that our entire nation faces. As you will see, the production possibilities curve is a simple but powerful economic model because it can demonstrate these related concepts.

A Two-Good Example

The example we will use is the choice between the production of smartphones and tablet devices. We assume for the moment that these are the only two goods that can be produced in the nation.

Panel (a) of Figure 2-2 gives the various combinations of smartphones and tablet devices, or tablets, that are possible. If all resources are devoted to smartphone production, 50 million per year can be produced. If all resources are devoted to production of tablets, 60 million per year can be produced. In between are various possible combinations.

Production Trade-Offs

The nation's production combinations are plotted as points *A, B, C, D, E, F,* and *G* in panel (b) of Figure 2-2. If these points are connected with a smooth curve, the nation's production possibilities curve (PPC) is shown, demonstrating the trade-off between the production of smartphones and tablets. These trade-offs occur *on* the PPC.

Notice the major difference in the shape of the production possibilities curves in Figure 2-1 and Figure 2-2. In Figure 2-1, we see there is a constant trade-off between grades in economics and in mathematics. In Figure 2-2, the trade-off between production of smartphones and tablet production is not constant, and therefore the PPC is a *bowed* curve. To understand why the production possibilities curve is typically bowed outward, you must understand the assumptions underlying the PPC.

FIGURE 2-2

The Trade-Off between Smartphones and Tablet Devices

The production of smartphones and tablet devices is measured in millions of units per year. The various combinations are given in panel (a) and plotted in panel (b). Connecting the points *A–G* with a relatively smooth line gives society's production possibilities curve for smartphones and tablets. Point *R* lies outside the production possibilities curve and is therefore unattainable at the point in time for which the graph is drawn. Point *S* lies inside the production possibilities curve and therefore entails unemployed or underemployed resources.

Panel (a)

Combination	Smartphones (millions per year)	Tablets (millions per year)
A	50.0	0
B	48.0	10
C	45.0	20
D	40.0	30
E	33.0	40
F	22.5	50
G	0.0	60

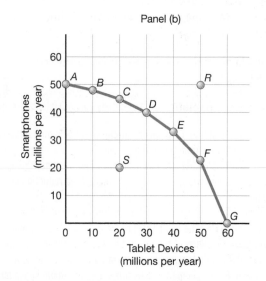

Panel (b)

Assumptions Underlying the Production Possibilities Curve

When we draw the curve that is shown in Figure 2-2, we make the following assumptions:

1. Resources are fully employed.

2. Production takes place over a specific time period—for example, one year.

3. The resource inputs, in both quantity and quality, used to produce smartphones or tablets are fixed over this time period.

4. Technology does not change over this time period.

Technology is defined as the total pool of applied knowledge concerning how goods and services can be produced by managers, workers, engineers, scientists, and artisans, using land, physical and human capital, and entrepreneurship. You can think of technology as the formula or recipe used to combine factors of production. (When better formulas are developed, more production can be obtained from the same amount of resources.) The level of technology sets the limit on the amount and types of goods and services that we can derive from any given amount of resources. The production possibilities curve is drawn under the assumptions that we use the best technology we currently have available and that this technology doesn't change over the time period under study.

How has the utilization of AI technology affected the manner in which city governments assess the trade-offs that they confront in allocating their available resources?

Technology
The total pool of applied knowledge concerning how goods and services can be produced.

AI | DECISION MAKING THROUGH DATA

City Management

The government of a major city must determine how to allocate scarce resources, such as labor and equipment, to a host of alternative purposes, including investigating criminal activity, clearing refuse from city properties, and directing congested traffic. A city government also typically confronts decisions about how to allocate available municipal-owned land among alternative uses, which might include choices among, say, a civic center, a hub for public transportation, or a building to house government offices. In short, city governments must, given the technology available to them, make choices along a varied set of trade-offs in providing services that involve a number of relevant opportunity costs.

In the past, one of the most significant challenges faced by city governments involved measuring the opportunity costs associated with such trade-offs. Today, application of big data techniques has reduced the scope of these measurement problems. Cities use sensors to track flows of people and vehicle traffic along walkways and over city streets. City workers utilize mobile devices with apps that regularly transmit data for digital analysis. Civil engineers in some cities fly sensor-equipped drones to collect data. Advances in machine-learning-based data analytics and low-cost information storage via cloud computing enable city governments to organize these large volumes of collected data. Cities use those data to compute opportunity costs associated with alternative resource allocations. In this way, data analytics employed by city governments, sometimes called "civic analytics," are enabling those governments to make better informed decisions about how to allocate available labor, equipment, and land.

FOR CRITICAL THINKING

Who ultimately funds the information-gathering and decision-making activities of city governments that big data techniques are helping to guide?

Sources are listed at the end of this chapter.

Being off the Production Possibilities Curve

Look again at panel (b) of Figure 2-2. Point *R* lies *outside* the production possibilities curve and is *impossible* to achieve during the time period assumed. By definition, the PPC indicates the *maximum* quantity of one good, given the quantity produced of the other good.

It is possible, however, to be at point *S* in Figure 2-2. That point lies beneath the PPC. If the nation is at point *S*, it means that its resources are not being fully utilized. This occurs, for example, during periods of relatively high unemployment. Point *S* and all such points inside the PPC are always attainable but imply unemployed or underemployed resources.

Efficiency

The production possibilities curve can be used to define the notion of efficiency. Whenever the economy is operating on the PPC, at points such as *A*, *B*, *C*, or *D*, we say that its production is efficient. Points such as *S* in Figure 2-2, which lie beneath the PPC, are said to represent production situations that are not efficient.

Efficiency can mean many things to many people. Even in economics, there are different types of efficiency. Here we are discussing *productive efficiency*. An economy is productively efficient whenever it is producing the maximum output with given technology and resources along the PPC.

A simple commonsense definition of efficiency is getting the most out of what we have. Clearly, we are not getting the most out of what we have if we are at point *S* in panel (b) of Figure 2-2. We can move from point *S* to, say, point *C*, thereby increasing the total quantity of smartphones produced without any decrease in the total quantity of tablets produced. Alternatively, we can move from point *S* to point *E*, for example, and have both more smartphones and more tablets. Point *S* is called an **inefficient point,** which is defined as any point below the production possibilities curve.

Efficiency
The case in which a given level of inputs is used to produce the maximum output possible. Alternatively, the situation in which a given output is produced at minimum cost.

Inefficient point
Any point below the production possibilities curve, at which the use of resources is not generating the maximum possible output.

The Law of Increasing Additional Cost

In the example given in Figure 2-1, the trade-off between a grade in mathematics and a grade in economics was one to one. The trade-off ratio was constant. That is, the production possibilities curve was a straight line. The curve in Figure 2-2 is a more general case. We have re-created the curve in Figure 2-2 as Figure 2-3. Each combination, *A* through *G*, of smartphones and tablets is represented on the PPC. Starting with the production of zero tablets, the nation can produce 50 million smartphones with its available resources and technology.

FIGURE 2-3

The Law of Increasing Additional Cost

Consider equal increments of production of tablets, as measured on the horizontal axis. All of the horizontal arrows—*aB*, *bC*, and so on—are of equal length (10 million). In contrast, the length of each vertical arrow—*Aa*, *Bb*, and so on—increases as we move down the production possibilities curve. Hence, the opportunity cost of going from 50 million tablets per year to 60 million (*Ff*) is much greater than going from zero units to 10 million (*Aa*). The opportunity cost of each additional equal increase in production of tablets rises.

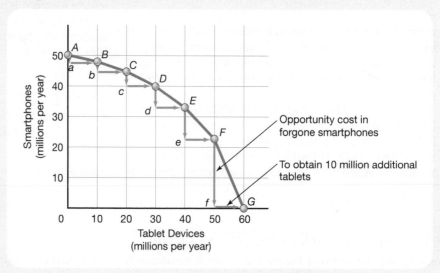

Increasing Additional Costs When we increase production of tablet devices from zero to 10 million per year, the nation has to give up in smartphones an amount shown by that first vertical arrow, *Aa*. In panel (a) of Figure 2-2, this distance is 2 million per year (50 million minus 48 million). Again, if we increase production of tablets by another 10 million units per year, we go from *B* to *C*. To do so, the nation has to give up the vertical distance *Bb*, or 3 million smartphones per year. By the time we go from 50 million to 60 million tablets, to obtain that 10 million increase, we have to forgo the vertical distance *Ff*, or 22.5 million smartphones. In other words, we see that the opportunity cost of the last 10 million tablets has increased to 22.5 million smartphones, compared to 2 million smartphones for the same increase in tablets when we started with none at all being produced.

What we are observing is called the **law of increasing additional cost.** When people take more resources and apply them to the production of any specific good, the opportunity cost increases for each additional unit produced.

Explaining the Law of Increasing Additional Cost The reason that as a nation we face the law of increasing additional cost (shown as a production possibilities curve that is bowed outward) is that certain resources are better suited for producing some goods than other goods. Generally, resources are not *perfectly* adaptable for alternative uses. When increasing the output of a particular good, producers must use less suitable resources than those already used in order to produce the additional output. Hence, the cost of producing the additional units increases.

With respect to our hypothetical example here, at first the computing specialists at smartphone firms would shift over to producing tablet devices. After a while, though, the workers who normally design and produce smartphones would be asked to help design and manufacture tablet components. Typically, they would be less effective at making tablets than the people who previously specialized in this task.

In general, *the more specialized the resources, the more bowed the production possibilities curve.* At the other extreme, if all resources are equally suitable for smartphone production or production of tablets, the curves in Figures 2-2 and 2-3 would approach the straight line shown in our first example in Figure 2-1.

Why is the addition of each extra given length of bicycle lane to an existing road usually subject to the law of increasing additional cost?

Law of increasing additional cost
The fact that the opportunity cost of additional units of a good generally increases as people attempt to produce more of that good. This accounts for the bowed-out shape of the production possibilities curve.

POLICY EXAMPLE

City Bicycle Lanes Encounter the Law of Increasing Additional Cost

In efforts to encourage people to pedal bicycles instead of driving polluting vehicles and to reduce the likelihood of bicycle collisions with vehicles, a number of cities have been adding bicycle lanes to existing roadways without changing their widths. Adding a 50-foot stretch of bicycle lane near an intersection to provide extra protection for a cyclist creates opportunity costs by reducing the widths of through and turn lanes for vehicles, which creates a new source of traffic congestion for all vehicles. Furthermore, the addition of another 50 feet of bicycle lane to the initial stretch farther from an intersection not only adds to vehicular traffic congestion along that new stretch but also can eliminate up to three parking spaces for vehicles. Thus, cities cannot avoid confronting the law of increasing additional cost whenever they consider adding or extending bicycle lanes along existing roadways.

FOR CRITICAL THINKING

Why might we anticipate a bowed shape for the production possibilities curve relating space taken up by a bicycle lane along a street to parking spaces along the street?

Sources are listed at the end of this chapter.

2.4 Explain why the economy faces a trade-off between consumption goods and capital goods

Economic Growth, Production Possibilities, and the Trade-Off between Present and Future

At any particular point in time, a society cannot be outside the production possibilities curve. *Over time*, however, it is possible to have more of everything. This occurs through economic growth.

Economic Growth and the Production Possibilities Curve

Figure 2-4 shows the production possibilities curve for smartphones and tablet devices shifting outward. The two additional curves shown represent new choices open to an economy that has experienced economic growth. Such economic growth occurs for many reasons, including increases in the number of workers and productive investment in equipment.

Scarcity still exists, however, no matter how much economic growth takes place. At any point in time, we will always be on some production possibilities curve. Thus, we will always face trade-offs. The more we have of one thing, the less we can have of others.

If economic growth occurs in the nation, the production possibilities curve between smartphones and tablets moves outward, as shown in Figure 2-4. This takes time and does not occur automatically. One reason it will occur involves the choice about how much to consume today.

The Trade-Off between the Present and the Future

The production possibilities curve and economic growth can be combined to examine the trade-off between present **consumption** and future consumption. When we consume today, we are using up what we call consumption of consumer goods—food and clothes, for example.

Consumption
The use of goods and services for personal satisfaction.

Why We Make Capital Goods
Why would we be willing to use productive resources to make things—physical capital, or capital goods—that we cannot consume directly? The reason is that capital goods enable us to produce larger quantities of consumer goods or to produce them less expensively than we otherwise could. Before fish are "produced" for the market, equipment such as fishing boats, nets, and poles is produced first. Imagine how expensive it would be to obtain fish for market without using these capital goods. Catching fish with one's hands is not an easy task. The cost per fish would be very high if capital goods weren't used.

FIGURE 2-4

Economic Growth Allows for More of Everything

If the nation experiences economic growth, the production possibilities curve between smartphones and tablets moves outward as shown. This output increase takes time, however, and it does not occur immediately. This means, therefore, that we can have more of both smartphones and tablets only after a period of time during which we have experienced economic growth.

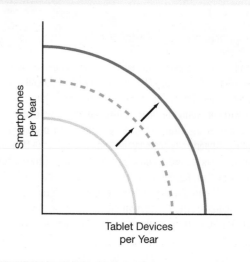

Forgoing Current Consumption Whenever we use productive resources to make capital goods, we are implicitly forgoing current consumption. We are waiting for some time in the future to consume the rewards that will be reaped from the use of capital goods. In effect, when we forgo current consumption to invest in capital goods, we are engaging in an economic activity that is forward-looking—we do not get instant utility or satisfaction from our activity.

The Trade-Off between Consumption Goods and Capital Goods To have more consumer goods in the future, we must accept fewer consumer goods today, because resources must be used in producing capital goods instead of consumer goods. In other words, an opportunity cost is involved. Every time we make a choice of more goods today, we incur an opportunity cost of fewer goods tomorrow. Every time we make a choice of more goods in the future, we incur an opportunity cost of fewer goods today. With the resources that we don't use to produce consumer goods for today, we invest in capital goods that will produce more consumer goods for us later. The trade-off is shown in Figure 2-5. On the left in panel (a), you can see this trade-off depicted as a production possibilities curve between capital goods and consumption goods.

Assume that we are willing to give up $1 trillion worth of consumption today. We will be at point *A* in the left-hand diagram of panel (a). This will allow the economy to grow. We will have more future consumption because we invested in more capital goods today. In the right-hand diagram of panel (a), we see two consumer goods represented, game apps and digital devices. The production possibilities curve will move outward if individuals in the economy decide to restrict consumption now and invest in capital goods.

FIGURE 2-5

Capital Goods and Growth

In panel (a), people choose not to consume $1 trillion, so they invest that amount in capital goods. As a result, more of all goods, such as digital devices and game apps, may be produced in the future, as shown in the right-hand diagram in panel (a). In panel (b), people choose even more capital goods (point *C*). The result is that the production possibilities curve (PPC) moves even more to the right on the right-hand diagram in panel (b).

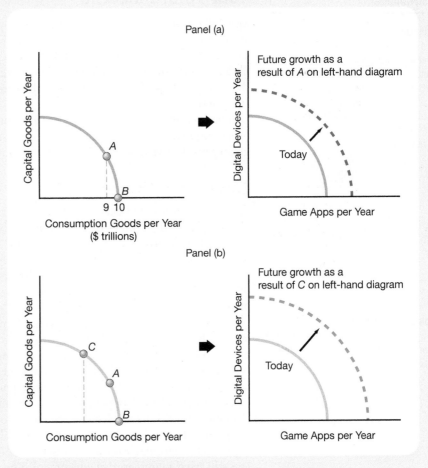

In panel (b) in Figure 2-5, we show the results of our willingness to forgo even more current consumption. We move from point A to point C in the left-hand side, where we have many fewer consumer goods today but produce many more capital goods. This leads to more future growth in this simplified model, and thus the production possibilities curve in the right-hand side of panel (b) shifts outward more than it did in the right-hand side of panel (a). In other words, the more we give up today, the more we can have tomorrow of all goods, such as digital devices and game apps, provided, of course, that the capital goods are productive in future periods.

WHAT HAPPENS WHEN...

new companies can handle the wastewater by-product from oil fracking at a lower opportunity cost than the oil-drilling firms that generate the wastewater as a by-product of unearthing the oil?

The fracking process typically involves blasting a mix of water, sand, and chemicals to release the oil from underground rock formations. A by-product of this process is large volumes of polluted wastewater. Safely handling the wastewater typically accounts for a significant cost of fracking, which is estimated to be equivalent to about 25 percent of a traditional oil drillers' overall expenses for a fracking project. Recently, new firms have developed techniques for transporting fracking wastewaters via pipelines to deep underground caverns for safe disposal at a much lower opportunity cost. Because these firms can perform the water-handling function at a lower opportunity cost than the fracking firms that generate the wastewater, they possess a comparative advantage. Thus, increasingly traditional drillers are specializing in unearthing the oil via fracking, and the new wastewater-management firms are specializing in handling the polluted wastewater by-product.

2.5 Distinguish between absolute and comparative advantage

Specialization
The organization of economic activity so that what each person (or region) consumes is not identical to what that person (or region) produces. An individual may specialize, for example, in law or medicine. A nation may specialize in the production of coffee, e-book readers, or digital cameras.

Comparative advantage
The ability to produce a good or service at a lower opportunity cost compared to other producers.

Comparative Advantage and Maximizing Your Future Income

Specialization involves working at a relatively well-defined, limited endeavor, such as accounting or teaching. Most individuals do specialize. For example, you could replace a cracked smartphone screen if you wanted to. Typically, though, you take your smartphone to a repair shop and let a technician replace the screen. You benefit by letting the technician specialize in replacing the screen and in doing other repairs on your smartphone.

The specialist normally will get the job finished sooner than you could and has the proper equipment to make the job go more smoothly. Specialization usually leads to greater productivity, not only for each individual but also for the nation.

Comparative Advantage

Specialization occurs because different individuals experience different costs when they engage in the same activities. Some individuals can accurately solve mathematical problems at lower cost than others who might try to solve the same problems. Thus, those who solve math problems at lower cost sacrifice production of fewer alternative items. Some people can develop more high-quality iPad applications than others while giving up less production of other items, such as clean houses and neatly manicured yards.

Comparative advantage is the ability to perform an activity *at a lower opportunity cost*. You have a comparative advantage in one activity whenever you have a lower opportunity cost of performing that activity. Comparative advantage is always a *relative* concept. You may be able to change the oil in your car. You might even be able to change it faster than the local mechanic. But if the opportunity cost you face by changing the oil exceeds the mechanic's opportunity cost, the mechanic has a comparative advantage in changing the oil. The mechanic faces a lower opportunity cost for that activity.

You may be convinced that everybody can do more of everything than you can during the same period of time and using the same resources. In this extreme situation, do you still have a comparative advantage? The answer is yes. You do not have to be a mathematical genius to figure this out. The market tells you so very clearly by offering you the highest income for the job for which you have a comparative advantage. Stated differently, to find your comparative advantage, simply find the job that maximizes your income. Be aware, though, that the decision as to how many years of higher education to pursue will influence the level of your future maximum income. Moreover, what you choose to specialize in while pursuing higher education will also determine your maximum income.

Absolute Advantage

Suppose you are the president of a firm and are convinced that you have the ability to do every job in that company faster than everyone else who works there. You might be able to enter data into a spreadsheet program faster than any of the other employees, file documents in order in a file cabinet faster than any of the file clerks, and wash windows faster than any of the window washers. Furthermore, you are able to manage the firm more effectively in less time than any other individual in the company.

Absolute Advantage versus Comparative Advantage
If all of these self-perceptions were really true, then you would have an **absolute advantage** in all of these endeavors. In other words, if you were to spend a given amount of time in any one of them, you could produce more than anyone else in the company. Nonetheless, you would not spend your time doing these other activities. Why not? Because your time advantage in undertaking the president's managerial duties is even greater.

Therefore, you would find yourself specializing in that particular task even though you have an *absolute* advantage in all these other tasks. Indeed, absolute advantage is irrelevant in predicting how you will allocate your time. Instead, you will specialize based on your *comparative* advantage. This will be so because you will find that allocating each hour of your time on the basis of comparative advantage will yield you the highest hourly reward.

Only *comparative advantage*, not absolute advantage, matters in determining how you will allocate your time. Comparative advantage determines your choice because it involves the highest-valued alternative in a decision about time allocation.

Comparative Advantage in Sports
The coaches of sports teams often have to determine the comparative advantage of an individual player who has an absolute advantage in every aspect of the sport in question. Babe Ruth, who could hit more home runs and pitch more strikeouts per game than other players on the Boston Red Sox, was a pitcher on that professional baseball team.

After Ruth was traded to the New York Yankees, the owner and the manager decided to make him an outfielder, even though he could also pitch more strikeouts per game than other Yankees. They wanted "The Babe" to concentrate on his hitting because a home-run king would bring in more paying fans than a good pitcher would. Babe Ruth had an absolute advantage in both aspects of the game of baseball, but his comparative advantage was in hitting homers rather than in practicing and developing his pitching game.

Scarcity, Self-Interest, and Specialization

In Chapter 1, you learned about the assumption of rational self-interest. To repeat, for the purposes of our analyses we assume that individuals are rational in that they will do what is in their own self-interest. They will not consciously carry out actions that will make them worse off. In this chapter, you learned that scarcity requires people to make choices. We *assume* that they make choices based on their self-interest. When people make choices, they attempt to maximize benefits net of opportunity cost. In so doing, individuals choose their comparative advantage and end up specializing.

Absolute advantage
The ability to produce more units of a good or service using a given quantity of labor or resource inputs. Equivalently, the ability to produce the same quantity of a good or service using fewer units of labor or resource inputs.

The Division of Labor

In any firm that includes specialized human and nonhuman resources, there is a **division of labor** among those resources. The best-known example comes from Adam Smith (1723–1790), who in *The Wealth of Nations* illustrated the benefits of a division of labor in the making of pins, as depicted in the following example:

> One man draws out the wire, another straightens it, a third cuts it, a fourth points it, a fifth grinds it at the top for receiving the head; to make the head requires two or three distinct operations; to put it on is a peculiar business, to whiten the pins is another; it is even a trade by itself to put them into the paper.

Making pins this way allowed 10 workers without very much skill to make almost 48,000 pins "of a middling size" in a day. One worker, toiling alone, could have made perhaps 20 pins a day. Therefore, 10 workers could have produced 200. Division of labor allowed for an increase in the daily output of the pin factory from 200 to 48,000! (Smith did not attribute all of the gain to the division of labor but credited also the use of machinery and the fact that less time was spent shifting from task to task.)

What we are discussing here involves a division of the resource called labor into different uses of labor. The different uses of labor are organized in such a way as to increase the amount of output possible from the fixed resources available. We can therefore talk about an organized division of labor within a firm leading to increased output.

Division of labor
The segregation of resources into different specific tasks. For instance, one digital-device assembler inserts touchscreen connectors, another attaches the screen, and so on.

Comparative Advantage and Trade among Nations

Most of our analysis of absolute advantage, comparative advantage, and specialization has dealt with individuals. Nevertheless, it is equally applicable to groups of people.

Trade among Regions   Consider the United States. The Plains states have a comparative advantage in the production of grains and other agricultural goods. Relative to the Plains states, the states to the east tend to specialize in industrialized production, such as automobiles. Not surprisingly, grains are shipped from the Plains states to the eastern states, and automobiles are shipped in the reverse direction. Such specialization and trade allow for higher incomes and standards of living.

If both the Plains states and the eastern states were separate nations, the same analysis would still hold, but we would call it international trade. Indeed, the European Union (EU) is comparable to the United States in area and population, but instead of one nation, the EU has 27. What U.S. residents call *interstate* trade, Europeans call *international* trade. There is no difference, however, in the economic results—both yield greater economic efficiency and higher average incomes.

International Aspects of Trade   Political problems that normally do not occur within a particular nation often arise between nations. For example, if California avocado growers develop a cheaper method of producing avocados than growers in southern Florida use, the Florida growers will lose out. They cannot do much about the situation except try to lower their own costs of production or improve their product.

If avocado growers in Mexico, however, develop a cheaper method of producing avocados, both California and Florida growers can (and likely will) try to raise political barriers that will prevent Mexican avocado growers from freely selling their product in the United States. U.S. avocado growers will use such arguments as "unfair" competition and loss of U.S. jobs. Certainly, avocado-growing jobs may decline in the United States, but there is no reason to believe that U.S. jobs will decline overall. Instead, former U.S. avocado workers will move into alternative employment—something that 1 million people do every *week* in the United States. If the argument of U.S. avocado growers had any validity, every time a region in the United States developed a better way to produce a product manufactured somewhere else in the country, U.S. employment would decline. That has never happened and never will.

When nations specialize in an area of comparative advantage and then trade with the rest of the world, the average standard of living in the world rises. In effect, international trade allows the world to move from inside the global production possibilities curve toward the curve itself, thereby improving worldwide economic efficiency. Thus, all countries that engage in trade can benefit from comparative advantage, just as regions in the United States benefit from interregional trade.

ECONOMICS IN YOUR LIFE

Extreme Specialization Leads One Person to Pursue Small-Rocket Launches

Peter Beck, founder of California-based aerospace company Rocket Lab, has developed a new business plan. It calls for launching thousands of small rockets carrying microsatellites about the size of shoeboxes that will be designed to perform various commercial communications functions. In seeking to implement this plan, Beck quickly encountered a problem that other aerospace companies also confront: Profitable airlines and other firms flying commercial aircraft already utilize much of the airspace above the most desirable U.S. locations from which to launch satellites into orbit. Beck has found that in most such locations, the opportunity costs of airspace are sufficiently high that Rocket Lab cannot squeeze in all of the lower-value launches required by its plan of operations.

After years of study, Rocket Lab finally has found the ideal place from which to conduct thousands of microsatellite launches. Although commercial aircraft fly to a handful of locations within the island nation of New Zealand, much of the country's airspace lies above empty lands that contain six times more sheep than people.

Rocket Lab now has built its first launch pads in New Zealand and has begun testing its first rockets in the nation's low-opportunity-cost airspace.

FOR CRITICAL THINKING

As more aerospace firms set up in New Zealand to launch satellites and other payloads beyond the earth's atmosphere, what is likely to happen to the opportunity cost of larger portions of the airspace above that nation? Explain briefly.

REAL APPLICATION

Assume you are hired as part of the management team for a new aerospace company in New Zealand. It, too, wishes to launch satellites along paths very close to those of Rocket Labs. What would you tell the president of that new company about future opportunity costs?

Sources are listed at the end of this chapter.

ISSUES & APPLICATIONS

There Is No Such Thing as Free Parking

non c/Shutterstock

CONCEPTS APPLIED

➤ Land

➤ Scarcity

➤ Opportunity Cost

As shown in Figure 2-6, the number of vehicles in relation to population is considerably higher in the United States than in other high-population countries. Indeed, in excess of 250 million vehicles exist within U.S. borders.

During a typical day, the average U.S. vehicle is in motion only about 70 minutes. Thus, all of these vehicles are parked an average of almost 23 hours per day. Determining how to allocate space for so many vehicles during such a large portion of each day is a substantial problem involving the allocation of scarce land resources.

FIGURE 2-6

Number of Vehicles per 1,000 People in Selected Nations

The number of vehicles in relation to population is higher in the United States than in other nations, which translates into substantial space requirements for vehicle parking in locations where U.S. residents live.
Source: U.S. Environmental Protection Agency.

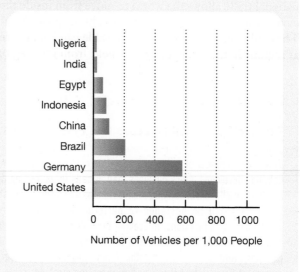

The Parking Space Requirements—and the Implied Trade-Offs

The minimum parking space requirement for a typical automobile is about 16 feet long and 8 feet wide. Of course, all of the required parking area for all of the more than 250 million U.S. vehicles is not confined to a single region occupied solely by these vehicles. People in rural areas, towns, and cities across the nation must determine how to allocate parcels of land that they own to space for parking the vehicles that they own. In rural areas, lands devoted to vehicle parking could be committed to such alternative uses as raising crops or livestock. In towns and cities, space allocated to vehicle parking otherwise could be sites for, say, residential or commercial buildings.

Opportunity Cost and the Allocation of Land to Parking Spaces

All of the various ways that land occupied by vehicles might alternatively be utilized indicates that people confront many potential trade-offs when deciding whether to set aside parking spaces. In each and every case in which an individual makes a choice regarding potentially allocating available space to parking, however, the single relevant trade-off is the perceived value of that space as compared with its opportunity cost.

That opportunity cost, in turn, is each individual's assessment of the value of the *single next-best* alternative use of the space. For one person, therefore, the opportunity cost of space devoted to parking might be its value if it otherwise were utilized for adding rooms to a building. For another person, the opportunity cost might be a perceived valuation if the space functioned as a flower garden. In every case in which land is utilized for parking, someone has determined that the value of the land for that purpose exceeds the relevant opportunity cost.

FOR CRITICAL THINKING

Why do you suppose that trying to assess the aggregate opportunity cost of all lands devoted to parking would require determining the opportunity costs of parking spaces by all of the owners of those lands? (*Hint:* Recall that the opportunity cost is the value of the single next-best alternative as evaluated by each individual who makes a choice.)

REAL APPLICATION

Assume you are a homeowner with a parking space. You discover that you can lease the land for $1,000 per year to someone who covets that space. Alternatively, you can build a small basketball court for your personal use. Of the two options, how do you determine which makes you better off?

Sources are listed at the end of this chapter.

What You Should Know

Here is what you should know after reading this chapter.

LEARNING OBJECTIVES

2.1 Evaluate why everyone, whether poor or affluent, faces the problem of scarcity *Even the richest people face scarcity because they have to make choices among alternatives. Despite their high levels of income or wealth, affluent people, like everyone else, want more than they can have (in terms of goods, power, prestige, and so on).*

2.2 Explain why the scarcity problem causes people to consider opportunity costs and trade-offs among choices *Opportunity cost is the highest-valued alternative that one must give up to obtain an item. The trade-offs people face can be represented by a production possibilities curve (PPC). Moving along a PPC from one point to another entails incurring an opportunity cost of allocating scarce resources toward the production of one good instead of another good.*

2.3 Discuss why obtaining increasing increments of any particular good typically entails giving up more and more units of other goods *When people allocate additional resources to producing more units of a good, they must increasingly employ resources that would be better suited for producing other goods. As a result, the law of increasing additional cost holds. Each additional unit of a good can be obtained only by giving up more and more of other goods. Hence, the production possibilities curve is bowed outward.*

2.4 Explain why the economy faces a trade-off between consumption goods and capital goods *If we allocate more resources to producing capital goods today, then the production possibilities curve will shift outward by more in the future, which means that we can have additional future consumption goods. The trade-off is that producing more capital goods today entails giving up consumption goods today.*

2.5 Distinguish between absolute and comparative advantage *A person has an absolute advantage if she can produce more of a good than someone else who uses the same amount of resources. An individual can gain from specializing in producing a good if she has a comparative advantage in producing that good, meaning that she can produce the good at a lower opportunity cost than someone else.*

KEY TERMS

scarcity, 27
production, 27
land, 27
labor, 27
physical capital, 28
human capital, 28
entrepreneurship, 28
goods, 28
economic goods, 28
services, 28

opportunity cost, 29
production possibilities
curve (PPC), 31
Key Figure
Figure 2-1, 30

technology, 33
efficiency, 34
inefficient point, 34
law of increasing
additional cost, 35
Key Figure
Figure 2-3, 34

consumption, 36
Key Figure
Figure 2-4, 36

specialization, 38
comparative advantage, 38
absolute advantage, 39
division of labor, 39

PROBLEMS

2-1. Define opportunity cost. What is your opportunity cost of attending a class at 11:00 A.M.? How does it differ from your opportunity cost of attending a class at 8:00 A.M.?

2-2. If you receive a ticket to a concert at no charge, what, if anything, is your opportunity cost of attending the concert? How does your opportunity cost change if miserable weather on the night of the concert requires you to leave much earlier for the concert hall and greatly extends the time it takes to get home afterward?

2-3. You and a friend decide to spend $100 each on concert tickets. Each of you alternatively could have spent the $100 to purchase a textbook, a meal at a highly rated local restaurant, or several Internet movie downloads. As you are on the way to the concert, your friend tells you that if she had not bought the concert ticket, she would have opted for a restaurant meal, and you reply that you otherwise would have downloaded several movies. Identify the relevant opportunity costs for you and your friend of the concert tickets that you purchased. Explain briefly.

2-4. After the concert discussed in Problem 2-3 is over and you and your friend are traveling home, you discuss how each of you might otherwise have used the four hours devoted to attending the concert. The four hours could have been used to study, to watch a streaming video of a sporting event, or to get some extra sleep. Your friend decides that if she had not spent four hours attending the concert, she would have chosen to study, and you reply that you otherwise would have watched the streaming video. Identify the relevant opportunity costs for you and your friend for allocating your four hours to attending the concert. Explain briefly.

2-5. Recently, a woman named Mary Krawiec attended an auction in Troy, New York. At the auction, a bank was seeking to sell a foreclosed property: a large Victorian house suffering from years of neglect in a neighborhood in which many properties had been on the market for years yet remained unsold. Her $10 offer was the highest bid in the auction, and she handed over a $10 bill for a title to ownership. Once she acquired the house, however, she became responsible for all taxes on the property and for an overdue water bill of $2,000.

In addition, to make the house habitable, she and her husband devoted months of time and unpaid labor to renovating the property. In the process, they incurred explicit expenses totaling $65,000. Why do you suppose that the bank was willing to sell the house to Ms. Krawiec for only $10? (*Hint:* Contemplate the bank's expected gain, net of all explicit and opportunity costs, if it had attempted to make the house habitable.)

2-6. The following table illustrates the points a student can earn on examinations in economics and biology if the student uses all available hours for study. Plot this student's production possibilities curve. Does the PPC illustrate the law of increasing additional cost?

Economics	Biology
100	40
90	60
80	75
70	85
60	93
50	98
40	100

2-7. Based on the information provided in Problem 2-6, what is the opportunity cost to this student of allocating enough additional study time on economics to move her grade up from a 90 to a 100?

2-8. Consider a change in the table in Problem 2-6. The student's set of opportunities is now as follows: Does the PPC illustrate the law of increasing additional cost? What is the opportunity cost to this student for the additional amount of study time on economics required to move her grade from 60 to 70? From 90 to 100?

Economics	Biology
100	40
90	50
80	60
70	70
60	80
50	90
40	100

2-9. Construct a production possibilities curve for a nation facing increasing opportunity costs for producing food and video games. Show how the PPC changes given the following events.

   a. A new and better fertilizer is invented.

   b. Immigration occurs, and immigrants' labor can be employed in both the agricultural sector and the video game sector.

   c. People invent a new programming language that is much less costly to code and is more memory-efficient.

   d. A heat wave and drought result in a 10 percent decrease in usable farmland.

Consider the following diagram when answering Problems 2-10, 2-11, and 2-12.

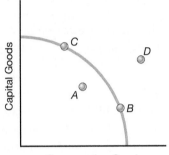

2-10. During a debate on the floor of the U.S. Senate, Senator Creighton states, "Our nation should not devote so many of its fully employed resources to producing capital goods because we already are not producing enough consumption goods for our citizens." Compared with the other labeled points on the diagram, which one could be consistent with the *current* production combination choice that Senator Creighton believes the nation has made?

2-11. In response to Senator Creighton's statement reported in Problem 2-10, Senator Long replies, "We must remain at our current production combination if we want to be able to produce more consumption goods in the future." Of the labeled points on the diagram, which one could depict the *future* production combination Senator Long has in mind?

2-12. Senator Borman interjects the following comment after the statements by Senators Creighton and Long reported in Problems 2-10 and 2-11: "In fact, both of my esteemed colleagues are wrong, because an unacceptably large portion of our nation's resources is currently unemployed." Of the labeled points on the diagram, which one is consistent with Senator Borman's position?

2-13. A nation's residents can allocate their scarce resources either to producing consumption goods or to producing human capital—that is, providing themselves with training and education. The table below displays the production possibilities for this nation:

Production Combination	Units of Consumption Goods	Units of Human Capital
A	0	100
B	10	97
C	20	90
D	30	75
E	40	55
F	50	30
G	60	0

   a. Suppose that the nation's residents currently produce combination A. What is the opportunity cost of increasing production of consumption goods by 10 units? By 60 units?

   b. Does the law of increasing additional cost hold true for this nation? Why or why not?

2-14. Like physical capital, human capital produced in the present can be applied to the production of future goods and services. Consider the table in Problem 2-13, and suppose that the nation's residents are trying to choose between combination C and combination F. Other things being equal, will the future production possibilities curve for this nation be located farther outward if the nation chooses combination F instead of combination C? Explain.

2-15. You can wash, fold, and iron a basket of laundry in two hours and prepare a meal in one hour. Your roommate can wash, fold, and iron a basket of laundry in three hours and prepare a meal in one hour. Who has the absolute advantage in laundry, and who has an absolute advantage in meal preparation? Who has the comparative advantage in laundry, and who has a comparative advantage in meal preparation?

2-16. Based on the information in Problem 2-15, should you and your roommate specialize in a particular task? Why? If so, who should specialize in which task? Show how much labor time you save if you choose to "trade" an appropriate task with your roommate as opposed to doing it yourself.

2-17. Using only the concept of comparative advantage, evaluate this statement: "A professor with a Ph.D. in physics should never mow his or her own lawn, because this would fail to take into account the professor's comparative advantage."

2-18. Country A and country B produce the same consumption goods and capital goods and currently have *identical* production possibilities curves. They also have the same resources at present, and they have access to the same technology.

 a. At present, does either country have a comparative advantage in producing capital goods? Consumption goods?

 b. Suppose that country A now chooses to produce more consumption goods, compared with country B. Other things being equal, which country will experience the larger outward shift of its PPC during the next year?

2-19. Suppose that in Figure 2-1, a student currently is allocating her study time in such a way that she is earning a C in mathematics and a C in economics. What is the opportunity cost, measured in terms of the resulting grade change, if this student wishes to reallocate her study time in order to raise her mathematics grade by one letter, from a C to a B?

2-20. Suppose that in Figure 2-1, a student currently is allocating her study time in such a way that she is earning a C in mathematics and a C in economics. If the student desires to boost her economics grade to an A, how must she alter the number of hours per week that she studies economics? How must she alter the number of hours per week that she studies mathematics?

2-21. Suppose that in Figure 2-2, the nation currently is producing combination D in the table and on the graph of the production possibilities curve. What is the opportunity cost of producing 5 million more smartphones and moving to production combination C?

2-22. Suppose that in Figure 2-2, the nation currently is producing combination D in the table and on the graph of the production possibilities curve. What is the opportunity cost of producing 20 million more tablet devices and moving to production combination F?

2-23. Suppose that in Figure 2-4, the nation currently has sufficient resources to produce combinations located along only the innermost production possibilities curve. In addition, suppose that the nation's residents have determined that smartphones function mainly as consumption goods while tablet devices function primarily as capital goods. If the nation produces no additional tablets this year, will the intermediate-shifted PPC resulting from minimal economic growth or the farthest-shifted PPC caused by more significant economic growth be more likely to apply next year?

2-24. Suppose that in Figure 2-4, the nation with otherwise the same background conditions as in Problem 2-23 currently has sufficient resources to produce combinations located along only the innermost production possibilities curve. If the nation produces no additional smartphones this year, will the intermediate-shifted PPC resulting from minimal economic growth or the farthest-shifted PPC caused by more significant economic growth be more likely to apply next year?

REFERENCES

BEHAVIORAL EXAMPLE: Why People with the Highest Hourly Opportunity Cost Allocate as Much Time to Leisure as Everyone Else

Hillary Hoffower, "A Woman Who Studied 600 Millionaires Found Five Major Differences in How They Spend Their Time and Energy Compared with the Average American," *Business Insider*, January 4, 2019.

Catherine Clifford, "Here's What Billionaires of the World Do with Their Free Time," CNBC (https://www.cnbc.com/2018/05/21/wealthx-billionaires-passions-include-sports-art-music.html), May 21, 2018.

Paul Smeets, Renee Bekkers, Ashley Whillans, and Michael Norton, "Time Use and Happiness of Millionaires," Harvard Business School Working Paper 18-111, 2018.

EXAMPLE: The Economic Explanation for Shrinking Jetliner Restrooms

Lewis Lazare, "American Airlines Adjusting Small Bathrooms on Some Planes," *Chicago Business Journal*, January 2, 2019.

Mary Schlangenstein, "Airline Bathrooms Are Getting Smaller—You're Not Imagining It," *Los Angeles Times*, July 10, 2018.

Joanna Whitehead, "Plane Toilets 'Shrinking in Size to Make Room for More Seats,'" *The Independent*, July 17, 2018.

AI—DECISION MAKING THROUGH DATA: City Management

Edward Krafcik, Ellory Monks, and Eyal Feder-Levy, "Smart City Predictions," Meeting of the Minds (https://meetingoftheminds.org/smart-cities-predictions-29579), January 17, 2019.

Skip Descant, "Big Data Can Help Solve Big City Problems, But Watch for the Potholes," Govtech.com (http://www.govtech.com/fs/data/Big-Data-Can-Help-Solve-Big-City-Problems-but-Watch-for-the-Potholes.html), March 28, 2018.

"Big Data and Local Government," *Government Computing*, June 1, 2018.

POLICY EXAMPLE: City Bicycle Lanes Encounter the Law of Increasing Additional Cost

Rich Calder, "Why De Blasio Won't Punish Vehicles Clogging Bike Lanes," *New York Post*, January 25, 2019.

Scott Calvert, "Creating Bike Lanes Isn't Easy. Just Ask Baltimore. Or Boulder. Or Seattle," *Wall Street Journal*, April 18, 2018.

David Sands, "Detroit's Bike Lanes Have Sparked Controversy. What's Next?" ModelMedia.com (http://www.modeldmedia.com/features/bike-lanes-detroit-complaints-052118.aspx), May 21, 2018.

ECONOMICS IN YOUR LIFE: Extreme Specialization Leads One Person to Pursue Small-Rocket Launches

"Rocket Lab to Launch Satellite for U.S. Defence Agency," Radio New Zealand (https://www.radionz.co.nz/news/national/380770/rocket-lab-to-launch-satellite-for-us-defence-agency), January 23, 2019.

"Is New Zealand the World's Best Rocket-Launching Site?" *Economist*, April 5, 2018.

Lauren Grush, "U.S. Space Startup Rocket Lab Sets New Date for First Commercial Launch," *The Verge*, May 25, 2018.

ISSUES & APPLICATIONS: There Is No Such Thing as Free Parking

"Parking Management Market Analysis 2019–2023," *MarketWatch* (https://www.marketwatch.com/press-release/parking-management-market-analysis-2019-2023-key-findings-global-trends-regional-study-key-players-profiles-and-future-prospects-2019-01-02), January 2, 2019.

Justin Fox, "America Has a Lot of Parking Spaces. It's a Problem," *Bloomberg*, July 22, 2018.

Christina Rogers, "American's Love Affair with Huge Vehicles Collides with Tiny Parking Spaces," *Wall Street Journal*, June 15, 2018.

3

Demand and Supply

samritk/Shutterstock

LEARNING OBJECTIVES

After reading this chapter, you should be able to:

3.1 Explain the law of demand

3.2 Distinguish between changes in demand and changes in quantity demanded

3.3 Explain the law of supply

3.4 Distinguish between changes in supply and changes in quantity supplied

3.5 Understand how the interaction of demand and supply determines the equilibrium price and quantity

During the past few years, a number of media reports have indicated that producers' sales of soft drinks have declined as consumers' purchases of bottled water have risen. The usual media interpretation is that these differing trends arise because increased health consciousness has induced consumers to opt away from sugary soft drinks in favor of more healthful bottled-water products. Usually not mentioned in these media stories is that dollar prices of soft drinks have risen and that dollar prices of bottled-water products have decreased. In this chapter, you will learn that the resulting reduction in the price of bottled water *relative* to soft drinks has played an important role in explaining the trends in soft drink sales and bottled-water consumption not contemplated in most media reports.

when the price of milk declined by more than one-third during the years following 2014, milk producers responded by cutting back on millions of gallons of production each year? Indeed, in one recent year, milk producers threw out more than 40 million gallons of milk instead of incurring higher transportation expenses to sell the milk at the lower prevailing prices.

If we use the economist's primary set of tools, *demand* and *supply*, we can develop a better understanding of why we sometimes observe relatively large decreases in the sale of items such as milk. We can also better understand why a decrease in the price of an item ultimately induces a decrease in the amount of that item that producers will offer for sale. Demand and supply are two ways of categorizing the influences on the prices of goods that you buy and the quantities available. In fact, demand and supply characterize much economic analysis of the world around us.

As you will see throughout this text, the operation of the forces of demand and supply takes place in *markets*. A **market** is an abstract concept summarizing all of the arrangements individuals have for exchanging with one another. Goods and services are sold in markets, such as the automobile market, the health care market, and the market for high-speed Internet access. Workers offer their services in the labor market. Companies, or firms, buy workers' labor services in the labor market. Firms also buy other inputs to produce the goods and services that you buy as a consumer. Firms purchase machines, buildings, and land. These markets are in operation at all times. One of the most important activities in these markets is the determination of the prices of all of the inputs and outputs that are bought and sold in our economy. To understand the determination of prices, you first need to look at the law of demand.

Market
All of the arrangements that individuals have for exchanging with one another. Thus, for example, we can speak of the labor market, the automobile market, and the credit market.

Demand

3.1 Explain the law of demand

Demand has a special meaning in economics. It refers to the quantities of specific goods or services that individuals, taken singly or as a group, will purchase at various possible prices, other things being constant. We can therefore talk about the demand for microprocessor chips, french fries, multifunction digital devices, children, and criminal activities.

Demand
A schedule showing how much of a good or service people will purchase at any price during a specified time period, other things being constant.

The Law of Demand

Associated with the concept of demand is the **law of demand,** which can be stated as follows:

> *When the price of a good goes up, people buy less of it, other things being equal. When the price of a good goes down, people buy more of it, other things being equal.*

Law of demand
The observation that there is a negative, or inverse, relationship between the price of any good or service and the quantity demanded, holding other factors constant.

The law of demand tells us that the quantity demanded of any commodity is inversely related to its price, other things being equal. In an inverse relationship, one variable moves up in value when the other moves down. The law of demand states that a change in price causes a change in the quantity demanded in the *opposite* direction.

Notice that we tacked on to the end of the law of demand the statement "other things being equal." We referred to this in Chapter 1 as the *ceteris paribus* assumption. It means, for example, that when we predict that people will buy fewer digital devices if their price goes up, we are holding constant the price of all other goods in the economy as well as people's incomes. Implicitly, therefore, if we are assuming that no other prices change when we examine the price behavior of digital devices, we are looking at the *relative* price of digital devices.

The law of demand is supported by millions of observations of people's behavior in the marketplace. Theoretically, it can be derived from an economic model based on rational behavior, as was discussed in Chapter 1. Basically, if nothing else changes and the price of a good falls, the lower price induces us to buy more because we can enjoy additional net gains that were unavailable at the higher price. If you examine your own behavior, you will see that it generally follows the law of demand.

Relative price
The money price of one commodity divided by the money price of another commodity; the number of units of one commodity that must be sacrificed to purchase one unit of another commodity.

Money price
The price expressed in today's dollars; also called the *absolute, nominal,* or *money price.*

Relative versus Money Prices and Your Future Consumer Choices

The **relative price** of any commodity is its price in terms of another commodity. The price that you pay in dollars and cents for any good or service at any point in time is called its **money price.**

The Relative Price of Houses and Cars You might hear from your grandparents, "My first new car cost only $3,200." The implication, of course, is that the price of cars today is outrageously high because the average new car may cost $37,000. That, however, is not an accurate comparison.

Consider what the price of the average house was when your grandparents bought their first car. Perhaps it was only $19,000. By comparison, then, given that the average price of houses today is about $300,000, the current price of a new car doesn't sound so far out of line, does it?

As a consumer, you will be faced with buying decisions about "big ticket" items, such as cars and houses. There is no reason to look at the past to see what the nominal (money) prices of those items were. Rather, you should make your buying decisions based on *relative* prices today. And, you will want to make those buying decisions based on what your current and future income will be.

What do you suppose has happened over recent years to the price of prepared food purchased at restaurants *relative to* the price of food purchased for preparation at home?

EXAMPLE

The Soaring Relative Price of Restaurant Meals

Since 2008, the average absolute price of food purchased for preparation at home has increased by about 16 percent. During the same period, the average absolute, or nominal, price of prepared food purchased at restaurants increased by 28 percent. Thus, the price of prepared food purchased at restaurants rose by 12 percent *relative to* the price of food purchased for preparation at home.

REAL APPLICATION

How might the law of demand help to explain why in one recent year, the number of prepared lunches sold by U.S. restaurants dropped by more than 400 million units from the previous year? How might you respond in the future to an even higher relative price of restaurant meals?

Sources are listed at the end of this chapter.

ECONOMICS IN YOUR LIFE
To contemplate the importance to buyers and sellers of considering the quality-adjusted price of restaurant soup-and-salad lunches, take a look at **Space-Constrained Restaurants Discover That Customers Care about Quality-Adjusted Lunch Prices** on page 67.

Comparing Relative Prices of Digital Storage Drives The point is that money prices during different time periods don't tell you much. You have to calculate relative prices. Consider an example of the price of 6-terabyte cloud servers versus the price of 6-terabyte external hard drives from last year and this year. In Table 3-1, we show the money prices of cloud servers and external hard drives for two years during which they have both gone down.

This means that in today's dollars we have to pay out less for both cloud servers and external hard drives. If we look, though, at the relative prices of cloud servers and external hard drives, we find that last year, cloud servers were twice as expensive as external hard drives, whereas this year they are only one and a half times as expensive. Conversely, if we compare external hard drives to cloud servers, last year the price of external hard drives was 50 percent of the price of cloud servers, but today the price of external hard drives is about 67 percent of the price of cloud servers. In the one-year period, although both prices have declined in money terms, the relative price of external hard drives has risen in relation to that of cloud servers.

Sometimes relative price changes occur because the quality of a product improves, thereby bringing about a decrease in the item's effective *price per constant-quality unit.* The price of an item may also increase simply because producers have reduced the item's quality. Thus, when evaluating the effects of price changes, we must always compare *price per constant-quality unit.*

CHAPTER 3 | Demand and Supply **51**

TABLE 3-1

Money Price versus Relative Price

The money prices of both 6-terabyte cloud servers and 6-terabyte external hard drives have fallen. The relative price of external hard drives, however, has risen (or, conversely, the relative price of cloud servers has fallen).

	Money Price		Relative Price	
	Price Last Year	Price This Year	Price Last Year	Price This Year
Cloud servers	$300	$210	$\frac{\$300}{\$150} = 2.0$	$\frac{\$210}{\$140} = 1.50$
External hard drives	$150	$140	$\frac{\$150}{\$300} = 0.50$	$\frac{\$140}{\$210} = 0.67$

Why might professional musicians regard 300-year-old concert violins with prices in the hundreds of thousands of dollars to have lower quality-adjusted prices than new concert violins with prices around a thousand dollars?

EXAMPLE

Assessing the Quality-Adjusted Prices of Old and New Concert Violins

To someone who is not a serious violinist, the thought of a thousand dollars for a newly manufactured violin that projects deep, melodious tones across a full range of low, medium, and high notes may seem like a high price. If so, *hundreds of thousands* of dollars for a 300-year-old instrument, such as a Stradivarius violin, surely would seem to be an even higher price. Nevertheless, in past years many of the best concert violinists have regarded very old, handmade violins that mimic aspects of the human voice to have quality-adjusted prices *lower* than the quality-adjusted prices of newly manufactured instruments priced at only about $1,000.

Recent comparisons conducted with blindfolded musicians playing violins and blocked from view by musically trained audiences may alter this perception of the relative quality-adjusted prices of modern versus 300-year-old concert violins. These comparisons reveal that most musicians playing and listening to the two types of violins judge that the latest modern concert violins offer richer sounds than the old instruments. Thus, if the quality-adjusted price reflects differences in perceived tones emitted by the two types of violins, in reality the quality-adjusted prices in the hundreds of thousands of dollars for the older instruments are considerably higher than the approximately thousand-dollar prices for the modern instruments.

FOR CRITICAL THINKING

If a concert violinist perceives that instruments that look very old enhance the experience of ticket-buying crowds, will that violinist be willing to pay more for an older violin?

Sources are listed at the end of this chapter.

The Demand Schedule

Let's take a hypothetical demand situation to see how the inverse relationship between the price and the quantity demanded looks (holding other things equal). We will consider the quantity of wireless earbuds demanded *per year*. Without stating the *time dimension*, we could not make sense out of this demand relationship because the numbers would be different if we were talking about the quantity demanded per month or the quantity demanded per decade.

In addition to implicitly or explicitly stating a time dimension for a demand relationship, we are also implicitly referring to *constant-quality units* of the good or service in question. We always express prices in constant-quality units to avoid the problem of comparing commodities that are in fact not truly comparable.

In panel (a) of Figure 3-1, we see that if the price is $1 apiece, 50 wireless earbuds will be bought each year by our representative individual, but if the price is $5 apiece, only 10 wireless earbuds will be bought each year. This reflects the law of demand. Panel (a) is also called simply demand, or a *demand schedule*, because it gives a schedule of quantities demanded per year at different possible prices.

FIGURE 3-1

The Individual Demand Schedule and the Individual Demand Curve

In panel (a), we show combinations A through E of the quantities of wireless earbuds demanded, measured in constant-quality units at prices ranging from $5 down to $1 apiece. These combinations are points on the demand schedule. In panel (b), we plot combinations A through E on a grid. The result is the individual demand curve for wireless earbuds.

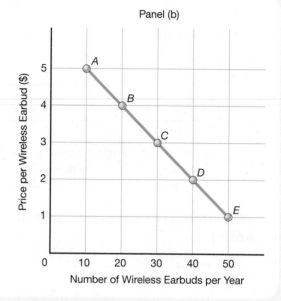

Panel (a)

Combination	Price per Constant-Quality Wireless Earbud	Quantity of Constant-Quality Wireless Earbuds per Year
A	$5	10
B	4	20
C	3	30
D	2	40
E	1	50

Demand curve

A graphical representation of the demand schedule. It is a negatively sloped line showing the inverse relationship between the price and the quantity demanded (other things being equal).

The Demand Curve Tables expressing relationships between two variables can be represented in graphical terms. To do this, we need only construct a graph that has the price per constant-quality wireless earbud on the vertical axis and the quantity measured in constant-quality wireless earbuds per year on the horizontal axis. All we have to do is take combinations A through E from panel (a) of Figure 3-1 and plot those points in panel (b). Now we connect the points with a smooth line, and *voilà*, we have a **demand curve.** It is downward sloping (from left to right) to indicate the inverse relationship between the price of wireless earbuds and the quantity demanded per year.

Our presentation of demand schedules and curves applies equally well to all commodities, including dental floss, bagels, textbooks, credit, and labor. Remember, the demand curve is simply a graphical representation of the law of demand.

What usually happens when charitable organizations say to prospective buyers, "Pay what you want"?

BEHAVIORAL EXAMPLE

Why Pay-What-You-Want Pricing Often Pays Off for Charitable Organizations

Charitable organizations are far more likely to offer items for sale at whatever price buyers are willing to pay, starting as low as $0 per unit. Behavioral economists have found that most individuals who go to the trouble to shop for items sold by charities have altruistic motivations for doing so. Hence, the buyer typically pays a price higher than the willingness to pay if the buyer had contemplated only purely self-interested preferences. Paying the higher price ensures that the buyer's altruistic desire will be satisfied purchasing an item offered by a charitable organization and sold under a "pay-what-you-want" arrangement. As a consequence, that buyer pays a price for a given quantity that lies at a point directly *above* the point on her demand curve at that quantity. The distance between these two points equals the amount per unit that the buyer wishes to ensure will be transmitted for a charitable purpose.

FOR CRITICAL THINKING

Why do you suppose that available evidence indicates that charitable organizations are more likely to offer "pay-what-you-want" pricing for items produced or obtained at relatively low cost per unit?

Sources are listed at the end of this chapter.

Individual versus Market Demand Curves The demand schedule shown in panel (a) of Figure 3-1 and the resulting demand curve shown in panel (b) are both given for an individual. As we shall see, the determination of price in the marketplace depends on, among other things, the **market demand** for a particular commodity. The way in which we measure a market demand schedule and derive a market demand curve for wireless earbuds or any other good or service is by summing (at each price) the individual quantities demanded by all buyers in the market. Suppose that the market demand for wireless earbuds consists of only two buyers: buyer 1, for whom we've already shown the demand schedule, and buyer 2, whose demand schedule is displayed in column 3 of panel (a) of Figure 3-2. Column 1 shows the price, and column 2 shows the quantity demanded by buyer 1 at each price. These data are taken directly from Figure 3-1. In column 3, we show the quantity demanded by buyer 2. Column 4 shows the total quantity demanded at each price, which is obtained by simply adding columns 2 and 3. Graphically, in panel (d) of Figure 3-2, we add the demand curves of buyer 1 [panel (b)] and buyer 2 [panel (c)] to derive the market demand curve.

There are, of course, numerous potential consumers of wireless earbuds. We'll simply assume that the summation of all of the consumers in the market results in a

Market demand
The demand of all consumers in the marketplace for a particular good or service. The summation at each price of the quantity demanded by each individual.

FIGURE 3-2

The Horizontal Summation of Two Demand Curves

Panel (a) shows how to sum the demand schedule for one buyer with that of another buyer. In column 2 is the quantity demanded by buyer 1, taken from panel (a) of Figure 3-1. Column 4 is the sum of columns 2 and 3. We plot the demand curve for buyer 1 in panel (b) and the demand curve for buyer 2 in panel (c). When we add those two demand curves horizontally, we get the market demand curve for two buyers, shown in panel (d).

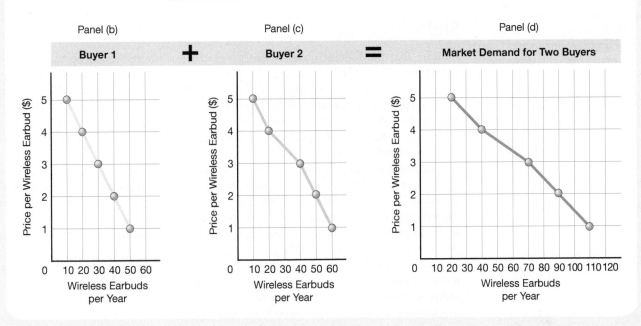

Panel (a)

(1) Price per Wireless Earbud	(2) Buyer 1's Quantity Demanded	(3) Buyer 2's Quantity Demanded	(4) = (2) + (3) Combined Quantity Demanded per Year
$5	10	10	20
4	20	20	40
3	30	40	70
2	40	50	90
1	50	60	110

The Market Demand Schedule for Wireless Earbuds

In panel (a), we add up the existing demand schedules for wireless earbuds on the part of all buyers. In panel (b), we plot the quantities from panel (a) on a grid. Connecting them produces the market demand curve for wireless earbuds.

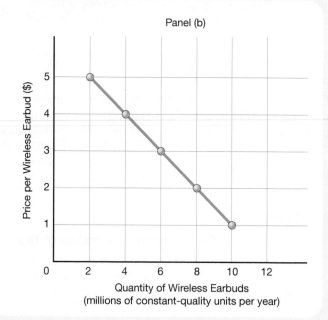

Panel (a)

Price per Constant-Quality Wireless Earbud	Total Quantity Demanded of Constant-Quality Wireless Earbuds per Year (millions)
$5	2
4	4
3	6
2	8
1	10

demand schedule, given in panel (a) of Figure 3-3, and a demand curve, given in panel (b). The quantity demanded is now measured in millions of units per year. Remember, panel (b) in Figure 3-3 shows the market demand curve for the millions of buyers of wireless earbuds. The "market" demand curve that we derived in Figure 3-2 was undertaken assuming that there were only two buyers in the entire market. That's why we assume that the "market" demand curve for two buyers in panel (d) of Figure 3-2 is not a smooth line, whereas the true market demand curve in panel (b) of Figure 3-3 is a smooth line with no kinks.

3.2 Distinguish between changes in demand and changes in quantity demanded

Shifts in Demand

Assume that the federal government gives every student registered in a college, university, or technical school in the United States a digital device that utilizes wireless earbuds. The demand curve presented in panel (b) of Figure 3-3 would no longer be an accurate representation of total market demand for wireless earbuds. What we have to do is shift the curve outward, or to the right, to represent the rise in demand that would result from this program. There will now be an increase in the number of wireless earbuds demanded at *each and every possible price*.

The demand curve shown in Figure 3-4 will shift from D_1 to D_2. Take any price, say, $3 per wireless earbud. Originally, before the federal government giveaway of digital devices, the amount demanded at $3 was 6 million wireless earbuds per year. After the government giveaway of digital devices, however, the new amount demanded at the $3 price is 10 million wireless earbuds per year. What we have seen is a shift in the demand for wireless earbuds.

Under different circumstances, the shift can also go in the opposite direction. What if colleges uniformly prohibited any of their students from using digital devices that utilize wireless earbuds? Such a regulation would cause a shift inward—to the left—of the demand curve for wireless earbuds. In Figure 3-4, the demand curve would shift to D_3. The quantity demanded would now be less at each and every possible price.

FIGURE 3-4 Shifts in the Demand Curve

If some factor other than price changes, we can show its effect by moving the entire demand curve, say, from D_1 to D_2. We have assumed in our example that this move was precipitated by the government's giving digital devices that utilize wireless earbuds to every registered college student in the United States. Thus, at *all* prices, a larger number of wireless earbuds would be demanded than before.

In contrast, curve D_3 represents reduced demand compared to curve D_1, caused by a prohibition of digital devices that utilize wireless earbuds on campus.

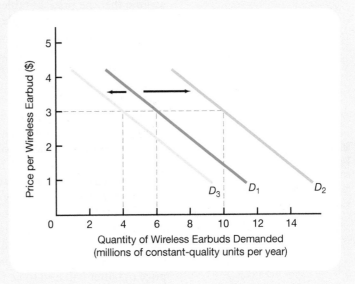

The Other Determinants of Demand

The demand curve in panel (b) of Figure 3-3 is drawn with other things held constant, specifically all of the other factors that determine how many wireless earbuds will be bought. There are many such determinants. We refer to these determinants as *ceteris paribus* **conditions,** and they include (1) consumers' incomes, (2) tastes and preferences, (3) the prices of related goods, (4) expectations regarding future prices and future incomes, and (5) market size (number of potential buyers). Let's examine each of these determinants more closely.

Income For most goods, an increase in income will lead to an increase in demand. That is, an increase in income will lead to a rightward shift in the position of the demand curve from, say, D_1 to D_2 in Figure 3-4. You can avoid confusion about shifts in curves by always relating a rise in demand to a rightward shift in the demand curve and a fall in demand to a leftward shift in the demand curve. Goods for which the demand rises when consumer income rises are called **normal goods.** Most goods, such as shoes, smartphones, and wireless earbuds, are "normal goods." For some goods, however, demand *falls* as income rises. These are called **inferior goods.** Beans might be an example. As households get richer, they tend to purchase fewer and fewer beans and purchase more and more fish. (The terms *normal* and *inferior* are merely part of the economist's specialized vocabulary. No value judgments are associated with them.)

Remember, a shift to the left in the demand curve represents a decrease in demand, and a shift to the right represents an increase in demand.

Tastes and Preferences A change in consumer tastes in favor of a good can shift its demand curve outward to the right. When extra-large, plastic-rimmed glasses became the rage a decade ago, the demand curve for them shifted outward to the right. When the rage died out, the demand curve shifted inward to the left. Fashions depend to a large extent on people's tastes and preferences. Economists have little to say about the determination of tastes. That is, they don't have any "good" theories of taste determination or why people buy one brand of product rather than others. (Advertisers, however, have various theories they use to try to cause consumers to prefer their products over those of competitors.)

Prices of Related Goods: Substitutes and Complements Demand schedules are always drawn with the prices of all other commodities held constant. That is to say, when

Ceteris paribus **conditions**
Determinants of the relationship between price and quantity that are unchanged along a curve. Changes in these factors cause the curve to shift.

Normal goods
Goods for which demand rises as income rises. Most goods are normal goods.

Inferior goods
Goods for which demand falls as income rises.

deriving a given demand curve, we assume that only the price of the good under study changes. For example, when we draw the demand curve for laptop computers, we assume that the price of tablet devices is held constant. When we draw the demand curve for home cinema speakers, we assume that the price of surround-sound amplifiers is held constant. When we refer to *related goods*, we are talking about goods for which demand is interdependent. If a change in the price of one good shifts the demand for another good, those two goods have interdependent demands.

There are two types of demand interdependencies: those in which goods are *substitutes* and those in which goods are *complements*. We can define and distinguish between substitutes and complements in terms of how the change in price of one commodity affects the demand for its related commodity.

Substitutes
Two goods are substitutes when a change in the price of one causes a shift in demand for the other in the same direction as the price change.

Butter and margarine are **substitutes.** Either can be consumed to satisfy the same basic want. Let's assume that both products originally cost $2 per pound. If the price of butter remains the same and the price of margarine falls from $2 per pound to $1 per pound, people will buy more margarine and less butter. The demand curve for butter shifts inward to the left. If, conversely, the price of margarine rises from $2 per pound to $3 per pound, people will buy more butter and less margarine. The demand curve for butter shifts outward to the right. In other words, an increase in the price of margarine will lead to an increase in the demand for butter, and an increase in the price of butter will lead to an increase in the demand for margarine.

For substitutes, a change in the price of a substitute will cause a change in demand **in the same direction.**

How has a significant decrease in the price of solar energy in China affected the demand for coal?

INTERNATIONAL EXAMPLE

In China, Lower-Priced Solar Energy Puts a Damper on the Demand for Coal

In recent decades, China's energy firms have consumed ever-larger quantities of coal to generate the energy required for the nation's substantial population and growing industries. During the past ten years, however, the prices of solar cells and panels that can be used to produce energy have plummeted. As a result, firms have substituted in favor of solar power as a source of energy. Over recent years, China's total consumption of coal, a key substitute item used to produce energy, has declined at a rate exceeding 4 percent per year.

FOR CRITICAL THINKING

What has happened to the position of China's market demand curve for coal? Explain briefly.

Sources are listed at the end of this chapter.

Complements
Two goods are complements when a change in the price of one causes an opposite shift in the demand for the other.

For **complements,** goods typically consumed together, the situation is reversed. Consider digital devices and online applications (apps). We draw the demand curve for apps with the price of digital devices held constant. If the price per constant-quality unit of digital devices decreases from, say, $500 to $300, that will encourage more people to purchase apps. They will now buy more apps, at any given app price, than before. The demand curve for apps will shift outward to the right. If, by contrast, the price of digital devices increases from $250 to $450, fewer people will purchase downloadable applications. The demand curve for apps will shift inward to the left.

To summarize, a decrease in the price of digital devices leads to an increase in the demand for apps. An increase in the price of digital devices leads to a decrease in the demand for apps.

Thus, for complements, a change in the price of a product will cause a change in demand **in the opposite direction** *for the other good.*

Expectations Consumers' expectations regarding future prices and future incomes will prompt them to buy more or less of a particular good without a change in its current money price. For example, consumers getting wind of a scheduled 100 percent increase in the price of wireless earbuds next month will buy more of them today at today's prices. Today's demand curve for wireless earbuds will shift from D_1 to D_2 in Figure 3-4. The opposite would occur if a decrease in the price of wireless earbuds was scheduled for next month (from D_1 to D_3).

Expectations of a rise in income may cause consumers to want to purchase more of everything today at today's prices. Again, such a change in expectations of higher future income will cause a shift in the demand curve from D_1 to D_2 in Figure 3-4.

Finally, expectations that goods will not be available at any price will induce consumers to stock up now, increasing current demand.

Market Size (Number of Potential Buyers) An increase in the number of potential buyers (holding buyers' incomes constant) at any given price shifts the market demand curve outward. Conversely, a reduction in the number of potential buyers at any given price shifts the market demand curve inward.

Changes in Demand versus Changes in Quantity Demanded

We have made repeated references to demand and to quantity demanded. It is important to realize that there is a difference between a *change in demand* and a *change in quantity demanded*.

Demand refers to a schedule of planned rates of purchase and depends on a great many *ceteris paribus* conditions, such as incomes, expectations, and the prices of substitutes or complements. Whenever there is a change in a *ceteris paribus* condition, there will be a change in demand—a shift in the entire demand curve to the right or to the left.

A *quantity demanded* is a specific quantity at a specific price, represented by a single point on a demand curve. When price changes, quantity demanded changes according to the law of demand, and there will be a movement from one point to another along the same demand curve. Look at Figure 3-5. At a price of $3 per wireless earbud, 6 million wireless earbuds per year are demanded. If the price falls to $1, quantity demanded increases to 10 million per year. This movement occurs because the current market price for the product changes. In Figure 3-5, you can see the arrow pointing down the given demand curve D.

FIGURE 3-5

Movement along a Given Demand Curve

A change in price changes the quantity of a good demanded. This can be represented as movement along a given demand schedule. If, in our example, the price of wireless earbuds falls from $3 to $1 apiece, the quantity demanded will increase from 6 million to 10 million wireless earbuds per year.

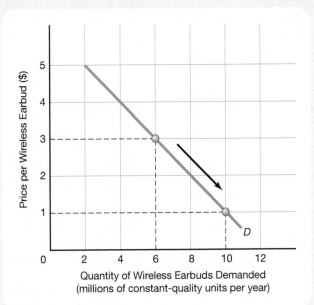

When you think of demand, think of the entire curve. Quantity demanded, in contrast, is represented by a single point on the demand curve.

A change or shift in demand is a movement of the entire curve. The only thing that can cause the entire curve to move is a change in a determinant other than the good's own price.

In economic analysis, we cannot emphasize too much the following distinction that must constantly be made:

A change in a good's own price leads to a change in quantity demanded for any given demand curve, other things held constant. This is a **movement** along *the curve.*

A change in any of the ceteris paribus *conditions for demand leads to a change in demand. This is a* **shift** *of the curve.*

In light of the numerous potential determinants of the demand for travel services, how might application of data-analytics techniques assist in predicting the position of the market demand curve for such a commodity?

 AI | DECISION MAKING THROUGH DATA

The Global Tourism Industry

The demand for tourism services within a nation depends, of course, on the prices of such services. Other determinants include the tourists' incomes, their tastes and preferences, prices of complements such as transportation services within a nation, prices of substitute items, and expectations of future prices of tourism services.

In addition, a fundamental *ceteris paribus* condition that ultimately influences the overall market demand for tourism services is the number of tourists who choose to visit that nation during a given period of time. Indeed, the starting point for predicting the position of the market demand curve for a nation's tourism services is to develop a prediction of the number of tourist arrivals to that nation. Global arrivals of international tourists have increased by 4,000 percent during the past sixty years. Automated collection of substantial data regarding elements that have influenced people to choose particular countries to visit has improved the accuracy of estimates of demands for tourism services within given intervals. Such estimates assist businesses and governments that provide tourist services in deciding how to allocate resources in advance of tourists' arrivals.

FOR CRITICAL THINKING

Once the predicted position of the demand for tourism services has been determined, would an anticipated increase in the incomes of tourists generate a movement along that curve or a shift in the position of the curve?

Sources are listed at the end of this chapter.

3.3 Explain the law of supply

Supply
A schedule showing the relationship between price and quantity supplied for a specified period of time, other things being equal.

Law of supply
The observation that the higher the price of a good, the more of that good sellers will make available over a specified time period, other things being equal.

Supply

The other side of the basic model in economics involves the quantities of goods and services that firms will offer for sale to the market. The **supply** of any good or service is the amounts that firms will produce and offer for sale under certain conditions during a specified time period.

The Law of Supply

The relationship between price and quantity supplied, called the **law of supply,** can be summarized as follows:

At higher prices, a larger quantity will generally be supplied than at lower prices, all other things held constant. At lower prices, a smaller quantity will generally be supplied than at higher prices, all other things held constant.

There is usually a direct relationship between price and quantity supplied. As the price rises, the quantity supplied rises. As the price falls, the quantity supplied falls in response. Producers are normally willing to produce and sell more of their product at a higher price than at a lower price, other things being constant. At $5 per wireless earbud, manufacturers would almost certainly be willing to supply a larger quantity than at $1 per wireless earbud, assuming, of course, that no other prices in the economy had changed. (See Figure 3-6.)

As with the law of demand, millions of instances in the real world have given us confidence in the law of supply. On a theoretical level, the law of supply is based on a model in which producers and sellers seek to make the most gain possible from their activities. For example, as a manufacturer attempts to produce more and more wireless earbuds over the same time period, it will eventually have to hire more workers, pay overtime wages (which are higher), and more heavily utilize its machines. Only if offered a higher price per wireless earbud will the manufacturer be willing to incur these higher costs. That is why the law of supply implies a direct relationship between price and quantity supplied.

The Supply Schedule

Just as we were able to construct a demand schedule, we can construct a *supply schedule*, which is a table relating prices to the quantity supplied at each price. A supply schedule can also be referred to simply as *supply*. It is a set of planned production rates that depends on the price of the product. We show the individual supply schedule for a hypothetical producer in panel (a) of Figure 3-6. At a price of $1 per wireless earbud, for example, this producer will supply 20,000 wireless earbuds per year. At a price of $5 per wireless earbud, this producer will supply 55,000 wireless earbuds per year.

Supply curve
The graphical representation of the supply schedule; a line (curve) showing the supply schedule, which generally slopes upward (has a positive slope), other things being equal.

The Supply Curve We can convert the supply schedule from panel (a) of Figure 3-6 into a **supply curve,** just as we earlier created a demand curve in Figure 3-1. All we do

---

The Individual Producer's Supply Schedule and Supply Curve for Wireless Earbuds

Panel (a) shows that at higher prices, a hypothetical supplier will be willing to provide a greater quantity of wireless earbuds. We plot the various price-quantity combinations in panel (a) on the grid in panel (b).

When we connect these points, we create the individual supply curve for wireless earbuds. It is positively sloped.

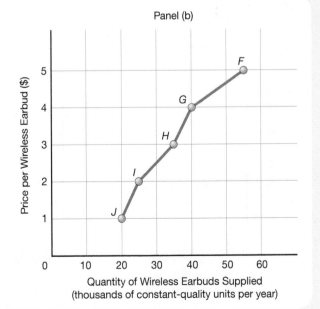

Panel (a)

Combination	Price per Constant-Quality Wireless Earbud	Quantity of Wireless Earbuds Supplied (thousands of constant-quality units per year)
F	$5	55
G	4	40
H	3	35
I	2	25
J	1	20

is take the price-quantity combinations from panel (a) of Figure 3-6 and plot them in panel (b). We have labeled these combinations *F* through *J*. Connecting these points, we obtain an upward-sloping curve that shows the typically direct relationship between price and quantity supplied. Again, we have to remember that we are talking about quantity supplied *per year*, measured in constant-quality units.

The Market Supply Curve Just as we summed the individual demand curves to obtain the market demand curve, we sum the individual producers' supply curves to obtain the market supply curve. Look at Figure 3-7, in which we horizontally sum two typical supply curves for manufacturers of wireless earbuds. Supplier 1's data are taken from Figure 3-6. Supplier 2 is added. The numbers are presented in panel (a). The graphical representation of supplier 1 is in panel (b), of supplier 2 in panel (c), and of the summation in panel (d). The result, then, is the supply curve for wireless earbuds for suppliers 1 and 2.

We assume that there are more suppliers of wireless earbuds, however. The total market supply schedule and total market supply curve for wireless earbuds are represented in Figure 3-8, with the curve in panel (b) obtained by adding all of the supply curves, such as those shown in panels (b) and (c) of Figure 3-7. Notice the difference

---

FIGURE 3-7

Horizontal Summation of Supply Curves

In panel (a), we show the data for two individual suppliers of wireless earbuds. Adding how much each is willing to supply at different prices, we come up with the combined quantities supplied in column 4. When we plot the values in columns 2 and 3 on grids from panels (b) and (c) and add them horizontally, we obtain the combined supply curve for the two suppliers in question, shown in panel (d).

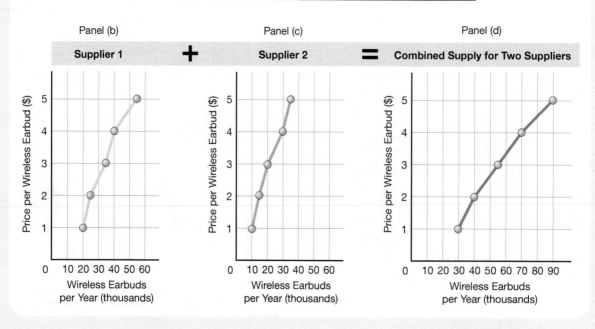

Panel (a)

(1) Price per Wireless Earbud	(2) Supplier 1's Quantity Supplied (thousands)	(3) Supplier 2's Quantity Supplied (thousands)	(4) = (2) + (3) Combined Quantity Supplied per Year (thousands)
$5	55	35	90
4	40	30	70
3	35	20	55
2	25	15	40
1	20	10	30

Panel (b) — **Supplier 1** **+** Panel (c) — **Supplier 2** **=** Panel (d) — **Combined Supply for Two Suppliers**

The Market Supply Schedule and the Market Supply Curve for Wireless Earbuds

In panel (a), we show the summation of all the individual producers' supply schedules. In panel (b), we graph the resulting supply curve.

It represents the market supply curve for wireless earbuds and is upward sloping.

Panel (a)

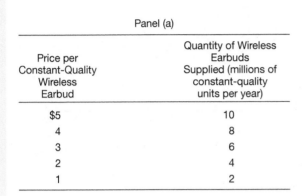

Price per Constant-Quality Wireless Earbud	Quantity of Wireless Earbuds Supplied (millions of constant-quality units per year)
$5	10
4	8
3	6
2	4
1	2

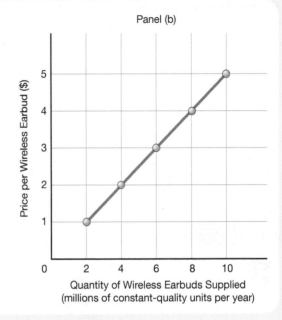

Panel (b)

Price per Wireless Earbud ($)

Quantity of Wireless Earbuds Supplied (millions of constant-quality units per year)

between the market supply curve with only two suppliers in Figure 3-6 and the one with many suppliers—the entire true market—in panel (b) of Figure 3-8. (For simplicity, we assume that the true total market supply curve is a straight line.)

Note what happens at the market level when price changes. If the price is $3, the quantity supplied is 6 million. If the price goes up to $4, the quantity supplied increases to 8 million per year. If the price falls to $2, the quantity supplied decreases to 4 million per year. Changes in quantity supplied are represented by movements along the supply curve in panel (b) of Figure 3-8.

Shifts in Supply

When we looked at demand, we found out that a change in anything relevant besides the price of the good or service caused the demand curve to shift inward or outward. The same is true for the supply curve. If something besides price changes and alters the willingness of suppliers to produce a good or service, we will see the entire supply curve shift.

Consider an example. There is a new method of manufacturing wireless earbuds that significantly reduces the cost of production. In this situation, producers of wireless earbuds will supply more product at *all* prices because their cost of so doing has fallen dramatically. Competition among manufacturers to produce more at each and every price will shift the supply curve outward to the right from S_1 to S_2 in Figure 3-9. At a price of $3, the number supplied was originally 6 million per year, but now the amount supplied (after the reduction in the costs of production) at $3 per wireless earbud will be 9 million a year. (This is similar to what has happened to the supply curve of digital devices in recent years as memory chip prices have fallen.)

Consider the opposite case. If the price of raw materials used in manufacturing wireless earbuds increases, the supply curve in Figure 3-9 will shift from S_1 to S_3. At each and every price, the quantity of wireless earbuds supplied will fall due to the increase in the price of raw materials.

3.4 Distinguish between changes in supply and changes in quantity supplied

FIGURE 3-9

Shifts in the Supply Curve

If the cost of producing wireless earbuds were to fall dramatically, the supply curve would shift rightward from S_1 to S_2 such that at all prices, a larger quantity would be forthcoming from suppliers.

In contrast, if the cost of production rose, the supply curve would shift leftward to S_3.

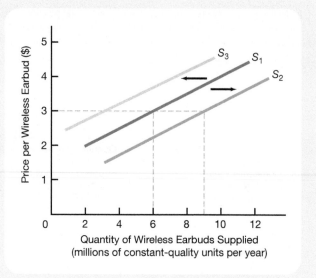

The Other Determinants of Supply

When a supply curve is drawn, only the price of the good in question changes, and it is assumed that other things remain constant. The other things assumed constant are the *ceteris paribus* conditions of supply. They include (1) technology and productivity, (2) the prices of resources (inputs) used to produce the product, (3) producers' price expectations, (4) taxes and subsidies, and (5) the number of firms in the industry. If *any* of these *ceteris paribus* conditions changes, there will be a shift in the supply curve.

Technology and Productivity A supply curve is drawn by assuming a given technology, or "state of the art." When the available production techniques change, the supply curve will shift. For example, when a better production technique for wireless earbuds becomes available, production costs will decrease, and the supply curve will shift to the right. A larger quantity will be forthcoming at each and every price because the cost of production is lower.

How has a technological improvement in the process of designing and manufacturing necklaces, bracelets, and earrings affected the supply of jewelry?

EXAMPLE

Technological Change Boosts Supply in the Jewelry Market

Crafting a piece of jewelry traditionally has been a highly labor-intensive process. Jewelers have applied years of training to the construction of pieces that exuded unique forms of rare beauty. Crafting a single piece of jewelry often required many weeks of careful thought and effort.

Recently, jewelers have discovered additive manufacturing—also known as "3D printing"—which involves using information technologies to guide machines that form products layer by layer. Utilizing this technique has fundamentally altered the economics of jewelry construction. Employees of a firm that utilizes such technology can design within a few days a piece of jewelry using an app powered by a digital device. Once that task is completed, however, printing each copy requires less than an hour.

A slight redesign usually requires a few more hours of time on the digital device, and then more copies can be printed. Not surprisingly, utilization of additive technology now is enabling the production of many more pieces of jewelry per year at any given price than was feasible in the past. As a consequence, the supply within the jewelry market has increased.

FOR CRITICAL THINKING

In what direction has the supply curve in the global jewelry market shifted? Explain briefly.

Sources are listed at the end of this chapter.

Prices of Inputs Used to Produce the Product If one or more input prices fall, production costs fall, and the supply curve will shift outward to the right. That is, more will be supplied at each and every price. The opposite will be true if one or more inputs become more expensive. For example, when we draw the supply curve of new tablet devices, we are holding the price of microprocessors (and other inputs) constant. When we draw the supply curve of blue jeans, we are holding the cost of cotton fabric fixed.

Price Expectations A change in the expectation of a future relative price of a product can affect a producer's current willingness to supply, just as price expectations affect a consumer's current willingness to purchase. For example, suppliers of wireless earbuds may withhold from the market part of their current supply if they anticipate higher prices in the future. The current amount supplied at each and every price will decrease.

WHAT HAPPENS WHEN...

both sellers **and** buyers anticipate that the price of an item will increase in the future?

When sellers expect that the price of the item they offer for sale in the market will rise in the future, they reduce the amount that they make available for sale today, and so supply decreases. At the same time, as discussed earlier in the chapter, buyers who also anticipate a higher price of that item will seek to purchase more units of the item today, and so demand increases. Thus, the market supply curve will shift leftward, and simultaneously the market demand curve will shift rightward.

Taxes and Subsidies Certain taxes, such as a per-unit tax, are effectively an addition to production costs and therefore reduce supply. If the supply curve is S_1 in Figure 3-8, a per-unit tax increase would shift it to S_3. A per-unit **subsidy** would do the opposite. Every producer would get a "gift" from the government for each unit produced. This per-unit subsidy would shift the curve to S_2.

Subsidy
A negative tax; a payment to a producer from the government, usually in the form of a cash grant per unit.

Number of Firms in the Industry In the short run, when firms can change only the number of employees they use, we hold the number of firms in the industry constant. In the long run, the number of firms may change. If the number of firms increases, supply will increase, and the supply curve will shift outward to the right. If the number of firms decreases, supply will decrease, and the supply curve will shift inward to the left.

Changes in Supply versus Changes in Quantity Supplied

We cannot overstress the importance of distinguishing between a movement along the supply curve—which occurs only when the price changes along a given supply curve—and a shift in the supply curve—which occurs only with changes in *ceteris paribus* conditions. A change in the price of the good in question always (and only) brings about a change in the quantity supplied along a given supply curve. We move to a different point on the existing supply curve. This is specifically called a *change in quantity supplied*. When price changes, quantity supplied changes—there is a movement from one point to another along the same supply curve.

When you think of *supply*, think of the entire curve. Quantity supplied is represented by a single point on the supply curve.

> *A change, or shift, in supply is a movement of the entire curve. The only thing that can cause the entire curve to move is a change in one of the* **ceteris paribus** *conditions.*

Consequently,

> *A change in price leads to a change in the quantity supplied, other things being constant. This is a* **movement along** *the curve.*

> *A change in any* **ceteris paribus** *condition for supply leads to a change in supply. This is a* **shift** *of the curve.*

3.5 Understand how the interaction of demand and supply determines the equilibrium price and quantity

Putting Demand and Supply Together

In the sections on demand and supply, we tried to confine each discussion to demand or supply only. You have probably already realized, however, that we can't view the world just from the demand side or just from the supply side. There is interaction between the two. In this section, we will discuss how they interact and how that interaction determines the prices that prevail in our economy and other economies in which the forces of demand and supply are allowed to work.

Let's first combine the demand and supply schedules and then combine the curves.

Demand and Supply Schedules Combined

Let's place panel (a) from Figure 3-3 (the market demand schedule) and panel (a) from Figure 3-8 (the market supply schedule) together in panel (a) of Figure 3-10. Column 1 displays the price. Column 2 shows the quantity supplied per year at any given price. Column 3 displays the quantity demanded. Column 4 is the difference between columns 2 and 3, or the difference between the quantity supplied and the quantity demanded. In column 5, we label those differences as either excess quantity supplied (called a *surplus*, which we shall discuss shortly) or excess quantity demanded (commonly known as a *shortage*, also discussed shortly).

For example, at a price of $1, only 2 million wireless earbuds would be supplied, but the quantity demanded would be 10 million. The difference would be 8 million, which we label excess quantity demanded (a shortage). At the other end, a price of $5 would elicit 10 million in quantity supplied. Quantity demanded would drop to 2 million, leaving a difference of +8 million units, which we call excess quantity supplied (a surplus).

Now, do you notice something special about the price of $3? At that price, both the quantity supplied and the quantity demanded per year are 6 million. The difference, then, is zero. There is neither excess quantity demanded (shortage) nor excess quantity supplied (surplus). Hence the price of $3 is very special. It is called the **market clearing price**—it clears the market of all excess quantities demanded or supplied. There are no willing consumers who want to pay $3 per wireless earbud but are turned away by sellers, and there are no willing suppliers who want to sell wireless earbuds at $3 who cannot sell all they want at that price. Another term for the market clearing price is the *equilibrium price*, the price at which there is no tendency for change. Consumers are able to get all they want at that price, and suppliers are able to sell all they want at that price.

Market clearing, or equilibrium, price
The price that clears the market, at which quantity demanded equals quantity supplied; the price where the demand curve intersects the supply curve.

Equilibrium

We can define **equilibrium** in general as a point at which quantity demanded equals quantity supplied at a particular price. There tends to be no movement of the price or the quantity away from this point unless demand or supply changes. Any movement away from this point will set into motion forces that will cause movement back to it. Therefore, equilibrium is a stable point. Any point that is not an equilibrium is unstable and will not persist.

The equilibrium point occurs where the supply and demand curves intersect. The equilibrium price is given on the vertical axis directly to the left of where the supply and demand curves cross. The equilibrium quantity is given on the horizontal axis directly underneath the intersection of the demand and supply curves.

Panel (b) in Figure 3-3 and panel (b) in Figure 3-8 are combined as panel (b) in Figure 3-10. The demand curve is labeled D, the supply curve S. We have labeled the intersection of the supply curve with the demand curve as point E, for equilibrium. That corresponds to a market clearing price of $3, at which both the quantity supplied and the quantity demanded are 6 million units per year. There is neither excess quantity supplied nor excess quantity demanded. Point E, the equilibrium point, always occurs at the intersection of the supply and demand curves. This is the price *toward which* the market price will automatically tend to gravitate, because there is no outcome more advantageous than this price for both consumers and producers.

Equilibrium
The situation in which quantity supplied equals quantity demanded at a particular price.

FIGURE 3-10

Putting Demand and Supply Together

In panel (a), we see that at the price of $3, the quantity supplied and the quantity demanded are equal, resulting in neither an excess quantity demanded nor an excess quantity supplied. We call this price the equilibrium, or market clearing, price. In panel (b), the intersection of the supply and demand curves is at *E*, at a price of $3 and a quantity of 6 million per year. At point *E*, there is neither an excess quantity demanded nor an excess quantity supplied. At a price of $1, the quantity supplied will be only 2 million per year, but the quantity demanded will be 10 million. The difference is excess quantity demanded at a price of $1. The price will rise, so we will move from point *A* up the supply curve and from point *B* up the demand curve to point *E*. At the other extreme, a price of $5 elicits a quantity supplied of 10 million but a quantity demanded of only 2 million. The difference is excess quantity supplied at a price of $5. The price will fall, so we will move down the demand curve and the supply curve to the equilibrium price, $3 per wireless earbud.

Panel (a)

(1) Price per Constant-Quality Wireless Earbud	(2) Quantity Supplied (wireless earbuds per year)	(3) Quantity Demanded (wireless earbuds per year)	(4) Difference (2) – (3) (wireless earbuds per year)	(5) Condition
$5	10 million	2 million	8 million	Excess quantity supplied (surplus)
4	8 million	4 million	4 million	Excess quantity supplied (surplus)
3	6 million	6 million	0	Market clearing price—equilibrium (no surplus, no shortage)
2	4 million	8 million	–4 million	Excess quantity demanded (shortage)
1	2 million	10 million	–8 million	Excess quantity demanded (shortage)

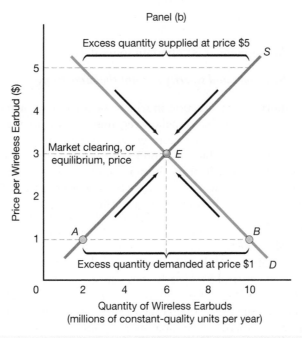

Panel (b)

Quantity of Wireless Earbuds
(millions of constant-quality units per year)

Shortages

The price of $3 depicted in Figure 3-10 arises in a situation of equilibrium. If there were a non-market-clearing, or disequilibrium, price, this price would put into play forces that would cause the price to change toward the market clearing price, at which equilibrium would again be sustained.

Shortage
A situation in which quantity demanded is greater than quantity supplied at a price below the market clearing price.

Look again at panel (b) in Figure 3-10. Suppose that instead of being at the equilibrium price of $3, for some reason the market price is $1. At this price, the quantity demanded of 10 million per year exceeds the quantity supplied of 2 million per year. We have an excess quantity demanded at the price of $1. This is usually called a **shortage.** Consumers of wireless earbuds would find that they could not buy all they wished at $1 apiece. Forces, though, will cause the price to rise: Competing consumers will bid up the price, and suppliers will increase output in response. (Remember, some buyers would pay $5 or more rather than do without wireless earbuds.) We would move from points *A* and *B* toward point *E*. The process would stop when the price again reached $3 per wireless earbud.

Why have vegetable prices increased in Britain?

INTERNATIONAL EXAMPLE

A British Vegetable Shortage Has Predictable Effects on Vegetable Prices

In a recent year, a heat wave in Britain resulted in sharp reductions in quantities supplied at initially prevailing prices of most vegetables. Because quantities supplied were smaller than quantities demanded at those prices, vegetable shortages emerged across Britain.

The effects of these shortages on prices were in accord with economic theory. Over a 12-month interval, the average price increases for selected vegetables were as follows: broccoli, 37 percent; cauliflower, 81 percent; carrots, 55 percent; lettuce, 22 percent; and onions, 55 percent. Thus, the vegetable shortages brought about higher equilibrium prices.

FOR CRITICAL THINKING

Once the prices of vegetables stopped rising and reached new market clearing levels, what must have been true of the relationship between quantities demanded and supplied in the affected British vegetable markets?

Sources are listed at the end of this chapter.

At this point, it is important to recall the following:

Shortages and scarcity are not the same thing.

A shortage is a situation in which the quantity demanded exceeds the quantity supplied at a price that somehow remains *below* the market clearing price. Our definition of scarcity was much more general and all-encompassing: a situation in which the resources available for producing output are insufficient to satisfy all wants. Any choice necessarily costs an opportunity, and the opportunity is lost. Hence, we will always live in a world of scarcity because we must constantly make choices, but we do not necessarily have to live in a world of shortages.

Surpluses

Surplus
A situation in which quantity supplied is greater than quantity demanded at a price above the market clearing price.

Now let's repeat the experiment with the market price at $5 rather than at the market clearing price of $3. Clearly, the quantity supplied will exceed the quantity demanded at that price. The result will be an excess quantity supplied at $5 per unit. This excess quantity supplied is often called a **surplus.** Given the curves in panel (b) in Figure 3-10, however, there will be forces pushing the price back down toward $3 per wireless earbud. Competing suppliers will cut prices and reduce output, and consumers will purchase more at these new lower prices. If the two forces of supply and demand are unrestricted, they will bring the price back to $3 per wireless earbud.

Shortages and surpluses are resolved in unfettered markets—markets in which price changes are free to occur. The forces that resolve them are those of competition: In the case of shortages, consumers competing for a limited quantity supplied drive up the price. In the case of surpluses, sellers compete for the limited quantity demanded, thus driving prices down to equilibrium. The equilibrium price is the only stable price, and the (unrestricted) market price tends to gravitate toward it.

ECONOMICS IN YOUR LIFE

Space-Constrained Restaurants Discover That Customers Care about Quality-Adjusted Lunch Prices

Blaine Hurst is the president of Panera Bread, a company that operates more than 2,000 small restaurants offering basic soup-and-sandwich meals to people taking short lunch or dinner breaks. Shortly after Hurst's appointment to his position, the quantity of restaurant lunches demanded decreased. Panera Bread was among many U.S. firms that consequently experienced a decline in sales.

Hurst quickly recognized that a fundamental problem was that customers of a typical Panera Bread outlet were spending lengthy intervals of time in lines to place orders at counters staffed by only a couple of employees. Naturally, the extra time that customers spend waiting in long lines is valuable to those consumers, so this waiting time had pushed up the quality-adjusted price of each meal. The result was a decrease in the quantity of restaurant lunches sold by the company.

Hurst responded by introducing self-order kiosks and an online facility for accepting remote digital orders. These innovations cut the average customer wait time at Panera Bread from 8 minutes to 1 minute. As a consequence, the total quantity of meals demanded by the company's customers increased.

FOR CRITICAL THINKING

Did the decline in the quality-adjusted price of soup-and-sandwich lunches offered by Panera Bread and other soup-and-salad restaurant chains generate a rightward shift in the demand curve or a downward movement along that curve? Explain.

REAL APPLICATION

As a future entrepreneur or manager, what lesson can you learn from the actions of this real-world manager?

Sources are listed at the end of this chapter.

ISSUES & APPLICATIONS

Explaining a Consumption Shift from Soft Drinks to Bottled Water: Tastes versus Relative Prices

CONCEPTS APPLIED

➤ *Ceteris Paribus* Conditions

➤ Tastes and Preferences

➤ Substitutes

In recent years, many media reporters and commentators have advanced the view that a change in one specific *ceteris paribus* condition accounts for observed changes in amounts consumed of two items that people frequently purchase and consume: bottled water and soft drinks. In doing so, these media analysts have ignored a change in another particularly important *ceteris paribus* condition that likely has been very relevant.

Falling Soft Drink Consumption and Rising Bottled-Water Consumption: The Usual Media Interpretation

As indicated in panel (a) of Figure 3-11, the per-person quantity of bottled water consumed has increased considerably since 2011. During the same period, the per-person quantity of soft drinks consumed has decreased. Indeed, in recent years the total annual U.S. purchase of bottled water has surpassed soft drink consumption. Hence, as shown in panel (a), the per-person quantity of bottled water consumed now exceeds the per-person quantity of soft drinks consumed.

Writers of media stories always point out these facts about the quantities of soft drinks and bottled water. Nearly all such stories also indicate that the reason for the altered purchases of the drinks surely involves a change in consumers' tastes and preferences. Consumers must have decided, media analysts argue, that bottled water is "more

Bottled Water versus Soft Drinks: Amounts Consumed and Index Measures of Money Prices

Panel (a) shows that since the beginning of the 2010 decade, purchases of bottled-water products increased at the same time that sales of soft drinks declined. Panel (b) indicates that over this period, the absolute price of soft drinks rose while the absolute price of bottled water decreased. The resulting decrease in the price of bottled water *relative to* soft drinks is an important element explaining the rise in bottled-water consumption and decrease in soft drink sales.

Sources: U.S. Department of Commerce; Bureau of Labor Statistics.

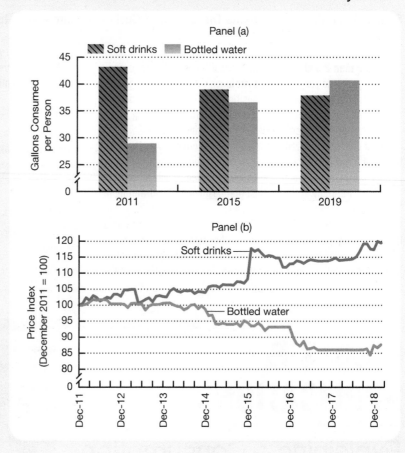

healthful" than soft drinks. This fact, the media analysts conclude, explains why the demand for bottled water has increased while the demand for soft drinks has decreased.

A Missing Element: A Decline in the Price of Bottled Water Relative to the Price of Soft Drinks

A key element that media reporters and commentators usually ignore in their coverage of changes in volumes of bottled water and soft drink purchases is the fact that many consumers undoubtedly regard bottled water and soft drinks as substitutes. Thus, a decrease in the price of bottled water relative to the price of soft drinks normally should be expected to induce consumers to substitute bottled water for soft drinks.

Panel (b) of Figure 3-11 displays index measures of the money prices of bottled water and soft drinks. Since 2011 the money price of bottled water generally has decreased, while the money price of soft drinks generally has increased. The more than 20 percent decline in the *relative*

price of bottled water since 2011 displayed in panel (b) surely has played an important role in explaining the rise in bottled-water consumption and fall in soft drink consumption shown in panel (a). Consumers' tastes and preferences regarding bottled water and soft drinks *might* have changed, but the decrease in the price of bottled water relative to soft drinks *definitely* did.

FOR CRITICAL THINKING

Why might economists find it harder to determine that the demand for an item has changed because of altered tastes and preferences than because of changes in the prices of substitutes? (*Hint:* Which is directly observable: market prices or people's tastes?)

REAL APPLICATION

Are there alternatives to bottled water that you, as a consumer, can purchase in a supermarket?

Sources are listed at the end of this chapter.

What You Should Know

LEARNING OBJECTIVES

3.1 **Explain the law of demand** *Other things being equal, individuals will purchase fewer units of a good at a higher price and will purchase more units at a lower price.*

3.2 **Distinguish between changes in demand and changes in quantity demanded** *The demand schedule shows quantities purchased at various possible prices. Graphically, the demand schedule is a downward-sloping demand curve. A change in the price generates a change in the quantity demanded, which is a movement along the demand curve. If any of the following ceteris paribus conditions of demand change, there is a change in demand, and the demand curve shifts to a new position: (1) income, (2) tastes and preferences, (3) the prices of related goods, (4) expectations, and (5) market size (the number of potential buyers).*

3.3 **Explain the law of supply** *According to the law of supply, sellers will produce and offer for sale more units of a good at a higher price, and they will produce and offer for sale fewer units of the good at a lower price.*

3.4 **Distinguish between changes in supply and changes in quantity supplied** *The supply schedule shows quantities produced and sold at various possible prices. On a graph, the supply schedule is a supply curve that slopes upward. A change in the price generates a change in the quantity supplied, which is a movement along the supply curve. If any of the following ceteris paribus conditions change, there is a change in supply, and the supply curve shifts to a new position: (1) input prices, (2) technology and productivity, (3) taxes and subsidies, (4) price expectations, and (5) the number of sellers.*

3.5 **Understand how the interaction of demand and supply determines the equilibrium price and quantity** *The equilibrium price of a good and the equilibrium quantity of the good that is produced and sold are determined by the intersection of the demand and supply curves. At this intersection point, the quantity demanded by buyers of the good just equals the quantity supplied by sellers, so there is neither an excess quantity of the good supplied (surplus) nor an excess quantity of the good demanded (shortage).*

KEY TERMS

market, 49
demand, 49
law of demand, 49
relative price, 50
money price, 50
demand curve, 52
market demand, 53
Key Figure
Figure 3-2, 53

ceteris paribus conditions, 55
normal goods, 55
inferior goods, 55
substitutes, 56
complements, 56
Key Figures
Figure 3-4, 55
Figure 3-5, 57

supply, 58
law of supply, 58
supply curve, 59
Key Figures
Figure 3-6, 59
Figure 3-7, 60

subsidy, 63
Key Figure
Figure 3-9, 62

market clearing, or
   equilibrium, price, 64
equilibrium, 64
shortage, 66
surplus, 66
Key Figure
Figure 3-11, 68

PROBLEMS

3-1. Suppose that in a recent market period, the following relationship existed between the price of tablet devices and the quantity supplied and quantity demanded.

Price	Quantity Demanded (Millions)	Quantity Supplied (Millions)
$330	100	40
$340	90	60
$350	80	80
$360	70	100
$370	60	120

Graph the supply and demand curves for tablet devices using the information in the table. What are the equilibrium price and quantity? If the industry price is $340, is there a shortage or surplus of tablet devices? How much is the shortage or surplus?

3-2. Suppose that in a later market period, the quantities supplied in the table in Problem 3-1 are unchanged. The amount demanded, however, has increased by 30 million at each price. Construct the resulting demand curve in the illustration you made for Problem 3-1. Is this an increase or a decrease in demand? What are the new equilibrium quantity and the new market price? Give two examples of changes in *ceteris paribus* conditions that might cause such a change.

3-3. Consider the market for cable-based Internet access service, which is a normal good. Explain whether the following events would cause an increase or a decrease in demand or an increase or a decrease in the quantity demanded.

   a. Firms providing wireless (an alternative to cable) Internet access services reduce their prices.

   b. Firms providing cable-based Internet access services reduce their prices.

   c. There is a decrease in the incomes earned by consumers of cable-based Internet access services.

   d. Consumers' tastes shift away from using wireless Internet access in favor of cable-based Internet access services.

3-4. In the market for wireless earbuds (a normal good), explain whether the following events would cause an increase or a decrease in demand or an increase or a decrease in the quantity demanded. Also explain what happens to the equilibrium quantity and the market clearing price.

   a. There is an increase in the price of carry cases for wireless earbuds.

   b. There is a decrease in the price of devices used to charge wireless earbuds.

   c. There is an increase in the number of consumers of wireless earbuds.

   d. A booming economy increases the income of the typical buyer of wireless earbuds.

   e. Consumers of wireless earbuds anticipate that the price of this good will decline in the future.

3-5. Give an example of a complement and a substitute in consumption for each of the following items.

   a. Bacon

   b. Tennis racquets

   c. Coffee

   d. Automobiles

3-6. Listed below are some changes in (shifts in) demand for various items. In each case, the change in demand has been caused by a change in the price of a substitute or of a complement. Explain whether the price of the substitute or complement must have increased or decreased.

   a. A rise in the demand for a dashboard global-positioning-system device follows a change in the price of automobiles, which are complements.

   b. A fall in the demand for e-book readers follows a change in the price of e-books, which are complements.

   c. A rise in the demand for tablet devices follows a change in the price of ultrathin laptop computers, which are substitutes.

   d. A fall in the demand for physical books follows a change in the price of e-books, which are substitutes.

3-7. Identify which of the following would generate an increase in the market demand for tablet devices, which are a normal good.

   a. A decrease in the incomes of consumers of tablet devices

   b. An increase in the price of ultrathin computers, which are substitutes

   c. An increase in the price of online apps, which are complements

   d. An increase in the number of consumers in the market for tablet devices

3-8. Identify which of the following would generate a decrease in the market demand for e-book readers, which are a normal good.

   a. An increase in the price of downloadable apps utilized to enhance the e-book reading experience, which are complements

   b. An increase in the number of consumers in the market for e-book readers

c. A decrease in the price of tablet devices, which are substitutes

d. A reduction in the incomes of consumers of e-book readers

3-9. Consider the following diagram of a market for one-bedroom rental apartments in a college community.

a. At a rental rate of $1,000 per month, is there an excess quantity supplied, or is there an excess quantity demanded? What is the amount of the excess quantity supplied or demanded?

b. If the present rental rate of one-bedroom apartments is $1,000 per month, through what mechanism will the rental rate adjust to the equilibrium rental rate of $800?

c. At a rental rate of $600 per month, is there an excess quantity supplied, or is there an excess quantity demanded? What is the amount of the excess quantity supplied or demanded?

d. If the present rental rate of one-bedroom apartments is $600 per month, through what mechanism will the rental rate adjust to the equilibrium rental rate of $800?

3-10. Consider the market for economics textbooks. Explain whether the following events would cause an increase or a decrease in supply or an increase or a decrease in the quantity supplied.

a. The market price of editorial services increases.

b. The market price of economics textbooks increases.

c. The number of publishers of economics textbooks increases.

d. Publishers expect that the market price of economics textbooks will increase next month.

3-11. Consider the market for smartphones. Explain whether the following events would cause an increase or a decrease in supply or an increase or a decrease in the quantity supplied. Illustrate each,

and show what would happen to the equilibrium quantity and the market clearing price.

a. The price of touch screens used in smartphones declines.

b. The price of machinery used to produce smartphones increases.

c. The number of manufacturers of smartphones increases.

d. There is a decrease in the market demand for smartphones.

3-12. If the price of flash memory chips used in manufacturing smartphones decreases, what will happen in the market for smartphones? How will the equilibrium price and equilibrium quantity of smartphones change?

3-13. Assume that the cost of aluminum used by soft drink companies increases. Which of the following correctly describes the resulting effects in the market for soft drinks distributed in aluminum cans? (More than one statement may be correct.)

a. The demand for soft drinks decreases.

b. The quantity of soft drinks demanded decreases.

c. The supply of soft drinks decreases.

d. The quantity of soft drinks supplied decreases.

3-14. In Figure 3-2, what are the effects of a price decrease from $4 per wireless earbud to $2 per wireless earbud on the quantities of wireless earbuds demanded by buyer 1 and by buyer 2 individually and combined?

3-15. In Figure 3-2, what are the effects of a price increase from $1 per wireless earbud to $3 per wireless earbud on the quantities demanded by buyer 1 and by buyer 2 individually and combined?

3-16. In Figure 3-4, the current position of the demand curve is D_1, and the price of a wireless earbud is $3. If there is an increase in the price of tablet devices that are complements to wireless earbuds, will the demand curve shift to D_2 or to D_3? What is the change in the amount of wireless earbuds demanded?

3-17. In Figure 3-4, the current position of the demand curve is D_1, and the price of a wireless earbud, which is a normal good, is $3. If there is an increase in consumer incomes, will the demand curve shift to D_2 or to D_3? What is the change in the amount of wireless earbuds demanded?

3-18. In Figure 3-7, what are the effects of a price decrease from $5 per wireless earbud to $3 per wireless earbud on the quantities supplied by supplier 1 and by supplier 2 individually and combined?

3-19. In Figure 3-7, what are the effects of a price increase from $2 per wireless earbud to $4 per wireless earbud on the quantities supplied by supplier 1 and by supplier 2 individually and combined?

3-20. In Figure 3-9, the current position of the supply curve is S_1, and the price of a wireless earbud is $3. If suppliers anticipate a higher price of wireless earbuds in the future, will the supply curve shift to S_2 or to S_3? What is the change in the amount of wireless earbuds supplied?

3-21. In Figure 3-9, the current position of the supply curve is S_1, and the price of a wireless earbud is $3. If the cost of inputs that suppliers utilize to produce wireless earbuds decreases, will the supply curve shift to S_2 or to S_3? What is the change in the amount of wireless earbuds supplied?

REFERENCES

EXAMPLE: The Soaring Relative Price of Restaurant Meals

Carmen Reinicke, "U.S. Restaurant Prices Jump the Most since 2011," *Bloomberg*, January 11, 2019.

"Here's How Much You Save by Cooking at Home," *Forbes*, June 10, 2018.

Jay Rayner, "If You Want to Eat Out, You Will Fork Out," *The Guardian*, March 15, 2018.

EXAMPLE: Assessing the Quality-Adjusted Prices of Old and New Concert Violins

"25 Best Violin Reviews," CMuse.org (https://www.cmuse.org/best-violin/), 2019.

Ian Sample, "Scientists Find Secret behind Sweet Sound of Stradivarius Violins," *Guardian*, May 21, 2018.

Tom Whipple, "Stradivarius Violins Really Do Have a Sweet Voice," *The Times*, May 22, 2018.

BEHAVIORAL EXAMPLE: Why Pay-What-You-Want Pricing Often Pays Off for Charitable Organizations

Sarah Gonzalez, "The Pay-What-You Want Experiment," National Public Radio Planet Money (https://www.npr.org/sections/money/2019/01/18/686665609/episode-889-the-pay-what-you-want-experiment), January 18, 2019.

Bruce Seaman, "Static and Dynamic Pricing Strategies: How Unique for Nonprofits?" In *Handbook of Research on Nonprofit Economics and Management*, Edited by Bruce Seaman and Dennis Young, 2nd Edition, Edward Elgar, Chapter 10, 2018.

Matthias Grieff and Henrik Egbert, "A Review of the Empirical Evidence on Pay-What-You-Want Pricing," *Economic and Business Review*, 2018.

INTERNATIONAL EXAMPLE: In China, Lower-Priced Solar Energy Puts a Damper on the Demand for Coal

"China Coal Imports Markets, 2012–2018 and 2019–2023," PRNewswire (https://www.prnewswire.com/news-releases/china-coal-imports-markets-2012-2018--2019-2023-300780871.html), January 18, 2019.

E. A. Crunden, "As United States Looks to Coal, China Invests in Renewable Energy," *Think Progress*, April 26, 2018.

Leanna Garfield, "China's Latest Energy Megaprojects Show That Coal Is Really on the Way Out," *Business Insider*, May 9, 2018.

AI—DECISION MAKING THROUGH DATA: The Global Tourism Industry

Shaolong Sun, Yunjie Wei, Kwok-Leung Tsui, and Shouyang Wang, "Forecasting Tourist Arrivals with Machine Learning and Internet Index Search," *Tourism Management*, 2019.

Oscar Claveria, Enric Monte, and Salvador Torra, "A Regional Perspective on the Accuracy of Machine Learning Forecasts of Tourism Demand Based on Data Characteristics," AQR Working Paper 201802, University of Barcelona, April 2018.

Saikumar Talari, "Envisioning Tourist Demand with Big Data," *Smart Data Collective*, April 6, 2018.

EXAMPLE: Technological Change Boosts Supply in the Jewelry Market

Jeff Graham, "What's the Difference between Synthetic, Simulated, and Created Gemstones?" International Gem Society (https://www.gemsociety.org/article/just-ask-jeff-what-is-the-difference-between-man-made-created-and-synthetic-materials/), 2019.

Ella Maclin, "The Effects of Modern Technology on the Jewelry Industry, *Thrive Global*, June 28, 2018.

Tracey Welson-Rossman, "3D Printing Poised to Revolutionize the Fashion Industry," *Forbes*, February 7, 2018.

INTERNATIONAL EXAMPLE: A British Vegetable Shortage Has Predictable Effects on Vegetable Prices

Kimberly Amadeo, "Why Food Prices Are Rising," *The Balance* (https://www.thebalance.com/why-are-food-prices-rising-causes-of-food-price-inflation-3306099), February 1, 2019

Sarah Butler, "Heatwave Pushes up U.K. Vegetable Prices as Yields Fall," *Guardian*, July 27, 2018.

"Vegetable Shortage Threatens Traditional Roast," *The Week*, July 16, 2018.

ECONOMICS IN YOUR LIFE: Space-Constrained Restaurants Discover That Customers Care about Quality-Adjusted Lunch Prices

"Rapid Pick-Up," Panera Bread (https://delivery.panerabread.com/menu/category/24), 2019.

Christopher Hall, "Kiosk Trailblazer Panera Bread Tapped as ICX Influencer of the Year," *Retail Customer Experience*, June 19, 2018.

Judy Motti, "Panera Bread, Wayfair Reap Benefits from Technologies That Enhance the Customer Experience," Kioskmarketplace.com (https://www.kioskmarketplace.com/articles/panera-wayfair-reap-benefits-from-technologies-that-enhance-the-customer-experience/), February 19, 2018.

ISSUES & APPLICATIONS: Explaining a Consumption Shift from Soft Drinks to Bottled Water: Tastes versus Relative Prices

"Consumers' Preferences for Bottled Water Is Growing," International Bottled Water Association (https://globenewswire.com/news-release/2019/01/08/1682157/0/en/Consumers-preference-for-bottled-water-is-growing-and-they-want-it-available-wherever-drinks-are-sold.html), January 8, 2019.

Kate Taylor, "People Are Drinking Less Pepsi and Coke Than Ever—And It Reveals the Power of the 'Biggest Marketing Trick of the Century,'" *Business Insider*, May 7, 2018.

Rachel Arthur, "'Bottled Water Is America's Favorite Drink!' Bottled Water Takes Top Spot in United States," *Beverage Daily*, June 1, 2018.

4 Extensions of Demand and Supply Analysis

Science History Images/Alamy Stock Photo

LEARNING OBJECTIVES

After reading this chapter, you should be able to:

4.1 Discuss the essential features of the price system

4.2 Evaluate the effects of changes in demand and supply on the market price and equilibrium quantity

4.3 Understand the rationing function of prices

4.4 Explain the effects of price ceilings

4.5 Explain the effects of price floors and government-imposed quantity restrictions

To restrict the overall rate of increase in prices of U.S. pharmaceuticals, the U.S. government sometimes intervenes in drug markets by placing upper limits, called *price ceilings*, on medication prices. For reasons you will learn about in this chapter, the consequence is that many of these markets experience periodic sustained shortages. When many consumers cannot obtain prescribed medications because of these shortages, their physicians often adjust by prescribing replacement drugs that perform similar functions. A common result of these adjustments to government-induced shortages of various medications, it turns out, is higher market clearing prices for the drugs that physicians prescribe as replacements. In this chapter, you will learn why this occurs.

DID YOU KNOW THAT...

in most U.S. cities during the past few years, construction of new middle-priced apartment units has lagged behind demolitions of old units, which has created significant shortages of apartments in the middle price range? In most regions that have experienced these shortages, apartment rental rates have risen considerably. As a consequence, the quantity of apartments demanded has declined, and shortages have diminished. In some areas, however, legally binding *price ceilings* prevent rental rates from increasing in response to an excess of quantity demanded over quantity supplied. The consequence has been that substantial shortages of middle-priced apartments have persisted.

What effects can a price ceiling have on the availability and consumption of a good or service? As you will learn in this chapter, we can use supply and demand analysis to answer this question. You will find that when a government sets a ceiling below the equilibrium price, the result will be a shortage. Similarly, you will learn how we can use supply and demand analysis to examine the "surplus" of various agricultural products, the "shortage" of gasoline in certain countries, and many other phenomena. All of these examples are part of our economy, which we characterize as a *price system*.

4.1 Discuss the essential features of the price system

Price system
An economic system in which relative prices are constantly changing to reflect changes in supply and demand for different commodities. The prices of those commodities are signals to everyone within the system as to what is relatively scarce and what is relatively abundant.

The Price System and Markets

In a **price system,** otherwise known as a *market system,* relative prices are constantly changing to reflect changes in supply and demand for different commodities. The prices of those commodities are the signals to everyone within the price system as to what is relatively scarce and what is relatively abundant. In this sense, prices provide information.

Indeed, it is the *signaling* aspect of the price system that provides the information to buyers and sellers about what should be bought and what should be produced. In a price system, there is a clear-cut chain of events in which any changes in demand and supply cause changes in prices that in turn affect the opportunities that businesses and individuals have for profit and personal gain. Such changes influence our use of resources.

Exchange and Markets

Voluntary exchange
An act of trading, done on a mutually agreed basis, in which both parties to the trade expect to be better off after the exchange.

The price system features **voluntary exchange,** acts of trading between individuals that make both parties to the trade subjectively better off. The prices we pay for the desired items are determined by the interaction of the forces underlying supply and demand. In our economy, exchanges take place voluntarily in markets. A market encompasses the exchange arrangements of both buyers and sellers that underlie the forces of supply and demand. Indeed, one definition of a market is that it is a low-cost institution for facilitating exchange. A market increases incomes by helping resources move to their highest-valued uses.

Transaction Costs

Transaction costs
All of the costs associated with exchange, including the informational costs of finding out the price and quality, service record, and durability of a product, plus the cost of contracting and enforcing that contract.

Individuals turn to markets because markets reduce the cost of exchanges. These costs are sometimes referred to as **transaction costs,** which are broadly defined as the costs associated with finding out exactly what is being transacted as well as the cost of enforcing contracts. If you were Robinson Crusoe and lived alone on an island, you would never incur a transaction cost. For everyone else, transaction costs are just as real as the costs of production. Today, high-speed networks have allowed us to reduce transaction costs by increasing our ability to process information and keep records.

Consider some simple examples of transaction costs. A club warehouse such as Sam's Club or Costco reduces the transaction costs of having to go to numerous specialty stores to obtain the items you desire. Financial institutions, such as commercial banks, have reduced the transaction costs of directing funds from savers to borrowers.

In general, the more organized the market, the lower the transaction costs. Among those who constantly attempt to lower transaction costs are the much-maligned middlemen.

Is there any evidence that transaction costs slow adjustments of prices from one market clearing level to another?

AI | DECISION MAKING THROUGH DATA

Transaction Costs and "Price Stickiness"

Over the years, many people in business and a number of observers of markets have argued that the presence of various transaction costs can slow adjustments of prices to final equilibrium levels. The result, they contend, has been that prices can tend to be "sticky"—that is, slow to adjust to their final market clearing values.

Alberto Cavallo of the Massachusetts Institute of Technology has sought to evaluate this argument. He has utilized data-analytics techniques to study data that companies' physical cash-register scanners and online systems automatically collect regarding prices of more than 250,000 individual products sold by 181 retailers in 31 nations. All told, Cavallo examined more than *60 million* different prices that firms posted and charged during an interval of about three years.

Cavallo's big data analysis of product prices has led him to conclude that transaction costs induce firms to make relatively few changes in prices over given intervals of time. When price changes do occur, they tend to be relatively large. He finds that the typical interval between price changes is about every nine months in the United States, which he interprets as a considerable degree of transaction-cost-generated "price stickiness."

FOR CRITICAL THINKING

Why can we anticipate that retailers' use of more machine learning to monitor consumers' visits to their websites and competitors' price adjustments could make prices less "sticky" in the future?

Sources are listed at the end of this chapter.

The Role of Middlemen

As long as there are costs of bringing together buyers and sellers, there will be an incentive for intermediaries linking ultimate sellers and buyers, normally called middlemen, to lower those costs. This means that middlemen specialize in lowering transaction costs. Whenever producers do not sell their products directly to the final consumer, by definition, one or more middlemen are involved. Farmers typically sell their output to distributors, who are usually called wholesalers, who then sell those products to retailers such as supermarkets.

Companies that provide middleman services have been thriving in our increasingly networked economy. Such middleman companies are called **platform firms.** These firms offer services that connect individuals to others with similar interests and that link people interested in purchasing particular products with companies that sell those products. Platform firms often provide such services via special network arrangements that they construct and operate on their own, such as via the Internet.

Platform firms
Companies whose services link people to other individuals who share their interests or who seek to buy firms' products, often via networks that the companies operate.

Changes in Demand and Supply

A key function of middlemen is to reduce transaction costs of buyers and sellers in markets for goods and services, and it is in markets that we see the results of changes in demand and supply. Market equilibrium can change whenever there is a *shock* caused by a change in a *ceteris paribus* condition for demand or supply. A shock to the supply and demand system can be represented by a shift in the supply curve, a shift in the demand curve, or a shift in both curves. Any shock to the system will result in a new set of supply and demand relationships and a new equilibrium. Forces will come into play to move the system from the old price-quantity equilibrium (now a disequilibrium) to the new equilibrium, where the new demand and supply curves intersect.

4.2 Evaluate the effects of changes in demand and supply on the market price and equilibrium quantity

FIGURE 4-1

Shifts in Demand and in Supply: Determinate Results

In panel (a), supply is unchanged at S. The demand curve shifts rightward from to D_1 to D_2. The equilibrium price and quantity rise from P_1, Q_1 to P_2, Q_2, respectively. In panel (b), the supply curve is unchanged at S. The demand curve shifts leftward from D_1 to D_3. Both equilibrium price and equilibrium quantity fall. In panel (c), demand now remains unchanged at D. The supply curve shifts from S_1 to S_2. The equilibrium price falls from P_1 to P_2. The equilibrium quantity increases, however, from Q_1 to Q_2. In panel (d), demand is unchanged at D. The supply curve shifts leftward from S_1 to S_3. The market clearing price increases from P_1 to P_3. The equilibrium quantity falls from Q_1 to Q_3.

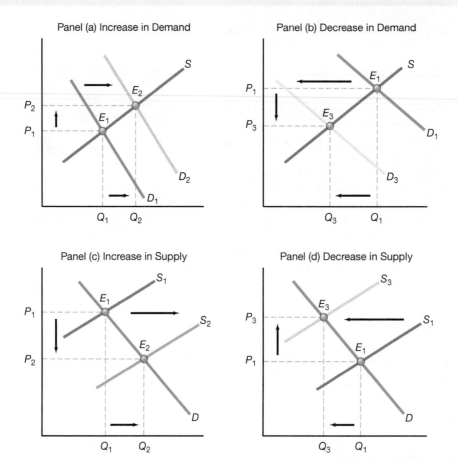

Effects of Changes in Either Demand or Supply

In many situations, it is possible to predict what will happen to both equilibrium price and equilibrium quantity when demand or supply changes. Specifically, whenever one curve is stable while the other curve shifts, we can tell what will happen to both price and quantity. Consider the possibilities in Figure 4-1. In panel (a), the supply curve remains unchanged, but demand increases from D_1 to D_2. Note that the results are an increase in the market clearing price from P_1 to P_2 and an increase in the equilibrium quantity from Q_1 to Q_2.

In panel (b) in Figure 4-1, there is a decrease in demand from D_1 to D_3. This results in a decrease in both the equilibrium price of the good and the equilibrium quantity. Panels (c) and (d) show the effects of a shift in the supply curve while the demand curve is unchanged. In panel (c), the supply curve has shifted rightward. The equilibrium price of the product falls, and the equilibrium quantity increases. In panel (d), supply has shifted leftward—there has been a supply decrease. The product's equilibrium price increases, and the equilibrium quantity decreases.

Situations in Which Both Demand and Supply Shift

Figure 4-1 shows determinate outcomes of a shift in the demand curve, holding the supply curve constant, and of a shift in the supply curve, holding the demand curve constant. We could also display cases in which both the supply and demand curves change. Depending on the directions that both curves shift, the outcome is indeterminate for either equilibrium price or equilibrium quantity.

Changes of Demand and Supply in the Same Direction When both demand and supply increase, the equilibrium quantity unambiguously rises, because the increase in demand and the increase in supply *both* tend to generate a rise in quantity. The change in the equilibrium price is uncertain without more information, because the increase in demand tends to increase the equilibrium price, whereas the increase in supply tends to decrease the equilibrium price.

Decreases in both demand and supply tend to generate a fall in quantity, so the equilibrium quantity falls. Again, the effect on the equilibrium price is uncertain without additional information, because a decrease in demand tends to reduce the equilibrium price, whereas a decrease in supply tends to increase the equilibrium price.

Changes of Demand and Supply in Opposite Directions We can be certain that when demand decreases and supply increases at the same time, the equilibrium price will fall, because *both* the decrease in demand and the increase in supply tend to push down the equilibrium price. The change in the equilibrium quantity is uncertain without more information, because the decrease in demand tends to reduce the equilibrium quantity, whereas the increase in supply tends to increase the equilibrium quantity.

If demand increases and supply decreases at the same time, both occurrences tend to push up the equilibrium price. Thus, the equilibrium price definitely rises. The increase in demand tends to raise the equilibrium quantity, whereas the decrease in supply tends to reduce the equilibrium quantity. Consequently, the change in the equilibrium quantity cannot be determined without more information.

Price Flexibility and Adjustment Speed

We have used as an illustration for our analysis a market in which prices are quite flexible. Some markets are indeed like that. In others, however, price flexibility may take the form of subtle adjustments such as hidden payments or quality changes. For example, although the published price of floral bouquets may stay the same, the freshness of the flowers may change, meaning that the price per constant-quality unit changes. The published price of French bread might stay the same, but the quality could go up or down, perhaps through use of a different recipe, thereby changing the price per constant-quality unit. There are many ways to implicitly change prices without actually changing the published price for a *nominal* unit of a product or service.

We must also note that markets do not always return to equilibrium immediately. There may be a significant adjustment time. A shock to the economy in the form of an oil embargo, a drought, or a long strike will not be absorbed overnight. This means that even in unfettered market situations, in which there are no restrictions on changes in prices and quantities, temporary excess quantities supplied or excess quantities demanded may appear. Our analysis simply indicates what the market clearing price and equilibrium quantity ultimately will be, given a demand curve and a supply curve.

Nowhere in the analysis is there any indication of the speed with which a market will get to a new equilibrium after a shock. The price may even temporarily overshoot the new equilibrium level. Remember this warning when we examine changes in demand and in supply due to changes in their *ceteris paribus* conditions.

What simultaneous events have generated changes in the equilibrium quantity of, and market clearing price for, vinyl records?

EXAMPLE

The Effects of a Simultaneous Decrease in the Supply of and an Increase in the Demand for Vinyl Records

The market clearing price of the machines used to press vinyl records has increased considerably in recent years. Indeed, the inflation-adjusted price of each hand-operated machine, which can press 400 vinyl records per day, has risen from about $400,000 per machine to more than $500,000. As shown in Figure 4-2, as the cost of this key input in the production of vinyl records has increased, the supply curve for vinyl records has shifted to the left of its original position.

During the same period, consumers have developed a renewed taste for "vinyl." Thus, as depicted in Figure 4-2, the demand for vinyl records has risen substantially. As a consequence, the market clearing price of a vinyl record unambiguously increased. On net, the equilibrium quantity of vinyl records also increased.

FOR CRITICAL THINKING

If some firms were to exit the market for vinyl records, what would happen to the market clearing price and equilibrium quantity? Explain briefly.

Sources are listed at the end of this chapter.

FIGURE 4-2

The Effects of a Simultaneous Decrease in the Supply of and Increase in the Demand for Vinyl Records

A renewed taste for phonograph-generated sounds has resulted in an increase in the demand for vinyl phonograph records, as shown by the shift in the demand curve from D_1 to D_2. At the same time, the higher cost of machines used to press vinyl records has generated decreases in the supply of vinyl records, depicted by the leftward shift in the supply curve from S_1 to S_2. On net, the equilibrium quantity of records has increased, from 11 million to about 25 million. The price of a vinyl record has increased from $30 to about $40.

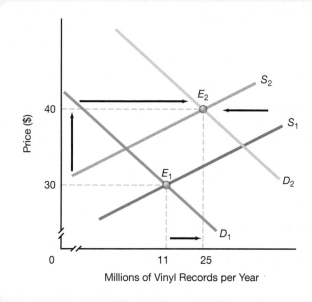

4.3 Understand the rationing function of prices

The Rationing Function of Prices

The synchronization of decisions by buyers and sellers that leads to equilibrium is called the *rationing function of prices*. Prices are indicators of relative scarcity. An equilibrium price clears the market. The plans of buyers and sellers, given the price, are not frustrated. It is the free interaction of buyers and sellers that sets the price that eventually clears the market. Price, in effect, rations a good to demanders who are willing and able to pay the highest price. Whenever the rationing function of prices is frustrated by government-enforced price ceilings that set prices below the market clearing level, a prolonged shortage results.

There are ways other than price to ration goods. *First come, first served* is one method. *Political power* is another. *Physical force* is yet another. Cultural, religious, and physical differences have been and are used as rationing devices throughout the world.

Rationing by Waiting Consider first come, first served as a rationing device. We call this *rationing by queues*, where *queue* means "line." Whoever is willing to wait in line the longest obtains the good that is being sold at less than the market clearing price. All who wait in line are paying a higher *total outlay* than the money price paid for the good. Personal time has an opportunity cost. To calculate the total outlay expended on the good, we must add up the money price plus the opportunity cost of the time spent waiting.

Rationing by waiting may occur in situations in which entrepreneurs are free to change prices to equate quantity demanded with quantity supplied but choose not to do so. This results in queues of potential buyers. It may seem that the price in the market is being held below equilibrium by some noncompetitive force. That is not true, however. Such queuing may arise in a free market when the demand for a good is subject to large or unpredictable fluctuations. Queuing also takes place when the additional costs to firms (and ultimately to consumers) of constantly changing prices or of holding sufficient inventories or providing sufficient excess capacity to cover peak demands are greater than the costs to consumers of waiting for the good.

Common examples are waiting in line to purchase a fast-food lunch and queuing to purchase a movie ticket a few minutes before the next showing.

Rationing by Random Assignment or Coupons *Random assignment* is another way to ration goods. You may have been involved in a rationing-by-random-assignment scheme in college if you were assigned a housing unit. Sometimes rationing by random assignment is used to fill slots in popular classes.

Rationing by *coupons* has also been used, particularly during wartime. In the United States during World War II, families were allotted coupons that allowed them to purchase specified quantities of rationed goods, such as meat and gasoline. To purchase such goods, they had to pay a specified price *and* give up a coupon.

The Essential Role of Rationing

In a world of scarcity, there is, by definition, competition for what is scarce. After all, any resources that are not scarce can be obtained by everyone at a zero price in as large a quantity as everyone wants. Air, for instance, can be burned in internal combustion engines. Once scarcity arises, there has to be some method to ration the available resources, goods, and services. The price system is one form of rationing. The others we mentioned are alternatives. Economists cannot say which system of rationing is "best." They can, however, say that rationing via the price system leads to the most efficient use of available resources. As explained in Appendix B (which follows this chapter), this means that generally in a freely functioning price system, all of the gains from mutually beneficial trade will be captured.

Why might consumers prefer water rationed via a positive per-unit price to water that is available at no charge?

INTERNATIONAL EXAMPLE

Customers of eWater Prefer Price Rationing over First Come, First Served at a Zero Price

A British company called eWater provides water to villages in the African nations of Gambia and Tanzania. The firm was started after its founder noticed that almost one out of three water pumps placed by governments and charitable organizations in villages without running water typically was inoperable. Use of the pumps and the water they dispensed were available on a first come, first served basis, at no explicit price. Consequently, townspeople had few incentives to take care of the pumps or to avoid wasting water. Indeed, unsupervised children sometimes even used the pumps as toys, treated the sinks like playground equipment, and

drained or splashed away large volumes of water. In some villages, so many pumps had worn out from overuse or misuse that few operating pumps remained, at which long lines for water often formed.

eWater dispensers release measured amounts of water when an electronic reader recognizes a tag displayed by an individual who has a digital account with eWater. The individual pays a shopkeeper to use a smartphone to credit this digital account. A small fraction of the fees that people pay to access the dispensers pays for the water they purchase. Another small fraction compensates shopkeepers for making space available for the

(Continued)

dispensers and preventing their misuse. The largest fraction funds regular maintenance of the dispensers.

Many are willing to pay to use eWater's dispensers because the machines operate consistently and because people do not have to wait long to access the water that they purchase and—as noticed by eWater employees—that they seek to avoid spilling. As a result, eWater's operations have expanded rapidly to serve more than 50,000 people from 500 water dispensers.

FOR CRITICAL THINKING

Why do you think that a number of people in Gambia and Tanzania are willing to pay to use eWater's dispensers instead of public pumps available at no charge?

Sources are listed at the end of this chapter.

4.4 Explain the effects of price ceilings

Price controls
Government-mandated minimum or maximum prices that may be charged for goods and services.

Price ceiling
A legal maximum price that may be charged for a particular good or service.

Price floor
A legal minimum price below which a good or service may not be sold. Legal minimum wages are an example.

Nonprice rationing devices
All methods used to ration scarce goods that are price-controlled. Whenever the price system is not allowed to work, nonprice rationing devices will evolve to ration the affected goods and services.

Price Ceilings

The rationing function of prices is prevented when governments impose price controls. **Price controls** often involve setting a **price ceiling**—the maximum price that may be allowed in an exchange. The world has had a long history of price ceilings applied to product prices, wages, rents, and interest rates. Occasionally, a government will set a **price floor**—a minimum price below which a good or service may not be sold. Price floors have most often been applied to wages and agricultural products. Let's first consider price ceilings.

Price Ceilings and Black Markets

As long as a price ceiling is below the market clearing price, imposing a price ceiling creates a shortage, as can be seen in Figure 4-3. At any price below the market clearing, or equilibrium, price of $1,000, there will always be a larger quantity demanded than quantity supplied—a shortage. Normally, whenever quantity demanded exceeds quantity supplied—that is, when a shortage exists—there is a tendency for the price to rise to its equilibrium level. But with a price ceiling, this tendency cannot be fully realized because everyone is forbidden to trade at the equilibrium price.

Nonprice Rationing Devices The result is fewer exchanges and **nonprice rationing devices.** Figure 4-3 shows the situation for portable electric generators after a natural disaster: The equilibrium quantity of portable generators demanded and supplied

---

FIGURE 4-3

Black Markets for Portable Electric Generators

The demand curve is *D*. The supply curve is *S*. The equilibrium price is $1,000. The government, however, steps in and imposes a maximum price of $600. At that lower price, the quantity demanded will be 15,000, but the quantity supplied will be only 5,000. There is a "shortage." If the price ceiling is fully enforced, the implicit supply curve becomes the vertical line *S'*, and the effective price (including time costs) tends to increase to $1,400. If black markets arise, as they generally will, the equilibrium black market price will end up somewhere between $600 and $1,400.

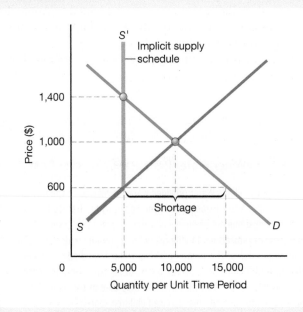

(or traded) would be 10,000 units, and the market clearing price would be $1,000 per generator. If the government, though, essentially imposes a price ceiling by requiring the price of portable generators to remain at the predisaster level, which the government determines was a price of $600, the equilibrium quantity offered is only 5,000.

Because frustrated consumers will be able to purchase only 5,000 units, there is a shortage. The most obvious nonprice rationing device to help clear the market is queuing, or physical lines, which we have already discussed. To avoid physical lines, waiting lists may be established.

Black Markets   Typically, an effective price ceiling leads to a **black market.** A black market is a market in which the price-controlled good is sold at an illegally high price through various methods. For example, if the price of gasoline is controlled at lower than the market clearing price, drivers who wish to fill up their cars may offer the gas station attendant a cash payment on the side (as happened in the United States in the 1970s and in China and India in the mid-2000s during price controls on gasoline).

If the price of beef is controlled at below its market clearing price, a customer who offers the butcher tickets for good seats to an upcoming football game may be allocated otherwise unavailable beef. Indeed, the true implicit price of a price-controlled good or service can be increased in an infinite number of ways, limited only by the imagination. (Black markets also occur when goods are made illegal.)

Black market
A market in which goods are traded at prices above their legal maximum prices or in which illegal goods are sold.

WHAT HAPPENS WHEN...

the New York City government effectively raises the legal minimum price of cigarettes within the city's boundaries to almost twice the average U.S. price?

For the United States as a whole, the average price of a pack of cigarettes is about $7. Various policies of the government of New York City, however, have raised the minimum legal price at which cigarettes can be sold above $13 per pack. One consequence has been black-market smuggling of cigarettes. Smugglers purchase cigarettes at lower prices in other cities and states and transport them into New York City to sell at a price that is lower than the higher minimum legal price. Current estimates indicate that more than half of the cigarettes consumed in New York City are purchased on the black market.

The Policy of Rent Ceilings

Hundreds of U.S. cities and towns, including most communities in California and New York City, operate under some kind of rent control. **Rent control** is a system under which the local government tells building owners how much they can charge their tenants for rent. In the United States, rent controls date back to at least World War II. The objective of rent control is to keep rents below levels that would be observed in a freely competitive market.

Rent control
Price ceilings on rents.

The Functions of Rental Prices   In any housing market, rental prices serve three functions: (1) to promote the efficient maintenance of existing housing and to stimulate the construction of new housing, (2) to allocate existing scarce housing among competing claimants, and (3) to ration the use of existing housing by current demanders. Rent controls interfere with all of these functions.

Rent Controls and Construction   Rent controls discourage the construction of new rental units. Rents are the most important long-term determinant of profitability, and rent controls artificially depress them. Consider some examples. In a recent year in Dallas, Texas, with a 16 percent rental vacancy rate but no rent control laws, 11,000 new rental housing units were built. In the same year in San Francisco, California, only 2,000 units were built, despite a mere 1.6 percent vacancy rate. The major difference? San Francisco has had stringent rent control laws. In New York City, most rental units being built are luxury units, which are exempt from controls.

Effects on the Existing Supply of Housing   When rental rates are held below equilibrium levels, property owners cannot recover the cost of maintenance, repairs, and capital improvements through higher rents. Hence, they curtail these activities. In the extreme situation, taxes, utilities, and the expenses of basic repairs exceed rental receipts. The result has been abandoned buildings from Santa Monica, California, to New York City. Some owners have resorted to arson, hoping to collect the insurance on their empty buildings before the city claims them to pay back taxes.

Rationing the Current Use of Housing   Rent controls also affect the current use of housing because they restrict tenant mobility. Consider a family whose children have gone off to college. That family might want to live in a smaller apartment. In a rent-controlled environment, however, giving up a rent-controlled unit can entail a substantial cost. In most rent-controlled cities, rents can be adjusted only when a tenant leaves. This means that a move from a long-occupied rent-controlled apartment to a smaller apartment can involve a hefty rent hike. In New York, this artificial preservation of the status quo came to be known as "housing gridlock."

Attempts to Evade Rent Ceilings

The distortions produced by rent ceilings lead to efforts by both property owners and tenants to evade the rules. These efforts lead to the growth of expensive government bureaucracies whose job it is to make sure that rent ceilings aren't evaded. In New York City, because rent on a rent-controlled apartment can be raised only if the tenant leaves, property owners have had an incentive to make life unpleasant for tenants in order to drive them out or to evict them on the slightest pretext. The city has responded by making evictions extremely costly for property owners. Eviction requires a tedious and expensive judicial proceeding.

Tenants, for their part, routinely try to sublet all or part of their rent-controlled apartments at fees substantially above the rent they pay to the owner. Both the city and the property owners try to prohibit subletting and often end up in the city's housing courts—an entire judicial system developed to deal with disputes involving rent-controlled apartments. The overflow and appeals from the city's housing courts sometimes clog the rest of New York's judicial system.

Who Loses and Who Gains from Rent Ceilings?

The big losers from rent ceilings are clearly property owners. There is, however, another group of losers—low-income individuals, especially single mothers, trying to find apartments. Some observers now believe that rent ceilings have worsened the problem of homelessness in cities such as New York.

Why Both Landlords and Some Tenants Lose

Often, owners of rent-controlled apartments charge "key money" before allowing a new tenant to move in. This is a large up-front cash payment, usually illegal but demanded nonetheless—just one aspect of the black market in rent-controlled apartments. Poor individuals have insufficient income to pay the hefty key money payment, nor can they assure the owner that their rent will be on time or even paid each month.

Because rent ceilings are usually below market clearing levels, apartment owners have little incentive to take any risk on low-income individuals as tenants. This is particularly true when a prospective tenant's chief source of income is public assistance. Indeed, a large number of litigants in the New York housing courts are single mothers on public assistance who have missed their rent payments due to emergency expenses or delayed welfare checks. Their appeals often end in evictions and a new home in a temporary public shelter—or on the streets.

Beneficiaries of Rent Controls

Who benefits from rent ceilings? Ample evidence indicates that upper-income professionals benefit the most. These people can use their mastery of the bureaucracy and their large network of friends and connections to exploit the rent ceilings. Consider that in New York City, a recent analysis found that about 2,300 of the city's rent-controlled apartments were occupied by people who earn more than $500,000 per year. More than 20,000 additional apartments were rented at below-market rates by people with annual incomes exceeding $199,000.

Price Floors and Quantity Restrictions

4.5 Explain the effects of price floors and government-imposed quantity restrictions

Another way that government can seek to control markets is by imposing price floors or *quantity restrictions*. Let's begin by examining the effects of price floors, which governments most commonly impose in agricultural and labor markets.

Price Floors and Price Supports in Agriculture

During the Great Depression, the federal government swung into action to help farmers. In 1933, it established a system of price supports for many agricultural products. Since then, there have been price supports for wheat, feed grains, cotton, rice, soybeans, sorghum, and dairy products, among other foodstuffs.

Implementing Agricultural Price Support The nature of the supports is quite simple: The government simply chooses a *support price* for an agricultural product and then acts to ensure that the price of the product never falls below the support level.

Figure 4-4 shows an example depicting market demand for and supply of peanuts. Without a price-support program, competitive forces would yield an equilibrium price of $400 per ton and an equilibrium quantity of 3 million tons per year. Clearly, if the government were to set the support price at or below $500 per ton, the quantity of peanuts demanded would equal the quantity of peanuts supplied at

---

FIGURE 4-4

Agricultural Price Supports

Free market equilibrium occurs at *E*, with an equilibrium price of $400 per ton and an equilibrium quantity of 3 million tons. When the government sets a support price at $500 per ton, the quantity demanded is 2.5 million tons and the quantity supplied is 4.5 million tons. The difference is the surplus, which the government buys.

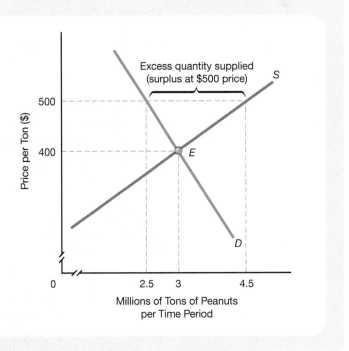

point *E*, because farmers could sell all they wanted at the market clearing price of $400 per ton.

An Effective Agricultural Price Floor

What happens, though, when the government sets the support price *above* the market clearing price, at $500 per ton? At a support price of $500 per ton, the quantity demanded is only 2.5 million tons, but the quantity supplied is 4.5 million tons. The 2-million-ton difference between them is called the *excess quantity supplied*, or *surplus*. As simple as this program seems, its existence creates a fundamental question: How can the government agency charged with administering the price-support program prevent market forces from pushing the actual price down to $400 per ton?

If production exceeds the amount that consumers want to buy at the support price, what happens to the surplus? Quite simply, if the price-support program is to work, the government has to buy the surplus—the 2-million-ton difference. As a practical matter, the government acquires the 2-million-ton surplus indirectly through a government agency. The government either stores the surplus or sells it to foreign countries at a greatly reduced price (or gives it away free of charge) under the Food for Peace program.

Who Benefits from Agricultural Price Supports?

Although agricultural price supports have traditionally been promoted as a way to guarantee "decent" earnings for low-income farmers, most of the benefits have in fact gone to the owners of very large farms. Price-support payments are made on a per-ton basis, not on a per-farm basis. Thus, traditionally, the larger the farm, the bigger the benefit from agricultural price supports. In addition, all of the benefits from price supports ultimately accrue to land-owners on whose land price-supported crops grow.

Keeping Price Supports Alive under a New Name Back in the early 1990s, Congress indicated an intention to phase out most agricultural subsidies by the early 2000s. Nevertheless, the federal government and several state governments have continued to support prices of a number of agricultural products, such as peanuts, through "marketing loan" programs. These programs advance funds to farmers to help them finance the storage of some or all of their crops. The farmers can then use the stored produce as collateral for borrowing or sell it to the government and use the proceeds to repay debts.

Marketing loan programs raise the effective price that farmers receive for their crops and commit federal and state governments to purchasing surplus production. Consequently, they lead to outcomes similar to those of traditional price-support programs.

The Main Beneficiaries of Agricultural Subsidies In 2014, Congress enacted the Agricultural Act, which perpetuated marketing loan programs and other subsidy and price-support arrangements for such farm products as wheat, corn, rice, peanuts, and soybeans. All told, the more than $20 billion in U.S. government payments for these and other products amounts to about 25 percent of the annual market value of all U.S. farm production.

The government seeks to cap the annual subsidy payment that an individual farmer can receive at $125,000 per year, but some farmers are able to garner higher annual amounts by engaging in conservation programs that provide subsidies as high as $450,000. The greatest share of total agricultural subsidies goes to the owners of the largest farming operations. At present, about 10 percent of U.S. farmers receive more than 70 percent of agricultural subsidies.

Under another subsidy program implemented under the 2014 law, the government provides additional subsidies to assist farmers in purchasing crop insurance policies. These policies provide farmers with extra payments if circumstances outside their control, such as too little or too much rain, harm their crops.

Price Floors in the Labor Market

The **minimum wage** is the lowest hourly wage rate that firms may legally pay their workers. Proponents favor higher minimum wages to ensure low-income workers a "decent" standard of living. Opponents counter that higher minimum wages cause increased unemployment, particularly among unskilled minority teenagers.

Minimum wage
A wage floor, legislated by government, setting the lowest hourly rate that firms may legally pay workers.

Minimum Wages in the United States The federal minimum wage started in 1938 at 25 cents an hour, about 40 percent of the average manufacturing wage at the time. After holding the minimum wage at $5.15 per hour from 1997 to 2007, Congress in 2009 established the current federal minimum wage of $7.25 per hour.

Many states and cities have their own minimum wage laws that exceed the federal minimum. A number of municipalities refer to their minimum wage rules as "living wage" laws. Governments of these municipalities seek to set minimum wages consistent with living standards they deem to be socially acceptable—that is, overall wage income judged to be sufficient to purchase basic items such as housing and food.

Economic Effects of a Minimum Wage What happens when the government establishes a floor on wages? The effects can be seen in Figure 4-5. We start off in equilibrium with the equilibrium wage rate of W_e and the equilibrium quantity of labor equal to Q_e. A minimum wage, W_m, higher than W_e, is imposed. At W_m, the quantity demanded for labor is reduced to Q_d, and some workers now become unemployed. Certain workers will become unemployed as a result of the minimum wage, but others will move to sectors where minimum wage laws do not apply. Wages will be pushed down in these uncovered sectors.

Explaining the Overall Decrease in Employment Note that the reduction in employment from Q_e to Q_d, or the distance from B to A, is less than the excess quantity of

ECONOMICS IN YOUR LIFE

To learn about why the mayor of a major U.S. city who had promoted a higher minimum wage while running for office changed her mind after she was elected, read **A Mayor Favors the Minimum Wage until Confronting Its Consequences** on page 87.

FIGURE 4-5

The Effect of Minimum Wages

The market clearing wage rate is W_e. The market clearing quantity of employment is Q_e, determined by the intersection of supply and demand at point E. A minimum wage equal to W_m is established. The quantity of labor demanded is reduced to Q_d. The reduction in employment from Q_e to Q_d is equal to the distance between B and A. That distance is smaller than the excess quantity of labor supplied at wage rate W_m. The distance between B and C is the increase in the quantity of labor supplied, to Q_s, that results from the higher minimum wage rate.

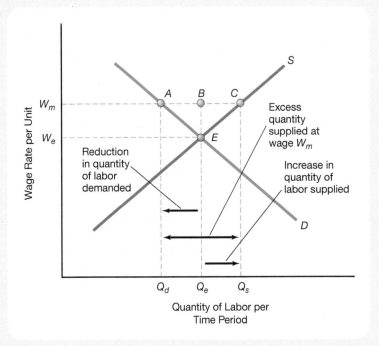

labor supplied at wage rate W_m. This excess quantity supplied is the distance between A and C, or the distance between Q_d and Q_s. The reason the reduction in employment is smaller than the excess quantity of labor supplied at the minimum wage is that the excess quantity of labor supplied also includes the *additional* workers who would like to work more hours at the new, higher minimum wage.

How have establishments of a $15-per-hour minimum wage in Los Angeles and a union salary requirement to adhere strictly to that limit in salary contracts affected employment of actors at the city's small theaters?

EXAMPLE

"99-Seat Theaters" in Los Angeles Adapt to a Minimum Wage Requirement

In Los Angeles, many struggling actors waiting for chances at parts in Hollywood movie productions have long kept themselves fed, clothed, and housed, and their career hopes alive, by performing at low wages in so-called 99-seat theaters—stages hosting productions of plays funded by ticket receipts received from small crowds of patrons. Recently, however, the city government established a minimum wage of $15 per hour. Shortly thereafter, Actor's Equity Association—a union in which actors who work in Hollywood films must have membership—ruled that actors performing at 99-seat theaters had to earn contract salaries offering hourly pay equivalent to at least $15.

The 99-seat theaters of Los Angeles have adjusted in four ways. A few theaters have switched to producing plays in which actors who are union members agree to perform as unpaid volunteers, which affords union-member actors an opportunity to promote their art and practice their skills at no charge to the theaters. Some theaters have instead adopted a policy of hiring only non-union actors. Theaters that hire unionized actors under contracts ensuring payment of the hourly minimum wage have stopped producing plays that require casts of more than nine or ten actors instead of the previous norm of nineteen or twenty actors. Reducing casts has permitted these theaters to stretch their existing budgets for actors over the smaller number of actors who now must be paid higher wages. A remaining handful of theaters have closed their doors. On net, the outcome for wage-earning actors has been a reduction in overall employment at the city's 99-seat theaters.

REAL APPLICATION

A certain percentage of those studying this textbook will attempt to become actors. You know that you need experience to become successful. How could you react to Los Angeles' higher minimum wage?

Sources are listed at the end of this chapter.

In the long run (a time period that is long enough to allow for full adjustment by workers and firms), some of the reduction in the quantity of labor demanded will result from a reduction in the number of firms, and some will result from changes in the number of workers employed by each firm. Economists estimate that a 10 percent increase in the inflation-adjusted minimum wage decreases total employment of those affected by 1 to 2 percent.

Your Summer Plans if the Minimum Wage Were, Say, $25 an Hour When you are young and inexperienced, generally the jobs you are eligible for pay no more than the minimum wage. Twenty years from now, presumably you will not be so concerned with what the minimum wage is. But assume that today the minimum wage jumps to $25 an hour. For some of you, that might affect your summer plans. Rather than going on a summer vacation, you might consider applying for a minimum wage job to save for graduate school. You might even decide to take part-time work during the school year. Hence, a higher minimum wage increases the number of job seekers like you. That is to say, the labor supply curve is indeed upward sloping.

What have behavioral researchers learned about the effects of imposing a minimum hourly wage above the market clearing wage rate?

BEHAVIORAL EXAMPLE

Experimental Evidence Verifies Predictions about the Effects of Imposing a Price Floor in a Labor Market

A recent experimental study conducted by John Horton of New York University randomly imposed minimum hourly wages on firms that posted job openings in an online labor market. As predicted by the theory of price floors, firms subjected to the minimum wage requirement responded by cutting back on hiring and by reducing the number of employment hours for hired workers. Thus, the additional workers who sought employment at the higher minimum wage imposed on the affected firms were not hired, and those workers who were hired were paid for fewer hours of work.

FOR CRITICAL THINKING

Why do you suppose economists have found that firms sometimes respond to minimum wage requirements to pay higher explicit dollar wages by reducing fringe benefits such as premiums for health insurance coverage?

Sources are listed at the end of this chapter.

Quantity Restrictions

Governments can impose quantity restrictions on a market. The most obvious restriction is an outright ban on the ownership or trading of a good. It is currently illegal to buy and sell human organs. It is also currently illegal to buy and sell certain psychoactive drugs such as cocaine, heroin, and methamphetamine. In some states, it is illegal to start a new hospital without obtaining a license for a particular number of beds to be offered to patients. This licensing requirement effectively limits the quantity of hospital beds in some states. From 1933 to 1973, it was illegal for U.S. citizens to own gold except for manufacturing, medicinal, or jewelry purposes.

Some of the most common quantity restrictions exist in the area of international trade. The U.S. government, as well as many foreign governments, imposes import quotas on a variety of goods. An **import quota** is a supply restriction that prohibits the importation of more than a specified quantity of a particular good in a one-year period. The United States has had import quotas on tobacco, sugar, and immigrant labor. For many years, there were import quotas on oil coming into the United States. There are also "voluntary" import quotas on certain goods. For instance, since the mid-2000s, the Chinese government has agreed to "voluntarily" restrict the amount of textile products China sends to the United States and the European Union.

Import quota
A physical supply restriction on imports of a particular good, such as sugar. Foreign exporters are unable to sell in the United States more than the quantity specified in the import quota.

ECONOMICS IN YOUR LIFE

A Mayor Favors the Minimum Wage until Confronting Its Consequences

Catherine Pugh has won the race to serve as mayor of the city of Baltimore. During the campaign, she supported a plan by the city council to begin a gradual increase in the citywide minimum hourly wage rate above Maryland's statewide requirement of $9.25 to a level of $15 by 2022. After the city council formally approved its minimum wage plan, however, Pugh exercised her mayoral power to veto the council's action. A key reason for her change of heart, Pugh states, is that major employers around the city told her that they would respond by reducing their hiring of new workers. Some firms indicated that if confronted with a higher minimum wage rate, they would reduce their existing workforces. Others would contemplate moving their operations to other locations in Maryland in which they could continue legally to pay workers lower wages, given that the statewide minimum wage floor is lower than Baltimore's.

FOR CRITICAL THINKING

Who unambiguously would have been harmed if the city council's plan had gone into effect?

REAL APPLICATION

Assume that you are the owner of a fast-food restaurant in a city that is going to increase its minimum wage to, say, $20 per hour. What would be some of the ways you could legally react to such a higher minimum wage?

Sources are listed at the end of this chapter.

ISSUES & APPLICATIONS

Why Shortages of Some Pharmaceuticals Generate Higher Prices for Other Drugs

Science History Images/Alamy Stock Photo

CONCEPTS APPLIED

➤ Price Controls

➤ Price Ceilings

➤ Nonprice Rationing Devices

At any given time, shortages exist in U.S. markets for more than 175 prescription drugs—shortages often caused by governmental price controls intended to hold down prices. The U.S. Food and Drug Administration (FDA) provides an online database to inform physicians of medications that their patients might find difficult to purchase at pharmacies. In this way, physicians can contemplate adjusting by prescribing alternative medications that perform similar functions. The result of such adjustments has been upward pressure on prices of the alternative medications.

Explaining Most Pharmaceuticals Shortages

Some pharmaceuticals shortages arise during the process of adjustment of markets to new equilibrium positions. In reality, most shortages of prescription medications arise because of government price controls.

Medicare and other government programs will not allow prices of drugs covered by their programs to rise to or above prespecified thresholds established for that year. Panel (a) of Figure 4-6 displays the outcome when the market clearing price of a drug, denoted "Medication A," rises to $50 per unit, which is above the government-prescribed threshold price of $40 per unit. Then the government's threshold price of $40 per unit becomes a price ceiling. Manufacturers typically respond by cutting back or even halting production until a new period begins with a higher government threshold price set at or above the $50-per-unit market clearing price. As a result, quantity supplied at the ceiling price drops below the quantity demanded, and a shortage of the drug results.

Upward Pressures on Prices of Replacement Drugs

Pharmaceuticals sellers usually respond to shortages with first-come, first-served nonprice rationing. Many physicians who learn from patients that they cannot obtain Medication A respond by writing prescriptions for replacement drugs that perform similar functions.

Suppose in our example that the closest replacement to Medication A is a drug called Medication B. Panel (b) of Figure 4-6 shows what happens when patients who are unable to obtain Medication A enter the market for Medication B. The increase in the number of consumers of Medication B causes an increase in the amount of that drug demanded at each possible price, so Medication B's demand curve shifts rightward, from D_1 to D_2. One result is an increase in the equilibrium quantity of Medication B, from 15,000 units to 18,000 units. The other outcome is an increase in the market clearing price of Medication B, from $35 per unit to $45 per unit—which we assume is below any government-established ceiling threshold for this market in the current year. In this

FIGURE 4-6

How a Shortage of Medication A Can Push Up the Price of a Substitute Medication B

In panel (a), the market clearing price of Medication A is $50 per unit. The legal ceiling price, however, is $40 per unit. At this ceiling price, the quantity of Medication A demanded by patients is 25,000 units, but the quantity supplied by manufacturers is only 15,000 units. Many patients' physicians respond to the resulting 10,000-unit shortage of Medication A by providing prescriptions for a substitute, Medication B. As a result, as

shown in panel (b), the demand for Medication B increases, from D_1 to D_2. The resulting upward movement along the supply curve generates an increase in the equilibrium quantity of Medication B, from 15,000 units to 18,000 units, and a rise in market clearing price of Medication B, from $35 per unit to $45 per unit.

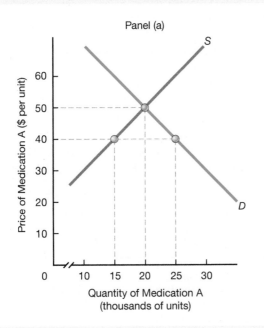
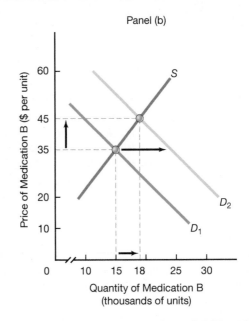

way, the shortage created by the government's price ceiling in the market for Medication A brings about a higher price for the replacement Medication B. Thus, the government's effort to limit the price in one pharmaceuticals market contributes to a higher price for another drug—a common event in real-world U.S. pharmaceuticals markets today.

FOR CRITICAL THINKING

If the demand for Medication B in panel (b) of Figure 4-6 were to rise sufficiently to push the market clearing price above a

governmental price ceiling, what events would occur in the market for Medication B? Explain briefly.

REAL APPLICATION

At some point in our lives, virtually all of us will become consumers of health care services, including the use of prescribed pharmaceuticals. Faced with a shortage of a prescribed drug, what are some of the ways you could react?

Sources are listed at the end of this chapter.

What You Should Know

Here is what you should know after reading this chapter.

LEARNING OBJECTIVES

4.1 **Discuss the essential features of the price system** *In the price system, prices respond to changes in supply and demand. Decisions on resource use depend on what happens to prices. Middlemen reduce transaction costs by bringing buyers and sellers together.*

KEY TERMS

price system, 74
voluntary exchange, 74
transaction costs, 74
platform firms, 75

LEARNING OBJECTIVES	KEY TERMS
4.2 Evaluate the effects of changes in demand and supply on the market price and equilibrium quantity *With a given supply curve, an increase in demand causes increases in the market price and equilibrium quantity, and a decrease in demand induces decreases in the market price and equilibrium quantity. With a given demand curve, an increase in supply causes a fall in the market price and an increase in the equilibrium quantity, and a decrease in supply causes a rise in the market price and a decline in the equilibrium quantity. When both demand and supply shift at the same time, we must know the direction and amount of each shift in order to predict changes in the market price and the equilibrium quantity.*	**Key Figure** Figure 4-1, 76
4.3 Understand the rationing function of prices *In the price system, prices ration scarce goods and services. Other ways of rationing include first come, first served; political power; physical force; random assignment; and coupons.*	
4.4 Explain the effects of price ceilings *Government-imposed price controls that require prices to be no higher than a certain level are price ceilings. If a government sets a price ceiling below the market price, then at the ceiling price the quantity of the good demanded will exceed the quantity supplied. There will be a shortage at the ceiling price. Price ceilings can lead to nonprice rationing devices and black markets.*	price controls, 80 price ceiling, 80 price floor, 80 nonprice rationing devices, 80 black market, 81 rent control, 81 **Key Figure** Figure 4-3, 80
4.5 Explain the effects of price floors and government-imposed quantity restrictions *Government-mandated price controls that require prices to be no lower than a certain level are price floors. If a government sets a price floor above the market price, then at the floor price the quantity of the good supplied will exceed the quantity demanded. There will be a surplus at the floor price. Quantity restrictions can take the form of outright bans or licensing and import restrictions that restrict the amount supplied.*	minimum wage, 85 import quota, 87 **Key Figures** Figure 4-4, 83 Figure 4-5, 85

PROBLEMS

4-1. In recent years, technological improvements have greatly reduced the costs of producing smartphones, and a number of new firms have entered the smartphone industry. At the same time, prices of substitutes for smartphones, such as various tablet devices, have declined considerably. Construct a supply and demand diagram of the market for smartphones. Illustrate the impacts of these developments, and evaluate the effects on the market price and equilibrium quantity.

4-2. Advances in research and development in the pharmaceutical industry have enabled manufacturers to identify potential cures more quickly and therefore at lower cost. At the same time, the aging of our society has increased the demand for new drugs. Construct a supply and demand diagram of the market for pharmaceutical drugs.

Illustrate the impacts of these developments, and evaluate the effects on the market price and the equilibrium quantity.

4-3. There are simultaneous changes in the demand for and supply of global-positioning-system (GPS) devices, with the consequences being an unambiguous increase in the market clearing price of these devices but no change in the equilibrium quantity. What changes in the demand for and supply of GPS devices could have generated these outcomes? Explain.

4-4. There are simultaneous changes in the demand for and supply of tablet devices, with the consequences being an unambiguous decrease in the equilibrium quantity of these devices but no change in the market clearing price. What changes in the demand for and supply of tablet devices could have generated these outcomes? Explain.

4-5. The following table depicts the quantity demanded and quantity supplied of studio apartments in a small college town.

Monthly Rent	Quantity Demanded	Quantity Supplied
$600	3,000	1,600
$650	2,500	1,800
$700	2,000	2,000
$750	1,500	2,200
$800	1,000	2,400

What are the market price and equilibrium quantity of apartments in this town? If this town imposes a rent control of $650 per month, how many studio apartments will be rented?

4-6. Suppose that the government places a ceiling on the price of a medical drug below the equilibrium price.

a. Show why there is a shortage of the medical drug at the new ceiling price.

b. Suppose that a black market for the medical drug arises, with pharmaceutical firms secretly selling the drug at higher prices. Illustrate the black market for this medical drug, including the implicit supply schedule, the ceiling price, the black market supply and demand, and the highest feasible black market price.

4-7. The table below illustrates the demand and supply schedules for seats on air flights between two cities:

Price	Quantity Demanded	Quantity Supplied
$200	2,000	1,200
$300	1,800	1,400
$400	1,600	1,600
$500	1,400	1,800
$600	1,200	2,000

What are the market price and equilibrium quantity in this market? Now suppose that federal authorities limit the number of flights between the two cities to ensure that no more than 1,200 passengers can be flown. Evaluate the effects of this quota if price adjusts. (*Hint:* What price per flight are the 1,200 passengers willing to pay?)

4-8. The consequences of decriminalizing illegal drugs have long been debated. Some claim that legalization will lower the price of these drugs and reduce related crime and that more people will use these drugs. Suppose some of these drugs are legalized so that anyone may sell them and use them. Now

consider the two claims—that price will fall and quantity demanded will increase. Based on positive economic analysis, are these claims sound?

4-9. In recent years, the government of Pakistan has established a support price for wheat of about $0.20 per kilogram of wheat. At this price, consumers are willing to purchase 10 billion kilograms of wheat per year, while Pakistani farmers are willing to grow and harvest 18 billion kilograms of wheat per year. The government purchases and stores all surplus wheat.

a. What are annual consumer expenditures on the Pakistani wheat crop?

b. What are annual government expenditures on the Pakistani wheat crop?

c. How much, in total, do Pakistani wheat farmers receive for the wheat they produce?

4-10. Consider the information in Problem 4-9 and your answers to that problem. Suppose that the market clearing price of Pakistani wheat in the absence of price supports is equal to $0.10 per kilogram. At this price, the quantity of wheat demanded is 12 billion kilograms. Under the government wheat price-support program, how much more is spent each year on wheat harvested in Pakistan than otherwise would have been spent in an unregulated market for Pakistani wheat?

4-11. Consider the diagram below, which depicts the labor market in a city that has adopted a "living wage law" requiring employers to pay a minimum wage rate of $11 per hour. Answer the questions that follow.

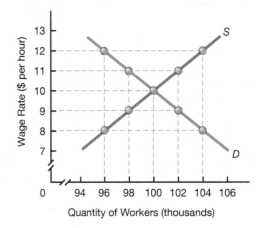

Quantity of Workers (thousands)

a. What condition exists in this city's labor market at the present minimum wage of $11 per hour? How many people are unemployed at this wage?

b. A city councilwoman has proposed amending the living wage law. She suggests reducing the minimum wage to $9 per hour. Assuming that the labor demand and supply curves were to remain in their present positions, how many people would be unemployed at a new $9 minimum wage?

c. A councilman has offered a counterproposal. In his view, the current minimum wage is too low and should be increased to $12 per hour. Assuming that the labor demand and supply curves remain in their present positions, how many people would be unemployed at a new $12 minimum wage?

4-12. A city has decided to impose rent controls, and it has established a rent ceiling below the previous equilibrium rental rate for offices throughout the city. How will the quantity of offices leased by building owners change?

4-13. In 2019, the government of a nation established a price support for wheat. The government's support price has been above the equilibrium price each year since, and the government has purchased all wheat over and above the amounts that consumers have bought at the support price. Every year since 2019, there has been an increase in the number of wheat producers in the market. No other factors affecting the market for wheat have changed. Predict what has happened every year since 2019, to each of the following:

a. Amount of wheat supplied by wheat producers

b. Amount of wheat demanded by all wheat consumers

c. Amount of wheat purchased by the government

4-14. The government of the state of Arizona decided to boost its own minimum wage by an additional $1.60 per hour above the minimum wage established by the federal government. This pushed the wage rate earned by Arizona teenagers above the equilibrium wage rate in the teen labor market. What is the predicted effect of this action by Arizona's government on each of the following?

a. The quantity of labor supplied by Arizona teenagers

b. The quantity of labor demanded by employers of Arizona teenagers

c. The number of unemployed Arizona teenagers

4-15. Consider Figure 4-1. The current demand and supply curves are D_1 and S_1, at which the equilibrium price and quantity are P_1 and Q_1. If there is a decrease in the price of an item that consumers regard as a substitute for this good, which curve shifts, and in which direction does it shift? What happens to the market clearing price and to the equilibrium quantity?

4-16. Consider Figure 4-1. The current demand and supply curves are D_1 and S_1, at which the equilibrium price and quantity are P_1 and Q_1. If firms adopt a cost-reducing technique for producing this good, which curve shifts, and in which direction does it shift? What happens to the market clearing price and to the equilibrium quantity?

4-17. Consider Figure 4-3. Suppose that the government reduces the ceiling price to $500 per unit. Would the shortage at the $500-per-unit ceiling price be greater than at the $600-per-unit price ceiling?

4-18. Suppose that in Figure 4-4, the government raises the floor price of peanuts above the displayed $500-per-ton floor price, to $600 per ton. Will the excess quantity of peanuts supplied increase or decrease as a consequence?

4-19. Suppose that in Figure 4-4, the government reduces the floor price of peanuts below the displayed $500-per-ton floor price, to $400 per ton. Will the excess quantity of peanuts supplied increase or decrease as a consequence?

4-20. Suppose that Figure 4-5 applies to the labor market in the state of Ohio, in which W_m is the minimum wage established by the federal government, and $Q_s - Q_d$ therefore is Ohio's excess quantity of labor supplied as a result of the federal wage minimum. What would happen to Ohio's excess quantity of labor supplied if the state were to decide to establish its own minimum wage at a level above the federal minimum?

REFERENCES

AI—DECISION MAKING THROUGH DATA: Reduced Transaction Costs and "Price Stickiness"

"Sticky Price Consumer Price Index," Federal Reserve Bank of St. Louis (https://fred.stlouisfed.org/series/STICK-CPIM157SFRBATL), 2019.

James Melton, "Bed Bath & Beyond Looks to Dynamic Pricing to Fuel Growth," *Internet Retailer* (https://www.digitalcommerce360.com/2018/04/18/bed-bath-beyond-looks-to-dynamic-pricing-to-fuel-growth/), April 18, 2018.

Alberto Cavallo, "Scraped Data and Sticky Prices," *Review of Economics and Statistics*, 2018.

EXAMPLE: The Effects of a Simultaneous Decrease in the Supply of and Increase in the Demand for Vinyl Records

Stephane Mlot, "Vinyl Record Sales Show No Signs of Slowing," Geek.com (https://www.geek.com/tech/vinyl-record-sales-show-no-signs-of-slowing-in-2019-1768561/), January 7. 2019.

Marsha Silva, "Vinyl Records Are Still Enjoying Double-Digit Growth," *Digital Music News*, July 9, 2018.

Anton Spice, "Physical Record Sales Are Out-Selling Digital Downloads Once More," *The Vinyl Factory*, March 23, 2018.

INTERNATIONAL EXAMPLE: Customers of eWater Prefer Price Rationing over First Come, First Served at a Zero Price

"Clean Drinking Water for Gambia," DW.com (https://www.dw.com/en/clean-drinking-water-for-gambia/a-6079864), 2019.

"Tanzania: Investing in Water and Sanitation Reaps Benefits for Poverty Alleviation," World Bank (https://www.worldbank.org/en/results/2018/04/02/tanzania-investing-in-water-and-sanitation-reaps-benefits-for-poverty-alleviation), April 2, 2018.

Johnny Wood, "Everything You Need to Know about Water," *World Economic Forum*, August 23, 2018.

EXAMPLE: "99-Seat Theaters" in Los Angeles Adapt to a Minimum Wage Requirement

"Save LA's Intimate Theater: I Love 99," ilove99.org, 2019.

Steven Leigh Morris, "Into the Woods: Old Sorrows and New Hopes for Theater in 2018," *This Stage Magazine*, January 11, 2018.

"LA 99 Seat Theater: Western Agreement," Actor's Equity (https://www.actorsequity.org/resources/contracts/LA99/), 2018.

BEHAVIORAL EXAMPLE: Experimental Evidence Verifies Predictions about the Effects of Imposing a Price Floor in a Labor Market

"Four Ways Minimum Wage Increase Might Affect Companies," Mitrefinch.com (https://mitrefinch.com/blog/4-ways-minimum-wage-increase-might-effect-companies-in-2019/), January 10, 2019.

Jeffrey Clemens, Lisa Kahn, and Jonathan Meer, "The Minimum Wage, Fringe Benefits, and Worker Welfare," National Bureau of Economic Research Working Paper No. 24635, 2018.

John Horton, "Price Floors and Employer Preferences: Evidence from a Minimum Wage Experiment," Working Paper, New York University, July 17, 2018.

ECONOMICS IN YOUR LIFE: A Mayor Favors the Minimum Wage until Confronting Its Consequences

Pamela Wood, "Advocates, Maryland Lawmakers Seek to Raise Minimum Hourly Wage to $15 by 2023," *Baltimore Sun*, January 14, 2019.

John Rydell, "Maryland Legislator to Consider Bill to Increase Minimum Wage to $15 per Hour," Fox5News Baltimore, February 27, 2018.

"Baltimore City Council Asks State to Raise Minimum Wage," *USA Today*, February 6, 2018.

ISSUES & APPLICATIONS: Why Shortages of Some Pharmaceuticals Generate Higher Prices for Other Drugs

U.S. Food and Drug Administration, "Drug Shortages" (https://www.fda.gov/Drugs/DrugSafety/DrugShortages/default.htm), 2019.

Catherine Hu, "The United States Is Running Out of Commonly Used Drugs Including Ones Used in Epidurals, and It's Put Us on 'the Brink of a Public Health Emergency,'" *Business Insider*, May 23, 2018.

Alexa Lardieri, "FDA Adds EpiPens to List of Drug Shortages," *U.S. News & World Report*, May 9, 2018.

Consumer Surplus, Producer Surplus, and Gains from Trade within a Price System

A key principle of economics is that the price system enables people to benefit from the voluntary exchange of goods and services. Economists measure the benefits from trade by applying the concepts of *consumer surplus* and *producer surplus*, which are defined in the sections that follow.

Consumer Surplus

Let's first examine how economists measure the benefits that consumers gain from engaging in market transactions in the price system. Consider Figure B-1, which displays a market demand curve, D. We begin by assuming that consumers face a per-unit price of this item given by P_A. Thus, the quantity demanded of this particular product is equal to Q_A at point A on the demand curve.

Willingness to Pay

Typically, we visualize the market demand curve as indicating the quantities that all consumers are willing to purchase at each possible price. The demand curve also tells

---

FIGURE B-1

Consumer Surplus

If the per-unit price is P_A, then at point A on the demand curve D, consumers desire to purchase Q_A units. To purchase Q_1 units of this item, consumers would have been willing to pay the price P_1 for the last unit purchased, but they have to pay only the per-unit price P_A, so they gain a surplus equal to $P_1 - P_A$ for the last of the Q_1 units purchased. Likewise, to buy the last of the Q_2 units, consumers would have been willing to pay the price P_2, so they gain the surplus equal to $P_2 - P_A$ for the last of the Q_2 units purchased. Summing these and all other surpluses that consumers receive from purchasing each of the Q_A units at the price P_A yields the total consumer surplus at this price, shown by the blue-shaded area.

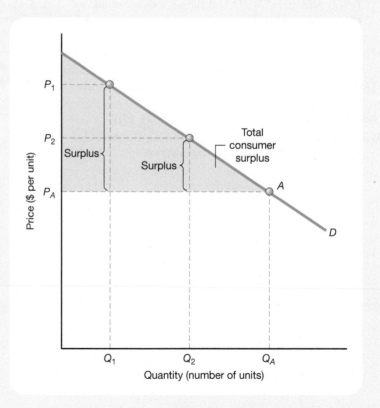

us the price that consumers are willing to pay for a unit of output at various possible quantities. For instance, if consumers buy Q_1 units of this good, they will be willing to pay a price equal to P_1 for the last unit purchased. If they have to pay only the price P_A for each unit they buy, however, consumers gain an amount equal to $P_1 - P_A$ for the last of the units Q_1 purchased. This benefit to consumers equals the vertical distance between the demand curve and the level of the market clearing price. Economists call this vertical distance a *surplus* value to consumers from being able to consume the last of the Q_1 units at the lower, market clearing price.

Likewise, if consumers purchase Q_2 units of this good, they will be willing to pay a price equal to P_2 for the last unit. Nevertheless, because they have to pay only the price P_A for each unit purchased, consumers gain an amount equal to $P_2 - P_A$. Hence, this is the surplus associated with the last of the Q_2 units that consumers buy.

Graphing Consumer Surplus

Of course, when consumers pay the same per-unit price P_A for every unit of this product that they purchase at point A, they obtain Q_A units. Thus, consumers gain surplus values—all of the vertical distances between the demand curve and the level of the market clearing price—for each unit consumed, up to the total of Q_A units. Graphically, this is equivalent to the blue-shaded *area under the demand curve but above the market clearing price* in Figure B-1. This entire area equals the total **consumer surplus,** which is the difference between the total amount that consumers *would have been willing to pay* for an item and the total amount that they actually pay. Note that "surplus" in this context is not the same as the "surplus" that arises when the government imposes a price floor. In economics, as in the rest of life, the same words can have different meanings depending on the context. Thus, it is always important to be aware of the context.

Consumer surplus
The difference between the total amount that consumers would have been willing to pay for an item and the total amount that they actually pay.

Producer Surplus

Consumers are not the only ones who gain from exchange. Producers (suppliers) gain as well. To consider how economists measure the benefits to producers from supplying goods and services in exchange, look at Figure B-2, which displays a market supply curve, S. Let's begin by assuming that suppliers face a per-unit price of this item given by P_B. Thus, the quantity supplied of this particular product is equal to Q_B at point B on the supply curve.

Willingness to Sell

The market supply curve tells us the quantities that all producers are willing to sell at each possible price. At the same time, the supply curve also indicates the price that producers are willing to accept to sell a unit of output at various possible quantities. For example, if producers sell Q_3 units of this good, they will be willing to accept a price equal to P_3 for the last unit sold. If they receive the price P_B for each unit they supply, however, producers gain an amount equal to $P_B - P_3$ for the last of the Q_3 units sold. This benefit to producers equals the vertical distance between the supply curve and the market clearing price, which is a *surplus* value from being able to provide the last of the Q_3 units at the higher, market clearing price.

Similarly, if producers supply Q_4 units of this good, they will be willing to accept a price equal to P_4 for the last unit. Producers actually receive the price P_B for each unit supplied, however, so they gain an amount equal to $P_B - P_4$. Hence, this is the surplus gained from supplying the last of the Q_4 units.

Graphing Producer Surplus

Naturally, when producers receive the same per-unit price P_B for each unit supplied at point B, producers sell Q_B units. Consequently, producers gain surplus values—all of the vertical distances between the level of the market clearing price and the supply

FIGURE B-2

Producer Surplus

If the per-unit price is P_B, then at point B on the supply curve S, producers are willing to supply Q_B units. To sell Q_3 units of this item, producers would have been willing to receive the price P_3 for the last unit sold, but instead they accept the higher per-unit price P_B, so they gain a surplus equal to $P_B - P_3$ for the last of the Q_3 units sold. Similarly, producers would have been willing to accept P_4 to provide Q_4 units, so they gain the surplus equal to $P_B - P_4$ for the last of the Q_4 units sold. Summing these and all other surpluses that producers receive from supplying each of the Q_B units at the price P_B yields the total producer surplus at this price, shown by the brown-shaded area.

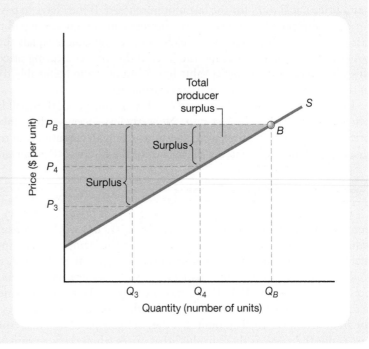

Producer surplus
The difference between the total amount that producers actually receive for an item and the total amount that they would have been willing to accept for supplying that item.

curve—for each unit supplied, up to the total of Q_B units. In Figure B-2 above, this is equivalent to the brown-shaded *area above the supply curve but below the market clearing price.* This area is the total **producer surplus,** which is the difference between the total amount that producers actually receive for an item and the total amount that they *would have been willing to accept* for supplying that item.

Gains from Trade within a Price System

The concepts of consumer surplus and producer surplus can be combined to measure the gains realized by consumers and producers from engaging in voluntary exchange. To see how, take a look at Figure B-3. The market demand and supply curves intersect at point E, and as you have learned, at this point, the equilibrium quantity is Q_E. At the market clearing price P_E, this is both the quantity that consumers are willing to purchase and the quantity that producers are willing to supply.

In addition, at the market clearing price P_E and the equilibrium quantity Q_E the blue-shaded area under the demand curve but above the market clearing price is the amount of consumer surplus. Furthermore, the brown-shaded area under the market clearing price but above the supply curve is the amount of producer surplus. The sum of *both* areas is the total value of the **gains from trade**—the sum of consumer surplus and producer surplus—generated by the mutually beneficial voluntary exchange of the equilibrium quantity Q_E at the market clearing price P_E.

Gains from trade
The sum of consumer surplus and producer surplus.

Consumer Surplus, Producer Surplus, and Gains from Trade

At point E, the demand and supply curves intersect at the equilibrium quantity Q_E and the market clearing price P_E. Total consumer surplus at the market clearing price is the blue-shaded area under the demand curve but above the market clearing price. Total producer surplus is the brown-shaded area below the market clearing price but above the supply curve. The sum of consumer surplus and producer surplus at the market clearing price constitutes the total gain to society from voluntary exchange of the quantity Q_E at the market clearing price P_E.

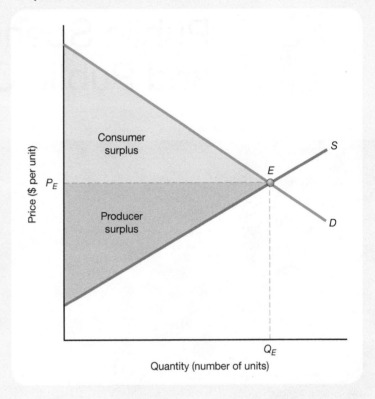

Price Controls and Gains from Trade

How do price controls affect gains from trade? Consider first the effects of imposing a ceiling price that is lower than the market clearing price. As you learned in an earlier chapter, the results are an increase in quantity demanded and a decrease in quantity supplied, so a shortage occurs. The smaller quantity supplied by firms is the amount actually produced and available in the market for the item in question. Thus, consumers are able to purchase fewer units, and this means that consumer surplus may be lower than it would have been without the government's price ceiling. Furthermore, because firms sell fewer units at the lower ceiling price, producer surplus definitely decreases. Thus, the government's imposition of the price ceiling tends to reduce gains from trade.

Now consider the effects of the establishment of a price floor above the market clearing price of a good. The effects of imposing such a floor price are an increase in the quantity supplied and a decrease in the quantity demanded. The smaller quantity demanded by consumers is the amount actually traded in the market. Thus, consumers purchase fewer units of the good, resulting in a reduction in consumer surplus. In addition, firms sell fewer units, so producer surplus may decrease. Hence, the establishment of a price floor also tends to reduce gains from trade.

5

Public Spending and Public Choice

Randall Runtsch/123RF GB Limited

LEARNING OBJECTIVES

After reading this chapter, you should be able to:

5.1 Explain how market failures such as externalities might justify economic functions of government

5.2 Distinguish between private goods and public goods and explain the nature of the free-rider problem

5.3 Describe political functions of government that entail its involvement in the economy

5.4 Analyze how public spending programs such as Medicare and spending on public education affect consumption incentives

5.5 Discuss the central elements of the theory of public choice

Many people assume that because governments often assist in providing or even directly produce particular goods or services, the actions of those governments are then "necessary" to make those items available for use. In fact, though, people regularly pay user charges for commodities provided by governments, such as fees for trash pickup by a city department or for entering or camping at a state park. Indeed, residents of Wisconsin have been learning that even though their state government's financing of the provision of services at their state parks has been slashed, those services have continued to be provided. In this chapter, you will learn about the important distinctions between private goods and public goods.

a nonprofit corporation manages all air traffic control in Canada? In contrast to the U.S. air traffic control system, which is managed by a U.S. government agency called the Federal Aviation Administration (FAA), Nav Canada is privately owned and operated. Some U.S. politicians have noticed that the FAA has struggled to function with antiquated technologies that commonly malfunction and create flight delays, whereas Nav Canada has put into place highly modern systems for tracking and directing flights. These politicians have called for the United States to follow Canada's example by shifting U.S. air-traffic control responsibilities away from the FAA to a private company that would function independently from the federal government.

Many of us think of "government" as a monolithic institution. Nevertheless, governmental decision making involves choices made by people who occupy roles as politicians, appointed officials, and employees of government agencies. We can assume that these human beings are, like any others, motivated by self-interest. In this chapter, you will learn that a key requirement of any economic analysis of governmental behavior is to account for government's distinctive *incentive structure*—that is, its unique system of rewards and punishments. First, however, you must understand the rationales for agents of government to undertake actions that can influence others' choices.

Market Failures and Externalities

Throughout the book so far, we have alluded to the advantages of a price system. High on the list is economic efficiency.

5.1 Explain how market failures such as externalities might justify economic functions of government

Advantages of a Price System

In its ideal form, a price system allows all resources to move from lower-valued uses to higher-valued uses via voluntary exchange, by which mutually advantageous trades take place.

Consumer Sovereignty In a price system, consumers are sovereign. That is to say, they have the individual freedom to decide what they wish to purchase. Politicians and even business managers do not ultimately decide what is produced. Consumers decide. Some proponents of the price system argue that this is its most important characteristic.

Benefits of Competition among Sellers and Buyers Competition among sellers is beneficial to consumers because the availability of more than one seller protects consumers from coercion by a single seller. Likewise, competition among buyers benefits sellers because the availability of multiple potential buyers protects sellers from coercion by one consumer.

Market Failures and Externalities

Sometimes the price system generates outcomes in which too few or too many resources go to specific economic activities. Such situations are **market failures.** Market failures prevent the price system from attaining economic efficiency and individual freedom. Market failures offer one of the strongest arguments in favor of certain economic functions of government, which we now examine.

In a pure market system, competition generates economic efficiency only when individuals know and must bear the true opportunity cost of their actions. In some circumstances, the price that someone actually pays for a resource, good, or service is higher or lower than the opportunity cost that all of society pays for that same resource, good, or service.

Market failure

A situation in which the market economy leads to too few or too many resources going to a specific economic activity.

Externalities Consider a hypothetical world in which there is no government regulation against pollution. You are living in a town that until now has had clean air. A steel mill moves into town. It produces steel and has paid for the inputs—land, labor, capital, and entrepreneurship. The price the mill charges for the steel reflects, in this example, only the costs that it incurs. In the course of production, however, the mill utilizes one input—clean air—by simply using it. This is indeed an input because in making steel, the furnaces emit smoke. The steel mill doesn't have to pay the cost of dirtying the air. Rather, the people in the community incur that cost in the form of dirtier clothes, dirtier cars and houses, and more respiratory illnesses.

The effect is similar to what would happen if the steel mill could take coal or oil or workers' services without paying for them. There is an **externality,** an external cost. Some of the costs associated with the production of the steel have "spilled over" to affect **third parties,** parties other than the buyer and the seller of the steel.

A fundamental reason that air pollution creates external costs is that the air belongs to everyone and hence to no one in particular. Lack of clearly assigned **property rights,** or the rights of an owner to use and exchange property, prevents market prices from reflecting all the costs created by activities that generate spillovers onto third parties.

How have external costs been created by production of pork in the state of North Carolina?

Externality
A consequence of an economic activity that spills over to affect third parties. Pollution is an externality.

Third parties
Parties who are not directly involved in a given activity or transaction.

Property rights
The rights of an owner to use and to exchange property.

EXAMPLE

Neighbors Are Not Hog Wild about a North Carolina Pig Farm

North Carolina residents who live close to a pig farm owned by Smithfield Foods are not key participants in the pork market in which the farm's hogs—about 4,700 are on the farm at any given time—are raised and sold. These neighbors do, however, have to deal with spillover effects created by the farm's large, open pools of manure, which employees regularly spray into lagoons, to be returned to the soil naturally. Neighbors of the farm must contend with foul odors and particulate pollution in the air that cause watery red eyes, sneezing, and coughing. Neighbors of this and other pig farms using similar production techniques regard these spillover effects

of hog production as external costs not taken into account by pork-producing firms when they decide how much pork to produce at given prices.

FOR CRITICAL THINKING

Could negative externalities be addressed if pork producers negotiated payments for the right to pollute air shared with properties owned by residential neighbors? Explain your reasoning.

Sources are listed at the end of this chapter.

External Costs in Graphical Form To consider how market prices fail to take into account external costs in situations in which third-party spillovers exist without a clear assignment of property rights, look at panel (a) in Figure 5-1. Here we show the demand curve for steel as D. The supply curve is S_1. The supply curve includes only the costs that the firms in the market have to pay. Equilibrium occurs at point E, with a price of $800 per ton and a quantity equal to 110 million tons per year.

Producing steel, however, also involves externalities—the external costs that people who reside near steel mills pay in the form of dirtier clothes, cars, and houses and increased respiratory disease due to the air pollution emitted from the mills. In this case, the producers of steel use clean air without having to pay for it. Let's include these external costs in our graph. Doing so will indicate what the full cost of steel production would really be if property rights to the air around the steel mill could generate payments for "owners" of that air. We do this by imagining that steel producers have to pay the "owners" of the air for the input—clean air—that the producers previously used at a zero price.

Recall from an earlier chapter that an increase in input prices shifts the supply curve upward and to the left. Thus, in panel (a) of the figure, the supply curve shifts from S_1 to S_2. External costs equal the vertical distance between A and E_1. In this example, if steel firms take into account these external costs, the equilibrium quantity falls to 100 million tons per year, and the price rises to $900 per ton. Equilibrium would shift from E to E_1. In contrast, if the price of steel does not account for external costs, third parties bear those costs—represented by the distance between A and E_1—in the form of dirtier clothes, houses, and cars and increased respiratory illnesses.

External Benefits in Graphical Form Externalities can also be positive. To demonstrate external benefits in graphical form, we will use the example of inoculations against communicable disease. In panel (b) of Figure 5-1, we show the demand curve as D_1 (without

ECONOMICS IN YOUR LIFE

To consider how an upsurge in pet travel on passenger planes is generating externalities, read **Fake "Service Pets" Create External Costs on Airline Flights** on page 114.

FIGURE 5-1

External Costs and Benefits

In panel (a), steel production generates external costs. If producers ignore pollution, the equilibrium quantity of steel will be 110 million tons. If producers had to pay all costs, the supply curve would shift the vertical distance $A—E_1$, to S_2. In panel (b), inoculations against communicable diseases generate external benefits. If each individual ignores these external benefits, the market clearing quantity will be 150 million. If buyers of inoculations took external benefits into account, however, the demand curve would shift to D_2. The new equilibrium quantity would be 200 million, and the equilibrium price of an inoculation would rise from $40 to $45.

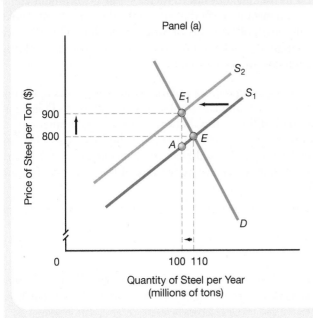

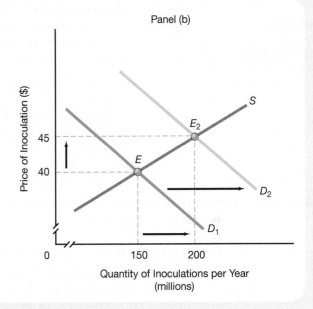

taking account of any external benefits) and the supply curve as S. The equilibrium price is $40 per inoculation, and the equilibrium quantity is 150 million inoculations.

We assume, however, that inoculations against communicable diseases generate external benefits to individuals who may not be inoculated but will benefit nevertheless because epidemics will not break out. If such external benefits were considered by those who purchase inoculations, the demand curve would shift from D_1 to D_2.

As a consequence of this shift in demand at point E_2, the new equilibrium quantity would be 200 million inoculations, and the new equilibrium price would be $45 per inoculation. If people who consider getting inoculations fail to take external benefits into account, individuals in society are not devoting enough resources to inoculations against communicable diseases.

Resource Misallocations of Externalities When there are external costs, the market will tend to *overallocate* resources to the production of the good or service in question, for those goods or services are implicitly priced deceptively low. In the steel example, too many resources will be allocated to steel production, because the steel mill owners and managers are not required to take account of the external cost that steel production is imposing on other individuals. In essence, the full cost of production is not borne by the owners and managers, so the price they charge the public for steel is lower than it would otherwise be. Of course, the lower price means that buyers are willing and able to buy more. More steel is produced and consumed than if the sellers and buyers were to bear external costs.

In contrast, when there are external benefits, the price is too low to induce suppliers to allocate resources to the production of that good or service (because the demand, which fails to reflect the external benefits, is too low). Thus, the market *underallocates* resources to producing the good or service. Hence, in a market system, too many of the goods that generate external costs are produced, and too few of the goods that generate external benefits are produced.

How the Government Can Correct Negative Externalities

In theory, the government can try to correct situations in which a lack of property rights allows third-party spillovers to create an externality. In the case of negative externalities, at least two avenues are open to the government: special taxes and legislative regulation or prohibition.

Effluent fee

A charge to a polluter that gives the right to discharge into the air or water a certain amount of pollution; also called a *pollution tax*.

Special Taxes In our example of the steel mill, the externality arises because using the air for waste disposal is costless to the firm but not to society. The government could attempt to tax the steel mill commensurate with the cost to third parties from smoke in the air. This, in effect, would be a pollution tax or an **effluent fee.** The ultimate effect would be to reduce the supply of steel and raise the price to consumers, ideally making the price equal to the full cost of production to society.

Regulation Alternatively, to correct a negative externality arising from steel production, the government could specify a maximum allowable rate of pollution. This regulation would require that the steel mill install pollution abatement equipment at its facilities, reduce its rate of output, or some combination of the two. Note that the government's job would not be simple, for it would have to determine the appropriate level of pollution, which would require extensive knowledge of both the benefits and the costs of pollution control.

WHAT HAPPENS WHEN...

governments require everyone to purchase health insurance?

Recently, both the federal government and a number of state governments have adopted rules requiring people to purchase various forms of insurance designed to fund health care expenses when they become ill or experience accidental injuries. Enforcement of such laws, which typically are intended to generate external benefits by ensuring that everyone obtains health care, boosts the amount of health insurance demanded at any given price. The results are a rightward shift in the market demand curve for health insurance, an upward movement along the market supply curve, and an increase in the equilibrium price of health insurance.

How the Government Can Correct Positive Externalities

What can the government do when the production of one good spills *benefits* over to third parties? It has several policy options: financing the production of the good or producing the good itself, regulation, and subsidies (negative taxes).

Government Financing and Production If the positive externalities seem extremely large, the government has the option of financing the desired additional production facilities so that the "right" amount of the good will be produced. Again consider inoculations against communicable diseases. The government could—and often does—finance campaigns to inoculate the population. It could (and does) even operate inoculation centers where inoculations are given at no charge.

Regulation In some cases involving positive externalities, the government can require by law that individuals in the society undertake a certain action. For example, regulations require that all school-age children be inoculated before entering public and private schools. Some people believe that a basic school education itself generates positive externalities. Perhaps as a result of this belief, we have regulations—laws— that require all school-age children to be enrolled in a public or private school.

Subsidies A subsidy is a negative tax. A subsidy is a per-unit payment made either to a business or to a consumer when the business produces or the consumer buys a good or a service. To generate more inoculations against communicable diseases, the government could subsidize everyone who obtains an inoculation by directly reimbursing those inoculated or by making per-unit payments to private firms that provide inoculations. Provision of a per-unit subsidy shifts the supply curve rightward, which generates a lower market clearing price and a higher equilibrium quantity.

The Other Economic Functions of Government

5.2 Distinguish between private goods and public goods and explain the nature of the free-rider problem

Besides correcting for externalities, the government performs many other economic functions that affect the way exchange is carried out. In contrast, the political functions of government have to do with deciding how income should be redistributed among households and selecting which goods and services have special merits and should therefore be treated differently. The economic and political functions of government can and do overlap.

Let's look at four more economic functions of government.

Providing a Legal System

The courts and the police may not at first seem like economic functions of government. Their activities nonetheless have important consequences for economic activities in any country. You and I enter into contracts constantly, whether they be oral or written, expressed or implied. When we believe that we have been wronged, we seek redress of our grievances through our legal institutions. Moreover, consider the legal system that is necessary for the smooth functioning of our economic system. Our system has defined quite explicitly the legal status of businesses, the rights of private ownership, and a method of enforcing contracts. All relationships among consumers and businesses are governed by the legal rules of the game.

In its judicial function, then, the government serves as the referee for settling disputes in the economic arena. In this role, the government often imposes penalties for violations of legal rules.

Much of our legal system is involved with defining and protecting property rights. One might say that property rights are really the rules of our economic game. When property rights are well defined, meaning that the government enforces those rights and allows their transferral, the owners of property have an incentive to use that property efficiently. Any mistakes in their decisions about the use of property have negative consequences that the owners suffer. Furthermore, when property rights are well defined, owners of property have an incentive to maintain that property so that if they ever desire to sell it, it will fetch a better price.

What happens when the government fails to establish clear rights to private property and fails to enforce owners' rights fully? In such situations, at least some individuals and firms will create spillover effects for other individuals. Thus, externalities will result. In these cases, however, externalities result from ambiguously assigned and weakly enforced property rights. The government, rather than the market, is at fault.

Promoting Competition

Many economists argue that the only way to attain economic efficiency is through competition. One of the roles of government is to serve as the protector of a competitive economic system. Congress and the various state governments have passed **antitrust legislation.** Such legislation makes illegal certain (but not all) economic activities that might restrain trade—that is, that might prevent free competition among actual and potential rival firms in the marketplace. The avowed aim of antitrust legislation is to reduce the power of **monopolies**—firms that can determine the market price of the goods they sell. A large number of antitrust laws have been passed that prohibit specific anticompetitive actions. Both the Antitrust Division of the U.S. Department of Justice and the Federal Trade Commission attempt to enforce these antitrust laws. Various state judicial agencies also expend efforts at maintaining competition.

Antitrust legislation
Laws that restrict the formation of monopolies and regulate certain anticompetitive business practices.

Monopoly
A firm that can determine the market price of a good. In the extreme case, a monopoly is the only seller of a good or service.

Providing Public Goods

The goods used in our examples up to this point have been **private goods.** When I use a tablet device, you cannot use the same one. So you and I are rivals for access to

Private goods
Goods that can be consumed by only one individual at a time. Private goods are subject to the principle of rival consumption.

that device, just as much as contenders for a sports world championship are. When I use the services of a tablet-device technician, that person cannot work at the same time for you. That is the distinguishing feature of private goods—their use is exclusive to the people who purchase them.

Principle of rival consumption
The recognition that individuals are rivals in consuming private goods because one person's consumption reduces the amount available for others to consume.

Private Goods and Rival Consumption The **principle of rival consumption** applies to most private goods. Rival consumption is easy to understand. Either you use such a private good or I use it.

Of course, private firms provide some goods and services that are not fully subject to the principle of rival consumption. For instance, you and a friend can both purchase tickets providing the two of you with the right to sit in a musical facility and listen to a concert during a specified period of time. Your friend's presence does not prohibit you from enjoying the music, nor does your presence prevent him from appreciating the concert. Nevertheless, the owner of the musical facility can prevent others who have not purchased tickets from entering the facility during the concert. Consequently, as long as nonpayers can be excluded from consuming an item, that item can also be produced and sold as a private good.

Public goods
Goods for which the principle of rival consumption does not apply and for which exclusion of nonpaying consumers is too costly to be feasible. They can be jointly consumed by many individuals at no additional cost and with no drop in quality or quantity. Furthermore, no one who fails to help pay for the good can be denied benefits.

Public Goods There is an entire class of goods that are not private goods. These are called **public goods.** Like fireworks displays, public goods are items to which the principle of rival consumption does not apply. Hence, many individuals simultaneously can consume public goods *jointly.* What truly distinguishes public goods from all private goods is that the costs required to exclude nonpayers from consuming public goods are so high that doing so is infeasible. National defense and police protection are examples. Suppose that your next-door neighbor were to pay for protection from a terrorist effort to explode a large bomb. If so, your neighbor's life and property could not be defended from such a threat without your life and property also receiving the same defense, even if you had failed to provide any payment for protection. Finding a way to avoid protecting you while still protecting your neighbor would be so expensive that such exclusion of defense for you and your property would be difficult.

Characteristics of Public Goods The combination of two fundamental characteristics of public goods sets them apart from all other goods:

1. *Public goods can be used by more and more people at no additional opportunity cost and without depriving others of any of the services of the goods.* Following expenditures on national defense, the defense protection you receive does not reduce the amount of protection bestowed on anyone else. The opportunity cost of your receiving national defense once it is in place is zero because after national defense is in place to protect you, it also protects others.

2. *It is difficult to design a collection system for a public good on the basis of how much individuals use it.* Nonpayers can often utilize a public good without incurring any monetary cost, because the cost of excluding them from using the good is so high. Those who provide the public good find that it is not cost-effective to prevent nonpayers from utilizing it. For instance, taxpayers who pay to provide national defense typically do not incur the costs that would be entailed in excluding nonpayers from benefiting from national defense.

The fundamental problem of public goods is that the private sector has a difficult, if not impossible, time providing them. Individuals in the private sector have little or no incentive to offer public goods. It is difficult for them to make a profit doing so, because it is too costly and, hence, infeasible to exclude nonpayers. Consequently, true public goods must necessarily be provided by government. (Note, though, that economists do not categorize something as a public good simply because the government provides it.)

Could big data be classified as a public good?

AI DECISION MAKING THROUGH DATA

Contemplating Big Data as a Public Good

A number of observers have advanced arguments that many forms of big data, such as large volumes of information obtained from the click-streams of people on the Internet, should be classified as public goods. Proponents of this view advance the argument that much information automatically collected about choices of many parties, such as individuals, firms, or governments, can readily be tracked electronically—both by human agents and by machine-guided apps. Furthermore, titles to ownership of such data are poorly defined, which enables virtually unhindered capture of these data from the Internet and other readily accessible communications networks. Finally, they contend that designing means of funding the process of compiling data in suitable form for universal availability might prove difficult. Based on these arguments, these proponents conclude that most forms of big data are public goods.

One problem with such arguments is that considerable amounts of data are collected under private contractual agreements. For instance, most consumers obtain access to a particular Internet site by agreeing to allow the operator access to and the right to use to all information. In addition, the prices that consumers pay for services compensate firms for taking actions to ensure confidentiality of the consumers' data. Thus, legal ownership of information implies control over who has access to much of the information contained in privately compiled datasets. In addition, access to almost all bits of data can be priced. Even on the Internet, anyone who has collected data can limit access to the data to people willing to pay for the information. Thus, while it is possible that certain large datasets might qualify, under very particular circumstances, as public goods, most large datasets are private goods subject to the principle of rival consumption.

REAL APPLICATION

Over 2 billion people use Facebook. Consequently, Facebook has access to enormous amounts of Internet usage data. Facebook allowed access to such data by Microsoft, Spotify, and Netflix. If you are a Facebook user, should you be worried?

Sources are listed at the end of this chapter.

Free Riders The nature of public goods leads to the **free-rider problem,** a situation in which some individuals take advantage of the fact that others will assume the burden of paying for public goods such as national defense. Suppose that citizens were taxed directly in proportion to how much they tell an interviewer that they value national defense. Some people who actually value national defense will probably tell interviewers that it has no value to them—they don't want any of it. Such people are trying to be free riders. We may all want to be free riders if we believe that someone else will provide the commodity in question that we actually value.

The free-rider problem often arises in connection with sharing the burden of international defense. A country may choose to belong to a multilateral defense organization, such as the North Atlantic Treaty Organization (NATO), but then consistently attempt to avoid contributing funds to the organization. The nation knows it would be defended by others in NATO if it were attacked but would rather not pay for such defense. In short, it seeks a free ride.

Free-rider problem
A problem that arises when individuals presume that others will pay for public goods so that, individually, they can escape paying for their portion without causing a reduction in production.

Ensuring Economywide Stability

Our economy sometimes faces the problems of undesired unemployment and rising prices. The government, especially the federal government, has made an attempt to solve these problems by trying to stabilize the economy by smoothing out the ups and downs in overall business activity. The notion that the federal government should undertake actions to stabilize business activity is a relatively new idea in the United States, encouraged by high unemployment rates during the Great Depression of the 1930s and subsequent theories about possible ways that government could reduce unemployment. In 1946, Congress passed the Full-Employment Act, a landmark law concerning government responsibility for economic performance. It established three goals for government stabilization policy: full employment, price stability, and economic growth. These goals have provided the justification for many government economic programs during the post–World War II period.

5.3 Describe political functions of government that entail its involvement in the economy

The Political Functions of Government

At least two functions of government are political or normative functions rather than economic ones like those discussed in the first part of this chapter. These two areas are (1) the provision of government-sponsored and prevention of government-inhibited goods and (2) income redistribution.

Government-Sponsored and Government-Inhibited Goods

Government-sponsored good

A good that has been deemed socially desirable through the political process. Museums are an example.

Through political processes, governments often determine that certain goods possess special merit and seek to promote their production and consumption. A **government-sponsored good** is defined as any good that the political process has deemed worthy of public support. Examples of government-sponsored goods in our society are sports stadiums, museums, ballets, plays, and operas. In these areas, the government's role is the provision of these goods to the people in society who would not otherwise purchase them at market clearing prices or who would not purchase an amount of them judged to be sufficient. This provision may take the form of government production and distribution of the goods. It can also take the form of reimbursement for spending on government-sponsored goods or subsidies to producers or consumers for part of the goods' costs.

Governments do indeed subsidize such goods as professional sports, operas, ballets, museums, and plays. In most cases, those goods would not be so numerous without subsidization.

To what extent is the provision of light rail passenger services in U.S. cities sponsored by governments?

POLICY EXAMPLE

Government Sponsorship Keeps Light Rail Systems in Operation

In recent years, so-called "light rail" systems, which typically include connecting bus vehicle services, have expanded existing operations considerably in a number of U.S. urban areas. Very few such systems could function without substantial government sponsorship, however.

Consider, for instance, Washington D.C.'s Metro light rail and bus service, which incurs about $3.1 billion per year in overall operating expenses. Passenger fares and station parking fees annually provide only about $0.8 billion toward covering these costs. Local city and state governments contribute more than $1.8 billion per year in funds raised from local taxpayers. Federal taxpayers provide the nearly $0.5 billion in additional financing required to keep the Metro system moving people through and around the nation's capital city.

Other operations of urban light rail systems also are heavily subsized by local, state, and federal governments. Many billions of dollars per year must be raised from taxpayers to keep these government-sponsored transportation services operating year after year.

FOR CRITICAL THINKING

Why do you suppose that light rail service cutbacks take place when governments reduce their sponsorship funding even if an affected operating authority responds by charging riders slightly higher fares?

Sources are listed at the end of this chapter.

Government-inhibited good

A good that has been deemed socially undesirable through the political process. Heroin is an example.

Government-inhibited goods are the opposite of government-sponsored goods. They are goods that, through the political process, have been deemed undesirable for human consumption. Heroin, cigarettes, gambling, and cocaine are examples. The government exercises its role with respect to these goods by taxing, regulating, or prohibiting their manufacture, sale, and use. Governments justify the relatively high taxes on alcohol and tobacco by declaring that they are socially undesirable. The best-known example of governmental exercise of power in this area is the stance against certain psychoactive drugs. Most psychoactives (except nicotine, caffeine, and alcohol) are either expressly prohibited, as is the case for heroin, cocaine, and opium, or heavily regulated, as in the case of prescription psychoactives.

Can policymakers seeking to inhibit consumption of nicotine generate equal rates of "success" by imposing the same inhibiting policies on people who smoke traditional cigarettes and on those who "vape" e-cigarettes?

BEHAVIORAL EXAMPLE

To Inhibit Nicotine Consumption, Should the Government Assume That All Consumers Behave the Same?

Even though nicotine is not a legally prohibited drug, various federal and state government agencies devote considerable resources toward inhibiting U.S. consumption. Most people who consume nicotine do so by smoking cigarettes, but an increasing number of nicotine consumers utilize e-cigarettes instead of or alongside traditional cigarette smoking. Government agencies are seeking to inhibit nicotine consumption of e-cigarettes via methods, such as taxation and regulation, that are analogous to those used to inhibit consumption of traditional cigarettes.

Recent behavioral research indicates, however, that the responses to government taxation or regulation likely depend on whether individuals consume nicotine via traditional cigarette smoking, e-cigarette "vaping," or both. For instance, Joachim Marti of Imperial College London, Johanna Maclean of Temple University, and John Buckell and Jody Sindelar of Yale University provide evidence that nicotine consumption choices differ across these three consumption methods. Motives to use e-cigarettes differ from those affecting consumption of nicotine via traditional cigarettes. The effects on nicotine consumption of taxing or regulating "vaping" thereby will not necessarily correspond to the effects of taxing or regulating traditional cigarette smoking. Thus, government agencies cannot assume that taxing or regulating users of e-cigarettes similarly to smokers of traditional cigarettes will yield the same outcomes with respect to inhibiting consumption of nicotine.

FOR CRITICAL THINKING

Why might imposing the same taxes on traditional cigarettes and e-cigarettes fail to generate the same changes in quantity demanded? (Hint: *Is someone who is limiting nicotine consumption by exclusively "vaping" likely to cut back as much in response to a tax-induced price increase than someone who regularly smokes traditional cigarettes?*)

Sources are listed at the end of this chapter.

Income Redistribution

Another relatively recent political function of government has been the explicit redistribution of income. This redistribution uses two systems: the progressive income tax (described in another chapter) and transfer payments. **Transfer payments** are payments made to individuals for which no services or goods are rendered in return. The two primary money transfer payments in our system are Social Security old-age and disability benefits and unemployment insurance benefits. Income redistribution also includes a large amount of income **transfers in kind,** which people must direct to spending on specified goods, in contrast to money transfers that they can allocate to spending on any items they desire. Some income transfers in kind are benefits provided for food purchases through the Supplemental Nutritional Assistance Program, for health care spending by Medicare and Medicaid, and for subsidized public housing.

The government has also engaged in other activities as a form of redistribution of income. For example, the provision of public education is at least in part an attempt to redistribute income by making sure that the poor have access to education.

Transfer payments
Money payments made by governments to individuals for which no services or goods are rendered in return. Examples are Social Security old-age and disability benefits and unemployment insurance benefits.

Transfers in kind
Payments that are in the form of actual goods and services, such as food stamps, subsidized public housing, and medical care, and for which no goods or services are rendered in return.

Public Spending and Transfer Programs

The size of the public sector can be measured in many different ways. One way is to count the number of public employees. Another is to look at total government outlays. Government outlays include all government expenditures on employees, rent, electricity, and the like. In addition, total government outlays include transfer payments, such as welfare and Social Security.

In Figure 5-2, you see that government outlays prior to World War I did not exceed 10 percent of annual national income. There was a spike during World War I, an increase during the Great Depression, and then a huge spike during World War II. After World War II, government outlays as a percentage of total national income rose steadily before dropping in the 1990s, rising again in the early 2000s, and then jumping sharply beginning in 2008.

How do federal and state governments allocate their spending? A typical federal government budget allocation is shown in panel (a) of Figure 5-3. The three largest categories are Medicare and other health-related spending, Social Security and other income security programs, and national defense, which together constitute 77.1 percent of the total federal budget.

The makeup of state and local expenditures is quite different. As panel (b) shows, education is the biggest category, accounting for 33.0 percent of all expenditures.

> **5.4** Analyze how public spending programs such as Medicare and spending on public education affect consumption incentives

FIGURE 5-2

Total Government Outlays over Time

Total government outlays (federal, state, and local combined) remained small until the 1930s, except during World War I. After World War II, government outlays did not fall back to their historical average and quite recently have risen back close to their World War II levels.

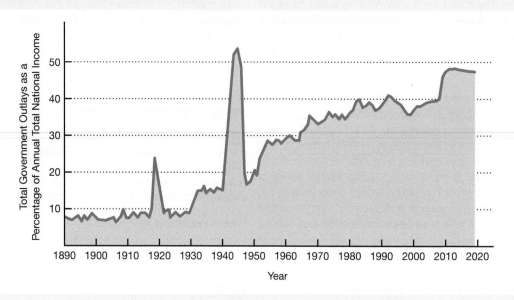

Sources: *Facts and Figures on Government Finance*, various issues; *Economic Indicators*, various issues.

FIGURE 5-3

Federal Government Spending Compared to State and Local Spending

The federal government's spending habits are quite different from those of the states and cities. In panel (a), you can see that the most important categories in the federal budget are Medicare and other health-related spending, Social Security and other income security programs, and national defense, which make up 77.1 percent.

In panel (b), the most important category at the state and local level is education, which makes up 33 percent. "Other" includes expenditures in such areas as health and hospitals, waste treatment, garbage collection, mosquito abatement, and the judicial system.

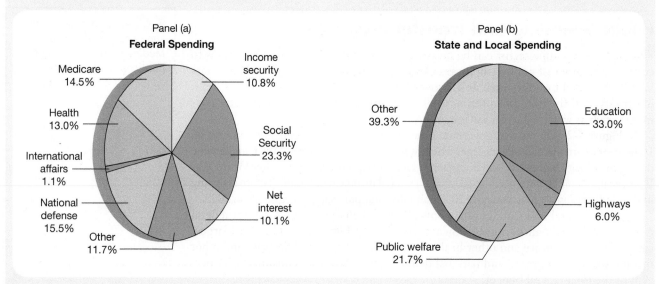

Sources: *Economic Report of the President, Economic Indicators.*

Publicly Subsidized Health Care: Medicare

Figure 5-3 shows that health-related spending is a significant portion of total government expenditures. Certainly, medical expenses are a major concern for many elderly people. Since 1965, that concern has been reflected in the existence of the Medicare program, which pays much of hospital and physicians' bills for U.S. residents over the age of 65 (and for those younger than 65 in some instances). In return for paying a tax on their earnings while in the workforce (2.9 percent of wages and salaries, plus 3.8 percent on certain income for high-income households), retirees are assured that the majority of their hospital and physicians' bills will be paid for with public monies.

The Simple Economics of Medicare To understand how, in fewer than 50 years, Medicare became the second-biggest domestic government spending program in existence, a bit of economics is in order. Consider Figure 5-4, which shows the demand for and supply of medical care.

The initial equilibrium price is P_0 and equilibrium quantity is Q_0. Perhaps because the government believes that Q_0 is not enough medical care for these consumers, suppose that the government begins paying a subsidy that eventually is set at M for each unit of medical care consumed. This will simultaneously tend to raise the price per unit of care received by providers (physicians, hospitals, and the like) and lower the perceived price per unit that consumers see when they make decisions about how much medical care to consume. As presented in the figure, the price received by providers rises to P_s, while the price paid by consumers falls to P_d. As a result, consumers of medical care want to purchase Q_m units, and suppliers are quite happy to provide it for them.

Medicare Incentives at Work We can now understand the problems that plague the Medicare system today. First, one of the things that people observed during the 20 years after the founding of Medicare was a huge upsurge in physicians' incomes and medical school applications, the spread of private for-profit hospitals, and the rapid proliferation of new medical tests and procedures. All of this was being encouraged by the rise in the price of medical services from P_0 to P_s, as shown in Figure 5-4, which encouraged entry into this market.

Second, government expenditures on Medicare have routinely turned out to be far in excess of the expenditures forecast at the time the program was put in place or was expanded. The reasons for this are easy to see. Bureaucratic planners often fail to

FIGURE 5-4

The Economic Effects of Medicare Subsidies

When the government pays a per-unit subsidy M for medical care, consumers pay the price of services P_d for the quantity of services Q_m. Providers receive the price P_s for supplying this quantity. Originally, the federal government projected that its total spending on Medicare would equal an amount such as the area $Q_0 \times (P_0 - P_d)$. Because actual consumption equals Q_m, however, the government's total expenditures equal $Q_m \times M$.

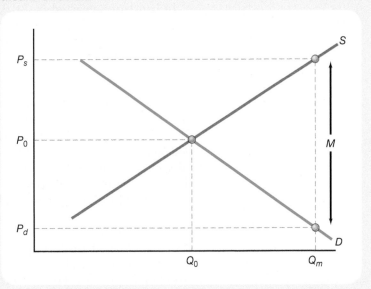

recognize the incentive effects of government programs. On the demand side, they fail to account for the huge increase in consumption (from Q_0 to Q_m) that will result from a subsidy like Medicare. On the supply side, they fail to recognize that the larger number of services can only be extracted from suppliers at a higher price, P_s.

Consequently, original projected spending on Medicare was an area like $Q_0 \times (P_0 - P_d)$, because original plans for the program only contemplated consumption of Q_0 and assumed that the subsidy would have to be only $P_0 - P_d$ per unit. In fact, consumption rises to Q_m, and the additional cost per unit of service rises to P_s, implying an increase in the per-unit subsidy to M. Hence, actual expenditures turn out to be the far larger number $Q_m \times M$. Every expansion of the program has followed the same pattern. Examples include the 2004 broadening of Medicare to cover obesity as a new illness eligible for coverage and the extension of Medicare to cover patients' prescription drug expenses and coverage of psychological services for the elderly beginning in 2006.

Third, total spending on medical services has soared, consuming far more income than initially expected. Originally, total spending on medical services was $P_0 \times Q_0$. In the presence of Medicare, spending rises to $P_s \times Q_m$.

Health Care Subsidies Continue to Grow Just how fast are Medicare subsidies growing? Medicare's cost has risen from 0.7 percent of U.S. national income in 1970 to more than 3.5 percent today, which amounts to nearly $550 billion per year. Because Medicare spending is growing much faster than total employer and employee contributions, future spending guarantees far outstrip the taxes to be collected in the future to pay for the system. (The current Medicare tax rate is 2.9 percent on all wages, with 1.45 percent paid by the employee and 1.45 percent paid by the employer. For certain income earned above $200,000 for individuals and $250,000 for married couples, a 3.8 percent Medicare tax rate applies.) Today, unfunded guarantees of Medicare spending in the future are estimated at more than $25 trillion (in today's dollars).

These amounts fail to reflect the costs of another federal health program called Medicaid. The Medicaid program is structured similarly to Medicare, in that the government also pays per-unit subsidies for health care to qualifying patients. Medicaid, however, provides subsidies only to people who qualify because they have lower incomes. At present, about 70 million people, or about one out of every five U.S. residents, qualify for Medicaid coverage. Medicaid is administered by state governments, but the federal government pays about 60 percent of the program's total cost from general tax revenues. The current cost of the program is more than $500 billion per year. In recent years, inflation-adjusted Medicaid spending has grown even faster than expenditures on Medicare, rising by more than 150 percent since 2000 alone.

In legislation enacted in 2010, the U.S. Congress further expanded by about $100 billion per year the annual growth of government health care spending, which already has been increasing at an average pace of about $125 billion per year.

Economic Issues of Public Education

In the United States, government involvement in health care is a relatively recent phenomenon. In contrast, state and local governments have assumed primary responsibility for public education for many years. Currently, these governments spend about $1 trillion on education—in excess of 5 percent of total U.S. national income. State and local sales, excise, property, and income taxes finance the bulk of these expenditures. In addition, each year the federal government provides tens of billions of dollars of support for public education through grants and other transfers to state and local governments.

The Now-Familiar Economics of Public Education State and local governments around the United States have developed a variety of complex mechanisms for funding public education. What all public education programs have in common, however, is the provision of educational services to primary, secondary, and college students at prices well below those that would otherwise prevail in the marketplace for these services.

So how do state and local governments accomplish this? The answer is that they operate public education programs that share some of the features of government-subsidized health care programs such as Medicare. Analogously to Figure 5-4, public schools provide educational services at a price below the market price. They are willing and able to produce the quantity of educational services demanded at this below-market price as long as they receive a sufficiently high per-unit subsidy provided by funds obtained from taxpayers.

The Incentive Problems of Public Education Since the 1960s, various measures of the performance of U.S. primary and secondary students have failed to improve even as public spending on education has risen. Some measures of student performance have even declined.

Many economists argue that the incentive effects that have naturally arisen with higher government subsidies for public education help to explain this lack of improvement in student performance. A per-pupil subsidy creates a difference between the relatively high per-unit costs of providing the number of educational services that parents and students are willing to purchase and lower valuations of those services. As a consequence, some schools have provided services, such as after-school babysitting and various social services, that have contributed relatively little to student learning.

A factor that complicates efforts to assess the effects of education subsidies is that in most locales, parents who are unhappy with the quality of services provided at the subsidized price cannot transfer their child to a different public school. Thus, the individual public schools typically face little or no competition from unsubsidized providers of educational services.

Decision Making as a Parent An alternative to public education is private education. The cost to parents, however, is not covered by taxes. No matter how much a parent may have paid in property taxes that go to funding public schools, additional family funds have to be paid for the use of private schools. Each parent has to make the evaluation of the additional benefits a private education might offer compared to the additional direct cost. This calculation must be undertaken within the individual family's budget constraint. For most U.S. families, private education is not an option.

Collective Decision Making: The Theory of Public Choice

> **5.5** Discuss the central elements of the theory of public choice

Governments consist of individuals. No government actually thinks and acts. Instead, government actions are the result of decision making by individuals in their roles as elected representatives, appointed officials, and salaried bureaucrats. Therefore, to understand how government works, we must examine the incentives of the people in government. We also must study the incentives of those, such as special-interest lobbyists, who would like to influence government decisions. At issue is the analysis of **collective decision making.**

Collective decision making involves the actions of voters, politicians, political parties, interest groups, and many other groups and individuals. The analysis of collective decision making is usually called the **theory of public choice.** It has been given this name because it involves hypotheses about how choices are made in the public sector, as opposed to the private sector. The foundation of public-choice theory is the assumption that individuals will act within the political process to maximize their *individual* (not collective) well-being. In that sense, the theory is similar to our analysis of the market economy, in which we also assume that individuals act as though they are motivated by self-interest.

To understand public-choice theory, it is necessary to point out other similarities between the private market sector and the public, or government, sector. Then we will look at the differences.

Collective decision making
How voters, politicians, and other interested parties act and how these actions influence nonmarket decisions.

Theory of public choice
The study of collective decision making.

Similarities in Market and Public-Sector Decision Making

In addition to the assumption of self-interest as the motivating force in both sectors, there are other similarities.

Opportunity Cost Everything that is spent by all levels of government plus everything that is spent by the private sector must add up to the total income available at any point in time. Hence, every government action has an opportunity cost, just as in the market sector.

Competition Although we typically think of competition as a private market phenomenon, it is also present in collective action. Given the scarcity constraint government faces, bureaucrats, appointed officials, and elected representatives will always be in competition for available government funds. Furthermore, the individuals within any government agency or institution will act as individuals do in the private sector: They will try to obtain higher wages, better working conditions, and higher job-level classifications. We assume that they will compete and act in their own interest, not society's.

Similarity of Individuals Contrary to popular belief, the types of individuals working in the private sector and working in the public sector are not inherently different. The difference, as we shall see, is that the individuals in government face a different **incentive structure** than those in the private sector. For example, the costs and benefits of being efficient or inefficient differ in the private and public sectors.

One approach to predicting government bureaucratic behavior is to ask what incentives bureaucrats face. Take the U.S. Postal Service (USPS) as an example. The bureaucrats running that government corporation are human beings with IQs not dissimilar to those possessed by workers in similar positions at Google or Apple. Yet the USPS does not function like either of these companies.

The difference can be explained in terms of the incentives provided for managers in the two types of institutions. When the bureaucratic managers and workers at Google make incorrect decisions, work slowly, produce shoddy programs, and are generally "inefficient," the profitability of the company declines. The owners—millions of shareholders—express their displeasure by selling some of their shares of company stock. The market value, as tracked on the stock exchange, falls. This induces owners of shares of stock to pressure managers to pursue strategies more likely to boost revenues and reduce costs.

What about the USPS? If a manager, a worker, or a bureaucrat in the USPS gives shoddy service, the organization's owners—the taxpayers—have no straightforward mechanism for expressing their dissatisfaction. Despite the postal service's status as a "government corporation," taxpayers as shareholders do not own shares of stock in the organization that they can sell.

Thus, to understand purported inefficiency in the government bureaucracy, we need to examine incentives and institutional arrangements—not people and personalities.

Differences between Market and Collective Decision Making

There are probably more dissimilarities between the market sector and the public sector than there are similarities.

Government Goods and Services at Zero Price The majority of goods that governments produce are furnished to the ultimate consumers without payment required. **Government**, or **political, goods** can be either private or public goods. The fact that they are furnished to the ultimate consumer free of charge does *not* mean that the cost to society of those goods is zero, however. It only means that the price *charged* is zero. The full opportunity cost to society is the value of the resources used in the production of goods produced and provided by the government.

For example, none of us pays directly for each unit of consumption of defense or police protection. Rather, we pay for all these items indirectly through the taxes that support our governments—federal, state, and local. This special feature of government can be looked at in a different way. There is no longer a one-to-one relationship between consumption of government-provided goods and services and payment for

---

Incentive structure
The system of rewards and punishments individuals face with respect to their own actions.

Government, or political, goods
Goods (and services) provided by the public sector; they can be either private or public goods.

these items. Indeed, most taxpayers will find that their tax bill is the same whether or not they consume government-provided goods.

Why do you suppose government spaceflight agencies such as the National Aeronautics and Space Administration (NASA) have jettisoned into space most launched rocket components, whereas private launch companies have developed techniques for reusing such materials?

POLICY EXAMPLE

Private Space Firms Recycle Rocket Boosters and Capsules That the Government Regards as Throwaways

Space shuttles that NASA flew and re-flew during a generation of suborbital spaceflight were among the only materials that NASA did not jettison in orbit, allow to disintegrate or crash, or leave on the moon. Virtually all other materials utilized over the course of seven decades of space missions effectively were scrapped after a single use. NASA's primary mission objectives involved speedily proving that various aspects of spaceflight and exploration were or were not feasible with available technology and given the agency's annual budget funded by taxpayers. Minimizing overall expenses by designing systems and equipment that could be used more than once were not key elements of NASA's planning or operations.

Private spaceflight companies, in contrast, incur ongoing expenses that reflect the full opportunity costs of all resources devoted to space travel instead of alternative purposes. The private resources dedicated to placing a satellite into orbit around the earth otherwise could be utilized to transport fresh lobsters to restaurants at various points around the planet.

United Parcel Service and FedEx react to having to pay all of the expenses entailed in transporting fresh lobsters to restaurants by reusing planes and trucks over the course of several years. In like manner, private firms such as SpaceX and United Launch Alliance are responding to incurring all relevant opportunity costs of allocating resources to spaceflight by reusing rocket parts, boosters, and capsules. For these firms, recycling these materials yields the lowest price that must be paid for private space travel.

FOR CRITICAL THINKING

Why might privately financed spaceflight add less each year to the clutter of abandoned materials in orbit as compared with past annual jettisons of materials by NASA and agencies funded by European and Asian governments?

Sources are listed at the end of this chapter.

Use of Force All governments can resort to using force in their regulation of economic affairs. For example, governments can use *expropriation*, which means that if you refuse to pay your taxes, your bank account and other assets may be seized by the Internal Revenue Service. In fact, you have no choice in the matter of paying taxes to governments. Collectively, we decide the total size of government through the political process, but individually, we cannot determine how much service we pay for during any one year.

Voting versus Spending In the private market sector, a dollar voting system is in effect. This dollar voting system is not equivalent to the voting system in the public sector. There are at least three differences:

1. In a political system, one person gets one vote, whereas in the market system, each dollar a person spends counts separately.

2. The political system is run by **majority rule,** whereas the market system is run by **proportional rule.**

3. The spending of dollars can indicate intensity of want, whereas because of the all-or-nothing nature of political voting, a vote cannot.

Political outcomes often differ from economic outcomes. Remember that economic efficiency is a situation in which, given the prevailing distribution of income, consumers obtain the economic goods they want. There is no corresponding situation when political voting determines economic outcomes. Thus, a political voting process is unlikely to lead to the same decisions that a dollar voting process would yield in the marketplace.

Indeed, consider the dilemma every voter faces. Usually, a voter is not asked to decide on a single issue (although this happens). Rather, a voter is asked to choose among candidates who present a large number of issues and state a position on each of them. Just consider the average U.S. senator, who has to vote on several thousand different issues during a six-year term. When you vote for that senator, you are voting for a person who must make thousands of decisions during the next six years.

Majority rule
A collective decision-making system in which group decisions are made on the basis of more than 50 percent of the vote. In other words, whatever more than half of the electorate votes for, the entire electorate has to accept.

Proportional rule
A decision-making system in which actions are based on the proportion of the "votes" cast and are in proportion to them. In a market system, if 10 percent of the "dollar votes" are cast for blue cars, 10 percent of automobile output will be blue cars.

ECONOMICS IN YOUR LIFE

Fake "Service Pets" Create External Costs on Airline Flights

Dexter is a peacock, a type of bird that can weigh up to 20 pounds and extend in length to 7 feet. To a woman who sought to bring Dexter aboard an airline flight, however, the bird should be classified as an "emotional-support animal." Indeed, the Air Carrier Access Act of 1986 allows people with physical disabilities or mental illnesses or other emotional problems who travel on passenger planes to be accompanied by service pets, such as guide dogs and emotional-support animals.

Unfortunately for a number of passengers, the presence of service pets within airline passenger cabins can create adverse spillover effects. People who have asthma problems and others who are allergic to various animals can find themselves wheezing during the durations of their flights. In some cases, emotional-support animals have even attacked passengers and trained service pets that airlines long have permitted for passengers with disabilities such as blindness.

A growing problem is a proliferation of firms that provide, typically for a fee of about $100, over-the-phone emotional-distress "diagnoses" and letters attesting to "needs" for in-flight service-pet accompaniment. In addition, anyone who wishes to try to take a pet on a flight and claim a physical disability that requires the pet's assistance can obtain an official-looking "service pet" vest at a price of about $40. Once planes are in the air with illegitimate "service pets," passengers can suffer the consequences.

FOR CRITICAL THINKING

Why do you suppose that proposals have surfaced for the U.S. Transportation Department to allow airlines to charge special fees to passengers who wish to board planes accompanied by service pets?

REAL APPLICATION

Airline companies are increasingly changing their rules about which animals they will accept as "service animals." If by chance you require a service animal to enjoy less stressful airline flights, then the change in rules may affect you. What might be your options if your particular service animal is no longer accepted?

Sources are listed at the end of this chapter.

ISSUES & APPLICATIONS

Randall Runtsch/123RF GB Limited

Residents of Wisconsin Learn That Services Provided by State Parks Are Not Public Goods

CONCEPTS APPLIED

➤ Public Goods

➤ Principle of Rival Consumption

➤ Government-Sponsored Goods

Because the land that state parks occupy typically is government-owned, most people think of the services provided by such parks as public goods. Residents of Wisconsin, however, have learned from recent experience that the services offered by their state's parks most assuredly do not qualify for classification as public goods—a fact that economists have long known.

Why the Services Provided by State Parks Are Not Public Goods

Although state parks are on publicly owned lands, the services that they provide visitors are not public goods. Undoubtedly, a few people find ways to sneak into any state park from time to time, but otherwise such parks have a straightforward way of collecting fees based on how often people visit: entrances with gates that prevent vehicle entry until occupants pay a specified fee. Furthermore, although numerous people can fit within the open spaces at many state parks, the fact is that more and more people cannot really utilize the services that such parks offer without depriving others of those services. As more vehicles enter a park's grounds, parking lots eventually fill up, roads become more heavily congested, and the most notable features of the park become crowded with people and hence less accessible to the latest people who pay to enter the park.

Furthermore, many services commonly offered by parks are subject to the principle of rival consumption. To be sure, once someone enters a picturesque park, at least some of the beauty can be enjoyed even if the park becomes increasingly congested. Nevertheless, if one family camps at a park's campsite, another family cannot camp there. If one couple takes a rowboat onto a park's lake, another couple cannot use the boat. Indeed, most state parks charge additional fees. Thus, the parks can readily exclude people who fail to pay for access to these types of park services.

How Wisconsin State Parks' Ties to Government Are Fraying

In Wisconsin, the state government has taken an additional step. In contrast to most states, in which state parks receive periodic grants from the government, Wisconsin recently ended most taxpayer support. The main aspect of Wisconsin state parks that merits the "state" descriptor is that their operations are overseen by a government agency because they occupy government-owned lands. The state's

parks must generate sufficient funds to finance most of their operations, however.

One funding idea that has gained attention recently is to permit limited advertising. In light of a lack of enthusiasm for billboards and similar forms of advertising that would detract from the natural beauty of Wisconsin parks, officials have contemplated instead the idea of granting "naming rights" for various facilities. Under a recent proposal, corporations or groups might, for instance, be granted the right, in exchange for periodic funding grants, to post the name of their company or organization at a campsite or other park facility.

FOR CRITICAL THINKING

In what way does the state of Wisconsin, by providing the lands occupied by state parks, make implicit grants even though the government transmits few payments explicitly? (*Hint:* Remember the concept of opportunity cost of any resource, including lands with alternative uses.)

REAL APPLICATION

The population is growing in the United States, average incomes are rising, and more U.S. residents are taking vacations. State park campgrounds are often booked months in advance and those tourists who show up for camping often cannot find a space. What business opportunity does this situation create?

Sources are listed at the end of this chapter.

What You Should Know

Here is what you should know after reading this chapter.

LEARNING OBJECTIVES

5.1 **Explain how market failures such as externalities might justify economic functions of government** *A market failure occurs when too many or too few resources are directed to a specific form of economic activity. One type of market failure is an externality, which is a spillover effect on third parties not directly involved in producing or purchasing a good or service. In the case of a negative externality, firms do not pay for the costs arising from spillover effects that their production of a good imposes on others, so they produce too much of the good in question. In the case of a positive externality, buyers fail to take into account the benefits that their consumption of a good yields to others, so they purchase too little of the good.*

5.2 **Distinguish between private goods and public goods and explain the nature of the free-rider problem** *Private goods are subject to the principle of rival consumption, meaning that one person's consumption of such a good reduces the amount available for another person to consume. In contrast, public goods can be consumed by many people simultaneously at no additional opportunity cost and with no reduction in quality or quantity. In addition, no individual can be excluded from the benefits of a public good even if that person fails to help pay for it.*

KEY TERMS

market failure, 99
externality, 100
third parties, 100
property rights, 100
effluent fee, 102
Key Figures
Figure 5-1, 101

antitrust legislation, 103
monopoly, 103
private goods, 103
principle of rival
  consumption, 104
public goods, 104
free-rider problem, 105

LEARNING OBJECTIVES	KEY TERMS

5.3 **Describe political functions of government that entail its involvement in the economy** *As a result of the political process, government may seek to promote the production and consumption of government-sponsored goods. The government may also seek to restrict the production and sale of goods that have been deemed socially undesirable, called government-inhibited goods. In addition, the political process may determine that income redistribution is socially desirable.*

government-sponsored good, 106
government-inhibited good, 106
transfer payments, 107
transfers in kind, 107

5.4 **Analyze how public spending programs such as Medicare and spending on public education affect consumption incentives** *Medicare subsidizes the consumption of medical services. As a result, the quantity consumed is higher, as is the price sellers receive per unit of those services. Subsidies for programs such as Medicare and public education also encourage people to consume services that are very low in per-unit value relative to the cost of providing them.*

Key Figures
Figure 5-2, 108
Figure 5-4, 109

5.5 **Discuss the central elements of the theory of public choice** *The theory of public choice applies to collective decision making, or the process through which voters and politicians interact to influence nonmarket choices. Certain aspects of public-sector decision making, such as scarcity and competition, are similar to those that affect private-sector choices. Others, however, such as legal coercion and majority-rule decision making, differ from those involved in the market system.*

collective decision making, 111
theory of public choice, 111
incentive structure, 112
government, or political, goods, 112
majority rule, 113
proportional rule, 113

PROBLEMS

5-1. Many people who do not smoke cigars are bothered by the odor of cigar smoke. If private contracting is impossible, will too many or too few cigars be produced and consumed? Taking *all* costs into account, is the market price of cigars too high or too low?

5-2. Suppose that repeated application of a pesticide used on orange trees causes harmful contamination of groundwater. The pesticide is applied annually in almost all of the orange groves throughout the world. Most orange growers regard the pesticide as a key input in their production of oranges.

   a. Use a diagram of the market for the pesticide to illustrate the implications of a failure of orange producers' costs to reflect the social costs of groundwater contamination.

   b. Use your diagram from part (a) to explain a government policy that might be effective in achieving the amount of orange production that fully reflects all social costs.

5-3. Draw a diagram of the market for oranges. Explain how the government policy you discussed in part (b) of Problem 5-2 is likely to affect the market price and equilibrium quantity in the orange market. In what sense do consumers of oranges now "pay" for dealing with the spillover costs of pesticide production?

5-4. Suppose the U.S. government determines that cigarette smoking creates social costs not reflected in the current market price and equilibrium quantity of cigarettes. A study has recommended that the government can correct for the externality effect of cigarette consumption by paying farmers *not* to plant tobacco used to manufacture cigarettes. It also recommends raising the funds to make these payments by increasing taxes on cigarettes. Assuming that the government is correct that cigarette smoking creates external costs, evaluate whether the study's recommended policies might help correct this negative externality.

5-5. A nation's government has determined that mass transit, such as bus lines, helps alleviate traffic congestion, thereby benefiting both individual auto commuters and companies that desire to move products and factors of production speedily along streets and highways. Nevertheless, even though several private bus lines are in service, the country's commuters are failing to take into account the positive externality associated with the use of mass transit.

   a. Discuss, in the context of demand-supply analysis, the essential implications of commuters' failure to take into account the positive externality associated with bus ridership.

b. Explain a government policy that might be effective in achieving the socially efficient use of bus services.

5-6. Draw a diagram of this nation's market for automobiles, which are a substitute for buses. Explain how the government policy you discussed in part (b) of Problem 5-5 is likely to affect the market price and equilibrium quantity in the country's auto market. How are auto consumers affected by this policy described in your answer to Problem 5-5?

5-7. Consider a nation with a government that does not provide people with property rights for a number of items and that fails to enforce the property rights it does assign for remaining items. Would externalities be more or less common in this nation than in a country such as the United States? Explain.

5-8. Many economists suggest that our nation's legal system is an example of a public good. Does the legal system satisfy the key properties of a public good? Explain your reasoning.

5-9. Displayed in the diagram below are conditions in the market for residential Internet access in a U.S. state. The government of this state has determined that access to the Internet improves the learning skills of children, which it has concluded is an external benefit of Internet access. The government has also concluded that if these external benefits were to be taken into account, 3 million residences would have Internet access. Suppose that the state government's judgments about the benefits of Internet access are correct and that it wishes to offer a per-unit subsidy just sufficient to increase total Internet access to 3 million residences. What per-unit subsidy should it offer? Use the diagram to explain how providing this subsidy would affect conditions in the state's market for residential Internet access.

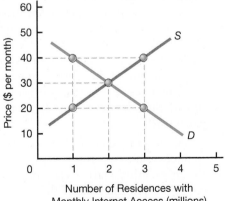

Number of Residences with Monthly Internet Access (millions)

5-10. A few years ago, the French government allocated the equivalent of more than $120 million in public funds to *Quaero* (Latin for "I search"), an Internet search engine analogous to Google or Yahoo. Does an Internet search engine satisfy the key characteristics of a public good? Why or why not? Based on your answer, is a publicly funded Internet search engine a public good or a government-sponsored good?

5-11. A government offers to let a number of students at public schools transfer to private schools under two conditions: It will transmit to private schools the same per-pupil subsidy it provides public schools, and the private schools will be required to admit the students at an out-of-pocket tuition rate below the market tuition rate. Will the economic outcome be the same as the one that would have arisen if the government instead simply provided students with grants to cover the current market tuition rate at the private school? (*Hint:* Does it matter if schools receive payments directly from the government or from consumers?)

5-12. After a government implements a voucher program, granting funds that families can spend at schools of their choice, numerous students in public schools switch to private schools. The program's per-unit subsidy is exactly equal to the external benefit from private educational services. Is anyone likely to lose out nonetheless? If so, who?

5-13. Suppose that the current price of a tablet device is $300 and that people are buying 1 million devices per year. The government decides to begin subsidizing the purchase of new tablet devices. The government believes that the appropriate price is $260 per tablet, so the program offers to send people cash for the difference between $260 and whatever the people pay for each tablet they buy.

a. If no consumers change their tablet-buying behavior, how much will this program cost the taxpayers?

b. Will the subsidy cause people to buy more, fewer, or the same number of tablets? Explain.

c. Suppose that people end up buying 1.5 million tablets once the program is in place. If the market price of tablets does not change, how much will this program cost the taxpayers?

d. Under the assumption that the program causes people to buy 1.5 million tablets and also causes the market price of tablets to rise to $320, how much will this program cost the taxpayers?

5-14. Scans of internal organs using magnetic resonance imaging (MRI) devices are often covered by subsidized health insurance programs such as Medicare. Consider the following table illustrating hypothetical quantities of individual MRI testing procedures demanded and supplied at various prices, and then answer the questions that follow.

Price	Quantity Demanded	Quantity Supplied
$100	100,000	40,000
$300	90,000	60,000
$500	80,000	80,000
$700	70,000	100,000
$900	60,000	120,000

a. In the absence of a government-subsidized health plan, what is the equilibrium price of MRI tests? What is the amount of society's total spending on MRI tests?

b. Suppose that the government establishes a health plan guaranteeing that all qualified participants can purchase MRI tests at an effective price (that is, out-of-pocket cost) to the individual of $100 per test. How many MRI tests would people desire to consume?

c. What is the per-unit price that induces producers to provide the number of MRI tests demanded at the government-guaranteed price of $100? What is society's total spending on MRI tests?

d. Under the government's coverage of MRI tests, what is the per-unit subsidy it provides? What is the total subsidy that the government pays to support MRI testing at its guaranteed price?

5-15. Suppose that, as part of an expansion of its State Care health system, a state government decides to offer a $50 subsidy to all people who, according to their physicians, should have their own blood pressure monitoring devices. Prior to this governmental decision, the market clearing price of blood pressure monitors in this state was $50, and the equilibrium quantity purchased was 20,000 per year.

a. After the government expands its State Care plan, people in this state desire to purchase 40,000 devices each year. Manufacturers of blood pressure monitors are willing to provide 40,000 devices at a price of $60 per device. What out-of-pocket price does each consumer pay for a blood pressure monitor?

b. What is the dollar amount of the increase in total expenditures on blood pressure monitors in this state following the expansion in the State Care program?

c. Following the expansion of the State Care program, what *percentage* of total expenditures on blood pressure monitors is paid by the government? What percentage of total expenditures is paid by consumers of these devices?

5-16. A government agency is contemplating launching an effort to expand the scope of its activities. One rationale for doing so is that another government agency might make the same effort and, if successful, receive larger budget allocations in future years. Another rationale for expanding the agency's activities is that this will make the jobs of its workers more interesting, which may help the government agency attract better-qualified employees. Nevertheless, the agency will have to convince more than half of the House of Representatives and the Senate to approve a formal proposal to expand its activities. In addition, to expand its activities, the agency must have the authority to force private companies it does not currently regulate to be officially licensed by agency personnel. Identify which aspects of this problem are similar to those faced by firms that operate in private markets and which aspects are specific to the public sector.

5-17. Suppose that panel (a) of Figure 5-1 applies to Pennsylvania's steel market. Suppose that steel manufacturers in this state adopt a new, equal-cost technique for producing steel that entails a smaller external cost. In the absence of any government action to correct the negative externality from steel production, would the overallocation of resources to steel production in Pennsylvania be larger or smaller following the adoption of the next steel-manufacturing technique?

5-18. Based on your answer to Problem 5-17, if Pennsylvania's government aims to correct the steel market's negative externality via an effluent fee, is the appropriate fee higher or lower now that steel producers have adopted the new technique? Why?

5-19. Consider panel (b) of Figure 5-1. Assume that a careful study of the likely transmission of influenza in light of a changed population distribution has revealed that the external benefits from inoculations are greater than currently displayed in the graph. In light of this information, is the underallocation of resources to the provision of flu-vaccine inoculations larger or smaller than indicated in panel (b)?

5-20. Based on your answer to Problem 5-19, if the government aims to correct the positive externality in the inoculation market via a per-unit subsidy to consumers, in the wake of the study, is the appropriate per-unit subsidy higher or lower than before?

5-21. An online video game has the technical capability for a large number of players to participate, as long as a game administrator works to ensure constant functionality of the game. Adding more players deprives no other participants of the entertainment services provided by the online game. It has been easy, however, to set up a system for excluding participation by anyone who fails to contribute $5 per month to a fund that ensures covering extra expenses generated by that player's participation. Is this game a public good?

5-22. Consider the market for a health care service displayed in Figure 5-4, in which the government currently pays a per-unit subsidy M. If the government raises the value of M to a larger dollar amount per unit of service, what will happen to the out-of-pocket price paid by consumers, the price required to induce suppliers to provide services, and the quantity of services provided? Will the government's total expense for this health care service rise or fall?

REFERENCES

EXAMPLE: Neighbors Are Not Hog Wild about a North Carolina Pig Farm

Greg Barnes, "Smithfield's Plans to Cover Hog Lagoons Could Spur North Carolina Biogas Industry," North Carolina Health News (https://www.northcarolinahealthnews.org/2019/01/04/smithfields-plans-to-cover-hog-lagoons-could-spur-n-c-biogas-industry/), January 4, 2019.

Valerie Bauerlein, "Residents Raise a Stink over Pig Farms in North Carolina," *Wall Street Journal*, May 29, 2018.

Craig Jarvis, "Jury Awards Hog Farm Neighbors Their Biggest Verdict Yet," *Raleigh News and Observer*, August 3, 2018.

AI—DECISION MAKING THROUGH DATA: Contemplating Big Data As a Public Good

Nestor Duch-Brown, Bertin Martens, and Frank Mueller-Langer, "The Economics of Ownership, Access, and Trade in Digital Data," JRC Digital Economy Working paper 2017-01 (https://papers.ssrn.com/sol3/papers.cfm?abstract_id=2914144), February 2017.

KaMariana Mazzucato, "Let's Make Private Data into a Public Good," *MIT Technology Review*, June 27, 2018.

Bing Song, "Big Data as the Next Public Good," *Washington Post*, May 2, 2018.

POLICY EXAMPLE: Government Sponsorship Keeps Light Rail Systems in Operation

Faiz Siddiqui, "Metro Plan Would Subsidize Uber and Lyft Fares to Fill Late-Night Service Gap," *Washington Post*, February 13, 2019.

Scott Calvert, "Washington D.C.'s Five Letter Problem: Metro," *Wall Street Journal*, February 22, 2018.

Shayndi Raice and Paul Overberg, "High-Speed Rail in the United States Remains Elusive," *Wall Street Journal*, March 4, 2019.

BEHAVIORAL EXAMPLE: To Inhibit Nicotine Consumption, Should the Government Assume That All Consumers Behave the Same?

U.S. Food and Drug Administration, "Vaporizers, E-Cigarettes, and other Electronic Nicotine Delivery Systems" (https://www.fda.gov/TobaccoProducts/Labeling/ucm456610.htm), 2019.

Joachim Marti, John Buckell, Johanna Catherine Maclean, and Jody Sindelar, "To 'Vape' or Smoke? A Discrete Choice Experiment among Adult Smokers," *Economic Inquiry*, 2018.

Public Health Law Center, Northeastern University, "U.S. E-Cigarette Regulations—50-State Review" (www.publichealthlawcenter.org/resources/us-e-cigarette-regulations-50-state-review), 2018.

POLICY EXAMPLE: Private Space Firms Recycle Rocket Boosters and Capsules That the Government Regards as Throwaways

Stephen Clark, "Scorched SpaceX Rocket Returns to Port in Florida, Ready to Launch a Fourth Time," SpaceFlightNow.com (https://spaceflightnow.com/2019/02/25/scorched-spacex-rocket-returns-to-port-in-florida-ready-to-launch-a-fourth-time/), February 25, 2019.

"Elon Musk's Next SpaceX Rocket Could Blast Off 100 Times," CNet.com (https://www.cnet.com/news/spacex-block-5-falcon-9-rocket-hopes-to-reuse-100-times/), April 3, 2018.

Claudia Geib, "Blue Origin Is Testing Reusable Rockets. Here's Why You Rarely See Them," *Futurism*, April 30, 2018.

ECONOMICS IN YOUR LIFE: Fake "Service Pets" Create External Costs on Airline Flights

U.S. Department of Transportation, "About the Air Carrier Access Act" (https://www.transportation.gov/airconsumer/passengers-disabilities), 2019.

David Leonhardt, "It's Time to End the Scam of Flying Pets," *New York Times*, February 4, 2018.

Scott McCartney, "On Planes, the Dogs Are Winning," *Wall Street Journal*, August 6, 2018.

ISSUES & APPLICATIONS: How Wisconsin's State Parks' Ties to Government Are Fraying

Wisconsin State Park System, "State Parks, Forests, Recreation Areas and Trails" (https://dnr.wi.gov/topic/parks/), 2019.

Mike McFadzen, "Wisconsin State Parks Position Themselves in Self-Funding Era," SilentSports.net (https://www.silentsports.net/2018/04/11/wisconsin-state-parks-position-themselves-in-self-funding-era-april-silent-alarm/), April 11, 2018.

James Rowen, "DNR Supports Park Land for Private Golfing?" *Urban Milwaukee*, January 13, 2018.

6

Funding the Public Sector

LEARNING OBJECTIVES

After reading this chapter, you should be able to:

6.1 Distinguish between average tax rates and marginal tax rates

6.2 Explain the structure of the U.S. income tax system

6.3 Understand the key factors influencing the relationship between tax rates and the tax revenues governments collect

6.4 Explain how the taxes governments levy on purchases of goods and services affect market prices and equilibrium quantities

Since 1935, when Congress established the Social Security Administration, U.S. residents from whom "contributions" are deducted as fixed percentages of their wages have been promised future payments beginning at an age as low as 62. Between now and 2030, the percentage of the U.S. population in this age group will increase from 16 percent to 22 percent. As the percentage of people in retirement increases, the percentage that is of working age correspondingly will shrink. Thus, promised aggregate benefit payouts will increase at the same time that total collected Social Security contributions will tend to decline. In this chapter, you will learn about why this fact is placing pressure on the viability of the Social Security promise to workers that the U.S. government has extended since 1935.

California taxpayers receiving the top 1 percent of incomes pay 48 percent of the state's total income taxes? Many of the earnings of these taxpayers are subject to a 13.3 percent income tax rate, which is highest among the income tax rates assessed across all U.S. states.

To fund pension payments to retired teachers and other former employees, California and its municipalities follow other state and local governments by assessing sales taxes; property taxes; hotel occupancy taxes; and electricity, gasoline, water, and sewage taxes. When a person dies, California, like the federal government and a number of other state governments, also collects estate taxes. Clearly, governments give considerable attention to their roles as tax collectors.

Paying for the Public Sector: Systems of Taxation

6.1 Distinguish between average tax rates and marginal tax rates

There are three sources of funding available to governments. One source is explicit fees, called *user charges*, for government services. The second and main source of government funding is taxes. Nevertheless, sometimes federal, state, and local governments spend more than they collect in taxes. To do this, they must rely on a third source of financing, which is borrowing. A government cannot borrow unlimited amounts, however. After all, a government, like an individual or a firm, can convince others to lend it funds only if it can provide evidence that it will repay its debts. A government must ultimately rely on taxation and user charges, the sources of its own current and future revenues, to repay its debts.

The Government Budget Constraint

Over the long run, therefore, taxes and user charges are any government's *fundamental* sources of revenues. The **government budget constraint** states that each dollar of public spending on goods, services, transfer payments, and repayments of borrowed funds during a given period must be provided by tax revenues and user charges collected by the government. This constraint indicates that the total amount a government plans to spend and transfer today and into the future cannot exceed all taxes and user charges that it currently earns and anticipates collecting in future years. Taxation dwarfs user charges as a source of government resources, so let's begin by looking at taxation from a government's perspective.

Government budget constraint
The limit on government spending and transfers imposed by the fact that every dollar the government spends, transfers, or uses to repay borrowed funds must ultimately be provided by the user charges and taxes it collects.

If market interest rates that state and local governments must pay on borrowed funds increase, what likely will happen to their spending on debt repayments in relation to their other expenditures?

POLICY EXAMPLE

State Governments Confront Higher Debt Repayment Expenses

Governments of a number of U.S. states are confronting several rising annual expenses, including higher Medicaid benefits and increased payments for previously underfunded pensions of retired state employees. Nevertheless, for California, Illinois, Connecticut, and New York and many city governments, another growing expense is debt repayments. Governments of these jurisdictions have taken in fewer taxes and user charges than they have spent, which has required them to borrow funds each year. By some estimates, total state and local government debts in the United States now exceed $3 trillion, or an amount equivalent to about 15 percent of the total indebtedness of the U.S. federal government. Each 0.1-percentage-point increase in the market interest rate that these entities must offer to finance their debts raises their future combined interest repayment expenses by $3 billion per year.

FOR CRITICAL THINKING

Who ultimately pays the debt repayment expenses owed by state and local governments?

Sources are listed at the end of this chapter.

Implementing Taxation with Tax Rates

In light of the government budget constraint, a major concern of any government is how to collect taxes. Jean-Baptiste Colbert, the seventeenth-century French finance minister, said the art of taxation was in "plucking the goose so as to obtain the largest amount of feathers with the least possible amount of hissing." In the United States, governments have designed a variety of methods of plucking the private-sector goose.

Tax base
The value of goods, services, wealth, or incomes subject to taxation.

Tax rate
The proportion of a tax base that must be paid to a government as taxes.

The Tax Base and the Tax Rate To collect a tax, a government typically establishes a **tax base,** which is the value of goods, services, wealth, or incomes subject to taxation. Then it assesses a **tax rate,** which is the proportion of the tax base that must be paid to the government as taxes.

As we discuss shortly, for the federal government and many state governments, incomes are key tax bases. Therefore, to discuss tax rates and the structure of taxation systems in more detail, let's focus for now on income taxation.

Why is the U.S. government applying AI technologies to analyze data on U.S. residents' transfers of and holdings of funds outside the United States?

AI | DECISION MAKING THROUGH DATA

Preserving National Tax Bases

A technique that U.S. residents and companies sometimes employ to reduce their tax burdens is to move abroad flows of revenues or incomes or stocks of wealth that otherwise would be subject to domestic taxation. Some of these actions involve legal tax *avoidance*. Others constitute illegal tax *evasion*. To maximize their tax bases, domestic governments must expend resources to determine which category applies.

Before a nation's government can evaluate whether funds that otherwise would be part of a domestic tax base have been shifted abroad, the government must be able to identify the funds that have been moved. Toward this end, the U.S. government has induced 110 foreign governments and almost 300,000 foreign companies to provide past and current data regarding flows and stocks of funds involving U.S. residents outside the United States. Government agencies are using AI-based data-analytics techniques to sift this information and separate taxable from nontaxable flows of funds transferred abroad. By identifying the taxable funds and those who have sought to evade paying taxes on these funds, the U.S. government can maximize the tax bases to which it can assess applicable tax rates.

FOR CRITICAL THINKING

Why do you suppose that the U.S. government's AI-directed efforts to boost the tax bills of firms earning incomes abroad have induced some firms to relocate to other countries?

Sources are listed at the end of this chapter.

Marginal and Average Tax Rate If somebody says, "I pay 28 percent in taxes," you cannot really tell what that person means unless you know whether he or she is referring to average taxes paid or the tax rate on the last dollars earned. The latter concept refers to the **marginal tax rate,** with the word *marginal* meaning "incremental."

The marginal tax rate is expressed as follows:

Marginal tax rate
The change in the tax payment divided by the change in income, or the percentage of *additional* dollars that must be paid in taxes. The marginal tax rate is applied to taxable income in the highest tax bracket reached.

$$\text{Marginal tax rate} = \frac{\text{change in taxes due}}{\text{change in taxable income}}$$

It is important to understand that the marginal tax rate applies only to the income in the highest **tax bracket** reached, with a tax bracket defined as a specified range of taxable income to which a specific and unique marginal tax rate is applied.

The marginal tax rate is not the same thing as the **average tax rate**, which is defined as follows:

Tax bracket
A specified interval of income to which a specific and unique marginal tax rate is applied.

Average tax rate
The total tax payment divided by total income. It is the proportion of total income paid in taxes.

$$\text{Average tax rate} = \frac{\text{total taxes due}}{\text{total taxable income}}$$

Taxation Systems

No matter how governments raise revenues—from income taxes, sales taxes, or other taxes—all of those taxes fit into one of three types of taxation systems: proportional, progressive, or regressive, according to the relationship between the tax rate and income. To determine whether a tax system is proportional, progressive, or regressive, we simply ask, what is the relationship between the average tax rate and the marginal tax rate?

Proportional Taxation **Proportional taxation** means that regardless of an individual's income, taxes comprise exactly the same proportion. In a proportional taxation system, the marginal tax rate is always equal to the average tax rate. If every dollar is taxed at 20 percent, then the average tax rate is 20 percent, and so is the marginal tax rate.

Under a proportional system of taxation, taxpayers at all income levels end up paying the same *percentage* of their income in taxes. With a proportional tax rate of 20 percent, an individual with an income of $10,000 pays $2,000 in taxes, while an individual making $100,000 pays $20,000. Thus, the identical 20 percent rate is levied on both taxpayers.

Progressive Taxation Under **progressive taxation,** as a person's taxable income increases, the percentage of income paid in taxes increases. In a progressive system, the marginal tax rate is above the average tax rate. If you are taxed 5 percent on the first $10,000 you earn, 10 percent on the next $10,000 you earn, and 30 percent on the last $10,000 you earn, you face a progressive income tax system. Your marginal tax rate is always above your average tax rate.

Regressive Taxation With **regressive taxation**, a smaller percentage of taxable income is taken in taxes as taxable income increases. The marginal rate is *below* the average rate. As income increases, the marginal tax rate falls, and so does the average tax rate. The U.S. Social Security tax is regressive. Once the legislated maximum taxable wage base is reached, no further Social Security taxes are paid. Consider a simplified hypothetical example: Suppose that every dollar up to $120,000 is taxed at 10 percent. After $120,000 there is no Social Security tax. Someone making $200,000 still pays only $12,000 in Social Security taxes. That person's average Social Security tax is 6 percent. The person making $120,000, by contrast, effectively pays 10 percent. The person making $1.2 million faces an average Social Security tax rate of only 1 percent in our simplified example.

How do marginal federal income tax rates vary with incomes of U.S. taxpayers?

Proportional taxation
A tax system in which, regardless of an individual's income, the tax bill comprises exactly the same proportion.

Progressive taxation
A tax system in which, as income increases, a higher percentage of the additional income is paid as taxes. The marginal tax rate exceeds the average tax rate as income rises.

Regressive taxation
A tax system in which as more dollars are earned, the percentage of tax paid on them falls. The marginal tax rate is less than the average tax rate as income rises.

EXAMPLE

Average Federal Income Tax Rates and U.S. Income Tax Progressivity

In the United States, the average income tax rate paid by the 20 percent of taxpayers with lowest incomes is about 3.7 percent. As incomes increase for the remaining 20-percent groupings, the average tax rate increases to approximately 8.4 percent, 13.6 percent, 17.4 percent, and 26.2 percent. Those taxpayers categorized within the top 1 percent of income earners pay an average tax rate of about 33.4 percent. Because the average percentage of income paid as taxes increases as taxpayers' incomes rise, the U.S. income tax system is progressive.

REAL APPLICATION

If you have a chance in the future to invest in a risky, but potentially profitable venture, what is most important to you—your average tax rate or your marginal tax rate? Why?

Sources are listed at the end of this chapter.

The Most Important Federal Taxes

6.2 Explain the structure of the U.S. income tax system

What types of taxes do federal, state, and local governments collect? The two pie charts in Figure 6-1 show the percentages of receipts from various taxes obtained by the federal government and by state and local governments. For the federal government, key taxes are individual income taxes, corporate income taxes, Social Security taxes, and excise taxes on items such as gasoline and alcoholic beverages. For state and local governments, sales taxes, property taxes, and personal and corporate income taxes are the main types of taxes.

The Federal Personal Income Tax

The most important tax in the U.S. economy is the federal personal income tax, which, as Figure 6-1 indicates, accounts for 50 percent of all federal revenues. All U.S. citizens, resident aliens, and most others who earn income in the United States are required to pay federal income taxes on all taxable income, including income earned abroad.

The rates that are paid rise as income increases, as can be seen in Table 6-1. Marginal income tax rates at the federal level have ranged from as low as 1 percent after the 1913 passage of the Sixteenth Amendment, which made the individual income tax constitutional, to as high as 94 percent (reached in 1944). There were 14 separate tax brackets prior to the Tax Reform Act of 1986, which reduced the number to three (now seven, as shown in Table 6-1).

FIGURE 6-1

Sources of Government Tax Receipts

As panel (a) shows, about 85.6 percent of federal revenues comes from income and Social Security and other social insurance taxes. State government revenues, shown in panel (b), are spread more evenly across sources, with less emphasis on taxes based on individual income.

Sources: Economic Report of the President; Economic Indicators, various issues.

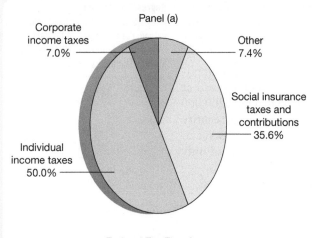

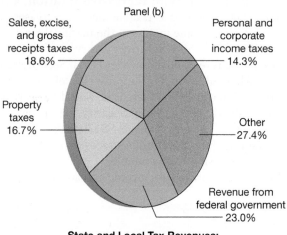

Federal Tax Receipts:
Fiscal Year 2020 Estimate

State and Local Tax Revenues:
Fiscal Year 2020 Estimate

TABLE 6-1

Federal Marginal Income Tax Rates

These rates applied in 2019.

Single Persons		Married Couples	
Marginal Tax Bracket	**Marginal Tax Rate**	**Marginal Tax Bracket**	**Marginal Tax Rate**
$0–$9,700	10.0%	$0–$19,400	10.0%
$9,701–$39,475	12.0%	$19,401–$78,950	12.0%
$39,476–$84,200	22.0%	$78,951–$168,400	22.0%
$84,201–$160,275	24.0%	$168,401–$321,450	24.0%
$160,276–$204,100	32.0%	$321,451–$408,200	32.0%
$204,101–$510,300	35.0%	$408,201–$612,350	35.0%
$510,301 AND UP	37.0%	$612,351 AND UP	37.0%

Source: U.S. Department of the Treasury.

The Treatment of Capital Gains

The difference between the purchase price and sale price of an asset, such as a share of stock or a plot of land, is called a **capital gain** if it is a profit and a **capital loss** if it is not. The federal government taxes capital gains, and as of 2020, there were several capital gains tax rates.

What appear to be capital gains are not always real gains. If you pay $100,000 for a financial asset in one year and sell it for 50 percent more 10 years later, your nominal capital gain is $50,000. But what if during those 10 years inflation has driven average asset prices up by 50 percent? Your *real* capital gain would be zero, but you would still have to pay taxes on that $50,000.

To counter this problem, many economists have argued that capital gains should be indexed to the rate of inflation. This is exactly what is done with the marginal tax brackets in the federal income tax code. Tax brackets for the purposes of calculating marginal tax rates each year are expanded at the rate of inflation, that is, the rate at which the average of all prices is rising. If the rate of inflation is 10 percent, therefore, each tax bracket is moved up by 10 percent. The same concept could be applied to capital gains and financial assets. So far, Congress has refused to enact such a measure.

Capital gain
A positive difference between the purchase price and the sale price of an asset. If a share of stock is bought for $5 and then sold for $15, the capital gain is $10.

Capital loss
A negative difference between the purchase price and the sale price of an asset.

WHAT HAPPENS WHEN...

the government raises the tax rate on capital gains derived from sales of financial assets?

People owe capital gains taxes only on gains that they actually receive following sales of those assets. Thus, when the government raises the tax rate on such capital gains, many taxpayers typically choose not to sell assets that have experienced price increases following an increase in the capital gains tax rate. As a consequence, capital gains taxes owed by these people will not increase, and actual capital gains taxes collected increase less than the government anticipated when it raised the tax rate.

The Corporate Income Tax

Figure 6-1 shows that corporate income taxes account for 7 percent of all federal taxes collected. They also make up about 2 percent of all state and local taxes collected. Corporations are generally taxed on the difference between their total revenues and their expenses. For many years, the federal corporate income tax structure imposed different marginal tax rates over varying levels of income, as for individual income taxes. Since 2018, however, corporations have been subject to a single, "flat" corporate income tax rate of 21 percent.

Making Decisions to Maximize Your Future Income When you are in a position to create a personal retirement "nest egg," you will have plenty of decisions to make. If you seek to place some of your funds in corporate stocks that generate dividends each year, you will be subject to *double taxation*. Therefore, particularly when you are younger, you might wish to consider only placing your funds in the stocks of corporations that do not pay dividends. Rather, you will favor corporations that retain earnings in order to have higher rates of growth.

Double Taxation Because individual stockholders must pay taxes on the dividends they receive, and those dividends are paid out of *after-tax* profits by the corporation, corporate profits are taxed twice. If you receive $1,000 in dividends, you have to declare them as income, and you must normally pay taxes on them. Before the corporation was able to pay you those dividends, it had to pay taxes on all its profits, including any that it put back into the company or did not distribute in the form of dividends.

Eventually, the new investment made possible by those **retained earnings**—profits not given out to stockholders—along with borrowed funds will be reflected in the

Retained earnings
Earnings that a corporation saves, or retains, for investment in other productive activities; earnings that are not distributed to stockholders.

value of the stock in that company. When you sell your stock in that company, you will have to pay taxes on the difference between what you paid for the stock and what you sold it for. In both cases, dividends and retained earnings (corporate profits) are taxed twice. In 2003, Congress reduced the double taxation effect somewhat by enacting legislation that allowed most dividends to be taxed at lower rates than are applied to regular income.

Who Really Pays the Corporate Income Tax? Corporations can function only as long as consumers buy their products, employees make their goods, stockholders (owners) buy their shares, and bondholders buy their bonds. Corporations per se do not do anything. We must ask, then, who really pays the tax on corporate income? This is a question of **tax incidence**. (The question of tax incidence applies to all taxes, including sales taxes and Social Security taxes.) The incidence of corporate taxation is the subject of considerable debate. Some economists suggest that corporations pass their tax burdens on to consumers by charging higher prices.

Tax incidence
The distribution of tax burdens among various groups in society.

Other economists argue that it is the stockholders who bear most of the tax. Still others contend that employees pay at least part of the tax by receiving lower wages than they would otherwise. Because the debate is not yet settled, we will not hazard a guess here as to what the correct conclusion may be. Suffice it to say that you should be cautious when you advocate increasing corporate income taxes. *People*, whether owners, consumers, or workers, end up paying all of the increase—just as they pay all of any tax.

Social Security and Unemployment Taxes

Each year, taxes levied on payrolls account for an increasing percentage of federal tax receipts. These taxes, which are distinct from personal income taxes, are for Social Security, retirement, survivors' disability, and old-age medical benefits (Medicare). The Social Security tax is imposed on earnings up to about $133,000 at a rate of 6.2 percent on employers and 6.2 percent on employees. That is, the employer matches your "contribution" to Social Security. (The employer's contribution is really paid by the employees, at least in part, in the form of a reduced wage rate.) Recall that a Medicare tax is imposed on all wage earnings at a combined rate of 2.9 percent. The 2010 federal health care law also added a 3.8 percent Medicare tax on certain income above $200,000.

Social Security Taxes Passage of the Federal Insurance Contributions Act (FICA) in 1935 brought Social Security taxes into existence. At that time, many more people paid into the Social Security program than the number who received benefits. Currently, however, older people drawing benefits make up a much larger share of the population. Consequently, in recent years, outflows of Social Security benefit payments have sometimes exceeded inflows of Social Security taxes. Various economists have advanced proposals to raise Social Security tax rates on younger workers or to reduce benefit payouts to older retirees and disabled individuals receiving Social Security payments. So far, however, the federal government has failed to address Social Security's deteriorating funding situation.

Unemployment Insurance Taxes There is also a federal unemployment insurance tax, which helps pay for wage and salary insurance that the government provides to unemployed workers. This tax rate is 0.6 percent on the first $7,000 of annual wages of each employee who earns more than $1,500. Only the employer makes this tax payment. This tax covers the costs of the unemployment insurance system. In addition to this federal tax, some states with an unemployment system impose their own tax of up to about 3 percent, depending on the past record of the particular employer. An employer who frequently lays off workers typically will have a slightly higher state unemployment tax rate than an employer who never lays off workers.

Tax Rates and Tax Revenues

6.3 Understand the key factors influencing the relationship between tax rates and the tax revenues governments collect

For most state and local governments, income taxes yield fewer revenues than taxes imposed on sales of goods and services. Figure 6-1 showed that sales taxes, gross receipts taxes, and excise taxes generate almost one-fifth of the total funds available to state and local governments. Thus, from the perspective of many state and local governments, a fundamental issue is how to set tax rates on sales of goods and services to extract desired total tax payments.

Sales Taxes

Governments levy **sales taxes** on the prices that consumers pay to purchase each unit of a broad range of goods and services. Sellers collect sales taxes and transmit them to the government. Sales taxes are a form of *ad valorem* **taxation,** which means that the tax is applied "to the value" of the good. Thus, a government using a system of *ad valorem* taxation charges a tax rate equal to a fraction of the market price of each unit that a consumer buys. For instance, if the tax rate is 8 percent and the market price of an item is $100, then the amount of the tax on the item is $8.

A sales tax is therefore a proportional tax with respect to purchased items. The total amount of sales taxes a government collects equals the sales tax rate times the sales tax base, which is the market value of total purchases.

Sales taxes
Taxes assessed on the prices paid on most goods and services.

***Ad valorem* taxation**
Assessing taxes by charging a tax rate equal to a fraction of the market price of each unit purchased.

Static Tax Analysis

There are two approaches to evaluating how changes in tax rates affect government tax collections. **Static tax analysis** assumes that changes in the tax rate have no effect on the tax base. Thus, this approach implies that if a state government desires to increase its sales tax collections, it can simply raise the tax rate. Multiplying the higher tax rate by the tax base thereby produces higher tax revenues.

Governments often rely on static tax analysis. Sometimes this yields unpleasant surprises. For instance, in recent years states such as Delaware and Maryland have imposed special tax rates on so-called "millionaires"—usually defined as people earning hundreds of thousands of dollars per year. Agencies of state governments implementing these special taxes have applied the special tax rate to incomes subject to the tax and projected that additional tax revenues of tens of millions of dollars would be collected. In fact, however, many earners of income subjected to these special taxes responded by changing their state of residency. Consequently, the tax base of the high earners decreased, and the state governments imposing these taxes experienced much smaller increases in tax collections than they had projected.

Static tax analysis
Economic evaluation of the effects of tax rate changes under the assumption that there is no effect on the tax base, meaning that there is an unambiguous positive relationship between tax rates and tax revenues.

ECONOMICS IN YOUR LIFE

To contemplate why the government of the state with the most high-income residents is giving up on raising tax rates assessed solely on the rich, take a look at **The Connecticut Government Decides to Avoid Striking Out on Its Income Tax Policy** on page 132.

Dynamic Tax Analysis

The problem with static tax analysis is that it ignores incentive effects created by new taxes or hikes in existing tax rates. According to **dynamic tax analysis**, a likely response to an increase in a tax rate is a *decrease* in the tax base. When a government pushes up its sales tax rate, for example, consumers have an incentive to cut back on their purchases of goods and services subjected to the higher rate, perhaps by buying them in a locale where there is a lower sales tax rate or perhaps no tax rate at all. As shown in Figure 6-2, the maximum sales tax rate varies considerably from state to state.

Consider someone who lives in a state bordering Oregon. In such a border state, the sales tax rate can be as high as 8 percent, so a resident of that state has a strong incentive to buy higher-priced goods and services in Oregon, where there is no sales tax. Someone who lives in a high-tax county in Alabama has an incentive to buy an item from an out-of-state firm. Such shifts in expenditures in response to higher relative tax rates will reduce a state's sales tax base and thereby result in lower sales tax collections than the levels predicted by static tax analysis.

Dynamic tax analysis
Economic evaluation of tax rate changes that recognizes that the tax base declines with ever-higher tax rates, so that tax revenues may eventually decline if the tax rate is raised sufficiently.

States with the Highest and Lowest Sales Tax Rates

A number of states allow counties and cities to collect their own sales taxes in addition to state sales taxes. This figure shows the maximum sales tax rates for selected states, including county and municipal taxes. Delaware, Montana, New Hampshire, and Oregon have no sales taxes.

Source: U.S. Department of Commerce.

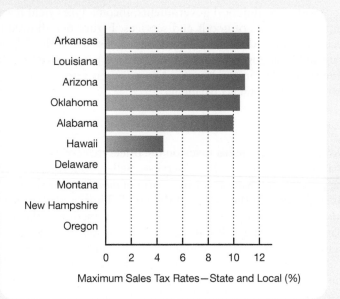

Dynamic tax analysis recognizes that increasing the tax rate could actually cause the government's total tax collections to *decline* if a sufficiently large number of consumers react to the higher sales tax rate by cutting back on purchases of goods and services included in the state's tax base. Some residents who live close to other states with lower sales tax rates might, for instance, drive across the state line to do more of their shopping. Other residents might place more orders with firms located in other tax jurisdictions where their state's sales tax does not apply.

Why do you suppose that some critics are predicting rules established by California's Franchise Tax Board for taxing sales generated by commercial spaceflights could lead to fewer rocket launches from that state?

POLICY EXAMPLE

If You Generate Sales from Moving Items from Our State to Outer Space, Pay Up!

Recently, the Franchise Tax Board of the state of California established the first set of rules governing taxation of sales associated with private spaceflights. Under these rules, rocket flights that originate in California and generate sales by launching people or property into outer space will be subject to taxation. The tax rate now assessed by the Franchise Tax Board varies with the number of miles into space that a flight traverses.

Experts in tax policy question whether the California agency's tax plan will generate as many tax revenues as the Franchise Tax Board anticipates will be forthcoming from taxable space launches. These observers note that no other state governments have adopted plans to impose per-mile tax rates on sales generated by spaceflights. In fact, critics employing dynamic tax analysis point out that several state governments now offer *subsidies*—negative tax rates—intended to induce companies

to base rocket-launching facilities within their states. The imposition of tax rates on sales derived from spaceflights, these critics argue, is likely to induce new companies to establish spaceflight operations outside California. Furthermore, some firms that currently launch rockets from facilities within California may be induced to move their operations to other states. The predicted outcomes are a smaller tax base and lower tax revenues than the Franchise Tax Board anticipates.

FOR CRITICAL THINKING

Did California's Franchise Tax Board rely on static or dynamic analysis? Explain briefly.

Sources are listed at the end of this chapter.

Maximizing Tax Revenues

Dynamic tax analysis indicates that whether a government's tax revenues ultimately rise or fall in response to a tax rate increase depends on exactly how much the tax base

FIGURE 6-3

Maximizing the Government's Sales Tax Revenues

Dynamic tax analysis predicts that ever-higher tax rates bring about declines in the tax base, so that at sufficiently high tax rates the government's tax revenues begin to fall off. This implies that there is a tax rate, 6 percent in this example, at which the government can collect the maximum possible revenues, T_{max}.

declines in response to the higher tax rate. On the one hand, the tax base may decline by a relatively small amount following an increase in the tax rate, so that tax revenues rise. For instance, in the situation we imagine a government facing in Figure 6-3, a rise in the tax rate from 5 percent to 6 percent causes tax revenues to increase. On the other hand, the tax base may decline so much that total tax revenues decrease. In Figure 6-3, for example, increasing the tax rate from 6 percent to 7 percent causes tax revenues to *decline*.

What is most likely is that when the tax rate is already relatively low, increasing the tax rate causes relatively small declines in the tax base. Within a range of relatively low sales tax rates, therefore, increasing the tax rate generates higher sales tax revenues, as illustrated along the upward-sloping portion of the curve depicted in Figure 6-3. If the government continues to push up the tax rate, however, people increasingly have an incentive to find ways to avoid purchasing taxable goods and services. Eventually, the tax base decreases sufficiently that the government's tax collections decline with ever-higher tax rates.

Consequently, governments that wish to maximize their tax revenues should not necessarily assess a high tax rate. In the situation illustrated in Figure 6-3, the government maximizes its tax revenues at T_{max} by establishing a sales tax rate of 6 percent. If the government were to raise the rate above 6 percent, it would induce a sufficient decline in the tax base that its tax collections would decline. If the government wishes to collect more than T_{max} in revenues to fund various government programs, it must somehow either expand its sales tax base or develop another tax.

Does bounded rationality limit dynamic responses to higher sales taxes?

BEHAVIORAL EXAMPLE

Increases in Complex Sales Taxes Generate Predictable Dynamic Responses by Consumers

A fundamental tenet of behavioral economics is that complexities confronted by people with limited time and capabilities induce them to exhibit bounded rationality: They operate based on simple rules of thumb instead of contemplating every element of each possible choice available to them. U.S. state and municipal sales taxes are among the complexities that people must face when they shop for goods and services. These taxes pose three sources of complexity. First, sales taxes typically are not included in posted prices and are applied only at the point of sale, which requires consumers to conduct their own careful calculations to determine overall tax-inclusive prices before buying. Second, certain items are exempt from taxation, and some are subject to different rates of taxation than others. Third, about 10,000 state and municipal sales tax jurisdictions exist, so an individual contemplating shopping in person, via catalogues, or online confronts a dizzying array of different sales tax rates.

(Continued)

Nevertheless, behavioral economists have found that people go to considerable lengths to shop for items with the lowest overall sales-tax-inclusive prices. Consider adjustments following states' or municipalities' announcements of plans to increase a sales tax rate. People within these jurisdictions often rush to buy goods they can store for later use and thereby avoid paying higher taxes for a time. In addition, people commonly increase their online and cross-tax-jurisdiction shopping, which indicates that they begin to devote more time to searching for items available in other jurisdictions at lower tax-inclusive prices. In spite of the complexities presented by sales taxes, people go to considerable lengths to limit the after-tax prices they pay for the items they buy.

6.4 Explain how the taxes governments levy on purchases of goods and services affect market prices and equilibrium quantities

Taxation from the Point of View of Producers and Consumers

Governments collect taxes on product sales at the source. They require producers to charge these taxes when they sell their output. This means that taxes on sales of goods and services affect market prices and quantities. Let's consider why this is so.

Taxes and the Market Supply Curve

Imposing taxes on final sales of a good or service affects the position of the market supply curve. To see why, consider panel (a) of Figure 6-4, which shows a gasoline market supply curve S_1 in the absence of taxation. At a price of $2.35 per gallon, gasoline producers are willing and able to supply 180,000 gallons of gasoline per week. If

---

FIGURE 6-4

The Effects of Excise Taxes on the Market Supply and Equilibrium Price and Quantity of Gasoline

Panel (a) shows what happens if the government requires gasoline sellers to collect and transmit a $0.40 unit excise tax on gasoline. To be willing to continue supplying a given quantity, sellers must receive a price that is $0.40 higher for each gallon they sell, so the market supply curve shifts vertically by the amount of the tax. As illustrated in panel (b), this decrease in market supply causes a reduction in the equilibrium quantity of gasoline produced and purchased. It also causes a rise in the market clearing price, to $2.75, so that consumers pay part of the tax. Sellers pay the rest in lower profits.

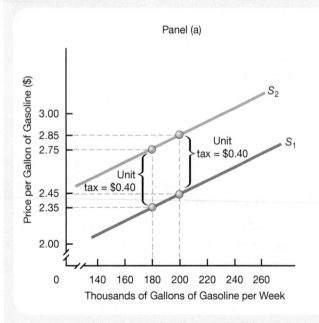

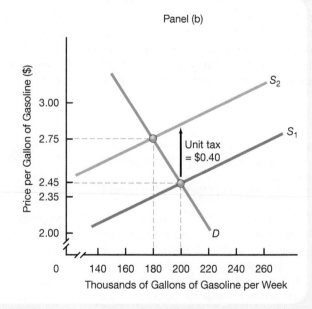

the price increases to $2.45 per gallon, firms increase production to 200,000 gallons of gasoline per week.

Both federal and state governments assess **excise taxes**—taxes on sales of particular commodities—on sales of gasoline. They levy gasoline excise taxes as a **unit tax**, or a constant tax per unit sold. On average, combined federal and state excise taxes on gasoline are about $0.40 per gallon.

Let's suppose, therefore, that a gasoline producer must transmit a total of $0.40 per gallon to federal and state governments for each gallon sold. Producers must continue to receive a net amount of $2.35 per gallon to induce them to supply 180,000 gallons each week, so they must now receive $2.75 per gallon to supply that weekly quantity. Likewise, gasoline producers now will be willing to supply 200,000 gallons each week only if they receive $0.40 more per gallon, or a total amount of $2.85 per gallon.

As you can see, imposing the combined $0.40 per gallon excise taxes on gasoline shifts the supply curve vertically by exactly that amount to S_2 in panel (a). Thus, the effect of levying excise taxes on gasoline is to shift the supply curve vertically by the total per-unit taxes levied on gasoline sales. Hence, there is a decrease in supply. (In the case of an *ad valorem* sales tax, the supply curve would shift vertically by a proportionate amount equal to the tax rate.)

Excise tax
A tax levied on purchases of a particular good or service.

Unit tax
A constant tax assessed on each unit of a good that consumers purchase.

How Taxes Affect the Market Price and Equilibrium Quantity

Panel (b) of Figure 6-4 shows how imposing $0.40 per gallon in excise taxes affects the market price of gasoline and the equilibrium quantity of gasoline produced and sold. In the absence of excise taxes, the market supply curve S_1 crosses the demand curve D at a market price of $2.45 per gallon. At this market price, the equilibrium quantity of gasoline is 200,000 gallons of gasoline per week.

The excise tax levy of $0.40 per gallon shifts the supply curve to S_2. At the original $2.45 per gallon price, there is now an excess quantity of gasoline demanded, so the market price of gasoline rises to $2.75 per gallon. At this market price, the equilibrium quantity of gasoline produced and consumed each week is 180,000 gallons.

What factors determine how much the equilibrium quantity of a good or service declines in response to taxation? The answer to this question depends on how responsive quantities demanded and supplied are to changes in price.

Who Pays the Tax?

In our example, imposing excise taxes of $0.40 per gallon of gasoline causes the market price to rise to $2.75 per gallon from $2.45 per gallon. Thus, the price that each consumer pays is $0.30 per gallon higher. Consumers pay three-fourths of the excise tax levied on each gallon of gasoline produced and sold in our example.

Gasoline producers must pay the rest of the tax. Their profits decline by $0.10 per gallon because costs have increased by $0.40 per gallon while consumers pay $0.30 more per gallon.

In the gasoline market, as in other markets for products subject to excise taxes and other taxes on sales, the shapes of the market demand and supply curves determine who pays most of a tax. The reason is that the shapes of these curves reflect the responsiveness to price changes of the quantity demanded by consumers and of the quantity supplied by producers.

In the example illustrated in Figure 6-4, the fact that consumers pay most of the excise taxes levied on gasoline reflects a relatively low responsiveness of quantity demanded by consumers to a change in the price of gasoline. Consumers pay most of the excise taxes on each gallon produced and sold because in this example the amount of gasoline they desire to purchase is relatively (but not completely) unresponsive to a change in the market price induced by excise taxes.

ECONOMICS IN YOUR LIFE

The Connecticut Government Decides to Avoid Striking Out on Its Income Tax Policy

In the game of baseball, failure to get on base after three swings that miss the pitched ball sends a batter off the field and fails to advance the score of the batter's team. Recently, the head of Connecticut's Department of Revenue Services, Kevin Sullivan, decided to avoid a likely tax-policy strikeout. Twice in recent years, the Connecticut government boosted the income tax rates assessed on the incomes of the highest-income residents of the state, which has the highest average income per capita in the United States. Both times, however, the higher tax rates failed to generate additional annual tax revenues, even though the total number of residents subject to the higher tax rates increased slightly.

The problem for the state government, Sullivan determined, is that its highest-income residents have undertaken dynamic responses to higher tax rates. These residents have chosen to earn less income subject to the higher tax rates. Thus, instead of recommending a third round of tax-rate increases for the state's richest residents, prior to his recent retirement, Sullivan developed a set of alternative proposals for boosting the state government's tax revenues. His successor is considering those ideas, but an increased income tax rate for the highest-income Connecticut residents remains a possibility in future years.

FOR CRITICAL THINKING

What happened to the tax base comprising the incomes of the richest Connecticut residents subject to higher tax rates? Explain briefly.

REAL APPLICATION

Assume that you have become a high-income-earning individual and that you are living in a state with an income tax. Detail the ways that you could react to an increase in that state's highest marginal tax rate.

Sources are listed at the end of this chapter.

ISSUES & APPLICATIONS

What Would It Take to Save Social Security as We Know It?

Andriy Popov/123RF GB Limited

CONCEPTS APPLIED

➤ Government Budget Constraint

➤ Tax Base

➤ Marginal Tax Rate

The government budget constraint states that a given period's flow of public expenditures must be funded by a corresponding flow of tax revenues, user charges, and borrowings. A significant expenditure program included within the federal government's budget constraint, Social Security, is on the verge of failing to satisfy this constraint.

For the Social Security program that provides payments to the elderly, the relevant interval of time is no more than two decades, because a current beneficiary who retires and begins receiving benefits at age 65 can be expected to continue receiving benefits until the age of 85. Many among the population bulge of so-called baby boomers born between the 1940s and 1960s are in the process of retiring. As they do so, the difference between collections of Social Security contributions from current taxpayers and payouts to retired beneficiaries will shrink. Indeed, most government projections indicate that Social Security outflows will exceed inflows within about a decade, so the government is running out of time to find ways to finance Social Security. How might the looming shortfall be avoided?

Alternatives for Maintaining Current Social Security Benefits

One approach to financing the Social Security program would be to collect more contributions from taxpayers during the coming years. A way to do so would be to subject more of each individual's annual earnings to taxation at the current 12.4 percent contribution rate than the first $133,000 currently subject to taxation. In this way, the tax base for Social Security would be expanded. All earnings of people who receive more than $133,000 in annual income would be taxed at the current rate, and total tax collections would increase.

Another way to boost Social Security tax collections would be to raise the program's contribution rate. Indeed, some recent proposals call for gradually increasing the contribution rate to nearly 15 percent over the next 25 years. One proposal combines elements of both ideas by subjecting all income to the Social Security contribution rate and raising the tax rate. Projections indicate that implementing this combined plan ultimately would increase by one-fifth the total contributions of lower- and middle-income earners and double the total Social Security taxes collected from higher-income earners.

Alternatives for Reducing Total Social Security Payouts

Critics of plans to boost Social Security tax collections argue that collecting more taxes—particularly via higher tax rates—would tax labor and thereby reduce incentives for businesses to hire workers and for people to offer to supply their labor. These critics offer two types of alternatives to tax increases. One proposal is to increase the ages at which older people qualify for Social Security benefits. Another is to raise age limits for benefits. Boosting the minimum benefit age from 62 to 64 and the normal benefit age from 65 to 70 would generate projected expenditure savings of at least $600 billion over a 20-year horizon. Implementing either or both proposals would begin addressing Social Security's problems on the spending side.

Some observers have proposed combinations of benefit reductions and tax increases. All observers, however, agree that action eventually will have to be taken before the government's Social Security program's financial inflows and outflows can be brought back into balance.

FOR CRITICAL THINKING

Why do you suppose that the baby-boom-generated population bulge has caused the Social Security budget constraint to fall out of balance?

REAL APPLICATION

If you are young, when you reach your 60s, the minimum retirement age to receive Social Security benefits probably will have risen. Moreover, it is not certain that Social Security payments for which you will be eligible will be as generous as they are today. How does this information affect your future?

Sources are listed at the end of this chapter.

What You Should Know

Here is what you should know after reading this chapter.

LEARNING OBJECTIVES

6.1 **Distinguish between average tax rates and marginal tax rates** *The average tax rate is the ratio of total tax payments to total income. The marginal tax rate is the change in tax payments induced by a change in total taxable income and thereby applies to the last dollar that a person earns. In a progressive tax system, the marginal tax rate increases as income rises, so that the marginal tax rate exceeds the average tax rate. In a regressive tax system, the marginal tax rate decreases as income rises, so that the marginal tax rate is less than the average tax rate. The marginal tax rate equals the average tax rate only under proportional taxation, in which the marginal tax rate does not vary with income.*

6.2 **Explain the structure of the U.S. income tax system** *The U.S. federal government raises most of its annual tax revenues from individual and corporate income taxes and also collects Social Security and unemployment taxes. State governments raise revenues through a variety of different taxes, including personal and corporate income taxes, sales and excise taxes, and property taxes.*

KEY TERMS

government budget
   constraint, 121
tax base, 122
tax rate, 122
marginal tax rate, 122
tax bracket, 122
average tax rate, 122
proportional taxation, 123
progressive taxation, 123
regressive taxation, 123

capital gain, 125
capital loss, 125
retained earnings, 125
tax incidence, 126

LEARNING OBJECTIVES

6.3 **Understand the key factors influencing the relationship between tax rates and the tax revenues governments collect** *Static tax analysis assumes that the tax base does not respond significantly to an increase in the tax rate, so it seems to imply that a tax rate hike must always boost a government's total tax collections. Dynamic tax analysis reveals, however, that increases in tax rates cause the tax base to decline. Thus, there is a tax rate that maximizes the government's tax revenues. If the government pushes the tax rate higher, tax collections decline.*

6.4 **Explain how the taxes governments levy on purchases of goods and services affect market prices and equilibrium quantities** *When a government imposes a per-unit tax on a good or service, a seller is willing to supply any given quantity only if the seller receives a price that is higher by exactly the amount of the tax. Hence, the supply curve shifts vertically by the amount of the tax per unit. In a market with typically shaped demand and supply curves, this results in a fall in the equilibrium quantity and an increase in the market price. To the extent that the market price rises, consumers pay a portion of the tax on each unit they buy. Sellers pay the remainder in lower profits.*

KEY TERMS

sales taxes, 127
ad valorem taxation, 127
static tax analysis, 127
dynamic tax analysis, 127
Key Figure
Figure 6-3, 129

excise tax, 131
unit tax, 131
Key Figure
Figure 6-4, 130

PROBLEMS

6-1. A senior citizen gets a part-time job at a fast-food restaurant. She earns $8 per hour for each hour she works, and she works exactly 25 hours per week. Thus, her total pretax weekly income is $200. Her total income tax assessment each week is $40. She pays $3 in taxes for the final hour she works each week.

 a. What is this person's average tax rate each week?

 b. What is the marginal tax rate for the last hour she works each week?

6-2. For purposes of assessing income taxes, there are three official income levels for workers in a small country: high, medium, and low. For the last hour on the job during a 40-hour workweek, a high-income worker pays a marginal income tax rate of 15 percent, a medium-income worker pays a marginal tax rate of 20 percent, and a low-income worker is assessed a 25 percent marginal income tax rate. Based only on this information, does this nation's income tax system appear to be progressive, proportional, or regressive?

6-3. Consider the table below when answering the questions that follow. Show your work, and explain briefly.

Christino		Jarius		Meg	
Income	Taxes Paid	Income	Taxes Paid	Income	Taxes Paid
$1,000	$200	$1,000	$200	$1,000	$200
$2,000	$300	$2,000	$400	$2,000	$500
$3,000	$400	$3,000	$600	$3,000	$800

 a. What is Christino's marginal tax rate?

 b. What is Jarius's marginal tax rate?

 c. What is Meg's marginal tax rate?

6-4. Refer to the table in Problem 6-3 when answering the following questions. Show your work, and explain briefly.

 a. Does Christino experience progressive, proportional, or regressive taxation?

 b. Does Jarius experience progressive, proportional, or regressive taxation?

 c. Does Meg experience progressive, proportional, or regressive taxation?

6-5. Suppose that a state has increased its sales tax rate every other year since 2012. Assume the state collected all sales taxes that residents legally owed. The table below summarizes its experience. What were total taxable sales in this state during each year displayed in the table?

Year	Sales Tax Rate	Sales Tax Collections
2012	0.03 (3 percent)	$9.0 million
2014	0.04 (4 percent)	$14.0 million
2016	0.05 (5 percent)	$20.0 million
2018	0.06 (6 percent)	$24.0 million
2020	0.07 (7 percent)	$29.4 million

6-6. The sales tax rate applied to all purchases within a state was 0.04 (4 percent) throughout 2019 but increased to 0.05 (5 percent) during all of 2020.

The state government collected all taxes due, but its tax revenues were equal to $40 million each year. What happened to the sales tax base between 2019 and 2020? What could account for this result?

6-7. The British government recently imposed a unit excise tax of about $154 per ticket on airline tickets for flights to or from London airports. In answering the following questions, assume normally shaped demand and supply curves.

   a. Use an appropriate diagram to predict effects of the ticket tax on the market clearing price of London airline tickets and on the equilibrium number of flights into and out of London.

   b. What do you predict is likely to happen to the equilibrium price of tickets for air flights into and out of cities that are in close proximity to London but are not subject to the new ticket tax? Explain your reasoning.

6-8. To raise funds aimed at providing more support for public schools, a state government has just imposed a unit excise tax equal to $4 for each monthly unit of cell services sold by each company operating in the state. The following diagram depicts the positions of the demand and supply curves for cell services *before* the unit excise tax was imposed. Use this diagram to determine the position of the new market supply curve now that the tax hike has gone into effect.

   a. Does imposing the $4-per-month unit excise tax cause the market price of cell services to rise by $4 per month? Why or why not?

   b. What portion of the $4-per-month unit excise tax is paid by consumers? What portion is paid by providers of cell services?

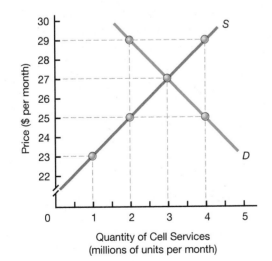

Quantity of Cell Services
(millions of units per month)

6-9. The following information applies to the market for a particular item in the *absence* of a unit excise tax:

Price ($ per unit)	Quantity Supplied	Quantity Demanded
4	50	200
5	75	175
6	100	150
7	125	125
8	150	100
9	175	75

   a. According to the information in the table, in the *absence* of a unit excise tax, what is the market price? What is the equilibrium quantity?

   b. Suppose that the government decides to subject producers of this item to a unit excise tax equal to $2 per unit sold. What is the new market price? What is the new equilibrium quantity?

   c. What portion of the tax is paid by producers? What portion of the tax is paid by consumers?

6-10. Between 2020 and 2021, a small business owner's income increased from $200,000 to $220,000. The annual state income taxes that she paid increased from $5,000 to $5,500. What was her average state income tax rate in each year?

6-11. In Problem 6-10, what was the individual's marginal state income tax rate in 2018? Did this individual experience proportional, progressive, or regressive taxation? Explain briefly.

6-12. Between 2020 and 2021, the income received by a company located in a city rose from $5,000,000 to $6,000,000. The annual city income taxes that the company paid increased from $250,000 to $500,000. What was the company's average city income tax rate in each year?

6-13. In Problem 6-12, what was the company's marginal city income tax rate in 2021? Did this company experience proportional, progressive, or regressive taxation? Explain briefly.

6-14. Consider Figure 6-3. Suppose that the government raises its sales tax rate from 4 percent to 6 percent. Does the direction of the effect on the government's tax revenues indicated by the figure's dynamic tax analysis accord with the prediction that would have been forthcoming from static tax analysis? Explain briefly.

6-15. Consider Figure 6-3. Suppose that the government raises its sales tax rate from 6 percent to 8 percent. Are the predictions of static tax analysis and dynamic tax analysis in agreement on the direction of the change of the government's tax revenues? Explain briefly.

REFERENCES

POLICY EXAMPLE: State Governments Confront Higher Debt Repayment Expenses

"State Debt Ranking Percent of GDP," USGovernmentSpending.com (https://www.usgovernmentdebt.us/state_debt_rank), 2019.

Romey Varghese, "California's $83 Billion of Bond Debt Isn't Enough for Some," *Bloomberg*, March 4, 2018.

Cole Lauterbatch, "Illinois Is 2018's Least Fiscally Stable State," Illinois News Network (https://www.ilnews.org/news/state_politics/report-illinois-is-s-least-fiscally-stable-state/article_2ae91cdc-23e5-11e8-aa11-0b64dc049cac.html), May 12, 2018.

AI—DECISION MAKING THROUGH DATA: Preserving National Tax Bases

"Advance Data and Analytics," Internal Revenue Service, U.S. Department of the Treasury (https://www.irs.gov/about-irs/strategic-goals/advance-data-analytics), 2019.

Deborah Planko, "Using Artificial Intelligence to Reduce Tax Fraud," NextGov.com (https://www.nextgov.com/ideas/2018/04/using-artificial-intelligence-reduce-tax-fraud/147807/), April 27, 2018.

Morgan Wright, "Government Robots, Chatbots Are Coming," *The Hill*, June 15, 2018.

EXAMPLE: Average Federal Income Tax Rates and U.S. Income Tax Progressivity

Tax Policy Center, *Briefing Book* (www.taxpolicycenter.org/briefing-book/are-federal-taxes-progressive), 2019.

"Who Pays Taxes in America?" Institute on Taxation and Economic Policy, April 2018.

Laura Saunders, "Top 2-Percent of Americans Will Pay 87 Percent of Income Tax," *Wall Street Journal*, April 6, 2018.

POLICY EXAMPLE: If You Generate Sales from Moving Items from Our State to Outer Space, Pay Up!

"State of California Franchise Tax Board," FTB.CA.gov (https://www.ftb.ca.gov), 2019.

Foon Rhee, "SpaceX Had a Big Launch, California Is Taxing It," *Sacramento Bee*, February 6, 2018.

Mark Whittington, "Can Republicans Stop California's Tax on Space Flight?" *Washington Examiner*, February 1, 2018.

BEHAVIORAL EXAMPLE: Increases in Complex Sales Taxes Generate Predictable Dynamic Responses by Consumers

Scott Baker and Lorenz Kueng, "Shopping for Lower Sales Tax Rates," Northwestern University, May 2018. "State Sales Tax Rates," Sales Tax Institute (https://www.salestaxinstitute.com/resources/rates), February 1, 2019.

Jared Walczak and Scott Drenkard, "State and Local Sales Tax Rates," Tax Foundation (https://taxfoundation.org/state-and-local-sales-tax-rates-2018/), February 13, 2018.

ECONOMICS IN YOUR LIFE: The Connecticut Government Decides to Avoid Striking Out on Its Income Tax Policy

"Connecticut Income Tax Brackets," Tax-Brackets.org (https://www.tax-brackets.org/connecticuttaxtable), 2019.

Greg Sullivan, "Connecticut Example Argues Against Millionaire Taxes," BizJournals.com (https://www.bizjournals.com/boston/news/2018/02/06/viewpoint-connecticut-example-argues-against.html), February 6, 2018.

Dan Caplinger, "Are You a Millionaire? You'll Pay Higher Taxes in These Four Places," *Motley Fool*, June 17, 2018.

ISSUES & APPLICATIONS: What Would It Take to Save Social Security as We Know It?

Office of the Chief Actuary, Social Security Administration, "Proposals Affecting Trust Fund Solvency" (https://www.ssa.gov/oact/solvency/), 2019.

"Social Security Says System's Costs Will Exceed Income This Year," CBS News (https://www.cbsnews.com/news/social-security-says-costs-will-exceed-income-this-year/), June 5, 2018.

Stephen Entin, "Social Security in Deficit: Why and What to Do About It," Tax Foundation (https://taxfoundation.org/social-security-deficit/), June 12, 2018.

7 The Macroeconomy: Unemployment, Inflation, and Deflation

Shutterstock

LEARNING OBJECTIVES

After reading this chapter, you should be able to:

7.1 Explain how the U.S. government calculates the official unemployment rate

7.2 Discuss the types of unemployment

7.3 Describe how price indexes are calculated and define the key types of price indexes

7.4 Evaluate who loses and who gains from inflation and distinguish between nominal and real interest rates

7.5 Understand key features of business fluctuations

Each month, media stories alert us to the latest value of the U.S. *unemployment rate*. This term refers to the percentage of people deemed eligible to be employed but who currently do not have a formal job. Formal work, in turn, constitutes occupying a full-time or part-time position of "employment" as defined by government statisticians. At one time or another, however, about one out of every five U.S. residents engages in so-called informal work, perhaps by earning extra income from providing accounting work for a company for a month. Some people who engage in informal work have positions that government statisticians deem sufficiently "official" to place them among employed people. Others, however, are categorized as either unemployed or not seeking jobs. As you will learn in this chapter, a consequence of widespread informal work is that it can bias official measures of the unemployment rate.

DID YOU KNOW THAT...

the Congressional Budget Office has estimated that work disincentives generated by the 2010 national health care law, the Affordable Care Act, reduced by about 200,000 per year the number of people seeking jobs? By inducing people to opt *not* to work, the law thereby brought about annual reductions in the U.S. *labor force*, which is the government's key measure of the number of people either employed or looking for work.

Understanding the determinants of the nation's total employment, of aggregate unemployment, and of the overall performance of either the national economy or the global economy is a central objective of macroeconomics. This branch of economics seeks to explain and predict movements in the average level of prices, unemployment, and total production of goods and services. This chapter introduces you to these key issues of macroeconomics.

7.1 Explain how the U.S. government calculates the official unemployment rate

Unemployment
The total number of adults (aged 16 years or older) who are willing and able to work and who are actively looking for work but have not found a job.

Labor force
Individuals aged 16 years or older who either have jobs or are looking and available for jobs; the number of employed plus the number of unemployed.

Unemployment

Unemployment is normally defined as the number of adults who are actively looking for work but do not have a job. Unemployment is costly in terms of lost output for the entire economy. At the end of the first decade of the twenty-first century, the unemployment rate rose by more than 4 percentage points and firms operated below 80 percent of their capacity. One estimate indicates that the amount of output that the economy lost due to idle resources was roughly 5 percent of the potential total production throughout the United States.

That was the equivalent of more than an inflation-adjusted $700 billion of schools, houses, restaurant meals, cars, and movies that *could have been* produced. It is no wonder that policymakers closely watch the unemployment figures published by the Department of Labor's Bureau of Labor Statistics.

On a more personal level, the state of being unemployed often results in hardship and failed opportunities as well as a lack of self-respect. Psychological researchers believe that being fired creates at least as much stress as the death of a close friend. The numbers that we present about unemployment can never fully convey its true cost to the people of this or any other nation.

Historical Unemployment Rates

The unemployment rate, defined as the proportion of the measured **labor force** that is unemployed, hit a low of 1.2 percent of the labor force at the end of World War II, after having reached 25 percent during the Great Depression in the 1930s. You can see in Figure 7-1 what has happened to the unemployment rate in the United States since 1890. The highest level ever was reached in the Great Depression, but the unemployment rate was also high during the Panic of 1893.

Employment, Unemployment, and the Labor Force

Figure 7-2 presents the population of individuals 16 years of age or older broken into three segments: (1) employed, (2) unemployed, and (3) not in the civilian labor force (a category that includes homemakers, full-time students, military personnel, persons in institutions, and retired persons). The employed and the unemployed, added together, make up the labor force. In 2020, the labor force amounted to 157.3 million + 6.1 million = 163.4 million people. To calculate the unemployment rate, we simply divide the number of unemployed by the number of people in the labor force and multiply by 100: 6.1 million/163.4 million × 100 = 3.7 percent.

FIGURE 7-1

More Than a Century of Unemployment

The U.S. unemployment rate dropped below 2 percent during World Wars I and II but exceeded 25 percent during the Great Depression.

During the period following 2007, the unemployment rate rose to about 10 percent.

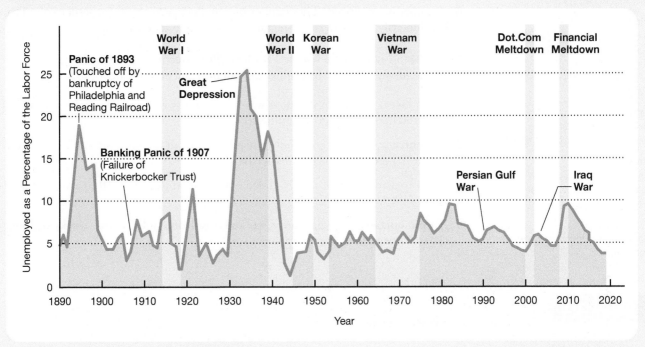

Source: U.S. Department of Labor, Bureau of Labor Statistics.

FIGURE 7-2

Adult Population

The population aged 16 and older can be broken down into three groups: people who are employed, those who are unemployed, and those not in the labor force.

Source: U.S. Department of Labor, Bureau of Labor Statistics.

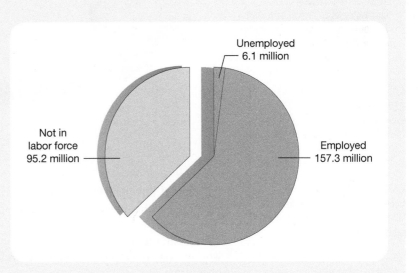

The Arithmetic Determination of Unemployment

Because there is a transition between employment and unemployment at any point in time—people are leaving jobs and others are finding jobs—there is a simple relationship between the employed and the unemployed. This fact can be seen in Figure 7-3. Job departures are shown at the top of the diagram, and job acquisitions are shown at

Stock
The quantity of something, measured at a given point in time—for example, an inventory of goods or a bank account. Stocks are defined independently of time, although they are assessed at a point in time.

Flow
A quantity measured per unit of time; something that occurs over time, such as the income you make per week or per year or the number of individuals who are fired every month.

Job loser
An individual in the labor force whose employment was involuntarily terminated.

Reentrant
An individual who used to work full-time but left the labor force and has now reentered it looking for a job.

Job leaver
An individual in the labor force who quits voluntarily.

the bottom. If the numbers of job departures and acquisitions are equal, the unemployment rate stays the same. If departures exceed acquisitions, the unemployment rate rises.

The number of unemployed is some number at any point in time. It is a **stock** of individuals who do not have a job but are actively looking for one. The same is true for the number of employed. The number of people departing jobs, whether voluntarily or involuntarily, is a **flow,** as is the number of people acquiring jobs.

Categories of Individuals Who Are without Work According to the Bureau of Labor Statistics, an unemployed individual will fall into any of four categories:

1. A **job loser,** whose employment was involuntarily terminated or who was laid off (40 to 60 percent of the unemployed)

2. A **reentrant,** who worked a full-time job before but has been out of the labor force (20 to 30 percent of the unemployed)

3. A **job leaver,** who voluntarily ended employment (less than 10 to around 15 percent of the unemployed)

4. A **new entrant,** who has never worked a full-time job for two weeks or longer (10 to 15 percent of the unemployed)

FIGURE 7-3

The Logic of the Unemployment Rate

Individuals who depart jobs but remain in the labor force are subtracted from the employed and added to the unemployed. When the unemployed acquire jobs, they are subtracted from the unemployed and added to the employed. In an unchanged labor force, if both flows are equal, the unemployment rate is stable. If more people depart jobs than acquire them, the unemployment rate increases, and vice versa.

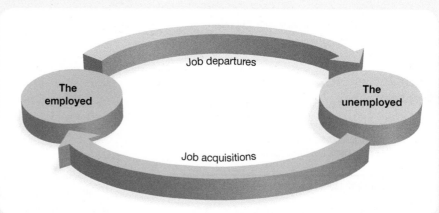

New entrant
An individual who has never held a full-time job lasting two weeks or longer but is now seeking employment.

ECONOMICS IN YOUR LIFE

To contemplate how the unemployment rate among teenagers has changed in recent years, take a look at **After Years of High Teen Unemployment Rates, U.S. Teenagers Are Finding Work Once More** on page 153.

Duration of Unemployment The overall average duration of unemployment for the past 25 years has been about 17 weeks. If you are out of a job for a week, your situation is typically much less serious than if you are out of a job for, say, 14 weeks. An increase in the duration of unemployment can raise the unemployment rate because workers stay unemployed longer, thereby creating a greater number of them at any given time.

When overall business activity goes into a downturn, the duration of unemployment tends to rise, thereby accounting for much of the increase in the estimated unemployment rate. In a sense, then, it is the increase in the *duration* of unemployment during a downturn in national economic activity that generates the bad news that concerns policymakers in Washington, D.C. Furthermore, the individuals who stay unemployed longer than six months are the ones who create pressure on Congress to "do something." What Congress does, typically, is extend and supplement unemployment benefits.

The Optimal Duration of Unemployment for You At some point in your future, you may become unemployed. Should you take the first job you are offered when you start your new job search? Probably not. After all, just about anyone can get a job in a fast-food restaurant. Presumably, you will have completed some higher education, obtained training in previous jobs, and are qualified for more than entry-level jobs. As with most decisions in your future, you will have to compare the potential benefits of searching longer for a better job opportunity compared with the income that you will have lost during this more extended search period.

What accounts for the fact that many people who have lost their jobs involuntarily are choosing *not* to apply for unemployment benefits?

EXAMPLE

Why Are Millions of Those Laid Off or Fired Opting Not to Apply for Unemployment Benefits?

Over the course of a two-year period just about a decade ago, unemployment rose by about 14 million. During that interval, workers' initial claims for unemployment benefits tracked closely the number of layoffs and discharges of workers by firms. Since the end of that period, however, the number of initial claims for unemployment benefits has dropped much faster than the number of layoffs and discharges. In recent years, the number of initial claims for unemployment benefits has averaged several millions below reported layoffs and discharges. Some observers have offered this fact as evidence that the state governments have unreasonably tightened their requirements for benefits and thereby deprived potentially deserving individuals of such benefits.

Actually, two other elements have contributed to the drop in initial claims for unemployment benefits. First, many previously discouraged workers had recently reentered the labor force and obtained jobs. Then when some of these workers have lost their positions, they have lacked a sufficiently long work history to meet unemployment-insurance requirements. Second, today's job losers are finding new positions faster than was true ten years ago. Thus, a larger number of today's job losers—including some of the new reentrants to the labor force who recently found but then quickly lost positions—are able to find jobs speedily and consequently do not apply for unemployment benefits.

REAL APPLICATION

How should you take into account unemployment benefits when deciding when to accept a job offer?

Sources are listed at the end of this chapter.

The Discouraged Worker Phenomenon Critics of the published unemployment rate calculated by the federal government believe that it fails to reflect the true numbers of **discouraged workers** and "hidden unemployed." Though there is no agreed-on method to measure discouraged workers, the Department of Labor defines them as people who have dropped out of the labor force and are no longer looking for a job because they believe that the job market has little to offer them. To what extent do we want to include in the measured labor force those individuals who voluntarily choose not to look for work? Should we include those who take only a few minutes a day to scan online job ads and then decide there are no good jobs?

Some economists argue that people who work part-time but are willing to work full-time should be classified as "semihidden" unemployed. Estimates range as high as 6 million workers at any one time. Offsetting this factor, though, is the *multiple-job holder*. An individual working 50 or 60 hours a week is still counted as only one full-time worker. And some people hold two or three jobs but still are counted as just one employed person.

Discouraged workers
Individuals who have stopped looking for a job because they are convinced that they will not find a suitable one.

Labor Force Participation The way in which we define unemployment and membership in the labor force will affect the **labor force participation rate.** It is defined as the proportion of noninstitutionalized (i.e., not in prisons, mental institutions, etc.) working-age individuals who are employed or seeking employment.

The U.S. labor force participation rate rose from about 59 percent in 1950 to 67 percent at the end of the 1990s. The labor force participation rate since has declined and currently is about 63 percent. The gender composition of the U.S. labor force has changed considerably during this time. In 1950, more than 83 percent of men and fewer than 35 percent of women participated in the U.S. labor force. Today, fewer than 70 percent of men and about 57 percent of women are U.S. labor force participants.

Labor force participation rate
The percentage of noninstitutionalized working-age individuals who are employed or seeking employment.

7.2 Discuss the types of unemployment

The Major Types of Unemployment

After economists adjust unemployment to take into account seasonal variations—for instance, more construction industry unemployment during winter months—they classify unemployment into three basic types: frictional, structural, and cyclical. Economists also seek to measure full employment and a concept known as the natural rate of unemployment.

Frictional Unemployment

Of the more than 163 million people in the labor force, in excess of 50 million will either change jobs or take new jobs during the year. In the process, at least 25 million persons will report themselves unemployed at one time or another each year. This continuous flow of individuals from job to job and in and out of employment is called **frictional unemployment.**

Frictional unemployment
Unemployment due to the fact that workers must search for appropriate job offers. This activity takes time, and so they remain temporarily unemployed.

There will always be some frictional unemployment as resources are redirected in the economy, because job-hunting costs are never zero, and workers never have full information about available jobs. To eliminate frictional unemployment, we would have to prevent workers from leaving their present jobs until they had already lined up other jobs at which they would start working immediately. We also would have to guarantee first-time job seekers a job *before* they started looking.

Structural Unemployment

Structural changes in our economy cause some workers to become unemployed for very long periods of time because they cannot find jobs that use their particular skills. This is called **structural unemployment.** Structural unemployment is not caused by general business fluctuations, although business fluctuations may affect it. Unlike frictional unemployment, structural unemployment is not related to the movement of workers from low-paying to high-paying jobs.

Structural unemployment
Unemployment of workers over lengthy intervals resulting from skill mismatches with position requirements of employers and from fewer jobs being offered by employers constrained by governmental business regulations and labor market policies.

At one time, economists thought about structural unemployment only from the perspective of workers. The concept applied to workers who did not have the ability, training, and skills necessary to obtain available jobs. Today, it still encompasses these workers. In addition, however, economists increasingly look at structural unemployment from the viewpoint of employers, many of whom face government mandates requiring them to take such steps as providing funds for social insurance programs for their employees and announcing plant closings months or even years in advance.

There is now considerable evidence that government labor market policies influence how many job positions businesses wish to create, thereby affecting structural unemployment. In the United States, many businesses appear to have adjusted to these policies by hiring more "temporary workers" or establishing short-term contracts with "private consultants." Such measures may have increased the extent of U.S. structural unemployment in recent years.

How have labor laws that have given rise to temporary work contracts in several European nations contributed to higher structural unemployment in those countries?

INTERNATIONAL EXAMPLE

Temporary Work Feeds Europe's Structural Unemployment Problem

Labor laws established by a number of European governments make it difficult and expensive for companies to fire workers who have been employed for lengthy periods. In some nations, such as Spain and France, government rules require firms to provide terminated employees with substantial severance payments. Firms have responded to such legal constraints by employing larger numbers of workers under temporary contracts exempt from some government labor rules. Naturally, many older workers already had been covered by permanent contracts, so firms' increased utilization of temporary contracts has most affected younger workers. Figure 7-4 displays the percentages of workers between the ages of 15 and 29 in selected European nations employed under such temporary agreements.

Because companies know that many of the younger workers whom they hire will not remain for more than a few months, they have little incentive to provide them with in-depth training. Indeed, firms assign to most temporary young employees menial tasks that are unlikely to provide skills that will help the workers land better-paying and longer-term jobs. As a consequence, many young workers afterward slip back into unemployment. This fact helps to explain why youth unemployment rates have exceeded 25 percent in France and Spain and contribute to relatively high overall levels of structural unemployment in other countries with similar labor laws.

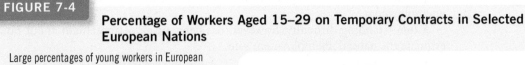

FOR CRITICAL THINKING

Why do you suppose that older workers might favor the labor laws that have given firms incentives to employ younger workers only on a temporary basis?

Sources are listed at the end of this chapter.

FIGURE 7-4

Percentage of Workers Aged 15–29 on Temporary Contracts in Selected European Nations

Large percentages of young workers in European nations are employed under short-term contracts.
Source: European Commission.

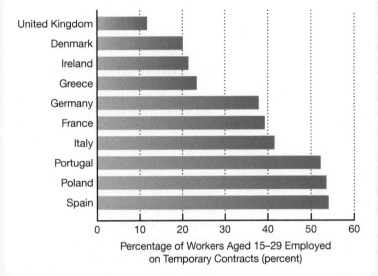

Cyclical Unemployment

Cyclical unemployment is related to business fluctuations. It is defined as unemployment associated with changes in business conditions—primarily recessions and depressions. The way to lessen cyclical unemployment would be to reduce the intensity, duration, and frequency of downturns in business activity. Economic policymakers attempt, through their policies, to reduce cyclical unemployment by keeping business activity on an even keel.

Cyclical unemployment
Unemployment resulting from business recessions that occur when aggregate (total) demand is insufficient to create full employment.

Full Employment and the Natural Rate of Unemployment

Does full employment mean that everybody has a job? Certainly not, for not everyone is looking for a job—full-time students and full-time homemakers, for example, are not. Is it always possible for everyone who is looking for a job to find one? No, because transaction costs in the labor market are not zero. Transaction costs are those associated with any activity whose goal is to enter into, carry out, or terminate contracts. In the labor market, these costs involve time spent looking for a job, being interviewed, negotiating the terms of employment, and the like.

Full Employment We will always have some frictional unemployment as individuals move in and out of the labor force, seek higher-paying jobs, and move to different

Full employment
An arbitrary level of unemployment that corresponds to "normal" friction in the labor market.

parts of the country. **Full employment** is therefore a concept that implies some sort of balance or equilibrium in an ever-shifting labor market. Of course, this general notion of full employment must somehow be put into numbers so that economists and others can determine whether the economy has reached the full-employment point.

The Natural Rate of Unemployment In trying to assess when a situation of balance has been attained in the labor market, economists estimate the **natural rate of unemployment,** the rate that is expected to prevail in the long run once all workers and employers have fully adjusted to any changes in the economy. If correctly estimated, the natural rate of unemployment should not include cyclical unemployment. Thus, the natural unemployment rate should include only frictional and structural unemployment.

Natural rate of unemployment
The rate of unemployment that is estimated to prevail in long-run macroeconomic equilibrium, when all workers and employers have fully adjusted to any changes in the economy.

A long-standing difficulty, however, has been a lack of agreement about how to estimate the natural unemployment rate.

7.3 Describe how price indexes are calculated and define the key types of price indexes

Inflation and Deflation

During World War II, you could buy bread for 8 to 10 cents a loaf and have milk delivered fresh to your door for about 25 cents a half gallon. The average price of a new car was less than $700, and the average house cost less than $3,000. Today, bread, milk, cars, and houses all cost more—a lot more. Prices are about 17 times what they were in 1940. Clearly, this country has experienced quite a bit of *inflation* since then. We define **inflation** as an upward movement in the average level of prices. The opposite of inflation is **deflation,** defined as a downward movement in the average level of prices. Notice that these definitions depend on the *average* level of prices. This means that even during a period of inflation, some prices can be falling if other prices are rising at a faster rate. The prices of electronic equipment have dropped dramatically since the 1960s, even though there has been general inflation.

Inflation
A sustained increase in the average of all prices of goods and services in an economy.

Deflation
A sustained decrease in the average of all prices of goods and services in an economy.

Inflation and the Purchasing Power of Money

By definition, the value of a dollar does not stay constant when there is inflation. The value of money is usually talked about in terms of **purchasing power.** A dollar's purchasing power is the real goods and services that it can buy. Consequently, another way of defining inflation is as a decline in the purchasing power of money. The faster the rate of inflation, the greater the rate of decline in the purchasing power of money.

Purchasing power
The value of money for buying goods and services. If your money income stays the same but the price of one good that you are buying goes up, your effective purchasing power falls.

One way to think about inflation and the purchasing power of money is to discuss dollar values in terms of *nominal* versus *real* values. The nominal value of anything is simply its price expressed in today's dollars. In contrast, the real value of anything is its value expressed in purchasing power, which varies with the overall price level. Let's say that you received a $100 bill from your grandparents this year. One year from now, the nominal value of that bill will still be $100. The real value will depend on what the purchasing power of money is after one year's worth of inflation. Obviously, if there is inflation during the year, the real value of that $100 bill will have diminished. For example, if you keep the $100 bill in your pocket for a year during which the rate of inflation is 3 percent, at the end of the year you will have to come up with $3 more to buy the same amount of goods and services that the $100 bill can purchase today.

To discuss what has happened to prices here and in other countries, we have to know how to measure inflation.

Measuring the Rate of Inflation

How can we measure the rate of inflation? It is easy to determine how much the price of an individual commodity has risen: If last year a compact fluorescent light bulb cost $6.00, and this year it costs $9.00, there has been a 50 percent rise in the price of that light bulb over a one-year period. We can express the change in the individual light bulb price in one of several ways: The price has gone up $3.00. The price is one and a half (1.5) times as high. The price has risen by 50 percent. An *index number* of this price rise is simply the second way (1.5) multiplied by 100, meaning that the index today would stand at 150. We multiply by 100 to eliminate decimals because it is easier to think in terms of percentage changes using whole numbers. This is the standard convention adopted for convenience in dealing with index numbers or price levels.

Computing a Price Index

The measurement problem becomes more complicated when it involves a large number of goods, especially if some prices have risen faster than others and some have even fallen. What we have to do is pick a representative bundle, a so-called market basket, of goods and compare the cost of that market basket of goods over time. When we do this, we obtain a **price index,** which is defined as the cost of a market basket of goods today, expressed as a percentage of the cost of that identical market basket of goods in some starting year, known as the **base year.**

$$\text{Price index} = \frac{\text{cost of market basket today}}{\text{cost of market basket in base year}} \times 100$$

In the base year, the price index will always be 100, because the year in the numerator and in the denominator of the fraction is the same. Therefore, the fraction equals 1, and when we multiply it by 100, we get 100. A simple numerical example is given in Table 7-1. In the table, there are only two goods in the market basket—corn and digital devices. The *quantities* in the basket are the same in the base year, 2012, and the current year, 2022. Only the *prices* change. Such a *fixed-quantity* price index is the easiest to compute because the statistician need only look at prices of goods and services sold every year rather than observing how much of these goods and services consumers actually purchase each year.

Price index
The cost of today's market basket of goods expressed as a percentage of the cost of the same market basket during a base year.

Base year
The year that is chosen as the point of reference for comparison of prices in other years.

TABLE 7-1

Calculating a Price Index for a Two-Good Market Basket

In this simplified example, there are only two goods—corn and digital devices. The quantities and base-year prices are given in columns 2 and 3. The 2012 cost of the market basket, calculated in column 4, comes to $1,300. The 2022 prices are given in column 5. The cost of the market basket in 2022, calculated in column 6, is $1,500. The price index for 2022 compared with 2012 is 115.38.

(1) Commodity	(2) Market Basket Quantity	(3) 2012 Price per Unit	(4) Cost of Market Basket in 2012	(5) 2022 Price per Unit	(6) Cost of Market Basket in 2022
Corn	100 bushels	$ 4	$ 400	$ 8	$ 800
Digital devices	2	450	900	350	700
		0			
Totals			$1,300		$1,500

Consumer Price Index (CPI)

A statistical measure of a weighted average of prices of a specified set of goods and services purchased by typical consumers in urban areas.

Producer Price Index (PPI)

A statistical measure of a weighted average of prices of goods and services that firms produce and sell.

GDP deflator

A price index measuring the changes in prices of all new goods and services produced in the economy.

Personal Consumption Expenditure (PCE) Index

A statistical measure of average prices that uses annually updated weights based on surveys of consumer spending.

Real-World Price Indexes Government statisticians calculate a number of price indexes. The most often quoted are the **Consumer Price Index (CPI)**, the **Producer Price Index (PPI)**, the **GDP deflator**, and the **Personal Consumption Expenditure (PCE) Index.** The CPI attempts to measure changes only in the level of prices of goods and services purchased by consumers. The PPI attempts to show what has happened to the average price of goods and services produced and sold by a typical firm. (There are also *wholesale price indexes* that track the price level for commodities that firms purchase from other firms.) The GDP deflator is the most general indicator of inflation because it measures changes in the level of prices of all new goods and services produced in the economy. The PCE Index measures average prices using weights from surveys of consumer spending.

The CPI The Bureau of Labor Statistics (BLS) has the task of identifying a market basket of goods and services of the typical consumer. Today, the BLS uses the time period 1982–1984 as its base of market prices. The BLS has indicated an intention to change the base to 1993–1995 but has yet to do so. It has, though, updated the expenditure weights for its market basket of goods to reflect consumer spending patterns in 2011–2012. All CPI numbers since that period reflect these expenditure weights.

Economists have known for years that there are possible problems in the CPI's market basket. Specifically, the BLS has been unable to account for the way consumers substitute less expensive items for higher-priced items. The reason is that the CPI is a fixed-quantity price index, meaning that the BLS implicitly ignores changes in consumption patterns that occur between years in which it revises the index. Until recently, the BLS has also been unable to take quality changes into account as they occur. Now, though, it is subtracting from certain list prices estimated effects of qualitative improvements and adding to other list prices to account for deteriorations in quality. An additional flaw is that the CPI usually ignores successful new products until long after they have been introduced. Despite these flaws, the CPI is widely followed because its level is calculated and published monthly.

WHAT HAPPENS WHEN...

innovative new products with novel features appear on the scene or previously existing products undergo significant improvements?

Every time firms introduce novel forms of products or improve existing products, the Consumer Price Index becomes more flawed. This problem arises because of the inability or unwillingness of the Bureau of Labor Statistics to update the set of items from which it samples the prices included in the CPI. As a consequence, the reported value of the CPI fails to reflect changes in the quality-adjusted prices of the new products, which tends to bias the value of the CPI upward.

The PPI There are a number of Producer Price Indexes, including one for foodstuffs, another for intermediate goods (goods used in the production of other goods), and one for finished goods. Most of the producer prices included are in mining, manufacturing, and agriculture. The PPIs can be considered general-purpose indexes for non-retail markets.

Although in the long run the various PPIs and the CPI generally show the same rate of inflation, that is not the case in the short run. Most often the PPIs increase before the CPI because it takes time for producer price increases to show up in the prices that consumers pay for final products. Changes in the PPIs are watched closely as a hint that CPI inflation is going to increase or decrease.

The GDP Deflator The broadest price index reported in the United States is the GDP deflator, where GDP stands for gross domestic product, or annual total national income. Unlike the CPI and the PPIs, the GDP deflator is *not* based on a fixed market basket of goods and services. The basket is allowed to change with people's consumption and investment patterns. In this sense, the changes in the GDP deflator reflect both price changes and the public's market responses to those price changes. Why? Because new expenditure patterns are allowed to show up in the GDP deflator as people respond to changing prices.

What can adjusting new house prices to reflect changes in the GDP deflator tell us about how much they *really* have risen?

EXAMPLE

Are Prices of New Houses Really Almost Fourteen Times Higher Than 50 Years Ago?

In 1968, the average price of a new house in the United States was $25,300. Today, this price is about $350,000. Because today's average price is about 13.8 times greater than the 1968 price, the price comparisons that media commentators typically have undertaken would imply that the prices of new houses have increased by that multiple over the past five decades.

By and large, however, media fail to adjust their price comparisons for the effects of changes in the GDP deflator. After using the GDP deflator, which currently is based on values of goods and services expressed in 2009, the inflation-adjusted price of a new house in 1968 was $115,000. The current inflation-adjusted price of a new house is about $308,000, which is about 2.7 times greater than the inflation-adjusted

price in 1968. Thus, the increase in the price of a new home in the United States during the past 50 years has been substantially smaller than implied by new-home price comparisons undertaken in media reports.

FOR CRITICAL THINKING

If claims that media commentators prefer to report the largest possible, attention-grabbing changes in numbers are correct, why might they prefer to report economic data that have not been adjusted for changes in the price level?

Sources are listed at the end of this chapter.

The PCE Index Another price index that takes into account changing expenditure patterns is the Personal Consumption Expenditure (PCE) Index. The Bureau of Economic Analysis, an agency of the U.S. Department of Commerce, uses continuously updated annual surveys of consumer purchases to construct the weights for the PCE Index. Thus, an advantage of the PCE Index is that weights in the index are updated every year. The Federal Reserve has used the rate of change in the PCE Index as its primary inflation indicator because Fed officials believe that the updated weights in the PCE Index make it more accurate than the CPI as a measure of consumer price changes. Nevertheless, the CPI remains the most widely reported price index, and the U.S. government continues to use the CPI to adjust the value of Social Security benefits to account for inflation.

Historical Changes in the CPI Between World War II and the early 1980s, the Consumer Price Index showed a fairly dramatic trend upward. Figure 7-5 shows the annual rate of change in the CPI since 1860. Prior to World War II, there were numerous periods of deflation interspersed with periods of inflation. Persistent year-in and year-out inflation seems to be a post–World War II phenomenon, at least in this country. As far back as before the American Revolution, prices used to rise during war periods but then would fall back toward prewar levels afterward. This occurred after the Revolutionary War, the War of 1812, the Civil War, and to a lesser extent World War I. Consequently, the overall price level in 1940 wasn't much different from 150 years earlier.

FIGURE 7-5

Inflation and Deflation in U.S. History

For 80 years after the Civil War, the United States experienced alternating inflation and deflation. Here we show them as reflected by changes in the price level. Since World War II, the periods of inflation have not been followed by periods of deflation. Even during peacetime, the price index has continued to rise. The shaded areas represent wartime.

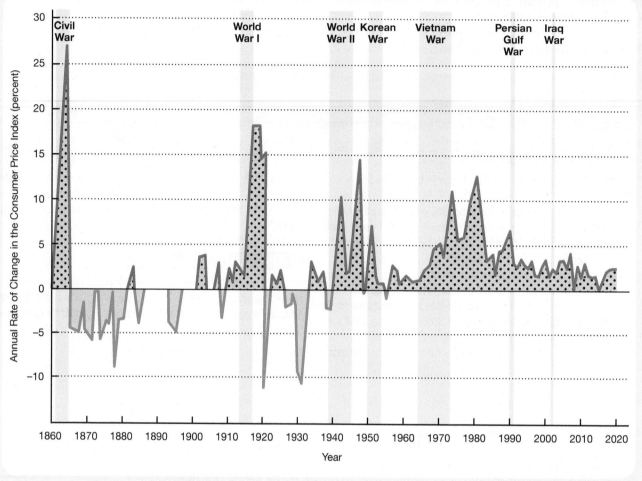

Source: U.S. Department of Labor, Bureau of Labor Statistics.

7.4 Evaluate who loses and who gains from inflation and distinguish between nominal and real interest rates

Anticipated Versus Unanticipated Inflation

To determine who is hurt by inflation and what the effects of inflation are in general, we have to distinguish between anticipated and unanticipated inflation. We will see that the effects on individuals and the economy are vastly different, depending on which type of inflation exists.

Anticipated inflation is the rate of inflation that most individuals believe will occur. If the rate of inflation this year turns out to be 5 percent, and that's about what most people thought it was going to be, we are in a situation of fully anticipated inflation.

Unanticipated inflation is inflation that comes as a surprise to individuals in the economy. For example, if the inflation rate in a particular year turns out to be 10 percent when, on average, people thought it was going to be 3 percent, there was unanticipated inflation—inflation greater than anticipated.

Some of the problems caused by inflation arise when it is unanticipated, because then many people are unable to protect themselves from its ravages. Keeping the

Anticipated inflation
The inflation rate that we believe will occur. When it does occur, we are in a situation of fully anticipated inflation.

Unanticipated inflation
Inflation at a rate that comes as a surprise, either higher or lower than the rate anticipated.

distinction between anticipated and unanticipated inflation in mind, we can easily see the relationship between inflation and interest rates.

Inflation, Interest Rates, and Borrowing Funds to Purchase a House or Car

Let's start in a hypothetical world in which there is no inflation and anticipated inflation is zero. In that world, you may be able to borrow funds—to buy a house or a car, for example—at a **nominal rate of interest** of, say, 4 percent. If you borrow the funds to purchase a house or a car and your anticipation of inflation turns out to be accurate, neither you nor the lender will have been fooled. Each dollar you pay back in the years to come will be just as valuable in terms of purchasing power as the dollar you borrowed.

What you ordinarily want to know when you borrow is the *real* rate of interest that you will have to pay. The **real rate of interest** is defined as the nominal rate of interest minus the anticipated rate of inflation. In effect, we can say that the nominal rate of interest is equal to the real rate of interest plus an *inflationary premium* to take account of anticipated inflation. That inflationary premium covers depreciation in the purchasing power of the dollars repaid by borrowers. (Whenever there are relatively high rates of anticipated inflation, we must add an additional factor to the inflationary premium. This factor is the product of the real rate of interest times the anticipated rate of inflation. Usually, this last term is omitted because the anticipated rate of inflation is not high enough to make much of a difference.)

What is the explanation for why people's inflation anticipations can be difficult to discern from opinion surveys?

Nominal rate of interest
The market rate of interest observed in contracts expressed in today's dollars.

Real rate of interest
The nominal rate of interest minus the anticipated rate of inflation.

BEHAVIORAL EXAMPLE

Why Might Surveys Fail to Reveal People's True Inflation Expectations?

One way that economic policymakers, media reporters, and others assess people's anticipations about inflation is on the basis of answers to opinion surveys regarding inflation expectations. Rates of inflation expected by people who are polled are averaged to obtain a survey estimate of the anticipated inflation rate.

A central tenet of behavioral economics is that people are unable to comprehend all relevant aspects of economic problems that they confront. Behavioral studies of surveyed inflation expectations indicate that such difficulties affect people's answers to inflation-expectation surveys. For instance, when asked to state the inflation rate they anticipate during the next year, people often respond by thinking in terms of prices of a small set of items of most immediate importance to them instead of answering in terms of the change they expect in the overall price level. Various studies have found that constraints on the ability of people to consider all relevant aspects of the problem of predicting the relevant inflation rate cause the expectations obtained by polltakers to be biased. Thus, inflation expectations indicated by surveys are not necessarily accurate representations of people's actual anticipations regarding inflation.

FOR CRITICAL THINKING

Why do you think that many observers prefer to gauge the public's anticipation of inflation by subtracting a measure of the real interest rate from the observed nominal interest rate? (Hint: Recall that by definition, the real interest rate equals the nominal interest rate minus the expected inflation rate.)

Sources are listed at the end of this chapter.

Does Inflation Necessarily Hurt Everyone?

Most people think that inflation is bad. After all, inflation means higher prices, and when we have to pay higher prices, are we not necessarily worse off? The truth is that inflation affects different people differently. Its effects also depend on whether it is anticipated or unanticipated.

Unanticipated Inflation: Creditors Lose and Debtors Gain In most situations, unanticipated inflation benefits borrowers because the nominal interest rate they are being charged does not fully compensate creditors for the inflation that actually occurred. In other words, the lender did not anticipate inflation correctly. Whenever inflation rates are underestimated for the life of a loan, creditors lose and debtors gain. Periods of considerable unanticipated (higher than anticipated) inflation occurred in the late 1960s and all of the 1970s. During those years, creditors lost and debtors gained.

Protecting against Inflation Lenders attempt to protect themselves against inflation by raising nominal interest rates to reflect anticipated inflation. Adjustable-rate mortgages in fact do just that: The interest rate varies according to what happens to interest rates in the economy. Workers can protect themselves from inflation by obtaining **cost-of-living adjustments (COLAs),** which are automatic increases in wage rates to take account of increases in the price level.

To the extent that you hold non-interest-bearing cash, you will lose because of inflation. If you have put $100 in a mattress and the inflation rate is 5 percent for the year, you will have lost 5 percent of the purchasing power of that $100. If you have your funds in a non-interest-bearing checking account, you will suffer the same fate. Individuals attempt to reduce the cost of holding cash by putting it into interest-bearing accounts, some of which pay nominal rates of interest that reflect anticipated inflation.

The Resource Cost of Inflation Some economists believe that the main cost of inflation is the opportunity cost of resources used to protect against distortions that inflation introduces as firms attempt to plan for the long run. Individuals have to spend time and resources to figure out ways to adjust their behavior in case inflation is different from what it has been in the past. That may mean spending a longer time working out more complicated contracts for employment, for purchases of goods in the future, and for purchases of raw materials to be delivered later.

Inflation requires that price lists be changed. This is called the **repricing, or menu, cost of inflation.** The higher the rate of inflation, the higher the repricing cost of inflation, because prices must be changed more often within a given period of time.

Cost-of-living adjustments (COLAs)
Clauses in contracts that allow for increases in specified nominal values to take account of changes in the cost of living.

Repricing, or menu, cost of inflation
The cost associated with recalculating prices and printing new price lists when there is inflation.

7.5 Understand key features of business fluctuations

Changing Inflation and Unemployment: Business Fluctuations

Some years unemployment goes up, and some years it goes down. Some years there is a lot of inflation, and other years there isn't. We have fluctuations in all aspects of our macroeconomy. The ups and downs in economywide economic activity are sometimes called **business fluctuations.** When business fluctuations are positive, they are called **expansions**—speedups in the pace of national economic activity. The opposite of an expansion is a **contraction,** which is a slowdown in the pace of national economic activity. The top of an expansion is usually called its *peak*, and the bottom of a contraction is usually called its *trough*.

Business fluctuations used to be called *business cycles*, but that term no longer seems appropriate because *cycle* implies regular or automatic recurrence, and we have never had automatic recurrent fluctuations in general business and economic activity. What we have had are contractions and expansions that vary greatly in length. For example, the 10 post–World War II expansions have averaged 57 months, but three of those exceeded 90 months, and two lasted less than 25 months.

If the contractionary phase of business fluctuations becomes severe enough, we call it a **recession.** An extremely severe recession is called a **depression.** Typically, at the beginning of a recession, there is a marked increase in the rate of unemployment, and the duration of unemployment increases. In addition, people's incomes start to decline. In times of expansion, the opposite occurs.

In Figure 7-6, you see that typical business fluctuations occur around a growth trend in overall national business activity shown as a straight upward-sloping line.

Business fluctuations
The ups and downs in business activity throughout the economy.

Expansion
A business fluctuation in which the pace of national economic activity is speeding up.

Contraction
A business fluctuation during which the pace of national economic activity is slowing down.

Recession
A period of time during which the rate of growth of business activity is consistently less than its long-term trend or is negative.

Depression
An extremely severe recession.

The Idealized Course of Business Fluctuations

A hypothetical business cycle would go from peak to trough and back again in a regular cycle. Real-world business cycles are not as regular as this hypothetical cycle.

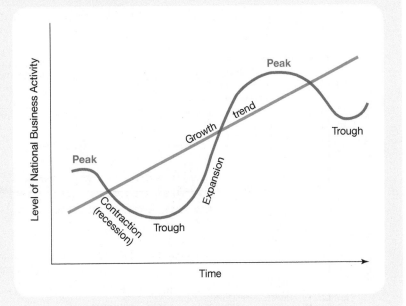

Starting out at a peak, the economy goes into a contraction (recession). Then an expansion starts that moves up to its peak, typically higher than the last one, and the sequence starts over again.

A Historical Picture of Business Activity in the United States

Figure 7-7 traces changes in U.S. business activity from 1880 to the present. Note that the long-term trend line is shown as horizontal, so all changes in business activity focus around that trend line. Major changes in business activity in the United States occurred during the Great Depression, World War II, and, most recently, the sharp 2008–2009 recession. Note that none of the actual business fluctuations in Figure 7-7 exactly mirror the idealized course of a business fluctuation shown in Figure 7-6.

Explaining Business Fluctuations: External Shocks

As you might imagine, because changes in national business activity affect everyone, economists for decades have attempted to understand and explain business fluctuations. For years, one of the most obvious explanations has been external events that tend to disrupt the economy. In many of the graphs in this chapter, you have seen that World War II was a critical point in this nation's economic history. A war is certainly an external shock—something that originates outside our economy.

In trying to help account for shocks to economic activity that may induce business fluctuations and thereby make fluctuations easier to predict, the U.S. Department of Commerce and private firms and organizations tabulate indexes (weighted averages) of **leading indicators.** These are events that economists have noticed typically occur *before* changes in business activity. For example, economic downturns often follow such events as a reduction in the average workweek, an increase in unemployment insurance claims, a decrease in the prices of raw materials, or a drop in the quantity of money in circulation.

How might Google searches for the term "jobs" provide a useful leading indicator of unemployment?

Leading indicators
Events that have been found to occur before changes in business activity.

FIGURE 7-7

National Business Activity, 1880 to the Present

Variations around the trend of U.S. business activity have been frequent since 1880.

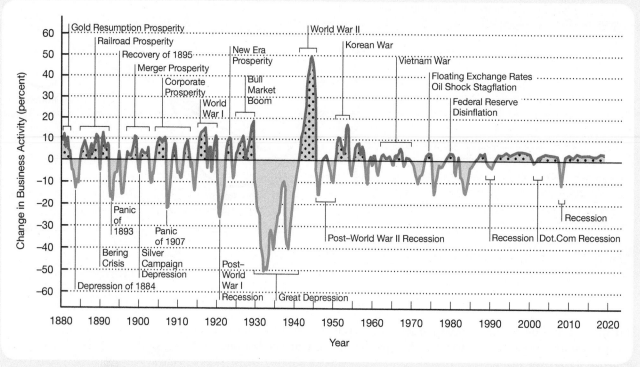

Sources: *American Business Activity from 1790 to Today,* 67th ed., AmeriTrust Co., January 1996, plus author's estimates.

 ## AI | DECISION MAKING THROUGH DATA

Google Job Searches to Predict Unemployment

The Google search engine processes at least 40,000 searches every second, which means that people—or the automated technologies that they utilize—engage in more than 1.25 *trillion* Google searches each year. A fraction of these searches include the keyword "jobs." Millions of people or their bots enter "jobs" into the search engine when they are seeking information about employment opportunities. A number of these people already know that they are going to lose their job and are about to join the ranks of the unemployed. Consequently, an uptick in the number of Google "jobs" searches presumably might provide a leading indicator of the unemployment rate.

To evaluate this idea, researchers utilize volumes of data on searches that Google makes available publicly at an Internet site (https://trends.google.com/trends/?hl=en). Google reports values for trend indexes for search terms. The value of the index for the word "jobs," for instance, indicates the likelihood that a random user in a particular area chooses to conduct a Google search using that particular keyword during a given week. A number of recent studies find evidence that the trend index value for Google "jobs" searches better predicts the unemployment rate than other commonly used leading indicators. Hence, the researchers conclude that the value of the Google "jobs" search trend index is a useful leading indicator for unemployment.

FOR CRITICAL THINKING

Why do you suppose researchers typically find evidence that values of search indexes for the terms "jobs center" and "collect unemployment" are almost as useful as leading indicators as the value of the search index for "jobs"?

Sources are listed at the end of this chapter.

To better understand the role of shocks in influencing business fluctuations, we need a theory of why national economic activity changes. The remainder of the macro chapters in this book develop the models that will help you understand the ups and downs of our business fluctuations.

ECONOMICS IN YOUR LIFE

After Years of High Teen Unemployment Rates, U.S. Teenagers Are Finding Work Once More

Thayer McCollum, a 17-year-old high school student in Loveland, Colorado, drinks chocolate milk, likes to listen to rock music, and has homework assignments to complete. In addition, however, McCollum has become "highly integral" to Avionics Specialists, LLC, an aeronautics firm headed by Jerry Stooksbury. Indeed, when the company agreed on short notice to produce an instrument panel for an airplane, Stooksbury called McCollum and asked him to rush over to the firm, where he would utilize mechanical-drawing software to lay out a schematic diagram for use by company machinists.

In 2010, a teenager like McCollum might well have been among the approximately 27 percent of teens who at that time were classified as unemployed. Now, however, the teen unemployment rate is close to 13 percent, its lowest level since 1969.

All currently employed teenagers such as McCollum and unemployed teens together are among almost one-third of young people counted as part of the U.S. labor force. Many more teenagers would have to decide to enter the labor force, however, to push the teen labor force participation rate up to its level in the late 1970s and early 1980s. At that time, about half of all U.S. teenagers were part of the labor force.

FOR CRITICAL THINKING

Why do you suppose that the drop in the overall U.S. unemployment rate to its lowest levels in more than 50 years contributed to an increase in the teen labor force participation rate and a decrease in the teen unemployment rate?

REAL APPLICATION

No one requires teenagers to seek higher education after they graduate from high school. How has the drop in teenage unemployment changed teenagers' perceived opportunity cost of going to college?

Sources are listed at the end of this chapter.

ISSUES & APPLICATIONS

How "Informal Work" Complicates Measuring Unemployment and the Labor Force

Shutterstock

CONCEPTS APPLIED

➤ Unemployment

➤ Labor Force

➤ Employment

Many people in the United States earn income from engaging in informal work. Government statisticians currently do not take into account such work when assessing whether a person is officially unemployed. In addition, the statisticians do not view these activities as qualifying a person for inclusion in the labor force. If informal work were taken into account, both the unemployment rate and the labor force participation rate would change.

Contemplating the Issue from a Working College Student's Perspective

Suppose that a department in your college already employs you in a part-time position. You decide, nonetheless, to engage in a tutoring "gig," both in person and online, during weekends in exchange for hourly wages. Engaging in this informal tutoring work adds both to your number of hours worked during the week and to your weekly income. Because you have a formal part-time job, government statisticians include you within both the labor force and the ranks of those counted as employed, and your informal work does not affect that classification.

Now assume that you are fired from the formal part-time position. If you respond by expanding informal tutoring enough to earn the same overall income, how government statisticians classify you will depend on whether you search for a new formal position. If you were to search for formal work, you would be categorized as unemployed and in the labor force. If you were to decide to halt your search without finding a formal part-time position, government statisticians would classify you as being outside the labor force. This action will contribute to a lower labor force participation rate. The latter choice would cut the measured labor force participation rate and thereby boost the measured unemployment rate.

Assessing the Actual Biases Created by Informal Work

Recent estimates indicate that more than 35 percent of working-age adults—the equivalent of about 90 million people—engage in some form of informal work each year. Many of these people have formal jobs. At any given time, however, a fraction of these individuals may have left their formal positions even though they continue to participate in informal work. Consistent with the example discussed above, the government currently counts these people as unemployed even though they engage in informal work. In addition, people who have informal jobs but no formal positions as far as government statisticians are concerned are classified as being outside the labor force.

Economists have estimated how much the measured unemployment rate and the labor force participation rate would change if government statisticians were to count informally employed people as in the labor force and employed. The midrange estimates indicate that accounting for informal work would boost the labor force participation rate by about 1.4 percentage points and reduce the unemployment rate by about 0.5 percentage point.

FOR CRITICAL THINKING

What would happen to current official measures of the unemployment rate and the labor force participation rate if the informal labor market were to collapse and people engaged in associated informal work lost their positions? (*Hint:* Do the official measures take into account those who perform these types of informal work?)

REAL APPLICATION

What are some of the drawbacks to engaging in informal work compared to formal work? Do these drawbacks weigh more heavily on you if you are younger or older? Why?

Sources are listed at the end of this chapter.

What You Should Know

Here is what you should know after reading this chapter.

LEARNING OBJECTIVES

7.1 **Explain how the U.S. government calculates the official unemployment rate** *The total number of workers who are officially unemployed consists of noninstitutionalized people aged 16 or older who are willing and able to work and who are actively looking for work but have not found a job. To calculate the unemployment rate, the government determines what percentage this quantity is part of the labor force, which consists of all noninstitutionalized people aged 16 years or older who either have jobs or are available for and actively seeking employment.*

7.2 **Discuss the types of unemployment** *Temporarily unemployed workers who are searching for appropriate job offers are frictionally unemployed. The structurally unemployed lack the skills currently required by prospective employers. People unemployed due to business contractions are cyclically unemployed.*

KEY TERMS

unemployment, 138
labor force, 138
stock, 140
flow, 140
job loser, 140
reentrant, 140
job leaver, 140
new entrant, 140
discouraged workers, 141
labor force participation rate, 141
Key Figure
Figure 7-3, 140

frictional unemployment, 142
structural unemployment, 142
cyclical unemployment, 143
full employment, 144
natural rate of unemployment, 144

7.3 Describe how price indexes are calculated and define the key types of price indexes *To calculate any price index, economists multiply 100 times the ratio of the cost of a market basket of goods and services in the current year to the cost of the same market basket in a base year. The Consumer Price Index (CPI) is a weighted average of prices of items purchased by a typical urban consumer. The Producer Price Index (PPI) is a weighted average of prices of goods produced and sold by a typical firm. The GDP deflator measures changes in the overall level of prices of all goods produced during a given interval. The Personal Consumption Expenditure (PCE) Index is a measure of average prices using weights from surveys of consumer spending.*

7.4 Evaluate who loses and who gains from inflation and distinguish between nominal and real interest rates *The nominal interest rate applies to contracts expressed in current dollars. The real interest rate equals the nominal interest rate minus the expected inflation rate.*

Creditors lose as a result of unanticipated inflation, because the real value of the interest payments received will turn out to be lower than they had expected. Borrowers gain when unanticipated inflation occurs, because the real value of interest and principal payments declines. Key costs of inflation include expenses of protecting against inflation, costs of altering business plans because of unexpected changes in prices, and menu costs of repricing goods and services.

7.5 Understand key features of business fluctuations *Business fluctuations are increases and decreases in business activity. A positive fluctuation is an expansion, which is an upward movement in business activity from a trough, or low point, to a peak, or high point. A negative fluctuation is a contraction, which is a drop in the pace of business activity from a previous peak to a new trough.*

PROBLEMS

7-1. Suppose that you are given the following information:

Total population	330.0 million
Adult, noninstitutionalized, nonmilitary population	260.0 million
Unemployment	8.5 million

a. If the labor force participation rate is 65 percent, what is the labor force?

b. How many workers are employed?

c. What is the unemployment rate?

7-2. Suppose that you are given the following information:

Labor force	206.2 million
Adults in the military	1.5 million
Nonadult population	48.0 million
Employed adults	196.2 million
Institutionalized adults	3.5 million
Nonmilitary, noninstitutionalized adults not in labor force	40.8 million

a. What is the total population?

b. How many people are unemployed, and what is the unemployment rate?

c. What is the labor force participation rate?

7-3. Suppose that the U.S. nonmilitary, noninstitutionalized adult population is 254 million, the number employed is 156 million, and the number unemployed is 8 million.

    a. What is the unemployment rate?

    b. Suppose there is a difference of 60 million between the adult population and the combined total of people who are employed and unemployed. How do we classify these 60 million people? Based on these figures, what is the U.S. labor force participation rate?

7-4. During the course of a year, the labor force consists of the same 1,000 people. Employers have chosen not to hire 20 of these people in the face of government regulations making it too costly to employ them. Hence, they remain unemployed throughout the year. At the same time, every month during the year, 30 different people become unemployed, and 30 other different people who were unemployed find jobs.

    a. What is the frictional unemployment rate?

    b. What is the unemployment rate?

    c. Suppose that a system of unemployment compensation is established. Each month, 30 new people (not including the 20 that employers have chosen not to employ) continue to become unemployed, but each monthly group of newly unemployed now takes two months to find a job. After this change, what is the frictional unemployment rate?

    d. After the change discussed in part (c), what is the unemployment rate?

7-5. Suppose that a nation has a labor force of 100 people. In January, Amy, Barbara, Carine, and Denise are unemployed. In February, those four find jobs, but Evan, Francesco, George, and Horatio become unemployed. Suppose further that every month, the previous four who were unemployed find jobs and four different people become unemployed. Throughout the year, however, three people—Ito, Jack, and Kelley—continually remain unemployed because firms facing government regulations view them as too costly to employ.

    a. What is this nation's frictional unemployment rate?

    b. What is its structural unemployment rate?

    c. What is its unemployment rate?

7-6. In a country with a labor force of 200, a different group of 10 people becomes unemployed each month, but becomes employed once again a month later. No others outside these groups are unemployed.

    a. What is this country's unemployment rate?

    b. What is the average duration of unemployment?

    c. Suppose that establishment of a system of unemployment compensation increases to two months the interval that it takes each group of job losers to become employed each month. Nevertheless, a different group of 10 people still becomes unemployed each month. Now what is the average duration of unemployment?

    d. Following the change discussed in part (c), what is the country's unemployment rate?

7-7. A nation's frictional unemployment rate is 1 percent. Its cyclical rate of unemployment is 3 percent, and its structural unemployment rate is 4 percent. What is this nation's overall rate of unemployment?

7-8. In 2019, the cost of a market basket of goods was $2,000. In 2021, the cost of the same market basket of goods was $2,100. Use the price index formula to calculate the price index for 2021 if 2019 is the base year.

7-9. Suppose that in 2020, a typical U.S. student attending a state-supported college bought 10 textbooks at a price of $100 per book and enrolled in 25 credit hours of coursework at a price of $360 per credit hour. In 2021, the typical student continued to purchase 10 textbooks and enroll in 25 credit hours, but the price of a textbook rose to $110 per book, and the tuition price increased to $400 per credit hour. The base year for computing a "student price index" using this information is 2020. What is the value of the student price index in 2020? In 2021? Show your work.

7-10. Between 2020 and 2021 in a particular nation, the value of the consumer price index—for which the base year is 2017—rose by 9.091 percent, to a value of 120 in 2021. What was the value of the price index in 2020?

7-11. Consider the following price indexes: 90 in 2020, 100 in 2021, 110 in 2022, 121 in 2023, and 150 in 2024. Answer the following questions.

    a. Which year is likely the base year?

    b. What is the inflation rate from 2021 to 2022?

    c. What is the inflation rate from 2022 to 2023?

    d. If the cost of a market basket in 2021 is $2,000, what is the cost of the same basket of goods and services in 2020? In 2024?

7-12. The real interest rate is 4 percent, and the nominal interest rate is 6 percent. What is the anticipated rate of inflation?

7-13. Currently, the price index used to calculate the inflation rate is equal to 90. The general expectation throughout the economy is that next year its value will be 99. The current nominal interest rate is 12 percent. What is the real interest rate?

7-14. At present, the nominal interest rate is 7 percent, and the expected inflation rate is 5 percent. The current year is the base year for the price index used to calculate inflation.

    a. What is the real interest rate?

    b. What is the anticipated value of the price index next year?

7-15. Suppose that in 2022, there is a sudden, unanticipated burst of inflation. Consider the situations faced by the following individuals. Who gains and who loses?

    a. A homeowner whose wages will keep pace with inflation in 2022 but whose monthly mortgage payments to a savings bank will remain fixed

    b. An apartment landlord who has guaranteed to his tenants that their monthly rent payments during 2022 will be the same as they were during 2021

    c. A banker who made an auto loan that the auto buyer will repay at a fixed rate of interest during 2022

    d. A retired individual who earns a pension with fixed monthly payments from her past employer during 2022

7-16. Consider the diagram below. The line represents the economy's growth trend, and the curve represents the economy's actual course of business fluctuations. For each part below, provide the letter label from the portion of the curve that corresponds to the associated term.

    a. Contraction

    b. Peak

    c. Trough

    d. Expansion

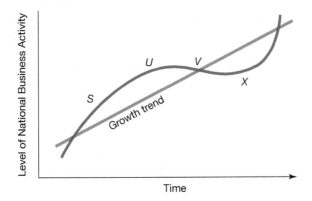

7-17. Suppose that in Figure 7-2, the number of people employed were to expand by 9.2 million, and the number of people unemployed were to rise by 7.1 million. What would be the new values of the labor force and of the unemployment rate?

7-18. Suppose that among the 15 million unemployed people in Problem 7-17, currently 6.9 million are frictionally unemployed, 5.9 million are cyclically unemployed, and 2.2 million are structurally unemployed. What is the natural rate of unemployment?

7-19. Consider Table 7-1. Suppose that the 2022 price of corn were to rise to $8.50 per bushel but that the price of a digital device were to fall to $300. The quantities of the two commodities remain the same, however. How would these changes affect the value of the 2022 price index?

7-20. The cost of a nation's market basket in the base year is $1,200, and the current year's price index equals 125. What is the cost of the market basket in the current year?

7-21. This year's value of the economy's price index is 100, and people anticipate that next year's value will be 103. The current nominal interest rate is 5 percent. What is the real interest rate?

7-22. This year is the base year for computing the nation's price index. The current nominal interest rate is 6 percent, and the real interest rate is 3.5 percent. What is the anticipated value of next year's price index?

REFERENCES

EXAMPLE: Why Are Millions of Those Laid Off or Fired Opting Not to Apply for Unemployment Benefits?

"Weekly Initial Claims," Federal Reserve Economic Data II, Federal Reserve Bank of St. Louis (https://fred.stlouisfed.org/categories/32240), 2019.

"United States Initial Jobless Claims," TradingEconomics.com (https://tradingeconomics.com/united-states/jobless-claims), 2019.

Joseph Lawler, "Fewer People Are on Unemployment Benefits Than Any Time in 44 Years," *Washington Examiner*, June 14, 2018.

INTERNATIONAL EXAMPLE: Temporary Work Feeds Europe's Structural Unemployment Problem

"Temporary Employment," Organization for Economic Cooperation and Development (https://data.oecd.org/emp/temporary-employment.htm), 2019.

"European Youth Unemployment in the Aftermath of the Great Recession," *IAB Forum*, July 2, 2018.

"Youth Unemployment," World Economic Forum (http://reports.weforum.org/global-risks-2018/youth-unemployment/), 2018.

EXAMPLE: Are Prices of New Houses Really Almost Fourteen Times Higher Than 50 Years Ago?

"Median Sales Price for New Houses Sold in the United States," Federal Reserve Economic Data II, Federal Reserve Bank of St. Louis (https://fred.stlouisfed.org/series/MSPNHSUS), 2019.

"Home Prices in the 100 Largest Metro Areas," Kiplinger (https://www.kiplinger.com/tool/real-estate/T010-S003-home-prices-in-100-top-u-s-metro-areas/index.php), January 2019.

Diana Olick, "Housing Confidence Hits Record High as Home Prices Skyrocket," CMBC (https://www.cnbc.com/2018/05/07/housing-confidence-hits-record-high-as-home-prices-skyrocket.html), May 7, 2018.

BEHAVIORAL EXAMPLE: Why Might Surveys Fail to Reveal People's True Inflation Expectations?

"University of Michigan Survey: Inflation Expectations," FRED2, Federal Reserve Bank of St. Louis (https://fred.stlouisfed.org/series/MICH), 2019.

Edda Claus and Viet Hoang Nguyen, "*Consumptor economicus*: How do consumers form expectations on economic variables?" *Journal of Economic Behavior and Organization*, 2018.

Charles Manski, "Survey Measurement of Probabilistic Macroeconomic Expectations: Progress and Promise," *NBER Macroeconomics Annual*, 2018.

AI—DECISION MAKING THROUGH DATA: Google Job Searches to Predict Unemployment

Maryam Dilmaghani, "What Does Google Trends Say about the Unemployment Rate?" *Journal of Economic Studies*, 2019.

Marcos Gonzalez-Fernandez and Carmen Gonzalez-Velasco, "Can Google Econometrics Predict Unemployment? Evidence from Spain," *Economics Letters*, 2018.

Alessia Naccarato, Stefano Falorsi, Silvia Loriga, and Andrea Pierini, "Combining Official and Google Trends Data to Forecast the Italian Youth Unemployment Rate ," *Technological Forecasting and Social Change*, 2018.

ECONOMICS IN YOUR LIFE: After Years of High Teen Unemployment Rates, U.S. Teenagers Are Finding Work Once More

U.S. Bureau of Labor Statistics, "Employment and Unemployment Among Youth Summary" (https://www.bls.gov/news.release/youth.nr0.htm), 2019.

Jennifer Levitz and Eric Morath, "Facing Historic Labor Shortages, Companies Snap up Teenagers," *Wall Street Journal*, April 16, 2018.

Nelson Schwartz, "New Milestones in Jobs Report Signal a Bustling Economy," *New York Times*, June 1, 2018.

ISSUES & APPLICATIONS: How "Informal Work" Complicates Measuring Unemployment and the Labor Force

Katharine Abraham, Brad Hershbein, and Susan Houseman, "Gig and Other Contract Work: Developing Better Measures in Household Surveys," American Economic Association Annual Meeting, 2019.

Marcela Escobari and Sandy Fernandez, "Measuring American Gig Workers Is Difficult, but Essential," *Brookings*, July 19, 2018.

Nicole Torres, "Are There Good Jobs in the Gig Economy?" *Harvard Business Review*, July-August 2018.

8 Measuring the Economy's Performance

LEARNING OBJECTIVES

After reading this chapter, you should be able to:

8.1 Describe the circular flow of income and output

8.2 Define gross domestic product (GDP) and explain its limitations

8.3 Explain the expenditure and income approaches to tabulating GDP

8.4 Discuss the key components of national income

8.5 Distinguish between nominal GDP and real GDP

Since 2015, the inflation-adjusted value of all newly produced goods and services calculated and published by China's government has risen by very nearly the same percentage during each quarter, or three-month interval. Indeed, from one three-month interval to the next, quarterly growth rates reported by China's government have rarely varied by more than one-tenth of 1 percentage point. This experience contrasts considerably with that of the United States. Over the same period, variations in U.S. quarterly rates of growth of the same basic measure of total national production of goods, known as *gross domestic product*, or *GDP*, have been up to *ten times* greater than those in China. To understand why many observers regard China's reported growth of aggregate production to be too "smooth" to be believable, you must first fully comprehend the concept of GDP and understand how economists tabulate GDP. Helping you to accomplish these tasks is the primary objective of this chapter.

National income accounting
A measurement system used to estimate national income and its components. One approach to measuring an economy's aggregate performance.

the female fraction of India's labor force is less than one-fourth, with the result that the earnings of women account for less than 17 percent of India's aggregate personal income each year? In contrast, the share of income generated by women who work in China exceeds 40 percent. To measure overall income flows in India, China, and other countries, national governments utilize what has become known as **national income accounting.** How this measurement is done is the main focus of this chapter. First, though, we need to look at the flow of income within an economy, for it is the flow of goods and services from businesses to consumers and of payments from consumers to businesses that constitutes economic activity.

8.1 Describe the circular flow of income and output

The Simple Circular Flow

The concept of a circular flow of income (ignoring taxes) involves two principles:

1. In every economic exchange, the seller receives exactly the same amount that the buyer spends.

2. Goods and services flow in one direction, and money payments flow in the other.

In the simple economy shown in Figure 8-1, there are only businesses and households. It is assumed that businesses sell their *entire* output in the current period to households and that households spend their *entire* income in the current period on consumer products. Households receive their income by selling the use of whatever factors of production they own, such as labor services.

FIGURE 8-1

The Circular Flow of Income and Product

Businesses provide final goods and services to households (upper clockwise loop), who in turn pay for them (upper counterclockwise loop). Payments flow in a counterclockwise direction and can be thought of as a circular flow. The dollar value of output is identical to total income because profits are defined as being equal to total business receipts minus business outlays for wages, rents, and interest. Households provide factor services to businesses and receive income (lower loops).

Profits Explained

We have indicated in Figure 8-1 that profit is a cost of production. You might be under the impression that profits are not part of the cost of producing goods and services, but profits are indeed a part of this cost because entrepreneurs must be rewarded for providing their services or they won't provide them. Their reward, if any, is profit. The reward—the profit—is included in the cost of the factors of production. If there were no expectations of profit, entrepreneurs would not incur the risk associated with the organization of productive activities. That is why we consider profits a cost of doing business. Just as workers expect wages, entrepreneurs expect profits.

Total Income or Total Output

The arrow that goes from businesses to households at the bottom of Figure 8-1 is labeled "Total income." What would be a good definition of **total income**? If you answered "the total of all individuals' incomes," you would be right. All income, however, is actually a payment for something, whether it be wages paid for labor services, rent paid for the use of land, interest paid for the use of capital, or profits paid to entrepreneurs. It is the amount paid to the resource suppliers. Therefore, total income is also defined as the annual *cost* of producing the entire output of **final goods and services.**

The arrow going from households to businesses at the top of Figure 8-1 represents the dollar value of output in the economy. This is equal to the total monetary value of all final goods and services for this simple economy. In essence, it represents the total business receipts from the sale of all final goods and services produced by businesses and consumed by households. Business receipts are the opposite side of household expenditures. When households purchase goods and services, those payments become a *business receipt*. Every transaction, therefore, simultaneously involves an expenditure and a receipt.

Product Markets Transactions in which households buy goods take place in the product markets—that's where households are the buyers and businesses are the sellers of consumer goods. *Product market* transactions are represented in the upper loops in Figure 8-1. Note that consumer goods and services flow to household demanders, while money flows in the opposite direction to business suppliers.

Factor Markets *Factor market* transactions are represented by the lower loops in Figure 8-1. In the factor market, households are the sellers. They sell resources such as labor, land, capital, and entrepreneurial ability. Businesses are the buyers in factor markets. Business expenditures represent receipts or, more simply, income for households. Also, in the lower loops of Figure 8-1, factor services flow from households to businesses, while the payments for these services flow in the opposite direction from businesses to households. Observe also the flow of money income (counterclockwise) from households to businesses and back again from businesses to households: It is an endless circular flow.

Why the Dollar Value of Total Output Must Equal Total Income

Total income represents the income received by households in payment for the production of goods and services. Why must total income be identical to the dollar value of total output? First, as Figure 8-1 shows, spending by one group is income to another. Second, it is a matter of simple accounting and the economic definition of profit as a cost of production. Profit is defined as what is *left over* from total business receipts after all other costs—wages, rents, interest—have been paid. If the dollar value of total output is $1,000 and the total of wages, rent, and interest for producing that output is $900, profit is $100. Profit is always the *residual* item that makes total income equal to the dollar value of total output.

Total income
The yearly amount earned by the nation's resources (factors of production). Total income therefore includes wages, rent, interest payments, and profits that are received by workers, landowners, capital owners, and entrepreneurs, respectively.

Final goods and services
Goods and services that are at their final stage of production and will not be transformed into yet other goods or services. For example, wheat ordinarily is not considered a final good because it is usually used to make a final good, bread.

8.2 Define gross domestic product (GDP) and explain its limitations

National Income Accounting

We have already mentioned that policymakers require information about the state of the national economy. Economists use historical statistical records on the performance of the national economy for testing their theories about how the economy really works. Thus, national income accounting is important. Let's start with the most commonly presented statistic on the national economy.

Gross Domestic Product (GDP)

Gross domestic product (GDP)
The total market value of all final goods and services produced during a year by factors of production located within a nation's borders.

Gross domestic product (GDP) represents the total market value of the nation's annual final product, or output, produced by factors of production located within national borders. We therefore formally define GDP as the total market value of all final goods and services produced in an economy during a year. We are referring here to the value of a *flow of production*. A nation produces at a certain rate, just as you receive income at a certain rate. Your income flow might be at a rate of $20,000 per year or $100,000 per year. Suppose you are told that someone earns $5,000. Would you consider this a good salary? There is no way to answer that question unless you know whether the person is earning $5,000 per month or per week or per day. Thus, you have to specify a time period for all flows. Income received is a flow.

You must contrast this flow with, for example, your total accumulated savings, which are a stock measured at a point in time, not over time. Implicit in just about everything we deal with in this chapter is a time period—usually one year. All the measures of domestic product and income are specified as *rates* measured in dollars per year.

Stress on Final Output

Intermediate goods
Goods used up entirely in the production of final goods.

GDP does not count **intermediate goods** (goods used up entirely in the production of final goods) because to do so would be to count them twice. For example, even though grain that a farmer produces may be that farmer's final product, it is not the final product for the nation. It is sold to make bread. Bread is the final product.

Value added
The dollar value of an industry's sales minus the value of intermediate goods (for example, raw materials and parts) used in production.

We can use a numerical example to clarify this point further. Our example will involve determining the value added at each stage of production. **Value added** is the dollar value contributed to a product at each stage of its production. In Table 8-1, we see the difference between total value of all sales and value added in the production of a donut. We also see that the sum of the values added is equal to the sale price to the final consumer. It is the 45 cents that is used to measure GDP, not the 97 cents. If we used the 97 cents, we would be double counting from stages 2 through 5, for each intermediate good would be counted at least twice—once when it was produced and again when the good it was used in making was sold. Such double counting would greatly exaggerate GDP.

To what extent has value added to overall U.S. production of goods and services by the manufacturing of physical items declined in recent decades?

EXAMPLE

A Reduced Role for Manufacturing of Physical Merchandise as a Source of Value Added in U.S. Production

Various forms of productive activity generate value added during the production of a final good or service. In the early 1950s, manufacturing of physical merchandise accounted for about 28 percent of the overall value added in final production of all items in the United States. This percentage has gradually declined over the past several decades. Today, physical manufacturing activities contribute less than 12 percent of total value added in production of final U.S. goods and services. Thus, the role of manufacturing of physical items as a source of total value added has declined considerably during the past several decades.

REAL APPLICATION

How might the reduced role of manufacturing in our economy influence your career choices?

Sources are listed at the end of this chapter.

TABLE 8-1

Sales Value and Value Added at Each Stage of Donut Production

(1) Stage of Production	(2) Dollar Value of Sales	(3) Value Added
Stage 1: Fertilizer and seed	$0.03	$0.03
Stage 2: Growing	0.07	0.04
Stage 3: Milling	0.12	0.05
Stage 4: Baking	0.30	0.18
Stage 5: Retailing	0.45	0.15

Total dollar value of all sales $0.97   Total value added $0.45

Stage 1: A farmer purchases 3 cents' worth of fertilizer and seed, which are used as factors of production in growing wheat.

Stage 2: The farmer grows the wheat, harvests it, and sells it to a miller for 7 cents. Thus, we see that the farmer has added 4 cents' worth of value. Those 4 cents represent income over and above expenses incurred by the farmer.

Stage 3: The miller purchases the wheat for 7 cents and adds 5 cents as the value added. That is, there is 5 cents for the miller as income. The miller sells the ground wheat flour to a donut-baking company.

Stage 4: The donut-baking company buys the flour for 12 cents and adds 18 cents as the value added. It then sells the donut to the final retailer.

Stage 5: The donut retailer sells donuts at 45 cents apiece, thus creating an additional value of 15 cents.

We see that the total value of the transactions involved in the production of one donut is 97 cents, but the total value added is 45 cents, which is exactly equal to the retail price. The total value added is equal to the sum of all income payments.

Gross Output (GO)

In recent years, some critics have argued that the avoidance of double counting is misguided. In their view, *all* aggregate business expenditures on intermediate inputs—supplies, raw materials, tools and equipment, and the like—should be included in any meaningful measure of the economy's total productive activity. The entirety of such purchases by firms from other firms, they contend, is required to transform resources across production stages. In their view, such business spending consequently should be summed in obtaining an overall U.S. output measure.

To assess the merits of this view, the U.S. Bureau of Economic Analysis now tracks an alternative to GDP, developed by Mark Skousen of Chapman University. This production measure, called **gross output (GO),** includes all forms of business-to-business expenditures. Not surprisingly, double counting business spending across all stages of production boosts the relative importance of such expenditures. Total business spending accounts for only about 25 percent of GDP, but total business expenditures make up more than 50 percent of gross output.

Exclusion of Financial Transactions, Transfer Payments, and Secondhand Goods

Remember that GDP is the measure of the dollar value of all final goods and services produced in one year. Many more transactions occur that have nothing to do with

Gross output
The total market value of all goods and services produced during a year by factors of production located within a nation's borders, including all forms of business-to-business expenditures and thereby double counting business spending across all stages of production.

final goods and services produced. There are financial transactions, transfers of the ownership of preexisting goods, and other transactions that should not (and do not) get included in our measure of GDP.

Financial Transactions

There are three general categories of purely financial transactions: (1) the buying and selling of securities, (2) government transfer payments, and (3) private transfer payments.

Securities When you purchase shares of existing stock in Apple, Inc., someone else has sold it to you. In essence, there was merely a *transfer* of ownership rights. You paid $100 to obtain the stock. Someone else received the $100 and gave up the stock. No production activity was consummated at that time, unless a broker received a fee for performing the transaction, in which case only the fee is part of GDP. The $100 transaction is not included when we measure GDP.

Government Transfer Payments Transfer payments are payments for which no productive services are concurrently provided in exchange. The most obvious government transfer payments are Social Security benefits and unemployment compensation. The recipients add nothing to *current* production in return for such transfer payments (although they may have contributed in the past to be eligible to receive them). Government transfer payments are not included in GDP.

Private Transfer Payments Are you receiving funds from your parents in order to attend school? Has a wealthy relative ever given you a gift of cash? If so, you have been the recipient of a private transfer payment. This payment is merely a transfer of funds from one individual to another. As such, it does not constitute productive activity and is not included in GDP.

Transfer of Secondhand Goods

If I sell you my two-year-old laptop computer, no current production is involved. I transfer to you the ownership of a computer that was produced years ago. In exchange, you transfer to me $350. The original purchase price of the computer was included in GDP in the year I purchased it. To include the price again when I sell it to you would be counting the value of the computer a second time.

Other Excluded Transactions

Many other transactions are not included in GDP for practical reasons:

- Household production—housecleaning, child care, and other tasks performed by people in their *own* households and for which they receive no payments through the marketplace

- Otherwise legal underground transactions—those that are legal but not reported and hence not taxed, such as paying housekeepers in cash that is not declared as income to the Internal Revenue Service

- Illegal underground activities—these include prostitution, illegal gambling, and the sale of illicit drugs

Recognizing the Limitations of GDP

Like any statistical measure, gross domestic product is a concept that can be both well used and misused. Economists find it especially valuable as an overall indicator of a nation's economic performance. It is important, however, to realize that GDP has significant weaknesses.

Might behavioral economists potentially offer an objective measure of aggregate welfare?

BEHAVIORAL EXAMPLE

Obstacles to Measuring Aggregate "Well-Being" alongside Gross Domestic Product

Policymakers and commentators often succumb to the temptation to try using GDP as a measure of aggregate welfare in spite of its various weaknesses even as just an indicator of a country's overall economic performance. Some economists have responded by seeking to develop quantitative index measures of welfare to use alongside GDP. Most proposed measures of a collective well-being typically have relied on people's answers to survey questions that ask respondents to rate their perceived levels of satisfaction or happiness along numerical scales, such as "1 = very happy" versus "5 = very unhappy." Such survey methods of eliciting measures of happiness suffer, however, from some long-recognized problems. One difficulty is that research has demonstrated that answers to such questions can be influenced simply by the order in which questions appear in the surveys. Answers also can be influenced by slight differences in the wording of questions.

More generally, index measures of well-being derived from subjective answers to survey questions are based on what people say rather than on data that arguably might objectively indicate true states of satisfaction or happiness. Some behavioral economists proposed utilizing recent research in *neuroeconomics*, in which economists use measures of blood pressure, body mass indexes, and heart rates to evaluate people's responses to changes in prices, incomes, and so on. The idea would be to conduct random surveys documenting how close such biometric measures are to healthful levels in order to objectively calculate a nation's aggregate welfare.

FOR CRITICAL THINKING

Why do you think that economists critical of biometric-based indexes as indicators of aggregate well-being argue that such measures do not necessarily relate to a nation's overall economic performance?

Sources are listed at the end of this chapter.

GDP Excludes Nonmarket Production Because it includes only the value of goods and services traded in markets, GDP excludes *nonmarket* production, such as the household services of homemakers discussed earlier. This can cause some problems in comparing the GDP of an industrialized country with the GDP of a highly agrarian nation in which nonmarket production is relatively more important.

It also causes problems if nations have different definitions of legal versus illegal activities. For instance, a nation with legalized gambling will count the value of gambling services, which has a reported market value as a legal activity. In a country where gambling is illegal, though, individuals who provide such services will not report the market value of gambling activities, and so they will not be counted in that country's GDP. This can complicate comparing GDP in the nation where gambling is legal with GDP in the country that prohibits gambling.

WHAT HAPPENS WHEN...

significantly larger numbers of people decide to pay others to perform various household tasks instead of engaging in these activities on their own?

When people mow their own yards, devote their own time to caring for their own children, and perform other household tasks on their own, no market transactions take place. No market values are assigned to these activities to include in measured GDP. In contrast, if people pay others to mow their lawns or care for young children, payments to those who perform the activities on their behalf yield dollar values for these activities that are measured in markets. These market transactions are included in GDP. Thus, if considerably larger numbers of people were to decide to pay others to perform such tasks, measured GDP would increase.

GDP Is Not a Direct Measure of Human Well-Being Although GDP is often used as a benchmark measure for standard-of-living calculations, it is not necessarily a good measure of the well-being of a nation. No measured figure of total national annual income can take account of changes in the degree of labor market discrimination, declines or improvements in personal safety, or the quantity or quality of leisure time. Measured GDP also says little about our environmental quality of life.

ECONOMICS IN YOUR LIFE

To consider how particular aspects of today's economy may be adding to the list of GDP limitations, read **Should Real GDP Be Supplemented or Even Replaced as the Primary Measure of Economic Performance?** on page 176.

A number of nations, such as those of Western Europe and the United States in past years and, more recently, China and India, have experienced greater pollution problems as their levels of GDP have increased. Hence, it is important to recognize the following point:

GDP is a measure of the value of production in terms of market prices and an indicator of economic activity. It is not a measure of a nation's overall welfare.

Nonetheless, GDP is a relatively accurate and useful measure of the economy's domestic economic activity, measured in current dollars. Understanding GDP is thus an important first step for analyzing changes in economic activity over time.

How might governmental statistical agencies use big data to supplement the GDP measure of economic activity?

AI | DECISION MAKING THROUGH DATA

Using New Information about Flows of Goods and Services

A host of digital devices, including Earth-orbiting satellites, smartphones, tablets, and traffic sensors, automatically collects huge volumes of data each day. Among these data are flows of goods and services as they are distributed from the firms that produce them to the households, firms, and governments that purchase them.

The United Kingdom's Office for National Statistics (ONS), which tabulates that nation's GDP, has established a "data science campus" at its headquarters office in south Wales. The campus's staff of economists and statisticians has been charged with developing ways to harvest the masses of data from digital devices and to utilize this information to track flows of goods and services and the prices of

transactions throughout the nation. Staff engaging in research at the ONS data science campus hope that applying machine learning to these data may improve existing GDP computations and assist in developing alternative measures of economic activity.

FOR CRITICAL THINKING

Why might staffers of the ONS data science campus seek to distinguish between GDP-style versus GO-style measures of economic activity by carefully accounting for value added at intermediate stages of production? (Hint: Recall that GDP counts only the final market values of items, while GO double-counts values added at intermediate production stages.)

Sources are listed at the end of this chapter.

8.3 Explain the expenditure and income approaches to tabulating GDP

Expenditure approach
Computing GDP by adding up the dollar value at current market prices of all final goods and services.

Income approach
Measuring GDP by adding up all components of national income, including wages, interest, rent, and profits.

Durable consumer goods
Consumer goods that have a life span of more than three years.

Nondurable consumer goods
Consumer goods that are used up within three years.

Two Main Methods of Measuring GDP

The definition of GDP is the total dollar value of all final goods and services produced during a year. How, exactly, do we go about actually computing this number?

The circular flow diagram presented in Figure 8-1 gave us a shortcut method for calculating GDP. We can look at the *flow of expenditures*, which consists of consumption, investment, government purchases of goods and services, and net expenditures in the foreign sector (net exports). In this **expenditure approach** to measuring GDP, we add the dollar value of all final goods and services. We could also use the *flow of income*, looking at the income received by everybody producing goods and services. In this **income approach,** we add the income received by all factors of production.

Deriving GDP by the Expenditure Approach

To derive GDP using the expenditure approach, we must look at each of the separate components of expenditures and then add them together. These components are consumption expenditures, investment, government expenditures, and net exports.

Consumption Expenditures How do we spend our income? As households or as individuals, we spend our income through consumption expenditure (*C*), which falls into three categories: **durable consumer goods**, **nondurable consumer goods**, and

services. Durable goods are *arbitrarily* defined as items that last more than three years. They include automobiles, furniture, and household appliances. Nondurable goods are all the rest, such as food and gasoline. Services are intangible commodities: nursing services, education, and the like.

Housing expenditures constitute a major proportion of anybody's annual expenditures. Rental payments on apartments are automatically included in consumption expenditure estimates. People who own their homes, however, do not make rental payments. Consequently, government statisticians estimate what is called the *implicit rental value* of existing owner-occupied homes. It is roughly equal to the amount of rent you would have to pay if you did not own the home but were renting it from someone else.

Gross Private Domestic Investment

We now turn our attention to **gross private domestic investment** (*I*) undertaken by businesses. When economists refer to investment, they are referring to additions to productive capacity. **Investment** may be thought of as an activity that uses resources today in such a way that they allow for greater production in the future and hence greater consumption in the future. When a business buys new equipment or builds a new data center, it is investing. It is increasing its capacity to produce in the future.

In estimating gross private domestic investment, government statisticians also add consumer expenditures on *new* residential structures because new housing represents an addition to our future productive capacity in the sense that a new house can generate housing services in the future.

The layperson's notion of investment often relates to the purchase of stocks and bonds. For our purposes, such transactions simply represent the *transfer of ownership* of assets called stocks and bonds. Thus, you must keep in mind the fact that in economics, investment refers *only* to *additions* to productive capacity, not to transfers of assets.

Fixed versus Inventory Investment

In our analysis, we will consider the basic components of investment. We have already mentioned the first one, which involves a firm's purchase of equipment or construction of a new factory. These are called **producer durables,** or **capital goods.** A producer durable, or a capital good, is simply a good that is purchased not to be consumed in its current form but to be used to make other goods and services. The purchase of equipment and factories—capital goods—is called **fixed investment.**

The other type of investment has to do with the change in inventories of raw materials and finished goods. Firms do not immediately sell off all their products to consumers. Some of this final product is usually held in inventory waiting to be sold. Firms hold inventories to meet future expected orders for their products. Inventories consist of all finished goods on hand, goods in process, and raw materials. When a firm increases its inventories, it is engaging in **inventory investment**.

The reason we can think of a change in inventories as being a type of investment is that an increase in such inventories provides for future increased consumption possibilities. When inventory investment is zero, the firm is neither adding to nor subtracting from the total stock of goods or raw materials on hand. Thus, if the firm keeps the same amount of inventories throughout the year, inventory *investment* has been zero.

Government Expenditures

In addition to personal consumption expenditures, there are government purchases of goods and services (*G*). The government buys goods and services from private firms and pays wages and salaries to government employees. Generally, we value goods and services at the prices at which they are sold. Many government goods and services, however, are not sold in the market. Therefore, we cannot use their market value when computing GDP.

Until recently, the values of all government-produced goods were considered equal to their *costs*. For example, the value of a newly built road was considered

Services
Mental or physical labor or assistance purchased by consumers. Examples are the assistance of physicians, lawyers, dentists, repair personnel, housecleaners, educators, retailers, and wholesalers; items purchased or used by consumers that do not have physical characteristics.

Gross private domestic investment
The creation of capital goods, such as factories and machines, that can yield production and hence consumption in the future. Also included in this definition are changes in business inventories and repairs made to machines or buildings.

Investment
Any use of today's resources to expand tomorrow's production or consumption.

Producer durables, or capital goods
Durable goods having an expected service life of more than three years that are used by businesses to produce other goods and services.

Fixed investment
Purchases by businesses of newly produced producer durables, or capital goods, such as production machinery and office equipment.

Inventory investment
Changes in the stocks of finished goods and goods in process, as well as changes in the raw materials that businesses keep on hand. Whenever inventories are decreasing, inventory investment is negative. Whenever they are increasing, inventory investment is positive.

equal to its construction cost for inclusion in GDP for the year it was built. In recent years, in contrast, national income accountants have "imputed" the values of many government-produced items. For instance, the accountants value public education, fire protection, and police services in terms of prices observed in markets for privately produced education, fire protection, and security services. Three decades ago, imputed values of such government-provided activities made up a negligible portion of GDP. Today, imputed values constitute about 15 percent of GDP.

Net Exports (Foreign Expenditures)   To obtain an accurate representation of GDP, we must include the foreign sector. As U.S. residents, we purchase foreign goods called *imports*. The goods that foreign residents purchase from us are our *exports*. To determine the *net* expenditures from the foreign sector, we subtract the value of imports from the value of exports to get net exports (X) for a year:

$$\text{Net exports } (X) = \text{total exports} - \text{total imports}$$

To understand why we subtract imports rather than ignoring them altogether, recall that we want to estimate *domestic* output, so we have to subtract U.S. expenditures on the goods produced in other nations.

Presenting the Expenditure Approach

We have just defined the components of GDP using the expenditure approach. When we add them all together, we get a definition for GDP, which is as follows:

$$GDP = C + I + G + X$$

where C = consumption expenditures
I = investment expenditures
G = government expenditures
X = net exports

The Historical Picture   To get an idea of the relationship among C, I, G, and X, look at Figure 8-2, which shows GDP, personal consumption expenditures, government purchases, and gross private domestic investment plus net exports since 1929. When we add up the expenditures of the household, business, government, and foreign sectors, we get GDP.

Depreciation and Net Domestic Product   We have used the terms *gross domestic product* and *gross private domestic investment* without really indicating what *gross* means. The dictionary defines it as "without deductions," the opposite of *net*. You might ask, deductions for what? The deductions are for something we call **depreciation**. In the course of a year, machines and structures wear out or are used up in the production of domestic product. For example, houses deteriorate as they are occupied, and machines need repairs or they will fall apart and stop working. Most capital, or durable, goods depreciate.

An estimate of the amount that capital goods have depreciated during the year is subtracted from gross domestic product to arrive at a figure called **net domestic product (NDP)**, which we define as follows:

$$NDP = GDP - \text{depreciation}$$

Depreciation is also called **capital consumption allowance** because it is the amount of capital stock that has been consumed over a one-year period. In essence, it equals the amount a business would have to put aside to repair and replace deteriorating machines. Because we know that

$$GDP = C + I + G + X$$

Depreciation
Reduction in the value of capital goods over a one-year period due to physical wear and tear and obsolescence; also called *capital consumption allowance.*

Net domestic product (NDP)
GDP minus depreciation.

Capital consumption allowance
Another name for depreciation, the amount that businesses would have to put aside in order to take care of deteriorating machines and other equipment.

FIGURE 8-2

GDP and Its Components

Here we see a display of gross domestic product, personal consumption expenditures, government purchases, and gross private domestic investment plus net exports for the years since 1929. (Note that the scale of the vertical axis changes as we move up the axis.) During the Great Depression of the 1930s, gross private domestic investment *plus* net exports was negative because we were investing very little at that time. Since the late 1990s, the sum of gross private domestic investment and net exports has been highly variable.

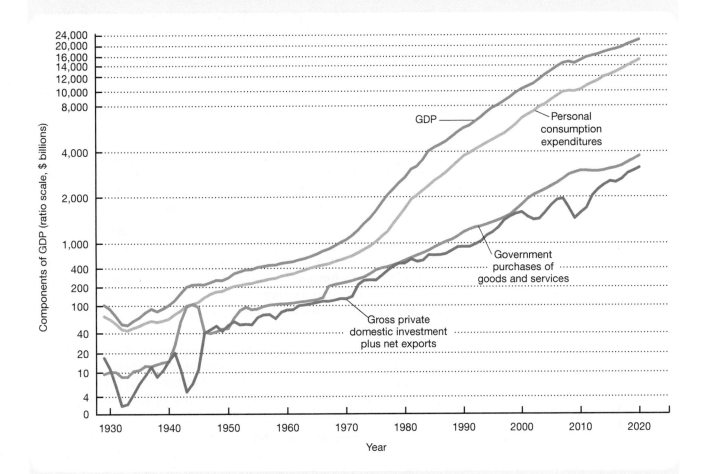

we know that the formula for NDP is

$$\text{NDP} = C + I + G + X - \text{depreciation}$$

Because net $I = I -$ depreciation, **net investment** measures *changes* in our capital stock over time and is positive nearly every year. Because depreciation does not vary greatly from year to year as a percentage of GDP, we get a similar picture of what is happening to our national economy by looking at either NDP or GDP data.

Net investment is an important variable to observe over time nonetheless. If everything else remains the same in an economy, changes in net investment can have dramatic consequences for future economic growth. Positive net investment by definition expands the productive capacity of our economy.

This capacity expansion means that there is increased capital, which will generate even more income in the future. When net investment is zero, we are investing just enough to offset depreciation. Our economy's productive capacity remains unchanged.

Net investment

Gross private domestic investment minus an estimate of the wear and tear on the existing capital stock. Net investment therefore measures the change in the capital stock over a one-year period.

Finally, when net investment is negative, we can expect negative economic growth prospects in the future. Negative net investment means that our productive capacity is actually declining—we are disinvesting. This actually occurred during the Great Depression.

Deriving GDP by the Income Approach

If you go back to the circular flow diagram in Figure 8-1, you see that product markets are at the top of the diagram and factor markets are at the bottom. We can calculate the value of the circular flow of income and product by looking at expenditures—which we just did—or by looking at total factor payments. Factor payments are called income. We calculate **gross domestic income (GDI)**, which we will see is identical to gross domestic product (GDP). Using the income approach, we have four categories of payments to individuals: wages, interest, rent, and profits.

Gross domestic income (GDI)
The sum of all income—wages, interest, rent, and profits—paid to the four factors of production.

1. *Wages.* The most important category is, of course, wages, including salaries and other forms of labor income, such as income in kind and incentive payments. Because GDI measures all income, there is no deduction from wages for Social Security taxes (whether paid by employees or employers).

2. *Interest.* Here interest payments do not equal the sum of all payments for the use of funds in a year. Instead, interest is expressed in *net* rather than in gross terms. The interest component of total income is only net interest received by households plus net interest paid to us by foreign residents. Net interest received by households is the difference between the interest they receive (from savings accounts, certificates of deposit, and the like) and the interest they pay (to banks for home mortgages, credit cards, and other loans).

3. *Rent.* Rent is all income earned by individuals for the use of their real (nonmonetary) assets, such as farms, houses, and stores. As explained in a previous chapter, we have to include here the implicit rental value of owner-occupied houses. Also included in this category are royalties received from copyrights, patents, and assets such as oil wells.

4. *Profits and nonincome expense items.* Our last category includes three business-related items. The first of these is total gross corporate profits. The second is *proprietors' income* earned from the operation of unincorporated businesses, which include sole proprietorships, partnerships, and producers' cooperatives. The third is *nonincome expense items.* Included among nonincome expense items are various taxes unrelated to incomes, such as sales taxes that firms collect from consumers and transmit to government agencies, net of any non-income-related subsidies that governments transmit to firms. The total of these taxes less subsidies is the net portion of GDI transmitted indirectly to the government sector via firms. Also included among nonincome expense items is depreciation, the part of GDI used to replace physical capital consumed in the process of production.

In principle, GDP and GDI should be the same. In practice, however, they usually differ slightly as a consequence of incomplete data and measurement errors. The resulting difference between GDP and GDI is called a *statistical discrepancy*, which in 2020 was about $24.4 billion.

Figure 8-3 shows a comparison between estimated gross domestic product and gross domestic income for 2020. Whether you decide to use the expenditure approach or the income approach, you will come out with the same number. There are sometimes statistical discrepancies, but they are usually relatively small.

FIGURE 8-3

Gross Domestic Product and Gross Domestic Income, 2020 (Dollar amounts in billions)

By using the two different methods of computing the output of the economy, we come up with gross domestic product and gross domestic income, which are by definition equal. One approach focuses on expenditures, or the flow of product. The other approach concentrates on income, or the flow of costs.

Sources: U.S. Department of Commerce and author's estimates.

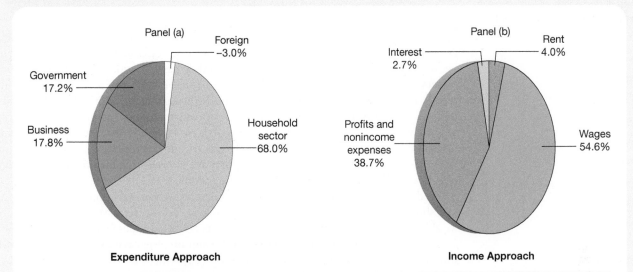

Expenditure Point of View—Product Flow		Income Point of View—Cost Flow	
Expenditure by Different Sectors:		**Domestic Income (at Factor Cost):**	
Household sector		*Wages*	
Personal consumption expenses	$15,086.7	All wages, salaries, and supplemental employee compensation	$12,115.0
Government sector		*Rent*	
Estimated value of goods and services	3,808.1	All rental income of individuals plus implicit rent on owner-occupied dwellings	887.2
Business sector		*Interest*	
Gross private domestic investment (including depreciation)	3,947.9	Net interest received by households	587.7
Foreign sector		*Profits and nonincome expense items*	
Net exports of goods and services	−669.2	Proprietorial income	1,474.5
		Corporate profits before taxes deducted	2,445.2
		Nonincome expense items	4,688.3
		Statistical discrepancy	−24.4
Gross domestic income	$22,173.5	Gross domestic product	$22,173.5

Other Components of National Income Accounting

> **8.4** Discuss the key components of national income

Gross domestic income or product does not really tell us how much income people have access to for spending purposes. To get to those kinds of data, we must make some adjustments, which we now do.

National Income (NI)

We know that net domestic product (NDP), or GDP minus depreciation, is the total market value of goods and services available to consume and to add to the capital

National income (NI)
The total of all factor payments to resource owners. It can be obtained from net domestic product (NDP) by adding net U.S. income earned abroad and adjusting for statistical discrepancies.

stock. Because U.S. residents earn income abroad and foreign residents earn income in the United States, we also add *net* U.S. income earned abroad and adjust for any statistical discrepancies. As before, such discrepancies arise from measurement errors, such as lost records of transactions, and uncollected data, such as unreported flows of incomes across the U.S. border. The result is what we define as **national income (NI)**—income earned by all U.S. factors of production.

Personal Income (PI)

National income does not actually represent what is available to individuals to spend because some people obtain income for which they have provided no concurrent good or service and others earn income but do not receive it. In the former category are mainly recipients of transfer payments from the government, such as Social Security, welfare, and food stamps. These payments represent shifts of funds within the economy by way of the government, with no goods or services concurrently rendered in exchange. For the other category, income earned but not received, the most obvious examples are corporate retained earnings that are plowed back into the business, contributions to social insurance, and corporate income taxes.

In addition, national income includes taxes on production and imports net of subsidies that should not count as part of income available to individuals to spend. Consequently, we also subtract taxes on production and imports net of subsidies from national income.

Personal income (PI)
The amount of income that households actually receive before they pay personal income taxes.

When transfer payments are added and when income earned but not received is subtracted, we end up with **personal income (PI)**—income *received* by the factors of production prior to the payment of personal income taxes.

Disposable Personal Income (DPI)

Disposable personal income (DPI)
Personal income after personal income taxes have been paid.

Everybody knows that you do not get to take home all your salary. To obtain **disposable personal income (DPI)**, we subtract all personal income taxes from personal income. This is the income that individuals have left for consumption and saving.

Deriving the Components of GDP

Table 8-2 shows how to derive the various components of GDP. It explains how to go from gross domestic product to net domestic product to national income to

TABLE 8-2

Going from GDP to Disposable Income, 2020

	Billions of Dollars
Gross domestic product (GDP)	22,173.5
Minus depreciation	−3,547.8
Net domestic product (NDP)	18,625.7
Plus net U.S. income earned abroad	+275.6
Plus statistical discrepancy	+74.3
National income (NI)	18,975.6
Minus corporate taxes, Social Security contributions, taxes on production and imports net of subsidies	−5,373.0
Plus net transfers and interest earnings	5,414.5
Personal income (PI)	19,017.1
Minus personal income taxes	−2,217.6
Disposable personal income (DPI)	16,799.5

Sources: U.S. Department of Commerce and author's estimates.

personal income and then to disposable personal income. In Appendix H, "National Income Accounts and Real GDP since 1929," you can see the historical record for GDP, NDP, NI, PI, and DPI for selected years since 1929.

We have completed our rundown of the different ways that GDP can be computed and of the different variants of the nation's income and product. What we have not yet touched on is the difference between the nation's income measured in this year's dollars and its income representing real goods and services.

Distinguishing between Nominal and Real Values

8.5 Distinguish between nominal GDP and real GDP

So far, we have shown how to measure *nominal* income and product. When we say "nominal," we are referring to income and product expressed in the current "face value" of today's dollar. Given the existence of inflation or deflation in the economy, we must also be able to distinguish between the **nominal values** that we will be looking at and the **real values** underlying them. Nominal values are expressed in current dollars. Real income involves our command over goods and services—purchasing power—and therefore depends on money income and a set of prices. Thus, real income refers to nominal income corrected for changes in the weighted average of all prices. In other words, we must make an adjustment for changes in the price level.

Consider an example. Nominal income *per person* in 1960 was only about $3,000 per year. In 2020, nominal income per person was about $66,600. Were people really that badly off in 1960? No, for nominal income in 1960 is expressed in 1960 prices, not in the prices of today. In today's dollars, the per-person income of 1960 would be about $18,000, or approximately 27 percent of today's income per person. This is a meaningful comparison between income in 1960 and income today. Next we will show how we can translate nominal measures of income into real measures by using an appropriate price index, such as the Consumer Price Index or the GDP deflator discussed in Chapter 7.

Nominal values
The values of variables such as GDP and investment expressed in current dollars, also called *money values;* measurement in terms of the actual market prices at which goods and services are sold.

Real values
Measurement of economic values after adjustments have been made for changes in the average of prices between years.

Correcting GDP for Price Changes

If a tablet device costs $200 this year, 10 tablet devices will have a market value of $2,000. If next year they cost $250 each, the same 10 tablet devices will have a market value of $2,500. In this case, there is no increase in the total quantity of tablet devices, but the market value will have increased by one-fourth. Apply this to every single good and service produced and sold in the United States, and you realize that changes in GDP, measured in *current* dollars, may not be a very useful indication of economic activity.

If we are really interested in variations in the *real* output of the economy, we must correct GDP (and just about everything else we look at) for changes in the average of overall prices from year to year. Basically, we need to generate an index that approximates the average prices and then divide that estimate into the value of output in current dollars to adjust the value of output to what is called **constant dollars,** or dollars corrected for general price level changes. This price-corrected GDP is called *real GDP.*

How much has correcting for price changes caused real GDP to differ from nominal GDP during the past few years?

Constant dollars
Dollars expressed in terms of real purchasing power, using a particular year as the base or standard of comparison, in contrast to current dollars.

EXAMPLE

Correcting GDP for Price Index Changes, 2010–2020

Let's take a numerical example to see how we can adjust GDP for changes in the price index. We must pick an appropriate price index in order to adjust for these price level changes. Let's use the GDP deflator to adjust our figures. Table 8-3 gives 11 years of GDP figures. Nominal GDP figures are shown in column 2. The price index (GDP deflator) is in column 3, with base year of 2012, when the GDP deflator equals 100. Column 4 shows real (inflation-adjusted) GDP in 2012 dollars.

The formula for real GDP is

$$Real\ GDP = \frac{nominal\ GDP}{price\ index} \times 100$$

The step-by-step derivation of real (constant-dollar) GDP is as follows: The base year is 2012, so the price index for that year must equal 100. In 2012, nominal GDP was $16,197.0 billion, and so was real GDP

(Continued)

expressed in 2012 dollars. In 2013, the price index increased to 101.75493. Thus, to correct 2013's nominal GDP for inflation, we divide the price index, 101.75493, into the nominal GDP figure of $16,784.9 billion and then multiply it by 100. The rounded result is $16,495.4 billion, which is 2013 GDP expressed in terms of the purchasing power of dollars in 2012. What about a situation when the price index is lower than in 2012? Look at 2010. Here the price index shown in column 3 is only 96.11058. That means that in 2010, the average of all prices was just over 96 percent of prices in 2012. To obtain 2010 GDP expressed in terms of 2012 purchasing power, we divide nominal GDP, $14,992.1 billion, by

96.11058 and then multiply by 100. The rounded result is a larger number—$15,598.8 billion. Column 4 in Table 8-3 is a better measure of how the economy has performed than column 2, which shows nominal GDP changes.

FOR CRITICAL THINKING

Based on the information in Table 8-3, how much inflation occurred between 2012 and 2020? Explain briefly.

Sources are listed at the end of this chapter.

Plotting Nominal and Real GDP

Nominal GDP and real GDP since 1970 are plotted in Figure 8-4. There is quite a big gap between the two GDP figures, reflecting the amount of inflation that has occurred. Note that the choice of a base year is arbitrary. We have chosen 2012 as the base year in our example. This happens to be the base year currently used by the government for the GDP deflator.

Per Capita Real GDP

Looking at changes in real GDP as a measure of economic growth may be deceiving, particularly if the population size has changed significantly. If real GDP over a 10-year period went up 100 percent, you might jump to the conclusion that the real income of a typical person in the economy had increased by that amount. But what if during the same period the population increased by 200 percent? Then what would you say? Certainly, the amount of real GDP per person, or *per capita real GDP*, would have fallen, even though *total* real GDP had risen. To account not only for price changes but also for population changes, we must first deflate GDP and then divide by the total population, doing this for each year. If we were to look at certain less developed

TABLE 8-3

Correcting GDP for Price Index Changes

To correct GDP for price index changes, we first have to pick a price index (the GDP deflator) with a specific year as its base. In our example, the base year is 2012. The price index for that year is 100. To obtain 2012 constant-dollar GDP, we divide the price index into nominal GDP and multiply by 100. In other words, we divide column 3 into column 2 and multiply by 100. This gives us column 4, which (taking into account rounding of the deflator) is a measure of real GDP expressed in 2012 purchasing power.

(1) Year	(2) Nominal GDP (billions of dollars per year)	(3) Price Index (base year 2012 = 100)	(4) = [(2) ÷ (3)] × 100 Real GDP (billions of dollars per year, in constant 2012 dollars)
2010	14,992.1	96.11058	15,598.8
2011	15,542.6	98.11825	15,840.7
2012	16,197.0	100.00000	16,197.0
2013	16,784.9	101.75493	16,495.4
2014	17,521.7	103.68001	16,899.8
2015	18,219.3	104.78870	17,386.7
2016	18,707.2	105.93460	17,659.2
2017	19,485.4	107.94818	18,050.7
2018	20,500.6	110.38889	18,571.3
2019	21,320.7	112.55338	18,942.7
2020	22,173.5	114.76030	19,321.6

Sources: U.S. Department of Commerce, Bureau of Economic Analysis, and author's estimates.

Nominal and Real GDP

Here we plot both nominal and real GDP. Real GDP is expressed in the purchasing power of 2012 dollars. The gap between the two represents price level changes.

Source: U.S. Department of Commerce.

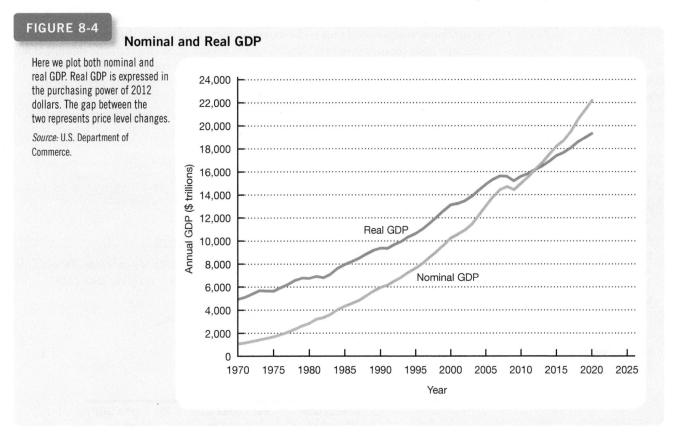

countries, we would find that in many cases, even though real GDP has risen over the past several decades, per capita real GDP has remained constant or fallen because the population has grown just as rapidly or even more rapidly.

Comparing GDP throughout the World

It is relatively easy to compare the standard of living of a family in Los Angeles with that of one living in Boston. Both families get paid in dollars and can buy the same goods and services at Walmart, McDonald's, and Costco. It is not so easy, however, to make a similar comparison between a family living in the United States and one in, say, Indonesia. The first problem concerns currency comparisons. Indonesian residents get paid in rupiah, their national currency, and buy goods and services with those rupiah. How do we compare the average standard of living measured in rupiah with that measured in dollars?

Foreign Exchange Rates In earlier chapters, you have encountered international examples that involved local currencies, but the dollar equivalent has always been given. The dollar equivalent is calculated by looking up the **foreign exchange rate** that is published daily in major newspapers throughout the world. If you know that you can exchange $1.33 per British pound, the exchange rate is 1.33 to 1 (or otherwise stated, a dollar is worth 0.75 pound). So, if British incomes per capita are, say, 39,760 pounds, that translates, at an exchange rate of $1.33 per pound, to $52,881. For years, statisticians calculated relative GDPs by simply adding up each country's GDP in its local currency and dividing by the respective dollar exchange rate.

Foreign exchange rate
The price of one currency in terms of another.

True Purchasing Power The problem with simply using foreign exchange rates to convert other countries' GDPs and per capita GDPs into dollars is that not all goods and services are bought and sold in a world market. Restaurant meals, housecleaning services, and home repairs do not get exchanged across countries. In countries that

Purchasing power parity
Adjustment in exchange rate conversions that takes into account differences in the true cost of living across countries.

have very low wages, those kinds of services are much cheaper than foreign exchange rate computations would imply. Government statistics claiming that per capita income in some poor country is only $900 a year seem shocking. Such a statistic, though, does not tell you the true standard of living of people in that country. Only by looking at what is called **purchasing power parity** can you hope to estimate other countries' true standards of living compared to ours.

Given that nations use different currencies, how can we compare nations' levels of real GDP per capita?

INTERNATIONAL EXAMPLE

Purchasing Power Parity Comparisons of World Incomes

A few years ago, the International Monetary Fund accepted the purchasing power parity approach as the correct one. It started presenting international statistics on each country's GDP relative to every other's based on purchasing power parity in U.S. dollars. The results were surprising. As you can see from Table 8-4, China's per capita GDP is higher based on purchasing power parity than when measured at market foreign exchange rates.

FOR CRITICAL THINKING

What is the percentage increase in China's per capita GDP when one switches from foreign exchange rates to purchasing power parity?

Sources are listed at the end of this chapter.

TABLE 8-4

Comparing GDP Internationally

Country	Annual GDP Based on Purchasing Power Parity (trillions of U.S. dollars)	Per Capita GDP Based on Purchasing Power Parity (U.S. dollars)	Per Capita GDP Based on Foreign Exchange Rates (U.S. dollars)
United States	19.4	59,532	59,532
Germany	4.2	50,639	44,470
Japan	5.5	43,279	38,428
United Kingdom	2.9	43,269	39,720
France	2.9	42,850	38,477
Italy	2.4	39,427	31,953
Russia	3.8	25,533	10,743
China	23.3	16,807	8,827
Brazil	3.2	15,484	9,821
Indonesia	3.2	12,284	3,847

Source: World Bank.

ECONOMICS IN YOUR LIFE

Should Real GDP Be Supplemented or Even Replaced as the Primary Measure of Economic Performance?

Diane Coyle, an economist at Britain's University of Manchester, has identified two fundamental difficulties with using real GDP as a nation's economic performance measure that she feels are particularly relevant today. First, the GDP deflator that is divided into nominal GDP to compute real GDP does not fully reflect *quality* changes generated by new

inventions and resulting innovations that take place over time. This failure for real GDP to account for changes in quality-adjusted prices, Coyle argues, makes real GDP values in different years hard to compare.

Second, a growing number of items, such as downloadable apps that people regularly utilize on a daily basis and from which they derive considerable benefits, are available for use at no *explicit* price. Thus, even though people have to give up bits of time to acquire such items, these services are available at virtually zero prices. To be sure, real GDP takes into account some of the value added by such services by including firms' real investment spending related to development of such products. Nevertheless, Coyle argues that annual consumption of such virtually "free" items creates a serious undercounting problem for real GDP.

Although Coyle views as promising efforts to apply AI technologies in using massive volumes of available online information to infer aggregate production, she views such ideas as too undeveloped to be employed at present. She concludes that policymakers should also consult supplementary performance measures, such as the recently introduced gross output (GO) measure, to supplement real GDP. In her view, an advantage of the GO measure is that it implicitly takes into account quality changes and the proliferation of virtually "free" items through its double counting of intermediate goods and services.

FOR CRITICAL THINKING

Why might economists experience difficulties in developing objective measures of quality-adjusted prices? (Hint: Do all people identically perceive quality characteristics of a good or service?)

REAL APPLICATION

You undoubtedly have downloaded "free" apps on your smartphone, tablet, or laptop. The producers and platforms that offer you these "free" apps eventually must recoup production costs. How do you help them do that?

Sources are listed at the end of this chapter.

ISSUES & APPLICATIONS

China's Incredibly Smooth Real GDP Growth

CONCEPTS APPLIED

➤ Gross Domestic Product

➤ Real GDP

➤ Limitations of GDP

At the end of one recent three-month interval, or quarter, China's government announced that the nation's real gross domestic product had increased during that period by 6.8 percent. Three months later, it announced that during the quarter that had followed, real GDP once more had risen by 6.8 percent. Then, three months hence, the government again announced a three-month growth rate equal to 6.8 percent. Indeed, as shown in Figure 8-5, China's officially announced quarterly rates of real GDP growth since 2015 have been strikingly close to this 6.8 percent figure.

The fact that most nations throughout history rarely have experienced such speedy yet virtually constant rates of real GDP growth has induced economists to take a closer look at how China's government measures the nation's GDP. Not all economists have come away convinced that they can rely on the nation's official GDP figures.

FIGURE 8-5

Quarterly Rates of Growth of Real GDP in China since 2015

Since 2015, growth of China's real GDP over three-month, or quarterly, intervals has remained within a narrow interval between 6.6 percent and 6.9 percent.

Source: Ministry of Finance of the People's Republic of China; author's estimates.

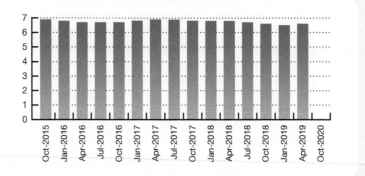

Cooking the Books versus Attaining Production Growth Targets

Observers have expressed concerns that China's government provides insufficient data on the components of the nation's GDP. Omissions of data on some elements of income and product complicate outsiders' efforts to ensure that those components sum to the reported nominal and, after price-level adjustments, real GDP.

Other observers suggest that China's national and regional governments, which own and manage many resources, constantly aim to achieve targeted quarterly rates of production growth. If growth is lagging during a given quarter, officials can marshal large volumes of government resources to hurry construction of public works, such as government buildings or hydroelectric equipment, to push real GDP toward the growth target. Such "real GDP targeting" on the part of China's government could yield the smooth reported quarterly real GDP growth.

Tracking Alternative Measures of China's Economic Performance

A number of economists have developed alternative measures of economic activity in China. These economists utilize data from a variety of other indicators, ranging from movie ticket sales and orders for bulldozers to rail cargo volume and satellite images of manufacturing locales, as supplementary measures.

A few of these economists have combined such measures to develop their own measures of overall economic activity in China, which they use to try evaluating the accuracy of real GDP figures released by China's government. Interestingly, over the past few years they have indicated average rates of growth very close to the rates of real GDP growth reported by the government. Rates of growth of the alternative production measures, however, display considerably more variability than the officially reported rates of growth of real GDP.

FOR CRITICAL THINKING

Why might officials of China's government confront different incentives regarding data measurement than private economists interested in predicting the nation's future economic performance?

REAL APPLICATION

Many younger Americans are learning to speak Chinese and contemplate living and working in China. If you are one of them, why should you be concerned with China's actual economic rate of growth?

Sources are listed at the end of this chapter.

What You Should Know

Here is what you should know after reading this chapter.

LEARNING OBJECTIVES

8.1 **Describe the circular flow of income and output** *The circular flow of income and output captures two principles: (1) In every transaction, the seller receives the same amount that the buyer spends; and (2) goods and services flow in one direction, and money payments flow in the other direction. Households ultimately purchase the nation's total output of final goods and services. They make these purchases using income—wages, rents, interest, and profits—earned from selling labor, land, capital, and entrepreneurial services, respectively. Hence, income equals the value of output.*

8.2 **Define gross domestic product (GDP) and explain its limitations** *A nation's gross domestic product is the total market value of its final output of goods and services produced within a given year using factors of production located within the nation's borders. Because GDP measures the value of a flow of production during a year in terms of market prices, it is not a measure of a nation's wealth.*

8.3 **Explain the expenditure and income approaches to tabulating GDP** *To calculate GDP using the expenditure approach, we sum consumption spending, investment expenditures, government spending, and net export expenditures. Thus, we add up the total amount spent on newly produced goods and services to obtain the dollar value of the output produced and purchased during the year.*

8.4 **Discuss the key components of national income** *To tabulate GDP using the income approach, we add total wages and salaries, rental income, interest income, profits, and nonincome expense items—depreciation and non-income-based taxes that firms transmit to the government—to obtain gross domestic income, which is equivalent to gross domestic product. Thus, the total value of all income earnings (equivalent to total factor costs) equals GDP.*

8.5 **Distinguish between nominal GDP and real GDP** *Nominal GDP is the value of newly produced output during the current year measured at current market prices. Real GDP adjusts the value of current output into constant dollars by correcting for changes in the overall level of prices from year to year. To calculate real GDP, we divide nominal GDP by the price index (the GDP deflator) and multiply by 100.*

KEY TERMS

national income
  accounting, 160
total income, 161
final goods and services, 161
Key Figure
Figure 8-1, 160

gross domestic product
  (GDP), 162
intermediate goods, 162
value added, 162
gross output (GO), 163

expenditure approach, 166
income approach, 166
durable consumer goods, 166
nondurable consumer
  goods, 166
services, 167
gross private domestic
  investment, 167
investment, 167
producer durables, or capital
  goods, 167
fixed investment, 167
inventory investment, 167
depreciation, 168
net domestic product
  (NDP), 168
capital consumption
  allowance, 168
net investment, 169
gross domestic income
  (GDI), 170
Key Figure
Figure 8-2, 169

national income (NI), 172
personal income (PI), 172
disposable personal income
  (DPI), 172

nominal values, 173
real values, 173
constant dollars, 173
foreign exchange rate, 175
purchasing power parity, 176
Key Figure
Figure 8-4, 175

PROBLEMS

8-1. Explain in your own words why the flow of gross domestic product during a given interval must always be equivalent to the flow of gross domestic income within that same period.

8-2. In the first stage of manufacturing each final unit of a product, a firm purchases a key input at a price of $4 per unit. The firm then pays a wage rate of $3 per unit for the time that labor is exerted, combining an additional $2 of inputs for each final unit of output produced. The firm sells every unit of the product for $10. What is the contribution of each unit of output to GDP in the current year?

8-3. Each year after a regular spring cleaning, Maria spruces up her home a little by repainting the walls of one room in her house. In a given year, she spends $25 on magazines to get ideas about wall textures and paint shades, $45 on newly produced texturing materials and tools, $35 on new paintbrushes and other painting equipment, and $175 on newly produced paint. Normally, she preps the walls, a service that a professional wall-texturing specialist would charge $200 to do, and applies two coats of paint, a service that a painter would charge $350 to do, on her own.

   a. When she purchases her usual set of materials and does all the work on her home by herself in a given spring, how much does Maria's annual spring texturing and painting activity contribute to GDP?

   b. Suppose that Maria hurt her back this year and is recovering from surgery. Her surgeon has instructed her not to do any texturing work, but he has given her the go-ahead to paint a room as long as she is cautious. Thus, she buys all the equipment required to both texture and paint a room. She hires someone else to do the texturing work but does the painting herself. How much would her spring painting activity add to GDP?

   c. As a follow-up to part (b), suppose that as soon as Maria bends down to dip her brush into the paint, she realizes that painting will be too hard on her back after all. She decides to hire someone else to do all the work using the materials she has already purchased. In this case, how much will her spring painting activity contribute to GDP?

8-4. Each year, Johan typically does all his own landscaping and yard work. He spends $200 per year on mulch for his flower beds, $225 per year on flowers and plants, $50 on fertilizer for his lawn, and $245 on gasoline and lawn mower maintenance. The lawn and garden store where he obtains his mulch and fertilizer charges other customers $500 for the service of spreading that much mulch in flower beds and $50 for the service of distributing fertilizer over a yard the size of Johan's. Paying a professional yard care service to mow his lawn would require an expenditure of $1,200 per year, but in that case Johan would not have to buy gasoline or maintain his own lawn mower.

   a. In a normal year, how much does Johan's landscaping and yard work contribute to GDP?

   b. Suppose that Johan has developed allergy problems this year and will have to reduce the amount of his yard work. He can wear a mask while running his lawn mower, so he will keep mowing his yard, but he will pay the lawn and garden center to spread mulch and distribute fertilizer. How much will all the work on Johan's yard contribute to GDP this year?

   c. As a follow-up to part (b), at the end of the year, Johan realizes that his allergies are growing worse and that he will have to arrange for all his landscaping and yard work to be done by someone else next year. How much will he contribute to GDP next year?

8-5. Consider the following hypothetical data for the U.S. economy in 2023 (all amounts are in trillions of dollars).

Consumption	14.0
Non-income-related taxes net of subsidies	0.8
Depreciation	1.3
Government spending	4.8
Imports	2.7
Gross private domestic investment	4.0
Exports	2.5

   a. Based on the data, what is GDP? NDP? NI?

   b. Suppose that in 2024, exports fall to $2.3 trillion, imports rise to $2.85 trillion, and gross private domestic investment falls to $4.25 trillion. What will GDP be in 2024, assuming that other values do not change between 2023 and 2024?

8-6. Look back at Table 8-3, which explains how to calculate real GDP in terms of 2012 constant dollars. Change the base year to 2010. Recalculate the price index, and then recalculate real GDP—that is, express column 4 of Table 8-3 in terms of 2010 dollars instead of 2012 dollars.

8-7. Consider the following hypothetical data for the U.S. economy in 2023 (in trillions of dollars), and assume that there are no statistical discrepancies, zero net incomes earned abroad, and zero taxes and subsidies for production.

Corporate profits before taxes deducted	3.0
Proprietorial income	2.0
Rent	1.0
Interest	0.8
Wages	15.2
Depreciation	3.3
Consumption	16.5
Exports	2.0
Net transfers and interest earnings	4.8
Nonincome expense items	5.0
Imports	2.8
Corporate taxes	1.5
Social Security contributions	2.5
Government spending	4.3

   a. What is gross domestic income? GDP?

   b. What is gross private domestic investment?

   c. What is personal income?

8-8. Which of the following are production activities that are included in GDP? Which are not?

   a. Mr. King performs the service of painting his own house instead of paying someone else to do it.

   b. Mr. King paints houses for a living.

   c. Mrs. King earns income from parents by taking baby photos in her digital photography studio.

   d. Mrs. King takes digital photos of planets and stars as part of her astronomy hobby.

   e. E*Trade charges fees to process Internet orders for stock trades.

   f. Mr. Ho spends $10,000 on shares of stock via an Internet trade order and pays a $10 brokerage fee.

   g. Mrs. Ho receives a Social Security payment.

   h. Ms. Hernandez makes a $300 payment for an Internet-based course on stock trading.

   i. Mr. Langham sells a used laptop computer to his neighbor.

8-9. Explain what happens to contributions to GDP in each of the following situations.

   a. A woman who makes a living charging for investment advice on her Internet site marries one of her clients, to whom she now provides advice at no charge.

   b. A man who had washed the windows of his own house every year decides to pay a private company to wash those windows this year.

   c. A company that had been selling used firearms illegally finally gets around to obtaining an operating license and performing background checks as specified by law prior to each gun sale.

8-10. Explain what happens to the official measure of GDP in each of the following situations.

   a. Air quality improves significantly throughout the United States, but there are no effects on aggregate production or on market prices of final goods and services.

   b. The U.S. government spends considerably less on antipollution efforts this year than it did in recent years.

   c. The quality of cancer treatments increases, so patients undergo fewer treatments, which hospitals continue to provide at the same price per treatment as before.

8-11. Which of the following activities of a digital device manufacturer during the current year are included in this year's measure of GDP?

   a. The firm makes a chip in June, uses it as a component in a device in August, and sells the device to a customer in November.

   b. A retail outlet of the firm sells a device completely built during the current year.

   c. A marketing arm of the company receives fee income during the current year when a buyer of one of its devices elects to use the device manufacturer as her Internet service provider.

8-12. A number of economists contend that official measures of U.S. gross private investment expenditures are understated. For instance, household spending on education, such as college tuition expenditures, is counted as consumption. Some economists suggest that these expenditures, which amount to 6 percent of GDP, should be counted as investment instead. Based on this 6 percent estimate and the GDP computations detailed in Figure 8-3, how many billions of dollars would shift from consumption to investment if this suggestion was adopted?

8-13. Consider the table below for the economy of a nation whose residents produce five final goods.

	2020		2024	
Good	**Price**	**Quantity**	**Price**	**Quantity**
Shampoo	$ 2	15	$ 4	20
External hard drives	200	10	250	10
Books	40	5	50	4
Milk	3	10	4	3
Candy	1	40	2	20

Assuming a 2020 base year:

a. What is nominal GDP for 2020 and 2024?

b. What is real GDP for 2020 and 2024?

8-14. Consider the following table for the economy of a nation whose residents produce four final goods.

Good	2022		2023	
	Price	Quantity	Price	Quantity
Computers	$1,000	10	$800	15
Bananas	6	3,000	11	1,000
Televisions	100	500	150	300
Cookies	1	10,000	2	10,000

Assuming a 2022 base year:

a. What is nominal GDP for 2022 and 2023?

b. What is real GDP for 2022 and 2023?

8-15. In the table for Problem 8-14, if 2023 is the base year, what is the price index for 2022? (Round decimal fractions to the nearest tenth.)

8-16. Suppose that early in a year, a hurricane hits a town in Florida and destroys a substantial number of homes. A portion of this stock of housing, which had a market value of $100 million (not including the market value of the land), was uninsured. The owners of the residences spent a total of $5 million during the rest of the year to pay salvage companies to help them save remaining belongings. A small percentage of uninsured owners had sufficient resources to spend a total of $15 million during the year to pay construction companies to rebuild their homes. Some were able to devote their own time, the opportunity cost of which was valued at $3 million, to work on rebuilding their homes. The remaining people, however, chose to sell their land at its market value and abandon the remains of their houses. What was the combined effect of these transactions on GDP for this year? (*Hint:* Which transactions took place in the markets for *final* goods and services?) In what ways, if any, does the effect on GDP reflect a loss in welfare for these individuals?

8-17. Suppose that in 2022, geologists discover large reserves of oil under the tundra in Alaska. These new reserves have a market value estimated at $50 billion at current oil prices. Oil companies spend $1 billion to hire workers and move and position equipment to begin exploratory pumping during that same year. In the process of loading some of the oil onto tankers at a port, one company accidentally spills some of the oil into a bay and by the end of the year pays $1 billion to other companies to clean it up. The oil spill kills thousands of birds, seals, and other wildlife. What was

the combined effect of these events on GDP for this year? (*Hint:* Which transactions took place in the markets for *final* goods and services?) In what ways, if any, does the effect on GDP reflect a loss in national welfare?

8-18. Consider the diagram below, and answer the following questions.

a. What is the base year? Explain.

b. Has this country experienced inflation or deflation since the base year? How can you tell?

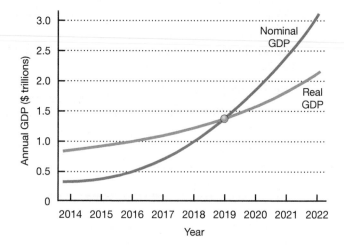

8-19. Suppose that in Figure 8-1, the sum total of all the goods and services produced during the relevant period—pairs of shoes, candy bars, digital devices, etc., all summed together—is 500 trillion units. The total value of this flow of output is $20 trillion. The total amount of factors of production—labor, land, capital, entrepreneurship, all summed together—is 1 billion units. What is the flow of income—that is, the sum of wages, rents, interest, and profits?

8-20. In Table 8-1, what is the total dollar amount that is added to the nation's gross domestic product? Why?

8-21. Suppose that U.S. consumption spending is $13 trillion, gross private domestic investment is $4.5 trillion, government spending is $5 trillion, and net exports are –$0.5 trillion. If interest income is $1 trillion, depreciation is $0.5 trillion, wages are $12 trillion, and rental income is $0.75 trillion, what is the net domestic product?

8-22. In Problem 8-21, what is net investment?

8-23. Consider Figure 8-4. Explain what is special about the year at which the two data plots cross, and why this is so.

8-24. Take a look at Table 8-4. Provide a possible explanation of why per capita GDP based on purchasing power parity is higher in China and Indonesia than GDP based on foreign exchange rates.

REFERENCES

EXAMPLE: A Reduced Role for Manufacturing of Physical Merchandise as a Source of Value Added in U.S. Production

Federal Reserve Economic Data, "Value Added by Private Industries: Manufacturing as a Percentage of GDP" (https://fred.stlouisfed.org/series/VAPGDPMA), 2019.

Justin Fox, "Shares of Real GDP Don't Give the Real Story of Manufacturing," *Bloomberg*, March 12, 2018.

Darrell West and Christian Lansang, "Global Manufacturing Scorecard: How the United States Compares with 18 Other Nations," *Brookings*, July 10, 2018.

BEHAVIORAL EXAMPLE: Obstacles to Measuring Aggregate "Well-Being" alongside Gross Domestic Product

"Measuring Well-Being and Progress: Well-Being Research," Organization for Economic Cooperation and Development (http://www.oecd.org/statistics/measuring-well-being-and-progress.htm), 2019.

Barbara Cavalletti and Matteo Corsi, "'Beyond GDP' Effects on National Subjective Well-Being of OECD Countries," *Social Indicators Research*, 2018.

Daniel Fehder, Michael Porter, and Scott Stern, "The Empirics of Social Progress: The Interplay between Subjective Well-Being and Societal Performance," *American Economic Review Papers and Proceedings*, 2018.

AI—DECISION MAKING THROUGH DATA: Using New Information about Flows of Goods and Services

"Data Science for the Public Good," Data Science Campus, United Kingdom (https://datasciencecampus.ons.gov.uk/about-us/), 2019.

"Economic Well-Being, United Kingdom," United Kingdom Office for National Statistics (https://www.ons.gov.uk/peoplepopulationandcommunity/personalandhousehold finances/incomeandwealth/bulletins/economicwellbeing/januarytomarch2018), 2018.

Jonathan Vanian, "United Kingdom Plans $1.3 Billion Artificial Intelligence Push," *Fortune*, April 25, 2018.

ECONOMICS IN YOUR LIFE: Should Real GDP Be Supplemented or Even Replaced as the Primary Measure of Economic Performance?

Rutger Hoekstra, *Replacing GDP by 2030*, Cambridge University Press, 2019.

Diane Coyle, "Why GDP Statistics Are Failing Us," U.S. Chamber of Commerce Foundation (https://www.uschamberfoundation.org/article/why-gdp-statistics-are-failing-us), 2018.

Mark Skousen, "If GDP Falters, Watch the Economy GO," *Wall Street Journal*, April 23, 2018.

ISSUES & APPLICATIONS: China's Incredibly Smooth Real GDP Growth

Tom Orlik, "China's Latest Official GDP Report Is Accurate. No, Really," *Bloomberg Businessweek*, January 25, 2019.

Edna Curran, with James Mayger and Jeff Kearns, "China's Wrinkle-Free Growth," *Bloomberg Businessweek*, April 23, 2018.

Peter Pham, "Is There a Secret Growth Hormone Added to China's Economy?" *Forbes*, May 6, 2018.

9 Global Economic Growth and Development

dinozzo/123RF GB Limited

LEARNING OBJECTIVES

After reading this chapter, you should be able to:

9.1 Define economic growth and recognize the importance of economic growth rates

9.2 Explain why productivity growth, saving, and new technologies are crucial for maintaining economic growth

9.3 Describe how immigration and property rights influence economic growth

9.4 Discuss the fundamental elements that contribute to a nation's economic development

What motivates much scientific and engineering work is a desire to find a new way of producing quantities of goods and services with fewer inputs or, equivalently, to utilize the same quantity of inputs to produce more goods and services. As you learned in an earlier chapter, success in such endeavors expands the productive possibilities for a nation's economy. In this chapter you will learn that such expansions translate into higher rates of economic growth measured by the rate of change of real GDP per capita.

Sometimes inventions that on the surface appear rather minor can lead to significant productivity improvements. Seemingly small inventions, such as new forms of colors for products, can generate substantial effects on productivity. Innovative development of new shades of color can generate surprisingly significant productivity growth and, as a result, contribute meaningfully to overall economic growth.

only about half of U.S. residents in their 30s today earn as much on average as their parents did when they were in their 30s? In contrast, forty years ago, when the rate of growth of per capita real GDP in the United States was considerably higher, nearly all U.S. residents in their 30s earned more than their parents had earned at that same age. In this chapter, you will learn the rate of growth of per capita real GDP is economists' primary measure of *economic growth.*

How Do We Define Economic Growth?

We can show economic growth graphically as an outward shift of a production possibilities curve, as is seen in Figure 9-1. If there is economic growth between 2022 and 2042, the production possibilities curve will shift outward toward the red curve. The distance that it shifts represents the amount of economic growth, defined as the increase in the productive capacity of a nation. Although it is possible to come up with a measure of a nation's increased productive capacity, it would not be easy. Therefore, we turn to a more readily obtainable definition of economic growth.

Most people have a general idea of what economic growth means. When a nation grows economically, its citizens must be better off in at least some ways, usually in terms of their material well-being. Typically, though, we do not measure the well-being of any nation solely in terms of its total output of real goods and services or in terms of real GDP without making some adjustments. After all, India has a real GDP more than 3 times as large as that of Italy. The population in India, though, is more than 20 times greater than that of Italy. Consequently, we view India as a poorer country and Italy as a richer country. Thus, when we measure economic growth, we must adjust for population growth. Our formal definition becomes this:

> **Economic growth** *occurs when there are increases in* **per capita** *real GDP,* *measured by the rate of change in per capita real GDP per year.*

Figure 9-2 presents the historical record of real GDP per person in the United States.

Problems in Definition

Our definition of economic growth says nothing about the *distribution* of output and income. A nation might grow very rapidly in terms of increases in per capita real GDP, while its poor people remain poor or become even poorer. Therefore, in assessing the

9.1 Define economic growth and recognize the importance of economic growth rates

Economic growth
Increases in per capita real GDP measured by its rate of change per year.

Economic Growth

If there is growth between 2022 and 2042, the production possibilities curve for the entire economy will shift outward from the blue line labeled 2022 to the red line labeled 2042. The distance that it shifts represents an increase in the productive capacity of the nation.

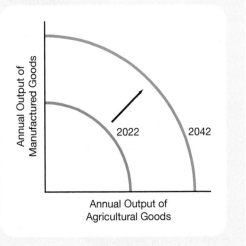

FIGURE 9-2

The Historical Record of U.S. Economic Growth

The graph traces per capita real GDP in the United States since 1900. Data are given in 2012 dollars.

Source: U.S. Department of Commerce.

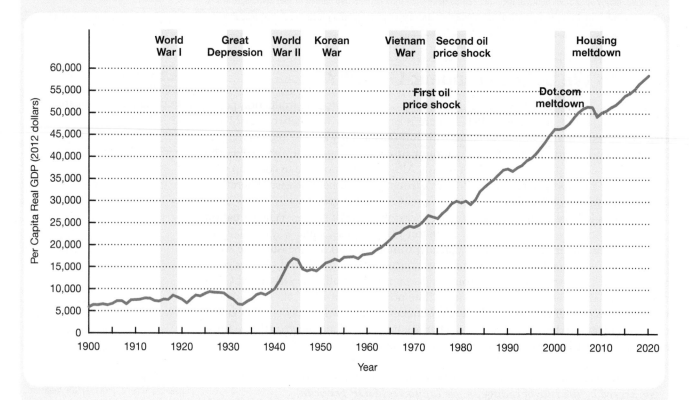

economic growth record of any nation, we must be careful to pinpoint which income groups have benefited the most from such growth. Another important consideration is how much economic growth differs across countries.

Real standards of living can go up without any positive economic growth. This can occur if individuals are, on average, enjoying more leisure by working fewer hours but producing as much as they did before. For example, if per capita real GDP in the United States remained at $59,000 a year for a decade, we still could not conclude that living standards for U.S. residents were the same at the end of the decade. What if, during that same 10-year period, average hours worked fell from 37 per week to 33 per week? That would mean that during the 10 years under study, individuals in the labor force were "earning" 4 more hours of leisure a week.

How much does economic growth differ across countries?

INTERNATIONAL EXAMPLE

Growth Rates around the World

Table 9-1 shows the average annual rate of growth of real GDP per person in selected countries since 1990. During this time period, the United States has been positioned in the middle range of the pack. Thus, even though we are one of the world's richest countries, in recent years our rate of economic growth has been in the lower range.

FOR CRITICAL THINKING

"The largest change is from zero to one." Does this statement have anything to do with relative growth rates in poorer versus richer countries?

Sources are listed at the end of this chapter.

TABLE 9-1

Per Capita Real GDP Growth Rates in Various Countries

Country	Average Annual Rate of Growth of Real GDP Per Capita, 1990–2020 (%)
Japan	0.7
France	0.9
Germany	1.5
Canada	1.5
Sweden	1.4
United States	1.6
Turkey	2.2
Chile	3.8
Malaysia	3.9
Indonesia	4.5
India	4.5
China	8.0

Sources: Penn World Tables and International Monetary Fund estimates.

Nothing so extreme as this example of leisure gain has occurred in this country, but something similar has. Average hours worked per week fell steadily until the 1960s, when they leveled off. That means that during much of the history of this country, the increase in per capita real GDP *understated* the growth in living standards that we were experiencing because we were enjoying more and more leisure as time passed.

Is Economic Growth Bad?

Some commentators on our current economic situation believe that the definition of economic growth ignores its negative effects. Some psychologists even contend that economic growth makes us worse off. They say that the more the economy grows, the more "needs" are created so that we feel worse off as we become richer. Our expectations are rising faster than reality, so we presumably always suffer from a sense of disappointment. Also, economists' measurement of economic growth does not take into account the spiritual and cultural aspects of the good life. As with all activities, both costs and benefits are associated with growth. You can see some of those listed in Table 9-2.

Any measure of economic growth that we use will be imperfect. Nonetheless, the measures that we do have allow us to make comparisons across countries and over

TABLE 9-2

Costs and Benefits of Economic Growth

Benefits	Costs
Reduction in illiteracy	Environmental pollution
Reduction in poverty	Breakdown of the family
Improved health	Isolation and alienation
Longer lives	Urban congestion
Political stability	

time and, if used judiciously, can enable us to gain important insights. Per capita real GDP, used so often, is not always an accurate measure of economic well-being, but it is a serviceable measure of productive activity.

The Importance of Growth Rates

Notice in Table 9-1 that the growth rates in real per capita income for most countries differ very little—generally by only a few percentage points. You might want to know why such small differences in growth rates are important. What does it matter if we grow at 3 percent rather than at 4 percent per year? The answer is that in the long run, it matters a lot.

A small difference in the rate of economic growth does not matter very much for next year or the year after. For the more distant future, however, it makes considerable difference. The power of *compounding* is impressive. Let's see what happens with three different annual rates of growth: 3 percent, 4 percent, and 5 percent. We start with $1 trillion per year of U.S. GDP at some time in the past. We then compound this $1 trillion, or allow it to grow at these three different growth rates. The difference is huge. In 50 years, $1 trillion per year becomes $4.38 trillion per year if compounded at 3 percent per year. Just one percentage point more in the growth rate, 4 percent, results in a real GDP of $7.11 trillion per year in 50 years, almost double the previous amount. Two percentage points' difference in the growth rate—5 percent per year— results in a real GDP of $11.5 trillion per year in 50 years, or nearly three times as much. Obviously, very small differences in annual growth rates result in great differences in cumulative economic growth. That is why nations are concerned if the growth rate falls even a little in absolute percentage terms.

Thus, when we talk about growth rates, we are talking about compounding. In Table 9-3, we show how $1 compounded annually grows at different interest rates. We see in the 3 percent column that $1 in 50 years grows to $4.38. We merely multiplied $1 trillion times 4.38 to get the growth figure in our earlier example. In the 5 percent column, $1 grows to $11.50 after 50 years. Again, we multiplied $1 trillion times 11.50 to get the growth figure for 5 percent in the preceding example.

TABLE 9-3

One Dollar Compounded Annually at Different Interest Rates

Here we show the value of a dollar at the end of a specified period during which it has been compounded annually at a specified interest rate. For example, if you took $1 today and invested it at 5 percent per year, it would yield $1.05 at the end of one year. At the end of 10 years, it would equal $1.63, and at the end of 50 years, it would equal $11.50.

Number of Years	Interest Rate						
	3%	4%	5%	6%	8%	10%	20%
1	1.03	1.04	1.05	1.06	1.08	1.10	1.20
2	1.06	1.08	1.10	1.12	1.17	1.21	1.44
3	1.09	1.12	1.16	1.19	1.26	1.33	1.73
4	1.13	1.17	1.22	1.26	1.36	1.46	2.07
5	1.16	1.22	1.28	1.34	1.47	1.61	2.49
6	1.19	1.27	1.34	1.41	1.59	1.77	2.99
7	1.23	1.32	1.41	1.50	1.71	1.94	3.58
8	1.27	1.37	1.48	1.59	1.85	2.14	4.30
9	1.30	1.42	1.55	1.68	2.00	2.35	5.16
10	1.34	1.48	1.63	1.79	2.16	2.59	6.19
20	1.81	2.19	2.65	3.20	4.66	6.72	38.30
30	2.43	3.24	4.32	5.74	10.00	17.40	237.00
40	3.26	4.80	7.04	10.30	21.70	45.30	1,470.00
50	4.38	7.11	11.50	18.40	46.90	117.00	9,100.00

The Rule of 70 Table 9-3 indicates that how quickly the level of a nation's per capita real GDP increases depends on the rate of economic growth. A formula called the **rule of 70** provides a shorthand way to calculate approximately how long it will take a country to experience a significant increase in per capita real GDP. According to the rule of 70, the approximate number of years necessary for a nation's per capita real GDP to increase by 100 percent—that is, to *double*—is equal to 70 divided by the average rate of economic growth. Thus, at an annual growth rate of 10 percent, per capita real GDP should double in about 7 years.

Rule of 70
A rule stating that the approximate number of years required for per capita real GDP to double is equal to 70 divided by the average rate of economic growth.

How can people's reactions to particularly deep and long-lasting economic contractions lead to changes in laws that contribute to reduced economic growth?

AI | DECISION MAKING THROUGH DATA

Lengthy, Deep Recessions and Long-Run Economic Growth

Stephen Broadberry of Oxford University and John Wallis of the University of Maryland recently have conducted a big-data-style analysis of eight centuries of data from 18 countries. They focus on how durations of contractions and rates of real-per-capita-GDP shrinkage (recessions) affect long-run economic growth. They find evidence that when nations experience particularly lengthy and deep recessions, their residents enact laws that require redistribution of diminished national incomes and stocks of wealth to those people most harmed by the recessions. During years that

follow, incomes continue to be redistributed, which causes people to become less willing to invest and to save. The result is lower subsequent rates of long-run economic growth.

REAL APPLICATION

Redistributive policies may include additional government-provided benefits to poorer individuals as well as higher taxes on richer individuals. How could such policies affect your future decisions to save and to invest?

Sources are listed at the end of this chapter.

As you can see in Table 9-3, at a 10 percent growth rate, in 7 years per capita real GDP would rise by a factor of 1.94, which is very close to 2, or very nearly the doubling predicted by the rule of 70. At an annual growth rate of 8 percent, the rule of 70 predicts that nearly 9 years will be required for a nation's per capita real GDP to double. Table 9-3 verifies that this prediction is correct. Indeed, the table shows that after 9 years an exact doubling will occur at a growth rate of 8 percent.

The rule of 70 implies that at lower rates of economic growth, much more time must pass before per capita real GDP will double. At a 3 percent growth rate, just over 23 (70 ÷ 3) years must pass before per capita real income doubles. At a rate of growth of only 1 percent per year, 70 (70 ÷ 1) years must pass. This means that if a nation's average rate of economic growth is 1 percent instead of 3 percent, 47 more years—about two generations—would be required for per capita real GDP to double. Clearly, the rule of 70 verifies that even very slight differences in economic growth rates are important.

Productivity Growth, Saving, and New Technologies: Fundamental Determinants of Economic Growth

9.2 Explain why productivity growth, saving, and new technologies are crucial for maintaining economic growth

Productivity growth, the national saving rate, and the pace of development of new technologies influence the rate of economic growth. Let's consider each element individually.

Productivity Increases: The Heart of Economic Growth

Productivity is an index of how much output can be produced with given amounts of inputs. **Labor productivity** normally is measured by dividing total real domestic output (real GDP) by the number of workers or the number of labor hours. By definition, labor productivity increases whenever average output produced per worker (or per hour worked) during a specified time period increases.

Labor productivity
Total real domestic output (real GDP) divided by the number of workers (output per worker).

FIGURE 9-3

Rates of Growth of U.S. Real GDP and of Labor and Capital Productivity since 1952

The path of the 5-year-average rate of growth of U.S. real GDP has closely paralleled the path of the 5-year-average rate of growth of the nation's labor and capital productivity.

Source: Bureau of Economic Analysis.

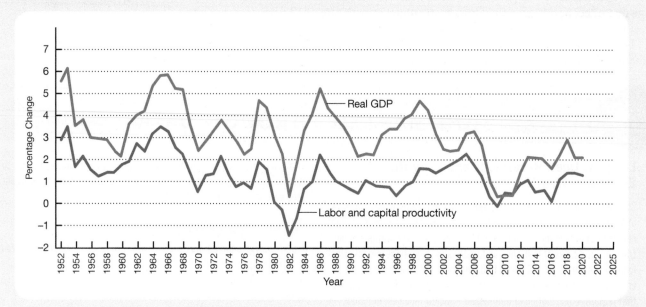

Clearly, there is a relationship between economic growth and increases in labor productivity. If you divide all resources into just capital and labor, economic growth can be defined simply as the cumulative contribution to per capita GDP growth of three components: the rate of growth of capital, the rate of growth of labor, and the rate of growth of capital and labor productivity. If everything else remains constant, improvements in labor and capital productivity ultimately lead to economic growth and higher living standards.

Figure 9-3 shows the importance of growth of labor and capital productivity for economic growth. To emphasize the long-run relationship between real GDP growth and the growth rate of labor and capital productivity, each point plotted displays average growth rates of real GDP and of labor and capital productivity over the preceding 5 years. As the figure indicates, the 5-year-average rate of growth of U.S. real GDP closely tracks the 5-year-average rate of growth of labor and capital productivity.

The Fundamental Role of Saving for Economic Growth

Alongside productivity growth, one of the most important factors that affect the rate of economic growth is the rate of saving. As a consequence, long-term living standards, measured by annual per capita real GDP, typically are closely related to the rate of saving.

A basic proposition in economics is that if you want more tomorrow, you have to consume less today.

> *To have more consumption in the future, you have to consume less today and save the difference between your income and your consumption.*

How might the patience of a nation's residents influence its rate of economic growth?

BEHAVIORAL EXAMPLE

Is Patience a Virtue for Economic Growth?

According to a fourteenth-century poem since quoted many times, "Patience is a virtue." Economists consider people's degrees of patience by measuring their "time preferences"—the relative weights that they place on the present versus the future when they make current choices. Typically, economists try to measure the time preferences that people exhibit via laboratory experiments or from evidence gleaned from observed decisions or survey data.

Recently, behavioral economists have evaluated how people's time preferences relate to determinants of economic growth, such as saving, investment, and innovation. These economists have found evidence of a positive relationship between patience and economic growth. Two explanations have been offered for this result. One is that when economic growth is higher, so that real GDP per capita is rising at a faster

pace, people feel more confident about the present and hence can place more emphasis on preparing for the future. Another is that people who innately have more patience are more likely to save. Higher rates of saving, of course, promote higher economic growth rates. This second rationalization suggests that, indeed, patience is a virtue for economic growth.

FOR CRITICAL THINKING

Why should we anticipate that a national population composed mainly of impatient people might be likely to experience a relatively low long-run rate of economic growth?

Sources are listed at the end of this chapter.

On a national basis, higher saving rates eventually yield higher living standards in the long run, all other things held constant. Although the U.S. saving rate has recently increased, concern has been growing that we still are not saving enough. Saving is important for economic growth because without saving, we cannot have investment. If there is no investment in our capital stock, there would be much less economic growth.

The relationship between the rate of saving (gross saving as a percentage of real GDP) and a measure of living standard (per capita real GDP) is shown in Figure 9-4. Among the nations with the highest rates of saving are China, Germany, Japan, and South Korea.

FIGURE 9-4

Relationship between Rate of Saving and Per Capita Real GDP

This diagram shows the relationship between per capita real GDP and the rate of saving expressed as the average share of annual real GDP saved.

Source: World Bank.

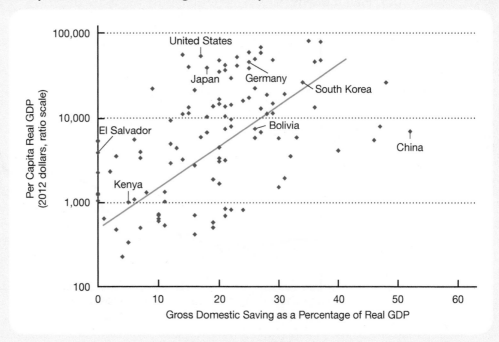

New Growth Theory and the Determinants of Economic Growth

The simple arithmetic definition of economic growth states that the rate of economic growth equals the per capita growth rates of capital and labor plus the per capita growth rate of their productivity. When you add these growth rates together, however, you still do not get the total U.S. economic growth rate. Proponents of what is now called **new growth theory** argue that the discrepancy arises from new technology, which they argue cannot simply be viewed as an outside factor without explanation. Therefore, technology must be understood in terms of what drives it. What are the forces that cause productivity to grow in the United States and elsewhere?

New growth theory
A theory of economic growth that examines the factors that determine why technology, research, innovation, and the like are undertaken and how they interact.

Technology: A Separate Factor of Production Consider some startling statistics about the growth in technology. Microprocessor speeds may increase from 5,000 megahertz to 25,000 megahertz by the year 2035. By that same year, the size of the thinnest circuit line within a transistor may decrease by 90 percent. The typical memory capacity (RAM) of digital devices will jump from 10 gigabytes, or more than 100 times the equivalent text in the Internal Revenue Code, to more than 1,000 gigabytes. Recent developments in phase-change memory technologies and in new techniques for storing bits of data on molecules and even individual atoms promise even greater expansions of digital memory capacities. Predictions are that computers may become as powerful as the human brain by 2030.

We now recognize that technology must be viewed as a separate factor of production that is sensitive to rewards. Indeed, one of the major foundations of new growth theory is that when rewards are greater, more technological advances will occur. A key determinant of the rewards from technological advance are research and development (R&D) activities that have as their goal the development of specific new materials, new products, and new machines.

Patents for New Technologies To protect new techniques developed through R&D, we have a system of **patents**, in which the federal government gives the patent holder the exclusive right to make, use, and sell an invention for a period of 20 years. One can argue that this special protection given to owners of patents encourages expenditures on R&D and therefore adds to long-term economic growth. Figure 9-5 shows that

Patent
A government protection that gives an inventor the exclusive right to make, use, or sell an invention for a limited period of time (currently, 20 years).

FIGURE 9-5

U.S. Patent Grants

The U.S. Patent and Trademark Office gradually began awarding more patent grants between the early 1980s and the mid-1990s. Since 1995, the number of patents granted each year has risen in most years, except the mid and late 2000s.

Source: U.S. Patent and Trademark Office.

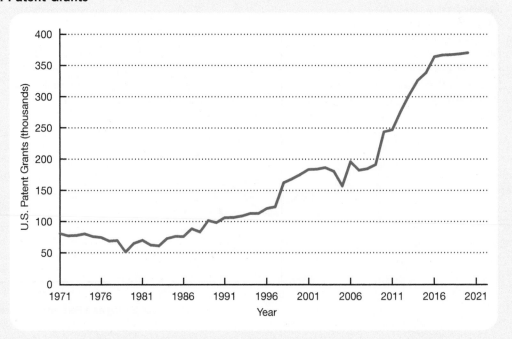

U.S. patent grants fell during the 1970s, increased steadily after 1982, surged following 1995, dropped in 2004 and 2005, and increased again starting in 2010.

As we discussed in an earlier chapter, positive externalities are benefits from an activity that are enjoyed by someone besides the instigator of the activity. In the case of R&D spending, a certain amount of the benefits go to other companies that do not have to pay for them. In addition, one country's R&D expenditures benefit other countries because they are able to import capital goods—say, computers and telecommunications networks—from technologically advanced countries and then use them as inputs in making their own industries more efficient. Furthermore, countries that import high-tech goods are able to imitate the technology. Economists David Coe of the International Monetary Fund and Elhanan Helpman of Harvard University have estimated that about a quarter of the global productivity gains of R&D investment in the top seven industrialized countries goes to other nations. For every 1 percent rise in the stock of R&D in the United States alone, productivity in the rest of the world increases by about 0.25 percent.

Do patents really contribute to more innovative activities that contribute to economic growth?

EXAMPLE

Do New Firms That Obtain Patents Really Engage in More Activities That Promote Economic Growth?

Some critics of U.S. patent policies argue that the U.S. Patent and Trademark Office (USPTO) awards too many patents. To assess whether this criticism is justified, researchers have sought to measure the benefits derived from receipt of patents by new firms, or "startups." They have found evidence that new firms that receive patents also have a substantially higher likelihood of receiving funding to pursue additional innovative activities. Success in obtaining a patent also is associated with substantially higher product sales. Startup firms that obtain new patents additionally produce output valued more highly in the marketplace than the output of new firms that fail to receive patents. Thus, in spite of some of the uncertainties associated with patents' benefits, recipient startups generally engage in additional innovative efforts of benefit to themselves and to the economic-growth process.

FOR CRITICAL THINKING

Why is innovative activity that actually yields higher-valued production required for new inventions to contribute to greater economic growth?

Sources are listed at the end of this chapter.

Innovation, Knowledge, and Human Capital

We tend to think of technological progress as, say, the invention of the microchip. But invention means little by itself. **Innovation**—the transformation of something new, such as an invention, into something that benefits the economy either by lowering production costs or by providing new goods and services—is required. Historically, technologies have moved relatively slowly from invention to innovation to widespread use. The dispersion of new technology remains for the most part slow and uncertain, however. Typically, thousands of raw ideas emerge each year at a large firm's R&D laboratories. Only a few hundred of these ideas develop into formal proposals for new processes or products. Of these proposals, the business selects perhaps a few dozen that it deems suitable for further study to explore their feasibility. After careful scrutiny, the firm concludes that only a handful of these ideas are inventions worthy of being integrated into actual production processes or launched as novel products. The firm is fortunate if one or two ultimately become successful marketplace innovations.

Innovation
Transforming an invention into something that is useful to humans.

The economist Paul Romer has added at least one other important factor that determines the rate of economic growth: the economy's store of ideas, which we call knowledge. Romer considers knowledge a factor of production that, like capital, has to be paid for by forgoing current consumption. Economies must therefore invest in knowledge just as they invest in machines. The major conclusion that Romer and other new growth theorists draw is this:

Economic growth can continue as long as we keep coming up with new ideas.

ECONOMICS IN YOUR LIFE
To contemplate further the important distinction between an initial invention and follow-up market innovations, read **A 50-Year-Old Invention Generates Unforeseen Modern Market Innovations** on page 198.

9.3 Describe how immigration and property rights influence economic growth

Indeed, knowledge, ideas, and productivity are all tied together. One of the threads is the quality of the labor force. Increases in the productivity of the labor force are a function of increases in human capital. Recall that human capital consists of the knowledge and skills that people in the workforce acquire through education, on-the-job training, and self-teaching. According to the new growth theorists, human capital has become as important as physical capital, because increases in human capital lead to more technological improvements, which in turn generate more economic growth.

Immigration, Property Rights, and Growth

New theories of economic growth have also shed light on two additional factors that play important roles in influencing a nation's rate of growth of per capita real GDP: immigration and property rights.

Population and Immigration as They Affect Economic Growth

There are several ways to view population growth as it affects economic growth. On the one hand, population growth can result in a larger labor force and increases in human capital, which contribute to economic growth. On the other hand, population growth can be seen as a drain on the economy because for any given amount of GDP, more population means lower per capita GDP.

Does immigration help spur economic growth? Yes, according to the late economist Julian Simon, who pointed out that "every time our system allows in one more immigrant, on average, the economic welfare of American citizens goes up. . . . Additional immigrants, both the legal and the illegal, raise the standard of living of U.S. natives and have little or no negative impact on any occupational or income class." He further argued that immigrants do not displace natives from jobs but rather create jobs through their purchases and by starting new businesses. Immigrants' earning and spending simply expand the economy.

Not all researchers agree with Simon, and few studies have tested the theories he and others have advanced. This area is currently the focus of much research. Such research is important in the political arena because illegal immigration has become a major source of controversy in the United States and elsewhere.

Property Rights and Entrepreneurship

If you were in a country where bank accounts and businesses were periodically confiscated by the government, how willing would you be to leave your financial assets in a savings account or to invest in a business? Certainly, you would be less willing than if such actions never occurred.

In general, the more securely private property rights are assigned, the more capital accumulation there will be. People will be willing to invest their savings in endeavors that will increase their wealth in future years. Attaining this outcome requires that property rights in their wealth be sanctioned and enforced by the government.

The legal structure of a nation is closely tied to the degree with which its citizens use their own entrepreneurial skills. In an earlier chapter, we identified entrepreneurship as the fifth factor of production. Entrepreneurs are the risk takers who seek out new ways to do things and create new products. To the extent that entrepreneurs are allowed to capture the rewards from their entrepreneurial activities, they will seek to engage in those activities. In countries where such rewards cannot be captured because of a lack of property rights, there will be less entrepreneurship. Typically, this results in fewer investments and a lower rate of growth.

WHAT HAPPENS WHEN...

national governments broaden and deepen the property rights available to their residents?

China, Eastern European nations, and Western African countries have enacted legal changes that have expanded the range of property rights available to residents and strengthened the legal force of existing property rights. In all of these nations, the legal assurance that returns from risky investments can be retained has contributed to increased investments in both human and physical capital. The consequences have been enlarged production possibilities that have generated increased economic growth in these countries.

Economic Development

How did developed countries travel paths of growth from extreme poverty to relative riches? That is the essential issue of **development economics**, which is the study of why some countries grow and develop and others do not and of policies that might help developing economies get richer. It is not enough simply to say that people in different countries are different and that is why some countries are rich and some countries are poor. Economists do not deny that different cultures have different work ethics, but they are unwilling to accept such a pat and fatalistic answer.

Look at any world map. About four-fifths of the countries you will see on the map are considered relatively poor. The goal of economists who study development is to help the more than 4.5 billion people today with low living standards join the more than 2.5 billion people who have at least moderately high living standards.

9.4 Discuss the fundamental elements that contribute to a nation's economic development

Development economics
The study of factors that contribute to the economic growth of a country.

Putting World Poverty into Perspective

Most U.S. residents cannot even begin to understand the reality of poverty in the world today. At least one-half, if not two-thirds, of the world's population lives at subsistence level, with just enough to eat for survival. Indeed, the World Bank estimates that nearly 10 percent of the world's people live on less than $2.00 per day. The official poverty line in the United States is above the annual income of at least half the human beings on the planet. This is not to say that we should ignore domestic problems with the poor and homeless simply because they are living better than many people elsewhere in the world. Rather, it is necessary for us to maintain an appropriate perspective on what are considered problems for this country relative to what are considered problems elsewhere.

The Relationship between Population Growth and Economic Development

The world's population is growing at the rate of about 2 people a second. That amounts to 172,800 a day or 63.1 million a year. Today, there are more than 7.5 billion people on earth. By 2050, according to the United Nations, the world's population will be close to leveling off at around 10 billion. Panel (a) of Figure 9-6 shows projected population growth. Panel (b) emphasizes an implication of panel (a), which is that almost all the growth in population is expected in developing nations. Many developed countries are expected to lose population over the next several decades.

Ever since the Reverend Thomas Robert Malthus wrote *An Essay on the Principle of Population* in 1798, excessive population growth has been a concern. Modern-day Malthusians are able to generate great enthusiasm for the concept that population growth is bad. Over and over, media commentators and a number of scientists tell us that rapid population growth threatens economic development and the quality of life.

Malthus Was Proved Wrong Malthus predicted that population would outstrip food supplies. This prediction has never been supported by the facts, according to

FIGURE 9-6

Expected Growth in World Population by 2050

Panel (a) displays the percentages of the world's population residing in the various continents by 2050 and shows projected percentage population changes for these continents and for selected nations. It indicates that Asia and Africa are expected to gain the most in population by the year 2050.

Panel (b) indicates that population will increase in developing countries before beginning to level off around 2050, whereas industrially advanced nations will grow very little in population in the first half of this century. *Source:* United Nations.

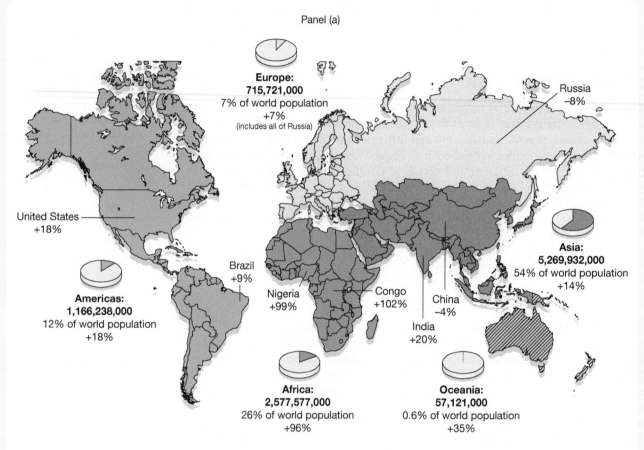

Panel (a)

Europe:
715,721,000
7% of world population
+7%
(includes all of Russia)

Russia
−8%

United States
+18%

Asia:
5,269,932,000
54% of world population
+14%

Brazil
+9%

Nigeria
+99%

Congo
+102%

China
−4%

India
+20%

Americas:
1,166,238,000
12% of world population
+18%

Africa:
2,577,577,000
26% of world population
+96%

Oceania:
57,121,000
0.6% of world population
+35%

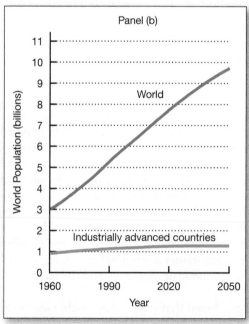

Panel (b)

economist Nicholas Eberstadt of the American Enterprise Institute for Public Policy Research. As the world's population has grown, so has the world's food stock, measured by calories per person. In addition, the price of food, corrected for inflation, has generally been falling for more than a century. The production of food has been expanding faster than the increase in demand caused by increased population.

Growth Leads to Smaller Families Furthermore, economists have found that as nations become richer, average family size declines. Otherwise stated, the more economic development occurs, the slower the population growth rate becomes. Population growth certainly has dropped throughout much of Europe and in Russia, where populations are actually declining. Predictions of birthrates in developing countries have often turned out to be overstated if those countries experience rapid economic growth. Past birthrate overpredictions have occurred for this reason in nations such as Chile, Hong Kong, Mexico, and Taiwan.

Research on population and economic development has revealed that social and economic modernization has been accompanied by a decline in childbearing significant enough to be called a demographic transition. Modernization reduces infant mortality, which in turn reduces the incentive for couples to have many children to make sure that a certain number survive to adulthood. Modernization also lowers the demand for children for a variety of reasons, not the least being that couples in more developed countries do not need to rely on their children to take care of them in old age.

The Stages of Development: Agriculture to Industry to Services

If we analyze the development of modern rich nations, we find that they went through three stages. First is the agricultural stage, when most of the population is involved in agriculture. Then comes the manufacturing stage, when much of the population becomes involved in the industrialized sector of the economy. Finally, there is a shift toward services. That is exactly what happened in the United States: The so-called tertiary, or service, sector of the economy continues to grow, whereas the manufacturing sector (and its share of employment) is declining in relative importance.

As noted in an earlier chapter, of particular significance is the requirement for specialization in a nation's comparative advantage. The doctrine of comparative advantage is particularly appropriate for the developing countries of the world. If trading is allowed among nations, a country is best off if it produces what it has a comparative advantage in producing and imports the rest. This means that many developing countries should continue to specialize in agricultural production or in labor-intensive manufactured goods.

Keys to Economic Development

According to one theory of development, a country must have a large natural resource base in order to develop. This theory goes on to assert that much of the world is running out of natural resources, thereby limiting economic growth and development. Only the narrowest definition of a natural resource, however, could lead to such an opinion. In broader terms, a natural resource is something occurring in nature that we can use for our own purposes. As emphasized by new growth theory, natural resources therefore include human capital—education and experience. Also, natural resources change over time. Several hundred years ago, for example, they did not include hydroelectric power—no one knew that such a natural resource existed or how to bring it into existence.

Natural resources by themselves are not a prerequisite for, or a guarantee of, economic development, as demonstrated by Japan's extensive development despite a lack of domestic oil resources and by Brazil's slow pace of development in spite of a vast array of natural resources. Resources must be transformed into something usable for either investment or consumption.

Economists have found that four factors seem to be highly related to the pace of economic development:

1. *Establishing a system of property rights.* As noted earlier, if you were in a country in which bank accounts and businesses were periodically confiscated by the government, you would be reluctant to leave some of your wealth in a savings account or to invest in a business. Confiscation of private property rarely takes place in developed countries. It has occurred in numerous developing countries, however. For example, private property has been nationalized in Venezuela and in Cuba. Economists have found that other things being equal, the more secure private property rights are, the more private capital accumulation and economic growth there will be.

2. *Developing an educated population.* Both theoretically and empirically, we know that a more educated workforce aids economic development because it allows individuals to build on the ideas of others. Thus, developing countries can advance more rapidly if they increase investments in education. Or, stated in the negative, economic development is difficult to sustain if a nation allows a sizable portion of its population to remain uneducated. Education allows impoverished young people to acquire skills that enable them to avoid poverty as adults.

3. *Letting "creative destruction" run its course.* The twentieth-century Harvard economist Joseph Schumpeter championed the concept of "creative destruction," through which new businesses ultimately create new jobs and economic growth in the course of destroying old jobs, old companies, and old industries. Such change is painful and costly, but it is necessary for economic advancement. Many governments in developing nations have had a history of supporting current companies and industries by discouraging new technologies and new companies from entering the marketplace. The process of creative destruction has not been allowed to work its magic in these countries.

4. *Limiting protectionism.* Open economies experience faster economic development than economies closed to international trade. Trade encourages people and businesses to discover ways to specialize so that they can become more productive and earn higher incomes. Increased productivity and subsequent increases in economic growth are the results. Thus, having fewer trade barriers promotes faster economic development.

ECONOMICS IN YOUR LIFE

An Old Invention Generates Unforeseen Modern Market Innovations

Today, Rick Durnford, captain of the ship *Maersk Detector*, will undertake a range of activities directed by images provided by C-Core, a company that has transformed facial recognition technology into a series of market innovations. Guided by satellite images and one of C-Core's remote-sensing recognition apps, Durnford and his crew have located a previously unidentified iceberg floating toward an offshore oil platform about 200 miles from Newfoundland, Canada. Durnford's crew proceeds to encircle the iceberg with thick polypropylene rope, which the *Maersk Detector* tows to a different location to proceed along a new course at safe distance from both the oil platform and ocean shipping.

C-Core's remote-sensing technology has yielded innovations beyond the realm of determining whether scatterings of white pixels in digital satellite images are 100-foot waves, pods of whales, or iceberg threats. Military and police authorities utilize one of its remote-sensing systems to detect ocean-going drug smugglers. Urban planners are adapting another of C-Core's systems to monitor how city buildings respond to tunneling for subway systems. Companies that operate offshore wind turbines are studying its potential for inspecting the turbines' underwater bases for potential structural weaknesses.

Five decades ago, no one could have envisioned how an invention intended to recognize human faces might lead to such market innovations. In fact, the innovations in remote sensing made possible by this earlier invention have expanded production possibilities and contributed to economic growth.

FOR CRITICAL THINKING

How might remote-sensing innovations that enable underwater structural inspections of offshore wind turbines make energy companies more willing to undertake additional investments in wind-turbine systems?

REAL APPLICATION

Marketing and retailing firms have pursued facial recognition technologies for the past half century. To what extent do those technologies make you better off? To what extent do they make you worse off?

Sources are listed at the end of this chapter.

ISSUES & APPLICATIONS

A Color Quest Demonstrates Why Innovation Is a Fundamental Contributor to Economic Growth

dinozzo/123RF GB Limited

CONCEPTS APPLIED

➤ Invention and Innovation

➤ Economic Growth

➤ Productivity Growth

Colors are fundamental features of many products. Hence, development of new product colors that can be applied to items using smaller amounts of chemical inputs can generate innovations that contribute to increased productivity growth and, ultimately, to economic growth.

Inventing New Shades of Color Is the Easy Part

In theory, creating a new color is not a difficult undertaking. Over the course of human history, inventors have developed a vast array of color shades.

Indeed, today at least 16.8 million shades of color can be displayed using electronic apps, some of which human eyes have difficulty distinguishing. More importantly from an economic standpoint, however, is the problem of transforming shades of color into a form that can be physically rendered by a printing device or other technique.

Why New Color Can Translate into Higher Productivity and Boost Economic Growth

Making colors transferable to a wide range of products, including cotton, linens, paints, paper, plastics, rayon, silk, velvet, and wool, requires combining chemicals to create pigments that successfully capture shades. Many inorganic chemicals used in the past to create color pigments, such as lead, cobalt, and cyanide, are now known to be unsafe for human use. Thus, modern efforts to invent new color shades intended to enhance productivity growth focus on finding shades that can be rendered in pigments using the smallest feasible set of organic chemicals that humans can use safely.

The development of pigments utilizing minimal organic-chemical resources to render most shades of black, green, and yellow has proved straightforward, as has

inventing organic pigments for subdued blue and red shades. Inventing organic pigments for bright shades of blue and red, however, has been much more challenging. Only a few years ago, after the expenditure of considerable time and effort, was a stable new organic bright blue pigment developed. Creation of this blue pigment enabled the application of bright blue shades to existing products using a smaller set of organic chemicals. Today, a global quest is under way to develop bright red shades that can be rendered in safe organic pigments using the smallest feasible set of combinations of organic chemicals. Success in this endeavor would boost productivity in transmitting novel colors to new products and, eventually, contribute to higher economic growth.

FOR CRITICAL THINKING

Why might rendering shades for products using the smallest feasible set of organic chemicals yield considerable productivity growth for a nation's economy? (*Hint:* Contemplate how many items produced by a nation's firms utilize different shades of color.)

REAL APPLICATION

What are the two benefits that you, as an individual, receive from companies using minimal inorganic (chemical) resources to create the colors of the products that you buy?

Sources are listed at the end of this chapter.

What You Should Know

Here is what you should know after reading this chapter.

LEARNING OBJECTIVES

9.1 Define economic growth and recognize the importance of economic growth rates
The rate of economic growth is the annual rate of change in per capita real GDP. This measure reflects growth in overall production of goods and services and population growth. It is an average measure that does not account for possible changes in the distribution of income or welfare costs or benefits. Economic growth compounds over time. Thus, over long intervals, small differences in growth can accumulate to produce large disparities in per capita incomes.

9.2 Explain why productivity growth, saving, and new technologies are crucial for maintaining economic growth *Fundamental elements contributing to economic growth include growth in a nation's labor productivity, which means that more output can be produced with the same labor inputs, and its saving rate, which enables expansion of investment in capital resources. New growth theory examines why individuals and businesses conduct research into inventing and developing new technologies and how this innovation process affects economic growth. A key implication of the theory is that ideas and knowledge are crucial elements of the growth process.*

9.3 Describe how immigration and property rights influence economic growth
Immigration increases a nation's population, which can have the effect of pushing down per capita GDP. Nevertheless, the resulting increase in labor resources and their employment in production contribute to economic growth. More secure property rights provide a foundation for capital accumulation and increased economic growth.

9.4 Discuss the fundamental elements that contribute to a nation's economic development
Key features shared by nations that attain higher levels of economic development are protection of property rights, significant opportunities for their residents to obtain training and education, policies that permit new companies and industries to replace older ones, and the avoidance of protectionist barriers that hinder international trade.

KEY TERMS

economic growth, 185
rule of 70, 189
Key Figures
Figure 9-1, 185
Figure 9-2, 186

labor productivity, 189
new growth theory, 192
patent, 192
innovation, 193
Key Figures
Figure 9-3, 190
Figure 9-4, 191
Figure 9-5, 192

development economics, 195
Key Figure
Figure 9-6, 196

PROBLEMS

9-1. The graph to the right shows a production possibilities curve for 2023 and two potential production possibilities curves for 2024, denoted 2024$_A$ and 2024$_B$.

    a. Which of the labeled points corresponds to maximum feasible 2020 production that is more likely to be associated with the curve denoted 2024$_A$?

    b. Which of the labeled points corresponds to maximum feasible 2020 production that is more likely to be associated with the curve denoted 2024$_B$?

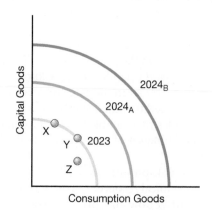

9-2. A nation's capital goods wear out over time, so a portion of its capital goods become unusable every year. Last year, its residents decided to produce no capital goods. It has experienced no growth in its population or in the amounts of other productive resources during the past year. In addition, the nation's technology and resource productivity have remained unchanged during the past year. Will the nation's economic growth rate for the current year be negative, zero, or positive?

9-3. In the situation described in Problem 9-2, suppose that vocational training during the past year enables the people of this nation to repair all capital goods so that they continue to function as well as new. All other factors are unchanged, however. In light of this single change to the conditions faced in this nation, will the nation's economic growth rate for the current year be negative, zero, or positive?

9-4. Consider the following data. What is the per capita real GDP in each of these countries?

Country	Population (millions)	Real GDP ($ billions)
A	10	55
B	20	60
C	5	70

9-5. Suppose that during the next 10 years, real GDP triples and population doubles in each of the nations in Problem 9-4. What will per capita real GDP be in each country after 10 years have passed?

9-6. Consider the following table displaying annual growth rates for nations X, Y, and Z, each of which entered 2020 with real per capita GDP equal to $20,000.

	Annual Growth Rate (%)			
Country	2020	2021	2022	2023
X	7	1	3	4
Y	4	5	7	9
Z	5	5	3	2

a. Which nation most likely experienced a sizable earthquake in late 2020 that destroyed a significant portion of its stock of capital goods, but was followed by speedy investments in rebuilding the nation's capital stock? What is this nation's per capita real GDP at the end of 2023, rounded to the nearest dollar?

b. Which nation most likely adopted policies in 2020 that encouraged a gradual shift in production from capital goods to consumption goods? What is this nation's per capita real GDP at the end of 2023, rounded to the nearest dollar?

c. Which nation most likely adopted policies in 2020 that encouraged a quick shift in production from consumption goods to capital goods? What is this nation's per capita real GDP at the end of 2023, rounded to the nearest dollar?

9-7. Per capita real GDP grows at a rate of 3 percent in country F and at a rate of 6 percent in country G. Both begin with equal levels of per capita real GDP. Use Table 9-3 to determine how much higher per capita real GDP will be in country G after 20 years. How much higher will real GDP be in country G than in country F after 40 years?

9-8. Since the early 1990s, the average rate of growth of per capita real GDP in Mozambique has been 3 percent per year, compared with a growth rate of 8 percent in China. Refer to Table 9-3. If a typical resident of each of these nations begins this year with a per capita real GDP of $3,000 per year and past growth rates persist, about how many more dollars' worth of real GDP per capita would the person in China be earning 10 years from now than the individual in Mozambique?

9-9. On the basis of the information in Problem 9-8 and reference to Table 9-3, about how many more dollars' worth of real GDP per capita would the person in China be earning 50 years from now than the individual in Mozambique?

9-10. In 2021, a nation's population was 10 million. Its nominal GDP was $40 billion, and its price index was 100. In 2022, its population had increased to 12 million, its nominal GDP had risen to $57.6 billion, and its price index had increased to 120. What was this nation's economic growth rate during the year?

9-11. Between the start of 2021 and the start of 2022, a country's economic growth rate was 4 percent. Its population did not change during the year, nor did its price level. What was the rate of increase of the country's nominal GDP during this one-year interval?

9-12. In 2021, a nation's population was 10 million, its real GDP was $1.21 billion, and its GDP deflator had a value of 121. By 2022, its population had increased to 12 million, its real GDP had risen to $1.5 billion, and its GDP deflator had a value of 125. What was the percentage change in per capita real GDP between 2021 and 2022?

9-13. A nation's per capita real GDP was $2,000 in 2020, and the nation's population was 5 million in that year. Between 2020 and 2021, the inflation rate in this country was 5 percent, and the nation's annual rate of economic growth was 10 percent. Its population remained unchanged. What was per capita real GDP in 2021? What was the *level* of real GDP in 2021?

9-14. Brazil has a population of about 210 million, with about 150 million over the age of 15. Of these, an estimated 25 percent, or 37.5 million people, are functionally illiterate. The typical literate individual reads only about two nonacademic books per year, which is less than half the number read by the typical literate U.S. or European resident. Answer the following questions solely from the perspective of new growth theory:

a. Discuss the implications of Brazil's literacy and reading rates for its growth prospects in light of the key tenets of new growth theory.

b. What types of policies might Brazil implement to improve its growth prospects? Explain.

9-15. Based on data in Table 9-1 and the rule of 70, if U.S. per capita real GDP continues to grow at the average rate it has experienced since 1990, about how many years will be required for it to double?

9-16. Based on data in Table 9-1 and the rule of 70, if India's per capita real GDP continues to grow at the average rate it has experienced since 1990, about how many years will be required for it to double?

9-17. Based on data in Table 9-1 and in Table 9-3, if China's per capita real GDP continues to grow at the average rate it has experienced since 1990, will its per capita real GDP be twice as high as it is today within a decade? Explain your reasoning.

REFERENCES

AI—DECISION MAKING THROUGH DATA: Lengthy, Deep Recessions and Long-Run Economic Growth

Stephen Broadberry and John Wallis, "Growing, Shrinking, and Long-Run Economic Performance: Historical Perspectives on Economic Development," Presented at Economic Development Workshop, Center for Economic Institutions, Hitotsubashi University, June 1, 2018.

Jerg Gutmann and Stefan Voigt, "The Rule of Law: Measurement and Deep Roots," *European Journal of Political Economy*, 2018.

A.G. Lisitsyn-Svetlanov, A.V. Mal'ko, and S.F. Afanas'ev, "The Rule of Law as a Factor of Economic Growth," *Herald of the Russian Academy of Sciences*, 2018.

BEHAVIORAL EXAMPLE: Is Patience a Virtue for Economic Growth?

James Andreoni, Michael Kuhn, John List, Anya Samek, Kevin Sokal, and Charles Sprenger, "Toward an Understanding of the Development of Time Preference: Evidence from Field Experiments," National Bureau of Economic Research Working Paper No. 25590, February 2019.

Vonseok Choi and Jong-soo Han, "Time Preference and Savings Behavior," *Applied Economics Letters*, 2018.

Mark Dodgson and David Gann, "The Missing Ingredient in Innovation: Patience," *World Economic Forum*, April 26, 2018.

EXAMPLE: Do New Firms That Obtain Patents Really Engage in More Activities That Promote Economic Growth?

"LexisNexis PatentAdvisor® Rolls Out Examiner Lottery Framework™, A Suite of Analytics to Guide Your Patent Prosecution Strategy with the USPTO," BizJournals.com (https://www.bizjournals.com/prnewswire/press_releases/2019/01/14/UN22719), January 14, 2019.

Amaia Altuzarra, "R&D and Patents: Is It a Two-Way Street?" *Economics of Innovation and New Tecnhology*, 2018.

Changkyu Choi and Myung Hoon Yi, "The Internet, R&D Expenditures, and Economic Growth," *Applied Economics Letters*, 2018.

ECONOMICS IN YOUR LIFE: A 50-Year-Old Invention Generates Unforeseen Modern Market Innovations

"International Ice Patrol Starts Operations, Informing for Icebergs," Safety4Sea.com (https://safety4sea.com/international-ice-patrol-starts-operations-informing-for-icebergs/), February 8, 2019.

C-Core, "Remote-Sensing Systems" (https://www.c-core.ca/remote-sensing-systems), 2019.

Bob Berwyn, "'Extreme' Iceberg Seasons Threaten Oil Rigs and Shipping as the Arctic Warms," *Inside Climate News*, March 28, 2018.

ISSUES & APPLICATIONS: A Color Quest Demonstrates Why Innovation Is a Fundamental Contributor to Economic Growth

Kerry Pianoforte, "Pigments Update," Coatings World (https://www.coatingsworld.com/contents/view_online-exclusives/2019-01-04/pigments-update-part-2), January 4, 2019.

Dave Gebhardt, "The Economics of Natural Color Pigments," Sensient Food Colors (https://sensientfoodcolors.com/en-us/research-development/economics-natural-color-pigments/), March 2018.

Zach Schonbrun, "The Quest for the Next Billion-Dollar Color," *Bloomberg Businessweek*, April 23, 2018.

10

Real GDP and the Price Level in the Long Run

scanrail/123RF GB Limited

LEARNING OBJECTIVES

After reading this chapter, you should be able to:

10.1 Discuss the concept of long-run aggregate supply and describe the effect of economic growth on the long-run aggregate supply curve

10.2 Explain why the aggregate demand curve slopes downward and list key factors that cause this curve to shift

10.3 Evaluate the meaning of long-run equilibrium for the economy as a whole and explain why economic growth can cause deflation

10.4 Evaluate likely reasons for persistent inflation in recent decades

Iceland is endowed with two resources in particular abundance: chilly outdoor temperatures and steam rising through rocky vents along tectonic faults. Until recently, the natural beauty associated with the country's unique geography and geology contributed to its economic performance primarily by attracting large numbers of foreign tourists. In recent years, however, the nation's natural endowments of cold climate and geothermal steam have generated a new form of productive activity. Firms have been constructing and staffing *data centers* housing equipment that global digital firms utilize to maintain online apps, to store large volumes of digital information, and to sustain stable Internet connectivity. The consequence has been an upsurge in Iceland's long-run capability to produce real GDP, which in this chapter you will learn has constituted an increase in the nation's *long-run aggregate supply*. You will also learn in this chapter about the resulting implications for Iceland's equilibrium real GDP and for its price level.

between 2007 and 2015, U.S. real GDP increased an average of about $200 billion per year, or only about 1.2 percent per year? As a consequence, during this period, the United States experienced the slowest overall growth in inflation-adjusted economic activity since the Great Depression of the 1930s. In contrast, since 2015, U.S. real GDP has increased an average of about $700 billion per year, or at a rate exceeding 2.5 percent per year. In this chapter, you will learn about how to analyze the essential implications of variations in real GDP growth using the tools of *aggregate supply* and *aggregate demand*.

10.1 Discuss the concept of long-run aggregate supply and describe the effect of economic growth on the long-run aggregate supply curve

Aggregate supply
The total of all planned production for the economy.

Long-run aggregate supply (*LRAS*) curve
A vertical line representing the real output of goods and services after full adjustment has occurred. It can also be viewed as representing the real GDP of the economy under conditions of full employment—the full-employment level of real GDP.

Base-year dollars
The value of a current sum expressed in terms of prices in a base year.

Endowments
The various resources in an economy, including both physical resources and such human resources as ingenuity and management skills.

Output Growth and the Long-Run Aggregate Supply Curve

Previously, we showed the derivation of the production possibilities curve (PPC). At any point in time, the economy can be inside or on the PPC but never outside it. Along the PPC, a country's resources are fully employed in the production of goods and services, and the sum total of the inflation-adjusted value of all final goods and services produced is the nation's real GDP. Economists refer to the total of all planned production for the entire economy as the **aggregate supply** of real output.

The Long-Run Aggregate Supply Curve

Put yourself in a world in which nothing has been changing, year in and year out. The price level has not changed. Technology has not changed. The prices of inputs that firms must purchase have not changed. Labor productivity has not changed. All resources are fully employed, so the economy operates on its production possibilities curve, such as the one depicted in panel (a) of Figure 10-1. This is a world that is fully adjusted and in which people have all the information they are ever going to have about that world. The **long-run aggregate supply (*LRAS*) curve** in this world is some amount of real GDP—say, $22 trillion of real GDP—which is the value of the flow of production of final goods and services measured in **base-year dollars.**

We can represent long-run aggregate supply by a vertical line at $22 trillion of real GDP. This is what you see in panel (b) of the figure. That curve, labeled *LRAS*, is a vertical line determined by technology and **endowments,** or resources that exist in

FIGURE 10-1

The Production Possibilities Curve and the Economy's Long-Run Aggregate Supply Curve

At a point in time, a nation's base of resources and its technological capabilities define the position of its production possibilities curve (PPC), as shown in panel (a). This defines the real GDP that the nation can produce when resources are fully employed, which determines the position of the long-run aggregate supply curve (*LRAS*) displayed in panel (b). Because people have complete information and input prices adjust fully in the long run, the *LRAS* is vertical.

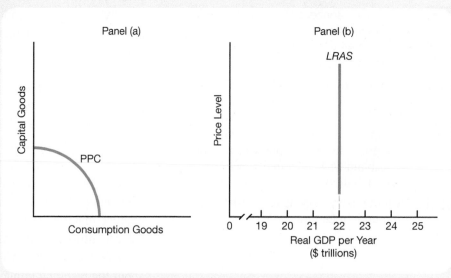

our economy. It is the full-information and full-adjustment level of real output of goods and services. It is the level of real GDP that will continue being produced year after year, forever, if nothing changes.

The *LRAS* Curve and Full-Employment Real GDP Another way of viewing the *LRAS* is to think of it as the full-employment level of real GDP. When the economy reaches full employment along its production possibilities curve, no further adjustments will occur unless a change occurs in the other variables that we are assuming to be stable.

Some economists suggest that the *LRAS* occurs at the level of real GDP consistent with the natural rate of unemployment, the unemployment rate that occurs in an economy with full adjustment in the long run. As we discussed in an earlier chapter, many economists like to think of the natural rate of unemployment as consisting of frictional and structural unemployment.

Why the *LRAS* Curve Is Vertical To understand why the *LRAS* is vertical, think about the long run. To an economist examining the economy as a whole, the long run is a sufficiently long period that all factors of production and prices, including wages and other input prices, can change.

A change in the level of prices of goods and services has no effect on real GDP per year in the long run, because higher prices will be accompanied by comparable changes in input prices. Suppliers will therefore have no incentive to increase or decrease their production of goods and services. Remember that in the long run, everybody has full information, and there is full adjustment to price level changes. (Of course, this is not necessarily true in the short run, as we shall discuss in a later chapter.)

Economic Growth and Long-Run Aggregate Supply

The determinants of growth in per capita real GDP are the annual growth rate of labor, the rate of year-to-year capital accumulation, and the rate of growth of the productivity of labor and capital. As time goes by, population gradually increases, and labor force participation rates may even rise. The capital stock typically grows as businesses add such capital equipment as new information-technology hardware. Furthermore, technology improves. Thus, the economy's production possibilities increase, and as a consequence, the production possibilities curve shifts outward, as shown in panel (a) of Figure 10-2.

FIGURE 10-2

The Long-Run Aggregate Supply Curve and Shifts in It

In panel (a), we show the meaning of economic growth. Over time, the production possibilities curve shifts outward. In panel (b), we demonstrate the same principle by showing the long-run aggregate supply curve initially as a vertical line at $21.3 trillion of real GDP per year. As our productive abilities increase, the *LRAS* moves outward to *LRAS*₂₀₂₄ at $23.1 trillion.

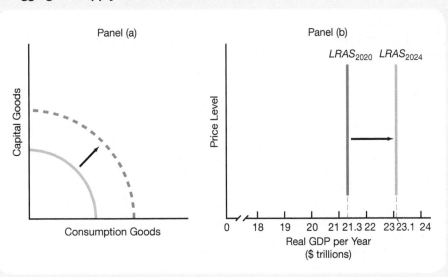

FIGURE 10-3

A Sample Long-Run Growth Path for Real GDP

Year-to-year shifts in the long-run aggregate supply curve yield a long-run trend path for real GDP growth. In this example, from 2022 onward, real GDP grows by a steady 3 percent per year.

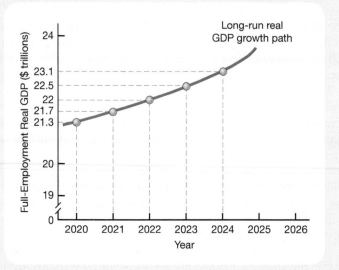

ECONOMICS IN YOUR LIFE

To contemplate a policy aimed at shifting Japan's *LRAS* curve rightward, take a look at **Why Japan's Government Aims to Increase Long-Run Aggregate Supply by *Reducing* People's Hours at Work** on page 216.

The result is economic growth: Aggregate real GDP and per capita real GDP increase. This means that in a growing economy such as ours, the *LRAS* will shift outward to the right, as in panel (b). We have drawn the *LRAS* for the year 2024 to the right of our original *LRAS* of $21.3 trillion of real GDP. We assume that between 2020 and 2024, real GDP increases to $23.1 trillion, to give us the position of the $LRAS_{2024}$ curve. Thus, it is to the right of the original *LRAS* curve.

We may conclude that in a growing economy, the *LRAS* shifts ever farther to the right over time. If the *LRAS* happened to shift rightward at a constant pace, real GDP would increase at a steady annual rate. As shown in Figure 10-3, this means that real GDP would increase along a long-run, or *trend*, path that is an upward-sloping line. Thus, the *LRAS* in Figure 10-2 shifts rightward from $21.3 trillion in 2020 to $23.1 trillion in 2024.

What types of public investments are some governments currently pursuing in hopes of obtaining big-data-generated increases in long-run aggregate supply?

AI | DECISION MAKING THROUGH DATA

Governments Seeking Growth in Long-Run Aggregate Supply

Considerable evidence indicates that the main source of growth in long-run aggregate supply is economic growth generated by increases in private firms' utilization of labor and capital resources and growth of productivity of these resources. Nevertheless, governments in China and the European Union are making multi-billion-dollar public-sector investments in AI techniques. These governments hope that research into new methods for conducting automated data analytics and development of novel forms of machine learning will contribute to increases in long-run aggregate supply. The governments are hoping that once they have provided an "AI infrastructure," private investments in human and physical

capital will follow and generate further increases in economic growth that will expand long-run aggregate supply.

FOR CRITICAL THINKING

Would governmental investments in an "AI infrastructure" likely yield significant additional increases in a nation's long-run aggregate supply if private firms were to utilize their own AI technologies independently of this infrastructure? (Hint: If private firms were to employ solely AI technologies that they had developed on their own initiative, could a governmental AI "infrastructure" influence the firms' production possibilities?)

Sources are listed at the end of this chapter.

Total Expenditures and Aggregate Demand

10.2 Explain why the aggregate demand curve slopes downward and list key factors that cause this curve to shift

In equilibrium, individuals, businesses, and governments purchase all the goods and services produced, valued in trillions of real dollars. As explained in earlier chapters, GDP is the dollar value of total expenditures on domestically produced final goods and services. Because all expenditures are made by individuals, firms, or governments, the total value of these expenditures must be what these market participants decide it shall be.

The Importance of Spending Decisions for the Level of Real GDP

The decisions of individuals, managers of firms, and government officials determine the annual dollar value of total expenditures. You can certainly see this in your role as an individual. You decide what the total dollar amount of your expenditures will be in a year. You decide how much you want to spend and how much you want to save. Thus, if we want to know what determines the total value of GDP, the answer is clear: the spending decisions of individuals like you, firms, and local, state, and national governments. In an open economy, we must also include foreign individuals, firms, and governments (foreign residents, for short) that decide to spend their inflation-adjusted incomes in the United States.

Simply stating that the dollar value of total expenditures in this country depends on what individuals, firms, governments, and foreign residents decide to do really doesn't tell us much, though. Two important issues remain:

1. What determines the total amount that individuals, firms, governments, and foreign residents want to spend?

2. What determines the equilibrium price level and the rate of inflation (or deflation)?

The *LRAS* tells us only about the economy's long-run real GDP. To answer these additional questions, we must consider another important concept. This is **aggregate demand,** which is the total of all *planned* real expenditures in the economy.

Aggregate demand
The total of all planned expenditures in the entire economy.

The Aggregate Demand Curve

The **aggregate demand curve,** *AD*, gives the various quantities of all final commodities demanded at various price levels, all other things held constant. Recall the components of GDP: consumption spending, investment expenditures, government purchases, and net foreign demand for domestic production. They are all components of aggregate demand. Throughout this chapter and the next, whenever you see the aggregate demand curve, realize that it is a shorthand way of talking about the components of GDP that are measured by government statisticians when they calculate total economic activity each year. In a later chapter, you will look more closely at the relationship between these components and, in particular, at how consumption spending depends on income.

Aggregate demand curve
A curve showing planned purchase rates for all final goods and services in the economy at various price levels, all other things held constant.

The aggregate demand curve gives the total amount, measured in base-year dollars, of *real* domestic final goods and services that will be purchased at each price level—everything produced for final use by households, businesses, the government, and foreign (non-U.S.) residents. It includes iPads, socks, shoes, medical and legal services, digital devices, and millions of other goods and services that people buy each year.

Depicting the Aggregate Demand Curve A graphical representation of the aggregate demand curve is seen in Figure 10-4. On the horizontal axis, real GDP is measured. For our measure of the price level, we use the GDP price deflator on the vertical axis.

The aggregate demand curve is labeled *AD*. If the GDP deflator is 110, aggregate quantity demanded is $22 trillion per year (point *A*). At the price level 115, it is $21 trillion per year (point *B*). At the price level 120, it is $20 trillion per year (point *C*).

FIGURE 10-4
The Aggregate Demand Curve

The aggregate demand curve, *AD*, slopes downward. If the price level is 110, we will be at point *A* with $22 trillion of real GDP demanded per year. As the price level increases to 115 and to 120, we move up the aggregate demand curve to points *B* and *C*.

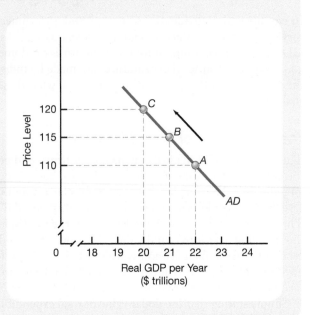

The higher the price level, the lower the total real amount of final goods and services demanded in the economy, everything else remaining constant, as shown by the arrow along *AD* in Figure 10-4. Conversely, the lower the price level, the higher the total real GDP demanded by the economy, everything else staying constant.

Planned Spending in the U.S. Economy Let's take the year 2020. Estimates based on U.S. Department of Commerce preliminary statistics reveal the following information:

- Nominal GDP was estimated to be $22,173.5 billion.

- The price level as measured by the GDP deflator was about 114.8 (base year is 2012, for which the index equals 100).

- Real GDP was approximately $19,321.6 billion in 2012 dollars.

What can we say about 2020? Given the dollar cost of buying goods and services and all of the other factors that go into spending decisions by individuals, firms, governments, and foreign residents, the total amount of planned spending on final goods and services by firms, individuals, governments, and foreign residents was $19,321.6 billion in 2020 (in terms of 2012 dollars).

What Happens When the Price Level Rises?

What if the price level in the economy rose to 160 tomorrow? What would happen to the amount of real goods and services that individuals, firms, governments, and foreigners wish to purchase in the United States? We know that when the price of one good or service rises, the quantity of it demanded will fall. But here we are talking about the *price level*—the average price of *all* goods and services in the economy.

The answer is still that the total quantities of real goods and services demanded would fall, but the reasons are different. When the price of one good or service goes up, the consumer substitutes other goods and services. For the entire economy, when the price level goes up, the consumer doesn't simply substitute one good for another, for now we are dealing with the demand for *all* goods and services in the nation. There are *economywide* reasons that cause the aggregate demand curve to slope downward.

They involve at least three distinct forces: the *real-balance effect*, the *interest rate effect*, and the *open economy effect*.

The Real-Balance Effect

A rise in the price level will have an effect on spending. Individuals, firms, governments, and foreign residents carry out transactions using money, a portion of which consists of currency and coins that you have in your pocket (or stashed away) right now. Because people use money to purchase goods and services, the amount of money that people have influences the amount of goods and services they want to buy.

An Example If you find a $100 bill on the sidewalk, the amount of money you have increases. Given your now greater level of money, or cash, balances—currency in this case—you will almost surely increase your spending on goods and services.

Similarly, if your pocket is picked while you are at the mall, your desired spending would be affected. For instance, if your wallet had $150 in it when it was stolen, the reduction in your cash balances—in this case, currency—would no doubt cause you to reduce your planned expenditures. You would ultimately buy fewer goods and services.

Contemplating the Real-Balance Effect This response is sometimes called the **real-balance effect** (or *wealth effect*) because it relates to the real value of your cash balances. While your *nominal* cash balances may remain the same, any change in the price level will cause a change in the *real* value of those cash balances—hence the real-balance effect on total planned expenditures.

When you think of the real-balance effect, just think of what happens to your real wealth if you have, say, a $100 bill hidden under your mattress. If the price level increases by 5 percent, the purchasing power of that $100 bill drops by 5 percent, so you have become less wealthy. You will reduce your purchases of all goods and services by some small amount.

The Interest Rate Effect

There is a more subtle but equally important effect on your desire to spend. A higher price level leaves people with too few money balances. Hence, they try to borrow more (or lend less) to replenish their real money holdings. This response drives up interest rates. Higher interest rates raise borrowing costs for consumers and businesses. They will borrow less and consequently spend less. The fact that a higher price level pushes up interest rates and thereby reduces borrowing and spending is known as the **interest rate effect.**

Higher interest rates make it more costly for people to finance purchases of houses and cars. Higher interest rates also make it less profitable for firms to install new equipment and to erect new office buildings. Whether we are talking about individuals or firms, a rise in the price level will cause higher interest rates, which in turn reduce the amount of goods and services that people are willing to purchase. Therefore, an increase in the price level will tend to reduce total planned expenditures. (The opposite occurs if the price level declines.)

The Open Economy Effect: The Substitution of Foreign Goods

Recall that GDP includes net exports—the difference between exports and imports. In an open economy, we buy imports from other countries and ultimately pay for them through the foreign exchange market. The same is true for foreign residents who purchase our goods (exports).

Given any set of exchange rates between the U.S. dollar and other currencies, an increase in the price level in the United States makes U.S. goods more expensive relative to foreign goods. Foreign residents have downward-sloping demand curves for U.S. goods. When the relative price of U.S. goods goes up, foreign residents buy fewer U.S. goods and more of their own. At home, relatively cheaper prices for foreign goods cause U.S. residents to want to buy more foreign goods instead of domestically produced goods. Thus, when the domestic price level rises, the result is a fall in exports and a rise in imports. That means that a price level increase tends to reduce net exports, thereby reducing the amount of real goods and services purchased in the United States. This is known as the **open economy effect.**

Real-balance effect
The change in expenditures resulting from a change in the real value of money balances when the price level changes, all other things held constant; also called the *wealth effect.*

Interest rate effect
One of the reasons that the aggregate demand curve slopes downward: Higher price levels increase the interest rate, which in turn causes businesses and consumers to reduce desired spending due to the higher cost of borrowing.

Open economy effect
One of the reasons that the aggregate demand curve slopes downward: A higher price level induces foreign residents to buy fewer U.S.-made goods and U.S. residents to buy more foreign-made goods, thereby reducing net exports and decreasing the amount of real goods and services purchased in the United States.

What Happens When the Price Level Falls?

What about the reverse? Suppose now that the GDP deflator falls to 100 from an initial level of 120. You should be able to trace the three effects on desired purchases of goods and services. Specifically, how do the real-balance, interest rate, and open economy effects cause people to want to buy more? You should come to the conclusion that the lower the price level, the greater the total planned spending on goods and services.

The aggregate demand curve, *AD*, shows the quantity of aggregate output that will be demanded at alternative price levels. It is downward sloping, just like the demand curve for individual goods. The higher the price level, the lower the real amount of total planned expenditures, and vice versa.

Demand for All Goods and Services versus Demand for a Single Good or Service

Even though the aggregate demand curve, *AD*, in Figure 10-4 looks similar to the one for individual demand, *D*, for a single good or service that you encountered in earlier chapters, the two are not the same. When we derive the aggregate demand curve, we are looking at the entire economic system. The aggregate demand curve, *AD*, differs from an individual demand curve, *D*, because we are looking at total planned expenditures on *all* goods and services when we construct *AD*.

Shifts in the Aggregate Demand Curve

Any time a nonprice determinant of demand for a particular item changes, the demand curve will shift inward to the left or outward to the right. The same analysis holds for the aggregate demand curve, except we are now talking about the non-price-level determinants of aggregate demand. So, when we ask the question, "What determines the position of the aggregate demand curve?" the fundamental proposition is as follows:

> *Any non-price-level change that increases aggregate spending (on domestic goods) shifts AD to the right. Any non-price-level change that decreases aggregate spending (on domestic goods) shifts AD to the left.*

The list of potential determinants of the position of the aggregate demand curve is long. Some of the most important "curve shifters" for aggregate demand are presented in Table 10-1.

TABLE 10-1

Determinants of Aggregate Demand

Aggregate demand consists of the demand for domestically produced consumption goods, investment goods, government purchases, and net exports. Consequently, any change in total planned spending on any one of these components of real GDP will cause a change in aggregate demand. Some possibilities are listed here.

Changes That Cause an Increase in Aggregate Demand	Changes That Cause a Decrease in Aggregate Demand
An increase in the amount of money in circulation	A decrease in the amount of money in circulation
Increased security about jobs and future income	Decreased security about jobs and future income
Improvements in economic conditions in other countries	Declines in economic conditions in other countries
A reduction in real interest rates (nominal interest rates corrected for inflation) not due to price level changes	A rise in real interest rates (nominal interest rates corrected for inflation) not due to price level changes
Tax decreases	Tax increases
A drop in the foreign exchange value of the dollar	A rise in the foreign exchange value of the dollar

WHAT HAPPENS WHEN...

a tax reduction is implemented at the same time that people experience improved economic security about jobs and future incomes?

In fact, both of these events have taken place in recent years. Both a tax reduction and improved economic security about jobs and future incomes generate increases in aggregate demand. Hence, the combined effect, which the U.S. economy actually experienced during those years, is a rightward shift in the position of the economy's aggregate demand curve.

Long-Run Equilibrium and the Price Level

10.3 Evaluate the meaning of long-run equilibrium for the economy as a whole and explain why economic growth can cause deflation

Equilibrium in a market for a particular good or service occurs where the demand and supply curves intersect. The same is true for the economy as a whole, as shown in Figure 10-5: The equilibrium price level occurs at the point where the aggregate demand curve *(AD)* crosses the long-run aggregate supply curve *(LRAS)*. At this equilibrium price level of 120, the total of all planned real expenditures for the entire economy is equal to actual real GDP produced by firms after all adjustments have taken place. Thus, the equilibrium depicted in Figure 10-5 is the economy's *long-run equilibrium*.

The Long-Run Equilibrium Price Level

Note in Figure 10-5 that if the price level were to increase to 140, actual real GDP of $22 trillion would exceed total planned real expenditures real GDP of $21 trillion. More goods and services would be produced than people wish to purchase. As a result, the price level would tend to fall.

In contrast, if the price level were 100, then $23 trillion of total planned real expenditures by individuals, businesses, and the government would exceed actual real GDP of $22 trillion. The price level would rise toward 120, and higher prices would induce individuals, businesses, and the government to cut back on planned real spending.

FIGURE 10-5

Long-Run Economywide Equilibrium

For the economy as a whole, long-run equilibrium occurs at the price level where the aggregate demand curve crosses the long-run aggregate supply curve. At this long-run equilibrium price level, which is 120 in the diagram, total planned real expenditures equal real GDP at full employment, which in our example is a real GDP of $22 trillion.

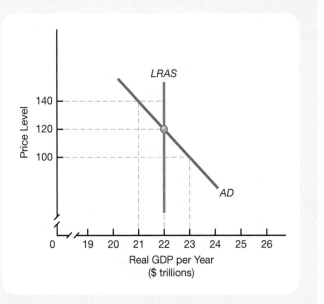

The Effects of Economic Growth on the Price Level

We now have a basic theory of how real GDP and the price level are determined in the long run when all of a nation's resources can change over time and all input prices can adjust fully to changes in the overall level of prices of goods and services that firms produce. Let's begin by evaluating the effects of economic growth on the nation's price level.

Economic Growth and Secular Deflation Take a look at panel (a) of Figure 10-6, which shows what happens, other things being equal, when the *LRAS* shifts rightward over time. If the economy were to grow steadily during, say, a 10-year interval, the long-run aggregate supply schedule would shift to the right, from $LRAS_1$ to $LRAS_2$. In panel (a), this results in a downward movement along the aggregate demand schedule. The equilibrium price level falls, from 120 to 80.

Thus, if all factors that affect total planned real expenditures are unchanged, so that the aggregate demand curve does not noticeably move during the 10-year period of real GDP growth, the growing economy in the example would experience deflation. This is known as **secular deflation,** or a persistently declining price level resulting from economic growth in the presence of relatively unchanged aggregate demand.

Secular deflation
A persistent decline in prices resulting from economic growth in the presence of stable aggregate demand.

Secular Deflation in the United States In the United States, between 1872 and 1894, the price of bricks fell by 50 percent, the price of sugar by 67 percent, the price of wheat by 69 percent, the price of nails by 70 percent, and the price of copper by nearly 75 percent. Founders of a late-nineteenth-century political movement called *populism* offered a proposal for ending deflation: They wanted the government to issue new money backed by silver. As noted in Table 10-1, an increase in the quantity of money in circulation causes the aggregate demand curve to shift to the right. In panel (b) of Figure 10-6, we see that the increase in the quantity of money would indeed have pushed the price level back upward, because the *AD* curve would shift from AD_1 to AD_2.

FIGURE 10-6

Secular Deflation versus Long-Run Price Stability in a Growing Economy

Panel (a) illustrates what happens when economic growth occurs without a corresponding increase in aggregate demand. The result is a decline in the price level over time, known as *secular deflation*. Panel (b) shows that, in principle, secular deflation can be eliminated if the aggregate demand curve shifts rightward at the same pace that the long-run aggregate supply curve shifts to the right.

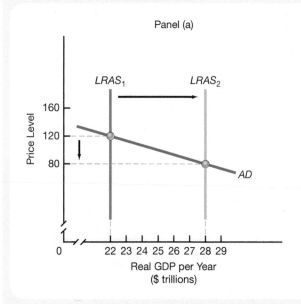

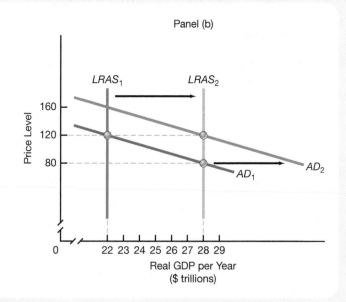

Why has the long-run equilibrium price level failed to increase very noticeably in nations that use euros as their circulating money?

INTERNATIONAL EXAMPLE

Explaining Low Inflation in the "Eurozone"

The rate of increase in the price level for the 19 countries that use euros as money—the "Eurozone"—has been much lower during the past few years than was true for a number of preceding years. One reason for this has been that the growth of the quantity of money in circulation has been lower than was observed in prior years. As a consequence, the Eurozone's aggregate demand curve has shifted only slightly to the right. Another reason is that overall growth of real GDP has been somewhat higher over the past few years than during many of the preceding years. Hence, the Eurozone's long-run aggregate supply curve shifted rightward at a slightly speedier pace than previously. The net effect was a decreased rate of growth in the price level.

FOR CRITICAL THINKING

What would happen to the Eurozone price level if the quantity of euros in circulation were to decline while the long-run aggregate supply curve continued to shift rightward? Explain briefly.

Sources are listed at the end of this chapter.

Nevertheless, money growth remained low for several more years. Not until the early twentieth century would the United States put an end to secular deflation, namely, by creating a new monetary system.

Causes of Inflation

10.4 Evaluate likely reasons for persistent inflation in recent decades

Of course, so far during your lifetime, deflation has not been a problem in the United States. Instead, what you have experienced is inflation. Figure 10-7 shows annual U.S. inflation rates for the past few decades. Clearly, inflation rates have been variable. The other obvious fact, however, is that inflation rates have been consistently *positive*. The price level in the United States has *risen* almost every year. For today's United States, secular deflation has not been a big political issue. If anything, it is secular *inflation* that has generally occurred.

FIGURE 10-7

Annual U.S. inflation rates rose considerably during the 1970s but declined to lower levels after the 1980s. The inflation rate has declined significantly in some years after creeping upward during the early and middle 2000s.

Sources: Economic Report of the President; Economic Indicators, various issues.

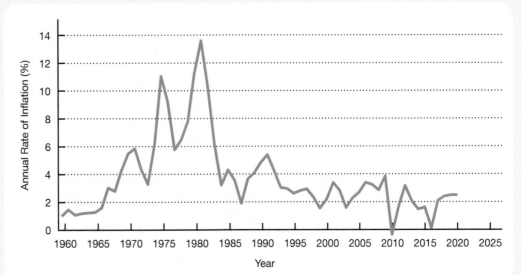

Inflation Rates in the United States

FIGURE 10-8

Explaining Persistent Inflation

As shown in panel (a), it is possible for a decline in long-run aggregate supply to cause a rise in the price level. Long-run aggregate supply *increases* in a growing economy, however, so this cannot explain the observation of persistent U.S. inflation. Panel (b) provides the actual explanation of persistent inflation in the United States and most other nations today, which is that increases in aggregate demand push up the long-run equilibrium price level. Thus, it is possible to explain persistent inflation if the aggregate demand curve shifts rightward at a faster pace than the long-run aggregate supply curve.

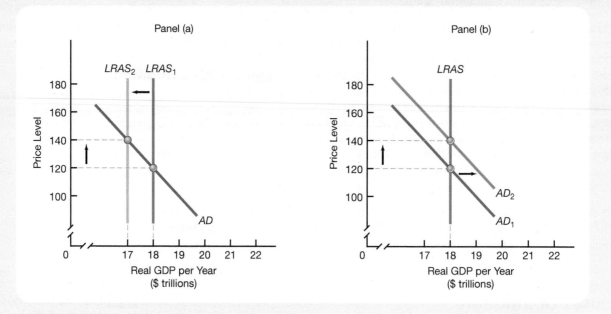

Supply-Side Inflation?

What causes such persistent inflation? The model of aggregate demand and long-run aggregate supply provides two possible explanations for inflation. One potential cause is depicted in panel (a) of Figure 10-8. This panel shows a rise in the price level caused by a *decline in long-run aggregate supply*. Hence, one possible reason for persistent inflation would be continual reductions in economywide production.

A leftward shift in the aggregate supply schedule could be caused by several factors, such as reductions in labor force participation, higher marginal tax rates on wages, or the provision of government benefits that give households incentives *not* to supply labor services to firms. Tax rates and government benefits have increased during recent decades, but so has the U.S. population. The significant overall rise in real GDP that has taken place during the past few decades tells us that population growth and productivity gains undoubtedly have dominated other factors. In fact, the aggregate supply schedule has actually shifted *rightward*, not leftward, over time. Consequently, this supply-side explanation for persistent inflation *cannot* be the correct explanation.

Demand-Side Inflation

This leaves only one other explanation for the persistent inflation that the United States has experienced in recent decades. This explanation is depicted in panel (b) of Figure 10-8. If aggregate demand increases for a given level of long-run aggregate supply, the price level must increase. The reason is that at an initial price level such as 120, people desire to purchase more goods and services than firms are willing and able to produce, given currently available resources and technology. As a result, the rise in aggregate demand leads only to a general rise in the price level, such as the increase to a value of 140, depicted in the figure.

FIGURE 10-9

Real GDP and the Price Level in the United States, 1970 to the Present

This figure shows the points where aggregate demand and aggregate supply have intersected each year from 1970 to the present.

The United States has experienced economic growth over this period, but not without inflation.

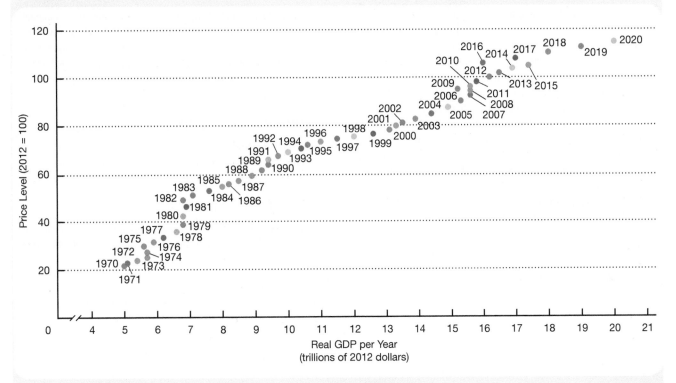

Sources: *Economic Report of the President; Economic Indicators*, various issues; author's estimates.

From a long-run perspective, we are left with only one possibility: Persistent inflation in a growing economy is possible only if the aggregate demand curve shifts rightward over time at a faster pace than the rightward progression of the long-run aggregate supply curve. Thus, in contrast to the experience of people who lived in the latter portion of the nineteenth century, when aggregate demand grew too slowly relative to aggregate supply to maintain price stability, your grandparents, parents, and you have lived in times when aggregate demand has grown too *speedily*. The result has been a continual upward drift in the price level, or long-term inflation.

Figure 10-9 shows that U.S. real GDP has grown in most years since 1970. Nevertheless, this growth has been accompanied by a higher price level every single year.

Why did the nation of Turkey recently experience significant inflation even as its long-run aggregate supply increased?

INTERNATIONAL EXAMPLE

Explaining Why Turkey's Growing Economy Experienced a Burst of Inflation

During some years, Turkey's real GDP increased at annual rates exceeding 5 percent as the nation experienced a significant increase in long-run aggregate supply. The quantity of money in circulation, however, began to grow at annual rates in excess of 20 percent. As a consequence, the nation's aggregate demand curve shifted outward at an even faster pace than the rightward shift of its long-run aggregate supply curve. The net effect was an increase in the country's equilibrium price level, or inflation. Indeed, the annual inflation rate in Turkey rose to nearly 20 percent.

FOR CRITICAL THINKING

What would have happened to Turkey's price level if the position of its aggregate demand curve had not changed while long-run aggregate supply increased?

Sources are listed at the end of this chapter.

ECONOMICS IN YOUR LIFE

Why Japan's Government Aims to Increase Long-Run Aggregate Supply by *Reducing* People's Hours at Work

Sanae Abuta, a Panasonic manager based in Osaka, Japan, has worked out a flexible schedule with her employer. On some days, she works from 9 A.M. until about 6 P.M. On other days, either she reports to work around 11 A.M., so that she can stay at home with her child, or she takes a lengthy mid-day break to take care of personal business. Sometimes she works from home all day. "I appreciate the flexibility," says Abuta. Panasonic has determined that her weekly productivity has increased since deciding to switch her from the previously standard full-day work schedule across the entire workweek.

Abuta and Panasonic have been encouraged to adopt this more flexible workweek by a program launched by the government of Japan. Note that the average annual rate of growth of real GDP in Japan has been close to 1 percent for about two decades. The government recently determined that a national business culture that had promoted being at work for large numbers of hours per week had actually contributed to lower output of goods and services per week worked. So many people had become so intent on being seen by their employers to be hard at work that they were reaching the point of physical and mental exhaustion. Indeed, the government now tabulates an annual report of companies with employees who experienced *karoshi*, or death attributed to overwork. By shaming employers into providing more flexible, health-promoting work schedules, Japan's government hopes to boost the average worker's output per hour worked and thereby increase the nation's annual long-run aggregate supply.

FOR CRITICAL THINKING

How might a flexible work schedule that totals to the same hourly workweek as a fixed schedule nonetheless contribute to an increase in the typical employee's weekly output of goods and services produced?

REAL APPLICATION

If your boss offered you a very flexible work arrangement, including working from home, are there any reasons that you might refuse this flexibility?

Sources are listed at the end of this chapter.

ISSUES & APPLICATIONS

How a Cold Climate and Access to Geothermal Steam Are Increasing Long-Run Aggregate Supply in Iceland

scanrail/123RF GB Limited

CONCEPTS APPLIED

➤ Aggregate Supply

➤ Endowments

➤ Long-Run Aggregate Supply Curve

Two key determinants of the position of an economy's long-run aggregate supply curve are its endowments of resources and the technology that it can utilize to combine resources in the production of final goods and services. Iceland has found itself in a unique situation in which its endowment of two particular resources has contributed to an expansion of its economy's technological capabilities and, hence, speedier rightward shifts in the position of its long-run aggregate supply curve.

A Chilly Climate and Tectonic Faults Fuel Proliferation of Icelandic Data Centers

The apps, streaming videos, financial information, and so on that people use on their digital devices to transmit online must be managed by data centers. These centers operate large numbers of digital servers, information-storage equipment, and communications networks. Keeping the centers operating effectively and without interruption 24 hours per day requires keeping the equipment cool and powering it with electricity.

Iceland is endowed with a cold climate, and its chilly airs can readily be channeled to rooms containing digital equipment that require steady streams of cool air to maintain effective and stable operations. In addition, the nation straddles a system of geologic faults, which in turn contain natural rocky vents that emit large volumes of hot steam that rises from deeper regions of the earth's crust. This steam, in turn, can be utilized to generate electricity. These resource endowments have earned Iceland the ranking as the best location in the world in which to locate data centers, which has set off a high-tech business boom for the nation's economy.

Implications for the Icelandic Long-Run Aggregate Supply, Real GDP, and Price Level

Global tech firms have constructed dozens of new data centers in Iceland, and a number of others are planned or in the process of being built. Thousands of new jobs have opened for Icelandic residents, who are utilizing the newly installed data centers to provide substantially larger volumes of services to users of digital information.

The long-run implications of these developments are depicted in Figure 10-10. Because Iceland's capability to produce final services has increased significantly, the position of its economy's long-run aggregate supply curve has shifted rightward, from a 2010 position given by $LRAS_1$ to the 2020 position given by $LRAS_2$. Thus, the nation's long-run equilibrium flow of real GDP per year has increased. The nation's aggregate demand curve has shifted rightward at a slightly greater pace than has its $LRAS$ curve. Hence, on net Iceland's equilibrium price level also has increased.

FOR CRITICAL THINKING

New immigrants to Iceland have arrived to fill data-center positions and have brought with them well-educated spouses and other family members. How might this wave of immigration change Iceland's resource endowments and thereby influence the position of its long-run aggregate supply curve in the future?

REAL APPLICATION

What factors would you have to consider if you were thinking about moving to another country to work?

Sources are listed at the end of this chapter.

FIGURE 10-10

Changes in the Positions of Iceland's *LRAS* and *AD* Curves

As Iceland's economy has benefited from its endowments of tectonic steam that fuels new data centers and a cold climate that keeps data centers' equipment cooled, its long-run aggregate supply has increased. The nation's *LRAS* curve has shifted rightward, from *LRAS*₁ at real GDP of $15.1 billion in 2010 to *LRAS*₂ at an estimated $27.5 billion by 2020. Aggregate demand has shifted farther rightward over the period, however, from *AD*₁ to *AD*₂, so on net the nation's price level has increased.

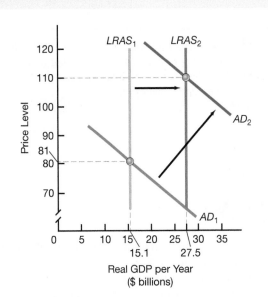

What You Should Know

Here is what you should know after reading this chapter.

LEARNING OBJECTIVES	KEY TERMS
10.1 Discuss the concept of long-run aggregate supply and describe the effect of economic growth on the long-run aggregate supply curve *The long-run aggregate supply curve is vertical at the amount of real GDP that firms plan to produce when they have full information and when complete adjustment of input prices to any changes in output prices has taken place. The production possibilities curve shifts rightward when the economy grows, and so does the nation's long-run aggregate supply curve. In a growing economy, the changes in full-employment real GDP defined by the shifting long-run aggregate supply curve show the nation's long-run, or trend, growth path.*	aggregate supply, 204 long-run aggregate supply (*LRAS*) curve, 204 base-year dollars, 204 endowments, 204 **Key Figures** Figure 10-1, 204 Figure 10-2, 205 Figure 10-3, 206
10.2 Explain why the aggregate demand curve slopes downward and list key factors that cause this curve to shift *The real-balance effect occurs when a rise in the price level reduces the real value of cash balances, which induces people to cut back on planned spending. The interest rate effect caused by a higher price level induces people to cut back on borrowing and spending. Finally, a rise in the price level at home causes domestic goods to be more expensive relative to foreign goods, so there is a fall in exports and a rise in imports, both of which cause domestic planned expenditures to fall. These three factors together account for the downward slope of the aggregate demand curve, which shifts if there is any autonomous change in total planned real expenditures at any given price level.*	aggregate demand, 207 aggregate demand curve, 207 real-balance effect, 209 interest rate effect, 209 open economy effect, 209 **Key Figure** Figure 10-4, 208
10.3 Evaluate the meaning of long-run equilibrium for the economy as a whole and explain why economic growth can cause deflation *In a long-run economywide equilibrium, the price level adjusts until total planned real expenditures equal actual real GDP. Thus, the long-run equilibrium price level is determined at the point where the aggregate demand curve intersects the long-run aggregate supply curve. If the aggregate demand curve is stationary during a period of economic growth, the long-run aggregate supply curve shifts rightward along the aggregate demand curve. The long-run equilibrium price level falls, so there is secular deflation.*	secular deflation, 212 **Key Figures** Figure 10-5, 211 Figure 10-6, 212
10.4 Evaluate likely reasons for persistent inflation in recent decades *Inflation can result from a fall in long-run aggregate supply, but in a growing economy, long-run aggregate supply generally rises. Thus, a much more likely cause of persistent inflation is a pace of aggregate demand growth that exceeds the pace at which long-run aggregate supply increases.*	**Key Figures** Figure 10-7, 213 Figure 10-8, 214

PROBLEMS

10-1. Many economists view the natural rate of unemployment as the level observed when real GDP is given by the position of the long-run aggregate supply curve. How can there be positive unemployment in this situation?

10-2. Suppose that the long-run aggregate supply curve is positioned at a real GDP level of $22 trillion in base-year dollars, and the long-run equilibrium price level (in index number form) is 115. What is the full-employment level of *nominal* GDP?

10-3. Continuing from Problem 10-2, suppose that the full-employment level of *nominal* GDP in the following year rises to $25.85 trillion. The long-run equilibrium price level, however, remains unchanged. By how much (in real dollars) has the long-run aggregate supply curve shifted to the right in the following year? By how much, if any, has the aggregate demand curve shifted to the right? (*Hint:* The equilibrium price level can stay the same only if *LRAS* and *AD* shift rightward by the same amount.)

10-4. Suppose that the position of a nation's long-run aggregate supply curve has not changed, but its long-run equilibrium price level has increased. Which of the following factors might account for this event?

   a. A rise in the value of the domestic currency relative to other world currencies

   b. An increase in the quantity of money in circulation

   c. An increase in the labor force participation rate

   d. A decrease in taxes

   e. A rise in real incomes of countries that are key trading partners of this nation

   f. Increased long-run economic growth

10-5. Identify the combined shifts in long-run aggregate supply and aggregate demand that could explain the following simultaneous occurrences.

   a. An increase in equilibrium real GDP and an increase in the equilibrium price level

   b. A decrease in equilibrium real GDP with no change in the equilibrium price level

   c. An increase in equilibrium real GDP with no change in the equilibrium price level

   d. A decrease in equilibrium real GDP and a decrease in the equilibrium price level

10-6. Suppose that during the past 3 years, equilibrium real GDP in a country rose steadily, from $450 billion to $500 billion, but even though the position of its aggregate demand curve remained unchanged, its equilibrium price level steadily declined, from 110 to 103. What could have accounted for these outcomes, and what is the term for the change in the price level experienced by this country?

10-7. Suppose that during a given year, the quantity of U.S. real GDP that can be produced in the long run rises from $21.9 trillion to $22.0 trillion, measured in base-year dollars. During the year, no change occurs in the various factors that influence aggregate demand. What will happen to the U.S. long-run equilibrium price level during this particular year?

10-8. Assume that the position of a nation's aggregate demand curve has not changed, but the long-run equilibrium price level has declined. Other things

being equal, which of the following factors might account for this event?

   a. An increase in labor productivity

   b. A decrease in the capital stock

   c. A decrease in the quantity of money in circulation

   d. The discovery of new mineral resources used to produce various goods

   e. A technological improvement

10-9. Suppose that there is a sudden rise in the price level. What will happen to economywide planned spending on purchases of goods and services? Why?

10-10. Assume that the economy is in long-run equilibrium with complete information and that input prices adjust rapidly to changes in the prices of goods and services. If there is a rise in the price level induced by an increase in aggregate demand, what happens to real GDP?

10-11. Consider the diagram below when answering the questions that follow.

   a. Suppose that the current price level is P_2. Explain why the price level will decline toward P_1.

   b. Suppose that the current price level is P_3. Explain why the price level will rise toward P_1.

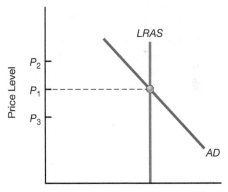

10-12. Explain whether each of the following events would cause a movement along or a shift in the position of the *LRAS* curve, other things being equal. In each case, explain the direction of the movement along the curve or shift in its position.

   a. Last year, businesses invested in new capital equipment, so this year the nation's capital stock is higher than it was last year.

   b. There has been an 8 percent increase in the quantity of money in circulation that has shifted the *AD* curve.

   c. A hurricane of unprecedented strength has damaged oil rigs, factories, and ports all along the nation's coast.

d. Inflation has occurred during the past year as a result of rightward shifts of the *AD* curve.

10-13. Explain whether each of the following events would cause a movement along or a shift in the *AD* curve, other things being equal. In each case, explain the direction of the movement along the curve or shift in its position.

a. Deflation has occurred during the past year.

b. Real GDP levels of all the nation's major trading partners have declined.

c. There has been a decline in the foreign exchange value of the nation's currency.

d. The price level has increased this year.

10-14. This year, a nation's long-run equilibrium real GDP and price level both increased. Which of the following combinations of factors might simultaneously account for *both* occurrences?

a. An isolated earthquake at the beginning of the year destroyed part of the nation's capital stock, and the nation's government significantly reduced its purchases of goods and services.

b. There was a technological improvement at the end of the previous year, and the quantity of money in circulation rose significantly during the year.

c. Labor productivity increased throughout the year, and consumers significantly increased their total planned purchases of goods and services.

d. The capital stock increased somewhat during the year, and the quantity of money in circulation declined considerably.

10-15. Explain how, if at all, each of the following events would affect equilibrium real GDP and the long-run equilibrium price level.

a. A reduction in the quantity of money in circulation

b. An income tax rebate (the return of previously paid taxes) from the government to households, which they can apply only to purchases of goods and services

c. A technological improvement

d. A decrease in the value of the home currency in terms of the currencies of other nations

10-16. For each question, suppose that the economy *begins* at the long-run equilibrium point *A* in the next diagram. Identify which of the other points on the diagram—points *B*, *C*, *D*, or *E*—could represent a *new* long-run equilibrium after the described events take place and move the economy away from point *A*.

a. Significant productivity improvements occur, and the quantity of money in circulation increases.

b. No new capital investment takes place, and a fraction of the existing capital stock depreciates and becomes unusable. At the same time, the government imposes a large tax increase on the nation's households.

c. More efficient techniques for producing goods and services are adopted throughout the economy at the same time that the government reduces its spending on goods and services.

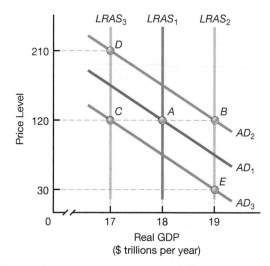

10-17. In Ciudad Barrios, El Salvador, the latest payments from relatives working in the United States have finally arrived. When the credit unions open for business, up to 150 people are already waiting in line. After receiving the funds their relatives have transmitted to these institutions, customers go off to outdoor markets to stock up on food or clothing or to appliance stores to purchase new refrigerators or televisions. Similar scenes occur throughout the developing world, as each year migrants working in higher-income, developed nations send around $200 billion of their earnings back to their relatives in less developed nations. Evidence indicates that the relatives, such as those in Ciudad Barrios, typically spend nearly all of the funds on current consumption.

a. Based on the information supplied, are developing countries' income inflows transmitted by migrant workers primarily affecting their economies' long-run aggregate supply curves or aggregate demand curves?

b. How are equilibrium price levels in nations that are recipients of large inflows of funds from migrants likely to be affected? Explain your reasoning.

10-18. In Figure 10-2, if the economy acquires a larger amount of capital goods in the current year, does a larger or smaller outward shift in the production possibilities curve result? Does the *LRAS* curve shift more or less far to the right? Why?

10-19. Consider Figure 10-4. What are the three effects of decreases in the price level, and do these generate upward or downward movements along the economy's aggregate demand curve?

10-20. Take a look at panel (a) of Figure 10-6. In the absence of a change in aggregate demand, what effect does economic growth have on the price level over time, other things being equal? Why?

10-21. Take a look at panel (b) of Figure 10-6. If the Federal Reserve seeks to prevent secular deflation from taking place as a consequence of economic growth, how should it change the quantity of money in circulation? How would this policy action prevent secular deflation?

10-22. Consider panel (a) of Figure 10-8. What type of variation in the position of the long-run aggregate supply curve could generate inflation—that is, an increase in the equilibrium price level? In a nation that generally experiences economic growth over the long run, would we anticipate that such a change in the position of the long-run aggregate supply curve could explain persistent inflation?

10-23. Take a look at panel (b) of Figure 10-8. What change in the position of the aggregate demand curve could generate inflation—that is, an increase in the equilibrium price level? What type of variation in the quantity of money placed into circulation by the Federal Reserve could generate such a change in the position of the aggregate demand curve?

REFERENCES

AI—DECISION MAKING THROUGH DATA: Governments Seeking Growth in Long-Run Aggregate Supply

Alex Verkhivker, "Why Artificial Intelligence Isn't Boosting the Economy—Yet," *Chicago Booth Review*, January 3, 2019.

European Commission, "The Age of Artificial Intelligence: Towards a European Stragegy for Human-Centric Machines," EPSC Strategic Notes, Issue 29, March 27, 2018 (https://ec.europa.eu/epsc/sites/epsc/files/epsc_strategicnote_ai.pdf).

Ouyang Shijia and Yang Cheng, "China Banking on AI for Innovation Edge," *China Daily*, May 18, 2018.

INTERNATIONAL EXAMPLE: Explaining Low Inflation in the "Eurozone"

Pan Pylas, "Eurozone Concerns Mount as Inflation Dips and Economy Slows," *U.S. News and World Report*, January 3, 2019.

Christophe Blot, Jerome Creel, and Paul Hubert, "Why Does the Recovery Show So Little Inflation," OFCE Policy Brief, Sciences Po, Paris, France (https://www.ofce.sciences-po.fr/pdf/pbrief/2018/OFCEpbrief33.pdf), March 15, 2018.

Tom Fairless, "The Riddle of the Eurozone's Missing Inflation," *Wall Street Journal*, May 6, 2018.

INTERNATIONAL EXAMPLE: Explaining Why Turkey's Growing Economy Experienced a Burst of Inflation

Cagan Koc, "Turkey Inflation Edges Up as Food Prices Soar," *Bloomberg*, February 4, 2019.

Yeliz Candemir, "Turkey Central Bank Vows to Take Action after Inflation Hits 18 Percent," *Wall Street Journal*, September 3, 2018.

Yen Nee Lee, "What Went Wrong for Turkey"? CNBC (https://www.cnbc.com/2018/08/13/turkey-crisis-economy-faces-weak-lira-inflation-debt-and-tariffs.html), August 13, 2018.

ECONOMICS IN YOUR LIFE: Why Japan's Government Aims to Increase Long-Run Aggregate Supply by *Reducing* People's Hours at Work

Nobuko Kobayashi, "Japan's Women Need More Than Jobs," *Bloomberg*, February 12, 2019.

Jeremy Berke, "Japan Is Facing a 'Death by Overwork' Problem," *Business Insider*, March 25, 2018.

"Japan Inc and the Government Are Trying to Tackle Overwork," *Economist*, March, 22, 2018.

ISSUES & APPLICATIONS: How a Cold Climate and Access to Geothermal Steam Are Increasing Long-Run Aggregate Supply in Iceland

"Iceland Economic Outlook," Focus-Economics.com (https://www.focus-economics.com/countries/iceland), February 26, 2019.

Richard Partington, "Tourists and Tech Bring Iceland Back from the Brink," *Guardian*, June 16, 2018.

Zeke Turner, "Iceland Takes Hard Look at Tech Boom Sparked by Its Cheap, Bountiful Power," *Wall Street Journal*, April 19, 2018.

11

Classical and Keynesian Macro Analyses

Album/Alamy Stock Photo

LEARNING OBJECTIVES

After reading this chapter, you should be able to:

11.1 Describe the short-run determination of equilibrium real GDP and the price level in the classical model

11.2 Discuss the essential features of Keynesian economics and explain the short-run aggregate supply curve

11.3 Explain what factors cause shifts in the short-run and long-run aggregate supply curves

11.4 Evaluate the effects of aggregate demand and supply shocks on equilibrium real GDP in the short run

11.5 Determine the causes of short-run variations in the inflation rate

I n recent years, observers of the economies of various nations have expressed concerns about alleged problems of "overcapacity," or the potential for the real values of goods and services that firms desire to produce each year persistently exceeding people's desired real expenditures on goods and services. At the same time, others have worried that the world as a whole could eventually experience difficulties with "undercapacity," or the possibility that people's desired real spending on items might outstrip the real aggregate value of goods and services produced. Economists have contemplated the potential issues of "overcapacity" and "undercapacity" for many years. These concerns particularly occupied an economist of the late eighteenth and early nineteenth centuries named Jean-Baptiste Say, who proposed that any such problems should be short-lived. In this chapter, you will learn about "Say's law" and the *classical* macroeconomic theory developed by Say and other economists of that period. In addition, you will learn about an alternative approach known as the *Keynesian* macroeconomic theory.

DID YOU KNOW THAT...

following more than a decade over which the price of a gallon of gasoline was persistently lower than the price of a gallon of milk, between 2010 and 2014 the price of a gallon of gasoline rose above the price of a gallon of milk? Many economists do not believe it was a coincidence that the interval during which the price of a gallon of gasoline was elevated corresponded to a period of reduced real GDP growth. In their view, gasoline is so widely used as an input in the production and distribution of new final goods and services that sudden increases in its price generate economywide *shocks* that tend to depress equilibrium real GDP. You will learn later in this chapter that sudden increases in prices of gasoline and prices of other sources of energy are categorized as *aggregate supply shocks*. First, however, you will learn about alternative perspectives on the short-term determinants of equilibrium real GDP.

The Classical Model

The classical model, which traces its origins to the 1770s, was the first systematic attempt to explain the determinants of the price level and the national levels of real GDP, employment, consumption, saving, and investment. Classical economists—Adam Smith, J. B. Say, David Ricardo, John Stuart Mill, Thomas Malthus, A. C. Pigou, and others—wrote from the 1770s to the 1930s. They assumed, among other things, that all wages and prices were flexible and that competitive markets existed throughout the economy.

11.1 Describe the short-run determination of equilibrium real GDP and the price level in the classical model

Say's Law

Every time you produce something for which you receive income, you generate the income necessary to make expenditures on other goods and services. That means that an economy producing $22 trillion of real GDP, measured in base-year dollars (the value of current goods and services expressed in terms of prices in a base year), simultaneously produces the income with which these goods and services can be purchased. As an accounting identity, *actual* aggregate output always equals *actual* aggregate income. Classical economists took this accounting identity one step further by arguing that total national supply creates its own national demand. They asserted what has become known as **Say's law**:

> *Supply creates its own demand. Hence, it follows that desired expenditures will equal actual expenditures.*

Say's law
A dictum of economist J. B. Say that supply creates its own demand. Producing goods and services generates the means and the willingness to purchase other goods and services.

The Implication of Say's Law What does Say's law really mean? It states that the very process of producing specific goods (supply) is proof that other goods are desired (demand). People produce more goods than they want for their own use only if they seek to trade them for other goods. Someone offers to supply something only because he or she has a demand for something else.

The implication of this, according to Say, is that no general glut, or overproduction, is possible in a market economy. From this reasoning, it seems to follow that full employment of labor and other resources would be the normal state of affairs in such an economy.

Say acknowledged that an oversupply of some goods might occur in particular markets. He argued that such surpluses would simply cause prices to fall, thereby decreasing production as the economy adjusted. The opposite would occur in markets in which shortages temporarily appeared.

Say's Law in a Modern Economy All this seems reasonable enough in a simple barter economy in which households produce most of the goods they want and trade for the rest. This is shown in Figure 11-1, in which there is a simple circular flow.

FIGURE 11-1

Say's Law and the Circular Flow

Here we show the circular flow of income and output. The very act of supplying a certain level of goods and services necessarily equals the level of goods and services demanded, in Say's simplified world.

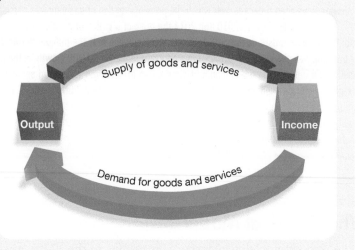

ECONOMICS IN YOUR LIFE

To contemplate the real-world implications of the relationship between household saving and private investment spending, take a look at **U.S. Household Saving Increases, and So Does Private Investment Spending** on page 237.

What about a more sophisticated economy, however, in which people work for others and money is used instead of barter? Can these complications create the possibility of unemployment? Does the fact that laborers receive money income, some of which can be saved, lead to unemployment? No, said the classical economists to these last two questions. They based their reasoning on a number of key assumptions.

Assumptions of the Classical Model

The classical model makes four major assumptions:

1. *Pure competition exists.* No single buyer or seller of a commodity or an input can affect its price.

2. *Wages and prices are flexible.* The assumption of pure competition leads to the notion that prices, wages, and interest rates are free to move to whatever level supply and demand dictate (as the economy adjusts). Although no *individual* buyer can set a price, the community of buyers or sellers can cause prices to rise or to fall to an equilibrium level.

3. *People are motivated by self-interest.* Businesses want to maximize their profits, and households want to maximize their economic well-being.

4. *People cannot be fooled by money illusion.* Buyers and sellers react to changes in relative prices. That is to say, they do not suffer from **money illusion**. For example, the assumption here is that you would never be fooled into thinking that a doubling of your wages would make you better off while at the same time the price level also doubled.

Money illusion
Reacting to changes in money prices rather than relative prices. If a worker whose wages double when the price level also doubles thinks he or she is better off, that worker is suffering from money illusion.

The classical economists concluded, after taking account of the four major assumptions, that the role of government in the economy should be minimal. They assumed that pure competition prevails, all prices and wages are flexible, and people are self-interested and do not experience money illusion. If so, they argued, then any problems in the macroeconomy will be temporary. The market will correct itself.

Equilibrium in the Credit Market

When income is saved, it is not reflected in product demand. It is a type of *leakage* from the circular flow of income and output because saving withdraws funds from the income stream. Therefore, total planned consumption spending *can* fall short of total current real GDP. In such a situation, it appears that supply does not necessarily create its own demand.

FIGURE 11-2

Equating Planned Saving and Planned Investment in the Classical Model

The curve showing planned investment is labeled "Planned investment." The planned saving curve is shown as an upward-sloping supply curve of saving. The equilibrating force here is, of course, the interest rate. At higher interest rates, people desire to save more. At higher interest rates, however, businesses wish to engage in less investment because it is less profitable to invest. In this model, at an interest rate of 5 percent, planned investment just equals planned saving, which is $3.8 trillion per year.

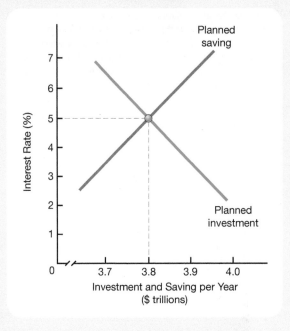

The Relationship between Saving and Investment The classical economists did not believe that the complicating factor of saving in the circular flow model of income and output was a problem. They contended that each dollar saved would be invested by businesses so that the leakage of saving would be matched by the injection of business investment. *Investment* here refers only to additions to the nation's capital stock. The classical economists believed that businesses as a group would intend to invest as much as households wanted to save.

The Equilibrium Interest Rate Equilibrium between the saving plans of consumers and the investment plans of businesses comes about, in the classical model, through the working of the credit market. In the credit market, the *price* of credit is the interest rate. At equilibrium, the price of credit—the interest rate—ensures that the amount of credit demanded to fund business investment equals the amount of credit supplied by savers. Planned investment just equals planned saving, so there is no reason to be concerned about the leakage of saving. This idea is illustrated graphically in Figure 11-2.

In the figure, the vertical axis measures the rate of interest in percentage terms, and the horizontal axis measures flows of desired saving and desired investment per unit time period. The desired saving curve is really a supply curve of saving. It shows that people wish to save more at higher interest rates than at lower interest rates.

In contrast, the higher the rate of interest, the less profitable it is to invest and the lower is the level of desired investment. Thus, the desired investment curve slopes downward. In this simplified model, the equilibrium rate of interest is 5 percent, and the equilibrium quantity of saving and investment is $3.8 trillion per year.

Equilibrium in the Labor Market

Now consider the labor market. If an excess quantity of labor is supplied at a particular wage level, the wage level must be above equilibrium. By accepting lower wages, unemployed workers will quickly be put back to work. We show equilibrium in the labor market in Figure 11-3.

FIGURE 11-3

Equilibrium in the Labor Market

The demand for labor is downward sloping. At higher wage rates, firms will employ fewer workers. The supply of labor is upward sloping. At higher wage rates, more workers will work longer, and more people will be willing to work. The equilibrium wage rate is $26 per hour with an equilibrium employment per year of 165 million workers.

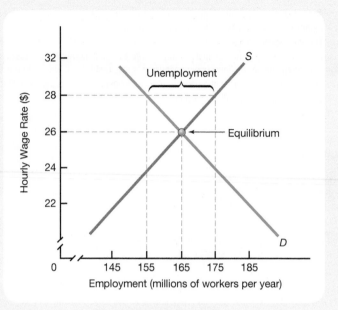

Assume that equilibrium exists at $26 per hour and 165 million workers employed. If the wage rate were $28 per hour, there would be unemployment—175 million workers would want to work, but businesses would want to hire only 155 million. In the classical model, this unemployment is eliminated rather rapidly by wage rates dropping back to $26 per hour, as seen in Figure 11-3.

WHAT HAPPENS WHEN...

the demand for labor suddenly increases in an economy that is experiencing unemployment?

Because the amount of labor unemployment is equal to the excess quantity supplied in the labor market, the classical theory indicates that normally unemployment will decline as a consequence of a decrease in the wage rate. If, however, the demand for labor happens to increase before a wage decrease can occur, then the labor demand curve shifts rightward, and the amount of labor demanded rises at any given wage rate. Thus, if this event should occur, as arguably occurred in the U.S. economy after 2016, then unemployment can decline without a reduction in the wage rate.

The Relationship between Employment and Real GDP Employment is not to be regarded simply as some isolated figure that government statisticians estimate. Rather, the level of employment in an economy determines its real GDP (output), other things held constant. A hypothetical relationship between input (number of employees) and the value of output (real GDP per year) is shown in Table 11-1. The row that has 165 million workers per year as the labor input is highlighted. That might be considered a hypothetical level of full employment, and it is related to a rate of real GDP, in base-year dollars, of $22 trillion per year.

Classical Theory, Vertical Aggregate Supply, and the Price Level

In the classical model, unemployment greater than the natural unemployment rate is impossible. Say's law, coupled with flexible interest rates, prices, and wages, would always tend to keep workers fully employed so that the aggregate supply curve, as shown in Figure 11-4, is vertical at the real GDP of $22 trillion, in base-year dollars. We have labeled the supply curve *LRAS*, which is the long-run aggregate supply curve. It is defined as the real GDP that would be produced in an economy with full

TABLE 11-1

The Relationship between Employment and Real GDP

Other things being equal, an increase in the quantity of labor input increases real GDP. In this example, if 165 million workers are employed, real GDP is $22 trillion in base-year dollars.

Labor Input per Year (millions of workers)	Real GDP per Year ($ trillions)
153	19
157	20
161	21
165	22
169	23
173	24

information and full adjustment of wages and prices year in and year out. *LRAS* therefore is related to the long-run rate of unemployment.

In the classical model, this happens to be the *only* aggregate supply curve. The classical economists made little distinction between the long run and the short run. Prices adjust so fast that the economy is essentially always on or quickly moving toward *LRAS*. Furthermore, because the labor market adjusts rapidly, real GDP is always at, or soon to be at, full employment. Full employment does not mean zero unemployment because there is always some frictional and structural unemployment, which corresponds to the natural rate of unemployment.

Effect of an Increase in Aggregate Demand in the Classical Model In this model, any change in aggregate demand will quickly cause a change in the price level. Consider starting at E_1, at price level 110, in Figure 11-4. If aggregate demand shifts to AD_2, the economy will tend toward point A, but because this is beyond full-employment real GDP, prices will rise, and the economy will find itself back on the vertical *LRAS* at

FIGURE 11-4

Classical Theory and Increases in Aggregate Demand

The classical theorists believed that Say's law and flexible interest rates, prices, and wages would always lead to full employment at real GDP of $22 trillion, in base-year dollars, along the vertical aggregate supply curve, *LRAS*. With aggregate demand AD_1, the price level is 110. An increase in aggregate demand shifts AD_1 to AD_2. At price level 110, the quantity of real GDP demanded per year would be $22.5 trillion at point A on AD_2. But $22.5 trillion in real GDP per year is greater than real GDP at full employment. Prices rise, and the economy moves from E_1 to E_2, at the higher price level of 120.

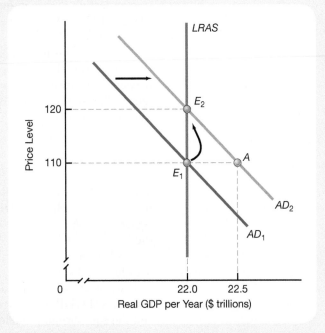

FIGURE 11-5

Effect of a Decrease in Aggregate Demand in the Classical Model

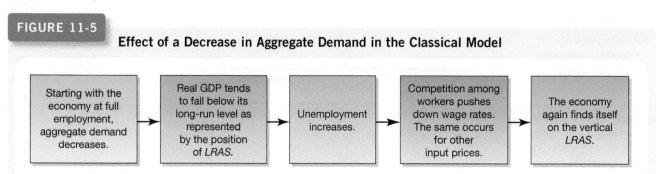

point E_2 at a higher price level, 120. The price level will increase as a result of the increase in AD because employers will end up bidding up wages for workers, as well as bidding up the prices of other inputs.

The level of real GDP per year clearly does not depend on the level of aggregate demand. Hence, we say that in the classical model, the equilibrium level of real GDP per year is completely *supply determined*. Changes in aggregate demand affect only the price level, not real GDP.

Effect of a Decrease in Aggregate Demand in the Classical Model The effect of a decrease in aggregate demand in the classical model is the converse of the analysis just presented for an increase in aggregate demand. You can simply reverse AD_2 and AD_1 in Figure 11-4. To help you see how this analysis works, consider the flowchart in Figure 11-5.

11.2 Discuss the essential features of Keynesian economics and explain the short-run aggregate supply curve

Keynesian Economics and the Keynesian Short-Run Aggregate Supply Curve

The classical economists' world was one of nearly fully utilized resources. There would only rarely be temporary bouts of unused capacity and short-term unemployment. But then in the 1930s, Europe and the United States entered a period of economic decline that seemingly could not be explained by the classical model. John Maynard Keynes developed an explanation that has since become known as the Keynesian model.

Keynes and his followers argued that prices, especially the price of labor (wages), were inflexible downward due to the existence of unions and long-term contracts between businesses and workers. This meant that prices were "sticky." Keynes contended that in such a world, which has large amounts of excess capacity and unemployment, an increase in aggregate demand will not raise the price level, and a decrease in aggregate demand will not cause firms to lower prices.

Demand-Determined Real GDP

This situation is depicted in Figure 11-6. For simplicity, Figure 11-6 does not show the point at which real GDP is at its long-run equilibrium. That is why the *short-run aggregate supply curve* (to be discussed later) never starts to slope upward and is simply the horizontal line labeled *SRAS*. Moreover, we do not show *LRAS* in Figure 11-6, either. It would be a vertical line at the level of real GDP per year that is consistent with full employment.

If we start out in equilibrium with aggregate demand at AD_1, the equilibrium level of real GDP per year, measured in base-year dollars, is $22 trillion at point E_1, and the equilibrium price level is 110. If there is a rise in aggregate demand, so that the aggregate demand curve shifts outward to the right to AD_2, the equilibrium price

FIGURE 11-6

Demand-Determined Equilibrium Real GDP at Less Than Full Employment

Keynes assumed that prices will not fall when aggregate demand falls and that there is excess capacity, so prices will not rise when aggregate demand increases. Thus, the short-run aggregate supply curve is simply a horizontal line at the given price level, 110, represented by *SRAS*. An aggregate demand shock that increases aggregate demand to AD_2 will increase the equilibrium level of real GDP per year to $22.5 trillion. An aggregate demand shock that decreases aggregate demand to AD_3 will decrease the equilibrium level of real GDP to $21.5 trillion. The equilibrium price level will not change.

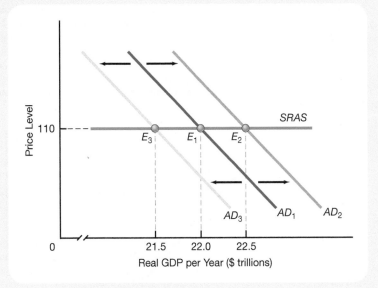

level at point E_2 will not change. Only the equilibrium level of real GDP per year will increase, to $22.5 trillion. Conversely, if there is a fall in aggregate demand that shifts the aggregate demand curve to AD_3, the equilibrium price level will again remain at 110 at point E_3, but the equilibrium level of real GDP per year will fall to $21.5 trillion.

Under such circumstances, the equilibrium level of real GDP per year is completely *demand determined*.

The Keynesian Short-Run Aggregate Supply Curve

The horizontal short-run aggregate supply curve represented in Figure 11-6 is often called the **Keynesian short-run aggregate supply curve**. According to Keynes, unions and long-term contracts are real-world factors that explain the inflexibility of *nominal* wage rates. Such stickiness of wages makes *involuntary* unemployment of labor a distinct possibility, because leftward movements along the Keynesian short-run aggregate supply curve reduce real production and, hence, employment. The classical assumption of everlasting full employment no longer holds.

Data from the 1930s offer evidence of a nearly horizontal aggregate supply curve. Between 1934 and 1940, the GDP deflator (base year × 100 in 2012) stayed in a range from about 7.4 to about 7.9, implying that the price level changed by less than 7 percent. Yet the level of real GDP measured in 2012 dollars varied between $0.9 trillion and about $1.3 trillion, or by nearly 45 percent. Thus, between 1934 and 1940, the U.S. short-run aggregate supply curve was almost flat.

Keynesian short-run aggregate supply curve
The horizontal portion of the aggregate supply curve in which there is excessive unemployment and unused capacity in the economy.

Output Determination Using Aggregate Demand and Aggregate Supply

The underlying assumption of the simplified Keynesian model is that the relevant range of the short-run aggregate supply schedule (*SRAS*) is horizontal, as depicted in panel (a) of Figure 11-7. There you see that short-run aggregate supply is fixed at price level 110. If aggregate demand is AD_1, then the equilibrium level of real GDP, in base-year dollars, is $22 trillion per year. If aggregate demand increases to AD_2, then the equilibrium level of real GDP increases to $23 trillion per year.

FIGURE 11-7

Real GDP Determination with Fixed versus Flexible Prices

In panel (a), the price level index is fixed at 110. An increase in aggregate demand from AD_1 to AD_2 moves the equilibrium level of real GDP from $22 trillion per year to $23 trillion per year in base-year dollars. In panel (b), *SRAS* is upward sloping. The same shift in aggregate demand yields an equilibrium level of real GDP of only $22.5 trillion per year and a higher price level index at 120.

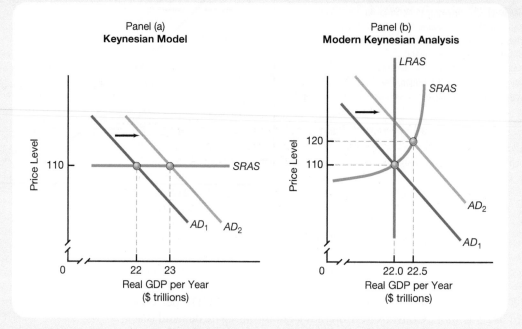

An Upward-Sloping Short-Run Aggregate Supply Curve The price level sometimes jumps upward or drops over the course of a few weeks or months. Hence, prices are not totally sticky. Modern Keynesian analysis recognizes that *some*—but not complete—price adjustment takes place in the short run. Panel (b) of Figure 11-7 displays a more general **short-run aggregate supply curve (SRAS)**. This curve represents the relationship between the price level and real GDP with incomplete price adjustment and in the absence of complete information in the short run. Allowing for partial price adjustment implies that *SRAS* slopes upward, and its slope is steeper after it crosses long-run aggregate supply, *LRAS*. This is because higher prices are required to induce firms to raise their production of goods and services to levels that temporarily exceed full-employment real GDP.

Short-run aggregate supply curve (SRAS)

The relationship between total planned economywide production and the price level in the short run, all other things held constant. If prices adjust incompletely in the short run, the curve is positively sloped.

With partial price adjustment in the short run, if aggregate demand is AD_1, then the equilibrium level of real GDP in panel (b) is also $22 trillion per year, at a price level of 110, too. An increase in aggregate demand to AD_2 such as occurred in panel (a) produces a different short-run equilibrium, however. Equilibrium real GDP increases to $22.5 trillion per year, which is less than in panel (a) because an increase in the price level to 120 causes some planned purchases of goods and services to decline.

Explaining the Short-Run Aggregate Supply Curve's Upward Slope In the modern Keynesian short run, when the price level rises partially, real GDP can be expanded beyond the level consistent with its long-run growth path, for a variety of reasons:

1. In the short run, most labor contracts implicitly or explicitly call for flexibility in hours of work at the given wage rate. Therefore, firms can use existing workers more intensively: They can get workers to work harder, to work more hours per day, and to work more days per week.

2. Existing capital equipment can be used more intensively. Machines can be worked more hours per day. Some can be made to operate faster. Maintenance can be delayed.

3. Finally, if wage rates are held constant, a higher price level leads to increased profits from additional production, which induces firms to hire more workers. The duration of unemployment falls, and thus the unemployment rate falls. Furthermore, people who were previously not in the labor force (homemakers and younger or older workers) can be induced to enter it.

All these adjustments cause real GDP to rise as the price level increases.

Shifts in the Aggregate Supply Curve

11.3 Explain what factors cause shifts in the short-run and long-run aggregate supply curves

Just as non-price-level factors can cause a shift in the aggregate demand curve, there are non-price-level factors that can cause a shift in the aggregate supply curve. The analysis here is more complicated than the analysis for the non-price-level determinants for aggregate demand, for here we are dealing with both the short run and the long run—*SRAS* and *LRAS*. Still, a change in anything other than the price level that affects the production of final goods and services can shift aggregate supply curves.

Shifts in Both Short- and Long-Run Aggregate Supply

There is a core class of events that causes a shift in both the short-run aggregate supply curve and the long-run aggregate supply curve. These include any change in our endowments of the factors of production. Any change in factors of production—labor, capital, or technology—that influences economic growth will shift *SRAS* and *LRAS*. Look at Figure 11-8. Initially, the two curves are $SRAS_1$ and $LRAS_1$. Now consider a situation in which large amounts of irreplaceable resources are lost *permanently* in a major oil spill and fire. This shifts $LRAS_1$ to $LRAS_2$ at $22.5 trillion of real GDP, measured in base-year dollars. $SRAS_1$ also shifts leftward horizontally to $SRAS_2$.

Shifts in *SRAS* Only

Some events, particularly those that are short lived, will temporarily shift *SRAS* but not *LRAS*. One of the most obvious is a change in production input prices, particularly those caused by external events that are not expected to last forever. Consider a major hurricane that temporarily shuts down a significant portion of U.S. oil

---

Shifts in Long-Run and Short-Run Aggregate Supply

Initially, the two aggregate supply curves are $SRAS_1$ and $LRAS_1$. An event that permanently reduces reserves of a key productive resource such as oil shifts $LRAS_1$ to $LRAS_2$ at $21.5 trillion of real GDP, in base-year dollars, and also shifts $SRAS_1$ horizontally leftward to $SRAS_2$. If, instead, a temporary increase in an input price occurred, $LRAS_1$ would remain unchanged, and only the short-run aggregate supply curve would shift, from $SRAS_1$ to $SRAS_2$.

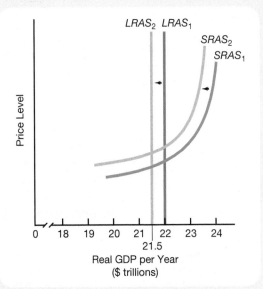

TABLE 11-2

Determinants of Aggregate Supply

The determinants listed here can affect short-run or long-run aggregate supply (or both), depending on whether they are temporary or permanent.

Changes That Cause an Increase in Aggregate Supply	Changes That Cause a Decrease in Aggregate Supply
Discoveries of new raw materials	Depletion of raw materials
Increased competition	Decreased competition
A reduction in international trade barriers	An increase in international trade barriers
Fewer regulatory impediments to business	More regulatory impediments to business
An increase in the supply of labor	A decrease in labor supplied
Increased training and education	Decreased training and education
A decrease in marginal income tax rates	An increase in marginal income tax rates
A reduction in input prices	An increase in input prices

production. Oil is an important input in many production activities. The resulting drop in oil production would cause at least a temporary increase in the price of this input. In this case, the long-run aggregate supply curve would remain at $LRAS_1$ in Figure 11-8.

The short-run aggregate supply curve *alone* would shift from $SRAS_1$ to $SRAS_2$, reflecting the increase in input prices—the higher price of oil. This is because the rise in the costs of production at each level of real GDP per year would require a higher price level to cover those increased costs.

We summarize the possible determinants of aggregate supply in Table 11-2. These determinants will cause a shift in the short-run or the long-run aggregate supply curve or both, depending on whether they are temporary or permanent.

11.4 Evaluate the effects of aggregate demand and supply shocks on equilibrium real GDP in the short run

Aggregate demand shock
Any event that causes the aggregate demand curve to shift inward or outward.

Aggregate supply shock
Any event that causes the aggregate supply curve to shift inward or outward.

Consequences of Changes in Aggregate Demand

We now have a basic model to apply when evaluating short-run adjustments of the equilibrium price level and equilibrium real GDP when there are shocks to the economy. Whenever there is a shift in the aggregate demand or short-run aggregate supply curves, the short-run equilibrium price level or real GDP level (or both) may change. These shifts are called **aggregate demand shocks** on the demand side and **aggregate supply shocks** on the supply side.

Why are the directions of some types of aggregate supply shocks becoming more difficult to assess?

AI | DECISION MAKING THROUGH DATA

Automated Trading Makes Aggregate Supply Shocks Murkier

Oil and derivative products such as gasoline are utilized to produce energy that warms buildings, powers vehicles, and provides energy to capital equipment across the nation. Thus, changes in the global price of oil can generate temporary aggregate supply shocks.

A recent complication in judging the magnitudes and even the directions of such shocks, however, has been so-called algorithmic trading on the part of oil investors—people who buy and sell titles to supplies of oil. A growing number of these investors are relying on machine-learning-guided apps to determine whether to offer to purchase or to sell shares of oil ownership. Most apps rely on similar signals provided by economic data to direct trading in these shares. As a result, prices of oil supplies have been exhibiting more frequent upward and downward swings. Both producers and consumers of oil have experienced difficulties making near-term determinations about which direction oil prices actually are moving. Thus, judging when oil-price movements may be generating aggregate supply shocks is more difficult than was true in years past.

FOR CRITICAL THINKING

Given that a smaller fraction of total energy production is powered by oil-related fuels, do you suppose that oil-price changes have become relatively more or less important sources of aggregate supply shocks in recent years?

Sources are listed at the end of this chapter.

When Aggregate Demand Falls While Aggregate Supply Is Stable

Now we can show what happens in the short run when aggregate supply remains stable but aggregate demand falls. The short-run outcome will be a rise in the unemployment rate. In Figure 11-9, you see that with AD_1, both long-run and short-run equilibrium are at $22 trillion (in base-year dollars) of real GDP per year (because $SRAS$ and $LRAS$ also intersect AD_1 at that level of real GDP). The long-run equilibrium price level is 110. A reduction in aggregate demand shifts the aggregate demand curve to AD_2. The new intersection with $SRAS$ is at $21.8 trillion per year, which is less than the long-run equilibrium level of real GDP. The difference between $22 trillion and $21.8 trillion is called a **recessionary gap,** defined as the difference between the short-run equilibrium level of real GDP and real GDP if the economy were operating at full employment on its $LRAS$.

In effect, at E_2, the economy is in short-run equilibrium at less than full employment. With too many unemployed inputs, input prices will begin to fall. Eventually, $SRAS$ will have to shift vertically downward.

Recessionary gap

The gap that exists whenever equilibrium real GDP per year is less than full-employment real GDP as shown by the position of the long-run aggregate supply curve.

Short-Run Effects When Aggregate Demand Increases

We can reverse the situation and have aggregate demand increase to AD_2, as is shown in Figure 11-10. The initial equilibrium conditions are exactly the same as in Figure 11-9. The move to AD_2 increases the short-run equilibrium from E_1 to E_2

FIGURE 11-9

The Short-Run Effects of Stable Aggregate Supply and a Decrease in Aggregate Demand: The Recessionary Gap

If the economy is at equilibrium at E_1, with price level 110 and real GDP per year of $22 trillion, a shift inward of the aggregate demand curve to AD_2 will lead to a new short-run equilibrium at E_2. The equilibrium price level will fall to 105, and the short-run equilibrium level of real GDP per year will fall to $21.8 trillion. There will be a recessionary gap of $200 billion.

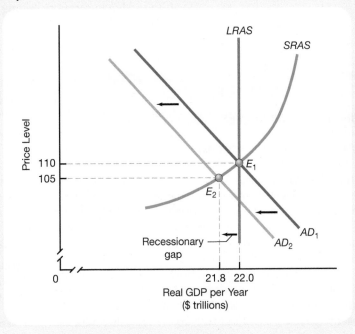

FIGURE 11-10

The Effects of Stable Aggregate Supply with an Increase in Aggregate Demand: The Inflationary Gap

The economy is at equilibrium at E_1. An increase in aggregate demand to AD_2 leads to a new short-run equilibrium at E_2, with the price level rising from 110 to 115 and equilibrium real GDP per year rising from $22 trillion to $22.2 trillion. The difference, $200 billion, is called the inflationary gap.

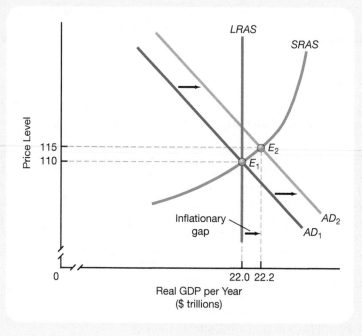

Inflationary gap

The gap that exists whenever equilibrium real GDP per year is greater than full-employment real GDP, as shown by the position of the long-run aggregate supply curve.

such that the economy is operating at $22.2 trillion of real GDP per year, which exceeds *LRAS*. This is a condition of an overheated economy, typically called an **inflationary gap**.

At E_2 in Figure 11-10, the economy is at a short-run equilibrium that is beyond full employment. In the short run, more can be squeezed out of the economy than in the long-run, full-information, full-adjustment situation. Firms will be operating beyond long-run capacity. Inputs will be working too hard. Input prices will begin to rise. That will eventually cause *SRAS* to shift vertically upward.

Can sudden uncertainty among households and firms generate aggregate demand and supply shocks?

BEHAVIORAL EXAMPLE

Uncertainty and Aggregate Demand Shocks

When suddenly confronted with considerable *uncertainty*—defined as a situation in which people cannot assess probabilities that events may occur—households and firms sometimes abruptly halt purchase and production plans. The effects of these behavioral responses can be simultaneous negative aggregate demand and aggregate supply shocks. Although a decline in aggregate demand at the same time as a fall in aggregate supply has an uncertain net effect on the equilibrium price level, the predicted unambiguous result is a reduction in equilibrium real GDP.

Benjamin Born of the University of Mannheim, Sebastian Breuer of the German Council of Economic Experts, and Steffen Elstner of the Rhine-Westphalia Institute for Economic Research have used uncertainty measures to estimate effects of uncertainty-induced aggregate demand and

supply shocks on U.S. real GDP and unemployment. Their estimates indicate that moderate increases in levels of uncertainty typically have relatively small effects on real GDP and unemployment. In contrast, a jump in uncertainty at the height of the severe recession at the end of the last decade accounted for 10 percent of that period's decrease in real GDP.

REAL APPLICATION

Suppose you read that a serious recession is just starting. You do not know what may happen to the market value of your investments. Nor do you know if you will keep your job. What might your response be?

Sources are listed at the end of this chapter.

Explaining Short-Run Variations in Inflation

11.5 Determine the causes of short-run variations in the inflation rate

In an earlier chapter, we noted that in a growing economy, the explanation for persistent inflation is that aggregate demand increases over time at a faster pace than the full-employment level of real GDP. Short-run variations in inflation, however, can arise as a result of both demand *and* supply factors.

Demand-Pull versus Cost-Push Inflation

Figure 11-10 presents a demand-side theory explaining a short-run jump in prices, sometimes called *demand-pull inflation*. Whenever the general level of prices rises in the short run because of increases in aggregate demand, we say that the economy is experiencing **demand-pull inflation**—inflation caused by increases in aggregate demand.

Demand-pull inflation
Inflation caused by increases in aggregate demand not matched by increases in aggregate supply.

An alternative explanation for increases in the price level comes from the supply side. Look at Figure 11-11. The initial equilibrium conditions are the same as in Figure 11-9. Now, however, there is a leftward shift in the short-run aggregate supply curve, from $SRAS_1$ to $SRAS_2$. Equilibrium shifts from E_1 to E_2. The price level increases from 110 to 115, while the equilibrium level of real GDP per year decreases from $22 trillion to $21.8 trillion. Persistent decreases in aggregate supply cause what is called **cost-push inflation**.

As the example of cost-push inflation shows, if the economy is initially in equilibrium on its *LRAS*, a decrease in *SRAS* will lead to a rise in the price level. Thus, any abrupt change in one of the factors that determine aggregate supply will alter the equilibrium level of real GDP per year and the equilibrium price level. If the economy is for some reason operating to the left of its *LRAS*, an increase in *SRAS* will lead to a simultaneous *increase* in the equilibrium level of real GDP per year and a *decrease* in the price level. You should be able to show this in a graph similar to Figure 11-11.

Cost-push inflation
Inflation caused by decreases in short-run aggregate supply.

When lower oil prices generate *positive* aggregate supply shocks that boost real GDP and *reduce* the price level—a "disinflation"—what does Europe's experience tell us about the persistence of these effects?

FIGURE 11-11   **Cost-Push Inflation**

If aggregate demand remains stable but $SRAS_1$ shifts to $SRAS_2$, equilibrium changes from E_1 to E_2. The price level rises from 110 to 115. If there are continual decreases in aggregate supply of this nature, the situation is called cost-push inflation.

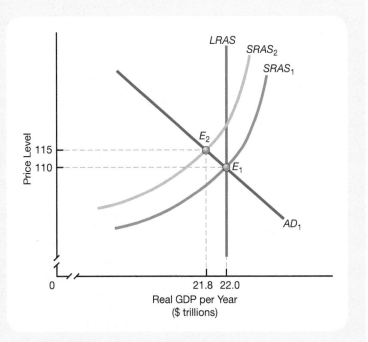

INTERNATIONAL EXAMPLE

How Long Lasting Are the Effects of Positive Aggregate Supply Shocks Caused by Lower Oil Prices?

In past decades, sudden increases in the price of oil have generated negative aggregate supply shocks—leftward shifts in the position of the short-run aggregate supply curve (*SRAS*)—that have reduced equilibrium real GDP. These *SRAS* shifts also have pushed up the equilibrium price level, thereby generating cost-push inflation. In more recent years, however, global oil prices have tended to exhibit sudden declines. The results have been positive aggregate supply shocks, or rightward shifts in the position of the short-run aggregate supply curve. These shifts, in turn, bring about increases in equilibrium real GDP and sudden reductions in the equilibrium price level, or *disinflations*, that contrast with the cost-push-inflation effects caused by higher oil prices.

These recent experiences have provided evidence regarding the lengths of the short-run effects of such decreases in oil prices. Research on European experiences with oil-price drops indicates that the resulting boosts in real GDP and disinflations typically last little longer than 6 to 12 months. Only rarely do the disinflationary effects of drops in global oil prices persist longer than one year.

FOR CRITICAL THINKING

Why does the long-run aggregate supply curve not shift in response to sudden but temporary jumps or drops in global oil prices?

Sources are listed at the end of this chapter.

Aggregate Demand and Supply in an Open Economy

In many of the international examples in the early chapters of this book, we had to translate foreign currencies into dollars when the open economy was discussed. We used the exchange rate, or the dollar price of other currencies. You learned in an earlier chapter that the open economy effect was one of the reasons why the aggregate demand curve slopes downward. When the domestic price level rises, U.S. residents want to buy cheaper-priced foreign goods. The opposite occurs when the U.S. domestic price level falls. Currently, the foreign sector of the U.S. economy constitutes more than 15 percent of all economic activities.

How a Stronger Dollar Affects Aggregate Supply Assume that the dollar becomes stronger in international foreign exchange markets. If last year the dollar could buy 40 *pesos*, the currency of the Philippines, but this year it buys 50 pesos, the dollar has become stronger. To the extent that U.S. companies import physical inputs and labor services from the Philippines, a stronger dollar leads to lower input prices.

For instance, if a U.S. firm purchases 5 million pesos' worth of inputs per year from a Philippines company, then before the strengthening of the dollar, that company paid $125,000 per year for those labor services. (Five million pesos divided by 40 pesos per dollar equals $125,000.) After the dollar's strengthening, however, the U.S. firm's Philippines-input expense drops to $100,000. (Five million pesos divided by 50 pesos per dollar equals $100,000.) This U.S. firm's cost reduction generated by the dollar's strengthening, as well as similar reductions in foreign-input expenses at other U.S. firms, will induce those firms to produce more final goods and services per year at any given price level.

Thus, a general strengthening of the dollar against the peso and other world currencies will lead the short-run aggregate supply curve to shift outward to the right, as shown in panel (a) of Figure 11-12. In that simplified model, equilibrium real GDP would rise, and the price level would decline. Employment would also tend to increase.

How a Stronger Dollar Affects Aggregate Demand A stronger dollar has another effect that we must consider. Foreign residents will find that U.S.-made goods are now more expensive, expressed in their own currency. Suppose that as a result of the dollar's strengthening, the dollar, which previously could buy 0.70 euro, can now buy 0.80 euro. Before the dollar strengthened, a U.S.-produced $10 downloadable music album cost a French resident 7.00 euros at the exchange rate of 0.70 euro per $1. After the dollar strengthens and the exchange rate changes to 0.80 euro per $1, that same $10 digital album will cost 8.00 euros. Conversely, U.S. residents will find that the stronger dollar makes imported goods less expensive.

FIGURE 11-12

The Two Effects of a Stronger Dollar

When the dollar increases in value in the international currency market, there are two effects. The first is lower prices for imported inputs, causing a shift in the short-run aggregate supply schedule outward and to the right, from $SRAS_1$ to $SRAS_2$ in panel (a). Equilibrium tends to move from E_1 to E_2 at a lower price level and a higher equilibrium real GDP per year. Second, a stronger dollar can also affect the aggregate demand curve because it will lead to lower net exports and cause AD_1 to shift inward to AD_2 in panel (b). Due to this effect, equilibrium will move from E_1 to E_2 at a lower price level and a lower equilibrium real GDP per year. On balance, the combined effects of the decrease in aggregate demand and increase in aggregate supply will be to push down the price level, but real GDP may rise or fall.

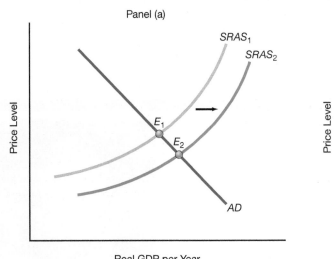

Panel (a)

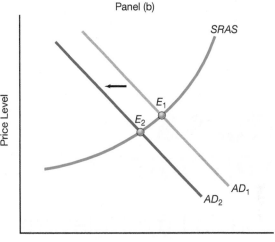

Panel (b)

The result for U.S. residents is fewer exports and more imports, or lower net exports (exports minus imports). If net exports fall, employment in export industries will fall: This is represented in panel (b) of Figure 11-12. After the dollar becomes stronger, the aggregate demand curve shifts inward from AD_1 to AD_2. The result is a tendency for equilibrium real GDP and the price level to fall and for unemployment to increase.

The Net Effects on Inflation and Real GDP We have learned, then, that a stronger dollar *simultaneously* leads to an increase in $SRAS$ and a decrease in AD. In such situations, the equilibrium price level definitely falls. A stronger dollar contributes to deflation.

The effect of a stronger dollar on real GDP depends on which curve—AD or $SRAS$—shifts more. If the aggregate demand curve shifts more than the short-run aggregate supply curve, equilibrium real GDP will decline. Conversely, if the aggregate supply curve shifts more than the aggregate demand curve, equilibrium real GDP will rise.

You should be able to redo this entire analysis for a weaker dollar.

ECONOMICS IN YOUR LIFE

U.S. Household Saving Increases, and So Does Private Investment Spending

Becky Groves is a 61-year-old social worker in Grand Junction, Colorado. In recent years, she has developed a stronger determination to save. "I don't buy as much junk, you know, trivial stuff that doesn't matter." Groves says. "I pay bills and buy food, and then I keep a little bit out and the rest just goes into savings." Over the past several years, many U.S. residents have opted to join Groves by spending less each week and saving more. A significant increase in the aggregate annual flow of personal saving on the part of U.S. households has resulted.

(Continued)

Consistent with the predictions of the classical model, funds that households do not spend eventually find their way to firms to utilize for investment expenditures—spending on new capital equipment, financing of research and development activities, and so on. Since 2016, when the annual flow of private investment spending was negative—meaning that business firms failed to offset depreciation of existing capital equipment—private investment expenditures have increased noticeably. The financing of this burst of investment spending ultimately has been provided by millions of people like Groves, who choose not to "buy as much junk" and choose to ensure that "the rest just goes into savings."

FOR CRITICAL THINKING

How could gradual increases in the interest rate contribute to an increase in household saving? (Hint: Does a nation's saving function slope upward or downward?)

REAL APPLICATION

When you are earning income, you can spend all that you earn after taxes or you can spend only part of it and save more. Under what circumstances would you be inclined to save more and what do you give up by so doing?

Sources are listed at the end of this chapter.

ISSUES & APPLICATIONS

Is Say's Law Relevant for Today's Economy?

Album/Alamy Stock Photo

CONCEPTS APPLIED

➤ Say's Law

➤ Classical Model

➤ Money Illusion

The dictum of economist Jean-Baptiste Say that "supply creates its own demand" is a basic building block of the classical model. Given that Say's thinking about aggregate demand and supply took place so long ago—around the turn of the nineteenth century—how could his ideas have any relevance for us today?

Say's Law and Modern Issues Regarding Alleged "Overcapacity" and "Undercapacity"

Many modern observers have expressed concerns about alleged "imbalances" among sectors of today's economy. They fret over whether industries that produce certain traditional items, including textiles or steel, may suffer from an "overcapacity" problem in which quantities supplied exceed amounts that people desire to purchase. The result could be temporary buildups of unsold inventories of produced goods.

At the same time, these modern observers worry that various high-tech industries might experience an "undercapacity" problem in which quantities demanded by consumers are greater than flows of production by firms. These observers commonly express concerns that resulting stresses could yield fewer produced items than desired, which could lead to unanticipated and undesired depletions of inventories of finished products.

The Equilibrating Role of Changes in the Price Level

Actually, commentators in Say's time expressed similar concerns. Nevertheless, these commentators realized that temporary buildups of inventories would lead to a decline of the price level. This decrease in the level of prices would generate an increase in desired real expenditures—a downward movement along the aggregate demand curve.

Real aggregate spending thereby would rise to an equality with the long-run aggregate supply of real GDP.

In contrast, in the event of an "undercapacity" situation in which households desire to purchase more items than is consistent with the economy's long-run aggregate supply, the result would be an increase in the price level. The rise in the price level would give people an incentive to reduce their desired real expenditures. Then equilibrium would be re-attained with real aggregate spending equal to the long-run aggregate supply of real GDP once more.

FOR CRITICAL THINKING

Could an "overcapacity" or "undercapacity" problem persist if the government were to enact policies that prevented the price level from changing in response? Explain your reasoning.

REAL APPLICATION

Under what circumstances have you probably experienced a situation of "undercapacity?"

Sources are listed at the end of this chapter.

What You Should Know

Here is what you should know after reading this chapter.

LEARNING OBJECTIVES

KEY TERMS

11.1 **Describe the short-run determination of equilibrium real GDP and the price level in the classical model** *The classical model assumes (1) pure competition, (2) flexible wages and prices, (3) self-interest, and (4) no money illusion. The short-run aggregate supply curve is vertical at full-employment real GDP. Variations in aggregate demand along aggregate supply generate changes in the equilibrium price level.*

Say's law, 223
money illusion, 224
Key Figures
Figure 11-2, 225
Figure 11-3, 226
Figure 11-4, 227
Figure 11-5, 228

11.2 **Discuss the essential features of Keynesian economics and explain the short-run aggregate supply curve** *If product prices and wages and other input prices are "sticky," the short-run aggregate supply schedule can be horizontal over much of its range. This is the Keynesian short-run aggregate supply curve. More generally, however, to the extent that there is incomplete adjustment of prices in the short run, the short-run aggregate supply curve slopes upward.*

Keynesian short-run aggregate supply curve, 229
short-run aggregate supply curve, 230
Key Figures
Figure 11-6, 229
Figure 11-7, 230

11.3 **Explain what factors cause shifts in the short-run and long-run aggregate supply curves** *Both the long-run aggregate supply curve and the short-run aggregate supply curve shift in response to changes in the availability of labor or capital or to changes in technology and productivity. A widespread temporary change in the prices of factors of production, however, can cause a shift in the short-run aggregate supply curve without affecting the long-run aggregate supply curve.*

Key Figure
Figure 11-8, 231
Key Table
Table 11-2, 232

11.4 **Evaluate the effects of aggregate demand and supply shocks on equilibrium real GDP in the short run** *An aggregate demand shock that causes the aggregate demand curve to shift leftward pushes equilibrium real GDP below the level of full-employment real GDP in the short run, so there is a recessionary gap. An aggregate demand shock that induces a rightward shift in the aggregate demand curve results in an inflationary gap, in which short-run equilibrium real GDP exceeds full-employment real GDP.*

aggregate demand shock, 232
aggregate supply shock, 232
recessionary gap, 233
inflationary gap, 234
Key Figures
Figure 11-9, 233
Figure 11-10, 234

11.5 **Determine the causes of short-run variations in the inflation rate** *Demand-pull inflation occurs when the aggregate demand curve shifts rightward along an upward-sloping short-run aggregate supply curve. Cost-push inflation occurs when the short-run aggregate supply curve shifts leftward along the aggregate demand curve. A strengthening of the dollar shifts the short-run aggregate supply curve rightward and the aggregate demand curve leftward, which causes deflation but has uncertain effects on real GDP.*

demand-pull inflation, 235
cost-push inflation, 235
Key Figure
Figure 11-11, 235

PROBLEMS

11-1. Consider a country whose economic structure matches the assumptions of the classical model. After reading a recent best-seller documenting a growing population of low-income elderly people who were ill prepared for retirement, most residents of this country decide to increase their saving at any given interest rate. Explain whether or how this could affect the following:

  a. The current equilibrium interest rate

  b. Current equilibrium real GDP

  c. Current equilibrium employment

  d. Current equilibrium investment

  e. Future equilibrium real GDP

11-2. Consider a country with an economic structure consistent with the assumptions of the classical model. Suppose that businesses in this nation suddenly anticipate higher future profitability from investments they undertake today. Explain whether or how this could affect the following:

  a. The current equilibrium interest rate

  b. Current equilibrium real GDP

  c. Current equilibrium employment

  d. Current equilibrium saving

  e. Future equilibrium real GDP

11-3. "There is *absolutely no distinction* between equilibrium in the classical model and the model of long-run macroeconomic equilibrium." Is this statement true or false? Support your answer.

11-4. Suppose that the Keynesian short-run aggregate supply curve is applicable for a nation's economy. Use appropriate diagrams to assist in answering the following questions:

  a. What are two events that can cause the nation's real GDP to increase in the short run?

  b. What are two events that can cause the nation's real GDP to increase in the long run?

11-5. What determines how much real GDP responds to changes in the price level along the short-run aggregate supply curve?

11-6. Suppose that there is a temporary, but significant, increase in oil prices in an economy with an upward-sloping *SRAS* curve. If policymakers wish to prevent the equilibrium price level from changing in response to the oil-price increase, should they increase or decrease the quantity of money in circulation? Why?

11-7. As in Problem 11-6, suppose that there is a temporary, but significant, increase in oil prices in an economy with an upward-sloping *SRAS* curve. In

this case, however, suppose that policymakers wish to prevent equilibrium real GDP from changing in response to the oil-price increase. Should they increase or decrease the quantity of money in circulation? Why?

11-8. Based on your answers to Problems 11-6 and 11-7, can policymakers stabilize *both* the price level *and* real GDP simultaneously in response to a short-lived but sudden rise in oil prices? Explain briefly.

11-9. Between early 2018 and late 2019, total planned expenditures by U.S. households substantially increased in response to changes in federal tax laws that resulted in a net tax reduction. Explain, from a short-run Keynesian perspective, the predicted effects of this event on the equilibrium U.S. price level and equilibrium U.S. real GDP. Be sure to discuss the spending gap that the Keynesian model indicates would result in the short run.

11-10. In the previous decade, a stock-market upturn and rising home prices generated a significant increase in U.S. household wealth that induced most U.S. residents to boost their planned real spending at any given price level. Explain, from a short-run Keynesian perspective, the predicted effects of this event on the equilibrium U.S. price level and equilibrium U.S. real GDP. Be sure to discuss the spending gap that the Keynesian model indicates would result in the short run.

11-11. For each question that follows, suppose that the economy *begins* at point A. Identify which of the other points on the diagram—point B, C, D, or E—could represent a *new* short-run equilibrium after the described events take place and move the economy away from point A. Briefly explain your answers.

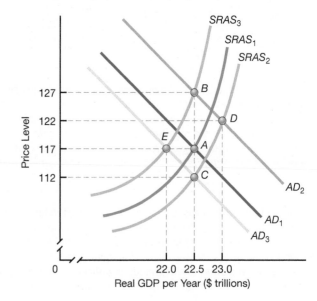

a. Most workers in this nation's economy are union members, and unions have successfully negotiated large wage boosts. At the same time, economic conditions suddenly worsen abroad, reducing real GDP and disposable income in other nations of the world.

b. A major hurricane has caused short-term halts in production at many firms and created major bottlenecks in the distribution of goods and services that had been produced prior to the storm. At the same time, the nation's central bank has significantly pushed up the rate of growth of the nation's money supply.

c. A strengthening of the value of this nation's currency in terms of other countries' currencies affects both the *SRAS* curve and the *AD* curve.

11-12. Consider an open economy in which the aggregate supply curve slopes upward in the short run. Firms in this nation do not import raw materials or any other productive inputs from abroad, but foreign residents purchase many of the nation's goods and services. What is the most likely short-run effect on this nation's economy if there is a significant downturn in economic activity in other nations around the world?

11-13. In Figure 11-2, if planned saving was less than planned investment, what would be true of the interest rate in relation to its equilibrium value? How would the interest rate adjust?

11-14. Consider Figure 11-3. Will all people who desire to work be employed if the current wage rate is $28 per hour? How many people will be employed and unemployed at this wage rate?

11-15. Take a look at Figure 11-4. If the Federal Reserve increases the quantity of money in circulation sufficiently to generate a rightward shift in the aggregate demand curve by $0.5 trillion, will actual equilibrium real GDP rise by this amount in the classical model? Explain.

11-16. Consider Figure 11-9. Suppose that businesses in this nation initially had been exporting significant amounts of domestically produced goods and services abroad. Assume that other nations of the world have experienced a sudden decline in economic conditions. What happens to the nation's aggregate demand curve? In the short run, will the nation experience an inflationary gap or a recessionary gap? Explain.

11-17. Consider Figure 11-10. Suppose that the real interest rate suddenly declines for reasons that do not relate to the price level. What happens to the nation's aggregate demand curve? In the short run, will the nation experience an inflationary gap or a recessionary gap? Explain.

11-18. Take a look at Figure 11-11. If this country's government decides to enact short-term barriers to international trade and substantial regulations of domestic businesses, what happens to the short-run equilibrium price level, and why? Is this an example of demand-pull or cost-push inflation? Explain.

REFERENCES

AI—DECISION MAKING THROUGH DATA: Automated Trading Makes Aggregate Supply Shocks Murkier

Irina Slav, "The Overlooked Factor Driving the Price of Oil," OilPrice.com (https://oilprice.com/Energy/Oil-Prices/The-Overlooked-Factor-Driving-The-Rally-In-Oil.html), January 7, 2019.

Amrith Ramkumar and Stephanie Yang, "The Oil Market Is Getting More Dangerous," *Wall Street Journal*, July 16, 2018.

U.S. Commodities Futures Trading Commission, "Sharp Price Movements in Commodity Futures Markets," Report by Staff of the Market Intelligence Branch, Division of Market Oversight (https://www.cftc.gov/sites/default/files/2018-06/SharpPriceMovementsReport0618.pdf), June 2018.

BEHAVIORAL EXAMPLE: Uncertainty and Aggregate Demand Shocks

Michael Clements, "Macroeconomic Uncertainty: Surveys versus Models?" *Macroeconomic Survey Expectations*, Springer, 2019.

Benjamin Born, Sebastian Breuer, and Steffen Elstner, "Uncertainty and the Great Recession," *Oxford Bulletin of Economics and Statistics*, 2018.

Stefano Fasani and Lorenza Rossi, "Are Uncertainty Shocks Aggregate Demand Shocks?" *Economics Letters*, 2018.

INTERNATIONAL EXAMPLE: How Long Lasting Are the Effects of Positive Aggregate Supply Shocks Caused by Lower Oil Prices?

Ana Maria Herrera, Mohamad Karaki, and Sandeep Kumar Rangaraju, "Oil Price Shocks and U.S. Economic Activity," *Energy Policy*, 2019.

Sangyup Choi, Davide Furceri, Prakash Loungani, Saurabh Mishra, and Marcos Poplawski-Ribeiro, "Oil Prices and Inflation Dynamics, Evidence from Advanced and Developing Countries," *Journal of International Money and Finance*, 2018.

Fédéric Holm-Hadulla and Kirstin Hubrich, "Macroeconomic Implications of Oil Price Fluctuations: A Regime-Switching Framework for the Euro Area," Federal Reserve Bank of Cleveland Conference on Inflation: Drivers and Dynamics, May 17–18, 2018.

ECONOMICS IN YOUR LIFE: U.S. Household Saving Increases, and So Does Private Investment Spending

"Personal Saving Rate," U.S. Bureau of Economic Analysis (https://www.bea.gov/data/income-saving/personal-saving-rate), 2019.

Evelyn Cheng, "Technology Companies Are Driving a Capital Spending Surge," CNBC (https://www.cnbc.com/2018/05/02/technology-companies-are-driving-a-capital-spending-surge.html), May 2, 2018.

*Paul Kiernan, "A Surprising Bulwark for the U.S. Economy: The Personal Saving Rate," *Wall Street Journal*, August 18, 2018.

ISSUES & APPLICATIONS: Is Say's Law Relevant for Today's Economy?

Harald Hagemann, "Say's Law," in *The Elgar Companion to John Maynard Keynes*, ed. Robert Dimand and Harald Hagemann, Chapter 34, Edward Elgar, 2019, pp. 218–223.

American Economic Association, "Beyond Say's Law: Reappraising Jean-Baptiste Say's Political Economy," Session at the AEA/ASSA Allied Social Science Annual Meetings (https://www.aeaweb.org/conference/2018/preliminary/1734?q=eNqrVipOLS7OzM8LqSxIVbKqhnGVrJQMlXSUUstS80qAbCOlWh2lxOLi_GQQxxwoU5JalAtkA1kpiZUQRklmbiqIVQtcMJAmGS0), January 6, 2018.

Alain Beraud and Guy Numa, "Beyond Say's Law: The Significance of Jean-Baptiste Say's Monetary Views," *Journal of the History of Economic Thought*, 2018.

12 Consumption, Real GDP, and the Multiplier

Aisyaqilumaranas/Shutterstock

LEARNING OBJECTIVES

After reading this chapter, you should be able to:

12.1 Explain the key determinants of consumption and saving in the Keynesian model

12.2 Identify the primary determinants of planned investment

12.3 Describe how equilibrium real GDP is established in the Keynesian model

12.4 Evaluate why autonomous changes in total planned expenditures have a multiplier effect on equilibrium real GDP

12.5 Understand the relationship between total planned expenditures and the aggregate demand curve

One of the most commonly watched bits of U.S. economic data is the change in real investment spending by businesses during the most recent 3-month interval. If the observed change in business investment expenditures is negative, some economists invariably boost their estimate of the probability of the near-term occurrence of an economic recession. In contrast, if the observed change in real investment spending is positive, many economists will raise their probability estimates for a more prolonged economic expansion. By the time you have finished reading this chapter, you will understand why economists pay such close attention to variations in business investment spending.

DID YOU KNOW THAT...

during a recent interval when after-tax, or *disposable*, incomes of U.S. households rose, economists found that households spent 89 cents of each additional dollar of disposable income and saved the remaining 11 cents? In this chapter, you will learn how an understanding of households' real consumption spending and saving decisions can assist in evaluating fluctuations in any country's real GDP.

12.1 Explain the key determinants of consumption and saving in the Keynesian model

Determinants of Planned Consumption and Planned Saving

To contemplate the determinants of planned consumption and planned saving in the Keynesian tradition, we will assume that the short-run aggregate supply curve within the current range of real GDP is horizontal. That is, we assume that it is similar to Figure 11-6. Thus, the equilibrium level of real GDP is demand determined. This is why Keynes wished to examine the elements of desired aggregate expenditures. Because of the Keynesian assumption of inflexible prices, inflation is not a concern in this analysis. Hence, real values are identical to nominal values.

Some Simplifying Assumptions in a Keynesian Model

To simplify the income determination model that follows, a number of assumptions are made:

1. Businesses pay no indirect taxes (for example, sales taxes).

2. Businesses distribute all of their profits to shareholders.

3. There is no depreciation (capital consumption allowance), so gross private domestic investment equals net investment.

4. The economy is closed—that is, there is no foreign trade.

Real disposable income
Real GDP minus net taxes, or after-tax real income.

Given all these simplifying assumptions, **real disposable income**, or after-tax real income, will be equal to real GDP minus net taxes—taxes paid less transfer payments received.

Another Look at Definitions and Relationships You can do only two things with a dollar of disposable income: Consume it or save it. If you consume it, it is gone forever. If you save the entire dollar, however, you will be able to consume it (and perhaps more if it earns interest) at some future time. That is the distinction between **consumption** and **saving**. Consumption is the act of using income for the purchase of consumption goods. **Consumption goods** are goods purchased by households for immediate satisfaction. (These also include services.) Consumption goods are such things as food and movies. By definition, whatever you do not consume you save and can utilize for consumption at some time in the future.

Consumption
Spending on new goods and services to be used up out of a household's current income. Whatever is not consumed is saved. Consumption includes such things as buying food and going to a concert.

Saving
The act of not consuming all of one's current income. Whatever is not consumed out of spendable income is, by definition, saved. *Saving* is an action measured over time (a flow), whereas *savings* are a stock, an accumulation resulting from the act of saving in the past.

Consumption goods
Goods bought by households to use up, such as food and movies.

Stocks and Flows: The Difference between Saving and Savings It is important to distinguish between *saving* and *savings*. *Saving* is an action that occurs at a particular rate—for example, $40 per week or $2,080 per year. This rate is a flow. It is expressed per unit of time, usually a year. Implicitly, then, when we talk about saving, we talk about a *flow*, or rate, of saving. *Savings*, by contrast, are a *stock* concept, measured at a certain point or instant in time. Your current *savings* are the result of past *saving*. You may currently have *savings* of $8,000 that are the result of four years' *saving* at a rate of $2,000 per year. Consumption is also a flow concept. You consume from after-tax income at a certain rate per week, per month, or per year.

Relating Income to Saving and Consumption A dollar of take-home income can be allocated either to consumption or to saving. Realizing this, we can see the relationship among saving, consumption, and disposable income from the following expression:

$$\text{Consumption} + \text{saving} \equiv \text{disposable income}$$

This is called an *accounting identity*, meaning that it has to hold true at every moment in time. (To indicate that the relationship is always true, we use the $\equiv$ symbol.)

From this relationship, we can derive the following definition of saving:

$$\text{Saving} \equiv \text{disposable income} - \text{consumption}$$

Hence, saving is the amount of disposable income that is not spent to purchase consumption goods.

Investment Spending **Investment** is also a flow concept. *Investment* as used in economics differs from the common use of the term. In common speech, it is often used to describe putting funds into the stock market or real estate. In economic analysis, investment primarily is defined to include expenditures on new machines and buildings—**capital goods**—that are expected to yield a future stream of income. This is called *fixed investment*. We also include changes in business inventories in our definition. This we call *inventory investment*.

Although saving could be influenced by income in the classical model, the key determinant of saving was the rate of interest. Specifically, the higher the rate of interest, the more people wanted to save and consequently the less people wanted to consume.

In contrast, according to Keynes, the interest rate is *not* the most important determinant of an individual's real saving and consumption decisions. In his view, the flow of income, not the interest rate, is the main determinant of consumption and saving.

Investment
Spending on items such as machines and buildings, which can be used to produce goods and services in the future. (It also includes changes in business inventories.) The investment part of real GDP is the portion that will be used in the process of producing goods *in the future*.

Capital goods
Producer durables; nonconsumable goods that firms use to make other goods.

How Income Flows Can Influence Consumption and Saving

When a person decides how much to consume and save today, Keynes reasoned, that individual must take into account both current and anticipated future incomes. After all, a higher income this year enables an individual *both* to purchase more final goods and services *and* to increase the flow of saving during the current year. Furthermore, a person's anticipation about the *future* flow of income likely influences how much of *current* income is allocated to consumption and how much to saving.

The Life-Cycle Theory of Consumption The most realistic and detailed theory of consumption, often called the **life-cycle theory of consumption**, considers how a person varies consumption and saving as income ebbs and flows during the course of an entire life span. This theory predicts that when an individual anticipates a higher income in the future, the individual will tend to consume more and save less in the current period than would have been the case otherwise. In contrast, when a person expects the flow of income to drop in the future, the individual responds in the present by allocating less of current income to consumption and more to saving.

Life-cycle theory of consumption
A theory in which a person bases decisions about current consumption and saving on both current income and anticipated future income.

The Permanent Income Hypothesis In a related theory, called the **permanent income hypothesis**, the income level that matters for a person's decision about current consumption and saving is *permanent income*, or expected average lifetime income. The permanent income hypothesis suggests that people increase their flow of consumption only if their anticipated average lifetime income rises. Thus, if a person's flow of income temporarily rises without an increase in average lifetime income, the person responds by saving the extra income and leaving consumption unchanged.

What other incentive besides higher after-tax income and interest returns might induce low-income individuals to increase their flows of real saving?

Permanent income hypothesis
A theory of consumption in which an individual determines current consumption based on anticipated average lifetime income.

BEHAVIORAL EXAMPLE

Using Lottery Prizes to Induce Low-Income People to Save More of Their Disposable Incomes

Considerable evidence shows that people with relatively low real disposable incomes tend also to save much smaller fractions of their incomes than do higher-income individuals. Some states have reacted by seeking to boost real saving flows of their low-income residents. Studies by these states revealed that reduced real disposable incomes and lower interest returns to saving have discouraged saving on the part of lower-income residents. Consequently, states have sought to identify other incentives that might encourage lower-income individuals to save.

Behavioral economists have considered a number of possible incentives. They have found that one of the more effective is automatic entry of savers into lotteries for prizes. Low-income individuals particularly respond to the possibility of winning a prize by increasing the fraction of their real disposable incomes that they allocate to real saving.

In light of such evidence, more than half of U.S. state governments have implemented laws permitting financial institutions based in their states to offer "prize-linked savings accounts." Such accounts offer lotteries for physical or financial prizes alongside traditional payments of interest returns as inducements to save.

FOR CRITICAL THINKING

Why do you suppose that the researchers found that offering low-income people accounts with more frequent automatic saving deductions from their real incomes also raised their real saving?

Sources are listed at the end of this chapter.

The Keynesian Theory of Consumption and Saving Keynes recognized that expectations about future income could affect current consumption and saving decisions. For purposes of developing a basic theory of consumption and saving, however, Keynes focused solely on the relationship between current income and current consumption and saving. Thus:

> *Keynes argued that real consumption and saving decisions depend primarily on a household's current real disposable income.*

Consumption function

The relationship between amount consumed and disposable income. A consumption function tells us how much people plan to consume at various levels of disposable income.

Dissaving

Negative saving; a situation in which spending exceeds income. Dissaving can occur when a household is able to borrow or use up existing assets.

The relationship between planned real consumption expenditures of households and their current level of real disposable income has been called the **consumption function**. It shows how much all households plan to consume per year at each level of real disposable income per year. Columns (1) and (2) of Table 12-1 illustrate a consumption function for a hypothetical household.

We see from Table 12-1 that as real disposable income rises, planned consumption also rises, but by a smaller amount, as Keynes suggested. Planned saving also increases with disposable income. Notice, however, that below an income of $60,000, the planned saving of this hypothetical household is actually negative. (See column 3.) The further that income drops below that level, the more the household engages in **dissaving**, either by going into debt or by using up some of its existing wealth.

Graphing the Numbers We now graph the consumption and saving relationships presented in Table 12-1. In the upper part of Figure 12-1, the vertical axis measures the level of planned real consumption per year, and the horizontal axis measures the level of real disposable income per year. In the lower part of the figure, the horizontal axis is again real disposable income per year, but now the vertical axis is planned real saving per year. All of these are on a dollars-per-year basis, which emphasizes the point that we are measuring flows, not stocks.

Consumption and Saving Functions As you can see, we have taken income-consumption and income-saving combinations *A* through *K* and plotted them. In the upper part of Figure 12-1, the result is called the *consumption function*. In the lower part, the result is called the *saving function*.

Mathematically, the saving function is the *complement* of the consumption function because consumption plus saving always equals disposable income. What is not consumed is, by definition, saved. The difference between actual disposable income and the planned rate of consumption per year *must* be the planned rate of saving per year.

TABLE 12-1

Real Consumption and Saving Schedules: A Hypothetical Case

Column 1 presents real disposable income from zero up to $120,000 per year. Column 2 indicates planned real consumption per year. Column 3 presents planned real saving per year. At levels of real disposable income below $60,000, planned real saving is negative. In column 4, we see the average propensity to consume, which is planned consumption divided by disposable income. Column 5 lists average propensity to save, which is planned saving divided by disposable income. Column 6 is the marginal propensity to consume, which shows the proportion of *additional* income that will be consumed. Finally, column 7 shows the proportion of *additional* income that will be saved, or the marginal propensity to save. (Δ represents "change in.")

Combination	(1) Real Disposable Income per Year (Y_d)	(2) Planned Real Consumption per Year (C)	(3) Planned Real Saving per Year ($S \equiv Y_d - C$) (1) − (2)	(4) Average Propensity to Consume ($APC \equiv C/Y_d$) (1) ÷ (2)	(5) Average Propensity to Save ($APS \equiv S/Y_d$) (3) ÷ (1)	(6) Marginal Propensity to Consume ($MPC \equiv \Delta C/\Delta Y_d$)	(7) Marginal Propensity to Save ($MPS \equiv \Delta S/\Delta Y_d$)
A	$ 0	$ 12,000	$−12,000	−	−	−	−
B	12,000	21,600	−9,600	1.8	−0.8	0.8	0.2
C	24,000	31,200	−7,200	1.3	−0.3	0.8	0.2
D	36,000	40,800	−4,800	1.133	−0.133	0.8	0.2
E	48,000	50,400	−2,400	1.05	−0.05	0.8	0.2
F	60,000	60,000	0	1.0	0.0	0.8	0.2
G	72,000	69,600	2,400	0.967	0.033	0.8	0.2
H	84,000	79,200	4,800	0.943	0.057	0.8	0.2
I	96,000	88,800	7,200	0.925	0.075	0.8	0.2
J	108,000	98,400	9,600	0.911	0.089	0.8	0.2
K	120,000	108,000	12,000	0.9	0.1	0.8	0.2

The 45-Degree Reference Line How can we find the rate of saving or dissaving in the upper part of Figure 12-1? We begin by drawing a line that is equidistant from both the horizontal and the vertical axes. This line is 45 degrees from either axis and is often called the **45-degree reference line**. At every point on the 45-degree reference line, a vertical line drawn to the income axis is the same distance from the origin as a horizontal line drawn to the consumption axis. Thus, at point *F*, where the consumption function intersects the 45-degree line, real disposable income equals planned real consumption.

45-degree reference line
The line along which planned real spending equals real GDP per year.

Point *F* is sometimes called the *break-even income point* because there is neither positive nor negative real saving. This can be seen in the lower part of Figure 12-1 as well. The planned annual rate of real saving at a real disposable income level of $60,000 is indeed zero.

Dissaving and Autonomous Consumption To the left of point *F* in either part of Figure 12-1, this hypothetical family engages in dissaving, either by going into debt or by consuming existing assets. The rate of real saving or dissaving in the upper part of the figure can be found by measuring the vertical distance between the 45-degree line and the consumption function. This simply tells us that if our hypothetical household sees its real disposable income fall to less than $60,000, it will not limit its consumption to this amount. It will instead go into debt or consume existing assets in some way to compensate for part of the lost income.

Autonomous Consumption Now look at the point on the diagram where real disposable income is zero but planned consumption is $12,000. This amount of real planned consumption, which does not depend at all on actual real disposable income,

The Consumption and Saving Functions

If we plot the combinations of real disposable income and planned real consumption from columns 1 and 2 in Table 12-1, we get the consumption function.

At every point on the 45-degree line, a vertical line drawn to the income axis is the same distance from the origin as a horizontal line drawn to the consumption axis. Where the consumption function crosses the 45-degree line at *F*, we know that planned real consumption equals real disposable income and there is zero saving. The vertical distance between the 45-degree line and the consumption function measures the rate of real saving or dissaving at any given income level.

If we plot the relationship between column 1 (real disposable income) and column 3 (planned real saving) from Table 12-1, we arrive at the saving function shown in the lower part of this diagram. (It is the complement of the consumption function presented above it.)

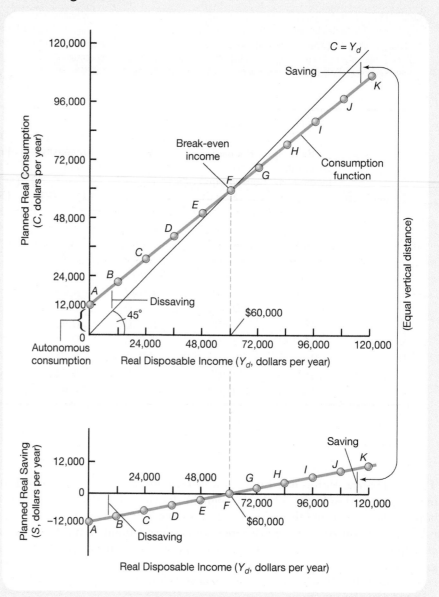

Autonomous consumption
The part of consumption that is independent of (does not depend on) the level of disposable income. Changes in autonomous consumption shift the consumption function.

is called **autonomous consumption**. The autonomous consumption of $12,000 is *independent* of disposable income. That means that no matter how low the level of real disposable income of our hypothetical household falls, the household will always attempt to consume at least $12,000 per year. (We are, of course, assuming here that the household's real disposable income does not equal zero year in and year out. There is certainly a limit to how long our hypothetical household could finance autonomous consumption without any income.)

The $12,000 of yearly consumption is determined by things other than the level of income. We don't need to specify what determines autonomous consumption. We merely state that it exists and that in our example it is $12,000 per year.

The Meaning of Autonomous Spending Just remember that the word *autonomous* means "existing independently." In our model, autonomous consumption exists independently of the hypothetical household's level of real disposable income. (Later we will review some of the determinants of consumption other than real disposable income.)

There are many possible types of autonomous expenditures. Hypothetically, we can assume that investment is autonomous—independent of income. We can assume that government expenditures are autonomous. We will do just that at various times in our discussions to simplify our analysis of income determination.

Average Propensity to Consume and to Save Let's now go back to Table 12-1, and this time let's look at columns 4 and 5: **average propensity to consume (APC)** and **average propensity to save (APS)**. They are defined as follows:

$$APC \equiv \frac{\text{real consumption}}{\text{real disposable income}}$$

$$APS \equiv \frac{\text{real saving}}{\text{real disposable income}}$$

Notice from column 4 in Table 12-1 that for this hypothetical household, the average propensity to consume decreases as real disposable income increases. This decrease simply means that the fraction of the household's real disposable income going to consumption falls as income rises. Column 5 shows that the average propensity to save, which at first is negative, finally hits zero at an income level of $60,000 and then becomes positive. In this example, the APS reaches a value of 0.1 at income level $120,000. This means that the household saves 10 percent of a $120,000 income.

It's quite easy for you to figure out your own average propensity to consume or to save. Just divide the value of what you consumed by your total real disposable income for the year, and the result will be your personal APC at your current level of income. Also, divide your real saving during the year by your real disposable income to calculate your own APS.

Marginal Propensity to Consume and to Save Now we go to the last two columns in Table 12-1: **marginal propensity to consume (MPC)** and **marginal propensity to save (MPS)**. The term *marginal* refers to a small incremental or decremental change (represented by the Greek letter delta, Δ, in Table 12-1). The marginal propensity to consume, then, is defined as

$$MPC \equiv \frac{\text{change in real consumption}}{\text{change in real disposable income}}$$

The marginal propensity to save is defined similarly as

$$MPS \equiv \frac{\text{change in real saving}}{\text{change in real disposable income}}$$

Marginal versus Average Propensities What do MPC and MPS tell you? They tell you what percentage of a given increase or decrease in real income will go toward consumption and saving, respectively. The emphasis here is on the word *change*. The marginal propensity to consume indicates how much you will change your planned real consumption if there is a change in your actual real disposable income.

If your marginal propensity to consume is 0.8, that does *not* mean that you consume 80 percent of *all* disposable income. The percentage of your total real disposable income that you consume is given by the average propensity to consume, or APC. As Table 12-1 indicates, the APC is not equal to 0.8 anywhere in its column. Instead, an MPC of 0.8 means that you will consume 80 percent of any *increase* in your disposable income. Hence, the MPC cannot be less than zero or greater than one. It follows that households increase their planned real consumption by between 0 and 100 percent of any increase in real disposable income that they receive.

Average propensity to consume (APC)
Real consumption divided by real disposable income. For any given level of real income, the proportion of total real disposable income that is consumed.

Average propensity to save (APS)
Real saving divided by real disposable income. For any given level of real income, the proportion of total real disposable income that is saved.

Marginal propensity to consume (MPC)
The ratio of the change in consumption to the change in disposable income. A marginal propensity to consume of 0.8 tells us that an additional $100 in take-home pay will lead to an additional $80 consumed.

Marginal propensity to save (MPS)
The ratio of the change in saving to the change in disposable income. A marginal propensity to save of 0.2 indicates that out of an additional $100 in take-home pay, $20 will be saved. Whatever is not saved is consumed. The marginal propensity to save plus the marginal propensity to consume must always equal 1, by definition.

ECONOMICS IN YOUR LIFE

To consider how economists can utilize data about observed changes in consumption spending to make conjectures about unobserved changes in real GDP, read **Why Earned Real Disposable Income and Current Saving Have Increased for Many Older People** on page 263.

Distinguishing the MPC from the APC Consider a simple example in which we show the difference between the average propensity to consume and the marginal propensity to consume. Assume that your consumption behavior is exactly the same as our hypothetical household's behavior depicted in Table 12-1. You have an annual real disposable income of $108,000. Your planned consumption rate, then, from column 2 of Table 12-1 is $98,400. Your average propensity to consume, then, is $98,400/$108,000 = 0.911. Now suppose that at the end of the year, your boss gives you an after-tax bonus of $12,000.

What would you do with that additional $12,000 in real disposable income? According to the table, you would consume $9,600 of it and save $2,400 ($12,000 − $9.600 = $2,400). In that case, your *marginal* propensity to consume would be $9,600/$12,000 = 0.8 and your marginal propensity to save would be $2,400/$12,000 = 0.2. What would happen to your *average* propensity to consume? To find out, we add $9,600 to $98,400 of planned consumption, which gives us a new consumption rate of $108,000. The average propensity to consume is then $108,000 divided by the new higher take-home salary of $120,000. Your APC drops from 0.911 to 0.9.

In contrast, your MPC remains, in our simplified example, 0.8 all the time. Look at column 6 in Table 12-1. The MPC is 0.8 at every level of income. (Therefore, the MPS is always equal to 0.2 at every level of income.) The constancy of MPC reflects the assumption that the amount you are willing to consume out of *additional* income will remain the same in percentage terms no matter what level of real disposable income is your starting point.

Some Relationships Consumption plus saving must equal income. Both your total real disposable income and the change in total real disposable income are either consumed or saved. The sums of the proportions of either measure that are consumed and saved must equal 1, or 100 percent. This allows us to make the following statements:

$$APC + APS \equiv 1 (= 100 \text{ percent of total income})$$

$$MPC + MPS \equiv 1 (= 100 \text{ percent of the } \textit{change} \text{ income})$$

The average propensities as well as the marginal propensities to consume and save must total 1, or 100 percent. Check the two statements by adding the figures in columns 4 and 5 for each level of real disposable income in Table 12-1. Do the same for columns 6 and 7.

Causes of Shifts in the Consumption Function A change in any other relevant economic variable besides real disposable income will cause the consumption function to shift. The number of such nonincome determinants of the position of the consumption function is almost unlimited. Real household **net wealth** is one determinant of the position of the consumption function. An increase in the real net wealth of the average household will cause the consumption function to shift upward. A decrease in real net wealth will cause it to shift downward. So far we have been talking about the consumption function of an individual or a household. Now let's move on to the national economy.

Net wealth
The stock of assets owned by a person, household, firm, or nation (net of any debts owed). For a household, net wealth can consist of a house, cars, personal belongings, stocks, bonds, bank accounts, and cash (minus any debts owed).

12.2 Identify the primary determinants of planned investment

Determinants of Investment

Investment, you will remember, consists of expenditures on new buildings and equipment and changes in business inventories. Historically, real gross private domestic investment in the United States has been extremely volatile over the years, relative to real consumption. If we were to look at net private domestic investment (investment after depreciation has been deducted), we would see that in the depths of the Great Depression and at the peak of the World War II effort, the figure was negative. In other words, we were eating away at our capital stock—we weren't even maintaining it by fully replacing depreciated equipment.

If we compare real investment expenditures historically with real consumption expenditures, we find that the latter are less variable over time than the former. Why is this so? One possible reason is that the real investment decisions of businesses are based on highly variable, subjective estimates of how the economic future looks.

The Planned Investment Function

Consider that at all times, businesses perceive an array of investment opportunities. These investment opportunities have rates of return ranging from zero to very high, with the number (or dollar value) of all such projects increasing if the rate of return rises. Because a project is profitable only if its rate of return exceeds the opportunity cost of the investment—the rate of interest—it follows that as the interest rate falls, planned investment spending increases, and vice versa. Even if firms use retained earnings (internal financing) to fund an investment, the lower the market rate of interest, the smaller the *opportunity cost* of using those retained earnings.

Thus, it does not matter in our analysis whether the firm must seek financing from external sources or can obtain such financing by using retained earnings. Whatever the method of financing, as the interest rate falls, more investment opportunities will be profitable, and planned investment will be higher.

It should be no surprise, therefore, that the investment function is represented as an inverse relationship between the rate of interest and the value of planned real investment. In Figure 12-2, a hypothetical investment schedule is given in panel (a) and plotted in panel (b). We see from this schedule that if, for example, the rate of interest is 5 percent, the dollar value of planned investment will be $3.8 trillion per year. Notice that planned investment is also given on a per-year basis, showing that it represents a flow, not a stock. (The stock counterpart of investment is the stock of capital in the economy measured in inflation-adjusted dollars at a point in time.)

FIGURE 12-2

Planned Real Investment

As shown in the hypothetical planned investment schedule in panel (a), the rate of planned real investment is inversely related to the rate of interest. If we plot the data pairs from panel (a), we obtain the investment function, *I*, in panel (b). It is negatively sloped.

Panel (a)

Annual Rate of Interest (%)	Planned Real Investment per Year ($ trillions)
10	3.3
9	3.4
8	3.5
7	3.6
6	3.7
5	3.8
4	3.9
3	4.0
2	4.1
1	4.2

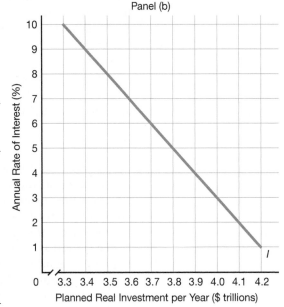

What Causes the Investment Function to Shift?

Because planned real investment is assumed to be a function of the rate of interest, any non-interest-rate variable that changes can have the potential of shifting the investment function. One of those variables is the expectations of businesses. If higher profits are expected, more machines and bigger plants will be planned for the future. More investment will be undertaken because of the expectation of higher profits. In this case, the investment function, *I*, in panel (b) of Figure 12-2, would shift outward to the right, meaning that more investment would be desired at all rates of interest.

Any change in productive technology can potentially shift the investment function. A positive change in productive technology would stimulate demand for additional capital goods and shift *I* outward to the right. Changes in business taxes can also shift the investment function. If they increase, we predict a leftward shift in the planned investment function because higher taxes imply a lower (after-tax) rate of return.

12.3 Describe how equilibrium real GDP is established in the Keynesian model

Determining Equilibrium Real GDP

We are interested in determining the equilibrium level of real GDP per year. When we examined the consumption function earlier in this chapter, however, it related planned real consumption expenditures to the level of real disposable income per year. We have already shown where adjustments must be made to GDP in order to get real disposable income. Real disposable income turns out to be less than real GDP because real net taxes (real taxes minus real government transfer payments) are usually about 20 to 25 percent of GDP. A representative average is about 22 percent, so disposable income, on average, has in recent years been around 78 percent of GDP.

Consumption as a Function of Real GDP

To simplify our model, assume that real disposable income, Y_d, differs from real GDP by the same absolute amount every year. Therefore, we can relatively easily substitute real GDP for real disposable income in the consumption function.

We can now plot any consumption function on a diagram in which the horizontal axis is no longer real disposable income but rather real GDP, as in Figure 12-3. Notice that there is an autonomous part of real consumption that is so labeled. The difference between this graph and the graphs presented earlier in this chapter is the change in the horizontal axis from real disposable income to real GDP per year. For the rest of this chapter, assume that the MPC out of real GDP equals 0.8, so that 20 percent of changes in real disposable income is saved. Of an additional after-tax $100 earned, an additional $80 will be consumed.

The 45-Degree Reference Line

As in the earlier graphs, Figure 12-3 shows a 45-degree reference line. The 45-degree line bisects the quadrant into two equal spaces. Thus, along the 45-degree reference line, planned real consumption expenditures, *C*, equal real GDP per year, *Y*. One can see, then, that at any point where the consumption function intersects the 45-degree reference line, planned real consumption expenditures will be exactly equal to real GDP per year, or $C = Y$.

Note that in this graph, because we are looking only at planned real consumption on the vertical axis, the 45-degree reference line is where planned real consumption, *C*, is always equal to real GDP per year, *Y*. Later, when we add real investment, government spending, and net exports to the graph, *all* planned real expenditures will be labeled along the vertical axis. In any event, real consumption and real GDP are equal at $1 trillion per year. That is where the consumption curve, *C*, intersects the 45-degree reference line. At that GDP level, all real GDP is consumed.

FIGURE 12-3

Consumption as a Function of Real GDP

This consumption function shows the rate of planned expenditures for each level of real GDP per year. Autonomous consumption is $0.2 trillion. Along the 45-degree reference line, planned real consumption expenditures per year, *C*, are identical to real GDP per year, *Y*. The consumption curve intersects the 45-degree reference line at a value of $1 trillion per year in base-year dollars (the value of current GDP expressed in prices in a base year).

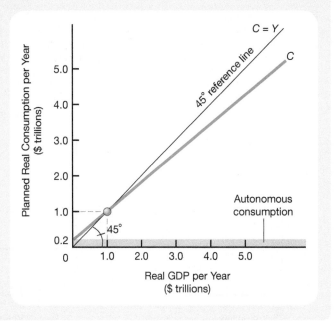

Adding the Investment Function

Another component of private aggregate demand is, of course, real investment spending, *I*. We have already looked at the planned investment function, which related real investment, which includes changes in inventories of final products, to the rate of interest.

Planned Investment and the Interest Rate In panel (a) of Figure 12-4, you see that at an interest rate of 5 percent, the rate of real investment is $3.8 trillion per year. The $3.8 trillion of real investment per year is *autonomous* with respect to real GDP—that is, it is independent of real GDP.

In other words, given that we have a determinant investment level of $3.8 trillion at a 5 percent rate of interest, we can treat this level of real investment as constant, regardless of the level of GDP. This is shown in panel (b) of Figure 12-4. The vertical distance of real investment spending is $3.8 trillion. Businesses plan on investing a particular amount—$3.8 trillion per year—and will do so no matter what the level of real GDP.

Combining Planned Investment and Consumption How do we add this amount of real investment spending to our consumption function? We simply add a line above the *C* line that we drew in Figure 12-3 that is higher by the vertical distance equal to $3.8 trillion of autonomous real investment spending. This is shown by the arrow in panel (c) of Figure 12-4.

Our new line, now labeled *C* + *I*, is called the *consumption plus investment line*. In our simple economy without real government expenditures and net exports, the *C* + *I* curve represents total planned real expenditures as they relate to different levels of real GDP per year. Because the 45-degree reference line shows all the points where planned real expenditures (now *C* + *I*) equal real GDP, we label it *C* + *I* = *Y*. Thus, in equilibrium, the sum of consumption spending (*C*) and investment spending (*I*) equals real GDP (*Y*), which is $20 trillion per year. Equilibrium occurs when total planned real expenditures equal real GDP (given that any amount of production of goods and services in this model in the short run can occur without a change in the price level).

Combining Consumption and Investment

In panel (a), we show that at an interest rate of 5 percent, real investment is equal to $3.8 trillion per year. In panel (b), investment is a constant $3.8 trillion per year. When we add this amount to the consumption line, we obtain in panel (c) the $C + I$ line, which is vertically higher than the C line by exactly $3.8 trillion. Real GDP is equal to $C + I$ at $20 trillion per year where total planned real expenditures, $C + I$, are equal to actual real GDP, for this is where the $C + I$ line intersects the 45-degree reference line, on which $C + I$ is equal to Y at every point.

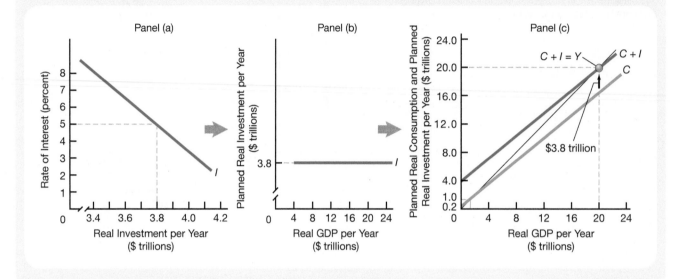

WHAT HAPPENS WHEN...

the planned investment function shifts?

The amount of planned real investment spending is added vertically to real consumption spending at any given level of real GDP to obtain the $C + I$ line. An increase in planned investment that generates an outward shift in the planned investment function causes the $C + I$ line to shift upward. This upward shift in the $C + I$ line, in turn, yields a point of intersection higher up along the 45-degree reference line. Hence, following an outward shift of the planned investment function, planned spending $C + I$ equals a higher real GDP flow Y.

Saving and Investment: Planned versus Actual

Figure 12-5 shows the planned investment curve as a horizontal line at $3.8 trillion per year in base-year dollars. Real investment is completely autonomous in this simplified model—it does not depend on real GDP.

The planned saving curve is represented by S. Because in our model whatever is not consumed is, by definition, saved, the planned saving schedule is the complement of the planned consumption schedule, represented by the C line in Figure 12-3. For better exposition, we look at only a part of the saving and investment schedules—annual levels of real GDP between $18 trillion and $22 trillion.

Why does equilibrium have to occur at the intersection of the planned saving and planned investment schedules? If we are at E in Figure 12-5, planned saving equals planned investment. All anticipations are validated by reality. There is no tendency for businesses to alter the rate of production or the level of employment because they are neither increasing nor decreasing their inventories in an unplanned way.

FIGURE 12-5

Planned and Actual Rates of Saving and Investment

Only at the equilibrium level of real GDP of $20 trillion per year will planned saving equal actual saving, planned investment equal actual investment, and hence planned saving equal planned investment.

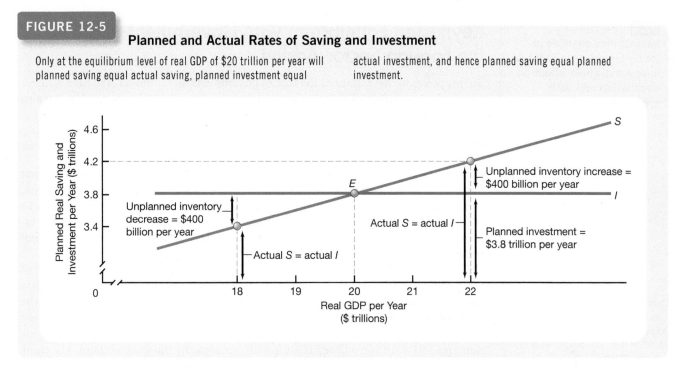

Unplanned Changes in Business Inventories If real GDP is $22 trillion instead of $20 trillion, planned investment, as usual, is $3.8 trillion per year. It is exceeded, however, by planned saving, which is $4.2 trillion per year.

A Mismatch between Actual and Anticipated Purchases The additional $0.4 trillion ($400 billion) in saving by households over and above planned investment represents less consumption spending. The fact that consumption is lower than planned will translate into unsold goods that accumulate as unplanned business inventory investment.

Thus, consumers will *actually* purchase fewer goods and services than businesses had *planned*. This will leave firms with unsold products, and their inventories will begin to rise above the levels they had planned.

How Businesses Adjust Unplanned business inventories will now rise at the rate of $400 billion per year, or $4.2 trillion in actual investment (including inventories) minus $3.8 trillion in planned investment by firms that had not anticipated an inventory buildup. This situation, though, cannot continue for long. Businesses will respond to the unplanned increase in inventories by cutting back production of goods and services and reducing employment, and we will move toward a lower level of real GDP.

Naturally, the adjustment process works in reverse if real GDP is less than the equilibrium level. For instance, if real GDP is $18 trillion per year, an unintended inventory decrease of $0.4 trillion ultimately brings about an increase in real GDP toward the equilibrium level of $20 trillion.

Every time the saving rate planned by households differs from the investment rate planned by businesses, there will be a shrinkage or an expansion in the circular flow of income and output in the form of unplanned inventory changes. Real GDP and employment will change until unplanned inventory changes are again zero—that is, until we have attained the equilibrium level of real GDP.

12.4 Evaluate why autonomous changes in total planned expenditures have a multiplier effect on equilibrium real GDP

Keynesian Equilibrium with Government and the Foreign Sector Added

To this point, we have ignored the role of government in our model. We have also left out the foreign sector of the economy. Let's think about what happens when we also consider these as elements of the model.

Government

To add real government spending, G, to our macroeconomic model, we assume that the level of resource-using government purchases of goods and services (federal, state, and local), *not* including transfer payments, is determined by the political process. In other words, G will be considered autonomous, just like real investment (and a relatively small component of real consumption). In the United States, resource-using federal government expenditures account for about 20 percent of real GDP.

Lump-sum tax

A tax that does not depend on income. An example is a $1,000 tax that every household must pay, irrespective of its economic situation.

The other side of the coin, of course, is that there are real taxes, which are used to pay for much of government spending. We will simplify greatly by assuming that there is a constant **lump-sum tax** of $3.4 trillion a year to finance a portion of the $4.4 trillion of government spending, yielding a difference—called a *government budget deficit*—of $1.0 trillion that must be borrowed in the credit market The lump-sum tax of $3.4 trillion will reduce disposable income by the same amount. We show this in Table 12-2 (column 2) , where we give the numbers for a complete model.

The Foreign Sector

For years, the media have focused attention on the nation's foreign trade deficit. We have been buying merchandise and services from foreign residents—real imports—the value of which exceeds the value of the real exports we have been selling to them. The difference between real exports and real imports is *real net*

TABLE 12-2

The Determination of Equilibrium Real GDP with Government and Net Exports Added

Figures are trillions of dollars.

(1) Real GDP	(2) Real Taxes	(3) Real Disposable Income	(4) Planned Real Consumption	(5) Planned Real Saving	(6) Planned Real Investment	(7) Real Government Spending	(8) Real Net Exports (exports minus imports)	(9) Total Planned Real Expenditures	(10) Unplanned Inventory Changes	(11) Direction of Change in Real GDP
16.0	3.4	12.6	10.0	2.6	3.8	4.4	−1.0	17.2	−1.2	Increase
17.0	3.4	13.6	10.8	2.8	3.8	4.4	−1.0	18.0	−1.0	Increase
18.0	3.4	14.6	11.6	3.0	3.8	4.4	−1.0	18.8	−0.8	Increase
19.0	3.4	15.6	12.4	3.2	3.8	4.4	−1.0	19.6	−0.6	Increase
20.0	3.4	16.6	13.2	3.4	3.8	4.4	−1.0	20.4	−0.4	Increase
21.0	3.4	17.6	14.0	3.6	3.8	4.4	−1.0	21.2	−0.2	Increase
22.0	3.4	18.6	14.8	3.8	3.8	4.4	−1.0	22.0	0	Neither (equilibrium)
23.0	3.4	19.6	15.6	4.0	3.8	4.4	−1.0	22.8	+0.2	Decrease
24.0	3.4	20.6	16.4	4.2	3.8	4.4	−1.0	23.6	+0.4	Decrease

FIGURE 12-6

The Equilibrium Level of Real GDP

The consumption function, with no government and thus no taxes, is shown as C. When we add autonomous investment, government spending, and net exports, we obtain $C + I + G + X$. We move from E_1 to E_2. Equilibrium real GDP is $22 trillion per year.

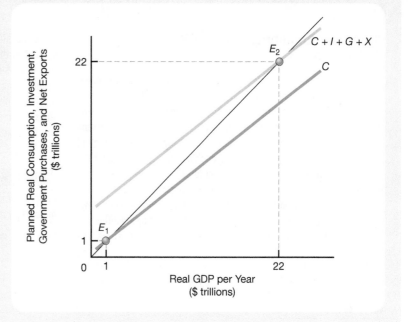

exports, which we will label X in our graphs. The level of real exports depends on international economic conditions, especially in the countries that buy our products. Real imports depend on economic conditions here at home. For simplicity, assume that real imports exceed real exports (real net exports, X, is negative) and furthermore that the level of real net exports is autonomous—independent of real national income. Assume a level of X of $-$1.0 trillion per year, as shown in column 8 of Table 12-2.

Determining the Equilibrium Level of GDP per Year

We are now in a position to determine the equilibrium level of real GDP per year under the continuing assumptions that the price level is unchanging; that investment, government, and the foreign sector are autonomous; and that planned consumption expenditures are determined by the level of real GDP. As can be seen in Table 12-2, total planned real expenditures of $22 trillion per year equal real GDP of $22 trillion per year, and this is where we reach equilibrium.

Remember that equilibrium *always* occurs when total planned real expenditures equal real GDP. Now look at Figure 12-6, which shows the equilibrium level of real GDP. There are two curves: one showing the consumption function, which is the exact duplicate of the one as it was in Figure 12-3, before we added the government and taxes, and the other being the $C + I + G + X$ curve, which intersects the 45-degree reference line (representing equilibrium) at $22 trillion per year.

Whenever total planned real expenditures differ from real GDP, there are unplanned inventory changes. When total planned real expenditures are greater than real GDP, inventory levels drop in an unplanned manner. To get inventories back up, firms seek to expand their production of goods and services, which increases real GDP. Real GDP rises toward its equilibrium level. Whenever total planned real expenditures are less than real GDP, the opposite occurs. There are unplanned inventory increases, causing firms to cut back on their production of goods and services in an effort to push inventories back down to planned levels. The result is a drop in real GDP toward the equilibrium level.

How is application of AI techniques promising to improve forecasts of equilibrium real GDP?

AI | DECISION MAKING THROUGH DATA

"Nowcast" Equilibrium Real GDP and Its Components

Businesspeople often seek economic forecasts regarding future movements in equilibrium real GDP and its components to better enable them to anticipate likely levels of consumer spending on their products. Knowing when economic booms are in the offing may help businesspersons plan expansions of production. In contrast, receiving forewarnings of pending decreases in real GDP would enable them to scale back their output rates. Nevertheless, professional forecasters have a very poor track record in predicting real GDP booms and busts.

Two recent developments promise forecasting improvements, however. One is the use of machine learning to "train" forecasting algorithms—connected lines of computer code—to learn from previous errors and avoid repeating those mistakes the next time around. The other development is the use of "real-time data," or up-to-the-second information, to consistently update these machine-learning-assisted forecasts. People using these techniques to make economic forecasts already are reporting improvements in their capabilities to forecast future recessions. It remains to be seen, though, if utilization of these new methods will yield advance forecasts of any sustained decline in equilibrium real GDP.

REAL APPLICATION

Under what circumstances in your future might more accurate business forecasting be beneficial for you?

Sources are listed at the end of this chapter.

12.5 Understand the relationship between total planned expenditures and the aggregate demand curve

The Multiplier, Total Expenditures, and Aggregate Demand

Look again at panel (c) of Figure 12-4. Assume for the moment that the only real expenditures included in real GDP are real consumption expenditures. Where would the equilibrium level of real GDP be in this case? It would be where the consumption function (C) intersects the 45-degree reference line, which is at $1 trillion per year. Now we add the autonomous amount of planned real investment, $3.8 trillion, and then determine what the new equilibrium level of real GDP will be. It turns out to be $20 trillion per year. Adding $3.8 trillion per year of investment spending increased equilibrium real GDP by *five* times that amount, or by $19 trillion per year.

The Multiplier Effect

Multiplier
The ratio of the change in the equilibrium level of real GDP to the change in autonomous real expenditures. The number by which a change in autonomous real investment or autonomous real consumption, for example, is multiplied to get the change in equilibrium real GDP.

What is operating here is a multiplier effect of changes in autonomous spending. The **multiplier** is the number by which a permanent change in autonomous real investment or autonomous real consumption is multiplied to get the change in the equilibrium level of real GDP. Any permanent increases in autonomous real investment or in any autonomous component of consumption will cause an even larger increase in real GDP. Any permanent decreases in autonomous real spending will cause even larger decreases in real GDP per year. To understand why this multiple expansion (or contraction) in equilibrium real GDP occurs, let's look at a simple numerical example.

An Example We'll use the same figures we used for the marginal propensity to consume and to save. MPC will equal 0.8, or $\frac{4}{5}$ and MPS will equal 0.2, or $\frac{1}{5}$. Now let's run an experiment and say that businesses decide to increase planned real investment permanently by $100 billion a year.

We see in Table 12-3 that during what we'll call the first round in column 1, investment is increased by $100 billion. This also means an increase in real GDP of $100 billion, because the spending by one group represents income for another, shown in column 2. Column 3 gives the resultant increase in consumption by households that received this additional $100 billion in income. This rise in consumption

TABLE 12-3

The Multiplier Process

We trace the effects of a *permanent* $100 billion increase in autonomous real investment spending on real GDP per year. If we assume a marginal propensity to consume of 0.8, such an increase will eventually elicit a $500 billion increase in equilibrium real GDP per year.

(1) Round	Assumption: MPC = 0.8, or $\frac{4}{5}$		
	(2) Annual Increase in Real GDP ($ billions)	(3) Annual Increase in Planned Real Consumption ($ billions)	(4) Annual Increase in Planned Real Saving ($ billions)
1 ($100 billion per year increase in I)	100.00 → 80.000	80.000	20.000
2	80.00 → 64.000	64.000	16.000
3	64.00 → 51.200	51.200	12.800
4	51.20 → 40.960	40.960	10.240
5	40.96 → 32.768	32.768	8.192
.	.	.	.
.	.	.	.
.	.	.	.
All later rounds	163.84	131.072	32.768
Totals	500.00	400.000	100.000

spending is found by multiplying the MPC by the increase in real GDP. Because the MPC equals 0.8, real consumption expenditures during the first round will increase by $80 billion.

The Multiplier Process That's not the end of the story, however. This additional household consumption is also spending, and it will provide $80 billion of additional income for other individuals. Thus, during the second round, we see an increase in real GDP of $80 billion. Now, out of this increased real GDP, what will be the resultant increase in consumption expenditures? It will be 0.8 times $80 billion, or $64 billion.

We continue these induced expenditure rounds and find that an initial increase in autonomous investment expenditures of $100 billion will eventually cause the equilibrium level of real GDP to increase by $500 billion. A permanent $100 billion increase in autonomous real investment spending has induced an additional $400 billion increase in real consumption spending, for a total increase in real GDP of $500 billion. In other words, equilibrium real GDP will change by an amount equal to five times the change in real investment.

The Multiplier Formula

It turns out that the autonomous spending multiplier is equal to 1 divided by the marginal propensity to save. In our example, the MPC was 0.8, or $\frac{4}{5}$. Therefore, because MPC + MPS = 1, the MPS was equal to 0.2, or $\frac{1}{5}$. When we divide 1 by $\frac{1}{5}$ we get 5. That was our multiplier. A $100 billion increase in real planned investment led to a $500 billion increase in the equilibrium level of real GDP. Our multiplier will always be the following:

$$\text{Multiplier} \equiv \frac{1}{1 - \text{MPC}} \equiv \frac{1}{\text{MPS}}$$

Determining the Multiplier with Either MPC or MPS You can always figure out the multiplier if you know either the MPC or the MPS. Let's consider an example. If MPS = 0.25, or $\frac{1}{4}$,

$$\text{Multiplier} = \frac{1}{\frac{1}{4}} = 4$$

Because MPC + MPS = 1, it follows that MPS = 1 − MPC. Hence, we can always figure out the multiplier if we are given the marginal propensity to consume. In this example, if the marginal propensity to consume is given as 0.75, or $\frac{3}{4}$,

$$\text{Multiplier} = \frac{1}{1 - \frac{3}{4}} = \frac{1}{\frac{1}{4}} = 4$$

How the Values of MPC and MPS Affect the Multiplier By taking a few numerical examples, you can demonstrate to yourself an important property of the multiplier:

The smaller the marginal propensity to save, the larger the multiplier.

Otherwise stated:

The larger the marginal propensity to consume, the larger the multiplier.

When the MPS is smaller and the MPC is larger, more of each additional dollar of disposable real income is spent by consumers. This greater spending generated a larger amount of real disposable income for people to spend in the next round of the multiplier process. Thus a smaller MPS and larger MPC translate into higher real GDP at every stage in the process and, consequently, a larger total increase in real GDP.

Demonstrate this to yourself by computing the multiplier when the marginal propensity to save equals $\frac{3}{4}$, $\frac{1}{2}$, and $\frac{1}{4}$. What happens to the multiplier as the MPS gets smaller?

When you have the multiplier, the following formula will then give you the change in equilibrium real GDP due to a permanent change in autonomous spending:

Change in equilibrium real GDP = multiplier × change in autonomous spending

The multiplier, as noted earlier, works for a *permanent* increase or a *permanent* decrease in autonomous spending per year. In our earlier example, if the autonomous component of real consumption had fallen permanently by $100 billion, the reduction in equilibrium real GDP would have been $500 billion per year.

Significance of the Multiplier

Depending on the size of the multiplier, it is possible that a relatively small permanent change in planned investment or in autonomous consumption can trigger a much larger change in equilibrium real GDP per year. In essence, the multiplier magnifies the fluctuations in yearly equilibrium real GDP initiated by changes in autonomous spending.

As was just noted, the larger the marginal propensity to consume, the larger the multiplier. If the marginal propensity to consume is $\frac{1}{2}$, the multiplier is 2. In that case, a $1 billion decrease in (autonomous) real investment will elicit a $2 billion decrease in equilibrium real GDP per year. Conversely, if the marginal propensity to consume is $\frac{9}{10}$, the multiplier will be 10. That same $1 billion decrease in planned real investment expenditures with a multiplier of 10 will lead to a $10 billion decrease in equilibrium real GDP per year.

Which governmental sources of changes in autonomous spending appear to contribute most to bringing about multiplier effects on U.S. real GDP?

POLICY EXAMPLE

Comparing the Relative Contributions of Government-Generated Multiplier Effects on Real GDP

Both the U.S. federal government and state and local governments periodically enact changes in their expenditures that bring about changes in U.S. autonomous spending. In addition, variations in government taxes and benefits also influence *autonomous* consumption spending by households that must transmit tax payments net of government-transmitted benefits.

Economists have found that the contributions of federal, state, and local government spending rarely account for more than relatively small fractions of ultimate multiplier effects on real GDP. In contrast, on average, changes in autonomous spending generated by variations in taxes net of benefits account for well over half of the eventual effects of governmental spending and taxation policies on U.S. real GDP.

FOR CRITICAL THINKING

Why might the fact that real consumption spending accounts for more than two-thirds of U.S. planned real expenditures help to explain why tax-and-benefit policy changes have the largest ultimate effects on real GDP?

Sources are listed at the end of this chapter.

How a Change in Real Autonomous Spending Affects Real GDP When the Price Level Can Change

So far, our examination of how changes in real autonomous spending affect equilibrium real GDP has considered a situation in which the price level remains unchanged. Thus, our analysis has indicated only how much the aggregate demand curve shifts in response to a change in investment, government spending, net exports, or lump-sum taxes.

Taking Aggregate Supply into Consideration Of course, when we take into account the aggregate supply curve, we must also consider responses of the equilibrium price level to a multiplier-induced change in aggregate demand. We do so in Figure 12-7.

The intersection of AD_1 and $SRAS$ is at a price level of 110 with equilibrium real GDP of $22 trillion per year. An increase in autonomous spending shifts the aggregate demand curve outward to the right to AD_2. If the price level remained at 110, the short-run equilibrium level of real GDP would increase to $22.5 trillion per year because, for the $100 billion increase in autonomous spending, the multiplier would be 5, as it was in Table 12-3.

FIGURE 12-7

Effect of a Rise in Autonomous Spending on Equilibrium Real GDP

A $100 billion increase in autonomous spending (investment, government, or net exports) moves AD_1 to AD_2. If the price index increases from 110 to 115, equilibrium real GDP goes up only to, say, $22.3 trillion per year instead of $22.5 trillion per year.

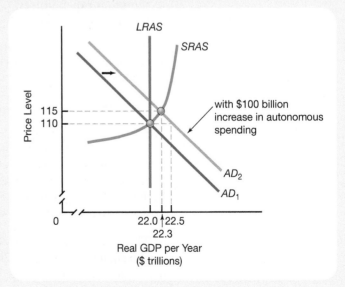

Accounting for a Price Level Change The price level does not stay fixed, however, because ordinarily the *SRAS* curve is positively sloped. In this diagram, the new short-run equilibrium level of real GDP is hypothetically $22.3 trillion. The ultimate effect on real GDP is smaller than the multiplier effect on nominal income because part of the additional income is used to pay higher prices. Not all is spent on additional goods and services, as is the case when the price level is fixed.

If the economy is at an equilibrium level of real GDP that is greater than *LRAS*, the implications for the eventual effect on real GDP are even more severe. Look again at Figure 12-7. The *SRAS* curve starts to slope upward more dramatically after $22 trillion of real GDP per year. Therefore, any increase in aggregate demand will lead to a proportionally greater increase in the price level and a smaller increase in equilibrium real GDP per year. The ultimate effect on real GDP of any increase in autonomous spending will be relatively small because most of the changes will be in the price level. Moreover, any increase in the short-run equilibrium level of real GDP will tend to be temporary because the economy is temporarily above *LRAS*—the strain on its productive capacity will raise the price level.

The Relationship between Aggregate Demand and the *C + I + G + X* Curve

A relationship clearly exists between the aggregate demand curves that you studied previously and the *C + I + G + X* curve developed in this chapter. After all, aggregate demand consists of consumption, investment, and government purchases, plus the foreign sector of our economy. There is a major difference, however, between the aggregate demand curve, *AD*, and the *C + I + G + X* curve: The latter is drawn with the price level held constant, whereas the former is drawn, by definition, with the price level changing. To derive the aggregate demand curve from the *C + I + G + X* curve, we must now allow the price level to change. Look at the upper part of Figure 12-8. Here we see the *C + I + G + X* curve at a price level equal to 100, and at $22 trillion of real GDP per year, planned real expenditures exactly equal real GDP. This gives us point *A* in the lower graph, for it shows what real GDP would be at a price level of 100.

Now let's assume that in the upper graph, the price level increases to 125. What are the effects?

1. A higher price level can decrease the purchasing power of any cash that people hold (the real-balance effect). This is a decrease in real wealth, and it causes consumption expenditures, *C*, to fall, thereby putting downward pressure on the *C + I + G + X* curve.

2. Because individuals attempt to borrow more to replenish their real cash balances, interest rates will rise, which will make it more costly for people to buy houses and cars (the interest rate effect). Higher interest rates also make it less profitable to install new equipment and to erect new buildings. Therefore, the rise in the price level indirectly causes a reduction in total planned spending on goods and services.

3. In an open economy, our higher price level causes foreign spending on our goods to fall (the open economy effect). Simultaneously, it increases our demand for others' goods. If the foreign exchange price of the dollar stays constant for a while, there will be an increase in imports and a decrease in exports, thereby reducing the size of *X*, again putting downward pressure on the *C + I + G + X* curve.

The result is that a new *C + I + G + X* curve at a price level equal to 125 generates an equilibrium at E_2 at $20 trillion of real GDP per year. This gives us point *B* in the lower part of Figure 12-8. When we connect points *A* and *B*, we obtain the aggregate demand curve, *AD*.

FIGURE 12-8

The Relationship between *AD* and the *C* + *I* + *G* + *X* Curve

In the upper graph, the *C* + *I* + *G* + *X* curve at a price level equal to 100 intersects the 45-degree reference line at E_1, or $22 trillion of real GDP per year. That gives us point *A* (price level = 100; real GDP = $22 trillion) in the lower graph. When the price level increases to 125, the *C* + *I* + *G* + *X* curve shifts downward, and the new level of real GDP at which planned real expenditures equal real GDP is at E_2 at $20 trillion per year. This gives us point *B* in the lower graph. Connecting points *A* and *B*, we obtain the aggregate demand curve.

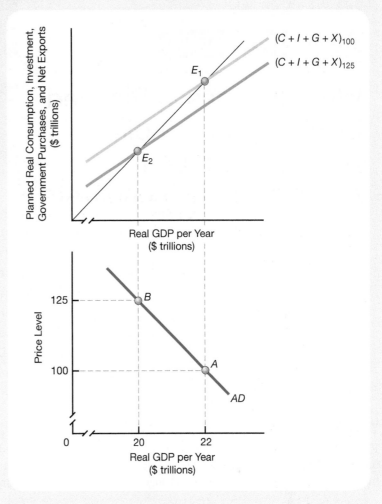

ECONOMICS IN YOUR LIFE

Why Earned Real Disposable Income and Current Saving Have Increased for Many Older People

Roberta Gordon is a 76-year-old woman who has started a new job. "I'm a working woman again," she says. In prior years, Gordon had jobs in fund raising, home health care, housecleaning, library management, and telemarketing. Currently, she earns an extra $50 per day handing out product samples at a grocery store. Gordon's personal marginal and average propensities to save during her prior years of work were very low. As a consequence, her accumulated personal savings available to utilize during retirement have turned out to be insufficient to fund desired real consumption spending now that she is older. Gordon additionally is seeking to save a larger fraction of her renewed flow of earned real disposable income than she did when she was younger.

Current estimates indicate that among the approximately 9,000 people who reach the age of 65 each day, at least 40 percent likewise have failed to amass sufficient personal savings to fund desired consumption spending in future years. Many of these people

envision working well into their seventies. Like Gordon, most are trying to save higher fractions of their real-disposable-income flows than they did in years past.

FOR CRITICAL THINKING

Why might the choices that Gordon and many other older individuals are making help to explain why the observed fraction of additional aggregate real U.S. disposable income allocated to saving has increased?

REAL APPLICATION

If the prospect of your having to work well into your seventies makes you uncomfortable, how can you avoid experiencing that situation? Alternatively, what are the positive aspects for your life if you do continue working into your seventies?

Sources are listed at the end of this chapter.

ISSUES & APPLICATIONS

Why Changes in Planned Investment Spending Receive So Much Attention from Economists

CONCEPTS APPLIED

➤ Real Investment Spending

➤ Planned Investment Function

➤ Multiplier Effect

Real investment spending accounts for a smaller fraction of aggregate desired expenditures than household consumption spending and government expenditures. Nevertheless, variations in the position of the planned investment function contribute more to the *volatility* of aggregate desired expenditures. Indeed, upward shifts in the position of the planned investment function often are credited with generating economic expansions. Downward shifts of this function, in contrast, often receive blame for bringing about economic contractions.

Why Recession Concerns Increased

Figure 12-9 displays percentage changes in U.S. real investment spending over several years. During the first eighteen months of the period, nearly all of these changes were negative.

Hence, the amount of real planned investment spending decreased. Interest rates barely changed during this period, so the most likely explanation for the investment decrease was a downward shift of the U.S. planned investment function.

FIGURE 12-9

Variations in U.S. Investment Spending since 2016

During most of the 2015–2016 interval, percentage changes in U.S. real investment spending were negative. The planned real investment function was shifting downward and, other things being equal, generating negative multiplier effects on equilibrium U.S. real GDP. Since late 2016, however, percentage changes in real investment spending have been positive. The planned investment function has been shifting upward and inducing positive multiplier effects on equilibrium real GDP.

Sources: Federal Reserve Economic Data, Federal Reserve Bank of St. Louis; author's estimates.

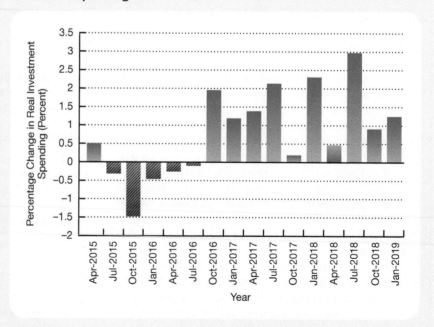

As you have learned, reductions in real planned investment exert negative multiplier effects on equilibrium real GDP by inducing cascading decreases in consumption spending. This is why during the early months displayed in Figure 12-9, some economists considerably increased their estimates of the probability that a recession could occur.

Why Recession Worries Largely Disappeared

As you can see, in every three-month interval following the first six in Figure 12-9, the percentage changes in real investment spending were positive. Hence, real investment spending increased. Interest rates rose slightly during the more recent period, which means that the U.S. planned investment function shifted upward considerably. Most economists agree that the likely reasons for this upward shift were improved business expectations regarding future profits and a reduction in federal business tax rates.

Of course, increases in real planned investment exert positive multiplier effects on equilibrium real GDP. Thus, during the more recent period, few economists raised concerns about any near-term recession likelihood.

FOR CRITICAL THINKING

How do you suppose that a reduction in business tax rates can cause the planned investment function to shift upward?

REAL APPLICATION

Assume that at some point in your life, you are running your own business. What are some of the types of planned investment that you might contemplate?

Sources are listed at the end of this chapter.

What You Should Know

Here is what you should know after reading this chapter.

LEARNING OBJECTIVES

12.1 **Explain the key determinants of consumption and saving in the Keynesian model** *In the Keynesian model, as real disposable income increases, so does the flow of real consumption expenditures. The portion of consumption unrelated to disposable income is autonomous consumption. The ratio of the flow of saving to disposable income is the average propensity to save (APS), and the ratio of consumption to disposable income is the average propensity to consume (APC). A change in saving divided by the corresponding change in disposable income is the marginal propensity to save (MPS), and a change in consumption divided by the corresponding change in disposable income is the marginal propensity to consume (MPC).*

KEY TERMS

real disposable income, 244
consumption, 244
saving, 244
consumption goods, 244
investment, 245
capital goods, 245
life-cycle theory of consumption, 245
permanent income hypothesis, 245
consumption function, 246
dissaving, 246
45-degree reference line, 247
autonomous consumption, 248
average propensity to consume (APC), 249
average propensity to save (APS), 249
marginal propensity to consume (MPC), 249
marginal propensity to save (MPS), 249
net wealth, 250
Key Figure
Figure 12-1, 248

12.2 **Identify the primary determinants of planned investment** *Planned investment varies inversely with the interest rate, so the investment schedule slopes downward. Changes in business expectations, productive technology, or business taxes cause the investment schedule to shift.*

LEARNING OBJECTIVES

12.3 **Describe how equilibrium real GDP is established in the Keynesian model** *In equilibrium, total planned real consumption, investment, government, and net export expenditures equal real GDP, so C + I + G + X = Y. This occurs at the point where the C + I + G + X curve crosses the 45-degree reference line. In a world without government spending and taxes, equilibrium also occurs when planned saving is equal to planned investment.*

12.4 **Evaluate why autonomous changes in total planned expenditures have a multiplier effect on equilibrium real GDP** *Any increase in autonomous expenditures causes a direct rise in real GDP. The resulting increase in disposable income in turn stimulates increased consumption by an amount equal to the marginal propensity to consume multiplied by the rise in disposable income that results. The ultimate expansion of real GDP is equal to the multiplier, 1/(1 − MPC), or 1/MPS, times the increase in autonomous expenditures.*

12.5 **Understand the relationship between total planned expenditures and the aggregate demand curve** *An increase in the price level induces households and businesses to cut back on spending. Thus, the C + I + G + X curve shifts downward following a rise in the price level, so that equilibrium real GDP falls. This yields the downward-sloping aggregate demand curve.*

KEY TERMS

Key Figure
Figure 12-5, 255

lump-sum tax, 256
Key Figure
Figure 12-6, 257

multiplier, 258
Key Figures
Figure 12-7, 261
Figure 12-8, 263
Key Table
Table 12-3, 259

PROBLEMS

12-1. Classify each of the following as either a stock or a flow.

a. Myung Park earns $850 per week.

b. Time Warner purchases $100 million in new telecommunications equipment this month.

c. Sally Schmidt has $1,000 in a savings account at a credit union.

d. XYZ, Inc., produces 200 units of output per week.

e. Giorgio Giannelli owns three private jets.

f. Apple's production declines by 750 digital devices per month.

g. Russia owes $25 billion to the International Monetary Fund.

12-2. Consider the table below when answering the following questions. For this hypothetical economy, the marginal propensity to save is constant at all levels of real GDP, and investment spending is autonomous. There is no government.

Real GDP	Consumption	Saving	Investment
$ 2,000	$2,200	$_____	$400
4,000	4,000	_____	_____
6,000	_____	_____	_____
8,000	_____	_____	_____
10,000	_____	_____	_____
12,000	_____	_____	_____

a. Complete the table. What is the marginal propensity to save? What is the marginal propensity to consume?

b. Draw a graph of the consumption function. Then add the investment function to obtain C + I.

c. Under the graph of C + I, draw another graph showing the saving and investment curves. Note that the C + I curve crosses the 45-degree reference line in the upper graph at the same level of real GDP where the saving and investment curves cross in the lower graph. (If not, redraw your graphs.) What is this level of real GDP?

d. What is the numerical value of the multiplier?

e. What is equilibrium real GDP without investment? What is the multiplier effect from the inclusion of investment?

f. What is the average propensity to consume at equilibrium real GDP?

g. If autonomous investment declines from $400 to $200, what happens to equilibrium real GDP?

12-3. Consider the table below when answering the following questions. For this economy, the marginal propensity to consume is constant at all levels of real GDP, and investment spending is autonomous. Equilibrium real GDP is equal to $8,000. There is no government.

Real GDP	Consumption	Saving	Investment
$ 2,000	$ 2,000	___	___
4,000	3,600	___	___
6,000	5,200	___	___
8,000	6,800	___	___
10,000	8,400	___	___
12,000	10,000	___	___

a. Complete the table. What is the marginal propensity to consume? What is the marginal propensity to save?

b. Draw a graph of the consumption function. Then add the investment function to obtain $C + I$.

c. Under the graph of $C + I$, draw another graph showing the saving and investment curves. Does the $C + I$ curve cross the 45-degree reference line in the upper graph at the same level of real GDP where the saving and investment curves cross in the lower graph, at the equilibrium real GDP of $8,000? (If not, redraw your graphs.)

d. What is the average propensity to save at equilibrium real GDP?

e. If autonomous consumption were to rise by $100, what would happen to equilibrium real GDP?

12-4. Calculate the multiplier for the following cases.

a. MPS = 0.25

b. MPC = $\frac{5}{6}$

c. MPS = 0.125

d. MPC = $\frac{6}{7}$

12-5. Given each of the following values for the multiplier, calculate both the MPC and the MPS.

a. 20

b. 10

c. 8

d. 5

12-6. The marginal propensity to consume is equal to 0.80. An increase in household wealth causes autonomous consumption to rise by $10 billion. By how much will equilibrium real GDP increase at the current price level, other things, including other forms of autonomous spending, being equal?

12-7. Assume that the multiplier in a country is equal to 4 and that autonomous real consumption spending is $1 trillion. If current real GDP is $22 trillion, what is the current value of real consumption spending?

12-8. The multiplier in a country is equal to 5, and households pay no taxes. At the current equilibrium real GDP of $14 trillion, total real consumption spending by households is $12 trillion. What is real autonomous consumption in this country?

12-9. At an initial point on the aggregate demand curve, the price level is 125, and real GDP is $22 trillion. When the price level falls to a value of 120, total autonomous expenditures increase by $250 billion, so that the $C + I + G + X$ curve shifts upward by $250 billion. The marginal propensity to consume is 0.75. What is the level of real GDP at the new point on the aggregate demand curve?

12-10. At an initial point on the aggregate demand curve, the price level is 100, and real GDP is $22 trillion. After the price level rises to 110, however, there is an upward movement along the aggregate demand curve, and real GDP declines to $14 trillion. If total planned spending declined by $200 billion in response to the increase in the price level, what is the marginal propensity to consume in this economy?

12-11. In an economy in which the multiplier has a value of 3, the price level has decreased from 115 to 110. As a consequence, there has been a movement along the aggregate demand curve from $22 trillion in real GDP to $22.9 trillion in real GDP.

a. What is the marginal propensity to save?

b. What was the amount of the change in planned expenditures generated by the decline in the price level?

12-12. Consider the diagram nearby, which applies to a nation with no government spending, taxes, and net exports. Use the information in the diagram to answer the following questions, and explain your answers.

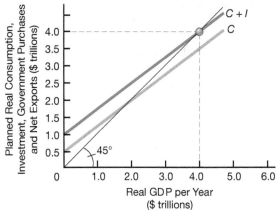

a. What is the marginal propensity to save?

b. What is the present level of planned investment spending for the present period?

c. What is the equilibrium level of real GDP for the present period?

d. What is the equilibrium level of saving for the present period?

e. If planned investment spending for the present period increases by $25 billion, what will be the resulting *change* in equilibrium real GDP? What will be the new equilibrium level of real GDP if other things, including the price level, remain unchanged?

12-13. Consider movements from points *F* to *K* in both panels of Figure 12-1. Use the resulting changes in planned real consumption and saving corresponding to the change in real disposable income to calculate the marginal propensities to consume and to save.

12-14. Take a look at Figure 12-5. If current real GDP for this nation's economy is $18 trillion per year, what are the values of planned real investment and actual real investment? What is the amount of the unplanned inventory change, and why does this fact imply that real GDP must change? To what new level will real GDP adjust?

12-15. Consider Table 12-2. What is the average propensity to consume at the equilibrium level of real GDP? What is the average propensity to save?

12-16. Take a look at Table 12-2 and consider the changes in planned real consumption and saving associated with an increase in real GDP from $18.0 trillion to $19.0 trillion to calculate the marginal propensity to consume.

12-17. Consider the current equilibrium real GDP level of $22.0 trillion displayed in Table 12-2. Based on your answer to Problem 12-16, if real government spending were to decrease by $1.0 trillion, what would be the resulting change in real GDP? What would be the new equilibrium level of real GDP? Verify that at the new level of government spending, this new equilibrium real GDP equals $C + I + G + X$.

12-18. Consider Figure 12-7, which applies to an economy in which the marginal propensity to consume is 0.8. Why does a $0.1 trillion increase in planned real investment spending cause the aggregate demand curve to shift rightward by exactly $0.5 trillion at the initial equilibrium price level of 110?

12-19. Following the rightward shift in the aggregate demand curve generated by the $0.1 trillion rise in real planned investment spending in Problem 12-18, why does the actual equilibrium level of real GDP increase by only $0.3 trillion instead of $0.5 trillion?

REFERENCES

BEHAVIORAL EXAMPLE: Using Lottery Prizes to Induce Low-Income People to Save More of Their Disposable Incomes

"Prize-Linked Savings Program," The Wisconsin Credit Union League (https://www.theleague.coop/products-solutions/solutions-directory/prize-linked-savings-savers-sweepstakes), 2019.

Matthew Frankel, "Prize-Linked Savings Accounts: A Smart Way to Build an Emergency Fund," *USA Today*, January 26, 2018.

Cazilla Loibl, Lauren Jones, and Emily Haisley, "Testing Strategies to Increase Saving in Individual Development Account Programs," *Journal of Economic Psychology*, 2018.

AI—DECISION MAKING THROUGH DATA: "Nowcast" Equilibrium Real GDP and Its Components

Oguzhan Cepni and Ibrahim Guney, "Nowcasting Emerging Markets GDP," *Applied Economics Letters*, 2019.

Brandyn Bok, Daniele Caratelli, Domenico Giannone, Argia M. Sbordone, and Andrea Tambalotti, "Macroeconomic Nowcasting and Forecasting with Big Data," *Annual Review of Economics*, 2018.

John Galbraith and Greg Tkacz, "Nowcasting with Payments System Data," *International Journal of Forecasting*, 2018.

POLICY EXAMPLE: Comparing the Relative Contributions of Government-Generated Multiplier Effects on Real GDP

Brookings Institution, "Hutchins Center Fiscal Impact Measure" (https://www.brookings.edu/interactives/hutchins-center-fiscal-impact-measure/), 2019.

Congressional Budget Office, "Outlook for the Budget and the Economy" (https://www.cbo.gov/topics/budget/outlook-budget-and-economy), 2019.

Michael Rainey, "Fiscal Policy Isn't Having Much Effect on the Economy: Brookings," *Fiscal Times*, April 30, 2018.

ECONOMICS IN YOUR LIFE: Why Earned Real Disposable Income and Current Saving Have Increased for Many Older People

Paul Davidson, "Older Workers Are Driving Job Growth as Boomers Remain in Workforce Longer," *USA Today*, January 9, 2019.

Angela Moore, "More Than 40 Percent of Americans Are at Risk of Going Broke in Retirement—And That's the Good News," MarketWatch, May 12, 2018.

Alana Semuels, "This Is What Life without Retirement Savings Is Like," *Atlantic*, February 22, 2018.

ISSUES & APPLICATIONS: Why Changes in Planned Investment Spending Receive So Much Attention from Economists

"Consumer, Business Spending Propel Solid GDP Growth," LPL Financial Research (https://lplresearch.com/2019/02/28/consumer-business-spending-propel-solid-gdp-growth/), February 28, 2019.

Sho Chandra, "Business Spending Is Poised to Surge in the United States," *Bloomberg*, May 7, 2018.

Caroline Valetkevitch, "U.S. Companies Seen Investing More after Tax Cuts," Reuters, May 17, 2018.

APPENDIX C

The Keynesian Model and the Multiplier

We can see the multiplier effect more clearly if we look at Figure C-1, in which we see only a small section of the graphs that we used in Chapter 12. We start with equilibrium real GDP of $21.5 trillion per year. This equilibrium occurs with total planned real expenditures represented by $C + I_1 + G + X$, where I_1 is the initial level of real investment spending. The $C + I_1 + G + X$ curve intersects the 45-degree reference line at $21.5 trillion per year. Now we increase real investment by $100 billion, which yields the curve labeled $C + I_2 + G + X$. The vertical shift represents that $100 billion increase in autonomous investment. With the higher level of planned expenditures per year, we are no longer in equilibrium at E. Inventories are falling. Production of goods and services will increase as firms try to replenish their inventories.

Eventually, real GDP will catch up with total planned expenditures. The new equilibrium level of real GDP is established at E_2 at the intersection of the new $C + I_2 + G + X$ curve and the 45-degree reference line, along which $C + I + G + X = Y$ (total planned expenditures equal real GDP). The new equilibrium level of real GDP is $22 trillion per year. Thus, the increase in equilibrium real GDP is equal to five times the permanent increase in planned investment spending.

FIGURE C-1

Graphing the Multiplier

We can translate Table 12-3 into graphic form by looking at each successive round of additional spending induced by an autonomous increase in planned investment of $100 billion. The total planned expenditures curve shifts from $C + I_1 + G + X$, with its associated equilibrium level of real GDP of $21.5 trillion, to a new curve labeled $C + I_2 + G + X$. The new equilibrium level of real GDP is $22 trillion. Equilibrium is again established.

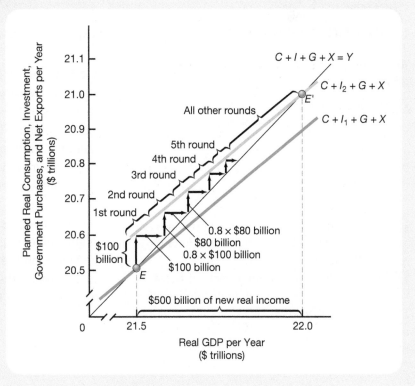

13 Fiscal Policy

LEARNING OBJECTIVES

After reading this chapter, you should be able to:

13.1 Use traditional Keynesian analysis to evaluate the effects of discretionary fiscal policies

13.2 Discuss ways in which indirect crowding out and direct expenditure offsets can reduce the effectiveness of fiscal policy actions

13.3 List and define fiscal policy time lags and explain why they complicate efforts to engage in fiscal "fine-tuning"

13.4 Describe how certain aspects of fiscal policy function as automatic stabilizers for the economy

In some years, increases in government spending accompany decreases in taxes, and together these events tend to push up total planned expenditures. In certain other years, government spending decreases at the same time that taxes increase, and the combined effect is a decrease in total planned spending. In remaining years, government spending and taxes move in the same direction and thereby exert contradictory effects on total planned expenditures. In this chapter, you will learn the tools required to assess the *net overall effect* of changes in government spending and taxes on total planned spending, on the position of the aggregate demand curve, and on the equilibrium price level and equilibrium real GDP.

a recent study of government grants and private gifts to charitable organizations found that every $10,000 grant that a government agency awards to such an organization generates a reduction in private gifts to that organization by about $7,500? The economists who conducted the study, A. Abigail Payne of McMaster University in Ontario, Canada, and James Andreoni of the University of California at San Diego, concluded that the government grants "crowd out" private charitable giving. On one hand, the authors argue, when people know that government agencies already are directing some of their tax dollars to charities, those people have less desire to make individual contributions. On the other hand, when charitable organizations receive taxpayer funds from the government, their incentive to seek private donations declines. In this chapter, you will learn that such *crowding-out effects* commonly occur as a consequence of government spending, whether such spending is directed to charitable organizations or is utilized to purchase goods and services.

Discretionary Fiscal Policy

The making of deliberate, discretionary changes in federal government expenditures or taxes (or both) to achieve certain national economic goals is the realm of **fiscal policy**. Some national goals are high employment (low unemployment), price stability, and economic growth. Fiscal policy can be thought of as a deliberate attempt to cause the economy to move to full employment and price stability more quickly than it otherwise might.

Fiscal policy has typically been associated with the economic theories of John Maynard Keynes and what is now called *traditional* Keynesian analysis. Recall that Keynes's explanation of the Great Depression was that there was insufficient aggregate demand. Because he believed that wages and prices were "sticky downward," he argued that the classical economists' picture of an economy moving automatically and quickly toward full employment was inaccurate. To Keynes and his followers, government had to step in to increase aggregate demand. Expansionary fiscal policy initiated by the federal government was the preferred way to ward off recessions and depressions.

Changes in Government Spending

In a previous chapter, we looked at the recessionary gap and the inflationary gap. The recessionary gap was defined as the amount by which the current level of real GDP falls short of the economy's *potential* production if it were operating on its *LRAS* curve. The inflationary gap was defined as the amount by which the short-run equilibrium level of real GDP exceeds the long-run equilibrium level as given by *LRAS*. Let us examine fiscal policy first in the context of a recessionary gap.

When There Is a Recessionary Gap The government, along with firms, individuals, and foreign residents, is one of the spending entities in the economy. When the government spends more, all other things held constant, the dollar value of total spending initially must rise. Look at panel (a) of Figure 13-1. We begin by assuming that some negative shock in the near past has left the economy at point E_1, which is a short-run equilibrium in which AD_1 intersects *SRAS* at $21.5 trillion of real GDP per year. There is a recessionary gap of $500 billion of real GDP per year—the difference between *LRAS* (the economy's long-run potential) and the short-run equilibrium level of real GDP per year.

When the government decides to spend more (expansionary fiscal policy), the aggregate demand curve shifts to the right to AD_2. Here we assume that the government knows exactly how much more to spend so that AD_2 intersects *SRAS* at $22 trillion, or at *LRAS*. Because of the upward-sloping *SRAS*, the price level rises from 110 to 120 as real GDP goes to $22 trillion per year.

13.1 Use traditional Keynesian analysis to evaluate the effects of discretionary fiscal policies

Fiscal policy
The discretionary changing of government expenditures or taxes to achieve national economic goals, such as high employment with price stability.

FIGURE 13-1

Expansionary and Contractionary Fiscal Policy: Changes in Government Spending

If there is a recessionary gap and short-run equilibrium is at E_1 in panel (a), additional government spending can presumably increase aggregate demand to AD_2. The new equilibrium is at E_2 at higher real GDP per year and a higher price level. In panel (b), the economy is at short-run equilibrium at E_1, which is at a higher real GDP than the *LRAS*. To reduce this inflationary gap, additional government spending can be used to decrease aggregate demand from AD_1 to AD_2. Eventually, equilibrium will fall to E_2, which is on the *LRAS*.

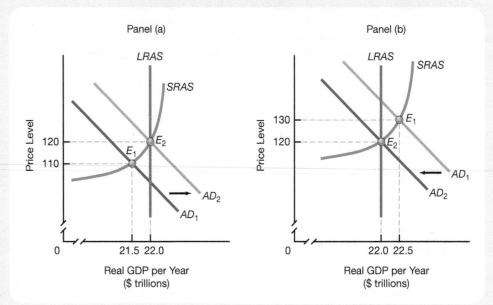

When There Is an Inflationary Gap The entire process shown in panel (a) of Figure 13-1 can be reversed, as shown in panel (b). There, we assume that a recent shock has left the economy at point E_1, at which an inflationary gap exists at the intersection of *SRAS* and AD_1. Real GDP cannot be sustained at \$22.5 trillion indefinitely, because this exceeds long-run aggregate supply, which in real terms is \$22 trillion. If the government recognizes this and reduces its spending (pursues a contractionary fiscal policy), this action reduces aggregate demand from AD_1 to AD_2. Equilibrium will fall to E_2 on the *LRAS*, where real GDP per year is \$22 trillion. The price level will fall from 130 to 120.

Changes in Taxes

The spending decisions of firms, individuals, and other countries' residents depend on the taxes levied on them. Individuals in their role as consumers look to their disposable (after-tax) income when determining their desired rates of consumption. Firms look at their after-tax profits when deciding on the levels of investment per year to undertake. Foreign residents look at the tax-inclusive cost of goods when deciding whether to buy in the United States or elsewhere. Therefore, holding all other things constant, an increase in taxes causes a reduction in aggregate demand because it reduces consumption, investment, or net exports.

When the Current Short-Run Equilibrium Is to the Left of *LRAS* Look at panel (a) in Figure 13-2. The aggregate demand curve AD_1 intersects *SRAS* at E_1, with real GDP at \$21.5 trillion, less than the *LRAS* of \$22 trillion. In this situation, a decrease in taxes shifts the aggregate demand curve outward to the right. At AD_2, equilibrium is established at E_2, with the price level at 120 and equilibrium real GDP at \$22 trillion per year.

When the Current Short-Run Equilibrium Is to the Right of *LRAS* Assume that aggregate demand is AD_1 in panel (b) of Figure 13-2. This aggregate demand curve intersects *SRAS* at E_1, which yields real GDP greater than *LRAS*. In this situation, an increase in

FIGURE 13-2

Expansionary and Contractionary Fiscal Policy: Changes in Taxes

In panel (a), the economy is initially at E_1, where real GDP is less than long-run equilibrium real GDP. Expansionary fiscal policy via a tax reduction can move aggregate demand to AD_2 so that the new equilibrium is at E_2 at a higher price level. Real GDP is now consistent with *LRAS*, which eliminates the recessionary gap. In panel (b), with an inflationary gap (in this case of $500 billion), taxes are increased. AD_1 moves to AD_2. The economy moves from E_1 to E_2, and real GDP is now at $22 trillion per year, the long-run equilibrium level.

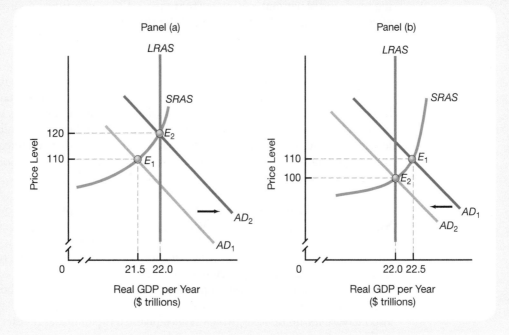

taxes shifts the aggregate demand curve inward to the left. For argument's sake, assume that it intersects *SRAS* at E_2, or exactly where *LRAS* intersects AD_2. In this situation, the level of real GDP falls from $22.5 trillion per year to $22 trillion per year. The price level falls from 110 to 100.

If the government were to seek to generate an *increase* in the amount of taxes, how might it seek to collect more business taxes legally owed but not paid?

BEHAVIORAL EXAMPLE

Trying to Reduce Government Deficits by "Behaviorally Nudging" Businesses into Paying Taxes

Evidence compiled by governments indicates that businesses are more likely than households to conceal failures to comply fully with tax laws and to evade full payment of taxes due under those laws. The reason is not that businesspeople are somehow more naturally inclined to break the law. Instead, numerous managers and employees typically are involved in ensuring satisfaction of requirements of highly detailed tax laws that apply to businesses. Human miscommunications and errors more commonly result. Furthermore, the individuals involved in complying with business taxation do not simply confront potential government penalties. They also face the possibility of losing their positions of employment when they err.

Traditionally, most efforts to induce compliance with business tax laws focus on enforcement through systems of penalties imposed upon noncomplying taxpaying firms. Recently, however, behavioral research has contemplated "nudges," or external governmental inducements, aimed at influencing decisions of the governmental officials who are responsible for monitoring firms' compliance with tax laws. Officials have been nudged to discuss new tax rules with business managers, to remind firms of key requirements, and to invite businesses to ask questions about tax rules. When such nudges have been used, the result has been a noticeable increase in the amount of taxes collected from firms.

FOR CRITICAL THINKING

If behavioral nudges discussed above were to generate a significant increase in a nation's aggregate tax collections, what would be the ultimate effects on the equilibrium price level and on equilibrium real GDP?

Sources are listed at the end of this chapter.

13.2 Discuss ways in which indirect crowding out and direct expenditure offsets can reduce the effectiveness of fiscal policy actions

Possible Offsets to Fiscal Policy

Fiscal policy does not operate in a vacuum. Important questions must be answered: If government spending rises by, say, $300 billion, how is the spending financed, and by whom? If taxes are increased, what does the government do with the taxes? What will happen if individuals anticipate higher *future* taxes because the government is spending more today without raising current taxes? These questions involve *offsets* to the effects of current fiscal policy. We consider them in detail here.

Indirect Crowding Out

Let's take the first example of fiscal policy in this chapter—an increase in government expenditures. If government expenditures rise and taxes are held constant, something has to give. Our government does not simply take goods and services when it wants them. It has to pay for them. When it pays for them and does not simultaneously collect the same amount in taxes, it must borrow. This means that an increase in government spending without raising taxes creates additional government borrowing from the private sector (or from other countries' residents).

Induced Interest Rate Changes If the government attempts to borrow in excess of $425 billion more per year from the private sector, as it has since 2015, it will have to offer a higher interest rate to lure the additional funds from savers. This is the interest rate effect of expansionary fiscal policy financed by borrowing from the public. Consequently, when the federal government finances increased spending by additional borrowing, it will push interest rates up. When interest rates go up, firms' borrowing costs rise, which induces them to cut back on planned investment spending. Borrowing costs also increase for households, which reduce planned expenditures on cars and homes.

Thus, a rise in government spending, holding taxes constant (that is, deficit spending), tends to crowd out private spending, dampening the positive effect of increased government spending on aggregate demand. This is called the **crowding-out effect**. In the extreme case, the crowding out may be complete, with the increased government spending having no net effect on aggregate demand. The final result is simply more government spending and less private investment and consumption. Figure 13-3 shows how the crowding-out effect occurs.

Crowding-out effect
The tendency of expansionary fiscal policy to cause a decrease in planned investment or planned consumption in the private sector. This decrease normally results from the rise in interest rates.

The Firm's Investment Decision To understand the crowding-out effect better, consider a firm that is contemplating borrowing $100,000 to expand its business. Suppose that the interest rate is 5 percent. The interest payments on the debt will be 5 percent times $100,000, or $5,000 per year ($417 per month). A rise in the interest rate to 8 percent will push the payments to 8 percent of $100,000, or $8,000 per year ($667 per month). The extra $250 per month in interest expenses will discourage

FIGURE 13-3

The Crowding-Out Effect, Step by Step

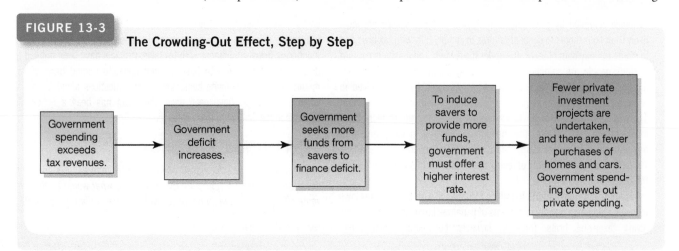

FIGURE 13-4

The Crowding-Out Effect

Expansionary fiscal policy that causes deficit financing initially shifts AD_1 to AD_2. Equilibrium initially moves toward E_2. Expansionary fiscal policy, however, pushes up interest rates, thereby reducing interest-sensitive spending. This effect causes the aggregate demand curve to shift inward to AD_3, and the new short-run equilibrium is at E_3.

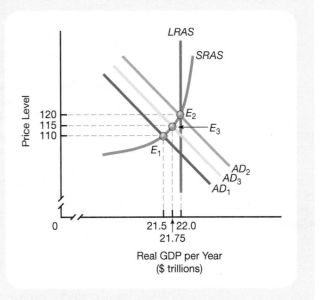

some firms from making the investment. Consumers face similar decisions when they purchase houses and cars. An increase in the interest rate causes their monthly payments to go up, thereby discouraging some of them from purchasing cars and houses.

Graphical Analysis You see in Figure 13-4 that the economy is in a situation in which, at point E_1, equilibrium real GDP is below the long-run level consistent with the position of the *LRAS* curve. Suppose, however, that government expansionary fiscal policy in the form of increased government spending (without increasing current taxes) attempts to shift aggregate demand from AD_1 to AD_2. In the absence of the crowding-out effect, real GDP would increase to $22 trillion per year, and the price level would rise to 120 (point E_2). With the (partial) crowding-out effect, however, as investment and consumption decline, partly offsetting the rise in government spending, the aggregate demand curve shifts inward to the left to AD_3.

The new short-run equilibrium is now at E_3, with real GDP of $21.75 trillion per year at a price level of 115. In other words, crowding out dilutes the effect of expansionary fiscal policy, and a recessionary gap remains.

Planning for the Future: Ricardian Equivalence

Economists have often implicitly assumed that people look at changes in taxes or changes in government spending only in the present. What if people actually think about the size of *future* tax payments? Does this have an effect on how they react to an increase in government spending with no current tax increases? Some economists believe that the answer is yes.

Current Tax Cuts and Future Debts What if people's horizons extend beyond this year? Don't we then have to take into account the effects of today's government policies on the future?

Consider an example. The government wants to reduce taxes by $200 billion today, as it did in 2008 and 2009 via tax "rebate" programs. Assume that government spending remains constant. Assume further that the government initially has a balanced budget. Thus, the only way for the government to pay for this $200 billion tax cut is to borrow $200 billion today. The public will owe $200 billion plus interest later. Realizing that a $200 billion tax cut today is mathematically equivalent to $200 billion plus interest later, people may wish to save the proceeds from the tax cut to meet future tax liabilities—payment of interest and repayment of debt.

Consequently, a tax cut may not affect total planned expenditures. A reduction in taxes without a reduction in government spending may therefore have no impact on aggregate demand. Similarly, an increase in taxes without an increase in government spending may not have a large (negative) impact on aggregate demand.

The Ricardian Equivalence Theorem Suppose that a decrease in taxes shifts the aggregate demand curve from AD_1 to AD_2 in Figure 13-4. If consumers partly compensate for a higher future tax liability by saving more, the aggregate demand curve shifts leftward, to a position such as AD_3. In the extreme case in which individuals fully take into account their increased tax liabilities, the aggregate demand curve shifts all the way back to AD_1, so that there is no effect on the economy. This is known as the **Ricardian equivalence theorem**, after the nineteenth-century economist David Ricardo, who first developed the argument publicly.

According to the Ricardian equivalence theorem, it does not matter how government expenditures are financed—by taxes or by borrowing. Is the theorem correct? Research indicates that Ricardian equivalence effects likely exist but has not provided much compelling evidence about their exact magnitudes.

Restrained Consumption Effects of Temporary Tax Changes

Recall that a person's consumption and saving decisions realistically depend on *both* current income *and* anticipated future income. On the basis of this fact, the theory of consumption known as the *permanent income hypothesis* proposes that an individual's current flow of consumption depends on the individual's permanent, or anticipated lifetime, income.

Sometimes, the government seeks to provide a short-term "stimulus" to economic activity through temporary tax cuts that last no longer than a year or two or by rebating lump-sum amounts back to taxpayers. According to the permanent income hypothesis, such short-term tax policies at best have minimal effects on total consumption spending. The reason is that *temporary* tax cuts or one-time tax rebates fail to raise the recipients' *permanent* incomes. Even after receiving such a temporary tax cut or rebate, therefore, people usually do not respond with significant changes in their consumption. Instead of spending the tax cut or rebate, they typically save most of the funds or use the funds to make payments on outstanding debts.

Thus, temporary tax cuts or rebates tend to have minimal effects on aggregate consumption, as the U.S. government has discovered when it has provided temporary tax rebates. For instance, all one-time federal tax rebates have only temporarily boosted real disposable income in the year that they were instituted. They had no perceptible effects on long-run flows of real consumption spending.

Direct Expenditure Offsets

Government has a distinct comparative advantage over the private sector in certain activities such as diplomacy and national defense. Otherwise stated, certain resource-using activities in which the government engages do not compete with the private sector. In contrast, some of what government does, such as public education, competes directly with the private sector. When government competes with the private sector, **direct expenditure offsets** to fiscal policy may occur. For example, if the government starts providing milk at no charge to students who are already purchasing milk, there is a direct expenditure offset. Government spending on milk increases, but direct household spending on milk decreases.

Normally, the impact of an increase in government spending on aggregate demand is analyzed by implicitly assuming that government spending is *not* a substitute for private spending. This is clearly the case for a cruise missile. Whenever government spending is a substitute for private spending, however, a rise in government spending causes a direct reduction in private spending to offset it.

Ricardian equivalence theorem
The proposition that an increase in the government budget deficit has no effect on aggregate demand.

Direct expenditure offsets
Actions on the part of the private sector in spending income that offset government fiscal policy actions. Any increase in government spending in an area that competes with the private sector will have some direct expenditure offset.

The Extreme Case In the extreme case, the direct expenditure offset is dollar for dollar, so we merely end up with a relabeling of spending from private to public. Assume that you have decided to spend $100 on groceries. Upon your arrival at the checkout counter, you find a U.S. Department of Agriculture official. She announces that she will pay for your groceries—but only the ones in the cart. Here increased government spending is $100. You leave the store in bliss. Just as you are deciding how to spend the $100, though, an Internal Revenue Service agent appears. He announces that as a result of the current budgetary crisis, your taxes are going to rise by $100. You have to pay on the spot. Increases in taxes have now been $100. We have a balanced-budget increase in government spending.

In this scenario, *total* spending does not change. We simply end up with higher government spending, which directly offsets exactly an equal reduction in consumption. Aggregate demand and GDP are unchanged. Otherwise stated, if there is a full direct expenditure offset, the government spending multiplier is zero.

The Less Extreme Case Much government spending has a private-sector substitute. When government expenditures increase, private spending tends to decline somewhat (but generally not dollar for dollar), thereby mitigating the upward impact on total aggregate demand. To the extent that there are some direct expenditure offsets to expansionary fiscal policy, predicted changes in aggregate demand will be lessened. Consequently, real GDP and the price level will be less affected.

How might the degree of crowding out be reduced by combining private and public support for certain forms of government spending projects?

INTERNATIONAL POLICY EXAMPLE

Do Private-Public Infrastructure Projects Generate Smaller Crowding-Out Effects?

In a number of countries, including Australia, Canada, and several European nations, infrastructure projects, such as the construction of roads and bridges, are directed by groups of private firms that design, build, and operate the projects. To induce the private companies to engage in these activities, governments often provide part of the initial construction funding. Firms are promised some or all fees that consumers pay for access during the periods that they operate the facilities.

Commonly cited rationales for such "public-private partnerships" in infrastructure spending are that the involvement of private firms may help provide more initial financing and greater efficiency in operations than governments might deliver. A possible macroeconomic effect, however, is the potential for the government expenditures on such projects to generate fewer direct private expenditure offsets. Profit-maximizing firms may seek construction of projects such as hospitals or stadiums in quantities consistent with meeting the desires of customers, such as

patients or sports fans. Partial government support for projects of these types, therefore, is less likely to prevent private companies from engaging in spending on additional projects if doing so is consistent with pursuit of additional profits. Thus, public-private partnerships in infrastructure spending may generate smaller direct expenditure offsets as compared with infrastructure projects designed, built, operated, and financed solely by governments.

FOR CRITICAL THINKING

Why might government construction of a single sports stadium designed for multiple types of sporting events generate a larger private expenditure offset than partial government support for smaller stadiums for specific sporting events?

Sources are listed at the end of this chapter.

The Supply-Side Effects of Changes in Taxes

We have talked about changing taxes and changing government spending, the traditional tools of fiscal policy. Let's now consider the possibility of changing *marginal* tax rates.

Altering Marginal Tax Rates Recall that the marginal tax rate is the rate applied to the last, or highest, bracket of taxable income. In our federal tax system, higher marginal tax rates are applied as income rises. In that sense, the United States has a progressive federal individual income tax system. Expansionary fiscal policy could involve reducing marginal tax rates. Advocates of such changes argue that lower tax rates will lead

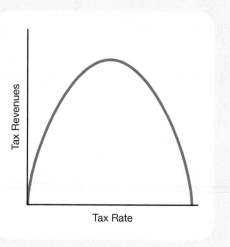

FIGURE 13-5

Laffer Curve

The Laffer curve indicates that tax revenues initially rise with a higher tax rate. Eventually, however, tax revenues decline as the tax rate increases.

to an increase in productivity. They contend that individuals will work harder and longer, save more, and invest more and that increased productivity will lead to more economic growth, which will lead to higher real GDP. The government, by applying lower marginal tax rates, will not necessarily lose tax revenues, for the lower marginal tax rates will be applied to a growing tax base because of economic growth—after all, tax revenues are the product of a tax rate times a tax base.

The relationship between tax rates and tax revenues is sometimes called the *Laffer curve*, named after economist Arthur Laffer, who explained the relationship to some journalists and politicians in 1974. It is reproduced in Figure 13-5. On the vertical axis are tax revenues, and on the horizontal axis is the marginal tax rate. As you can see, total tax revenues initially rise but then eventually fall as the tax rate continues to increase after reaching some unspecified tax-revenue-maximizing rate at the top of the curve.

WHAT HAPPENS WHEN...

a sudden, deep recession takes place after a nation's government has just begun to operate at the very top of its economy's Laffer curve?

The Laffer curve relates tax revenues collected by a nation's government to the tax rate, *other things being equal*. One element that is held unchanged along a given Laffer curve is a nation's flow of real GDP and, hence, the flow of taxable real income. If the nation's flow of equilibrium real GDP were to decrease substantially during a sudden, deep recession, then the flow of taxable real income would decrease at any given

tax rate. This means that the Laffer curve becomes shallower between its two endpoints. The government thereby would be able to collect fewer real tax revenues at any given tax rate, including the top tax rate at which the government's tax revenues are maximized. Consequently, a sudden, deep recession generates an immediate decrease in a government's tax revenues.

Supply-Side Economics and Your Response to Changing Marginal Income Tax Rates   People who support the notion that reducing tax rates does not necessarily lead to reduced tax revenues are called supply-side economists. **Supply-side economics** involves changing the tax structure to reduce disincentives that otherwise tend to decrease productivity. Due to a resulting shift in the aggregate supply curve to the right, there can be greater real GDP without upward pressure on the price level.

Supply-side economics
The theory that creating incentives for individuals and firms to increase productivity will cause the aggregate supply curve to shift outward.

Consider the supply-side effects of changes in marginal tax rates on income from labor. An increase in tax rates reduces the opportunity cost of leisure, thereby inducing individuals to reduce their work effort and to consume more leisure. An increase in tax rates, however, will also reduce spendable income, thereby shifting the demand curve for leisure inward to the left, which tends to increase work effort. The outcome of these two effects on the choice of leisure (and thus work) depends on which of them is stronger. Supply-side economists argue that the first effect often dominates: Increases in marginal tax rates cause people to work less, and decreases in marginal tax rates induce workers to work more.

In your own decision making, you certainly are more interested in your after-tax income than in your before-tax income. After all, you are only able to spend what you take home after taxes. Consequently, you might be willing to work longer hours if your marginal income tax rate is, say, 10 percent than if it is 50 percent.

ECONOMICS IN YOUR LIFE

To consider the supply-side rationale for an Italian tax proposal, take a look at **The Italian Government Contemplates a "Flat Tax"—for High-Income People Willing to Move to Italy** on page 282.

Discretionary Fiscal Policy in Practice: Coping with Time Lags

13.3 List and define fiscal policy time lags and explain why they complicate efforts to engage in fiscal "fine-tuning"

We can discuss fiscal policy in a relatively precise way. We draw graphs with aggregate demand and supply curves to show what we are doing. We could in principle estimate the offsets that we just discussed. Even if we were able to measure all of these offsets exactly, however, would-be fiscal policymakers still face a problem: The conduct of fiscal policy involves a variety of time lags.

Policy Time Lags

Policymakers must take time lags into account. Not only is it difficult to measure economic variables, but it also takes time to collect and assimilate such data. Consequently, policymakers must contend with the **recognition time lag**, the months that may elapse before national economic problems can be identified.

After an economic problem is recognized, a solution must be formulated. Thus, there will be an **action time lag** between the recognition of a problem and the implementation of policy to solve it. For fiscal policy, the action time lag is particularly long. Such policy must be approved by Congress and is subject to political wrangling and infighting. The action time lag can easily last a year or two. Then it takes time to actually implement the policy. After Congress enacts fiscal policy legislation, it takes time to decide such matters as who gets new federal construction contracts.

Finally, there is the **effect time lag**: After fiscal policy is enacted, it takes time for the policy to affect the economy. To demonstrate the effects, economists need only shift curves on a whiteboard or screen, but in the real world, such effects take quite a while to work their way through the economy.

Recognition time lag
The time required to gather information about the current state of the economy.

Action time lag
The time between recognizing an economic problem and implementing policy to solve it. The action time lag is quite long for fiscal policy, which requires congressional approval.

Effect time lag
The time that elapses between the implementation of a policy and the results of that policy.

Problems Posed by Time Lags

Because the various fiscal policy time lags are long, a policy designed to stimulate equilibrium real GDP such as tax cuts might not produce results until aggregate demand is already rising for other reasons and the economy perhaps is experiencing inflation, in which case the fiscal policy action would contribute to higher inflation. Or a fiscal policy designed to eliminate inflation might not produce effects until the economy is in a recession. In that case, too, fiscal policy could make economic problems worse rather than better.

Furthermore, because fiscal policy time lags tend to be *variable* (each lasting anywhere from one to three years), policymakers have a difficult time fine-tuning the economy. Clearly, fiscal policy is more guesswork than science.

How might application of automated data analytics reduce time lags in fiscal policy?

AI | DECISION MAKING THROUGH DATA

Reducing Policy Time Lags

To implement fiscal policy actions in a timely manner, national governments first must be able to track their own past and current revenues and expenditures. Most governments, however, regularly have experienced delays of weeks or even months in the availability of such information. These delays have contributed considerably to time lags in fiscal policymaking.

A number of national governments are in the process of implementing real-time fiscal monitoring systems that use data-analytics techniques. These systems automatically record government revenue and expenditure transactions instantaneously. Utilization of such systems should enable governments to possess immediate knowledge of their own budgetary situations and thereby help to reduce such policy time lags.

FOR CRITICAL THINKING

Even if the use of big data enables government officials to better monitor their own budgets, why might they still experience time lags in deciding on and implementing appropriate discretionary policy actions? (Hint: Does just one policymaker always make fiscal policy changes?)

Sources are listed at the end of this chapter.

Why Actual Fiscal Multipliers Are Smaller Than the Keynesian Multiplier

You learned earlier about the Keynesian spending multiplier, which has a value equal to 1 divided by the difference between 1 and the marginal propensity to consume (MPC). For instance, if the economy's MPC is 0.80, then the Keynesian spending multiplier equals $1/(1 - MPC) = 1/(1 - 0.80) = 1/0.20 = 5$. This value, however, indicates the *maximum feasible* effect on real GDP of a change in government spending. For instance, you have seen that when a fiscal policy action alters the position of the aggregate demand curve, the equilibrium price level changes. As a consequence, equilibrium real GDP changes by a smaller amount than the Keynesian spending multiplier predicts.

This chapter has brought to light other considerations that must be taken into account when assessing actual fiscal multipliers, which are significantly smaller than the Keynesian spending multiplier.

The Impact Fiscal Multiplier The actual immediate effect of discretionary fiscal policy actions on real GDP is measured by the **impact fiscal multiplier**. In contrast to the Keynesian multiplier, the impact fiscal multiplier measures the direct, current effect on equilibrium real GDP of an increase in government spending after accounting for direct fiscal offsets and any other short-term crowding out of private spending.

Most studies indicate that the average value of the immediate impact fiscal multiplier is about 1. This value implies that an inflation-adjusted increase in government spending of $1 typically adds, after accounting for direct fiscal offsets and short-term crowding-out effects, about $1 to total desired real expenditures.

Impact fiscal multiplier
The actual immediate multiplier effect of a fiscal policy action after taking into consideration direct fiscal offsets and other short-term crowding out of private spending.

The Cumulative Fiscal Multiplier The full effects of discretionary increases in real government expenditures on real GDP do not occur immediately. Increases in interest rates caused by higher government borrowing to finance additional spending often take time to occur, as do the induced reductions in private spending. Hence, the fullest extent of crowding-out effects typically is reached only after a number of months. In addition, the existence of policy time lags—in particular, the effect time lag—implies that the complete adjustments of equilibrium real GDP to discretionary fiscal policy actions can be assessed only after the passage of time.

For these reasons, a complete evaluation of the ultimate effects of fiscal policy actions on real GDP focuses on the value of the **cumulative fiscal multiplier**, which applies to a long-run period after all influences of fiscal policy actions on equilibrium real GDP have taken place. Estimates of the cumulative fiscal multiplier

Cumulative fiscal multiplier
The multiplier effect of a fiscal policy action that applies to a long-run period after all influences on equilibrium real GDP have been taken into account.

indicate that its value normally is very small. Indeed, most estimates are close to zero. Thus, after direct fiscal offsets, crowding-out effects, and long-run adjustments operating through adjustments to changes in the price level are taken into account, discretionary fiscal policy actions typically generate little net change in equilibrium real GDP.

Automatic Stabilizers

13.4 Describe how certain aspects of fiscal policy function as automatic stabilizers for the economy

Not all changes in taxes (or in tax rates) or in government spending (including government transfers) constitute discretionary fiscal policy. There are several types of automatic (or nondiscretionary) fiscal policies. Such policies do not require new legislation on the part of Congress. Specific automatic fiscal policies—called **automatic, or built-in, stabilizers**—include the tax system itself, unemployment compensation, and income transfer payments.

Automatic, or built-in, stabilizers
Special provisions of certain federal programs that cause changes in desired aggregate expenditures without the action of Congress and the president. Examples are the federal progressive tax system and unemployment compensation.

The Tax System as an Automatic Stabilizer

You know that if you work less, you are paid less, and therefore you pay fewer taxes. The amount of taxes that our government collects falls automatically during a recession. Basically, as observed in the U.S. economy during the severe 2007–2009 recession, incomes and profits fall when business activity slows down, and the government's tax revenues drop, too. Some economists consider this an automatic tax cut, which therefore may stimulate aggregate demand. It thereby may reduce the extent of any negative economic fluctuation.

The progressive nature of the federal personal and corporate income tax systems magnifies any automatic stabilization effect that might exist. If your hours of work are reduced because of a recession, you still pay some federal personal income taxes. But because of our progressive system, you may drop into a lower tax bracket, thereby paying a lower marginal income tax rate. As a result, your disposable income falls by a smaller percentage than your before-tax income falls.

Unemployment Compensation and Income Transfer Payments

Like our tax system, unemployment compensation payments stabilize aggregate demand. Throughout the course of business fluctuations, unemployment compensation reduces *changes* in people's disposable income. When business activity drops, most laid-off workers automatically become eligible for unemployment compensation from their state governments. Their disposable income therefore remains positive, although at a lower level than when they were employed. During boom periods, there is less unemployment, and consequently fewer unemployment payments are made to the labor force. Less purchasing power is being added to the economy because fewer unemployment checks are paid out. In contrast, during recessions the opposite is true.

Income transfer payments act similarly as an automatic stabilizer. When a recession occurs, more people become eligible for income transfer payments, such as Supplemental Security Income and Temporary Assistance for Needy Families. Therefore, those people do not experience as dramatic a drop in disposable income as they otherwise would have.

Stabilizing Impact

The key stabilizing impact of our tax system, unemployment compensation, and income transfer payments is their ability to mitigate changes in disposable income,

FIGURE 13-6

Automatic Stabilizers

Here we assume that as real GDP rises, tax revenues rise and government transfers fall, other things remaining constant. Thus, as the economy expands from Y_f to Y_1, a budget surplus automatically arises. As the economy contracts from Y_f to Y_2, a budget deficit automatically arises. Such automatic changes tend to reduce the magnitude of fluctuations in real GDP.

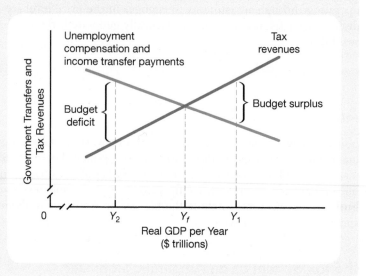

consumption, and the equilibrium level of real GDP. If disposable income is prevented from falling as much as it otherwise would during a recession, the downturn will be moderated. In contrast, if disposable income is prevented from rising as rapidly as it otherwise would during a boom, the boom is less likely to get out of hand. Unemployment compensation and income transfer payments thus provide automatic stabilization to the economy. We present the argument graphically in Figure 13-6.

ECONOMICS IN YOUR LIFE

The Italian Government Contemplates a "Flat Tax"—for High-Income People Willing to Move to Italy

Fabrizio Pagani, the Italian Minister of Economy and Finance, has unveiled a new tax plan aimed at inducing people who currently live outside Italy to move their official residence to Italy. Under the proposal, anyone who relocates to Italy would be able to pay a lump-tax of about $123,000 per year irrespective of the amount of the individual's annual income earnings. Naturally, Pagani anticipates that particularly high-income people might be willing to pay "only" $123,000 in taxes to take Italy up on the offer.

Italy's current ratio of real tax revenues collected to the nation's real GDP is now 43 percent, considerably higher than the U.S. ratio of 25 percent. The problem that Pagani confronts is that tax rates on earned incomes of Italian residents are so much higher than those faced by U.S. residents that the typical Italian resident chooses to work almost 30 percent fewer hours per year than the typical U.S. resident. The result is that Italy's higher tax rates are applied to a lower amount of total earned income derived from fewer hours of work. Thus, the

Italian government's collected tax revenues are insufficient to cover its flow of spending. Pagani hopes that the plan might bring in enough additional tax collections at the annual $123,000-per-person lump-sum tax to make a dent in Italy's annual budget deficit of nearly $50 billion.

FOR CRITICAL THINKING

About how many thousands of people (to the nearest thousand) would have to agree to move to Italy and pay its lump-sum tax to generate $1 billion of additional annual tax collections for the Italian government? Explain briefly.

REAL APPLICATION

In what ways might you react if you faced Italy's high average tax rate of 43 percent?

Sources are listed at the end of this chapter.

ISSUES & APPLICATIONS

Assessing Overall Effects of Discretionary U.S. Fiscal Policy Actions on Aggregate Demand

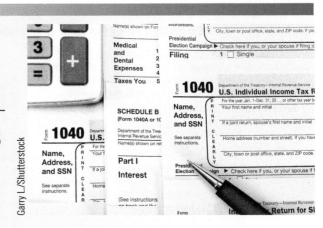

CONCEPTS APPLIED

➤ Fiscal Policy

➤ Changes in Government Spending

➤ Changes in Taxes

Sometimes, discretionary changes in government spending and taxes shift the aggregate demand curve in the same direction. At other times, however, these policy changes generate effects that work in opposing directions. Consequently, only an assessment of the *net* effects of discretionary fiscal policy actions can determine whether simultaneous changes in government spending and taxes shift the aggregate demand curve rightward or leftward.

Reinforcing versus Contradictory Fiscal Policy Actions

As you learned in this chapter, discretionary increases in government spending and decreases in taxes shift the aggregate demand curve rightward. Discretionary decreases in government spending and increases in taxes shift the aggregate demand curve leftward.

Hence, if the government raises government spending and reduces taxes simultaneously, it unambiguously generates an increase in aggregate demand, and if it cuts government spending and increases taxes at the same time, it unambiguously brings about a decrease in aggregate demand. If it increases or decreases government spending and taxes simultaneously, the net effects on aggregate demand could be positive or negative, depending on the *net* relative effects that the discretionary policy actions have on the aggregate demand curve's position.

Estimates of the Net Effects of Discretionary Fiscal Policies in Recent Years

Both government and private economists have estimated the net effects of U.S. discretionary fiscal policy actions on aggregate demand. Figure 13-7 displays the government's assessment of the net effects, which have generally been supported by private economists' estimates.

During 2009 and 2010, the government raised spending while reducing taxes, and the figure indicated that both policy actions unambiguously contributed to higher real GDP at any given price level. Tax increases were implemented between 2011 and 2014, and both actions contributed to decreases in aggregate demand. Government spending increased only slightly during those years, which tended to raise aggregate demand. The estimated *net* effects for those years, however, are negative. In the years since 2014, government spending increased as tax revenues continued to rise. The overall estimated *net* effects on aggregate demand during these most recent years are positive.

FOR CRITICAL THINKING

Given that a recessionary gap existed in 2009 and 2010, were the estimated percentage changes in aggregate demand consistent with discretionary fiscal policy aimed at reducing this gap?

REAL APPLICATION

When the federal government engages in expansionary fiscal policy, how might you become the beneficiary of that policy?

Sources are listed at the end of this chapter.

FIGURE 13-7

Estimated Net Effects of Discretionary Fiscal Policy on Aggregate Demand since 2008

This figure displays estimates of the net effects of discretionary fiscal policy actions on aggregate demand. Displayed are estimated percentage changes in real GDP induced by all discretionary fiscal policies given an unchanged price level. Hence, positive percentage changes translate into rightward effects on the position of the aggregate demand curve, and negative percentage changes indicate leftward effects on the position of this curve.

Source: Office of Management and Budget; author's estimates.

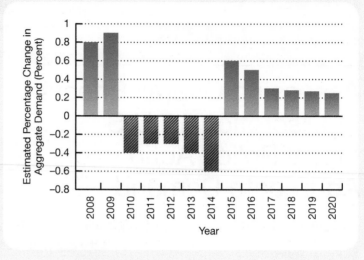

What You Should Know

Here is what you should know after reading this chapter.

LEARNING OBJECTIVES

13.1 Use traditional Keynesian analysis to evaluate the effects of discretionary fiscal policies
In short-run Keynesian analysis, an increase in government spending or tax decrease shifts the aggregate demand curve outward and thereby closes a recessionary gap in which current real GDP is less than the long-run level of real GDP. Likewise, a reduction in government spending or a tax increase shifts the aggregate demand curve inward and closes an inflationary gap in which current real GDP exceeds the long-run level of real GDP.

13.2 Discuss ways in which indirect crowding out and direct expenditure offsets can reduce the effectiveness of fiscal policy actions *Indirect crowding out occurs when the government must borrow from the private sector because government spending exceeds tax revenues. To obtain the necessary funds, the government must offer a higher interest rate, thereby driving up market interest rates. This reduces, or crowds out, interest-sensitive private spending. Increased government spending may also substitute directly for private expenditures and thereby offset the increase in total planned expenditures that the government had intended to bring about.*

13.3 List and define fiscal policy time lags and explain why they complicate efforts to engage in fiscal "fine-tuning" *Efforts to use fiscal policy to bring about changes in aggregate demand are complicated by policy time lags. One of these is the recognition time lag, which is the time required to collect information about the economy's current situation. Another is the action time lag, the period between recognition of a problem and implementation of a policy intended to address it. Finally, there is the effect time lag, which is the interval between the implementation of a policy and its having an effect on the economy.*

KEY TERMS

fiscal policy, 271
Key Figures
Figure 13-1, 272
Figure 13-2, 273

crowding-out effect, 274
Ricardian equivalence
theorem, 276
direct expenditure offsets, 276
supply-side economics, 278
Key Figures
Figure 13-3, 274
Figure 13-4, 275
Figure 13-5, 278

recognition time lag, 279
action time lag, 279
effect time lag, 279
impact fiscal multiplier, 280
cumulative fiscal
multiplier, 280

13.4 Describe how certain aspects of fiscal policy function as automatic stabilizers for the economy *Income taxes diminish automatically when economic activity drops, and unemployment compensation and income transfer payments increase. Thus, when there is a decline in real GDP, the automatic reduction in income tax collections and increases in unemployment compensation and income transfer payments tend to minimize the reduction in total planned expenditures that would otherwise have resulted.*

automatic, or built-in, stabilizers, 281
Key Figure
Figure 13-6, 282

PROBLEMS

13-1. Suppose that Congress and the president decide that the nation's economic performance is weakening and that the government should "do something" about the situation. They make no tax changes but do enact new laws increasing government spending on a variety of programs.

a. Prior to the congressional and presidential action, careful studies by government economists indicated that the Keynesian multiplier effect of a rise in government expenditures on equilibrium real GDP per year is equal to 3. In the 12 months since the increase in government spending, however, it has become clear that the actual ultimate effect on real GDP will be less than half of that amount. What factors might account for this?

b. Another year and a half elapses following passage of the government spending boost. The government has undertaken no additional policy actions, nor have there been any other events of significance. Nevertheless, by the end of the second year, annual real GDP has returned to its original level, and the price level has increased sharply. Provide a possible explanation for this outcome.

13-2. Suppose that Congress enacts a significant tax cut with the expectation that this action will stimulate aggregate demand and push up real GDP in the short run. In fact, however, neither real GDP nor the price level changes significantly as a result of the tax cut. What might account for this outcome?

13-3. Explain how time lags in discretionary fiscal policymaking could thwart the efforts of Congress and the president to stabilize real GDP in the face of an economic downturn. Is it possible that these time lags could actually cause discretionary fiscal policy to *destabilize* real GDP?

13-4. Determine whether each of the following is an example of a situation in which a direct expenditure offset to fiscal policy occurs.

a. In an effort to help rejuvenate the nation's railroad system, a new government agency buys unused track, locomotives, and passenger and freight cars, many of which private companies would otherwise have purchased and put into regular use.

b. The government increases its expenditures without raising taxes. To cover the resulting budget deficit, it borrows more funds from the private sector, thereby pushing up the market interest rate and discouraging private planned investment spending.

c. The government finances the construction of a classical music museum that otherwise would never have received private funding.

13-5. Determine whether each of the following is an example of a situation in which there is indirect crowding out resulting from an expansionary fiscal policy action.

a. The government provides a subsidy to help keep an existing firm operating, even though a group of investors otherwise would have provided a cash infusion that would have kept the company in business.

b. The government reduces its taxes without decreasing its expenditures. To cover the resulting budget deficit, it borrows more funds from the private sector, thereby pushing up the market interest rate and discouraging private planned investment spending.

c. Government expenditures fund construction of a high-rise office building on a plot of land where a private company otherwise would have constructed an essentially identical building.

13-6. The U.S. government is in the midst of spending more than $1 billion on seven buildings containing more than 100,000 square feet of space to be used for the study of infectious diseases. Prior to the government's decision to construct these buildings, a few universities had been planning to build essentially the same facilities using privately obtained funds. After construction on the government buildings began, however, the universities dropped their plans. Evaluate whether the government's $1 billion expenditure is actually likely to push U.S. real GDP above the level it would have reached in the absence of the government's construction spree.

13-7. Determine whether each of the following is an example of a discretionary fiscal policy action.

   a. A recession occurs, and government-funded unemployment compensation is paid to laid-off workers.

   b. Congress votes to fund a new jobs program designed to put unemployed workers to work.

   c. The Federal Reserve decides to reduce the quantity of money in circulation in an effort to slow inflation.

   d. Under powers authorized by an act of Congress, the president decides to authorize an emergency release of funds for spending programs intended to head off economic crises.

13-8. Determine whether each of the following is an example of an automatic fiscal stabilizer.

   a. A federal agency must extend loans to businesses whenever an economic downturn begins.

   b. As the economy heats up, the resulting increase in equilibrium real GDP per year immediately results in higher income tax payments, which dampen consumption spending somewhat.

   c. As the economy starts to recover from a severe recession and more people go back to work, government-funded unemployment compensation payments begin to decline.

   d. To stem an overheated economy, the president, using special powers granted by Congress, authorizes emergency impoundment of funds that Congress had previously authorized for spending on government programs.

13-9. Consider the first diagram, in which the current short-run equilibrium is at point *A*, and answer the questions that follow.

   a. What type of gap exists at point *A*?

   b. If the marginal propensity to save equals 0.20, what change in government spending financed by borrowing from the private sector that shifts the aggregate demand curve by a sufficient horizontal distance could eliminate the gap identified in part (a)? Explain.

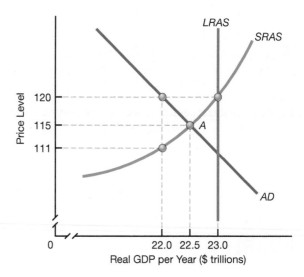

13-10. Consider the second diagram, in which the current short-run equilibrium is at point *A*, and answer the questions that follow.

   a. What type of gap exists at point *A*?

   b. If the marginal propensity to consume equals 0.75, what change in government spending financed by borrowing from the private sector that shifts the aggregate demand curve by a sufficient horizontal distance could eliminate the gap identified in part (a)? Explain.

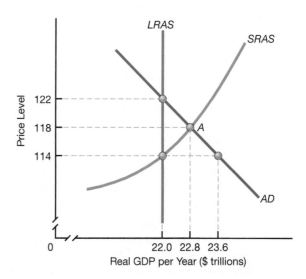

13-11. Currently, a government's budget is balanced. The marginal propensity to consume is 0.80. The government has determined that each additional $10 billion it borrows to finance a budget deficit pushes up the market interest rate by 0.1 percentage point. It has also determined that every 0.1-percentage-point change in the market interest rate generates a change in planned investment expenditures equal to $2 billion. Finally, the government knows that to close a recessionary gap and take into account the resulting change in the price level, it must generate a net rightward shift in the aggregate demand curve equal to $200 billion. Assuming that there are no direct expenditure offsets to fiscal policy, how much should the government increase its expenditures? (*Hint:* How much private investment spending will each $10 billion increase in government spending crowd out?)

13-12. A government is currently operating with an annual budget deficit of $40 billion. The government has determined that every $10 billion reduction in the amount it borrows each year would reduce the market interest rate by 0.1 percentage point. Furthermore, it has determined that every 0.1-percentage-point change in the market interest rate generates a change in planned investment expenditures in the opposite direction equal to $5 billion. The marginal propensity to consume is 0.75. Finally, the government knows that to eliminate an inflationary gap and take into account the resulting change in the price level, it must generate a net leftward shift in the aggregate demand curve equal to $40 billion. Assuming that there are no direct expenditure offsets to fiscal policy, how much should the government increase taxes? (*Hint:* How much new private investment spending is induced by each $10 billion decrease in government spending?)

13-13. Assume that the Ricardian equivalence theorem is not relevant. Explain why an income-tax-rate cut should affect short-run equilibrium real GDP.

13-14. Suppose that Congress enacts a lump-sum tax cut of $750 billion. The marginal propensity to consume is equal to 0.75. Assuming that Ricardian equivalence holds true, what is the effect on equilibrium real GDP? On saving?

13-15. In May and June of 2008, the federal government issued one-time tax rebates—checks returning a small portion of taxes previously paid—to millions of U.S residents, and U.S. real disposable income temporarily jumped by nearly $500 billion. Household real consumption spending did not increase in response to the short-lived increase in real disposable income. Explain how the logic of the permanent income hypothesis might help to account for this apparent non-relationship between real consumption and real disposable income in the late spring of 2008.

13-16. It is late 2023, and the U.S. economy is showing signs of slipping into a potentially deep recession. Government policymakers are searching for

income-tax-policy changes that will bring about a significant and lasting boost to real consumption spending. According to the logic of the permanent income hypothesis, should the proposed income-tax-policy changes involve tax increases or tax reductions, and should the policy changes be short-lived or long-lasting?

13-17. Recall that the Keynesian spending multiplier equals $1/(1 - MPC)$. Suppose that in panel (a) of Figure 13-1, the government determined that the amount by which the *AD* curve had to be shifted directly rightward from point E_1 was equal to $1.0 trillion. If the government decided that a $0.2 trillion increase in real government spending was required to generate this shift, what must be the value of the MPC?

13-18. Recall that the Keynesian spending multiplier equals $1/(1 - MPC)$. Suppose that in panel (b) of Figure 13-1, the government knows that the MPC is equal to 0.75 and that the amount of the horizontal distance that the *AD* curve had to be shifted directly leftward from point E_1 was equal to $1.0 trillion. What is the reduction in real government spending required to have generated this shift?

13-19. Recall that the Keynesian spending multiplier equals $1/(1 - MPC)$. Suppose that in Figure 13-4, the MPC is equal to 0.9. In addition, the amount of the horizontal leftward shift from AD_2 to AD_3 caused by a crowding-out effect on planned investment spending was $0.5 trillion, or $500 billion. How much investment spending was crowded out?

13-20. Every 1-percentage-point increase in the marginal income tax rate induces some workers to supply less labor, which cuts real GDP by $0.2 trillion. At the same time, each 1-percentage-point increase in the marginal income tax rate causes spendable income to drop, which induces some workers to supply labor that yields $0.1 trillion more in real GDP. Is the net outcome consistent with the supply-side theory? Why?

13-21. A government has found that 2 months elapse before it can identify a problem to address with a policy action. It has found that 1 month is required to determine the appropriate policy action. Finally, it has concluded that the total time required between the initial presence of the problem and the effects of a policy action to be realized is 12 months. What is the remaining policy time lag and its duration?

13-22. In Figure 13-6, explain why a budget deficit naturally tends to arise at a real GDP level such as Y_2 to the left of Y_f.

REFERENCES

BEHAVIORAL EXAMPLE: Trying to Reduce Government Deficits by "Behaviorally Nudging" Businesses into Paying Taxes

Mathias Sinning and Katja Fels, "Nudging Businesses to Pay Their Taxes," *RWI Impact Notes* (https://www.econstor.eu/bitstream/10419/192970/1/1048330826.pdf), 2019.

Nicholas Biddle, Katja Fels, and Mathias Sinning, "Behavioral Insights and Business Taxation: Evidence from Two Randomized Controlled Trials," *Journal of Behavioral and Experimental Finance*, 2018.

Christian Gillitzer and Mathias Sinning, "Nudging Businesses to Pay Their Taxes: Does Timing Matter?" IZA Institute of Labor Economics Discussion Paper No. 11599, June 2018.

INTERNATIONAL POLICY EXAMPLE: Do Private-Public Infrastructure Projects Generate Smaller Crowding-Out Effects?

World Bank, "Infrastructure and Public-Private Partnerships" (https://www.worldbank.org/en/topic/publicprivatepartnerships), 2019.

Annibel Rice, Ranjitha Shivaram, and Adie Tomer, "Modernizing Infrastructure Policies to Advance Public-Private Partnerships," Brookings, May 22, 2018.

U.S. Chamber of Commerce, "Modernizing America's Infrastructure Requires Public-Private Partnerships" (https://www.uschamber.com/issue-brief/modernizing-americas-infrastructure-requires-public-private-partnerships), January 17, 2018.

AI—DECISION MAKING THROUGH DATA: Reducing Policy Time Lags

Gerald Evans, William Biles, and Ki-Hwan Bae, *Analytics, Operations, and Strategic Decision Making in the Public Sector*, IGI Global, 2019.

Government Finance Officers Association, "Budget Monitoring" (www.gfoa.org/budget-monitoring), 2019.

Robin Wigglesworth, "Can Big Data Revolutionize Policymaking by Governments?" *Financial Times*, January 31, 2018.

ECONOMICS IN YOUR LIFE: The Italian Government Contemplates a "Flat Tax"—for High-Income People Willing to Move to Italy

Daniel Mitchell, "Can a Flat Tax Rescue Italy?" Austrian Economics Center (https://www.austriancenter.com/can-flat-tax-rescue-italy-economy), January 14, 2019.

Edward Lazear, "Government Spending Discourages Work," *Wall Street Journal*, February 26, 2018.

Matthew Michaels, "Italy Wants to Attract Super-Rich People with a Low Tax Rate," *Business Insider* (https://www.businessinsider.com/italy-flat-tax-silvio-berlusconi-italian-election-2018-2), March 2, 2018.

ISSUES & APPLICATIONS: Assessing Overall Effects of Discretionary U.S. Fiscal Policy Actions on Aggregate Demand

U.S. Congressional Budget Office, "The Budget and Economic Outlook, 2019–2029" (https://www.cbo.gov/system/files?file=2019-01-54918-Outlook.pdf), 2019.

David Cashin, Jamie Lenney, Byron Lutz, and William Peterman, "Fiscal Policy and Aggregate Demand in the United States Before, During, and Following the Great Recession," *International Tax and Public Finance*, 2018.

John McClelland, "How the 2017 Tax Act Affects the CBO's Projections," U.S. Congressional Budget Office (https://www.cbo.gov/publication/53787), April 20, 2018.

Fiscal Policy: A Keynesian Perspective

The traditional Keynesian approach to fiscal policy differs in three ways from that presented in Chapter 13. First, it emphasizes the underpinnings of the components of aggregate demand. Second, it assumes that government expenditures are not substitutes for private expenditures and that current taxes are the only taxes taken into account by consumers and firms. Third, the traditional Keynesian approach focuses on the short run and so assumes that as a first approximation, the price level is constant.

Changes in Government Spending

Figure D-1 measures real GDP along the horizontal axis and total planned real expenditures (aggregate demand) along the vertical axis. The components of aggregate demand are real consumption (C), investment (I), government spending (G), and net exports (X). The height of the schedule labeled $C + I + G_1 + X$ shows total planned real expenditures (aggregate demand) as a function of real GDP, given an initial amount of real government spending G_1. This schedule slopes upward because consumption depends positively on real GDP. Everywhere along the 45-degree reference line, planned real spending equals real GDP.

At Y^*, where the $C + I + G_1 + X$ line intersects the 45-degree line, planned real spending is consistent with actual real GDP per year. At any income less than Y^*, planned spending exceeds real GDP, and so real GDP and thus real spending will tend to rise. At any level of real GDP greater than Y^*, planned spending is less than real GDP, and so real GDP and thus spending will tend to decline. Given the determinants of C, I, G, and X, total real spending (aggregate demand) will be Y^*.

FIGURE D-1

The Impact of Higher Government Spending on Aggregate Demand

Government spending increases, causing $C + I + G_1 + X$ to move to $C + I + G_2 + X$. Equilibrium real GDP per year increases to Y^{**}.

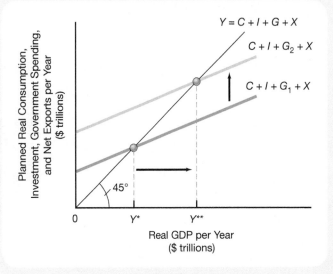

The Keynesian approach assumes that changes in government spending cause no direct offsets in either consumption or investment spending because G is not a substitute for C, I, or X. Hence, a rise in government spending from G_1 to G_2 causes the $C + I + G + X$ line to shift upward by the full amount of the rise in government spending, yielding the line $C + I + G_2 + X$. The rise in real government spending causes real GDP to rise, which in turn causes consumption spending to rise, which further increases real GDP. Ultimately, aggregate demand rises to the level Y^{**}, where planned spending again equals real GDP. A key conclusion of the traditional Keynesian analysis is that total spending rises by *more* than the original rise in government spending because consumption spending depends positively on real GDP.

Changes in Taxes

According to the Keynesian approach, changes in current taxes affect aggregate demand by changing the amount of real disposable (after-tax) income available to consumers. A rise in taxes reduces disposable income and thus reduces real consumption. Conversely, a tax cut raises disposable income and thus causes a rise in consumption spending. The effects of a tax increase are shown in Figure D-2. Higher taxes cause consumption spending to decline from C_1 to C_2, causing total spending to shift downward to $C_2 + I + G + X$. In general, the decline in consumption will be less than the increase in taxes because people will also reduce their saving to help pay the higher taxes.

The Balanced-Budget Multiplier

One interesting implication of the Keynesian approach concerns the impact of a balanced-budget change in government real spending. Suppose that the government increases spending by \$1 billion and pays for it by raising current taxes by \$1 billion. Such a policy is called a *balanced-budget increase in real spending*. The higher spending tends to push aggregate demand *up* by *more* than \$1 billion while the higher taxes tend to push aggregate demand *down* by *less* than \$1 billion. Thus, a most remarkable thing happens: A balanced-budget increase in G causes total spending to rise by *exactly* the

FIGURE D-2

The Impact of Higher Taxes on Aggregate Demand

Higher taxes cause consumption to fall to C_2. Equilibrium real GDP per year decreases to Y''.

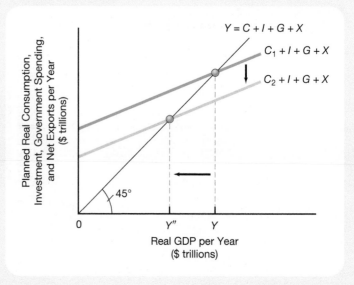

amount of the rise in *G*—in this case, $1 billion. We say that the *balanced-budget multiplier* is equal to 1. Similarly, a balanced-budget reduction in government spending will cause total spending to fall by exactly the amount of the government spending cut.

The Fixed Price Level Assumption

The final key feature of the traditional Keynesian approach is that it typically assumes that as a first approximation, the price level is fixed. Recall that nominal GDP equals the price level multiplied by real GDP. If the price level is fixed, an increase in government spending that causes nominal GDP to rise will show up exclusively as a rise in *real* GDP. This will in turn be accompanied by a decline in the unemployment rate because the additional real GDP can be produced only if additional factors of production, such as labor, are utilized.

PROBLEMS

D-1. Assume that equilibrium real GDP is $22.2 trillion and full-employment equilibrium (*FE*) is $22.55 trillion. The marginal propensity to save is $\frac{1}{7}$. Answer the questions using the data in the following graph.

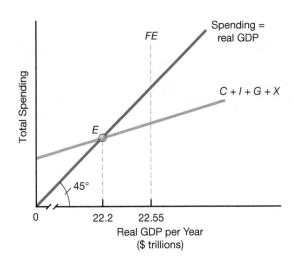

a. What is the marginal propensity to consume?

b. By how much must new investment or government spending increase to achieve full employment if taxes are unchanged?

c. By how much must government cut personal taxes to attain the full-employment equilibrium if its spending is unchanged?

D-2. Assume that MPC $= \frac{4}{5}$ when answering the following questions.

a. If government expenditures rise by $2 billion, by how much will the aggregate expenditure curve shift upward? By how much will equilibrium real GDP per year change?

b. If taxes increase by $2 billion, by how much will the aggregate expenditure curve shift downward? By how much will equilibrium real GDP per year change?

D-3. Assume that MPC $= \frac{4}{5}$ when answering the following questions.

a. If government expenditures rise by $1 billion, by how much will the aggregate expenditure curve shift upward?

b. If taxes rise by $1 billion, by how much will the aggregate expenditure curve shift downward?

c. If both taxes and government expenditures rise by $1 billion, by how much will the aggregate expenditure curve shift? What will happen to the equilibrium level of real GDP?

d. How does your response to the second question in part (c) change if MPC $= \frac{3}{4}$? If MPC $= \frac{1}{2}$?

14 Deficit Spending and the Public Debt

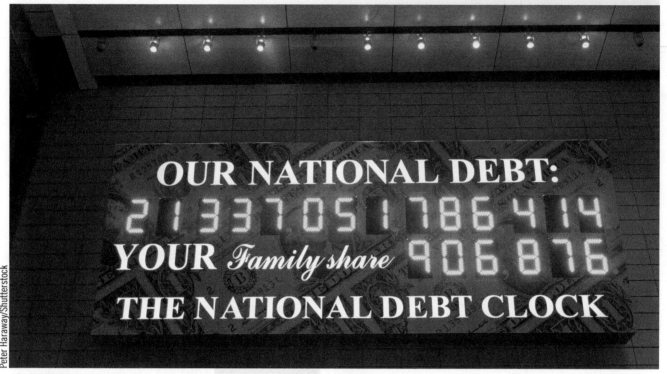

OUR NATIONAL DEBT:
21337051786414
YOUR *Family share* 906,876
THE NATIONAL DEBT CLOCK

Peter Haraway/Shutterstock

LEARNING OBJECTIVES

After reading this chapter, you should be able to:

14.1 Explain how federal government budget deficits occur and define the public debt

14.2 Evaluate circumstances under which the public debt could be a burden to future generations

14.3 Analyze the macroeconomic effects of government budget deficits

14.4 Describe possible ways to reduce the government budget deficit

At any given point during the past 250 years, most of the world's governments have been indebted to holders of bonds that the governments issued in previous years. Consequently, portions of the taxes that these governments collect each year have gone toward transmitting interest and principal to holders of government bonds. Rarely in history, however, have all of the world's governments collectively had so much debt outstanding in relation to annual global production of goods and services. Indeed, by most measures, the aggregate indebtedness of all national governments currently exceeds 60 percent of global GDP. In what ways could today's unusually large government debt create a "burden" on the world's residents? After reading this chapter, you will be able to address this question.

in each year since 2003, the U.S. federal government has transmitted more than $80 billion per year in overpayments—that is, taxpayer-provided funds to which recipients were not legally entitled—to households and businesses? The federal government has continued to transmit such overpayments in spite of the fact that its expenditures have exceeded its revenues every year since 2001. The government anticipates that it will continue to spend more than it receives indefinitely. Should you be worried about this? The answer, as you will see in this chapter, is both yes and no. First, let's examine what the government does when it spends more than it receives.

Public Deficits and Debts

A **government budget deficit** exists if the government spends more than it receives in taxes during a given period of time. The government has to finance this shortfall somehow. Barring any resort to money creation, the U.S. Treasury sells IOUs on behalf of the U.S. government, in the form of securities that are normally called bonds. In effect, the federal government asks U.S. and foreign households, businesses, and governments to lend funds to the government to cover its deficit. For example, if the federal government spends $500 billion more than it receives in revenues, the Treasury will obtain that $500 billion by selling $500 billion of new Treasury bonds. Those who buy the Treasury bonds (lend funds to the U.S. government) will receive interest payments over the life of the bond plus eventual repayment of the entire amount lent. In return, the U.S. Treasury receives immediate purchasing power. In the process, it also adds to its indebtedness to bondholders.

Distinguishing between Deficits and Debts

You have already learned about flows. GDP, for instance, is a flow because it is a dollar measure of the total amount of final goods and services produced within a given period of time, such as a year.

The federal deficit is also a flow. Suppose that the current federal deficit is $500 billion. Consequently, the federal government is currently spending at a rate of $500 billion *per year* more than it is collecting in taxes and other revenues.

Of course, governments do not always spend more each year than the revenues they receive. If a government spends an amount exactly equal to the revenues it collects during a given period, then during this interval the government operates with a **balanced budget**. If a government spends less than the revenues it receives during a given period, then during this interval it experiences a **government budget surplus**.

The Public Debt

You have also learned about stocks, which are measured at a point in time. Stocks change between points in time as a result of flows. For instance, household savings is a stock of accumulated household wealth. Suppose that total household savings turns out to equal $75 trillion at the end of 2021 and then increases to $75.5 trillion at the end of 2022. This means that there would be a net flow of household saving equal to $0.5 trillion during 2022.

Likewise, the total accumulated **public debt** is a stock measured at a given point in time, and it changes from one time to another as a result of government budget deficits or surpluses. Suppose, for instance, as of January 1, 2021, one measure of the public debt was about $18.0 trillion. Then during 2021, the federal government operated at a deficit of about $1.0 trillion. As a consequence, as of January 1, 2022, this measure of the public debt had increased to about $19.0 trillion.

Your Deficits and Your Debts

If the only debt that you have is with one or more credit cards, and you pay them off monthly, you run a monthly deficit, but you do not have any debt. That is to say, at the end of each month you have no outstanding debt.

14.1 Explain how federal government budget deficits occur and define the public debt

Government budget deficit
An excess of government spending over government revenues during a given period of time.

Balanced budget
A situation in which the government's spending is exactly equal to the total taxes and other revenues it collects during a given period of time.

Government budget surplus
An excess of government revenues over government spending during a given period of time.

Public debt
The total value of all outstanding federal government securities.

But, if you only pay part of your credit card debt each month, at the end of each month you are racking up a larger and larger debt. So we can say that you are running monthly deficits and you are increasing your personal debt because you do not pay off those deficits completely.

Government Finance: Spending More Than Tax Collections

Following four consecutive years—1998 through 2001—of official budget surpluses, the federal government began to experience budget deficits once more beginning in 2002. Since then, government spending has increased considerably, and tax revenues have failed to keep pace. Consequently, the federal government has operated with a deficit. Indeed, after 2009 the federal budget deficit widened dramatically—to inflation-adjusted levels not seen since World War II.

The Historical Record of Federal Budget Deficits Figure 14-1 charts inflation-adjusted expenditures and revenues of the federal government since 1940. The *real* annual budget deficit is the arithmetic difference between real expenditures and real revenues during years in which the government's spending has exceeded its revenues. As you can see, this nation has experienced numerous years of federal budget deficits. Indeed, the annual budget surpluses of 1998 through 2001 were out of the ordinary. The 1998 budget surplus was the first since 1968, when the government briefly operated with a surplus. Before the 1998–2001 budget surpluses, the U.S. government had not experienced back-to-back annual surpluses since the 1950s.

Indeed, since 1940 the U.S. government has operated with an annual budget surplus for a total of only 13 years. In all other years, it has collected insufficient taxes and other revenues to fund its spending. Every year this has occurred, the federal government has borrowed to finance its additional expenditures.

FIGURE 14-1

Inflation-Adjusted Federal Budget Deficits and Surpluses since 1940

Federal budget deficits (expenditures in excess of receipts, in red) have been much more common than federal budget surpluses (receipts in excess of expenditures, in green).

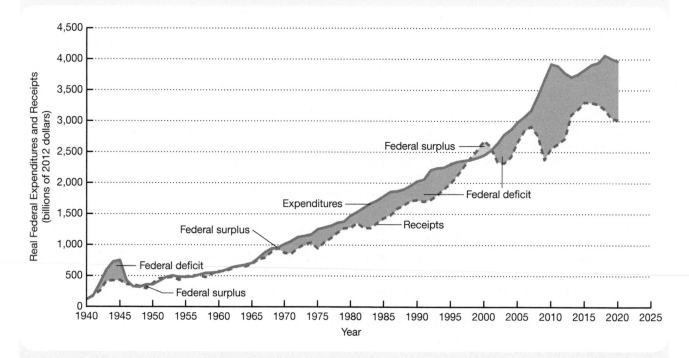

Source: Office of Management and Budget.

FIGURE 14-2

The Federal Budget Deficit Expressed as a Percentage of GDP

During the early 2000s, the federal budget deficit rose as a share of GDP and then declined somewhat until 2007. Next it increased dramatically until 2010. (Note that the negative values for the 1998–2001 period designate budget surpluses as a percentage of GDP during those years.)

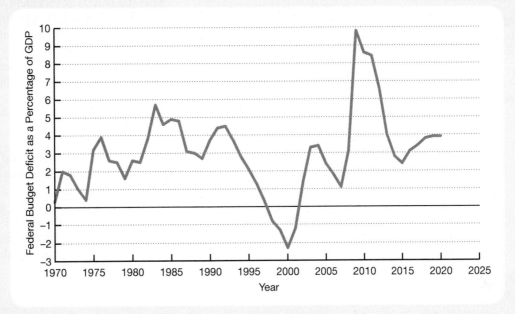

Sources: *Economic Report of the President; Economic Indicators*, various issues; estimates after 2020.

Even though Figure 14-1 accounts for inflation, it does not give a clear picture of the size of the federal government's deficits or surpluses in relation to overall economic activity in the United States. Figure 14-2 provides a clearer view of the size of government deficits or surpluses relative to the size of the U.S. economy by expressing them as percentages of GDP. As you can see, the federal budget deficit rose to nearly 6 percent of GDP in the early 1980s. It then fell back, increased once again during the late 1980s and early 1990s, and then declined steadily into the budget surplus years of 1998–2001. Each year since 2008, the annual government budget deficit has exceeded 2 percent of GDP.

The Resurgence of Federal Government Deficits Why has the government's budget slipped from a surplus equal to nearly 2.5 percent of GDP into a deficit in excess of 2 percent of GDP? The answer is that the government has been spending more than its revenues. Spending has increased at a faster pace since the beginning of this century than during any other decade since World War II.

The more complex answer also considers government revenues. In 2001, Congress and the executive branch slightly reduced income tax rates, and in 2003 they also cut federal capital gains tax rates and estate tax rates. Because tax rates were reduced toward the end of a recession, when real income growth was relatively low, government tax revenues were stagnant for a time.

When economic activity began to expand into the middle of the first decade of this century, tax revenues started rising at a pace closer to the rapid rate of growth of government spending. Then, later in that decade, economic activity dropped significantly. Thus, annual tax collections declined at the same time that annual federal expenditures increased. Since 2011, tax revenues have increased but have continued to be less than government spending. Tax revenues also have remained below government spending since 2017, when the federal income tax base was restructured and certain tax rates were decreased.

14.2 Evaluate circumstances under which the public debt could be a burden to future generations

Gross public debt
All federal government debt irrespective of who owns it.

Net public debt
Gross public debt minus all government interagency borrowing.

Evaluating the Rising Public Debt

All federal public debt, taken together, is called the **gross public debt**. We arrive at the **net public debt** when we subtract from the gross public debt the portion that is held by government agencies (in essence, what the federal government owes to itself). For instance, if the Social Security Administration holds U.S. Treasury bonds, the U.S. Treasury makes debt payments to another agency of the government. On net, therefore, the U.S. government owes these payments to itself.

The net public debt increases whenever the federal government experiences a budget deficit. That is, the net public debt increases when government outlays are greater than total government receipts.

Accumulation of the Net Public Debt

Table 14-1 displays, for various years since 1940, real values, in base-year 2012 dollars, of the federal budget deficit, the total and per capita net public debt (the amount owed on the net public debt by a typical individual), and the net interest cost of the public debt in total and as a percentage of GDP. It shows that the level of the real net public debt and the real net public debt per capita grew following the early 1980s and rose again very dramatically after 2010. Thus, the real, inflation-adjusted amount that a typical individual owes to holders of the net public debt has varied considerably over time.

TABLE 14-1

The Federal Deficit, Our Public Debt, and the Interest We Pay on It

The inflation-adjusted net public debt in column 3 is defined as total federal debt *excluding* all loans between federal government agencies. Per capita net public debt shown in column 4 is obtained by dividing the net public debt by the population.

(1) Year	(2) Federal Budget Deficit (billions of 2012 dollars)	(3) Net Public Debt (billions of 2012 dollars)	(4) Per Capita Net Public Debt (2012 dollars)	(5) Net Interest Costs (billions of 2012 dollars)	(6) Net Interest as a Percentage of GDP
1940	51.6	546.6	4,273.7	11.9	0.9
1945	524.1	2,286.6	16,347.3	30.1	1.45
1950	22.4	1,585.2	10,408.5	34.7	1.68
1955	19.1	1,447.1	8,722.9	31.2	1.23
1960	1.7	1,333.4	7,376.8	38.8	1.37
1965	8.4	1,369.4	7,047.7	45.0	1.26
1970	12.2	1,243.2	6,061.4	62.8	1.47
1975	142.6	1,254.9	5,809.4	73.7	1.52
1980	164.0	1,576.5	6,980.4	116.7	1.92
1985	365.8	2,584.1	10,897.0	223.1	3.22
1990	326.0	3,548.9	14,195.7	258.5	3.23
1995	213.9	4,701.9	17,636.6	302.8	3.24
2000	−284.1*	4,097.4	14,509.0	268.0	2.34
2005	364.0	5,252.4	17,706.6	210.4	1.38
2010	1,345.6	9,375.3	34,413.2	203.9	1.26
2015	415.6	12,435.6	38,861.5	211.6	1.24
2019	964.2	15,084.9	45,948.4	439.5	2.32
2020	949.8	15,585.0	47,313.2	463.7	2.40

Sources: U.S. Department of the Treasury; Office of Management and Budget.
Note: Data for 2020 are estimates.
*A surplus

The net public debt levels reported in Table 14-1 do not provide a basis of comparison with the overall size of the U.S. economy. Panel (a) of Figure 14-3 does this by displaying the net public debt as a percentage of GDP. We see that after World War II, this ratio fell steadily until the early 1970s (except for a small rise in the late 1950s) and then leveled off until the 1980s. After that, the ratio of the net public debt to GDP more or less continued to rise to around 50 percent of GDP, before dropping slightly in the late 1990s. The ratio has been rising once again since 2001 and has jumped dramatically since 2010.

Annual Interest Payments on the Public Debt

Columns 5 and 6 of Table 14-1 show an important consequence of the net public debt. This is the interest that the government must pay to those who hold the bonds it has issued to finance past budget deficits. Those interest payments started rising dramatically around 1975 and then declined into the middle of the first decade of this century. Deficits increased to higher levels in the following years, however. So have the accumulated net public debt and the annual flows of *net* interest payments on that debt, exclusive of interest payments on debt held by government agencies. From an economic standpoint amount, such payments to government agencies involve shuffling of funds within the government as a whole.

Panel (b) of Figure 14-3 provides actual and projected net interest costs of the public debt as a percentage of GDP reported by the U.S. government. Panel (b) indicates

---

FIGURE 14-3

The Official Net Public Debt as a Percentage of GDP and Annual Net Interest Payments on the Debt

As shown in panel (a), the net public debt grew dramatically during World War II, declined after the war until the 1970s, then drifted upward before declining between the mid-1990s and early 2000s, and increased slightly afterward and then more considerably in recent years. Panel (b) displays actual and projected future amounts of annual net interest payments on the public debt since 2014, which are projected to double in dollar amounts between now and 2025 and to reach nearly 3 percent of GDP by that year.

Source: U.S. Department of the Treasury.

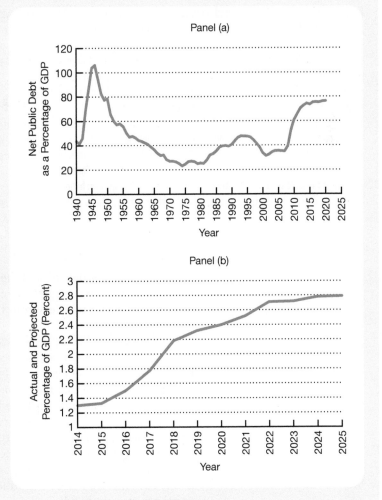

that as a percentage of GDP, the net interest expense is expected to be close to 3 percent by 2025. Note, however, that these projections do not take into account possible increases in market interest rates in the coming years. The dollar amount of the government's annual interest expense is expected to more than double by 2025. In that year, the government's net interest cost is projected to reach nearly $800 billion—an annual expenditure roughly the same as the government anticipates will be spent on the entire U.S. Medicare program. If rates of interest required to be paid on debts issued rise in future years, then annual interest payments will turn out to be higher, both as percentages of GDP and in dollar amounts.

If U.S. residents were the sole owners of the government's debts, the interest payments on the net public debt would go only to U.S. residents. In this situation, we would owe the debt to ourselves, with most people being taxed so that the government could pay interest. During the 1970s, however, the share of the net public debt owned by foreign individuals, businesses, and governments started to rise, reaching 20 percent in 1978. From there it declined until the late 1980s, when it began to rise rapidly. Today, foreign residents, businesses, and governments hold more than 50 percent of the net public debt. Thus, we do not owe our government debt just to ourselves.

Why is the U.S. Treasury Department contemplating following the examples of other nations' governments by issuing 50-year or perhaps even 100-year bonds to fund its growing accumulation of debt?

INTERNATIONAL POLICY EXAMPLE

Could U.S. Taxpayers Gain from the Treasury Borrowing over Longer Stretches of Time?

In the past, interest rates dropped so much in several nations that the governments of these nations decided to try to "lock in" new borrowing at relatively lower rates. The governments of Canada, Italy, and the United Kingdom have introduced 50-year bonds, and the governments of Argentina, Belgium, and Ireland issued 100-year bonds. By issuing debts over such long intervals, these nations' governments sought to minimize their taxpayers' future annual net interest payments.

Currently, the U.S. Treasury's longest bond-borrowing interval is 30 years. Nevertheless, the Treasury Department has been undertaking careful study of extending this maximum borrowing interval out to 40, 50, or perhaps even 100 years. One concern for the Treasury Department is that if market interest rates were to increase suddenly after it began issuing such long-term bonds, continuing to issue these bonds would "lock in" the relatively higher rates.

If so, overall costs to taxpayers could be higher than if the Treasury were to continue issuing debts over spans no longer than 30 years. Nevertheless, serious consideration is being given to the idea of issuing Treasury bonds with 50-year maturities.

REAL APPLICATION

Assume that you have some savings that you wish to place in U.S. Treasury bonds. You have the choice of buying a 1-year bond or a 50-year bond. What are the benefits and risks if you choose a 1-year bond? A 50-year bond?

Sources are listed at the end of this chapter.

Burdens of the Public Debt

Do current budget deficits and the accumulating public debt create social burdens? One perspective on this question considers possible burdens on future generations. Another focuses on transfers from U.S. residents to residents of other nations.

How Today's Budget Deficits Might Burden Future Generations If the federal government wishes to purchase goods and services valued at $300 billion, it can finance this expenditure either by raising taxes by $300 billion or by selling $300 billion in bonds. Many economists maintain that the second option, deficit spending, would lead to a higher level of national consumption and a lower level of national saving than the first option.

The reason, say these economists, is that if people are taxed, they will have to forgo private consumption now as society substitutes government goods for private goods. If the government does not raise taxes but instead sells bonds to finance the $300 billion in expenditures, the public's disposable income remains the same. Members of the public have merely shifted their allocations of assets to include $300 billion in additional government bonds.

Two possible circumstances could cause people to treat government borrowing differently than they treat taxes. One is if people fail to realize that their liabilities (in the form of higher future taxes due to increased interest payments on the public debt) have *also* increased by $300 billion. Another is if people believe that they can consume the governmentally provided goods without forgoing any private consumption because the bill for the government goods will be paid by *future* taxpayers.

The Crowding-Out Effect But if full employment exists, and society raises its present consumption by adding consumption of government-provided goods to the original quantity of privately provided goods, then something must be *crowded out*. In a closed economy, investment expenditures on capital goods must decline. The mechanism by which investment is crowded out is an increase in the interest rate. Deficit spending increases the total demand for credit but leaves the total supply of credit unaltered. The rise in interest rates causes a reduction in the growth of investment and capital formation, which in turn slows the growth of productivity and improvement in society's living standard.

This perspective suggests that deficit spending can impose a burden on future generations in two ways. First, unless the deficit spending is allocated to purchases that lead to long-term increases in real GDP, future generations will have to be taxed at a higher rate. That is, only by imposing higher taxes on future generations will the government be able to retire the higher public debt resulting from the present generation's consumption of governmentally provided goods. Second, the increased level of spending by the present generation crowds out investment and reduces the growth of capital goods, leaving future generations with a smaller capital stock and thereby reducing their wealth.

WHAT HAPPENS WHEN...

financing a larger percentage of government spending by issuing bonds domestically and abroad ends up crowding out investment spending?

Investment expenditures go toward both maintaining the existing stock of capital goods and generating an increase in the stock of these goods. Thus, if a larger share of bond-financed government spending crowds out investment expenditures, the stock of capital goods fails to grow as much and potentially could even shrink. The result would be reduced economic growth, which might cause the debts created by the issuance of government bonds to become burdensome for future generations.

Paying off the Public Debt in the Future Suppose that after years of running substantial deficits financed by selling bonds to U.S. residents, the public debt has become so large that each adult person's implicit share of the net public debt liability is $70,000. Assume that all of the debt is owed to ourselves. Suppose further that the government chooses (or is forced) to pay off the debt at that time. Will that generation be burdened with our government's overspending?

It is true that every adult will have to come up with $70,000 in taxes to pay off the debt, but then the government will use these funds to pay off the bondholders. Sometimes the bondholders and taxpayers will be the same people. Thus, *some* people will be burdened because they owe $70,000 and own less than $70,000 in government bonds. Others, however, will receive more than $70,000 for the bonds they own. Nevertheless, as a generation within society, they could—if all government debt were issued within the nation's borders—pay and receive about the same amount of funds.

Of course, there could be a burden on some low-income adults who will find it difficult or impossible to obtain $70,000 to pay off the tax liability. Still, nothing says that taxes to pay off the debt must be assessed equally. Indeed, it seems likely that a special tax would be levied, based on the ability to pay.

Our Debt to Foreign Residents So far we have been assuming that we owe all of the public debt to ourselves. As we saw earlier, though, that is not the case. What about the more than 50 percent owned by foreign residents?

It is true that if foreign residents buy U.S. government bonds, we do not owe that debt to ourselves. Thus, when debts held by foreign residents come due, future U.S. residents will be taxed to repay these debts plus accumulated interest. Portions of the incomes of future U.S. residents will then be transferred abroad. In this way, a potential burden on future generations may result.

Note that this transfer of income from U.S. residents to residents of other nations will not necessarily be a burden. It is important to realize that if the rate of return on projects that the government funds by operating with deficits exceeds the interest rate paid to foreign residents, both foreign residents and future U.S. residents will be better off. If funds obtained by selling bonds to foreign residents are expended on wasteful projects, however, a burden will be placed on future generations.

We can apply the same reasoning to the problem of current investment and capital creation being crowded out by current deficits. If deficits lead to slower growth rates, future generations will be poorer. If the government expenditures are really investments, and if the rate of return on such public investments exceeds the interest rate paid on the bonds, however, both present and future generations will be economically better off.

> **14.3** Analyze the macroeconomic effects of government budget deficits

Growing U.S. Government Deficits: Implications for U.S. Economic Performance

Many economists argue that it is no accident that foreign residents hold such a large portion of the U.S. public debt. Their reasoning suggests that a U.S. trade deficit—a situation in which the value of U.S. imports of goods and services exceeds the value of its exports—will often accompany a government budget deficit. In addition, most economists contend that government budget deficits can have significant implications, as well, for the overall economy.

Trade Deficits and Government Budget Deficits

Figure 14-4 shows U.S. trade deficits and surpluses compared with federal budget deficits and surpluses. In the early 1980s, imports of goods and services began to consistently exceed exports of those items on an annual basis in the United States. At the same time, the federal budget deficit rose dramatically. Both deficits increased once again in the early 2000s. Then, during the economic turmoil of the late 2000s, the budget deficit exploded while the trade deficit shrank somewhat.

Overall, however, it appears that larger trade deficits tend to accompany larger government budget deficits.

Domestic Deficits Partly Financed Abroad Intuitively, there is a reason why we would expect federal budget deficits to be associated with trade deficits. You might call this the unpleasant arithmetic of trade and budget deficits.

Suppose that, initially, the government's budget is balanced. Government expenditures are matched by an equal amount of tax collections and other government revenues. Now assume that the federal government begins to operate with a budget deficit. It increases its spending, collects fewer taxes, or both. Assume further that domestic consumption and domestic investment do not decrease relative to GDP. Where, then, do the funds come from to finance the government's budget deficit? A portion of these funds *must* come from abroad. That is to say, dollar holders abroad ultimately will purchase newly created government bonds. This is the first link in the relationship between government budget deficits and trade deficits.

FIGURE 14-4

The Related U.S. Deficits

The United States exported more than it imported until the mid-1970s. Then it started experiencing large trade deficits, as shown in this diagram. The federal budget has been in deficit most years since the 1960s.

The question is, has the federal budget deficit created the trade deficit?

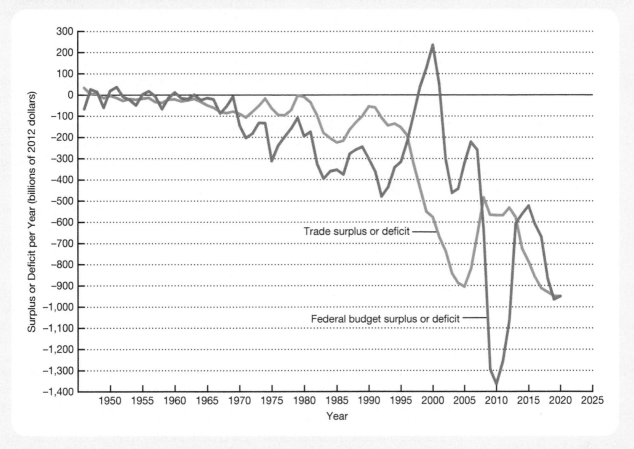

Sources: *Economic Report of the President; Economic Indicators*, various issues; author's estimates.

Why the Two Deficits Tend to Be Related

The second link relating government budget deficits to trade deficits arises because foreign dollar holders will choose to hold the new U.S. government bonds only if there is an economic inducement to do so, such as an increase in U.S. interest rates. Given that private domestic spending and other factors are unchanged, interest rates will indeed rise whenever there is an increase in deficits financed by increased borrowing.

When foreign dollar holders purchase new U.S. government bonds, they will have fewer dollars to spend on U.S. items, including U.S. export goods. Hence, when our nation's government operates with a budget deficit, we should expect to see foreign dollar holders spending more on U.S. government bonds and less on U.S.-produced goods and services. As a consequence of the U.S. government deficit, therefore, we should generally anticipate a decline in U.S. exports relative to U.S. imports, or a higher U.S. trade deficit.

The Macroeconomic Consequences of Budget Deficits

We have seen that one consequence of higher U.S. government budget deficits tends to be higher international trade deficits. Higher budget deficits, such as the much higher deficits of recent years (especially during the recession at the end of the last decade), are also likely to have broader consequences for overall economic performance.

When evaluating additional macroeconomic effects of government deficits, two important points must be kept well in mind. First, given the level of government expenditures, the main alternative to the deficit is higher taxes. Therefore, the effects of a deficit should be compared to the effects of higher taxes, not to zero. Second, it is important to distinguish between the effects of deficits when full employment exists and the effects when substantial unemployment exists.

Short-Run Macroeconomic Effects of Higher Budget Deficits   How do increased government budget deficits affect the economy in the short run? The answer depends on the initial state of the economy. Recall that higher government spending and lower taxes that generate budget deficits typically add to total planned expenditures, even after taking into account direct and indirect expenditure offsets. When there is a recessionary gap, the increase in aggregate demand can eliminate the recessionary gap and push the economy toward its full-employment real GDP level. In the presence of a short-run recessionary gap, therefore, government deficit spending can influence both real GDP and employment.

If the economy is at the full-employment level of real GDP, however, increased total planned expenditures and higher aggregate demand generated by a larger government budget deficit create an inflationary gap. Although greater deficit spending temporarily raises equilibrium real GDP above the full-employment level, the price level also increases.

Long-Run Macroeconomic Effects of Higher Budget Deficits   In a long-run macroeconomic equilibrium, the economy has fully adjusted to changes in all factors. These factors include changes in government spending and taxes and, consequently, the government budget deficit. Although increasing the government budget deficit raises aggregate demand, in the long run equilibrium real GDP remains at its full-employment level. Further increases in the government deficit via higher government expenditures or tax cuts can only be inflationary. They have no effect on equilibrium real GDP, which remains at the full-employment level in the long run.

The fact that long-run equilibrium real GDP is unaffected in the face of increased government deficits has an important implication:

> *In the long run, higher government budget deficits have no effect on equilibrium real GDP per year. Ultimately, therefore, government spending in excess of government receipts simply redistributes a larger share of real GDP per year to government-provided goods and services.*

Thus, if the government operates with higher deficits over an extended period, the ultimate result is a shrinkage in the share of privately provided goods and services. By continually spending more than it collects in taxes and other revenue sources, the government takes up a larger portion of economic activity.

14.4 Describe possible ways to reduce the government budget deficit

How Could the Government Reduce All of Its Red Ink?

There have been many suggestions about how to reduce the government deficit. One way to reduce the deficit is to increase tax collections.

Why does recent behavioral research indicate that if people were better informed about the size of our deficits and the net public debt, the former might begin to shrink, and the latter might grow less rapidly?

BEHAVIORAL EXAMPLE

One Way to Generate Lower Government Deficits Might Be to Better Inform People about the Debt

Behavioral studies consistently find that people substantially underestimate the magnitude of the net public debt in relation to the volume of economic activity. Furthermore, these studies indicate that informing people about the ratio of the inflation-adjusted net public debt to real GDP affects attitudes regarding the "appropriate" amount of annual government expenditures. When people learn that the ratio of the inflation-adjusted net public debt to real GDP is higher than they had realized, their preferences about taxation typically are not altered, but their preferences shift toward a desire for lower government spending. Thus, in nations in which elected government officials determine spending levels, providing more complete information about the relative magnitude of the net public

debt likely would shrink the annual government deficit. The result would be reduced growth of the net public debt.

FOR CRITICAL THINKING

Why does generating a shrinkage of the current government deficit fail to bring about a corresponding shrinkage in the current magnitude of the net public debt? (Hint: Recall that the current net public debt has accumulated as a consequence of past deficits.)

Sources are listed at the end of this chapter.

Increasing Taxes for Everyone

From an arithmetic point of view, a federal budget deficit can be wiped out by simply increasing the amount of taxes collected. Let's see what this would require. Projections for 2020 are instructive. The Office of Management and Budget put the 2020 federal budget deficit at about $1 trillion. To have prevented this deficit from occurring by raising taxes, in 2020 the government would have had to collect nearly $8,000 in additional taxes from *every worker* in the United States. Needless to say, reality is such that we will never see annual federal budget deficits wiped out by one-time tax increases.

Taxing the Rich

Some people suggest that the way to eliminate the deficit is to raise taxes on the rich. What does it mean to tax the rich more? If you talk about taxing "millionaires," you are referring to those who pay taxes on more than $1 million in income per year. There are fewer than 300,000 of them. Even if you were to double the taxes they now pay, the reduction in the deficit would be relatively trivial. Changing marginal tax rates at the upper end will produce similarly unimpressive results. The Internal Revenue Service (IRS) has determined that an increase in the top marginal tax rate from 40 percent to 50 percent would raise, at best, only about $40 billion in additional taxes. (This assumes that people do not figure out a way to avoid the higher tax rate.) Extra revenues of $40 billion per year represent only about 4 percent of the estimated 2020 federal budget deficit.

The reality is that the data do not support the notion that tax increases can completely *eliminate* deficits. Although eliminating a deficit in this way is possible arithmetically, politically just the opposite has occurred. When more tax revenues have been collected, Congress has usually responded by increasing government spending.

Reducing Expenditures

Reducing expenditures is another way to decrease the federal budget deficit. Figure 14-5 shows various components of government spending as a percentage of total expenditures. There you see that military spending (national defense) as a share of total federal expenditures has risen slightly in some recent years, though it remains much lower than in most previous years.

During the period from the conclusion of World War II until 1972, military spending was the most important aspect of the federal budget. Figure 14-5 shows that it no longer is, even taking into account the war on terrorism that began in late 2001. **Entitlements**, which are legislated federal government payments that anyone who

ECONOMICS IN YOUR LIFE

To consider how some nations' governments are reducing their deficits by selling off some of their assets, read **Government-Pension Expenditures Appear to Have Become Noncontrollable in Brazil** on page 305.

Entitlements
Guaranteed benefits under a government program such as Social Security, Medicare, or Medicaid.

FIGURE 14-5

Components of Federal Expenditures as Percentages of Total Federal Spending

Although military spending as a percentage of total federal spending has risen and fallen with changing national defense concerns, national defense expenditures as a percentage of total spending have generally trended downward since the mid-1950s. Social Security and other income security programs and Medicare and other health programs now account for larger shares of total federal spending than any other programs.

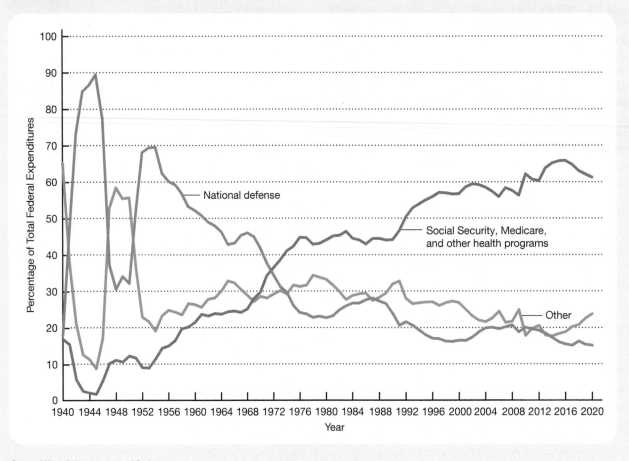

Source: Office of Management and Budget.

qualifies is entitled to receive, are now the most important component of the federal budget. These include payments for Social Security and other income security programs and for Medicare and other health programs such as Medicaid. Entitlements are consequently often called **noncontrollable expenditures**, or nondiscretionary expenditures unrelated to national defense that automatically change without any direct action by Congress.

Noncontrollable expenditures
Government spending that changes automatically without action by Congress.

Can governmental adoption of big-data techniques significantly reduce the deficit?

AI | DECISION MAKING THROUGH DATA

Cutting Government Spending and Trimming the Federal Deficit

Recently, personnel in the Department of Health and Human Services (HHS) utilized data-analytics methods to uncover efforts by more than 300 individuals to defraud the federal Medicare program of nearly $1 billion. The HHS personnel discovered that previously, those people had found ways to hide their requests for unauthorized reimbursements in the masses of data that HHS accumulates every year. The HHS application of big data and machine-learning techniques to the huge volumes of data enabled them to uncover unusual patterns in Medicare claims submissions that revealed the fraudulent activity.

Various departments overseeing HHS and other federal agencies are in the process of transmitting large quantities of data to cloud storage. This effort is coordinated under rules established by the Federal Risk and Authorization Management Program. One key objective of this program is to enable agencies to follow the HHS example and uncover other improper payouts and wasteful duplicative expenditures, with an aim to trim the annual federal government deficit.

FOR CRITICAL THINKING

Why is the net amount trimmed from the annual federal deficit likely to be smaller than the amount of fraudulent payments and duplicative spending eliminated via application of AI techniques? (Hint: Can the federal government employ AI methods at zero cost?)

Sources are listed at the end of this chapter.

Entitlements Help to Feed Deficit Spending

In 1960, spending on entitlements represented about 20 percent of the total federal budget. Today, entitlement expenditures make up more than 60 percent of total federal spending. Consider Social Security, Medicare, and Medicaid. In constant 2012 dollars, in 2020 Social Security, Medicare, and Medicaid represented about $3.1 trillion of estimated federal expenditures. (This calculation excludes military and international payments and interest on the government debt.)

Entitlement payments for Social Security, Medicare, and Medicaid now exceed all other domestic spending. Entitlements are growing faster than any other part of the federal government budget. During the past two decades, real spending on entitlements (adjusted for inflation) grew between 7 and 8 percent per year, while the economy grew less than 3 percent per year. Social Security payments are growing in real terms at about 6 percent per year, but Medicare and Medicaid are growing at double-digit rates. The passage of Medicare prescription drug benefits in 2003 and the new federal health care legislation in 2010 simply added to the already rapid growth of these health care entitlements.

ECONOMICS IN YOUR LIFE

Government-Pension Expenditures Appear to Have Become Noncontrollable in Brazil

Michel Temer, when he was president of Brazil, was trying to confront a serious problem. During recent years, Brazil's annual government deficit quadrupled, to about $50 billion. A significant contributor to the sudden increase has been the public pension system. Most people in government positions retire at age 55, and some can retire as early as age 50. Surviving spouses receive the full pensions of deceased retirees. If the surviving spouses themselves are retired public workers, they can continue to receive their own pensions as well.

Temer's advisors provided reports showing that the public pension system pays out $60 billion more each year than it receives. Almost half of the national government's annual expenditures currently are directed toward funding most of this enlarged public pension deficit. The failure to cover this entitlement overrun accounts for the sharp increase in Brazil's government budget deficit. Temer was convinced that the government could bring down its deficit only if he convinced fellow Brazilians who have worked in the public sector to give up some of their entitlements. Given that Temer himself collected a public pension for more than 20 years after retiring as a public prosecutor at age 56, his pleas rang a bit hollow in some Brazilian public employees' ears.

FOR CRITICAL THINKING

What do you suppose has happened to Brazil's net public debt in recent years? Explain your reasoning.

REAL APPLICATION

Suppose that you take a job with a local, state, or federal government. You are told that you can retire at age 50. Assume further that no such generous pension plan exists in the private sector. How would you determine whether to stay in the public sector or to move into the private sector?

Sources are listed at the end of this chapter.

ISSUES & APPLICATIONS

The World Is Awash in Government Debt

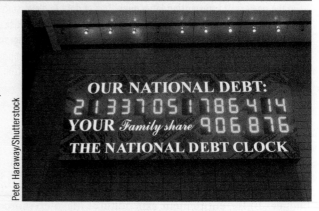

OUR NATIONAL DEBT:
21337051786414
YOUR *Family share* 906876
THE NATIONAL DEBT CLOCK

Peter Haraway/Shutterstock

CONCEPTS APPLIED

➤ Net Public Debt

➤ Net Interest Cost of the Public Debt

➤ Entitlements

As Figure 14-6 indicates, both for the world's most advanced nations and for those that are classified as having either emerging or developed economies, current levels of public indebtedness are at heights not observed for more than two decades. Indeed, combined net public indebtedness of the most advanced nations as a percentage of the countries' total gross domestic product is at its highest level in more than 60 years. The latest percentage for governments of emerging and developing nations displayed in the figure is at its highest level ever.

FIGURE 14-6

The Combined Level of Public Debt as a Percentage of Combined GDP per Year for Advanced Nations and for Emerging and Developing Nations since 2001

The combined public debt as a percentage of the combined GDP for the world's most advanced nations, including governments of the European Union countries, Japan, and the United States, rose rapidly during the late 2000s and has remained above 100 percent each year since 2011. For the world's emerging and developing countries, the percentage has gradually increased since 2011 to a current level that is the highest yet recorded.

Source: International Monetary Fund.

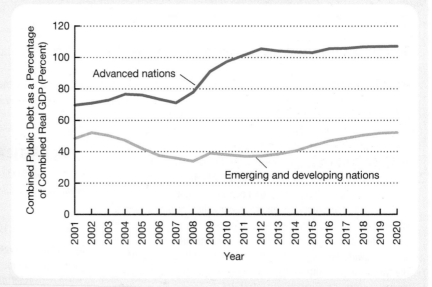

The Redistribution Effect of Global Public Indebtedness

The combined total of the net public debts of *all* of the world's governments is greater than $65 trillion. This amount exceeds 60 percent of all common measures of the annual value of *global* economic activity.

Of course, the combined debts of the world's governments are financed by all of the world's taxpayers, who repay the principal amounts of the debts and pay associated net interest costs. Those taxpayers who do not hold government bonds, however, transmit interest payments on the debts to those who do hold these bonds. Thus, the existence of such high debt levels across the world's nations implies substantial transfers of income from non-bondholding taxpayers to those who do own these bonds. To the extent that people in some nations hold more of the net public debts of other countries than do other countries' residents, transfers of income from the latter group to the former set of nations also occurs.

The Potential Burden of Greater Government Debt

Of course, governments may undertake spending with rates of return that are lower than the interest rates paid on their debts and lower than rates that crowded-out private investment projects otherwise would have yielded. If so, the significant combined net public indebtedness of the world's nations could create a global burden. The result would be reduced growth of the world economy.

This burden would not primarily be borne by the world's current adult residents, however. Instead, it would fall mainly on the world's younger residents and on future generations yet unborn, who would experience reduced rates of economic growth.

FOR CRITICAL THINKING

Why would either a particularly low rate of return on bond-financed global public spending or significant crowding out of private investment expenditures by such public spending yield lower global economic growth? (Hint: What exactly is purchased by private investment spending?)

REAL APPLICATION

Imagine that your outstanding debt is growing faster than your actual and expected income per year. What are the implications of this situation for you personally?

Sources are listed at the end of this chapter.

What You Should Know

Here is what you should know after reading this chapter.

LEARNING OBJECTIVES

14.1 **Explain how federal government budget deficits occur and define the public debt** *A budget deficit occurs whenever the flow of government expenditures exceeds the flow of government revenues during a period of time. Accumulated budget deficits are a stock, called the public debt. The gross public debt is the stock of total government bonds, and the net public debt is the difference between the gross public debt and the amount of government agencies' holdings of government bonds.*

14.2 **Evaluate circumstances under which the public debt could be a burden to future generations** *People taxed at a higher rate must forgo private consumption as society substitutes government goods for private goods. Any current crowding out of investment as a consequence of additional debt accumulation can reduce capital formation and future economic growth. Furthermore, if capital invested by foreign residents who purchase some of the U.S. public debt has not been productively used, future generations will be worse off.*

14.3 **Analyze the macroeconomic effects of government budget deficits** *Higher government deficits contribute to a rise in total planned expenditures and aggregate demand. If there is a short-run recessionary gap, higher government deficits can thereby push equilibrium real GDP toward the full-employment level. If the economy is already at the full-employment level of real GDP, however, then a higher deficit creates a short-run inflationary gap.*

14.4 **Describe possible ways to reduce the government budget deficit** *Suggested ways to reduce the deficit are to increase taxes, particularly on the rich, and to reduce expenditures, particularly on entitlements, defined as guaranteed benefits under government programs such as Social Security and Medicare.*

KEY TERMS

government budget deficit, 293
balanced budget, 293
government budget surplus, 293
public debt, 293
Key Figures
Figure 14-1, 294
Figure 14-2, 295

gross public debt, 296
net public debt, 296
Key Figure
Figure 14-3, 297

Key Figure
Figure 14-4, 301

entitlements, 303
noncontrollable
  expenditures, 304
Key Figure
Figure 14-5, 304

PROBLEMS

14-1. In 2023, government spending is $5.0 trillion, and taxes collected are $4.1 trillion. What is the federal government deficit in that year?

14-2. Suppose that the Office of Management and Budget provides the estimates of federal budget receipts, federal budget spending, and GDP shown below, all expressed in billions of dollars. Calculate the implied estimates of the federal budget deficit as a percentage of GDP for each year.

Year	Federal Budget Receipts	Federal Budget Spending	GDP
2023	4,132.0	5,008.8	24,925.2
2024	4,305.2	5,199.1	25,947.1
2025	4,447.3	5,407.1	27,010.9
2026	4,603.0	5,644.9	28,145.4

14-3. It may be argued that the effects of a higher public debt are the same as the effects of a higher deficit. Why?

14-4. What happens to the net public debt if the federal government operates next year with the following:

a. A budget deficit?

b. A balanced budget?

c. A budget surplus?

14-5. What is the relationship between the gross public debt and the net public debt?

14-6. Explain how each of the following will affect the net public debt, other things being equal.

a. Previously, the government operated with a balanced budget, but recently there has been a sudden increase in federal tax collections.

b. The government had been operating with a very small annual budget deficit until three hurricanes hit the Atlantic Coast, and now government spending has risen substantially.

c. The Government National Mortgage Association, a federal government agency that purchases certain types of home mortgages, buys U.S. Treasury bonds from another government agency.

14-7. Explain in your own words why there is likely to be a relationship between federal budget deficits and U.S. international trade deficits.

14-8. Suppose that the share of U.S. GDP going to domestic consumption remains constant. Initially, the federal government was operating with a balanced budget, but this year it has increased its spending well above its collections of taxes and other sources of revenues. To fund its deficit spending, the government has issued bonds. So far, very few foreign residents have shown any interest in purchasing the bonds.

a. What must happen to induce foreign residents to buy the bonds?

b. If foreign residents desire to purchase the bonds, what is the most important source of dollars to buy them?

14-9. Suppose that the economy is experiencing the short-run equilibrium position depicted at point A in the first diagram. Then the government raises its spending and thereby runs a budget deficit in an effort to boost equilibrium real GDP to its long-run equilibrium level of $22 trillion (in base-year dollars). Explain the effects of an increase in the government deficit on equilibrium real GDP and the equilibrium price level. In addition, given that many taxes and government benefits vary with real GDP, discuss what change we might expect to see in the budget deficit as a result of the effects on equilibrium real GDP.

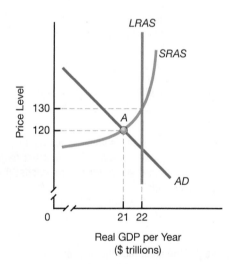

14-10. Suppose that the economy is experiencing the short-run equilibrium position depicted at point B in the second diagram. Explain the short-run effects of an increase in the government deficit on equilibrium real GDP and the equilibrium price level. What will be the long-run effects?

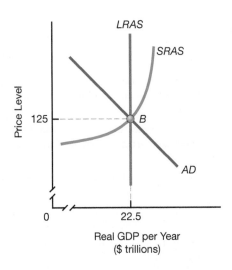

14-11. To eliminate the deficit (and halt the growth of the net public debt), a politician suggests that "we should tax the rich." The politician makes a simple arithmetic calculation in which he applies a higher tax rate to the total income reported by "the rich" in a previous year. He says that the government could thereby solve the deficit problem by taxing "the rich." What is the major fallacy in such a claim?

14-12. Refer back to Problem 14-11. If the politician defines "the rich" as people with annual taxable incomes exceeding $1 million per year, what is another difficulty with the politician's reasoning, given that "the rich" rarely earn a combined taxable income exceeding $1 trillion, yet the federal deficit has regularly exceeded $1 trillion in recent years?

14-13. In each of the past few years, the federal government has regularly borrowed funds to pay for at least one-third of expenditures that tax revenues were insufficient to cover. More than 60 percent of all federal expenditures now go for entitlement spending. What does this fact imply about how the government is paying for most of its discretionary expenditures?

14-14. Take a look at Figure 14-1. During the brief green-shaded intervals, is the amount of the U.S. net public debt more likely to be increasing or decreasing? Explain your reasoning.

14-15. Consider Figure 14-2. The years immediately after 2008 stand out as having the highest values in the figure. The main reason is that the dollar magnitudes of the federal government's deficits were very large during these years. How might the fact that a significant economic contraction occurred during these years provide another explanation for why the percentages for these years were so high?

14-16. Take a look at the most recent years of data on the net public debt displayed in Figure 14-3, and then examine the most recent years of data on federal budget deficits shown in Figure 14-2. Why do you suppose that the net public debt as a percentage of GDP has grown more rapidly in most years since 2008?

14-17. A fraction of the funds borrowed by the federal government between 2008 and 2015 were utilized to fund public investments in a number of solar power companies that produced little output and halted operations. These businesses provided no repayments to the government. In what sense might this fraction of deficit spending arguably have imposed a "burden" on future generations?

14-18. The long-run effect of higher government budget deficits on the equilibrium annual flow of real GDP is zero. Who, therefore, benefits in the long run from higher government deficits?

REFERENCES

INTERNATIONAL POLICY EXAMPLE: Could U.S. Taxpayers Gain from the Treasury Borrowing over Longer Stretches of Time?

Michael Rainey, "Is It Time to Start Selling 100-Year Bonds?" *Fiscal Times*, February 5, 2019.

Pablo Rosendo Gonzalez, "Just 99 Years to Go as Argentine Century Bond Hits Record," *Bloomberg*, June 28, 2018.

U.S. Department of the Treasury, "Minutes of the Meeting of the Treasury Borrowing Advisory Committee of the Securities Industry and Financial Markets Association," May 2, 2018.

BEHAVIORAL EXAMPLE: One Way to Generate Lower Government Deficits Might Be to Better Inform People about the Debt

"Be Informed: National Debt," JustFacts.com (https://www.just-facts.com/nationaldebt.asp), February 11, 2019.

Committee for a Responsible Federal Budget, "Updating the U.S. Budget Outlook," March 2, 2018.

Christopher Roth and Johannes Wohlfart, "Public Debt and the Demand for Government Spending and Taxation," Working Paper, University of Oxford, 2018.

AI—DECISION MAKING THROUGH DATA: Cutting Government Spending and Trimming the Federal Deficit

"Today's Application of AI within Government," Inside HPC (https://insidehpc.com/2019/02/government-ai-applications/), February 12, 2019.

Jack Corrigan, "HHS Is Using Data to Fight Opioid Abuse, Fraud, and Just about Everything Else," Nextgov.com (https://www.nextgov.com/analytics-data/2018/07/hhs-using-data-fight-opioid-abuse-fraud-and-just-about-everything-else/149226/), July 5, 2018.

Matt Leonard, "Government Leans into Machine Learning," GCN.com (https://gcn.com/articles/2018/08/17/machine-learning.aspx), August 19, 2018.

ECONOMICS IN YOUR LIFE: Government-Pension Expenditures Appear to Have Become Noncontrollable in Brazil

Wellton Maximo and Pedro Rafael Vilela, "Pension Reform Among Priorities of Government," *Agencia Brazil*, January 3, 2019.

"Michel Temer Is Trying to Fix Brazil's Pension Systems," *Economist*, February 15, 2018.

Rachel Gamarski, "Brazil's Lost Fiscal Decade Is a Time Bomb Awaiting the Next President," *Bloomberg*, April 30, 2018.

ISSUES & APPLICATIONS: The World Is Awash in Government Debt

International Monetary Fund, "Fiscal Monitor" (https://www.imf.org/en/Publications/FM/Issues/2019/04/XX/fiscal-monitor-april-2019), April 2019.

Jeff Desjardins, "This Chart Shows What $63 Trillion of World Debt Looks Like" (https://www.weforum.org/agenda/2018/05/63-trillion-of-world-debt-in-one-visualization), *World Economic Forum*, May 9, 2018.

Josh Zumbrun, "Since 1880, Global Government Debts Have Rarely Been So High," *Wall Street Journal*, April 18, 2018.

15 Money, Banking, and Central Banking

rrodrickbeiler/Fotolia

LEARNING OBJECTIVES

After reading this chapter, you should be able to:

15.1 Define the functions of money, identify key properties that money must possess, and explain official definitions of the money supply

15.2 Understand why financial intermediaries such as banks exist

15.3 Describe the basic structure and functions of the Federal Reserve System

15.4 Determine the maximum potential extent that the money supply will change following a Federal Reserve monetary policy action

15.5 Explain the essential features of federal deposit insurance

Every year, the Federal Reserve, the U.S. central bank often called "the Fed"—which is responsible for determining the quantity of money in circulation—transmits to the U.S. Treasury tens of billions of dollars, payments called "remittances." The source of these Fed remittances to the Treasury is the profit that the Fed has received from creating money during the previous 12 months. What is money, and what functions does it perform? How does the Fed "create" money, and how does the Fed generate such significant profits that the Treasury can then apply to help finance its own operations alongside funds raised from the various taxes that the Treasury collects? Read this chapter, and you will learn the answers to these questions.

DID YOU KNOW THAT...

J.P. Morgan Chase, one of the nation's largest banks, recently revealed that more than 950 of its employees devote their time to producing about 20,000 pages of documentation required to comply with 750 rules laid down by 21 government entities, including the Federal Reserve? In 2010, Congress granted the Federal Reserve's Board of Governors increased responsibilities to establish new bank regulations affecting institutions such as J.P. Morgan Chase, which has contributed to these institutions' regulatory reporting requirements and expenses. Regulating such institutions is among several of the Federal Reserve's responsibilities, but the most important of its duties is determining the quantity of money in circulation within the U.S. economy.

15.1 Define the functions of money, identify key properties that money must possess, and explain official definitions of the money supply

Money
Any medium that is universally accepted in an economy both by sellers of goods and services as payment for those goods and services and by creditors as payment for debts.

Medium of exchange
Any item that sellers will accept as payment.

Barter
The direct exchange of goods and services for other goods and services without the use of money.

Functions and Measures of Money

Money has been important to society for thousands of years. In the fourth century B.C.E., Aristotle claimed that everything had to "be accessed in money, for this enables men always to exchange their services, and so makes society possible." Money is indeed a part of our everyday existence. Nevertheless, we have to be careful when we talk about money. Often we hear a person say, "I wish I had more money," instead of "I wish I had more wealth," thereby confusing the concepts of money and wealth. Economists use the term **money** to mean anything that people generally accept in exchange for goods and services. Table 15-1 provides a list of some items that various civilizations have used as money. The best way to understand how these items served this purpose is to examine the functions of money.

Money traditionally has four functions. The one that most people are familiar with is money's function as a *medium of exchange*. Money also serves as a *unit of accounting*, a *store of value* or *purchasing power*, and a *standard of deferred payment*. Anything that serves these four functions is money. Anything that could serve these four functions could be considered money.

Money as a Medium of Exchange

When we say that money serves as a **medium of exchange**, we mean that sellers will accept it as payment in market transactions. Without some generally accepted medium of exchange, we would have to resort to *barter*. In fact, before money was used, transactions took place by means of barter. **Barter** is simply a direct exchange of goods for goods. In a barter economy, the shoemaker who wants to obtain a dozen water glasses must seek out a glassmaker who at exactly the same time is interested in obtaining a pair of shoes. For this to occur, there has to be a high likelihood of a *double coincidence*

TABLE 15-1

Examples of Money

This is a partial list of items that have been used as money. Native Americans used *wampum*, beads made from shells. Fijians used whale teeth. The early colonists in North America used tobacco. And cigarettes were used in post–World War II Germany and in Poland during the breakdown of Communist rule in the late 1980s.

Boar tusk	Goats	Rice
Boats	Gold	Round stones with centers removed
Cigarettes	Horses	Rum
Copper	Iron	Salt
Corn	Molasses	Silver
Cows	Polished beads (wampum)	Tobacco
Feathers	Pots	Tortoise shells
Glass	Red woodpecker scalps	Whale teeth

Source: Author's research.

of wants for each specific item to be exchanged. If there isn't, the shoemaker must go through several trades in order to obtain the desired dozen glasses—perhaps first trading shoes for jewelry, then jewelry for some pots and pans, and then the pots and pans for the desired glasses.

Money facilitates exchange by reducing the transaction costs associated with means-of-payment uncertainty. That is, the existence of money means that individuals no longer have to hold a diverse collection of goods as an exchange inventory. As a medium of exchange, money allows individuals to specialize in producing those goods for which they have a comparative advantage and to receive money payments for their labor. Money payments can then be exchanged for the fruits of other people's labor. The use of money as a medium of exchange permits more specialization and the inherent economic efficiencies that come with it (and hence greater economic growth).

Money as a Unit of Accounting

A **unit of accounting** is a way of placing a specific price on economic goods and services. It is the common denominator, the commonly recognized measure of value. The dollar is the unit of accounting in the United States. It is the yardstick that allows individuals easily to compare the relative value of goods and services. Accountants at the U.S. Department of Commerce use dollar prices to measure national income and domestic product. A business uses dollar prices to calculate profits and losses. A typical household budgets regularly anticipated expenses using dollar prices as its unit of accounting.

Another way of describing money as a unit of accounting is to say that it serves as a *standard of value* that allows people to compare the relative worth of various goods and services. This allows for comparison shopping, for example.

What "new" form of money will Zimbabwe's government accept from the nation's residents?

Unit of accounting
A measure by which prices are expressed; the common denominator of the price system; a central property of money.

INTERNATIONAL EXAMPLE

What Once Was Old Money Is Now "New" Money in Zimbabwe

At different points in time throughout history, residents of African countries have used livestock as money. In modern times, of course, central banks in these nations have issued circulating currencies as the primary form of money. Nevertheless, the government of the East African nation of Zimbabwe recently announced that it is accepting a "new" form of money. As payment for certain government services, such as fees for public schools, people can transfer to the government goats, cattle, and other livestock. Thus, livestock money has made a comeback in this part of the African continent.

FOR CRITICAL THINKING

In principle, what functions of money can goats, cattle, and other livestock perform? Explain your reasoning.

Sources are listed at the end of this chapter.

Money as a Store of Value

One of the most important functions of money is that it serves as a **store of value** or purchasing power. The money you have today can be set aside to purchase things later on. If you have $1,000 in your checking account, you can choose to spend it today on goods and services, spend it tomorrow, or spend it a month from now. In this way, money provides a way to transfer value (wealth) into the future.

Store of value
The ability to hold value over time; a necessary property of money.

Money as a Standard of Deferred Payment

The fourth function of the monetary unit is as a **standard of deferred payment**. This function involves the use of money both as a medium of exchange and as a unit of accounting. Debts are typically stated in terms of a unit of accounting, and they are paid with a monetary medium of exchange. That is to say, a debt is specified in a dollar

Standard of deferred payment
A property of an item that makes it desirable for use as a means of settling debts maturing in the future; an essential property of money.

amount and paid in currency (or by debit card or check). A corporate bond, for example, has a face value—the dollar value stated on it, which is to be paid upon maturity. The periodic interest payments on that corporate bond are specified and paid in dollars, and when the bond comes due (at maturity), the corporation pays the face value in dollars to the holder of the bond.

Properties of Money

Money is an asset—something of value—that accounts for part of personal wealth. Wealth in the form of money can be exchanged for other assets, goods, or services. Although money is not the only form of wealth that can be exchanged for goods and services, it is the most widely and readily accepted one.

Liquidity

The degree to which an asset can be acquired or disposed of without much danger of any intervening loss in *nominal* value and with small transaction costs. Money is the most liquid asset.

Money—The Most Liquid Asset Money's attribute as the most readily tradable asset is called **liquidity**. We say that an asset is *liquid* when it can easily be acquired or disposed of without high transaction costs and with relative certainty as to its value. Money is by definition the most liquid asset. People can easily convert money to other asset forms. Therefore, most individuals hold at least a part of their wealth in the form of the most liquid of assets, money. You can see how assets rank in liquidity relative to one another in Figure 15-1.

When we hold money, however, we incur a cost for this advantage of liquidity. Because cash in your pocket and many checking or debit account balances do not earn interest, that cost is the interest yield that could have been obtained had the asset been held in another form—for example, in the form of stocks and bonds.

> *The cost of holding money (its opportunity cost) is measured by the alternative interest yield obtainable by holding some other asset.*

Transactions deposits

Checkable and debitable account balances in commercial banks and other types of financial institutions, such as credit unions and savings banks. Any accounts in financial institutions from which you can easily transmit debit-card and check payments without significant restrictions.

Fiduciary monetary system

A system in which money is issued by the government and its value is based uniquely on the public's faith that the currency represents command over goods and services and will be accepted in payment for debts.

Monetary Standards, or What Backs Money In the past, many different monetary standards have existed. For example, commodity money, which is a physical good that may be valued for other uses it provides, has been used (see Table 15-1). The main forms of commodity money were gold and silver. Today, though, most people throughout the world accept coins, paper currency, and balances held on deposit as **transactions deposits** (debitable—related to debit cards—and checkable accounts with banks and other financial institutions) in exchange for items sold, including labor services.

These forms of money, however, raise a question: Why are we willing to accept as payment something that has no intrinsic value? After all, you could not sell checks or debit cards to very many producers for use as a raw material in manufacturing. The reason is that payments in the modern world arise from a **fiduciary monetary system**. This concept refers to the fact that the value of the payments rests on the public's confidence that such payments can be exchanged for goods and services. *Fiduciary* comes from the Latin *fiducia*, which means "trust" or "confidence."

FIGURE 15-1

Degrees of Liquidity

The most liquid asset is cash. Liquidity decreases as you move from right to left.

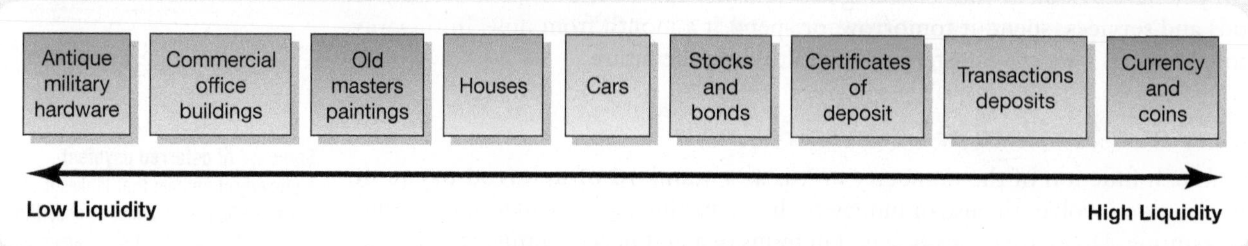

| Antique military hardware | Commercial office buildings | Old masters paintings | Houses | Cars | Stocks and bonds | Certificates of deposit | Transactions deposits | Currency and coins |

Low Liquidity ——————————————————————————————→ High Liquidity

In our fiduciary monetary system, there is no legal requirement for money, in the form of currency or transactions deposits, to be convertible to a fixed quantity of gold, silver, or some other precious commodity. The bills are just pieces of paper. Coins have a value stamped on them that today is usually greater than the market value of the metal in them. Nevertheless, currency and transactions deposits are money because of their acceptability and predictability of value.

Acceptability Transactions deposits and currency are money because they are accepted in exchange for goods and services. They are accepted because people have confidence that these items can later be exchanged for other goods and services. This confidence is based on the knowledge that such exchanges have occurred in the past without problems.

Predictability of Value Money retains its usefulness even if its purchasing power is declining year in and year out, as during periods of inflation, if it still retains the characteristic of predictability of value. If you anticipate that the inflation rate is going to be around 3 percent during the next year, you know that any dollar you receive a year from now will have a purchasing power equal to 3 percent less than that same dollar today. Thus, you will not necessarily refuse to accept money in exchange simply because you know that its value will decline by the rate of inflation during the next year.

ECONOMICS IN YOUR LIFE
To consider the possibility that the Federal Reserve might create its own *digital* currency, read **Contemplating Digital Currency at the Federal Reserve** on page 330.

Defining Money

Money is important. Changes in the total **money supply**—the amount of money in circulation—and changes in the rate at which the money supply increases or decreases affect important economic variables. Examples of such variables are the rate of inflation, interest rates, and (at least in the short run) employment and the level of real GDP. Economists have struggled to reach agreement about how to define and measure money, however. There are two basic approaches: the **transactions approach**, which stresses the role of money as a medium of exchange, and the **liquidity approach**, which stresses the role of money as a temporary store of value.

The Transactions Approach to Measuring Money: M1 According to the transactions approach to measuring money, the money supply consists of currency, transactions deposits, and traveler's checks not issued by banks. One key designation of the money supply, including currency, transactions deposits, and traveler's checks not issued by banks, is **M1**. The various elements of M1 for a typical year are presented in panel (a) of Figure 15-2.

The largest component of U.S. currency is paper bills called Federal Reserve notes, which are designed and printed by the U.S. Bureau of Engraving and Printing. U.S. currency also consists of coins minted by the U.S. Treasury. Federal Reserve banks (to be discussed shortly) issue paper notes throughout the U.S. banking system.

Individuals transfer ownership of deposits in financial institutions by using debit cards and checks. Hence, debitable and checkable transactions deposits are normally acceptable as a medium of exchange. The **depository institutions** that offer transactions deposits are numerous and include commercial banks and almost all **thrift institutions**—savings banks, savings and loan associations (S&Ls), and credit unions.

Traveler's checks are paid for by the purchaser at the time of transfer. The total quantity of traveler's checks outstanding issued by institutions other than banks is part of the M1 money supply. American Express and other institutions issue traveler's checks.

Is paper currency maintaining its traditional role as a key part of nations' money supplies?

Money supply
The amount of money in circulation.

Transactions approach
A method of measuring the money supply by looking at money as a medium of exchange.

Liquidity approach
A method of measuring the money supply by looking at money as a temporary store of value.

M1
The money supply, measured as the total value of currency plus transactions deposits plus traveler's checks not issued by banks.

Depository institutions
Financial institutions that accept deposits from savers and lend funds from those deposits out at interest.

Thrift institutions
Financial institutions that receive most of their funds from the savings of the public. They include savings banks, savings and loan associations, and credit unions.

Traveler's checks
Financial instruments obtained from a bank or a nonbanking organization and signed during purchase that can be used in payment upon a second signature by the purchaser.

FIGURE 15-2

Composition of the U.S. M1 and M2 Money Supply, 2020

Panel (a) shows estimates of the M1 money supply, of which the largest component (about 54 percent) is transactions deposits. M2 consists of M1 plus three other components, the most important of which is savings deposits at all depository institutions.

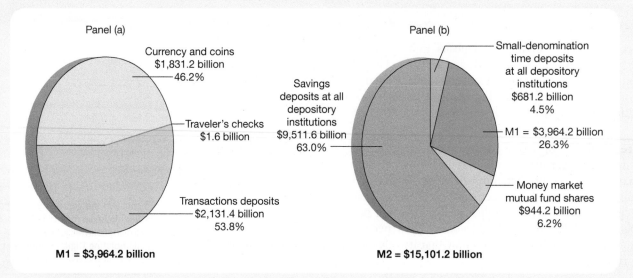

Sources: *Federal Reserve Bulletin; Economic Indicators,* various issues; author's estimates.

Currency Remains Entrenched as a Key Component of National Money Supplies

For more than four decades, media observers and many economists have speculated that paper currency ultimately will disappear. Nevertheless, U.S. currency, which the Federal Reserve purchases from the U.S. Bureau of Engraving and Printing and then distributes to private banks from Federal Reserve banks, has remained a significant part of the M1 measure of money.

Paper currency also continues to be a mainstay component of money supplies in other nations of the world. Central banks of more than 140 countries purchase their currency notes from private printers, such as the British firm De La Rue and the Australian company CCL Secure. These firms recently have reported that their printing runs of currency notes for all these nations continue to grow at an annual rate of at least 3 percent. The main change has been the inclusion of security features, such as color-shifting ink, three-dimensional ribbons, and holographic images to frustrate criminals' efforts to counterfeit currency.

FOR CRITICAL THINKING

Can you think of any reasons why people might prefer to use currency for certain transactions instead of deposit transfers that leave electronic records at depository institutions?

Sources are listed at the end of this chapter.

The Liquidity Approach to Measuring Money: M2 The liquidity approach to defining and measuring the U.S. money supply views money as a temporary store of value and so includes all of M1 *plus* several other highly liquid assets. Panel (b) of Figure 15-2 shows the components of **M2**—money as a temporary store of value. These components include the following:

M2

M1 plus (1) savings deposits at all depository institutions, (2) small-denomination time deposits, and (3) balances in retail money market mutual funds.

1. *Savings deposits.* Total *savings deposits*—deposits with no set maturities—are the largest component of the M2 money supply.

2. *Small-denomination time deposits.* With a *time deposit,* the funds must be left in a financial institution for a given period before they can be withdrawn without penalty. To be included in the M2 definition of the money supply, time deposits must be less than $100,000—hence, the designation *small-denomination time deposits.*

3. *Money market mutual fund balances.* Many individuals keep part of their assets in the form of shares in *money market mutual funds*—highly liquid funds that investment companies obtain from the public. All money market mutual fund balances except those held by large institutions (which typically use them more like large time deposits) are included in M2 because they are very liquid.

When all of these assets are added together, the result is M2, as shown in panel (b) of Figure 15-2.

Other Money Supply Definitions Economists and other researchers have come up with additional definitions of money. Some businesspeople and policymakers prefer a monetary aggregate known as *MZM*. The MZM aggregate is the so-called money-at-zero-maturity money stock. Obtaining MZM entails adding to M1 those deposits without set maturities, such as savings deposits, that are included in M2. MZM includes *all* money market funds but excludes all deposits with fixed maturities, such as small-denomination time deposits.

Financial Intermediation and Banks

15.2 Understand why financial intermediaries such as banks exist

Most nations, including the United States, have a banking system that encompasses two types of institutions. One type consists of privately owned profit-seeking institutions, such as commercial banks and thrift institutions. The other type of institution is a **central bank**, which typically serves as a banker's bank and as a bank for the national treasury or finance ministry.

Central bank
A banker's bank, usually an official institution that also serves as a bank for a nation's government treasury. Central banks normally regulate commercial banks.

Direct versus Indirect Financing

When individuals choose to hold some of their savings in new bonds issued by a corporation, their purchases of the bonds are in effect direct loans to the business. This is an example of *direct finance*, in which people lend funds directly to a business. Business financing is not always direct. Individuals might choose instead to hold a time deposit at a bank. The bank may then lend to the same company. In this way, the same people can provide *indirect finance* to a business. The bank makes this possible by *intermediating* the financing of the company.

Financial Intermediation

Banks and other financial institutions are all in the same business—transferring funds from savers to investors. This process is known as **financial intermediation**, and its participants, such as banks and savings institutions, are **financial intermediaries**. The process of financial intermediation is illustrated in Figure 15-3.

Financial intermediation
The process by which financial institutions accept savings from businesses, households, and governments and lend the savings to other businesses, households, and governments.

Asymmetric Information, Adverse Selection, and Moral Hazard Why might people wish to deposit their funds in a bank instead of lending them directly to a business? One important reason is **asymmetric information**—the fact that the business may have better knowledge of its own current and future prospects than potential lenders do. For instance, the business may know that it intends to use borrowed funds for projects with a high risk of failure that would make repaying the loan difficult.

This potential for borrowers to use the borrowed funds in high-risk projects is known as **adverse selection**. Alternatively, a business that had intended to undertake low-risk projects may change management after receiving a loan, and the new managers may use the borrowed funds in riskier ways. The possibility that a borrower might engage in behavior that increases risk after borrowing funds is called **moral hazard**.

To minimize the possibility that a business might fail to repay a loan, people thinking about lending funds directly to the business must study the business carefully before making the loan, and they must continue to monitor its performance

Financial intermediaries
Institutions that transfer funds between ultimate lenders (savers) and ultimate borrowers.

Asymmetric information
Information possessed by one party in a financial transaction but not by the other party.

Adverse selection
The tendency for high-risk projects and clients to be overrepresented among borrowers.

Moral hazard
The possibility that a borrower might engage in riskier behavior after a loan has been obtained.

The Process of Financial Intermediation

The process of financial intermediation is depicted here. Note that ultimate lenders and ultimate borrowers are the same economic units—households, businesses, and governments—but not necessarily the same individuals. Whereas individual households can be net lenders or borrowers, households as an economic unit typically are net lenders. Specific businesses or governments similarly can be net lenders or borrowers. As economic units, both are net borrowers.

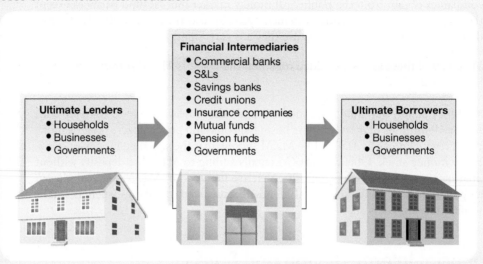

Ultimate Lenders
- Households
- Businesses
- Governments

Financial Intermediaries
- Commercial banks
- S&Ls
- Savings banks
- Credit unions
- Insurance companies
- Mutual funds
- Pension funds
- Governments

Ultimate Borrowers
- Households
- Businesses
- Governments

afterward. Alternatively, they can choose to avoid the trouble by holding deposits with financial intermediaries, which then specialize in evaluating the creditworthiness of business borrowers and in keeping tabs on their progress until loans are repaid. Thus, adverse selection and moral hazard both help explain why people use financial intermediaries.

Larger Scale and Lower Management Costs Another important reason that financial intermediaries exist is that they make it possible for many people to pool their funds, thereby increasing the size, or *scale*, of the total amount of savings managed by an intermediary. This centralization of management reduces costs and risks below the levels savers would incur if all were to manage their savings alone.

Pension fund companies, which are institutions that specialize in managing funds that individuals save for retirement, owe their existence largely to their abilities to provide such cost savings to individual savers. Likewise, *investment companies*, institutions that manage portfolios of financial instruments called mutual funds on behalf of shareholders, exist largely because of cost savings from their greater scale of operations. In addition, *government-sponsored financial institutions*, such as the Federal National Mortgage Association, seek to reduce overall lending costs by pooling large volumes of funds from investors in order to buy groups of mortgage loans.

Financial Institution Liabilities and Assets Every financial intermediary has its own sources of funds, which are **liabilities** of that institution. When you place $100 in your transactions deposit at a bank, the bank creates a liability—it owes you $100—in exchange for the funds deposited. A commercial bank gets its funds from transactions and savings accounts, and an insurance company gets its funds from insurance policy premiums.

Each financial intermediary has a different primary use of its **assets**. For example, a credit union usually makes small consumer loans, whereas a savings bank makes mainly mortgage loans. Table 15-2 lists the assets and liabilities of typical financial intermediaries. Be aware, though, that the distinctions between different types of financial institutions are becoming more and more blurred. As laws and regulations change, there will be less need to make any distinction. All may ultimately be treated simply as financial intermediaries.

How has the advent of big data techniques affected the banking industry?

Liabilities
Amounts owed; the legal claims against a business or household by nonowners.

Assets
Amounts owned; all items to which a business or household holds legal claim.

TABLE 15-2

Financial Intermediaries and Their Assets and Liabilities

Financial Intermediary	Assets	Liabilities
Commercial banks, savings and loan associations, savings banks, and credit unions	Car loans and other consumer debt, business loans, government securities, home mortgages	Transactions deposits, savings deposits, various other time deposits
Insurance companies	Mortgages, stocks, bonds, real estate	Insurance contracts, annuities, pension plans
Pension and retirement funds	Stocks, bonds, mortgages, time deposits	Pension plans
Money market mutual funds	Short-term credit instruments such as large-denomination certificates of deposit, Treasury bills, and high-grade commercial paper	Fund shares with limited checking privileges
Government-sponsored financial institutions	Home mortgages	Mortgage-backed securities issued to investors

AI | DECISION MAKING THROUGH DATA

AI in the Banking Industry

The utilization of machine-learning techniques and of AI apps offers ways in which banks may be able to improve their operations, reduce their costs, and boost their profits. For instance, the increased ability of banks to automatically monitor data in real time enables them to assess values of actual and potential assets and liabilities at almost any moment. This capability increasingly is allowing banks contemplating making mortgage loans to evaluate values of real estate without requiring the services of appraisers. The result is a decrease in banks' expenses and reduction in time required to make lending decisions. AI apps also assist in assessing the risk associated with particular loans, thereby reducing losses to banks resulting from frauds or defaults.

In spite of these potential benefits, banks have been slow to integrate big data techniques into their operations. Some critics of government policies blame a vast web of banking regulations and associated compliance costs that banks face. Nevertheless, banks gradually are using additional data, more analytic methods, and emerging AI apps in the normal course of their business, which ultimately should reshape their operations as financial intermediaries.

FOR CRITICAL THINKING

Why do you think that banks find that having access to more data about potential borrowers improves the likelihood of repayments? (Hint: *Recall the asymmetric-information problems that banks face as lenders.*)

Sources are listed at the end of this chapter.

Transmitting Payments via Debit-Card Transactions

Since 2006, the dollar volume of payments transmitted using debit cards has exceeded the value of checking transactions. To see how a debit-card transaction clears, take a look at Figure 15-4. Suppose that Bank of America has provided a debit card to a college student named Jill Jones, who in turn uses the card to purchase $200 worth of clothing from Macy's, which has an account at Citibank. The debit-card transaction generates an electronic record, which the debit-card system transmits to Citibank.

The debit-card system also automatically uses the electronic record to determine the bank that issued the debit card used to purchase the clothing. It transmits this information to Bank of America. Then Bank of America verifies that Jill Jones is an account holder, deducts $200 from her transactions deposit account, and transmits these funds electronically, via the debit-card system, to Citibank. Finally, Citibank credits $200 to Macy's transactions deposit account, and payment for the clothing purchase is complete.

FIGURE 15-4

How a Debit-Card Transaction Clears

A college student named Jill Jones uses a debit card issued by Bank of America to purchase clothing valued at $200 from Macy's, which has an account with Citibank. The debit-card transaction creates an electronic record that is transmitted to Citibank. The debit-card system forwards this record to Bank of America, which deducts $200 from Jill Jones's transactions deposit account. Then the debit-card system transmits the $200 payment to Citibank, which credits the $200 to Macy's account.

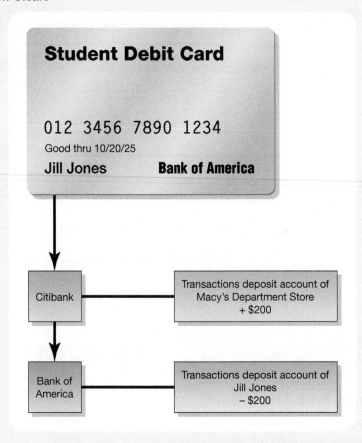

The Federal Reserve System: The U.S. Central Bank

The Federal Reserve System, which serves as the nation's central bank, is one of the key banking institutions in the United States. It is partly a creature of government and partly privately owned.

The Federal Reserve System

The Fed
The Federal Reserve System; the central bank of the United States.

The Federal Reserve System, also known simply as **the Fed**, is the most important regulatory agency in the U.S. monetary system and is considered the monetary authority. The Fed was established by the Federal Reserve Act, signed on December 13, 1913, by President Woodrow Wilson.

Organization of the Federal Reserve System Figure 15-5 shows how the Federal Reserve System is organized. It is managed by the Board of Governors, composed of seven full-time members appointed by the U.S. president with the approval of the Senate. The chair of the Board of Governors is the leading official of the Board of Governors and of the Federal Reserve System. Since 2018, Jerome Powell has held this position.

The 12 Federal Reserve district banks have a total of 25 branches. The boundaries of the 12 Federal Reserve districts and the cities in which Federal Reserve banks are located are shown in Figure 15-6. The Federal Open Market Committee (FOMC) determines the future growth of the money supply and other important variables. This committee is composed of the members of the Board of Governors, the president of the New York Federal Reserve Bank, and presidents of four other Federal Reserve banks, rotated periodically. The chair of the Board of Governors also chairs the FOMC.

FIGURE 15-5

Organization of the Federal Reserve System

The 12 Federal Reserve district banks are headed by 12 separate presidents. The main authority of the Fed resides with the Board of Governors of the Federal Reserve System, whose seven members are appointed for 14-year terms by the president of the United States and confirmed by the Senate.

Open market operations are carried out through the Federal Open Market Committee (FOMC), consisting of the seven members of the Board of Governors plus five presidents of the district banks (always including the president of the New York bank, with the others rotating).

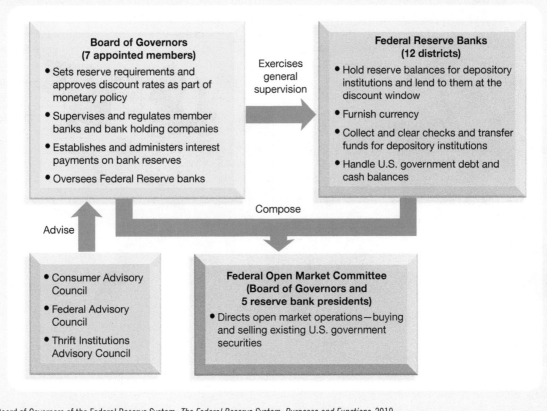

Source: Board of Governors of the Federal Reserve System, *The Federal Reserve System: Purposes and Functions*, 2019.

Depository Institutions Depository institutions—all financial institutions that accept deposits—constitute our monetary system, consisting of about 4,500 commercial banks, 750 savings and loan associations and savings banks, and about 5,500 credit unions. All depository institutions may purchase services from the Federal Reserve System on an equal basis. Also, almost all depository institutions are required to keep a certain percentage of their deposits in reserve at the Federal Reserve district banks or as vault cash. This percentage depends on the bank's volume of business.

Functions of the Federal Reserve System

The Federal Reserve performs several functions:

1. ***The Fed supplies the economy with fiduciary currency.*** The Federal Reserve banks supply the economy with paper currency called Federal Reserve notes, which are printed at the Bureau of Engraving and Printing in Washington, D.C. Each of these notes is an obligation (liability) of the Federal Reserve System, *not* the U.S. Treasury.

2. ***The Fed holds depository institutions' reserves and pays interest on these reserves.*** The 12 Federal Reserve district banks hold the reserves (other than vault cash) of depository institutions and transmit interest payments on these reserves.

FIGURE 15-6

The Federal Reserve System

The Federal Reserve System is divided into 12 districts, each served by one of the Federal Reserve district banks, located in the cities indicated. The Board of Governors meets in Washington, D.C.

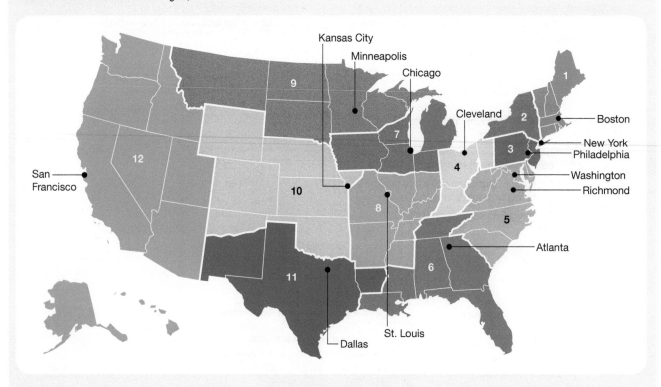

Source: Board of Governors of the Federal Reserve System.

3. *The Fed acts as the government's fiscal agent.* The Federal Reserve is the primary banker and fiscal agent for the federal government. Consequently, the U.S. Treasury has a transactions account with the Federal Reserve, which helps the government collect some tax revenues and aids in the purchase and sale of government securities.

4. *The Fed supervises depository institutions.* The Fed (along with the Comptroller of the Currency, the Federal Deposit Insurance Corporation, and the National Credit Union Administration) is a supervisor and regulator of depository institutions.

5. *The Fed conducts monetary policy.* To understand how the Fed manages the money supply, we must examine more closely its reserve-holding function and the way in which depository institutions aid in expansion and contraction of the money supply. We will do this later in this chapter.

6. *The Fed intervenes in foreign currency markets.* Sometimes the Fed attempts to keep the value of the dollar from changing. It does this by buying and selling U.S. dollars in foreign exchange markets.

Lender of last resort
The Federal Reserve's role as an institution that is willing and able to lend to a temporarily illiquid bank that is otherwise in good financial condition to prevent the bank's illiquid position from leading to a general loss of confidence in that bank or in others.

7. *The Fed acts as the "lender of last resort."* As **lender of last resort**, the Fed stands ready to lend to any temporarily illiquid but otherwise financially healthy banking institution. In this way, the Fed seeks to prevent illiquidity at a few banks from leading to a general loss of depositors' confidence in the overall soundness of the banking system.

Does the Fed's willingness to serve as a lender of last resort induce banks to become less liquid?

BEHAVIORAL EXAMPLE

Banks' Behavioral Response to Establishment of the Federal Reserve as the Last-Resort Lender

Before the Federal Reserve was founded in 1913, U.S. banks operated their own systems for clearing interbank payments across regions of the nation. To help ensure that sufficient funds were always available to back payment claims, each bank that participated in these systems held deposits with other banks. Indeed, a typical bank held funds on deposit with other banks that were equivalent to about 15 percent of its assets, which it held alongside other highly liquid assets such as cash in its vault.

After the Federal Reserve was established to serve in part as lender of last resort, banks altered their behavior. Because banks knew that the Fed stood willing to lend funds if emergency situations arose, following the Fed's establishment they immediately cut back by about two-thirds on extra funds that they held on deposit with other institutions. Over the years that

followed, most of these deposits held at other banks disappeared entirely, and banks also reduced holdings of other liquid assets, including vault cash. As a consequence, the founding of the Federal Reserve made the U.S. banking system less liquid.

REAL APPLICATION

If a parent or friend promised to replenish your bank account with a zero-interest loan if you were to overdraw the account, why might you be tempted to hold fewer funds in that account?

Sources are listed at the end of this chapter.

Fractional Reserve Banking, the Federal Reserve, and the Money Supply

> **15.4** Determine the maximum potential extent that the money supply will change following a Federal Reserve monetary policy action

As early as 1000 B.C.E., uncoined gold and silver were being used as money in Mesopotamia. Goldsmiths weighed and assessed the purity of those metals. Later they started issuing paper notes indicating that the bearers held gold or silver of given weights and purity on deposit with the goldsmith. These notes could be transferred in exchange for goods and became the first paper currency. The gold and silver on deposit with the goldsmiths were the first bank deposits. Eventually, goldsmiths realized that inflows of gold and silver for deposit always exceeded the average amount of gold and silver withdrawn at any given time—often by a predictable ratio.

These goldsmiths started making loans by issuing to borrowers paper notes that exceeded in value the amount of gold and silver the goldsmiths actually kept on hand. They charged interest on these loans. This constituted the earliest form of what is now called **fractional reserve banking**. We know that goldsmiths operated this way in Delphi, Didyma, and Olympia in Greece as early as the seventh century B.C.E. In Athens, fractional reserve banking was well developed by the sixth century B.C.E.

Fractional reserve banking
A system in which depository institutions hold reserves that are less than the amount of total deposits.

Depository Institution Reserves

In a fractional reserve banking system, banks do not keep sufficient funds on hand to cover 100 percent of their depositors' accounts. Also, the funds held by depository institutions in the United States are not kept in gold and silver, as they were with the early goldsmiths. Instead, the funds are held as **reserves** in the form of cash in banks' vaults and deposits that banks hold on deposit with Federal Reserve district banks.

The fraction of deposits that banks hold as reserves is called the **reserve ratio**. There are two determinants of the size of this ratio. One is the quantity of reserves that the Federal Reserve requires banks to hold, which are called *required reserves*. The other determinant of the reserve ratio is whatever additional amount of reserves that banks voluntarily hold, known as *excess reserves*.

To show the relationship between reserves and deposits at an individual bank, let's examine the **balance sheet**, or statement of assets owned and liabilities (amounts owed to others), for a particular depository institution. Balance Sheet TB displays a balance sheet for a depository institution called Typical Bank. Liabilities for this institution consist solely of $1 million in transactions deposits. Assets consist of $100,000 in reserves and $900,000 in loans to customers. Total assets of $1 million equal total liabilities of $1 million. Because Typical Bank has $100,000 of reserves and $1 million

Reserves
In the U.S. Federal Reserve System, deposits held by Federal Reserve district banks for depository institutions, plus depository institutions' vault cash.

Reserve ratio
The fraction of transactions deposits that banks hold as reserves.

Balance sheet
A statement of the assets and liabilities of any business entity, including financial institutions and the Federal Reserve System. Assets are what is owned; liabilities are what is owed.

BALANCE SHEET TB

Typical Bank

Assets		Liabilities	
Reserves	$100,000	Transactions deposits	$1,000,000
Loans	$900,000		
Total	$1,000,000	Total	$1,000,000

of transactions deposits, its reserve ratio is 10 percent. Thus, Typical Bank is part of a system of fractional reserve banking, in which it holds only 10 percent of its deposits as reserves.

Fractional Reserve Banking and Money Expansion

Under fractional reserve banking, the Federal Reserve can add to the quantity of money in circulation by bringing about an expansion of deposits within the banking system. To understand how the Fed can create money within the banking system, we must look at how depository institutions respond to Fed actions that increase reserves in the entire system.

Open market operations
The purchase and sale of existing U.S. government securities (such as bonds) in the open private market by the Federal Reserve System.

Let's consider the effect of a Fed **open market operation**, which is a Fed purchase or sale of existing U.S. government securities in the open market—the private secondary market in which people exchange securities that have not yet matured. Assume that the Fed engaged in an *open market purchase* by buying a $100,000 U.S. government security from a bond dealer. The Fed does this by electronically transferring $100,000 to the bond dealer's transactions deposit account at Bank 1. Thus, as shown in Balance Sheet 15-1, Bank 1's transactions deposit liabilities increase by $100,000.

BALANCE SHEET 15-1

Bank 1

Assets		Liabilities	
Reserves	+$10,000	Transactions deposits	+$100,000
Loans	+$90,000		
Total	+$100,000	Total	+$100,000

Let's suppose that the reserve ratio for Bank 1 and all other depository institutions is 10 percent. As shown in Balance Sheet 15-1, therefore, Bank 1 responds to this $100,000 increase in transactions deposits by adding 10 percent of this amount, or $10,000, to its reserves. The bank allocates the remaining $90,000 of additional deposits to new loans, so its loans increase by $90,000.

Effect on the Money Supply At this point, the Fed's purchase of a $100,000 U.S. government security from a bond dealer has increased the money supply immediately by $100,000. This occurs because transactions deposits held by the public—bond dealers are part of the public—are part of the money supply. Hence, the addition of $100,000 to deposits with Bank 1, with no corresponding deposit reduction elsewhere in the banking system, raises the money supply by $100,000. (If another member of the public, instead of the Fed, had purchased the bond, that person's transactions deposit would have been reduced by $100,000, so there would have been no change in the money supply.)

The process of money creation does not stop here. The borrower who receives the $90,000 loan from Bank 1 will spend these funds, which will then be deposited in other banks. In this instance, suppose that the $90,000 spent by Bank 1's borrower is deposited in a transactions deposit account at Bank 2. At this bank, as shown in Balance Sheet 15-2, transactions deposits and hence the money supply increase by $90,000. Bank 2 adds 10 percent of these deposits, or $9,000, to its reserves. It uses the remaining $81,000 of new deposits to add $81,000 to its loans.

BALANCE SHEET 15-2

Bank 2

Assets		Liabilities	
Reserves	+$9,000	Transactions deposits	+$90,000
Loans	+$81,000		
Total	+$90,000	Total	+$90,000

Continuation of the Deposit Creation Process Look at Bank 3's account in Balance Sheet 15-3. Assume that the borrower receiving the $81,000 loan from Bank 2 spends these funds, which then are deposited in an account at Bank 3. Transactions deposits and the money supply increase by $81,000. Reserves of Bank 3 rise by 10 percent of this amount, or $8,100. Bank 3 uses the rest of the newly deposited funds, or $72,900, to increase its loans.

BALANCE SHEET 15-3

Bank 3

Assets		Liabilities	
Reserves	+$8,100	Transactions deposits	+$81,000
Loans	+$72,900		
Total	+$81,000	Total	+$81,000

This process continues to Banks 4, 5, 6, and so forth. Each bank obtains smaller and smaller increases in deposits because banks hold 10 percent of new deposits as reserves. Thus, each succeeding depository institution makes correspondingly smaller loans. Table 15-3 shows new deposits, reserves, and loans for the remaining depository institutions.

Effect on Total Deposits and the Money Supply In this example, deposits and the money supply increased initially by the $100,000 that the Fed paid the bond dealer in exchange for a U.S. government security. Deposits and the money supply were further increased by a $90,000 deposit in Bank 2, and they were again increased by an

TABLE 15-3

Maximum Money Creation with 10 Percent Reserve Ratio

This table shows the maximum new loans that banks can make, given the Fed's electronic transfer of $100,000 to a transactions deposit account at Bank 1. The reserve ratio is 10 percent.

Bank	New Deposits	New Reserves	Maximum New Loans
1	$100,000 (from Fed)	$10,000	$90,000
2	90,000	9,000	81,000
3	81,000	8,100	72,900
4	72,900	7,290	65,610
·	·	·	·
·	·	·	·
·	·	·	·
All other banks	656,100	65,610	590,490
Totals	$1,000,000	$100,000	$900,000

$81,000 deposit in Bank 3. Eventually, total deposits and the money supply increase by $1 million, as shown in Table 15-3. This $1 million expansion of deposits and the money supply consists of the original $100,000 created by the Fed, plus an extra $900,000 generated by deposit-creating bank loans. The deposit creation process is portrayed graphically in Figure 15-7.

FIGURE 15-7

The Multiple Expansion in the Money Supply Due to $100,000 in New Reserves When the Reserve Ratio Is 10 Percent

The banks are all aligned in decreasing order of new deposits created. Bank 1 receives the $100,000 in new reserves and lends out $90,000. Bank 2 receives the $90,000 and lends out $81,000. The process continues through Banks 3 to 19 and then the rest of the banking system. Ultimately, assuming no leakages into currency, the $100,000 of new reserves results in an increase in the money supply of $1 million, or 10 times the new reserves, because the reserve ratio is 10 percent.

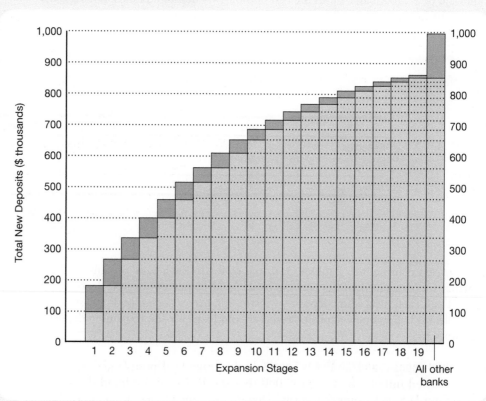

You should be able to work through the foregoing example to show the reverse process when there is a *decrease* in reserves because the Fed engages in an *open market sale* by selling a $100,000 U.S. government security. The result is a multiple contraction of deposits and, therefore, of the total money supply in circulation.

The Money Multiplier

In the example just given, a $100,000 increase in reserves generated by the Fed's purchase of a security yielded a $1 million increase in transactions deposits and, hence, the money supply. Thus, deposits and the money supply increased by a multiple of 10 times the initial $100,000 increase in overall reserves. Conversely, a $100,000 decrease in reserves generated by a Fed sale of a security will yield a decrease in total deposits of $1 million—that is, a multiple of 10 times the initial $100,000 decrease in overall reserves.

We can now make a generalization about the extent to which the total money supply will change when the banking system's reserves are increased or decreased. The **money multiplier** gives the change in the money supply due to a change in reserves. In our example, the value of the money multiplier is 10.

Money multiplier
A number that, when multiplied by a change in reserves in the banking system, yields the resulting change in the money supply.

Potential versus Actual Money Multipliers If we assume, as in our example, that all loan proceeds are deposited with banks, we obtain the **potential money multiplier**— the *maximum* possible value of the money multiplier:

Potential money multiplier
The reciprocal of the reserve ratio, assuming no leakages into currency. It is equal to 1 divided by the reserve ratio.

$$\text{Potential money multiplier} = \frac{1}{\text{reserve ratio}}$$

That is, the potential money multiplier is equal to 1 divided by the fraction of transactions deposits that banks hold as reserves. In our example, the reserve ratio was 10 percent, or 0.10 expressed as a decimal fraction. Thus, in the example, the value of the potential money multiplier was equal to 1 divided by 0.10, which equals 10.

What happens if the entire amount of a loan from a depository institution is not redeposited? When borrowers want to hold a portion of their loans as currency outside the banking system, these funds cannot be held by banks as reserves from which to make loans. The greater the amount of cash leakage, the smaller the *actual* money multiplier. Typically, borrowers do hold a portion of loan proceeds as currency, so the actual money multiplier usually is smaller than the potential money multiplier.

WHAT HAPPENS WHEN...

a central bank increases the required reserve ratio?

An increase in the required reserve ratio causes the value of the potential money multiplier to decrease. Other things being equal, this fact will cause the quantity of money in circulation to decline. Indeed, varying the required reserve ratio to influence the potential money multiplier and money supply is a key way in which some central banks, such as the People's Bank of China, conduct monetary policy.

Real-World Money Multipliers The potential money multiplier is rarely exactly attained for the banking system as a whole. Furthermore, each definition of the money supply, M1 or M2, will yield a different actual money multiplier.

In most years, the actual M1 multiplier has been in a range between 1 and 3. The actual M2 multiplier showed an upward trend until recently, rising from 6.5 in the 1960s to over 12 in the mid-2000s. Since then, however, it has dropped to about 4.

15.5 Explain the essential features of federal deposit insurance

Federal Deposit Insurance

As you have seen, fractional reserve banking enables the Federal Reserve to use an open market purchase (or sale) of U.S. government bonds to generate an expansion (or contraction) of deposits. The change in the money supply is a multiple of the open market purchase (or sale). Another effect of fractional reserve banking is to make depository institutions somewhat fragile. After all, the institutions have only a fraction of reserves on hand to honor their depositors' requests for withdrawals.

Bank run

Attempt by many of a bank's depositors to convert transactions and time deposits into currency out of fear that the bank's liabilities may exceed its assets.

If many depositors simultaneously rush to their bank to withdraw all of their transactions and time deposits—a phenomenon called a **bank run**—the bank would be unable to satisfy their requests. The result would be the failure of that depository institution. Widespread bank runs could lead to the failure of many institutions.

Seeking to Limit Bank Failures with Deposit Insurance

When businesses fail, they create hardships for creditors, owners, and customers. When a depository institution fails, however, an even greater hardship results, because many individuals and businesses depend on the safety and security of banks. As Figure 15-8 shows, during the 1920s an average of about 600 banks failed each year. In the early 1930s, during the Great Depression, that average soared to nearly 3,000 failures each year.

Federal Deposit Insurance Corporation (FDIC)

A government agency that insures the deposits held in banks and most other depository institutions. All U.S. banks are insured this way.

In 1933, at the height of these bank failures, the **Federal Deposit Insurance Corporation (FDIC)** was founded to insure the funds of depositors and remove the reason for ruinous runs on banks. In 1934, federal deposit insurance was extended to deposits in savings and loan associations and mutual savings banks, and in 1971 it was offered for deposits in credit unions.

FIGURE 15-8

Bank Failures

A tremendous number of banks failed prior to the creation of federal deposit insurance in 1933. Thereafter, bank failures were few until the mid-1980s. Annual failure rates jumped again in the early and late 2000s.

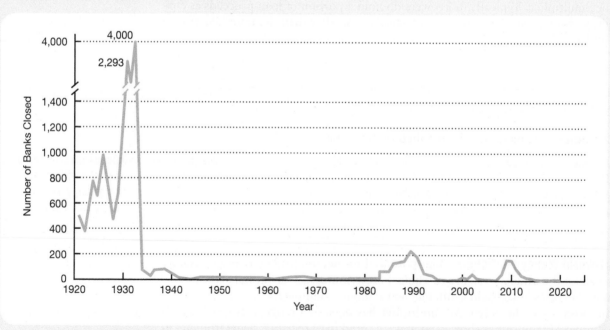

Source: Federal Deposit Insurance Corporation.

As can be seen in Figure 15-8, bank failure rates dropped dramatically after passage of the early federal legislation. The long period from 1935 until the 1980s was relatively quiet. From World War II to 1984, fewer than nine banks failed per year. From 1995 until 2008, failures again averaged about nine per year. Since 2009, however, more than 400 banks have failed, and some remain in weakened states. We will examine the reasons for this shortly. First, though, we need to understand how deposit insurance works.

The Rationale for Deposit Insurance

In our fractional reserve banking system, banks do not hold 100 percent of their depositors' funds as cash. Instead, banks lend out most of their deposit funds to borrowers. Consequently, all depositors cannot withdraw all their funds simultaneously. Hence, the intent of the legislation enacted in the 1930s was to assure depositors that they could have their deposits converted into cash when they wished, no matter how serious the financial situation of the bank.

Federal deposit insurance provided this assurance. The FDIC charged depository institutions premiums based on their total deposits, and these premiums went into funds that would reimburse depositors in the event of bank failures. By insuring deposits, the FDIC bolstered depositors' trust in the banking system and provided depositors with the incentive to leave their deposits with the bank, even in the face of widespread talk of bank failures. In 1933, it was sufficient for the FDIC to cover each account up to $2,500. The current maximum is $250,000 per depositor per institution.

How Deposit Insurance Causes Increased Risk Taking by Bank Managers

Until the 1990s, all insured depository institutions paid the same small fee for coverage. Although deposit insurance premiums for a while were adjusted somewhat in response to the riskiness of a depository institution's assets, they never reflected all of the relative risk. Indeed, between the late 1990s and the late 2000s, very few depository institutions paid *any* deposit insurance premiums. This lack of correlation between risk and premiums can be considered a fundamental flaw in the deposit insurance scheme. When covered by deposit insurance, bank managers do not have to pay higher insurance premiums if they make riskier loans. The managers have an incentive to invest in more assets of higher yield, and therefore necessarily higher risk, than they would if there were no deposit insurance.

Artificially Low Insurance Premiums Another problem with the insurance scheme is that the premium rate is artificially low. Depository institution managers are able to obtain deposits at less than full cost (because depositors will accept a lower interest payment on insured deposits). Consequently, managers can increase their profits by using insured deposits to purchase higher-yield, higher-risk assets. The gains to risk taking accrue to the managers and stockholders of the depository institutions. The losses go to the deposit insurer (and, as we will see, ultimately to taxpayers).

A Regulatory Solution To combat these flaws in the financial industry and in the deposit insurance system, a vast regulatory apparatus oversees depository institutions. The FDIC and other federal deposit insurance agencies possess regulatory powers to offset the risk-taking temptations to depository institution managers.

These regulatory powers include the ability to require higher capital investment; to regulate, examine, and supervise bank affairs; and to enforce regulatory decisions. Higher capital requirements were imposed in the early 1990s and then adjusted somewhat shortly after the turn of the century, but the last jump in bank failures revealed that basic flaws remain.

Deposit Insurance, Adverse Selection, and Moral Hazard

As a deposit insurer, the FDIC effectively acts as a government-run insurance company. This means that the FDIC's operations expose the federal government to the same kinds of asymmetric information problems that other financial intermediaries face.

Adverse Selection in Deposit Insurance One of these problems is *adverse selection*, which is often a problem when insurance is involved because people or firms that are relatively poor risks are sometimes able to disguise that fact from insurers. It is instructive to examine the way this works with the deposit insurance provided by the FDIC. Deposit insurance shields depositors from the potential adverse effects of risky decisions and so makes depositors willing to accept riskier investment strategies by their banks. Clearly, protection of depositors from risks potentially encourages more high-flying, risk-loving entrepreneurs to become managers of banks. The possible consequences for the FDIC—and for taxpayers—are larger losses.

Moral Hazard in Deposit Insurance Moral hazard is also an important phenomenon in the presence of insurance contracts, such as the deposit insurance provided by the FDIC. Insured depositors know that they will not suffer losses if their bank fails. Hence, they have little incentive to monitor their bank's investment activities or to punish their bank by withdrawing their funds if the bank assumes too much risk. This means that insured banks have incentives to take on more risks than they otherwise would.

Federal Insurance Deposit Affects Your Behavior

Do you or will you ever care about how federal deposit insurance creates a moral hazard in the banking community? Probably not. All you need to know is that your deposits are insured by an agency of the federal government. This means that you will never investigate the behavior of bank managers in any banking institution. In other words, because you know that you cannot lose your deposits due to bad banking practices, you rationally choose to spend *no* time investigating banks in which you put your deposits.

ECONOMICS IN YOUR LIFE

Contemplating Digital Currency at the Federal Reserve

Jerome Powell, chair of the Federal Reserve's Board of Governors, is concerned. A flurry of proposals has surfaced for central banks to introduce digital currencies. Some of these proposals call for the Fed to issue a digital currency *alongside* its existing physical currency, thereby giving the public a choice between alternative forms of Fed-issued money to use as a medium of exchange. Others call for the Fed to *replace* paper currency with digital currency. Under the latter proposal, the Fed effectively would require U.S. residents to end the use of the physical currency commonly utilized in small transactions and sometimes used to finance purchases of illegal items or to avoid reporting of transactions subject to various forms of taxation.

Powell is concerned that digital currencies issued by central banks would become targets for cyber attacks, counterfeiting, and theft. In addition, he states, Fed issuance of a digital currency would enable the central bank to track exchanges that people make, thus raising serious privacy concerns that likely would reduce its appeal. "We're not looking at this at the Fed, that the Fed would do a digital currency," sums up Powell in congressional testimony. "That's not something we're looking at."

FOR CRITICAL THINKING

Central banks pay no interest on paper currency, but in principle how could a central bank easily pay annual interest to holders of its digital currency?

REAL APPLICATION

If the Fed simultaneously issued physical currency and digital currency, would you benefit in any way from opting to use the Fed's digital currency?

Sources are listed at the end of this chapter.

ISSUES & APPLICATIONS

The Fed Provides the U.S. Treasury with More Funds

CONCEPTS APPLIED

➤ Money and the Federal Reserve

➤ Open Market Operations

➤ Reserves and the Fed's Balance Sheet

Each year, the Fed transmits payments called remittances to the U.S. Treasury. The inflation-adjusted amounts of the Fed's annual remittances, which amount to nearly all of the profits received by the Fed, generate tens of billions of dollars of annual revenues for the U.S. Treasury.

Central Bank Profits

Governments have profited from money creation throughout history. The Fed also profits from creating money. The Fed's interest receipts on securities and other interest-bearing holdings on the asset side of its balance sheet are higher than the Fed's expenses.

These expenses include the interest that the Fed pays banks on reserves and the costs of printing and distributing U.S. currency, on which the Fed pays no interest. The expenses also include wages and salaries paid to Fed officials and staff. The differential between the Fed's interest earnings and its expenses generates the Fed's annual profits, nearly all of which it is obliged under U.S. law to turn over as remittances to the U.S. Treasury each year.

Why the Fed's Remittances to the Treasury Recently Have Increased—But Eventually May Shrink

During and after the financial crisis and recession of 2007–2009, the Fed conducted very large open market operations that added significant accounts to its portfolio of securities and other assets. Thus, interest receipts on the Fed's assets rose considerably, but the Fed paid comparatively little interest to banks on their reserve holdings and continued to pay no interest on currency. Thus, the Fed's inflation-adjusted profits soared by nearly 200 percent, and hence so did its annual remittances to the Treasury.

The Fed forecasts that market interest rates will rise in future years, which will increase significantly the annual amounts of interest that it will have to pay banks on their reserve holdings. As a consequence, the Fed's annual expenses will increase considerably, and its annual profits and remittances to the Treasury may decline.

FOR CRITICAL THINKING

Given that the Latin-derived word "seignior" refers to government officials, why do you suppose that economists refer to the profits that central banks such as the Fed receive from money creation as "seigniorage"?

REAL APPLICATION

Why might it ever matter to you that the Fed pays interest on reserves?

Sources are listed at the end of this chapter.

What You Should Know

LEARNING OBJECTIVES

KEY TERMS

15.1 Define the functions of money, identify key properties that money must possess, and explain official definitions of the money supply *Money is a medium of exchange that people use to make payments for goods, services, and financial assets. It is also a unit of accounting for quoting prices in terms of money values. In addition, money is a store of value, so people can hold money for future use in exchange. Finally, money is a standard of deferred payment, enabling lenders to make loans and buyers to repay those loans with money. A good will function as money only if people are widely willing to accept the good in exchange for other goods and services. People will use money only if its value is relatively predictable. The narrow definition of the money supply, called M1, includes only currency, transactions deposits, and traveler's checks. A broader definition, called M2, is equal to M1 plus savings deposits, small-denomination time deposits, and noninstitutional holdings of money market mutual fund balances.*

money, 312
medium of exchange, 312
barter, 312
unit of accounting, 313
store of value, 313
standard of deferred
  payment, 313
liquidity, 314
transactions deposits, 314
fiduciary monetary
  system, 314
money supply, 315
transactions approach, 315
liquidity approach, 315
M1, 315
depository institutions, 315
thrift institutions, 315
traveler's checks, 315
M2, 316
Key Figure
Figure 15-1, 314

15.2 Understand why financial intermediaries such as banks exist *Financial intermediaries help reduce problems stemming from the existence of asymmetric information. Adverse selection arises when uncreditworthy individuals and firms seek loans. Moral hazard problems exist when an individual or business that has been granted credit begins to engage in riskier practices. Financial intermediaries may also permit savers to benefit from economies of scale, which is the ability to reduce the costs and risks of managing funds by pooling funds and spreading costs and risks across many savers.*

central bank, 317
financial intermediation, 317
financial intermediaries, 317
asymmetric information, 317
adverse selection, 317
moral hazard, 317
liabilities, 318
assets, 318
Key Figures
Figure 15-3, 318
Figure 15-4, 320

15.3 Describe the basic structure and functions of the Federal Reserve System *The Federal Reserve System consists of 12 district banks overseen by the Board of Governors. The Fed's main functions are supplying fiduciary currency, holding banks' reserves and clearing payments, acting as the government's fiscal agent, supervising banks, regulating the money supply, intervening in foreign exchange markets, and acting as a lender of last resort.*

The Fed, 320
lender of last resort, 322
Key Figure
Figure 15-6, 322

PROBLEMS

15-1. Until 1946, residents of the island of Yap used large doughnut-shaped stones as financial assets. Although prices of goods and services were not quoted in terms of the stones, the stones were often used in exchange for particularly large purchases, such as livestock. To make the transaction, several individuals would insert a large stick through a stone's center and carry it to its new owner. A stone was difficult for any one person to steal, so an owner typically would lean it against the side of his or her home as a sign to others of accumulated purchasing power that would hold value for later use in exchange. Loans would often be repaid using the stones. Which of the functions of money did the stones perform?

15-2. During the late 1970s, prices quoted in terms of the Israeli currency, the shekel, rose so fast that grocery stores listed their prices in terms of the U.S. dollar and provided customers with dollar-shekel conversion tables that they updated daily. Although people continued to buy goods and services and make loans using shekels, many Israeli citizens converted shekels to dollars to avoid a reduction in their wealth due to inflation. In what way did the U.S. dollar function as money in Israel during this period?

15-3. During the 1945–1946 Hungarian hyperinflation, when the rate of inflation reached 41.9 *quadrillion* percent per month, the Hungarian government discovered that the real value of its tax receipts was falling dramatically. To keep real tax revenues more stable, it created a good called a "tax pengö," in which all bank deposits were denominated for purposes of taxation. Nevertheless, payments for

goods and services were made only in terms of the regular Hungarian currency, whose value tended to fall rapidly even though the value of a tax pengö remained stable. Prices were also quoted only in terms of the regular currency. Lenders, however, began denominating loan payments in terms of tax pengös. In what ways did the tax pengö function as money in Hungary in 1945 and 1946?

15-4. Considering the following data (expressed in billions of U.S. dollars), calculate M1 and M2.

Currency	2,050
Savings deposits	10,500
Small-denomination time deposits	1,000
Traveler's checks outside banks and thrifts	10
Total money market mutual funds	800
Institution-only money market mutual funds	1,800
Transactions deposits	2,140

15-5. Considering the following data (expressed in billions of U.S. dollars), calculate M1 and M2.

Transactions deposits	1,025
Savings deposits	3,300
Small-denomination time deposits	950
Money market deposit accounts	5,950
Noninstitution money market mutual funds	900
Traveler's checks outside banks and thrifts	25
Currency	2,050
Institution-only money market mutual funds	1,250

15-6. Identify whether each of the following amounts is counted in M1 only, M2 only, both M1 and M2, or neither.

   a. $50 billion in U.S. Treasury bills

   b. $15 billion in small-denomination time deposits

   c. $5 billion in traveler's checks not issued by a bank

   d. $20 billion in money market deposit accounts

15-7. Identify whether each of the following items is counted in M1 only, M2 only, both M1 and M2, or neither.

   a. A $1,000 balance in a transactions deposit at a mutual savings bank

   b. A $100,000 time deposit in a New York bank

   c. A $10,000 time deposit an elderly widow holds at her credit union

   d. A $50 traveler's check not issued by a bank

   e. A $50,000 savings deposit

15-8. Match each of the rationales for financial intermediation listed below with at least one of the following financial intermediaries: insurance company, pension fund, savings bank. Explain your choices.

   a. Adverse selection

   b. Moral hazard

   c. Lower management costs generated by larger scale

15-9. Identify whether each of the following events poses an adverse selection problem or a moral hazard problem in financial markets.

   a. A manager of a savings and loan association responds to reports of a likely increase in federal deposit insurance coverage. She directs loan officers to extend mortgage loans to less credit-worthy borrowers.

   b. A loan applicant does not mention that a legal judgment in his divorce case will require him to make alimony payments to his ex-wife.

   c. An individual who was recently approved for a loan to start a new business decides to use some of the funds to take a Hawaiian vacation.

15-10. In what sense is currency a liability of the Federal Reserve System?

15-11. In what respects is the Fed like a private banking institution? In what respects is it more like a government agency?

15-12. Take a look at the map of the locations of the Federal Reserve districts and their headquarters in Figure 15-6. Today, the U.S. population is centered just west of the Mississippi River—that is, about half of the population is either to the west or the east of a line running roughly just west of this river. Can you reconcile the current locations of Fed districts and banks with this fact? Why do you suppose the Fed has its current geographic structure?

15-13. Draw an empty bank balance sheet, with the heading "Assets" on the left and the heading "Liabilities" on the right. Then place the following items on the proper side of the balance sheet:

   a. Loans to a private company

   b. Borrowings from a Federal Reserve district bank

   c. Deposits with a Federal Reserve district bank

   d. U.S. Treasury bills

   e. Vault cash

   f. Transactions deposits

15-14. Draw an empty bank balance sheet, with the heading "Assets" on the left and the heading "Liabilities" on the right. Then place the following items on the proper side of the balance sheet.

   a. Borrowings from another bank in the interbank loans market

   b. Deposits this bank holds in an account with another private bank

   c. U.S. Treasury bonds

   d. Small-denomination time deposits

   e. Mortgage loans to household customers

   f. Money market deposit accounts

15-15. The reserve ratio is 11 percent. What is the value of the potential money multiplier?

15-16. The Federal Reserve purchases $1 million in U.S. Treasury bonds from a bond dealer, and the dealer's bank credits the dealer's account. The reserve ratio is 15 percent. Assuming that no currency leakage occurs, how much will the bank lend to its customers following the Fed's purchase?

15-17. Suppose that the value of the potential money multiplier is equal to 4. What is the reserve ratio?

15-18. Consider a world in which there is no currency and depository institutions issue only transactions deposits. The reserve ratio is 20 percent. The central bank sells $1 billion in government securities. What ultimately happens to the money supply?

15-19. Assume a 1 percent reserve ratio and no currency leakages. What is the potential money multiplier? How will total deposits in the banking system ultimately change if the Federal Reserve purchases $5 million in U.S. government securities?

15-20. Consider Figure 15-1, which focuses on liquidity. How might limited acceptability of old masters paintings in exchange and difficulties in predicting the values of these paintings from year to year help to explain their relatively low liquidity? How might these characteristics affect the likelihood that these assets could function as forms of money?

15-21. Does Figure 15-3 depict direct finance or indirect finance? Explain. How could the figure be revised to illustrate the alternative form of finance?

15-22. Consider Figure 15-4. Explain how Jill Jones's debit-card transaction affects the assets and liabilities of Citibank and of Bank of America. Why does this transaction leave unchanged the total quantity of deposits in the banking system and, consequently, the money supply?

15-23. Consider Figure 15-7. Describe the basic shape that this figure would take if the Fed had instead generated a multiple contraction in the money supply by removing $100,000 in reserves from the banking system via an open market sale.

15-24. In Problem 15-23, what would be the amount of the potential money multiplier that applies to a $100,000 decrease in reserves in Figure 15-7 caused by a Fed open market sale of that amount? How much would the money supply potentially decrease as a result of this sale?

REFERENCES

INTERNATIONAL EXAMPLE: What Once Was Old Money Is Now "New" Money in Zimbabwe

Steve Hanke, "Zimbabwe's Monetary Death Spiral," *Forbes*, January 16, 2019.

Kat Lonsdorf and Ari Shapiro, "Mugabe's Gone, but Zimbabwe Still Has a Serious Cash Shortage," National Public Radio (https://www.npr.org/2018/07/28/632986144/mugabes-gone-but-zimbabwe-still-has-a-serious-cash-shortage), July 28, 2018.

Tatira Zwinoira, "Rural Households Turn to Barter Trade," *Newsday*, April 6, 2018.

INTERNATIONAL EXAMPLE: Currency Remains Entrenched as a Key Component of National Money Supplies

Board of Governors of the Federal Reserve System, "Federal Reserve Note Print Order," (https://www.federalreserve.gov/paymentsystems/coin_currency_orders.htm), 2019.

CCL Secure, "Our Expertise" (https://cclsecure.com/our-expertise/), 2019.

De La Rue, "Cash Supply Chain: Security Features," (https://www.delarue.com/markets-and-solutions/cash-supply-chain/security-features), 2019.

AI—DECISION MAKING THROUGH DATA: The Banking Industry

Ron Shevlin, "The Artificial Intelligence Gap between Megabanks, Community Banks, and Credit Unions," January 14, 2019.

John Manning, "How Artificial Intelligence Is Disrupting the Banking Industry," *International Banker*, July 4, 2018.

Laura Noonan, "Artificial Intelligence in Banking: The Reality behind the Hype," *Financial Times*, April 12, 2018.

BEHAVIORAL EXAMPLE: Banks' Behavioral Response to Establishment of the Federal Reserve as the Last-Resort Lender

Tarishi Matsuoka and Makoto Watanabe, "Banking Panics and the Lender of Last Resort in a Monetary Economy," CESifo Working Paper 7451, 2019.

Haelim Anderson, Charles Calomiris, Matthew Jaremski, and Gary Richardson, "Liquidity Risk, Bank Networks, and the Value of Joining the Federal Reserve System," *Journal of Money, Credit, and Banking*, 2018.

Mark Carlson and David Wheelock, "Did the Founding of the Federal Reserve Affect the Vulnerability of the Interbank System to Systemic Risk?" *Journal of Money, Credit, and Banking*, 2018.

ECONOMICS IN YOUR LIFE: Contemplating Digital Currency at the Federal Reserve

Christian Barontini and Henry Holden, "Proceeding with Caution—A Survey on Central Bank Digital Currency," Bank for International Settlements, 2019.

Fred Imbert, "Fed Chairman Powell Says Cryptocurrencies Present Big Risks to Investors," CNBC (https://www.cnbc.com/2018/07/18/fed-chairman-rips-into-cryptocurrencies-cites-big-risk-to-investors.html), July 18, 2018.

Jeffrey Tucker, "Governments and Central Banks: Leave That Crypto Alone," *Forbes*, July 26, 2018.

ISSUES & APPLICATIONS: The Fed Provides the U.S. Treasury with More Funds

Board of Governors of the Federal Reserve System, "Federal Reserve Board Announces Reserve Bank Income and Transfers to the Treasury" (https://www.federalreserve.gov/newsevents/pressreleases/other20180110a.htm), January 10, 2019.

Dan Caplinger, "The Federal Reserve Is Surprisingly Profitable," *USA Today*, January 30, 2018.

Igor Concharov, Vasso Ioannidou, and Martin Schmalz, "(Why) Do Central Banks Care about Their Profits?" University of Lancaster and University of Michigan, Presented at American Economic Association Annual Meetings, January 6, 2019.

16 Domestic and International Dimensions of Monetary Policy

Tananuphong Kumar/123RF GB Limited

LEARNING OBJECTIVES

After reading this chapter, you should be able to:

16.1 Identify the key factors that influence the quantity of money that people desire to hold

16.2 Describe how Federal Reserve monetary policy actions influence market interest rates

16.3 Evaluate how expansionary and contractionary monetary policy actions affect equilibrium real GDP and the price level in the short run

16.4 Understand the equation of exchange and its importance in the quantity theory of money and prices

16.5 Explain how the Federal Reserve has implemented credit policy since 2008

Since late 2008, the Federal Reserve has paid banks interest on the excess reserves that they hold with Federal Reserve banks. Before the Fed offered interest on these reserves, total holdings of excess reserves across the entire banking system rarely amounted to much more $2 billion. By paying the interest on their excess reserves, however, for a time the Fed induced more than a thousand-fold increase in their holdings, to in excess of *$2 trillion*. Why has the Fed given banks an incentive to hold so many more excess reserves? How much in annual interest payments has the Fed transmitted to banks, and how much interest does it project having to pay in future years? In this chapter you will find out the answers to these questions.

in the past ten years, the number of highest-denomination currency notes held by Japanese individuals and companies has risen by nearly 25 percent and that annual sales of safes in which to store such notes are more than six times higher? Holdings of high-denomination currency notes and sales of safes also have increased in a number of European nations, such as Germany, Serbia, and Switzerland. In all of these countries, annual interest rates on some bonds and paid by banks on funds held in various deposit accounts have dropped below zero percent. That is, people and firms get back fewer funds than the amount they had initially placed on deposit. In contrast, currency earns no interest, which means that at least people in Japan and these European nations can be assured that after the passage of time they will have as much currency as when they placed the funds in their safes.

In this chapter, you will learn about how and why interest rates dropped to negative levels in Japan and several European nations. First, though, you must learn how interest rates influence how much money private individuals and firms desire to hold—that is, about their *demand for money*.

The Demand for Money

In the previous chapter, we saw how the Federal Reserve's open market operations can increase or decrease the money supply. Our focus was on the effects of the Fed's actions on the banking system. In this chapter, we widen our discussion to see how Fed monetary policy actions have an impact on the broader economy by influencing market interest rates. First, though, you must understand the factors that determine how much money people desire to hold—in other words, you must understand the demand for money.

All of us engage in a flow of transactions. We buy and sell things all of our lives. Because we use money—dollars—as our medium of exchange, however, all *flows* of nonbarter transactions involve a *stock* of money. We can restate this as follows:

To use money, one must hold money.

Given that everybody must hold money, we can now talk about the *demand* to hold it. People do not demand to hold money just to look at pictures of past leaders. They hold it to be able to use it to buy goods and services.

The Demand for Money: What People Wish to Hold

People have certain motivations that cause them to want to hold **money balances**. Individuals and firms could try to do without non-interest-bearing money balances. Life, though, is inconvenient without a ready supply of money balances. Thus, the public has a demand for money, motivated by several factors.

The Transactions Demand The main reason people hold money is that money can be used to purchase goods and services. People are paid at specific intervals (once a week, once a month, and the like), but they wish to make purchases more or less continuously. To free themselves from having to buy goods and services only on payday, people find it beneficial to hold money. The benefit they receive is convenience: They willingly forgo interest earnings in order to avoid the inconvenience of cashing in nonmoney assets such as bonds every time they wish to make a purchase. Thus, people hold money to make regular, *expected* expenditures because of the **transactions demand**. As nominal GDP rises, people will want to hold more money because they will be making more transactions.

The Precautionary Demand The transactions demand involves money held to make *expected* expenditures. People also hold money for the **precautionary demand** to make *unexpected* purchases or to meet emergencies. When people hold money for the

16.1 Identify the key factors that influence the quantity of money that people desire to hold

Money balances
Synonymous with money, money stock, money holdings.

Transactions demand
Holding money as a medium of exchange to make payments. The level varies directly with nominal GDP.

Precautionary demand
Holding money to meet unplanned expenditures and emergencies.

precautionary demand, they incur a cost in forgone interest earnings that they compare to the benefit of having cash on hand. The higher the rate of interest, the lower the precautionary money balances people wish to hold.

The Asset Demand Remember that one of the functions of money is to serve as a store of value. People can hold money balances as a store of value, or they can hold bonds or stocks or other interest-earning assets. The desire to hold money as a store of value leads to the **asset demand** for money. People choose to hold money rather than other assets for two reasons: its liquidity and the lack of risk.

Asset demand
Holding money as a store of value instead of other assets such as corporate bonds and stocks.

The disadvantage of holding money balances as an asset, of course, is the interest earnings forgone. Each individual or business decides how much money to hold as an asset by looking at the opportunity cost of holding money. The higher the interest rate—which is the opportunity cost of holding money—the lower the money balances people will want to hold as assets. Conversely, the lower the interest rate offered on alternative assets, the higher the money balances people will want to hold as assets.

The Demand for Money Curve

Assume for simplicity's sake that the amount of money demanded for transactions purposes is proportionate to income. That leaves the precautionary and asset demands for money, both determined by the opportunity cost of holding money. If we assume that the interest rate represents the cost of holding money balances, we can graph the relationship between the interest rate and the quantity of money demanded.

In Figure 16-1, the demand for money curve shows a familiar downward slope. The horizontal axis measures the quantity of money demanded, and the vertical axis is the interest rate. The rate of interest is the cost of holding money. At a higher interest rate, a lower quantity of money is demanded, and vice versa.

To see this, imagine two scenarios. In the first one, you can earn 20 percent a year if you put your funds into purchases of U.S. government securities. In the other scenario, you can earn 1 percent if you put your funds into purchases of U.S. government securities. If you have $1,000 average cash balances in a non-interest-bearing checking account, in the first scenario over a one-year period, your opportunity cost would be 20 percent of $1,000, or $200. In the second scenario, the opportunity cost that you would incur would be 1 percent of $1,000, or $10. Under which scenario would you hold more funds in your checking account instead of securities?

FIGURE 16-1

The Demand for Money Curve

If we use the interest rate as a measure of the opportunity cost of holding money balances, the demand for money curve, M_d, is downward sloping, similar to other demand curves.

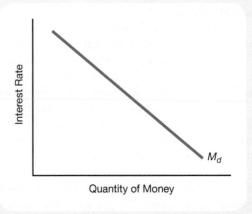

How the Fed Influences Interest Rates

16.2 Describe how Federal Reserve monetary policy actions influence market interest rates

When the Fed takes actions that alter the rate of growth of the money supply, it is seeking to influence investment, consumption, and total aggregate expenditures. In taking these monetary policy actions, the Fed in principle has four tools at its disposal: open market operations, changes in the reserve ratio, changes in the interest rates paid on reserves, and discount rate changes. The discount rate and interest rates paid on reserves will be discussed later in this chapter. Let's consider the effects of open market operations, the tool that the Fed regularly employs on a day-to-day basis.

Open Market Operations

As we saw in the previous chapter, the Fed changes the amount of reserves in the banking system by its purchases and sales of government bonds issued by the U.S. Treasury. To understand how these actions by the Fed influence the market interest rate, we start out in an equilibrium in which all individuals, including the holders of bonds, are satisfied with the current situation. There is some equilibrium level of interest rate (and bond prices).

Now, if the Fed wants to conduct open market operations, it must somehow induce individuals, businesses, and foreign residents to hold more or fewer U.S. Treasury bonds. The inducement must take the form of making people better off. So, if the Fed wants to buy bonds, it will have to offer to buy them at a higher price than exists in the marketplace. If the Fed wants to sell bonds, it will have to offer them at a lower price than exists in the marketplace. Thus, an open market operation must cause a change in the price of bonds.

Graphing the Sale of Bonds The Fed sells some of the bonds it has on hand. This is shown in panel (a) of Figure 16-2. Notice that the supply of bonds in the private market is shown here as a vertical line with respect to price. The demand for bonds is downward sloping. If the Fed offers more bonds it owns for sale, the supply curve shifts from S_1 to S_2. People will not be willing to buy the extra bonds at the initial equilibrium bond price, P_1. They will be satisfied holding the additional bonds at the new equilibrium price, P_2.

FIGURE 16-2

Determining the Price of Bonds

In panel (a), the Fed offers more bonds for sale. The price drops from P_1 to P_2. In panel (b), the Fed purchases bonds. This is the equivalent of a reduction in the supply of bonds available for private investors to hold. The price of bonds must rise from P_1 to P_3 to clear the market.

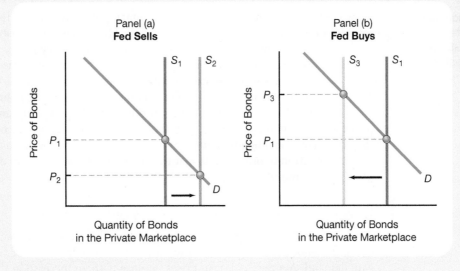

The Fed's Purchase of Bonds The opposite occurs when the Fed purchases bonds. You can view this purchase of bonds as a reduction in the stock of bonds available for private investors to hold. In panel (b) of Figure 16-2, the original supply curve is S_1. The new supply curve of outstanding bonds will end up being S_3 because of the Fed's purchases of bonds. To get people to give up these bonds, the Fed must offer them a more attractive price. The price will rise from to P_1 to P_3.

Relationship between the Price of Existing Bonds and the Rate of Interest

The price of existing bonds and the rate of interest are inversely related. Assume that the average yield on bonds is 5 percent. You decide to purchase a bond. A local corporation agrees to sell you a bond that will pay you $50 a year forever. What is the price you are willing to pay for the bond? It is $1,000. Why? Because $50 divided by $1,000 equals 5 percent, which is as good as the best return you can earn elsewhere. You purchase the bond. The next year something happens in the economy, and you can now obtain bonds that have effective yields of 10 percent. (In other words, the prevailing interest rate in the economy is now 10 percent.) What will happen to the market price of the existing bond that you own, the one you purchased the year before? It will fall.

If you try to sell the bond for $1,000, you will discover that no investors will buy it from you. Why should they when they can obtain the same $50-a-year yield from someone else by paying only $500? Indeed, unless you offer your bond for sale at a price that is no higher than $500, no buyers will be forthcoming. Hence, an increase in the prevailing interest rate in the economy has caused the market value of your existing bond to fall.

The important point to be understood is this:

> *The market price of **existing** bonds (and all fixed-income assets) is inversely related to the rate of interest prevailing in the economy.*

As a consequence of the inverse relationship between the price of existing bonds and the interest rate, the Fed is able to influence the interest rate by engaging in open market operations. A Fed open market sale that reduces the equilibrium price of bonds brings about an increase in the interest rate. A Fed open market purchase causes both an increase in the equilibrium price of bonds and a decrease in the interest rate.

16.3 Evaluate how expansionary and contractionary monetary policy actions affect equilibrium real GDP and the price level in the short run

Effects of an Increase in the Money Supply

Now that we've seen how the Fed's monetary policy actions influence the market interest rate, we can ask a broader question: How does monetary policy influence real GDP and the price level? To understand how monetary policy works in its simplest form, we are going to run an experiment in which you increase the money supply in a very direct way. Assume that the government has given you hundreds of millions of dollars in just-printed bills. You then fly around the country in a helicopter, dropping the money out of the window. People pick it up and put it in their pockets. Some deposit the money in their transactions deposit accounts. As a result, they now have too much money—not in the sense that they want to throw it away but rather in relation to other assets that they own. There are a variety of ways to dispose of this "new" money.

Direct Effect of an Increase in the Money Supply

The simplest thing that people can do when they have excess money balances is to go out and spend them on goods and services. Here they have a direct impact on aggregate demand. Aggregate demand rises because with an increase in the money supply, at any given price level people now want to purchase more output of real goods and services.

Indirect Effect of an Increase in the Money Supply

Not everybody will necessarily spend the newfound money on goods and services. Some people may wish to deposit a portion or all of those excess money balances in banks.

Banks' Lending Responses and Aggregate Demand
The recipient banks now discover that they have higher reserves than they wish to hold. As you learned in an earlier chapter, one thing that banks can do to get higher-interest-earning assets is to lend out the excess reserves.

Banks, however, cannot induce people to borrow more funds than they were borrowing before unless the banks lower the interest rate that they charge on loans. This lower interest rate encourages people to take out those loans. Businesses will therefore engage in new investment with the funds loaned. Individuals will engage in more consumption of durable goods such as housing, autos, and home entertainment centers. In both ways, the increased loans generate a rise in aggregate demand. More people will be involved in more spending—even those who did not pick up any of the money that was originally dropped out of your helicopter.

Low Interest Rates and Quantitative Easing
What happens if the market interest rate on bonds falls to zero, as has occurred in recent years? In that case, monetary policy traditionally must rely on the direct effect of a change in bank reserves and, through the money multiplier effect, the quantity of money in circulation. Monetary policy cannot depend on the indirect effect of an interest rate that is already at zero. A policy action in which the Federal Reserve conducts open market purchases to increase bank reserves without seeking to alter the interest rate, which is already zero, is called **quantitative easing**.

Quantitative easing
Federal Reserve open market purchases intended to generate an increase in bank reserves at a zero interest rate.

Graphing the Effects of an Expansionary Monetary Policy

To consider the effects of an expansionary monetary policy on real GDP and the price level, look at Figure 16-3. We start out in a situation in which the economy is

FIGURE 16-3

Expansionary Monetary Policy with Underutilized Resources

If we start out with equilibrium at E_1, expansionary monetary policy will shift AD_1 to AD_2. The new equilibrium will be at E_2.

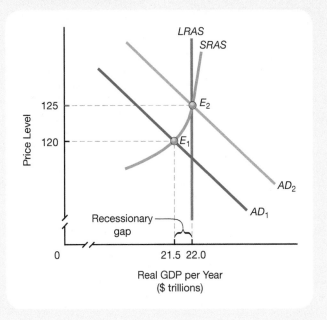

operating at less than full employment. You see a recessionary gap in the figure, which is measured as the horizontal difference between the long-run aggregate supply curve, *LRAS*, and the current equilibrium. Short-run equilibrium is at E_1, with a price level of 120 and real GDP of $21.5 trillion. The *LRAS* curve is at $22 trillion. Assume now that the Fed increases the money supply. Because of the direct and indirect effects of this increase in the money supply, aggregate demand shifts outward to the right to AD_2. The new equilibrium is at an output rate of $2 trillion of real GDP per year and a price level of 125. Here expansionary monetary policy can move the economy toward its *LRAS* curve sooner than otherwise.

Graphing the Effects of Contractionary Monetary Policy

Assume that there is an inflationary gap as shown in Figure 16-4. There you see that the short-run aggregate supply curve, *SRAS*, intersects aggregate demand, AD_1, at E_1. This is to the right of the *LRAS* of real GDP per year of $22 trillion. Contractionary monetary policy can eliminate this inflationary gap. Because of both the direct and indirect effects of monetary policy, the aggregate demand curve shifts inward from AD_1 to AD_2. Equilibrium is now at E_2, which is at a lower price level, 120. Equilibrium real GDP has now fallen from $22.5 trillion to $22 trillion.

Note that contractionary monetary policy involves a reduction in the money supply, with a consequent decline in the price level (deflation). In the real world, contractionary monetary policy more commonly involves reducing the *rate of growth* of the money supply, thereby reducing the rate of increase in the price level (inflation). Similarly, real-world expansionary monetary policy typically involves increasing the rate of growth of the money supply.

Why might application of AI techniques threaten the jobs held by the Federal Reserve's large advisory staff?

FIGURE 16-4

Contractionary Monetary Policy with Overutilized Resources

If we begin at short-run equilibrium at point E_1, contractionary monetary policy will shift the aggregate demand curve from AD_1 to AD_2. The new equilibrium will be at point E_2.

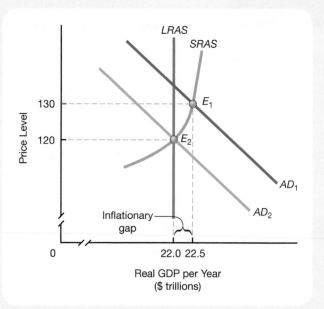

AI | DECISION MAKING THROUGH DATA

Reducing or Replacing the Staffs of Central Banks

In recent years, a number of officials and staff employees at central banks have, like businesspersons and other government officials, become increasingly interested in big data techniques. Several central banks have organized conferences exploring utilization of these techniques. Attendees of the conferences have included advisers to central banks' governing boards that make final decisions about monetary policy actions that influence interest rates, bond prices, real GDP, and the price level. In the meantime, the Fed and other central banks already have been hiring new staffers to implement big data and machine-learning operations relating to the payment services that they provide to depository institutions.

Some observers argue that these institutions' access to growing volumes of past and real-time data and the utilization of AI-guided data analytics ultimately could render central banks' advisory staffs obsolete. These observers contend, for instance, that nearly all of the Fed's 22,000 economists, statisticians, and other support staff could be replaced by digital equipment directing AI apps that would compile and analyze millions of bits of data per second. At the Fed, they conclude, such automated systems could deliver continuously updated economic summaries and forecasts to top Federal Reserve officials at a fraction of the current expense. Those few officials who have legal authority to direct the Fed's policymaking would then make policy decisions as they always have.

FOR CRITICAL THINKING

Why do you suppose that some Fed critics have suggested that the Fed itself could be replaced by digital equipment and AI apps?

Sources are listed at the end of this chapter.

Open Economy Transmission of Monetary Policy

So far we have discussed monetary policy in a closed economy. When we move to an open economy, with international trade and the international purchases and sales of all assets including dollars and other currencies, monetary policy becomes more complex. Consider first the effect of monetary policy on exports.

The Net Export Effect of Expansionary Monetary Policy To see how a change in monetary policy can affect net exports, suppose that the Federal Reserve implements an expansionary policy that reduces the market interest rate. The lower U.S. interest rate, in turn, tends to discourage foreign purchases of U.S. financial assets, such as U.S. government securities.

A Dollar Depreciation If residents of foreign countries decide that they want to purchase fewer U.S. government securities or other U.S. assets, they will require fewer U.S. dollars with which to purchase these U.S. assets. As a consequence, the demand for dollars decreases in foreign exchange markets. The international price of the dollar therefore falls. This is called a *depreciation* of the dollar.

A dollar depreciation tends to boost net exports because it makes our exports cheaper in terms of foreign currency and imports more expensive in terms of dollars. Foreign residents demand more of our goods and services, and we demand fewer of theirs.

A Positive Net Export Effect The preceding reasoning implies that when expansionary monetary policy reduces the U.S. interest rate at the current price level, there will be a positive net export effect because foreign residents will want fewer U.S. financial instruments such as bonds and stocks. Hence, they will demand fewer dollars, thereby causing the international price of the dollar to decline.

This fall in the dollar's international value makes our exports less expensive for the rest of the world. Consequently, foreign residents demand a larger quantity of our exports. The decline in the dollar's value also means that foreign goods and services are more expensive in the United States, so we therefore demand fewer imports. We come up with this conclusion:

> *Expansionary monetary policy causes interest rates to fall. Such a decrease will induce international outflows of funds. The resulting decrease in the demand for dollars reduces the international value of the dollar. U.S. exports become more expensive abroad, and U.S. imports become less expensive. The net export effect of expansionary monetary policy will be in the same direction as the monetary policy effect, thereby amplifying the effect of such policy.*

The Net Export Effect of Contractionary Monetary Policy Now assume that the Federal Reserve wants to pursue a contractionary monetary policy. In so doing, it will cause interest rates to increase in the short run, as discussed earlier. Rising interest rates will induce people to desire to hold more U.S. bonds and stocks, so funds flow into the United States. The demand for dollars will increase, and the international price of the dollar will rise. Foreign goods will now be less expensive for U.S. residents, and imports will rise. Foreign residents will desire fewer of our exports, and exports will fall. The result will be a decrease in net exports. Again, the international consequences reinforce the domestic consequences of monetary policy, in this case by inducing a reduction in aggregate demand.

On a broader level, the Fed's ability to control the rate of growth of the money supply may be hampered as U.S. money markets become less isolated. With the push of a computer button, billions of dollars can change hands halfway around the world. If the Fed reduces the growth of the money supply, individuals and firms in the United States can obtain liquidity from other sources. Indeed, as world markets become increasingly integrated, U.S. residents, who can already hold U.S. bank accounts denominated in foreign currencies, more regularly conduct transactions using other nations' currencies.

| **16.4** Understand the equation of exchange and its importance in the quantity theory of money and prices |

Monetary Policy and Inflation

Most media discussions of inflation focus on the short run. The price index can fluctuate in the short run because of events such as oil price shocks, labor union strikes, or discoveries of large amounts of new natural resources. In the long run, however, empirical studies show that excessive growth in the money supply results in inflation.

If the supply of money rises relative to the demand for money, people have more money balances than desired. They adjust their mix of assets to reduce money balances in favor of other items. This ultimately causes their spending on goods and services to increase. The result is a rise in the price level, or inflation.

The Equation of Exchange and the Quantity Theory

Equation of exchange
The formula indicating that the number of monetary units (M_s) times the number of times each unit is spent on final goods and services (V) is identical to the price level (P) times real GDP (Y).

Income velocity of money (V)
The number of times per year a dollar is spent on final goods and services; identically equal to nominal GDP divided by the money supply.

A simple way to show the relationship between changes in the quantity of money in circulation and the price level is through the **equation of exchange**, developed by U.S. economist Irving Fisher (note that $\equiv$ refers to an identity or truism):

$$M_s V \equiv PY$$

where M_s = actual money balances held by the nonbanking public
V = **income velocity of money**, which is the number of times, on average per year, each monetary unit is spent on final goods and services
P = price level or price index
Y = real GDP per year

Consider a numerical example involving the entire economy. Assume that in this economy, the total money supply, M_s, is \$16.5 trillion; real GDP, Y, is \$22 trillion (in base-year dollars); and the price level, P, is 1.5 (150 in index number terms). Using the equation of exchange,

$$M_s V \equiv PY$$
$$\$16.5 \text{ trillion} \times V \equiv 1.5 \times \$22 \text{ trillion}$$
$$V \equiv 2.0$$

Thus, each dollar is spent an average of 2 times per year.

The Equation of Exchange as an Identity The equation of exchange must always be true—it is an *accounting identity*. The equation of exchange states that the total amount of funds spent on final output, $M_s V$, is equal to the total amount of funds *received* for final output, PY. Thus, a given flow of funds can be viewed from either the buyers' side or the producers' side. The value of goods purchased is equal to the value of goods sold.

If Y represents real GDP and P is the price level, PY equals the dollar value of national output of goods and services or *nominal* GDP. Thus,

$$M_s V \equiv PY \equiv \text{nominal GDP}$$

The Quantity Theory of Money and Prices If we now make some assumptions about different variables in the equation of exchange, we come up with the simplified theory of why the price level changes, called the **quantity theory of money and prices**. If we assume that the velocity of money, V, is constant and that real GDP, Y, is also constant, the simple equation of exchange tells us that a change in the money supply can lead only to an equiproportional change in the price level.

Continue with our numerical example. Y is \$22 trillion. V equals 2.0. If the money supply increases by 20 percent, to \$19.8 trillion, the only thing that can happen is that the price level, P, has to go up from 1.5 to 1.8. In other words, the price level must also increase by 20 percent. Otherwise the equation is no longer in balance. An increase in the money supply of 20 percent results in a rise in the price level (inflation) of 20 percent.

Quantity theory of money and prices
The hypothesis that changes in the money supply lead to equiproportional changes in the price level.

ECONOMICS IN YOUR LIFE

To contemplate the lengths to which Indonesia's central bank has gone to try to limit inflation, take a look at **A Central Bank Takes Inflation Control to an Entirely Different Level** on page 353.

WHAT HAPPENS WHEN...

the Federal Reserve increases the quantity of money in circulation at the same time that the income velocity of money is declining at an even faster pace?

If an increase in the quantity of money brought about by the Fed takes place during an interval in which the income velocity of money is decreasing at a faster rate, on net, the left-hand side of the equation of exchange declines. This means that the right-hand side of the equation of exchange also must decrease. Hence, the net effect will be a reduction in nominal GDP.

Empirical Verification There is considerable evidence of the empirical validity of the relationship between monetary growth and high rates of inflation. Figure 16-5 tracks the correspondence between money supply growth and the rates of inflation in various countries around the world.

Why do economists often point to Zimbabwe as one of the best recent examples of a strong relationship between a nation's annual rate of money growth and its annual inflation rate?

FIGURE 16-5

The Relationship between Money Supply Growth Rates and Rates of Inflation

If we plot rates of inflation and rates of monetary growth for different countries, we come up with a scatter diagram that reveals an obvious direct relationship. If you were to draw a line through the "average" of the points in this figure, it would be upward sloping, showing that an increase in the rate of growth of the money supply leads to an increase in the rate of inflation.

Sources: International Monetary Fund and national central banks. Data are for latest available periods.

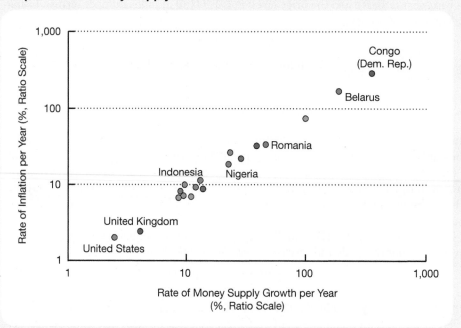

INTERNATIONAL POLICY EXAMPLE

Zimbabwe Switches to Using the U.S. Dollar as Its Money—for a While

Between 1980 and 2008, Zimbabwe's government declared the *Zimbabwe dollar* to be the only legal form of money in payment for goods, services, and settlement of debts. From the late 1990s through 2008, however, the government increased the annual rate of growth of the quantity of Zimbabwe dollars in circulation from about 20 percent to more than *200 million* percent. The average inflation rate in Zimbabwe rose to about *231 million* percent by the summer of 2008, and in the middle of November of that year some estimates have indicated that the nation's annualized inflation rate reached more than *79 billion* percent. At that point, the government eliminated the Zimbabwe dollar and declared the U.S. dollar to be the new official form of money.

In the mid-2010s, however, residents of Zimbabwe began buying more goods abroad. When they paid for the imported items with U.S. dollars, the quantity of U.S. dollars in circulation within Zimbabwe began to shrink. In response to this negative annual rate of growth of the quantity of money in

circulation, Zimbabwe's inflation rate also became negative—that is, the nation began to experience *deflation*. In 2016, the nation's government sought to combat this deflation by issuing a new form of money called *Zimbabwe bond notes*, which the government allowed people to use to purchase items and settle debts only within Zimbabwe. The country's residents had to continue utilizing only U.S. dollars to pay for imports. Since late 2018, the annualized rate of growth of the total quantity of money in circulation—U.S. dollars plus Zimbabwe bond notes—has risen to a substantially positive level, which has raised the nation's annual rate of inflation significantly.

REAL APPLICATION

Imagine a situation in which the rate of inflation in the United States increased to 25 percent per year. How could you react?

Sources are listed at the end of this chapter.

16.5 Explain how the Federal Reserve has implemented credit policy since 2008

Monetary Policy Transmission and Credit Policy at Today's Fed

Earlier in this chapter, we talked about the direct and indirect effects of monetary policy. The direct effect is simply that an increase in the money supply causes people to have excess money balances. To get rid of these excess money balances, people increase their expenditures. The indirect effect, depicted in Figure 16-6 as the interest-rate-based money transmission mechanism, occurs because some people have decided to purchase interest-bearing assets with their excess money balances. This causes the

FIGURE 16-6

FIGURE 16-6

The Interest-Rate-Based Money Transmission Mechanism

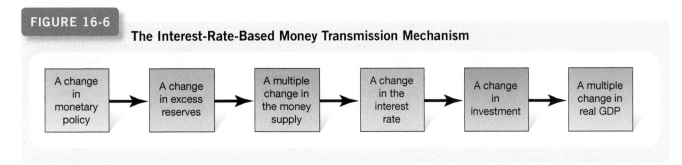

price of such assets—bonds—to go up. Because of the inverse relationship between the price of existing bonds and the interest rate, the interest rate in the economy falls. This lower interest rate induces people and businesses to spend more than they otherwise would have spent.

An Interest-Rate-Based Transmission Mechanism

The indirect, interest-rate-based transmission mechanism can be seen explicitly in Figure 16-7. In panel (a), you see that an increase in the money supply reduces the interest rate. The economywide demand curve for money is labeled M_d in panel (a). At first, the money supply is at M_s, a vertical line determined by the Federal Reserve. The equilibrium interest rate is r_1. This occurs where the money supply curve intersects the money demand curve.

Now assume that the Fed increases the money supply, say, via open market operations. This will shift the money supply curve outward to the right to M'_s. People find

FIGURE 16-7

Adding Monetary Policy to the Aggregate Demand–Aggregate Supply Model

In panel (a), we show a demand for money function, M_d. It slopes downward to show that at lower rates of interest, a larger quantity of money will be demanded. The money supply is given initially as M_s, so the equilibrium rate of interest will be r_1. At this rate of interest, we see from the planned investment schedule given in panel (b) that the

quantity of planned investment demanded per year will be I_1. After the shift in the money supply to M'_s, the resulting increase in investment from I_1 to I_2 shifts the aggregate demand curve in panel (c) outward from AD_1 to AD_2. Equilibrium moves from E_1 to E_2, at real GDP of $22 trillion per year.

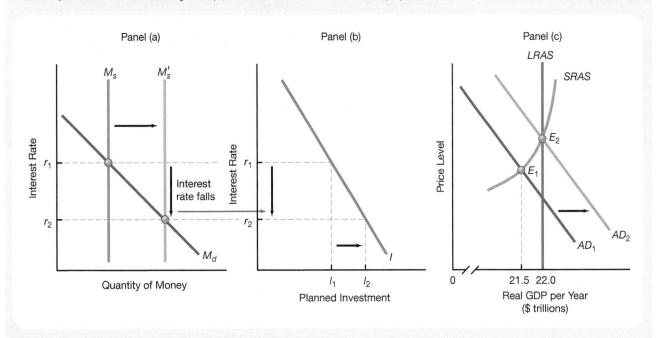

themselves with too much cash (liquidity). They buy bonds. When they buy bonds, they bid up the prices of bonds, thereby lowering the interest rate. The interest rate falls to r_2, where the new money supply curve M'_s intersects the money demand curve M_d. This reduction in the interest rate from r_1 to r_2 has an effect on planned investment, as can be seen in panel (b). Planned investment per year increases from I_1 to I_2. An increase in investment will increase aggregate demand, as shown in panel (c). Aggregate demand increases from AD_1 to AD_2. Equilibrium in the economy increases from real GDP per year of \$21.5 trillion, which is not on the *LRAS*, to equilibrium real GDP per year of \$22 trillion, which is on the *LRAS*.

Targeting the Federal Funds Rate As we have seen, the Fed can influence interest rates only by actively entering the market for federal government securities (usually Treasury bills). So, if the Fed wants to raise "the" interest rate, it essentially must engage in contractionary open market operations. That is to say, it must sell more Treasury securities than it buys, thereby reducing total reserves in the banking system and, hence, the money supply. This tends to boost the rate of interest. Conversely, when the Fed wants to decrease "the" rate of interest, it engages in expansionary open market operations, thereby increasing reserves and the money supply. But what interest rate is the Fed attempting to change?

In reality, more than one interest rate matters for Fed policymaking. Three interest rates are particularly relevant.

Federal funds market
A private market (made up mostly of banks) in which banks can borrow reserves from other banks that want to lend them. Federal funds are usually lent for overnight use.

1. ***The Federal Funds Rate.*** In normal times, depository institutions wishing to borrow funds rarely seek to borrow directly from the Fed. In years past, this was because the Fed would not lend them all they wanted to borrow. Instead, the Fed encouraged banks to obtain funds in the **federal funds market** when they wanted to expand their reserves. The federal funds market is an interbank market in reserves where one bank borrows the excess reserves—resources held voluntarily over and above required reserves—of another. The generic term *federal funds* refers to the borrowing or lending of reserve funds that are usually repaid within the same 24-hour period.

   Depository institutions that borrow in the federal funds market pay an interest rate called the **federal funds rate**. Because the federal funds rate is a ready measure of the cost that banks must incur to raise funds, the Federal Reserve often uses it as a yardstick by which to measure the effects of its policies. Consequently, the federal funds rate is closely watched as an indicator of the Fed's intentions.

Federal funds rate
The interest rate that depository institutions pay to borrow reserves in the interbank federal funds market.

2. ***The Discount Rate.*** When the Fed does lend reserves directly to depository institutions, the rate of interest that it charges is called the **discount rate**. When depository institutions borrow reserves from the Fed at this rate, they are said to be borrowing through the Fed's "discount window." Borrowing from the Fed increases reserves and thereby expands the money supply, other things being equal.

   Since 2003, the Fed has set the discount rate above the federal funds rate. The differential has ranged from 0.25 percentage point to 1.0 percentage point. An increase in this differential reduces depository institutions' incentive to borrow from the Fed and thereby generates a reduction in discount window borrowings.

Discount rate
The interest rate that the Federal Reserve charges for reserves that it lends to depository institutions. It is sometimes referred to as the *rediscount rate* or, in Canada and England, as the *bank rate*.

3. ***The Interest Rate on Reserves.*** In October 2008, Congress granted the Fed authority to pay interest on both required reserves and excess reserves of depository institutions. Initially, the Fed paid different rates of interest on required and excess reserves, but since 2009 the Fed has paid the same interest rate on both categories of reserves.

Varying the interest rate on reserves alters the incentives that banks face when deciding whether to hold any additional reserves they obtain as excess reserves or to lend those reserves out to other banks in the federal funds market. If the Fed raises the interest rate it pays on reserves and thereby reduces the differential between the federal funds rate and the interest rate on reserves, banks have less incentive to lend reserves in the federal funds market. Thus because the interest rate on reserves has been close to the federal funds rate, it is not surprising that excess reserves in the U.S. banking system currently amount to more than $2 trillion, as discussed in more detail later in this chapter.

Establishing the Fed Policy Strategy The policy decisions that determine open market operations by which the Fed pursues its announced objective for the federal funds rate are made by the Federal Open Market Committee (FOMC). Every six to eight weeks, the voting members of the FOMC—the seven Fed board governors and five regional bank presidents—determine the Fed's general strategy of open market operations.

The FOMC outlines its strategy in a document called the **FOMC Directive**. This document lays out the FOMC's general economic objectives, establishes short-term federal funds rate objectives, and specifies target ranges for money supply growth. After each meeting, the FOMC issues a brief statement to the media, which then publish stories about the Fed's action or inaction and what it is likely to mean for the economy. Typically, these stories have headlines such as "Fed Cuts Key Interest Rate," "Fed Acts to Push Up Interest Rates," or "Fed Decides to Leave Interest Rates Alone."

FOMC Directive
A document that summarizes the Federal Open Market Committee's general policy strategy, establishes near-term objectives for the federal funds rate, and specifies target ranges for money supply growth.

The Trading Desk The FOMC leaves the task of implementing the Directive to officials who manage an office at the Federal Reserve Bank of New York known as the **Trading Desk**. The media spend little time considering how the Fed's Trading Desk conducts its activities, taking for granted that the Fed can implement the policy action that it has announced to the public. The Trading Desk's open market operations typically are confined to a one-hour interval each weekday morning.

Trading Desk
An office at the Federal Reserve Bank of New York charged with implementing monetary policy strategies developed by the Federal Open Market Committee.

The Taylor Rule In 1990, John Taylor of Stanford University suggested a relatively simple equation that the Fed might use for the purpose of selecting a federal funds rate target. This equation would direct the Fed to set the federal funds rate target based on an estimated long-run *real* interest rate, the current deviation of the actual inflation rate from the Fed's inflation objective, and the proportionate gap between actual real GDP per year and a measure of *potential* real GDP per year. Taylor and other economists have applied his equation, which has become known as the **Taylor rule**, to actual Fed policy choices. They have concluded that the Taylor rule's recommendations for federal funds rate target values come close to the actual targets the Fed should contemplate selecting over time.

Taylor rule
An equation that specifies a federal funds rate target based on an estimated long-run real interest rate, the current deviation of the actual inflation rate from the Federal Reserve's inflation objective, and the gap between actual real GDP per year and a measure of potential real GDP per year.

Plotting the Taylor Rule on a Graph The Federal Reserve Bank of St. Louis now regularly tracks target levels for the federal funds rate predicted by a basic Taylor-rule equation. Figure 16-8 displays paths of both the actual federal funds rate (the orange line) and the Taylor-rule recommendation if the Fed's inflation objective (the green line) is 0 percent inflation.

Assessing the Stance of Fed Policy with the Taylor Rule Suppose that the actual federal funds rate is *below* the rate implied by a 0 percent inflation goal. In this situation, the Taylor rule implies that the Fed's policymaking is expansionary. As a consequence, the actual inflation rate will rise above 0 percent. Since 2010, the actual federal funds rate has been below the level consistent with a 0 percent inflation rate. This implies that Fed policymaking has been sufficiently expansionary to be expected to yield a long-run inflation rate in excess of 0 percent per year.

Until just after the beginning of this century, the actual federal funds rate remained close to the Taylor-rule predictions over time. In recent years, however, the Fed has failed to set its federal funds rate target in a manner consistent with the Taylor rule.

Is central bank policymaking a precise science or an example of behavioral sluggishness and overreaction?

FIGURE 16-8

Actual Federal Funds Rates and Values Predicted by a Taylor Rule

This figure displays both the actual path of the federal funds rate since 2006 and the target paths specified by a Taylor-rule equation for a Federal Reserve annual inflation objective of 0 percent.

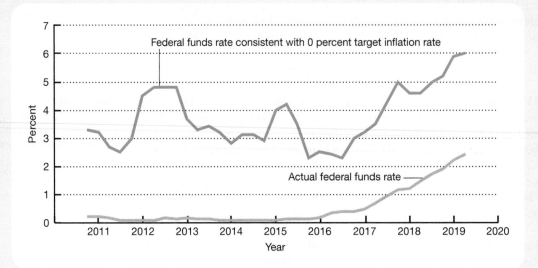

Source: Federal Reserve Bank of St. Louis; *Monetary Trends,* various issues.

BEHAVIORAL EXAMPLE

Do Central Bank Policymakers Shape Global Events or, Like Many Other People, React to Them?

Officials at the Federal Reserve and other central banks commonly discuss their activities using precise, scientific terminology. These officials often make statements such as the following paraphrased example: "We seek to actively adjust policy instruments with an aim to achieve values for intermediate economic and financial targets that we have found to be consistent with attainment of ultimate economic objectives." Studies of central banks' policy actions, however, do not always support the notion that central bank officials actually conduct policies that shape economic outcomes in this manner.

For instance, some behavioral economists have found evidence that officials of the central banks of New Zealand, Norway, and Sweden have persistently failed to make timely use of readily available information about events that affect their nations' economies. The consequence is that those officials typically react belatedly to such events and add to variability within their economies instead of reducing it. Based on a separate analysis of Federal Reserve policymaking, other behavioral economists have concluded that a key determinant of Fed policymaking is the average overall price of shares traded in stock markets. The Fed reacts particularly strongly, this evidence indicates, to *decreases* in average stock prices—so strongly that about 20 percent of the Fed policy response to a stock-market drop is an overreaction in relation to the effect of the drop on overall economic activity.

Thus, central bank policymaking does not necessarily exhibit scientific precision. Central bank officials can be so slow to respond to some events that they *contribute* to economic volatility, and they sometimes persistently overreact to other occurrences in ways that also add to variability in nationwide economic conditions.

FOR CRITICAL THINKING

Do you suppose that people who currently have positions as central bank officials respond to economic events any more speedily or with any more scientific precision than people now in business who previously worked as central bank policymakers?

Sources are listed at the end of this chapter.

Credit Policy at Today's Fed

Credit policy
Federal Reserve policymaking involving direct lending to financial and nonfinancial firms.

Federal Reserve policymakers continue to announce a target value for the federal funds rate. During and following the late-2000s financial meltdown, however, the Fed pursued a new approach to policymaking, called **credit policy**, under which it directly extended credit to specific banks, other financial intermediaries, and even nonfinancial companies. When Fed officials initiated this new policy approach in 2008, they indicated their intention to make it a temporary undertaking. In reality, the Fed has continued credit policy alongside traditional monetary policy.

The Credit Policy Approach in Practice When hundreds of banking institutions found themselves struggling to avoid severe illiquidity and bankruptcy in 2008, the Fed introduced a number of programs through which it provided credit directly to these institutions. The Fed auctioned funds to banking institutions and also bought many debt securities held by a number of these institutions.

In addition, the Fed purchased some of the debts of auto finance companies and then later allowed the companies to obtain bank charters so that they could receive direct loans from the Fed's discount window. The Fed also provided short-term emergency financing arrangements for nonfinancial firms, such as Caterpillar, Inc. and Toyota. (Note that the Fed had engaged in none of these varied forms of credit policy activities prior to 2008.)

In recent years, the Fed has cut by about half these extensions of credit to institutions and firms. Nevertheless, many of the debts that it purchased from banks and other firms have long *maturities*—periods of time before full repayments are due. This situation is quite different from the situation prior to 2008, when only a small portion of the Fed's assets had lengthy maturities.

Furthermore, a number of the debts the Fed has purchased from private institutions are relatively risky mortgage obligations. This state of affairs is also quite different from the situation in preceding years, when the bulk of the Fed's assets, about 80 percent of which were U.S. government securities, carried very low risks of loss.

How the Fed Has Financed the Credit It Has Extended In an important sense, the Fed's credit policy has more closely resembled that of a private bank than a central bank. Like a private banking institution, the Fed has extended credit by lending out funds that it obtains from depositors. Unlike private banks, however, the Fed holds deposits of banking institutions instead of deposits of households and firms. These deposits consist of the reserve deposits that banks hold with Federal Reserve banks.

To engage in its active and substantial credit policy, the Fed had to induce private banks to maintain substantial reserve deposits with the Federal Reserve banks. A key inducement has been the interest rate the Fed pays on reserves. The Fed's policy has been to pay an interest rate on reserves that is higher than the market clearing federal funds rate. Thus, banks have earned more by setting funds aside in reserve deposit accounts at Federal Reserve banks than by lending to other banks in the federal funds market. This means that the Fed essentially has paid banks a per-unit *subsidy* to keep trillions of dollars on deposit with the Fed.

All such funds held at Federal Reserve banks do not remain idle, though. Just as private banks can use the deposits of households and firms to fund loans and purchases of securities, the Fed can use the reserve deposits of private banks to fund its own lending and securities-buying activities. Between 2008 and 2017, total reserve deposits at Federal Reserve banks rose from less than $50 billion to in excess of *$2.5 trillion*. A large portion of these funds financed the Fed's credit policy—lending to domestic and foreign banks, nonfinancial companies, and central banks and buying risky, longer-term mortgage obligations.

Arguments in Favor of the Fed's Credit Policy Three arguments supported the Federal Reserve's credit policy:

1. *Giving Banks Time to Recover from the Financial Meltdown.* The original rationale for initiating the credit policy was to address the deteriorating condition of the U.S. banking industry that began in 2007. As more and more banks weakened during 2008 and 2009, the Fed created an array of lending programs aimed at countering the fact that institutions were less willing to lend to one another in private markets. These new Fed lending programs made banks much more liquid than they would have been otherwise, which ensured their ability to withstand bank

runs. The Fed's lending programs also succeeded in keeping many otherwise insolvent banks—those for which the value of assets dropped below the value of liabilities—afloat until they could become more economically viable. A few large institutions ultimately could not continue as stand-alone banks, and hundreds of smaller community banks failed. Nevertheless, the programs provided "breathing space" until other financial institutions could acquire those banks and their lower-valued assets.

2. *Making Financial Markets and Institutions More Liquid and Solvent.* The Fed's purchases of debt securities also helped make financial markets and institutions more liquid and solvent. At the height of the financial crisis, the Fed's purchases of debt securities from companies such as Ford Motor Company and Harley-Davidson, Inc. ensured that these otherwise profitable and solvent firms remained liquid. The Fed's later purchases of mortgage-obligation debt securities removed many high-risk assets from banks' balance sheets and thereby improved the banks' longer-term solvency prospects.

3. *Contributing to International Financial Liquidity.* Finally, the credit extended by the Fed to foreign private banks and central banks enabled these institutions to maintain holdings of U.S. dollars. This credit policy action helped ensure liquidity in international financial markets.

Thus, the Fed's credit policy activities did much to help prevent banks, firms, and financial markets from becoming illiquid, which undoubtedly forestalled possible bank runs in 2008 and 2009. Its credit policy actions also prevented a number of bank failures.

Arguments against the Fed's Credit Policy Critics of the Fed's credit policy have offered three arguments against it.

1. *Providing an Incentive for Institutions to Operate Less Efficiently.* Critics point out that the Fed is capable of creating as much liquidity as desired via open market purchases. These critics worry that the Fed encourages institutions to which it directs credit to operate with less attention to minimizing operating costs than they would otherwise.

2. *Reducing Incentives to Screen and Monitor in Order to Limit Asymmetric Information Problems.* Critics of the Fed argue that preventing insolvencies via this credit policy interferes with the functions of private institutions and markets in identifying and addressing asymmetric information problems. If banks know the Fed will bail them out, critics suggest, banks will do poorer jobs of screening and monitoring borrowers. Hence, in the longer term, the Fed's credit policy could broaden the scope of asymmetric information problems.

3. *Making Monetary Policy Less Effective.* Critics suggest that the Fed has pursued its credit policy so vigorously that its performance in the realm of monetary policy has worsened. They point out that while the Fed was providing credit to many individual institutions and firms, difficulties in predicting how these actions would affect the money supply contributed to substantial swings in monetary aggregates. In fact, although quantitative easing policies when the interest rate was near zero raised bank reserves to more than $2.5 trillion, the Fed's payment of interest on reserves induced banks to hold those reserves idle at Federal Reserve banks. Thus, the reserve ratio increased, and the money multiplier fell. On net, therefore, the money supply failed to grow very much in response to the Fed's quantitative easing. Indeed, over some intervals the money supply even declined.

Since 2017, the Fed has cut back on the extent of its credit policy. The Fed has gradually reduced its holdings of private loans. As the value of private assets it holds has decreased, the quantity of excess bank reserves held as liabilities at Federal Reserve banks has declined by nearly $1 trillion. Nevertheless, the Fed has yet to exit fully from its credit-policy-related activities.

ECONOMICS IN YOUR LIFE

A Central Bank Takes Inflation Control to an Entirely Different Level

Bank Indonesia, the Indonesian central bank, has demonstrated that it understands the equation of exchange. Recently, the central bank demonstrated that it could bring about a reduction in the nation's annual inflation rate by reducing the rate of growth of the money supply.

Suharman Tabrani, an official based at one of Bank Indonesia's 500 field offices spread across the nation's 34 provinces, recently mobilized his office's unit of the central bank's Regional Inflation Control Team. Data collected by central bank statisticians indicated a sudden jump in the price of chilies—a significant consumption good in Indonesia—within the jurisdiction of Tabrani's office. In addition to the usual central bank task of utilizing changes in the money supply to influence the nation's inflation rate, officials at Bank Indonesia have the power to investigate sudden increases in the prices of individual items with an aim to hold down inflation directly. Indeed, Bank Indonesia's inflation-control unit has marshaled police powers to examine whether sellers of chilies have conspired to push up prices across a number of provinces. The unit quickly determined that a chili-pricing conspiracy had indeed generated higher chili prices

across much of Indonesia. As Bank Indonesia filed charges against the sellers for illegally boosting prices of the key food item, it began to investigate whether prices of fuels not subsidized by the government were rising too rapidly.

FOR CRITICAL THINKING

Why do you suppose that critics of Bank Indonesia's Regional Inflation Control Team argue that it could much more effectively decrease the overall inflation rate by further reducing growth of the nation's money supply?

REAL APPLICATION

Suppose that you become an adviser to the Fed. You notice that the prices of running shoes, snowboards, BMX bicycles, and streaming services are rising much faster than the prices of other goods and services. Would you tell the Fed to launch an investigation into these rising individual prices to bring down the overall rate of inflation? Why or why not?

Sources are listed at the end of this chapter.

ISSUES & APPLICATIONS

The Increasing Interest Cost of the Federal Reserve's Credit Policy and Quantitative Easing

Tananuphong Kummaru/123RF GB Limited

CONCEPTS APPLIED

➤ Credit Policy

➤ Quantitative Easing

➤ Interest Rate on Reserves

To implement the credit policy and quantitative easing that the Fed utilized to expand the asset side of its balance sheet during the years following the U.S. 2007–2009 financial crisis, the Fed induced banks to hold large amounts of excess reserves. The Fed's inducement to banks was payment of an interest rate on reserves beginning in late 2008. Initially, the Fed's annual interest payments on excess reserves were small in relation to the Fed's total expenses. During the coming years, however, the Fed projects that its annual interest payments on excess reserves will increase to its most significant single expense item.

Why the Fed's Initially "Small" Annual Interest Payments on Reserves Will Increase

The Fed began paying banks interest on excess reserves in late 2008. Its goal was to induce banks to hold all of the reserves that the Fed had created via its credit policy and quantitative easing. But by that time, the Fed's policy actions already had pushed market interest rates very low. As a consequence, the Fed initially only had to pay an annual interest rate on excess reserves of about 0.25 percent to give banks sufficient incentive to hold all of the excess reserves that its policy actions created.

Thus, the Fed "only" had to pay about $3 billion per year in interest on the more than $2 trillion in excess reserves that it created to implement its credit policy and engage in its quantitative easing. This total annual payment to banks was "small" in relation to the Fed's overall expenses and much smaller than the interest revenues that the Fed earned each year.

How Much Does the Fed Anticipate It Will Have to Pay Banks on Their Excess Reserves in Future Years?

The Federal Reserve currently projects that market interest rates will rise during the next several years. Fed policy-making can be consistent with these higher rates of interest only if the Fed pushes up the interest rate that it pays on excess reserves and thereby increases its total annual interest payments on these reserves.

Consequently, the Fed projects that its annual payments of interest to banks on their excess reserve holdings will rise considerably. In 2019, its payments of interest on reserves amounted to nearly $20 billion. The Fed currently projects that these payments potentially could rise to as much as *$50 billion* per year.

FOR CRITICAL THINKING

Why do you think the Fed projects that the profits it receives and transmits to the U.S. Treasury likely will decrease in future years?

REAL APPLICATION

Assume that the Fed does increase the interest rate it pays for reserves sufficiently to induce banks to maintain high reserves. Could that have any effect on you?

Sources are listed at the end of this chapter.

What You Should Know

Here is what you should know after reading this chapter.

LEARNING OBJECTIVES	KEY TERMS
16.1 Identify the key factors that influence the quantity of money that people desire to hold *People desire to hold more money to make transactions when nominal GDP increases. In addition, money is a store of value that people may hold alongside bonds, stocks, and other interest-earning assets. The opportunity cost of holding money as an asset is the interest rate, so the quantity of money demanded declines as the market interest rate increases.*	money balances, 337 transactions demand, 337 precautionary demand, 337 asset demand, 338 **Key Figure** Figure 16-1, 338
16.2 Describe how Federal Reserve monetary policy actions influence market interest rates *When the Fed sells U.S. government bonds, it must offer them for sale at a lower price to induce buyers to purchase the bonds. The market price of existing bonds and the prevailing interest rate in the economy are inversely related, so the market interest rate rises when the Fed sells bonds.*	**Key Figure** Figure 16-2, 339
16.3 Evaluate how expansionary and contractionary monetary policy actions affect equilibrium real GDP and the price level in the short run *An expansionary monetary policy action increases the money supply and causes a decrease in market interest rates. The aggregate demand curve shifts rightward, which can eliminate a short-run recessionary gap in real GDP. In contrast, a contractionary monetary policy action reduces the money supply and causes an increase in market interest rates. This results in a leftward shift in the aggregate demand curve, which can eliminate a short-run inflationary gap.*	quantitative easing, 341 **Key Figures** Figure 16-3, 341 Figure 16-4, 342

PROBLEMS

16-1. Let's denote the price of a nonmaturing bond (called a *consol*) as P_b. The equation that indicates this price is $P_b = I/r$, where I is the annual net income the bond generates and r is the nominal market interest rate.

  a. Suppose that a bond promises the holder $500 per year forever. If the nominal market interest rate is 5 percent, what is the bond's current price?

  b. What happens to the bond's price if the market interest rate rises to 10 percent?

16-2. On the basis of Problem 16-1, imagine that initially the market interest rate is 5 percent and at this interest rate you have decided to hold half of your financial wealth as bonds and half as holdings of non-interest-bearing money. You notice that the market interest rate is starting to rise, however, and you become convinced that it will ultimately rise to 10 percent.

  a. In what direction do you expect the value of your bond holdings to go when the interest rate rises?

  b. If you wish to prevent the value of your financial wealth from declining in the future, how should you adjust the way you split your wealth between bonds and money? What does this imply about the demand for money?

16-3. You learned in an earlier chapter that if there is an inflationary gap in the short run, then in the long run a new equilibrium arises when input prices and expectations adjust upward, causing the short-run aggregate supply curve to shift upward and to the left and pushing equilibrium real GDP per year back down to its long-run value. In this chapter, however, you learned that the Fed can eliminate an inflationary gap in the short run by undertaking a policy action that reduces aggregate demand.

  a. Propose one monetary policy action that could eliminate an inflationary gap in the short run.

  b. In what way might society gain if the Fed implements the policy you have proposed instead of simply permitting long-run adjustments to take place?

16-4. You learned in an earlier chapter that if a recessionary gap occurs in the short run, then in the long run a new equilibrium arises when input prices and expectations adjust downward, causing the short-run aggregate supply curve to shift downward and to the right and pushing equilibrium real GDP per year back up to its long-run value. In this chapter, you learned that the Federal Reserve can eliminate a recessionary gap in the short run by undertaking a policy action that increases aggregate demand.

  a. Propose one monetary policy action that could eliminate the recessionary gap in the short run.

  b. In what way might society gain if the Fed implements the policy you have proposed instead of simply permitting long-run adjustments to take place?

16-5. Suppose that the economy currently is in long-run equilibrium. Explain the short- and long-run adjustments that will take place in an aggregate demand–aggregate supply diagram if the Fed expands the quantity of money in circulation.

16-6. Explain why the net export effect of a contractionary monetary policy reinforces the impact that monetary policy has on equilibrium real GDP per year in the short run.

16-7. Suppose that, initially, the U.S. economy was in an aggregate demand–aggregate supply equilibrium at point A along the aggregate demand curve AD in the diagram. Now, however, the value of the U.S. dollar suddenly appreciates relative to foreign currencies. This appreciation happens to have no measurable effects on either the short-run or the long-run aggregate supply curve in the United States. It does, however, influence U.S. aggregate demand.

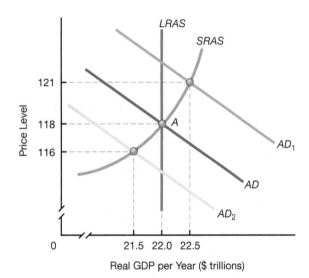

a. Explain in your own words how the dollar appreciation will affect net export expenditures in the United States.

b. Of the alternative aggregate demand curves depicted in the figure—AD_1 versus AD_2—which could represent the aggregate demand effect of the U.S. dollar's appreciation? What effects does the appreciation have on real GDP and the price level?

c. What policy action might the Federal Reserve take to prevent the dollar's appreciation from affecting equilibrium real GDP in the short run?

16-8. Suppose that the quantity of money in circulation is fixed but the income velocity of money doubles. If real GDP remains at its long-run potential level, what happens to the equilibrium price level?

16-9. Suppose that following adjustment to the events in Problem 16-8, the Fed cuts the money supply in half. How does the price level compare with its value before the income velocity and the money supply changed?

16-10. Consider the following data: The money supply is $1 trillion, the price level equals 2, and real GDP is $5 trillion in base-year dollars. What is the income velocity of money?

16-11. Consider the data in Problem 16-10. Suppose that the money supply increases by $100 billion and real GDP and the income velocity remain unchanged.

    a. According to the quantity theory of money and prices, what is the new equilibrium price level after full adjustment to the increase in the money supply?

    b. What is the percentage increase in the money supply?

    c. What is the percentage change in the price level?

    d. How do the percentage changes in the money supply and price level compare?

16-12. Assuming that the Fed judges inflation to be the most significant problem in the economy and that it wishes to employ all of its policy instruments except interest on reserves, what should the Fed do with its policy tools?

16-13. Suppose that the Fed implements each of the policy changes you discussed in Problem 16-12. Now explain how the net export effect resulting from these monetary policy actions will reinforce their effects that operate through interest rate changes.

16-14. Imagine working at the Trading Desk at the New York Fed. Explain whether you would conduct open market purchases or sales in response to each of the following events. Justify your recommendation.

    a. The latest FOMC Directive calls for an increase in the target value of the federal funds rate.

    b. For a reason unrelated to monetary policy, the Fed's Board of Governors has decided to raise the differential between the discount rate and the federal funds rate. Nevertheless, the FOMC Directive calls for maintaining the present federal funds rate target.

16-15. Suppose that to implement a credit policy intended to expand liquidity of the U.S. housing market, the Fed desires to increase its assets by purchasing a number of mortgage-backed securities. How might the Fed adjust the interest rate that it pays banks on reserves in order to induce them to hold the reserves required for funding this credit policy action? What will happen to the Fed's liabilities if it implements this policy action?

16-16. Suppose that to finance its credit policy, the Fed pays an annual interest rate of 3 percent on bank reserves. During the course of the current year, banks hold $1 trillion in reserves. What is the total amount of interest the Fed pays banks during the year?

16-17. During three intervals between 2008 and 2015, the Federal Reserve engaged in policy actions involving expanding its assets that it termed "quantitative easing." Total reserves in the banking system increased during each interval. Hence, the Federal Reserve's liabilities to banks increased, and at the same time its assets rose as it purchased more assets—many of which were securities with private market values that had dropped considerably. The money multiplier declined, so the net increase in the money supply was negligible. Indeed, during a portion of the overall period, the money supply actually declined before rising near its previous value. Evaluate whether the Fed's "quantitative easing" was a monetary policy or credit policy action.

16-18. Consider the two panels of Figure 16-2. Suppose that instructions in the latest FOMC Directive call for a monetary policy action aimed at pushing down the rate of interest prevailing in the economy. Use the appropriate panel of the figure to assist in explaining whether officials at the Federal Reserve Bank of New York's Trading Desk should buy or sell existing bonds.

16-19. Take a look at the two panels of Figure 16-2, and also consider Figure 16-1. Suppose that instructions in the latest FOMC Directive call for a monetary policy action aimed at inducing individuals and businesses to demand a smaller quantity of money. Use the appropriate panel of Figure 16-2 to assist in explaining whether officials at the Federal Reserve Bank of New York's Trading Desk should buy or sell bonds.

16-20. Take a look at Figure 16-3. Discuss a policy action that the Trading Desk at the Federal Reserve Bank of New York could undertake in order to bring about the increase in aggregate demand displayed in this figure.

16-21. Consider Figure 16-3. Discuss a policy action that the Trading Desk at the Federal Reserve Bank of New York could undertake in order to generate the decrease in aggregate demand displayed in this figure.

16-22. Take a look at Figure 16-6. Suppose that a multiple reduction in real GDP is the final outcome that the Fed desires in the last box in the figure. Explain the required directions of effects—that is, increases or decreases—that must occur in the preceding boxes in the figure in order to yield this desired decrease in real GDP.

16-23. Consider Figure 16-7. Discuss a specific monetary policy action that the Fed's Trading Desk could implement in order to induce the effects traced out by this figure.

REFERENCES

AI—DECISION MAKING THROUGH DATA: Reducing or replacing the staffs of central banks

Emily Witt and Jannick Blaschke, "ECB Data for Analysis and Decision-Making: Data Governance and Technology," European Central Bank, 2019.

Glassdoor.com, "Technical Lead of Big Data/AI in Data Services, Community Services Technology Group Federal Reserve Bank of New York" (https://www.glassdoor.com/job-listing/technical-lead-of-big-data-ai-in-data-services-common-services-technology-group-federal-reserve-bank-of-new-york-JV_IC1132348_KO0,79_KE80,112.htm?jl=2811465280), 2018.

Bank of Italy, "Harnessing Big Data and Machine Learning Technologies for Central Banks" (https://www.bancaditalia.it/pubblicazioni/altri-atti-convegni/2018-bigdata/index.html), March 27, 2018.

INTERNATIONAL POLICY EXAMPLE: Zimbabwe Switches to Using the U.S. Dollar as Its Money—for a While

Paul Wallace, "No Currency, Just a Currency Crisis: Zimbabwe's Woes Deepen," *Bloomberg*, January 15, 2019.

Colls Ndlovu, "Solution to the Cash Crisis in Zim," *Financial Times*, July 27, 2018.

"We Will Phase Out Bond Notes, Replace Them With USD Before Introducing Local Currency: Chamisa," *Zimbabwe Mail*, May 28, 2018.

BEHAVIORAL EXAMPLE: Do Central Bank Policymakers Shape Global Events or, Like Many Other People, React to Them?

Hilde Bjørnland, Leif Anders Thorsrud, and Sepideh Kahyati Zahiri, "Do Central Banks Respond Timely to Developments in the Global Economy?" *Oxford Bulletin of Economics and Statistics*, 2019.

Daniel Masciandaro and Davide Romelli, "Behavioral Monetary Policymaking: Economics, Political Economy, and Psychology," University of Bocconi Working Paper No. 105, January 2019.

Anna Cieslak and Annette Vissing-Jorgensen, "The Economics of the Fed Put," Working Paper, Duke University and University of California at Berkeley, 2018.

ECONOMICS IN YOUR LIFE: A Central Bank Takes Inflation Control to an Entirely Different Level

Bank Indonesia, "Inflation Control" (https://www.bi.go.id/en/moneter/inflasi/bi-dan-inflasi/Contents/Pengendalian.aspx), 2019.

Bank Indonesia, "Inflation Is Controlled Supported by Food Price Correction" (https://www.bi.go.id/en/ruang-media/siaran-pers/Pages/sp_203518.aspx), February 5, 2018.

The Business Times, "Indonesia to Regulate Non-Subsidized Fuel Prices to Control Inflation," April 10, 2018.

ISSUES & APPLICATIONS: The Increasing Interest Cost of the Federal Reserve's Credit Policy and Quantitative Easing

Board of Governors of the Federal Reserve System, "Decisions Regarding Monetary Policy Implementation" (https://www.federalreserve.gov/newsevents/pressreleases/monetary20181219a1.htm), 2019.

Donald Dutkowsky and David VanHoose, "Breaking Up Isn't Hard to Do: Interest on Reserves and Monetary Policy," *Journal of Economics and Business*, 2018.

Sarah Chaney and Kate Davidson, "Fed Sent Lower Remittances to U.S. Treasury in 2018: The Fed's Expenses Are Rising as It Raises Short-Term Interest Rates," *Wall Street Journal*, January 10, 2019.

APPENDIX E

Monetary Policy: A Keynesian Perspective

According to the traditional Keynesian approach to monetary policy, changes in the money supply can affect the level of aggregate demand only through their effect on interest rates. Moreover, interest rate changes act on aggregate demand solely by changing the level of real planned investment spending. Finally, the traditional Keynesian approach argues that there are plausible circumstances under which monetary policy may have little or no effect on interest rates and thus on aggregate demand.

Figure E-1 measures real GDP per year along the horizontal axis and total planned expenditures (aggregate demand) along the vertical axis. The components of aggregate demand are real consumption (C), investment (I), government spending (G), and net exports (X). The height of the schedule labeled $C + I_1 + G + X$ shows total real planned expenditures (aggregate demand) as a function of real GDP per year. This schedule slopes upward because consumption depends positively on real GDP. All along the line labeled $Y = C + I + G + X$, real planned spending equals real GDP per year. At point Y^*, where the $C + I_1 + G + X$ line intersects this 45-degree reference line, real planned spending is consistent with real GDP.

At any real GDP level less than Y^*, spending exceeds real GDP, so real GDP and thus spending will tend to rise. At any level of real GDP greater than Y^*, real planned spending is less than real GDP, so real GDP and thus spending will tend to decline. Given the determinants of $C, I, G,$ and X, total spending (aggregate demand) will be Y^*.

FIGURE E-1

An Increase in the Money Supply

An increase in the money supply increases real GDP by lowering interest rates and thus increasing investment from I_1 to I_2.

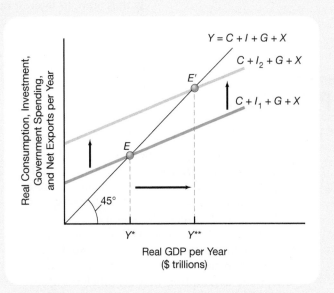

Increasing the Money Supply

According to the Keynesian approach, an increase in the money supply pushes interest rates down. This induces firms to increase the level of investment spending from I_1 to I_2. As a result, the $C + I_1 + G + X$ line shifts upward in Figure E-1 by the full amount of the rise in investment spending, thus yielding the line $C + I_2 + G + X$. The rise in investment spending causes real GDP to rise, which in turn causes real consumption spending to rise, further increasing real GDP. Ultimately, aggregate demand rises to Y^{**}, where spending again equals real GDP. Because consumption spending increases, total spending rises by *more* than the original rise in investment spending because consumption spending depends positively on real GDP.

Decreasing the Money Supply

Not surprisingly, contractionary monetary policy works in exactly the reverse manner. A reduction in the money supply pushes interest rates up. Firms respond by reducing their investment spending, and this pushes real GDP downward. Consumers react to the lower real GDP by scaling back on their real consumption spending, which further depresses real GDP. Thus, the ultimate decline in real GDP is larger than the initial drop in investment spending. Indeed, because the change in real GDP is a multiple of the change in investment, Keynesians note that changes in investment spending (similar to changes in government spending) have a *multiplier* effect on the economy.

Arguments against Monetary Policy

It might be thought that this multiplier effect would make monetary policy a potent tool in the Keynesian arsenal, particularly when it comes to getting the economy out of a recession. In fact, however, many traditional Keynesians argue that monetary policy is likely to be relatively ineffective as a recession fighter.

According to their line of reasoning, although monetary policy has the potential to reduce interest rates, changes in the money supply have little *actual* impact on interest rates. Instead, during recessions, people try to build up as much as they can in liquid assets to protect themselves from risks of unemployment and other losses of income. When the monetary authorities increase the money supply, individuals are willing to allow most of it to accumulate in their bank accounts. This desire for increased liquidity thus prevents interest rates from falling very much, which in turn means that there will be almost no change in investment spending and thus little change in aggregate demand.

PROBLEMS

E-1. Suppose that each 0.1-percentage-point decrease in the equilibrium interest rate induces a $10 billion increase in real planned investment spending by businesses. In addition, the investment multiplier is equal to 5, and the money multiplier is equal to 4. Furthermore, every $20 billion increase in the money supply brings about a 0.1-percentage-point reduction in the equilibrium interest rate. Use this information to answer the following questions under the assumption that all other things are equal.

a. How much must real planned investment increase if the Federal Reserve desires to bring about a $100 billion increase in equilibrium real GDP?

b. How much must the money supply change for the Fed to induce the change in real planned investment calculated in part (a)?

c. What dollar amount of open market operations must the Fed undertake to bring about the money supply change calculated in part (b)?

E-2. Suppose that each 0.1-percentage-point increase in the equilibrium interest rate induces a $5 billion decrease in real planned investment spending by businesses. In addition, the investment multiplier is equal to 4, and the money multiplier is equal to 3. Furthermore, every $9 billion decrease in the money supply brings about a 0.1-percentage-point increase in the equilibrium interest rate. Use this information to answer the following questions under the assumption that all other things are equal.

a. How much must real planned investment decrease if the Federal Reserve desires to bring about an $80 billion decrease in equilibrium real GDP?

b. How much must the money supply change for the Fed to induce the change in real planned investment calculated in part (a)?

c. What dollar amount of open market operations must the Fed undertake to bring about the money supply change calculated in part (b)?

E-3. Assume that the following conditions exist:

a. All banks are fully loaned up—there are no excess reserves, and desired excess reserves are always zero.

b. The money multiplier is 3.

c. The planned investment schedule is such that at a 6 percent rate of interest, investment is $1,200 billion; at 5 percent, investment is $1,225 billion.

d. The investment multiplier is 3.

e. The initial equilibrium level of real GDP is $18 trillion.

f. The equilibrium rate of interest is 6 percent.

Now the Fed engages in expansionary monetary policy. It buys $1 billion worth of bonds, which increases the money supply, which in turn lowers the market rate of interest by 1 percentage point. Determine how much the money supply must have increased, and then trace out the numerical consequences of the associated reduction in interest rates on all the other variables mentioned.

E-4. Assume that the following conditions exist:

a. All banks are fully loaned up—there are no excess reserves, and desired excess reserves are always zero.

b. The money multiplier is 4.

c. The planned investment schedule is such that at a 4 percent rate of interest, investment is $1,400 billion. At 5 percent, investment is $1,380 billion.

d. The investment multiplier is 5.

e. The initial equilibrium level of real GDP is $19 trillion.

f. The equilibrium rate of interest is 4 percent.

Now the Fed engages in contractionary monetary policy. It sells $2 billion worth of bonds, which reduces the money supply, which in turn raises the market rate of interest by 1 percentage point. Determine how much the money supply must have decreased, and then trace out the numerical consequences of the associated increase in interest rates on all the other variables mentioned.

17 Stabilization in an Integrated World Economy

primagefactory/123RF GB Limited

LEARNING OBJECTIVES

After reading this chapter, you should be able to:

17.1 Explain why the actual unemployment rate might depart from its natural rate

17.2 Describe an inverse relationship between inflation and unemployment

17.3 Understand the rational expectations hypothesis and its policy implications

17.4 Distinguish among modern approaches to active policymaking

17.5 Evaluate the implications of behavioral economics for macro policymaking

Since the 1950s, many policymakers have used as a guide a relationship called the *Phillips curve*—a hypothesized inverse relationship between the inflation rate and the unemployment rate. In theory, if such a relationship exists, policymakers could trade off higher inflation for a lower unemployment rate. During the last decade, however, this proposed inverse relationship has failed to exist in the United States. In this chapter, you will learn about the explanation behind why an inverse relationship between the inflation rate and the unemployment rate might, nevertheless, hold true. In addition, you will learn about the reality of the relationship between the U.S. inflation rate and the U.S. unemployment rate during the last decade.

the annual inflation rate in Venezuela recently has exceeded 100,000 percent, meaning that the price level in that nation was more than three times higher at the end of a typical day than it was at the beginning? If this inflation rate seems high, consider the plight of residents of Hungary during the summer of 1946, when they confronted an annualized inflation rate of 41,900,000,000,000,000 percent!

In Venezuela recently and in Hungary more than seven decades ago, government institutions allowed so much inflation partly in hopes of stimulating economic activity that would assist in reducing significant unemployment problems. Even in the United States today, it is commonplace to read media reports of politicians and economic policymakers arguing for slightly higher inflation to boost labor employment. In this chapter you will study the basis for such claims. First, though, you must learn about the argument for *active policymaking* intended to improve the economic performances of nations.

Active versus Passive Policymaking and the Natural Rate of Unemployment

17.1 Explain why the actual unemployment rate might depart from its natural rate

If it is true that monetary and fiscal policy actions aimed at exerting significant stabilizing effects on overall economic activity are likely to succeed, then this would be a strong argument for **active (discretionary) policymaking**. This is the term for actions that monetary and fiscal policymakers undertake in reaction to or in anticipation of a change in economic performance. On the other side of the debate is the view that the best way to achieve economic stability is through **passive (nondiscretionary) policymaking**, in which there is no deliberate stabilization policy at all. Policymakers follow a rule and do not attempt to respond in a discretionary manner to actual or potential changes in economic activity.

Does the application of AI-guided data-analytics techniques mean bad news for the ways that officials at the Federal Reserve and other central banks conduct active (discretionary) monetary policymaking?

Active (discretionary) policymaking
All actions on the part of monetary and fiscal policymakers that are undertaken in response to or in anticipation of some change in the overall economy.

Passive (nondiscretionary) policymaking
Policymaking that is carried out in response to a rule. It is therefore not in response to an actual or potential change in overall economic activity.

 AI | DECISION MAKING THROUGH DATA

Applying AI May Yield Results That Central Bankers Do Not Desire

Central banking institutions such as the European Central Bank and the Federal Reserve have been contemplating the use of techniques involving automated data collection and analysis as a supplement to the methods already in place at these institutions to guide active (discretionary) policymaking. Economists at central banks such as the Bank of England and Sweden's Riksbank, for instance, have investigated using automated data collection from Twitter and other social networks as guides for discretionary monetary policymaking.

So far, however, those who are evaluating results from experiments with big data techniques have reached mixed conclusions about whether the currently used policymaking methods should be supplemented or replaced. For instance, research by some central bank economists has

found that if policymakers had based their actions on movements in simple indexes of economic news, they would have done a better job of meeting their policy goals than by paying close attention to their own methods. Additionally, other research has indicated that rather than using analysis of automatically collected data to *supplement* standard central bank policymaking methods, it might be better to *replace* those traditional methods with the data-analytics techniques.

FOR CRITICAL THINKING

Why is it important to evaluate past performances of policymakers by taking into account only information that was available to them at the time they made their decisions? Explain briefly.

Sources are listed at the end of this chapter.

To take a stand on this debate concerning active versus passive policymaking, you first must know the potential trade-offs that policymakers believe they face. Then you must see what the data actually show. One possible policy trade-off may be between price stability and unemployment. Before exploring that, however, we need to look at the economy's natural, or long-run, rate of unemployment.

The Natural Rate of Unemployment

Recall that there are different types of unemployment: frictional, cyclical, structural, and seasonal. *Frictional unemployment* arises because individuals take the time to search for the best job opportunities. Much unemployment is of this type, except when the economy is in a recession or a depression, when cyclical unemployment rises.

The Role of Structural Unemployment Note that we did not say that frictional unemployment was the *sole* form of unemployment during normal times. *Structural unemployment* is caused by a variety of "rigidities" throughout the economy. Structural unemployment results from factors including these:

1. Government-imposed minimum wage laws, laws restricting entry into occupations, and welfare and unemployment insurance benefits that reduce incentives to work

2. Union activity that sets wages above the equilibrium level and also restricts the mobility of labor

Such factors reduce individuals' abilities or incentives to choose employment rather than unemployment.

The Natural Unemployment Rate Frictional unemployment and structural unemployment both exist even when the economy is in long-run equilibrium—they are a natural consequence of costly information (the need to conduct a job search) and the existence of rigidities such as those noted above. Because these two types of unemployment arise naturally from imperfect and costly information, they are components of what economists call the **natural rate of unemployment**. As we discussed in an earlier chapter, the natural rate of unemployment is defined as the rate of unemployment that would exist in the long run after everyone in the economy fully adjusted to any changes that have occurred. Figure 17-1 displays both the actual unemployment rate and estimates of the natural rate of unemployment compiled by the Congressional Budget Office.

Real GDP per year tends to return to the level implied by the long-run aggregate supply curve (*LRAS*). Thus, whatever rate of unemployment the economy tends to return to in long-run equilibrium can be called the natural rate of unemployment.

Natural rate of unemployment
The rate of unemployment that is estimated to prevail in long-run macroeconomic equilibrium, when all workers and employers have fully adjusted to any changes in the economy.

Departures from the Natural Rate of Unemployment

The unemployment rate has a strong tendency to stay at and return to the natural rate. It is possible for other factors, such as changes in private spending or fiscal and monetary policy actions to move the actual unemployment rate away from the natural rate, at least in the short run. Deviations of the actual unemployment rate from the natural rate are called *cyclical unemployment* because they are observed over the course of nationwide business fluctuations. During recessions, the overall unemployment rate exceeds the natural rate, so cyclical unemployment is positive. During periods of economic booms, the overall unemployment rate can go below the natural rate. At such times, cyclical unemployment is negative.

To see how departures from the natural rate of unemployment can occur, let's consider two examples. In Figure 17-2, we begin in equilibrium at point E_1 with the associated price level 117 and real GDP per year of $22 trillion.

The Impact of Expansionary Policy Now imagine that the government decides to use fiscal or monetary policy to stimulate the economy. Further suppose, for reasons that will soon become clear, that this policy surprises decision makers

FIGURE 17-1

The Actual U.S. Unemployment Rate and Congressional Budget Office Estimates of the Natural Rate of Unemployment

As you can see, the actual U.S. rate of unemployment has exhibited considerable variability in recent decades. Congressional Budget Office estimates of the natural unemployment rate have exhibited considerably less short-term variation but instead have changed more gradually over time.

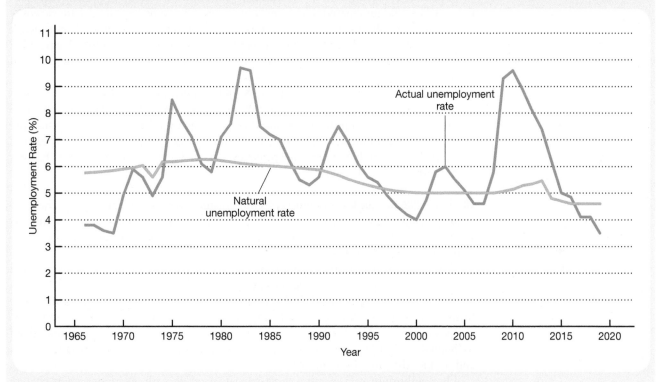

Sources: Economic Report of the President; Economic Indicators, various issues; author's estimates; Congressional Budget Office.

FIGURE 17-2

Impact of an Increase in Aggregate Demand on Real GDP and Unemployment

Point E_1 is an initial short-run and long-run equilibrium. An expansionary monetary or fiscal policy shifts the aggregate demand curve outward to AD_2. The price level rises from 117 to 120 at point E_2, and real GDP per year increases to $22.4 trillion in base-year dollars. The unemployment rate is now below its natural rate at the short-run equilibrium point E_2. As expectations of input owners are revised, the short-run aggregate supply curve shifts from $SRAS_1$ to $SRAS_2$ because of higher prices and higher input costs. Real GDP returns to the *LRAS* level of $22 trillion per year, at point E_3. The price level increases to 122. The unemployment rate returns to the natural rate.

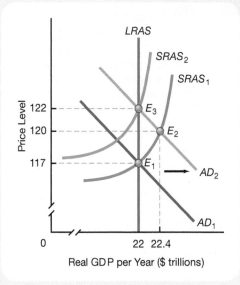

throughout the economy in the sense that they did not anticipate that the policy would occur.

As shown in Figure 17-2, the expansionary policy action causes the aggregate demand curve to shift from AD_1 to AD_2. The price level rises from 117 to 120. Real GDP, measured in base-year dollars, increases from $2 trillion to $22.4 trillion.

In the labor market, individuals find that conditions have improved markedly relative to what they anticipated. Firms seeking to expand output want to hire more workers. To accomplish this, they recruit more actively and possibly ask workers to work overtime, so individuals in the labor market find more job openings and more possible hours they can work. Consequently, the average duration of unemployment falls, and so does the unemployment rate.

The $SRAS$ curve does not stay at $SRAS_1$ indefinitely, however. Input owners, such as workers and owners of capital and raw materials, revise their expectations. The short-run aggregate supply curve shifts to $SRAS_2$ as input prices rise. We find ourselves at a new equilibrium at E_3, which is on the $LRAS$. Long-run real GDP per year is $22 trillion again, but at a higher price level, 122. The unemployment rate returns to its original, natural level.

The Consequences of Contractionary Policy Instead of expansionary policy, the government could have decided to engage in contractionary (or deflationary) policy. As shown in Figure 17-3, the sequence of events would have been in the opposite direction of those in Figure 17-2.

Beginning from an initial equilibrium E_1, an unanticipated reduction in aggregate demand puts downward pressure on both prices and real GDP. The price level falls from 120 to 118, and real GDP declines from $22 trillion to $21.7 trillion. Fewer firms are hiring, and those that are hiring offer fewer overtime possibilities. Individuals looking for jobs find that it takes longer than predicted. As a result, unemployed individuals remain unemployed longer. The average duration of unemployment rises, and so does the rate of unemployment.

The equilibrium at E_2 is only a short-run situation, though. As input owners change their expectations about future prices, $SRAS_1$ shifts to $SRAS_2$, and input prices fall. The new long-run equilibrium is at E_3, which is on the long-run aggregate supply curve, $LRAS$. In the long run, the price level declines further, to 116, as real GDP returns to $22 trillion. Thus, in the long run the unemployment rate returns to its natural level.

FIGURE 17-3

Impact of a Decline in Aggregate Demand on Real GDP and Unemployment

Starting from equilibrium at E_1, a decline in aggregate demand to AD_2 leads to a lower price level, 118, and real GDP declines to $21.7 trillion. The unemployment rate will rise above the natural rate of unemployment. Equilibrium at E_2 is temporary, however. At the lower price level, the expectations of input owners are revised. $SRAS_1$ shifts to $SRAS_2$. The new long-run equilibrium is at E_3, with real GDP equal to $22 trillion and a price level of 116. The actual unemployment rate is once again equal to the natural rate of unemployment.

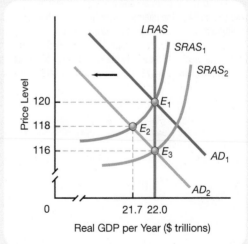

The Phillips Curve: A Rationale for Active Policymaking?

17.2 Describe an inverse relationship between inflation and unemployment

Let's recap what we have just observed. In the short run, an *unanticipated increase* in aggregate demand causes the price level to rise and the unemployment rate to fall. Conversely, in the short run, an *unanticipated decrease* in aggregate demand causes the price level to fall and the unemployment rate to rise. Moreover, although not shown explicitly in Figure 17-2 and Figure 17-3, two additional points are true:

1. The greater the unanticipated increase in aggregate demand, the greater the amount of inflation that results in the short run, and the lower the unemployment rate.

2. The greater the unanticipated decrease in aggregate demand, the greater the deflation that results in the short run, and the higher the unemployment rate.

The Negative Short-Run Relationship between Inflation and Unemployment

Figure 17-4 summarizes these predictions. The inflation rate (*not* the price level) is measured along the vertical axis, and the unemployment rate is measured along the horizontal axis. Panel (a) shows the unemployment rate at a natural rate denoted U_N that is assumed to be 5 percent at point A. At this point, the actual inflation rate and expected inflation rate are both equal to 0 percent. Panel (b) of Figure 17-4 depicts the effects of unanticipated changes in aggregate demand. In panel (b), an unanticipated increase in aggregate demand causes the price level to rise—the inflation rate rises to 3 percent per year—and causes the unemployment rate to fall to 4 percent. Thus, the economy moves upward to the left from A to B.

Conversely, in the short run, unanticipated decreases in aggregate demand cause the price level to fall and the unemployment rate to rise above the natural rate. In panel (b), the price level declines—the *deflation* rate is 1 percent—and the unemployment rate rises to 8 percent. The economy moves from point A to point C. If we look at both increases and decreases in aggregate demand, we see that high inflation rates tend to be associated with low unemployment rates (as at B) and that low (or negative) inflation rates tend to be accompanied by high unemployment rates (as at C).

FIGURE 17-4

The Phillips Curve

Unanticipated changes in aggregate demand produce a negative relationship between the inflation rate and unemployment. In panel (a), U_N is the natural rate of unemployment, and the rate of inflation is zero at this unemployment rate at point A. Panel (b) indicates that a higher inflation rate at point B is associated with a lower unemployment rate. Deflation at point C is associated with a higher unemployment rate.

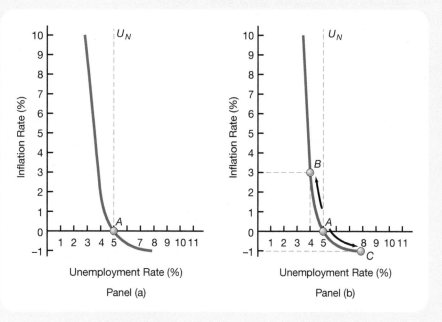

Is There a Trade-Off?

Phillips curve

A curve showing the relationship between unemployment and changes in wages or prices. It was long thought to reflect a trade-off between unemployment and inflation.

The apparent negative relationship between the inflation rate and the unemployment rate shown in panels (a) and (b) of Figure 17-4 has come to be called the **Phillips curve**, after A. W. Phillips, who discovered that a similar relationship existed historically in Great Britain. Although Phillips presented his findings only as an empirical regularity, economists quickly came to view the relationship as representing a *trade-off* between inflation and unemployment.

In particular, policymakers who favored active policymaking believed that they could *choose* alternative combinations of unemployment and inflation. Thus, it seemed that a government that disliked unemployment could select a point like *B* in panel (b) of Figure 17-4, with a positive inflation rate but a relatively low unemployment rate. Conversely, a government that feared inflation could choose a stable price level at *A*, but only at the expense of a higher associated unemployment rate. Indeed, the Phillips curve seemed to suggest that it was possible for discretionary policymakers to fine-tune the economy by selecting the policies that would produce the exact mix of unemployment and inflation that suited current government objectives. As it turned out, matters are not so simple.

The Importance of Expectations

The reduction in unemployment that takes place as the economy moves from *A* to *B* in Figure 17-4 occurs because the wage offers encountered by unemployed workers are unexpectedly high. As far as the workers are concerned, these higher *nominal* wages appear, at least initially, to be increases in *real* wages. It is this perception that induces them to reduce the duration of their job search. This is a sensible way for the workers to view the world if aggregate demand fluctuates up and down at random, with no systematic or predictable variation one way or another.

If activist policymakers attempt to exploit the apparent trade-off in the Phillips curve, however, according to economists who support passive policymaking, aggregate demand will no longer move up and down in an *unpredictable* way.

The Effects of an Unanticipated Policy Consider, for example, Figure 17-5. If the Federal Reserve attempts to reduce the unemployment rate to 4 percent, it must increase

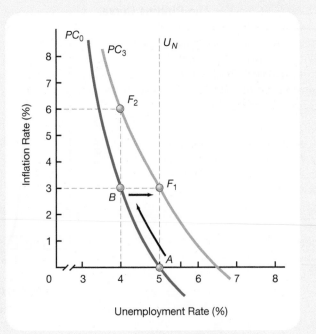

FIGURE 17-5

A Shift in the Phillips Curve

When there is a change in the expected inflation rate, the Phillips curve (*PC*) shifts to incorporate the new expectations. PC_0 shows expectations of zero inflation. PC_3 reflects a higher expected inflation rate, such as 3 percent.

the rate of growth of the money supply enough to produce an inflation rate of 3 percent. If this is an unanticipated one-shot action in which the rate of growth of the money supply is first increased and then returned to its previous level, the inflation rate will temporarily rise to 3 percent, and the unemployment rate will temporarily fall to 4 percent.

Proponents of passive policymaking contend that past experience with active policies indicates that after the money supply stops growing, the inflation rate will soon return to zero and unemployment will return to 5 percent, its natural rate. Thus, an unanticipated temporary increase in money supply growth will cause a movement from point A to point B, and the economy will move on its own back to A.

Adjusting Expectations and a Shifting Phillips Curve

Why do those advocating passive policymaking argue that variations in the unemployment rate from its natural rate typically are temporary? If, for instance, activist Federal Reserve policymakers wish to prevent the unemployment rate from returning to $U_N = 5$ percent in Figure 17-5, they will conclude that the money supply must grow fast enough to keep the inflation rate at 3 percent. But if the Fed does this, argue those who favor passive policymaking, all of the economic participants in the economy—workers and job seekers included—will come to *expect* that inflation rate to continue. This, in turn, will change their expectations about wages.

An Example

Consider again an example in which the expected inflation rate is zero. In this situation, a 3 percent rise in nominal wages meant a 3 percent anticipated rise in real wages, and this was sufficient to induce some individuals to take jobs rather than remain unemployed. It was this expectation of a rise in real wages that reduced job search duration and caused the unemployment rate to drop from $U_N = 5$ percent to 4 percent.

If the expected inflation rate becomes 3 percent, though, a 3 percent rise in nominal wages means *no* rise in *real* wages. Once workers come to expect the higher inflation rate, rising nominal wages will no longer be sufficient to entice them out of unemployment. As a result, as the *expected* inflation rate moves up from 0 percent to 3 percent, the unemployment rate will move up also.

Implications for the Phillips Curve

In terms of Figure 17-5, as authorities initially increase aggregate demand, the economy moves from point A to point B. If the authorities continue the stimulus in an effort to keep the unemployment rate down, workers' expectations will adjust, causing the unemployment rate to rise. In this second stage, the economy moves from B to point F_1. The unemployment rate returns to the natural rate, $U_N = 5$ percent, but the inflation rate is now 3 percent instead of zero.

Once the adjustment of expectations has taken place, any further short-run adjustments to future unanticipated policy actions will take place along a curve such as PC_3, such as a movement from F_1 to F_2. This new curve is also a Phillips curve, differing from the first, PC_0, in that the actual inflation rate consistent with a 4 percent unemployment rate is higher, at 6 percent, because the expected inflation rate is higher. Of course, if future changes in policies generating a rise in the inflation rate from 3 percent to 6 percent are fully anticipated, instead of a movement from F_1 to F_2, yet another outward shift in the Phillips curve would take place.

WHAT HAPPENS WHEN...

a current decline in the *actual* inflation rate along a nation's Phillips curve is followed by a reduction in the *expected* inflation rate?

A current reduction in the *actual* inflation rate generates a downward movement along the Phillips curve, which is accompanied by an increase in the unemployment rate. In contrast, the subsequent decline in the *expected* inflation rate causes the Phillips curve to shift inward, which thereby brings about a decrease in the unemployment rate. Thus, the actual inflation rate unambiguously declines, but on net the unemployment rate tends to adjust back toward its natural level.

17.3 Understand the rational expectations hypothesis and its policy implications

Rational expectations hypothesis
A theory stating that people combine the effects of past policy changes on important economic variables with their own judgment about the future effects of current and future policy changes.

Rational Expectations, the Policy Irrelevance Proposition, and Real Business Cycles

You already know that economists assume that economic participants act *as though* they were rational and calculating. We assume that firms rationally maximize profits when they choose today's rate of output and that consumers rationally maximize satisfaction when they choose how much of what goods to consume today. One of the pivotal features of current macro policy research is the assumption that economic participants think rationally about the future as well as the present. This relationship was developed by Robert Lucas, who won the Nobel Prize in 1995 for his work. In particular, there is widespread agreement among many macroeconomics researchers that the **rational expectations hypothesis** extends our understanding of the behavior of the macroeconomy. This hypothesis has two key elements:

1. Individuals base their forecasts (expectations) about the future values of economic variables on all readily available past and current information.

2. These expectations incorporate individuals' understanding about how the economy operates, including the operation of monetary and fiscal policy.

In essence, the rational expectations hypothesis holds that Abraham Lincoln was correct when he said, "You can fool all the people some of the time. You can even fool some of the people all of the time. But you can't fool *all* of the people *all* the time."

If we further assume that there is pure competition in all markets and that all prices and wages are flexible, we obtain what many call the *new classical* approach to evaluating the effects of macroeconomic policies. To see how rational expectations operate in the new classical perspective, let's take a simple example of the economy's response to a change in monetary policy.

Flexible Wages and Prices, Rational Expectations, and Policy Irrelevance

Consider Figure 17-6, which shows the long-run aggregate supply curve (*LRAS*) for the economy, as well as the initial aggregate demand curve (*AD*$_1$) and the short-run aggregate supply curve (*SRAS*$_1$). The money supply is initially given by $M_1 =$ \$15 trillion, and the price level and real GDP are equal to 110 and \$22 trillion, respectively. Consequently, point *A* represents the initial long-run equilibrium.

Suppose now that the money supply is *unexpectedly* increased to $M_2 =$ \$18 trillion, thereby causing the aggregate demand curve to shift outward to *AD*$_2$. Given the location of the short-run aggregate supply curve, this increase in aggregate demand will cause the price level and real GDP to rise to 130 and \$22.3 trillion, respectively. The new short-run equilibrium is at *B*. Because real GDP is *above* the long-run equilibrium level of \$22 trillion, unemployment must be below long-run levels (the natural rate), and so workers will soon respond to the higher price level by insisting on higher nominal wages. The resulting increase in firms' labor expenses will cause the short-run aggregate supply curve to shift upward vertically. As indicated by the upward-sloping black arrow, the economy moves from point *B* to a new long-run equilibrium at *C*.

The price level thus continues its rise to 132, even as real GDP declines back down to \$22 trillion (and unemployment returns to the natural rate). So, as we have seen before, even though an increase in the money supply can raise real GDP and lower unemployment in the short run, it has no effect on either variable in the long run.

Anticipated Policy and the Policy Irrelevance Proposition What if people *anticipate* the policy action discussed above? Let's look again at Figure 17-6 to consider the answer to this question. In the initial equilibrium at point *A* of the figure, the

FIGURE 17-6

Responses to Anticipated and Unanticipated Increases in Aggregate Demand

A $3 trillion increase in the money supply causes the aggregate demand curve to shift rightward. If people *anticipate* the increase in the money supply and insist on higher nominal wages, the short-run aggregate supply curve shifts leftward immediately, from $SRAS_1$ to $SRAS_2$. There is a direct movement, indicated by the green arrow, from point *A* to point *C*. In contrast, an *unanticipated* increase in the money supply causes an initial upward movement along $SRAS_1$ from point *A* to point *B*, indicated by the upward-sloping black arrow. In the long run, workers recognize that the price level has increased and demand higher wages, causing the *SRAS* curve to shift leftward, resulting in a movement from point *B* to point *C*.

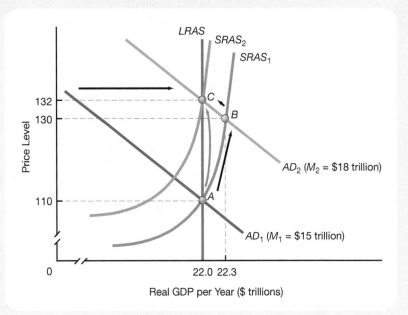

short-run aggregate supply curve $SRAS_1$ corresponds to a situation in which the expected money supply and the actual money supply are equal. When the money supply changes in a way that is *anticipated* by economic participants, the aggregate supply curve will shift to reflect this anticipated change in the money supply. The new short-run aggregate supply curve $SRAS_2$ results. According to the rational expectations hypothesis, the short-run aggregate supply curve will shift upward *simultaneously* with the rise in aggregate demand. As a result, the economy will move directly from point *A* to point *C*, without passing through *B*, as depicted by the green arrow in Figure 17-6.

The *only* response to the rise in the money supply is a rise in the price level from 110 to 132. Neither output nor unemployment changes at all. This conclusion—that fully anticipated monetary policy is irrelevant in determining the levels of real variables—is called the **policy irrelevance proposition**:

> *Under the assumption of rational expectations on the part of decision makers in the economy,* anticipated *monetary policy cannot alter either the rate of unemployment or the level of real GDP. Regardless of the nature of the anticipated policy, the unemployment rate will equal the natural rate, and real GDP will be determined solely by the economy's long-run aggregate supply curve.*

Policy irrelevance proposition
The conclusion that policy actions have no real effects in the short run if the policy actions are anticipated and none in the long run even if the policy actions are unanticipated.

Another Challenge to Policy Activism: Real Business Cycles

When confronted with the policy irrelevance proposition, many economists began to reexamine the first principles of macroeconomics with fully flexible wages and prices.

The Distinction between Real and Monetary Shocks Some economists argue that real, as opposed to purely monetary, forces might help explain aggregate economic fluctuations. These shocks may take any of the following forms:

- Technological advances that improve productivity

- Changes in the composition of the labor force

- Changes in prices of and availability of a key resource, such as oil and other key inputs used in producing energy

As you learned in a previous chapter, these shocks generate shifts in the position of the economy's aggregate supply curve. That is, these real-resource-generated shocks are aggregate supply shocks.

Most economists agree that such real shocks to aggregate supply constitute one important source of variations in the price level and real GDP. Some, however, view these real shocks as the *predominant* causes of such variations. They contend that shocks to technology and productivity, to the composition of the labor force, or to prices of and availabilities of key inputs are both frequent and significant. These economists argue, therefore, that business fluctuations largely amount to *real business cycles* caused by aggregate supply shocks.

Activist monetary and fiscal policies, of course, generate effects on aggregate demand and cannot fully offset the effects of an aggregate supply shock on *both* the price level *and* real GDP. Thus, if the real-business-cycle theory is correct, the scope for activist monetary and fiscal policymaking is limited.

Stagflation Recall from earlier chapters what happens in the event of a negative aggregate supply shock that causes the *SRAS* curve to shift leftward along the aggregate demand curve: The equilibrium price level rises, and equilibrium real GDP simultaneously declines. If these effects persist over additional periods, then the decline in real GDP will be associated with lower employment and a higher unemployment rate. Inflation also will result. Such a situation involving lower real GDP and increased inflation is called **stagflation**.

Stagflation
A situation characterized by lower real GDP, lower employment, and a higher unemployment rate during the same period that the rate of inflation increases.

The most recent period of minor stagflation in the United States occurred between 2008 and 2016. Contributing to the stagflation episode during those years were sharp increases in global oil prices. In addition, the government implemented steep increases in various marginal tax rates and placed a host of new federal regulations on firms. All these factors together acted to reduce long-run aggregate supply and hence contributed to stagflation. Increases in oil supplies, cuts in marginal tax rates, and deregulation since 2016 helped to end this stagflation episode.

17.4 Distinguish among modern approaches to active policymaking

Modern Approaches to Justifying Active Policymaking

The policy irrelevance proposition and the idea that real shocks are important causes of business fluctuations undermine the desirability of trying to stabilize economic activity with activist policies. Both criticisms of activist policies arise from combining the rational expectations hypothesis with the assumptions of pure competition and flexible wages and prices. It should not be surprising, therefore, to learn that economists who see a role for activist policymaking argue that market clearing models of the economy cannot explain business cycles. They contend that the "sticky" wages and prices assumed in Keynesian theory remain important in today's economy. To explain how aggregate demand shocks and policies can influence a nation's real GDP and unemployment rate, these economists, often called *new Keynesians*, have tried to refine the theory of aggregate supply.

Small Menu Costs and Sticky Prices

One approach to explaining why many prices might be sticky in the short run supposes that much of the economy is characterized by imperfect competition and that it is costly for firms to change their prices in response to changes in demand. The costs associated with changing prices are called *menu costs*. These include the costs of renegotiating contracts, printing price lists (such as menus), and informing customers of price changes.

Small menu costs
Costs that deter firms from changing prices in response to demand changes—for example, the costs of renegotiating contracts or printing new price lists.

Many such costs may not be very large, so economists call them **small menu costs**. Some of the costs of changing prices, however, such as those incurred by renegotiating deals with customers, may be significant.

How has a nation's government potentially contributed to small menu costs?

BEHAVIORAL EXAMPLE

What Happens When the Government Requires Prices to End with Zeroes

In 1991, the government of Israel, which uses the *shekel* as money, eliminated the 0.01-shekel coin that functioned like the U.S. penny, and in 2008 it eliminated the 0.05-shekel coin that functioned like the U.S. nickel. To prevent businesses from being able to post prices that consumers could not pay with the coins still made available by the government, in 2014 a law was passed requiring all prices in Israel to end with a zero.

Behavioral research has shown that one result of implementing this law was that because prices that previously had ended with a "nine"—for instance, 0.99 shekel or 99 shekels—had become illegal, prices now most commonly end with a "ninety"—for example, 0.90 shekel or 90 shekels.

Another implication is a widening of the differential change in price that must be made to adjust menus and price lists. The potential effect has been to increase the susceptibility of businesses' pricing decisions to the presence of small menu costs, resulting in greater price stickiness.

REAL APPLICATION

Assume that a law is passed in the United States requiring all posted retail prices to end in a zero (0). How would your economic life change?

Sources are listed at the end of this chapter.

Real GDP and the Price Level in a Sticky-Price Economy

According to the new Keynesians, sticky prices strengthen the argument favoring active policymaking as a means of preventing substantial short-run swings in real GDP and, as a consequence, employment.

New Keynesian Inflation Dynamics To see why the idea of price stickiness strengthens the case for active policymaking, consider panel (a) of Figure 17-7. If a significant portion of all prices do not adjust rapidly, then in the short run the aggregate supply curve effectively is horizontal, as assumed in the traditional Keynesian theory discussed in an earlier chapter. This means that a decline in aggregate demand, such as the shift from

FIGURE 17-7

Short- and Long-Run Adjustments in the New Keynesian Sticky-Price Theory

In panel (a), when prices are sticky, the short-run aggregate supply curve is horizontal at a price level of 118. Hence, the short-run effect of a fall in aggregate demand from AD_1 to AD_2 generates the largest possible decline in real GDP, from $22 trillion at point E_1 to $21.7 trillion at point E_2. In the long run, producers incur menu costs of reducing prices to boost their profits, which shifts the *SRAS* curve downward. The price level falls to 116 and real GDP returns to $22 trillion at point E_3. In panel (b), instead of waiting for long-run adjustments to occur, policymakers engage in expansionary policies that shift the aggregate demand curve back to its original position, thereby shortening or even eliminating a recession.

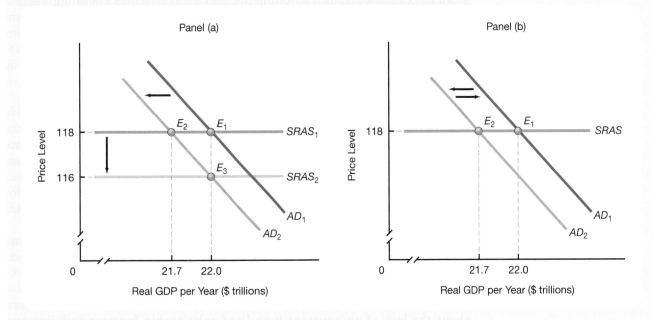

Just How Exploitable Is the New Keynesian Phillips Curve? Not all economists are persuaded that the new Keynesian theory is correct. They point out that basic theory already indicates that when prices are *flexible*, higher inflation expectations should reduce short-run aggregate supply. Such a decline in aggregate supply should, in turn, contribute to increased inflation.

Even if one were convinced that new Keynesian theory is correct, a fundamental issue is whether the new Keynesian theory has truly identified *exploitable* relationships. At the heart of this issue is just how often firms adjust their prices.

Why do temporary changes in inflation complicate efforts by policymakers to apply new Keynesian inflation dynamics to the formulation of policy actions?

POLICY EXAMPLE

Separating Temporary Inflation Variations from a Policy-Relevant Trend in Inflation Dynamics

Since new Keynesian inflation dynamics was first fully developed, policymakers have sought ways to apply the theory to dampen cyclical fluctuations by offsetting deviations of the unemployment rate from its natural level. There is a key difficulty that policymakers have faced in this endeavor, however. It is that the relationship between the actual inflation rate, firms' real per-unit costs, and the expected future inflation rate has exhibited considerable variability over time. This apparent changeability of the relationship has made it difficult for policymakers to identify appropriate actions to implement in any given period.

Recent studies provided a possible solution. These studies found ways of identifying temporary changes in the actual inflation rate that are unrelated to either inflation-adjusted per-unit costs incurred by firms

or the expected future inflation rate. Once these temporary variations in the actual inflation rate have been taken into account, what remains is a *trend*, or longer-term, new Keynesian inflation dynamics relationship. Such a trend relationship, the studies indicate, can provide a better guidepost for the formulation of appropriate policy actions.

FOR CRITICAL THINKING

Why do you think that instability in a relationship that policymakers try to use as a guidepost complicates the policymakers' efforts to formulate appropriate policy actions? Explain briefly.

Sources are listed at the end of this chapter.

17.5 Evaluate the implications of behavioral economics for macro policymaking

Behavioral Economics and Macroeconomic Policymaking

A central feature of behavioral economics is the concept of *bounded rationality*. This is the hypothesis that people are limited in their ability to consider every conceivable choice available to them. Behavioral economists propose that bounded rationality constrains individuals to rely upon simple rules of thumb to choose among the set of options that the individuals happen to identify.

What are the consequences for macroeconomic policymaking if consumers and producers are constrained by bounded rationality?

Habit Formation, Real Consumption, and Policy Effects on Aggregate Demand

Habit formation

An inclination for household choices, such as decisions to purchase goods and services, to become automatic, or habitual, through frequent repetition.

Psychologists have long studied people's **habit formation**, or the tendency for households to make certain behaviors, such as purchases of goods and services, automatic, or habitual, through frequent repetition. In recent years, economists have considered the effects of habit formation for aggregate desired real consumption spending. These economists have proposed that when people use rules of thumb to determine their desired real consumption expenditures, higher *past* consumption spending tends to be associated with more *current* consumption expenditures.

Behavioral economists argue that once people get into the habit of spending more of their real disposable income on goods and services, they tend to continue to do so in the present. Habit formation thereby implies that policies that boost current spending also cause future spending to be higher. Habit formation, therefore, strengthens the argument that policy changes can exert significant longer-term effects on aggregate demand.

Rational Inattention, Infrequent Information, and Aggregate Supply

Individuals subject to bounded rationality have difficulties taking into account all available information. A consequence might be that people experience **rational inattention**, meaning that because of the problems that households and firms confront in acquiring information, they opt to do so infrequently. This fact means that for much of the time, people do not go to the trouble to update their knowledge about the state of the economy.

This theory implies that during the periods between informational updates, people make decisions on the basis of incomplete knowledge. Proponents of the theory contend that from a macroeconomic policy perspective, one key example of imperfectly informed choices involves the pricing of goods and services. During the intervals between informational updates, firms fail to adjust product prices. Thus, consistent with the new Keynesian theory of inflation dynamics, prices of goods and services can remain unchanged during these periods. These intervals could be sufficiently long for macroeconomic policymakers to exploit with activist policies.

In addition, the rational-inattention theory indicates that people will not always possess enough information to alter their inflation expectations. During periods between updates to people's base of knowledge about economic conditions, expectations about inflation will fail to reflect fully actual changes in the inflation rate. As you learned earlier in this chapter, the result would be a downward-sloping Phillips curve along which policymakers might seek to generate movements—at least during short-run intervals between the public's informational updates.

> **Rational inattention**
> Choosing to acquire information infrequently and to make decisions based on incomplete knowledge of the state of the economy during the intervals between updates.

Summing Up: Economic Factors Favoring Active versus Passive Policymaking

To many people who have never taken a principles of economics course, it seems apparent that the world's governments should engage in active policymaking aimed at achieving high and stable real GDP growth and a low and stable unemployment rate. As you have learned in this chapter, the advisability of policy activism is not so obvious.

Several factors are involved in assessing whether policy activism is really preferable to passive policymaking. Table 17-1 summarizes the issues involved in evaluating the case for active policymaking versus the case for passive policymaking.

The current state of thinking on the relative desirability of active or passive policymaking may leave you somewhat frustrated. On the one hand, most economists agree that active policymaking is unlikely to exert sizable long-run effects on any nation's economy. Most also agree that aggregate supply shocks contribute to business cycles. Consequently, it is generally agreed that there are limits on the effectiveness of monetary and fiscal policies. On the other hand, a number of economists continue to argue that there is evidence indicating stickiness of prices and wages. They argue, therefore, that monetary and fiscal policy actions can offset, at least in the short run and perhaps even in the long run, the effects that aggregate demand shocks would otherwise have on real GDP and unemployment.

These diverging perspectives help explain why economists reach differing conclusions about the advisability of pursuing active or passive approaches to macroeconomic policymaking. Different interpretations of evidence on the issues summarized in Table 17-1 will likely continue to divide economists for years to come.

TABLE 17-1

Issues That Must Be Assessed in Determining the Desirability of Active versus Passive Policymaking

Economists who contend that active policymaking is justified argue that for each issue listed in the first column, there is evidence supporting the conclusions listed in the second column. In contrast, economists who suggest that passive policymaking is appropriate argue that for each issue in the first column, there is evidence leading to the conclusions in the third column.

Issue	Support for Active Policymaking	Support for Passive Policymaking
Phillips curve inflation–unemployment trade-off	Stable in the short run; perhaps predictable in the long run	Varies with inflation expectations; at best fleeting in the short run and nonexistent in the long run
Aggregate demand shocks	Induce short-run and perhaps long-run effects on real GDP and unemployment	Have little or no short-run effects and certainly no long-run effects on real GDP and unemployment
Aggregate supply shocks	Can, along with aggregate demand shocks, influence real GDP and unemployment	Cause movements in real GDP and unemployment and hence explain most business cycles
Pure competition	Is not typical in most markets, where imperfect competition predominates	Is widespread in markets throughout the economy
Price flexibility	Is uncommon because factors such as small menu costs induce firms to change prices infrequently	Is common because firms adjust prices quickly when demand changes
Wage flexibility	Is uncommon because labor market adjustments occur relatively slowly	Is common because nominal wages adjust speedily to price changes, making real wages flexible
Rational behavior of consumers and producers	Is atypical, which results in habit persistence that strengthens longer-term aggregate demand effects of policies and rational inattention that yields stickiness of prices and of inflation expectations	Is typical because people can readily adjust current desired real consumption spending to changes in real GDP and speedily adjust product prices and update inflation expectations

ECONOMICS IN YOUR LIFE

Rethinking "Inflation Targeting" at the Fed

John Williams, president of the Federal Reserve Bank of New York, is frustrated by the Fed's performance over the preceding several years. Each month, the Fed has announced an "inflation target"—an annualized rate of inflation that it states it has determined to be consistent with attaining its broader objectives for real GDP and the unemployment rate. During a 6-year period, however, the actual inflation rate has ended up at a level lower than the announced monthly inflation target in about 94 percent of the months.

Williams thinks that he has a solution, which he calls "flexible price level targeting." Under his proposal, suppose that the Fed's inflation target is, for instance, 2 percent. At the end of any month during which the Fed fails to generate a rise in the price level to a value 2 percentage points higher than before, it would in the following month be obliged to boost the price level at the end of the next month that is sufficiently higher to make up for its earlier target "miss." In effect, if the Fed were to deliver an annualized inflation rate below 2 percent in

the first month, it would have to aim for an inflation rate higher than 2 percent in the second month to ensure attaining a 2 percent inflation rate over the full two-month period. This procedure, Williams argues, would guarantee that the Fed would actually achieve the annual inflation rate deemed to be consistent with its ultimate economic goals.

FOR CRITICAL THINKING

How might the theory of the short-run Phillips curve be applied to motivate the idea of the Fed aiming to achieve a particular inflation target in order to attain a desired rate of unemployment?

REAL APPLICATION

If the Fed succeeds in raising the rate of inflation, are you necessarily worse off? Why or why not?

Sources are listed at the end of this chapter.

ISSUES & APPLICATIONS

The Breakdown of the U.S. Relationship between Inflation and Unemployment

CONCEPTS APPLIED

➤ Active (Discretionary) Policymaking

➤ New Keynesian Inflation Dynamics

➤ Phillips Curve

Evidence favoring the existence of either new Keynesian inflation dynamics or, more generally, the theory of the short-run Phillips curve would strengthen the case for active (discretionary) policymaking. In recent years, however, such evidence has been difficult to discern in the U.S. experience with inflation and unemployment.

A Decade of No Response of the Inflation Rate to a Drop in the Unemployment Rate

Take a look at Figure 17-9. The figure shows that over the course of the most recent decade, the U.S. unemployment rate has decreased to nearly half of its initial level, from about 9 percent to 3.5 percent.

According to the theories of new Keynesian inflation dynamics and of the short-run Phillips curve, the significant decrease in the unemployment rate should have brought about a noticeable increase in the inflation rate. In fact, the annual U.S. inflation rate remained in a range between 1 percent and just over 2 percent throughout the decade. Thus, during the decade, the U.S. relationship between the inflation rate and the unemployment rate broke down. No apparent inflation–unemployment trade-off has existed.

Alternative Interpretations of the Evidence from the Recent Decade

Two interpretations of this recent U.S. experience have been offered. Proponents of passive (nondiscretionary) policymaking favor the first of these interpretations. It indicates an absence of a relationship between the inflation rate and the unemployment rate. Hence, no policy actions intended to trade off higher inflation for lower unemployment should be pursued.

Proponents of active (discretionary) policymaking favor the second interpretation. It indicates that the failure of the inflation rate to rise as the unemployment rate has decreased was only a temporary departure from the Phillips curve trade-off between inflation and unemployment. According to this view, elements such as declining inflation expectations generated a reduction in the unemployment rate independently from changes in the actual inflation rate. If this second interpretation is correct, then in the near future a more apparent short-run trade-off between the U.S. inflation rate and the U.S. unemployment rate eventually should exist once more.

FOR CRITICAL THINKING

If the interpretation offered by proponents of passive (nondiscretionary) policymaking is correct, then if the unemployment rate were to rise during the next few years, would you expect the inflation rate to change in response? If so, would the inflation rate rise or fall?

REAL APPLICATION

Assume that you have become part of the 22,000-strong staff of the Federal Reserve System. Why might you be more likely to support active (discretionary) policymaking?

Sources are listed at the end of this chapter.

The Recent Non-Relationship between the Inflation Rate and Unemployment Rate in the United States

Both the theory of the Phillips curve and of new Keynesian inflation dynamics predict that a decrease in the unemployment rate should generate an increase in the annual inflation rate. During the most recent decade, however, the annual U.S. inflation rate has remained between 1 percent and just over 2 percent in spite of a significant decline in the U.S. unemployment rate from about 9 percent to less than 5 percent.

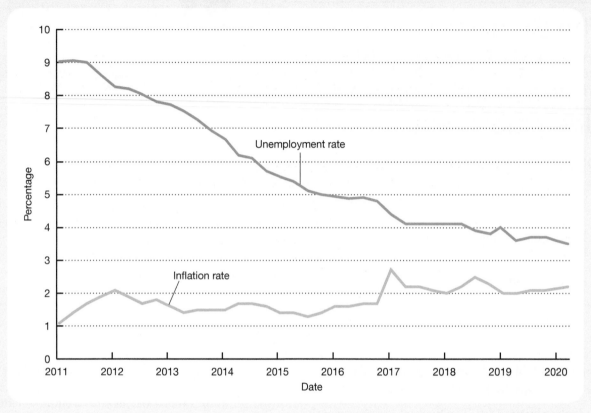

Source: Federal Reserve Bank of St. Louis.

What You Should Know

Here is what you should know after reading this chapter.

LEARNING OBJECTIVES

17.1 **Explain why the actual unemployment rate might depart from its natural rate** *An unexpected increase in aggregate demand can cause real GDP to rise in the short run, which results in a reduction in the unemployment rate below the natural rate of unemployment. Likewise, an unanticipated reduction in aggregate demand can push down real GDP in the short run, thereby causing the actual unemployment rate to rise above the natural unemployment rate.*

KEY TERMS

active (discretionary) policymaking, 363
passive (nondiscretionary) policymaking, 363
natural rate of unemployment, 364
Key Figures
Figure 17-1, 365
Figure 17-2, 365
Figure 17-3, 366

17.2 **Describe an inverse relationship between inflation and unemployment** *An unexpected increase in aggregate demand that causes a drop in the unemployment rate also induces inflation. Thus, there should be an inverse relationship between the inflation rate and the unemployment rate. If people anticipate that efforts to exploit this Phillips curve trade-off will boost inflation, the Phillips curve will shift outward.*

Phillips curve, 368
Key Figures
Figure 17-4, 367
Figure 17-5, 369

17.3 **Understand the rational expectations hypothesis and its policy implications** *The rational expectations hypothesis suggests that people form expectations of inflation using all available past and current information and an understanding of how the economy functions. If pure competition prevails, wages and prices are flexible, and people completely anticipate the actions of policymakers, so real GDP remains unaffected by anticipated policy actions. Technological changes and labor market shocks such as variations in the composition of the labor force can induce business fluctuations, called real business cycles, which weaken the case for active policymaking.*

rational expectations
  hypothesis, 370
policy irrelevance
  proposition, 371
stagflation, 372
Key Figure
Figure 17-6, 371

17.4 **Distinguish among modern approaches to active policymaking** *New Keynesian approaches suggest that firms may be slow to change prices in the face of variations in demand. Thus, the short-run aggregate supply curve is horizontal, and changes in aggregate demand have the largest possible effects on real GDP in the short run. If prices and wages are sufficiently inflexible in the short run that there is an exploitable trade-off between inflation and real GDP, discretionary policy actions can stabilize real GDP.*

small menu costs, 372
new Keynesian inflation
  dynamics, 374
Key Figures
Figure 17-7, 373
Figure 17-8, 375

17.5 **Evaluate the implications of behavioral economics for macro policymaking** *Bounded rationality tends to strengthen the case for activist policymaking. Habit formation on the part of households can cause current desired real consumption spending to depend on past consumption. As a result, policy actions have longer-term effects on aggregate demand. Rational inattention, or the infrequent updating of information about the economy, helps to explain sticky product prices and slowly adjusting inflation expectations.*

habit formation, 376
rational inattention, 377

PROBLEMS

17-1. Suppose that the government altered the computation of the unemployment rate by including people in the military as part of the labor force.

   a. How would this affect the measured unemployment rate?

   b. How would such a change affect estimates of the natural rate of unemployment?

   c. If this computational change were made, would it in any way affect the logic of the short-run and long-run Phillips curve analysis and its implications for policymaking? Why might the government wish to make such a change?

17-2. The natural rate of unemployment depends on factors that affect the behavior of both workers and firms. Make lists of possible factors affecting workers and firms that you believe are likely to influence the natural rate of unemployment.

17-3. Suppose that more unemployed people who are classified as part of frictional unemployment decide to stop looking for work and start their own businesses instead. What is likely to happen to each of the following, other things being equal?

   a. The natural unemployment rate

   b. The economy's Phillips curve

17-4. Suppose that people who previously had held jobs become cyclically unemployed at the same time the inflation rate declines. Would the result be a movement along or a shift of the short-run Phillips curve? Explain your reasoning.

17-5. Suppose that people who previously had held jobs become structurally unemployed due to establishment of new government regulations during a period in which the inflation rate remains unchanged. Would the result be a movement along or a shift of the short-run Phillips curve? Explain your reasoning.

17-6. Suppose that the greater availability of online job placement services generates a reduction in frictional unemployment during an interval in which the inflation rate remains unchanged. Would the result be a movement along or a shift of the short-run Phillips curve? Explain your reasoning.

17-7. Consider a situation in which a future president has appointed Federal Reserve leaders who conduct monetary policy much more erratically than in past years. The consequence is that the quantity of money in circulation varies in a much more unsystematic and, hence, hard-to-predict manner. According to the policy irrelevance proposition, is it more or less likely that the Fed's policy actions will cause real GDP to change in the short run? Explain.

17-8. People called "Fed watchers" earn their living by trying to forecast what policies the Federal Reserve will implement within the next few weeks and months. Suppose that Fed watchers discover that the current group of Fed officials is following very systematic and predictable policies intended to reduce the unemployment rate. The Fed watchers then sell this information to firms, unions, and others in the private sector. If pure competition prevails, prices and wages are flexible, and people form rational expectations, are the Fed's policies enacted after the information sale likely to have their intended effects on the unemployment rate?

17-9. Suppose that economists were able to use U.S. economic data to demonstrate that the rational expectations hypothesis is true. Would this be sufficient to support the policy irrelevance proposition?

17-10. Both the traditional Keynesian theory discussed in a previous chapter and the new Keynesian theory considered in this chapter indicate that the short-run aggregate supply curve is horizontal.

a. In terms of their *short-run* implications for the price level and real GDP, is there any difference between the two approaches?

b. In terms of their *long-run* implications for the price level and real GDP, is there any difference between the two approaches?

17-11. Consider the diagram, which is drawn under the assumption that the new Keynesian sticky-price theory of aggregate supply applies. Assume that at present, the economy is in long-run equilibrium at point *A*. Answer the following questions.

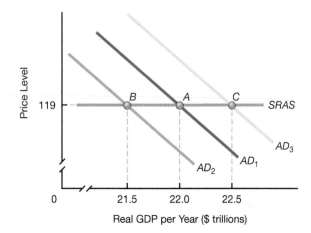

a. Suppose that there is a sudden increase in desired investment expenditures. Which of the alternative aggregate demand curves—AD_2 or AD_3—will apply after this event occurs? Other things being equal, what will happen to the equilibrium price level and to equilibrium real GDP in the *short run*? Explain.

b. Other things being equal, after the event and adjustments discussed in part (a) have taken place, what will happen to the equilibrium price level and to equilibrium real GDP in the *long run*? Explain.

17-12. Normally, when aggregate demand increases, firms find it more profitable to raise prices than to leave prices unchanged. The idea behind the small-menu-cost explanation for price stickiness is that firms will leave their prices unchanged if their profit gain from adjusting prices is less than the menu costs they would incur if they change prices. If firms anticipate that a rise in demand is likely to last for a long time, does this make them more or less likely to adjust their prices when they face small menu costs? (*Hint:* Profits are a flow that firms earn from week to week and month to month, but small menu costs are a one-time expense.)

17-13. The policy relevance of new Keynesian inflation dynamics based on the theory of small menu costs and sticky prices depends on the exploitability of the implied relationship between inflation and real GDP. Explain in your own words why the average time between price adjustments by firms is a crucial determinant of whether policymakers can actively exploit this relationship to try to stabilize real GDP.

17-14. Consider Figure 17-2. Explain whether the cyclical unemployment rate is positive, zero, or negative at point E_2, after the shift in the aggregate demand curve from AD_1 to AD_2. In addition, explain whether the cyclical unemployment rate is positive, zero, or negative at point E_3, following the shift in the short-run aggregate supply curve from $SRAS_1$ to $SRAS_2$.

17-15. Take a look at Figure 17-3. Explain whether the cyclical unemployment rate is positive, zero, or negative at point E_2, after the shift in the aggregate demand curve from AD_1 to AD_2. In addition, explain whether the cyclical unemployment rate is positive, zero, or negative at point E_3, following the shift in the short-run aggregate supply curve from $SRAS_1$ to $SRAS_2$.

17-16. Consider panel (b) of Figure 17-4, and suppose that the economy initially operates at point *A*, at which the inflation rate is 0 percent and the unemployment rate is 5 percent, which is the natural rate of unemployment. Then the inflation rate decreases to –1 percent. Does additional cyclical, frictional, or structural unemployment account for the resulting rise in the unemployment rate at point *C*? Explain briefly.

17-17. Take a look at panel (b) of Figure 17-4, and suppose that the economy initially operates at point *A*, at which the inflation rate is 0 percent and the unemployment rate is 5 percent, which is the natural rate of unemployment. Then the inflation rate increases to 3 percent. Does reduced cyclical,

frictional, or structural unemployment account for the resulting decrease in the unemployment rate at point *B*? Explain briefly.

17-18. Consider Figure 17-5, and suppose that the economy initially operates at point *A*, at which the inflation rate is 0 percent and the unemployment rate is 5 percent, which is the natural rate of unemployment. In the long run, will an increase in the inflation rate to 3 percent result in the economy operating at point *B* or at point F_1? Explain your reasoning.

REFERENCES

AI—DECISION MAKING THROUGH DATA: Yielding Results that Central Bankers do not Desire

"Computing Platforms for Big Data and Machine Learning," Conference Organized by the Bank of Italy and Bank for International Settlements (https://www.bis.org/ifc/events/boibis_jan19_ws_prog.pdf), January 14, 2019.

"Putting Big Data into Action," *Central Banking: Big Data in Central Banks Focus Report*, 2018, pp. 86–93.

Emma Glass, "Big Data in Central Banks: 2018 Survey Results," CentralBanking.com (https://www.centralbanking.com/central-banks/economics/data/3661931/big-data-in-central-banks-2018-survey-results), August 2, 2018.

BEHAVIORAL EXAMPLE: What Happens When the Government Requires Prices to End with Zeroes

Michael Guta, "Prices Ending in .99 Help Online Merchants Sell More, Study Finds," *Small Business Trends*, January 9, 2019.

Haipeng Allan Chen, Daniel Levy, and Avichai Snir, "End of 9-Endings and Price Perceptions," Working Paper, Texas A&M University, 2018.

Matthew Hudson, "Odd-Even Pricing in Retail," *The Balance Small Business*, July 22, 2018.

POLICY EXAMPLE: Separating Temporary Inflation Variations from a Policy-Relevant Trend in Inflation Dynamics

Laurence Ball and Sandeep Mazumder, "A Phillips Curve with Anchored Expectations and Short-Term Unemployment," *Journal of Money, Credit, and Banking*, 2019.

Kristin Forbes, Lewis Kirkham, and Konstantinos Theodoridis, "A Trendy Approach to UK Inflation Dynamics," Centre for Economic Policy Research Working Paper No. 12652, 2018.

Takashi Kano, "Trend Inflation and Exchange Rate Dynamics: A New Keynesian Approach," Hitotsubashi University, June 2018.

ECONOMICS IN YOUR LIFE: Rethinking "Inflation Targeting" at the Fed

Kristie Engemann, "The Fed's Inflation Target: Why 2 Percent?" Federal Reserve Bank of St. Louis *Open Vault Blog*, January 16, 2019.

Pedro Nicolaci da Costa, "An Effort to Boost the Economy That Was Once Radical Is About to Get a Fair Hearing at the Fed," *Business Insider*, May 15, 2018.

Tate Lacy, "Price Level Targeting: A Step in the Right Direction," *Cato at Liberty*, Cato Institute, June 12, 2018.

ISSUES & APPLICATIONS: The Breakdown of the U.S. Relationship between Inflation and Unemployment

David Simon, "Economic Data Are Clear: Phillips Curve Points in the Wrong Direction," RealClearMarkets.com (https://www.realclearmarkets.com/articles/2019/02/01/economic_data_are_clear_phillips_curve_points_in_the_wrong_direction_103597.html), February 1, 2019.

James Bullard, "The Case of the Disappearing Phillips Curve," 2018 ECB Forum on Central Banking, Sintra, Portugal, June 19, 2018.

Ramesh Ponnuru, "Inflation, Unemployment, and Thermostats," *National Review*, May 25, 2018.

18 Policies and Prospects for Global Economic Growth

Anton_Ivanov/Shutterstock

LEARNING OBJECTIVES

After reading this chapter, you should be able to:

18.1 Explain why population growth can have uncertain effects on economic growth

18.2 Understand why the existence of dead capital retards economic growth

18.3 Describe the growth shift from advanced nations to developing and emerging countries

18.4 Discuss the sources of international investment funds for developing nations

18.5 Identify the key functions of the World Bank and the International Monetary Fund

Four decades ago, many social scientists warned that people of the twenty-first century likely would experience extremely high levels of poverty. In fact, however, even as the global population has increased during the years since, the number of world residents classified by the World Bank as impoverished has steadily declined. In this chapter, you will learn about a global economic-growth shift away from advanced to less developed nations that has helped to bring about this reduction in global poverty. That said, you will also learn about a number of continuing impediments to economic growth in much of the developing world.

since 2008, the average number of days required to obtain a U.S. construction permit has increased from 40 to 81? In addition, the average number of days required to enforce a contract has risen from 300 to 420. Furthermore, the average cost of registering property as a percentage of the property's value has increased from 0.5 percent to 2.4 percent. The result? It is now harder to build, transfer, and use capital resources most efficiently. You will learn in this chapter that economists have consistently found in their studies of the economic development of nations that difficulties in efficient utilization of capital resources have been associated with decreased economic growth rates. First, however, let's consider the role performed by labor resources in economic development and growth.

Labor Resources and Economic Growth

> **18.1** Explain why population growth can have uncertain effects on economic growth

Currently, the world's population increases by more than 70 million people each year. A common assumption is that high population growth in a less developed nation hinders the growth of its per capita GDP. Certainly, this has been the presumption in China, where until recently the government imposed an absolute limit of one child per female resident. In fact, however, the relationship between population growth and economic growth is not really so clear-cut.

Basic Arithmetic of Population Growth and Economic Growth

Does a larger population raise or lower per capita real GDP? If a country has fixed borders and an unchanged level of aggregate real GDP, a higher population directly reduces per capita real GDP. After all, if there are more people, then dividing a constant amount of real GDP by a larger number of people reduces real GDP per capita.

This basic arithmetic works for growth rates too. We can express the growth rate of per capita real GDP in a nation as

$$\text{Rate of growth of per capita real GDP} = \text{rate of growth in real GDP} - \text{rate of growth of population}$$

Hence, if real GDP grows at a constant rate of 4 percent per year and the annual rate of population growth increases from 2 percent to 3 percent, the annual rate of growth of per capita real GDP will decline, from 2 percent to 1 percent.

How Population Growth Can Contribute to Economic Growth The arithmetic of the relationship between economic growth and population growth can be misleading. Certainly, it is a mathematical fact that the rate of growth of per capita real GDP equals the difference between the rate of growth in real GDP and the rate of growth of the population. Economic analysis, however, indicates that population growth can, under certain circumstances, affect the rate of growth of real GDP. Thus, these two growth rates generally are not independent.

Recall from an earlier chapter that a higher rate of labor force participation by a nation's population contributes to increased growth of real GDP. If population growth is also accompanied by growth in the rate of labor force participation, then population growth can positively contribute to *per capita* real GDP growth. Even though population growth by itself tends to reduce the growth of per capita real GDP, greater labor force participation by an expanded population can boost real GDP growth sufficiently to more than compensate for the increase in population. On balance, the rate of growth of per capita real GDP can thereby increase.

Whether Population Growth Hinders or Contributes to Economic Growth Depends on Where You Live On net, does an increased rate of population growth detract from or add to the rate of economic growth? Table 18-1 indicates that the answer depends on

TABLE 18-1

Population Growth and Growth in Per Capita Real GDP in Selected Nations since 1990

Country	Average Annual Population Growth Rate (%)	Average Annual Rate of Growth of Per Capita Real GDP (%)
Central African Republic	2.0	0.0
Chile	1.1	3.7
China	0.7	8.2
Congo Democratic Republic	2.8	−1.9
Egypt	1.6	2.5
Haiti	1.5	0.4
Indonesia	1.4	3.6
Liberia	3.0	−0.5
Madagascar	2.9	−1.0
Malaysia	2.0	3.8
Togo	2.5	−0.1
United States	0.9	1.5

Source: United Nations, Penn World Tables, International Monetary Fund.

which nation one considers. In some nations that have experienced relatively high rates of population growth, such as Egypt, Indonesia, and Malaysia, and, to a lesser extent, Chile and China, economic growth has accompanied population growth. In contrast, in nations such as the Congo Democratic Republic, Liberia, and Togo, there has been a negative relationship between population growth and per capita real GDP growth. Other factors apparently must affect how population growth and economic growth ultimately interrelate.

The Role of Economic Freedom

Economic freedom
The rights to own private property and to exchange goods, services, and financial assets with minimal government interference.

A crucial factor influencing economic growth is the relative freedom of a nation's residents. Particularly important is the degree of **economic freedom**—the rights to own private property and to exchange goods, services, and financial assets with minimal government interference—available to the residents of a nation.

Approximately two-thirds of the world's people reside in about three dozen nations with governments unwilling to grant residents significant economic freedom. The economies of these nations, even though they have the majority of the world's population, produce less than 20 percent of the world's total output. Only 17 nations, with 15 percent of the world's people, grant their residents high degrees of economic freedom. These nations together account for about 80 percent of total world output. All of the countries that grant considerable economic freedom have experienced positive rates of economic growth, and most are close to or above the world's average rate of economic growth.

The Role of Political Freedom

Interestingly, *political freedom*—the right to openly support and democratically select national leaders—appears to be less important than economic freedom in determining economic growth. Some countries that grant considerable economic freedom to their citizens have relatively severe restrictions on their residents' freedoms of speech and the press.

When nondemocratic countries have achieved high standards of living through consistent economic growth, they tend to become more democratic over time. This suggests that economic freedom may stimulate economic growth (some suggest that China is a counterexample), which then leads to more political freedom.

Capital Goods and Economic Growth

A fundamental problem developing countries face is **dead capital**. This term, coined by economist Hernando de Soto, refers to a capital resource lacking clear title of ownership. Dead capital may actually be put to some productive purpose, but individuals and firms face difficulties in exchanging, insuring, and legally protecting their rights to this resource.

Thus, dead capital is a resource that people cannot readily allocate to its *most efficient* use. As economists have dug deeper into the difficulties confronting residents of the world's poorest nations, they have found that dead capital is among the most significant impediments to growth of per capita incomes in these countries.

How are governmental inefficiencies hindering national investments in capital equipment that could enable utilization of AI techniques to combat the dead capital problem confronting private individuals and firms?

> **18.2** Understand why the existence of dead capital retards economic growth

Dead capital
Any capital resource that lacks clear title of ownership.

AI | DECISION MAKING THROUGH DATA

Developing Nations Could Face Big Problems

Studies undertaken by multinational institutions such as the United Nations and the World Bank have concluded that greater use of data analytics by businesses and governments of developing nations could offer substantial economic-growth payoffs. Indeed, these institutions now offer training programs in data analytics for government officials in developing countries. A key assumption, however, is that developing nations will put into place the capital equipment required to utilize the apps and machine-learning programs required to store, process, and analyze large volumes of data. In reality, some governmental inefficiencies have hindered capital investments necessary to enable employment of AI technologies in many developing countries. Developing nations will have to overcome dead capital problems and government inefficiencies holding up investments in capital equipment.

FOR CRITICAL THINKING

How might inefficiencies that weaken the delivery of education to residents of some developing nations also delay reaping gains from applications of big data techniques in businesses and governments?

Sources are listed at the end of this chapter.

Dead Capital and Inefficient Production

Physical structures used to house both business operations and labor resources are forms of capital goods. Current estimates indicate that unofficial, nontransferable physical structures valued at more than $20 trillion are found in developing nations around the world.

People in developing countries do not officially own this huge volume of capital goods, so they cannot easily trade these resources. Consequently, it is difficult for many of the world's people to use capital goods in ways that will yield the largest feasible output of goods and services.

Dead Capital and Economic Growth Recall from Chapter 2 that when we take into account production choices over time, any society faces a trade-off between consumption goods and capital goods. Whenever we make a choice to produce more consumption goods today, we incur an opportunity cost of fewer goods in the future. Hence, when we make a choice to seek more future economic growth to permit consumption of more goods in the future, we must allocate more resources to producing capital goods today. Making this choice entails incurring an opportunity cost

ECONOMICS IN YOUR LIFE

To contemplate the scope of a dead capital problem experienced by one of the world's more advanced nations, take a look at **Japan's Dead Capital Problem** on page 396.

today because society must allocate fewer resources to the current production of consumption goods.

This growth trade-off applies to any society, whether in a highly industrialized nation or a developing country. In a developing country, however, the inefficiencies of dead capital greatly reduce the rate of return on investment by individuals and firms. The resulting disincentives to invest in new capital goods can greatly hinder economic growth.

Government Inefficiencies, Investment, and Growth A major factor contributing to the problem of dead capital in many developing nations is significant and often highly inefficient and corrupt government regulation. Governments in many of the world's poorest nations place tremendous obstacles in the way of entrepreneurs interested in owning capital goods and directing them to profitable opportunities.

Overzealously administered regulations and inefficiencies created by corrupt government officials impede private resource allocation to capital goods. In a nation with a stifling government bureaucracy regulating the uses of capital goods, newly created capital will all too likely become dead capital.

How might insights from behavioral economics help developing nations fight corruption by confronting regulatory officials with some competition?

BEHAVIORAL EXAMPLE

Could Regulatory Competition Reduce Government Corruption That Undermines Economic Growth?

More than a decade ago, the United Nations ratified an agreement called the Convention Against Corruption that was intended to convince member countries to adopt national and international anticorruption laws. Economic researchers have found evidence that such reforms do reduce corruption and contribute to economic growth. Nevertheless, official corruption remains widespread in many countries, and such corruption continues to contribute to economic-growth-reducing dead capital problems.

Dmitry Ryvikin of Florida State University and Danila Serra of Southern Methodist University argue that one way of reducing the level of official corruption in developing nations might be to add an element of competition to government regulatory processes. Experimental subjects were placed in roles in which some of them had to obtain a license from other subjects who had the ability to withhold those licenses unless they received bribes. Only then could the former subjects interact within a market setting to earn profits for their business. These researchers found that if several different regulators

had the authority to grant the same licenses, those "competitive" regulators were less able to demand bribes in exchange for the business licenses. Although multiple regulators were allowed to try to collude to coordinate bribe-taking activity, competition ultimately undercut such collusion and thereby caused the extent of organized regulatory corruption to diminish. The researchers argue that implementing regulatory competition could be a means by which developing nations might reduce real-world corruption that undermines economic growth.

FOR CRITICAL THINKING

If implementation of these researchers' proposal reduced bribery of government officials, why might we anticipate the result to be a diminishment of dead capital problems that hinder economic growth?

Sources are listed at the end of this chapter.

18.3 Describe the growth shift from advanced nations to developing and emerging countries

A Recent Shift in Global Growth Trends

In a number of developing countries, residents have found that greater economic freedom, increased property-rights protection, and reduced government interference with business formation and operation promote higher economic growth. Economists commonly classify developing countries that have adopted successful growth-promoting policies and begun a transition toward a more advanced economic status as **emerging nations**. Among the developing nations typically placed within this category are China, India, Mexico, and Poland.

The continuing rise of emerging nations during recent decades has contributed to a redistribution of global economic growth. By and large, emerging nations such as China and India have experienced rapid rates of growth of per capita real GDP. At the same time, already advanced nations such as the United States and countries in Western Europe have observed diminishing rates of growth. Before considering the

Emerging nations

Developing countries that have adopted policy changes that have generated sufficiently increased economic growth to move the nations closer to advanced-nation status.

longer-term implications of this growth redistribution, let's take a look at the changing patterns of year-to-year economic growth for emerging and developing nations versus advanced countries.

Changing Growth Rates: Emerging and Developing versus Advanced Nations

Figure 18-1 displays average annual rates of growth of per capita real GDP since 1981 for all emerging and developing countries combined and for all advanced nations combined. These year-to-year average rates of growth exhibit considerable variability. Nevertheless, Figure 18-1 reveals a gradual shift in global growth patterns for these two groups of countries.

The figure shows that during the 1980s, the average annual economic growth rate for advanced countries exceeded that of developing and emerging nations. Indeed, the average year-to-year rates of growth in per capita real GDP in advanced nations were higher in almost every year of that decade.

Economic growth rates for the two groups of countries followed a similar pattern during the 1990s. Over this decade, annual rates of growth remained higher in advanced nations in most years.

Since 2000, an entirely new growth pattern has arisen, as emerging nations began to experience increased economic growth. The average annual rate of economic growth for these countries and developing nations rose to levels above the average annual growth rate for advanced nations. In fact, emerging and developing nations have observed a higher average rate of growth of per capita real GDP than advanced nations in each year since 2000.

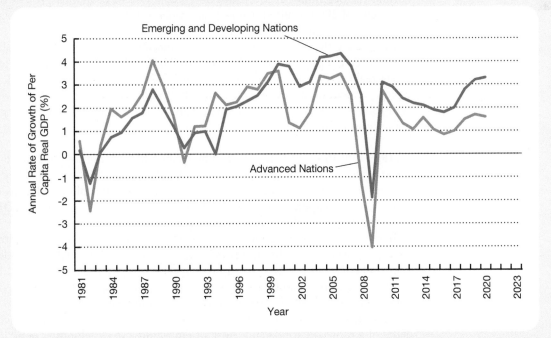

FIGURE 18-1

Annual Rates of Economic Growth in Advanced Nations versus Emerging and Developing Nations since 1981

Between the early 1980s and the beginning of this century, annual rates of growth of per capita real GDP in advanced nations remained above or close to growth rates in emerging and developing nations. Since 2000, however, the annual rate of economic growth in emerging and developing nations consistently has remained above the growth rate experienced by advanced nations.

Source: International Monetary Fund, World Bank, author's estimates.

FIGURE 18-2

A Global Growth Shift

This figure shows that average annual growth rates in the world's advanced nations have declined. In contrast, the current young generation in emerging and developing countries has experienced a higher average annual rate of economic growth than was experienced by a generation born in those parts of the world at the beginning of the 1980s.

Source: International Monetary Fund, World Bank, author's estimates.

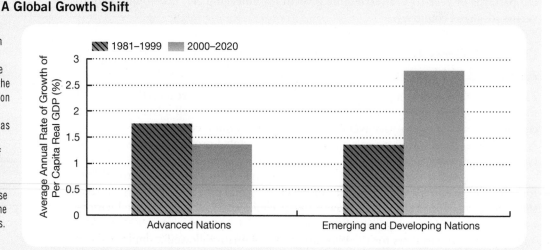

An Economic Growth Reversal: 1981–1999 versus 2000–2020

How has the change in global growth patterns of growth in per capita real GDP altered longer-term economic-growth trends for advanced nations vis-à-vis emerging and developing countries? Figure 18-2 provides the answer to this question by comparing average rates of per capita real GDP growth over longer intervals.

Average Economic Growth Rates prior to 2000 Figure 18-2 contrasts average rates of growth for the two groups of countries for two periods: 1981–1999 and 2000–2020. The blue bars display average growth rates for the groups of nations for the earlier period. They indicate that a typical resident of an emerging or developing country born at the beginning of the 1980s observed a rate of economic growth that by the beginning of 2000 resulted in a per capita real GDP about 28 percent larger than it was when that generation was born.

In contrast, the typical resident of an advanced nation born at the start of the 1980s experienced a higher rate of economic growth that brought about a 2000 level of per capita real GDP that was 37 percent larger. Naturally, these amounts indicate that a typical resident of an advanced nation, who would have begun the 1980s with higher per capita real GDP, pulled even further ahead of a resident of an emerging or developing country by 1999.

Average Growth Rates after 2000 The orange bars in Figure 18-2 display average growth rates for the two groups of nations for the 2000–2020 interval. They show that the typical resident born in an advanced nation in 2000 observed a lower annual growth in per capita real GDP. As a consequence, per capita real GDP for this advanced-nation resident was only 32 percent larger by 2020.

In contrast, a typical resident born in an emerging or developing country in 2000 has experienced a *larger* annual growth rate of per capita real GDP. As a result, between 2000 and 2020 this person's per capita real GDP rose by about 65 percent. Hence, by 2020 the per capita real GDP of an emerging or developing nation rose *closer* to the per capita real GDP of an average advanced-nation resident.

Clearly, Figure 18-2 indicates that the longer-term growth experiences of residents of advanced nations and those of emerging and developing countries born in 2000 essentially reversed in relation to those of residents born at the beginning of the 1980s. As more developing nations opted for greater economic freedom, more protections of property rights, and reduced government interference with business formation and operations, the list of emerging nations has lengthened. Economic growth rates in these nations increased, resulting in higher average growth across the entire set of emerging and developing countries. In contrast, advanced nations experienced generally slower average annual rates of economic growth that only recently have increased slightly.

Private International Financial Flows as a Source of Global Growth

Given the large volume of inefficiently employed capital goods in developing nations, what can be done to promote greater global growth? One approach is to rely on private markets to find ways to direct capital goods toward their best uses in most nations. Another is to entrust the world's governments with the task of developing and implementing policies that enhance economic growth in developing nations. Let's begin by considering the market-based approach to promoting global growth.

Private Investment in Developing Nations

Since 2005, at least $300 billion per year in private funds flowed to developing nations in the form of loans or purchases of bonds or stocks. Of course, in some years, international investors stopped lending to developing countries or sold off government-issued bonds and private-company stocks of those countries. When these international outflows of funds are taken into account, the *net* flows of funds to developing countries have averaged just over $150 billion per year since 2005. This is nearly 10 percent of the annual net investment within the United States.

Nearly all the funds that flow into developing countries do so to finance investment projects in those nations. Economists group these international flows of investment funds into three categories:

- Loans from banks and other sources

- **Portfolio investment**, or purchases of less than 10 percent of the shares of ownership in a company

- **Foreign direct investment**, or the acquisition of stocks to obtain more than a 10 percent share of a firm's ownership

Figure 18-3 displays percentages of each type of international investment financing provided to developing nations since 1988. As you can see, three decades ago, bank loans accounted for the bulk of international funding of investment in the world's less developed nations. Today, direct ownership shares in the form of portfolio investment and foreign direct investment together account for most international investment financing.

Obstacles to International Investment

There is an important difficulty with depending on international flows of funds to finance capital investment in developing nations. The markets for loans, bonds, and stocks in developing countries are particularly susceptible to problems relating to *asymmetric information*. International investors are well aware of the informational problems to which they are exposed in developing nations, so many stand ready to withdraw their financial support at a moment's notice.

Asymmetric Information as a Barrier to Financing Global Growth Recall that asymmetric information in financial markets exists when institutions that make loans or investors who hold bonds or stocks have less information than those who seek to use the funds. *Adverse selection* problems arise when those who wish to

---

18.4 Discuss the sources of international investment funds for developing nations

Portfolio investment
The purchase of less than 10 percent of the shares of ownership in a company in another nation.

Foreign direct investment
The acquisition of more than 10 percent of the shares of ownership in a company in another nation.

FIGURE 18-3

Sources of International Investment Funds

Since 1988, international funding of capital investment in developing nations has shifted from lending by banks to ownership shares via portfolio investment and foreign direct investment.

Source: International Monetary Fund (including estimates).

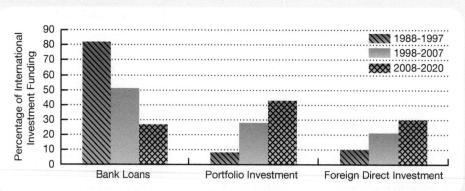

obtain funds for the least worthy projects are among those who attempt to borrow or issue bonds or stocks. If banks and investors have trouble identifying these higher-risk individuals and firms, they may be less willing to channel funds to even creditworthy borrowers. Another asymmetric information problem is *moral hazard*. This is the potential for recipients of funds to engage in riskier behavior after receiving financing.

In light of the adverse selection problem, anyone thinking about funding a business endeavor in any locale must study the firm carefully before extending financial support. The potential for moral hazard requires someone who has purchased the firm's bonds or stocks to continue to monitor the company's performance after providing financial support.

By definition, financial intermediation is still relatively undeveloped in less advanced regions of the world. Consequently, individuals interested in financing potentially profitable investments in developing nations typically cannot rely on financial intermediaries based in these countries. Asymmetric information problems may be so great in some developing nations that very few private lenders or investors will wish to direct their funds to capital investment projects. In some countries, therefore, concerns about adverse selection and moral hazard can be a significant obstacle to economic growth.

Incomplete Information and International Financial Crises Those who are willing to contemplate making loans or buying bonds or stocks issued in developing nations must either do their own careful homework or follow the example of other lenders or investors whom they regard as better informed. Many relatively unsophisticated lenders and investors, such as relatively small banks and individual savers, rely on larger lenders and investors to evaluate risks in developing nations.

International financial crisis
The rapid withdrawal of foreign investments and loans from a nation.

This state of affairs has led some economists to suggest that a herding mentality can influence international flows of funds. In extreme cases, they contend, the result can be an **international financial crisis**. This is a situation in which lenders rapidly withdraw loans made to residents of developing nations and investors sell off bonds and stocks issued by firms and governments in those countries.

An international financial crisis began in 2008. Unlike the crisis that started in 1997 and radiated outward from Southeast Asia, Central Asia, and Latin America, the 2008 crisis began in the United States. It then spread to Europe before adversely affecting most developing nations. Although economies of several Asian nations weathered the crisis relatively well, the world economy shrank for the first time in decades. The result was a temporary decline in flows of private funds to developing nations.

WHAT HAPPENS WHEN...

governments and central banks limit the amount of information that banks and other financial firms can reveal concerning the risks of loans extended to companies in developing nations?

During the financial crisis that occurred beginning in 2008, several governments and central banks, such as the U.S. government and the Federal Reserve, placed restrictions on information that U.S. financial institutions could divulge about sources of risks to international loans. These limits on openness added to the informational asymmetries that international investors confronted in trying to assess adverse selection and moral hazard risks. Investors responded by reducing flows of funds to companies based in a number of developing countries. This experience indicates that restrictions on information about lending risks encountered during financial crises typically magnify the scope of asymmetric information problems, which tends to further hinder investment flows during such crises.

International Institutions and Policies for Global Growth

18.5 Identify the key functions of the World Bank and the International Monetary Fund

There has long been a recognition that adverse selection and moral hazard problems can both reduce international flows of private funds to developing nations and make these flows relatively variable. Since 1945, the world's governments have taken an active role in supplementing private markets. Two international institutions, the World Bank and the International Monetary Fund, have been at the center of government-directed efforts to attain higher rates of global economic growth.

The World Bank

The **World Bank** specializes in extending relatively long-term loans for capital investment projects that otherwise might not receive private financial support. When the World Bank was first formed in 1945, it provided assistance in the post–World War II rebuilding period. In the 1960s, the World Bank broadened its mission by widening its scope to encompass global antipoverty efforts.

Today, the World Bank makes loans to about 100 developing nations containing roughly half the world's population. Governments and firms in these countries typically seek loans from the World Bank to finance specific projects, such as better irrigation systems, road improvements, and better hospitals.

The World Bank is actually composed of five separate institutions:

- International Development Association
- International Bank for Reconstruction and Development
- International Finance Corporation
- Multinational Investment Guarantee Agency
- International Center for Settlement of Investment Disputes

These World Bank organizations each have between 150 and 188 member nations, and on their behalf, the approximately 10,000 people employed by World Bank institutions coordinate the funding of investment activities undertaken by various governments and private firms in developing nations. Figure 18-4 displays the current regional distribution of about $50 billion yearly in World Bank lending. Although the World Bank raises some of its funds in private financial markets, governments of the world's wealthiest countries provide most of the funds that the World Bank lends each year. The U.S. government funds about half of all loans that the World Bank extends.

World Bank
A multinational agency that specializes in making loans to about 100 developing nations in an effort to promote their long-term development and growth.

The International Monetary Fund

The **International Monetary Fund (IMF)** is an international organization that aims to promote global economic growth by fostering financial stability. Currently, the IMF has more than 180 member nations.

International Monetary Fund (IMF)
A multinational organization that aims to promote world economic growth through more financial stability.

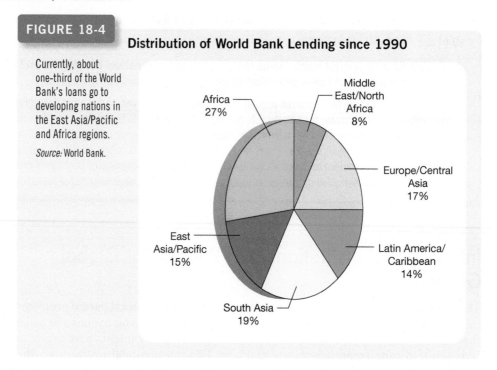

FIGURE 18-4

Distribution of World Bank Lending since 1990

Currently, about one-third of the World Bank's loans go to developing nations in the East Asia/Pacific and Africa regions.

Source: World Bank.

Quota subscription
A nation's account with the International Monetary Fund, denominated in special drawing rights.

When a country joins the IMF, it deposits funds into an account called its **quota subscription**. These funds are measured in terms of an international unit of accounting called *special drawing rights (SDRs)*, which have a value based on a weighted average of a basket of five key currencies: the euro, the pound sterling, the yen, the yuan, and the dollar. At present, one SDR is equivalent to about $1.37.

The IMF assists developing nations primarily by making loans to their governments. Originally, the IMF's primary function was to provide short-term loans, and it continues to offer these forms of assistance.

After the 1970s, however, nations' demands for short-term credit declined, and the IMF adapted by expanding its other lending programs. It now provides certain types of credit directly to poor and heavily indebted countries, either as long-term loans intended to support growth-promoting projects or as short- or long-term assistance aimed at helping countries experiencing problems in repaying existing debts. Under these funding programs, the IMF seeks to assist any qualifying member experiencing an unusual fluctuation in exports or imports, a loss of confidence in its own financial system, or spillover effects from financial problems originating elsewhere.

The World Bank and the IMF: Problems and Proposals

Among the World Bank's client nations, meager economic growth in recent decades shows up in numerous ways. Many residents of nations receiving World Bank assistance live on less than $2 per day. Hundreds of millions of people in nations receiving its financial support will never attend school, and tens of thousands of people in these countries die of preventable diseases every day. Thus, there is an enormous range of areas where World Bank funds might be put to use.

The International Monetary Fund also continues to deal with an ongoing string of major international financial crisis situations. Countries most notably involved in such crises in recent years have included Ireland, Iceland, Portugal, Spain, Greece, and Cyprus.

Asymmetric Information and the World Bank and IMF Like any other lenders, the World Bank and IMF encounter adverse selection and moral hazard problems. In an effort to address these problems, both institutions impose conditions that borrowers must meet to receive funds.

Officials of these organizations do not publicly announce all terms of lending agreements, however, so it is largely up to the organizations to monitor whether borrower nations are wisely using funds donated by other countries. In addition, the

World Bank and IMF tend to place very imprecise initial conditions on the loans they extend. They typically toughen conditions only after a borrowing nation has violated the original arrangement. By giving nations that are most likely to try to take advantage of vague conditions a greater incentive to seek funding, this policy worsens the adverse selection problem the World Bank and IMF face.

Rethinking Long-Term Development Lending Since the early 1990s, one of the main themes of development economics has been the reform of market processes in developing nations. Markets work better at promoting growth when a developing nation has more effective institutions, such as basic property rights, well-run legal systems, and uncorrupt government agencies.

Hence, there is considerable agreement that a top priority of the World Bank and the IMF should be to identify ways to put basic market foundations into place by guaranteeing property and contract rights. Doing so would require constructing legal systems that can credibly enforce laws protecting these rights. Another key requirement is simplifying the processes for putting capital goods to work most efficiently in developing countries.

Could "microlenders" do a better job than the World Bank or the International Monetary Fund in providing financial assistance to residents of developing nations who are adversely affected by natural disasters?

INTERNATIONAL EXAMPLE

Backing Up Microlenders That Provide Loans to Developing Nations' Residents after Natural Disasters

A common complaint about financial assistance that the World Bank and IMF provide to developing countries whose residents experience natural disasters is that such loans typically are granted to national governments rather than to individuals. Bureaucratic red tape delays the transmission of funding, and governmental inefficiencies and corruption siphon off portions of the loans for unrelated purposes. Hence, people who would most benefit from access to funds to rebuild following such disasters often receive assistance slowly and in relatively meager amounts.

In recent years, "microlenders"—firms that extend small-denomination, short-term loans collateralized by farm animals or equipment—have sought to assist residents of disaster-prone developing nations. Their operations have been hindered, however, by the firms' inability to expand their lending capabilities speedily in the wake of sudden disasters. Recently, the British and German governments established a central financing authority, called the Global Parametrics Natural Disaster Fund, to stand ready to grant short-term loans to microlenders. The microlenders, in turn, evaluate the short-term funding requirements of victims of earthquakes, famines, floods,

or windstorms; assess the victims' creditworthiness; and grant them loans that they will be able to repay. Once the microlenders receive victims' repayment of the disaster loans, the microlenders repay principal and interest on loans they had received from the Global Parametrics fund. In this way, delays and inefficiencies associated with World Bank and IMF lending are avoided entirely. Instead, private microlenders earn sufficient profits to specialize in assisting disaster victims in developing nations, and the victims obtain the short-term credit that they require to recover their financial footing in the wake of disasters.

REAL APPLICATION

Someday, you may be a victim of a natural disaster, such as a hurricane or a flood. Why will you not be seeking the help of a "microlender" in this time of financial need?

Sources are listed at the end of this chapter.

Alternative Institutional Structures for Limiting Financial Crises In recent years, economists have advanced a wide variety of proposals on the appropriate role for the International Monetary Fund in anticipating and reacting to international financial crises. Many of these proposals share common features, such as more frequent and in-depth releases of information both by the IMF and by countries that borrow from this institution. Nearly all economists also recommend improved financial and accounting standards for those receiving funds from the World Bank and the IMF, as well as other changes that might help reduce moral hazard problems in such lending.

Nevertheless, proposals for change diverge sharply. The IMF and its supporters have suggested maintaining its current structure but working harder to develop so-called early warning systems of financial crises so that aid can be provided to head off crises before they develop. Some economists have proposed establishing an international system of rules restricting capital outflows that might threaten international financial stability.

Other economists call for more dramatic changes. For instance, one proposal suggests creating a board composed of finance ministers of member nations to be directly in charge of day-to-day management of the IMF. Another recommends providing government incentives, in the form of tax breaks and subsidies, for increased private-sector lending that would supplement or even replace loans now made by the IMF.

ECONOMICS IN YOUR LIFE

Japan's Dead Capital Problem

In the wake of a tsunami wave that flattened much of the northeastern landscape of several of Japan's islands, Rie Nakaya has discovered that she had inherited a severely damaged house in a newly created wasteland of flattened buildings. She found out when the government began sending her regular bills to pay property taxes owed on the land. Nevertheless, a formal legal record of title to her family's ancestral home does not exist, and obtaining such a title will require her to pay 0.4 percent of the assessed value of the house and surrounding property prior to the tsunami. In addition, she would have to pay a substantial fee to have any title change officially notarized.

Titles of ownerships to many properties in Japan have never been formally established. Furthermore, even a number of properties for which formal legal titles were granted a couple of centuries ago have not had those titles updated in more than 150 years. Because of the steep costs required to formally record changes in ownership, people long ago stopped going to the trouble to register changes of ownership with the government.

Thus, Nakaya has found that she is a resident of an advanced economy with a significant dead capital problem. Japan's government judges the property as sufficiently "owned" by her to hold her responsible for paying taxes on it. Yet Nakaya is unable to contemplate improving or eventually trying to sell the property until she first incurs considerable expenses to establish her formal ownership. Indeed, for Nakaya, the informally inherited property has become more like a "zombie" that is not quite economically dead yet not quite economically alive, either.

FOR CRITICAL THINKING

What likely motivates many people to abandon lands that they informally inherit from departed relations?

REAL APPLICATION

At some point in your life, you might purchase real property—vacant land or land with a house or a condo. Why will you not be worried about the question of who has title to this real property once you purchase it?

Sources are listed at the end of this chapter.

Issues & Applications

A Positive Effect of the Global Economic Growth Shift: A Lower World Poverty Rate

Anton_Ivanov/Shutterstock

CONCEPTS APPLIED

➤ Basic Arithmetic of Economic Growth

➤ Population Growth and Economic Growth

➤ Economic Freedom

The global growth shift has involved a decrease in average growth rates in advanced nations, such as the United States, nations of Western Europe, and Japan, and a rise in average growth rates among emerging and developing nations. Because many of the world's poorest people inhabit the latter regions, this global growth shift has had a positive spillover onto the world poverty rate.

A Measure of the World Poverty Rate

The World Bank classifies a resident of the world as being in absolute poverty when that person must subsist on an inflation-adjusted amount, based on a 2011 base year, of $1.90 or less per day. Based on this measure of poverty, in 1981 about 1.9 billion of the world's residents were impoverished.

We can use this poverty measure to calculate the *world poverty rate*, which is the percentage of global residents who live in the state of absolute poverty as defined by the World Bank. In 1981, the world's population was 4.4 billion, so the world poverty rate according to this measure was about 42 percent.

The Positive Poverty Effect of the Global Growth Shift

Since 1981, the world's population has increased by more than 70 percent. Back in 1981, when many observers contemplated the basic arithmetic of economic growth, they anticipated that population growth of this magnitude would result in a higher poverty rate than 42 percent decades hence. Thus, reporters from the early 1980s warned of the potential for even more widespread poverty in their future—that is, today.

As Figure 18-5 shows, such warnings turned out to be misguided. This was so because the earlier predictions oversimplified the relationship between population and economic growth. An upswing in economic freedom across many emerging and developing nations in recent decades enabled a larger share of the increased human population to be directed to boosting per capita real GDP using productive labor and employing a larger amount of capital resources. As a consequence, since 1981 the number of people in poverty has declined even as the global population has risen, and the world poverty rate has decreased considerably.

FOR CRITICAL THINKING

How could increased economic freedom have enabled the increased global population to have produced more real GDP per capita?

REAL APPLICATION

You might be a younger person working in a popular city, such as New York or San Francisco. You might believe that, although you are not living in poverty, you have trouble making ends meet. You might, for example, have to share an apartment or a rented house with several roommates. What options do you have to improve your standard of living?

Sources are listed at the end of this chapter.

FIGURE 18-5

The World Poverty Rate since 1981

The absolute number of people subsisting on an inflation-adjusted (2011 base year) amount of $1.90 or below per day has declined as the global population has increased and economic growth in emerging and developing nations has risen. As a consequence, the world poverty rate has steadily decreased during the past several decades.

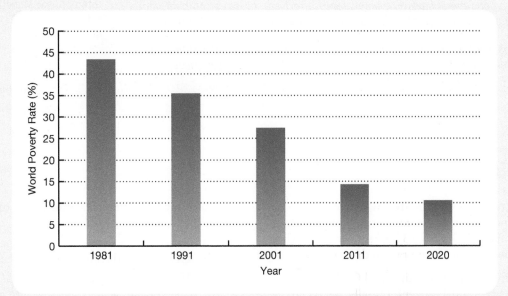

Sources: World Bank and United Nations; author's estimates.

What You Should Know

Here is what you should know after reading this chapter.

LEARNING OBJECTIVES	KEY TERMS
18.1 Explain why population growth can have uncertain effects on economic growth *Increased population growth has contradictory effects on economic growth. On the one hand, for a given growth rate of real GDP, increased population growth tends to reduce growth of per capita real GDP. On the other hand, if increased population growth is accompanied by higher labor force participation, the growth rate of real GDP can increase.*	economic freedom, 386
18.2 Understand why the existence of dead capital retards economic growth *Relatively few people in less developed countries establish legal ownership of capital goods. Unofficially owned resources are known as dead capital. Inability to trade, insure, and enforce rights to dead capital makes it difficult to employ these resources most efficiently, and this tends to limit economic growth.*	dead capital, 387
18.3 Describe the growth shift away from advanced nations to developing and emerging countries *During the decades preceding the turn of the current century, advanced nations such as the United States and countries of Western Europe experienced higher average rates of economic growth than the world's developing and emerging countries. Since 2000, however, the average rate of growth of per capita real GDP in emerging and developing countries has become significantly greater than in advanced nations.*	emerging nations, 388 **Key Figures** Figure 18-1, 389 Figure 18-2, 390
18.4 Discuss the sources of international investment funds for developing nations *International flows of funds to developing nations promote global economic growth. Asymmetric information problems, such as adverse selection and moral hazard problems, hinder international flows of funds and thereby slow economic growth in developing nations.*	portfolio investment, 391 foreign direct investment, 391 international financial crisis, 392 **Key Figure** Figure 18-3, 392
18.5 Identify the key functions of the World Bank and the International Monetary Fund *Adverse selection and moral hazard problems faced by private investors can both limit and destabilize international flows of funds to developing countries. The World Bank finances capital investment in countries that have trouble attracting funds from private sources. The International Monetary Fund attempts to stabilize international financial flows by extending loans to countries caught up in international financial crises.*	World Bank, 393 International Monetary Fund (IMF), 393 quota subscription, 394

PROBLEMS

18-1. A country's real GDP is growing at an annual rate of 3.1 percent, and the current rate of growth of per capita real GDP is 0.3 percent per year. What is the population growth rate in this nation?

18-2. The annual rate of growth of real GDP in a developing nation is 0.3 percent. Initially, the country's population was stable from year to year. Recently, however, a significant increase in the nation's birthrate has raised the annual rate of population growth to 0.5 percent.

a. What was the rate of growth of per capita real GDP before the increase in population growth?

b. If the rate of growth of real GDP remains unchanged, what is the new rate of growth of per capita real GDP following the increase in the birthrate?

18-3. A developing country has determined that each additional $1 billion of net investment in capital goods adds 0.01 percentage point to its long-run average annual rate of growth of per capita real GDP.

    a. Domestic entrepreneurs recently began to seek official approval to open a range of businesses employing capital resources valued at $20 billion. If the entrepreneurs undertake these investments, by what fraction of a percentage point will the nation's long-run average annual rate of growth of per capita real GDP increase, other things being equal?

    b. After weeks of effort trying to complete the first of 15 stages of bureaucratic red tape necessary to obtain authorization to start their businesses, a number of entrepreneurs decide to drop their investment plans completely, and the amount of official investment that actually takes place turns out to be $10 billion. Other things being equal, by what fraction of a percentage point will this decision reduce the nation's long-run average annual rate of growth of per capita real GDP from what it would have been if investment had been $20 billion?

18-4. Consider the estimates that the World Bank has assembled for the following nations:

Country	Legal Steps Required to Start a Business	Days Required to Start a Business	Cost of Starting a Business as a Percentage of Per Capita GDP
Angola	14	146	838%
Bosnia-Herzegovina	12	59	52%
Morocco	11	36	19%
Togo	14	63	281%
Uruguay	10	27	47%

Rank the nations in order, starting with the one you would expect to have the highest rate of economic growth, other things being equal. Explain your reasoning.

18-5. Suppose that every $500 billion of dead capital reduces the average rate of growth in worldwide per capita real GDP by 0.1 percentage point. If there is $10 trillion in dead capital in the world, by how many percentage points does the existence of dead capital reduce average worldwide growth of per capita real GDP?

18-6. Assume that each $1 billion in net capital investment generates 0.3 percentage point of the average percentage rate of growth of per capita real GDP, given the nation's labor resources. Firms have been investing exactly $6 billion in capital goods each year, so the annual average rate of growth of per capita real GDP has been 1.8 percent. Now a government that fails to consistently adhere to the rule of law has come to power, and firms must pay $100 million in bribes to gain official approval for every $1 billion in investment in capital goods. In response, companies cut back their total investment spending to $4 billion per year. If other things are equal and companies maintain this rate of investment, what will be the nation's new average annual rate of growth of per capita real GDP?

18-7. During the past year, several large banks extended $200 million in loans to the government and several firms in a developing nation. International investors also purchased $150 million in bonds and $350 million in stocks issued by domestic firms. Of the stocks that foreign investors purchased, $100 million were shares that amounted to less than a 10 percent interest in domestic firms. This was the first year this nation had ever permitted inflows of funds from abroad.

    a. Based on the investment category definitions discussed in this chapter, what was the amount of portfolio investment in this nation during the past year?

    b. What was the amount of foreign direct investment in this nation during the past year?

18-8. Last year, $100 million in outstanding bank loans to a developing nation's government were not renewed, and the developing nation's government paid off $50 million in maturing government bonds that had been held by foreign residents. During that year, however, a new group of banks participated in a $125 million loan to help finance a major government construction project in the capital city. Domestic firms also issued $50 million in bonds and $75 million in stocks to foreign investors. All of the stocks issued gave the foreign investors more than 10 percent shares of the domestic firms.

    a. What was gross foreign investment in this nation last year?

    b. What was net foreign investment in this nation last year?

18-9. Identify which of the following situations currently faced by international investors are examples of adverse selection and which are examples of moral hazard.

    a. Among the governments of several developing countries that are attempting to issue new bonds this year, it is certain that a few will fail to collect taxes to repay the bonds when they mature. It is difficult, however, for investors considering buying government bonds to predict which governments will experience this problem.

b. Foreign investors are contemplating purchasing stock in a company that, unknown to them, may have failed to properly establish legal ownership over a crucial capital resource.

c. Companies in a less developed nation have already issued bonds to finance the purchase of new capital goods. After receiving the funds from the bond issue, however, the company's managers pay themselves large bonuses instead.

d. When the government of a developing nation received a bank loan three years ago, it ultimately repaid the loan but had to reschedule its payments after officials misused the funds for unworthy projects. Now the government, which still has many of the same officials, is trying to raise funds by issuing bonds to foreign investors, who must decide whether or not to purchase them.

18-10. Identify which of the following situations currently faced by the World Bank or the International Monetary Fund are examples of adverse selection and which are examples of moral hazard.

a. The World Bank has extended loans to the government of a developing country to finance construction of a canal with a certain future flow of earnings. Now, however, the government has decided to redirect those funds to build a casino that may or may not generate sufficient profits to allow the government to repay the loan.

b. The IMF is considering extending loans to several nations that failed to fully repay loans they received from the IMF during the past decade but now claim to be better credit risks. Currently, the IMF is not sure in advance which of these nations are unlikely to fully repay new loans.

c. The IMF recently extended a loan to a government directed by democratically elected officials that would permit the nation to adjust to an abrupt reduction in private flows of funds from abroad. A coup has just occurred, however, in response to newly discovered corruption within the government's elected leadership. The new military dictator has announced tentative plans to disburse some of the funds in equal shares to all citizens.

18-11. For each of the following situations, explain which of the policy issues discussed in this chapter relates to the stance the institution has taken.

a. The World Bank offers to make a loan to a company in an impoverished nation at a lower interest rate than the company had been about to agree to pay to borrow the same amount from a group of private banks.

b. The World Bank makes a loan to a company in a developing nation that has not yet received formal approval to operate there, even though the government approval process typically takes 15 months.

c. The IMF extends a loan to a developing nation's government, with no preconditions, to enable the government to make already overdue payments on a loan it had previously received from the World Bank.

18-12. For each of the following situations, explain which of the policy issues discussed in this chapter relates to the stance the institution has taken.

a. The IMF extends a long-term loan to a nation's government to help it maintain publicly supported production of goods and services that the government otherwise would have turned over to private companies.

b. The World Bank makes a loan to companies in an impoverished nation in which government officials typically demand bribes equal to 50 percent of companies' profits before allowing them to engage in any new investment projects.

c. The IMF offers to make a loan to banks in a country in which the government's rulers commonly require banks to extend credit to finance high-risk investment projects headed by the rulers' friends and relatives.

18-13. Answer the following questions concerning proposals to reform long-term development lending programs currently offered by the IMF and World Bank.

a. Why might the World Bank face moral hazard problems if it were to offer to provide funds to governments that promise to allocate the funds to major institutional reforms aimed at enhancing economic growth?

b. How does the IMF face an adverse selection problem if it is considering making loans to governments in which the ruling parties have already shown predispositions to try to "buy" votes by creating expensive public programs in advance of elections? How might following an announced rule in which the IMF cuts off future loans to governments that engage in such activities reduce this problem and promote increased economic growth in nations that do receive IMF loans?

18-14. Consider Table 18-1. Based on the basic arithmetic of economic growth, what were the average annual rates of real GDP growth since 1990 for those nations experiencing positive rates of annual growth of per capita real GDP?

18-15. Take a look at Table 18-1. Based on the basic arithmetic of economic growth, what were the average annual rates of real GDP growth since 1990 for those nations experiencing negative rates of annual growth of per capita real GDP?

18-16. Consider Figure 18-1. Average rates of population growth have been higher over the entire period covered by the figure in nearly all emerging and developing nations than in advanced nations. What does this tell us about a comparison of the average rate of growth of real GDP since 2000 in emerging and developing nations compared with advanced nations?

18-17. Take a look at Figure 18-1, and read the related text that discusses the exact values of the average growth rates displayed in the figure. Over the entire interval since 2000, which group of countries has experienced a higher rate of economic growth: emerging and developing nations or advanced nations?

18-18. Suppose that a foreign resident is contemplating buying 5 percent of the shares of a company based in a developing nation but is experiencing difficulty determining whether the firm is riskier than others in that country. What type of investment is this foreign resident considering, and what type of asymmetric information problem is he or she experiencing?

18-19. Suppose that a foreign resident has bought 20 percent of the shares of a company based in a developing nation but is experiencing difficulty determining whether the firm has responded to this purchase by engaging in riskier behavior. What type of investment has this foreign resident undertaken, and what type of asymmetric information problem is she or he experiencing?

REFERENCES

AI—DECISION MAKING THROUGH DATA: Developing Nations Could Face Big Problems

Daniel Araya, "Who Will Lead in the Age of Artificial Intelligence?" *Brookings*, February 26, 2019

United Nations, "Leveraging Big Data for Sustainable Development," March 29, 2018.

World Bank, "Artificial Intelligence for Economic Development," March 1, 2018.

BEHAVIORAL EXAMPLE: Could Regulatory Competition Reduce Government Corruption That Undermines Economic Growth?

"CPIA Transparency, Accountability, and Corruption in the Public Sector Rating," World Bank (https://data.worldbank.org/indicator/iq.cpa.tran.xq), 2019.

Mustafa Kamal, Ebney Ayaj Rana, and Abu Wahid, "Economic Reform and Corruption: Evidence from Panel Data," *Australian Economic Papers*, 2018.

Dmitry Ryvkin and Danila Serra, "Corruption and Competition among Bureaucrats: An Experimental Study," *Journal of Economic Behavior and Organization*, 2018.

INTERNATIONAL EXAMPLE: Backing Up Microlenders That Provide Loans to Developing Nations' Residents after Natural Disasters

T. S. Anand Kumar and Jeyanth Newport, "Role of Microfinance in Disaster Mitigation," *Disaster Prevention and Management*, 2019.

Jasper Cox, "Fund Aims to Make the Market for Climate Insurance," *Global Capital*, April 30, 2018.

"Global Parametrics Natural Disaster Fund to Be Seeded by DFID," Artemis.bm (http://www.artemis.bm/blog/2018/02/26/global-parametrics-natural-disaster-fund-to-be-seeded-by-dfid/), February 28, 2018.

ECONOMICS IN YOUR LIFE: Japan's Dead Capital Problem

Emiko Jozuka, "Japan Has So Many Vacant Homes It's Giving Them Away," CNN.com (https://www.cnn.com/2018/12/05/asia/japan-vacant-akiya-ghost-homes/index.html), January 14, 2019.

"A Startling Amount of Land in Japan Has No Official Owner," *Economist*, March 17, 2018.

Eric Johnson, "Issue of Abandoned Land Slowing Rural Development in Japan," *The Japan Times*, June 1, 2018.

ISSUES & APPLICATIONS: A Positive Effect of the Global Economic Growth Shift: A Lower World Poverty Rate

World Bank, "Poverty Headcount at $1.90 per Day (2011 PPP)," (http://data.worldbank.org/indicator/SI.POV.DDAY), 2019.

World Economic Situation and Prospects, United Nations, 2018.

Homi Kharas, Kristofer Hamel, and Martin Hofer, "The Start of a New Poverty Narrative," *Brookings* (https://www.brookings.edu/blog/future-development/2018/06/19/the-start-of-a-new-poverty-narrative/), June 19, 2018.

19 Demand and Supply Elasticity

ChameleonsEye/Shutterstock

LEARNING OBJECTIVES

After reading this chapter, you should be able to:

19.1 Calculate price elasticity of demand

19.2 Explain the relationship between price elasticity of demand and total revenues

19.3 Describe the factors that determine the price elasticity of demand

19.4 Explain the cross price elasticity of demand and the income elasticity of demand

19.5 Classify supply elasticities and explain how the length of time for adjustment affects the price elasticity of supply

Various taxes imposed on air travel add about 10 percent to the price of a typical ticket for a flight operated by a U.S. airline. Naturally, a higher ticket price induces, via the law of demand, a reduction in the quantity of airline tickets demanded. In this chapter, you will learn about the *price elasticity of demand*, which measures the proportionate response in quantity demanded to a proportionate change in price. You will also learn how the reaction of consumers to an increase in the price of tickets caused by taxes on tickets provides information about the price elasticity of demand in the market for air travel. More generally, you will learn about both demand and supply elasticities and about associated applications of these concepts.

during a recent holiday season, the prices paid by people who used ride-sharing services provided by firms such as Uber and Lyft decreased by 10 to 50 percent, which resulted in such a substantial increase in the quantity of rides demanded that on net these companies' total revenues *increased*? Firms such as Uber and Lyft must constantly take into account consumers' responses to changing fees and prices. If Apple reduces its prices by 10 percent, will consumers respond by buying so many more digital devices that the company's revenues rise? At the other end of the spectrum, can Ferrari dealers "get away" with a 2 percent increase in prices? That is, will Ferrari purchasers respond so little to the relatively small increase in price that the total revenues received for Ferrari sales will not fall and may actually rise? The only way to answer these questions is to know how responsive consumers in the real world will be to changes in prices. Economists have a special name for quantity responsiveness—*elasticity*, which is the subject of this chapter.

Price Elasticity

19.1 Calculate price elasticity of demand

To begin to understand what elasticity is all about, just keep in mind that it means "responsiveness." Here we are concerned with the price elasticity of demand. We wish to know the extent to which a change in the price of, say, petroleum products will cause the quantity demanded to change, other things held constant. We want to determine the percentage change in quantity demanded in response to a percentage change in price.

Price Elasticity of Demand

We will formally define the **price elasticity of demand**, which we will label E_p, as follows:

Price elasticity of demand (E_p)
The responsiveness of the quantity demanded of a commodity to changes in its price; defined as the percentage change in quantity demanded divided by the percentage change in price.

$$E_p = \frac{\text{percentage change in quantity demanded}}{\text{percentage change in price}}$$

What will price elasticity of demand tell us? It will tell us the *relative* amount by which the quantity demanded will change in response to a change in the price of a particular good.

Consider an example in which a 10 percent rise in the price of oil leads to a reduction in quantity demanded of 2 percent. Putting these numbers into the formula, we find that the price elasticity of demand for oil in this case equals the percentage change in quantity demanded divided by the percentage change in price, or

$$E_p = \frac{-2\%}{+10\%} = -0.2$$

An elasticity of -0.2 means that a 1 percent *increase* in the price would lead to a mere 0.2 percent *decrease* in the quantity demanded. If you were now told, in contrast, that the price elasticity of demand for oil was -2, you would know that a 1 percent increase in the price of oil would lead to a 2 percent decrease in the quantity demanded.

How can we use observed percentage changes in the price and quantity demanded of an item to compute the price elasticity of demand for that item?

EXAMPLE

The Price Elasticity of Demand for Freshman Enrollments at Private Colleges

Recently, the annual percentage increase in the average inflation-adjusted tuition rates of private colleges was 1.5 percent. The associated number of freshman enrollments for that year decreased by 1.9 percent.

Other things being equal, the price elasticity of demand for freshman college enrollments is equal to the percentage change in quantity demanded divided by the percentage change in price, or

$$E_p = \frac{-1.9\%}{1.5\%} = -1.27$$

Thus, for this year, a 1 percent increase in the price of freshman enrollments at private colleges generated a 1.27 percent decrease in the quantity demanded of college enrollments.

REAL APPLICATION

Imagine you were someone contemplating higher education. How could you react to increases in the tuition prices of private colleges?

Sources are listed at the end of this chapter.

Relative Quantities Only Notice that in our elasticity formula, we talk about *percentage* changes in quantity demanded divided by *percentage* changes in price. We focus on relative amounts of price changes, because percentage changes are independent of the units chosen. This means that it doesn't matter if we measure price changes in terms of cents, dollars, or hundreds of dollars. It also doesn't matter whether we measure quantity changes in ounces, grams, or pounds.

Always Negative The law of demand states that quantity demanded is *inversely* related to the relative price. An *increase* in the price of a good leads to a *decrease* in the quantity demanded. If a *decrease* in the relative price of a good should occur, the quantity demanded would *increase* by some percentage. The point is that price elasticity of demand will always be negative. By convention, however, *we will ignore the minus sign in our discussion from this point on.*

Basically, the greater the *absolute* price elasticity of demand (disregarding the sign), the greater the demand responsiveness to relative price changes—a small change in price has a great impact on quantity demanded. Conversely, the smaller the absolute price elasticity of demand, the smaller the demand responsiveness to relative price changes—a large change in price has little effect on quantity demanded.

Calculating Elasticity

To calculate the price elasticity of demand, we must compute percentage changes in quantity demanded and in price. To calculate the percentage change in quantity demanded, we might divide the absolute change in the quantity demanded by the original quantity demanded:

$$\frac{\text{change in quantity demanded}}{\text{original quantity demanded}}$$

To find the percentage change in price, we might divide the change in price by the original price:

$$\frac{\text{change in price}}{\text{original price}}$$

There is an arithmetic problem, though, when we calculate percentage changes in this manner. The percentage change, say, from 2 to 3—50 percent—is not the same as the percentage change from 3 to 2—$33\frac{1}{3}$ percent. In other words, it makes a difference where you start. One way out of this dilemma is simply to use average values.

To compute the price elasticity of demand, we take the *average* of the two prices and the two quantities over the range we are considering and compare the change with these averages. Thus, the formula for computing the price elasticity of demand is as follows:

$$E_p = \frac{\text{change in quantity}}{\text{sum of quantities}/2} \div \frac{\text{change in price}}{\text{sum of prices}/2}$$

We can rewrite this more simply if we do two things: (1) We can let Q_1 and Q_2 equal the two different quantities demanded before and after the price change and let P_1 and P_2 equal the two different prices. (2) Because we will be dividing a percentage by a percentage, we simply use the ratio, or the decimal form, of the percentages. Therefore,

$$E_p = \frac{\Delta Q}{(Q_1 + Q_2)/2} \div \frac{\Delta P}{(P_1 + P_2)/2}$$

where the Greek letter Δ (delta) stands for "change in."

How can we use this formula to calculate the price elasticity of demand for a specific product such as Tesla vehicles?

INTERNATIONAL POLICY EXAMPLE

The Price Elasticity of Demand for Tesla Vehicles in Hong Kong

For a number of years, many governments have provided substantial subsidies for purchases of electric vehicles. Recently, however, the Hong Kong government temporarily eliminated all subsidies offered to purchasers of Tesla vehicles. As a consequence, the price of a Tesla vehicle increased from about $75,000 to $130,000. This price increase caused the quantity of Tesla vehicles demanded in Hong Kong to decrease from about 500 per month to about 30.

Assuming that other things were equal, we can calculate the price elasticity of demand for Tesla vehicles during the period before and after the elimination of Hong Kong's Tesla subsidies:

$$E_p = \frac{\text{change in } Q}{\text{sum of quantities}/2} \div \frac{\text{change in } P}{\text{sum of quantities}/2}$$

$$= \frac{500 \text{ vehicles} - 30 \text{ vehicles}}{(500 \text{ vehicles} + 30 \text{ vehicles})/2}$$

$$\div \frac{(\$130,000 \text{ per vehicle} - \$75,000 \text{ per vehicle})}{(\$130,000 \text{ per vehicle} + \$75,000 \text{ per vehicle})/2}$$

$$= \frac{470 \text{ vehicles}}{530 \text{ vehicles}/2} \div \frac{\$65,000 \text{ per vehicle}}{\$205,000 \text{ per vehicle}/2}$$

$$= 2.8$$

The price elasticity of 2.8 means that each 1 percent increase in price generated a 2.8 percent decrease in the quantity of Tesla vehicles purchased. Thus, the quantity of Tesla vehicles demanded was relatively responsive to an increase in the per-vehicle price created by the Hong Kong government's subsidy elimination.

There have been attempts in the United States to eliminate federal and state subsidies for Tesla vehicles. In the future, we might likewise be able to utilize observed changes in quantities demanded following eliminated U.S. subsidies to calculate the U.S. price elasticity of demand for these vehicles.

FOR CRITICAL THINKING

Would the estimated price elasticity of demand for Tesla vehicles have been different if we had not used the average-values formula? How?

Sources are listed at the end of this chapter.

Price Elasticity Ranges

We have names for the varying ranges of price elasticities, depending on whether a 1 percent change in price causes more or less than a 1 percent change in the quantity demanded.

- We say that a good has an **elastic demand** whenever the price elasticity of demand is greater than 1. A change in price of 1 percent causes a greater than 1 percent change in the quantity demanded.

Elastic demand
A demand relationship in which a given percentage change in price will result in a larger percentage change in quantity demanded.

Unit elasticity of demand

A demand relationship in which the quantity demanded changes exactly in proportion to the change in price.

Inelastic demand

A demand relationship in which a given percentage change in price will result in a less-than-proportionate percentage change in the quantity demanded.

ECONOMICS IN YOUR LIFE

To contemplate how the effect of a new tax on changes in the price and quantity demanded of soft drinks enabled an inference about the price elasticity of demand for soft drinks, take a look at **Imposing a Philadelphia Soft Drinks Tax Reveals Information about the Price Elasticity of Demand** on page 417.

Perfectly inelastic demand

A demand that exhibits zero responsiveness to price changes. No matter what the price is, the quantity demanded remains the same.

Perfectly elastic demand

A demand that has the characteristic that even the slightest increase in price will lead to zero quantity demanded.

- In a situation of **unit elasticity of demand**, a change in price of 1 percent causes exactly a 1 percent change in the quantity demanded.

- In a situation of **inelastic demand**, a change in price of 1 percent causes a change of less than 1 percent in the quantity demanded.

When we say that a commodity's demand is elastic, we are indicating that consumers are relatively responsive to changes in price. When we say that a commodity's demand is inelastic, we are indicating that its consumers are relatively unresponsive to price changes. When economists say that demand is inelastic, it does not necessarily mean that quantity demanded is *totally* unresponsive to price changes. Remember, the law of demand implies that there will always be some responsiveness in quantity demanded to a price change. The question is how much. That's what elasticity attempts to determine.

Extreme Elasticities

There are two extremes in price elasticities of demand. One extreme represents total unresponsiveness of quantity demanded to price changes, which is referred to as **perfectly inelastic demand**, or zero elasticity. The other represents total responsiveness, which is referred to as infinitely or **perfectly elastic demand**.

We show perfect inelasticity in panel (a) of Figure 19-1. Notice that the quantity demanded per year is 8 million units, no matter what the price. Hence, for any price change, the quantity demanded will remain the same, and thus the change in the quantity demanded will be zero. Look back at our formula for computing elasticity. If the change in the quantity demanded is zero, the numerator is also zero, and a non-zero number divided into zero results in a value of zero, too. This is true at any point along the demand curve. Hence, there is perfect inelasticity.

At the opposite extreme is the situation depicted in panel (b) of Figure 19-1. Here we show that at a price of 30 cents, an unlimited quantity will be demanded over the relevant range of quantities. At a price that is only slightly above 30 cents, no quantity will be demanded. There is perfect, or infinite, responsiveness at each point along this curve, and hence we call the demand schedule in panel (b) perfectly elastic.

FIGURE 19-1

Extreme Price Elasticities

In panel (a), we show complete price unresponsiveness. The demand curve is vertical at the quantity of 8 million units per year. This means that the price elasticity of demand is zero. In panel (b), we show complete price responsiveness. At a price of 30 cents, in this example, consumers will demand an unlimited quantity of the particular good in question, over the relevant range of quantities. This is a case of infinite price elasticity of demand.

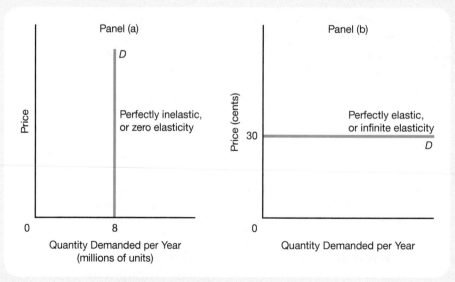

Extreme Price Elasticities and Your Analysis of Politicians

While it is easy to show extreme elasticities in a graph, in the real world rarely do we observe such extreme elasticities for any good or service. If you carefully analyze politicians' statements about taxes, as one example, you will often discover underlying assumptions of extreme price elasticities. When taxes are raised on just about anything, including income, people react. A big increase in a tax on luxury items often results in a reduction in the quantity demanded and thus lower tax revenues than predicted by politicians. An increase in a state income tax on the "rich" often leads to fewer revenues than predicted. Rich people figure out ways to avoid those taxes, even if it means moving to a no-tax or lower-tax state.

WHAT HAPPENS WHEN...

a government requires firms to collect a per-unit tax on sales of a product for which demand is highly elastic?

Governments commonly require firms to add per-unit taxes to the prices they charge for items, to collect the taxes, and to transmit the taxes to the governments' revenue departments. Firms thereby wish to receive a higher overall price for the taxed items to be willing to supply any given number of units. This fact means that the imposition of such taxes shifts market supply curves upward and to the left. If the demand for an item subject to a newly imposed per-unit tax to be collected by firms that sell the taxed item is very elastic, the resulting upward and leftward shift of the market supply curve yields a relatively small increase in the market clearing price. Thus, consumers pay a rather small fraction of the per-unit tax. In contrast, the firms required to collect the taxes must pay a large fraction of the tax. Essentially, the per-unit tax becomes a new "cost of doing business" for these firms.

Elasticity and Total Revenues

> **19.2** Explain the relationship between price elasticity of demand and total revenues

Suppose that you are an employee of a firm in the industry that provides apps for making restaurant reservations using digital devices. How would you know when a rise in the market clearing price of app-enabled restaurant reservations will result in an increase in the total revenues, or the total receipts, of firms in the industry? It is commonly thought that the way for total receipts to rise is for the price per unit to increase. Is it possible, however, that a rise in price per unit could lead to a *decrease* in total revenues? The answer to this question depends on the price elasticity of demand.

Let's look at Figure 19-2. In panel (a), column 1 shows the price of app-enabled restaurant reservations in dollars per reservation, and column 2 represents thousands of reservations per month. In column 3, we multiply column 1 times column 2 to derive total revenue because total revenue is always equal to the number of units (quantity) sold times the price per unit. In column 4, we calculate values of elasticity. Notice what happens to total revenues throughout the schedule. They rise steadily as the price rises from $1 to $5 per reservation. When the price rises further to $6 per reservation, total revenues remain constant at $3 million. At prices per reservation higher than $6, total revenues fall as price increases. Indeed, if prices are above $6 per reservation, total revenues will increase only if the price *declines*, not if the price rises.

Labeling Elasticity

The relationship between price and quantity on the demand schedule is given in columns 1 and 2 of panel (a) in Figure 19-2. In panel (b), the demand curve, *D*, representing that schedule is drawn. In panel (c), the total revenue curve representing the data in column 3 is drawn. Notice first the level of these curves at small quantities. The demand curve is at a maximum height, but total revenue is zero, which makes sense according to this demand schedule—at a price of $11 per reservation and above, no units will be purchased, and therefore total revenue will be zero. As price is lowered, we travel down the demand curve, and total revenues increase until price is $6 per

FIGURE 19-2

The Relationship between Price Elasticity of Demand and Total Revenues for App-Enabled Restaurant Reservation

In panel (a), we show the elastic, unit-elastic, and inelastic sections of the demand schedule according to whether a reduction in price increases total revenues, causes them to remain constant, or causes them to decrease, respectively. In panel (b), we show these regions graphically on the demand curve. In panel (c), we show them on the total revenue curve.

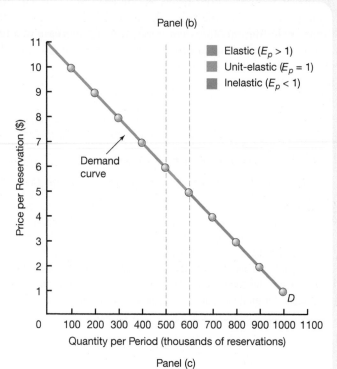

Panel (b)

Elastic ($E_p > 1$)
Unit-elastic ($E_p = 1$)
Inelastic ($E_p < 1$)

Panel (a)

(1) Price, P, per Restaurant Reservation Service	(2) Quantity Demanded, D (thousands of reservations)	(3) Total Revenue ($ millions) = (1) × (2)	(4) Elasticity, E_p = $\dfrac{\text{Change in } Q}{(Q_1 + Q_2)/2} \div \dfrac{\text{Change in } P}{(P_1 + P_2)/2}$
$11	0	0	
			21.000
10	100	1.0	
			6.330
9	200	1.8	
			3.400 } Elastic
8	300	2.4	
			2.143
7	400	2.8	
			1.144
6	500	3.0	
			1.000 } Unit-elastic
5	600	3.0	
			.692
4	700	2.8	
			.467
3	800	2.4	} Inelastic
			.294
2	900	1.8	
			.158
1	1000	1.0	

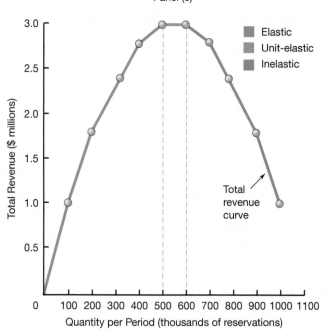

Panel (c)

Elastic
Unit-elastic
Inelastic

restaurant reservation, remain constant from $6 to $5 per reservation, and then fall at lower unit prices. Corresponding to those three sections, demand is elastic, unit-elastic, and inelastic. Hence, we have three relationships among the three types of price elasticity and total revenues.

- *Elastic demand.* A negative relationship exists between changes in price and changes in total revenues. That is to say, along the elastic range of market demand for an item, total revenues will rise if the market price decreases. Total revenues will fall if the market price increases.

- *Unit-elastic demand.* Changes in price do not change total revenues. When price increases along the unit-elastic range of market demand, total revenues will not change, nor will total revenues change if the market price decreases.

- *Inelastic demand.* A positive relationship exists between changes in price and total revenues. When price increases along the inelastic range of market demand, total revenues will go up. When the market price decreases, total revenues will fall. We therefore conclude that if demand is inelastic, price and total revenues move in the *same* direction.

Graphic Presentation

The elastic, unit-elastic, and inelastic areas of the demand curve are shown in Figure 19-2, in panel (a). For prices from $11 per app-enabled restaurant reservation to $6 per reservation, as price decreases, total revenues rise from zero to $3 million. Demand is elastic. When price changes from $6 to $5, however, total revenues remain constant at $3 million. Demand is unit-elastic. Finally, when price falls from $5 to $1, total revenues decrease from $3 million to $1 million. Demand is inelastic.

In panels (b) and (c) of Figure 19-2, we have labeled the sections of the demand curve accordingly, and we have also shown how total revenues first rise, then remain constant, and finally fall.

The Elasticity-Revenue Relationship

The relationship between price elasticity of demand and total revenues brings together some important microeconomic concepts. Total revenues, as we have noted, are the product of price per unit times the number of units purchased. The law of demand states that along a given demand curve, price and quantity will move in opposite directions: One increases as the other decreases. Consequently, what happens to the product of price times quantity depends on which of the opposing changes exerts a greater force on total revenues. Responsiveness of quantity demanded to a change in price, of course, is just what price elasticity of demand is designed to measure.

The relationship between price elasticity of demand and total revenues is summarized in Table 19-1.

How are firms using AI techniques to apply price elasticity of demand to boost their total revenues?

TABLE 19-1

Relationship between Price Elasticity of Demand and Total Revenues		Effect of Price Change on Total Revenues (TR)	
Price Elasticity of Demand (E_p)		Price Decrease	Price Increase
Inelastic	($E_p < 1$)	TR↓	TR↑
Unit-elastic	($E_p = 1$)	No change in TR	No change in TR
Elastic	($E_p > 1$)	TR↑	TR↓

AI DECISION MAKING THROUGH DATA

In the Pursuit of "Price Optimization"

In principle, the inverse-U-shaped relationship between price elasticity of demand and total revenues provides a means for firms to engage in so-called price optimization. This concept refers to identifying a price that increases total revenues as part of the primary objective of maximizing profits obtainable in a market.

Companies in industries ranging from online retailers to grocers are utilizing AI-guided data-analytics techniques to try to infer the revenue-increasing price. Studies of online data on quantities produced by their industry competitors are enabling the firms to infer the appropriate quantities to produce in an effort to induce prices to adjust toward revenue-boosting levels. If all firms competing in these industries were able to infer these quantities and simultaneously act on these inferences, the result would be a market quantity consistent with their combined best interests: jointly maximized profits for all firms.

FOR CRITICAL THINKING

If the demand is relatively elastic for a particular retail item and all firms respond to AI guidance with an aim to boost their revenues and profits, should each one increase or decrease its production rate? Explain briefly.

Sources are listed at the end of this chapter.

19.3 Describe the factors that determine the price elasticity of demand

Determinants of the Price Elasticity of Demand

We know that theoretically the price elasticity of demand ranges numerically from zero (completely inelastic) to infinity (completely elastic). What we would like to do now is to come up with a list of the determinants of the price elasticity of demand. The price elasticity of demand for a particular commodity at any price depends, at a minimum, on the following factors:

- The existence and number of substitutes
- The share of a consumer's total budget devoted to purchases of that commodity
- The length of time allowed for adjustment to changes in the price of the commodity

Existence of Substitutes

The closer the substitutes for a particular commodity and the more substitutes there are, the greater will be its price elasticity of demand. At the limit, if there is a perfect substitute, the elasticity of demand for the commodity will be infinity. Thus, even the slightest increase in the commodity's price will cause a dramatic reduction in the quantity demanded: Quantity demanded will fall to zero.

Keep in mind that in this extreme example, we are really talking about two goods that the consumer believes are exactly alike and equally desirable, such as dollar bills whose only difference is their serial numbers. When we talk about less extreme examples, we can speak only in terms of the number and the similarity of substitutes that are available.

Thus, we will find that the more narrowly we define a good, the closer and greater will be the number of substitutes available. For example, the demand for one specific diet soft drink may be relatively elastic because consumers can switch to other low-calorie liquid refreshments. The demand for diet drinks (as a single group), however, is relatively less elastic because there are fewer substitutes.

Share of the Budget

We know that the greater the share of a person's total budget that is spent on a commodity, the greater that person's price elasticity of demand is for that commodity. A key reason that the demand for pepper is very inelastic is because individuals spend so little on it relative to their total budgets. In contrast, the demand for items such as transportation and housing is far more elastic because they occupy a large part of people's budgets—changes in their prices cannot easily be ignored without sacrificing a lot of other alternative goods that could be purchased.

Consider a numerical example. A household spends $40,000 a year. It purchases $4 of pepper per year and $4,000 of transportation services. Now consider the spending power of this family when the price of pepper and the price of transportation both double. If the household buys the same amount of pepper, it will now spend $8. It will thus have to reduce other expenditures by $4. This $4 represents only 0.01 percent of the entire household budget. By contrast, if transportation costs double, the family will have to spend $8,000, or $4,000 more on transportation, if it is to purchase the same quantity. That increased expenditure on transportation of $4,000 represents 10 percent of total expenditures that must be switched from other purchases.

We would therefore predict that the household will react differently if the price of pepper doubles than it will if transportation prices double. It will reduce its transportation purchases by a proportionately greater amount.

Time for Adjustment

When the price of a commodity changes and that price change persists, more people will learn about it. Further, consumers will be better able to revise their consumption patterns the longer the time period they have to do so. In fact, the longer the time they do take, the less costly it will be for them to engage in this revision of consumption patterns. Consider a price decrease. The longer the price decrease persists, the greater will be the number of new uses that consumers will discover for the particular commodity, and the greater will be the number of new users of that particular commodity.

It is possible to make a very strong statement about the relationship between the price elasticity of demand and the time allowed for adjustment:

> *The longer any price change persists, the greater the elasticity of demand, other things held constant. Elasticity of demand is greater in the long run than in the short run.*

Short-Run versus Long-Run Adjustments Let's consider an example. Suppose that the price of electricity goes up 50 percent. How do you adjust in the short run? You can turn the lights off more often, you can stop using devices powered by electricity as much as you usually do, and similar measures. Otherwise it's very difficult to cut back on your consumption of electricity.

In the long run, though, you can devise other methods to reduce your consumption. Instead of using only electric heaters, the next time you have a house built you will install solar panels. You will purchase LED bulbs because they use less electricity. The more time you have to think about it, the more ways you will find to cut your electricity consumption.

Demand Elasticity in the Short Run and in the Long Run We would expect, therefore, that the short-run demand curve for electricity would be relatively less elastic (in the price range around P_e), as demonstrated by D_1 in Figure 19-3. The long-run demand curve, however, will exhibit more elasticity (in the neighborhood of P_e), as demonstrated by D_3. Indeed, we can think of an entire family of demand curves such as those depicted in the figure. The short-run demand curve is for the period when there is little time for adjustment. As more time is allowed, the demand curve goes first to D_2 and then all the way to D_3. Thus, in the neighborhood of P_e, elasticity differs for each of these curves. It is greater for the less steep curves (but slope alone does not measure elasticity for the entire curve).

Economists have consistently found that estimated price elasticities of demand are greater in the long run than in the short run, as seen in Table 19-2. There you see that estimates indicate that the long-run price elasticity of demand for vacation air travel is 2.7, whereas the estimate for the short run is 1.1. Throughout the table, you see that all estimates of long-run price elasticities of demand exceed their short-run counterparts.

How to Define the Short Run and the Long Run We've mentioned the short run and the long run. Is the short run one week, two weeks, one month, two months? Is the long

FIGURE 19-3

Short-Run and Long-Run Price Elasticity of Demand

Consider a situation in which the market price is P_e and the quantity demanded is Q_e. Then there is a price increase to P_1. In the short run, as evidenced by the demand curve D_1, we move from equilibrium quantity demanded, Q_e to Q_1. After more time is allowed for adjustment, the demand curve rotates at original price P_e to D_2. Quantity demanded falls again, now to Q_2. After even more time is allowed for adjustment, the demand curve rotates at price P_e to D_3. At the higher price P_1 in the long run, the quantity demanded falls all the way to Q_3.

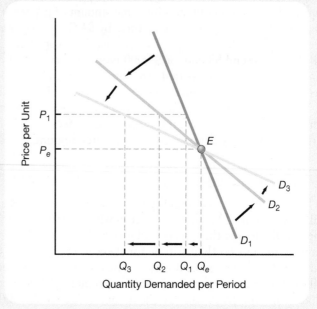

run three years, four years, five years? There is no single answer. The long run is the period of time necessary for consumers to make a *full* adjustment to a given price change, all other things held constant. In the case of the demand for electricity, the long run will be however long it takes consumers to switch over to cheaper sources of heating, to buy houses and appliances that are more energy-efficient, and so on. The long-run price elasticity of demand for electricity therefore relates to a period of at least several years. The short run—by default—is any period less than the long run.

TABLE 19-2

Price Elasticities of Demand for Selected Goods

Here are estimated demand elasticities for selected goods. All of them are negative, although we omit the minus sign. Estimates of both short-run and long-run price elasticities of demand are given where available. The long run is associated with the time necessary for consumers to adjust fully to any given price change. (Note: "N.A." indicates that no estimate is available.)

Category	Estimated Elasticity	
	Short Run	Long Run
Air travel (business)	0.4	1.2
Air travel (vacation)	1.1	2.7
Beef	0.6	N.A.
Cheese	0.3	N.A.
Electricity	0.1	1.7
Fresh tomatoes	4.6	N.A.
Gasoline	0.2	0.5
Hospital services	0.1	0.7
Intercity bus service	0.6	2.2
Physician services	0.1	0.6
Private education	1.1	1.9
Restaurant meals	2.3	N.A.
Tires	0.9	1.2

The Cross Price and Income Elasticities of Demand

19.4 Explain the cross price elasticity of demand and the income elasticity of demand

You have learned how to calculate the price elasticity of demand, how to evaluate the relationship between price elasticity of demand and total revenues, and how to assess determinants of the price elasticity of demand. Now let's contemplate additional key demand elasticity concepts.

Cross Price Elasticity of Demand

Earlier, we discussed the effect of a change in the price of one good on the demand for a related good. We defined substitutes and complements in terms of whether a reduction in the price of one caused a decrease or an increase, respectively, in the demand for the other. If the price of Internet digital movie downloads is held constant, the number of individual movies purchased (at any price) will certainly be influenced by the price of a close substitute, such as subscriptions to streaming video services. If the price of digital apps is held constant, the amount of apps demanded (at any price) will certainly be affected by changes in the price of digital devices. (These goods are complements.)

Measuring the Cross Price Elasticity of Demand What we now need to do is come up with a numerical measure of the responsiveness of the amount of an item demanded to the prices of related goods. This is called the **cross price elasticity of demand (E_{xy})**, which is defined as the percentage change in the amount of a particular item demanded at the item's current price (a shift in the demand curve) divided by the percentage change in the price of the related good. In equation form, the cross price elasticity of demand between good X and good Y is

Cross price elasticity of demand (E_{xy})
The percentage change in the amount of an item demanded (holding its price constant) divided by the percentage change in the price of a related good.

$$E_{xy} = \frac{\text{percentage change in the amount of good X demanded}}{\text{percentage change in price of good Y}}$$

Alternatively, the cross price elasticity of demand between good Y and good X would use the percentage change in the amount of good Y demanded as the numerator and the percentage change in the price of good X as the denominator.

Substitutes and Complements The cross price elasticity of demand is very useful to economists in evaluating whether consumers regard goods and services as substitutes in consumption. In addition, the cross price elasticity can be utilized to consider whether items are complements.

Substitutes and the Cross Price Elasticity of Demand When two goods are substitutes, the cross price elasticity of demand will be positive. For example, when the price of portable hard drives goes up, the amount of flash memory drives demanded at their current price will rise. The demand curve for flash drives will shift horizontally rightward in response as consumers shift away from the now relatively more expensive portable hard drives to flash memory drives. A producer of flash memory drives could benefit from knowing the numerical estimate of the cross price elasticity of demand between portable hard drives and flash memory drives.

For example, if the price of portable hard drives goes up by 10 percent and the producer of flash memory drives knows that the cross price elasticity of demand is 1, the flash drive producer can estimate that the amount of flash memory drives demanded will also go up by 10 percent at any given price of flash memory drives. Plans for increasing production of flash memory drives can then be made.

Complements and the Cross Price Elasticity of Demand When two related goods are complements, the cross price elasticity of demand will be negative (and we will *not* disregard the minus sign). For example, when the price of digital devices declines while all other determinants of demand are unchanged, the amount of printers demanded will rise. Because digital devices and printers often are used together, as prices of digital devices decrease, the number of printers purchased at any given price of printers will naturally increase. Any manufacturer of printers must take this into account in making production plans.

If goods are completely unrelated, their cross price elasticity of demand will, by definition, be zero.

Income Elasticity of Demand

Previously, we discussed the determinants of demand. One of those determinants was income. We can apply our understanding of elasticity to the relationship between changes in income and changes in the amount of a good demanded at that good's current price.

Measuring the Income Elasticity of Demand We measure the responsiveness of the amount of an item demanded at that item's current price to a change in income by the **income elasticity of demand (E_i)**:

Income elasticity of demand (E_i)
The percentage change in the amount of a good demanded, holding its price constant, divided by the percentage change in income. The responsiveness of the amount of a good demanded to a change in income, holding the good's relative price constant.

$$E_i = \frac{\text{percentage change in amount of a good demanded}}{\text{percentage change in income}}$$

holding the item's relative price constant.

Income elasticity of demand refers to a *horizontal shift* in the demand curve in response to changes in income, whereas price elasticity of demand refers to a *movement along* the curve in response to price changes.

> *Thus, income elasticity of demand is calculated at a given price, and price elasticity of demand is calculated at a given income.*

Calculating the Income Elasticity of Demand To get the same income elasticity of demand over the same range of values regardless of the direction of change (increase or decrease), we can use the same formula that we used in computing the price elasticity of demand. When doing so, we have

$$E_i = \frac{\text{change in quantity}}{\text{sum of quantities}/2} \div \frac{\text{change in income}}{\text{sum of incomes}/2}$$

A simple example will demonstrate how income elasticity of demand can be computed. Table 19-3 gives the relevant data. The product in question is digital apps. We assume that the price of digital apps remains constant relative to other prices. In period 1, six apps per month are purchased. Income per month is $4,000. In period 2, monthly income increases to $6,000, and the number of apps demanded per month increases to eight. We can apply the following calculation:

$$E_i = \frac{2/[\,(6+8)/2\,]}{\$2,000/[\,(\$4,000 + \$6,000)/2\,]} = \frac{2/7}{2/5} = 0.71$$

Hence, measured income elasticity of demand for digital apps for the individual represented in this example is 0.71.

You have just been introduced to three types of elasticities. All three elasticities are important in influencing the consumption of most goods. Reasonably accurate estimates of these elasticities can go a long way toward making accurate forecasts of quantities demanded of goods or services.

TABLE 19-3

How Income Affects Quantity of Digital Apps Demanded

Period	Number of Digital Apps Demanded per Month	Income per Month
1	6	$4,000
2	8	$6,000

Price Elasticity of Supply

The **price elasticity of supply** (E_s) is defined similarly to the price elasticity of demand. Supply elasticities are generally positive. The reason is that at higher prices, larger quantities will generally be forthcoming from suppliers. The definition of the price elasticity of supply is as follows:

$$E_s = \frac{\text{percentage change in quantity supplied}}{\text{percentage change in price}}$$

> **19.5** Classify supply elasticities and explain how the length of time for adjustment affects the price elasticity of supply

Price elasticity of supply (E_s)
The responsiveness of the quantity supplied of a commodity to a change in its price—the percentage change in quantity supplied divided by the percentage change in price.

Classifying Supply Elasticities

Just as with demand, there are different ranges of supply elasticities. They are similar in definition to the ranges of demand elasticities.

If a 1 percent increase in price elicits a greater than 1 percent increase in the quantity supplied, we say that at the particular price on the supply schedule, *supply is elastic*. The most extreme elastic supply is called **perfectly elastic supply**—the slightest reduction in price will cause quantity supplied to fall to zero.

If, conversely, a 1 percent increase in price elicits a less than 1 percent increase in the quantity supplied, we refer to that as an *inelastic supply*. The most extreme inelastic supply is called **perfectly inelastic supply**—no matter what the price, the quantity supplied remains the same.

If the percentage change in the quantity supplied is just equal to the percentage change in the price, we call this *unit-elastic supply*.

Figure 19-4 shows two supply schedules, S and S'. You can tell at a glance, even without reading the labels, which one is perfectly elastic and which one is perfectly inelastic. As you might expect, most supply schedules exhibit elasticities that are somewhere between zero and infinity.

How did behavioral economists recently collect sufficient data to determine the price elasticity of exercise time supplied at gyms in exchange for cash payments?

Perfectly elastic supply
A supply characterized by a reduction in quantity supplied to zero when there is the slightest decrease in price.

Perfectly inelastic supply
A supply for which quantity supplied remains constant, no matter what happens to price.

BEHAVIORAL EXAMPLE

Getting Paid to Work Out

In a recent experimental study, behavioral economists offered 690 people cash payments aimed at inducing them to supply additional exercise workouts at a gymnasium. Everyone who participated in the experiment received a $30 payment, but participants who exercised at the gym an average of 1.33 times per week over a 6-week interval received an additional $30. The study determined that receipt of this additional payment induced these people to increase the number of exercise workouts supplied by about 1.47 workouts per week.

We can calculate the price elasticity of supply of gym-exercise workouts:

$$\begin{aligned}
E_s &= \frac{\text{change in } Q}{\text{sum of quantities}/2} \div \frac{\text{change in } P}{\text{sum of quantities}/2} \\[6pt]
&= \frac{1.47 \text{ workouts} - 1.33 \text{ workouts}}{(1.47 \text{ workouts} + 1.33 \text{ workouts})/2} \\[6pt]
&\quad \div \frac{(\$60 \text{ per workout} - \$30 \text{ per workout})}{(\$60 \text{ per workout} + \$30 \text{ per workout})/2} \\[6pt]
&= \frac{0.14 \text{ workouts}}{2.80 \text{ workouts}/2} \div \frac{\$30 \text{ per workout}}{\$90 \text{ per workout}/2} \\[6pt]
&= 0.15
\end{aligned}$$

Thus, the price elasticity of supply was equal to 0.15, meaning that a 1 percent increase in dollar payments for workouts that participants supplied at the gym induced about 0.15 additional gym workouts per week.

FOR CRITICAL THINKING

Why do you suppose that developers have designed apps that allow people to give themselves incentives to exercise by providing payments for supplying gym workouts but that impose penalties for failing to do so?

Sources are listed at the end of this chapter.

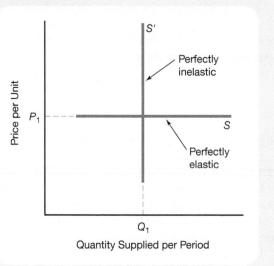

FIGURE 19-4

The Extremes in Supply Curves

Here we have drawn two extremes of supply schedules: S is a perfectly elastic supply curve; S' is a perfectly inelastic one. In the former, an unlimited quantity will be supplied within the relevant range of quantities at price P_1. In the latter, no matter what the price, the quantity supplied will be Q_1. An example of S' might be the supply curve for fresh (unfrozen) fish on the morning the boats come in.

Price Elasticity of Supply and Length of Time for Adjustment

We pointed out earlier that the longer the time period allowed for adjustment, the greater the price elasticity of demand. It turns out that the same proposition applies to supply. The longer the time for adjustment, the more elastic the supply curve. Consider why this is true:

1. *The longer the time allowed for adjustment, the more resources can flow into (or out of) an industry through expansion (or contraction) of existing firms.* As an example, suppose that there is a long-lasting, significant increase in the demand for gasoline. The result is a sustained rise in the market price of gasoline. Initially, gasoline refiners will be hampered in expanding their production with the operating refining equipment available to them. Over time, however, some refining companies might be able to recondition old equipment that had fallen into disuse. They can also place orders for construction of new gasoline-refining equipment, and once the equipment arrives, they can also put it into place to expand their gasoline production. Given sufficient time, therefore, existing gasoline refiners can eventually respond to higher gasoline prices by adding new refining operations.

2. *The longer the time allowed for adjustment, the entry (or exit) of firms increases (or decreases) production in an industry.* Consider what happens if the price of gasoline remains higher than before as a result of a sustained rise in gasoline demand. Even as existing refiners add to their capability to produce gasoline by retooling old equipment, purchasing new equipment, and adding new refining facilities, additional businesses may seek to earn profits at the now-higher gasoline prices. Over time, the entry of new gasoline-refining companies adds to the productive capabilities of the entire refining industry, and the quantity of gasoline supplied increases.

We therefore talk about short-run and long-run price elasticities of supply. The short run is defined as the time period during which full adjustment has not yet taken place. The long run is the time period during which firms have been able to adjust fully to the change in price.

FIGURE 19-5

Short-Run and Long-Run Price Elasticity of Supply

Consider a situation in which the price is P_e and the quantity supplied is Q_e. In the immediate run, we hypothesize a vertical supply curve, S_1. With the price increase to P_1, therefore, there will be no change in the short run in quantity supplied, which will remain at Q_e. Given some time for adjustment, the supply curve will rotate to S_2. The new amount supplied will increase to Q_1. The long-run supply curve is shown by S_3. The amount supplied again increases to Q_2.

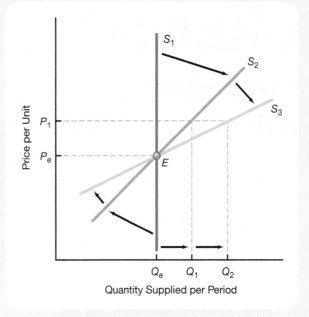

A Graphic Presentation We can show a whole set of supply curves similar to the ones we generated for demand. As Figure 19-5 shows, when nothing can be done in the immediate run, the supply curve is vertical, S_1. As more time is allowed for adjustment, the supply curve rotates around point E to S_2 and then to S_3, becoming more elastic as it rotates around point E.

ECONOMICS IN YOUR LIFE

Imposing a Philadelphia Soft Drinks Tax Reveals Information about the Price Elasticity of Demand

The Pennsylvania Supreme Court upheld a special tax on sugary drinks implemented by Philadelphia's Mayor James Kenney and its city council. The 1.5-cent-per-ounce tax was imposed with an aim to fund universal pre-kindergarten programs and provide supplemental funding for various other city expenditures, such as contributions to benefits for city workers.

Imposition of the tax generated a proportionate price increase of about 35 percent. Over the months following implementation of the new tax, purchases of sugary soft drinks within Philadelphia declined by about 45 percent. These facts reveal that the price elasticity of demand for soft drinks is approximately equal to 45 percent/35 percent, or about 1.3. Thus, Philadelphia's imposition of the sugary-drinks tax has revealed that city residents' demand for soft drinks is elastic.

FOR CRITICAL THINKING

Why might the fact that the demand for soft drinks is elastic help to explain why Philadelphia's revenues from the sugary drinks tax have turned out to be about 15 percent lower than predicted by Mayor Kenney and the city council?

REAL APPLICATION

Assume that you are living in Philadelphia and like sugary drinks. You continue to buy almost the same quantity of such drinks. Does that mean that the law of demand is wrong?

Sources are listed at the end of this chapter.

ISSUES & APPLICATIONS

Tax-Induced Increases in Airline Ticket Prices, the Price Elasticity of Demand, and Airline Revenues

ChameleonsEye/Shutterstock

CONCEPTS APPLIED

➤ Price Elasticity of Demand

➤ Inelastic Demand

➤ Elastic Demand

Taxes on air travel add more than 10 percent to the price of a typical passenger ticket. A few years ago, the U.S. Department of Transportation adopted a rule requiring airlines to clearly list all applicable taxes on tickets available for purchase. In the process of evaluating the various implications for the airline industry of this regulatory change, Sebastien Bradley of Drexel University and Naomi Feldman of the Federal Reserve contemplated issues involving the price elasticity of demand.

Higher Airline Prices and the Price Elasticity of Demand for Tickets

In their analysis of the effects of the requirement to reveal information about the amount of the taxes, Bradley and Feldman found that the quantity of tickets demanded became more responsive to changes in the overall, tax-inclusive, out-of-pocket price. To show this, Bradley and Feldman estimated the price elasticity of demand for airline tickets, which they showed increased after airlines had to reveal tax information to consumers.

Just how responsive is the quantity of airline tickets demanded to a tax-induced increase in the overall price of airline tickets? The answer the researchers found is that a 1 percent increase in the ticket price generated by higher ticket taxes reduces the quantity of tickets demanded by about 8 percent. Thus, the price elasticity of demand is approximately equal to 8, so the demand for airline tickets is elastic.

Effects on Airline Revenues

A higher price of airline tickets tends to push up revenues in the airline industry, other things being equal. At the same time, however, a decrease in the number of airline tickets sold tends to reduce the industry's revenues. Which

of these effects predominates depends on the value of the price elasticity of demand.

As you have learned, along the elastic range of a demand curve, an increase in price should result in a net decrease in revenues. This is exactly what Bradley and Feldman found to be true for the airline industry. Indeed, their conclusion is that every $5 increase in the total out-of-pocket price of an airline ticket brought about by a tax increase generates a 2.4 percent reduction in airline revenues.

FOR CRITICAL THINKING

Suppose that economists were to divide consumers into two groups based on how quickly they had to decide about purchase of an airline ticket versus other modes of travel. Which group likely would have a higher price elasticity of demand: the group with more or less time to decide? Explain.

REAL APPLICATION

If there is a significant increase in airline ticket taxes, how do you determine whether alternative modes of transportation might be acceptable to you?

Sources are listed at the end of this chapter.

What You Should Know

LEARNING OBJECTIVES

19.1 **Calculate price elasticity of demand** *The price elasticity of demand is the percentage change in quantity demanded divided by the percentage change in price. Over the elastic range of a demand curve, the price elasticity of demand exceeds 1. Over the inelastic range of a demand curve, the price elasticity of demand is less than 1. Finally, over the unit-elastic range of a demand curve, the price elasticity of demand equals 1.*

19.2 **Explain the relationship between price elasticity of demand and total revenues** *Total revenues equal the price multiplied by the number of units purchased. Along a demand curve, price and quantity changes move in opposite directions, so the effect of a price change on total revenues depends on the responsiveness of quantity demanded to a price change. If demand is elastic, a price increase reduces total revenues, but if demand is inelastic, a price increase raises total revenues. If demand is unit-elastic, a price increase leaves total revenues unchanged.*

19.3 **Describe the factors that determine the price elasticity of demand** *Price elasticity of demand is greater with more close substitutes, when a larger portion of a person's budget is spent on the good, or if there is more time to adjust to a price change.*

19.4 **Explain the cross price elasticity of demand and the income elasticity of demand** *Cross price elasticity of demand is the percentage change in the amount demanded divided by the percentage change in the price of a related item, and income elasticity is the percentage change in the amount demanded divided by the percentage change in income.*

19.5 **Classify supply elasticities and explain how the length of time for adjustment affects the price elasticity of supply** *The price elasticity of supply equals the percentage change in quantity supplied divided by the percentage change in price. If the price elasticity of supply exceeds 1, supply is elastic, and if the price elasticity of supply is less than 1, supply is inelastic. Supply is unit-elastic if the price elasticity of supply equals 1. Supply is more likely to be elastic when sellers have more time to adjust to price changes.*

KEY TERMS

price elasticity of demand
(E_p), 403
elastic demand, 405
unit elasticity of demand, 406
inelastic demand, 406
perfectly inelastic demand, 406
perfectly elastic demand, 406
Key Figure
Figure 19-1, 406

Key Figure
Figure 19-2, 408

Key Figure
Figure 19-3, 412

cross price elasticity of
demand (E_{xy}), 413
income elasticity of demand
(E_i), 414

price elasticity of supply
(E_s), 415
perfectly elastic supply, 415
perfectly inelastic supply, 415
Key Figure
Figure 19-5, 417

PROBLEMS

19-1. When the price of shirts emblazoned with a college logo is $20, consumers buy 150 per week. When the price declines to $19, consumers purchase 200 per week. Based on this information, calculate the price elasticity of demand for logo-emblazoned shirts.

19-2. Table 19-2 indicates that the short-run price elasticity of demand for tires is 0.9. If an increase in the price of petroleum (used in producing tires) causes the market prices of tires to rise from $50 to $60, by what percentage would you expect the quantity of tires demanded to change?

19-3. The diagram depicts the demand curve for "miniburgers" in a nationwide fast-food market. Use the information in this diagram to answer the questions that follow.

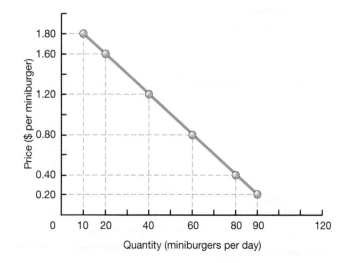

a. What is the price elasticity of demand along the range of the demand curve between a price of $0.20 per miniburger and a price of $0.40 per miniburger? Is demand elastic or inelastic over this range?

b. What is the price elasticity of demand along the range of the demand curve between a price of $0.80 per miniburger and a price of $1.20 per miniburger? Is demand elastic or inelastic over this range?

c. What is the price elasticity of demand along the range of the demand curve between a price of $1.60 per miniburger and a price of $1.80 per miniburger? Is demand elastic or inelastic over this range?

19-4. In a local market, the monthly price of Internet access service decreases from $20 per account to $10 per account, and the total quantity of monthly accounts across all Internet access providers increases from 100,000 to 200,000. What is the price elasticity of demand? Is demand elastic, unit-elastic, or inelastic?

19-5. At a price of $57.50 to play 18 holes on local golf courses, 1,200 consumers pay to play a game of golf each day. A rise in the price to $62.50 causes the number of consumers to decline to 800. What is the price elasticity of demand? Is demand elastic, unit-elastic, or inelastic?

19-6. It is very difficult to find goods with perfectly elastic or perfectly inelastic demand. We can, however, find goods that lie near these extremes. Characterize demands for the following goods as being near perfectly elastic or near perfectly inelastic.

a. Corn grown and harvested by a small farmer in Iowa

b. Heroin for a drug addict

c. Water for a desert hiker

d. One of several optional textbooks in a pass-fail course

19-7. In the market for handmade guitars, when the price of guitars is $800, annual revenues are $640,000. When the price falls to $700, annual revenues decline to $630,000. Over this range of guitar prices, is the demand for handmade guitars elastic, unit-elastic, or inelastic?

19-8. Suppose that over a range of prices, the price elasticity of demand varies from 15.0 to 2.5. Over another range of prices, the price elasticity of demand varies from 1.5 to 0.75. What can you say about total revenues and the total revenue curve over these two ranges of the demand curve as price falls?

19-9. Based solely on the information provided below, characterize the demands for the following goods as likely to be more elastic or more inelastic.

a. A 45-cent box of salt that you buy once a year

b. A type of high-powered ski boat that you can rent from any one of a number of rental agencies

c. A specific brand of bottled water

d. Automobile insurance in a state that requires autos to be insured but has only a few insurance companies

e. A 75-cent guitar pick for the lead guitarist of a major band

19-10. The value of cross price elasticity of demand between goods X and Y is 1.25, while the cross price elasticity of demand between goods X and Z is −2.0. Characterize X and Y and X and Z as substitutes or complements.

19-11. Suppose that the cross price elasticity of demand between eggs and bacon is −0.5. What would you expect to happen to purchases of bacon if the price of eggs rises by 10 percent?

19-12. A 5 percent increase in the price of digital apps reduces the amount of tablet devices demanded by 3 percent. What is the cross price elasticity of demand? Are tablet devices and digital apps complements or substitutes?

19-13. An individual's income rises from $80,000 per year to $84,000 per year, and as a consequence the person's purchases of movie downloads rise from 48 per year to 72 per year. What is this individual's income elasticity of demand?

19-14. Assume that the income elasticity of demand for hot dogs is −1.25 and that the income elasticity of demand for lobster is 1.25. What will happen to each good's demand curve as income goes up?

19-15. At a price of $25,000, producers of midsized automobiles are willing to manufacture and sell 75,000 cars per month. At a price of $35,000, they are willing to produce and sell 125,000 a month. Using the same type of calculation method used to compute the price elasticity of demand, what is the price elasticity of supply? Is supply elastic, unit-elastic, or inelastic?

19-16. An increase in the market price of men's haircuts, from $15 per haircut to $25 per haircut, initially causes a local barbershop to have its employees work overtime to increase the number of daily haircuts provided from 35 to 45. When the $25

market price remains unchanged for several weeks and all other things remain equal as well, the barbershop hires additional employees and provides 65 haircuts per day. What is the short-run price elasticity of supply? What is the long-run price elasticity of supply?

19-17. Consider panel (a) of Figure 19-1. Use the basic definition of the price elasticity of demand to explain why the value of the price elasticity of demand is zero for the extremely rare situation of vertical demand curve.

19-18. Take a look at Figure 19-2. Work out the calculation for the price elasticity of demand between prices of $11 per reservation and $10 per reservation to prove that the value is 21.

19-19. Consider Figure 19-2. Work out the calculation for the price elasticity of demand between prices of $1 per reservation and $2 per reservation to prove that the value is 0.158.

19-20. Take a look at Figure 19-2. Work out the calculation for the price elasticity of demand between prices of $6 per reservation and $5 per reservation to prove that the value is 1.

19-21. Consider Figure 19-3. Following a price increase, is the quantity demanded more responsive to the price increase immediately, after an initial passage of time, and then after even more time has passed? Why is this so?

19-22. Take a look at Figure 19-5. Following a price increase, is the quantity supplied more responsive to the price increase immediately, after an initial passage of time, and then after even more time has passed? Why is this so?

REFERENCES

EXAMPLE: The Price Elasticity of Demand for Freshman Enrollments at Private Colleges

College Board, "Trends in College Pricing" (https://trends.college-board.org/college-pricing), 2019.

Laura Krantz, "For Small, Private Colleges, Fewer Students Means More Worries," *Boston Globe*, March 31, 2018.

James Paterson, "Small Colleges Hit Hard by Shrinking Enrollments," *Education Dive* (https://www.educationdive.com/news/small-colleges-hit-hard-by-shrinking-enrollments/530154/), August 15, 2018.

INTERNATIONAL POLICY EXAMPLE: The Price Elasticity of Demand for Tesla Vehicles in Hong Kong

Annie Gaus, "With More Electric Cars on the Way, Where Does That Leave Tesla?" *The Street*, January 15, 2019.

Fred Lambert, "Hong Kong Brings Back Some Electric Vehicle Incentives That Made Tesla So Popular in the Region," *Electrek*, February 28, 2018.

Alice Woodhouse, "Tesla Sales Drop in Hong Kong after Tax Break Is Removed," *Financial Times*, February 5, 2018.

AI—DECISION MAKING THROUGH DATA: In the Pursuit of "Price Optimization"

Rahul Sharma, "Price Optimization: How Machine Learnings Puts AI into Retail," InkHive.com (https://inkhive.com/2019/01/31/price-optimization-machine-learning-puts-ai-retail/), January 31, 2019.

Raghav Bharadwa, "Artificial Intelligence for High Frequency Pricing, Inventory, and Margins Optimization," *TechEmergence* (https://www.techemergence.com/artificial-intelligence-high-frequency-retail-pricing-inventory-margins-optimization/), July 25, 2018.

"How AI Powers Pricing Optimization to Drive Maximum Profitability for Grocers," Daisy Intelligence (www.daisyintelligence.com/how-ai-powers-pricing-optimization-to-drive-maximum-profitability-for-grocers/), April 18, 2018.

BEHAVIORAL EXAMPLE: Getting Paid to Work Out

Wendy Bumgardner, "How to Get Paid to Walk," VeryWelFit.com (https://www.verywellfit.com/walking-apps-that-earn-rewards-3434997), January 31, 2019.

Mariana Carrera, Heather Royer, Mark Stehr, Justin Sydnor, "Can Financial Incentives Help People Trying to Establish New Habits? Experimental Evidence with New Gym Members," *Journal of Health Economics*, 2018.

Josh Patoka, "Fourteen Apps That Will Pay You to Work Out," WellKeptWallet.com (https://wellkeptwallet.com/apps-pay-you-to-workout/), September 9, 2019.

ECONOMICS IN YOUR LIFE: Imposing a Philadelphia Soft Drinks Tax Reveals Information about the Price Elasticity of Demand

"Philadelphia Beverage Tax," City of Philadelphia (https://www.phila.gov/services/payments-assistance-taxes/business-taxes/philadelphia-beverage-tax/), 2019.

John Bacon, "Push for Soda Taxes across U.S.A. Notches Win in Philly," *USA Today*, July 18, 2018.

Adam Smeltz, "Soda Tax Stands in Philadelphia, But Does It Have Pop in Pittsburgh?" *Pittsburgh Post-Gazette*, July 21, 2018.

ISSUES & APPLICATIONS: Tax-Induced Increases in Airline Ticket Prices, the Price Elasticity of Demand, and Airline Revenues

"The Full Fare Advertising Law," TheTravelNet.com (https://www.thetravelnet.com/university/articles/sdetails/rules-and-regulations/the-full-fare-advertising-law), 2019.

U.S. Department of Transportation, "Advertising Rules" (https://www.transportation.gov/airconsumer/advertising), 2019.

Sebastien Bradley and Naomi Feldman, "Hidden Baggage: Behavioral Responses to Changes in Airline Ticket Tax Disclosure," Financial and Economics Discussion Series, Divisions of Research and Statistics and Monetary Affairs, Board of Governors of the Federal Reserve System, July 2018.

20 Consumer Choice

Foxy burrow/Shutterstock

After reading this chapter, you should be able to:

20.1 Distinguish between total and marginal utility and discuss why marginal utility ultimately falls as a person consumes more of an item

20.2 Explain why an optimal choice of how much to consume entails equalizing the marginal utility per dollar spent across all items

20.3 Describe the substitution and real-income effects of a price change

20.4 Discuss why bounded rationality may prevent reaching a true consumer optimum

These days, people who have not purchased a new vehicle for several years commonly express surprise at the suddenly expanded array of digital features included as part of the overall "package" that they purchase when they pay the vehicle's price. Automakers include these features in an effort to induce people to make such purchases. In this chapter, you will learn how adding "infotainment systems" and other digital systems to vehicles can indeed give individuals incentives to add a new vehicle to the set of goods and services bought during a given interval. In addition, you will learn ways in which expansions of the array of digital features included within vehicles can induce *some* consumers to *forgo* a new vehicle purchase.

the number of U.S. residents who pay fees for memberships with firms that offer them access to exercise facilities currently exceeds 55 million people, an increase of nearly 10 million from a decade ago? This substantial increase in gym memberships took place even as the average price of a gym membership increased at a rate exceeding 15 percent per year over that period.

In an earlier chapter, you learned that the price of a particular item, such as gym memberships, is a key determinant of the quantity of that item demanded. That is, you learned about the law of demand, which implies that at a lower price, there will be a higher quantity demanded, other things being equal. You also learned, however, that the amount of an item demanded also depends on other elements, such as tastes and incomes. Understanding the various elements that influence the amount of an item demanded is useful because it allows us to make better sense of the world and even generate predictions about it. One way of deriving the law of demand involves an analysis of the logic of consumer choice in a world of limited resources. In this chapter, therefore, we discuss what is called *utility analysis*.

20.1 Distinguish between total and marginal utility and discuss why marginal utility ultimately falls as a person consumes more of an item

Utility
The want-satisfying power of a good or service.

Utility Theory

When you buy something, you do so because of the satisfaction you expect to receive from having and using that good. For everything that you like to have, the more you have of it, the higher the level of total satisfaction you receive. Another term that can be used for satisfaction is **utility,** or want-satisfying power. This property is common to all goods that are desired. The concept of utility is purely subjective, however. There is no way that you or I can measure the amount of utility that a consumer might be able to obtain from a particular good, for utility does not imply "useful" or "utilitarian" or "practical." Thus, there can be no accurate scientific assessment of the utility that someone might receive by consuming a fast-food dinner or a movie relative to the utility that another person might receive from that same good or service.

Tastes and Preferences and Utility

The utility that individuals receive from consuming a good depends on their tastes and preferences. These tastes and preferences are normally assumed to be given and stable for a particular individual. An individual's tastes determine how much utility that individual derives from consuming a good, and this in turn determines how that individual allocates his or her income to purchases of that good. But we cannot explain why tastes are different between individuals. For example, we cannot explain why some people like yogurt but others do not.

Analyzing Utility We can analyze in terms of utility the way consumers decide what to buy, just as physicists have analyzed some of their problems in terms of what they call force. No physicist has ever seen a unit of force, and no economist has ever seen a unit of utility. In both cases, however, these concepts have proved useful for analysis.

Utility analysis
The analysis of consumer decision making based on utility maximization.

Throughout this chapter, we will be discussing **utility analysis,** which is the analysis of consumer decision making based on utility maximization—that is, making choices with the aim of attaining the highest feasible satisfaction.

Utility and Utils Economists once believed that utility could be measured. In fact, there is a philosophical school of thought based on utility theory called *utilitarianism*, developed by the English philosopher Jeremy Bentham (1748–1832). Bentham held that society should seek the greatest happiness for the greatest number. He sought to apply an arithmetic formula for measuring happiness. He and his followers developed the notion of measurable utility and invented the **util** to measure it. For the moment, we will assume that we can measure satisfaction using this representative unit. Our assumption will allow us to quantify the way we examine consumer behavior.

Util
A representative unit by which utility is measured.

Thus, the first chocolate bar that you eat might yield you 4 utils of satisfaction. The first peanut cluster might yield 6 utils, and so on. Today, no one really believes that we can actually measure utils, but the ideas forthcoming from such analysis will prove useful in understanding how consumers choose among alternatives.

Total and Marginal Utility Consider the satisfaction, or utility, that you receive each time you download and utilize digital apps. Obviously, one only downloads an app to use it, but we shall focus on the act of downloading that is required to utilize the app. To make the example straightforward, let's say that there are thousands of apps to choose from each year and that each of them is of the same quality. Let's say that you normally download and utilize one app per week. You could, of course, download two, or three, or four per week. Presumably, each time you download and utilize another app per week, you will get additional satisfaction, or utility. The question that we must ask, though, is, given that you are already downloading and using one app per week, will the next one downloaded and utilized during that week give you the same amount of additional utility?

That additional, or incremental, utility is called **marginal utility,** where *marginal* means "incremental" or "additional." (Marginal changes also refer to decreases, in which cases we talk about *decremental* changes.) The concept of marginality is important in economics because we can think of people comparing additional (marginal) benefits with additional (marginal) costs.

Marginal utility
The change in total utility due to a one-unit change in the quantity of a good or service consumed.

Applying Marginal Analysis to Utility The example in Figure 20-1 will clarify the distinction between total utility and marginal utility. The table in panel (a) shows the total utility and the marginal utility of downloading and using digital apps each week. Marginal utility is the difference between total utility derived from one level of consumption and total utility derived from another level of consumption within a given time interval. A simple formula for marginal utility is this:

$$\text{Marginal utility} = \frac{\text{change in total utility}}{\text{change in number of units consumed}}$$

In our example, when a person has already downloaded and utilized two digital apps in one week and then downloads and uses another, total utility increases from 16 utils to 19 utils. Therefore, the marginal utility (of downloading and utilizing one more app after already having downloaded and used two in one week) is equal to 3 utils.

Graphical Analysis

We can transfer the information in panel (a) onto a graph, as we do in panels (b) and (c) of Figure 20-1. Total utility, which is represented in column 2 of panel (a), is transferred to panel (b).

Total utility continues to rise until four digital apps are downloaded and utilized per week. This measure of utility remains at 20 utils through the fifth app, and at the sixth app per week it falls to 18 utils. We assume that at some quantity consumed per unit time period, boredom with consuming more digital apps begins to set in. Thus, at some quantity consumed, the additional utility from consuming an additional app begins to fall, so total utility first rises and then declines in panel (b).

Marginal Utility If you look carefully at panels (b) and (c) of Figure 20-1, the notion of marginal utility becomes clear. In economics, the term *marginal* always refers to a *change* in the total. The marginal utility of consuming three downloaded digital apps per week instead of two apps per week is the increment in total utility and is equal to 3 utils per week. All of the points in panel (c) are taken from column 3 of the table in panel (a).

Notice that marginal utility falls throughout the graph. A special point occurs after four apps are downloaded and used per week because the total utility curve in panel (b) is unchanged after the consumption of the fourth app. That means that the consumer receives no additional (marginal) utility from downloading and using five apps rather than four. This is shown in panel (c) as *zero* marginal utility. After that point, marginal utility becomes negative.

FIGURE 20-1

Total and Marginal Utility of Downloading and Utilizing Digital Apps

If we were able to assign specific values to the utility derived from downloading and utilizing digital apps each week, we could obtain a marginal utility schedule similar in pattern to the one shown in panel (a). In column 1 is the number of apps downloaded and used per week. Column 2 is the total utility derived from each quantity. Column 3 shows the marginal utility derived from each additional quantity, which is defined as the change in total utility due to a change of one unit of using downloaded apps per week. Total utility from panel (a) is plotted in panel (b). Marginal utility is plotted in panel (c), where you see that it reaches zero where total utility hits its maximum at between 4 and 5 units.

Panel (a)

(1) Number of Digital Apps Downloaded and Utilized per Week	(2) Total Utility (utils per week)	(3) Marginal Utility (utils per week)
0	0	
		10 (10 − 0)
1	10	
		6 (16 − 10)
2	16	
		3 (19 − 16)
3	19	
		1 (20 − 19)
4	20	
		0 (20 − 20)
5	20	
		−2 (18 − 20)
6	18	

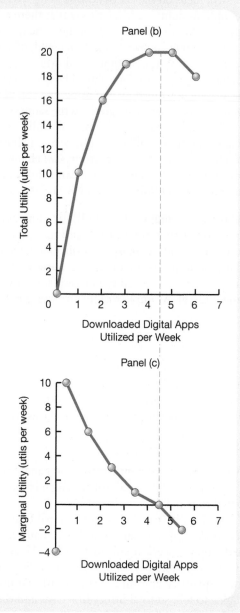

Panel (b)

Panel (c)

WHAT HAPPENS WHEN...

consuming an additional unit of a good or service leaves total utility unchanged?

When consumption of one more unit of an item does not yield a change in the level of total utility, then the additional utility from that unit consumed must be zero. Marginal utility for that unit, therefore, equals zero.

Negative Marginal Utility In our example, when marginal utility becomes negative, it means that the consumer is tired of consuming digital apps and would require some form of compensation to consume any more. When marginal utility is negative, an additional unit consumed actually lowers total utility by becoming a nuisance.

Rarely does a consumer face a situation of negative marginal utility. Whenever this point is reached, goods in effect become "bads." Consuming more units actually causes total utility to *fall* so that marginal utility is negative. A rational consumer will stop consuming at the point at which marginal utility becomes negative, even if the good is available at a price of zero.

How do economists recommend that people avoid negative marginal utility from overconsumption of calories across a large array of food choices confronted each day?

BEHAVIORAL EXAMPLE

Rational Rationing of Calories to Prevent Negative Marginal Utility from Food Consumption

Many people indicate in surveys of their food consumption that they regularly discover when they step on a scale to measure their weight that they have been eating "too much" food. These people, of course, take into account the enjoyment of food consumption. Additionally, after the fact, they observe the effects of higher caloric ingestion on body weight. They believe that they experienced *negative* marginal utility from the overconsumption of food. Thus, on net, their total utility has been *reduced* by food consumption.

Behavioral economists have found that when people decide how many calories to consume prior to a meal or snack break, they tend to focus on the utility that they derive from near-term enjoyment from consuming the calories and forget about implications for utility that they will experience based on their changed body weight. The straightforward way for people to avoid such mistakes, these economists contend, is to aim for a truly overall consumer optimum encompassing available food choices. Such an all-encompassing optimum can be reached, they argue, by careful arrangement of the array of choices for each specific meal and snack breaks. For instance, instead of choosing from among the full array of foods available for a lunch break, an individual can limit a lunch to a salad chosen from among the widest possible set of low-calorie, healthful salad choices. Furthermore, an individual can allow for a choice of one higher-calorie dessert item at, say, one meal per day to help ensure attainment of utility related to the pure enjoyment of consumption. By maintaining but limiting choices among foods over the course of each day, therefore, an individual can maximize overall utility from food consumption relating *both* to eating enjoyment *and* to satisfaction with one's body weight.

REAL APPLICATION

Assume that you are a person concerned about being overweight or becoming overweight. How might you change your method of shopping for food to improve the probability that you don't "overeat"?

Sources are listed at the end of this chapter.

Diminishing Marginal Utility

Notice that in panel (c) of Figure 20-1, marginal utility is continuously declining. This property has been named the principle of **diminishing marginal utility.** There is no way that we can prove diminishing marginal utility. Nevertheless, diminishing marginal utility has even been called a law. This supposed law concerns a psychological, or subjective, utility that you receive as you consume more and more of a particular good.

Diminishing marginal utility
The principle that as more of any good or service is consumed, its *extra* benefit declines. Otherwise stated, increases in total utility from the consumption of a good or service become smaller and smaller as more is consumed during a given time period.

The Law of Diminishing Marginal Utility Stated formally, the law of diminishing marginal utility is as follows:

> *As an individual consumes more of a particular commodity, the total level of utility, or satisfaction, derived from that consumption usually increases. Eventually, however, the rate at which it increases diminishes as more is consumed.*

Take a hungry individual at a dinner table. The first serving is greatly appreciated, and the individual derives a substantial amount of utility from it. Consumption of the second serving does not have quite as much pleasurable impact as the first one, and consumption of the third serving is likely to be even less satisfying. This individual experiences diminishing marginal utility of food until he or she stops eating, and this is true for most people. All-you-can-eat restaurants count on this fact. A second helping of ribs may provide some marginal utility, but the third helping would have only a little or even negative marginal utility.

Marginal Utility Cannot Persistently Increase Consider for a moment the opposite possibility—increasing marginal utility. Under such a situation, the marginal utility after consuming, say, one hamburger would increase. Consuming the second hamburger would yield more utility to you, and consuming the third would yield even more.

Thus, if increasing marginal utility existed, each of us would consume only one good or service! Rather than observing that "variety is the spice of life," we would see that monotony in consumption was preferred. We do not observe such single-item consumption, and therefore we have great confidence in the concept of diminishing marginal utility.

20.2 Explain why an optimal choice of how much to consume entails equalizing the marginal utility per dollar spent across all items

Consumer optimum
A choice of a set of goods and services that maximizes the level of satisfaction for each consumer, subject to limited income.

Optimizing Consumption Choices

Every consumer has a limited income, so choices must be made. Suppose that a consumer has made all of his or her choices about what to buy and in what quantities. If the total level of satisfaction, or utility, from that set of choices is as great as it can be, we say that the consumer has *optimized*. When the consumer has attained an optimum consumption set of goods and services, we say that he or she has reached **consumer optimum.**

Why might consumers be willing to rely on machine learning to assist them in narrowing down their choices?

 AI | DECISION MAKING THROUGH DATA

An Aid for Attaining a Consumer Optimum

In years past, people would joke about shopping at malls until they dropped. Today, it is possible to utilize electronic devices to shop constantly, truly to the point of dropping from physical and mental fatigue. People usually prefer being able to decide from among a wider range of potential choices. Nevertheless, the ability to use digital devices to increase the array of options—including a rapidly growing set of digital products and app-guided home services—impinges on a key consumer decision variable: allocation of available time.

In recognition of this fact, research scientists at a number of companies are working to develop machine-learning apps that enable an individual's digital devices to search online and narrow the range of choices, even during intervals when that individual is not paying attention to those devices. A machine-learning shopping app could, for instance, search among a vast set of clothing items available online.

The app could narrow the set of choices based on preference settings while that individual is taking in a concert or working to earn income. Afterward, the consumer could utilize planned shopping time to select from this narrowed set. Of course, the consumer would have to select a machine-learning app and choose among available machine-learning preference settings. Nevertheless, the allowed reallocation of time likely would move many people to positions of consumer optimum at higher levels of satisfaction than before the advent of machine-learning shopping apps.

FOR CRITICAL THINKING

How might the advent of machine-learning shopping apps undermine an oft-repeated media claim that consumers can be harmed by having to confront "too many choices"?

Sources are listed at the end of this chapter.

A Two-Good Example

Consider a simple two-good example that appears in Table 20-1. During a given period, a consumer's income is $26. The consumer has to choose between spending income on downloads of digital apps at $5 per app and on purchasing wireless earbuds

TABLE 20-1

Total and Marginal Utility from Consuming Digital Apps and Wireless Earbuds on an Income of $26

(1) Digital Apps per Period	(2) Total Utility of Digital Apps per Period (utils)	(3) Marginal Utility (utils) (MU_d)	(4) Marginal Utility per Dollar Spent (MU_d/P_d) (price = $5)	(5) Wireless Earbuds per Period	(6) Total Utility of Wireless Earbuds per Period (utils)	(7) Marginal Utility (utils) (MU_e)	(8) Marginal Utility per Dollar Spent (MU_e/P_e) (price = $3)
0	0	–	–	0	0	–	–
1	50.0	50.0	10.0	1	25	25	8.3
2	95.0	45.0	9.0	2	47	22	7.3
3	135.0	40.0	8.0	3	65	18	6.0
4	171.5	36.5	7.3	4	80	15	5.0
5	200.0	28.5	5.7	5	89	9	3.0

at $3 each. Let's say that when the consumer has spent all income on digital apps and wireless earbuds, the last dollar spent on a wireless earbud yields 3 utils of utility but the last dollar spent on apps yields 10 utils. Wouldn't this consumer increase total utility if fewer dollars were spent on wireless earbuds and allocated to apps?

Conditions for a Consumer Optimum The answer is yes. More dollars spent downloading apps will reduce marginal utility per last dollar spent, whereas fewer dollars spent on the consumption of wireless earbuds will increase marginal utility per last dollar spent. Nevertheless, the loss in utility from spending fewer dollars purchasing fewer wireless earbuds is more than made up by spending additional dollars on more digital apps. As a consequence, total utility increases.

The consumer optimum—where total utility is maximized—occurs when the satisfaction per last dollar spent on both wireless earbuds and digital apps per week is equal for the two goods. Thus, the amount of goods consumed depends on the prices of the goods, the income of the consumer, and the marginal utility derived from the amounts of each good consumed.

Utility Derived from Consuming Two Items Table 20-1 presents information on utility derived from consuming various quantities of digital apps and wireless earbuds. Columns 4 and 8 show the marginal utility per dollar spent on apps and wireless earbuds, respectively. If the prices of both goods are zero, individuals will consume each as long as their respective marginal utility is positive (at least five units of each and probably much more).

It is also true that a consumer with unlimited income will continue consuming goods until the marginal utility of each is equal to zero. When the price is zero or the consumer's income is unlimited, there is no effective constraint on consumption.

A Two-Good Consumer Optimum

Consumer optimum is attained when the marginal utility of the last dollar spent on each good yields the same utility and income is completely exhausted. In the situation in Table 20-1, the individual's income is $26. From columns 4 and 8 of Table 20-1, equal marginal utilities per dollar spent occur at the consumption level of four digital apps and two wireless earbuds (the marginal utility per dollar spent equals 7.3).

ECONOMICS IN YOUR LIFE

To contemplate why some people are willing to pay up to $2,000 for a pair of blue jeans, take a look at **Boutique Sellers Offer $2,000 Japanese-Made Jeans That Some Consumers Truly Are Happy to Buy** on page 435.

TABLE 20-2

Steps to Consumer Optimum

In each purchase situation described here, the consumer always purchases the good with the higher marginal utility per dollar spent. For example, at the time of the third purchase, the marginal utility per last dollar spent on digital apps is 8, but it is 8.3 for wireless earbuds, and

$16 of income remains, so the next purchase will be a wireless earbud. Here the price of digital apps is $P_d =$ $5, the price of wireless earbuds is $P_c =$ $3, MU_d is the marginal utility of consumption of digital apps, and MU_e is the marginal utility of consumption of wireless earbuds.

| | Choices | | | | | |
| | Digital Apps | | Wireless Earbuds | | | |
Purchase	Unit	MU_d/P_d	Unit	MU_e/P_e	Buying Decision	Remaining Income
1	First	10.0	First	8.3	First digital app	$26 − $5 = $21
2	Second	9.0	First	8.3	Second digital app	$21 − $5 = $16
3	Third	8.0	First	8.3	First wireless earbud	$16 − $3 = $13
4	Third	8.0	Second	7.3	Third digital app	$13 − $5 = $8
5	Fourth	7.3	Second	7.3	Fourth digital app and second wireless earbud	$8 − $5 = $3 $3 − $3 = $0

Equalizing Marginal Utility per Dollar Spent Notice that the marginal utility per dollar spent for both goods is also (approximately) equal at the consumption level of three apps and one wireless earbud, but here total income is not completely exhausted. Likewise, the marginal utility per dollar spent is (approximately) equal at five apps and three wireless earbuds, but the expenditures necessary for that level of consumption ($34) exceed the individual's income.

Steps Required to Attain the Consumer Optimum Table 20-2 shows the steps taken to arrive at consumer optimum. Using the first digital app would yield a marginal utility per dollar of 10 (50 units of utility divided by $5 per digital app), while consuming the first wireless earbud would yield a marginal utility per dollar of only 8.3 (25 units of utility divided by $3 per wireless earbud). Because it yields the higher marginal utility per dollar, the app is purchased. This leaves $21 of income. Consuming the second digital app yields a higher marginal utility per dollar (9, versus 8.3 for a wireless earbud), so this app is also purchased, leaving an unspent income of $16. Purchasing and consuming the first wireless earbud now yield a higher marginal utility per dollar than the next digital app (8.3 versus 8), so the first wireless earbud is purchased. This leaves income of $13 to spend. The process continues until all income is exhausted and the marginal utility per dollar spent is equal for both goods.

To restate, consumer optimum requires the following:

A consumer's money income should be allocated so that the last dollar spent on each good purchased yields the same amount of marginal utility (when all income is spent), because this rule yields the largest possible total utility.

A Little Math

We can state the rule of consumer optimum in algebraic terms by examining the ratio of marginal utilities and prices of individual products. The rule simply states that a consumer maximizes personal satisfaction when allocating money income in such a way that the last dollars spent on good A, good B, good C, and so on, yield equal amounts of marginal utility. Marginal utility (MU) from good A is indicated by

"*MU* of good A." For good B, it is "*MU* of good B." Our algebraic formulation of this rule, therefore, becomes

$$\frac{MU \text{ of good A}}{\text{Price of good A}} = \frac{MU \text{ of good B}}{\text{price of good B}} = \cdots = \frac{MU \text{ of good Z}}{\text{price of good Z}}$$

The letters A, B, . . . , Z indicate the various goods and services that the consumer might purchase.

We know, then, that in order for the consumer to maximize utility, the marginal utility of good A divided by the price of good A must equal the marginal utility of any other good divided by its price. Note, though, that the application of the rule of equal marginal utility per dollar spent does not necessarily describe an explicit or conscious act on the part of consumers. Rather, this is a *model* of consumer optimum.

Why might some people be willing to spend $100 on a designer-brand version of a plain white T-shirt instead of paying $7 for an otherwise rather ordinary plain white T-shirt?

EXAMPLE

Why a Consumer Optimum Can Encompass a $100 Plain White Cotton T-Shirt

A minuscule fraction of annual U.S. consumer spending is directed toward purchases of designer plain white cotton T-shirts that are priced at $100 or more per unit. Among brands of plain white T-shirts with three-figure dollar prices are Handvaerk, Kotn, and Prada, which typically contain the finest Egyptian cotton and are specially designed and assembled for the most comfortable fits.

The theory of the consumer optimum indicates why some individuals are willing to place such high-priced, high-quality T-shirts into their shopping bags. For these consumers, it must be true that the last dollar spent on, say, a plain white Prada T-shirt generates the same amount of marginal utility as the last dollar spent on any other item in the shopping bag. Thus, people who purchase such T-shirts at prices of $100 or more must derive considerable additional utility from doing so.

REAL APPLICATION

When you observe others' behavior, you see that some people purchase what appears to be outrageously expensive plain cotton T-shirts as well as similarly high-priced designer goods. You may observe others who purchase relatively expensive cars. What type of analysis would you be undertaking if you judged such purchases as frivolous or unnecessary or stupid?

Sources are listed at the end of this chapter.

How a Price Change Affects Consumer Optimum

20.3 Describe the substitution and real-income effects of a price change

Consumption decisions are summarized in the law of demand, which states that the amount purchased is inversely related to price. We can now see why by using utility analysis.

A Consumer's Response to a Price Change

When a consumer has optimally allocated all her income to purchases, the marginal utility per dollar spent at current prices of goods and services is the same for each good or service she buys. No consumer will, when optimizing, buy 10 units of a good per unit of time when the marginal utility per dollar spent on the tenth unit of that good is less than the marginal utility per dollar spent on a unit of some other item.

A Price Change and the Consumer Optimum If we start out at a consumer optimum and then observe a good's price decrease, we can predict that consumers will respond to the price decrease by consuming more of that good. This is because before the price change, the marginal utility per dollar spent on each good or service consumed was the same. Now, when a specific good's price is lower, it is possible to consume more of that good while continuing to equalize the marginal utility per dollar spent on that good with the marginal utility per dollar spent on other goods and services.

The purchase and consumption of additional units of the lower-priced good will cause the marginal utility from consuming the good to fall. Eventually, it will fall to the point at which the marginal utility per dollar spent on the good is once again equal to the marginal utility per dollar spent on other goods and services. At this point, the consumer will stop buying additional units of the lower-priced good.

An Example of a Price Change A hypothetical demand curve for digital apps for a typical consumer during a specific time interval is presented in Figure 20-2. Suppose that at point A, at which the price per digital app is $5, the marginal utility of the last app consumed during the period is MU_A. At point B, at which the price is $4 per app, the marginal utility is represented by MU_B.

With the consumption of more digital apps, the marginal utility of the last unit of these additional digital apps is lower—MU_B must be less than MU_A. What has happened is that at a lower price, the number of digital app downloads per week increased from four to five. At a higher consumption rate, the marginal utility falls in response to the rise in digital app consumption so that the marginal utility per dollar spent is equalized across all purchases.

The Substitution Effect

Substitution effect

The tendency of people to substitute cheaper commodities for more expensive commodities.

What is happening as the price of digital app downloads falls is that consumers are substituting the now relatively cheaper digital apps for other goods and services, such as wireless earbuds, restaurant meals, and live concerts. We call this the **substitution effect** of a change in the price of a good because it occurs when consumers substitute relatively cheaper goods for relatively more expensive ones.

We assume that people desire a variety of goods and pursue a variety of goals. This means that few, if any, goods are irreplaceable in meeting demand. We are generally able to substitute one product for another to satisfy demand. This is commonly referred to as the **principle of substitution.**

Principle of substitution

The principle that consumers shift away from goods and services that become priced relatively higher in favor of goods and services that are now priced relatively lower.

An Example Let's assume now that there are several goods, not exactly the same, and perhaps even very different from one another, but all contributing to consumers' total utility. If the relative price of one particular good falls, individuals will substitute in favor of the now lower-priced good and against the other goods that they might have been purchasing. Conversely, if the price of that good rises relative to the price of the other goods, people will substitute in favor of them and not buy as much of the now

---

FIGURE 20-2

Digital App Prices and Marginal Utility

When consumers respond to a reduction in the price of digital apps from $5 per app to $4 per app by increasing consumption, marginal utility falls. The movement is from point A, at which marginal utility is MU_A, to point B, at which marginal utility is MU_B, which is less than MU_A. This brings about the equalization of the marginal utility per dollar spent across all purchases.

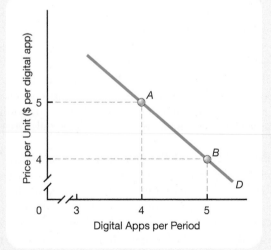

higher-priced good. An example is the growth in purchases of tablet devices, or digital tablets, since the early 2010s. As the relative price of tablets has plummeted, people have substituted away from other, now relatively more expensive goods in favor of purchasing additional digital tablets.

Purchasing Power and Real Income If the price of some item that you purchase goes down while your money income and all other prices stay the same, your ability to purchase goods goes up. That is to say, your effective **purchasing power** has increased, even though your money income has stayed the same. If you purchase 20 e-books per year at $10 per e-book, your total outlay for e-books is $200. If the price goes down by 50 percent, to $5.00 per e-book, you would have to spend only $100 per year to purchase the same number of e-books. If your money income and the prices of other goods remain the same, it would be possible for you to continue purchasing 20 e-books per year *and* to purchase more of other goods. You will feel richer and will indeed probably purchase more of a number of goods, including perhaps even more e-books.

The converse will also be true. When the price of one good you are purchasing goes up, without any other change in prices or income, the purchasing power of your income drops. You will have to reduce your purchases of either the now higher-priced good or other goods (or a combination).

In general, this **real-income effect** is usually quite small. After all, unless we consider broad categories, such as housing or food, a change in the price of one particular item that we purchase will have a relatively small effect on our total purchasing power. Thus, we anticipate that the substitution effect will be more important than the real-income effect in causing us to purchase more of goods that have become cheaper and less of goods that have become more expensive.

The Demand Curve Revisited

Linking the law of diminishing marginal utility and the rule of equal marginal utilities per dollar gives us a negative relationship between the quantity demanded of a good or service and its price. As the relative price of digital apps goes up, for example, the quantity demanded will fall, and as the relative price of digital apps goes down, the quantity demanded will rise. Figure 20-2 showed this demand curve for digital apps. As the price of digital apps falls, the consumer can maximize total utility only by purchasing more apps, and vice versa.

In other words, the relationship between price and quantity desired is simply a downward-sloping demand curve. Note, though, that this downward-sloping demand curve (the law of demand) is derived under the assumption of constant tastes and incomes. You must remember that we are keeping these important determining variables constant when we look at the relationship between price and quantity demanded.

Marginal Utility, Total Utility, and the Diamond-Water Paradox Even though water is essential to life and diamonds are not, water is relatively cheap and diamonds are relatively expensive. This relative market valuation of diamonds over water sometimes is called the "diamond-water paradox."

Understanding the Paradox The diamond-water paradox is easily understood when we make the distinction between total utility and marginal utility. The total utility of water greatly exceeds the total utility derived from diamonds. What determines the price, though, is what happens on the margin. We have relatively few diamonds, so the marginal utility of the last diamond consumed is relatively high. The opposite is true for water. Total utility does not determine what people are willing to pay for a unit of a particular commodity—marginal utility does.

Look at the situation graphically in Figure 20-3. We show the demand curve for diamonds, labeled $D_{diamonds}$. The demand curve for water is labeled D_{water}. We plot quantity in terms of kilograms per unit time period on the horizontal axis. On the vertical axis, we plot price in dollars per kilogram. We use kilograms as our common

Purchasing power
The value of money for buying goods and services. If your money income stays the same but the price of one good that you are buying goes up, your effective purchasing power falls, and vice versa.

Real-income effect
The change in people's purchasing power that occurs when, other things being constant, the price of one good that they purchase changes. When that price goes up, real income, or purchasing power, falls, and when that price goes down, real income increases.

FIGURE 20-3

The Diamond-Water Paradox

We pick kilograms as a common unit of measurement for both water and diamonds. To demonstrate that the demand for and supply of water are immense, we have put a break in the horizontal quantity axis. Although the demand for water is much greater than the demand for diamonds, the marginal valuation of water is given by the marginal value placed on the *last* unit of water consumed. To find that, we must know the supply of water, which is given as S_1. At that supply, the price of water is P_{water}. But the supply for diamonds is given by S_2. At that supply, the price of diamonds is $P_{diamonds}$. The total valuation that consumers place on water is tremendous relative to the total valuation consumers place on diamonds. What is important for price determination, however, is the marginal valuation, or the marginal utility received.

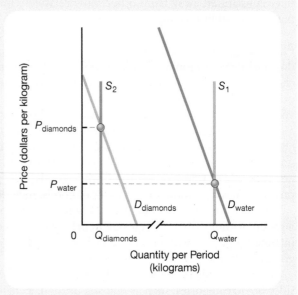

unit of measurement for water and for diamonds. We could just as well have used pounds or liters.

Why the Price of Diamonds Exceeds the Price of Water Notice in Figure 20-3 that the demand for water is many, many times the demand for diamonds (even though we really can't show this in the diagram). We draw the supply curve of water as S_1 at a quantity of Q_{water}. The supply curve for diamonds is given as S_2 at quantity $Q_{diamonds}$.

At the intersection of the supply curve of water with the demand curve of water, the price per kilogram is P_{water}. The intersection of the supply curve of diamonds with the demand curve of diamonds is at $P_{diamonds}$. Notice that $P_{diamonds}$ exceeds P_{water}. Diamonds sell at a higher price than water.

20.4 Discuss why bounded rationality may prevent reaching a true consumer optimum

Behavioral Economics and Consumer Choice Theory

Utility analysis has long been appealing to economists because it makes clear predictions about how individuals will adjust their consumption of different goods and services based on the prices of those items and their incomes. Traditionally, another attraction of utility analysis for many economists has been its reliance on the assumption that consumers behave *rationally*, or that they do not intentionally make decisions that would leave them worse off. Proponents of behavioral economics have doubts about the rationality assumption, which causes them to question the utility-based theory of consumer choice.

Does Behavioral Economics Better Predict Consumer Choices?

Advocates of behavioral economics question whether utility theory is supported by the facts, which they argue are better explained by applying the assumption of *bounded rationality*. Recall that this assumption states that human limitations prevent people from examining every possible choice available to them and thereby thwart their efforts to effectively pursue long-term personal interests.

As evidence favoring the bounded rationality assumption, proponents of behavioral economics point to real-world examples that they claim violate rationality-based utility theory. For instance, economists have found that when purchasing electric appliances such as refrigerators, people sometimes buy the lowest-priced, energy-inefficient models even though the initial purchase-price savings often fail to compensate for higher future energy costs. There is also evidence that people who live in earthquake- or flood-prone regions commonly fail to purchase sufficient insurance against these events. In addition, experiments have shown that when people are placed in situations in which strong emotions come into play, they may be willing to pay different amounts for items than they would pay in calmer settings.

These and other observed behaviors, behavioral economists suggest, indicate that consumers do not behave as if they are rational. If the rationality assumption does not apply to actual behavior, they argue, it follows that utility-based consumer choice theory cannot, either.

Consumer Choice Theory Remains Alive and Well

In spite of the doubts expressed by proponents of behavioral economics, most economists continue to apply the assumption that people behave *as if* they act rationally with an aim to maximize utility. These economists continue to employ utility theory because of a fundamental strength of this approach: It yields clear-cut predictions regarding consumer choices that receive support from real-world evidence.

In contrast, if the rationality assumption is rejected, any number of possible human behaviors might be considered. To proponents of behavioral economics, ambiguities about actual outcomes make the bounded rationality approach to consumer choice more realistic than utility-based consumer choice theory. Nevertheless, a major drawback is that no clearly testable predictions emerge from the many alternative behaviors that people might exhibit if they fail to behave *as if* they are rational.

Certainly, arguments among economists about the "reasonableness" of rational consumers maximizing utility are likely to continue. So far, however, the use of utility-based consumer choice theory has allowed economists to make a wide array of predictions about how consumers respond to changes in prices, incomes, and other factors. In general, these key predictions continue to be supported by the actual choices that consumers make.

ECONOMICS IN YOUR LIFE

Boutique Sellers Offer $2,000 Japanese-Made Jeans That Some Consumers Truly Are Happy to Buy

Kiya Babzani is the co-owner of several U.S.-based Self Edge boutiques that specialize in the sale of denim clothing, such as blue jean trousers and jackets. When asked about which denim clothing items are the "best," Babzani answers, "If someone wants the best denim, they will be led to Japanese denim." Babzani and other retailers agree that Japanese producers, including Iron Heart and Pure Blue Japan, stand out because of the perceived high quality of their denim and various product details. One Japanese jeans seller, Momotaro, stands out among consumers for carefully designed fade lines, specially colored seam threads, and hand-stitched and invisible fabric-connecting rivets.

Buyers of the "best" Japanese denim products are willing to pay unusually high prices. Some Momotaro trouser lines, for instance, are priced as high as $2,000 per pair. At a consumer optimum, of course, buyers of these jeans derive the same utility per dollar spent as they perceive for any other item that they purchase from their incomes. These buyers are willing to pay such a high price for each pair of Momotaro jeans only because they derive considerable additional utility per pair of jeans that they purchase.

FOR CRITICAL THINKING

Under what specific consumer-optimum circumstances would a regular consumer of Momotaro jeans have been willing to pay $90,000 for a sports car on the same day that she bought her latest pair of Momotaro jeans priced at $2,000?

REAL APPLICATION

Suppose that you end up with a very high annual income. Suppose further that there are several lines of designer shoes that you like. In spite of your high income, will you still shop "for the best deal" for those brands that you prefer?

Sources are listed at the end of this chapter.

ISSUES & APPLICATIONS

How Much "Intermittently Functioning" High-Tech Automotive Gadgetry Fits into a Consumer Optimum

Foxy burrow/Shutterstock

Concepts Applied

➤ Consumer Optimum

➤ Marginal Utility

➤ Diminishing Marginal Utility

A car, a sport-utility vehicle, or a pickup truck amounts to an agglomeration of product features, including an engine to power the vehicle, a drive-train system to propel it along roads and streets, body and interior designs, a color scheme, and so on. An individual's decision about whether to include the purchase of particular vehicle within a consumer optimum equates the ratio of the marginal utility per dollar derived from the set of characteristics embodied within a single vehicle to the price of that vehicle. For many people, the expanding range of digital features being incorporated within vehicles' embodied arrays of characteristics is complicating decisions about whether to include a new vehicle within the consumer optimum.

Diminishing Marginal Utility from Expanded Sets of Digital Automotive Features?

Each year, automakers expand the array of digital-instrument clusters included within the vehicles that they offer for sale. So-called infotainment systems tucked into automotive dashboards include widening ranges of Bluetooth-integration, GPS-navigation, USB-connectivity, user-interface, and voice-recognition systems. Many vehicles include wireless systems that enable drivers to interact with apps that provide various forms of user aids.

For most people, expansion of the number of digital systems included within vehicles boosts the total utility that they derive from a vehicle purchase. For some, adding certain digital features also boosts the *marginal* utility derived from a vehicle purchase. For all consumers, however, further expansion of such features eventually results in total utility increasing at a diminishing rate. That is, the law of diminishing marginal utility prevails, so that marginal utility ultimately diminishes as the number of digital systems added to a typical vehicle increases.

Varying Effects on Marginal Utility per Dollar Spent and Vehicle Decisions within a Consumer Optimum

Naturally, automakers have added digital systems with the intent of pushing up the marginal utility per dollar spent for more consumers. Their hope is to raise for these additional individuals the marginal utility per dollar spent on a vehicle relative to the marginal utility per dollar spent on other items. If so, more people would choose to add a new vehicle alongside the set of items to be included within a consumer optimum.

Nevertheless, two problems have interfered with attainment of the automakers' aims. The first of these is that as the range of systems included within vehicles has increased, more people have experienced difficulties learning to operate the systems effectively. Encountering such difficulties reduces the marginal utility that these consumers derive from buying a vehicle. The second problem is that the automakers have had troubles producing error-free digital systems. Naturally, individuals who struggle to operate systems that are new or whose digital features will function only intermittently are less likely to experience higher marginal utility. As a consequence, adding to the range of digital features in vehicles on net has *reduced* the marginal utility per dollar spent on vehicles for some consumers, many of whom have responded by choosing *not* to include a new vehicle purchase within their consumer optimum. Thus, while expansions in vehicles' digital systems have generated more new vehicle purchases by some consumers, another result has been fewer purchases by other consumers.

FOR CRITICAL THINKING

How might some individuals' marginal utility per dollar spent be reduced by the inclusion of wireless systems that report

data on driving speeds and vehicle movements accessible by insurers or police agencies?

REAL APPLICATION

Learning how to use the numerous digital systems for a particular brand of automobile does take time. Once learned, however, most consumers can retain their proficiency in using such digital systems. In what ways might you avoid incurring the learning costs of future new digital systems in cars?

Sources are listed at the end of this chapter.

What You Should Know

Here is what you should know after reading this chapter.

LEARNING OBJECTIVES

20.1 Distinguish between total and marginal utility and discuss why marginal utility ultimately falls as a person consumes more of an item *Total utility is the total satisfaction that an individual derives from consuming a given amount of a good or service during a given period. Marginal utility, the additional satisfaction that a person gains by consuming an additional unit of the good or service, eventually declines with increased consumption.*

20.2 Explain why an optimal choice of how much to consume entails equalizing the marginal utility per dollar spent across all items *An individual optimally allocates available income to consumption of all goods and services when the marginal utility per dollar spent on the last unit consumed of each good is equalized. Thus, a consumer optimum occurs (1) when the ratio of the marginal utility derived from an item to the price of that item is equal across all items that the person consumes and (2) when the person spends all available income.*

20.3 Describe the substitution and real-income effects of a price change *The substitution effect of a change in the price of a good or service arises because the price change induces people to substitute among goods. The real-income effect occurs because the price change alters the purchasing power of people's incomes.*

20.4 Discuss why bounded rationality may prevent reaching a true consumer optimum *If people experience bounded rationality, they face limitations in considering all possible choices consistent with pursuing their long-term interests. Consequently, they may fail to reach a true consumer optimum. If so, a number of possible behaviors and choices might be feasible, in contrast to the clear-cut predictions from utility-maximization theory.*

KEY TERMS

utility, 424
utility analysis, 424
util, 424
marginal utility, 425
diminishing marginal
   utility, 427
Key Figure
Figure 20-1, 426

consumer optimum, 428

substitution effect, 432
principle of substitution, 432
purchasing power, 433
real-income effect, 433
Key Figures
Figure 20-2, 432
Figure 20-3, 434

PROBLEMS

20-1. The campus pizzeria sells a single pizza for $12. If you order a second pizza, however, the pizzeria charges a price of only $5 for the additional pizza. Explain how an understanding of marginal utility helps to explain the pizzeria's pricing strategy.

20-2. As an individual consumes more units of an item, the person eventually experiences diminishing marginal utility. This means that to increase marginal utility, the person must consume less of an item. Explain the logic of this behavior using the example in Problem 20-1.

20-3. Where possible, complete the missing cells in the table below.

Number of Cheese-burgers	Total Utility of Cheese-burgers	Marginal Utility of Cheese-burgers	Bags of French Fries	Total Utility of French Fries	Marginal Utility of French Fries
0	0	—	0	0	—
1	20	—	1	—	10
2	36	—	2	—	8
3	—	12	3	—	2
4	—	8	4	21	—
5	—	4	5	21	—

20-4. From the data in Problem 20-3, if the price of a cheeseburger is $2, the price of a bag of french fries is $1, and you have $6 to spend (and you spend all of it), what is the utility-maximizing combination of cheeseburgers and french fries?

20-5. Return to Problem 20-4. Suppose that the price of cheeseburgers falls to $1. Determine the new utility-maximizing combination of cheeseburgers and french fries.

20-6. Suppose that you observe that total utility rises as more of an item is consumed. What can you say for certain about marginal utility? Can you say for sure that it is rising or falling or that it is positive or negative?

20-7. You determine that your daily consumption of soft drinks is 3 and your daily consumption of tacos is 4 when the prices per unit are 50 cents and $1, respectively. Explain what happens to your consumption bundle, and, after your consumption choices adjust, to the marginal utility of soft drinks and the marginal utility of tacos, when the price of soft drinks rises to 75 cents.

20-8. At a consumer optimum, for all goods purchased, marginal utility per dollar spent is equalized. A high school student is deciding between attending Western State University and Eastern State University. The student cannot attend both universities simultaneously. Both are fine universities, but the reputation of Western is slightly higher, as is the tuition. Use the rule of consumer optimum to explain how the student will go about deciding which university to attend.

20-9. In the graph, consider the movements that take place from one point to the next (A to B to C and so on) along the total utility curve as the individual successively increases consumption by one more unit, and answer the questions that follow.

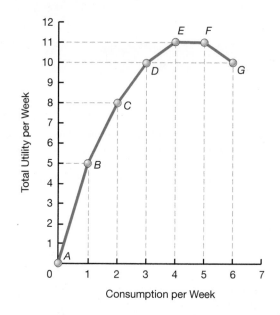

a. Which one-unit increase in consumption from one point to the next along the total utility curve generates the highest marginal utility?

b. Which one-unit increase in consumption from one point to the next along the total utility curve generates zero marginal utility?

c. Which one-unit increase in consumption from one point to the next along the total utility curve generates negative marginal utility?

20-10. Draw a marginal utility curve corresponding to the total utility curve depicted in Problem 20-9.

20-11. Refer to the second table. If the subscription price for a sports app is $2 per week, the subscription price of a game app is $1 per week, and a student has $9 per week to spend, what quantities will she purchase at a consumer optimum?

Quantity of Sports Apps per Week	Marginal Utility (utils)	Quantity of Game Apps per Week	Marginal Utility (utils)
1	1,200	1	1,700
2	1,000	2	1,400
3	800	3	1,100
4	600	4	800
5	400	5	500
6	100	6	200

20-12. Refer to the third table for a different consumer, and assume that each week this consumer buys only weekly subscriptions to economic statistics apps and subscriptions to office productivity apps. The price of a subscription to each type of economic statistics app is $2 per week, and the price of a subscription to each office productivity app is $60 per week. If the consumer's available income is $128 per week, what quantity of each item will the individual purchase each week at a consumer optimum?

Quantity of Subscriptions to Economic Statistics Apps per Week	Total Utility (utils)	Quantity of Subscriptions to Office Productivity Apps per Week	Total Utility (utils)
1	40	1	400
2	60	2	700
3	76	3	850
4	86	4	950
5	91	5	1,000
6	93	6	1,025

20-13. In Problem 20-12, if the consumer's income rises to $190 per week, what new quantities characterize the new consumer optimum?

20-14. At a consumer optimum involving goods A and B, the marginal utility of good A is twice the marginal utility of good B. The price of good B is $3.50. What is the price of good A?

20-15. At a consumer optimum involving goods X and Y, the marginal utility of good X equals 3 utils. The price of good Y is three times the price of good X. What is the marginal utility of good Y?

20-16. At a consumer optimum involving goods A and B, the marginal utility of good A is 2 utils, and the

marginal utility of good B is 8 utils. How much greater or smaller is the price of good B compared with the price of good A?

20-17. At a consumer optimum involving goods X and Y, the price of good X is $3 per unit, and the price of good Y is $9 per unit. How much greater or smaller is the marginal utility of good Y than the marginal utility of good X?

20-18. The marginal utility that an individual would experience if she were to consume the first unit of a digital app is 15 utils, and the marginal utility that she would experience if she were to consume a second unit is 18 utils. If one app is the amount that the individual decides to consume, what is the person's total utility?

20-19. Take a look at Figure 20-1. Suppose that the individual currently consumes 5 digital apps. What happens to the person's total utility if he were to reduce his consumption to 4 units? Why does this fact imply that the marginal utility curve cuts through the horizontal axis of panel (c) between the fourth and fifth app consumed?

20-20. Consider Figure 20-1. If this individual were to contemplate consuming a seventh digital app and experience a total utility of 15 utils as a consequence, what would be the resulting marginal utility? Would the points on the total utility and marginal utility graphs in panels (a) and (b) lie higher or lower to the right of the current endpoints of those graphs?

20-21. Take a look at Table 20-1. Suppose that the price of each digital app rises to $5.97. At the same time, the price of each wireless earbud falls to $2.70. Income remains unchanged at $26. Rework the marginal-utility-per-dollars-spent columns and round each amount to the nearest one-tenth. What are the quantities of digital apps and wireless earbuds now purchased by this consumer?

20-22. At the optimal quantities of digital apps and wireless earbuds determined in your answer to Problem 20-21, after rounding to the nearest 10 cents, is the $26 income all spent at the new consumer optimum?

20-23. Consider Figure 20-2, and suppose that the initial point is *A*. Explain why a decrease in the price of each digital app from $5 to $4 results in a change in the marginal utilities of digital apps in a direction that is consistent with re-attainment of a new consumer optimum at point *B*.

REFERENCES

BEHAVIORAL EXAMPLE: Rational Rationing of Calories to Prevent Negative Marginal Utility from Food Consumption

"Making Trade-Offs to Reduce Fat and Sugar," American Heart Association (https://atgprod.heart.org/HEARTORG/HealthyLiving/WeightManagement/LosingWeight/Making-Trade-offs-to-Reduce-Fat-and-Sugar_UCM_320187_Article.jsp), 2019.

Bloomberg Businessweek Critic, "It's the Obesity, Stupid," January 16, 2018.

Christopher Payne and Rob Barnett, *The Economists' Diet*, Touchstone, 2018.

AI—DECISION MAKING THROUGH DATA: An Aid for Attaining a Consumer Optimum

Brian Uzzi, "How AI Could Make Your Life Easier This Year," CNN.com (https://www.cnn.com/2019/01/10/perspectives/artificial-intelligence-predictions-2019/index.html), January 10, 2019.

Mark Osborn, "Using AI to Serve 'Right Here, Right Now' Consumers," *Consumer Goods Technology*, March 16, 2018.

"Artificial Intelligence Resolves Paradox of Consumer Choice," Zenith (https://www.zenithmedia.com/insights/global-intelligence-issue-05-2018/artificial-intelligence-resolves-paradox-of-consumer-choice/), April 17, 2018.

EXAMPLE: Why a Consumer Optimum Can Encompass a $100 Plain White Cotton T-Shirt

"Designer T-Shirts," Farfetch (https://www.farfetch.com/shopping/men/t-shirts-vests-2/items.aspx), 2019.

"The Top Five Most Expensive T-Shirts in the World," MoneyInc (https://moneyinc.com/the-top-five-most-expensive-t-shirts-in-the-world/), 2019.

"Most Expensive T-Shirt Brands in the World," SuccessStory (https://successstory.com/spendit/most-expensive-t-shirt-brands-in-the-world), 2019.

ECONOMICS IN YOUR LIFE: Boutique Sellers Offer $2,000 Japanese-Made Jeans That Some Consumers Truly Are Happy to Buy

"Momotaro," Heddels.com (https://www.heddels.com/brand/momotaro/), 2019.

Suryatapa Bhattacharya, "The Hottest Jeans Cost $2,000 and Are Made in Japan," *Wall Street Journal*, June 5, 2018.

Kelly Wetherille, "Why Japanese Jeans and Denim Are Trending and Which Labels You Should Be Wearing," *South China Morning Post*, April 27, 2018.

ISSUES & APPLICATIONS: How Much "Intermittently Functioning" High-Tech Automotive Gadgetry Fits into a Consumer Optimum?

Jim Ciminillo, "Keep the Car, Ditch the Touchpad," NBC News (https://nbc25news.com/news/auto-matters/2019-lexus-es-keep-the-car-ditch-the-touchpad-retake), March 15, 2019.

Chester Dawson, "In Car Makers' Digital Dash, Little Room for Error," *Wall Street Journal*, March 27, 2018.

Matthew DeBord, "Car Owners Find This Feature in Modern Cars Most Frustrating," *Business Insider*, July 21, 2018.

More Advanced Consumer Choice Theory

It is possible to analyze consumer choice verbally, as we did for the most part in Chapter 20. The theory of diminishing marginal utility can be fairly well accepted on intuitive grounds and by introspection. If we want to be more formal and perhaps more elegant in our theorizing, however, we can translate our discussion into a graphical analysis with what we call *indifference curves* and the *budget constraint*. Here we discuss these terms and their relationship and demonstrate consumer equilibrium in geometric form.

On Being Indifferent

What does it mean to be indifferent? It usually means that you don't care one way or the other about something—you are equally disposed to either of two alternatives. With this interpretation in mind, we will turn to choices between two accessories for tablet devices that a consumer uses heavily and thereby regularly wears out each year: wireless earbuds and stylus pens. In panel (a) of Figure F-1, we show several combinations of wireless earbuds and stylus pens per year that a representative consumer

FIGURE F-1

Combinations That Yield Equal Levels of Satisfaction

A, B, C, and *D* represent combinations of wireless earbuds and stylus pens per year that give an equal level of satisfaction to this

consumer. In other words, the consumer is indifferent among these four combinations.

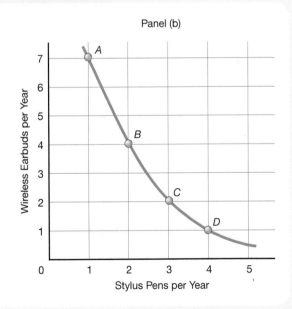

	Panel (a)	
Combination	Wireless Earbuds per Year	Stylus Pens per Year
A	7	1
B	4	2
C	2	3
D	1	4

considers equally satisfactory. That is to say, for each combination, *A*, *B*, *C*, and *D*, this consumer will have exactly the same level of total utility.

The simple numerical example that we have used happens to concern the consumption of wireless earbuds and stylus pens (both of which we assume this consumer wishes to utilize) per year. This example is used to illustrate general features of indifference curves and related analytical tools that are necessary for deriving the demand curve. Obviously, we could have used any two commodities. Just remember that we are using a *specific* example to illustrate a *general* analysis.

We plot these combinations graphically in panel (b) of Figure F-1, with stylus pens per year on the horizontal axis and wireless earbuds per year on the vertical axis. These are our consumer's indifference combinations—the consumer finds each combination as acceptable as the others. These combinations lie along a smooth curve that is known as the consumer's **indifference curve.** Along the indifference curve, every combination of the two goods in question yields the same level of satisfaction. Every point along the indifference curve is equally desirable to the consumer. For example, one wireless earbud per year and four stylus pens will give our representative consumer exactly the same total satisfaction as consuming four wireless earbuds per year and two stylus pens per year.

Indifference curve

A curve composed of a set of consumption alternatives, each of which yields the same total amount of satisfaction.

Properties of Indifference Curves

Indifference curves have special properties relating to their slope and shape.

Downward Slope The indifference curve shown in panel (b) of Figure F-1 slopes downward. That is, the indifference curve has a negative slope. Now consider Figure F-2. Here we show two points, *A* and *B*. Point *A* represents four wireless earbuds per year and two stylus pens per year. Point *B* represents five wireless earbuds per year and six stylus pens per year. Clearly, *B* is always preferred to *A* for a consumer who desires both wireless earbuds and stylus pens, because *B* represents more of everything. If *B* is always preferred to *A*, it is impossible for points *A* and *B* to be on the same indifference curve because the definition of the indifference curve is a set of combinations of two goods that are preferred equally.

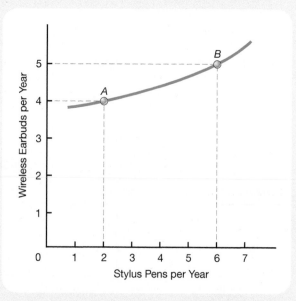

FIGURE F-2

Indifference Curves: Impossibility of an Upward Slope

Point *B* represents a consumption of more stylus pens per year and more wireless earbuds per year than point *A*. *B* is always preferred to *A*. Therefore, *A* and *B* cannot be on the same *positively* sloped indifference curve. An indifference curve shows *equally preferred* combinations of the two goods.

Implications of a Straight-Line Indifference Curve

This straight-line indifference curve indicates that the consumer will always be willing to give up the same number of wireless earbuds to get one more stylus pen per year. For example, the consumer at point *A* consumes five wireless earbuds and no stylus pens per year. She is willing to give up one wireless earbud in order to get one stylus pen per year. At point *C*, however, the consumer obtains only one wireless earbud and four stylus pens per year. Because of the straight-line indifference curve, this consumer is willing to give up the last wireless earbud in order to get one more stylus pen per year, even though she already has four.

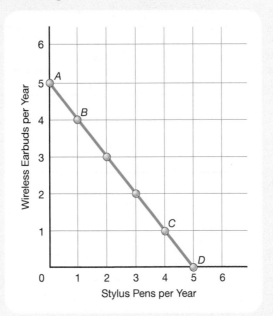

Curvature The indifference curve that we have drawn in panel (b) of Figure F-1 is special. Notice that it is curved. Why didn't we just draw a straight line, as we have usually done for a demand curve?

Imagining a Straight-Line Indifference Curve To find out why we don't consider straight-line indifference curves, consider the implications. We show such a straight-line indifference curve in Figure F-3. Start at point *A*. The consumer obtains no stylus pens and five wireless earbuds per year. Now the consumer wishes to go to point *B*. She is willing to give up only one wireless earbud in order to get one stylus pen. Now let's assume that the consumer is at point *C*, obtaining one wireless earbud and four stylus pens per year. If the consumer wants to go to point *D*, she is again willing to give up one wireless earbud in order to get one more stylus pen per year.

In other words, no matter how many wireless earbuds the consumer obtains, she is willing to give up one wireless earbud to get one stylus pen—which does not seem plausible. Doesn't it make sense to hypothesize that the more times the consumer obtains wireless earbuds per year, the less she will value an *additional* wireless earbud that year? Presumably, when the consumer has five wireless earbuds and no stylus pens per year, she should be willing to give up *more than* one wireless earbud in order to get one stylus pen. Therefore, a straight-line indifference curve as shown in Figure F-3 no longer seems plausible.

Convexity of the Indifference Curve In mathematical jargon, an indifference curve is convex with respect to the origin. Let's look at this in panel (a) of Figure F-1. Starting with combination *A*, the consumer has one stylus pen but seven wireless earbuds per year. To remain indifferent, the consumer would have to be willing to give up three wireless earbuds to obtain one more stylus pen (as shown in combination *B*). To go from combination *C* to combination *D*, however, notice that the consumer would have to be willing to give up only one wireless earbud for an additional stylus pen per year. The quantity of the substitute considered acceptable changes as the rate of consumption of the original item changes.

Consequently, the indifference curve in panel (b) of Figure F-1 will be convex when viewed from the origin at zero quantity.

Calculating the Marginal Rate of Substitution

As we move from combination *A* to combination *B*, we are still on the same indifference curve. To stay on that curve, the number of wireless earbuds decreases by three and the number of stylus pens increases by one. The marginal rate of substitution is 3:1. A three-unit decrease in wireless earbuds requires an increase in one stylus pen to leave the consumer's total utility unaltered.

(1) Combination	(2) Wireless Earbuds per Year	(3) Stylus Pens per Year	(4) Marginal Rate of Substitution of Wireless Earbuds for Stylus Pens
A	7	1	
B	4	2	3:1
C	2	3	2:1
D	1	4	1:1

The Marginal Rate of Substitution

Instead of using marginal utility, we can talk in terms of the *marginal rate of substitution* between wireless earbuds and stylus pens per year. We can formally define the consumer's marginal rate of substitution as follows:

> *The marginal rate of substitution is equal to the change in the quantity of one good that just offsets a one-unit change in the consumption of another good, such that total satisfaction remains constant.*

We can see numerically what happens to the marginal rate of substitution in our example if we rearrange panel (a) of Figure F-1 into Table F-1. Here we show wireless earbuds in the second column and stylus pens in the third. Now we ask the question, what change in the number of wireless earbuds per year will just compensate for a three-unit change in the consumption of stylus pens per year and leave the consumer's total utility constant? The movement from *A* to *B* increases the number of stylus pens by one. Here the marginal rate of substitution is 3:1—a three-unit decrease in wireless earbuds requires an increase of one stylus pen to leave the consumer's total utility unaltered. Thus, the consumer values the three wireless earbuds as the equivalent of one stylus pen.

We do this for the rest of the table and find that as wireless earbuds decrease, the marginal rate of substitution goes from 3:1 to 2:1 to 1:1. The marginal rate of substitution of wireless earbuds for stylus pens per year falls as the consumer obtains more stylus pens. That is, the consumer values each successive stylus pen obtained less and less in terms of wireless earbuds. The first stylus pen is valued at three wireless earbuds. The last (fourth) stylus pen is valued at only one wireless earbud. The fact that the marginal rate of substitution falls is sometimes called the *law of substitution*.

In geometric language, the slope of the consumer's indifference curve (actually, the negative of the slope of the indifference curve) measures the consumer's marginal rate of substitution.

The Indifference Map

Let's now consider the possibility of having both more stylus pens *and* more wireless earbuds per year. When we do this, we can no longer stay on the same indifference curve that we drew in Figure F-1. That indifference curve was drawn for equally satisfying combinations of stylus pens and wireless earbuds per year. If the individual can now obtain more of both, a new indifference curve will have to be drawn, above and to

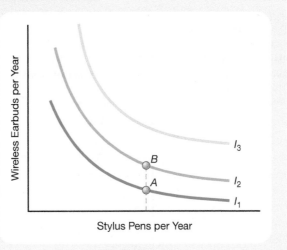

FIGURE F-4

A Set of Indifference Curves

An infinite number of indifference curves can be drawn. We show three possible ones. Realize that a higher indifference curve represents the possibility of higher rates of consumption of both goods. Hence, a higher indifference curve is preferred to a lower one because more is preferred to less. Look at points *A* and *B*. Point *B* represents more wireless earbuds than point *A*. Therefore, bundles on indifference curve I_2 have to be preferred over bundles on I_1 because the number of stylus pens per year is the same at points *A* and *B*.

the right of the one shown in panel (b) of Figure F-1. Alternatively, if the individual faces the possibility of having fewer of both stylus pens and wireless earbuds per year, an indifference curve will have to be drawn below and to the left of the one in panel (b) of Figure F-1. We can map out a whole set of indifference curves corresponding to these possibilities.

Figure F-4 shows three possible indifference curves. Indifference curves that are higher than others necessarily imply that for every given quantity of one good, more of the other good can be obtained on a higher indifference curve. Looked at one way, if one goes from curve I_1 to I_2, it is possible to obtain the same number of stylus pens *and* more wireless earbuds each year. This is shown as a movement from point *A* to point *B* in Figure F-4. We could do it the other way. When we move from a lower to a higher indifference curve, it is possible to obtain the same number of wireless earbuds *and* to get more stylus pens each year. Thus, the higher an indifference curve is for a consumer, the greater that consumer's total level of satisfaction.

The Budget Constraint and the Consumer Optimum

Our problem here is to find out how to maximize consumer satisfaction. To do so, we must consult not only our *preferences*—given by indifference curves—but also our *market opportunities*, which are given by our available income and prices, called our **budget constraint.** We might want more of everything, but for any given budget constraint, we have to make choices, or trade-offs, among possible goods. Everyone has a budget constraint. That is, everyone faces a limited consumption potential. How do we show this graphically? We must find the prices of the goods in question and determine the maximum consumption of each allowed by our budget.

For example, let's assume that there is a $5 price for each wireless earbud and that a stylus pen costs $10. Let's also assume that our representative consumer has a total tablet-accessories budget of $30 per year. What is the maximum number of wireless earbuds this individual can consume? Six. And the maximum number of stylus pens per year that she can obtain? Three. So now, as shown in Figure F-5, we have two points on our budget line, which is sometimes called the *consumption possibilities curve*. These anchor points of the budget line are obtained by dividing money income by the price of each product. The first point is at *b* on the vertical axis. The

Budget constraint
All of the possible combinations of goods that can be purchased (at fixed prices) with a specific budget.

The Budget Constraint

The line bb_1 represents this individual's budget constraint. Assuming that wireless earbuds cost $5 each, stylus pens cost $10 each, and the individual has a budget of $30 per year, a maximum of six wireless earbuds or three stylus pens can be bought each year. These two extreme points are connected to form the budget constraint. All combinations within the colored area and on the budget constraint line are feasible.

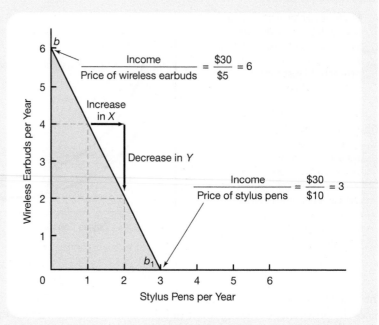

second point is at b_1 on the horizontal axis. The budget line is linear because prices are constant.

Any combination along line bb_1 is possible. In fact, any combination in the colored area is possible. We will assume, however, that there are sufficient goods available that the individual consumer completely uses up the available budget, and we will consider as possible only those points along bb_1.

Slope of the Budget Constraint

The budget constraint is a line that slopes downward from left to right. The slope of that line has a special meaning. Look carefully at the budget line in Figure F-5. Remember from our discussion of graphs in Appendix A that we measure a negative slope by the ratio of the decrease in Y over the run in X. In this case, Y is wireless earbuds per year and X is stylus pens per year. In Figure F-5, the decrease in Y is -2 wireless earbuds per year (a drop from 4 to 2) for an increase in X of one stylus pen per year (an increase from 1 to 2). Therefore, the slope of the budget constraint is $-2/1$, or -2. This slope of the budget constraint represents the *rate of exchange* between wireless earbuds and stylus pens.

Now we are ready to determine how the consumer achieves the optimum consumption rate.

Consumer Optimum Revisited

Consumers will try to attain the highest level of total utility possible, given their budget constraints. How can this be shown graphically? We draw a set of indifference curves similar to those in Figure F-4, and we bring in scarcity—the budget constraint bb_1. Both are drawn in Figure F-6. Because a higher level of total satisfaction is represented by a higher indifference curve, we know that the consumer will strive to be on the highest indifference curve possible. The consumer cannot get to indifference curve I_2, however, because the budget will be exhausted before any combination of wireless earbuds and stylus pens represented on indifference curve I_2 is attained. This

FIGURE F-6

Consumer Optimum

A consumer reaches an optimum when he or she ends up on the highest indifference curve possible, given a limited budget. This occurs at the tangency between an indifference curve and the budget constraint. In this diagram, the tangency is at E_1.

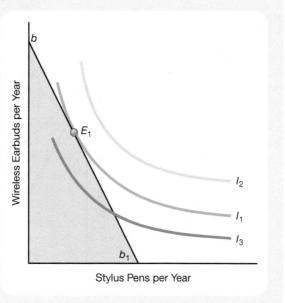

consumer can maximize total utility, subject to the budget constraint, only by being at point E_1 on indifference curve I_1 because here the consumer's income is just being exhausted. Mathematically, point E_1 is called the *tangency point* of the curve I_1 to the straight line bb_1.

Consumer optimum is achieved when the marginal rate of substitution (which is subjective) is just equal to the feasible rate of exchange between wireless earbuds and stylus pens. This rate is the ratio of the two prices of the goods involved. It is represented by the absolute value of the slope of the budget constraint (i.e., ignoring the negative signs). At point E_1, the point of tangency between indifference curve I_1 and budget constraint bb_1, the rate at which the consumer *wishes* to substitute wireless earbuds for stylus pens (the numerical value of the slope of the indifference curve) is just equal to the rate at which the consumer *can* substitute wireless earbuds for stylus pens (the slope of the budget line).

Deriving the Demand Curve

We are now in a position to derive the demand curve using indifference curve analysis. In panel (a) of Figure F-7, we show what happens when the price of stylus pens decreases, holding both the price of wireless earbuds and income constant. If the price of stylus pens decreases, the budget line rotates from bb_1 to bb_2.

The two optimum points are given by the tangency at the highest indifference curve that just touches those two budget lines. This is at E_1 and E_2. Those two points give us two price-quantity pairs. At point E_1, the price of stylus pens is $10. The quantity demanded is 2. Thus, we have one point that we can transfer to panel (b) of Figure F-7. At point E_2, we have another price-quantity pair. The price has fallen to $5, and the quantity demanded has increased to 5. We therefore transfer this other point to panel (b). When we connect these two points (and all the others in between), we derive the demand curve for stylus pens, which slopes downward.

Deriving the Demand Curve

In panel (a), we show the effects of a decrease in the price of stylus pens from $10 to $5. At $10, the highest indifference curve touches the budget line bb_1 at point E_1. The number of stylus pens purchased is two. We transfer this combination—price, $10; quantity demanded, 2—down to panel (b). Next we decrease the price of stylus pens to $5. This generates a new budget line, or constraint, which is bb_2. Consumer optimum is now at E_2. The optimum quantity of stylus pens demanded at a price of $5 is 5. We transfer this point—price, $5; quantity demanded, 5—down to panel (b). When we connect these two points, we have a demand curve, D, for stylus pens.

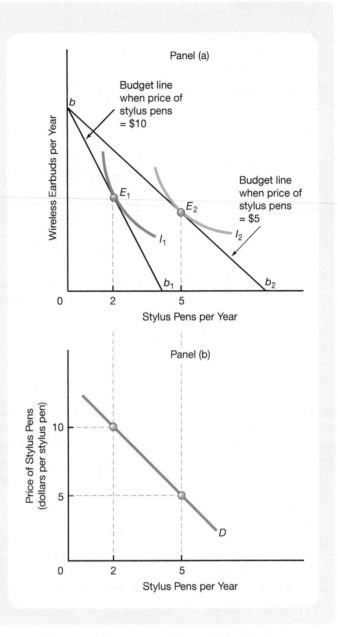

What You Should Know

Here is what you should know after reading this chapter.

LEARNING OBJECTIVES

On Being Indifferent *Along an indifference curve, the consumer experiences equal levels of satisfaction. That is to say, along any indifference curve, which typically slopes downward and is convex to the origin, every combination of the two goods in question yields exactly the same level of satisfaction. To measure the marginal rate of substitution, we find out how much of one good has to be given up in order to allow the consumer to consume one more unit of the other good while still remaining on the same indifference curve. The marginal rate of substitution falls as one moves down an indifference curve.*

KEY TERMS

indifference curve, 442
Key Figure
Figure F-1, 441

The Budget Constraint and the Consumer Optimum *Indifference curves represent preferences. A budget constraint represents opportunities—how much can be purchased with a given level of income. The slope of the budget constraint is the rate of exchange between two goods, which is the ratio of their dollar prices. Consumer optimum is obtained when the highest feasible indifference curve is just tangent to the budget constraint line. At that point, the consumer reaches the highest feasible indifference curve.*

budget constraint, 445
Key Figure
Figure F-5, 446

Deriving the Demand Curve *A decrease in the price of an item causes the budget line to rotate outward. This generates a new consumer optimum, at which the individual chooses to consume more units of the item. Hence, a decrease in price generates an increase in quantity demanded, or a movement down along a derived demand curve.*

Key Figure
Figure F-7, 448

PROBLEMS

F-1. Consider the indifference curve illustrated in Figure F-1. Explain, in economic terms, why the curve is convex to the origin.

F-2. Your classmate tells you that he is indifferent between three soft drinks and two hamburgers or two soft drinks and three hamburgers.

  a. Draw a rough diagram of an indifference curve containing your classmate's consumption choices.

  b. Suppose that your classmate states that he is also indifferent between two soft drinks and three hamburgers or one soft drink and four hamburgers, but that he prefers three soft drinks and two hamburgers to one soft drink and four hamburgers. Use your diagram from part (a) to reason out whether he can have these preferences.

F-3. The table below represents Sue's preferences for bottled water and soft drinks, the combination of which yields the same level of utility.

Combination of Bottled Water and Soft Drinks	Bottled Water per Month	Soft Drinks per Month
A	5	11
B	10	7
C	15	4
D	20	2
E	25	1

Calculate Sue's marginal rate of substitution of soft drinks for bottled water at each rate of consumption of water (or soft drinks). Relate the marginal rate of substitution to marginal utility.

F-4. Using the information provided in Problem F-3, illustrate Sue's indifference curve, with water on the horizontal axis and soft drinks on the vertical axis.

F-5. Sue's monthly budget for bottled water and soft drinks is $23. The price of bottled water is $1 per

bottle, and the price of soft drinks is $2 per bottle. Calculate the slope of Sue's budget constraint. Given this information and the information provided in Problem F-3, find the combination of goods that satisfies Sue's utility-maximization problem in light of her budget constraint.

F-6. Using the indifference curve diagram you constructed in Problem F-4, add in Sue's budget constraint using the information in Problem F-5. Illustrate the utility-maximizing combination of bottled water and soft drinks.

F-7. Suppose that at a higher satisfaction level than in Problem F-3, Sue's constant-utility preferences are as shown in the table below. Calculate the slope of Sue's new budget constraint using the information provided in Problem F-5. Supposing now that the price of a soft drink falls to $1, find the combination of goods that satisfies Sue's utility-maximization problem in light of her budget constraint.

Combination of Bottled Water and Soft Drinks	Bottled Water per Month	Soft Drinks per Month
A	5	22
B	10	14
C	15	8
D	20	4
E	25	2

F-8. Illustrate Sue's new budget constraint and indifference curve in a diagram from the data in Problem F-3. Illustrate also the utility-maximizing combination of goods.

F-9. Given your answers to Problems F-5 and F-7, are Sue's preferences for soft drinks consistent with the law of demand?

F-10. Using your answer to Problem F-8, draw Sue's demand curve for soft drinks.

21

Rents, Profits, and the Financial Environment of Business

Rawpixel.com/Shutterstock

LEARNING OBJECTIVES

After reading this chapter, you should be able to:

21.1 Understand the concept of economic rent

21.2 Distinguish among the main organizational forms of business and explain the difference between accounting profits and economic profits

21.3 Discuss how the interest rate performs a key role in allocating resources and calculate the present discounted value of a payment to be received at a future date

21.4 Identify the main sources of corporate funds and differentiate between stocks and bonds

S tock indexes are measures of values of groups of shares of ownership, or stocks, in companies. Such indexes are calculated as averages of the current prices of the companies' shares determined through daily trading in stock markets. During the past 15 years, the number of stock indexes has grown rapidly—so rapidly that today more stock indexes are in existence than the number of companies that issue the underlying stocks. Why are people who buy and sell shares of stock tracking more stock indexes than the number of different underlying stocks of companies whose shares they can buy or sell? You will find out the answer to this question by reading this chapter.

out of the many thousands of new U.S. businesses that open this year as either *sole proprietorships* owned by one person or *partnerships* owned by two or more people, about half will not be operating next year? Fewer than 20 percent of these recently opened sole proprietorships and partnerships will still be operating concerns a decade from now.

What are the pros and cons that people must weigh when they decide to establish businesses in the form of either a sole proprietorship or a partnership? In this chapter, you will learn about these pros and cons. First, however, you must learn about the important function of *economic rent*.

Economic Rent

When you hear the term *rent*, you are accustomed to having it mean the payment made to property owners for the use of land or dwellings. The term *rent* has a different meaning in economics. **Economic rent** is payment to the owner of a resource in excess of its *opportunity cost*—that is, the minimum payment that would be necessary to call forth production of that amount (and quality) of the resource.

Determining Land Rent

Economists originally used the term *rent* to designate payment for the use of land. What was thought to be important about land that could yield *economic* rents was that its supply was completely inelastic. That is, the supply curve for land was thought to be a vertical line, so that no matter what the prevailing market price for land, the quantity supplied would remain the same.

The concept of economic rent is associated with the British economist David Ricardo (1772–1823). Here is how Ricardo analyzed economic rent for land. He first simplified his model by assuming that all land is equally productive. Then Ricardo assumed that the quantity of land in a country is *fixed* so that land's opportunity cost is equal to zero. Graphically, then, in terms of supply and demand, we draw the supply curve for land vertically (zero price elasticity). In Figure 21-1, the supply curve of land is represented by S. If the demand curve is D_1, it intersects the supply curve, S, at price P_1.

> **21.1** Understand the concept of economic rent

Economic rent
A payment for the use of any resource over and above its opportunity cost.

FIGURE 21-1

Economic Rent

If, indeed, the supply curve of land were completely price-inelastic in the long run, it would be depicted by S. The same quantity of land is forthcoming at any constant-quality price. Thus, at the quantity in existence, Q_1, any and all revenues are economic rent. If demand is D_1, the price will be P_1. If demand is D_2, price will rise to P_2. Economic rent would be $P_1 \times Q_1$ and $P_2 \times Q_1$, respectively.

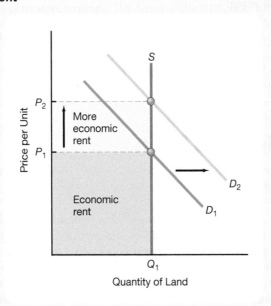

more co-owners, called partners. They share the responsibilities of operating the firm and its profits, and they are *each* legally responsible for *all* of the debts incurred by the firm. In this sense, a partnership may be viewed as a proprietorship with more than one owner.

Advantages of Partnerships. The first advantage of a partnership is that it is *easy to form*. In fact, it is almost as easy to form as a proprietorship. Second, partnerships, like proprietorships, often help *limit the costs of monitoring job performance*. This is particularly true when interpersonal skills are important for successful performance and in lines of business in which, even after the fact, it is difficult to measure performance objectively. Thus, attorneys and physicians often organize themselves as partnerships. A third advantage of the partnership is that it *permits more effective specialization* in occupations in which, for legal or other reasons, the multiple talents required for success are unlikely to be uniform across individuals. Finally, the income of the partnership is treated as personal income and thus is *subject only to personal taxation*.

Disadvantages of Partnerships. Partnerships also have their disadvantages. First, the *partners each have unlimited liability*. Thus, the personal assets of *each* partner are at risk due to debts incurred on behalf of the partnership by *any* of the partners. Second, *decision making is generally more costly* in a partnership than in a proprietorship. More people are involved in making decisions, and they may have differences of opinion that must be resolved before action is possible. Finally, *dissolution of the partnership* often occurs when a partner dies or voluntarily withdraws or when one or more partners wish to remove someone from the partnership. This creates potential uncertainty for creditors and employees.

Corporation A **corporation** is a legal entity that may conduct business in its own name just as an individual does. The owners of a corporation are called *shareholders* because they own shares of the profits earned by the firm. By law, shareholders have **limited liability,** meaning that if the corporation incurs debts it cannot pay, the shareholders' personal property is shielded from claims by the firm's creditors. Corporations account for fewer than 20 percent of all U.S. firms. Nevertheless, because of corporations' large size—typically, average annual sales exceeding $4 million per year—they are responsible for in excess of 80 percent of all business revenues in the United States.

Advantages of Corporations. Perhaps the greatest advantage of corporations is that their owners (the shareholders) have *limited liability*. The liability of shareholders is limited to the value of their shares. The second advantage is that, legally, the corporation *continues to exist* even if one or more owners cease to be owners. A third advantage of the corporation stems from the first two: Corporations are well positioned to *raise large sums of financial capital*. People are able to buy ownership shares or lend funds to the corporation, knowing that their liability is limited to the amount of funds they invest and confident that the corporation's existence does not depend on the life of any one of the firm's owners.

Disadvantages of Corporations. The chief disadvantage of the corporation is that corporate income is subject to *double taxation*. The profits of the corporation are subject first to corporate taxation. Then, if any of the after-tax profits are distributed to shareholders as **dividends,** such payments are treated as personal income to the shareholders and subject to personal taxation. Because the corporate income is also taxed at the corporate level, owners of corporations generally pay higher taxes on corporate income than on other forms of income.

A second disadvantage of the corporation is that corporations are potentially subject to problems associated with the *separation of ownership and control*. The owners and

Corporation
A legal entity that may conduct business in its own name just as an individual does. The owners of a corporation, called shareholders, own shares of the firm's profits and have the protection of limited liability.

Limited liability
A legal concept in which the responsibility, or liability, of the owners of a corporation is limited to the value of the shares in the firm that they own.

Dividends
Portion of a corporation's profits paid to its owners (shareholders).

managers of a corporation are typically different persons and may have different incentives. The problems that can result are discussed later in the chapter.

Your Future as a Business Owner Would you like to have the limited liability benefit of a corporation without the disadvantage of double taxation? If so, there is a business organization you can use, called a **limited liability company, or LLC**—a hybrid form of business enterprise that offers the limited liability of a corporation and the tax advantages of a partnership. Many states allow for LLCs that have only one member. When considering starting a business, you should also consider the LLC as perhaps the most advantageous legal organization.

Limited liability company (LLC)
A hybrid form of business enterprise that offers the limited liability of a corporation and the tax advantages of a partnership.

The Profits of a Firm

To most people, a firm's profit is a simple concept. They regard profit as the difference between the amount of revenues the firm takes in and the amount it spends for wages, materials, and so on.

Accounting Profit In a bookkeeping sense, the following formula could be used:

$$\text{Accounting profit} = \text{total revenues} - \text{explicit costs}$$

In this formula, **explicit costs** are expenses that must actually be paid out by the firm. This definition of profit is known as **accounting profit.** This profit definition is appropriate when used by accountants to determine a firm's taxable income.

Explicit costs
Costs that business managers must take account of because they must be paid. Examples are wages, taxes, and rent.

Accounting profit
Total revenues minus total explicit costs.

Implicit Costs Economists certainly are interested in how firm managers react to changes in explicit costs. In addition, however, they are interested in how managers respond to changes in **implicit costs,** defined as expenses that the managers do not have to pay out of pocket but are costs to the firm nonetheless because they represent an opportunity cost. They do not involve any direct cash outlay by the firm and must therefore be measured by the *opportunity cost principle*. That is to say, they are measured by what the resources (land, capital) currently used in producing a particular good or service could earn in other uses. Consequently, a better definition of implicit cost is the opportunity cost of using factors that a producer does not buy or hire but already owns.

Economists use the full opportunity cost of all resources (including both explicit and implicit costs) as the figure to subtract from revenues to obtain a definition of profit.

Implicit costs
Expenses that managers do not have to pay out of pocket and hence normally do not explicitly calculate, such as the opportunity cost of factors of production that are owned. Examples are owner-provided capital and owner-provided labor.

WHAT HAPPENS WHEN...

factors of production that a producer already owns could be leased to other firms at a higher price than previously?

If a firm could lease the factors of production that it owns to other producers at a higher price, then the opportunity cost of using those factors increases. Consequently, the implicit costs to the firm of using those factors of production for its own operations increase.

Opportunity Cost of Capital

Firms enter or remain in an industry if they earn, at minimum, a **normal rate of return.** People will not invest their wealth in a business unless they expect to obtain a positive normal (competitive) rate of return—that is, unless their invested wealth pays off.

Normal rate of return
The amount that must be paid to an investor to induce investment in a business. Also known as the *opportunity cost of capital.*

Attracting Capital Resources Any business wishing to attract capital must expect to pay at least the same rate of return on that capital as all other businesses (of similar risk) are willing to pay. Put another way, when a firm requires the use of a resource in producing a particular product, it must bid against alternative users of that resource. Thus, the firm must offer a price that is at least as much as other potential users are offering to pay.

Taking into Account the Opportunity Cost of Capital For example, if individuals can invest their wealth in almost any video-game firm and get a rate of return of 10 percent per year, each firm in the video-game industry must *expect* to pay 10 percent as the normal rate of return to present and future investors. This 10 percent is a *cost to the firm*, the **opportunity cost of capital.** The opportunity cost of capital is the amount of income, or yield, that could have been earned by investing in the next-best alternative.

Capital will not stay in firms or industries in which the expected rate of return falls below its opportunity cost—that is, what could be earned elsewhere. If a firm owns some capital equipment, it can either use it or lease it out and earn a return. If the firm uses the equipment for production, part of the cost of using that equipment is the forgone revenue that the firm could have earned had it leased out that equipment.

Opportunity Cost of Owner-Provided Labor and Capital

Single-owner proprietorships often grossly exaggerate their profit rates because they understate the opportunity cost of the labor that the proprietor provides to the business. Here we are referring to the opportunity cost of labor. For example, you may know people who run a small grocery store. These people will sit down at the end of the year and figure out what their "profits" are. They will add up all their sales and subtract what they had to pay to other workers, what they had to pay to their suppliers, what they had to pay in taxes, and so on. The end result they will call "profit." They normally will not, however, explicitly have figured into their costs the salary that they could have made if they had worked for somebody else in a similar type of job.

Proprietors as Residual Claimants By working for themselves, proprietors become residual claimants—they receive what is left after all explicit costs have been accounted for. Part of the costs, however, should include the salary the owner-operator could have received working for someone else.

Your So-Called Profits May Not Be as High as You Think Assume that you are a skilled auto mechanic working 14 hours a day, six days a week, at your own service station. Compare this situation to how much you could earn working 84 hours a week as a trucking company mechanic. As a self-employed auto mechanic, you might have an opportunity cost of about $35 an hour. For your 84-hour week in your own service station, you are forfeiting $2,940. Unless your service station shows accounting profits of more than that per week, you are incurring losses in an economic sense.

A Firm's Overall Opportunity Cost Another way of looking at the opportunity cost of running a business is that opportunity cost consists of all explicit and implicit costs. Accountants take account only of explicit costs. Therefore, accounting profit ends up being the residual after only explicit costs are subtracted from total revenues.

This same analysis can apply to owner-provided capital, such as land or buildings. The fact that the owner owns the building or the land with which he or she operates a business does not mean that it is "free." Rather, use of the building and land still has an opportunity cost—the value of the next-best alternative use for those assets.

Accounting Profits versus Economic Profits

The term *profits* in economics means the income that entrepreneurs earn, over and above all costs including their own opportunity cost of time, plus the opportunity cost

---

Opportunity cost of capital
The normal rate of return, or the available return on the next-best alternative investment. Economists consider this a cost of production, and it is included in our cost examples.

FIGURE 21-2

Simplified View of Economic and Accounting Profit

We see on the right column that accounting profit is the difference between total revenues and total explicit accounting costs. Conversely, we see on the left column that economic profit is equal to total revenues minus economic costs. Economic costs equal explicit accounting costs plus all implicit costs, including a normal rate of return on invested capital.

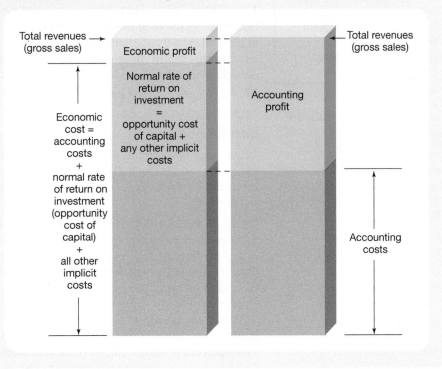

of the capital they have invested in their business. Profits can be regarded as total revenues minus total costs—which is how accountants think of them—but we must now include *all* costs. Our definition of **economic profits** will be the following:

> Economic profits = total revenues − total opportunity cost of all inputs used

or

> Economic profits = total revenues − (explicit + implicit costs)

Remember that implicit costs include a normal rate of return on invested capital. We show this relationship in Figure 21-2.

Economic profits
Total revenues minus total opportunity costs of all inputs used, or the total of all implicit and explicit costs.

The Goal of the Firm: Profit Maximization

When we examined the theory of consumer demand, utility (or satisfaction) maximization by the individual provided the basis for the analysis. In the theory of the firm and production, *profit maximization* is the underlying hypothesis of our predictive theory. The goal of the firm is to maximize economic profits, and the firm is expected to make the positive difference between total revenues and total costs as large as it can.

Our justification for assuming profit maximization by firms is similar to our assumption concerning utility maximization by individuals (see Chapter 20). To obtain labor, capital, and other resources required to produce commodities, firms must first obtain financing from investors. Investors typically monitor managers' performances to ensure that the funds they provide are not misused. Investors also are interested in the earnings on these funds and the risk of obtaining lower returns or losing the funds they have invested. Firms that can provide relatively higher risk-corrected returns will therefore have an advantage in obtaining the financing needed to continue or expand production. Over time, we would expect a policy of profit maximization to become the dominant mode of behavior for firms that survive.

21.3 Discuss how the interest rate performs a key role in allocating resources and calculate the present discounted value of a payment to be received at a future date

Financial capital
Funds used to purchase physical capital goods, such as buildings and equipment, and patents and trademarks.

Interest
The payment for current rather than future command over resources; the cost of obtaining credit.

Interest

Interest is the price paid by debtors to creditors for the use of loanable funds. Often businesses go to credit markets to obtain so-called **financial capital** in order to invest in physical capital and rights to patents and trademarks from which they hope to make a satisfactory return. In other words, in our society, the production of capital goods is often facilitated by the existence of credit markets. These are markets in which borrowing and lending take place.

Interest and Credit

When you obtain credit, you actually obtain funds to have command over resources today. We can say, then, that **interest** is the payment for current rather than future command over resources. Thus, interest is the payment for obtaining credit.

Paying for Credit with Interest If you borrow $100 from me, you have command over $100 worth of goods and services today. I no longer have that command. You promise to pay me back $100 plus interest at some future date. The interest that you pay is usually expressed as a percentage of the total loan, calculated on an annual basis. If at the end of one year you pay me back $105, the annual interest rate is $5 ÷ $100, or 5 percent.

When you go out into the marketplace to obtain credit, you will find that the interest rate charged differs greatly. A loan to buy a house (a mortgage) may cost you 4 to 6 percent in annual interest. An installment loan to buy an automobile may cost you 6 to 8 percent in annual interest. The federal government, when it wishes to obtain credit (issue U.S. Treasury securities), may have to pay only 0.2 to 3 percent in annual interest.

Determinants of the Interest Rate Variations in the rate of annual interest that must be paid for credit depend on the following factors.

1. *Length of loan.* In many (but not all) cases, the longer the loan will be outstanding, other things being equal, the greater will be the interest rate charged.

2. *Risk.* The greater the risk of nonrepayment of the loan, other things being equal, the greater the interest rate charged. Risk is assessed on the basis of the creditworthiness of the borrower and whether the borrower provides collateral for the loan. Collateral consists of any asset that will automatically become the property of the lender should the borrower fail to comply with the loan agreement.

3. *Handling charges.* It takes resources to set up a loan. Papers have to be filled out and filed, credit references have to be checked, collateral has to be examined, and so on. The larger the amount of the loan, the smaller the handling (or administrative) charges as a percentage of the total loan. Therefore, we would predict that, other things being equal, the larger the loan, the lower the interest rate.

Real versus Nominal Interest Rates

Nominal rate of interest
The market rate of interest expressed in today's dollars.

We have been assuming that there is no inflation. In a world of inflation—a persistent rise in an average of all prices—the **nominal rate of interest** will be higher than it would be in a world with no inflation. Nominal, or market, rates of interest rise to take account of the anticipated rate of inflation. If, for example, no inflation is expected, the nominal rate of interest might be 5 percent for home mortgages. If the rate of inflation goes to 4 percent a year and stays there, everybody will anticipate that inflation rate. The nominal rate of interest will rise to about 9 percent to take account of the anticipated rate of inflation.

We can therefore say that the nominal, or market, rate of interest is approximately equal to the real rate of interest plus the anticipated rate of inflation, or

$$i_n = i_r + \text{anticipated rate of inflation}$$

where i_n equals the nominal rate of interest and i_r equals the real rate of interest. In short, you can expect to see high nominal rates of interest in periods of high inflation rates. The **real rate of interest** may not necessarily be high, though. We must first correct the nominal rate of interest for the anticipated rate of inflation before determining whether the real interest rate is in fact higher than normal.

Real rate of interest
The nominal rate of interest minus the anticipated rate of inflation.

The Allocative Role of Interest

Earlier, we talked about the price system and the role that prices play in the allocation of resources. Interest is a price that allocates loanable funds (credit) to consumers and to businesses. Within the business sector, interest allocates funds to different firms and therefore to different investment projects. An investment, or capital, project with a rate of return—an annual payoff as a percentage of the investment—higher than the market rate of interest in the credit market will be undertaken, given an unrestricted market for loanable funds.

For example, suppose that the expected rate of return on the purchase of a new factory or of intellectual property—patents or copyrights—in some industry is 10 percent. If funds can be acquired for 6 percent, the investment project will proceed. If, however, that same project had an expected rate of return of only 4 percent, it would not be undertaken.

In sum, the interest rate allocates funds to industries whose investments yield the highest (risk-adjusted) returns. In these industries, resources will be the most productive.

It is important to realize that the interest rate performs the function of allocating financial capital and that this ultimately allocates real physical capital to various firms for investment projects.

Interest Rates and Present Value

Businesses make investments in which they often incur large costs today but don't make any profits until some time in the future. Somehow they have to be able to compare their investment cost today with a stream of future profits. How can they relate present cost to future benefits?

Linking the Present with the Future Interest rates are used to link the present with the future. After all, if you have to pay $105 at the end of the year when you borrow $100, that 5 percent interest rate gives you a measure of the premium on the earlier availability of goods and services. If you want to have things today, you have to pay the 5 percent interest rate in order to have current purchasing power.

The question could be put this way: What is the present value (the value today) of $105 that you could receive one year from now? That depends on the market rate of interest, or the rate of interest that you could earn in some appropriate savings institution, such as in a savings account.

Present Value To make the arithmetic simple, let's assume that the rate of interest is 5 percent. Now you can figure out the **present value (PV)** of $105 to be received one year from now. You figure it out by asking, What sum must I put aside today at the market interest rate of 5 percent to receive $105 one year from now? Mathematically, we represent this equation as

$$(1 + 0.05)\text{PV}_1 = \$105$$

where PV_1 is the sum that you must set aside now.

Present value (PV)
The value of a future amount expressed in today's dollars; the most that someone would pay today to receive a certain sum at some point in the future.

Let's solve this simple equation to obtain PV_1:

$$PV_1 = \frac{\$105}{1.05} = \$100$$

That is, $100 will accumulate to $105 at the end of one year with a market rate of interest of 5 percent. Thus, the present value of $105 one year from now, using a rate of interest of 5 percent, is $100. This means that at a 5 percent interest rate, $100 today is economically equivalent to $105 one year from now. The formula for present value of any sums to be received one year from now thus becomes

$$PV_1 = \frac{FV_1}{1 + i}$$

where

PV_1 = present value of a sum one year hence

FV_1 = future sum paid or received one year hence

i = market rate of interest

What happens to a state's budgetary allocations when the interest rate used to calculate the discounted present value of promised public pensions decreases?

POLICY EXAMPLE

State Governments Discover That a Change in the Interest Rate Affects Discounted Present Value

States' public pension systems promise future payments to current government employees. To determine whether a public pension system is "fully funded," a state calculates the discounted present value of its future pension-payment promises. The state achieves a fully funded status if the total amount of interest-earning assets held is at least equal to the calculated discounted present value of promised future pension payments. Otherwise, the state's public pension system is underfunded. Then the state eventually must direct more tax dollars into its pension fund.

Since the mid-2000s, many states, such as Connecticut, have calculated the discounted present value of promised pension payments based on higher interest rates than those actually observed in financial markets. Only in recent years have a number of these states reduced the interest rates that they utilize in their discounted-present-value computations to market levels. When states have done so, calculated discounted present values of promised future pension payments have

soared. In Connecticut, a recent 1.6-percentage-point reduction in the interest rate used by the government to calculate the discounted present value of promised pension payments increased pension underfunding by $9 billion. When Connecticut responded by allocating more tax dollars toward funding its future pension payouts, fewer tax dollars were available each year to provide *current* services in areas such as education and public safety.

FOR CRITICAL THINKING

Why do you think that since states began using lower interest rates to calculate discounted present values of future promised payments, the total extent of underfunding of states' pension systems rose from 15 percent to 28 percent?

Sources are listed at the end of this chapter.

Present Values for More Distant Periods The present-value formula for figuring out today's worth of dollars to be received at a future date can now be determined. How much would have to be put in the same savings account today to have $105 *two years* from now if the account pays a rate of 5 percent per year compounded annually?

After one year, the sum that would have to be set aside, which we will call PV_2, would have grown to $PV_2 \times 1.05$. This amount during the second year would increase to $PV_2 \times 1.05 \times 1.05$, or $PV_2 \times (1.05)^2$. To find the PV_2 that would grow to $105 over two years, let

$$PV_2 \times (1.05)^2 = \$105$$

and solve for PV_2:

$$PV_2 = \frac{\$105}{(1.05)^2} = \$95.24$$

TABLE 21-1

Present Value of a Future Dollar

This table shows how much a dollar received at the end of a certain number of years in the future is worth today. For example, at 5 percent a year, a dollar to be received 20 years in the future is worth 37.7 cents today. If received in 50 years, it isn't even worth a dime today. To find out how much $10,000 a certain number of years from now is worth today, just multiply the figures in the table by 10,000. For example, $10,000 received at the end of 10 years discounted at a 5 percent rate of interest would have a present value of $6,140.

	Discounted Present Values of $1				
Year	3%	5%	8%	10%	20%
1	.971	.952	.926	.909	.833
2	.943	.907	.857	.826	.694
3	.915	.864	.794	.751	.578
4	.889	.823	.735	.683	.482
5	.863	.784	.681	.620	.402
6	.838	.746	.630	.564	.335
7	.813	.711	.583	.513	.279
8	.789	.677	.540	.466	.233
9	.766	.645	.500	.424	.194
10	.744	.614	.463	.385	.162
15	.642	.481	.315	.239	.0649
20	.554	.377	.215	.148	.0261
25	.478	.295	.146	.0923	.0105
30	.412	.231	.0994	.0573	.00421
40	.307	.142	.0460	.0221	.000680
50	.228	.087	.0213	.00852	.000109

Thus, the present value of $105 to be paid or received two years hence, discounted at an interest rate of 5 percent per year compounded annually, is equal to $95.24. In other words, $95.24 put into a savings account yielding 5 percent per year compounded interest would accumulate to $105 in two years.

The General Formula for Discounting The general formula for **discounting** becomes

$$PV_t = \frac{FV_t}{(1 + i)^t}$$

where t refers to the number of periods in the future the money is to be paid or received.

Table 21-1 gives the present value of $1 to be received in future years at various interest rates. The interest rate used to derive the present value is called the **rate of discount.**

Discounting
The method by which the present value of a future sum or a future stream of sums is obtained.

Rate of discount
The rate of interest used to discount future sums back to present value.

Corporate Financing Methods

21.4 Identify the main sources of corporate funds and differentiate between stocks and bonds

When the Dutch East India Company was founded in 1602, it raised financial capital by selling shares of its expected future profits to investors. The investors thus became the owners of the company, and their ownership shares eventually became known as "shares of stock," or simply *stocks*. The company also issued notes of indebtedness, which involved borrowing funds in return for interest paid on the funds, plus eventual repayment of the principal amount borrowed. In modern parlance, these notes of indebtedness are called *bonds*. As the company prospered over time, some of its revenues were used to pay lenders the interest and principal owed them. Of the profits that remained, some were paid to shareholders in the form of dividends. Some were retained by the company for reinvestment in further enterprises.

The methods of financing used by the Dutch East India Company four centuries ago—stocks, bonds, and reinvestment—remain the principal methods of financing for today's corporations.

Stocks

Share of stock
A legal claim to a share of a corporation's future profits. If it is *common stock,* it incorporates certain voting rights regarding major policy decisions of the corporation. If it is *preferred stock,* its owners are accorded preferential treatment in the payment of dividends but do not have any voting rights.

A **share of stock** in a corporation is simply a legal claim to a share of the corporation's future profits. If there are 100,000 shares of stock in a company and you own 1,000 of them, you own the right to 1 percent of that company's future profits. If the stock you own is *common stock,* you also have the right to vote on major policy decisions affecting the company, such as the selection of the corporation's board of directors. Your 1,000 shares would entitle you to cast 1 percent of the votes on such issues.

If the stock you own is *preferred stock,* you own a share of the future profits of the corporation but do *not* have regular voting rights. You do, however, get something in return for giving up your voting rights: preferential treatment in the payment of dividends. Specifically, the owners of preferred stock generally must receive at least a certain amount of dividends in each period before the owners of common stock can receive *any* dividends.

Bonds

Bond
A legal claim against a firm, usually entitling the owner of the bond to receive a fixed annual coupon payment, plus a lump-sum payment at the bond's maturity date. Bonds are issued in return for funds lent to the firm.

A **bond** is a legal claim against a firm, entitling the owner of the bond to receive a fixed annual *coupon* payment, plus a lump-sum payment at the maturity date of the bond. Bonds are issued in return for funds lent to the firm. The coupon payments represent interest on the amount borrowed by the firm, and the lump-sum payment at maturity of the bond generally equals the amount originally borrowed by the firm.

Bonds are *not* claims on the future profits of the firm. Legally, bondholders must be paid whether the firm prospers or not. To help ensure this, bondholders generally receive their coupon payments each year, along with any principal that is due, before *any* shareholders can receive dividend payments.

What nation's government issues bonds that you can buy only in an electronic format?

INTERNATIONAL POLICY EXAMPLE

A Government Bond Designed for a Generation of Smartphone Users

Many parts of the African continent have never been served by old-fashioned telephone landlines. Instead, smartphones have been at the vanguard of most African residents' experiences with telecommunications. This fact helps to explain why so many people in Kenya have readily adopted digital payment systems and a form of mobile currency called M-Pesa held in electronic deposit accounts at banks.

Holders of such accounts now also can utilize their smartphones to purchase 3-year "M-Akiba" bonds from Kenya's government. In the Kiswahili language spoken by most Kenyan residents, "akiba" is the word for saving, and to give people an incentive to accumulate savings in the form of bonds, the government sells the bonds in denominations as small as about $30. The government offers interest at an annual rate

almost 3 percentage points above bank deposit rates, and it pays interest directly into their mobile-money accounts with banks. A smartphone-based market in M-Akiba bonds formed soon after the government announced that it would allow bond trading.

REAL APPLICATION

When you contemplate the purchase of bonds with your savings, how do the rate of inflation and your marginal income tax rate enter into your decision making?

Sources are listed at the end of this chapter.

Reinvestment

Reinvestment
Profits (or depreciation reserves) used to purchase new capital equipment.

Reinvestment takes place when the firm uses some of its profits to purchase new capital equipment rather than paying the profits out as dividends to shareholders. Although sales of stock are an important source of financing for new firms, reinvestment and borrowing are the primary means of financing for existing firms. Indeed, reinvestment by established firms is such an important source of financing that it dominates the other two sources of corporate finance, amounting to roughly 75 percent of new financial capital for corporations in recent years. Also, small businesses, which are the source of much current economic growth, commonly cannot rely on the stock market to raise investment funds.

The Markets for Stocks and Bonds

Economists often refer to the "market for wheat" or the "market for labor," but these are concepts rather than actual places. For **securities** (stocks and bonds), however, there really are markets—centralized, physical locations where exchange takes place. The most prestigious of these markets are the New York Stock Exchange (NYSE) and the New York Bond Exchange, both located in New York City. More than 2,500 stocks are traded on the NYSE, which is sometimes called the "Big Board." Numerous other stock and bond markets, or exchanges, exist throughout the United States and in various financial capitals of the world, such as London and Tokyo.

Even though the NYSE is traditionally the most prestigious of U.S. stock exchanges, it is no longer the largest. Since the mid-2000s, this title has belonged to the National Association of Securities Dealers Automated Quotations (NASDAQ), which began in 1971 as a tiny electronic network linking about 100 securities firms. Currently, the NASDAQ market links about 500 dealers, and NASDAQ is home to about 3,000 stocks, including those of such companies as Amazon, Apple, Facebook, and Google.

In the past, traders arranged trades of shares of stock on the floors of exchanges. Today, about 90 percent of exchanges occur electronically and involve people located hundreds or thousands of miles distant from each other.

The Theory of Efficient Markets At any point in time, there are tens of thousands, even millions, of persons looking for any bit of information that will enable them to forecast correctly the future prices of stocks. Responding to any information that seems useful, these people try to buy low and sell high. The result is that all publicly available information that might be used to forecast stock prices gets taken into account by those with access to the information and the knowledge and ability to learn from it, leaving no *predictable* profit opportunities. Because so many people are involved in this process, it occurs quite swiftly. Indeed, there is some evidence that *all* information entering the market is fully incorporated into stock prices within less than a minute of its arrival. One view is that any information about specific stocks will prove to have little value by the time it reaches you.

Consequently, stock prices tend to drift upward following a *random walk*, which is to say that the best forecast of tomorrow's price is today's price plus the effect of any upward drift. This is called the **random walk theory.** Although large values of the random component of stock price changes are less likely than small values, nothing else about the magnitude or direction of a stock price change can be predicted.

How are financial firms reducing expenses incurred in trading securities?

Securities
Stocks and bonds.

ECONOMICS IN YOUR LIFE
To contemplate the advantages of speedier access to information in financial markets, read **What New Microwave Towers Have to Do with Modern Financial Markets** on page 465.

Random walk theory
The theory that there are no predictable changes in securities prices that can be used to "get rich quick."

 AI | DECISION MAKING THROUGH DATA

Supplementing or Replacing Human Financial Trading

During the past two decades, financial firms such as banks and hedge funds have reduced the expenses that they incur in trading securities by substantially decreasing their employment of human traders. The firms no longer pay large numbers of people significant salaries to engage in trades that sometimes generate losses

alongside gains. Instead, the firms increasingly rely on automated trading algorithms residing on digital devices connected to electronic trading networks.

Because so many financial firms now operate with smaller staffs, the firms sometimes struggle to find people possessing the talents required to design ever more efficient trading algorithms. Some financial firms have developed innovative ways to find new employees

(Continued)

possessing such talent. For instance, a hedge fund called Quantopian developed an online securities-trading platform that provides interested people with the tools required to develop and utilize their own trading algorithms. More than 120,000 people have done so, and Quantopian can apply big data techniques to track the relative trading performances of all of these algorithms. Periodically, Quantopian selects the best-performing algorithms for its own staff to use for its own trading. Quantopian pays the developers of the winning algorithms a licensing fee equal to 10 percent of the profits that the developers' algorithms generate for the hedge fund.

FOR CRITICAL THINKING

Why might the design of trading algorithms that speed the execution of stock trades contribute to stock market efficiency?

Sources are listed at the end of this chapter.

Inside information

Information that is not available to the general public about what is happening in a corporation.

Inside Information Isn't there any way to "beat the market"? The answer is yes—but normally only if you have **inside information** that is not available to the public. Suppose that your best friend is in charge of new product development at Google, the world's largest digital-information firm. Your friend tells you that the company's smartest programmer has just come up with major new apps that millions of users of digital devices will want to buy. No one but your friend and the programmer—and now you—is aware of this. You could indeed make a killing using this information by purchasing shares of Google and then selling them (at a higher price) as soon as the new products are publicly announced.

There is one problem: Stock trading based on inside information such as this is illegal, punishable by substantial fines and even imprisonment. Unless you happen to have a stronger-than-average desire for a long vacation in a federal prison, then you might be better off investing in Google after the new program is publicly announced.

Why are many efforts by groups of stock shareholders to "punish" firms for operating in ways that currently maximize profits but that the groups regard as socially unacceptable unlikely to succeed?

EXAMPLE

Why Trying to Induce Companies to "Do the Right Thing" by "Punishing" Their Stocks Often Fails

Sometimes, a group of stockholders seeks to coordinate its stock trading to induce companies to pursue particular objectives, such as using more environmentally friendly production methods that would not yield maximized profits. One approach employed by such groups is to publicly single out and try to "punish" a specific firm that uses inputs or technologies that the groups believe are damaging to the environment. The groups seek to do so by announcing and following through on sales of large amounts of the firm's shares, with an aim to push down the firm's stock price.

A problem with this strategy is that if a coordinating group follows through with such a strategy and manages to push down the price of the targeted firm's stock, the result is predictable profit opportunities for other stock traders. These other traders know that if the "punished" firm sticks with its current profit-maximizing production approach, its shares of stock will possess the same underlying profit-based value reflected in its original share price. The individual traders' anticipation that the

stock price should rise back to its previous level gives those traders a strong incentive to purchase the targeted firm's stock. After all, these traders will expect to earn profits by buying at the new low price and selling at a higher price later! Indeed, if, as usually occurs, numerous traders respond to this incentive, then the market demand for the firm's stocks increases. Thus, the reactions of these individual traders help to more speedily push the equilibrium share price back up.

REAL APPLICATION

Assume that you read in the financial news section of an online news blog that Friends of the Planet has singled out TrashMaker Corporation for the latter's environmentally inappropriate manufacturing system. You already own some shares of stock in this company in your portfolio of investments. What should you do?

Sources are listed at the end of this chapter.

ECONOMICS IN YOUR LIFE

What New Microwave Towers Have to Do with Modern Financial Markets

Stěphane Tyč, co-founder of McKay Brothers LLC, a company that operates a high-speed network for financial traders, has completed the process of obtaining permission to erect a 350-foot-tall microwave tower in Chicago. Tyč and other company managers plan to place the tower on leased land. The location is across the street from a data center operated by the Chicago Mercantile Exchange (CME), one of the major U.S. exchanges for financial trading. Tyč's land-leasing and tower-building arrangement follows on the heels of the erection of microwave towers in another location across the street from the CME's data center by another company called World Class Wireless. The latter company is owned by Jump Trading LLC and Virtu Financial Inc., other financial-trading firms.

Why are Tyč's company and World Class Wireless placing microwave towers so close to CME's data center? The answer is that doing so cuts a few milliseconds off the time required for an offer to buy or sell a financial asset to be processed by the CME's communications system. Traders of the assets know that the theory of efficient markets

indicates that all relevant information is processed within a short interval after it becomes available. Nevertheless, they also know that a tiny fraction of a second can sometimes make a difference in profiting from the information available within that interval. This fact explains why they are competing to speed their access to the CME's data centers.

CRITICAL THINKING QUESTIONS

How might winning a bid to sell a financial asset a few microseconds faster than another firm enable a trader at a financial firm to earn a profit perhaps just a few minutes after buying the asset?

REAL APPLICATION

Given what you just learned in this feature above, should you place your savings with the financial trading firms mentioned? Why or why not?

Sources are listed at the end of this chapter.

ISSUES & APPLICATIONS

Rawpixel.com/Shutterstock

Explaining the Growth in the Number of Widely Used "Stock Indexes"

CONCEPTS APPLIED

➤ Securities

➤ Efficient Markets

➤ Random Walk Theory

Securities trading has been revolutionized in recent years by the widespread acceptance of the theory of efficient markets. A consequence has been an increase in the utilization of stock *indexes* even as the number of individual stocks traded on exchanges has decreased.

Stock Indexes

A stock index is a measure of the average value of a group of stocks, which typically is calculated as a simple average or as a specially adjusted or weighted average of the prices of stocks within the particular group. For instance, the Dow Jones Industrial Average is a stock index that sums the prices of thirty selected individual stocks. This sum then is divided by a number that adjusts this average to account for special events that had nothing to do with the underlying prices of those thirty stocks.

Traditionally, people have used stock indexes to judge the performances of money managers. For instance, consider a manager who is actively trading a few stocks. If that manager generates a higher return than a stock index indicates could have been earned on a broad set of stocks, the manager has performed better than someone who simply held that broad group of stocks. In addition, stock indexes for different industries or countries allow comparisons of varying overall performances of those industries' or countries' stocks. Furthermore, people have utilized stock indexes to create securities, such as stock index futures contracts, that offer returns based on movements in the underlying stock indexes.

The Decline of Individual Stocks and the Rise of Stock Indexes

Figure 21-3 displays a substantial increase in the number of widely used stock indexes. Accounting for much of this increase has been the decisions by many financial traders to end efforts to trade individual stocks actively with an aim to earn profits. Some traders instead are buying groups of stocks with average performances tracked by a stock market index. Other traders are trying to make sure that the overall portfolio of stocks they hold yield an average return that moves in conjunction with a broad stock market index.

Thus, most observers argue that the increase in the number of stock indexes—to a level that now exceeds the number of individual stocks included in these indexes— reflects growing acceptance of the theory of efficient markets. An increasing number of traders are doing no more than seeking to keep up with average performances of multiple stocks. Many fewer traders are buying and selling individual stocks with an aim to try to "beat the market."

FOR CRITICAL THINKING

Based on the efficient markets theory, might you conclude that a manager of funds has done "as well as could be expected" by earning a return on a portfolio of stocks that matches the performance of a broad stock index? Explain.

REAL APPLICATION

If you believe the efficient market hypothesis, how should you allocate your savings?

Sources are listed at the end of this chapter.

FIGURE 21-3

The Number of Individual Stocks versus the Number of Stock Indexes

During recent years, the number of individual stocks traded on exchanges has declined even as the number of stock indexes with values based on weighted averages of the prices of individual stocks has increased.

Sources: Securities and Exchange Commission; author's estimates.

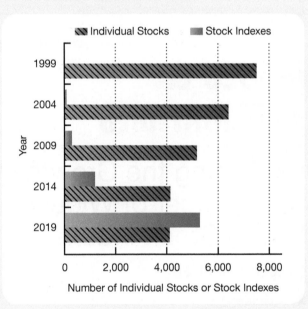

What You Should Know

Here is what you should know after reading this chapter.

LEARNING OBJECTIVES	KEY TERMS
21.1 **Understand the concept of economic rent** *Owners of a resource with a perfectly inelastic supply curve are paid economic rent, which is a payment for the use of any resource that exceeds the opportunity cost of the resource. The economic rents received by the owners of such a resource reflect the maximum market value.*	economic rent, 451 **Key Figure** Figure 21-1, 451

21.2 Distinguish among the main organizational forms of business and explain the difference between accounting profits and economic profits *The three primary forms of businesses are proprietorships owned by a single person, partnerships with two or more owners, and corporations with owners whose liability is limited to the value of their shares. A firm's accounting profits equal its total revenues minus its total explicit costs, which are expenses directly paid out by the firm. Economic profits equal accounting profits minus implicit costs, which are expenses that managers do not have to pay out of pocket.*

21.3 Discuss how the interest rate performs a key role in allocating resources and calculate the present discounted value of a payment to be received at a future date *Interest is a payment for the ability to use resources today instead of in the future. The nominal interest rate equals the real interest rate plus the anticipated inflation rate. The present value of a future payment is equal to the future amount divided by the quantity 1 plus the appropriate rate of interest, which is called the rate of discount.*

21.4 Identify the main sources of corporate funds and differentiate between stocks and bonds *Stocks are ownership shares, promising a share of profits, sold to investors. Common stocks embody voting rights regarding the major decisions of the firm. Preferred stocks typically have no voting rights but enjoy priority status in the payment of dividends. Bonds are notes of indebtedness that pay interest in the form of annual coupon payments, plus repayment of the original principal amount upon maturity.*

PROBLEMS

21-1. Which of the following individuals would you expect to have a high level of economic rent, and which would you expect to have a low level of economic rent? Explain why for each.

   a. Bob has a highly specialized medical skill possessed by very few individuals.

   b. Sally has never attended school. She is 25 years old and is an internationally known supermodel.

   c. Tim is a high school teacher and sells insurance part time.

21-2. Which of the following individuals would you expect to have a high level of economic rent, and which would you expect to have a low level of economic rent? Explain why for each.

   a. Emily quit high school at age 17, and she has since worked for several years as a cashier in fast-food restaurants.

   b. Demetrius earned a Ph.D. in financial economics, and he is among a handful of experts who specialize in assessing the values of highly complex securities traded in bond markets.

   c. Xin was a child prodigy on the violin, and after years of developing her skills, she is now rated among the most talented performing violinists in the world.

21-3. In which of the following situation(s) will owners who supply factors of production be most likely to earn economic rents?

   a. Highly elastic supply of the factor; highly elastic demand for the factor

   b. Highly elastic supply of the factor; highly inelastic demand for the factor

   c. Highly inelastic supply of the factor; highly inelastic demand for the factor

21-4. A British pharmaceutical company spent several years and considerable funds on the development of a treatment for HIV patients. Now, with the protection afforded by patent rights, the company has the potential to reap enormous gains. The government, in response, has threatened to tax away any economic rents the company may earn. Is this a sensible policy? Why or why not? (*Hint:* Contrast the short-run and long-run effects of taxing away the economic rents.)

21-5. Write a brief explanation of the differences among a sole proprietorship, a partnership, and a corporation. In addition, list one advantage and one disadvantage of a proprietorship, a partnership, and a corporation.

21-6. After graduation, you face a choice. One option is to work for a multinational consulting firm and earn a starting salary (benefits included) of $40,000. The other option is to use $5,000 in savings to start your own consulting firm. You could earn an interest return of 5 percent on your savings. You choose to start your own consulting firm. At the end of the first year, you add up all of your expenses and revenues. Your total includes $12,000 in rent, $1,000 in office supplies, $20,000 for office staff, and $4,000 in telecommunications expenses. What are your total explicit costs and total implicit costs?

21-7. Suppose, as in Problem 21-6, that you have now operated your consulting firm for a year. At the end of the first year, your total revenues are $77,250. Based on the information in Problem 21-6, what is the accounting profit, and what is your economic profit?

21-8. An individual leaves a college faculty, where she was earning $80,000 a year, to begin a new venture. She invests her savings of $20,000, which were earning 10 percent annually. She then spends $40,000 renting office equipment, hires two students at $30,000 a year each, rents office space for $24,000, and has other variable expenses of $80,000. At the end of the year, her revenues are $400,000. What are her accounting profit and her economic profit for the year?

21-9. Classify the following items as either financial capital or physical capital.

a. A computer server owned by an information-processing company

b. $100,000 set aside in an account to purchase a computer server

c. Funds raised through a bond offer to expand plant and equipment

d. A warehouse owned by a shipping company

21-10. Explain the difference between the dividends of a corporation and the profits of a proprietorship or partnership, particularly in their tax treatment.

21-11. The owner of Internet City is trying to decide whether to remain a proprietorship or to incorporate. Suppose that the corporate tax rate on profits is 20 percent and the personal income tax rate is 30 percent. For simplicity, assume that all corporate profits (after corporate taxes are paid) are distributed as dividends in the year they are earned and that such dividends are subject to tax at the personal income tax rate.

a. If the owner of Internet City expects to earn $100,000 in before-tax profits this year, regardless of whether the firm is a proprietorship or a corporation, which method of organization should be chosen?

b. What is the dollar value of the after-tax advantage of the form of organization determined in part (a)?

c. Suppose that the corporate form of organization has cost advantages that will raise before-tax profits by $50,000. Should the owner of Internet City incorporate?

d. Based on parts (a) and (c), by how much will after-tax profits change due to incorporation?

e. Suppose that tax policy is changed to completely exempt from personal taxation the first $40,000 per year in dividends. Would this change in policy affect the decision made in part (a)?

f. How can you explain the fact that even though corporate profits are subject to double taxation, most business in the United States is conducted by corporations rather than by proprietorships or partnerships?

21-12. Explain how the following events would likely affect the relevant interest rate.

a. A major bond-rating agency has improved the risk rating of a developing nation.

b. The government has passed legislation requiring bank regulators to significantly increase the paperwork required when a bank makes a loan.

21-13. Suppose that the interest rate in Japan is only 2 percent, while the comparable rate in the United States is 4 percent. Japan's rate of inflation is 0.5 percent, while the U.S. inflation rate is 3 percent. Which economy has the higher real interest rate?

21-14. You expect to receive a payment of $104 one year from now.

a. Your rate of discount is 4 percent. What is the present value of the payment to be received?

b. Suppose that your rate of discount rises to 5 percent. What is the present value of the payment to be received?

21-15. Outline the differences between common stock and preferred stock.

21-16. Explain the basic differences between a share of stock and a bond.

21-17. Suppose that one of your classmates informs you that he has developed a method of forecasting stock market returns based on past trends. With a monetary investment from you, he claims that the two of you could profit handsomely from this forecasting method. How should you respond to your classmate?

21-18. Suppose that you are trying to decide whether to spend $1,000 on stocks issued by Wild Internet or on bonds issued by the same company. There is a 50 percent chance that the value of the stock will rise to $2,200 at the end of the year and a 50 percent chance that the stock will be worthless at the end of the year. The bonds promise an interest rate of 20 percent per year, and it is certain that the bonds and interest will be repaid at the end of the year.

a. Assuming that your time horizon is exactly one year, will you choose the stocks or the bonds?

b. By how much is your expected end-of-year wealth reduced if you make the wrong choice?

c. Suppose the odds of success improve for Wild Internet: Now there is a 60 percent chance that the value of the stock will be $2,200 at year's end and only a 40 percent chance that it will be worthless. Should you now choose the stocks or the bonds?

d. By how much did your expected end-of-year wealth rise as a result of the improved outlook for Wild Internet?

21-19. Take a look at Figure 21-1. Suppose that $Q_1 = 10$ acres and $P_1 = \$2,000$ per acre. What is the dollar amount of economic rents received during the current period, and why is this amount classified as economic rents?

21-20. Reconsider Figure 21-1 and the data provided in Problem 21-19, and suppose that $P_2 = \$2,800$ per acre. By how much do economic rents change when the rental rate on land rises from P_1 to P_2 in the figure?

21-21. Consider Figure 21-2. Explain why the figure indicates that if the normal rate of return on investment were to remain unchanged while accounting profit increased, economic profit also would increase.

21-22. Take a look at Figure 21-2. Explain why the figure implies that if the amount of accounting profit were to shrink to zero while the normal rate of return on investment remained unchanged, economic profit necessarily would become negative.

21-23. Take a look at Table 21-1. Suppose that you are planning your retirement. The appropriate interest rate for computing the present values of future dollars to be received is 8 percent, and you plan to "cash in" all of what you save for retirement this year in exactly 30 years. How many dollars would you have to save this year to ensure being able to have a total of $50,000 accumulated 30 years from now?

21-24. Reconsider Table 21-1, and assume that as in Problem 21-23, you wish to save enough this year to have $50,000 available for your planned retirement 30 years into the future. How many dollars would you have to save this year to ensure that a total amount of $50,000 would be accumulated 30 years into the future if the interest rate appropriate for discounting decreases to 3 percent?

REFERENCES

POLICY EXAMPLE: State Governments Discover That a Change in the Interest Rate Affects Discounted Present Value

David Walker, "Connecticut Needs to Defuse Its Retirement Debt Bomb," *Hartford Courant*, January 13, 2019.

Marc Fitch, "Change in Pension Discount Rates Increases Liabilities $9 Billion on Balance Sheet," Yankee Institute for Public Policy, May 25, 2018.

Heather Gillers, "Pension Funds Still Making Promises They Probably Can't Keep," *Wall Street Journal*, May 8, 2018.

INTERNATIONAL POLICY EXAMPLE: A Government Bond Designed for a Generation of Smartphone Users

Government of Kenya, "How to Invest in M-Akiba," (http://www.m-akiba.go.ke/index.php/how-to-invest), 2019.

Yomi Kazeem, "World's First Mobile-Only Government Bond in Kenya Is Popular But Missed Its Target, *QuartzAfrica*, June 21, 2018.

Evans Osano and Tamara Cook, "The Story of Kenya's M-Akiba: Selling Treasury Bonds via Mobile," *fsdAfrica*, May 11, 2018.

AI—DECISION MAKING THROUGH DATA: Supplementing or Replacing Human Financial Trading

"Become an Expert in Quant Finance," Quantopian (https://www. quantopian.com), 2019.

"FactSet and Quantopian Announce Plans to Launch Financial Data Analysis Platform to Help Investment Industry Capitalize on Rapid Data Growth," *Global Newswire*, April 21, 2018.

Liz Moyer, "A Steve Cohen–backed Trading Firm Is Rolling Out Data for Quant Wannabees," CNBC, April 26, 2018.

EXAMPLE: Why Trying to Induce Companies to "Do the Right Thing" by "Punishing" Their Stocks Often Fails

"Boycotts List," EthicalConsumer.com (https://www.ethicalconsumer. org/ethicalcampaigns/boycotts), 2019.

James Mackintosh, "If You Want to Do Good, Expect to Do Badly," *Wall Street Journal*, June 28, 2018.

C. J. Polychroniou, "Are Fossil Fuel Divestment Campaigns Working?" *Global Policy*, May, 29, 2018.

ECONOMICS IN YOUR LIFE: What New Microwave Towers Have to Do with Modern Financial Markets

"About McKay Brothers LLC," McKay Brothers (https://www. mckay-brothers.com/about-us/), 2019.

Brian Lewis, Nick Baker, and John McCormick, "HFT Traders Dust Off Century-Old Search of Market Edge," *Bloomberg*, June 18, 2018.

Gregory Meyer, Nicole Bullock, and Joe Rennison, "How High-Frequency Trading Hit a Speed Bump," *Financial Times*, January 1, 2018.

ISSUES & APPLICATIONS: Explaining the Growth in the Number of Widely Used "Stock Indexes"

"Market Indexes: Major Markets," MarketWatch (https://www. marketwatch.com/tools/marketsummary/indices/indices. asp?indexid=1&groupid=37), 2019.

Tom Bailey, "There Are Now 70 Times More Stock Market Indices Than Listed Stocks in the World," *Money Observer*, January 24, 2018.

Harvey Sax, "There Are Now More Indices Than Stocks," The Insiders Fund, February 6, 2018.

22

The Firm: Cost and Output Determination

Andriy Popow/123RF GB Limited

Imagine a future world of retailing in which clothing purchases scanned at a retailer's fully networked cash register are transmitted to an AI-managed system that compiles, processes, and analyzes the latest clothing buying trends. This AI system automatically utilizes its analysis of these trends to adjust the retailer's clothing inventory plan over the coming weeks and months. In light of this revised plan, the system also automatically adjusts orders for new clothing items to be provided by suppliers over the course of the coming months.

In fact, for a growing number of retailers of clothing, as well as of grocery items and other merchandise, this imagined future setting has become today's reality. In this chapter, you will learn that production and cost incentives motivate these retailers to develop and put into place sophisticated AI systems for automatic tracking of merchandise sales.

DID YOU KNOW THAT...

many ranchers have sensors implanted within the stomachs of their livestock? Data from the sensors can be wirelessly downloaded each day and analyzed both to monitor the health of individual animals and to assess the general well-being of herds. At the first sign of a single animal's illness or spreading sickness within herds, ranchers can initiate speedy treatments and thereby limit overall veterinary expenses and losses resulting from livestock deaths. Incurring a small cost for each sensor purchased thereby helps to minimize a ranch's total costs.

How are a firm's costs related to its production process, and what are the main determinants of those costs? To understand the answer to this question, you must learn about the nature of the costs that firms incur in their productive endeavors. First, though, you must contemplate firms' use of inputs in their production of goods and services.

22.1 Discuss the difference between the short run and the long run from the perspective of a firm

Short Run Versus Long Run

In an earlier chapter, we discussed short-run and long-run price elasticities of supply and demand. As you will recall, for consumers, the long run means the time period during which all adjustments to a change in price can be made, and anything shorter than that is considered the short run. For suppliers, the long run is the time in which all adjustments can be made, and anything shorter than that is the short run. Now that we are discussing firms only, we will maintain a similar distinction between the short and the long run, but we will be more specific.

The Short Run

Short run
The time period during which at least one input, such as plant size, cannot be changed.

Plant size
The size of the facilities that a firm owns and operates to produce its output. Plant size can be defined by square footage, maximum capacity, and other measures of the scale of production of goods or services.

In the theory of the firm, the **short run** is defined as any time period so short that there is at least one input, such as current **plant size,** that the firm cannot alter. In other words, during the short run, a firm makes do with whatever equipment and facilities it already has, no matter how much more it wants to produce because of increased demand for its product. We consider the floor space and equipment, the size or amount of which cannot be varied in the short run, as *fixed* resources. In agriculture and in some other businesses, land may be a fixed resource.

There are, of course, variable resources that the firm can alter when it wants to change its rate of production. These are called *variable inputs* or *variable factors of production*. Typically, the variable inputs of a firm are its labor and its purchases of raw materials. In the short run, in response to changes in demand, the firm can, by definition, change only the amounts of its variable inputs.

The Long Run

Long run
The time period during which all factors of production can be varied.

The **long run** can now be considered the period of time in which *all* inputs can be varied. Specifically, in the long run, the firm can alter its plant size. How long is the long run? That depends on each individual industry. For Wendy's or McDonald's, the long run may be four or five months, because that is the time it takes to add new franchises. For a steel company, the long run may be several years, because that's how long it takes to plan and build a new plant. An electric utility might require more than a decade to build a new plant.

Short run and *long run* in our discussion are terms that apply to planning decisions made by managers. Managers routinely take account of both the short-run and the long-run consequences of their behavior. While always making decisions about what to do today, tomorrow, and next week—the short run as it were—they keep an eye on the long-run net benefits of all short-run actions. As an individual, you have long-run plans, such as going to graduate school or having a successful career, and you make a series of short-run decisions with these long-run plans in mind.

A Firm's Production

22.2 Describe production at a firm and explain why the marginal product of labor eventually declines as more units of labor are employed

A firm takes numerous inputs, combines them using a technological production process, and ends up with an output. There are, of course, a great many factors of production, or inputs. Keeping the quantity of land fixed, we classify production inputs into two broad categories—capital and labor.

The Relationship between Output and Inputs

The relationship between output and these two inputs is as follows:

Output per time period = some function of capital and labor inputs

We have used the word *production* but have not defined it. **Production** is any process by which resources are transformed into goods or services. Production includes not only making things but also transporting them, retailing, repackaging them, and so on. Notice that the production relationship tells nothing about the worth or value of the inputs or the output.

Production
Any activity that results in the conversion of resources into products.

The Production Function: A Numerical Example The relationship between maximum output and the quantity of capital and labor used in the production process is sometimes called the **production function.** The production function is a technological relationship between inputs and output.

Properties of the Production Function The production function specifies the *maximum* possible output that can be produced with a given amount of inputs. It also specifies the minimum amount of inputs necessary to produce a given level of output. Firms that are inefficient or wasteful in their use of capital and labor will obtain less output than the production function will show. No firm can obtain more output than the production function allows, however. The production function also depends on the technology available to the firm. It follows that an improvement in technology that allows the firm to produce more output with the same amount of inputs (or the same output with fewer inputs) results in a new production function.

How has a railroad company recently reconfigured—and then undone that reconfiguration—the relationship between its output and its inputs?

Production function
The relationship between inputs and maximum output. A production function is a technological, not an economic, relationship.

EXAMPLE

A Railroad Company Rediscovers How to Obtain Maximum Feasible Production from Available Inputs

For railway firms such as CSX Transportation, output is measured by freight hauled per mile per unit of time. Until early 2017, CSX had utilized hump yards to sort freight cars. In these areas filled with connecting tracks spread across hills, a car earmarked for transferral to a group intended for the same destination was pushed over a hill. Gravity sent the car down a hill to be routed through switches to an appropriate track containing the desired grouping of cars.

Then CSX altered the way that it combined groups of freight cars into trains that locomotives pull from one locale to another. The company's managers adopted a different process called preblocking and flat switching. Under this process, cars containing shipments intended for particular destinations were identified in advance. Locomotives were used to move the cars through switches on level terrain into groupings on designated tracks. The managers' view was that preblocking and flat switching would yield more rail output per unit of time.

In fact, CSX quickly discovered that preblocking and flat switching turned out to be a much more time-consuming method of sorting freight cars. Following months of reduced production flows, CSX promptly reversed course and integrated hump yards back into its operations. Thus, CSX's experiment with preblocking and flat switching actually proved that the traditional hump-yard approach to organizing and assembling trains of freight cars really is the most effective method to achieve maximum feasible rail output per unit of time.

FOR CRITICAL THINKING

Was CSX's railway output consistent with the quantity specified by its production function when the company used preblocking and flat switching? (Hint: Recall that the production function specifies the maximum *output that can be produced given quantities of inputs.)*

Sources are listed at the end of this chapter.

We will use a variety of production examples in this chapter, and the first will involve the production of cloud computing services. Panel (a) of Figure 22-1 shows a production function relating maximum output of cloud computing services in column 2 to the quantity of labor in column 1. Zero workers per week produce no service output. Five workers per week of input provide services that yield a total output of 290 units of cloud computing services per week. (Ignore for the moment the rest of that panel.) Panel (b) of Figure 22-1 displays this production function. It relates to the short run, because plant size is fixed, and it applies to a single firm.

Total Product Panel (b) shows a total product curve, or the maximum feasible service output when we add successive equal-sized units of labor while holding all other inputs constant. The graph of the production function in panel (b) is not a straight line. It peaks between nine and ten workers per week and then starts to go down.

FIGURE 22-1

The Production Relationship and Marginal Product: A Hypothetical Case

Marginal product is the addition to the total product that results when one additional worker is hired (for a week in this example). Thus, in panel (a), the marginal product of adding the fourth worker is 60 units of cloud computing services. With four workers, 240 units of services are produced, but with three workers, only 180 units are produced. The difference is 60 units of output. In panel (b), we plot the numbers from columns 1 and 2 of panel (a). In panel (c), we plot the numbers from columns 1 and 4 of panel (a). When we go from 0 to 1, marginal product is 50 units of output. When we go from one worker to two workers, marginal product increases to 60, and when we go from two workers to three workers, marginal product rises again, to 70 units. After three workers, marginal product declines, but it is still positive. Total product (output) reaches its peak at about ten workers, so after ten workers, marginal product is negative. When we move from ten to eleven workers, marginal product becomes −10 units of output per week.

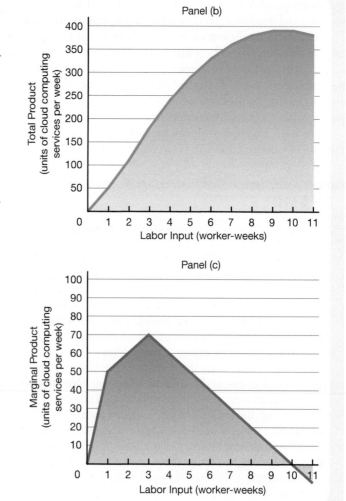

Panel (a)

(1) Input of Labor (number of worker-weeks)	(2) Total Product (output in units of cloud computing services per week)	(3) Average Product (total product ÷ number of worker-weeks) [units of cloud computing services per week]	(4) Marginal Product (output in units of cloud computing services per week)
0	—	—	
			50
1	50	50.00	
			60
2	110	55.00	
			70
3	180	60.00	
			60
4	240	60.00	
			50
5	290	58.00	
			40
6	330	55.00	
			30
7	360	51.43	
			20
8	380	47.50	
			10
9	390	43.33	
			0
10	390	39.00	
			−10
11	380	34.55	

Average and Marginal Product To understand the shape of the total product curve, let's examine columns 3 and 4 of panel (a) of Figure 22-1—that is, average and marginal products. **Average product** is the total product divided by the number of worker-weeks. You can see in column 3 of panel (a) of Figure 22-1 that the average product of labor first rises and then steadily falls after four workers are hired.

Marginal means "additional," so the **marginal product** of labor is the *change* in total product that occurs when a worker is added to a production process for a given interval. (Keep in mind that we always measure output of goods and services in terms of amounts of services or material quantities of goods, not in dollar terms.) The marginal product of labor therefore refers to the *change in output caused by a one-unit change in the labor input* as shown in column 4 of panel (a) of Figure 22-1.

Average product
Total product divided by the variable input.

Marginal product
The output that is due to the addition of one more unit of a variable factor of production. The change in total product occurring when a variable input is increased and all other inputs are held constant.

Diminishing Marginal Product

Note that in Figure 22-1, when four workers instead of three are employed each week, marginal product declines. The concept of diminishing marginal product applies to many situations. If you put a seat belt across your lap, a certain amount of safety is obtained. If you add another seat belt over your shoulder, some additional safety is obtained, but less than when the first belt was secured. When you use three seat belts rather than two over your shoulder, the amount of *additional* safety obtained is even smaller.

Measuring Diminishing Marginal Product How do we measure diminishing marginal product? First, we limit the analysis to only one variable factor of production (or input)—let's say the factor is labor. Every other factor of production, such as physical equipment, must be held constant. Only in this way can we calculate the marginal product from utilizing more workers with the fixed factors, including equipment, and know when we reach the point of diminishing marginal product.

Initially Increasing Marginal Product The marginal product of labor may increase rapidly at the very beginning. Suppose that a firm starts with no workers, and only two pieces of equipment. When the firm hires one worker instead of zero, that individual can use both of the firm's pieces of equipment for producing output, so production jumps. Then, when the firm hires two workers instead of just one, each of the two individuals can utilize a piece of equipment to produce output, and production leaps upward again. Indeed, the marginal product from hiring two workers instead of one may be greater than hiring one worker instead of zero. This is the situation displayed in Figure 22-1, in which hiring two workers instead of one yields a marginal product of 60 units of service output, which exceeds the 50 units of output gained when one worker is hired instead of zero.

Diminishing Marginal Product Beyond some point, marginal product must begin to diminish as more workers are hired—*not* because additional workers are less qualified but because each worker has, on average, less equipment with which to work (remember, all other inputs are fixed). In Figure 22-1, when four workers instead of three are hired to use two pieces of equipment, the fourth worker must perform subsidiary tasks, such as reconfiguring computer servers or redirecting computational flows. Total production of services rises, but not by as much as was the case when three workers rather than two were hired. Consequently, as you can see in column 4 of panel (a) of Figure 22-1, the marginal product when four workers instead of three are hired is 60 units, which is lower than the 70 units of output gained when three workers are hired instead of two. In fact, eventually the firm's plant will become so crowded that workers will start to get in each other's way. At that point, marginal product becomes negative, and total production declines.

Using these ideas, we can define the **law of diminishing marginal product:**

> *As successive equal increases in a variable factor of production are added to fixed factors of production, there will be a point beyond which the extra, or marginal, product that can be attributed to each additional unit of the variable factor of production will decline.*

Law of diminishing marginal product
The observation that after some point, successive equal-sized increases in a variable factor of production, such as labor, added to fixed factors of production will result in smaller increases in output.

The law of diminishing marginal product is a statement about the relationships between inputs and outputs that we have observed across firms operating in industries producing wide varieties of goods and services.

An Example of the Law of Diminishing Marginal Product Production of cloud computing services provides an example of the law of diminishing marginal product. With a fixed amount of plant space available to workers, digital equipment, and computer software and digital apps, the addition of more workers eventually yields successively smaller increases in output. After a while, when all the equipment and software are being used, additional workers will have to start producing services and troubleshooting quality problems manually. Output will not rise as much as when workers were added before this point, because the digital equipment and software are all in use. The marginal product of adding a worker, given a specified amount of capital, must eventually be less than that for the previous workers.

Graphing the Marginal Product of Labor A hypothetical set of numbers illustrating the law of diminishing marginal product is presented in panel (a) of Figure 22-1. The numbers are presented graphically in panel (c). Marginal productivity (additional output from adding more workers during a week) first increases, then decreases, and finally becomes negative.

When one worker is hired, total output goes from 0 to 50. Thus, marginal product is 50 units of cloud computing services per week. When two workers instead of one are hired, total product goes from 50 to 110 units of output per week. Marginal product therefore increases to 60 units of cloud computing services per week. When three workers rather than two are hired, total product again increases, from 110 to 180 units of output per week, so marginal product rises once more, to 70 units per week. Then when four workers are hired instead of three, total product rises from 180 to 240 units per week. This represents a marginal product of only 60 units of cloud computing services per week. Therefore, the point of diminishing marginal product occurs *after* three workers are hired.

The Point of Saturation Notice that after ten workers per week, marginal product becomes negative. This means that eleven workers instead of ten would reduce total product. Sometimes this is called the *point of saturation*, indicating that given the amount of fixed inputs, there is no further positive use for more of the variable input. We have entered the region of negative marginal product.

22.3 Explain the short-run cost curves a typical firm faces

Short-Run Costs to the Firm

You will see that costs are the extension of the production ideas just presented. Let's consider the costs the firm faces in the short run. To make this example simple, assume that there are only two factors of production, capital and labor. Our definition of the short run will be the time during which capital is fixed but labor is variable.

In the short run, a firm incurs certain types of costs. We label all costs incurred **total costs.** Then we break total costs down into total fixed costs and total variable costs, which we will explain shortly. Therefore,

Total costs
The sum of total fixed costs and total variable costs.

$$\text{Total costs} (\text{TC}) = \text{total fixed costs} (\text{TFC}) + \text{total variable costs} (\text{TVC})$$

Remember that these total costs include both explicit and implicit costs, including the normal rate of return on investment.

After we have looked at the elements of total costs, we will find out how to compute average and marginal costs.

Total Fixed Costs

Let's look at an ongoing business such as Apple. The decision makers in that corporate giant can look around and see facilities, thousands of parts, huge buildings, and a multitude of other components of plant and equipment that have already been acquired and are in place. As long as Apple intends to produce positive amounts of digital devices, it has to take into account expenses to replace some worn-out equipment, no matter how many devices it produces. The opportunity costs of any fixed resources that Apple owns will all be the same regardless of the rate of output. In the short run, these costs are the same for Apple no matter how many digital devices it produces.

We also have to point out that the opportunity cost (or normal rate of return) of capital must be included along with other costs. Remember that we are dealing in the short run, during which capital is fixed. This leads us to a very straightforward definition of fixed costs: All costs that do not vary—that is, all costs that do not depend on the rate of production—are called **fixed costs.**

Let's now take as an example the fixed costs incurred by a producer of wireless earbuds. This firm's total fixed costs will usually include the cost of the rent for its plant and equipment and the insurance it has to pay. We see in panel (a) of Figure 22-2 that total fixed costs per hour are $10. In panel (b), these total fixed costs are represented by the horizontal line at $10 per hour. They are invariant to changes in the daily output of wireless earbuds—no matter how many are produced, fixed costs will remain at $10 per hour.

Fixed costs
Costs that do not vary with output. Fixed costs typically include such expenses as rent on a building. These costs are fixed for a certain period of time (in the long run, though, they are variable).

Total Variable Costs

Total **variable costs** are costs whose magnitude varies with the rate of production. Wages are an obvious variable cost. The more the firm produces, the more labor it has to hire. Therefore, the more wages it has to pay. Parts are another variable cost. To manufacture wireless earbuds, for example, lithium battery input must be bought. The more wireless earbuds that are made, the more lithium material that must be bought. A portion of the rate of depreciation (wear and tear) on equipment that is used in the production process can also be considered a variable cost if depreciation depends partly on how long and how intensively the equipment is used. Total variable costs are given in column 3 in panel (a) of Figure 22-2. These are translated into the total variable cost curve in panel (b). Notice that the total variable cost curve lies below the total cost curve by the vertical distance of $10. This vertical distance, of course, represents total fixed costs.

Why are airline companies around the globe incurring higher total fixed costs in hopes of achieving larger reductions in total variable costs and hence lower total costs?

Variable costs
Costs that vary with the rate of production. They include wages paid to workers and purchases of materials.

EXAMPLE

Airline Companies Hope to Reduce Their Total Costs at the Expense of Higher Total Fixed Costs

The world's airline firms have incurred higher fixed expenses. They have upgraded the tracking and telecommunications systems used to coordinate planned and actual flights, to assign employees to tasks and locations, and to ticket and direct passengers. In 2008, such fixed systems expenses were equal to about 1.3 percent of airline firms' total costs. Today, they amount to about 2.7 percent of total costs.

This decision by airline companies to incur higher fixed maintenance expenses on tracking and telecommunications systems has raised their total fixed costs. Nevertheless, the ultimate aim of incurring higher total fixed costs has been to generate a net reduction in *total* costs by cutting total *variable* costs. Prior to the systems upgrades, many of the world's airline firms had experienced persistent and sometimes catastrophic breakdowns in their information-technology systems. These breakdowns

caused substantial upswings in the firms' total variable costs. Thus, airline companies are increasing the fixed costs of maintaining their information-technology systems. Their aim is to reduce the number of breakdowns in these systems and thereby bring about a more-than-offsetting reduction in their total variable costs. If they succeed, on net their total costs will decrease.

FOR CRITICAL THINKING

Are the hourly wages that an airline pays to its maintenance workers fixed costs or variable costs?

Sources are listed at the end of this chapter.

FIGURE 22-2

Cost of Production: An Example of Wireless Earbuds

In panel (a), the derivations of columns 4 through 9 are given in parentheses in each column heading. For example, in column 6, average variable costs are derived by dividing column 3, total variable costs, by column 1, total output per hour. Note that marginal cost (MC) in panel (c) intersects average variable costs (AVC) at the latter's minimum point. Also, MC intersects average total costs (ATC) at that latter's minimum point. It is a little more difficult to see that MC equals AVC and ATC at their respective

minimum points in panel (a) because we are using discrete one-unit changes. You can see, though, that the marginal cost of going from 4 units per hour to 5 units per hour is $2 and increases to $3 when we move to 6 units per hour. Somewhere in between, it equals AVC of $2.60, which is in fact the minimum average variable cost. The same analysis holds for ATC, which hits its respective minimum at 7 units per day at $4.28 per unit. MC goes from $4 to $5 and just equals ATC somewhere in between.

Panel (a)

(1)	(2)	(3)	(4)	(5)	(6)	(7)	(8)	(9)
Total Output (Q/hour)	Total Fixed Costs (TFC)	Total Variable Costs (TVC)	Total Costs (TC) (4) = (2) + (3)	Average Fixed Costs (AFC) (5) = (2) ÷ (1)	Average Variable Costs (AVC) (6) = (3) ÷ (1)	Average Total Costs (ATC) (7) = (4) ÷ (1)	Total Costs (TC) (4)	Marginal Cost (MC) (9) = $\frac{\text{Change in (8)}}{\text{Change in (1)}}$
0	$10	$ 0	$10	—	—	—	$10	
1	10	5	15	$10.00	$5.00	$15.00	15	$5
2	10	8	18	5.00	4.00	9.00	18	3
3	10	10	20	3.33	3.33	6.67	20	2
4	10	11	21	2.50	2.75	5.25	21	1
5	10	13	23	2.00	2.60	4.60	23	2
6	10	16	26	1.67	2.67	4.33	26	3
7	10	20	30	1.43	2.86	4.28	30	4
8	10	25	35	1.25	3.12	4.38	35	5
9	10	31	41	1.11	3.44	4.56	41	6
10	10	38	48	1.00	3.80	4.80	48	7
11	10	46	56	.91	4.18	5.09	56	8

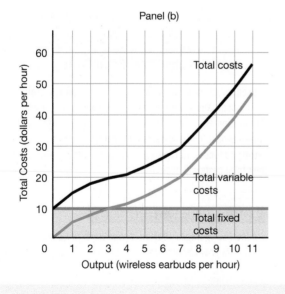

Panel (b)

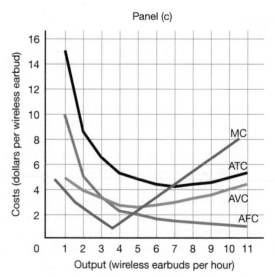

Panel (c)

Short-Run Average Cost Curves

In panel (b) of Figure 22-2, we see total costs, total variable costs, and total fixed costs. Now we want to look at average cost. With the average cost concept, we are measuring cost per unit of output. It is a matter of simple arithmetic to figure the averages of these three cost concepts. We can define them as follows:

$$\text{Average total costs (ATC)} = \frac{\text{total costs (TC)}}{\text{output } (Q)}$$

$$\text{Average variable costs (AVC)} = \frac{\text{total variable costs (TVC)}}{\text{output } (Q)}$$

$$\text{Average fixed costs (AFC)} = \frac{\text{total fixed costs (TFC)}}{\text{output } (Q)}$$

The arithmetic is done in columns 5, 6, and 7 in panel (a) of Figure 22-2. The numerical results are translated into a graphical format in panel (c). Because total costs (TC) equal variable costs (TVC) plus fixed costs (TFC), the difference between average total costs (ATC) and average variable costs (AVC) will always be identical to average fixed costs (AFC). That means that average total costs and average variable costs move together as output expands.

Now let's see what we can observe about the three average cost curves in Figure 22-2.

Average Fixed Costs (AFC) **Average fixed costs** continue to fall throughout the output range. In fact, if we were to continue panel (c) of Figure 22-2 farther to the right, we would find that average fixed costs would get closer and closer to the horizontal axis. That is because total fixed costs remain constant. As we divide this fixed number by a larger and larger number of units of output, the resulting AFC becomes smaller and smaller. In business, this is called "spreading the overhead."

Average fixed costs
Total fixed costs divided by the number of units produced.

Average Variable Costs (AVC) We assume a particular form of the curve for **average variable costs.** The form that it takes is U-shaped: First it falls; then it starts to rise. (It is possible for the AVC curve to take other shapes in the long run.)

Average variable costs
Total variable costs divided by the number of units produced.

Average Total Costs (ATC) This curve has a shape similar to that of the AVC curve. Nevertheless, it falls even more dramatically in the beginning and rises more slowly after it has reached a minimum point. It falls and then rises because **average total costs** are the vertical summation of AFC and AVC. Thus, when AFC and AVC are both falling, ATC must fall too. At some point, however, AVC starts to increase while AFC continues to fall. Once the increase in the AVC curve outweighs the decrease in the AFC curve, the ATC curve will start to increase and will develop a U shape, just like the AVC curve.

Average total costs
Total costs divided by the number of units produced.

How are firms reducing their average total costs by training employees to utilize "augmented reality" in their performance of various tasks?

 AI | DECISION MAKING THROUGH DATA

Using Augmented Reality

Most people know about how conditions of *virtual reality*—apparent immersion in an imagined artificial world—can be created by using headsets and visual gear in combination with digital devices and apps. For firms, however, *augmented reality*—overlaying large volumes of useful data across sensual perceptions of the real world—so far has proved far more practical in terms of generating reductions in average total costs.

Augmented-reality glasses and headsets can be used to save on fuel and labor costs by providing delivery workers with instructions regarding the shortest and speediest routes to their destinations. Once on site, these workers can use apps to project images of bulky

(*Continued*)

items such as appliances over visual views of doorways in order to determine the most efficient way to pass the items through those spaces. Physicians are using augmented-reality glasses to overlay digital images on patients' physical bodies. Doing so speeds surgery times and thereby reduces time-related expenses while reducing errors and thereby eliminating related costs. Manufacturers such as Boeing already are using augmented-reality techniques to give assembly workers step-by-step instructions for putting together product components and for checking to ensure that assembly has been properly completed. The faster assembly that results cuts labor costs, and the more accurate assembly eliminates expenses that product failures

otherwise would generate. In some cases, firms have found that their average total costs have been reduced by as much as 25 percent through the utilization of augmented-reality techniques.

FOR CRITICAL THINKING

How do cost-reducing applications of virtual-reality technologies affect the position of a firm's average total cost curve?

Sources are listed at the end of this chapter.

Marginal Cost

Marginal costs
The change in total costs due to a one-unit change in production rate.

We have stated repeatedly that the basis of decisions is always on the margin—choice in economics is always determined at the margin. This dictum also holds true within the firm. Firms, according to the analysis we use to predict their behavior, are very concerned with their **marginal costs.** Because the term *marginal* means "additional" or "incremental" (or "decremental," too) here, *marginal costs* refer to costs that result from a one-unit change in the production rate. For example, if the production of 10 wireless earbuds per hour costs a firm $48 and the production of 11 wireless earbuds costs $56 per hour, the marginal cost of producing 11 rather than 10 wireless earbuds per hour is $8.

Marginal costs can be measured by using the formula

$$\text{Marginal cost} = \frac{\text{change in total cost}}{\text{change in output}}$$

We show the marginal costs of production of wireless earbuds per hour in column 9 of panel (a) in Figure 22-2, computed according to the formula just given. In our example, we have changed output by one unit every time, so the denominator in that particular formula always equals one.

This marginal cost schedule is shown graphically in panel (c) of Figure 22-2. Just as average variable costs and average total costs initially decrease with rising output and then increase, it must also be true that marginal cost first falls with greater output and then rises. The U shape of the marginal cost curve is a result of increasing and then diminishing marginal product. At lower levels of output, the marginal cost curve declines. The reasoning is that as marginal product increases with each addition of output, the marginal cost of this last unit of output must fall.

Conversely, when diminishing marginal product sets in, marginal product decreases (and eventually becomes negative). It follows that the marginal cost must rise when the marginal product begins its decline. These relationships are clearly reflected in the geometry of panels (b) and (c) of Figure 22-2.

In summary:

> *Over the range of output along which marginal product rises, marginal cost will fall. At the output at which marginal product starts to fall (after reaching the point of diminishing marginal product), marginal cost will begin to rise.*

The Relationship between Average and Marginal Costs

Let us now examine the relationship between average costs and marginal costs. There is always a definite relationship between averages and marginals. Consider the example of 10 football players with an average weight of 250 pounds. An eleventh player is added. His weight is 300 pounds. That represents the marginal weight. What happens now to the average weight of the team? It must increase. That is, when the marginal player weighs more than the average, the average must increase. Likewise, if the marginal player weighs less than 250 pounds, the average weight will decrease.

Average Variable Costs and Marginal Costs There exists a similar relationship between average variable costs and marginal costs. As shown in Figure 22-2, when marginal costs are less than average costs, the latter must fall. Conversely, when marginal costs are greater than average costs, the latter must rise.

When you think about it, the relationship makes sense. The only way average variable costs can fall is if the extra cost of the marginal unit produced is less than the average variable cost of all the preceding units. For example, if the average variable cost for two units of production is $4.00 a unit, the only way for the average variable cost of three units to be less than that of two units is for the variable costs of producing three units rather than two—the marginal cost—to be less than the average of the previous units. In this particular case, if average variable cost falls to $3.33 a unit, total variable cost for the three units would be three times $3.33, or about $10.00. Total variable cost for two units is two times $4.00 (average variable cost), or $8.00. The marginal cost is therefore $10.00 minus $8.00, or $2.00, which is less than the variable cost of $3.33.

A similar type of computation can be carried out for rising average variable costs. The only way average variable costs can rise is if the variable cost of additional units is more than that for units already produced. But the additional cost is the marginal cost. In this particular case, the marginal costs have to be higher than the average variable costs.

Average Total Costs and Marginal Costs There is also a relationship between marginal costs and average total costs. Remember that average total cost is equal to total costs divided by the number of units produced. Also remember that marginal cost does not include any fixed costs. Fixed costs are, by definition, fixed and cannot influence marginal costs. Our example can therefore be repeated, substituting *average total costs* for *average variable costs*.

These rising and falling relationships can be seen in panel (c) of Figure 22-2, where MC intersects AVC and ATC at their respective minimum points.

Minimum Cost Points

At what rate of output of wireless earbuds per hour does our representative firm experience the minimum average total costs? Column 7 in panel (a) of Figure 22-2 shows that the minimum average total cost is $4.28, which occurs at an output rate of seven wireless earbuds per hour. We can also find this minimum cost by finding the point in panel (c) of Figure 22-2 where the marginal cost curve intersects the average total cost curve. This should not be surprising. When marginal cost is below average total cost, average total cost falls. When marginal cost is above average total cost, average total cost rises. At the point where average total cost is neither falling nor rising, marginal cost must then be equal to average total cost. When we represent this graphically, the marginal cost curve will intersect the average total cost curve at the latter's minimum.

The same analysis applies to the intersection of the marginal cost curve and the average variable cost curve. When are average variable costs at a minimum? According to panel (a) of Figure 22-2, average variable costs are at a minimum of $2.60 at an output rate of about five wireless earbuds per hour. This is where the marginal cost curve intersects the average variable cost curve in panel (c) of Figure 22-2.

ECONOMICS IN YOUR LIFE

To contemplate how a technological improvement affects a firm's cost curves, take a look at **Returning to the Days of Sailing Ships with High-Tech Wind Cylinders** on page 489.

WHAT HAPPENS WHEN...

total fixed cost increases at a firm?

Naturally, when total fixed cost increases at a firm, its total cost, which includes total fixed cost, increases at each possible output rate. Average fixed cost equals total fixed cost divided by quantity, so the AFC curve shifts upward. The average total cost curve adds AFC to average variable cost, so the ATC curve also shifts upward.

The Relationship between Diminishing Marginal Product and Cost Curves

There is a unique relationship between output and the shape of the various cost curves we have drawn. To illustrate this fact, let's return to our example involving production of cloud computing services from Figure 22-1. Columns 1 and 2 in panel (a) of Figure 22-3 display labor input and total product levels considered in Figure 22-1, which are graphed as the total product curve displayed in panel (b) of the figure. Columns 3 and 4 list for each labor input level the corresponding values of average product and marginal product. As will be explained below, columns 5 and 6 display resulting values for average variable costs and marginal costs. It turns out, you will see, that if wage rates are constant, the shapes of the average cost and marginal cost curves in panel (d) of Figure 22-3 are both reflections of and consequences of the law of diminishing marginal product. Let's consider why this is so.

Average Costs and Average Product

In this example, labor is the only variable input. Furthermore, each unit of labor can be purchased at a constant wage rate, W, of $1,000 per worker per week. Under these assumptions, it is straightforward for us to calculate average variable costs at each quantity of labor.

Computing Average Variable Costs Recall that the definition of average variable cost is

$$AVC = \frac{\text{total variable costs}}{\text{total output}}$$

As we move from zero labor input to one unit in panel (a) of Figure 22-3, output increases from zero to 50 units of cloud computing services. The total variable costs equal the $1,000 wage per worker per week, times the number of workers (1). Because the average product (AP) of one worker (column 3) is 10, we can write the total product, 50, as the average product, 50, times the number of workers, 1. Thus, we see that

$$AVC = \frac{\$1,000 \times 1}{50 \times 1} = \frac{\$1,000}{50} = \frac{W}{AP}$$

Consequently, the first value of average variable cost in column 6 is $20 per unit of cloud computing services per week, which is equal to the $1,000 weekly wage rate divided by the average product of 50 units of services for the first unit of labor in column 3.

When two workers are employed, the total variable cost of labor is equal to $1,000 per worker per week multiplied by two workers per week, or $2,000 per week. Column 2 indicates that two workers produce a total product of 110 units of cloud computing services per week, which equals the average product of 55 units of output per week times the number of workers (2). Thus, average variable cost when two workers are employed is

$$AVC = \frac{\$1,000 \times 2}{55 \times 2} = \frac{\$1,000}{55} = \frac{W}{AP}$$

Hence, the second value of average variable in column 5 is $18.18 per unit of cloud computing services per week, which is equal to the $1,000 wage rate divided by the average product of 55 units of service output for the first unit of labor in column 3. Performing successive AVC computations at each quantity of labor yields the remaining values in column 5.

Panel (d) of Figure 22-3 plots these average variable costs listed in column 5 of panel (a). The result, as you can see, is the familiarly U-shaped average variable cost curve. Panel (c) displays the values of average product in column 4 of panel (a). We see that the average product increases, reaches a maximum, and then declines.

FIGURE 22-3

The Relationship between Output and Costs

As the number of workers employed each week increases, the total number of units of cloud computing services produced each week rises, as shown in panels (a) and (b). In panel (c), marginal product (MP) first rises and then falls. Average product (AP) follows. The near mirror image of panel (c) is shown in panel (d), in which MC and AVC first fall and then rise.

Panel (a)

(1) Labor Input	(2) Total Product (units of cloud computing services per week)	(3) Average Product (units of services per week) (3) = (2) ÷ (1)	(4) Marginal Product	(5) Average Variable Cost (5) = $1,000 ÷ (3)	(6) Marginal Cost (6) = $1,000 ÷ (4)
0	0	—	—	—	—
1	50	50	50	$20.00	$20.00
2	110	55	60	18.18	16.67
3	180	60	70	16.67	14.29
4	240	60	60	16.67	16.67
5	290	58	50	17.24	20.00
6	330	55	40	18.18	25.00
7	360	51	30	19.61	33.33

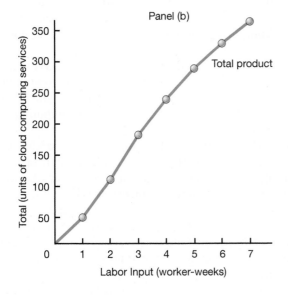

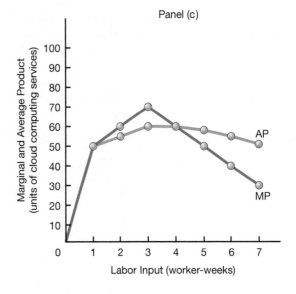

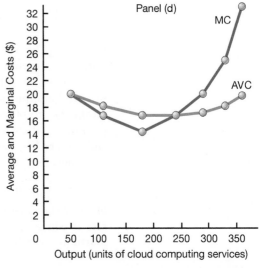

Evaluating the Shapes of the AVC and ATC Curves Because AVC $= W/\text{AP}$, average variable cost decreases as average product increases, and increases as average product decreases. AVC reaches its minimum when average product reaches its maximum.

Finally, we know that ATC $=$ AVC $+$ AFC. Thus, the average total cost curve inherits the relationship between the average variable cost and average product.

Marginal Cost and Marginal Product

It must also be the case that marginal cost declines when marginal product rises and increases when marginal product falls. Recall that marginal cost is defined as

$$\text{MC} = \frac{\text{change in total cost}}{\text{change in output}}$$

Because the price of labor is assumed to be constant, the change in total cost depends solely on the unchanged price of labor, W. The change in output is simply the marginal product (MP) of the one-unit increase in labor. Therefore,

$$\text{Marginal cost} = \frac{W}{\text{MP}}$$

Computing Marginal Cost Note in panel (a) of Figure 22-3 that when we go from zero labor input to one unit, output increases by 50 units of cloud computing services. Each of those 50 units of output has a marginal cost of $20. Now the second unit of labor is hired, and this individual costs the wage rate of $1,000 per week. Output increases by 60 units of cloud computing services. Thus, the marginal cost is $1,000 $\div$ 60 $=$ $16.67.

Column 6 of Figure 22-3 includes these and other marginal cost values. We see, for instance, that adding another unit of labor yields 70 additional units of cloud service output, so marginal cost declines once more, to $1,000 $\div$ 70 $=$ $14.29. The following unit of labor yields a marginal product of only 60 units of cloud computing services, so marginal cost increases to $1,000 $\div$ 60 $=$ $16.67.

Panel (d) of Figure 22-3 shows the points that lie along the resulting marginal cost curve. As you can see in comparing the marginal product (MP) and marginal cost (MC) curves in panels (c) and (d), the marginal cost of each extra unit of output declines as long as marginal product is rising, and then it increases as long as marginal product is falling. This means that initially, when marginal product is increasing, marginal cost falls (we are dividing the $1,000 weekly wage by larger numbers), and later, when marginal product is falling, marginal cost must increase (we are dividing the $1,000 weekly wage by smaller numbers). So, as marginal product increases, marginal cost decreases, and as marginal product decreases, marginal cost must increase. Thus, when marginal product reaches its maximum, marginal cost necessarily reaches its minimum.

Explaining the Shape of the Marginal Cost Curve Thus, when marginal product initially rises from 50 units of cloud service output per unit of labor to 70 units of output per unit of labor, marginal cost correspondingly declines from $20 per unit of cloud computing services to $14.29 per unit. Then when marginal product diminishes to 60 units of output per unit of labor and then to 50 units of output per unit of labor, marginal cost increases to $16.67 per unit of cloud service output and then to $20 per unit.

Hence, in panel (b) of Figure 22-3, which shows the values of marginal cost from column 5 at corresponding cloud service output rates from column 2, the marginal cost curve initially slopes downward as the firm hires the first, second, and third units of labor. The marginal cost curve slopes upward for output rates beyond the output rate at which the marginal product of labor begins to diminish, which is when the fourth unit of labor is employed.

All of the foregoing can be restated in relatively straightforward terms:

The shapes of firms' short-run cost curves reflect changes in marginal product. Given any constant price of the variable input, marginal costs decline as long as the marginal product of the variable resource is rising. At the point at which marginal product begins to diminish, marginal costs begin to rise as the marginal product of the variable input begins to decline.

The result is a marginal cost curve that slopes down, hits a minimum, and then slopes up.

Long-Run Cost Curves

The long run is defined as a time period during which full adjustment can be made to any change in the economic environment. Thus, in the long run, *all* factors of production are variable.

22.4 Describe the long-run cost curves a typical firm faces and define a firm's minimum efficient scale

The Firm's Planning Horizon

Long-run curves are sometimes called *planning curves*, and the long run is sometimes called the **planning horizon.** We start our analysis of long-run cost curves by considering a single firm contemplating the construction of a single plant. The firm has three alternative plant sizes from which to choose on the planning horizon. Each particular plant size generates its own short-run average total cost curve. Now that we are talking about the difference between long-run and short-run cost curves, we will label all short-run curves with an *S* and long-run curves with an *L*. Short-run average (total) costs will be labeled SAC. Long-run average cost curves will be labeled LAC.

Panel (a) of Figure 22-4 shows short-run average cost curves for three successively larger plants. Which is the optimal size to build, if we can choose only among these three?

Planning horizon
The long run, during which all inputs are variable.

FIGURE 22-4

Finding the Optimal Plant Size and the Long-Run Average Cost Curve

If the anticipated sustained rate of output per unit time period is Q_1, the optimal plant to build is the one corresponding to SAC_1 in panel (a) because average cost is lower, at C_1. If the sustained rate of output increases toward the higher level Q_2, however, it will be more profitable to have a plant size corresponding to SAC_2 at $AC = C_3$. If we draw all the possible short-run average cost curves that correspond to different plant sizes and then draw the envelope (a curve tangent to each member of a set of curves) to these various curves, SAC_1–SAC_8, we obtain the long-run average cost (LAC) curve as shown in panel (b).

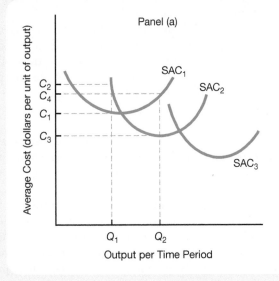

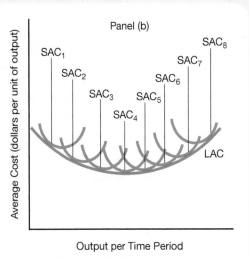

That depends on the anticipated normal, sustained rate of output per time period. Assume for a moment that the anticipated normal, sustained rate is Q_1. If a plant of size 1 is built, average cost will be C_1. If a plant of size 2 is built, we see on SAC_2 that average cost will be C_2, which is greater than C_1. Thus, if the anticipated rate of output is Q_1, the appropriate plant size is the one from which SAC_1 was derived.

If the anticipated sustained rate of output per time period increases from Q_1 to a higher level such as Q_2, however, and a plant of size 1 is selected, average cost will be C_4. If a plant of size 2 is chosen, average cost will be C_3, which is clearly less than C_4.

In choosing the appropriate plant size for a single-plant firm during the planning horizon, the firm will pick the size whose short-run average cost curve generates an average cost that is lowest for the expected rate of output.

Long-Run Average Cost Curve

If we now assume that the entrepreneur faces an infinite number of choices of plant sizes in the long run, we can conceive of an infinite number of SAC curves similar to the three in panel (a) of Figure 22-4. We are not able, of course, to draw an infinite number, but we have drawn quite a few in panel (b) of Figure 22-4. We then draw the "envelope" to all these various short-run average cost curves. The resulting envelope is the **long-run average cost curve.** This long-run average cost curve is sometimes called the **planning curve,** for it represents the various average costs attainable at the planning stage of the firm's decision making. It represents the locus (path) of points giving the lowest unit cost of producing any given rate of output.

Note that the LAC curve is *not* tangent to each individual SAC curve at the latter's minimum points, except at the minimum point of the LAC curve. Then and only then are minimum long-run average costs equal to minimum short-run average costs.

Why the Long-Run Average Cost Curve Is U-Shaped

Notice that the long-run average cost curve, LAC, in panel (b) of Figure 22-4 is U-shaped, similar to the U shape of the short-run average cost curve developed earlier in this chapter. The reason behind the U shape of the two curves is not the same, however. The short-run average cost curve is U-shaped because of the law of diminishing marginal product. The law cannot apply to the long run, however, because in the long run, all factors of production are variable. There is no point of diminishing marginal product because there is no fixed factor of production.

Why, then, do we see the U shape in the long-run average cost curve? The reasoning has to do with economies of scale, constant returns to scale, and diseconomies of scale. When the firm is experiencing **economies of scale,** the long-run average cost curve slopes downward—an increase in scale and production leads to a fall in unit costs. When the firm is experiencing **constant returns to scale,** the long-run average cost curve is at its minimum point, such that an increase in scale of production does not change unit costs. When the firm is experiencing **diseconomies of scale,** the long-run average cost curve slopes upward—an increase in scale and production increases unit costs. These three sections of the long-run average cost curve are broken up into panels (a), (b), and (c) in Figure 22-5.

Reasons for Economies of Scale
We shall examine three of the many reasons why a firm might be expected to experience economies of scale: specialization, the dimensional factor, and improvements in productive equipment.

Specialization As a firm's scale of operation increases, the opportunities for specialization in the use of resource inputs also increase. This is sometimes called *increased division of tasks* or *operations.* Cost reductions generated by productivity enhancements from such division of labor or increased specialization are well known. When we consider managerial staffs, we also find that larger enterprises may be able to put together more highly specialized staffs.

Long-run average cost curve
The locus of points representing the minimum unit cost of producing any given rate of output, given current technology and resource prices.

Planning curve
The long-run average cost curve.

Economies of scale
Decreases in long-run average costs resulting from increases in output.

Constant returns to scale
No change in long-run average costs when output increases.

Diseconomies of scale
Increases in long-run average costs that occur as output increases.

FIGURE 22-5

Economies of Scale, Constant Returns to Scale, and Diseconomies of Scale Shown with the Long-Run Average Cost Curve

The long-run average cost curve slopes downward when there are economies of scale, as shown in panel (a). The LRAC curve's slope is constant (so that the LRAC curve is flat) when the firm is experiencing

constant returns to scale, as shown in panel (b). The LRAC curve slopes upward when the firm is experiencing diseconomies of scale, as shown in panel (c).

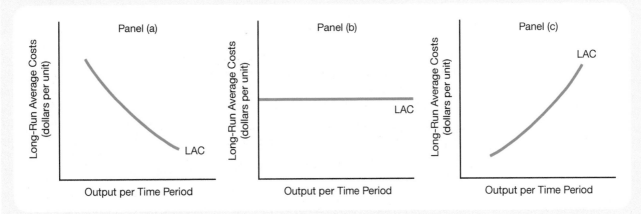

Dimensional Factor Large-scale firms often require proportionately less input per unit of output simply because certain inputs do not have to be doubled in order to double the output. Consider an oil-storage firm's cost of storing oil. The cost of storage is related to the cost of steel that goes into building the storage container. Other things being equal, the amount of steel required, however, goes up less than in proportion to the volume (storage capacity) of the container (because the volume of a container increases more than proportionately with its surface area).

Improvements in Productive Equipment The larger the scale of the enterprise, the more the firm is able to take advantage of larger-volume (output capacity) types of equipment. Small-scale operations may not be able to profitably use large-volume devices that can be more efficient per unit of output. Also, smaller firms often cannot use technologically more advanced equipment because they are unable to spread out the high cost of such sophisticated devices over a large output.

For any of these three reasons, the firm may experience economies of scale, which means that equal percentage increases in output result in a decrease in average cost. Thus, output can double, but total costs will less than double. Hence, average cost falls. Note that the factors listed for causing economies of scale are all *internal* to the firm. They do not depend on what other firms are doing or what is happening in the economy.

Why is a Chinese producer of electric-vehicle batteries counting on government policies to help it experience economies of scale?

INTERNATIONAL POLICY EXAMPLE

Government Policies May Ensure Economies of Scale for a Chinese Battery Manufacturer

China's Contemporary Amperex Technology, Limited, or CATL, has just completed the finishing touches on a massive production facility for manufacturing electric-vehicle (EV) batteries. Only the U.S. firm Tesla has a larger factory. When CATL combines battery production at the new plant with output at its existing facilities, however, CATL will be able to produce more EV batteries per unit of time than any other global manufacturer.

Nevertheless, CATL will confront an immediate problem for the first several years of operations at its new plant. Companies and individuals in China and the rest of the world do not purchase a sufficiently large number of EV batteries for CATL to increase output and move down and along its long-run average cost curve. Fortunately for the company, however, China's government is committed to a 600 percent increase in national

(Continued)

electric-vehicle production and consumption by 2025. Furthermore, the government is in the process of gradually banning vehicles with internal-combustion engines from streets of major cities throughout the nation. In future years, therefore, CATL is anticipating lower average costs as it expands its production of EV batteries as inputs in vehicular products that likely will be purchased to satisfy the government's regulatory requirements.

FOR CRITICAL THINKING

Is CATL's long-run average cost of producing EV batteries currently higher or lower than it will be in future years following implementation of China's government's planned policies? Explain briefly.

Sources are listed at the end of this chapter.

Why a Firm Might Experience Diseconomies of Scale One of the basic reasons that a firm can expect to run into diseconomies of scale is that there are limits to the efficient functioning of management. This is so because larger levels of output imply successively larger *plant* size, which in turn implies successively larger *firm* size. Thus, as the level of output increases, more people must be hired, and the firm gets bigger. As this happens, however, the support, supervisory, and administrative staff and the general paperwork of the firm all increase. As the layers of supervision grow, the costs of information and communication grow more than proportionately. Hence, the average unit cost will start to increase.

Some observers of corporate giants claim that many of them have been experiencing some diseconomies of scale. Witness the difficulties that firms such as Hewlett-Packard and Nokia have experienced in recent years. Some analysts say that the profitability declines they have encountered are at least partly a function of their size relative to their smaller, more flexible competitors, which can make decisions more quickly and then take advantage of changing market conditions more rapidly.

Minimum Efficient Scale

Economists and statisticians have obtained actual data on the relationship between changes in all inputs and changes in average cost. It turns out that for many industries, the long-run average cost curve does not resemble the curve shown in panel (b) of Figure 22-4. Rather, it more closely resembles Figure 22-6. What you observe there is a small portion of declining long-run average costs (economies of scale) and then a wide range of outputs over which the firm experiences essentially constant economies of scale.

FIGURE 22-6

Minimum Efficient Scale

This long-run average cost curve reaches a minimum point at *A*. After that point, long-run average costs remain horizontal, or constant, and then rise at some later rate of output. Point *A* is called the minimum efficient scale for the firm because that is the point at which it reaches minimum costs. It is the lowest rate of output at which average long-run costs are minimized. At point *B*, diseconomies of scale arise, so long-run average cost begins to increase with further increases in output.

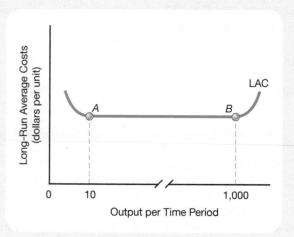

At the output rate when economies of scale end and constant economies of scale start, the **minimum efficient scale (MES)** for the firm is encountered. It occurs at point *A*. The minimum efficient scale is defined as the lowest rate of output at which long-run average costs are minimized. In any industry with a long-run average cost curve similar to the one in Figure 22-6, larger firms will have no cost-saving advantage over smaller firms as long as the smaller firms have at least obtained the minimum efficient scale at point *A*.

Minimum efficient scale (MES)
The lowest rate of output per unit time at which long-run average costs for a particular firm are at a minimum.

What issues are U.S. trucking companies confronting as they assess whether their minimum efficient scale of transportation services includes delivering bulky items directly to consumers' homes?

EXAMPLE

Long-Haul Trucking Firms Seek to Attain a Minimum Efficient Scale Encompassing "Last-Mile Deliveries"

For many years, nationwide and regional long-haul trucking firms have derived economies of scale from directing trucks and cargoes across roadways connecting sprawling networks of loading docks at depots and warehouses. Today, these trucking firms are searching for ways to expand their operating scales by extending their transportation services over the "last mile"—stretches of roadways connecting depots and warehouses to individual households.

Consumers' houses often are positioned on streets along which truckers experience difficulties navigating, and the houses do not have loading docks for receiving large items such as refrigerators or sofas. Hence, trucking firms' quests to attain business success over the last mile hinge on whether they can at least maintain existing average costs of moving such bulky items over streets and into houses. Some trucking firms are making transfers to local delivery firms that already have

expertise in home deliveries. Other trucking firms are experimenting with setting up their own home-delivery services. It remains to be seen whether either approach will enable large trucking firms to attain a minimum efficient scale that encompasses last-mile deliveries to consumers' homes.

FOR CRITICAL THINKING

Why do you think that some trucking firms have determined that including last-mile deliveries within their least-cost scale of operations would require providing very large volumes of delivery services within densely populated cities? (Hint: Why might there be economies of scale in home deliveries, particularly in urban areas?)

Sources are listed at the end of this chapter.

ECONOMICS IN YOUR LIFE

Returning to the Days of Sailing Ships with High-Tech Wind Cylinders

For more than two millennia, humans relied on wind pressure against sails to maneuver freight-carrying ships across the world's oceans. Since the beginning of the twentieth century, most of the world's seaborne freight instead has been transported by ships powered with carbon-based fuels. Nevertheless, Tommy Thomassen, a chief technical officer at the Danish shipping firm Maersk Tankers, has been involved in supervising a renewed effort to harness winds to power the company's ships. Maersk's new "sails" are 100-foot-tall cylinders manufactured from durable lightweight composite materials. The cylinders readily spin in the wind and provide forward or reverse thrust that eases burdens on the ships' engines.

"This technology has a significant potential to cut fuel consumption by 7 to 10 percent on the ships [on which] it will be installed," says Thomassen. Planned improvements in the new sailing-cylinders' design promise future fuel savings closer to 10 percent. Given this

projection and the fact that Maersk currently spends more than $2 billion per year on fuels, Maersk's managers intend to have the cylinders installed in its newest fleet of tanker ships.

CRITICAL THINKING QUESTIONS

Does Maersk's use of sailing cylinders reduce its total fixed costs or its total variable costs? Explain.

REAL APPLICATION

Suppose that you and some friends have started a long-distance trucking business. You are considering adding wind-resistance-reducing equipment to your trucks. How will you decide whether to go ahead with this project?

Sources are listed at the end of this chapter.

ISSUES & APPLICATIONS

Retailers Employ AI and Robots in Pursuit of Economies of Scale

Andriy Popov/123RF GB Limited

CONCEPTS APPLIED

➤ Long-Run Average Cost

➤ Economies of Scale

➤ Minimum Efficient Scale

Handling inventories of unsold items generates expenses for retailers. The firms must compensate employees for the time and effort of placing the goods on shelves in storage facilities. Then employees must be paid to unpack the items, price them, and place them on display for sale. Retailers commonly find themselves paying workers to shift items to other shelves or even different storage areas after they remain unsold for longer periods than expected. From time to time, retailers also incur expenses to alter quantities of shelving equipment and storage facility space in response to ebbs and flows in inventory accumulations or depletions.

Clothing Sellers Employ AI Technologies to Reduce Long-Run Average Cost

Some clothing retailers are employing AI technologies to minimize automatically the expenses associated with inventory management at higher operating scales. Firms that relied on seasonal rules of thumb or past sales patterns now track sales in real time and utilize machine learning to determine how to stock shelves at the lowest feasible average cost. Some clothiers even use weather forecasts to incorporate how variations in weather conditions will likely affect consumers' buying patterns or suppliers' shipments.

By having the most appropriate items in place on their shelves, selling those items quickly, and automatically placing orders for the next set of most saleable items, clothing retailers are finding that they can cut their inventory expenses even as they expand their sales. In doing so, the firms reduce their long-run average costs as they increase their scales of operations, thereby generating scale economies.

Grocers Add Robots to the High-Tech Mix

Like clothes sellers, grocers are making use of AI technologies. In the case of grocers, AI applications are being directed primarily at operating rapidly growing online food-ordering systems. Machine-learning systems track order flows and determine appropriate quantities of frozen, refrigerated, and nonrefrigerated food items to order

for warehouse storage. These systems also adjust automatically to changes in online order flows to alter these food allocations and electronically transmit instructions for shipments to grocery stores.

The grocery order-fulfillment process adds robots to the retail process. Robots dedicated to specific tasks, such as sorting produce or loading boxes of frozen foods, are the recipients of electronic messages from grocers' AI systems. The robots automatically move items across warehouse floors to loading docks. At this point—for now—humans take over the process of shipping and unloading at retail outlets. For grocers expanding their operations to include online-order fulfillments, this combination of AI and robots is essential to minimizing grocers' costs at each scale of retail operations.

FOR CRITICAL THINKING

Why is it likely every bit as important, from a cost standpoint, for clothiers to know when upcoming orders for items should be raised or lowered considerably as it is to smooth out inventories over periods of steady sales?

REAL APPLICATION

Perhaps you have read that AI-guided and robot-implemented systems will permanently reduce the need for human beings in the workforce. Should you be worried?

Sources are listed at the end of this chapter.

What You Should Know

Here is what you should know after reading this chapter.

LEARNING OBJECTIVES	KEY TERMS
22.1 Discuss the difference between the short run and the long run from the perspective of a firm *The short run for a firm is a period during which at least one input, such as plant size, cannot be altered. Inputs that cannot be changed in the short run are fixed inputs, whereas inputs that can be adjusted in the short run are variable inputs. The long run is a period in which a firm can vary all inputs.*	short run, 472 plant size, 472 long run, 472
22.2 Describe production at a firm and explain why the marginal product of labor eventually declines as more units of labor are employed *The production function is the relationship between inputs and the maximum output, or total product, that a firm can produce. Typically, a firm's marginal product—the output resulting from the addition of one more unit of a variable factor of production—increases with the first few units of the variable input that it employs. Eventually, as the firm adds more and more units of the variable input, the marginal product begins to decline. This is the law of diminishing marginal product.*	production, 473 production function, 473 average product, 475 marginal product, 475 law of diminishing marginal product, 475 **Key Figure** Figure 22-1, 474
22.3 Explain the short-run cost curves a typical firm faces *The expenses for a firm's fixed inputs are its fixed costs, and the expenses for its variable inputs are variable costs. The total costs of a firm are the sum of its fixed costs and variable costs. Average fixed cost equals total fixed cost divided by total product. Average variable cost equals total variable cost divided by total product, and average total cost equals total cost divided by total product. Finally, marginal cost is the change in total cost resulting from a one-unit change in production.*	total costs, 476 fixed costs, 477 variable costs, 477 average fixed costs, 479 average variable costs, 479 average total costs, 479 marginal costs, 480 **Key Figures** Figure 22-2, 478 Figure 22-3, 483
22.4 Describe the long-run cost curves a typical firm faces and define a firm's minimum efficient scale *The typically U-shaped long-run average cost curve is traced out by the short-run average cost curves corresponding to various plant sizes. Along the downward-sloping range of a firm's long-run average cost curve, the firm experiences economies of scale, meaning that its long-run production costs decline as it raises its output scale. In contrast, along the upward-sloping portion of the long-run average cost curve, the firm encounters diseconomies of scale, so that its long-run costs of production rise as it increases its output scale. The minimum point of the long-run average cost curve occurs at the firm's minimum efficient scale, which is the lowest rate of output at which the firm can achieve minimum long-run average cost.*	planning horizon, 485 long-run average cost curve, 486 planning curve, 486 economies of scale, 486 constant returns to scale, 486 diseconomies of scale, 486 minimum efficient scale (MES), 489 **Key Figures** Figure 22-5, 487 Figure 22-6, 488

PROBLEMS

22-1. The academic calendar for a university is August 15 through May 15. A professor commits to a contract that binds her to a teaching position at this university for this period. Based on this information, explain the short run and long run that the professor faces.

22-2. The short-run production function for a manufacturer of wireless earbuds is shown in the table below. Based on this information, answer the following questions.

Input of Labor (workers per week)	Total Output of Wireless Earbuds
0	0
1	25
2	60
3	85
4	105
5	115
6	120

   a. Calculate the average product at each quantity of labor.

   b. Calculate the marginal product of labor at each quantity of labor.

   c. At what point does marginal product begin to diminish?

22-3. During the past year, a firm produced 10,000 laptop computers. Its total costs were $5 million, and its fixed costs were $2 million. What are the average variable costs of this firm?

22-4. During the previous month, a firm produced 250 tablet devices at an average variable cost of $40 and at an average fixed cost of $10. What were the firm's total costs during the month?

22-5. For the firm discussed in Problem 22-4, the total cost of producing 249 units was $12,425. What was the marginal cost incurred by the firm in producing the final tablet device that month?

22-6. The cost structure of a manufacturer of microchips is described in the table that follows. The firm's fixed costs equal $10,000 per day. Calculate the average variable cost, average fixed cost, and average total cost at each output level.

Output (microchips per day)	Total Cost of Output ($ thousands)
0	10
25	60
50	95
75	150
100	220
125	325
150	465

22-7. The diagram displays short-run cost curves for a facility that produces liquid crystal display (LCD) screens for cell phones:

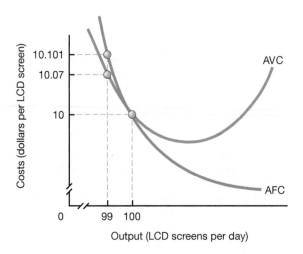

   a. What are the daily total fixed costs of producing LCD screens?

   b. What are the total variable costs of producing 100 LCD screens per day?

   c. What are the total costs of producing 100 LCD screens per day?

   d. What is the marginal cost of producing 100 LCD screens instead of 99? (*Hint:* To answer this question, you must first determine the total costs—or, alternatively, the total variable costs—of producing 99 LCD screens.)

22-8. A watch manufacturer finds that at 1,000 units of output, its marginal costs are below average total costs. If it produces an additional watch, will its average total costs rise, fall, or stay the same?

22-9. At its current short-run level of production, a firm's average variable costs equal $20 per unit, and its average fixed costs equal $30 per unit. Its total costs at this production level equal $2,500.

   a. What is the firm's current output level?

   b. What are its total variable costs at this output level?

   c. What are its total fixed costs?

22-10. In an effort to reduce their total costs, many companies are now replacing paychecks with payroll cards, which are stored-value cards onto which the companies can download employees' wages and salaries electronically. If the only factor of production that a company varies in the short run is the number of hours worked by people already on its payroll, would shifting from paychecks to payroll cards reduce the firm's total fixed costs or its total variable costs? Explain your answer.

22-11. During autumn months, passenger railroads across the globe deal with a condition called slippery rail. It results from a combination of water, leaf oil, and pressure from the train's weight, which creates a slippery black ooze that prevents trains from gaining traction.

a. One solution for slippery rail is to cut back trees from all of a rail firm's rail network on a regular basis, thereby helping to prevent the problem from developing. If incurred, would this railroad expense be a better example of a fixed cost or a variable cost? Why?

b. Another way of addressing slippery rail is to wait until it begins to develop. Then the company purchases sand and dumps it on the slippery tracks so that trains already en route within the rail network can proceed. If incurred, would this railroad expense be a better example of a fixed cost or a variable cost? Why?

22-12. In the short run, a firm's total costs of producing 100 units of output equal $10,000. If it produces one more unit, its total costs will increase to $10,150.

a. What is the marginal cost of producing 101 instead of 100 units of output?

b. What is the firm's average total cost of producing 100 units?

c. What is the firm's average total cost of producing 101 units?

22-13. Suppose that a firm's only variable input is labor, and the constant hourly wage rate is $20 per hour. The last unit of labor hired enabled the firm to increase its hourly production from 250 units to 251 units. What was the marginal cost of producing 251 units of output instead of 250?

22-14. Suppose that a firm's only variable input is labor. The firm increases the number of employees from four to five, thereby causing weekly output to rise by two units and total costs to increase from $3,000 per week to $3,300 per week.

a. What is the marginal product of hiring five workers instead of four?

b. What is the weekly wage rate earned by the fifth worker?

22-15. Suppose that a company currently employs 1,000 workers and produces 1 million units of output per month. Labor is its only variable input, and the company pays each worker the same monthly wage. The company's current total variable costs equal $2 million.

a. What are average variable costs at this firm's current output level?

b. What is the average product of labor?

c. What monthly wage does the firm pay each worker?

22-16. A manufacturing firm with a single plant is contemplating changing its plant size. It must choose from among seven alternative plant sizes. In the table below, plant size A is the smallest it might build, and size G is the largest. Currently, the firm's plant size is B.

a. At plant site B, is this firm currently experiencing economies of scale or diseconomies of scale?

b. What is the firm's minimum efficient scale?

Plant Size	Average Total Cost ($)
A (smallest)	4,250
B	3,600
C	3,100
D	3,100
E	3,100
F	3,250
G (largest)	4,100

22-17. An electricity-generating company confronts the following long-run average total costs associated with alternative plant sizes. It is currently operating at plant size G.

Plant Size	Average Total Cost ($)
A (smallest)	2,000
B	1,800
C	1,600
D	1,550
E	1,500
F	1,500
G (largest)	1,500

a. What is this firm's minimum efficient scale?

b. If damage caused by a powerful hurricane generates a reduction in the firm's plant size from its current size to B, would there be a leftward or rightward movement along the firm's long-run average total cost curve?

22-18. Take a look at Figure 22-1. Suppose that the firm decided to consider employing a 12th unit of labor, which it has determined would result in a decrease in total product to 370 units of output. If it were to do this, what would be the resulting average product of labor and marginal product of labor?

22-19. Consider Figure 22-2. If this firm were to boost its output to 12 units of output and thereby raise its total variable costs to $54, what would be the resulting average fixed cost, average variable cost, average total cost, and marginal cost?

22-20. Consider Figure 22-3. If the firm were to employ an 8th unit of labor, its total product would rise to 380 units of output. What would be the resulting values of the average product of labor and of the marginal product of labor?

22-21. In Problem 22-20, if the firm were to employ the 8th unit of labor and produce 380 units of output, what would be the average variable cost and the marginal cost?

22-22. Take a look at Figure 22-4. Suppose that the firm boosts its scale of operations from a level consistent with short-run average cost curve SAC_3 to short-run average cost curve SAC_5. Explain what happens with respect to economies or diseconomies of scale.

22-23. Consider Figure 22-6. Suppose that the current scale of output for a typical firm facing this LAC curve, which applies to all firms in this industry, is between points A and B, at about 500 units per period. If a new firm entering the industry desires to produce at the minimum efficient scale, would it wish to produce 10 units per period, 500 units per period, or 1,000 units per period? Explain.

REFERENCES

EXAMPLE: A Railroad Company Rediscovers How to Obtain Maximum Feasible Production from Available Inputs

Jim Foote, "Look Ahead: CSX Eyes to Keep Low Operating Ratios," *Jacksonville Business Journal*, January 2, 2019.

John Kingston, "Hump Yards, Dwell Times, and Velocity," *Freight Waves*, May 16, 2018.

Sandy Mazza, "CSX's Radnor Yard Revises Rail Car Sorting to Move Goods Faster," *Nashville Tennessean*, July 6, 2018.

INTERNATIONAL EXAMPLE: Airline Companies Hope to Reduce Their Total Costs at the Expense of Higher Total Fixed Costs

"Aircraft Operating Costs," Federal Aviation Administration (https://www.faa.gov/regulations_policies/policy_guidance/benefit_cost/media/econ-value-section-4-op-costs.pdf), 2019.

Adam Kress, "New 'Honeywell Connected Aircraft Report' Reveals Airline Industry on Cusp of Major Investment Wave," Honeywell Aerospace (https://aerospace.honeywell.com/en/press-release-listing/2018/june/new-honeywell-connected-aircraft-report-reveals-airline-industry-on-cusp-of-major-investment-wave), June 19, 2018.

Adam Levine-Weinberg, "American Airlines Suffers the Latest Airline Information Technology Meltdown," Motley Fool, June 19, 2018.

AI—DECISION MAKING THROUGH DATA: Using Augmented Reality

Lorne Fade, "How Businesses Today Are Implementing Virtual and Augmented Reality," *Forbes*, January 3, 2019.

Kayla Matthews, "Five Ways Augmented Reality Is Changing the Manufacturing Industry," Manufacturing.net (https://www.manufacturing.net/article/2018/06/5-ways-ar-changing-manufacturing-industry), June 22, 2018.

Sara Murthi and Amitabh Varshney, "How Augmented Reality Will Make Surgery Safer," *Harvard Business Review*, March 20, 2018.

INTERNATIONAL POLICY EXAMPLE: Government Policies May Ensure Economies of Scale for a Chinese Battery Manufacturer

"CATL Adds 100MWh Battery to 'China's Largest' Mixed Renewables Power Plant," *Energy Storage News*, February 6, 2019.

Jie Ma, David Stringer, Zoey Zhang, and Sohee Kim with Elisabeth Behrmann, "Electronic Battery Makers Should Fear this Factory," *Bloomberg Businessweek*, February 12, 2018.

James Temple, "China's Ambition to Power the World's Electric Cars Took a Huge Leap Forward this Week," *MIT Technology Journal*, June 13, 2018.

EXAMPLE: Long-Haul Trucking Firms Seek to Attain a Minimum Efficient Scale Encompassing "Last-Mile Deliveries"

Rich Sherman, "Is Last-Mile Delivery the Pothole in the Road to E-Commerce Growth?" SupplyChainBrain.com (https://www.supplychainbrain.com/articles/29343-is-last-mile-delivery-the-pothole-in-the-road-to-e-commerce-growth), February 6, 2019.

Jennifer Smith, "Truckers Seek New Routes into 'Last Mile,'" *Wall Street Journal*, April 13, 2018.

Cyndia Zwahlen, "Consumer-Friendly Last-Mile Delivery Comes to Heavy Goods," Trucks.com (https://www.trucks.com/2018/09/10/consumer-friendly-last-mile-delivery-heavy-goods/), September 10, 2018.

ECONOMICS IN YOUR LIFE: Returning to the Days of Sailing Ships with High-Tech Wind Cylinders

Kyunghee Park and Jason Clenfield, "How the Cargo Industry Is Cleaning Up Its Filthy Act," *Bloomberg*, January 17, 2019.

Pilita Clark, "Shipping Group's Trial Use of Wind Power to Cut Tankers' Fuel Bills," *Financial Times*, March 17, 2017.

Costas Paris, "Maersk Tanker Tests Wind Power to Cut Soaring Fuel Costs," *Wall Street Journal*, August 30, 2018.

ISSUES & APPLICATIONS: Retailers Employ AI and Robots in Pursuit of Economies of Scale

Amanda Baltazar, "How Grocers Are Reimagining the Future with AI," WinsightGroceryBusiness.com (https://www.winsight-grocerybusiness.com/technology/how-grocers-are-reimagining-future-ai), January 28, 2019.

Alexandra Suich Bass, "GrAIt Expectations: Non-Tech Businesses Are Beginning to Use Artificial Intelligence at Scale," *Economist*, March 31, 2018.

Corinna Underwood, "Robots in Retail—Examples of Real Industry Applications," TechEmergence, September 11, 2018.

23 Perfect Competition

penta/123RF GB Limited

LEARNING OBJECTIVES

After reading this chapter, you should be able to:

23.1 Identify the characteristics of a perfectly competitive market structure

23.2 Discuss how a perfectly competitive firm decides how much output to produce

23.3 Understand how the short-run supply curve for a perfectly competitive firm is determined

23.4 Explain how the equilibrium price is determined in a perfectly competitive market

23.5 Describe what factors induce firms to enter or exit a perfectly competitive industry

Over time, federal, state, and local governments have implemented a steadily growing set of regulatory requirements that U.S. companies must satisfy. Among these are restrictions on the lowest wages that firms can legally pay employees. Although the federal minimum wage standard has not been changed for several years, a number of state and city governments have raised their minimum wage requirements. Among the firms most heavily affected by such minimum wage increases are restaurants. In this chapter, you will learn why requirements for restaurants to pay higher minimum wages have contributed to a reduction in the number of competing firms. First, though, you must learn about one particularly important approach to analyzing how firms compete, which is known as the theory of perfect competition.

23.1 Identify the characteristics of a perfectly competitive market structure

Perfect competition
A market structure in which the decisions of *individual* buyers and sellers have no effect on market price.

Perfectly competitive firm
A firm that is such a small part of the total *industry* that it cannot affect the price of the product it sells.

Price taker
A perfectly competitive firm that must take the price of its product as given because the firm cannot influence its price.

Characteristics of a Perfectly Competitive Market Structure

We are interested in studying how a firm acting within a perfectly competitive market structure makes decisions about how much to produce. In a situation of **perfect competition,** each firm is such a small part of the total industry that it cannot affect the price of the product in question. That means that each **perfectly competitive firm** in the industry is a **price taker**—the firm takes price as a given, something determined *outside* the individual firm.

What It Means for a Firm to Be a Price Taker

The definition of a perfectly competitive firm is obviously idealized, for in one sense the individual firm *has* to set prices. How can we ever have a situation in which firms regard prices as set by forces outside their control? The answer is that even though every firm sets its own prices, a firm in a perfectly competitive situation will find that it will eventually have no customers at all if it sets its price above the competitive price.

The best example is in agriculture. Although the individual farmer can set any price for a bushel of wheat, if that price doesn't coincide with the market price of a bushel of similar-quality wheat, no one will purchase the wheat at a higher price. Nor would the farmer be inclined to reduce revenues by selling below the market price. The firm can sell all the units that it wishes to produce at the market price.

Characteristics of Perfect Competition

Let's examine why a firm in a perfectly competitive industry is a price taker.

1. *There are large numbers of buyers and sellers.* When this is the case, the quantity demanded by one buyer or the quantity supplied by one seller is negligible relative to the market quantity. No one buyer or seller has any influence on the market clearing price.

2. *The product sold by the firms in the industry is homogeneous—that is, indistinguishable across firms.* The product sold by each firm in the industry is a perfect substitute for the product sold by every other firm. Buyers are able to choose from a large number of sellers of a product that the buyers regard as being the same.

3. *Both buyers and sellers have access to all relevant information.* Consumers are able to find out about lower prices charged by competing firms. Firms are able to find out about cost-saving innovations that can lower production costs and prices, and they are able to learn about profitable opportunities in other industries.

4. *Any firm can enter or leave the industry without serious impediments.* Firms in a competitive industry are not hampered in their ability to obtain and allocate resources. In pursuit of profit-making opportunities, they reallocate labor and capital to whatever business venture gives them their highest expected rate of return on their investment.

How is the use of AI techniques making the U.S. gasoline retailing industry more nearly perfectly competitive than in years past?

ECONOMICS IN YOUR LIFE

To contemplate the relative incentives for entry into the agricultural industry confronted by urban versus rural farmers, read **For Urban Farmers, Industry Entry May Be Relatively Unimpeded but Still Entails an Expense** on page 513.

AI | DECISION MAKING THROUGH DATA

Accessing All Relevant Information for "Dynamic Pricing"

In the past, a market feature that cast doubt on the classification of some industries as perfectly competitive was that firms lacked access to all relevant information. Consider, for instance, the retail gasoline industry. A given grade of gasoline is virtually identical across various outlets, and the many retail outlets can easily enter or exit the industry. Nevertheless, companies purchase fuels from various refining firms and use a dizzying array of distribution networks to transport gasoline to their retail outlets. Furthermore, economists have documented that the prices of products derived from minerals, such as gasoline refined from oil, are among the most likely to exhibit considerable variability. In the past, these facts have complicated gasoline retailers' efforts to be assured of access to all relevant information.

These days, however, utilization of AI-guided "dynamic pricing" is altering this state of affairs. Many gasoline sellers are establishing digital links from their retail outlets to networks that instantaneously provide and process, using machine-learning tools, real-time information updates. These sellers receive relevant information about prices on refiners' different grades of fuel, costs that distributors confront in transporting gasoline, and prices on the pumps at competing firms. As a consequence, in recent years the U.S. retail gasoline industry has been transformed into a more nearly perfectly competitive industry.

REAL APPLICATION

You might be surveyed someday on whether you know the price per gallon of gasoline that you purchased for your car. You might be one of those individuals who cannot remember that price. Does that mean that the retail market for gasoline is not competitive?

Sources are listed at the end of this chapter.

Profit-Maximizing Choices of a Perfectly Competitive Firm

> **23.2** Discuss how a perfectly competitive firm decides how much output to produce

When we discussed substitutes in a previous chapter, we pointed out that the more substitutes there are and the more similar they are to the commodity in question, the greater is the price elasticity of demand. Here we assume that the perfectly competitive firm is producing a homogeneous (indistinguishable across all of the industry's firms) commodity that has perfect substitutes. That means that if the individual firm raises its price one penny, it will lose all of its business. This, then, is how we characterize the demand schedule for a perfectly competitive firm: It is the going market price as determined by the forces of market supply and market demand—that is, where the market demand curve intersects the market supply curve.

> *The demand curve for the product of an individual firm in a perfectly competitive industry is perfectly elastic at the going market price.*

Remember that with a perfectly elastic demand curve, any increase in price leads to zero quantity demanded.

We show the market demand and supply curves in panel (a) of Figure 23-1. Their intersection occurs at the price of $5. The commodity in question is wireless earbuds. Assume for the purposes of this exposition that all of these wireless earbuds are perfect substitutes for all others. At the going market price of $5 apiece, the demand curve for wireless earbuds produced by an individual firm that sells a very, very small part of total industry production is shown in panel (b). At the market price, this firm can sell all the hourly output it wants. At the market price of $5 each, which is where the demand curve for the individual producer lies, consumer demand for the wireless earbuds of that one producer is perfectly elastic.

This can be seen by noting that if the firm raises its price, consumers, who are assumed to know that this supplier is charging more than other producers, will buy elsewhere, and the producer in question will have no sales at all. Thus, the demand curve for that producer is perfectly elastic. We label the individual producer's demand curve *d*, whereas the *market* demand curve is always labeled *D*.

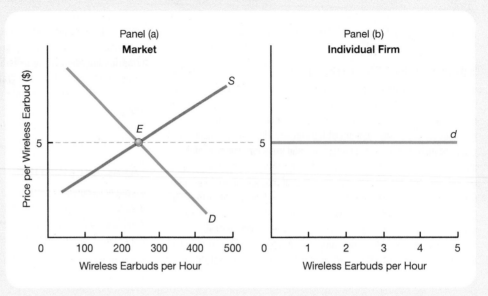

FIGURE 23-1

The Demand Curve for a Producer of Wireless Earbuds

At $5—where market demand, *D*, and market supply, *S*, intersect—the individual firm faces a perfectly elastic demand curve, *d*. If the firm raises its price even one penny, it will sell no wireless earbuds. [Notice the difference in the quantities of wireless earbuds represented on the horizontal axes of panels (a) and (b).]

How Much Should the Perfect Competitor Produce?

As we have shown, from the perspective of a perfectly competitive firm deciding how much to produce, the firm has to accept the price of the product as a given. If the firm raises its price, it sells nothing. If it lowers its price, it earns lower revenues per unit sold than it otherwise could. The firm has one decision left: How much should it produce? We will apply our model of the firm to this question to come up with an answer. We'll use the *profit-maximization model*, which assumes that firms attempt to maximize their total profits—the positive difference between total revenues and total costs. This also means that firms seek to minimize any losses that arise in times when total revenues may be less than total costs.

Total revenues
The price per unit times the total quantity sold.

Total Revenues Every firm has to consider its *total revenues*. **Total revenues** are defined as the quantity sold multiplied by the price per unit. (They are the same as total receipts from the sale of output.)

Look at Figure 23-2. The information in panel (a) comes from panel (a) of Figure 22-2, but we have added some essential columns for our analysis. Column 3 is the market price, *P*, of $5 per wireless earbud. Column 4 shows the total revenues, or TR, as equal to the market price, *P*, times the total output per hour, or *Q*. Thus, TR = *P* × *Q*.

We are assuming that the market supply and demand schedules intersect at a price of $5 and that this price holds for all the firm's production. We are also assuming that because our maker of wireless earbuds is a small part of the market, it can sell all that it produces at that price. Thus, panel (b) of Figure 23-2 shows the total revenue curve as a straight green line. For every additional wireless earbud sold, total revenue increases by $5.

Comparing Total Costs with Total Revenues Total costs are given in column 2 of panel (a) of Figure 23-2 and plotted in panel (b). Remember, the firm's costs always include a normal rate of return on investment. So, whenever we refer to total costs, we are talking *not* about accounting costs but about economic costs. When the total cost curve is above the total revenue curve, the firm is experiencing losses. When total costs are less than total revenues, the firm is making profits.

By comparing total costs with total revenues, we can figure out the number of wireless earbuds the individual competitive firm should produce per hour. Our analysis rests on the assumption that the firm will attempt to maximize total profits. In panel (a) of Figure 23-2, we see that total profits reach a maximum at a production rate of

Panel (a)

(1) Total Output and Sales per Hour (Q)	(2) Total Costs (TC)	(3) Market Price (P)	(4) Total Revenues (TR) (4) = (3) x (1)	(5) Total Profit (TR – TC) (5) = (4) – (2)	(6) Average Total Cost (ATC) (6) = (2) ÷ (1)	(7) Average Variable Cost (AVC)	(8) Marginal Cost (MC) (8) = Change in (2) Change in (1)	(9) Marginal Revenue (MR) (9) = Change in (4) Change in (1)
0	$10	$5	$ 0	–$10	—	—		
1	15	5	5	–10	$15.00	$5.00	$5	$5
2	18	5	10	–8	9.00	4.00	3	5
3	20	5	15	–5	6.67	3.33	2	5
4	21	5	20	–1	5.25	2.75	1	5
5	23	5	25	2	4.60	2.60	2	5
6	26	5	30	4	4.33	2.67	3	5
7	30	5	35	**5**	4.28	2.86	4	5
8	35	5	40	**5**	4.38	3.12	5	5
9	41	5	45	4	4.56	3.44	6	5
10	48	5	50	2	4.80	3.80	7	5
11	56	5	55	–1	5.09	4.18	8	5

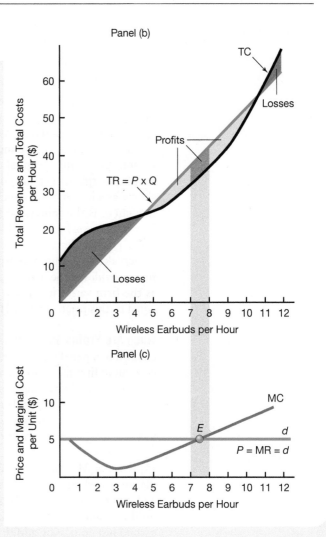

Panel (b)

Panel (c)

FIGURE 23-2

Profit Maximization

Profit maximization occurs where marginal revenue equals marginal cost. Panel (a) indicates that this point occurs at a rate of sales of between seven and eight wireless earbuds per hour. In panel (b), we find maximum profits where total revenues exceed total costs by the largest amount. This occurs at a rate of production and sales per hour of seven or eight wireless earbuds. In panel (c), the marginal cost curve, MC, intersects the marginal revenue curve at the same rate of output and sales of somewhere between seven and eight wireless earbuds per hour.

Profit-maximizing rate of production
The rate of production that maximizes total profits, or the difference between total revenues and total costs. Also, it is the rate of production at which marginal revenue equals marginal cost.

between seven and eight wireless earbuds per hour. We can see this graphically in panel (b) of the figure. The firm will maximize profits where the total revenue curve lies above the total cost curve by the greatest amount. That occurs at a rate of output and sales of between seven and eight wireless earbuds per hour. This rate is called the **profit-maximizing rate of production.** (If output were continuously divisible or there were extremely large numbers of wireless earbuds, we would get a unique profit-maximizing output.)

Using Marginal Analysis to Determine the Profit-Maximizing Rate of Production

It is possible—indeed, preferable—to use marginal analysis to determine the profit-maximizing rate of production. We end up with the same results derived in a different manner, one that focuses more on where decisions are really made—on the margin. Managers examine changes in costs and relate them to changes in revenues. In fact, whether the question is how much more or less to produce, how many more workers to hire or fire, or how much more to study or not study, we compare changes in costs with changes in benefits, where change is occurring at the margin.

Marginal revenue
The change in total revenues resulting from a one-unit change in output (and sale) of the product in question.

Marginal Revenue The change in total revenues attributable to changing the rate of production of an item by one unit is **marginal revenue.** Hence, a more formal definition of marginal revenue is

$$\text{Marginal revenue} = \frac{\text{change in total revenues}}{\text{change in output}}$$

In a perfectly competitive market, the marginal revenue curve is exactly equivalent to the individual firm's demand curve, d, which is a line horizontal at the market clearing price. Each time the firm produces and sells one more unit, total revenues rise by an amount equal to the (constant) market price of the good. Thus, in Figure 23-1, the demand curve, d, for the individual producer is at a price of $5. So is the marginal revenue curve, for marginal revenue in this case also equals $5.

The marginal revenue curve for our competitive producer of wireless earbuds is shown as a line at $5 in panel (c) of Figure 23-2. Notice again that the marginal revenue curve is the individual firm's demand curve, d. The fact that MR, P, and d are identically equal for an individual firm is a general feature of a perfectly competitive industry. The demand curve, d, for the individual firm shows the quantity that consumers desire to purchase from this firm at each price—which is *any* quantity that the firm provides at the market price. The market clearing price per unit does not change as the firm varies its output, so the average revenue and marginal revenue also are equal to this price. Thus, MR is identically equal to P along the firm's demand curve.

When Are Profits Maximized? Now we add the marginal cost curve, MC, taken from column 8 in panel (a) of Figure 23-2. As shown in panel (c) of that figure, the marginal cost curve first falls and then starts to rise, eventually intersecting the marginal revenue curve and then rising above it. Notice that the numbers for both the marginal cost schedule, column 8 in panel (a), and the marginal revenue schedule, column 9 in panel (a), are printed *between* the rows on which the quantities appear. This indicates that we are looking at a *change* between one rate of output and the next rate of output.

Equalizing Marginal Revenue and Marginal Cost In panel (c) of Figure 23-2, the marginal cost curve intersects the marginal revenue curve somewhere between seven and eight wireless earbuds per hour. The firm has an incentive to produce and sell until the amount of the additional revenue received from selling one more wireless earbud just equals the additional costs incurred for producing and selling that wireless earbud. This is how the firm maximizes profit. Whenever marginal cost is less than marginal revenue, the firm will always make more profit by increasing production.

Now consider the possibility of producing at an output rate of 10 wireless earbuds per hour. The marginal cost at that output rate is higher than the marginal revenue. The firm would be spending more to produce that additional output than it would be receiving in revenues. It would be foolish to continue producing at this rate.

The Profit-Maximizing Output Rate How much should the firm, then, produce? It should produce at point E in panel (c) of Figure 23-2, where the marginal cost curve intersects the marginal revenue curve from below. The firm should continue production until the cost of increasing output by one more unit is just equal to the revenues obtainable from that extra unit. This is a fundamental rule in economics:

Profit maximization occurs at the rate of output at which marginal revenue equals marginal cost.

For a perfectly competitive firm, this rate of output is at the intersection of the demand schedule, d, which is identical to the MR curve, and the marginal cost curve, MC. When MR exceeds MC, each additional unit of output adds more to total revenues than to total costs, so the additional unit should be produced. When MC is greater than MR, each unit produced adds more to total cost than to total revenues, so this unit should not be produced. Therefore, profit maximization occurs when MC equals MR. In our particular example, our profit-maximizing, perfectly competitive producer of wireless earbuds will produce at a rate of between seven and eight wireless earbuds per hour.

Marginal Analysis in Your Economic Life You can implicitly and explicitly use marginal analysis for your personal choices and actions. Whenever you engage in any activity, whether it be working for payment, enjoying streaming series, or exercising at the gym, marginal analysis is applicable. Your rule of thumb should always be:

Undertake any activity up to the point at which the marginal benefit equals the marginal cost.

Short-Run Supply under Perfect Competition

23.3 Understand how the short-run supply curve for a perfectly competitive firm is determined

In a previous chapter, you learned that in a market with many buyers and sellers, the equilibrium price and quantity arise when the total quantity of the product demanded equals the total quantity supplied. In a perfectly competitive market, the quantity supplied is determined along an industry supply curve, which in turn depends on the supply curves of all the firms in the market. To understand how to obtain supply curves for perfectly competitive firms and for the industry as a whole, you first must understand the determination of firms' economic profits.

Short-Run Profits

To find what our competitive individual producer of wireless earbuds is making in terms of profits in the short run, we have to add the average total cost curve to panel (c) of Figure 23-2. We take the information from column 6 in panel (a) and add it to panel (c) to get Figure 23-3. Again the profit-maximizing rate of output is between seven and eight wireless earbuds per hour. If we have production and sales of seven per hour, total revenues will be $35 per hour. Total costs will be $30 per hour, leaving a profit of $5 per hour. If the rate of output and sales is eight wireless earbuds per hour, total revenues will be $40 and total costs will be $35, again leaving a profit of $5 per hour.

A Graphical Depiction of Maximum Profits In Figure 23-3, the lower boundary of the rectangle labeled "Profits" is determined by the intersection of the profit-maximizing quantity line represented by vertical dashes at the point at which MR = MC and on

FIGURE 23-3

Measuring Total Profits

Profits are represented by the blue-shaded area. The height of the profit rectangle is given by the difference between average total costs and price ($5), where price is also equal to average revenue. This is found by the vertical difference between the ATC curve and the price, or average revenue, line *d*, at the profit-maximizing rate of output of between seven and eight wireless earbuds per hour.

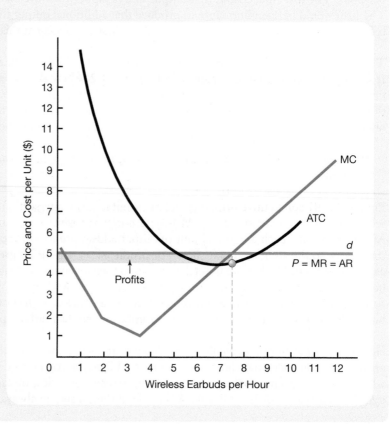

the average total cost curve. Why? Because the ATC curve gives us the cost per unit, whereas the price ($5), represented by *d*, gives us the revenue per unit. The difference is profit per unit.

Thus, the height of the rectangular box representing profits equals profit per unit, and the length equals the amount of units produced. When we multiply these two quantities, we get total profits. Note, as pointed out earlier, that we are talking about *economic profits* because a normal rate of return on investment plus all opportunity costs is included in the average total cost curve, ATC.

A Graphical Depiction of Minimum Losses It is also certainly possible for the competitive firm to make short-run losses, as shown in Figure 23-4 following a shift in the firm's demand from d_1 to d_2. The going market price has fallen from $5 to $3 per wireless earbud because of changes in market demand conditions. The firm will still do the best it can by producing where marginal revenue equals marginal cost.

We see in Figure 23-4 that the marginal revenue (d_2) curve is intersected (from below) by the marginal cost curve at an output rate of about $5\frac{1}{2}$ wireless earbuds per hour. The firm is clearly not making profits because average total costs at that output rate are greater than the price of $3 per wireless earbud. The losses are shown by the shaded area. By producing where marginal revenue equals marginal cost, however, the firm is minimizing its losses. That is, losses would be greater at any other output.

The Short-Run Break-Even Price and the Short-Run Shutdown Price

In Figure 23-4, the firm is sustaining economic losses. Will the owners sell its assets to someone else and thereby *go out of business*? In the long run it will if economic losses persist.

In the short run, however, the firm will not necessarily go out of business. In the short run, as long as the total revenues from continuing to produce output exceed the

FIGURE 23-4

Minimization of Short-Run Losses

In situations in which average total costs exceed price, which in turn is greater than or equal to average variable cost, profit maximization is equivalent to loss minimization. Losses are minimized at the output rate at which marginal cost equals marginal revenue. Losses are shown by the red-shaded area.

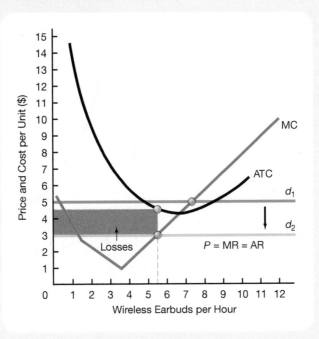

associated total variable costs, the firm will remain in business and continue to produce.

In the short run, a firm can choose temporarily to *shut down* and halt production, but it still is in business. Now how can a firm that is sustaining economic losses in the short run tell whether it is still worthwhile *not* to shut down? The firm must compare the total revenues that it receives if it continues producing with the resulting total variable costs that it thereby incurs. Looking at the problem on a per-unit basis, as long as average variable cost (AVC) is covered by average revenues (price), the firm is better off continuing to produce. If average variable costs are exceeded even a little bit by the price of the product, staying in production produces some revenues in excess of variable costs. The logic is fairly straightforward:

> *As long as the price per unit sold exceeds the average variable cost per unit produced, the earnings of the firm's owners will be higher if it continues to produce in the short run than if it shuts down.*

Calculating the Short-Run Break-Even Price   Look at demand curve d_1 in Figure 23-5. It just touches the minimum point of the average total cost curve, which is exactly where the marginal cost curve intersects the average total cost curve. At that price, which is about $4.30, the firm will be making exactly zero short-run *economic* profits. That price is called the **short-run break-even price,** and point E_1 therefore occurs at the short-run break-even price for a competitive firm. It is the point at which marginal revenue, marginal cost, and average total cost are all equal (that is, at which $P = MC$ and $P = ATC$). The break-even price is the one that yields zero short-run *economic* profits or losses.

Short-run break-even price
The price at which a firm's total revenues equal its total costs. At the break-even price, the firm is just making a normal rate of return on its capital investment. (It is covering its explicit and implicit costs.)

Calculating the Short-Run Shutdown Price   To calculate the firm's shutdown price, we must introduce the average variable cost (AVC) to our graph. In Figure 23-5, we have plotted the AVC values from column 7 in panel (a) of Figure 23-2. For the moment, consider two possible demand curves, d_1 and d_2, which are also the firm's respective

FIGURE 23-5

Short-Run Break-Even and Shutdown Prices

We can find the short-run break-even price and the short-run shutdown price by comparing price with average total costs and average variable costs. If the demand curve is d_1, profit maximization occurs at output E_1, where MC equals marginal revenue (the d_1 curve). Because the ATC curve includes all relevant opportunity costs, point E_1 is the break-even point, and zero economic profits are being made. The firm is earning a normal rate of return. If the demand curve falls to d_2, profit maximization (loss minimization) occurs at the intersection of MC and MR (the d_2 curve), or E_2. Below this price, it does not pay for the firm to continue in operation because its average variable costs are not covered by the price of the product.

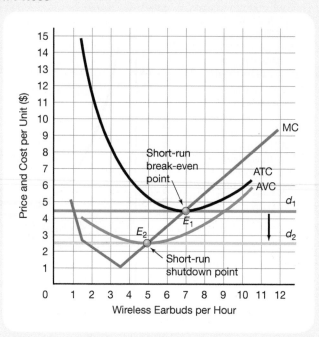

marginal revenue curves. If demand is d_1, the firm will produce at E_1, where that curve intersects the marginal cost curve. If demand falls to d_2, the firm will produce at E_2. The special feature of the hypothetical demand curve, d_2, is that it just touches the average variable cost curve at the latter's minimum point, which is also where the marginal cost curve intersects it. This price is the **short-run shutdown price.** Why? Below this price, the firm would be paying out more in variable costs than it is receiving in revenues from the sale of its product. Each unit it sold would generate losses that could be avoided if it shut down operations.

The intersection of d_2, the marginal cost curve, and the average variable cost curve is labeled E_2. The resulting short-run shutdown price is valid only for the short run because, of course, in the long run the firm will not stay in business if it is earning less than a normal rate of return (zero economic profits).

Short-run shutdown price

The price that covers average variable costs. It occurs just below the intersection of the marginal cost curve and the average variable cost curve.

WHAT HAPPENS WHEN...

a new regulation causes the marginal cost curve and, hence, the average total cost and variable cost curves to shift upward, thereby altering the short-run break-even and shutdown prices?

When a perfectly competitive firm's marginal cost, average total cost, and average variable cost curves shift upward, naturally the points at which the ATC and AVC curves cross the marginal cost curves shift upward as well. The short-run break-even price thereby increases. Consequently, following implementation of the regulation, the lowest price

at which it would be able to ensure at least a zero economic profit will be higher. In addition, the short-run shutdown price increases. Thus, the lowest price at which the firm will be able to earn sufficient revenues to at least cover its variable cost also will be higher than was the case before the regulation was implemented.

The Meaning of Zero Economic Profits   The fact that we labeled point E_1 in Figure 23-5 the break-even point may have disturbed you. At point E_1, price is just equal to average total cost. If this is the case, why would a firm continue to produce if it were making no profits whatsoever?

Accounting Profits versus Economic Profits If we again make the distinction between accounting profits and economic profits, you will realize that at that price, the firm has zero economic profits but positive accounting profits. Recall that accounting profits are total revenues minus total explicit costs. Such accounting, however, ignores the reward offered to investors—the opportunity cost of capital—plus all other implicit costs.

In economic analysis, the average total cost curve includes the full opportunity cost of capital. Indeed, the average total cost curve includes the opportunity cost of *all* factors of production used in the production process. At the short-run break-even price, economic profits are, by definition, zero. Accounting profits at that price are not, however, equal to zero. They are positive.

An Example of Zero Economic Profits Consider an example. A manufacturer of homogeneous nanotube chips sells chips at some price. The owners of the firm have supplied all the funds in the business. They have not borrowed from anyone else, and they explicitly pay the full opportunity cost to all factors of production, including any managerial labor that they themselves contribute to the business. Their salaries show up as a cost in the books and are equal to what they could have earned in the next-best alternative occupation.

At the end of the year, the owners find that after they subtract all explicit costs from total revenues, accounting profits are $100,000. If their investment was $1 million, the rate of return on that investment is 10 percent per year. We will assume that this turns out to be equal to the risk-adjusted market rate of return.

This $100,000, or 10 percent rate of return, is actually, then, a competitive, or normal, rate of return on invested capital in all industries with similar risks. If the owners had made only $50,000, or 5 percent on their investment, they would have been able to make higher profits by leaving the industry. The 10 percent rate of return is the opportunity cost of capital. Accountants show it as a profit. Economists call it a cost. We include that cost in the average total cost curve, similar to the one shown in Figure 23-5. At the short-run break-even price, average total cost, including this opportunity cost of capital, will just equal that price. The firm will be making zero economic profits but a 10 percent *accounting profit*.

The Perfect Competitor's Short-Run Supply Curve

As you learned in a previous chapter, the relationship between a product's price and the quantity produced and offered for sale is a supply curve. What does the supply curve for the individual firm look like? Actually, we have been looking at it all along. We know that when the price of wireless earbuds is $5, the firm will supply seven or eight of them per hour. If the price falls to $3, the firm will supply five or six wireless earbuds per hour. If the price falls below the minimum point along the average variable cost, the firm will shut down. Hence, in Figure 23-6, the firm's supply curve is the marginal cost curve above the short-run shutdown point. This is shown as the solid part of the marginal cost curve.

> *By definition, then, a firm's short-run supply curve in a competitive industry is its marginal cost curve at and above the point of intersection with the average variable cost curve.*

The Short-Run Industry Supply Curve

In a previous chapter, we indicated that the market supply curve was the summation of individual supply curves. At the beginning of this chapter, we drew a market supply curve in Figure 23-1. Now we want to derive more precisely a market, or industry, supply curve to reflect individual producer behavior in that industry.

Determining the Industry First we must ask, What is an industry? It is merely a collection of firms producing a particular product.

FIGURE 23-6

FIGURE 23-6

The Individual Firm's Short-Run Supply Curve

The individual firm's short-run supply curve is the portion of its marginal cost curve at and above the minimum point on the average variable cost curve.

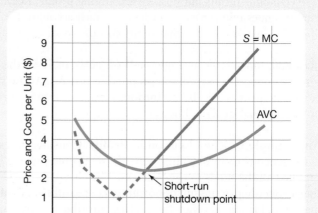

Therefore, we have a way to figure out the total supply curve of any industry: As discussed in a previous chapter, we add the quantities that each firm will supply at every possible price. In other words, we sum the individual supply curves of all the competitive firms *horizontally*. The individual supply curves, as we just saw, are simply the marginal cost curves of each firm.

Constructing the Industry Supply Curve Consider doing this for a hypothetical world in which there are only two producers of wireless earbuds in the industry, firm A and firm B. These two firms' marginal cost curves are given in panels (a) and (b) of Figure 23-7. The marginal cost curves for the two separate firms are presented as MC_A in panel (a)

FIGURE 23-7

Deriving the Industry Supply Curve

Marginal cost curves at and above minimum average variable cost are presented in panels (a) and (b) for firms A and B. We horizontally sum the two quantities supplied, 7 units by firm A and 10 units by firm B, at a price of $6. This gives us point *F* in panel (c). We do the same thing for the quantities supplied at a price of $10. This gives us point *G*.

When we connect those points, we have the industry supply curve, *S*, which is the horizontal summation—represented by the Greek letter sigma (Σ)—of the firms' marginal cost curves above their respective minimum average variable costs.

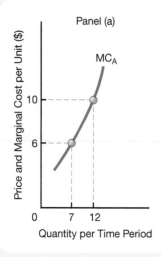

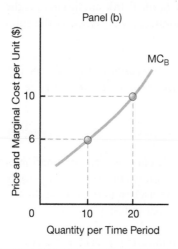

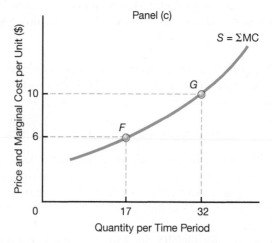

and MC_B in panel (b). Those two marginal cost curves are drawn only for prices above the minimum average variable cost for each respective firm. In panel (a), for firm A, at a price of $6 per unit, the quantity supplied would be 7 units. At a price of $10 per unit, the quantity supplied would be 12 units. In panel (b), we see the two different quantities that would be supplied by firm B corresponding to those two prices. Now, at a price of $6, we add horizontally the quantities 7 and 10 to obtain 17 units. This gives us one point, *F*, in panel (c), for our short-run **industry supply curve**, *S*. We obtain the other point, *G*, by doing the same horizontal adding of quantities at a price of $10 per unit.

When we connect all points such as *F* and *G*, we obtain the industry supply curve *S*, which is also marked Σ*MC* (where the capital Greek sigma, Σ, is the symbol for summation), indicating that it is the horizontal summation of the marginal cost curves (at and above the respective minimum average variable cost of each firm). Because the law of diminishing marginal product makes marginal cost curves rise as output rises, the short-run supply curve of a perfectly competitive industry must be upward sloping.

Industry supply curve
The set of points showing the minimum prices at which given quantities will be forthcoming; also called the *market supply curve*.

Factors That Influence the Industry Supply Curve

As you have just seen, the industry supply curve is the horizontal summation of all of the individual firms' marginal cost curves at and above their respective minimum average variable cost points. This means that anything that affects the marginal cost curves of the firm will influence the industry supply curve. Therefore, the individual factors that will influence the supply schedule in a competitive industry can be summarized as the factors that cause the variable costs of production to change. These are factors that affect the individual marginal cost curves, such as changes in the individual firm's productivity, in factor prices (such as wages paid to labor and prices of raw materials), in per-unit taxes, and in anything else that would influence the individual firm's marginal cost curve.

You learned in an earlier chapter that all of these are *ceteris paribus* conditions of supply. Because they affect the position of the marginal cost curve for the individual firm, they affect the position of the industry supply curve. A change in any of these will shift the firms' marginal cost curves and thus shift the industry supply curve.

Price Determination under Perfect Competition

23.4 Explain how the equilibrium price is determined in a perfectly competitive market

How is the market, or "going," price established in a competitive market? This price is established by the interaction of all the suppliers (firms) and all the demanders (consumers).

The Market Clearing Price

The market demand schedule, *D*, in panel (a) of Figure 23-8 represents the demand schedule for the entire industry, and the supply schedule, *S*, represents the supply schedule for the entire industry. The market clearing price, P_e, is established by the forces of supply and demand at the intersection of *D* and the short-run industry supply curve, *S*. Even though each individual firm has no control or effect on the price of its product in a competitive industry, the interaction of *all* the producers and buyers determines the price at which the product will be sold.

We say that the price P_e and the quantity Q_e in panel (a) of Figure 23-8 constitute the competitive solution to the resource allocation problem in that particular industry. It is the equilibrium at which quantity demanded equals quantity supplied, and both suppliers and demanders are doing as well as they can. The resulting individual firm demand curve, *d*, is shown in panel (b) of Figure 23-8 at the price P_e.

Market Equilibrium and the Individual Firm

In a purely competitive industry, the individual producer takes price as a given and chooses the output level that maximizes profits. We see in panel (b) of Figure 23-8

FIGURE 23-8

Industry Demand and Supply Curves and the Individual Firm Demand Curve

The industry demand curve is represented by D in panel (a). The short-run industry supply curve is S and is equal to ΣMC. The intersection of the demand and supply curves at E determines the equilibrium or market clearing price at P_e. The demand curve faced by the individual firm in panel (b) is perfectly elastic at the market clearing price determined in panel (a). If the producer has a marginal cost curve MC, its profit-maximizing output level is at q_e. For ATC_1, economic profits are zero. For ATC_2, profits are positive. For ATC_3, profits are negative.

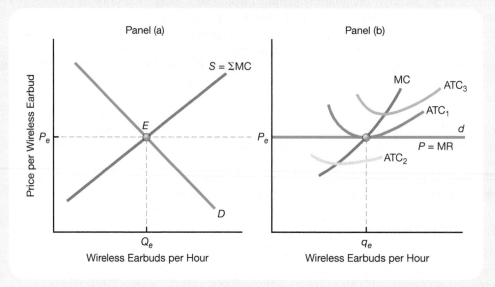

that this is at q_e. If the producer's average costs are given by ATC_1, the short-run break-even price arises at q_e. If its average costs are given by ATC_3, then at q_e, ATC exceeds price, and the firm is incurring losses. Alternatively, if average costs are given by ATC_2, the firm will be making economic profits at q_e. In the former case, we would expect, over time, that some firms will cease production (exit the industry), causing supply to shift inward. In the latter case, we would expect new firms to enter the industry to take advantage of the economic profits, thereby causing supply to shift outward. We now turn to these long-run considerations.

23.5 Describe what factors induce firms to enter or exit a perfectly competitive industry

The Long-Run Industry Situation: Exit and Entry

In the long run in a competitive situation, firms will be making zero economic profits. (Actually, this is true only for identical firms. Throughout the remainder of the discussion, we assume firms have the same cost structures.) We surmise, therefore, that in the long run a perfectly competitive firm's marginal revenue curve—which is horizontal at the market clearing price—will just touch its average total cost curve. How does this occur? It comes about through an adjustment process that depends on economic profits and losses.

Exit and Entry of Firms

Look back at both Figure 23-3 and Figure 23-4. The existence of either profits or losses is a signal to owners of capital both inside and outside the industry. If an industry is characterized by firms showing economic profits as represented in Figure 23-3, these economic profits signal owners of capital elsewhere in the economy that they, too, should enter this industry. In contrast, if some firms in an industry are suffering economic losses as represented in Figure 23-4, these economic losses signal resource owners outside the industry to stay out. In addition, these economic losses signal resource owners within the industry not to reinvest and if possible to leave the industry. It is in this sense that we say that profits direct resources to their highest-valued use.

In the long run, capital will flow into industries in which profitability is highest and will flow out of industries in which profitability is lowest.

Allocation of Capital and Market Signals The price system therefore allocates capital according to the relative expected rates of return on alternative investments. Hence, entry restrictions (such as limits on the numbers of taxicabs and banks permitted to enter the taxi service and banking industries) will hinder economic efficiency by not allowing resources to flow to their highest-valued use. Similarly, exit restrictions (such as laws that require firms to give advance notice of closings) will act to trap resources (temporarily) in sectors in which their value is below that in alternative uses. Such laws will also inhibit the ability of firms to respond to changes in both the domestic and international marketplaces.

Not every industry presents an immediate source of economic profits. In a brief period of time, it may be impossible for a firm that produces tractors to switch to the production of digital devices, even if there are very large profits to be made. Over the long run, however, we would expect to see owners of some other resources switch to producing digital devices. In a market economy, investors provide firms in the more profitable industry with more investment funds, which they take from firms in less profitable industries. (Also, positive economic profits induce existing firms to use internal investment funds for expansion.) Consequently, resources useful in the production of more profitable goods, such as labor, will be bid away from lower-valued opportunities. Investors and other suppliers of resources respond to market **signals** about their highest-valued opportunities.

How have some cargo-ship companies responded to market signals by adding human passengers alongside shipping containers?

Signals
Compact ways of conveying to economic decision makers information needed to make decisions. An effective signal not only conveys information but also provides the incentive to react appropriately. Economic profits and economic losses are such signals.

INTERNATIONAL EXAMPLE

Reallocating Quarters and Deck Space Transforms Ocean Freighters into Partial Cruise Ships

During the past decade, the number of passengers carried by ocean cruise lines has increased by more than 50 percent, to about 27 million per year. As demands for travel over ocean-going cruise routes have increased, so have the market clearing prices of cruises. Traditionally, cruise lines have responded to this signal by adding in excess of 60 new ships and thereby expanding their combined fleet to more than 300 ships capable of carrying about a half million passengers at any given moment.

Owners of cargo ships also have responded to the price signal. With only a few adjustments in space allocations, a typical ship that normally carries only a crew and shipping containers can temporarily provide rooms and deck space for about a dozen passengers on routes traversing both the Atlantic and Pacific Oceans. Scheduled cargo-ship-based passenger cruises

range from short trips between Australia and New Zealand to lengthy trips between Singapore and Houston. By shifting their available resources to accommodate passengers who wish to sight-see, the cargo-ship owners have entered another industry to boost the overall rate of return on their nautical investments.

FOR CRITICAL THINKING

Why do you suppose that as market clearing prices of traditional passenger cruises have continued to increase, owners of cargo ships have considered permanently reallocating more ship space to additional passenger quarters?

Sources are listed at the end of this chapter.

Tendency toward Equilibrium Market adjustment to changes in demand will occur regardless of the wishes of the managers of firms in less profitable markets. They can either attempt to alter their product line to respond to the new demands, be replaced by managers who are more responsive to new conditions, or see their firms go bankrupt.

In addition, when we say that in a competitive long-run equilibrium situation firms will be making zero economic profits, we must realize that at a particular point in time it would be pure coincidence for a firm to be making *exactly* zero economic profits. Real-world information is not as precise as the curves we use to simplify our analysis. Things change all the time in a dynamic world, and firms, even in a very competitive situation, may for many reasons not be making exactly zero economic profits. We say that there is a *tendency* toward that equilibrium position, but firms are adjusting constantly to changes in their cost curves and in the market demand curves.

Long-Run Industry Supply Curves

In panel (a) of Figure 23-8, we drew the summation of all of the portions of the individual firms' marginal cost curves at and above each firm's respective minimum average variable costs as the upward-sloping supply curve of the entire industry. We should be aware that a relatively inelastic supply curve may be appropriate only in the short run. After all, one of the prerequisites of a competitive industry is freedom of entry.

Remember that our definition of the long run is a period of time in which all adjustments can be made. The **long-run industry supply curve** is a supply curve showing the relationship between quantities supplied by the entire industry at different prices after firms have been allowed to either enter or leave the industry, depending on whether there have been positive or negative economic profits. Also, for simplicity, we shall draw the long-run industry supply curve under the assumption that firms are identical and that entry and exit have been completed. This means that along the long-run industry supply curve, firms in the industry earn zero economic profits.

The long-run industry supply curve can take one of three shapes, depending on whether input prices stay constant, increase, or decrease as the number of firms in the industry changes. To this point, we have assumed that input prices remained constant to the *firm* regardless of the firm's rate of output. When we look at the entire *industry*, however, when all firms are expanding and new firms are entering, they may simultaneously bid up input prices.

Constant-Cost Industries In principle, there are industries that use such a small percentage of the total supply of inputs required for industrywide production that firms can enter the industry without bidding up input prices. In such a situation, we are dealing with a **constant-cost industry.** Its long-run industry supply curve is therefore horizontal and is represented by S_L in panel (a) of Figure 23-9.

We can work through the case in which constant costs prevail. We start out in panel (a) with demand curve D_1 and supply curve S_1. The equilibrium price is P_1. Market demand shifts rightward to D_2. In the short run, the equilibrium price rises to P_2. This generates positive economic profits for existing firms in the industry. Such economic profits induce capital to flow into the industry. The existing firms expand or

Long-run industry supply curve

A market supply curve showing the relationship between prices and quantities after firms have been allowed the time to enter into or exit from an industry, depending on whether there have been positive or negative economic profits.

Constant-cost industry

An industry whose total output can be increased in the long run without an increase in input prices. Its long-run supply curve is horizontal.

FIGURE 23-9

Constant-Cost, Increasing-Cost, and Decreasing-Cost Industries

In panel (a), we show a situation in which the demand curve shifts from D_1 to D_2. Price increases from P_1 to P_2. In time, the short-run supply curve shifts outward because entry occurs in response to positive profits, and the equilibrium changes from E_2 to E_3. The market clearing price is again P_1. If we connect points such as E_1 and E_3, we come up with the long-run supply curve S_L. This is a constant-cost industry. In

panel (b), costs are increasing for the industry, and therefore the long-run supply curve, S_L', slopes upward and long-run prices rise from P_1 to P_2. In panel (c), costs are decreasing for the industry as it expands, and therefore the long-run supply curve, S_L'', slopes downward such that long-run prices decline from P_1 to P_2.

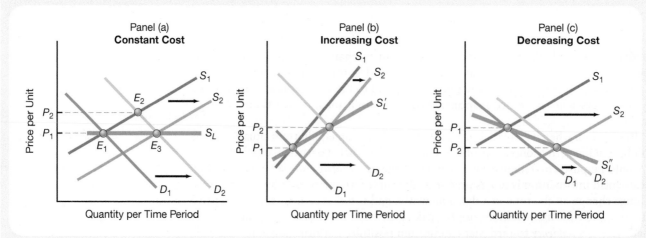

new firms enter (or both). The short-run supply curve shifts outward to S_2. The new intersection with the new demand curve is at E_3. The new equilibrium price is again P_1. The long-run supply curve, labeled S_L, is obtained by connecting the intersections of the corresponding pairs of demand and short-run supply curves, E_1 and E_3.

In a constant-cost industry, long-run supply is perfectly elastic. Any shift in demand is eventually met by just enough entry or exit of suppliers that the long-run price is constant at P_1. Retail trade is often given as an example of such an industry because output can be expanded or contracted without affecting input prices. Banking is another example.

Increasing-Cost Industries In an **increasing-cost industry,** expansion by existing firms and the addition of new firms cause the price of inputs specialized to that industry to be bid up. As costs of production rise, the ATC curve and the firms' MC curves shift upward, causing short-run supply curves (each firm's marginal cost curve) to shift vertically upward. Hence, industry supply shifts out by less than in a constant-cost industry. The result is a long-run industry supply curve that slopes upward, as represented by S_L' in panel (b) of Figure 23-9. Examples are residential construction and coal mining—both use specialized inputs that cannot be obtained in ever-increasing quantities without causing their prices to rise.

Increasing-cost industry
An industry in which a long-run increase in industry output is accompanied by an increase in input prices, such that the long-run industry supply curve slopes upward.

Decreasing-Cost Industries An expansion in the number of firms in an industry can lead to a reduction in input prices and a downward shift in the ATC and MC curves. When this occurs, the long-run industry supply curve will slope downward. An example, S_L'', is given in panel (c) of Figure 23-9. This is a **decreasing-cost industry.**

What is the shape of the long-run industry supply curve in the industry composed of delivery firms that transport restaurant meals to consumers who pre-order those meals online?

Decreasing-cost industry
An industry in which an increase in output in the long run leads to a reduction in input prices, such that the long-run industry supply curve slopes downward.

EXAMPLE

Assessing the Long-Run Industry Supply Curve in the Growing Third-Party Food Delivery Industry

Recent years have witnessed rapid growth in the demand for third-party food delivery services provided by firms that specialize in picking up pre-ordered meals at restaurants and making deliveries to people's homes. Younger people have been the main source of this demand growth. About 80 percent of people who transmit online orders to food delivery services are under the age of 45, and about half of those customers are younger than 35. Thus, most observers—and recent and potential new entrants to the industry—anticipate that higher demand for such services will continue for years to come.

As firms such as GrubHub, Uber Eats, and DoorDash have been joined in the industry by many other new entrants seeking to compete in the industry, the market supply of food delivery services also has

increased. Available evidence to date indicates that the market clearing price of food delivery services has remained steady as market demand and short-run supply curves have shifted rightward. Thus, the long-run supply curve for this industry has been horizontal, so that the food delivery service industry is a constant-cost industry.

FOR CRITICAL THINKING

If a future technological change were to cause the price of food delivery services to drop below its existing level following entry of new firms even as market demand continued to increase, what type of industry would exist?

Sources are listed at the end of this chapter.

Long-Run Equilibrium

In the long run, the firm can change the scale of its plant, adjusting its plant size in such a way that it has no further incentive to change. It will do so until profits are maximized.

The Firm's Long-Run Situation Figure 23-10 shows the long-run equilibrium of the perfectly competitive firm. Given a price of P and a marginal cost curve, MC, the firm produces at output q_e. Because economic profits must be zero in the long run, the firm's short-run average costs (SAC) must equal P at q_e, which occurs at minimum SAC. In addition, because we are in long-run equilibrium, any economies of scale

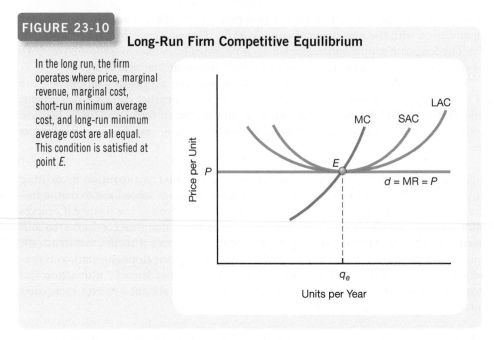

FIGURE 23-10

Long-Run Firm Competitive Equilibrium

In the long run, the firm operates where price, marginal revenue, marginal cost, short-run minimum average cost, and long-run minimum average cost are all equal. This condition is satisfied at point *E*.

must be exhausted, so we are on the minimum point of the long-run average cost curve (LAC). In other words, the long-run equilibrium position is where "everything is equal," which is at point *E* in Figure 23-10. There, *price* equals *marginal revenue* equals *marginal cost* equals *average cost* (minimum, short-run, and long-run).

Perfect Competition and Minimum Average Total Cost Look again at Figure 23-10. In long-run equilibrium, the perfectly competitive firm finds itself producing at output rate q_e. At that rate of output, the price is just equal to the minimum long-run average cost as well as the minimum short-run average cost. In this sense, perfect competition results in the production of goods and services using the least costly combination of resources. This is an important attribute of a perfectly competitive long-run equilibrium, particularly when we wish to compare the market structure of perfect competition with other market structures that are less than perfectly competitive. We will examine these other market structures in later chapters.

Competitive Pricing: Marginal Cost Pricing

In a perfectly competitive industry, each firm produces where its marginal cost curve intersects its marginal revenue curve from below. Thus, perfectly competitive firms always sell their goods at a price that just equals marginal cost. This is said to be the optimal price of this good because the price that consumers pay reflects the opportunity cost to society of producing the good. Recall that marginal cost is the amount that a firm must spend to purchase the additional resources needed to expand output by one unit. Given competitive markets, the amount paid for a resource will be the same in all of its alternative uses. Thus, MC reflects relative resource input use. That is, if the MC of good 1 is twice the MC of good 2, one more unit of good 1 requires twice the resource input of one more unit of good 2.

Marginal cost pricing
A system of pricing in which the price charged is equal to the opportunity cost to society of producing one more unit of the good or service in question. The opportunity cost is the marginal cost to society.

Marginal Cost Pricing The perfectly competitive firm produces up to the point at which the market price just equals the marginal cost. Herein lies the element of the optimal nature of a competitive solution, which is called **marginal cost pricing.**

Matching the Consumer's Marginal Benefit Under marginal cost pricing, the marginal benefit to consumers, given by the price that they are willing to pay for the last unit of the good purchased, just equals the marginal cost to society of producing the last unit. If the marginal benefit exceeds the marginal cost—that is, if

$P >$ MC—too little is being produced in that people value additional units more than the cost to society of producing them. If $P <$ MC, the opposite is true.

Thus, the perfectly competitive firm sells its product at a price that just equals the cost to society—the opportunity cost—for that is what the marginal cost curve represents. But note here that it is the self-interest of firm owners that causes price to equal the marginal cost to society.

The Efficiency of Marginal Cost Pricing When an individual pays a price equal to the marginal cost of production, the cost to the user of that product is equal to the sacrifice or cost to society of producing that quantity of that good as opposed to more of some other good. (We are assuming that all marginal social costs are accounted for.) The competitive solution, then, is called *efficient*, in the economic sense of the word. Economic efficiency means that it is impossible to increase the output of any good without lowering the *value* of the total output produced in the economy. No juggling of resources, such as labor and capital, will result in an output that is higher in total value than the value of all of the goods and services already being produced. In an efficient equilibrium, it is impossible to make one person better off without making someone else worse off. All resources are used in the most advantageous way possible, and society therefore enjoys an efficient allocation of productive resources. All goods and services are sold at their opportunity cost, and marginal cost pricing prevails throughout.

Market Failure Although perfect competition does offer many desirable results, situations arise when perfectly competitive markets cannot efficiently allocate resources. Either too many or too few resources are used in the production of a good or service. These situations are instances of **market failure**. Externalities arising from failures to fully assign property rights and public goods are examples. For reasons discussed in later chapters, perfectly competitive markets cannot efficiently allocate resources in these situations, and alternative allocation mechanisms may be called for. In some cases, alternative market structures or government intervention *may* improve the economic outcome.

Market failure
A situation in which an unrestrained market operation leads to either too few or too many resources going to a specific economic activity.

ECONOMICS IN YOUR LIFE

For Urban Farmers, Industry Entry May Be Relatively Unimpeded but Still Entails a Key Expense

The functioning of agricultural markets often is a good example of the theory of perfect competition in action. After all, farmers are aplenty, and the gain or loss of a few farmers from the market typically would be unnoticed. All farmers usually have access to very similar information. One farmer's product is usually interchangeable with the product raised by another, and each farmer's production is a tiny fraction of total industry output.

Tommy Garcia-Prats, who farms an urban lot next to busy train tracks in Houston, Texas, grows fruits and vegetables. To do so, he has incurred a cost of entering into the agricultural industry. Because urban land has many alternative uses, the opportunity cost of allocating the land he farms to agricultural use is rather high. For this reason, Garcia-Prats incurs a significant expense to lease the land that he uses. Nevertheless, Garcia-Prats already is located in a city full of people who wish to buy his fruits, vegetables, and other produce. Thus, the entry expense related to establishing links to consumers of his products is small. Rural farmers, in contrast, must incur a larger expense in developing sales networks in city markets. On net, the total

entry expense that Garcia-Prats and other urban farmers face is about the same as the overall entry cost farmers in rural areas confront. This fact is why Garcia-Prats has been able to enter and compete with rural farmers with lower land-related expenses, and it explains why other urban farmers continue to enter the industry.

FOR CRITICAL THINKING

Why do you suppose that some enterprising urban farmers are growing their crops on the tops of buildings?

REAL APPLICATION

Assume that you have access to funds that would allow you to enter the vegetable-growing business. You have the choice of purchasing the rights to grow your vegetables in an urban setting or a rural setting. How will you decide where to grow your vegetables?

Sources are listed at the end of this chapter.

ISSUES & APPLICATIONS

Higher Minimum Wage Rates and Long-Run Equilibrium in the Restaurant Industry

penta/123RF GB Limited

CONCEPTS APPLIED

➤ Signals

➤ Firm Entry

➤ Firm Exit

Market signals convey information and provide incentives for owners of firms to react appropriately in making decisions. For a number of restaurant owners, actions by municipalities around the nation to enact substantial increases in minimum wage rates have signaled that an industry exit might be appropriate.

Minimum Wages and the Relatively High Cost of Restaurant Labor

Most people assume that the majority of a restaurant's expenses are the costs of the food ingredients used to prepare meals. In fact, most restaurants spend about the same amount on labor as they do on food. Each type of expense usually accounts for one-third or more of a restaurant's total costs.

In a long-run competitive equilibrium, a restaurant owner who is just willing to continue operations and remain an active competitor earns an *economic* profit equal to zero. Naturally, an action by a local municipality to raise the minimum wage rate that must be paid to part of the restaurant's workforce signals a potential disruption to that equilibrium. In some cases, such a wage-rate increase signals that the appropriate reaction is to close the restaurant.

Measuring the Effect of a Higher Minimum Wage on Restaurant Closures

Dara Lee Luca of Mathematica Policy Research and Michael Luca of Harvard University have studied the effects of increases in minimum wage rates on restaurant closures. After careful analysis, they determined that restaurants receiving online customer ratings at or below the average also happen to be on the edge of leaving the industry prior to a minimum wage increase. Luca and Luca find that for such restaurants, a one-dollar-per-hour increase in the minimum wage rate raises by 14 percentage points the probability of exit from the industry. Thus, some owners already near a tipping point regarding continuing to operate within the restaurant industry view a minimum wage hike as a signal to which an appropriate reaction is to contemplate exiting the industry.

FOR CRITICAL THINKING

If an increase in the minimum wage rate induces a number of restaurants to leave the industry, what is the effect on the equilibrium price of a restaurant meal? Explain briefly.

REAL APPLICATION

You might eventually own a nationally franchised group of fast-food restaurants. If your state or municipality raises the minimum wage to $20 per hour, what are your options?

Sources are listed at the end of this chapter.

What You Should Know

LEARNING OBJECTIVES

KEY TERMS

23.1 Identify the characteristics of a perfectly competitive market structure *A perfectly competitive industry has four key characteristics: (1) there are many buyers and sellers, (2) firms produce and sell a homogeneous product, (3) information is accessible to both buyers and sellers, and (4) there are insignificant barriers to industry entry or exit. These characteristics imply that each firm takes the market price as given and outside its control.*

perfect competition, 496
perfectly competitive firm, 496
price taker, 496

23.2 Discuss how a perfectly competitive firm decides how much output to produce *A perfectly competitive firm sells the amount that it wishes at the market price, so the additional revenue from selling an additional unit of output is the market price. Thus, the firm's marginal revenue equals the market price, and its marginal revenue curve is the firm's perfectly elastic demand curve. The firm maximizes economic profits when marginal cost equals marginal revenue, so long as the market price is not below the short-run shutdown price, where the marginal cost curve crosses the average variable cost curve.*

total revenues, 498
profit-maximizing rate of
   production, 500
marginal revenue, 500
Key Figures
Figure 23-1, 498
Figure 23-2, 499

23.3 Understand how the short-run supply curve for a perfectly competitive firm is determined *If the market price is below the short-run shutdown price, the firm's total revenues fail to cover its variable costs. The firm would be better off halting production and minimizing its economic loss in the short run. If the market price is above the short-run shutdown price, however, the firm produces the rate of output where marginal revenue—the market price—equals marginal cost. Thus, the range of the firm's marginal cost curve above the short-run shutdown price is the firm's short-run supply curve, which gives the firm's combinations of market prices and production choices.*

short-run break-even price, 503
short-run shutdown price, 504
industry supply curve, 507
Key Figures
Figure 23-3, 502
Figure 23-4, 503
Figure 23-5, 504
Figure 23-6, 506
Figure 23-7, 506

23.4 Explain how the equilibrium price is determined in a perfectly competitive market *The short-run supply curve for a perfectly competitive industry is obtained by summing the quantities supplied by all firms at each price. At the equilibrium market price, the total amount of output supplied by all firms is equal to the total amount of output demanded by all buyers.*

Key Figure
Figure 23-8, 508

23.5 Describe what factors induce firms to enter or exit a perfectly competitive industry *The long-run industry supply curve in a perfectly competitive industry shows the relationship between prices and quantities after firms have entered or left the industry in response to economic profits or losses. In a constant-cost industry, total output can increase in the long run without a rise in input prices, so the long-run industry supply curve is horizontal. In an increasing-cost industry, input prices increase with a long-run rise in industry output, so the long-run industry supply curve slopes upward. In a decreasing-cost industry, input prices decline as industry output increases in the long run, and the long-run industry supply curve slopes downward.*

signals, 509
long-run industry supply
   curve, 510
constant-cost industry, 510
increasing-cost industry, 511
decreasing-cost industry, 511
marginal cost pricing, 512
market failure, 513
Key Figure
Figure 23-10, 512

PROBLEMS

23-1. Explain why each of the following examples is not a perfectly competitive industry.

   a. One firm produces a large portion of the industry's total output, but there are many firms in the industry, and their products are indistinguishable. Firms can easily exit and enter the industry.

   b. There are many buyers and sellers in the industry. Consumers have equal information about the prices of firms' products, which differ moderately in quality from firm to firm.

   c. Many taxicabs compete in a city. The city's government requires all taxicabs to provide identical service. Taxicabs are nearly identical, and all drivers must wear a designated uniform. The government also enforces a binding limit on the number of taxicab companies that can operate within the city's boundaries.

23-2. Consider a market for online movie rentals. The market supply curve slopes upward, the market demand curve slopes downward, and the equilibrium rental price equals $3.50. Consider each of the following events, and discuss the effects they will have on the market clearing price and on the demand curve faced by the individual online rental firm.

   a. People's tastes change in favor of going to see more movies at cinemas with their friends and family members.

   b. More online movie-rental firms enter the market.

   c. There is a significant increase in the price to consumers of *purchasing* movies online.

23-3. Consider the diagram, which applies to a perfectly competitive firm, which at present faces a market clearing price of $20 per unit and produces 10,000 units of output per week.

   a. What is the firm's current average revenue per unit?

   b. What are the present economic profits of this firm? Is the firm maximizing economic profits? Explain.

   c. If the market clearing price drops to $12.50 per unit, should this firm continue to produce in the short run if it wishes to maximize its economic profits (or minimize its economic losses)? Explain.

   d. If the market clearing price drops to $7.50 per unit, should this firm continue to produce in the short run if it wishes to maximize its economic profits (or minimize its economic losses)? Explain.

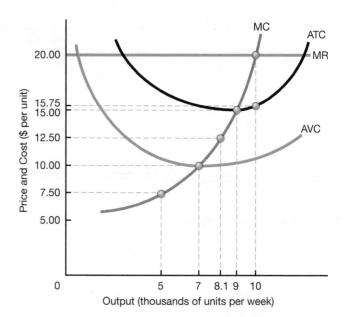

23-4. The table represents the hourly output and cost structure for a local pizzeria. The market is perfectly competitive, and the market price of a pizza in the area is $10. Total costs include all opportunity costs. Fixed costs equal zero.

Total Hourly Output and Sales of Pizzas	Total Hourly Variable Cost ($)
0	5
1	9
2	11
3	12
4	14
5	18
6	24
7	32
8	42
9	54
10	68

   a. Calculate the total revenue and total economic profit for this pizzeria at each rate of output.

   b. Assuming that the pizzeria always produces and sells at least one pizza per hour, does this appear to be a situation of short-run or long-run equilibrium?

   c. Calculate the pizzeria's marginal cost and marginal revenue at each rate of output. Based on marginal analysis, what is the profit-maximizing rate of output for the pizzeria?

d. Draw a diagram depicting the short-run marginal revenue and marginal cost curves for this pizzeria, and illustrate the determination of its profit-maximizing output rate.

23-5. Consider the information provided in Problem 23-4. Suppose the market price drops to only $5 per pizza. In the short run, should this pizzeria continue to make pizzas, or will it maximize its economic profits (that is, minimize its economic loss) by shutting down?

23-6. Until today, a perfectly competitive producer of construction bricks manufactured and sold 10,000 bricks per week at a market price that was just equal to the minimum average variable cost of producing each brick. Today, all the firm's costs are the same, but the market price of bricks has declined.

a. Until today, if this firm has positive fixed costs, did the firm earn economic profits, economic losses, or zero economic profits yesterday?

b. To maximize economic profits today, how many bricks should this firm produce today?

23-7. Suppose that a firm in a perfectly competitive industry finds that at its current output rate, marginal revenue exceeds the minimum average total cost of producing any feasible rate of output. Furthermore, the firm is producing an output rate at which marginal cost is less than the average total cost at that rate of output. Is the firm maximizing its economic profits? Why or why not?

23-8. A perfectly competitive industry is initially in a short-run equilibrium in which all firms are earning zero economic profits but in which firms are operating below their minimum efficient scale. Explain the long-run adjustments that will take place for the industry to attain long-run equilibrium with firms operating at their minimum efficient scale.

23-9. Two years ago, a large number of firms entered a market in which existing firms had been earning positive economic profits. By the end of last year, the typical firm in this industry had begun earning negative economic profits. No other events occurred in this market during the past two years.

a. Explain the adjustment process that occurred last year.

b. Predict what adjustments will take place in this market beginning this year, other things being equal.

23-10. The minimum feasible long-run average cost for firms in a perfectly competitive industry is $40 per unit. If every firm in the industry currently is producing an output consistent with a long-run equilibrium, what is the marginal cost incurred by each firm? What is the market price?

23-11. In several markets for digital devices that can be viewed as perfectly competitive, steady increases in demand for the required minerals ultimately have generated long-run reductions in the market prices of these devices. Describe in words the types of adjustments that must have occurred in these markets to have brought about this outcome, and evaluate whether such digital-device industries are increasing-, constant-, or decreasing-cost industries.

23-12. In several perfectly competitive markets for minerals used as inputs in digital devices, persistent increases in demand eventually have generated long-run increases in the market prices of these devices. Describe in words the types of adjustments that must have occurred in these markets to have brought about this outcome, and evaluate whether such digital-device industries are increasing-, constant-, or decreasing-cost industries.

23-13. Suppose that the firm with the costs and revenues tabulated in Figure 23-2 is contemplating whether to produce 12 units of output. If it were to produce this many units, what (if anything) would happen to the market price? What would be the firm's marginal revenue for the 12th unit produced? What would be the firm's total revenues per hour?

23-14. Consider the firm discussed in Problem 23-13. If the firm were to produce the 12th unit and thereby incur hourly total costs of $65, what would be its marginal cost? Based on this answer and your answers to Problem 23-13, would producing 12 units maximize the firm's profits? What would be its hourly economic profits?

23-15. Take a look at Figure 23-3. This figure uses the data in the table from Figure 23-2, which indicates that the area of the blue rectangle displaying hourly economic profits is $5 per period. What prevents this firm from continuing to produce the same number of units per hour but raising the price that it charges for each unit in order to enlarge the area of the profit rectangle?

23-16. Consider Figure 23-5, and suppose that the price per unit corresponding to the position of d_1 is at $4.50 per unit and that the quantity at point E_1 is exactly 7 units per hour. Calculate total revenues, total costs, and economic profits at point E_1 and explain why it is called the short-run break-even point.

23-17. Take a look at Figure 23-5, and suppose that the price per unit corresponding to the position of d_2 is at $2.50 per unit and that the quantity at point E_2 is exactly 5 units per hour. Calculate total revenues and total variable costs at point E_2 and explain why it is called the short-run shutdown point.

23-18. Consider Figure 23-8. Why does the output rate in panel (b) remain at q_e units per hour even if the position of the AC curve shifts from AC_1 to AC_3 following an increase in fixed costs, and how do we know that economic profits then become negative?

REFERENCES

AI—DECISION MAKING THROUGH DATA: Accessing All Relevant Information for "Dynamic Pricing"

"Dynamic Pricing: Hard to Compete with AI on Pricing," Coresight Research (https://www.fungglobalretailtech.com/research/dynamic-pricing-hard-compete-ai-pricing/), 2019.

"Dynamic Pricing: In-Depth Guide to Improved Margins," AIMultiple.com (https://blog.aimultiple.com/dynamic-pricing/), 2019.

Bill Waid, "AI-Enabled Personalization: The New Frontier in Dynamic Pricing," *Forbes*, July 9, 2018.

INTERNATIONAL EXAMPLE: Reallocating Quarters and Deck Space Transforms Ocean Freighters into Partial Cruise Ships

"Cargo Ship Voyages," CargoShipVoyages.com (https://www.cargoshipvoyages.com), 2019.

Chris Leadbeater, "The Budget Cruise to New York—Across the Atlantic on a Cargo Ship," *Telegraph*, May 11, 2018.

Friedel Rother, "How to Travel by Cargo Ship Around the World," TransitionsAbroad.com (https://www.transitionsabroad.com/listings/travel/articles/travel-by-cargo-ship-around-the-world.shtml), October 26, 2018.

EXAMPLE: Assessing the Long-Run Industry Supply Curve in the Growing Third-Party Food Delivery Industry

Marc Vartabedian, "Food Delivery Startups Cook Up New Model That's All about the Kitchen," *Wall Street Journal*, January 28, 2019.

Edison Trends, "In U.S. Food Delivery Wars, Grubhub Leads in Market Share with Uber Eats Close Behind; DoorDash Growing Fastest" (https://medium.com/edison-discovers/in-us-food-delivery-wars-grubhub-leads-in-market-share-with-uber-eats-close-behind-doordash-f1d9ffc7b8e5), August 16, 2018.

Sarah Whitten, "As Competition in the Food Delivery World Heats Up, Restaurants Turn to Third Parties to Keep Up," CNBC, March 16, 2018.

ECONOMICS IN YOUR LIFE: For Urban Farmers, Industry Entry May Be Relatively Unimpeded but Still Entails a Key Expense

Miguel Altieri, "How Urban Agriculture Can Improve Food Security in U.S. Cities," Phys.org (https://phys.org/news/2019-02-urban-agriculture-food-cities.html), February 13, 2019.

Cat Modlin-Jackson, "In Houston, the Promise and the Challenge of Urban Farming," *Urban Edge*, Rice-Kinder Institute for Urban Research, August 16, 2018.

Laurie Winkless, "The Rise of the Urban Rooftop," *Forbes*, August 10, 2018.

ISSUES & APPLICATIONS: Higher Minimum Wage Rates and Long-Run Equilibrium in the Restaurant Industry

Alexa Lardieri, "New York Restaurants Struggle to Adapt to Higher Wages," *U.S. News & World Report*, January 16, 2019.

Brittany De Lea, "Minimum Wage Hikes Sending Restaurants the Way of the Shopping Mall?" Fox Business, January 15, 2018.

Dara Lee Luca and Michael Luca, "Survival of the Fittest: The Impact of the Minimum Wage on Firm Exit," Harvard Business School Working Paper, August 13, 2018.

24 Monopoly

Paul/Fotolia

LEARNING OBJECTIVES

After reading this chapter, you should be able to:

24.1 Identify situations that can give rise to monopoly

24.2 Describe the demand and marginal revenue conditions a monopolist faces

24.3 Discuss how a monopolist determines how much output to produce, what price to charge, and the amount of its profits

24.4 Understand price discrimination

24.5 Explain the social cost of monopolies

raditionally, city governments have restrained competition in the provision of taxi services by issuing a limited number of taxicab licenses. The governments make these licenses available to taxicab firms at prices that those firms are willing to pay. Because limits on the number of taxicab licenses have restrained the quantity of taxi services provided to consumers, the result has been higher fares that consumers have to pay for rides provided by taxicab firms. Consequently, taxicab firms have been willing to pay relatively high prices to obtain licenses from city government. In this chapter, you will learn why in recent years the prices that taxicab firms have been willing to pay city governments for licenses have declined considerably.

DID YOU KNOW THAT...

in 36 U.S. states, health care providers seeking to open new hospitals confront "certificate of need" laws that require proving that new facilities will not create "too much competition" for existing hospitals? Such laws require approval from regulatory panels, which sometimes include members who have financial interests in existing hospitals. Without such approval, licenses to operate proposed new facilities cannot be obtained. Regulatory approvals often require years of persistent and costly effort. Evidence indicates that certificate-of-need laws deter many health care providers from applying for a license. Many economists argue that the regulatory requirements associated with satisfying certificate-of-need laws for hospitals lie behind the fact that some fast-growing cities and towns are served by only a single hospital. Read on to learn how such legal protections might enable an established hospital to operate as the single seller—a *monopoly*—in a local health care market.

24.1 Identify situations that can give rise to monopoly

Defining and Explaining the Existence of Monopoly

The word *monopoly* probably brings to mind notions of a business that gouges the consumer and gets rich in the process. If we are to succeed in analyzing and predicting the behavior of imperfectly competitive firms, however, we will have to be more objective in our definition. Although most monopolies in the United States are relatively large, our definition will be equally applicable to small businesses: A **monopolist** is the *single supplier* of a good or service for which there is no close substitute.

Monopolist
The single supplier of a good or service for which there is no close substitute. The monopolist therefore constitutes its entire industry.

The Monopolist as the Industry

In a monopoly market structure, the firm (the monopolist) and the industry are one and the same. Occasionally, there may be a problem in identifying an industry and therefore determining if a monopoly exists. For example, should we think of aluminum and steel as separate industries, or should we define the industry in terms of basic metals? Our answer depends on the extent to which aluminum and steel can be substituted in the production of a wide range of products.

As we shall see in this chapter, a seller prefers to have a monopoly rather than to face competitors. In general, we think of monopoly prices as being higher than prices under perfect competition and of monopoly profits as typically being higher than profits under perfect competition (which are, in the long run, merely equivalent to a normal rate of return). How does a firm obtain a monopoly in an industry? Basically, there must be *barriers to entry* that enable firms to receive monopoly profits in the long run. Barriers to entry are restrictions on who can start a business or who can stay in a business.

Barriers to Entry

For any amount of monopoly power to continue to exist in the long run, the market must be closed to entry in some way. Either legal means or certain aspects of the industry's technical or cost structure may prevent entry. We will discuss several of the barriers to entry that have allowed firms to reap monopoly profits in the long run (even if they are not pure monopolists in the technical sense).

Economies of Scale Sometimes it is not profitable for more than one firm to exist in an industry. This is true if one firm would have to produce such a large quantity in order to realize lower unit costs that there would not be sufficient demand to warrant a second producer of the same product.

The Phenomenon of Economies of Scale A situation in which demand is insufficient to allow for more than one producer in a market may arise because of economies of scale. Recall that economies of scale exist whenever proportional increases in output yield proportionately smaller increases in total costs, and per-unit costs drop.

When economies of scale exist, larger firms (with higher output rates) have an advantage. These larger firms experience lower per-unit costs. Their lower expenses enable them to charge lower prices and thereby drive smaller firms out of business.

Natural Monopoly When economies of scale occur over a wide range of outputs, a **natural monopoly** may develop. A natural monopoly is the first firm to take advantage of persistent declining long-run average costs as scale increases. The natural monopolist is able to underprice its competitors and eventually force all of them out of the market.

Figure 24-1 shows a downward-sloping long-run marginal cost curve (LMC). Recall that when marginal costs are falling, average costs are greater than marginal costs. Thus, when the long-run marginal cost curve slopes downward, the long-run average cost curve (LAC) will be above the LMC.

In our example, long-run average costs are falling over such a large range of production rates that we would expect only one firm to survive as a natural monopolist. It would be the first one to take advantage of the decreasing average costs. That is, it would construct the large-scale facilities first. As its average costs fell, it would lower prices and get an ever-larger share of the market. Once that firm had driven all other firms out of the industry, it would raise its price to maximize profits.

Legal or Governmental Restrictions

Governments and legislatures can also erect barriers to entry. These include licenses, franchises, tariffs, and specific regulations that tend to limit entry.

Licenses, Franchises, and Certificates of Convenience It is illegal to enter many industries without a government license, or a "certificate of convenience and public necessity." For example, in some states you cannot form an electrical utility to compete with the electrical utility already operating in your area. You would first have to obtain a certificate of convenience and public necessity from the appropriate authority, which is usually the state's public utility commission. Yet public utility commissions in these states rarely, if ever, issue a certificate to a group of investors who want to compete directly in the same geographic area as an existing electrical utility. Hence, entry into the industry in a particular geographic area is prohibited, and long-run monopoly profits conceivably could be earned by the electrical utility already serving the area.

Natural monopoly
A monopoly that arises from the peculiar production characteristics in an industry. It usually arises when there are large economies of scale relative to the industry's demand such that one firm can produce at a lower average cost than can be achieved by multiple firms.

ECONOMICS IN YOUR LIFE
To contemplate how a state government can prevent entry into a market through legal restrictions, take a look at **So, You Want to Provide Dietary Advice in Florida? Get a License!** on page 533.

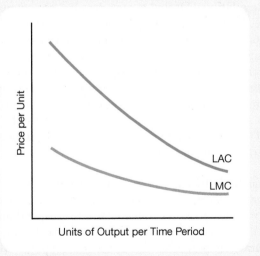

FIGURE 24-1

The Cost Curves That Might Lead to a Natural Monopoly

Whenever long-run marginal costs (LMC) are less than long-run average costs (LAC), then long-run average costs will be falling. A natural monopoly might arise when this situation exists over most output rates. The first firm to establish low-average-cost capacity would be able to take advantage of declining average total costs. This firm would drive out all rivals by charging a lower price than the others could sustain at their higher average costs.

Price per Unit

LAC

LMC

Units of Output per Time Period

To enter interstate (and also many intrastate) markets for pipelines, television and radio broadcasting, and transmission of natural gas, to cite a few such industries, it is often necessary to obtain similar permits. Because these franchises or licenses are restricted, long-run monopoly profits might be earned by the sellers already in the industry.

How does a U.S. city's restriction on licensing of food trucks protect its restaurant owners from competition?

POLICY EXAMPLE

Chicago's Licensing Barriers to Entry Limit Consumers' Access to Mobile Food Treats

During the past decade, the number of food trucks serving barbecue, burgers, cookies, tacos, and other tasty bites to residents of the cities of Portland, Seattle, and Austin has risen from fewer than 1 truck per 100,000 residents to more than 3 trucks per 100,000 residents. Data also indicate an increase in the number of food trucks selling items in many other cities and towns across the United States.

In Chicago, in contrast, the number of food trucks per 100,000 residents has not increased perceptibly over the past decade. The reason is that over this period, Chicago has licensed only about 70 food trucks to serve the city's population of about 2.7 million. By sharply restricting the number of food trucks permitted to operate legally within the city, Chicago protects the city's restaurants from additional competition that undoubtedly would arise if more people were allowed to sell food items from trucks parked along the city's streets.

FOR CRITICAL THINKING

Are the profits of Chicago restaurants higher or lower than they otherwise would be if Chicago were to permit many more food trucks to operate within the city?

Sources are listed at the end of this chapter.

Patents A patent is issued to an inventor to provide protection from having the invention copied or stolen for a period of 20 years. Suppose that engineers working for Apple discover a way to build a digital device that requires half the parts of a regular device and weighs only half as much. If Apple is successful in obtaining a patent on this discovery, it can (in principle) prevent others from copying it. The patent holder has a monopoly. It is the patent holder's responsibility to defend the patent, however. This means that Apple—like other patent owners—must expend resources to prevent others from imitating its invention. If the costs of enforcing a particular patent are greater than the benefits, though, the patent may not bestow any monopoly profits on its owner. The policing costs would be too high.

Regulations During recent decades, government regulation of the U.S. economy has increased, especially along the dimensions of safety and quality. U.S. firms incur hundreds of billions of dollars in expenses each year to comply with federal, state, and local government regulations of business conduct relating to workplace conditions, environmental protection, product safety, and various other activities. These large fixed costs of complying with regulations can be spread over a greater number of units of output by larger firms than by smaller firms, thereby putting the smaller firms at a competitive disadvantage. Entry will also be deterred to the extent that the scale of operation of a potential entrant must be sufficiently large to cover the average fixed costs of compliance.

Tariffs
Taxes on imported goods.

Tariffs Tariffs are special taxes that are imposed on certain imported goods. Tariffs make imports more expensive relative to their domestic counterparts, encouraging consumers to switch to the relatively cheaper domestically made products. If the tariffs are high enough, domestic producers may be able to act together like a single firm and gain monopoly advantage as the sole suppliers. Many countries have tried this protectionist strategy by using high tariffs to shut out foreign competitors.

The Demand Curve a Monopolist Faces

24.2 Describe the demand and marginal revenue conditions a monopolist faces

A *pure monopolist* is the sole supplier of *one* product. A pure monopolist faces the demand curve for the entire market for that good or service.

> *The monopolist faces the industry demand curve because the monopolist is the entire industry.*

Because the monopolist faces the industry demand curve, which is by definition downward sloping, its choice regarding how much to produce is not the same as for a perfect competitor. When a monopolist changes output, it does not automatically receive the same price per unit that it did before the change.

Profits to Be Made from Increasing Production

How do firms benefit from changing production rates? What happens to price in each case? Let's first review the situation among perfect competitors.

Marginal Revenue for the Perfect Competitor Recall that a firm in a perfectly competitive industry faces a perfectly elastic demand curve. That is because the perfectly competitive firm is such a small part of the market that it cannot influence the price of its product. It is a *price taker*. If the forces of supply and demand establish that the price per constant-quality pair of shoes is $50, the individual firm can sell all the pairs of shoes it wants to produce at $50 per pair. The per-unit price is $50, and the marginal revenue is also $50.

Let us again define marginal revenue:

> *Marginal revenue equals the change in total revenue due to a one-unit change in the quantity produced and sold.*

In the case of a perfectly competitive industry, each time a single firm changes production by one unit, total revenue changes by the going price, and price is unchanged.

Marginal Revenue for the Monopolist What about a monopoly firm? We begin by considering a situation in which a monopolist charges every buyer the same price for each unit of its product. Because a monopoly is the entire industry, the monopoly firm's demand curve is the market demand curve. The market demand curve slopes downward, just like the other demand curves that we have seen. Therefore, to induce consumers to buy more of a particular product, given the industry demand curve, the monopoly firm must lower the price. Thus, the monopoly firm moves *down* the demand curve. If all buyers are to be charged the same price, the monopoly must lower the price on *all* units sold in order to sell more. It cannot lower the price on just the *last* unit sold in any given time period in order to sell a larger quantity.

Put yourself in the shoes of a monopoly ferryboat owner. You have a government-bestowed franchise, and no one can compete with you. Your ferryboat goes between two islands. If you are charging $8 per crossing, a certain quantity of your services will be demanded. Let's say that you are ferrying 3 people per hour each way at that price. If you decide that you would like to ferry more individuals, you must lower your price—you must move *down* the existing demand curve for ferrying services. To calculate the marginal revenue of your change in price, you must first calculate the total revenues you received at $8 per passenger per crossing and then calculate the total revenues you would receive at, say, $7 per passenger per crossing.

Perfect Competition versus Monopoly It is sometimes useful to compare monopoly markets with perfectly competitive markets. The monopolist is constrained by the demand curve for its product, just as a perfectly competitive firm is constrained by its

FIGURE 24-2

Demand Curves for the Perfect Competitor and the Monopolist

The perfect competitor in panel (a) faces a perfectly elastic demand curve, *d*. The monopolist in panel (b) faces the entire industry demand curve, which slopes downward.

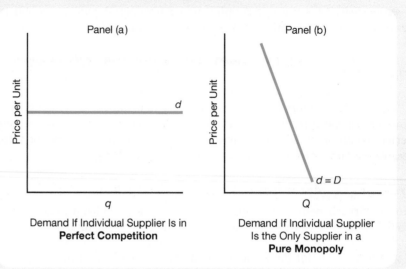

Panel (a)

Price per Unit

d

q

Demand If Individual Supplier Is in
Perfect Competition

Panel (b)

Price per Unit

d = D

Q

Demand If Individual Supplier
Is the Only Supplier in a
Pure Monopoly

demand. The key difference is the nature of the demand curve each type of firm faces. We see this in Figure 24-2.

Here we see the fundamental difference between the monopolist and the perfect competitor. The perfect competitor doesn't have to worry about lowering price to sell more. In a perfectly competitive situation, the perfectly competitive firm accounts for such a small part of the market that the price it receives is independent of its output rate. This is not true for the monopolist.

The more the monopolist wants to sell, the lower the price it has to charge on the last unit (and on *all* units put on the market for sale). To sell the last unit, the monopolist has to lower the price because it is facing a downward-sloping demand curve, and the only way to move down the demand curve is to lower the price. As long as this price must be the same for all units, the extra revenues the monopolist receives from selling one more unit are smaller than the extra revenues received from selling the next-to-last unit.

The Monopolist's Marginal Revenue: Less Than Price

An essential point is that for the monopolist, marginal revenue is always less than price. To understand why, look at Figure 24-3, which shows a unit increase in output sold due to a reduction from $8 to $7 in the price of ferry crossings provided by a monopolistic ferry company. The new $7 price is the price received for the last unit, so selling this unit contributes $7 to revenues. That is equal to the vertical column (area A). Area A is one unit wide by $7 high.

Price times the last unit sold, however, is *not* the net addition to *total* revenues received from selling that last unit. Why? Because price had to be reduced on the three previous units sold in order to sell the larger quantity—four ferry crossings. The reduction in price is represented by the vertical distance from $8 to $7 on the vertical axis. We must therefore subtract area B from area A to come up with the *change* in total revenues due to a one-unit increase in sales. Clearly, the change in total revenues—that is, marginal revenue—must be less than price because marginal revenue is always the difference between areas A and B in Figure 24-3. Thus, at a price of $7, marginal revenue is $4 per unit because there is a $1 per unit price reduction on three previous units. Hence, marginal revenue, $4, is less than price, $7.

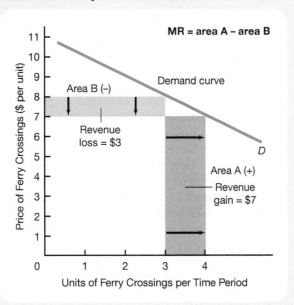

FIGURE 24-3

Marginal Revenue: Always Less Than Price

The price received for the last unit sold is equal to $7. The revenues received from selling this last unit are equal to $7 times one unit, or the orange-shaded area of the vertical column. If a single price is being charged for all units, however, total revenues do not go up by the amount of the area represented by that column. The price had to be reduced on all three units that were previously being sold at an $8 price. Thus, we must subtract the green-shaded area B, which is equal to $3, from area A, which is equal to $7, in order to derive marginal revenue. Marginal revenue of $4 is therefore less than the $7 price.

Elasticity and Monopoly

The monopolist faces a downward-sloping market demand curve. This fact means that the monopolist cannot charge just *any* price with no changes in quantity (a common misconception) because, depending on the price charged, a different quantity will be demanded.

Earlier we defined a monopolist as the single seller of a well-defined good or service with no *close* substitute. This does not mean, however, that the demand curve for a monopoly is vertical or exhibits zero price elasticity of demand. After all, consumers have limited incomes and unlimited wants. The market demand curve, which the monopolist alone faces in this situation, slopes downward because individuals compare the marginal satisfaction they will receive to the cost of the commodity to be purchased. Take the example of a particular type of vehicle, such as a sport utility vehicle (SUV). Even if miraculously there were absolutely no substitutes whatsoever for that SUV, the market demand curve would still slope downward. At lower prices, people will purchase more of those SUVs, perhaps buying SUVs for other family members.

Furthermore, the demand curve for the SUV slopes downward because there are at least several *imperfect* substitutes, such as other types of SUVs, used SUVs, crossover SUVs, hybrid SUVs, and fully electric SUVs. The more such substitutes there are, and the better these substitutes are, the more elastic will be the monopolist's demand curve, all other things held constant.

Costs and Monopoly Profit Maximization

To find the rate of output at which the perfect competitor would maximize profits, we had to add cost data. We will do the same now for the monopolist. We assume that profit maximization is the goal of the pure monopolist, just as it is for the perfect competitor. The perfect competitor, however, has only to decide on the profit-maximizing rate of output because price is given. The perfect competitor is a price taker.

24.3 Discuss how a monopolist determines how much output to produce, what price to charge, and the amount of its profits

Price Searching to Maximize Monopoly Profits

Price searcher

A firm that must determine the price-output combination that maximizes profit because it faces a downward-sloping demand curve.

For the pure monopolist, we must seek a profit-maximizing *price-output combination* because the monopolist is a **price searcher.** We can determine this profit-maximizing price-output combination with either of two equivalent approaches—by looking at total revenues and total costs or by looking at marginal revenues and marginal costs. We shall examine both approaches.

The Total Revenues–Total Costs Approach

Suppose that the government of a small town located in a remote desert area grants a single satellite television company the right to offer services within its jurisdiction. It enforces rules that prevent other firms from offering television services. We show demand (weekly rate of output and price per unit), revenues, costs, and other data in panel (a) of Figure 24-4. In column 3, we see total revenues for this satellite TV service monopolist, and in column 4, we see total costs. We can transfer these two columns to panel (b). The fundamental difference between the total revenue and total cost diagram in panel (b) and one we showed for a perfect competitor in an earlier chapter is that the total revenue line is no longer straight. Rather, it curves. For any given demand curve, in order to sell more, the monopolist must lower the price. This reflects the fact that the basic difference between a monopolist and a perfect competitor has to do with the demand curve for the two types of firms. The monopolist faces a downward-sloping demand curve.

Profit maximization involves maximizing the positive difference between total revenues and total costs. This occurs at an output rate of between 9 and 10 units per week.

The Marginal Revenue–Marginal Cost Approach

Profit maximization will also occur where marginal revenue equals marginal cost. This is as true for a monopolist as it is for a perfect competitor, although the monopolist will charge a price in excess of marginal revenue.

Equalizing Marginal Revenue and Marginal Cost When we transfer marginal cost and marginal revenue information from columns 6 and 7 in panel (a) to panel (c) in Figure 24-4, we see that marginal revenue equals marginal cost at a weekly quantity of satellite TV services of between 9 and 10 units. Profit maximization must occur at the same output as in panel (b).

Why Produce Where Marginal Revenue Equals Marginal Cost? If the monopolist produces past the point where marginal revenue equals marginal cost, marginal cost will exceed marginal revenue. That is, the incremental cost of producing any more units will exceed the incremental revenue. It would not be worthwhile, as was true also in perfect competition. Furthermore, just as in the case of perfect competition, if the monopolist produces less than that, it is not making maximum profits.

Look at output rate Q_1 in Figure 24-5. Here the monopolist's marginal revenue is at A, but marginal cost is at B. Marginal revenue exceeds marginal cost on the last unit sold. The profit for that *particular* unit, Q_1, is equal to the vertical difference between A and B, or the difference between marginal revenue and marginal cost. The monopolist would be foolish to stop at output rate Q_1 because if output is increased, marginal revenue will still exceed marginal cost, and therefore total profits will be increased by selling more. In fact, the profit-maximizing monopolist will continue to increase output and sales until marginal revenue equals marginal cost, which is at output rate Q_m.

The monopolist won't produce at rate Q_2 because here, as we see, marginal costs are C and marginal revenues are F. The difference between C and F represents the *reduction* in total profits from producing that additional unit. Total profits will rise as the monopolist reduces its rate of output back toward Q_m.

FIGURE 24-4

Monopoly Costs, Revenues, and Profits

In panel (a), we give demand (weekly satellite television services and price), revenues, costs, and other relevant data. As shown in panel (b), the satellite TV monopolist maximizes profits where the positive difference between TR and TC is greatest. This is at an output rate of between 9 and 10 units per week. Put another way, profit maximization occurs where marginal revenue equals marginal cost, as shown in panel (c). This is at the same weekly service rate of between 9 and 10 units. (The MC curve must cut the MR curve from below.)

Panel (a)

(1) Output (units)	(2) Price per Unit	(3) Total Revenues (TR) (3) = (2) x (1)	(4) Total Costs (TC)	(5) Total Profit (5) = (3) − (4)	(6) Marginal Cost (MC)	(7) Marginal Revenue (MR)
0	$8.00	$ .00	$10.00	−$10.00		
					$4.00	$7.80
1	7.80	7.80	14.00	−6.20		
					3.50	7.40
2	7.60	15.20	17.50	−2.30		
					3.25	7.00
3	7.40	22.20	20.75	1.45		
					3.05	6.60
4	7.20	28.80	23.80	5.00		
					2.90	6.20
5	7.00	35.00	26.70	8.30		
					2.80	5.80
6	6.80	40.80	29.50	11.30		
					2.75	5.40
7	6.60	46.20	32.25	13.95		
					2.85	5.00
8	6.40	51.20	35.10	16.10		
					3.20	4.60
9	6.20	55.80	38.30	17.50		
					4.40	4.20
10	6.00	60.00	42.70	17.30		
					6.00	3.80
11	5.80	63.80	48.70	15.10		
					9.00	3.40
12	5.60	67.20	57.70	9.50		

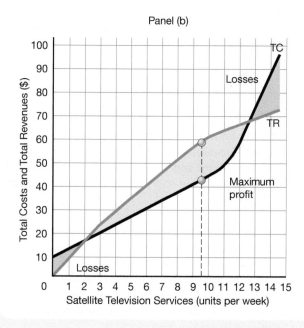

Panel (b)

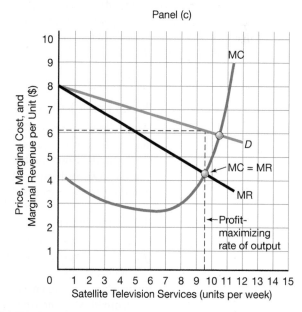

Panel (c)

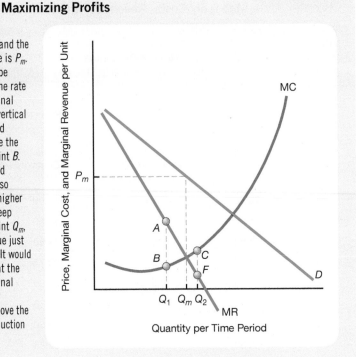

FIGURE 24-5

Maximizing Profits

The profit-maximizing production rate is Q_m, and the profit-maximizing price is P_m. The monopolist would be unwise to produce at the rate Q_1 because here marginal revenue would be the vertical distance to point A, and marginal cost would be the vertical distance to point B. Marginal revenue would exceed marginal cost, so profit would rise with higher output. The firm will keep producing until the point Q_m, where marginal revenue just equals marginal cost. It would be foolish to produce at the rate Q_2, for here marginal cost exceeds marginal revenue. It would behoove the monopolist to cut production back to Q_m.

WHAT HAPPENS WHEN...

the demand curve faced by a monopolist shifts rightward and the monopolist wishes to determine how many units to produce to maximize economic profits?

The marginal revenue curve is derived from the demand curve for the monopolist's product. Hence, a rightward shift in the demand curve brings about a rightward shift in the monopolist's marginal revenue curve. The monopolist must take this fact into account following an increase in the demand for the product that it sells. The firm must then search anew for the profit-maximizing, *higher* rate of output at which marginal revenue equals marginal cost.

What Price to Charge for Output?

How does the monopolist set prices? We know the quantity is set at the point at which marginal revenue equals marginal cost. The monopolist then finds out how much can be charged—how much consumers are willing and able to pay—for that particular quantity, Q_m, in Figure 24-5. The monopolist does so by identifying the price corresponding to the quantity Q_m on its demand curve.

The Monopoly Price We know that the demand curve shows the *maximum* price for which a given quantity can be sold. This means that our monopolist knows that to sell Q_m, it can charge only P_m because that is the price at which that specific quantity, Q_m, is demanded. This price is found by drawing a vertical line from the quantity, Q_m, to the market demand curve. Where that line hits the market demand curve, the price is determined. We find that price by drawing a horizontal line from the demand curve to the price axis. Doing that gives us the profit-maximizing price, P_m.

In our example, at a profit-maximizing quantity of satellite TV services of between 9 and 10 units in Figure 24-4, the firm can charge a maximum price of just over $6 and still sell all the services it provides, all at the same price.

The basic procedure for finding the profit-maximizing price-quantity combination for the monopolist is first to determine the profit-maximizing rate of output, by either the total revenue–total cost method or the marginal revenue–marginal cost method. Then it is possible to determine by use of the demand curve, D, the maximum price that can be charged to sell that output.

Real-World Informational Limitations Don't get the impression that just because we are able to draw an exact demand curve in Figures 24-4 and 24-5, real-world monopolists have such perfect information. The process of price searching by a less-than-perfect competitor is just that—a process. A monopolist can only estimate the actual demand curve and therefore can make only an educated guess when it sets its profit-maximizing price. This is not a problem for the perfect competitor because price is given already by the intersection of market demand and market supply. The monopolist, in contrast, reaches the profit-maximizing output-price combination by trial and error.

How might new data-analytics techniques be assisting monopoly firms in their efforts to search for the profit-maximizing price from one point in time to the next?

 AI | DECISION MAKING THROUGH DATA

Using "Dynamic Clustering Analysis" to Maximize Profits

Traditionally, a fundamental problem faced by a monopoly firm that continuously searches for the profit-maximizing price is ascertaining the position and shape of the demand curve for its product at any given time. Today, a number of companies are experimenting with utilizing apps that learn from experience via "dynamic clustering analysis" of data from previous and on-going customer transactions.

Among firms using such AI apps are electricity providers. When a producer of electricity experiences flows of customer transactions at past and current prices, the apps separate the information into clusters of transactions called "microgrids." The app analyzes the data to infer information about customers' demands for its product. The firm requires

this information, of course, to determine the position and shape of its marginal revenue curve over time. By equating inferred values of marginal revenue at any given time with its known marginal cost, the firm can determine its profit-maximizing output. Then the firm can utilize the information about its customers' demand for its product to search for, determine, and establish its current profit-maximizing price.

FOR CRITICAL THINKING

Why is the "dynamic"—meaning "in motion over time"—nature of demand a fundamental aspect of any monopoly's problem in searching for the price that maximizes its profit during a given period?

Sources are listed at the end of this chapter.

Calculating Monopoly Profit

We have talked about the monopolist's profit. We have yet to indicate how much profit the monopolist makes, which we do in Figure 24-6.

The Graphical Depiction of Monopoly Profits We have actually shown total profits in column 5 of panel (a) in Figure 24-4. We can also find total profits by adding an average total cost curve to panel (c) of that figure, as shown in Figure 24-6. When we add the average total cost curve, we find that the profit a monopolist makes is equal to the green-shaded area—or total revenues $(P_m \times Q_m)$ minus total costs $(\text{ATC} \times Q_m)$.

Given the demand curve and that all units are sold at the same price, a monopolist cannot make greater profits than those shown by the green-shaded area. The monopolist is maximizing profits where marginal cost equals marginal revenue. If the monopolist produces less than that, it will forfeit some profits. If the monopolist produces more than that, it will also forfeit some profits.

Just Because You Have a Monopoly Does Not Mean You Will Be Guaranteed Profits The term *monopoly* conjures up the notion of a greedy firm ripping off the public and making exorbitant profits. Just because you somehow have a monopoly does not guarantee high profits. Numerous monopolies have gone bankrupt. Figure 24-7 shows the monopolist's demand curve as D and the resultant marginal revenue curve as MR. It does not matter at what rate of output this particular monopolist operates. Total costs cannot be covered.

FIGURE 24-6

Monopoly Profit

We find monopoly profit by subtracting total costs from total revenues at a quantity of satellite TV services of between 9 and 10 units per week, labeled Q_m, which is the profit-maximizing rate of output for the satellite TV monopolist. The profit-maximizing price is therefore slightly more than $6 per week and is labeled P_m. Monopoly profit is given by the green-shaded area, which is equal to total revenues ($P_m \times Q_m$) minus total costs ($ATC \times Q_m$). This diagram is similar to panel (c) of Figure 24-4, with the short-run average total cost curve (ATC) added.

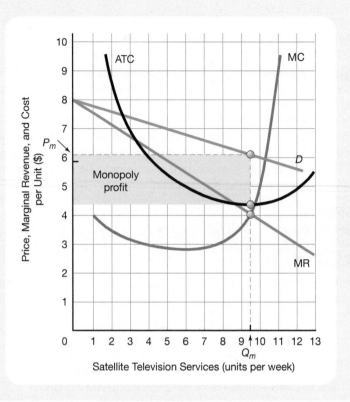

Look at the position of the average total cost curve. It lies everywhere above D. Thus, there is no price-output combination that will allow the monopolist even to cover costs, much less earn profits. This monopolist will, in the short run, suffer economic losses as shown by the red-shaded area. The graph in Figure 24-7, which

FIGURE 24-7

Monopolies: Not Always Profitable

Some monopolists face the situation shown here. The average total cost curve, ATC, is everywhere above the demand curve, D. In the short run, the monopolist will produce where $MC = MR$ at point A. Output Q_m will be sold at price P_m, but average total cost per unit is C_1. Losses are the red-shaded rectangle. Eventually, the monopolist will go out of business.

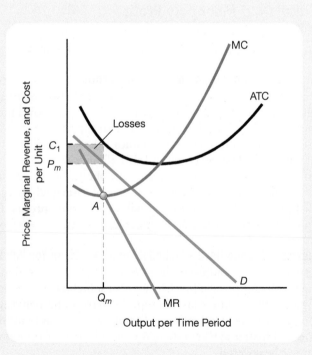

applies to many inventions, depicts a situation of monopoly. The owner of a patented invention or discovery has a pure legal monopoly, but the demand and cost curves are such that production is not profitable. Every year at inventors' conventions, one can see many inventions that have never been put into production because they were deemed "uneconomic" by potential producers and users.

On Making Higher Profits: Price Discrimination

24.4 Understand price discrimination

In a perfectly competitive market, each buyer is charged the same price for every constant-quality unit of the particular commodity (corrected for differential transportation charges). Because the product is homogeneous and we also assume full knowledge on the part of the buyers, a difference in price cannot exist. Any seller of the product who tried to charge a price higher than the going market price would find that no one would purchase it from that seller.

In this chapter, we have assumed until now that the monopolist charged all consumers the same price for all units. A monopolist, however, may be able to charge different people different prices or different unit prices for successive units sought by a given buyer. When there is no difference in the marginal cost of producing and distributing an item, such strategies are called **price discrimination.** A firm will engage in price discrimination whenever feasible to increase profits. A price-discriminating firm is able to charge some customers more than other customers.

It must be made clear at the outset that charging different prices to different people or for different units to reflect differences in costs of production does not amount to price discrimination. This is **price differentiation:** differences in price that reflect differences in marginal cost.

We can also say that a uniform price does not necessarily indicate an absence of price discrimination. Charging all customers the same price when production costs vary by customer is actually a situation of price discrimination.

Price discrimination

Selling a given product at more than one price, with the price difference being unrelated to differences in marginal cost.

Price differentiation

Establishing different prices for similar products to reflect differences in marginal cost in providing those commodities to different groups of buyers.

Necessary Conditions for Price Discrimination

Three conditions are necessary for price discrimination to exist:

1. The firm must face a downward-sloping demand curve.

2. The firm must be able to readily (and cheaply) identify buyers or groups of buyers with predictably different elasticities of demand.

3. The firm must be able to prevent resale of the product or service among customers.

How can companies utilize AI techniques to engage in price discrimination?

AI | DECISION MAKING THROUGH DATA

Price Discrimination via "Personalized Pricing"

One of the necessary conditions for the existence of price discrimination is for firms to be able to easily and inexpensively identify buyers or groups of buyers with predictably different price elasticities of demand. AI techniques including big data analysis and machine learning are enabling a larger array of companies to utilize information about customers gleaned from purchase patterns and visits to Internet sites.

Indeed, some companies have begun using such techniques to engage in "personalized pricing," or charging different prices to individual consumers. Personalized pricing is most readily implemented online via websites that do not provide price lists but instead require consumers to enter personalized requests for information about prices of listed products. After correlating the personalized requests with previous data about the customer, an automated system calculates the appropriate profit-maximizing price to quote to that individual.

REAL APPLICATION

If you regularly purchase items online via Amazon, how can you check to see if the company is engaging in personalized price discrimination?

Sources are listed at the end of this chapter.

24.5 Explain the social cost of monopolies

The Social Cost of Monopolies

Let's run a little experiment. We will start with a purely competitive industry with numerous firms, each one unable to affect the price of its product. The supply curve of the industry is equal to the horizontal sum of the marginal cost curves of the individual producers above their respective minimum average variable costs. In panel (a) of Figure 24-8, we show the market demand curve and the market supply curve in a perfectly competitive situation. The perfectly competitive price in equilibrium is equal to P_e, and the equilibrium quantity at that price is equal to Q_e. Each individual perfect competitor faces a demand curve (not shown) that is coincident with the price line P_e. No individual supplier faces the market demand curve, D.

Comparing Monopoly with Perfect Competition

Now let's assume that a monopolist comes in and buys up every single perfect competitor in the industry. In so doing, we'll assume that monopolization does not affect any of the marginal cost curves or demand. We can therefore redraw D and S in panel (b) of Figure 24-8, exactly the same as in panel (a).

The Monopolist's Price and Quantity How does this monopolist decide how much to charge and how much to produce? If the monopolist is profit maximizing, it is going to look at the marginal revenue curve, MR, and produce at the output where marginal revenue equals marginal cost.

What, though, is the marginal cost curve in panel (b) of Figure 24-8? It is S, because we said that S was equal to the horizontal summation of the portions of the individual marginal cost curves above each firm's respective minimum average variable cost. The monopolist therefore produces quantity Q_m, and sells it at price P_m.

FIGURE 24-8

The Effects of Monopolizing an Industry

In panel (a), we show a perfectly competitive situation in which equilibrium is established at the intersection of D and S at point E. The equilibrium price is P_e and the equilibrium quantity is Q_e. Each individual perfectly competitive producer faces a demand curve that is perfectly elastic at the market clearing price, P_e. What happens if the industry is suddenly monopolized? We assume that the costs stay the same. All that changes is that the monopolist now faces the entire downward-sloping demand curve. In panel (b), we draw the marginal revenue curve, MR. Marginal cost is S because that is the horizontal summation of all the individual marginal cost curves. The monopolist therefore produces at Q_m and charges price P_m. This price P_m in panel (b) is higher than P_e in panel (a), and Q_m is less than Q_e.

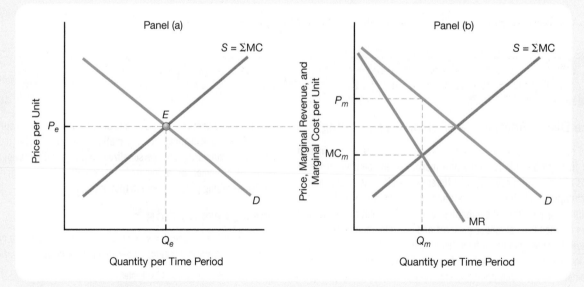

Monopoly versus Perfect Competition Notice that Q_m is less than Q_e and that P_m is greater than P_e. Hence, a monopolist produces a smaller quantity and sells it at a higher price. This is the reason usually given when economists criticize monopolists. Monopolists raise the price and restrict production, compared to a perfectly competitive situation.

For a monopolist's product, consumers pay a price that exceeds the marginal cost of production. Resources are misallocated in such a situation—too few resources are being used in the monopolist's industry, and too many are used elsewhere. (See Appendix G on deadweight loss at the end of this chapter.)

Implications of Higher Monopoly Prices

Notice from Figure 24-8 that by setting $MR = MC$, the monopolist produces at a rate of output where P is greater than MC (compare P_m to MC_m). The marginal cost of a commodity (MC) represents what society had to give up in order to obtain the last unit produced. Price, by contrast, represents what buyers are willing to pay to acquire that last unit.

Underproduction at a Higher Price Because the price of a good indicates the amount that buyers are willing to pay for the last unit produced, that price represents society's valuation of that unit. The monopoly outcome of P exceeding MC means that the value to society of the last unit produced is greater than its cost (MC).

As we have pointed out before, these differences between monopoly and perfect competition arise not because of differences in costs but rather because of differences in the demand curves the individual firms face. The monopolist faces a downward-sloping demand curve. The individual perfect competitor faces a perfectly elastic demand curve.

A Key Assumption Before we leave the topic of the cost to society of monopolies, we must repeat that our analysis is based on a heroic assumption: The monopolization of the perfectly competitive industry does not change the cost structure. If monopolization results in higher marginal cost, the net cost of monopoly to society is even greater.

Conversely, if monopolization results in cost savings, the net cost of monopoly to society is less than we infer from our analysis. Indeed, we could have presented a hypothetical example in which monopolization led to such a dramatic reduction in cost that society actually benefited. Such a situation is a possibility in industries in which economies of scale exist for a very great range of outputs.

ECONOMICS IN YOUR LIFE

So, You Want to Provide Dietary Advice in Florida? Get a License!

For several years, Heather Del Castillo operated a dietary advice business in California. Del Castillo developed a nationwide base of clients who paid her fees to obtain her advice regarding maintaining a healthful diet. To these clients, she came to be regarded as a full-time, paid "health coach."

Then Del Castillo's military husband was transferred to a base in Florida, and she moved her business to that state. After a Florida-licensed dietician learned about Del Castillo's dietary advice business and reported its existence to the state's Department of Health, she received an order to shut down her business and pay a $750 fine. In Florida, anyone offering dietary advice must obtain a state-issued license. The requirements include holding a bachelor's degree in dietetics, completing a 900-hour internship, passing a state examination, and paying a $290 license fee. The Florida government's rationale for the licensing requirement is to protect public health, but from Del Castillo's point of view, its main purpose appears to be to protect existing diet advisers from competition.

FOR CRITICAL THINKING

What is the effect of Florida's licensing requirement on the quantity of dietary advice services provided by sellers located in that state?

REAL APPLICATION

Onerous licensing statutes for the provision of different services exist in many states, and these statutes are increasing in number and complexity. How could you protect yourself from a situation similar to what Heather Del Castillo faced in Florida?

Sources are listed at the end of this chapter.

ISSUES & APPLICATIONS

The Unraveling of Taxicab Monopolies

Paul/Fotolia

CONCEPTS APPLIED

➤ Monopoly

➤ Barriers to Entry

➤ Government Restrictions

In most cities, taxicab firms must buy licenses conferring the legal right to operate taxis within a city's jurisdiction. City governments typically have strictly limited the number of licenses available for purchase. In this way, these governments have established barriers to entry that have restrained competition. The development and growth of ride-sharing services such as Uber and Lyft have provided new forms of competition. The result has been declines in the prices that firms are willing to pay city governments to obtain taxicab licenses.

The Great Run-Up in Prices of Taxicab Licenses

As you have learned in this chapter, barriers to entry enable monopoly firms to restrain their output and search for the profit-maximizing price. In the past, limitations on the number of available taxicab licenses have enabled taxicab firms to engage in exactly this behavior. In the years leading up to around 2013, increased growth of demand for auto transportation services within U.S. cities enabled

taxicab firms to raise the inflation-adjusted prices of their services even as cities continued to restrain the numbers of taxicabs on city streets and highways.

As a consequence, taxicab firms' profits increased, and the prices that they were willing to pay city governments for licenses rose. Figure 24-9 shows that in New York City, the inflation-adjusted prices of "medallions"—physical proof of ownership of licenses to operate individual taxicabs or mini-fleets of such vehicles—rose by more than one-third between 2009 and 2013.

FIGURE 24-9

Inflation-Adjusted Prices of New York City Taxicab Medallions

Until 2013, government restrictions that created a barrier to entry into New York City's taxicab market gave companies incentives to pay higher prices for medallions. After that year, taxicab companies responded to the entry of firms such as Uber and Lyft that provide ride-sharing services by reducing the prices they were willing to pay for medallions.

Sources: New York City Taxi and Medallion Commission and author's estimates.

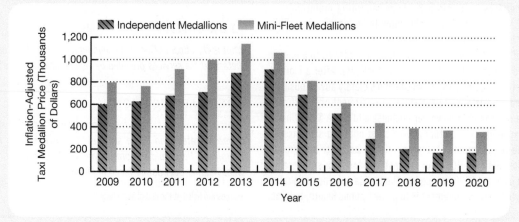

New Competition and a Drop in Prices Taxicab Firms Are Willing to Pay for Licenses

Since around 2013, Uber, Lyft, and other ride-sharing services have considerably expanded their fleets of ride-sharing services that can be arranged via mobile apps. Initially, city governments and licensed taxicab firms engaged in legal actions to prevent this new competition in the provision of auto passenger transportation services. These efforts failed in most locales, however.

One result has been greater volumes of passengers transported by a larger number of vehicles at lower fares. Another result is that the profits earned by traditional taxicab firms consequently decreased. These firms have responded by reducing the prices that they are willing to pay cities for licenses to operate taxicabs. As Figure 24-9 indicates, inflation-adjusted prices of New York City taxicab medallions have been steadily declining.

FOR CRITICAL THINKING

How do you suppose that the substantial increase in profits by traditional taxicab firms between 2009 and 2013 affected the incentive for non–taxi drivers to offer services through ride-sharing firms such as Uber and Lyft?

REAL APPLICATION

Because of competition from Uber, Lyft, and other ride-sharing services, the cost of obtaining a "medallion" to offer legal taxi services has fallen just about everywhere in the United States. Does that mean you should be more interested in purchasing a taxi "medallion" than you would have been when they were sold at much higher prices?

Sources are listed at the end of this chapter.

What You Should Know

Here is what you should know after reading this chapter.

LEARNING OBJECTIVES	KEY TERMS
24.1 Identify situations that can give rise to monopoly *Monopoly, a situation in which a single firm produces and sells a good or service, can occur when there are significant barriers to market entry. Examples of barriers to entry include (1) ownership of important resources for which there are no close substitutes, (2) economies of scale for ever-larger ranges of output, and (3) governmental restrictions.*	monopolist, 520 natural monopoly, 521 tariffs, 522
24.2 Describe the demand and marginal revenue conditions a monopolist faces *A monopolist faces the entire market demand curve. When it reduces the price of its product, it is able to sell more units at the new price, which boosts revenues, but it also sells other units at this lower price, which reduces revenues somewhat. Thus, the monopolist's marginal revenue at any given quantity is less than the price at which it sells that quantity. Its marginal revenue curve slopes downward and lies below the demand curve.*	**Key Figures** Figure 24-2, 524 Figure 24-3, 525
24.3 Discuss how a monopolist determines how much output to produce, what price to charge, and the amount of its profits *A monopolist is a price searcher that seeks to charge the price that maximizes its economic profits. It produces to the point at which marginal revenue equals marginal cost. The monopolist then charges the maximum price that consumers are willing to pay for that quantity. The monopolist's profits equal the difference between the price its charges and its average total cost times the quantity that it sells.*	price searcher, 526 **Key Figures** Figure 24-4, 527 Figure 24-5, 528 Figure 24-6, 530 Figure 24-7, 530
24.4 Understand price discrimination *A price-discriminating monopolist sells its product at more than one price, with the price difference being unrelated to differences in costs. To be able to price discriminate successfully, a monopolist must be able to sell some of its output at higher prices to consumers with less elastic demand.*	price discrimination, 531 price differentiation, 531
24.5 Explain the social cost of monopolies *A monopoly is able to charge the highest price that people are willing to pay. This price exceeds marginal cost. If the monopolist's marginal cost curve corresponds to the sum of the marginal cost curves for the number of firms that would exist if the industry were perfectly competitive instead, then the monopolist produces and sells less output than perfectly competitive firms would have produced and sold.*	**Key Figure** Figure 24-8, 532

PROBLEMS

24-1. The following table depicts the daily output, price, and costs of a monopoly dry cleaner located near the campus of a remote college town.

Output (suits cleaned)	Price per Suit ($)	Total Costs ($)
0	8.00	3.00
1	7.50	6.00
2	7.00	8.50
3	6.50	10.50
4	6.00	11.50
5	5.50	13.50
6	5.00	16.00
7	4.50	19.00
8	4.00	24.00

a. Compute revenues and profits at each output rate.

b. What is the profit-maximizing rate of output?

c. Calculate the dry cleaner's marginal revenue and marginal cost at each output level. What is the profit-maximizing level of output?

24-2. A manager of a monopoly firm notices that the firm is producing output at a rate at which average total cost is falling but is not at its minimum feasible point. The manager argues that surely the firm must not be maximizing its economic profits. Is this argument correct?

24-3. Use the first graph to answer the questions that follow.

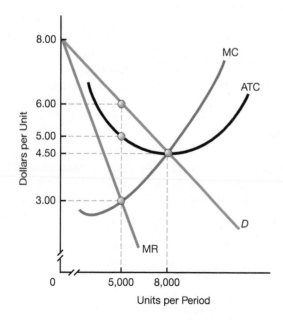

a. What is the monopolist's profit-maximizing output?

b. At the profit-maximizing output rate, what are average total cost and average revenue?

c. At the profit-maximizing output rate, what are the monopolist's total cost and total revenue?

d. What is the maximum profit?

e. Suppose that the marginal cost and average total cost curves in the diagram also illustrate the horizontal summation of the firms in a perfectly competitive industry in the long run. What would the equilibrium price and output be if the market were perfectly competitive? Explain the economic cost to society of allowing a monopoly to exist.

24-4. The marginal revenue curve of a monopoly crosses its marginal cost curve at $30 per unit and an output of 2 million units. The price that consumers are willing to pay for this output is $40 per unit. If it produces this output, the firm's average total cost is $43 per unit. What is the profit-maximizing (loss-minimizing) output? What are the firm's economic profits (or economic losses)?

24-5. A monopolist's maximized rate of economic profits is $5,000 per week. Its weekly output is 500 units, and at this output rate, the firm's marginal cost is $15 per unit. The price at which it sells each unit is $40 per unit. At these profit and output rates, what are the firm's average total cost and marginal revenue?

24-6. Currently, a monopolist's profit-maximizing output is 200 units per week. It sells its output at a price of $60 per unit and collects $30 per unit in revenues from the sale of the last unit produced each week. The firm's total costs each week are $9,000. Given this information, what are the firm's maximized weekly economic profits and its marginal cost?

24-7. Consider the revenue and cost conditions for a monopolist that are depicted in the second figure.

a. If price exceeds AVC, what is this producer's profit-maximizing (or loss-minimizing) output?

b. What are the firm's economic profits (or losses)?

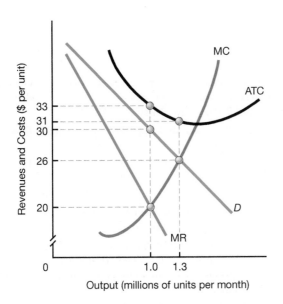

24-8. For each of the following examples, explain how and why a monopoly would try to price discriminate.

  a. Air transport for businesspeople and tourists

  b. Serving food on weekdays to businesspeople and retired people. (*Hint:* Which group has more flexibility during a weekday to adjust to a price change and, hence, a higher price elasticity of demand?)

  c. A theater that shows the same movie to large families and to individuals and couples. (*Hint:* For which set of people will the overall expense of a movie be a larger part of their budget, so that demand is relatively more elastic?)

24-9. A monopolist's revenues vary directly with price. Is it maximizing its economic profits? Why or why not? (*Hint:* Recall that the relationship between revenues and price depends on price elasticity of demand.)

24-10. A new competitor enters the industry and competes with a second firm, which had been a monopolist. The second firm finds that although demand is not perfectly elastic, it is now more elastic. What will happen to the second firm's marginal revenue curve and to its profit-maximizing price?

24-11. A monopolist's marginal cost curve has shifted upward. What is going to happen to the monopolist's price, output rate, and economic profits?

24-12. Demand has fallen. What is going to happen to the monopolist's price, output rate, and economic profits?

24-13. Suppose that in Figure 24-4, the monopolist knows that if it were to reduce the price of its product to $5.40 per unit, the quantity demanded—and hence its output—would rise to 13 units per week. What would be the marginal revenue that the monopolist would derive from producing and selling a 13th unit?

24-14. Consider the information from Problem 24-13. If the total costs of producing 13 units were equal to $72.70 per week, would the marginal revenue of producing the 13th unit (your answer to Problem 24-13) be greater or less than the marginal cost of producing that unit? How would the firm's weekly economic profits be affected if the firm were to produce the 13th unit?

24-15. Take a look at Figure 24-5. Suppose that Q_1 is equal to 25 units of output per time period. If the vertical distance to point A is $10 per unit and the vertical distance to point B is $4 per unit, then by how much does producing the 25th unit of output affect the firm's economic profits?

24-16. Look again at Figure 24-5. Suppose that Q_2 is equal to 35 units of output per time period. If the vertical distance to point C is $6 per unit and the vertical distance to point B is $3 per unit, then by how much does producing the 35th unit of output affect the firm's economic profits?

24-17. Take a look at Figure 24-6. Suppose that Q_m is 9.5 units per week, that P_m is $6.10 per unit, and that the average total cost of producing the 9.5 units is $4.26 per unit. What is the dollar amount of maximized monopoly profits displayed by the green area?

24-18. Suppose that initially the data in Problem 24-17 apply, but then an increase in fixed costs occurs. As a result, the ATC curve in Figure 24-6 shifts upward. Consequently, the average total cost of producing 9.5 units of output rises to $5 per unit. Does the monopolist's profit-maximizing weekly output rise, fall, or remain the same? What is the new amount of maximized weekly economic profits?

REFERENCES

POLICY EXAMPLE: Chicago's Licensing Barriers to Entry Limit Consumers' Access to Mobile Food Treats

Andrew Wimer, "Will the Illinois Supreme Court Free Chicago's Food Trucks?" *Forbes*, February 1, 2019.

"Mobile Food Truck Licenses," City of Chicago Business Affairs and Consumer Protection Department (https://www.cityofchicago.org/city/en/depts/bacp/supp_info/mobile_food_vendorlicenses.html), 2019.

Samantha Bomkamp, "Food Truck Case Against Chicago Heads to State Supreme Court," *Chicago Tribune*, May 30, 2018.

AI—DECISION MAKING THROUGH DATA: Using "Dynamic Clustering Analysis" to Maximize Profits

Bingqian Du, Chuan Wu, and Zhiyi Huang, "Learning Resource Allocation and Pricing for Cloud Profit Maximization," Working Paper, University of Hong Kong, 2019.

Fernando Bernstein, Sajad Modaresi, and Denis Sauré, "A Dynamic Clustering Approach to Data-Driven Assortment Personalization," Working Paper, Duke University and University of Chile, August 2018.

Hao Liu, Nadali Mahmoudi, and Kui Chen, "Microgrids Real-Time Pricing Based on Clustering Techniques," *Energies*, 2018.

AI—DECISION MAKING THROUGH DATA: Price Discrimination via "Personalized Pricing"

"Personalized Pricing: Will It Work?" FocusingFuture.com (http://www.focusingfuture.com/business-solutions/personalized-pricing/), 2019.

Justus Haucap, Werner Reinartz, and Nico Wiegand, "When Customers Are—and Aren't—Okay with Personalized Prices," *Harvard Business Review*, May 31, 2018.

Noah Smith, "Big Data Might Lead to Higher Prices," *Bloomberg*, March 9, 2018.

ECONOMICS IN YOUR LIFE: So, You Want to Provide Dietary Advice in Florida? Get a License!

Academy of Nutrition and Dietetics Commission on Dietetic Registration, "State Licensure: Do I Need to Be Licensed?" (https://www.cdrnet.org/state-licensure), 2019.

Florida Dietetic and Nutrition Practice Council, "Licensing: Application and License Requirements" (http://www.floridahealth.gov/licensing-and-regulation/dietetic-nutrition/licensing/index.html), 2019.

Shoshana Weissmann and C. Jarrett Dieterle, "Why Do You Need a College Degree to Give Diet Advice?" *Wall Street Journal*, February 1, 2018.

ISSUES & APPLICATIONS: The Unraveling of Taxicab Monopolies

"Medallion Transfers," New York City Taxi and Limousine Commission (https:www1.nyc.gov/site/tlc/businesses/medallion-transfers.page), 2020.

Barry Ritholtz, "Taxi Cab Owners and Regulators Created Uber," *Bloomberg*, May 4, 2018.

Ameena Walker, "In New York City, 139 Prized Yellow Taxi Medallions Hit the Auction Block," *Curbed New York*, June 11, 2018.

APPENDIX G

Consumer Surplus and the Deadweight Loss Resulting from Monopoly

You have learned that a monopolist produces fewer units than would otherwise be produced in a perfectly competitive market and that it sells these units at a higher price. It seems that consumers surely must be worse off under monopoly than they would be under perfect competition. This appendix shows that, indeed, consumers are harmed by the existence of a monopoly in a market that otherwise could be perfectly competitive.

Consumer Surplus in a Perfectly Competitive Market

Consider the determination of consumer surplus in a perfectly competitive market (for consumer surplus, see Appendix B). Take a look at the market diagram depicted in Figure G-1. In the figure, we assume that all firms producing in this market incur no fixed costs. We also assume that each firm faces the same marginal cost, which does not vary with its output. These assumptions imply that the marginal cost curve is horizontal and that marginal cost is the same as average total cost at any level of output. Thus, if many perfectly competitive firms operate in this market, the horizontal summation of all firms' marginal cost curves, which is the market supply curve, is this same horizontal curve, labeled MC = ATC.

Under perfect competition, the point at which this market supply curve crosses the market demand curve, D, determines the equilibrium quantity, Q_{pc}, and the market clearing price, P_{pc}. Thus, in a perfectly competitive market, consumers obtain Q_{pc} units at the same per-unit price of P_{pc}. Consumers gain surplus values—vertical distances

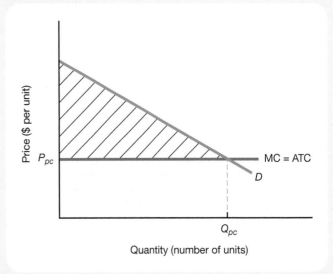

FIGURE G-1

Consumer Surplus in a Perfectly Competitive Market

If all firms in this market incur no fixed costs and face the same, constant marginal costs, then the marginal cost curve, MC, and the average total cost curve, ATC, are equivalent and horizontal. Under perfect competition, the horizontal summation of all firms' marginal cost curves is this same horizontal curve, which is the market supply curve, so the market clearing price is P_{pc}, and the equilibrium quantity is Q_{pc}. The total consumer surplus in a perfectly competitive market is the striped area.

between the demand curve and the level of the market clearing price—for each unit consumed, up to the total of Q_{pc} units. This totals to the entire striped area under the demand curve above the market clearing price. Consumer surplus is the difference between the total amount that consumers would have been willing to pay and the total amount that they actually pay, given the market clearing price that prevails in the perfectly competitive market.

How Society Loses from Monopoly

Now let's think about what happens if a monopoly arises in this market, perhaps because a government licenses the firms to conduct joint operations as a single producer. These producers respond by acting as a single monopoly firm, which searches for the profit-maximizing quantity and price.

Implications of Monopoly for Consumer Surplus

In this altered situation, which is depicted in Figure G-2, the new monopolist (which we assume is unable to engage in price discrimination) will produce to the point at which marginal revenue equals marginal cost. This rate of output is Q_m units. The demand curve indicates that consumers are willing to pay a price per unit equal to P_m for this quantity of output. Consequently, as you learned in this chapter, the monopolist will produce fewer units of output than the quantity, Q_{pc}, that firms would have produced in a perfectly competitive market. The monopolist also charges a higher price than the market clearing price, P_{pc}, that would have prevailed under perfect competition.

Recall that the monopolist's maximized economic profits equal its output times the difference between price and average total cost, or the yellow-shaded rectangular area (labeled monopoly profits) equal to $Q_m \times (P_m - \text{ATC})$. By setting its price at P_m, therefore, the monopolist is able to transfer this portion of the competitive level of consumer surplus to itself in the form of monopoly profits. Consumers are still able to purchase Q_m units of output at a per-unit price, P_m, below the prices they would otherwise have been willing to pay. Hence, the blue-shaded triangular area above this monopoly-profit rectangle is consumer surplus that remains in the new monopoly situation.

Losses Generated by Monopoly

If firms are able to act as a single monopoly, then the monopolist will produce only Q_m units at the point at which marginal revenue equals marginal cost and charge the price P_m. Economic profits, $Q_m \times (P_m - \text{ATC})$, equal the yellow-shaded rectangular area (labeled monopoly profits), which is a portion of the competitive level of consumer surplus (the original striped area) transferred to the monopolist. Consumers can now purchase Q_m units of output at a per-unit price, P_m below the prices they otherwise would have been willing to pay, so the blue-shaded triangular area (labeled total consumer surplus under monopoly) above this monopoly-profit rectangle remains consumer surplus. The green-shaded triangular area (labeled deadweight loss) is a loss in consumer surplus that results from the monopoly producing Q_m units instead of the Q_{pc} units that would have been produced under perfect competition. This is called a *deadweight loss* because it is a portion of the competitive level of consumer surplus that no one in society can obtain under monopoly.

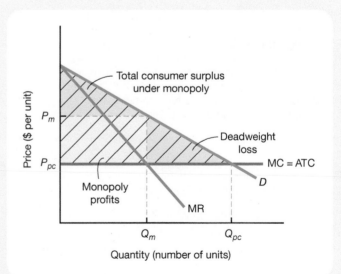

Deadweight Loss

Once the monopoly is formed, what happens to the light-green–shaded (labeled deadweight loss) portion of the competitive consumer surplus? The answer is that this portion of consumer surplus is lost to society. The monopolist's failure to produce the additional $Q_{pc} - Q_m$ units of output that would have been forthcoming in a perfectly competitive market eliminates this portion of the original consumer surplus. This lost consumer surplus resulting from monopoly production and pricing is called a **deadweight loss** because it is a portion of the competitive level of consumer surplus that no one in society can obtain in the presence of monopoly.

Thus, as a result of monopoly, consumers are worse off in two ways. First, the monopoly profits that result constitute a transfer of a portion of consumer surplus away from consumers to the monopolist. Second, the failure of the monopoly to produce as many units as would have been produced under perfect competition eliminates consumer surplus that otherwise would have been a benefit to consumers. No one in society, not even the monopoly, can obtain this deadweight loss.

Deadweight loss
The portion of consumer surplus that no one in society is able to obtain in a situation of monopoly.

25 Monopolistic Competition

LEARNING OBJECTIVES

After reading this chapter, you should be able to:

25.1 Discuss the key characteristics of a monopolistically competitive industry

25.2 Contrast the output and pricing decisions of monopolistically competitive firms with those of perfectly competitive firms

25.3 Explain why brand names and advertising are important features of monopolistically competitive industries

25.4 Describe the fundamental properties of information products and evaluate how the prices of these products are determined under monopolistic competition

As you know, many companies advertise their products. In years past, the bulk of advertisements were transmitted via newspapers, magazines, radio, and television. Today, however, the fastest growing and now one of the most important means of delivering ads to intended audiences is digital advertising via the Internet and other communications networks. What is the economic explanation for advertising? What accounts for the recent shift away from more traditional forms of advertising to advertising transmitted in digital formats? In this chapter, you will find out the answers to these questions.

there are more than 86,000 real-estate brokerage firms and in excess of 2 million realtors in the United States? Most of these brokerages and realtors advertise services that they seek to differentiate from those provided by competitors. In addition to the usual "location, location, location" admonition commonly associated with the real estate industry, another that is often on the lips of many realtors is "perception, perception, perception."

Product heterogeneity—variations in product characteristics—and advertising did not show up in our analysis of perfect competition. They play large roles, however, in industries that cannot be described as perfectly competitive but cannot be described as pure monopolies, either. A combination of consumers' preferences for variety and competition among producers has led to similar but *differentiated* products in the marketplace. This situation has been described as *monopolistic competition,* the subject of this chapter.

Monopolistic Competition

25.1 Discuss the key characteristics of a monopolistically competitive industry

In the 1920s and 1930s, economists realized that both the perfectly competitive model and the pure monopoly model did not seem to yield very accurate predictions regarding various industries. Theoretical and empirical research was instituted to develop some sort of middle ground. Two separately developed models of **monopolistic competition** resulted. At Harvard, Edward Chamberlin published *Theory of Monopolistic Competition* in 1933. The same year, Britain's Joan Robinson published *The Economics of Imperfect Competition*. In this chapter, we will outline the theory as presented by Chamberlin.

Chamberlin defined monopolistic competition as a market structure in which a relatively large number of producers offer similar but differentiated products. Monopolistic competition therefore has the following features:

Monopolistic competition
A market situation in which a large number of firms produce similar but not identical products. Entry into the industry is relatively easy.

1. Significant numbers of sellers in a highly competitive market

2. Differentiated products

3. Sales promotion and advertising

4. Easy entry of new firms in the long run

Even a cursory look at the U.S. economy leads to the conclusion that monopolistic competition is an important form of market structure in the United States. Indeed, that is true of all developed economies.

Number of Firms

In a perfectly competitive industry, there is an extremely large number of firms. In pure monopoly, there is only one. In monopolistic competition, there are a large number of firms, but not so many as in perfect competition. This fact has several important implications for a monopolistically competitive industry.

1. *Small share of market.* With so many firms, each firm has a relatively small share of the total market.

2. *Lack of collusion.* With so many firms, it is very difficult for all of them to get together to collude—to cooperate in setting a pure monopoly price (and output). Collusive pricing in a monopolistically competitive industry is nearly impossible. Also, barriers to entry are minor, and the flow of new firms into the industry makes collusive agreements less likely. The large number of firms makes the monitoring and detection of cheating very costly and extremely difficult. This difficulty is compounded by differentiated products and high rates of innovation. Collusive agreements are easier for a homogeneous product than for differentiated ones.

3. *Independence.* Because there are so many firms, each one acts independently of the others. No firm attempts to take into account the reaction of all of its rival firms—that would be impossible with so many rivals. Thus, an individual producer does not try to take into account possible reactions of rivals to its own output and price changes.

Product Differentiation

Perhaps the most important feature of the monopolistically competitive market is **product differentiation**. We can say that each individual manufacturer of a product has an absolute monopoly over its own product, which is slightly differentiated from other similar products. This means that the firm has some control over the price it charges. Unlike the perfectly competitive firm, it faces a downward-sloping demand curve.

Similar but Distinguishable Goods and Services
Consider the abundance of brand names for smartphones, tablet devices, apps, and most other consumer goods and a great many services. We are not obliged to buy just one type of video game, just one type of jeans, or just one type of footwear.

We can usually choose from a number of similar but differentiated products. The greater a firm's success at product differentiation, the greater the firm's pricing options.

Why are some movie theaters now offering luxury dinners to patrons?

ECONOMICS IN YOUR LIFE

To contemplate methods in which cruise ship lines are finding ways to differentiate their products, take a look at **A Fleet of Cruise Ships Turns to "Star Fleet" and Other Themes to Differentiate Their Services** on page 555.

Product differentiation
The distinguishing of products by brand name, color, and other minor attributes. Product differentiation occurs in other than perfectly competitive markets in which products are, in theory, homogeneous, such as wheat or corn.

EXAMPLE

A New Wave of Product Differentiation Sweeps the Movie Theater Industry

During the 1920s, before the massive U.S. business downturn now known as the Great Depression, many owners of movie theaters chose not to incur the expenses associated with offering sales of food or drinks. During the downturn, however, consumers whose incomes had plummeted flocked to theaters at which they could also purchase low-priced snacks. Ultimately, nearly all of the theaters that survived the Great Depression were those that differentiated their products by offering food and drink concessions.

Today, film chains and independent theaters are competing to further differentiate their products. In addition to offerings that extend well beyond popcorn and other snacks, many theaters now offer wide varieties of food offerings ranging from items on movie-themed menus to luxury dinners. A number have switched from traditional seats to luxury recliners, replaced traditional film screens with virtual-reality systems, and added child play areas. Product differentiation is a fundamental characteristic of the modern movie theater industry.

> **FOR CRITICAL THINKING**
>
> *How might offering cocktails and other drinks, unique food items, alternative viewing options, or more comfortable seats assist a movie theater in distinguishing its service product from those of competitors showing the same films?*

Sources are listed at the end of this chapter.

Product Substitutability and Price Elasticity of Demand
Each separate differentiated product has numerous similar substitutes. This clearly has an impact on the price elasticity of demand for the individual firm. Recall that one determinant of price elasticity of demand is the availability of substitutes: The greater the number and closeness of substitutes available, other things being equal, the greater the price elasticity of demand.

If the consumer has a vast array of alternatives that are just about as good as the product under study, a relatively small increase in the price of that product will lead many consumers to switch to one of the many close substitutes. Thus, the ability of a firm to raise the price above the price of *close* substitutes is very small. At a given price, the demand curve is highly elastic compared to a monopolist's demand curve. In the extreme case, with perfect competition, the substitutes are perfect because we are dealing with only one particular undifferentiated product. In that case, the individual firm faces a perfectly elastic demand curve.

Sales Promotion and Advertising

Monopolistic competition differs from perfect competition in that no individual firm in a perfectly competitive market will advertise. A perfectly competitive firm, by definition, can sell all that it wants to sell at the going market price anyway. Why, then, would it spend even one penny on advertising? Furthermore, by definition, the perfect competitor is selling a product that is identical to the product that all other firms in the industry are selling. Any advertisement that induces consumers to buy more of that product will, in effect, be helping all the competitors, too. A perfect competitor therefore cannot be expected to incur any advertising costs (except when all firms in an industry collectively agree to advertise to urge the public to buy more beef or drink more milk, for example).

The monopolistic competitor, however, has at least *some* pricing power. Because consumers regard the monopolistic competitor's product as distinguishable from the products of the other firms, the firm can search for the most profitable price that consumers are willing to pay for its differentiated product. Advertising, therefore, may result in increased profits. Advertising is used to increase demand and to differentiate one's product. How much advertising should be undertaken? It should be carried to the point at which the additional revenue from one more dollar of advertising just equals that one dollar of additional cost.

Ease of Entry

For any current monopolistic competitor, potential competition is always lurking in the background. The easier—that is, the less costly—entry is, the more a current monopolistic competitor must worry about losing business.

A good example of a monopolistic competitive industry is the app industry. Many small firms provide different programs for many applications. The fixed capital costs required to enter this industry are small. All you need are skilled programmers. In addition, there are few legal restrictions. The firms in this industry also engage in extensive advertising in more than 150 publications directed toward programmers.

What accounts for a difference in the number of "sickness certificates" issued by Norwegian physicians to patients at government-funded emergency centers versus patients at monopolistically competitive private practices?

BEHAVIORAL EXAMPLE

Why Physicians in Norway Behave Differently While Working in Second Jobs at Private Practices

A number of physicians in Norway have two jobs. One job entails employment in emergency centers. A governmental regulatory structure protects Norwegian emergency centers from competition. The other job involves working as physicians in private medical practices. These practices engage in substantial competition with each other for patients, as evidenced by a significant number of such practices, sales promotion and advertising, and easy entry (or exit) of practices in the long run.

Kurt Brekke of the Norwegian School of Economics, Tor Helge Holmas and Karin Monstad of the Uni Research Rokkan Centre, and Odd Rune Straume of the University of Bergen have studied "sickness certificates." These are official forms that physicians working in the two types of jobs issue to patients to provide to employers as excuses for work absences. The researchers find evidence, after controlling for different amounts of time spent in each type of work and for other differences, that these physicians issue about 10 percent more sickness certificates to patients whom they treat in the highly competitive private medical practices than they issue to emergency-center patients. The researchers argue that the physicians issue more sickness certificates while working at private practices in an effort to distinguish themselves from competitors. In effect, the issuance of sickness certificates that enable patients to justify missed hours or days of work functions as a form of sales promotion in a health care industry comprising monopolistically competitive private practices.

FOR CRITICAL THINKING

Why do you suppose that Norwegian physicians in the private sector have adapted individually unique ways of utilizing phone apps that patients use to obtain information about health care recommendations?

Sources are listed at the end of this chapter.

25.2 Contrast the output and pricing decisions of monopolistically competitive firms with those of perfectly competitive firms

Price and Output for the Monopolistic Competitor

Now that we are aware of the assumptions underlying the monopolistic competition model, we can analyze the price and output behavior of each firm in a monopolistically competitive industry. We assume in the analysis that follows that the desired product type and quality have been chosen. We further assume that the budget and the type of promotional activity have already been chosen and do not change.

The Individual Firm's Demand and Cost Curves

Because the individual firm is not a perfect competitor, its demand curve slopes downward, as in all three panels of Figure 25-1. Hence, it faces a marginal revenue curve that is also downward sloping and below the demand curve. To find the profit-maximizing rate of output and the profit-maximizing price, we go to the output where the marginal cost (MC) curve intersects the marginal revenue (MR) curve from below. That gives us the profit-maximizing output rate. Then we draw a vertical line up to the demand curve. That gives us the price that can be charged to sell exactly that quantity produced. This is what we have done in Figure 25-1. In each panel, a marginal cost curve intersects the marginal revenue curve at *A*. The profit-maximizing rate of output is *q*, and the profit-maximizing price is *P*.

FIGURE 25-1

Short-Run and Long-Run Equilibrium with Monopolistic Competition

In panel (a), the typical monopolistic competitor is shown making economic profits. In this situation, there would be entry into the industry, forcing the demand curve for the individual monopolistic competitor leftward. Eventually, firms would find themselves in the situation depicted in panel (c), where zero *economic* profits are being made. In panel (b), the typical firm is in a monopolistically competitive industry making economic losses. In this situation, firms would leave the industry. Each remaining firm's demand curve would shift outward to the right. Eventually, the typical firm would find itself in the situation depicted in panel (c).

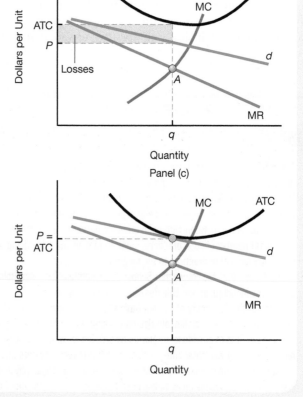

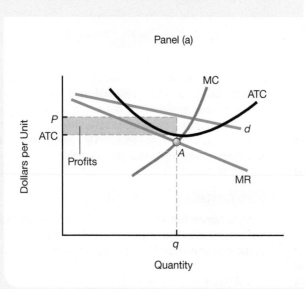

Short-Run Equilibrium

In the short run, it is possible for a monopolistic competitor to make economic profits—profits over and above the normal rate of return or beyond what is necessary to keep that firm in that industry. We show such a situation in panel (a) of Figure 25-1. The average total cost (ATC) curve is drawn below the demand curve, d, at the profit-maximizing rate of output, q. Economic profits are shown by the blue-shaded rectangle in that panel.

Losses in the short run are clearly also possible. They are presented in panel (b) of Figure 25-1. Here the average total cost curve lies everywhere above the individual firm's demand curve, d. The losses are indicated by the pink-shaded rectangle.

Just as with any market structure or any firm, in the short run it is possible to observe either economic profits or economic losses. In either case, the price does not equal marginal cost but rather is above it.

The Long Run: Zero Economic Profits

The long run is where the similarity between perfect competition and monopolistic competition becomes more obvious. In the long run, because so many firms produce substitutes for the product in question, any economic profits (but not accounting profits) will disappear with competition. They will be reduced to zero either through entry by new firms seeing a chance to make a higher rate of return than elsewhere or by changes in product quality and advertising outlays by existing firms in the industry. (Profitable products will be imitated by other firms.)

As for economic losses in the short run, they will disappear in the long run because the firms that suffer them will leave the industry. They will go into another business where the expected rate of return is at least normal. Panels (a) and (b) of Figure 25-1 therefore represent only short-run situations for a monopolistically competitive firm. In the long run, the individual firm's demand curve d will just touch the average total cost curve at the particular price that is profit maximizing for that particular firm. This is shown in panel (c) of Figure 25-1.

A word of warning: This is an idealized, long-run equilibrium situation for each firm in the industry. It does not mean that even in the long run we will observe every single firm in a monopolistically competitive industry making *exactly* zero economic profits, or *just* a normal rate of return. We live in a dynamic world. All we are saying is that if this model is correct, the rate of return will *tend toward* normal—economic profits will *tend toward* zero.

Comparing Perfect Competition with Monopolistic Competition

If both the monopolistic competitor and the perfect competitor make zero economic profits in the long run, how are they different? The answer lies in the fact that the demand curve for the individual perfect competitor is perfectly elastic. Such is not the case for the individual monopolistic competitor—its demand curve is less than perfectly elastic. This firm has some control over price. Price elasticity of demand is not infinite.

Perfect versus Monopolistic Competition We see the two situations in Figure 25-2. Both panels show average total costs just touching the respective demand curves at the particular price at which the firm is selling the product. Notice, however, that the perfect competitor's average total costs are at a minimum.

Average total costs are not minimized for the monopolistic competitor. The equilibrium rate of output is to the left of the minimum point on the average total cost curve where price is greater than marginal cost. The monopolistic competitor cannot expand output to the point of minimum costs without lowering price, and then marginal cost would exceed marginal revenue. A monopolistic competitor at profit maximization charges a price that exceeds marginal cost. In this respect it is similar to the monopolist.

FIGURE 25-2

Comparison of the Perfect Competitor with the Monopolistic Competitor

In panel (a), the perfectly competitive firm has zero economic profits in the long run. The price is set equal to marginal cost, and the price is P_1. The firm's demand curve is just tangent to the minimum point on its average total cost curve. With the monopolistically competitive firm in panel (b), there are also zero economic profits in the long run. The price is greater than marginal cost, though. The monopolistically competitive firm does not find itself at the minimum point on its average total cost curve. It is operating at a rate of output, q_2, to the left of the minimum point on the ATC curve.

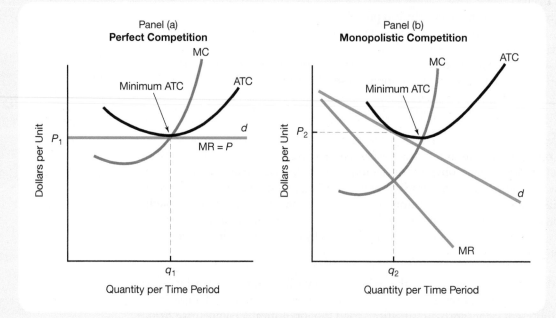

Social "Waste" versus "Differentness" It has been argued that monopolistic competition involves *waste* because minimum average total costs are not achieved and price exceeds marginal cost. There are too many firms, each with excess capacity, producing too little output. According to critics of monopolistic competition, society's resources are being wasted.

Chamberlin had an answer to this criticism. He contended that the difference between the average cost of production for a monopolistically competitive firm in an open market and the minimum average total cost represented what he called the cost of producing "differentness." Chamberlin did not consider this difference in cost between perfect competition and monopolistic competition a waste. In fact, he argued that it is rational for consumers to have a taste for differentiation. Consumers willingly accept the resultant increased production costs in return for more choice and variety of output.

What does a big data analysis reveal about the role of monopolistic competition in explaining significant variations of prices across many similar but distinguishable products?

AI | DECISION MAKING THROUGH DATA

Analysis of Billions of Prices

Considerable evidence has accumulated over the years that prices of similar products sold by large retail stores can vary considerably. Some critics argue that governments should enact regulations to eliminate such price differences. The critics allege that the differences are evidence of widespread success by monopoly firms to vary prices to different consumers of the same product based upon those consumers' differences in willingness to pay (price discrimination). Other observers have suggested that perhaps the price differences mainly reflect variations in costs of distributing and transporting items to various locales.

An alternative explanation has been offered, however, by a big data study conducted by University of Chicago economists Günter Hitsch, Ali

Hortaçsuh, and Xiliang Lin. These researchers examined about 2 *billion* prices of 50,000 products sold at about 17,000 stores operated by 81 companies owning retail chains. The retail-chain firms exhibited considerable competition within local markets. The study found evidence that prices tended to be the same across stores owned by the same retail-chain companies, so differences in prices did not appear to be explained by diverging regional distribution or transportation costs. Instead, the researchers conclude that variations in prices of comparable products mainly reflect differences across the retail chains caused by differences in consumers' preferences for the retailers' similar but distinguishable products. Thus, the researchers' analysis of billions of prices indicates that monopolistic competition involving differentiated products accounts for most price variations.

FOR CRITICAL THINKING

Why might consumers be willing to pay a higher price for a particular firm's product that is "different" from a close substitute sold by a competing company?

Sources are listed at the end of this chapter.

Brand Names and Advertising

> **25.3** Explain why brand names and advertising are important features of monopolistically competitive industries

Because "differentness" has value to consumers, monopolistically competitive firms regard their brand names as valuable. Firms use trademarks—words, symbols, and logos—to distinguish their product brands from goods or services sold by other firms. Consumers associate these trademarks with the firms' products. Thus, companies regard their brands as valuable private (intellectual) property, and they engage in advertising to maintain the differentiation of their products from those of other firms.

Brand Names and Trademarks

A firm's on-going sales generate current profits and, as long as the firm is viable, the prospect of future profits. A company's value in the marketplace depends largely on its current profitability and perceptions of its future profitability.

Table 25-1 gives the market values of firms possessing the world's most valuable product brands. Brand names, symbols, logos, and unique color schemes such as the color combinations trademarked by FedEx relate to consumers' perceptions of product differentiation and hence to the market values of firms. Companies protect their trademarks from misuse by registering them with the U.S. Patent and Trademark Office. Once its trademark application is approved, a company has the right to seek legal damages if someone makes unauthorized use of its brand name, spreads false rumors about the company, or engages in other untruthful activities that can reduce the value of its brand.

TABLE 25-1

Values of Firms with the Top Ten Brands

The market value of a company is equal to the number of shares of stock issued by the company times the market price of each share. To a large extent, the company's value reflects the value of its brand.

Brand	Estimated Value ($ billions)
Amazon	315.5
Apple	309.5
Google	309.0
Microsoft	251.2
Visa	177.9
Facebook	159.0
Alibaba	131.2
Tencent	130.9
McDonald's	130.4
AT&T	108.4

Source: Brand Z Most Valuable Brands Study, 2019.

Advertising

To help ensure that consumers differentiate their product brands from those of other firms, monopolistically competitive firms commonly engage in advertising. Advertising comes in various forms, and the nature of advertising can depend considerably on the types of products that firms wish to distinguish from competing brands.

Direct marketing

Advertising targeted at specific consumers, typically in the form of postal mailings, telephone calls, or e-mail messages.

Mass marketing

Advertising intended to reach as many consumers as possible, typically through television, newspaper, radio, or magazine ads.

Interactive marketing

Advertising that permits a consumer to follow up directly by searching for more information and placing direct product orders.

Search good

A product with characteristics that enable an individual to evaluate the product's quality in advance of a purchase.

Experience good

A product that an individual must consume before the product's quality can be established.

Credence good

A product with qualities that consumers lack the expertise to assess without assistance.

Informational advertising

Advertising that emphasizes transmitting knowledge about the features of a product.

Methods of Advertising Figure 25-3 shows the current distribution of advertising expenses among the various advertising media. Today, as in the past, firms primarily rely on two approaches to advertising their products. One is **direct marketing**, in which firms engage in personalized advertising using postal mailings, phone calls, and e-mail messages (excluding so-called banner and pop-up ads on websites). The other is **mass marketing**, in which firms aim advertising messages at as many consumers as possible via media such as television, newspapers, radio, and magazines.

A third advertising method is called **interactive marketing**. This advertising approach allows a consumer to respond directly to an advertising message. Often the consumer is able to search for more detailed information and place an order as part of the response. Sales booths and some types of Internet advertising, such as banner ads and video clips with links to sellers' web pages, are forms of interactive marketing.

Search, Experience, and Credence Goods The qualities and characteristics of a product determine how the firm should advertise that product. Some types of products, known as **search goods**, possess qualities that are relatively easy for consumers to assess in advance of their purchase. Clothing and music are common examples of items that have features a consumer may assess, or perhaps even sample, before purchasing.

Other products, known as **experience goods**, are products that people must actually consume before they can determine their qualities. Soft drinks, restaurant meals, and haircutting services are examples of experience goods.

A third category of products, called **credence goods**, includes goods and services with qualities that might be difficult for consumers who lack specific expertise to evaluate without assistance. Products such as pharmaceuticals and services such as health care and legal advice are examples of credence goods.

Informational versus Persuasive Advertising The forms of advertising that firms use vary considerably depending on whether the item being marketed is a search good or an experience good. If the item is a search good, a firm is more likely to use **informational advertising** that emphasizes the features of its product. A video trailer for the latest movie starring Scarlett Johansson will include snippets of the film, which help potential buyers assess the quality of the movie.

FIGURE 25-3

Distribution of U.S. Advertising Expenses

Direct marketing accounts for more than half of advertising expenses in the United States.

Sources: Advertising Today; Direct Marketing Today; and Internet Advertising Bureau.

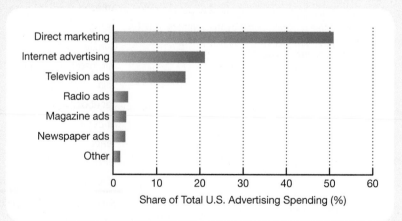

In contrast, if the product is an experience good, a firm is more likely to engage in **persuasive advertising** intended to induce a consumer to try the product and, as a consequence, discover a previously unknown taste for it. For example, a soft-drink ad is likely to depict happy people drinking the clearly identified product during breaks from enjoyable outdoor activities on a hot day.

Persuasive advertising
Advertising that is intended to induce a consumer to purchase a particular product and discover a previously unknown taste for the item.

If a product is a credence good, producers commonly use a mix of informational and persuasive advertising. For instance, an ad for a pharmaceutical product commonly provides both detailed information about the product's curative properties and side effects and suggestions to consumers to ask physicians for help in assessing the drug.

Advertising as Signaling Behavior Recall from an earlier chapter that *signals* are compact gestures or actions that convey information. For example, high profits in an industry are signals that resources should flow to that industry. Individual companies also can explicitly engage in signaling behavior. A firm can do so by establishing brand names or trademarks and then promoting them heavily. Such activity is a signal to prospective consumers that this is a company that plans to stay in business. Before the modern age of advertising, U.S. banks needed a way to signal their financial soundness. To do this, they constructed large, imposing bank buildings using marble and granite. Stone structures communicated permanence. The effect was to give bank customers confidence that they were not doing business with fly-by-night operations.

When Apple advertises its brand name heavily, it incurs substantial costs. The only way it can recoup those costs is by selling many Apple products over a long period of time. Heavy advertising in the company's brand name thereby signals to buyers of digital devices that Apple intends to stay in business a long time and wants to develop a loyal customer base—because loyal customers are repeat customers.

Information Products and Monopolistic Competition

A number of industries sell **information products**, which entail relatively high fixed costs associated with the use of knowledge and other information-intensive inputs as key factors of production. Once the first unit has been produced, however, it is possible to produce additional units at a relatively low per-unit cost. Most information products can be put into digital form. Good examples are operating systems for digital devices, online games, digital music and videos, educational and training software, electronic books and encyclopedias, and office productivity software.

25.4 Describe the fundamental properties of information products and evaluate how the prices of these products are determined under monopolistic competition

Information product
An item that is produced using information-intensive inputs at a relatively high fixed cost but distributed for sale at a relatively low marginal cost.

Special Cost Characteristics of Information Products

Creating the first copy of an information product often entails incurring a relatively sizable up-front cost. Once the first copy is created, however, making additional copies can be very inexpensive. For instance, a firm that sells an online game can simply make properly formatted copies of the original digital file of the game available for consumers to download, at a price, via the Internet.

Costs of Producing Information Products To think about the cost conditions faced by the seller of an information product, consider the production and sale of an online game. The company that creates an online game must devote many hours of labor to developing and editing its content. Each hour of labor and each unit of other resources devoted to performing this task entail an opportunity cost. The sum of all these up-front costs constitutes a relatively sizable *fixed cost* that the company must incur to generate the first copy of the online game.

Once the company has developed the online game in a form that is readable by digital devices, the marginal cost of making and distributing additional copies is very low. In the case of an online game, it is simply a matter of incurring a minuscule cost to place the required files on the company's website.

Cost Curves for an Information Product Suppose that a manufacturer decides to produce and sell an online game. Creating the first copy of the game requires incurring a total fixed cost equal to $250,000. The marginal cost that the company incurs to deliver a copy of the game online is a constant amount equal to $2.50 per game.

Figure 25-4 displays the firm's cost curves for this information product. By definition, average fixed cost is total fixed cost divided by the quantity produced and sold. Hence, the average fixed cost of the first copy of the online game is $250,000. If the company sells 5,000 copies, however, the average fixed cost drops to $50 per game. If the total quantity sold is 50,000, average fixed cost declines to $5 per game. The average fixed cost (AFC) curve slopes downward over the entire range of possible quantities of the online game delivered to consumers.

Average variable cost equals total variable cost divided by the number of units of a product that a firm sells. If this company sells only one copy, then the total variable cost it incurs is the per-unit cost of $2.50, and this is also the average variable cost of producing one unit. Because the per-unit cost of producing the online game is a constant $2.50, producing two games entails a total variable cost of $5.00, and the average variable cost of producing two games is $5.00 ÷ 2 = $2.50. Thus, as shown in Figure 25-4, the average variable cost of producing and selling this online game is always equal to the constant marginal cost of $2.50 per game that the company incurs. The average variable cost (AVC) curve is the same as the marginal cost (MC) curve, which for this company is the horizontal line depicted in Figure 25-4.

Short-Run Economies of Operation By definition, average total cost equals the sum of average fixed cost and average variable cost. The average total cost (ATC) curve for this online game company slopes downward over its entire range.

Recall from a previous chapter that along the downward-sloping range of an individual firm's *long-run* average cost curve, the firm experiences *economies of scale*. For the producer of an information product such as an online game, the *short-run* average total cost curve slopes downward. Consequently, sellers of information products typically experience **short-run economies of operation**. The average total cost of producing and selling an information product declines as more units of the product are sold. Short-run economies of operation are a distinguishing characteristic of information products that sets them apart from most other goods and services.

Short-run economies of operation
A distinguishing characteristic of an information product arising from declining short-run average total cost as more units of the product are sold.

FIGURE 25-4

Cost Curves for a Producer of an Information Product

The total fixed cost of producing an online game is $250,000. If the producer sells 5,000 copies, average fixed cost falls to $50 per copy. If quantity sold rises to 50,000, average fixed cost decreases to $5 per copy. Thus, the producer's average fixed cost (AFC) curve slopes downward. If the per-unit cost of delivering each copy of the game online is $2.50, then both the marginal cost (MC) and average variable cost (AVC) curves are horizontal at $2.50 per copy. Adding the AFC and AVC curves yields the ATC curve. Because the ATC curve slopes downward, the producer of this information product experiences short-run economies of operation.

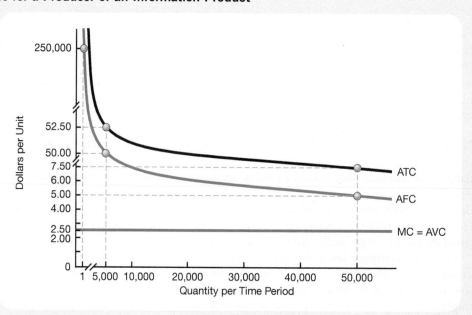

Monopolistic Competition and Information Products

In the example depicted in Figure 25-4, the information product is an online game. There are numerous online games among which consumers can choose. Hence, there are many products that are close substitutes in the market for these games. Yet no two online games are exactly the same. This means that the particular online game product sold by the company in our example is distinguishable from other competing products.

For the sake of argument, therefore, let's suppose that this company participates in a monopolistically competitive market for this online game. Panels (a) and (b) of Figure 25-5 display a possible demand curve for the online game manufactured and sold by this particular company.

Marginal Cost Pricing and Information Products What if the company making this particular online game were to behave *as if* it were a perfectly competitive firm by setting the price of its product equal to marginal cost? Panel (a) of Figure 25-5 provides the answer to this question.

Economic Losses In panel (a) of Figure 25-5, the company sets the price of the online game equal to marginal cost. It will charge only $2.50 per game it sells. Naturally, a larger number of people desire to purchase online games at this price, and given the demand curve in the figure, the company could sell 20,000 copies of this game.

The company would face a problem, however. At a price of $2.50 per online game, it would earn $50,000 in revenues on sales of 20,000 copies. The average fixed cost of 20,000 copies equals $250,000/20,000, or $12.50 per game. Adding this to the constant $2.50 average variable cost implies an average total cost of selling 20,000 copies of $15 per game. Under marginal cost pricing, therefore, the company would earn an average loss of $12.50 (price − average total cost = $2.50 − $15.00 = −$12.50) per online game for all 20,000 copies sold. The company's total economic loss from selling 20,000 online games at a price equal to marginal cost would amount to $250,000.

FIGURE 25-5

The Infeasibility of Marginal Cost Pricing of an Information Product

In panel (a), if the firm with the average total cost and marginal cost curves shown in Figure 25-4 sets the price of the online game equal to its constant marginal cost of $2.50 per copy, then consumers will purchase 20,000 copies. This yields $50,000 in revenues. The firm's average total cost of 20,000 games is $15 per copy, so its total cost of selling that number of copies is $15 × 20,000 = $300,000. Marginal cost pricing thereby entails a $250,000 loss, which is the total fixed cost of producing the online game. Panel (b) illustrates how the price of the game is ultimately determined under monopolistic competition. Setting a price of $27.50 per game induces consumers to buy 10,000 copies, and the average total cost of producing this number of copies is also $27.50. Consequently, total revenues equal $275,000, which just covers the sum of the $250,000 in total fixed costs and $25,000 (the 10,000 copies times the constant $2.50 average variable cost) in total variable costs. The firm earns zero economic profits.

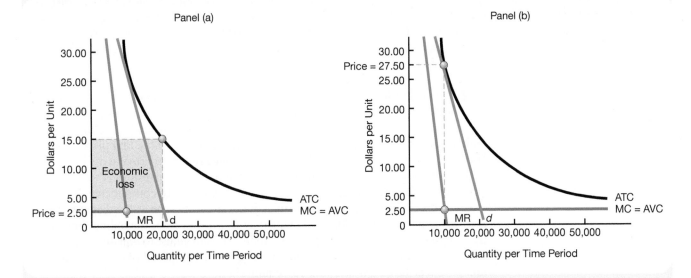

Hence, the company would fail to recoup any part of the $250,000 total fixed cost of producing the game. If the company had planned to set its price equal to the online game's marginal cost, it would never have developed the game in the first place!

Infeasibility of Marginal Cost Pricing The failure of marginal cost pricing to allow firms selling information products to cover the fixed costs of producing those products is intrinsic to the nature of such products. In the presence of short-run economies of operation in producing information products, marginal cost pricing is simply not feasible in the marketplace.

Recall that marginal cost pricing is associated with perfect competition. An important implication of this example is that markets for information products cannot function as perfectly competitive markets. Imperfect competition is the rule, not the exception, in the market for information products.

The Case in Which Price Equals Average Total Cost Panel (b) of Figure 25-5 illustrates how the *price* of the online game is ultimately determined in a monopolistically competitive market. After all entry or exit from the market has occurred, the price of the game will equal the producer's average cost of production, including all implicit opportunity costs. The price charged for the game generates total revenues sufficient to cover all explicit and implicit costs and therefore is consistent with earning a normal return on invested capital.

Given the demand curve depicted in Figure 25-5, at a price of $27.50 per online game, consumers are willing to purchase 10,000 copies. The company's average total cost of offering 10,000 copies for sale is also equal to $27.50 per game. Consequently, the price of each copy equals the average total cost of producing the game.

At a price of $27.50 per game, the company's revenues from selling 10,000 copies equal $275,000. This amount of revenues is just sufficient to cover the company's total fixed cost (including the opportunity cost of capital) of $250,000 and the $25,000 total variable cost it incurs in producing 10,000 copies at an average variable cost of $2.50 per game. Thus, the company earns zero economic profits.

WHAT HAPPENS WHEN...

an author who independently sells an information product—a self-help e-book—and initially earns zero economic profits experiences a large increase in the demand for downloads of the item?

A rightward shift in the author's marginal revenue curve accompanies the rightward shift in the e-book demand curve facing the author. Hence, marginal revenue will now equal marginal cost at a larger profit-maximizing quantity of e-book downloads, and the author will search for a new profit-maximizing price that buyers are willing to pay. The position of the downward-sloping average total cost curve will not have changed. The price therefore will be determined along the new demand curve at a level above the average total cost of providing the larger quantity of downloads. Consequently, the new profit-maximizing price will exceed average total cost, and the author will earn positive economic profits.

Long-Run Equilibrium for an Information Product Industry When competition drives the price of an information product to equality with average total cost, sellers charge the minimum price required to cover their production costs, including the relatively high initial costs they must incur to develop their products in the first place. Consumers thereby pay the lowest price necessary to induce sellers to provide the item.

The situation illustrated in panel (b) of Figure 25-5 corresponds to a long-run equilibrium for this particular firm in a monopolistically competitive market for online games. If this and other companies face a situation such as the diagram depicts, there is no incentive for additional companies to enter or leave the online game industry. Consequently, the product price naturally tends to adjust to equality with average total cost as a monopolistically competitive industry composed of sellers of information products moves toward long-run equilibrium.

ECONOMICS IN YOUR LIFE

Cruise Ships Turn to "Star Fleet" and Other Themes to Differentiate Their Services

Michael Lazaroff, executive director of Entertainment Cruise Productions, looks around the cruise ship in satisfaction. For this Western Caribbean cruise, a number of the ship's passengers are costumed as Andorians, Klingons, Orions, and Vulcans—fictitious extraterrestrial beings from the *Star Trek* series of television shows and movies. Most, however, have donned "Star Fleet" uniforms and are imagining serving on crews of starships instead of being passengers on an ocean cruise liner. William Shatner, the actor who played the role of Captain James T. Kirk in the original *Star Trek* television series, is serving as official host of the cruise, and other actors from the various series also have been signed to make appearances. The ship's elevators have been renamed "starship turbolifts," its restaurants are serving character-themed dishes, and its lounge has been redecorated as a live-performance "holodeck." The ship's auditorium will be featuring *Star Trek* television episodes and movies every night during the cruise.

Lazaroff's "*Star Trek:* The Cruise" is the latest among about 600 "theme cruises" operated by passenger shipping lines. Additional cruise themes are focused on magic acts, rock groups, other television shows, and a variety of alternative sources of inspiration for differentiation of passenger shippers' products: ocean cruises. Lazaroff is particularly pleased with the profitability of "*Star Trek:* The Cruise."

The average fare paid by each of the 2,300 passengers for this six-day cruise is $2,400, more than double the typical price for a comparable, but otherwise ordinary, Western Caribbean cruise. Indeed, this cruise is such a success that Lazaroff already has booked another actor, George Takei, who played the role of Lieutenant Sulu in the original *Star Trek* television series, to serve as host for two more *Star Trek*–themed cruises. Other cruise lines have responded with "superfan cruises" revolving around movies, popular music, professional sports teams, and the like.

FOR CRITICAL THINKING

Are themed cruises likely to be more or less substitutable as compared with traditional oceanic cruises?

REAL APPLICATION

Assume that someday you become the manager of a local restaurant. Would you ever consider "borrowing" the product differentiation techniques of cruise ships for your restaurant?

Sources are listed at the end of this chapter.

ISSUES & APPLICATIONS

U.S. Industries That Differentiate Their Products via Digital Advertising

Denys Prykhodov/Shutterstock

CONCEPTS APPLIED

➤ Monopolistic Competition

➤ Product Differentiation

➤ Advertising

A fundamental distinguishing characteristic of monopolistic competition is product differentiation. A key mechanism that firms utilize to differentiate the products is advertising. During the past decade, U.S. companies have opted to increase the amount of advertising in digital formats. Such ads typically appear on Internet sites and social network pages and are distributed via e-mail, text, and other messages transmitted electronically by firms to customers' digital devices.

The Allure of Digital Advertising

During the early years of digital advertising, companies placed on websites ads that were little different from those appearing in newspapers and magazines. Indeed, some digital ads were simply adapted from ads that appeared in the static paper medium.

Over time, however, companies learned that they could incorporate forms of interactive marketing into their digital advertising. By clicking on ads, viewers could receive informational advertising that provided details about firms' products. Alternatively, viewers could observe commercial messages aimed at persuading them to try the products. Eventually, ads began offering to connect viewers to sites on which they could place online orders.

Digital Ad Spending on the Upswing

As the nature of digital advertising shifted from traditional mass and direct marketing techniques to encompass interactive marketing approaches, the overall extent of digital advertising expanded. Associated spending on digital ads increased markedly. Today, U.S. firms spend more than $100 billion annually on digital advertising.

Figure 25-6 displays how these expenditures are distributed across various types of industries in the United States. Retailing firms that are heavily involved in monopolistically competitive product differentiation are the top spenders on digital ads. Clearly, though, a wide variety of U.S. companies also spend heavily on digital advertising in an effort to differentiate their products.

FOR CRITICAL THINKING

Why might firms perceive that the interactive capabilities of digital advertising could offer more opportunities for immediate boosts to revenues and profits than other forms of advertising?

REAL APPLICATION

You are now in charge of digital advertising for an online dating platform. Would you be better off advertising the vast scope of your platform or, assuming it's true, the narrow focus of your dating service?

Sources are listed at the end of this chapter.

FIGURE 25-6

Percentages of Digital Advertising Expenditures by U.S. Industries

Taken together, retailing, automotive, financial, and telecommunications industries account for more than half of U.S. digital advertising expenditures. Nevertheless, a wide variety of industries utilize digital ads to engage in product differentiation.

Source: eMarketer

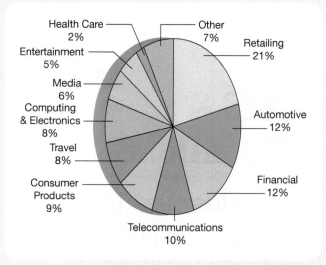

Health Care 2%
Entertainment 5%
Media 6%
Computing & Electronics 8%
Travel 8%
Consumer Products 9%
Telecommunications 10%
Other 7%
Retailing 21%
Automotive 12%
Financial 12%

What You Should Know

LEARNING OBJECTIVES

25.1 Discuss the key characteristics of a monopolistically competitive industry *A monopolistically competitive industry consists of a large number of firms that sell differentiated products that are close substitutes. Firms can easily enter or exit the industry. Monopolistically competitive firms can increase their profits if they can successfully distinguish their products from those of their rivals. Thus, they have an incentive to advertise.*

25.2 Contrast the output and pricing decisions of monopolistically competitive firms with those of perfectly competitive firms *In the short run, a monopolistically competitive firm produces to the point at which marginal revenue equals marginal cost. The price it charges can exceed both marginal cost and average total cost in the short run. The resulting economic profits induce new firms to enter the industry. In the long run, therefore, monopolistically competitive firms earn zero economic profits, but price exceeds marginal cost.*

25.3 Explain why brand names and advertising are important features of monopolistically competitive industries *Monopolistically competitive firms engage in advertising. Informational advertising is used for a search good with features that consumers can evaluate prior to purchase. Persuasive advertising is used for an experience good, with features that are apparent only when consumed. An advertising mix is used for a credence good with characteristics that consumers cannot readily assess unaided.*

25.4 Describe the fundamental properties of information products and evaluate how the prices of these products are determined under monopolistic competition *Providing an information product entails high fixed costs but a relatively low per-unit cost. Hence, the average total cost curve for a firm that sells an information product slopes downward, meaning that the firm experiences short-run economies of operation. In a long-run equilibrium, price adjusts to equality with average total cost.*

KEY TERMS

monopolistic
  competition, 543
product differentiation, 544

Key Figures
Figure 25-1, 546
Figure 25-2, 548

direct marketing, 550
mass marketing, 550
interactive marketing, 550
search good, 550
experience good, 550
credence good, 550
informational advertising, 550
persuasive advertising, 551

information product, 551
short-run economies of
  operation, 552
Key Figures
Figure 25-4, 552
Figure 25-5, 553

PROBLEMS

25-1. Explain why the following are examples of monopolistic competition.

   a. There are a number of fast-food restaurants in town, and they compete fiercely. Some restaurants cook their hamburgers over open flames. Others fry their hamburgers. In addition, some serve broiled fish sandwiches, while others serve fried fish sandwiches. A few serve ice cream cones for dessert, while others offer frozen ice cream pies.

   b. There are a vast number of colleges and universities across the country. Each competes for top

students. All offer similar courses and programs, but some have better programs in business, while others have stronger programs in the arts and humanities. Still others are academically stronger in the sciences.

25-2. Consider the diagram depicting the demand and cost conditions faced by a monopolistically competitive firm.

   a. What are the total revenues, total costs, and economic profits experienced by this firm?

   b. Is this firm more likely in short- or long-run equilibrium? Explain.

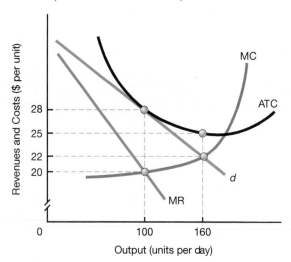

25-3. In a perfectly competitive market, price equals marginal cost, but this condition is not satisfied for the firm with the revenue and cost conditions depicted in Problem 25-2. In the long run, what would happen if the government decided to require the firm in Problem 25-2 to charge a price equal to marginal cost at the firm's long-run output rate?

25-4. Based on your answer to Problem 25-3, is the firm with the revenue and cost conditions depicted in Problem 25-2 charging a price in excess of the minimum price necessary to induce it to provide this good in long-run equilibrium? Explain your reasoning.

25-5. The table depicts the prices and total costs a local used-book store faces. The bookstore competes with a number of similar stores, but it capitalizes on its location and the word-of-mouth reputation of the coffee it serves to its customers. Calculate the store's total revenue, total profit, marginal revenue, and marginal cost at each level of output, beginning with the first unit. Based on marginal analysis, what is the approximate profit-maximizing level of output for this business?

Output	Price per Book ($)	Total Costs ($)
0	6.00	2.00
1	5.75	5.25
2	5.50	7.50
3	5.25	9.60
4	5.00	12.10
5	4.75	15.80
6	4.50	20.00
7	4.00	24.75

25-6. Calculate total average costs for the bookstore in Problem 25-5. Illustrate the store's short-run equilibrium by calculating demand, marginal revenue,

average total costs, and marginal costs. What is its total profit?

25-7. Suppose that after long-run adjustments take place in the used-book market, the business in Problem 25-5 ends up producing 4 units of output. What are the market price and economic profits of this monopolistic competitor in the long run?

25-8. It is a typical Christmas electronics shopping season, and makers of ultra-high-definition TVs (UHDTVs) are marketing the latest available models through their own websites as well as via retailers such as Best Buy and Walmart. Each manufacturer offers its own unique versions of UHDTVs in differing arrays of shapes and sizes. As usual, each is hoping to maintain a stream of economic profits earned since it first introduced these most recent models late last year or perhaps just a few months before Christmas. Nevertheless, as sales figures arrive at the headquarters of companies such as LG, Samsung, Panasonic, and Sony, it is clear that most of the companies will end up earning only a normal rate of return this year.

a. How can makers of UHDTVs earn economic profits during the first few months after the introduction of new models?

b. What economic forces result in the dissipation of economic profits earned by manufacturers of UHDTVs?

25-9. Classify each of the following as an example of direct, interactive, mass marketing, or a combination of these advertising methods.

a. The sales force of a pharmaceutical company visits physicians' offices to promote new medications and to answer questions about treatment options and possible side effects.

b. A mortgage company targets a list of specific low-risk borrowers for a barrage of e-mail messages touting its low interest rates and fees.

c. An online bookseller pays fees to an Internet search engine to post banner ads relating to each search topic chosen by someone conducting a search. In part, this helps promote the bookseller's brand, but clicking on the banner ad also directs the person to a web page displaying books on the topic that are available for purchase.

d. A national rental car chain runs advertisements on all of the nation's major television networks.

25-10. Classify each of the following as an example of direct, interactive, and/or mass marketing.

a. A cosmetics firm pays for full-page display ads in a number of top women's magazines.

b. A magazine distributor mails a fold-out flyer advertising its products to the addresses of all individuals it has identified as possibly interested in magazine subscriptions.

    c. An online gambling operation arranges for pop-up ads to appear on a digital device's screen every time a person uses a media player to listen to digital music or play video files, and clicking on the ads directs an individual to its Web gambling site.

    d. A car dealership places advertisements in newspapers throughout the region where potential customers reside.

25-11. Categorize each of the following as an experience good, a search good, or a credence good or service, and justify your answer.

    a. A heavy-duty filing cabinet

    b. A restaurant meal

    c. A wool overcoat

    d. Psychotherapy

25-12. Categorize each of the following as an experience good, a search good, or a credence good or service, and justify your answer.

    a. Services of a carpet cleaning company

    b. A new cancer treatment

    c. Athletic socks

    d. A silk necktie

25-13. In what ways do credence goods share certain characteristics of both experience goods and search goods? How do credence goods differ from both experience goods and search goods? Why does advertising of credence goods commonly contain both informational and persuasive elements? Explain your answers.

25-14. Is each of the following items more likely to be the subject of an informational or a persuasive advertisement? Why?

    a. An office copying machine

    b. An automobile loan

    c. A deodorant

    d. A soft drink

25-15. Discuss the special characteristics of an information product, and explain the implications for a producer's short-run average and marginal cost curves. In addition, explain why having a price equal to marginal cost is not feasible for the producer of an information product.

25-16. A firm sells all of its e-books relating to do-it-yourself topics (home plumbing, gardening, and the like) at the same price. At present, the company can earn a maximum annual profit of $25,000 when it sells 10,000 copies within a year's time. The firm incurs a 50-cent expense each time a consumer downloads a copy, but the company must spend $100,000 per year developing new editions of the e-books. Under marginal cost pricing, it could sell 100,000 copies.

    a. In the short run, what is the profit-maximizing price of e-books relating to do-it-yourself topics?

    b. At the profit-maximizing quantity, what is the average total cost of producing e-books?

25-17. Take a look at panel (a) of Figure 25-1, and assume that it initially applies to a typical firm in a monopolistically competitive industry. Explain how it might be possible for this firm temporarily to find itself in a situation such as that depicted in panel (b) during the process of adjustment from panel (a) to a final long-run equilibrium as shown in panel (c).

25-18. Take a look at panel (b) of Figure 25-1, and assume that it initially applies to a typical firm in a monopolistically competitive industry. Explain how it might be possible for this firm temporarily to find itself in a situation such as that depicted in panel (a) during the process of adjustment from panel (b) to a final long-run equilibrium as shown in panel (c).

25-19. In what fundamental ways does the monopolistic competitor in panel (b) of Figure 25-2 behave similarly to the perfectly competitive firm in panel (a) in a long-run equilibrium? In what fundamental ways does the monopolistically competitive firm behave differently?

25-20. At every point along the AFC curve in Figure 25-4, what is true of the explicit dollar amount of this firm's total fixed costs at any given point that one might select, such as the three points displayed along the AFC curve in the figure?

25-21. Take a look at panel (a) of Figure 25-5. Suppose that during the relevant time period, the firm's marginal and average variable costs remain unchanged. If the firm had to set the price of its information product equal to marginal cost, what would be the amount of its *economic* profit or loss following the increase in its total fixed costs?

REFERENCES

EXAMPLE: A New Wave of Product Differention Sweeps the Movie Theater Industry

David Bloom, "Cinemark's CEO on VR, Esports, and the Future of Movie Theaters," *Forbes*, February 25, 2019.

Erich Schwartzel, "Comfiest Seat in the House: Struggling Movie Theaters Go Upscale to Survive," *Wall Street Journal*, April 9, 2018.

Alissa Wilkinson, "Why Movie Theaters Are Trading Popcorn and Soda for Chimichangas and Custom Cocktails," Vox (https://www.vox.com/the-goods/2018/9/20/17870760/movie-theater-concessions-dinner-movie-alamo-regal-amc-metrograph), September 23, 2018.

BEHAVIORAL EXAMPLE: Why Physicians in Norway Behave Differently While Working in Second Jobs at Private Practices

European Commission, "Norway: Sickness Benefit and Attendance Allowance" (http://ec.europa.eu/social/main.jsp?catId=1123&langId=en&intPageId=4706), 2019.

"Self-Certified Sickness Absence," New in Norway (http://www.nyinorge.no/en/Ny-i-Norge-velg-sprak/New-in-Norway/Work/Employment/Self-certified-sickness-absenceSick-leave/), 2019.

Kurt Brekke, Tor Helge Homas, Karin Monstad, and Odd Rune Straume, "Competition and Physician Behavior: Does the Competitive Environment Affect the Propensity to Issue Sickness Certificates?" Presentation at Conference on Innovation Economics for Antitrust Lawyers, 2018.

AI—DECISION MAKING THROUGH DATA: Based on Analysis of Billions of Prices

Kay Matthews, "Six Industries That Could See Some Big Changes from Big Data," InsideBigData.com (https://insidebigdata.com/2019/01/25/6-industries-that-could-see-some-big-changes-from-big-data-in-2019/), January 25, 2019.

Leandro Guissoni, Juan Sanchez, and Jonny Rodrigues, "Price and In-Store Promotions in an Emerging Market," *Marketing Intelligence and Planning*, 2018.

Günter Hitsch, Ali Hortaçsuh, and Xiliang Lin, "Prices and Promotions in U.S. Retail Markets: Evidence from Big Data," Marketing Analytics and Big Data Conference Presentation, Columbia University, 2018.

ECONOMICS IN YOUR LIFE: Cruise Ships Turn to "Star Fleet" and Other Themes to Differentiate Their Services

"Star Trek: The Cruise—The Unconventional Voyage," Entertainment Cruise Productions (http://www.startrekthecruise.com), 2019.

Aisha Al-Muslim, "Cruising with Your Idols—and 2,000 Other Superfans," *Wall Street Journal*, August 21, 2018.

Robin Raven, "Geek Road Trip: Five Nerdy Cruises That Let You Geek Out on the High Seas," Syfi.com (https://www.syfy.com/syfywire/geek-road-trip-5-nerdy-cruises-that-let-you-geek-out-on-the-high-seas), August 1, 2018.

ISSUES & APPLICATIONS: U.S. Industries That Differentiate Their Products via Digital Advertising

Dave Chaffey, "Eight Trends in Digital Advertising," Smart Insights (https://www.smartinsights.com/managing-digital-marketing/marketing-innovation/business-critical-digital-marketing-trends/), January 8, 2019.

Dana Feldman, "U.S. TV Ad Spending Drops as Digital Ad Spending Climbs," *Forbes*, March 28, 2018.

"Which Industries Spend the Most on U.S. Digital Advertising?" MarketingCharts(https://www.marketingcharts.com/advertising-trends/spending-and-spenders-105020), July 18, 2018.

26 Oligopoly and Strategic Behavior

dennizn/Shutterstock

LEARNING OBJECTIVES

After reading this chapter, you should be able to:

26.1 Outline the fundamental characteristics of oligopoly

26.2 Explain alternative methods of measuring industry concentration

26.3 Understand how to apply game theory to evaluate the pricing strategies of oligopolistic firms

26.4 Identify features of an industry that help or hinder efforts to form a cartel that seeks to restrain output and earn economic profits

26.5 Discuss network effects and the functions and forms of two-sided markets

In some industries, companies called *platform* firms specialize in linking groups called *end users*. For instance, the radio and television industries link audiences to advertisers who sponsor entertainment programming, and online dating sites link different individuals interested in potentially romantic encounters. In a number of these industries, a few platform firms account for the bulk of industry output and sales. In such industries, decisions made by one firm can affect the choices of others. How do economists examine industries, called *oligopolies*, which are neither purely monopolistic nor perfectly or monopolistically competitive? What special features of industries containing platform firms might make them particularly likely to become oligopolies? In this chapter, you will learn the answers to these questions.

several people recently were sentenced for breaking into a large Canadian stockpile of maple syrup and stealing 3,000 tons of the sticky fluid valued at more than $15 million to sneak across the U.S. border? The storehouse from which the perpetrators pilfered this maple syrup contained barrels of syrup that had been produced by firms throughout Canada. The companies had agreed to withhold the syrup from sale in the market and coordinate distribution of the remaining output. By limiting and coordinating sales of maple syrup production, these firms operated a *cartel*, which is a collusive arrangement under which several firms essentially seek to replicate the production and pricing of a monopolist. A cartel is one possible manner in which a handful of competitors in a market sometimes may attempt to interact. The type of industry structure involving a few competitors, known as an *oligopoly*, is the subject of the present chapter.

26.1 Outline the fundamental characteristics of oligopoly

Oligopoly
A market structure in which there are very few sellers. Each seller knows that the other sellers will react to its changes in prices, quantities, and qualities.

Oligopoly

An important market structure that we have yet to discuss is one in which a few large firms constitute essentially an entire industry. They are not perfectly competitive in the sense that we have used the term. They are not even monopolistically competitive. Also, because there are several of them, a pure monopoly does not exist. We call such a situation an **oligopoly**, which consists of a small number of *interdependent* sellers. Each firm in the industry knows that other firms will react to its changes in prices, quantities, and qualities. An oligopoly market structure can exist for either a homogeneous or a differentiated product.

Characteristics of Oligopoly

Oligopoly is characterized by a small number of interdependent firms that constitute the entire market.

Small Number of Firms How many is "a small number of firms"? More than two but less than a hundred? The question is not easy to answer. Basically, though, oligopoly exists when the top few firms in the industry account for an overwhelming percentage of total industry output.

Oligopolies often involve three to five big companies that produce the bulk of industry output. Between World War II and the 1970s, three firms—General Motors, Chrysler, and Ford—produced and sold nearly all the output of the U.S. automobile industry. Among manufacturers of chewing gum and cigarettes, four large firms produce and sell almost the entire output of each industry.

Strategic dependence
A situation in which one firm's actions with respect to price, quality, advertising, and related changes may be strategically countered by the reactions of one or more other firms in the industry. Such dependence can exist only when there is a small number of major firms in an industry.

Interdependence All markets and all firms are, in a sense, interdependent. Only when a few large firms produce most of the output in an industry, however, does the question of **strategic dependence** of one on the others' actions arise. In this situation, when any one firm changes its output, its product price, or the quality of its product, other firms notice the effects of its decisions. The firms recognize that they are interdependent and that any action by one firm with respect to output, price, quality, or product differentiation will cause a reaction by other firms. A model of such mutual interdependence is difficult to build, but examples of such behavior are not hard to find in the real world. Oligopolists in the cigarette industry, for example, are constantly reacting to each other.

Recall that in the model of perfect competition, each firm ignores the behavior of other firms because each firm is able to sell all that it wants at the going market price. At the other extreme, the pure monopolist does not have to worry about the reaction of current rivals because there are none. In an oligopolistic market structure, the managers of firms are like generals in a war: *They must attempt to predict the reaction of rival firms.* It is a strategic game.

Why Oligopoly Occurs

Why are some industries composed chiefly of a few large firms? What causes an industry that might otherwise be competitive to tend toward oligopoly? We can provide some partial answers here.

Economies of Scale Perhaps the most common reason that has been offered for the existence of oligopoly is economies of scale. Recall that economies of scale exist when a doubling of output results in less than a doubling of total costs. When economies of scale exist, the firm's long-run average total cost curve will slope downward as the firm produces more and more output. Average total cost can be reduced by continuing to expand the scale of operation to the *minimum efficient scale*, or the output rate at which long-run average cost is minimized. Smaller firms in a situation in which the minimum efficient scale is relatively large will have average total costs greater than those incurred by large firms. Little by little, they will go out of business or be absorbed into larger firms.

Legal Barriers to Entry It is possible that certain legal barriers to entry have prevented more competition in oligopolistic industries. These include any governmental restrictions that limit entry into an industry, which include licenses, franchises, tariffs, and specific regulations that push up the costs of entering an industry.

Oligopoly by Merger Another reason that oligopolistic market structures may sometimes develop is that firms merge. A *merger* is the joining of two or more firms under single ownership or control. The merged firm naturally becomes larger, enjoys greater economies of scale as output increases, and may ultimately have a greater ability to influence the market price for the industry's output.

There are two key types of mergers, vertical and horizontal. A **vertical merger** occurs when one firm merges with either a firm from which it purchases an input or a firm to which it sells its output. Vertical mergers occur, for example, when a coal-using electrical utility purchases a coal-mining firm or when a shoe manufacturer purchases retail shoe outlets.

> **Vertical merger**
> The joining of a firm with another to which it sells an output or from which it buys an input.

Obviously, vertical mergers cannot *create* oligopoly as we have defined it. That can indeed occur, though, via a **horizontal merger**, which involves firms selling a similar product. If two shoe manufacturing firms merge, that is a horizontal merger. If a group of firms, all producing steel, merge into one, that is also a horizontal merger.

> **Horizontal merger**
> The joining of firms that are producing or selling a similar product.

Oligopoly, Efficiency, and Resource Allocation

Although oligopoly is not the dominant form of market structure in the United States, oligopolistic industries do exist. To the extent that oligopolists have *market power*—the ability to *individually* affect the *market* price for the industry's output—they lead to resource misallocations, just as monopolies do. Oligopolists charge prices that exceed marginal cost. What about oligopolies that occur because of economies of scale? Consumers might actually end up paying lower prices than if the industry were composed of numerous smaller firms.

All in all, there is no definite evidence of serious resource misallocation in the United States because of oligopolies. In any event, *the more U.S. firms face competition from the rest of the world, the less any current oligopoly will be able to exercise market power.*

Measuring Industry Concentration

> **26.2** Explain alternative methods of measuring industry concentration

As we have stated, oligopoly is a market structure in which a few interdependent firms produce a large part of total output in an industry. This situation is often called one of high *industry concentration*. Before we show the concentration statistics in the United States, let's determine how industry concentration can be measured.

TABLE 26-1

Computing the Four-Firm Concentration Ratio

Firm	Annual Sales ($ millions)	
1	150 ⎫	
2	100 ⎪	
3	80 ⎬ = 400	Total number of
4	70 ⎭	firms in industry = 25
5 through 25	50	
Total	450	

Four-firm concentration ratio = 400/450 = 88.9%

Concentration Ratios

The most common way to compute industry concentration is to determine the percentage of total sales or production accounted for by the top four or top eight firms in an industry. This gives the four- or eight-firm **concentration ratio**, also known as the *industry concentration ratio*. An example of an industry with 25 firms is given in Table 26-1. We can see in that table that the four largest firms account for almost 90 percent of total output in the hypothetical industry. This is an example of an oligopoly because a few firms will recognize the interdependence of their output, pricing, and quality decisions.

Table 26-2 shows the four-firm *domestic* concentration ratios for various industries. Can we find any way to show or determine which industries to classify as oligopolistic? There is no definite answer. If we arbitrarily picked a four-firm concentration ratio of 79 percent, we could infer that cigarettes and breakfast cereals were oligopolistic. We would, though, always be dealing with an arbitrary definition.

Concentration ratio
The percentage of all sales contributed by the leading four or leading eight firms in an industry; sometimes called the *industry concentration ratio.*

TABLE 26-2

Four-Firm Domestic Concentration Ratios for Selected U.S. Industries

Industry	Share of Total Sales Accounted for by the Top Four Firms (%)
Cigarettes	98
Breakfast cereals	80
Primary aluminum	77
Computer storage devices	76
Household vacuum cleaners	71
Soft drinks	58
Printing and publishing	42
Commercial banking	32

Source: U.S. Bureau of the Census.

What is the four-firm concentration ratio in the world's tire industry?

INTERNATIONAL EXAMPLE

The Four-Firm Concentration Ratio in the Global Tire Industry

In a recent year, a few companies accounted for a significant share of total global dollar sales of tires. Percentage sales shares for the top firms were as follows: Bridgestone, 14.2 percent; Michelin, 13.1 percent; Goodyear, 9.7 percent; Continental, 8.2 percent; and Pirelli, 3.8 percent. A number of smaller firms accounted for the remaining global tire sales. Consequently, the four-firm concentration ratio for the global tire industry was 14.2 percent + 13.1 percent + 9.7 percent + 8.2 percent, or 45.2 percent.

FOR CRITICAL THINKING

What was the five-firm concentration ratio in the global tire industry?

Sources are listed at the end of this chapter.

The Herfindahl-Hirschman Index

A problem with using concentration ratios is that these measures of industry concentration can fail to reflect differences in the relative sizes of firms within an industry. To understand why this is so, consider Table 26-3, which applies to two fictitious industries, called Industry A and Industry B.

Limitation of the Concentration Ratio Table 26-3 indicates that in Industry A, the four-firm concentration ratio is the sum of the percentage sales shares of the only four firms in the industry, which equals 81.25% + 6.25% + 6.25% + 6.25% = 100%. If we compute the four-firm concentration for Industry B, we obtain 25% + 25% + 25% + 25% = 100%.

Thus, even though the top firm in Industry A has far more than half of all sales in that industry, whereas the top firm in Industry B has 25 percent of all sales, the four-firm concentration ratios are the same for the two industries. This example shows that using concentration ratios can potentially fail to reflect considerable variations in the distribution of firm sizes within industries.

Defining and Computing the Herfindahl-Hirschman Index To account for variations in sizes of firms when measuring industry concentration, economists use the **Herfindahl-Hirschman Index (HHI)**, which is equal to the sum of the squared percentage sales shares of all firms in an industry. For a monopoly, in which only one firm has 100 percent of all industry sales, the value of the HHI equals $100^2 = 10,000$. Consequently, 10,000 is the maximum feasible level of the HHI for any industry.

Herfindahl-Hirschman Index (HHI)
The sum of the squared percentage sales shares of all firms in an industry.

TABLE 26-3

Dollar Sales and Percentage Sales Shares for Two Industries

	Industry A				Industry B		
Firm	Annual Sales ($ millions)	Sales Share (%)	Squared Sales Share	Firm	Annual Sales ($ millions)	Sales Share (%)	Squared Sales Share
1	65	81.25	6,601.6	1	20	25.00	625.0
2	5	6.25	39.1	2	20	25.00	625.0
3	5	6.25	39.1	3	20	25.00	625.0
4	5	6.25	39.1	4	20	25.00	625.0
	Total sales = 80	Total percentage = 100.00	HHI = 6,718.9		Total sales = 80	Total percentage = 100.00	HHI = 2,500.0

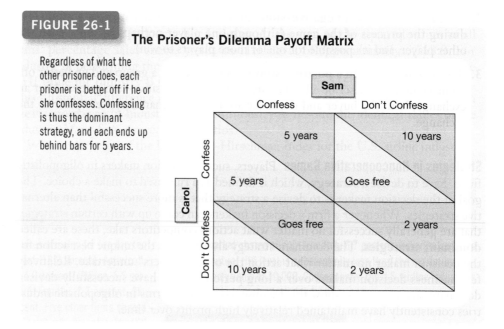

FIGURE 26-1

The Prisoner's Dilemma Payoff Matrix

Regardless of what the other prisoner does, each prisoner is better off if he or she confesses. Confessing is thus the dominant strategy, and each ends up behind bars for 5 years.

To confess is a dominant strategy for Sam. To confess is also a dominant strategy for Carol. The situation is exactly symmetrical. This is the prisoner's dilemma. The prisoners know that both of them will be better off if neither confesses. Yet it is in each individual prisoner's interest to confess, even though the *collective* outcome of each prisoner's pursuit of his or her own interest is inferior for both.

Applying Game Theory to Pricing Strategies

We can apply game strategy to two firms—oligopolists—that have to decide on their pricing strategy. Each can choose either a high or a low price. Their payoff matrix is shown in Figure 26-2. If they both choose a high price, each will make $6 million, but if they both choose a low price, each will make only $4 million. If one sets a high price and the other a low one, the low-priced firm will make $8 million, but the high-priced firm will make only $2 million. As in the prisoner's dilemma, in the absence of collusion, they will end up choosing low prices.

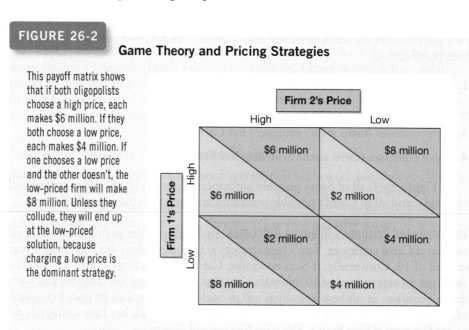

FIGURE 26-2

Game Theory and Pricing Strategies

This payoff matrix shows that if both oligopolists choose a high price, each makes $6 million. If they both choose a low price, each makes $4 million. If one chooses a low price and the other doesn't, the low-priced firm will make $8 million. Unless they collude, they will end up at the low-priced solution, because charging a low price is the dominant strategy.

Opportunistic Behavior

In the prisoner's dilemma, it is clear that cooperative behavior—both parties standing firm without admitting to anything—leads to the best outcome for both players. Each prisoner (player), however, stands to gain by cheating. Such action is called **opportunistic behavior**. Our daily economic activities involve the potential for the prisoner's dilemma all the time. We could engage in opportunistic behavior. You could write a check for a purchase knowing that it is going to bounce because you have just closed that bank account. When you agree to perform a specific task for pay, you could perform your work in a substandard way. When you go to buy a product, the seller might be able to cheat you by selling you a defective item.

In short, if all of us—sellers and buyers—engaged in opportunistic behavior all of the time, we would constantly be acting in a noncooperative manner. That is not the way most of us behave, however. Why not? Because most of us engage in *repeat transactions*. Manufacturers would like us to keep purchasing their products. Sellers would like us to keep coming back to their stores. As sellers of labor services, we all would like to keep our jobs, get promotions, or be hired away by another firm at a higher wage rate. Therefore, we engage in **tit-for-tat strategic behavior**. A consumer using a tit-for-tat strategy may, for instance, continue to purchase items from a firm each period as long as the firm provides products of the same quality and abides by any guarantees. If the firm fails in any period to provide high-quality products and honor its product guarantees, the consumer purchases items elsewhere.

Is oligopolistic interdependence too complicated for real-world managers of firms to analyze?

Opportunistic behavior
Actions that focus solely on short-run gains because long-run benefits of cooperation are perceived to be smaller.

Tit-for-tat strategic behavior
In game theory, cooperation that continues as long as the other players continue to cooperate.

BEHAVIORAL EXAMPLE

Success in Game Theory Does Not Necessarily Require Complex Thinking

Behavioral economists often emphasize bounded rationality as a constraint on the capabilities to pursue self-interest. This perspective raises the issue of whether managers of oligopoly firms that participate in strategic interactions with small numbers of market competitors might be bogged down in the complexities of game theory decision making. If so, they might end up failing to minimize costs. Thus, they might make non-profit-maximizing output and price choices.

Research by David Gill and Victoria Prowse of Purdue University indicates that such failures are less likely as long as managers of oligopoly firms do not "overthink" their strategic responses to competitors' actions. Gill and Prowse have measured the response times of experimental subjects in games that required repeated responses to other subjects' choices in an effort to boost their earnings from participating in the game. The researchers found that the experimental subjects who received the lowest earnings were those who took the longest times to make their strategic decisions. These subjects, Gill and Prowse conclude, engaged in "overthinking" that moved them further from choices consistent with equilibrium outcomes. In contrast, subjects who responded quickly to choices made by other subjects tended to move more speedily to equilibrium choices consistent with higher earnings.

The implication is that real-world managers of oligopoly firms who undertake direct and speedy reactions to competitors' choices rather than "overthinking" strategic interactions will incur fewer costs, receive higher revenues, and be more profitable. These firms will develop the "edge" required to survive. If so, worries about firms becoming bogged down due to oligopolistic interdependence may be overstated.

FOR CRITICAL THINKING

How might the results of Gill and Prowse's study support claims commonly made by company managers who are widely recognized as successful businesspeople that they have succeeded by making rapid "gut" decisions?

Sources are listed at the end of this chapter.

The Cooperative Game: A Collusive Cartel

Some years ago, an investigation into collusive behavior by a small group of large global producers of vitamins secretly recorded an audio clip of a leading businessperson saying, "Our customers are our enemies." This quote sums up a cooperative game among producers, who work together to obtain the largest feasible profits by extracting jointly profit-maximizing prices from consumers.

26.4 Identify features of an industry that help or hinder efforts to form a cartel that seeks to restrain output and earn economic profits

Collusive Production and Pricing and the Seeds of a Cartel's Undoing

If all the firms in an industry can find a way to cooperatively determine how much to produce to maximize their combined profits, then they can form a **cartel** and jointly act as a single producer. That is, they *collude*. They act together to attain the same outcome that a monopoly firm would aim to achieve: producing to the point at which marginal revenue derived from the *market* demand curve is equal to marginal cost.

Cartel

An association of producers in an industry that agree to set common prices and output quotas to prevent competition.

Collusive Price and Output Determination by Firms in a Cartel To operate a profit-maximizing cartel, firms that are members must be willing and able to set up and maintain an arrangement for coordinating overall cartel production at a common price. If the firms are able to accomplish this task, they can all charge the same profit-maximizing price that a monopoly would have charged. Then they can share in the maximized monopoly profits.

The Pre-Cartel, Noncoordinated Market To understand how a cartel functions, consider Figure 26-3, in which initially the market operates in a long-run equilibrium under conditions of perfect competition. In the absence of collusion among the firms, the market supply curve, S, in panel (a) is the sum of the marginal cost curves above the short-run shutdown point of all firms operating in the market, including the one depicted in panel (b). During a given week, the pre-cartel equilibrium price, $5 per unit, equalizes the total quantity demanded with the quantity supplied at 250,000 units at point E in panel (a). Each individual firm's marginal revenue is equal to this market clearing price at any given quantity that it might produce. In the absence of collusion, therefore, the firm depicted in panel (b) produces the individually profit-maximizing output of 5,000 units, at which the firm's marginal revenue at the market clearing price, denoted MR_{firm} in panel (b), equals marginal cost at point E.

In this long-run, pre-cartel equilibrium situation, the market clearing price equals its minimum average total cost. Consequently, the firm's maximized economic profit is

---

FIGURE 26-3

Weekly Price and Output Determination in a Long-Run Perfectly Competitive Equilibrium versus a Collusive Cartel

At point E in panel (a), the perfectly competitive equilibrium price and quantity are $5 per unit and 250,000 units, respectively. At point E in panel (b), a firm earns a zero maximum economic profit producing 5,000 units. At point M in panel (a), all firms collude to reduce industry output to 150,000 units, which requires the firm in panel (b) to reduce its output to 3,000 units at point M, which yields $3,000 in economic profits—the cross-hatched area. The firm in panel (b) will be tempted, however, to cheat on the cartel agreement by boosting output to 7,000 units at point C and receiving $4,000 in additional profit—the blue-shaded area.

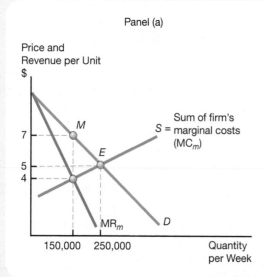

Panel (a)

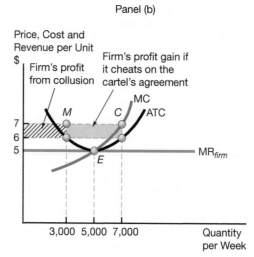

Panel (b)

equal to zero. Hence, there is no incentive for this firm to leave the industry, nor is there an incentive for any other firm facing the same cost conditions to enter the industry.

Boosting Economic Profits via a Collusive Cartel Price Now suppose that after some time has passed in which all firms have received zero economic profits per week, the manager of the firm depicted in panel (b) of Figure 26-3 invites managers of other competing firms to dinner. In an after-dinner presentation, the firm's manager offers the following proposal.

Instead of determining profit-maximizing outputs independently, this manager proposes, the firms in the market will coordinate their production. They will do so by computing the potential *market* marginal revenue curve, denoted MR_m in panel (a), and regarding the horizontal sum of their marginal costs as the overall marginal cost, MC_m, of a joint cartel enterprise in which each firm effectively will operate as a subsidiary unit. To maximize the economic profits available to the cartel in the market as a whole, the cooperating firms must produce the combined output of 150,000 units per week, at which the market marginal revenue equals the cartel's overall marginal cost, at $4.00 per unit. Consumers are willing to pay the price of $7 per unit for this quantity at point M in panel (a), and all firms must agree to establish this price, which exceeds the perfectly competitive price of $5 per unit.

Profit-Maximizing Collusion Requires Reducing Total Production The proposed cartel production rate, 150,000 units in panel (a), is 100,000 units, or 40 percent, lower than the perfectly competitive market output of 250,000 units. Hence, the firms in the cartel can achieve the output of 150,000 units at the collusive price of $7 per unit if each firm cuts its output by 40 percent. The firm in panel (b) thereby reduces its own production by 40 percent, from 5,000 units to 3,000 units at point M. All other firms likewise would decrease their output rates by 40 percent to ensure that the sum of total units produced across all firms would be equal to 150,000 units in panel (a).

Under this collusive arrangement, the firm depicted in panel (b) would receive during each week an economic profit equal to the difference between the cartel price of $7 per unit and the average cost of producing 3,000 units multiplied by the 3,000 units it sells. This profit would be equal to the area of the cross-hatched rectangle in panel (b), which equals ($7 per unit − $6 per unit) × 3,000 units = $3,000. By participating in the cartel and colluding with the other firms in production and pricing decisions, the firm thereby would raise its economic profits from zero to a *positive* amount. The manager making the after-dinner presentation points out that by following this firm's example, each of the other participating firms likewise could raise its economic profits above the zero long-run economic profits available under perfect competition.

The Temptation to Cheat on a Cartel Agreement Suppose that following the after-dinner speech, the managers of all firms in the market agree to implement the collusive arrangement that has been proposed. A problem arises immediately for every colluding firm. As soon as all firms begin to restrain production by 40 percent and charge the market-profit-maximizing, cartel price of $7 per unit, each firm in the cartel has an incentive to cheat on the agreement.

To see why, consider the firm in panel (b) of Figure 26-3. This firm now could maximize its *own* profits by regarding the $7-per-unit cartel price as its available marginal revenue under the cartel agreement and producing to the point at which this marginal revenue equals marginal cost, at 7,000 units of output each week at point C in panel (b). At this "cheating" output rate, the firm would earn economic profits equal to the sum of areas of the two shaded rectangles in panel (b). The amount of this economic profit is ($7 per unit − $6 per unit) × 7,000 units = $7,000 per week. The firm thereby would be able to add the area of the blue-shaded rectangle, $4,000 in additional profit, and more than double its economic profit, from $3,000 per week to $7,000 per week. Hence, if all other cartel members honor their agreement to restrain production, this firm will be tempted to increase its economic profit by reneging on its promise to the rest of the cartel and increasing its production.

The fact that this firm, and likewise every other cartel member, would be tempted to cheat on the cartel agreement means that the cartel can attain the objective of higher economic profits for all members only if firms can be prevented from cheating. After all, if cheating firms were to raise their production, total quantity in the market would rise, which would result in a movement downward along the market demand curve and a reduction in the price that consumers would be willing to pay. Then revenues and profits would decline at *all* firms, and the cartel agreement would begin to unravel.

Enforcing a Cartel Agreement

There are four conditions that make it more likely that firms will be able to coordinate their efforts to restrain output and detect cheating, thereby reducing the temptation for participating firms to cheat:

1. *A small number of firms in the industry.* If an industry consists of only a few firms, it is easier to assess how much each firm should restrain production to yield the monopoly output and hence maximum industry profits. In addition, it is easier for each cartel member to monitor other firms' output rates for signs of cheating. For instance, when a cartel has only a few members, they might agree to keep their sales rates a certain percentage below pre-cartel levels. Failure to do so could be regarded as evidence of cheating.

2. *Relatively undifferentiated products.* If, as in the example depicted in Figure 26-3, cartel members sell homogeneous products, typically it can be easy for them to agree on how much each firm should reduce its production. In contrast, if each firm sells a highly differentiated good, then some members can reasonably claim that the prices and quantities sold of their products should differ from those of other firms' products to reflect differences in costs of production. Thus, a firm with a differentiated good can reasonably claim that it is selling at a lower price for its differentiated good because its good is less valued by consumers—when in fact the firm may simply be using this claim as an excuse to cheat on the cartel agreement.

3. *Easily observable prices.* One way to attempt to make sure that a producer is abiding by a cartel agreement is to look at the prices at which it actually sells its output. If the terms of industry transactions are publicly available, cartel members can more readily spot a firm's efforts to cheat.

4. *Little variation in prices.* If the industry's market is susceptible to frequent shifts in demand for firms' products or in prices of key inputs, the firms' prices will tend to fluctuate. Establishing a cartel agreement and monitoring cheating consequently will be more difficult. Hence, stable demand and cost conditions help a cartel form and continue to operate effectively.

Sometimes cartels prevent cheating on prices by using mechanisms that masquerade as contracts that are favorable to buyers. For example, all members of a cartel might agree to offer buyers contracts that permit a buyer to switch to another seller if that seller offers the product at a lower price. Naturally, if a customer can provide evidence that a lower price is available from another firm claiming to participate in the cartel, this fact would constitute evidence that the other firm is cheating. In this way, cartel members use their customers to police other cartel participants!

Why Cartel Agreements Usually Break Down

Studies have shown that it is very rare for cartel agreements to last more than 10 years. In many cases, cartel agreements break down more quickly than that. Even industries that usually satisfy the four conditions listed above have difficulty keeping cartels together over time.

One reason that cartels tend to break down is that the economic profits that existing firms obtain from holding prices above competitive levels provide an incentive for new firms to enter the market. Effectively, market entrants can earn profits by acting as a cheating cartel firm would behave. Their entry then provides incentives to cartel members to reduce their own prices and boost their production, and ultimately the cartel unravels.

Variations in overall economic activity also tend to make cartels unsustainable. During general business downturns, market demands tend to decline across all industries as consumers' incomes fall. Profits of firms participating in a cartel do, as well. This increases the incentive for individual firms to cheat on a cartel agreement.

WHAT HAPPENS WHEN...

the market demand curve shifts leftward in an industry with a cartel whose member firms have restrained production in order to charge the profit-maximizing monopoly price?

The reduction in market demand for an industry with a profit-maximizing cartel causes the industry marginal revenue curve to shift leftward along with the demand curve. The profit-maximizing quantity and price both decline. The member firms of the cartel will have to respond by working out a new agreement for restraining production and sales to a combined output consistent with the required new, lower level of production. They will have to agree to sell their product at a lower price and to receive lower profits.

Network Effects and Two-Sided Markets

A feature sometimes present in oligopolistic industries is **network effects**, or situations in which a consumer's willingness to use an item depends on how many others use it. Commonplace examples are Facebook and Twitter. Membership with one of these social media companies is not particularly useful if no one else is a member. Once many people are participants, the benefits that others gain from maintaining memberships increase.

26.5 Discuss network effects and the functions and forms of two-sided markets

Network effect
A situation in which a consumer's willingness to purchase a good or service is influenced by how many others also buy or have bought the item.

Network Effects and Market Feedback

Industries in which firms produce goods or services subject to network effects can experience sudden surges in growth, but the fortunes of such industries can also undergo significant and sometimes sudden reversals.

Positive Market Feedback When network effects are an important characteristic of an industry's product, an industry can experience **positive market feedback**. This is the potential for a network effect to arise when an industry's product catches on with consumers. Increased use of the product by some consumers then induces other consumers to purchase the product.

Negative Market Feedback Network effects can also result in **negative market feedback**, in which a speedy downward spiral of product sales occurs for a product subject to network effects. If a sufficient number of consumers cut back on their use of the product, others are induced to reduce their consumption as well, and the product can rapidly become a "has-been."

ECONOMICS IN YOUR LIFE

To consider how companies in the cosmetics industry seek to take advantage of network effects, take a look at **Searching for Cosmetics Products with Network Effects** on page 576.

Positive market feedback
A tendency for a good or service to come into favor with additional consumers because other consumers have chosen to buy the item.

Negative market feedback
A tendency for a good or service to fall out of favor with more consumers because other consumers have stopped purchasing the item.

Network Effects and Industry Concentration

In some industries, a few firms can potentially reap most of the benefits of positive market feedback. Suppose that firms in an industry sell differentiated products that are subject to network effects. If the products of two or three firms catch on, these firms will capture the bulk of the sales due to industry network effects.

A good example is the market for online auction services. An individual is more likely to use the services of an auction site if there is a significant likelihood that many other potential buyers or sellers also trade items at that site. Hence, there is a network effect present in the online auction industry, in which eBay and Overstock account for more than 80 percent of total sales. eBay in particular has experienced positive market feedback, and its share of sales of online auction services has increased to more than 50 percent.

Consequently, in an industry that produces and sells products subject to network effects, a small number of firms may be able to secure the bulk of the payoffs resulting from positive market feedback. In such an industry, oligopoly is likely to emerge as the prevailing market structure.

Two-Sided Markets, Network Effects, and Oligopoly

Two-sided market
A market in which an intermediary firm provides services that link groups of producers and consumers.

Network effects are especially important to firms operating in **two-sided markets**. In such markets, an intermediary firm provides services that link other groups of producers and consumers. When you watch TV and streaming-video programming, your provider links you and others among the audience to advertisers. The TV and streaming-video industry operates in a two-sided market.

Types of Two-Sided Markets Figure 26-4 depicts the basic structure of a two-sided market, in which economists typically call the intermediary a *platform firm* and the groups of producers and consumers that it links—groups A and B in the figure—*end users of the platform*. Thus, in the TV and streaming-video industry, a provider is a platform, and the two groups of end users are the advertisers and the audience.

Two-sided markets are of four types:

1. *Audience-seeking markets.* TV and streaming-video, radio, newspaper, and streaming-music and other Internet-portal industries fall into this group of two-sided markets, in which media platforms link advertisers to audiences.

2. *Matchmaking markets.* Operating in these two-sided markets are platform firms such as real estate agents, companies providing Web auction services, online dating firms, and ride-sharing firms Uber and Lyft.

3. *Transaction-based markets.* Banks, credit- and debit-card companies, and other firms that finalize transactions between groups such as retailers and cardholders function as platforms within these two-sided markets.

4. *Shared-input markets.* In shared-input markets, groups of end users utilize a key input obtained from a platform firm in order to interact with one another. For instance, Google's Android operating system has served as a platform that provides a key input for digital devices sold to consumer end users by firms such as Samsung. In addition, broadband-Internet-access firms are platforms that provide a key interactive-communications input for use by online firms and their customers.

FIGURE 26-4

A Two-Sided Market

In a two-sided market, a platform firm provides a good or service that links two groups of end users, such as those among groups A and B in the figure. The platform establishes prices that are not necessarily the same for the two groups.

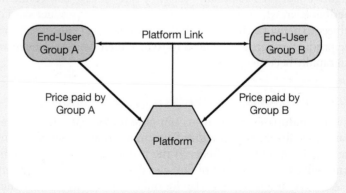

Network Effects in Two-Sided Markets Network effects are a common feature of two-sided markets. In an audience-seeking market, the perceived benefit received by each advertiser increases as the audience size grows. At the same time, even audience members who pay no attention to ads benefit from an expansion of a TV or streaming-video provider's content made possible by a rise in the number of advertisers.

In a matchmaking market, a platform's task of matching an end user in one group to an end user in another is simplified when both groups are larger, which causes each end user to experience a greater benefit when group sizes increase. For instance, a person using an online dating site to try to find a date this Friday evening perceives a greater benefit if the dating site can search among a larger group for someone with desired characteristics.

Network effects also arise in transaction-based and shared-input markets. In the credit-card industry, for example, retailers benefit when more consumers use a credit card accepted by the retailers, and likewise consumers gain when a larger number of retailers accept a credit card carried by the consumers. For a company like Google, which provides a shared input such as an operating system, sellers of digital devices with that operating system gain when a larger number of consumers use it. In addition, consumers who use the operating system benefit when it functions on more digital devices.

Is compiling and utilizing large volumes of data creating network effects that are contributing to more concentrated industries?

 AI | DECISION MAKING THROUGH DATA

Developing a New Source of Industry Concentration

Contemplate the germ of an idea that took form in the minds of a set of entrepreneurs about three decades ago: an online digital platform linking a set of consumer end users to numerous third-party providers of goods and services hosted by the platform. A key aspect of the idea was that the more links to third-party providers that the platform could provide, the more users it would be able to attract, which in turn would induce more third-party providers to set up links—a network externality. Today, of course, an array of recognizable firms, including Amazon, Facebook, and Google, has transformed this idea into reality.

As online platform firms have evolved, the accumulation of data has played an expanding role in their operations. These companies have found that the data collected regarding user interactions with both their online platform and with third-party providers assists them in tailoring platform offerings to the preferences of the end users. Applying collected user data in this way enables the firms to provide more and stronger links to their platforms—and to generate yet more data. Hence, in the regular course of their operations, these platform firms also are benefiting from a new form of network effect driven largely by the acquisition of data and the deployment of new techniques in data analytics. Many commentators and policymakers already are calling this a "big data network effect" that likely contributes to oligopolistic concentration in industries containing these platform firms.

FOR CRITICAL THINKING

How might the use of AI techniques to better attune platforms' services to end users' preferences enhance the emerging "big data network effect"?

Sources are listed at the end of this chapter.

Two-Sided Oligopolistic Pricing The presence of network effects in two-sided markets means a few firms are often able to capture most of the payoffs associated with market feedback. Thus, oligopoly is the most common industry structure in these markets.

> *Oligopolistic platform firms setting prices in a two-sided market must consider group differences in network-effect responses to price changes.*

In a number of two-sided markets, platform firms maximize profits by charging an explicit price of zero to one group of end users. Many online media sites, for instance, charge fees to advertisers but post news articles and videos for consumer audiences at no explicit charge. In a few cases, platform firms may even establish *negative* prices, or *subsidies*, for one of the end-user groups. For instance, Apple sometimes pays subsidies to developers of apps that function with the company's iOS–based operating system, because the availability of more iOS–based apps increases consumers' willingness to purchase Apple devices.

TABLE 26-4

Comparing Market Structures

Market Structure	Number of Sellers	Unrestricted Entry and Exit	Ability to Set Price	Long-Run Economic Profits Possible	Product Differentiation	Nonprice Competition	Examples
Perfect competition	Numerous	Yes	None	No	None	None	Agriculture, roofing nails
Monopolistic competition	Many	Yes	Some	No	Considerable	Yes	Toothpaste, toilet paper, soap, retail trade
Oligopoly	Few	Partial	Some	Yes	Frequent	Yes	Recorded music, college textbooks
Pure monopoly	One	No (for entry)	Considerable	Yes	None (product is unique)	None	Some electric companies, some local telephone companies

Of course, platform firms in two-sided markets must also take into account strategic interactions. For example, when choosing subsidies to pay app developers and the prices to charge buyers of Apple devices, Apple must consider how Google will set developer subsidies and how Samsung will price its devices.

Comparing Market Structures

Now that we have looked at perfect competition, pure monopoly, monopolistic competition, and oligopoly, we are in a position to compare the attributes of these four different market structures. The attributes of perfect competition, pure monopoly, monopolistic competition, and oligopoly can be compared. We do this in summary form in Table 26-4, in which we compare the number of sellers, their ability to set price, and the degree of product differentiation and also give some examples of each of the four market structures.

ECONOMICS IN YOUR LIFE

Searching for Cosmetics Products with Network Effects

Recently, Colin Welch, a managing director at TSG Consumer Partners LLC, oversaw the sale of the firm's share of ownership in IT Cosmetics to one of the largest firms in the cosmetics industry, L'Oréal. The key attraction of this acquisition for L'Oréal was that the products of IT Cosmetics had developed a significant social media presence, a characteristic that L'Oréal itself had lacked. Welch notes that careful attention of IT Cosmetics to social media likes, follows, and reviews had allowed that firm to expand meager annual sales prior to 2010 to almost $182 million a few years later. In contrast, L'Oréal's own sales had remained relatively flat during the same period.

Welch knows that L'Oréal is not the only major cosmetics firm seeking to acquire new brands that are benefiting from positive market feedback arising from network effects generated by substantial attention on social media. Other large cosmetics companies, such as Estée Lauder and Shiseido, Asia's largest, are in the midst of a frenzy of acquiring small brands of makeup and other skin-care products. These companies also are acquiring smaller firms deemed subject to network effects that are likely to yield positive market feedback in future years.

FOR CRITICAL THINKING

Why do you suppose that the largest cosmetics companies have engaged in bidding wars to acquire smartphone apps that can be used to match cosmetics to skin tones or to provide guidance for applying cosmetics?

REAL APPLICATION

Let's say that you have just been named the head manager of a small cosmetics firm. How will network effects influence the way you manage this firm?

Sources are listed at the end of this chapter.

ISSUES & APPLICATIONS

Why Platform Firms Must Balance Getting *More* Customers vis-à-vis Getting the *Right* Customers

dennizn/Shutterstock

CONCEPTS APPLIED

➤ Network Effects

➤ Oligopoly

➤ Market Feedback

The presence of network effects can contribute to the development and persistence of an oligopoly in an industry of platform firms, because such effects can enable a small number of firms to benefit from favorable market feedback. Just because the existence of network effects *can* enable platform firms to induce their products to "catch on" with consumers does *not* mean, however, that this outcome necessarily occurs. Platform firms must maintain a careful balance between seeking to obtain as many customers as possible versus striving to obtain the "right" customers.

More Customers Definitely Can Promote Favorable Market Feedback

New platform firms tend to focus much effort on attracting larger numbers of customers. The advantage to such a strategy is very clear: Having more customers increases the likelihood that platform firms will be able to experience favorable market feedback.

Other things being equal, platform firms operating in audience-seeking markets, for instance, will be better able to link advertisers to desired audiences of viewers, listeners, or readers when such audiences are larger. Likewise, in matchmaking markets, having a larger base of consumers searching for matches raises the chance that any particular customer will find a good match.

The Importance of Getting the "Right" Customers

Nevertheless, seeking to build an ever-larger platform by attracting ever-growing numbers of consumers ultimately can be shortsighted. After all, any given audience member will favor smaller platforms with more entertainment options that he or she prefers to view, hear, or read than bigger platforms with fewer desirable offerings. Similarly, a typical consumer in a matchmaking market will find

smaller platforms providing more good matches more attractive than larger platforms that provide fewer favorable matches.

Thus, while platform firms certainly can potentially improve the likelihood of favorable market feedback by seeing to boosting numbers of customers, attaining ever-higher customer numbers does not guarantee this outcome. Also important to achieving favorable market feedback are efforts by platforms to ensure that the members of the groups they seek to link are highly likely to find such linkages desirable. That is, the platforms must balance adding more customers with landing the "right" customers.

FOR CRITICAL THINKING

Why do you think that OpenTable, a restaurant-reservation platform, almost failed when it initially sought many *nationwide* fine-dining restaurants but then recovered when it better linked consumers to *nearby* restaurants?

REAL APPLICATION

Suppose that you want to create a news-feed app. In deciding what types of stories to put on this news app, how would you proceed?

Sources are listed at the end of this chapter.

What You Should Know

LEARNING OBJECTIVES

KEY TERMS

26.1 **Outline the fundamental characteristics of oligopoly** *Oligopoly is a situation in which a few firms produce most of an industry's output. To measure the extent to which a few firms account for an industry's production and sales, economists use concentration ratios, which are the top few firms' percentages of total sales. An important characteristic of oligopoly is strategic dependence, meaning that one firm's decisions about its production, price, product quality, or advertising can bring about responses by other firms.*

oligopoly, 562
strategic dependence, 562
vertical merger, 563
horizontal merger, 563

26.2 **Explain alternative methods of measuring industry concentration** *One fundamental measure of the extent to which a few firms account for an industry's production and sales is the concentration ratio, which is the top few firms' percentages of total sales. The other fundamental measure of industry concentration is the Herfindahl-Hirschman Index, which is the sum of the squared percentage sales shares of all firms in an industry.*

concentration ratio, 564
Herfindahl-Hirschman Index
    (HHI), 565

26.3 **Understand how to apply game theory to evaluate the pricing strategies of oligopolistic firms** *Game theory is the analytical framework used to evaluate how two or more firms compete for payoffs that depend on the strategies that others employ. When firms work together for a common objective such as maximizing industry profits, they participate in cooperative games, but when they cannot work together, they engage in noncooperative games. One important type of game is the prisoner's dilemma, in which the inability to cooperate in determining prices of their products can cause firms to choose lower prices than they otherwise would prefer.*

reaction function, 566
game theory, 566
cooperative game, 566
noncooperative game, 566
zero-sum game, 566
negative-sum game, 567
positive-sum game, 567
strategy, 567
dominant strategies, 567
prisoner's dilemma, 567
payoff matrix, 567
opportunistic behavior, 569
tit-for-tat strategic
    behavior, 569
Key Figures
Figure 26-1, 568
Figure 26-2, 568

26.4 **Identify features of an industry that help or hinder efforts to form a cartel that seeks to restrain output and earn economic profits** *A cartel is an organization of firms in an industry that collude to earn economic profits by producing a combined output consistent with monopoly profit maximization. Four conditions make a collusive cartel agreement easier to create and enforce: (1) a small number of firms in the industry, (2) relatively undifferentiated products, (3) easily observable prices, and (4) little variation in prices.*

cartel, 570
Key Figure
Figure 26-3, 570

26.5 **Discuss network effects and the functions and forms of two-sided markets** *Network effects arise when a consumer's demand for an item is affected by how many other consumers also use it. In a two-sided market, a platform firm links groups called end users. When network effects differ for end users, the platform establishes differing prices. When the extents of network effects differ for the groups of end users, the platform typically establishes contrasting prices for the different groups. When one group is particularly susceptible to network effects, the platform firm may charge an explicit price of zero or perhaps even a negative price to that group and generate revenues solely by charging a positive price to the other group.*

network effect, 573
positive market feedback, 573
negative market feedback, 573
two-sided market, 574
Key Table
Table 26-4, 576

PROBLEMS

26-1. Suppose that the distribution of sales within an industry is as shown in the first table.

Firm	Share of Total Market Sales
A	15%
B	14
C	12
D	11
E	10
F	10
G	8
H	7
All others	13
Total	100%

a. What is the four-firm concentration ratio for this industry?

b. What is the eight-firm concentration ratio for this industry?

26-2. The second table shows recent worldwide market shares of producers of inkjet printers.

Firm	Share of Worldwide Market Sales
Brother	3%
Canon	17
Dell	6
Epson	18
Hewlett-Packard	41
Lexmark	13
Samsung	1
Other	1

a. In this year, what was the four-firm concentration ratio in the inkjet-printer industry?

b. In this year, what was the seven-firm concentration ratio in the inkjet-printer industry?

26-3. If there are 13 "All others" in the industry in Problem 26-1, each of which has a share of sales equal to 1 percent, what is the value of the Herfindahl-Hirschman Index for this industry?

26-4. What is the approximate value of the industry's Herfindahl-Hirschman Index in Problem 26-2?

26-5. Characterize each of the following as a positive-sum game, a zero-sum game, or a negative-sum game.

a. Office workers contribute $10 each to a pool of funds, and whoever best predicts the winners in a professional sports playoff wins the entire sum.

b. After three years of fighting with large losses of human lives and materiél, neither nation involved in a war is any closer to its objective than it was before the war began.

c. Two collectors who previously owned incomplete and nearly worthless sets of trading cards exchange several cards, and as a result both end up with completed sets with significant market value.

26-6. Characterize each of the following as a positive-sum game, a zero-sum game, or a negative-sum game.

a. You play a card game in your dorm room with three other students. Each player brings $5 to the game to bet on the outcome, winner take all.

b. Two nations exchange goods in a mutually beneficial transaction.

c. A thousand people buy $1 lottery tickets with a single payoff of $800.

26-7. Last weekend, Bob attended the university football game. At the opening kickoff, the crowd stood up. Bob therefore realized that he would have to stand up as well to see the game. For the crowd (not the football team), explain the outcomes of a cooperative game and a noncooperative game. Explain what Bob's "tit-for-tat strategic behavior" would be if he wished to see the game.

26-8. Consider two strategically dependent firms in an oligopolistic industry, Firm A and Firm B. Firm A knows that if it offers extended warranties on its products but Firm B does not, it will earn $6 million in profits, and Firm B will earn $2 million. Likewise, Firm B knows that if it offers extended warranties but Firm A does not, it will earn $6 million in profits, and Firm A will earn $2 million. The two firms know that if they both offer extended warranties on their products, each will earn $3 million in profits. Finally, the two firms know that if neither offers extended warranties, each will earn $5 million in profits.

a. Set up a payoff matrix that fits the situation faced by these two firms.

b. What is the dominant strategy for each firm in this situation? Explain.

26-9. Take a look back at the data regarding the inkjet-printer industry in Problem 26-2, and answer the following questions.

a. Suppose that consumer demands for inkjet printers, the prices of which are readily observable in office supply outlets and at Internet sites, are growing at a stable pace. Discuss whether circumstances are favorable to an effort by firms in this industry to form a cartel.

b. If the firms successfully establish a cartel, why will there naturally be pressures for the cartel to break down, either from within or from outside?

26-10. Explain why network effects can cause the demand for a product *either* to expand *or* to contract relative to what it would be if there were no network effects.

26-11. List three products that you think are subject to network effects. For each product, indicate whether, in your view, all or just a few firms within the industry that produces each product experience market feedback effects. In your view, are any market feedback effects in these industries currently positive or negative?

26-12. Consider the following list, and classify each item according to the appropriate type of two-sided market—audience-making, matchmaking, shared-input, or transaction-based—and write a one-sentence answer justifying your classification. (*Hint:* You may wish to check out the firms' websites to assist in answering this question.)

    a. Realtor.com

    b. NYTimes.com

    c. Linux.com

    d. Paypal.com

26-13. Consider the following list, and classify each item according to the appropriate type of two-sided market—audience-making, matchmaking, shared-input, or transaction-based—and write a one-sentence answer justifying your classification. (*Hint:* You may wish to check out the firms' websites to assist in answering this question.)

    a. Mastercard.com

    b. FreeBSD.com

    c. Plentyoffish.com

    d. WSJ.com

26-14. Suppose that a company based in Dallas, Texas, confronts only four other rival firms. Its own market share is 35 percent, which ties it with the other largest producer and seller in the industry. The other three firms each have a 10 percent market share. What is the four-firm concentration ratio for this industry?

26-15. In Problem 26-14, what is the value of the Herfindahl-Hirschman Index?

26-16. Suppose that a firm located in Cleveland, Ohio, has entered the same industry as the Dallas company discussed in Problem 26-14. The new firm captures a 5 percent market share, and the market share of one of the smallest three original incumbents declines to 5 percent as well. After the Cleveland firm's entry into the industry, what are the values of the four-firm concentration ratio and of the Herfindahl-Hirschman Index?

26-17. Consider Figure 26-2. Suppose conditions in the industry change in such a way that the amount that each firm makes if it charges a high price when the other firm charges a low price increases from $2 million to $3 million. Is the firm's pricing decision altered by this change and, if so, in what way? Explain briefly.

26-18. Take a look at Figure 26-3. What is the total dollar amount of the typical perfectly competitive firm's economic incentive to join the proposed cartel, assuming that after the fact no firms cheat on the specified cartel agreement? Explain your reasoning.

26-19. Consider Figure 26-3, and suppose that this typical firm has agreed to participate in the proposed cartel. What is the total dollar amount of the firm's economic incentive to cheat on the cartel agreement, assuming that all other firms continue to abide by the agreement? Explain your reasoning.

REFERENCES

INTERNATIONAL EXAMPLE: The Four-Firm Concentration Ratio in the U.S. Global Tire Industry

"Top 10 Largest Tire Manufacturing Companies in the World," The Daily Records (http://www.thedailyrecords.com/2018-2019-2020-2021/world-famous-top-10-list/highest-selling-brands-products-companies-reviews/largest-tyre-manufacturing-companies-world-best-famous/12751/), January 2, 2019.

Sudeep Chakravarty, "The World's 15 Largest Tire Manufacturers by Revenue," *Market Watch*, September 19, 2018.

Anthony Deem, "Tire Industry Financial Outlook," Tire Review (http://www.tirereview.com/tire-industry-financial-outlook-2018/), May 2, 2018.

EXAMPLE: The HHI for the U.S. Airline Industry

"Airline Domestic Market Share," U.S. Bureau of Transportation Statistics (https://www.transtats.bts.gov), 2019.

"Major Canadian and U.S. Airlines," NationsOnline.org (https://www.nationsonline.org/oneworld/Airlines/airlines_north_america.htm), 2019.

"Top 100 U.S. Airlines, Ranked by Passenger and Cargo Volumes," Aeroweb (http://www.fi-aeroweb.com/Top-100-US-Airlines.html), 2019.

BEHAVIORAL EXAMPLE: Success in Game Theory Does Not Necessarily Require Complex Thinking

"Game Theory," EconomicsOnline (https://www.economicsonline.co.uk/Business_economics/Prisoner%27s_dilemma.html), 2019.

Joel Balbien, "Game Theory Gives Entrepreneurs an Edge," *Pacific Coast Business Times*, February 2, 2018.

David Gill and Victoria Prowse, "Using Response Times to Measure Strategic Complexity and the Value of Thinking in Games," Purdue University, 2018.

AI—DECISION MAKING THROUGH DATA: Developing a New Source of Industry Concentration

Jessica Rutledge, "'Data-opolies' and More," Lexology.com (https://www.lexology.com/library/detail.aspx?g=b408f28e-87d9-4762-ac3f-615c0048544f), January 29, 2019.

Jay Pil Choi, Doh-Shin Jeon, and Byung-Cheol Kim, "Privacy and Personal Data Collection with Information Externalities," Toulouse School of Economics Working Paper No. 18-887, January 2018.

Gigi Levy Weiss, "Network Effects Are Becoming Even More Important on Emerging Platforms," *Forbes*, March 18, 2018.

ECONOMICS IN YOUR LIFE: Searching for Cosmetics Products with Network Effects

"IT Cosmetics," L'Oréal (https://www.loreal.com/brand/l'oréal-luxe/it-cosmetics), 2019.

Suzana Rose, "IT Cosmetics Sells Out to L'Oréal for $1.2 Billion," Crueltyfreekitty.com (https://www.crueltyfreekitty.com/news/loreal-buys-it-cosmetics/), May 22, 2018.

Jennifer Weill, "L'Oréal Ramps Up Acquisitions," WWD (https://wwd.com/beauty-industry-news/color-cosmetics/loreal-ramps-up-acquisitions-1202683474/), May 29, 2018.

ISSUES & APPLICATIONS: Why Platform Firms Must Balance Getting *More* Customers vis-à-vis Getting the *Right* Customers

"Find Your Table for Any Occasion," OpenTable.com, 2019.

David Evans and Richard Schmalensee, "Debunking the 'Network Effects' Bogeyman," *Regulation*, 2018.

27

Regulation and Antitrust Policy in a Globalized Economy

iqoncept/123RF GB Limited

LEARNING OBJECTIVES

After reading this chapter, you should be able to:

27.1 Distinguish between economic regulation and social regulation

27.2 Recognize the practical difficulties in regulating the prices charged by natural monopolies

27.3 Explain the main rationales for regulation of industries that are not inherently monopolistic

27.4 Identify alternative theories aimed at explaining the behavior of regulators

27.5 Understand the foundations of antitrust regulations and enforcement

Many drugs have been prescribed for decades, because the physicians who continue to prescribe them perceive that doing so has benefited their patients. The Food and Drug Administration (FDA), the U.S. regulator of pharmaceuticals' production and distribution, first granted authorization for many of these drugs prior to 1962. Under FDA rules in place at that time, drug manufacturers only had to demonstrate that the medications were *safe* to use. As authorizations to produce these old drugs have come up for renewal in more recent years, manufacturers have had to meet a higher regulatory standard. They must also prove to the FDA that the medications definitely provide *benefits* to people who take them. When the FDA re-approves drugs on these grounds, it grants manufacturers the legal right to sell the old drugs as "new" medications. In this chapter, you will learn why a consequence has been that the prices of long-standing drugs that the FDA has re-labeled as "new" have jumped to significantly higher levels.

since 1991, the U.S. federal government has established more than 1,200 regulations that Congress has required the president to designate as "major" regulations—meaning that each has been projected to have an annual economic cost in excess of $100 million? Before you can understand the economic effects of government business rules on the economy, you must first learn about the ways in which U.S. businesses are regulated.

Forms of Industry Regulation

27.1 Distinguish between economic regulation and social regulation

The U.S. government began regulating social and economic activity early in the nation's history. The amount of government regulation began increasing in the twentieth century and has grown considerably since 1970. Figure 27-1 displays two common measures of regulation in the United States. Panel (a) shows that regulatory spending by federal agencies (in 2012 dollars) was stable in the 1980s and 1990s before rising considerably between 2000 and 2015. Panel (b) of Figure 27-1 depicts the number of pages in the *Federal Register*, a government publication that lists all *new* regulatory rules. According to this measure, the scope of new federal regulations increased sharply during the 1970s, dropped off in the 1980s, generally increased until 2016, and has declined to lower levels in recent years.

There are two basic types of government regulation. One is *economic regulation* of natural monopolies and of specific nonmonopolistic industries. For instance, some

FIGURE 27-1

Measures of Regulation

Panel (a) shows that federal government regulatory spending exceeds $50 billion per year. State and local spending is not shown. As panel (b) shows, the number of pages in the *Federal Register* per year rose sharply in the 1970s, dropped off somewhat in the 1980s, generally increased until 2016, and decreased in recent years.

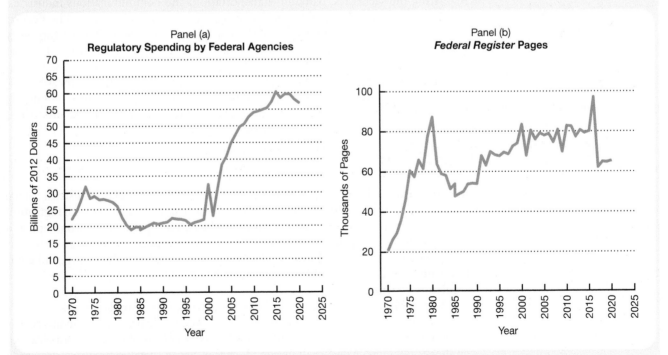

Sources: Institute for University Studies; *Federal Register*, various issues.

state commissions regulate the prices and quality of services provided by electrical power companies, which are considered natural monopolies that experience lower long-run average costs as their output increases. Financial services industries and interstate transportation industries are examples of nonmonopolistic industries that are subjected to considerable government regulation. The other form of government regulation is *social regulation*, which covers all industries. Examples include various occupational, health, and safety rules that federal and state governments impose on most businesses.

Economic Regulation

Initially, most economic regulation in the United States was aimed at controlling prices in industries considered to be natural monopolies. Over time, federal and state governments have also sought to influence the characteristics of products or processes of firms in a variety of industries without inherently monopolistic features.

Regulation of Natural Monopolies
The regulation of natural monopolies has tended to emphasize restrictions on product prices. Various public utility commissions throughout the United States regulate the rates (prices) of electrical utility companies and some telephone operating companies. This *rate regulation*, as it is usually called, officially has been aimed at preventing such industries from earning monopoly profits.

Regulation of Nonmonopolistic Industries
The prices charged by firms in many other industries that do not have steadily declining long-run average costs, such as financial services industries, have also been subjected to regulations. Every state in the United States, for instance, has a government agency devoted to regulating the prices that insurance companies charge.

More broadly, government regulations establish rules pertaining to production, product (or service) features, and entry and exit within a number of specific nonmonopolistic industries. The federal government is heavily involved, for instance, in regulating the securities, banking, transportation, and communications industries. The Securities and Exchange Commission regulates securities markets. The Federal Reserve, Office of the Comptroller of the Currency, and Federal Deposit Insurance Corporation regulate commercial banks and savings banks. The National Credit Union Administration supervises credit unions. The Federal Aviation Administration supervises the airline industry, and the Federal Motor Carrier Safety Administration regulates the trucking industry. The Federal Communications Commission has oversight powers relating to broadcasting and telephone and communications services.

Social Regulation

In contrast to economic regulation, which covers only particular industries, social regulation applies to all firms in the economy. In principle, the aim of social regulation is a better quality of life through improved products, a less polluted environment, and better working conditions. Since the 1970s, an increasing array of government resources has been directed toward regulating product safety, advertising, and environmental effects. Table 27-1 lists some major federal agencies involved in these broad regulatory activities.

The *possible* benefits of social regulations are many. For example, the water supply in some cities is known to be contaminated with potentially hazardous chemicals, and air pollution contributes to many illnesses. Society might well benefit from cleaning up these pollutants. As we shall discuss, however, broad social regulations also entail costs that we all pay, and not just as taxpayers who fund the regulatory activities of agencies such as those listed in Table 27-1.

TABLE 27-1

Federal Agencies Engaged in Social Regulation

Agency	Jurisdiction	Date Formed	Major Regulatory Functions
Federal Trade Commission (FTC)	Product markets	1914	Intended to prevent misleading advertising, unfair trade practices, and monopolistic actions and to protect consumer rights.
Food and Drug Administration (FDA)	Food and pharmaceuticals	1906	Regulates the quality and safety of foods, health and medical products, pharmaceuticals, cosmetics, and animal feed.
Equal Employment Opportunity Commission (EEOC)	Labor markets	1964	Investigates discrimination claims based on age, gender, race, religion, and other employment conditions.
Environmental Protection Agency (EPA)	Environment	1970	Develops and enforces environmental standards for air, water, waste, and noise.
Occupational Safety and Health Administration (OSHA)	Health and safety	1970	Regulates workplace safety and health conditions.
Consumer Product Safety Commission (CPSC)	Consumer product safety	1972	Responsible for protecting consumers from products posing general hazards or dangers to children.
Mining Safety and Health Administration	Mining and oil drilling safety	1977	Establishes and enforces operational safety rules for mines and oil rigs.

Regulating Natural Monopolies

27.2 Recognize the practical difficulties in regulating the prices charged by natural monopolies

At one time, much government regulation of business purportedly aimed to solve the so-called monopoly problem. Of particular concern was implementing appropriate regulations for natural monopolies.

The Theory of Natural Monopoly Regulation

Recall from an earlier chapter that a natural monopoly arises whenever a single firm can produce all of an industry's output at a lower per-unit cost than other firms attempting to produce less than total industry output. In a natural monopoly, therefore, economies of large-scale production exist, leading to a single-firm industry.

The Unregulated Natural Monopoly Like any other firm, an unregulated natural monopolist will produce to the point at which marginal revenue equals marginal cost. Panel (a) of Figure 27-2 depicts a situation in which a monopolist faces the market demand curve, D, and the marginal revenue curve, MR. The monopolist searches along the demand curve for the profit-maximizing price and quantity. The profit-maximizing quantity is at point A, at which the marginal revenue curve crosses the long-run marginal cost curve, LMC, and the unregulated monopolist maximizes profits by producing the quantity Q_m. Consumers are willing and able to pay the price per unit P_m for this quantity at point F. This price is above marginal cost, so it leads to a socially inefficient allocation of resources by restricting production to a rate below that at which price equals marginal cost.

Profit Maximization and Regulation through Marginal Cost Pricing

The profit-maximizing natural monopolist produces at the point in panel (a) at which marginal costs equal marginal revenue. This is point A, which gives the quantity of production Q_m. The per-unit price is P_m at point F. If a regulatory commission attempted to require equating price with long-run marginal cost, production would have to be at the point where the long-run marginal cost (LMC) curve intersects the demand schedule. This is shown at point B in panel (b). The quantity produced would be Q_1, and the per-unit price would be P_1. Average costs would be AC_1, however, so losses would equal the shaded area.

The Impracticality of Marginal Cost Pricing

What would happen if the government were to require the monopolist in Figure 27-2 to produce to the point at which price equals marginal cost, which is point B in panel (b)? Then it would produce a larger output rate, Q_1. Consumers, however, would pay only the price per unit P_1 for this quantity, which would be less than the average cost of producing this output rate, AC_1. Consequently, requiring the monopolist to engage in marginal cost pricing would yield a loss for the firm equal to the shaded rectangular area in panel (b). The profit-maximizing monopolist would go out of business rather than face such regulation, which would deprive consumers of the product.

Average Cost Pricing

Regulators cannot practically force a natural monopolist to engage in marginal cost pricing. Thus, regulation of natural monopolies has often taken the form of allowing the firm to set price at the point at which the long-run average cost (LAC) curve intersects the demand curve. In panel (b) of Figure 27-2, this is point C. In this situation, the regulator forces the firm to engage in *average cost pricing*, with average cost including what the regulators deem a "fair" rate of return on investment. For instance, a regulator might impose **cost-of-service regulation**, which requires a natural monopoly to charge only prices that reflect the actual average cost of providing products to consumers. Alternatively, although in a similar vein, a regulator might use **rate-of-return regulation**, which allows firms to set prices that ensure a normal return on investment.

Cost-of-service regulation
Regulation that allows prices to reflect only the actual average cost of production and no monopoly profits.

Rate-of-return regulation
Regulation that seeks to keep the rate of return in an industry at a competitive level by not allowing prices that would produce economic profits.

WHAT HAPPENS WHEN...

a natural monopoly subject to a regulatory requirement to utilize average cost pricing experiences a decline in the demand for its product?

Under a requirement for a natural monopoly to engage in average cost pricing, the intersection of the demand curve with the long-run average cost curve determines the price to be charged by the firm. When the demand for the natural monopolist's product declines and thereby shifts leftward, the result is a movement upward along the firm's long-run average cost curve. Thus, the regulatory requirement necessitates a required increase in the price of the natural monopolist's product following a reduction in demand.

Natural Monopolies No More?

Traditionally, a feature common to the electricity, natural gas, and telecommunications industries has been that they utilize large networks of wires or pipelines to transmit their products to consumers. Governments concluded that the average costs of providing electricity, natural gas, and telecommunications declined as output rates of firms in these industries increased. Consequently, governments treated these industries as natural monopolies and established regulatory commissions to subject the industries to forms of cost-of-service and rate-of-return regulation.

Electricity and Natural Gas: Separating Production from Delivery Today, numerous producers of natural gas vie to market their product in a number of cities across the country. In nearly half of U.S. states, there is active competition in the provision of electricity and natural gas.

What circumstances led to this transformation? The answer is that regulators of electricity and natural gas companies figured out that the function of *producing* electricity or natural gas did not necessarily have to be combined with the *delivery* of the product. Since the mid-1980s, various regulators have gradually implemented policies that have separated production of electricity and natural gas from the distribution of these items to consumers. Thus, in a growing number of U.S. locales, multiple producers now pay to use wire and pipeline networks to get their products to buyers.

What has happened to prices and average costs in the health insurance industry since it has been subjected to a particular type of cost-of-service regulation?

POLICY EXAMPLE

Cost-of-Service Regulation of the U.S. Health Insurance Industry Fails to Contain Either Costs or Prices

Little evidence exists to support the idea that the health insurance industry is a natural monopoly. The U.S. Affordable Care Act of 2010 nonetheless attempts to apply a form of cost-of-service regulation to health insurance policies sold to certain self-employed individuals and income groups. The legislation places a limit on insurers' medical claims costs as a percentage of revenues derived from the prices that consumers pay for the policies. One aim was to try to ensure that the insurers' average claims costs would not rise above a certain percentage of policy prices. The other was to limit increases in prices of insurance policies.

In fact, however, increases in demand for health insurance associated with the law's implementation have caused policy prices, which the law did nothing to constrain directly, to rise. Insurers' medical claims costs simultaneously increased at a pace consistent with maintaining the law's limit on those costs as a percentage of insurers' revenues. Thus, imposing this particular type of cost-of-service regulation on the health insurance industry failed to prevent increases either in average claims costs or in policy prices.

FOR CRITICAL THINKING

For an industry that actually was a natural monopoly, would imposing a regulation requiring price to equal average cost necessarily prevent both price and average cost from rising if demand were to increase? Explain briefly.

Sources are listed at the end of this chapter.

Telecommunications Services Meet the Internet As the production and sale of electricity and natural gas began to become more competitive undertakings, regulators started to apply the same principles to telecommunications services. At the same time, other forces reshaped the cost structure of the telecommunications industry. First, significant technological advances drastically reduced the costs of providing wireless telecommunications. Second, Internet phone service became more widely available. Most cable television companies that provide Internet access now offer Internet-based telephone services as well. Many other companies also offer Web phone services for purchase by anyone who already has access to the Internet.

Are Natural Monopolies Relics of the Past? Clearly, the scope of the government's role as regulator of natural monopolies has decreased with the unraveling of conditions that previously created this particular market structure. In many U.S. electricity and natural gas markets, government agencies now apply traditional cost-of-service or rate-of-return regulations primarily to landline and pipeline owners. Otherwise, the government's main role in many regional markets is to serve as a "traffic cop," enforcing property rights and rules governing the regulated networks that serve competing electricity and natural gas producers.

In telecommunications, there are competing views on natural monopoly and the role of regulation. According to one perspective, any natural monopoly rationale for a governmental regulatory role is dissipating rapidly as more and more households and businesses substitute cellular and Internet-based phone services for wired phone services. Under the alternative view, network effects contribute to the potential for a natural monopoly problem that regulators must continue to address.

27.3 Explain the main rationales for regulation of industries that are not inherently monopolistic

Regulating Nonmonopolistic Industries

Traditionally, one of the fundamental purposes of governments has been to provide a coordinated system of safeguarding the interests of their citizens. Not surprisingly, protecting consumer interests is the main rationale offered for governmental regulatory functions.

Rationales for Consumer Protection in Nonmonopolistic Industries

The Latin phrase *caveat emptor*, or "let the buyer beware," was once the operative principle in most consumer dealings with businesses. The phrase embodies the idea that the buyer alone is ultimately responsible for assessing a producer and the quality of the items it sells before agreeing to purchase the firm's product. Today, in contrast, various federal agencies require companies to meet specific minimal standards in their dealings with consumers. For instance, a few years ago, the U.S. Federal Trade Commission assessed a $5 billion penalty on Facebook because the company failed to abide by a privacy agreement it previously had established with its customers. Such a government action would have been unheard of a few decades ago.

In some industries, federal agencies dictate the rules of the game for firms' interactions with consumers. The Federal Aviation Administration (FAA), for example, oversees almost every aspect of the delivery of services by airline companies. The FAA regulates the process by which tickets for flights are sold and distributed, oversees all flight operations, and even establishes rules governing the procedures for returning luggage after flights are concluded.

How has the growing use of artificial-intelligence-guided production of goods and delivery of services raised novel consumer-protection concerns?

AI | DECISION MAKING THROUGH DATA

Applying a Human Regulatory Touch to Firms' AI Systems

Many science fiction novels and stories have speculated about the potential for AI systems to pose all manner of threats to humans. Although most such speculations focus on dangers to humans' physical existence, observers of firms' utilization of real-world AI systems are concerned about potential economic threats. The potential exists, they fret, for multiple apps that guide companies' AI systems to come into conflict after years of rewriting of app codes. Resulting collapses in production or halts in services, they argue, could cause economic damages to consumers.

In fact, some companies that use AI systems already are hiring engineers—sometimes called "robot psychologists"—who possess specialized training in diagnosing and correcting AI system failures. Not all firms utilizing AI systems have such specialists on their staffs. For this reason, some observers concerned about the possibility of economic harm from AI-system breakdowns are calling for government agencies to develop expertise in assessing the potential for AI-generated breakdowns. They argue that such agencies should begin requiring companies to take precautionary actions to protect consumers from the harms that could result from such failures.

FOR CRITICAL THINKING

Why do you suppose that the field of "robot psychology" is an example of one in which firms' increased utilization of capital-based resources is creating a new category of jobs for human beings?

Sources are listed at the end of this chapter.

Reasons for Government-Orchestrated Consumer Protection Two rationales are commonly advanced for extensive government involvement in overseeing and supervising nonmonopolistic industries.

Market Failures One rationale for government involvement in nonmonopolistic industries, which you encountered in a previous chapter, is the possibility of *market failures*. For example, the presence of negative externalities such as pollution may induce governments to regulate industries that create such externalities.

Asymmetric Information The second common rationale for regulation of nonmonopolistic industries is *asymmetric information*. In the context of many producer-consumer interactions, this term refers to situations in which a producer has information about a product that the consumer lacks. For instance, administrators of your college or university may know that another school in your vicinity offers better-quality degree programs in certain fields. If so, it would not be in the interest of your college or university to transmit this information to applicants who are interested in pursuing degrees in those fields.

For certain products, asymmetric information problems can pose special difficulties for consumers trying to assess product quality in advance of purchase. In unregulated financial markets, for example, individuals contemplating buying a company's stock or a municipality's bond might struggle to assess the associated risks of financial loss. If the air transportation industry were unregulated, a person might have trouble determining if one airline's planes were less safe than those of competing airlines. In an unregulated market for pharmaceuticals, parents might worry about whether one company's childhood-asthma medication could have more dangerous side effects than medications sold by other firms.

ECONOMICS IN YOUR LIFE

To contemplate how a proposed governmental regulation intended to be informative arguably actually provided false information to consumers, take a look at **When a Regulation Requiring the Label "Added Sugars" Actually Means Nothing of the Sort** on page 599.

Asymmetric Information and Product Quality In extreme cases, asymmetric information can create situations in which most of the available products are of low quality. A commonly cited example is the market for used automobiles. Current owners of cars that *appear* to be in good condition know the autos' service records. Some owners know that their cars have been well maintained and really do run great. Others, however, have not kept their autos in good repair and thus are aware that they will be susceptible to greater-than-normal mechanical or electrical problems.

An Example Suppose that in your local used-car market, half of all used cars offered for sale are high-quality autos. The other half are low-quality cars, commonly called "lemons," that are likely to break down within a few months or perhaps even weeks.

In addition, suppose that a consumer is willing to pay $20,000 for a particular car model if it is in excellent condition but is willing to pay only $10,000 if it is a lemon. Finally, suppose that people who own truly high-quality used cars are only willing to sell at a price of at least $20,000, but people who own lemons are willing to sell at any price at or above $10,000.

Willingness to Pay Because there is a 50–50 chance that a given car up for sale is of either quality, the average amount that a prospective buyer is willing to pay equals $\left(\frac{1}{2} \times \$20,000\right) + \left(\frac{1}{2} \times \$10,000\right) = \$15,000$. Owners of low-quality used cars are willing to sell them at this price, but owners of high-quality used cars are not.

In this example, only lemons will be traded, at the "lemon" price of $10,000. This fact is so because owners of cars in excellent condition will not sell their cars at a price that prospective buyers are willing to pay.

The Lemons Problem Economists refer to the possibility that asymmetric information can lead to a general reduction in product quality in an industry as the **lemons problem**. This problem does not apply only to the used-car industry. In principle, any product with qualities that are difficult for consumers to fully assess is susceptible to the same problem. *Credence goods*—items such as pharmaceuticals, health care, and professional services with features that consumers have trouble assessing on their own—also may be particularly vulnerable to the lemons problem.

Market Solutions to the Lemons Problem Firms offering truly high-quality products for sale can address the lemons problem in a variety of ways. They can offer product guarantees and warranties. In addition, to help consumers separate high-quality producers from incompetent or unscrupulous competitors, the high-quality producers may work together to establish industry standards.

In some cases, firms in an industry may even seek external product certification. They may, for example, solicit scientific reports supporting proposed industry standards and bearing witness that products of certain firms in the industry meet those standards. To legitimize a product-certification process, firms may hire outside companies or groups to issue such reports. In addition, firms may seek external product evaluations from independent reviewers, such as *Consumer Reports*, *PC Magazine*, TripAdvisor, or Yelp.

Implementing Consumer Protection Regulation

Governments offering asymmetric information and lemons problems as rationales for regulation presumably have concluded that private market solutions such as warranties, industry standards, and product certification are insufficient. To address asymmetric information problems, governments may offer legal remedies to consumers or enforce licensing requirements in an effort to provide minimum product standards. In some cases, governments go well beyond simple licensing requirements by establishing a regulatory apparatus for overseeing all aspects of an industry's operations.

Liability Laws and Government Licensing Sometimes liability laws, which specify penalties for product failures, provide consumers with protections similar to guarantees and warranties. When the Federal Trade Commission (FTC) charged Facebook with violating privacy guarantees to its customers, the FTC used powers granted to it by the 1914 FTC Act to investigate deceptive practices by firms. The FTC Act effectively made Facebook's privacy guarantees legally enforceable. Although the FTC applied the law in this particular case, any consumer could have filed suit for damages under the terms of the statute.

Lemons problem
The potential for asymmetric information to bring about a general decline in product quality in an industry.

Federal and state governments also get involved in consumer protection by issuing licenses granting only "qualifying" firms the legal right to produce and sell certain products. For instance, governments of nearly half the states give the right to sell caskets only to people who have a mortuary or funeral director's license, allegedly to ensure that bodies of deceased individuals are handled with care and dignity.

Although government licensing may successfully limit the sale of low-quality goods, licensing requirements also often limit the number of providers. As you learned earlier, such requirements can ease efforts by established firms to act as monopolists. In addition, if governments rely on the expertise of established firms for assistance in drafting licensing requirements, these firms certainly have strong incentives to recommend low standards for themselves but high standards for prospective entrants.

Direct Economic and Social Regulation In some instances, governments determine that liability laws and licensing requirements are insufficient to protect the interests of consumers. A government may decide that asymmetric information problems in banking are so severe that without an extensive banking regulatory apparatus, consumers will lose confidence in banks, and banking crises may ensue. It may rely on similar rationales to establish economic regulation of other financial services industries. Eventually, it may apply consumer protection rationales to justify the economic regulation of additional industries such as trucking or air transportation.

The government may establish an oversight authority to make certain that consumers are protected from incompetent producers of foods and pharmaceuticals. Eventually, the government may determine that a host of other products should meet government consumer protection standards. It may also decide that people who produce the products also require government agencies to ensure workplace safety. In this way, widespread social regulation emerges, as it has in the United States and almost all developed nations.

How You React to Regulatory "Overkill" with Respect to Product Safety Warnings Virtually every product sold in the United States contains safety warnings. The regulations concerning these safety warnings are complicated. Also, product producers wish to protect themselves from liability lawsuits. Consequently, the safety warnings have become so long that you and probably everyone you know simply ignore them. Thus, compared to, say, a one-sheet safety statement that you might read and that might be useful, you end up reading nothing. The result of these extensive consumer safety statements is that products are used less safely than they otherwise would have been.

Incentives and Costs of Regulation

> **27.4** Identify alternative theories aimed at explaining the behavior of regulators

Abiding by government regulations is a costly undertaking for firms. Consequently, businesses engage in a number of activities intended to avoid the true intent of regulations or to bring about changes in the regulations that government agencies establish.

Creative Response and Feedback Effects: Results of Regulation

Sometimes individuals and firms respond to a regulation in a way that conforms to the letter of the law but undermines its spirit. When they do so, they engage in **creative response** to regulations.

One type of creative response has been labeled a *feedback effect*. Individuals' behaviors may change after a regulation has been put into effect. If a regulation requires fluoridated water, then parents know that their children's teeth have significant protection against tooth decay. Consequently, the feedback effect is that parents become less concerned about how many sweets their children eat.

Why might "paternalistic lies" sometimes told by government agencies that implement regulatory "nudges" generate feedback effects undermining consumer behaviors that such lies are intended to induce?

Creative response
Behavior on the part of a firm that allows it to comply with the letter of the law but violate the spirit, significantly lessening the law's effects.

BEHAVIORAL EXAMPLE

Regulatory Nudges Predicated on Paternalistic Lies

Many governmental regulatory interventions have come in the form of "nudges," or regulatory constraints on the range of choices available to targeted consumers. Such nudges are intended to limit consumers to decisions that the government has deemed most desirable. In a sense, a governmental regulatory agency engaging in such nudges takes on the role of a parent who behaves paternalistically toward targeted consumers whom the agency effectively treats like children. When a paternalistic regulator fails to inform consumers that it has reduced their set of feasible choices, it implicitly behaves deceitfully. Some regulatory agencies even explicitly tell lies to induce the consumers to make a governmentally favored choice. One example is a regulatory claim that a government-favored light bulb always generates energy savings when, in fact, consumers who turn those types of bulbs on and off many times per day use more energy, rather than less.

Matthew James Lupoli of the University of California at San Diego, Emma Edelman Levine of the University of Chicago, and Adam Eric Greenberg of the University of California at Los Angeles have conducted experiments intended to gauge the behavioral effects of paternalistic lies. They find that such lies cause recipients to believe that the paternalistic liars violate the recipients' autonomy, inaccurately perceive their preferences, and fail to act in their best interests. Unintended reactions by the recipients can undermine the responses intended by the paternalistic liars. Efforts on the part of paternalistic liars, such as deceiving regulatory agencies, to offset resulting feedback effects can only be partly successful. Thus, government agencies' paternalistic lies meant to strengthen the intended behavioral responses to regulatory nudges will always at least partially undermine the intended effects of the nudges.

REAL APPLICATION

When Congress passed legislation limiting the sale of incandescent light bulbs, how could you have reacted?

Sources are listed at the end of this chapter.

Explaining Regulators' Behavior

Those charged with enforcing government regulations operate outside the market, so their decisions are determined by nonmarket processes. A number of theories have emerged to describe the behavior of regulators. These theories explain how regulation can harm consumers by generating higher prices and fewer product choices while benefiting producers by reducing competitive forces and allowing higher profits. Two of the best-known theories of regulatory behavior are the *capture hypothesis* and the *share-the-gains, share-the-pains theory*.

Capture hypothesis
A theory of regulatory behavior that predicts that regulators will eventually be captured by special interests of the industry being regulated.

The Capture Hypothesis Regulators often end up becoming champions of the firms they are charged with regulating. According to the **capture hypothesis**, regardless of why a regulatory agency was originally established, eventually special interests of the industry it regulates will capture it. After all, the people who know the most about a regulated industry are the people already in the industry. Thus, people who have been in the industry and have allegiances and friendships with others in the industry will most likely be asked to regulate the industry.

According to the capture hypothesis, individual consumers of a regulated industry's products and individual taxpayers who finance a regulatory agency have interests too diverse to be greatly concerned with the industry's actions. In contrast, special interests of the industry are well organized and well defined. These interests also have more to offer political entrepreneurs within a regulatory agency, such as future employment with one of the regulated firms. Therefore, regulators have a strong incentive to support the position of a well-organized special-interest group within the regulated industry.

Share-the-gains, share-the-pains theory
A theory of regulatory behavior that holds that regulators must take account of the demands of three groups: legislators, who established and oversee the regulatory agency; firms in the regulated industry; and consumers of the regulated industry's products.

"Share the Gains, Share the Pains" The **share-the-gains, share-the-pains theory** offers a somewhat different view of regulators' behavior. This theory focuses on the specific aims of regulators. It proposes that a regulator's main objective is simply to keep his or her job as a regulator. To do so, the regulator must obtain the approval of both the legislators who originally established and continue to oversee the regulatory agency and the regulated industry. The regulator must also take into account the views of the industry's customers.

In contrast to the capture hypothesis, which holds that regulators must take into account only industry special interests, the share-the-gains, share-the-pains theory contends that regulators must worry about legislators and consumers as well. After all, if industry customers who are hurt by improper regulation complain to legislators, the regulators might lose their jobs. Whereas the capture theory predicts that regulators will quickly allow electric utilities to raise their rates in the face of higher fuel costs, the share-the-gains, share-the-pains theory predicts a slower, more measured regulatory response. Ultimately, regulators will permit an increase in utility rates, but the allowed adjustment will not be as speedy or complete as predicted by the capture hypothesis. The regulatory agency is not completely captured by the industry. It also has to consider the views of consumers and legislators.

The Benefits and Costs of Regulation

As noted earlier, regulation offers many *potential* benefits. *Actual* benefits, however, are difficult to measure. Putting a dollar value on safer products, a cleaner environment, and better working conditions is a difficult proposition. Furthermore, the benefits of most regulations accrue to society over a long time.

The Direct Costs of Regulation to Taxpayers Measuring the costs of regulation is also a challenging undertaking. After all, about 5,000 new federal and state regulations are issued each year. One cost, though, is certain: U.S. federal taxpayers' inflation-adjusted expenditures are about $57 billion per year for staffing regulatory agencies with more than 300,000 employees and funding their various activities. Figure 27-3 displays the distribution of total federal government outlays for economic and social regulation of various areas of the economy.

The *total* cost of regulation is much higher than just the explicit government outlays to fund the administration of various regulations, however. After all, businesses must expend resources complying with regulations, developing creative responses to regulations, and funding special-interest lobbying efforts directed at legislators and regulatory officials. Sometimes companies find that it is impossible to comply with one regulation without violating another, and determining how to avoid the resulting legal entanglements can entail significant expenditures.

The Total Social Cost of Regulation According to the Office of Management and Budget, annual expenditures that U.S. businesses must make solely to comply with regulations issued by various federal agencies amount to more than $700 billion per year. Nevertheless, this estimate encompasses only the *explicit* costs of satisfying regulatory demands placed on businesses. It ignores relevant opportunity costs. After all, owners, managers, and employees of companies could be doing other things with their time and resources than complying with regulations. Economists estimate that

FIGURE 27-3

The Distribution of Federal Regulatory Spending

This figure shows the areas of the economy to which about $57 billion of inflation-adjusted taxpayer-provided funds currently are utilized to finance economic and social regulation.

Source: Office of Management and Budget.

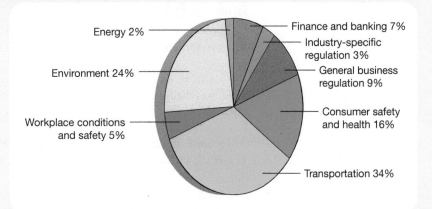

- Energy 2%
- Environment 24%
- Workplace conditions and safety 5%
- Finance and banking 7%
- Industry-specific regulation 3%
- General business regulation 9%
- Consumer safety and health 16%
- Transportation 34%

the additional opportunity costs of complying with federal regulations may be as high as $300 billion per year. A portion of this amount is passed on to consumers in the form of higher prices.

All told, therefore, the total social cost associated with satisfying federal regulations in the United States probably exceeds $1 trillion per year. This figure, of course, applies only to federal regulations. It does not include the explicit and implicit opportunity costs associated with regulations issued by 50 different state governments and tens of thousands of municipalities. The annual cost of regulation throughout the United States likely exceeds $1.75 trillion per year.

What are the effects on housing prices of requiring newly constructed homes to have solar panels?

POLICY EXAMPLE

California Seeks to Reduce Homeowners' Energy Costs at the Expense of Higher House Prices

California's Building Standard Commission establishes rules governing construction of new homes in the state. Recently, this regulator required that all new one-, two-, and three-level houses must contain sufficient solar panels to yield an estimated annual energy-expense reduction for a typical house buyer of about $633 per year. After multiplying this annual cost savings by 30, the regulator projected $19,000 in total savings to a buyer over a 30-year period.

At the current price of solar panels, the rule is anticipated to push up the price of a new house by about $10,000, so the commission claims that a typical buyer will come out ahead over 30 years. A fact that the regulator ignores, however, is that the average buyer of a new house sells it about 13 years later. Hence, an average homebuyer actually experiences an overall energy-expense reduction equal to $633 per year over 13 years of ownership. The resulting average $8,300 cost savings (which ignores discounting) is less than the projected average $10,000 house-price increase. Thus, the regulation causes a typical buyer to incur a *higher* net cost of owning a new house.

FOR CRITICAL THINKING

Why must private costs incurred to satisfy a government regulation ultimately fall on firms and individuals of the goods or services subjected to the regulation?

Sources are listed at the end of this chapter.

27.5 Understand the foundations of antitrust regulations and enforcement

Antitrust Policy

An expressed aim of the U.S. government is to foster competition. To this end, Congress has made numerous attempts to legislate against business practices that Congress has perceived to be anticompetitive. This is the general idea behind antitrust legislation. If the courts can prevent collusion among sellers of a product, there will be no restriction of output, and monopoly prices will not result. Instead, prices of goods and services will be close to their marginal social opportunity costs.

Antitrust Policy in the United States

Congress has enacted four key antitrust laws, which are summarized in Table 27-2. The most important of these is the original U.S. antitrust law, called the Sherman Act.

The Sherman Antitrust Act of 1890 The Sherman Antitrust Act, which was passed in 1890, was the first attempt by the federal government to control the growth of monopoly in the United States. The most important provisions of that act are as follows:

Section 1: Every contract, combination in the form of a trust or otherwise, or conspiracy, in restraint of trade or commerce among the several states, or with foreign nations, is hereby declared to be illegal.

Section 2: Every person who shall monopolize, or attempt to monopolize, or combine or conspire with any other person or persons to monopolize any part of the trade or commerce. . . shall be guilty of a misdemeanor [now a felony].

TABLE 27-2		
Key U.S. Antitrust Laws	Sherman Antitrust Act of 1890	Forbids any contract, combination, or conspiracy to restrain trade or commerce. Holds any person who attempts to monopolize trade or commerce criminally liable.
	Clayton Act of 1914	Prohibits specific business practices deemed to restrain trade or commerce. Bans price discrimination when price differences are not due to actual differences in selling or transportation costs and forbids a firm from selling goods on the condition of dealing exclusively with that company.
	Federal Trade Commission Act of 1914 (and 1938 Amendment)	Outlawed business practices that reduce the extent of competition and established the Federal Trade Commission with authority to issue cease and desist orders in situations involving "unfair methods of competition in commerce."
	Robinson-Patman Act of 1936	Bans selected discriminatory price cuts by chain stores that allegedly drive smaller competitors from the marketplace and forbids specific forms of price discrimination alleged to reduce competition substantially.

Notice how vague this act really is. No definition is given for the terms *restraint of trade* or *monopolize*. Despite this vagueness, however, the act was used to prosecute the infamous Standard Oil Trust of New Jersey. This company was charged with and convicted of violations of Sections 1 and 2 of the Sherman Antitrust Act in 1906. At the time it controlled more than 80 percent of the nation's oil-refining capacity. In addressing the company's legal appeal, the U.S. Supreme Court ruled that Standard Oil's predominance in the oil market created "a *prima facie* presumption of intent and purpose to control and maintain dominancy. . . not as a result from normal methods of industrial development, but by means of combinations." Here the word *combination* meant entering into associations and preferential arrangements with the intent of restraining competition. The Supreme Court forced Standard Oil of New Jersey to break up into many smaller companies that would have no choice but to compete.

The Sherman Act applies today just as it did more than a century ago. Recently, Chunghwa Picture Tubes, LG, and Sharp admitted that they had violated the Sherman Act by conspiring to fix the prices of liquid crystal display panels by holding down production. These companies paid $500 million in fines for this Sherman Act violation.

Other Important Antitrust Legislation Table 27-2 lists three other important antitrust laws. In 1914, Congress passed the Clayton Act to clarify some of the vague provisions of the Sherman Act by identifying specific business practices that were to be legally prohibited.

Congress also passed the Federal Trade Commission Act in 1914. In addition to establishing the Federal Trade Commission to investigate unfair trade practices, this law enumerated certain business practices that, according to Congress, involved overly aggressive competition. A 1938 amendment to this law expressly prohibited "unfair acts or practices in commerce" and empowered the FTC to regulate advertising and marketing practices by U.S. firms.

The Robinson-Patman Act of 1936 amended the Clayton Act by singling out specific business practices, such as selected price cuts, aimed at driving smaller competitors out of business. The act is often referred to as the "Chain Store Act" because it was intended to protect *independent* retailers and wholesalers from "unfair competition" by chain stores.

Exemptions from Antitrust Laws Numerous laws exempt the following industries and business practices from antitrust legislation:

- Labor unions

- Public utilities—electric, gas, and telephone companies

- Professional baseball

- Cooperative activities among U.S. exporters

- Hospitals

- Public transit and water systems

- Suppliers of military equipment

- Joint publishing arrangements in a single city by two or more newspapers

International Discord in Antitrust Policy

What, if anything, should U.S. antitrust authorities do if AT&T decides that it wishes to merge with British Telecommunications or if China's Dalian Wanda wants to acquire AMC Entertainment Holdings? What, if anything, should they do if Time Warner, the largest U.S. entertainment company, attempts to merge with London-based EMI, one of the world's largest recorded-music companies? These are not just rhetorical questions, as U.S. and European antitrust authorities learned when these issues actually surfaced. Growing international linkages among markets for many goods and services have increasingly made antitrust policy a global undertaking.

The international dimensions of antitrust pose a problem for U.S. antitrust authorities in the Department of Justice and the Federal Trade Commission. In the United States, the overriding goal of antitrust policies has traditionally been protecting the interests of consumers. This is also a formal objective of European Union (EU) antitrust authorities. In the EU, however, policymakers are also required to reject any business combination that "creates or strengthens a dominant position as a result of which effective competition would be significantly impeded."

This additional clause has sometimes created tension between U.S. and EU policymaking. In the United States, increasing dominance of a market by a single firm arouses the concern of antitrust authorities. Nevertheless, U.S. authorities typically will remain passive if they determine that the increased market dominance arises from factors such as exceptional management and greater cost efficiencies that ultimately benefit consumers by reducing prices. In contrast, under EU rules antitrust authorities are obliged to block *any* business combination that increases the dominance of any producer. They must do so regardless of what factors might have caused the business's preeminence in the marketplace or whether the antitrust action might have adverse implications for consumers.

Antitrust Enforcement

How are antitrust laws enforced? In the United States, most enforcement continues to be based on the Sherman Act. The Supreme Court has defined the offense of **monopolization** as involving the following elements: "(1) the possession of monopoly power in the relevant market and (2) the willful acquisition or maintenance of that power, as distinguished from growth or development as a consequence of a superior product, business acumen [shrewdness], or historical accident."

Monopolization
The possession of monopoly power in the relevant market and the willful acquisition or maintenance of that power, as distinguished from growth or development as a consequence of a superior product, business acumen, or historical accident.

The Relevant Market The Sherman Act does not define monopoly. To assess whether a monopolistic capability might exist, antitrust authorities seek to define a market and then to measure the degree of concentration in that market. They begin by determining the **relevant market** within which firms' products are in competition.

The relevant market consists of two elements. One is the relevant *product* market, which involves products that are closely substitutable for one another. The second element is the relevant *geographic* market, which involves a particular set of firms whose substitutable products actually are available to consumers in a particular area, ranging from a limited region to the entire nation. Combining the two elements yields the market in which firms in an industry compete.

Once the relevant market has been determined, antitrust enforcement focuses on the degree of competition within that market. The two federal enforcement agencies, the Antitrust Division of the U.S. Department of Justice and the Federal Trade Commission (FTC), utilize the Herfindahl-Hirschman Index, or HHI, for this purpose.

Relevant market
A group of firms' products that are closely substitutable and available to consumers within a particular geographic area.

HHI Limits for Merger Evaluations Recall that the HHI is equal to the sum of the squared shares of total sales or output by all firms in an industry. Thus, once the relevant market has been determined, antitrust enforcers compute the HHI for all firms within the industry defined by the scope of that market.

When assessing whether a proposed horizontal merger among two or more firms competing in a relevant market might create a monopoly pricing capability, enforcers consider *both* the resulting change in the HHI *and* the level of the postmerger HHI. Under current U.S. antitrust enforcement guidelines, *either* a combined HHI *change* greater than 200 and postmerger HHI in excess of 1,500 *or* a combined HHI *change* exceeding 100 and a postmerger HHI above 2,500 raise antitrust concerns. The Justice Department's Antitrust Division or the FTC can follow up on such concerns by trying to determine the predicted effects of the merger on overall industry output and on the equilibrium price in the relevant market.

Merger Enforcement Actions If the antitrust enforcement authority's position is that the proposed merger would lead to a substantial output reduction and price increase, then the authority files a lawsuit seeking to block the merger. The firms proposing the merger can respond either by dropping their merger plan or by defending the plan in court.

At this point, it is up to a court to determine whether the merger legally can proceed, must be abandoned, or can be allowed under certain conditions. Sometimes, for instance, a merger is permitted on the condition that merging firms sell parts of their operations to other firms in the same industry.

How might merger evaluations and other antitrust enforcement actions sometimes be led astray by HHI values that exclude the market shares of illegal competitors?

INTERNATIONAL POLICY EXAMPLE

Relevant Illegal Competition Complicates Merger Evaluations in Latin America

In many parts of the world, sellers that governments have not legally authorized to participate in the market nonetheless are major competitors whose combined activities can capture large market shares. Nevertheless, government agencies charged with antitrust enforcement typically define relevant markets only in terms of the market shares of legally authorized firms.

For instance, current estimates indicate that almost one-third of all buyers of cable and satellite television services in Latin America purchase services from providers that are not legally authorized to operate. In the South American nation of Peru, unauthorized sellers provide about 50 percent of all subscription television services. The HHI value calculated for a relevant market that government antitrust officials define solely in terms of legally authorized sellers of these services consequently is biased significantly by exclusion of these competitors. The unauthorized presence of illegal sellers of television subscription services constitutes economically relevant competition for the legally authorized sellers—and certainly is relevant to about half of Peruvian subscribers to these services.

FOR CRITICAL THINKING

Does the failure of antitrust authorities to include illegal but economically relevant competitors when computing an industry HHI for merger analysis yield an HHI value that is biased upward or downward? Explain briefly.

Sources are listed at the end of this chapter.

Product Packaging and Antitrust Enforcement

A particular problem in U.S. antitrust enforcement is determining whether a firm has engaged in "willful acquisition or maintenance" of market power. Actions that appear to some observers to be good business look like antitrust violations to others. To illustrate why quandaries can arise in antitrust enforcement, let's consider two examples: *versioning* and *bundling*.

Versioning
Selling a product in slightly altered forms to different groups of consumers.

Product Versioning A firm engages in product **versioning** when it sells an item in slightly altered forms to different groups of consumers. A typical method of versioning is to remove certain features from an item and offer what remains as a somewhat stripped-down version of the product at a different price.

The Mechanics of Versioning Consider an office-productivity software program, such as Adobe Acrobat or Microsoft Word. Firms selling such programs typically offer both a "professional" version containing a full range of features and a "standard" version providing only basic functions.

One perspective on this practice regards it as a form of price discrimination, or selling essentially the same product at different prices to different consumers. People who desire to use the full range of features in Adobe Acrobat or Microsoft Word are likely to be computing professionals. Compared to the demand by most other consumers, their demand for the full-featured version of an office-productivity software program is likely to be less elastic. In principle, therefore, Adobe and Microsoft can earn higher profits by offering "professional" versions at higher prices and selling a "standard" version at a lower price.

Price Discrimination versus Versioning Price discrimination—charging varying prices to different consumers when the price differences are not a result of different production or transportation costs—is illegal under the Clayton Act of 1914. Are Adobe, Microsoft, and other companies engaging in illegal price discrimination? An alternative perspective on versioning indicates that they are not. According to this point of view, consumers regard "professional" and "standard" versions of software packages as imperfect substitutes. Consequently, each version is a distinctive product sold in a unique market. If so, versioning increases overall consumer satisfaction because consumers who are not computing professionals are able to utilize certain features of software products at a lower price.

So far, antitrust authorities in the United States and elsewhere have adopted this view of the economic effects of versioning. These authorities have not perceived versioning to constitute a form of price discrimination.

Bundling
Offering two or more products for sale as a set.

Tie-in sales
Purchases of one product that are permitted by the seller only if the consumer buys another good or service from the same firm.

Product Bundling Antitrust authorities have been less tolerant of another form of product packaging, known as **bundling**, which involves the joint sale of two or more products as a set. Antitrust authorities usually are not concerned if a firm allows consumers to purchase the products either individually or as a set. They are more likely to investigate a firm's business practices, however, when the firm allows consumers to purchase one product only when it is bundled with another. Antitrust officials often view this form of bundling as a method of price discrimination known as **tie-in sales**, in which a firm requires consumers who wish to buy one of its products to purchase another item the firm sells as well.

A Hypothetical Illustration of Product Bundling to Engage in Price Discrimination To understand this reasoning about tie-in sales, consider a situation in which one group of consumers is willing to pay $100 for an operating system for a digital device but only $50 for an app-maintenance system. A second group of consumers is willing to pay only $50 for the same operating system but is willing to pay $100 for the same app-maintenance system.

If the same company that sells both types of systems offers the operating system at a price above $50, then only consumers in the first group will buy the operating system. Likewise, if it sells the app-maintenance system at a price above $50, then only the second group of consumers will purchase that program. If the firm, however, sells both products as a bundled set, it can charge $150 and generate sales of both products to both groups. One interpretation is that the first group pays $100 for the operating system, but for the second group, the operating system's price is $50. At the same time, the first group has paid $50 for the app-maintenance system, while the second group perceives the price of this system to be $100. In theory, bundling might thereby effectively enable the company selling these systems to engage in price discrimination by charging different prices to different groups.

Real-World Allegations of Bundling Intended to Attain a Monopoly Alternatively, offering two or more products for sale only as a bundle might assist a firm to extend an existing monopoly position involving one bundled product to other items it includes within the bundle. Europe's primary antitrust enforcement agency, the European Commission, recently sought to apply this interpretation in a lawsuit against Google. The European Commission claimed that Google sought to use product bundling to maintain near-monopoly power—market shares exceeding 80 percent in the production and sale of its Android operating system and distribution of apps for Android-based digital devices.

According to the European Commission, Google bundled the sale of Android-compatible apps with the sales of its operating system in an effort to restrain competition for both the operating system and apps compatible only with that product. Doing so, the European Commission claims, has allowed Google to maintain market shares exceeding 80 percent in the European market for digital-device operating systems and 90 percent in the market for apps. The status of this antitrust case currently is unresolved.

ECONOMICS IN YOUR LIFE

When a Regulation Requiring the Label "Added Sugars" Actually Means Nothing of the Sort

Each year, David and Susan Folino collect sap from trees in their Vermont forest, boil the sap to remove water and obtain a thick syrup, and sell the resulting product to consumers. For years, they have marketed their product as "pure maple syrup." Recently, however, the U.S. Food and Drug Administration (FDA) determined that they and all others who produce syrup using the same process must include a label indicating that the syrup includes "added sugars." The Folinos became concerned that consumers would take those words at face value and conclude that sugars are indeed added to their syrup products. The Folinos worried that consumers surely would confuse their natural products with other artificially sweetened toppings. The consequence would be decreased sales and reduced profits.

In response to complaints by the Folinos and other syrup producers, the FDA initially decided to have labels keep the "added sugars" warning but direct consumers to information about what that term meant to the FDA. Ultimately, though, the FDA backtracked on its "added sugars" labeling requirement for both syrup and honey. The FDA now will require only that the actual sugar content of the products be marked clearly on the products' labels.

FOR CRITICAL THINKING

In light of the fact that artificially sweetened toppings are lower-priced substitutes for natural maple syrup, why might the Folinos have been justified in their concerns that the FDA's requirement could reduce syrup demand?

REAL APPLICATION

The FDA regulates the labeling of gluten-free foods as well as non–genetically modified organisms (GMOs) in other foods. Do you still have to be careful about the labeling of such foods?

Sources are listed at the end of this chapter.

ISSUES & APPLICATIONS

How Have FDA Regulatory Rules Dramatically Pushed Up Prices of Old Drugs That Now Are "New"?

iqoncept/123RF GB Limited

CONCEPTS APPLIED

➤ Direct Costs of Regulation

➤ Total Social Cost of Regulation

➤ Benefits of Regulation

A few years ago, the FDA re-approved continued sale of a long-produced drug that prevents frequent urination. Its price then increased by more than 1,100 percent. Shortly thereafter, the Food and Drug Administration re-approved a drug that physicians have long prescribed to treat symptoms of gout. The price of the medication promptly increased by 2,300 percent. More recently, the FDA re-approved a drug that has long been known to help prevent premature births. The drug's price subsequently rose by about 2,600 percent.

How Old Drugs Become "New"

Each of the above medications entered the U.S. pharmaceuticals market before 1962. At that time, obtaining FDA approval required proving only that a drug is safe. Today, drug makers must also prove that their products provide the intended beneficial effects.

Thus, when the manufacturers of the drugs that prevent frequent urination, treat gout symptoms, and help prevent premature births filed for re-approval of these long-standing medications, the firms had to provide formal evidence that the drugs actually benefit patients. In each case, the pharmaceutical that had long been used to treat each problem became "new" from a regulatory point of view.

The Economic Benefit to a Drug Producer of Proving That a Long-Standing Drug Really Does Benefit Patients

Following FDA re-approval, the drug makers could pull the original versions of the medications from the market. The firms could then re-package the pharmaceuticals as "new" drugs for which the companies had sole authorization to produce as the only government-authorized sellers.

As the only firms granted the right to manufacture and sell these "new" generic drugs, the manufacturers were able to act as monopolies and search for higher, profit-maximizing prices. The monopoly prices yielded as a result of the FDA rules and charged to consumers turned out to be substantially higher than the prices of the original forms of the drugs. For consumers of the drugs, of course, the results have been significantly higher treatment costs.

FOR CRITICAL THINKING

How can the FDA's legal power to authorize firms to produce specific drugs enable the FDA to create monopoly producers of such pharmaceuticals?

REAL APPLICATION

Assume that you are a regular purchaser of a medication that has been on the market for decades, but has now been "re-approved." The price of that medication has risen dramatically. Will you and others who take this drug continue to purchase the same quantity as before?

Sources are listed at the end of this chapter.

What You Should Know

Here is what you should know after reading this chapter.

LEARNING OBJECTIVES	KEY TERMS
27.1 Distinguish between economic regulation and social regulation *There are two basic forms of government regulation of business: economic regulation and social regulation. Economic regulation applies to specific industries. Social regulations affect nearly all businesses and encompass a broad range of objectives concerning such issues as product safety, environmental quality, and working conditions.*	**Key Figure** Figure 27-1, 583
27.2 Recognize the practical difficulties in regulating the prices charged by natural monopolies *A natural monopoly's long-run marginal cost is less than long-run average total cost, so requiring marginal cost pricing causes an economic loss. Hence, regulators normally aim for a natural monopoly's price to equal average total cost, so it earns zero economic profits. In recent years, uncoupling production of electricity, natural gas, and telecommunications from their distribution has enabled regulators to promote competition in these industries.*	cost-of-service regulation, 586 rate-of-return regulation, 586 **Key Figure** Figure 27-2, 586
27.3 Explain the main rationales for regulation of industries that are not inherently monopolistic *The two most common rationales for regulation of nonmonopolistic industries relate to addressing market failures and protecting consumers from problems arising from information asymmetries. Asymmetric information can also create a lemons problem, which occurs when uncertainty about product quality leads to markets containing mostly low-quality items.*	lemons problem, 590
27.4 Identify alternative theories aimed at explaining the behavior of regulators *The capture theory of regulator behavior predicts that regulators will eventually find themselves supporting the positions of the firms that they regulate. The share-the-gains, share-the-pains theory predicts that a regulator will try to satisfy all constituencies, at least in part. The costs of regulation, which include both the direct costs to taxpayers of funding regulatory agencies and the explicit and implicit opportunity costs that businesses must incur to comply, are easier to quantify in dollar terms than the benefits.*	creative response, 591 capture hypothesis, 592 share-the-gains, share-the-pains theory, 592 **Key Figure** Figure 27-3, 593
27.5 Understand the foundations of antitrust regulations and enforcement *There are four key antitrust laws, the most important of which is the Sherman Antitrust Act of 1890, which forbids attempts to monopolize an industry. The Supreme Court has defined monopolization as possessing or seeking monopoly pricing power in the "relevant market." Authorities charged with enforcing antitrust laws evaluate concentration of production or sales within a defined relevant market as compared with regulatory threshold concentration levels. In recent years, antitrust officials have raised questions about whether product packaging, either in the form of different versions or as bundled sets, is a type of price discrimination involving tie-in sales.*	monopolization, 596 relevant market, 597 versioning, 598 bundling, 598 tie-in sales, 598

PROBLEMS

27-1. Local cable television companies are sometimes granted monopoly rights to service a particular territory of a metropolitan area. The companies typically pay special taxes and licensing fees to local municipalities. Why might a municipality give monopoly rights to a cable company?

27-2. A local cable company, the sole provider of cable television service, is regulated by the municipal government. The owner of the company claims that she is normally opposed to regulation by government, but asserts that regulation is necessary because local residents would not want a large number of different cables crisscrossing the city. Why do you think the owner is defending regulation by the city?

27-3. The table below depicts the cost and demand structure a natural monopoly faces.

Quantity	Price ($)	Long-Run Total Cost ($)
0	100	0
1	95	92
2	90	177
3	85	255
4	80	331
5	75	406
6	70	480

a. Calculate total revenues, marginal revenue, and marginal cost at each output level. If this firm is allowed to operate as a monopolist, what will be the quantity produced and the price charged by the firm? What will be the amount of monopoly profit? [*Hint:* Recall that marginal revenue equals the change in total revenues ($P \times Q$) from each additional unit and that marginal cost equals the change in total costs from each additional unit.]

b. If regulators require the firm to practice marginal cost pricing, what quantity will it produce, and what price will it charge? What is the firm's profit under this regulatory framework? [*Hint:* Recall that average total cost equals total cost divided by quantity and that profits equal $(P - ATC) \times Q$.]

c. If regulators require the firm to practice average cost pricing, what quantity will it produce, and what price will it charge? What is the firm's profit under this regulatory framework?

27-4. As noted in the chapter, separating the *production* of electricity from its *delivery* has led to considerable deregulation of producers.

a. Briefly explain which of these two aspects of the sale of electricity remains susceptible to natural monopoly problems.

b. Suppose that the potential natural monopoly problem you identified in part (a) actually arises. Why is marginal cost pricing not a feasible solution? What makes average cost pricing a feasible solution?

c. Discuss two approaches that a regulator could use to try to implement an average-cost-pricing solution to the problem identified in part (a).

27-5. Are lemons problems likely to be more common in some industries and less common in others? Based on your answer to this question, should

government regulatory activities designed to reduce the scope of lemons problems take the form of economic regulation or social regulation? Take a stand, and support your reasoning.

27-6. Research into genetically modified crops has led to significant productivity gains for countries such as the United States that employ these techniques. Countries such as the European Union's member nations, however, have imposed controls on the import of these products, citing concern for public health. Is the European Union's regulation of genetically modified crops social regulation or economic regulation?

27-7. Do you think that the regulation described in Problem 27-6 is more likely an example of the capture hypothesis or the share-the-gains, share-the-pains theory? Why?

27-8. Prices of tickets for seats on commercial passenger planes are typically in the hundreds of dollars, whereas trips often can be made by automobile at lower cost. Accident rates per person per trip in the airline industry are considerably lower than auto accident rates per person per trip. Based on these facts, discuss how regulatory costs and benefits may help to explain why government regulations require children to be placed in safety seats in automobiles but not on commercial passenger planes.

27-9. Several years ago, the U.S. government created a "Do Not Call Registry" and forbade marketing firms from calling people who placed their names on this list. Today, an increasing number of companies are sending mail solicitations to individuals inviting them to send back an enclosed postcard for more information about the firms' products. What these solicitations fail to mention is that they are worded in such a way that someone who returns the postcard gives up protection from telephone solicitations, even if they are on the government's "Do Not Call Registry." In what type of behavior are these companies engaging? Explain your answer. (*Hint:* Are these firms meeting the letter of the law but violating its spirit?)

27-10. Suppose that a business has developed a very high-quality product and operates more efficiently in producing that product than any other potential competitor. As a consequence, at present it is the only seller of this product, for which there are few close substitutes. Is this firm in violation of U.S. antitrust laws? Explain.

27-11. Consider the following fictitious sales data (in thousands of dollars) for both e-books and physical books. Firms have numbers instead of names, and Firm 1 generates only e-book sales. Suppose that antitrust authorities' initial evaluation of whether a single firm may possess "monopoly power" is whether its share of sales in the relevant market exceeds 70 percent.

	E-Book Sales		Physical Book Sales		Combined Book Sales	
Firm	Sales	Firm	Sales	Firm	Sales
1	$ 750	2	$4,200	2	$ 4,250
2	50	3	2,000	3	2,050
3	50	4	1,950	4	2,000
4	50	5	450	1	750
5	50	6	400	5	500
6	50			6	450
Total	$1,000		$9,000		$10,000

a. Suppose that the antitrust authorities determine that selling physical books and e-bookselling are individually separate relevant markets. Does an initial evaluation suggest that any single firm has monopoly power, as defined by the antitrust authorities?

b. Suppose that in fact there is really only a single book industry, in which firms compete in selling both physical books and e-books. According to the antitrust authorities' initial test of the potential for monopoly power, is there actually cause for concern?

27-12. Consider the data from Problem 27-11. Suppose that antitrust authorities have determined that there are separate relevant markets for e-books and physical books. In addition, these authorities perceive that a monopoly situation exists that can be challenged on legal grounds if the value of the Herfindahl-Hirschman Index exceeds 5,000. On the basis of this criterion, do the antitrust authorities conclude that there are grounds for a legal challenge in either market? Explain.

27-13. Consider the data from Problem 27-11. Suppose that antitrust authorities have determined that the relevant market includes both e-books and physical books. These authorities perceive that a monopoly situation exists that can be challenged on legal grounds if the value of the Herfindahl-Hirschman Index exceeds 5,000. On the basis of this criterion, do the antitrust authorities conclude that there are grounds for a legal challenge? Explain.

27-14. A package delivery company provides both overnight and second-day delivery services. It charges almost twice as much to deliver an overnight package to any world location as it does to deliver the same package to the same location in two days. Often, second-day packages arrive at company warehouses in destination cities by the next day, but drivers intentionally do not deliver these packages until the following day. What is this business practice called? Briefly summarize alternative perspectives concerning whether this activity should or should not be viewed as a form of price discrimination.

27-15. A firm that sells both Internet-security software and computer antivirus software will sell the antivirus software as a stand-alone product. It will only sell the Internet-security software to consumers in a combined package that also includes the antivirus software. What is this business practice called?

27-16. A few years ago, a food retailer called Whole Foods sought to purchase Wild Oats, a competitor in the market for organic foods. When the Federal Trade Commission (FTC) sought to block this merger on antitrust grounds, FTC officials argued that such a merger would dramatically increase concentration in the market for "premium organic foods." Whole Foods' counterargument was that it considered itself to be part of the broadly defined supermarket industry that includes retailers such as Albertsons, Kroger, and Safeway. What key issue of antitrust regulation was involved in this dispute? Explain.

27-17. A bank in Austin, Texas, has allowed its state banking license, under which it had been regulated by the Federal Deposit Insurance Corporation, a U.S. bank regulator, to expire. It has switched to a federal banking license, under which it is now regulated by the Office of the Comptroller of the Currency, another bank regulator. Do these regulators subject the bank to social or economic regulation?

27-18. Take a look at both panels of Figure 27-1. Suppose that we are willing to accept both federal regulatory spending per year and the annual number of *Federal Register* pages as measures of the extent of government regulation of businesses. Based on these measures, does any period unambiguously appear to stand out as one in which the extent of regulation declined?

27-19. Suppose that in panel (a) of Figure 27-2, the vertical distances to points F and A are $10 per unit and $2 per unit, and Q_m is 1,000 units. To measure the degree of monopoly power, economists often examine the differential between price and marginal cost as a percentage of the price. What would be the value of this measure of monopoly power for the natural monopolist depicted in panel (a) of the figure?

27-20. Consider panel (b) of Figure 27-2. The quantity Q_1 is 2,000 units, the price P_1 is $2 per unit, the average cost AC_1 is $4 per unit, and the vertical distance to point C is $6 per unit. What is the dollar amount of the losses earned by this natural monopolist when its price is equal to its marginal cost of producing Q_1 units?

27-21. The manager of a Pittsburgh shop wishes to sell on eBay a used telescope that is in good condition. The manager knows that prospective buyers perceive a 50–50 chance that the telescope is in good condition. If it is, buyers are willing to pay $1,000, but if it is in poor condition, they will pay only $200. What is the average amount a buyer will be willing to pay? Is there a lemons problem? Explain.

27-22. Manufacturing firms based in Columbus, Ohio, and Erie, Pennsylvania, have proposed a merger. If they were to merge, the resulting value of the Herfindahl-Hirschman Index in the nationwide market for the product they produce would rise from 1,400 to 1,800. Under current U.S. antitrust guidelines, would this proposed merger raise concerns for the U.S. Justice Department or Federal Trade Commission?

REFERENCES

POLICY EXAMPLE: Cost-of-Service Regulation of the U.S. Health Insurance Industry Fails to Contain Either Costs or Prices

Steve Cicala, Ethan Lieber, and Victoria Marone, "Regulating Markups in U.S. Health Insurance," *American Economic Journal: Applied Economics*, 2019.

Stuart Altman and Robert Mechanic, "Health Care Cost Control: Where Do We Go from Here?" *Health Affairs*, July 13, 2018.

AI—DECISION MAKING THROUGH DATA: Applying a Human Regulatory Touch to Firms' AI Systems

Steve Lohr, "How Do You Govern Machines That Can Learn? Policymakers Are Trying to Figure That Out," *New York Times*, January 20, 2019.

Kevin Bennett, "Can Robots Be Lazy or Mean?" *Psychology Today*, June 29, 2018.

Edd Gent, "Why Google DeepMind Is Putting AI on the Psychologist's Couch," SingularityHub (https://singularityhub.com/2018/02/12/google-deepmind-wants-to-put-ai-on-the-psychologists-couch/#sm.001o38na5149kdpd11e07drhq2pxg), February 12, 2018.

BEHAVIORAL EXAMPLE: Regulatory Nudges Predicated on Paternalistic Lies

Julian Jessop and Andy Mayer, "Nudge Economics—Can Paternalism Ever Be Libertarian?" Institute of Economic Affairs (https://iea.org.uk/debate-nudge-economics-can-paternalism-ever-be-libertarian/), January 15, 2019.

"When Lying Helps, and When It Hurts," Chicago Booth (https://newswise.com/articles/when-lying-helps-and-when-it-hurts), August 15, 2018.

Matthew James Lupoli, Emma Edelman Levine, and Adam Eric Greenberg, "Paternalistic Lies," *Organizational Behavior and Human Decision Processes*, 2018.

POLICY EXAMPLE: California Seeks to Reduce Homeowners' Energy Costs at the Expense of Higher House Prices

"2019 Building Energy Efficiency Standards," California Energy Commission (https://www.energy.ca.gov/title24/2019standards/), 2019.

Avery Anapol, "California Officials Give Final Approval to Requiring Solar Panels on New Homes," *The Hill*, December 6, 2018.

Natasha Bach, "California Becomes the First State to Require Solar Panels on New Homes. Here's How It Will Reduce Utility Costs," *Fortune*, December 6, 2018.

INTERNATIONAL POLICY EXAMPLE: Relevant Illegal Competition Complicates Merger Evaluations in Latin America

Jonathan Franklin, "The Insidious Device Revolutionizing Piracy in Latin America," *Americas Quarterly*, January 23, 2019.

Juan Fernandez Gonzalez, "Piracy, Unregulated Practices Cost Peru's Pay-TV Industry Dearly," Rapid TV News (https://www.rapidtvnews.com/2018052452237/pirate-unregulated-practices-cost-peru-s-pay-tv-industry-dearly.html#axzz5WCqpUyFW), May 24, 2018.

Christian Rojas and Arturo Briceño, "The Effects of Piracy on Competition: Evidence from Subscription TV," *International Journal of Industrial Organization*, 2018.

ECONOMICS IN YOUR LIFE: When a Regulation Requiring the Label "Added Sugars" Actually Means Nothing of the Sort

"Industry Resources on the Changes to the Nutrition Facts Label," U.S. Food and Drug Administration (https://www.fda.gov/Food/GuidanceRegulation/GuidanceDocumentsRegulatoryInformation/LabelingNutrition/ucm513734.htm#AddedSugars), 2019.

Elizabeth Crawford, "FDA Will Not Require 'Added Sugars' Call-Out on Pure Honey, Maple Syrup," Foodnavigator-USA.com (https://www.foodnavigator-usa.com/Article/2018/09/07/FDA-will-not-require-added-sugars-call-out-on-pure-honey-maple-syrup#), September 7, 2018.

Betsy McKay, "In Vermont, Pure Outrage Over Pure Syrup," *Wall Street Journal*, June 26, 2018.

ISSUES & APPLICATIONS: How Have FDA Regulatory Rules Dramatically Pushed Up Prices of Old Drugs That Now Are "New"?

Food and Drug Administration, "Drug Registration and Listing System" (https://www.fda.gov/Drugs/GuidanceComplianceRegulatoryInformation/DrugRegistrationandListing/default.htm), 2019.

Jennifer Barrett, "FDA Goals: Speed Up Generic Drug Approvals, Enhance Competition," *Pharmacy Times*, April 4, 2018.

Food and Drug Administration, "Drug Registration and Listing System" (https://www.fda.gov/Drugs/GuidanceComplianceRegulatoryInformation/DrugRegistrationandListing/default.htm), 2019.

Sheila Kaplan, "FDA Names and Shames Drug Makers to Encourage Generic Competition," *New York Times*, March 17, 2018.

28 The Labor Market

Nikita Anokhin/Shutterstock

LEARNING OBJECTIVES

After reading this chapter, you should be able to:

28.1 Understand why a firm's marginal revenue product curve is its labor demand curve

28.2 Describe how equilibrium wage rates are determined for perfectly competitive firms

28.3 Contrast wage determination under monopoly and perfect competition

28.4 Explain how a monopsonist determines how much labor to employ and what wage rate to pay

28.5 Discuss the goals, strategies, and current status of labor unions

n 1948, the percentage of U.S. male residents who were employed exceeded 80 percent, but by 2007 this percentage had declined to 70 percent. Since 2008, the percentage has fallen to 65 percent. The general downward trend in the percentage of men who are working has many causes, but the recent sharp drop largely is attributable to a significant decline in the supply of labor by young men aged 21 to 30. In this chapter, you will learn how the wider availability of lower-priced and higher-quality video games has contributed to this recent decline in the amount of labor supplied by young men at the prevailing wage rate. In addition, you will learn about how, other things being equal, the resulting overall drop in labor supply has affected U.S. employment and wages.

the total wages earned during the course of a typical year by an experienced welder or plumber often exceed those of an average college graduate? An average college graduate's annual earnings normally peak between $60,000 and $65,000 per year. In contrast, an experienced welder or plumber can anticipate peak annual earnings in excess of $70,000.

The wage rate that an individual can anticipate earning during the course of a typical year of employment depends on the conditions in markets for various labor skills. A key determinant of such market conditions is the demand for labor by firms that utilize such skills. The demand for any particular form of labor or for other types of inputs by businesses can be studied in much the same manner as we studied the demand for output. Our analysis will always end with the same conclusion: A firm will hire employees up to the point beyond which it isn't profitable to hire any more. It will hire employees to the point at which the marginal benefit of hiring a worker will just equal the marginal cost. Indeed, in every situation, it is most profitable to carry out an activity up to the point at which the marginal benefit equals the marginal cost. Remembering that guideline will help you in analyzing decision making at the firm level, which is where we will begin our discussion of the demand for labor.

28.1 Understand why a firm's marginal revenue product curve is its labor demand curve

The Demand for Labor in a Perfectly Competitive Labor Market

We will start our analysis under the assumption that the market for input factors is perfectly competitive. We will further assume that the output market is perfectly competitive. This provides a benchmark against which to compare other situations, in which labor markets or product markets are not perfectly competitive.

Competition in the Product Market

Let's take as our example a firm that sells wireless earbuds in a perfectly competitive market. The firm also buys labor (its variable input), which does not require any special skills, in a perfectly competitive market. A firm that hires labor under perfectly competitive conditions hires only a minuscule proportion of all the workers who are potentially available to the firm. By "potentially available," we mean all the workers in a geographic area who possess the skills demanded by our perfect competitor.

In such a market, it is always possible for the individual firm to hire extra workers without having to offer a higher wage. Thus, the supply of labor to the firm is perfectly elastic at the going wage rate established by the forces of supply and demand in the entire labor market. The firm is a *price taker* in the labor market.

Marginal Product

Look at panel (a) of Figure 28-1. In column 1, we show the number of workers per week that the firm can employ. In column 2, we show total product (TP) per week, the total production of wireless earbuds that different quantities of the labor input (in combination with a fixed amount of other inputs) will generate in a week's time. In column 3, we show the additional output gained when the company adds workers to its existing manufacturing facility.

Marginal product (MP) of labor
The change in output resulting from the addition of one more worker. The MP of the worker equals the change in total output accounted for by hiring the worker, holding all other factors of production constant.

This column, the **marginal product (MP) of labor**, represents the extra (additional) output attributed to employing additional units of the variable input factor. If this firm employs seven workers rather than six, the MP is 325 units of output. The law of diminishing marginal product predicts that additional units of a variable factor will, after some point, cause the MP to decline, other things held constant.

We are assuming that all other nonlabor factors of production are held constant. So, if our manufacturing firm wants to add one more worker to its production line, it has to crowd all the existing workers a little closer together because it does not increase

FIGURE 28-1

Marginal Revenue Product

In panel (a), the marginal revenue product (MRP) in column 4 is the additional revenue the firm receives for that additional output. For this perfectly competitive firm, marginal revenue equals the product price, which is $5 per unit. At a weekly wage of $1,000, the profit-maximizing firm will employ 12 workers, for which the marginal revenue product is just equal to the weekly wage rate. Panel (b) displays the number of workers the firm will want to hire at the wage rate established by the forces of supply and demand in the entire labor market. This firm hires labor in a perfectly competitive labor market and therefore faces the perfectly elastic supply curve *s* at a constant marginal factor cost (MFC) of $1,000 per week. The firm's labor demand curve is represented by MRP, and the labor supply curve that the firm faces is *s*. Profit maximization occurs at the point of intersection, at which MRP ≡ MFC.

Panel (a)

(1) Labor Input (workers per week)	(2) Total Product (TP) (wireless earbuds per week)	(3) Marginal Product (MP) (wireless earbuds per week)	(4) Marginal Revenue (MR = P = $5) x MP = Marginal Revenue Product (MRP) ($ per additional worker)	(5) Wage Rate ($ per week) = Marginal Factor Cost (MFC) = Change in Total Costs ÷ Change in Labor
6	2,175			
		325	$1,625	$1,000
7	2,500			
		300	1,500	1,000
8	2,800			
		275	1,375	1,000
9	3,075			
		250	1,250	1,000
10	3,325			
		225	1,125	1,000
11	3,550			
		200	1,000	1,000
12	3,750			
		175	875	1,000
13	3,925			

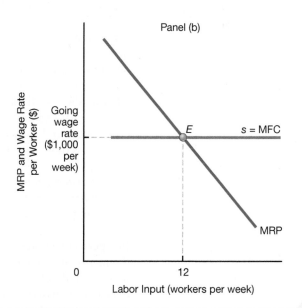

Panel (b)

its capital stock (the production equipment). Therefore, as we add more workers, each one has a smaller and smaller fraction of the available capital stock with which to work. If one worker uses one machine, adding another worker usually won't double the output because the machine can run only so fast and for so many hours per day. In other words, MP declines because of the law of diminishing marginal product.

Marginal Revenue Product

We now need to translate into a dollar value the volume of production of the good or service that results from hiring an additional worker. This is done by multiplying the marginal product by the marginal revenue of the firm. Because this firm sells wireless earbuds in a perfectly competitive market, marginal revenue is equal to the price of the product. If employing seven workers rather than six yields an MP of 325 and the marginal revenue is $5 per wireless earbud, the **marginal revenue product (MRP)** is $1,675 (325 × $5). The MRP is shown in column 4 of panel (a) of Figure 28-1. *The marginal revenue product represents the incremental worker's contribution to the firm's total revenues.*

Marginal revenue product (MRP)
The marginal product (MP) times marginal revenue (MR). The MRP gives the additional revenue obtained from a one-unit change in labor input.

When a firm operates in a perfectly competitive product market, the marginal product times the product price is also referred to as the *value of marginal product (VMP)*. Because price and marginal revenue are the same for a perfectly competitive firm, the VMP is also the MRP for such a firm.

Marginal Factor Cost   In column 5 of panel (a) of Figure 28-1, we show the wage rate, or *marginal factor cost*, of each worker. The marginal cost of workers is the extra cost incurred in employing an additional unit of that factor of production. We call that cost the **marginal factor cost (MFC)**. Otherwise stated,

Marginal factor cost (MFC)
The cost of using an additional unit of an input. For example, if a firm can hire all the workers it wants at the going wage rate, the marginal factor cost of labor is that wage rate.

$$\text{Marginal factor cost} = \frac{\text{change in total cost}}{\text{change in amount of resource used}}$$

Each worker is paid the same competitively determined wage of $1,000 per week, so the MFC is the same for all workers. Also, because the firm is buying labor in a perfectly competitive labor market, the wage rate of $1,000 per week really represents the supply curve of labor to the firm. That supply curve is perfectly elastic because the firm can purchase all labor at the same wage rate, considering that it is a minuscule part of the entire labor-purchasing market. (Recall the definition of perfect competition.) We show this perfectly elastic supply curve as *s* in panel (b) of Figure 28-1.

General Rule for Hiring   Nearly every optimizing rule in economics involves comparing marginal benefits with marginal cost. Because the benefit from added workers is extra output and consequently more revenues, the general rule for the hiring decision of a firm is this:

> *The firm hires workers up to the point at which the additional cost associated with hiring the last worker is equal to the additional revenue generated by hiring that worker.*

In a perfectly competitive market, this is the point at which the wage rate just equals the marginal revenue product. If the firm were to hire more workers, the additional wages would not be covered by additional increases in total revenue. If the firm were to hire fewer workers, it would be forfeiting the contributions that those workers otherwise could make to total profits.

Therefore, referring to columns 4 and 5 in panel (a) of Figure 28-1, we see that this firm would certainly employ at least seven workers because the MRP is $1,675 per week while the MFC is only $1,000 per week. The firm would continue to add workers up to the point at which MFC = MRP because as workers are added, they contribute more to revenue than to cost.

The MRP Curve: Demand for Labor We can also use panel (b) of Figure 28-1 to find how many workers our firm should hire. First, we draw a line at the going wage rate, which is determined by demand and supply in the labor market. The line is labeled *s* to indicate that it is the supply curve of labor for the *individual* firm purchasing labor in a perfectly competitive labor market. That firm can purchase all the labor it wants of equal quality at $1,000 per worker. This perfectly elastic supply curve, *s*, intersects the marginal revenue product curve at 12 workers per week. At the intersection, *E*, in panel (b) in Figure 28-1, the wage rate is equal to the marginal revenue product. The firm maximizes profits where its demand curve for labor, which is its MRP curve, intersects the firm's supply curve for labor, shown as *s*.

The firm in our example would not hire 13 workers, because using 13 rather than 12 would add only $875 to revenue but $1,000 to cost. If the price of labor should fall to, say, $875 per worker per week, the firm would hire an additional worker. Thus, the quantity of labor demanded increases as the wage decreases.

Derived Demand for Labor

We have identified an individual firm's demand for labor curve, which shows the quantity of labor that the firm will wish to hire at each wage rate, as its MRP curve. Under conditions of perfect competition in both product and labor markets, MRP is determined by multiplying MP times the product's price. This suggests that the demand for labor is a **derived demand**. Factors of production are rented or purchased not because they give any intrinsic satisfaction to the firms' owners but because they can be used to manufacture output that is expected to be sold at a profit.

Derived demand
Input factor demand derived from demand for the final product being produced.

Product Price and the Demand for Labor We know that an increase in the market demand for a given product raises the product's price (all other things held constant). A rise in this price, in turn, increases the marginal revenue product, or demand for the resource.

Figure 28-2 illustrates the effective role played by changes in product demand in a perfectly competitive product market. The MRP curve shifts whenever there is a change in the price of the final product that the workers are producing.

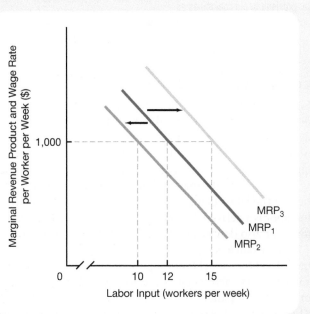

FIGURE 28-2

Demand for Labor, a Derived Demand

If we start with the marginal revenue product curve MRP$_1$ at the going wage rate of $1,000 per week, 12 workers will be hired. If the price of wireless earbuds goes down, the marginal revenue product curve will shift to MRP$_2$, and the number of workers hired will fall, in this case to 10. If the price of wireless earbuds goes up, the marginal revenue product curve will shift to MRP$_3$, and the number of workers hired will increase, in this case to 15.

How a Firm's Hiring Responds to a Product Price Change Suppose, for example, that the market price of wireless earbuds declines. In that case, the MRP curve will shift to the left from MRP_1 to MRP_2. We know that $MRP \equiv MP \times MR$. If marginal revenue (here the price of each unit sold) falls, so does the demand for labor. At the initial equilibrium, therefore, the price of labor (here the MFC) becomes greater than MRP. At the same going wage rate, the firm will hire fewer workers. This is because at various levels of labor use, the marginal revenue product of labor is now lower. Thus, the firm would reduce the number of workers hired. Conversely, if marginal revenue (the output price) rises, the demand for labor will also rise, and the firm will want to hire more workers at each and every possible wage rate.

We just pointed out that $MRP \equiv MP \times MR$. Clearly, then, a change in marginal productivity, or in the marginal product of labor, will shift the MRP curve. If the marginal productivity of labor decreases, the MRP curve, or demand curve, for labor will shift inward to the left. Again, this is because at every quantity of labor used, the MRP will be lower. A lower amount of labor will be demanded at every possible wage rate.

What accounts for a derived demand for the services of old German coal mines that has nothing to do with coal?

INTERNATIONAL EXAMPLE

A Newly Derived Demand for German Coal Mines Relates to Energy but Not to Coal

Decades ago, the demand for the services provided by German coal mines and workers within those spaces carved from the interior of the planet's crust was derived from the demand for energy that the burning of coal produced. In these times, in an effort to minimize release of gases generated by the burning of coal, electricity producers in Germany increasingly rely on the sun's rays and winds to generate energy via solar cells and wind turbines. As a consequence, the derived demand for the services of coal mines and people who operate the mines has been diminished relative to past levels.

A newly derived demand for the services of coal is still energy-related but has nothing to do with any remaining coal deposits. Problems for the production of solar- and wind-generated energy arise when there are days that are cloudy and calm. On such days, backup power sources are required. German engineers have identified the spaces provided by old coal mines as an ideal backup source. The engineers place a large pool of water on the land above the mine and another substantial pool of water at the base of the coal mine, up to 4,000 feet beneath the surface. On cloudy and calm days, the upper pool can be drained into the lower pool. As the water drains, it passes through turbines and spins them, which generates electricity. Almost all of the power is utilized to substitute for solar- and wind-generated power, but a small part of it is used to keep batteries that will power pumping water from the lower pool back to the upper pool to repeat the process until the appearance of sunny and windy days.

FOR CRITICAL THINKING

How might an increase in demand for tourist destinations along with a higher demand for solar and wind energy have induced conversion of some German mines into lakes surrounded by cottages, solar panels, and wind turbines?

Sources are listed at the end of this chapter.

Constructing the Market Labor Demand Curve

Given that the market demand curve for labor is made up of the individual firms' downward-sloping demand curves for labor, we can safely infer that the market demand curve for labor will look like *D* in panel (b) of Figure 28-3: It will slope downward. That market demand curve for labor in the wireless earbud industry shows the quantities of labor demanded by all of the firms in the industry at various wage rates.

Nevertheless, the market demand curve for labor is *not* a simple horizontal summation of the labor demand curves of all individual firms. Remember that the demand for labor is a derived demand. Even if we hold labor productivity constant, the demand for labor also depends on the price of the final output.

For instance, suppose that we start at a weekly wage rate of $1,300 and employment level 6 in panel (a) of Figure 28-3. If we sum all such employment levels—point *a* in panel (a)—across 200 firms, we get a market quantity of labor demanded of 1,200, or point *A* in panel (b), at the wage rate of $1,300. A decrease in the wage rate to $1,000 per week would induce individual firms' employment levels to increase to a quantity demanded of 20 *if the product price did not change.*

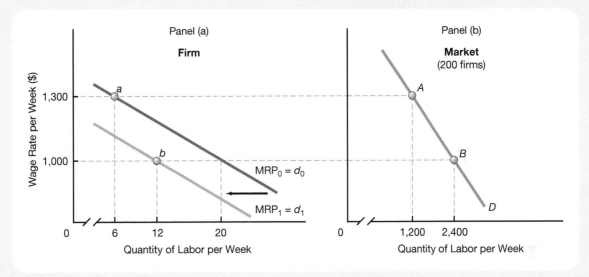

FIGURE 28-3

Derivation of the Market Demand Curve for Labor

The market demand curve for labor is not simply the horizontal summation of each individual firm's demand curve for labor. If weekly wage rates fall from $1,300 to $1,000, all 200 firms will increase employment and therefore output, causing the price of the product to fall.

This causes the marginal revenue product curve of each firm to shift inward, from d_0 to d_1 in panel (a). The resulting market demand curve, D, in panel (b) is therefore less elastic around weekly wage rates from $1,000 to $1,300 than it would be if the output price remained constant.

As all 200 firms simultaneously increase employment, total industry output also increases at the present price. Indeed, this would occur at *any* price, meaning that the industry product supply curve will shift rightward, and the market clearing price of the product must fall. The fall in the output price in turn causes a downward shift of each firm's MRP curve (d_0) to MRP_1 (d_1) in panel (a). Thus, each firm's employment of labor increases to 12 rather than to 20 at the wage rate of $1,000 per week. A summation of all such 200 employment levels gives us 2,400—point B—in panel (b).

Wage Determination in a Perfectly Competitive Labor Market

28.2 Describe how equilibrium wage rates are determined for perfectly competitive firms

Having developed the demand curve for labor (and all other variable inputs) in a particular industry, let's turn to the labor supply curve. By adding supply to the analysis, we can determine the equilibrium wage rate that workers earn in an industry. We can think in terms of a supply curve for labor that slopes upward in a particular industry.

At higher wage rates, more workers will want to enter that particular industry. The individual firm, however, does not face the entire *market* supply curve. Rather, in a perfectly competitive case, the individual firm is such a small part of the market that it can hire all the workers it wants at the going wage rate. We say, therefore, that the *industry* faces an upward-sloping supply curve but that the individual *firm* faces a perfectly elastic supply curve for labor.

Labor Market Equilibrium

The demand curve for labor in the wireless earbud industry is D in Figure 28-4, and the supply curve of labor is S. The equilibrium wage rate of $1,000 per week is established at the intersection of the two curves. The quantity of workers both supplied and demanded at that rate is Q_1. If for some reason the wage rate fell to $900 a week, in our hypothetical example, there would be an excess number of workers demanded at that wage rate. Conversely, if the wage rate rose to $1,100 a week, there would be an

FIGURE 28-4

The Equilibrium Wage Rate in the Wireless Earbud Industry

The industry demand curve for labor is D. We put in a hypothetical upward-sloping labor supply curve for the wireless earbud industry, S. The intersection is at point E, giving an equilibrium wage rate of $1,000 per week and an equilibrium quantity of labor demanded of Q_1. At a wage above $1,000 per week, there will be an excess quantity of workers supplied. At a wage below $1,000 per week, there will be an excess quantity of workers demanded.

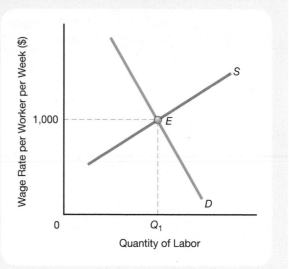

excess quantity of workers supplied at that wage rate. In either case, competition would quickly force the wage back to the equilibrium level.

We have just found the equilibrium wage rate for the entire wireless earbud industry. The individual firm must take that equilibrium wage rate as given in the perfectly competitive model used here because the individual firm is a very small part of the total demand for labor. Thus, each firm purchasing labor in a perfectly competitive market can purchase all of the input it wants at the going market price.

Shifts in the Market Demand for and the Supply of Labor

Just as we have discussed shifts in the supply curve and the demand curve for various products in other chapters, we can discuss the effects of shifts in supply and demand in labor markets.

Reasons for Labor Demand Curve Shifts Many factors can cause the demand curve for labor to shift. We have already discussed a number of them. Clearly, because the demand for labor or any other variable input is a derived demand, the labor demand curve will shift if there is a shift in the demand for the final product. There are two other important determinants of the position of the demand curve for labor: changes in labor's productivity and changes in the price of related factors of production (substitute inputs and complementary inputs).

1. *Changes in the demand for the final product.* The demand for labor is derived from the demand for the final product. The marginal revenue product is equal to marginal product times marginal revenue. Therefore, any change in the demand for the final product will change its price and hence the MRP of the input. The rule of thumb is as follows:

   A change in the demand for the final product that labor is producing will shift the market demand curve for labor in the same direction.

2. *Changes in labor productivity.* The second part of the MRP equation is MP, which relates to labor productivity. We can surmise, then, that other things being equal:

   A change in labor productivity will shift the market labor demand curve in the same direction.

Labor productivity can increase because labor has more capital or land to work with, because of technological improvements, or because labor's quality has improved. Such considerations explain why the real standard of living of workers in the United States is higher than in most other countries. U.S. workers generally work with a larger capital stock, have more natural resources, are in better physical condition, and are better trained than workers in many countries. Hence the demand for labor in the United States is, other things held constant, greater.

3. *Change in the price of related factors.* Labor is not the only resource that firms use. Some resources are substitutes and some are complements in the production process. If we hold output constant, we have the following general rule:

A change in the price of a substitute input will cause the demand for labor to change in the same direction.

Thus, if the price of an input for which labor can substitute as a factor of production decreases, the demand for labor falls. For instance, if the price of mechanized ditch-digging equipment decreases, the demand for workers who, in contrast, can use only shovels to dig ditches decreases.

Suppose that a particular type of capital equipment and labor are complementary. In general, we predict the following:

A change in the price of a complementary input will cause the demand for labor to change in the opposite direction.

If the price of capital equipment goes up but it must be used with labor, fewer pieces of equipment will be purchased and therefore fewer workers will be used.

Of course, the preceding reasoning we have applied to the demand for labor applies as well to any other variable input.

Determinants of the Supply of Labor Labor supply curves may shift in a particular industry for a number of reasons. For example, if wage rates for factory workers in the tablet industry go up dramatically, the supply curve of factory workers in the smartphone industry will shift inward to the left as these workers move to the tablet industry.

Changes in working conditions in an industry can also affect its labor supply curve. If employers in the smartphone industry discover a new production technique that makes working conditions much more pleasant, the supply curve of labor to the smartphone industry will shift outward to the right.

Job flexibility also determines the position of the labor supply curve. For example, when an industry allows workers more flexibility, such as the ability to work at home via networked digital devices, the workers are likely to provide more hours of labor. That is to say, their supply curve will shift outward to the right. Some industries in which firms offer *job sharing*, particularly to people raising families, have found that the supply curve of labor has shifted outward to the right.

Labor Demand of a Monopolist and Overall Input Utilization

28.3 Contrast wage determination under monopoly and perfect competition

So far we've considered only perfectly competitive markets, both in selling the final product and in buying factors of production. We will continue our assumption that the firm purchases its factors of production in a perfectly competitive factor market. Now, however, we will assume that the firm sells its product in an *imperfectly* competitive output market. In other words, we are considering the output market structures of monopoly, oligopoly, and monopolistic competition. In all such cases, the firm, be it a monopolist, an oligopolist, or a monopolistic competitor, faces a downward-sloping demand curve for its product.

Throughout the rest of this chapter, we will simply refer to a monopoly situation for ease of analysis. The analysis holds for all industry structures that are less than perfectly competitive. In any event, the fact that our firm now faces a downward-sloping demand curve for its product means that if it wants to sell more of its product (at a uniform price), it has to lower the price, *not just on the last unit, but on all preceding units.* The *marginal revenue* received from selling an additional unit is continuously falling (and is less than price) as the firm attempts to sell more and more. This relationship between marginal revenue and output is certainly different from our earlier discussions in this chapter in which the firm could sell all it wanted at a constant price. Why? Because the firm we discussed until now was a perfect competitor.

Constructing the Monopolist's Input Demand Curve

In reconstructing our demand schedule for an input, we must account for the facts that (1) the marginal product falls because of the law of diminishing marginal product as more workers are added and (2) the price (and marginal revenue) received for the product sold also falls as more is produced and sold. That is, for the monopolist, we have to account for both the diminishing marginal product and the diminishing marginal revenue. Marginal revenue is always less than price for the monopolist. The marginal revenue curve always lies below the downward-sloping product demand curve.

Marginal Revenue Product for a Perfectly Competitive Firm
Marginal revenue for the perfect competitor is equal to the price of the product because all units can be sold at the going market price. In our example involving the production of wireless earbuds, we assumed that the perfect competitor could sell all it wanted at $5 per unit. A one-unit change in sales always led to a $5 change in total revenues. Hence, marginal revenue was always equal to $5 for that perfect competitor. Multiplying this unchanging marginal revenue by the marginal product of labor then yielded the perfectly competitive firm's marginal revenue product.

Marginal Revenue Product for a Monopoly Firm
The monopolist, however, cannot simply calculate marginal revenue by looking at the price of the product. To sell the additional output from an additional unit of input, the monopolist has to cut prices on all previous units of output. As output is increasing, then, marginal revenue is falling.

The underlying concept is, of course, the same for both the perfect competitor and the monopolist. We are asking exactly the same question in both cases: When an additional worker is hired, what is the benefit? In either case, the benefit is obviously the change in total revenues due to the one-unit change in the variable input, labor. In our discussion of the perfect competitor, we were able simply to multiply the marginal product by the *constant* per-unit price of the product because the price of the product never changed (for the perfect competitor, $P \equiv MR$).

Labor Demand for a Monopolist
A single monopolist ends up hiring fewer workers than would all of the perfectly competitive firms added together. To see this, we must consider the marginal revenue product for the monopolist, which varies with each one-unit change in the monopolist's labor input.

The Monopolist's Marginal Revenue Product
We consider the monopolist's marginal revenue product in panel (a) of Figure 28-5. Column 5 in panel (a), "Marginal Revenue Product," gives the monopolist a quantitative notion of how additional workers and additional production generate additional revenues.

The marginal revenue product curve for this monopolist has been plotted in panel (b) of the figure. To emphasize the lower elasticity of the monopolist's MRP curve (MRP_m)

FIGURE 28-5

A Monopolist's Marginal Revenue Product

The monopolist hires just enough workers to make marginal revenue product equal to the going wage rate. If the going wage rate is $1,000 per week, as shown by the labor supply curve, s, in panel (b), the monopolist would want to hire 10 workers per week. That is the profit-maximizing amount of labor. The labor demand curve for a perfectly competitive industry from Figure 28-4 is also plotted (D). The monopolist's MRP curve will always be less elastic around the going wage rate than it would be if marginal revenue were constant.

Panel (a)

(1)	(2)	(3)	(4)	(5)	(6)
Labor Input (workers per week)	Marginal Product (MP) (wireless earbuds per week)	Price of Product (P)	Marginal Revenue (MR)	Marginal Revenue Product (MRP$_m$) = (2) x (4)	Wage Rate
8	300	$5.20	$4.40	$1,320	$1,000
9	275	5.10	4.20	1,155	1,000
10	250	5.00	4.00	1,000	1,000
11	225	4.90	3.80	855	1,000
12	200	4.80	3.60	720	1,000
13	175	4.70	3.40	595	1,000

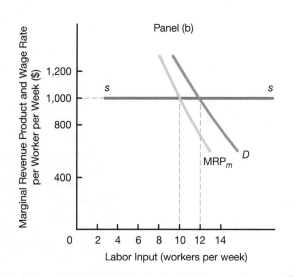

around the wage rate $1,000, the labor demand curve for a perfectly competitive industry (labeled D) has been plotted on the same graph in Figure 28-5.

The Monopolist's Demand for Labor Recall that this curve is not simply the sum of the marginal revenue product curves of all perfectly competitive firms, because when competitive firms together increase employment, their output expands and the product price declines. Nevertheless, at any given wage rate, the quantity of labor demanded by the monopoly is still less than the quantity of labor demanded by a perfectly competitive industry.

Why does MRP_m represent the monopolist's input demand curve? As always, our profit-maximizing monopolist will continue to hire labor as long as additional profits result. Profits are made as long as the additional cost of more workers is outweighed by the additional revenues made from selling the output of those workers. When the wage rate equals these additional revenues, the monopolist stops hiring. That is, the firm stops hiring when the wage rate is equal to the marginal revenue product because additional workers would add more to cost than to revenue.

Why the Monopolist Hires Fewer Workers

Because we have used the same numbers as in Figure 28-1, we can see that the monopolist hires fewer workers per week than firms in a perfectly competitive market would. That is to say, if we could magically change the wireless earbud industry in our example from one in which there is perfect competition in the output market to one in which there is monopoly in the output market, the amount of employment would fall. Why? Because the monopolist must take account of the declining product price that must be charged in order to sell a larger number of wireless earbuds. Remember that every firm hires up to the point at which marginal benefit equals marginal cost. The marginal benefit to the monopolist of hiring an additional worker is not simply the additional output times the price of the product. Rather, the monopolist faces a reduction in the price charged on *all* units sold in order to be able to sell more.

The monopolist therefore ends up hiring fewer workers than all of the perfect competitors taken together, assuming that all else remains the same for the two hypothetical examples. This, however, should not come as a surprise. In considering product markets, by implication we saw that a monopolized wireless earbud industry would produce less output than a competitive one. Therefore, the monopolized industry would hire fewer workers.

The Utilization of Other Factors of Production

The analysis in this chapter has been given in terms of the demand for the variable input labor. The same analysis holds for any other variable factor input. We could have talked about the demand for fertilizer or the demand for the services of tractors by a farmer instead of the demand for labor and reached the same conclusions. The entrepreneur will hire or buy any variable input up to the point at which its price equals the marginal revenue product.

A further question remains: How much of each variable factor should the firm utilize when all the variable factors are combined to produce the product? We can answer this question by looking at either the cost-minimizing side of the question or the profit-maximizing side.

Cost Minimization and Factor Utilization
From the cost-minimization point of view, how can the firm minimize its total costs for a given output? Assume that you are an entrepreneur attempting to minimize costs. Consider a hypothetical situation in which if you spend $1 more on labor, you would get 20 more units of output, but if you spend $1 more on capital equipment, you would get only 10 more units of output. What would you want to do in such a situation? You would wish to hire more workers or sell off some of your equipment, for you are not getting as much output per *last* dollar spent on capital equipment as you are per *last* dollar spent on labor. You would want to employ factors of production so that the marginal products per last dollar spent on each are equal. Thus, the least-cost, or cost-minimization, rule will be as follows:

> *To minimize total costs for a particular rate of production, the firm will hire factors of production up to the point at which the marginal product per last dollar spent on each factor of production is equalized.*

That is,

$$\frac{\text{MP of labor}}{\substack{\text{price of labor} \\ \text{(wage rate)}}} = \frac{\text{MP of capital}}{\substack{\text{price of capital (cost per} \\ \text{unit of service)}}} = \frac{\text{MP of land}}{\substack{\text{price of land (rental} \\ \text{rate per unit)}}}$$

All we are saying here is that the cost-minimizing firm will always utilize *all* resources in such combinations that cost will be minimized for any given output rate. This is commonly called the *least-cost combination of resources.*

How does the cost-minimization rule for employment of resources explain a change in the mix of human and robotic inputs that home builders are using in house construction?

EXAMPLE

Someday, You May Purchase a Largely Robot-Constructed House

Many home builders are shifting significant portions of construction off the sites where houses will be located. Instead, home modules—parts of houses such as walls and sections of roofing—are fabricated using robotic capital located many miles from home sites. After the modules have been shipped to the sites where the houses will stand, human workers complete final on-site assembly over a few weeks' time.

When home builders evaluate whether to employ human labor versus off-site robots, they consider the cost-minimizing rule for inputs:

$$\frac{\text{MP of a construction worker's labor}}{\text{price of a construction worker's labor}} = \frac{\text{MP of robotic capital}}{\text{price of robotic capital}}$$

In recent years, the price of a typical construction worker's hourly labor has soared, which has reduced the left-hand ratio in this relationship. At the same time, the price of modular-construction robots has

declined, which has raised the right-hand ratio. Builders have brought the relationship back into balance by employing fewer human construction workers and thereby raising the marginal product of a typical construction worker's labor and pushing the left-hand ratio up. In addition, they have utilized larger numbers of module-producing robots and consequently reduced the marginal product of robots and pushed the right-hand ratio back down. Hence, builders have minimized their costs by substituting robotic capital for human labor.

FOR CRITICAL THINKING

Why might an employer choose not *to hire some job candidates offering relatively high levels of marginal product if the price of the product the employer sells decreases considerably?*

Sources are listed at the end of this chapter.

Profit Maximization Revisited If a firm wants to maximize profits, how much of each factor should be hired (or bought)? As you have learned, the firm will never utilize a factor of production unless the marginal benefit from hiring that factor is at least equal to the marginal cost. What is the marginal benefit? As we have pointed out several times, the marginal benefit is the change in total revenues due to a one-unit change in utilization of the variable input. What is the marginal cost? In the case of a firm buying in a perfectly competitive market, it is the price of the variable factor— the wage rate if we are referring to labor.

The profit-maximizing combination of resources for the firm will be where, in a perfectly competitive market structure,

$$\text{MRP of labor} = \text{price of labor (wage rate)}$$

$$\text{MRP of capital} = \text{price of capital (cost per unit of service)}$$

$$\text{MRP of land} = \text{price of land (rental rate per unit)}$$

To attain maximum profits, the marginal revenue product of each of a firm's resources must be exactly equal to its price. If the MRP of labor is $20 and its price is only $15, the firm will expand its employment of labor.

There is an exact match between the profit-maximizing combination of resources and the least-cost combination of resources discussed above. In other words, either rule can be used to yield the same cost-minimizing rate of utilization of each variable resource.

ECONOMICS IN YOUR LIFE

To contemplate a choice between using humans or robots to make judgments about whether tennis balls land on or outside lines on tennis courts, take a look at **Why Tennis Clubs Are Replacing Human Line Judges with Robots** on page 625.

28.4 Explain how a monopsonist determines how much labor to employ and what wage rate to pay

Monopsonist
The only buyer in a market.

Monopsony: A Buyer's Monopoly

Let's assume that a firm is a perfect competitor in the product market. The firm cannot alter the price of the product it sells, and it faces a perfectly elastic demand curve for its product. We also assume that the firm is the only buyer of a particular input. Although this situation may not occur often, it is useful to consider. Let's think in terms of a factory town, like those that used to be dominated by textile mills or those in the mining industry. Such a single buyer of labor is called a **monopsonist**, the only buyer in the market.

What does this situation mean to a monopsonist in terms of the costs of hiring extra workers? It means that if the monopsonist wants to hire more workers, it has to offer higher wages. Our monopsonist firm cannot hire all the labor it wants at the going wage rate. Instead, it faces an upward-sloping supply curve. If it wants to hire more workers, it has to raise wage rates, including the wages of all its current workers (assuming a non-wage-discriminating monopsonist). It therefore has to take account of these increased costs when deciding how many more workers to hire.

Marginal Factor Cost

The monopsonist faces an upward-sloping supply curve of the input in question because, as the only buyer, it faces the entire market supply curve. Each time the monopsonist buyer of labor, for example, wishes to hire more workers, it must raise wage rates. Thus, the marginal cost of another unit of labor is rising. In fact, the marginal cost of increasing its workforce will always be greater than the wage rate. This is because the monopsonist must pay the same wage rate to everyone in order to obtain another unit of labor. Consequently, the higher wage rate has to be offered not only to the last worker but also to *all* its other workers. We call the additional cost to the monopsonist of hiring one more worker the marginal factor cost (MFC).

The marginal factor cost of hiring the last worker is therefore that worker's wages plus the increase in the wages of all other existing workers. Recall that the marginal factor cost is equal to the change in total variable costs due to a one-unit change in the one variable factor of production—in this case, labor. In a perfectly competitive labor market, marginal factor cost was simply the competitive wage rate because the employer could hire all workers at the same wage rate.

Derivation of a Marginal Factor Cost Curve

Panel (a) of Figure 28-6 shows the quantity of labor purchased, the wage rate per hour, the total cost of the quantity of labor supplied per hour, and the marginal factor cost per hour for the additional labor bought.

We translate the columns from panel (a) to the graph in panel (b) of the figure. We show the supply curve as *S*, which is taken from columns 1 and 2. The marginal factor cost curve (MFC) is taken from columns 1 and 4. The MFC curve must be above the supply curve whenever the supply curve is upward sloping. If the supply curve is upward sloping, the firm must pay a higher wage rate to attract a larger amount of labor. This higher wage rate must be paid to all workers. Thus, the increase in total costs due to an increase in the labor input will exceed the wage rate. (Recall that in a perfectly competitive input market, in contrast, the supply curve facing the firm is perfectly elastic and the marginal factor cost curve is identical to the supply curve.)

Employment and Wages under Monopsony

To determine the number of workers that a monopsonist desires to hire, we compare the marginal benefit to the marginal cost of each hiring decision. The marginal cost is the marginal factor cost (MFC) curve, and the marginal benefit is the marginal revenue product (MRP) curve. In Figure 28-7, we assume competition in the output market and monopsony in the input market. A monopsonist finds its profit-maximizing quantity of labor demanded at *A*, where the marginal revenue product is just equal to the marginal factor cost. The monopsonist will therefore desire to hire exactly Q_m workers.

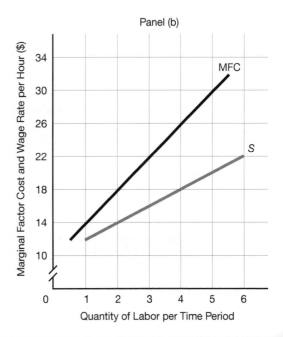

FIGURE 28-6

Derivation of a Marginal Factor Cost Curve

The supply curve, S, in panel (b) is taken from columns 1 and 2 of panel (a). The marginal factor cost curve (MFC) is taken from columns 1 and 4. It is the increase in the total wage bill resulting from a one-unit increase in labor input.

Panel (a)

(1) Quantity of Labor Supplied to Management	(2) Required Hourly Wage Rate	(3) Total Wage Bill (3) = (1) × (2)	(4) Marginal Factor Cost $(MFC) = \dfrac{\text{Change in (3)}}{\text{Change in (1)}}$
0	—	—	
			$12
1	$12	$12	
			16
2	14	28	
			20
3	16	48	
			24
4	18	72	
			28
5	20	100	
			32
6	22	132	

Panel (b)

The Input Price Paid by a Monopsony How much is the firm going to pay these workers? The monopsonist sets the wage rate so that it will get exactly the quantity, Q_m, supplied to it by its "captive" labor force. We find that wage rate is W_m. There is no reason to pay the workers any more than W_m because at that wage rate, the firm can get exactly the quantity it wants. The actual quantity used is determined by the intersection of the marginal factor cost curve and the marginal revenue product curve for labor—that is, at the point at which the marginal revenue from expanding employment just equals the marginal cost of doing so (point A in Figure 28-7).

FIGURE 28-7

Wage and Employment Determination for a Monopsonist

The monopsonist firm looks at a marginal cost curve, MFC, that slopes upward and lies above its labor supply curve, *S.* The marginal benefit of hiring additional workers is given by the firm's MRP curve (its demand-for-labor curve). The intersection of MFC with MRP, at point *A,* determines the number of workers hired. The firm hires Q_m workers but has to pay them only W_m to attract them.

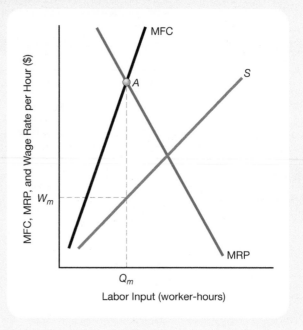

Monopsonistic exploitation

Paying a price for the variable input that is less than its marginal revenue product; the difference between marginal revenue product and the wage rate.

Notice that the profit-maximizing wage rate paid to workers W_m is lower than the marginal revenue product. That is to say, workers are paid a wage that is less than their contribution to the monopsonist's revenues. This is sometimes referred to as **monopsonistic exploitation** of labor.

In principle, how might firms such as Uber and Lyft utilize big data capabilities to engage in monopsonistic exploitation of labor?

AI | DECISION MAKING THROUGH DATA

Monopsonistic Decisions for Hiring Service Providers

In recent years, a number of companies, such as Uber and Lyft, have been founded on the basis of serving as platforms linking individuals willing to provide short-term labor services, such as a ride in a vehicle from one location to another, to people desiring to purchase those services. Such firms specialize in matching buyers' service requests with service providers.

During their normal course of operations, these companies collect voluminous data about geographic preferences of buyers of these services and the locations of service providers. Some observers have argued that the application of data-analytics techniques to such large volumes of information about providers of labor services within specific areas

could enable a platform firm to infer those workers' marginal factor costs. In principle, a platform firm thereby might be able to assign tasks automatically to service providers to the point at which the workers' marginal factor cost equals the firm's marginal revenue product. If so, the firm could engage in monopsonistic exploitation of the providers of these labor services.

FOR CRITICAL THINKING

How legitimate would concerns be about the possibility of monopsonistic exploitation of labor via platform firms' application of data analytics if providers of labor services can choose among a large number of potential employers?

Sources are listed at the end of this chapter.

Bilateral Monopoly The organization of workers into a union (which we discuss next) normally creates a monopoly supplier of labor, which gives the union some power to bargain for higher wages. What happens when a monopsonist meets a monopolist? This situation is called **bilateral monopoly**, defined as a market structure in which a single buyer faces a single seller. An example of bilateral monopoly is a players' union facing an organized group of team owners, as has occurred in professional baseball and football. To analyze bilateral monopoly, we would have to look at the interaction of both sides, buyer and seller. The equilibrium wage rate turns out to be uncertain.

Bilateral monopoly
A market structure consisting of a monopolist and a monopsonist.

We have studied the pricing of labor in various situations, including perfect competition in both the output and input markets and monopoly in both the output and input markets. Figure 28-8 shows four possible situations graphically.

FIGURE 28-8

Pricing and Employment under Various Market Conditions

In panel (a), the firm operates in perfect competition in both the input and output markets. It purchases labor up to the point where the going rate W_e is equal to MRP_c. It hires quantity Q_e of labor. In panel (b), the firm is a perfect competitor in the input market but has a monopoly in the output market. It purchases labor up to the point where W_e is equal to MRP_m. In panel (c), the firm is a monopsonist in the input market and a perfect competitor in the output market. It hires labor up to the point where $MFC = MRP_c$. It will hire quantity Q_1 and pay wage rate W_c. Panel (d) shows a situation in which the firm is both a monopolist in the market for its output and a monopsonist in its labor market. It hires the quantity of labor Q_2 at which $MFC = MRP_m$ and pays the wage rate W_m.

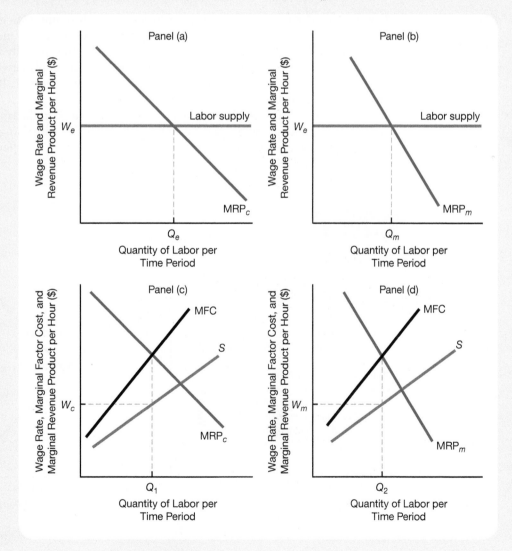

28.5 Discuss the goals, strategies, and current status of labor unions

Labor unions
Worker organizations that seek to secure economic improvements for their members. They also seek to improve the safety, health, and other benefits (such as job security) of their members.

Collective bargaining
Negotiation between the management of a company and the management of a union for the purpose of reaching a mutually agreeable contract that sets wages, fringe benefits, and working conditions for all employees in all the unions involved.

Labor Unions

An important economic element of some labor markets is the presence and activities of **labor unions**, which are organizations that seek to secure economic gains for members. One key rationale for forming a union has been for members to earn more than they would in a competitive labor market by obtaining a type of monopoly power. Because the entire supply of a particular group of workers is controlled by a single source, when a union bargains as a single entity with management, a monopoly element enters into the determination of employment and wages.

Union Goals, Strategies, and Constraints

Unions seek to engage in **collective bargaining**, in which representatives of all union members negotiate with business management about wages and hours of work. Through collective bargaining, unions establish the wages below which no individual worker may legally offer his or her services. Each year, union representatives and management negotiate collective bargaining contracts covering wages as well as working conditions and fringe benefits for about 5 million workers. If approved by the members, a union labor contract sets wage rates, maximum workdays, working conditions, fringe benefits, and other matters, usually for the next two or three years.

Setting Wages and Rationing Employment One of the goals of unions is to set minimum wages. The effects of setting a wage rate higher than a competitive market clearing wage rate can be seen in Figure 28-9. The market for labor initially is perfectly competitive. The market demand curve is D, and the market supply curve is S. The market clearing wage rate is W_e. The equilibrium quantity of labor is Q_e. If a union is formed and establishes by collective bargaining a minimum wage rate that exceeds W_e, an excess quantity of labor will be supplied (assuming no change in the labor demand schedule). If the minimum wage established by union collective bargaining is W_U, the quantity supplied will be Q_S. The quantity demanded will be Q_D. The difference is the excess quantity supplied, or surplus.

FIGURE 28-9

Unions Must Ration Jobs

The market clearing wage rate is W_e at point E, at which the equilibrium quantity of labor is Q_e. If the union succeeds in obtaining wage rate W_U, the quantity of labor demanded will be Q_D, at point A on the labor demand curve, but the quantity of labor supplied will be Q_S, at point B on the labor supply curve. The union must ration a limited number of jobs among a greater number of workers. The surplus of labor is equivalent to a shortage of jobs at that wage rate.

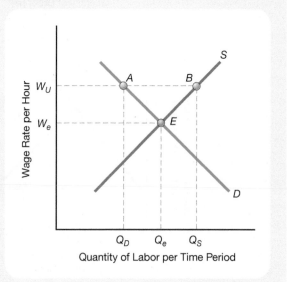

Hence, the following point becomes clear:

One of the major roles of a union that establishes a wage rate above the market clearing wage rate is to ration available jobs among the excess number of workers who wish to work in the unionized industry.

Note also that the surplus of labor is equivalent to a shortage of jobs at wage rates above equilibrium.

To ration jobs, the union may use a seniority system, lengthen the apprenticeship period to discourage potential members from joining, or institute other rationing methods. This has the effect of shifting the supply of labor curve to the left in order to support the higher wage, W_U. There is a trade-off here that any union's leadership must face: Higher wages inevitably mean a reduction in total union employment—fewer union positions. When facing higher wages, management may replace part of the workforce with machinery or may even seek to hire nonunion workers.

Three Possible Union Goals If we view unions as monopoly sellers of a service, we can identify three different goals that they may pursue: ensuring employment for all members of the union, maximizing aggregate income of workers, and maximizing wage rates for some workers.

1. *Employing All Members in the Union* Assume that the union has a certain number of members. In light of the demand curve that the union faces, the only way it can "sell" all of those workers' services is to accept the wage rate that firms are willing to pay to hire all of these workers. As in any market, the demand curve tells the maximum price that can be charged to sell any particular quantity of a good or service. Here the service happens to be labor.

2. *Maximizing Member Income* If the union is interested in maximizing the gross income of its members, it will desire that aggregate wage payments received by the union be as large as possible. To attain this outcome, the union will search along the demand curve for the combination of the number of workers employed and corresponding wage rate at which the multiplication of the two yields the largest total wage payments to all union members.

3. *Maximizing Wage Rates for Certain Workers* Assume that the union wants to maximize wage rates for a subset of union members—perhaps those with the most seniority. Then the union will have to agree to the wage rate at which firms will be willing to employ that subset of its members. This will require deciding which workers should be unemployed and which workers should work and for how many hours they should be employed.

Government Constraints on Unions Key legal constraints under which unions operate are specified by the Taft-Hartley Act of 1947 (the Labor Management Relations Act). In general, the Taft-Hartley Act outlawed certain labor practices of unions, such as imposing make-work rules and forcing unwilling workers to join a particular union. Among other things, it allowed individual states to pass their own **right-to-work laws**. A right-to-work law makes it illegal for union membership to be a requirement for continued employment in any establishment.

The Taft-Hartley Act also made a **closed shop** illegal. A closed shop requires union membership before employment can be obtained. A **union shop**, however, is legal. A union shop does not require membership as a prerequisite for employment, but it can, and usually does, require that workers join the union after a specified amount of time on the job. (Even a union shop is illegal in states with right-to-work laws.)

What have been the effects on states' union memberships following recent passages of right-to-work laws?

Right-to-work laws
Laws that make it illegal to require union membership as a condition of continuing employment in a particular firm.

Closed shop
A business enterprise in which employees must belong to the union before they can be hired and must remain in the union after they are hired.

Union shop
A business enterprise that may hire nonunion members, conditional on their joining the union by some specified date after employment begins.

POLICY EXAMPLE

In Twenty-Eight U.S. States, "Right to Work" Means No Mandatory Union "Dues" and Shrinking Union Memberships

Kentucky became the twenty-eighth state to adopt a "right-to-work" law. Such laws forbid requiring any worker to join a union as a condition of employment. As a consequence, unions in Kentucky that previously had operated under union shop rules suddenly confronted a new reality: Those unions could no longer rely on collections of mandatory "dues," or membership fees, from workers unless those workers voluntarily opted to remain members. If Kentucky workers who previously had been required to be union members decide that they do not perceive the benefits derived from union membership to be sufficiently high to justify paying dues to a union, they can halt payments and end their memberships. Michigan unions have experienced a decline in memberships of about 5 percent since Michigan adopted a right-to-work law in 2013. Since Wisconsin adopted such a law in 2013, the state's unions have lost about 40 percent of their members.

FOR CRITICAL THINKING

Why do you suppose that some unions in Michigan and Wisconsin have reduced their membership dues since the passage of right-to-work laws in those states?

Sources are listed at the end of this chapter.

The Current Status of U.S. Labor Unions

As shown in Figure 28-10, union membership has been declining in the United States since the 1960s. At present, only slightly over 10 percent of U.S. workers are union members. Less than 7 percent of workers in the private sector belong to unions.

A Decline in Manufacturing Employment A large part of the explanation for the decline in union membership has to do with the shift away from manufacturing. Six decades ago, workers in manufacturing industries, transportation, and utilities, which traditionally have been among the most heavily unionized industries, constituted more than half of private nonagricultural employment. Today, that fraction is less than one-fifth.

The relative decline in manufacturing employment also helps to explain a redistribution in union membership in favor of service industries. Among today's largest U.S. unions are the Service Employees International Union with 2 million members and the United Food and Commercial Workers Union with 1.3 million members.

FIGURE 28-10

Decline in Union Membership

Numerically, union membership in the United States has increased dramatically since the 1930s, but as a percentage of the labor force, union membership peaked around 1960 and has been falling ever since. Most recently, the absolute number of union members has also diminished.

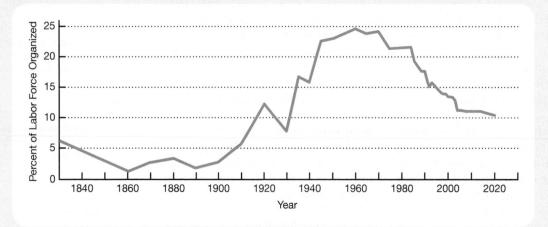

Sources: L. Davis et al., *American Economic Growth* (New York: HarperCollins, 1972), p. 220; U.S. Department of Labor, Bureau of Labor Statistics.

The Rise of Public-Sector Unions During the 1950s, municipal workers in New York City and other municipalities won the right to organize unions. In 1962, the federal government also granted its employees this right.

The percentage of unionized workers who are in the public sector has grown steadily since. Indeed, by 2009 more than half of all unionized workers in the United States were government employees.

ECONOMICS IN YOUR LIFE

Why Tennis Clubs Are Replacing Human Line Judges with Robots

French inventor Grégoire Gentil is happy about the market performance of his new product, called the In/Out. A plastic strap can attach the device to one end of the net on a tennis court. Once a button is pressed, the In/Out uses an artificial-intelligence app to scan the court and identify its lines, and players can use it to judge whether balls that hit the surface during play are within, on, or outside the lines. The device is not as accurate as alternative court-monitoring systems that have price tags ranging from $10,000 to $60,000 each. The In/Out's price, however, is only $200 per unit.

Gentil knows that when a tennis club is deciding upon its cost-minimizing combination of human judges and robotic devices such as the In/Out, the club equalizes resources' ratios of marginal product to price per unit. The much lower price of the In/Out tends to push up its ratio, and a tennis club responds by adjusting its combination of resources in a way that reduces the marginal product per In/Out device. Gentil is pleased that the adjustment that brings about this decrease is the utilization of more In/Out devices in relation to other

resources. The consequence for Gentil, naturally, is that tennis clubs' purchases of his device have increased considerably.

FOR CRITICAL THINKING

Will a tennis club that chooses for the first time to utilize In/Out devices on its courts tend to adjust the number of line judges that it employs within its cost-minimizing combination of resources in an upward or downward direction? Explain your reasoning.

REAL APPLICATION

Assume that you are a tennis player who frequently participates in tournaments. Would you rather have your tennis club use the In/Out device, a much more expensive "monitoring system," or human line judges?

Sources are listed at the end of this chapter.

ISSUES & APPLICATIONS

Video Games, U.S. Labor Supply, and Equilibrium Employment and Wages

Nikita Anokhin/Shutterstock

CONCEPTS APPLIED

➤ Determinants of the Supply of Labor

➤ Labor Market Equilibrium

➤ Wage Determination in a Perfectly Competitive Labor Market

The supply of labor by U.S. males between the ages of 21 and 30 has declined sharply since 2000. In that year, 8 percent of men in this age group chose not to supply labor. Today, this percentage is about twice as large, and annual hours worked by young men in this age group have declined by 12 percent. One reason for the reduced employment of young men, it turns out, is the availability of lower-priced and higher-quality video games.

Lower-Priced, Higher-Quality Video Games and the Supply of Labor by Young Men

Mark Aguiar of Princeton University, Mark Bils of the University of Rochester, and Kerwin Charles and Erik Hurst of the University of Chicago have studied the labor supply effects of lower prices and higher quality of video games. These researchers provide evidence that many young men have substituted time that otherwise could be spent on wage-earning work with leisure time devoted to playing video games.

The researchers estimate that young men spend at least 6 hours per week playing these games instead of supplying labor. This time allocation accounts, they estimate, for at least 23 percent of the decrease in the number of weekly hours of labor that young men supply at prevailing wages.

Implications for Labor Supply, Employment, and the Market Clearing Wage Rate

What can we predict about the labor market effects of the reduction in young men's labor supply on labor market equilibrium? As shown in Figure 28-11, as more young men exit the labor market, the labor supply curve shifts leftward, from S_1 to S_2. This shift causes a movement leftward along the labor demand curve, D. Equilibrium employment declines from Q_1 to Q_2 units of labor per week. The equilibrium weekly wage rate rises, from W_1 to W_2. Thus, other things being unchanged, because more young men are playing video games instead of supplying their labor, U.S. employment in that age group is lower and wages are higher than they would be otherwise.

FOR CRITICAL THINKING

Why might we expect that the availability of any lower-priced and higher-quality item that an individual consumes during leisure time is likely to reduce that person's willingness to supply labor at any given wage rate?

REAL APPLICATION

Assume that you are a young male in the 21- to 30-year-old age bracket. Further suppose that you do indeed devote large chunks of your time playing, say, Fortnite: Battle Royale. You obviously derive immense pleasure from so doing. What are the short-run and long-term costs of such behavior?

Sources are listed at the end of this chapter.

FIGURE 28-11

Effects of a Decrease in Young Men's Supply of Labor

The effect of a decrease in the amount of labor supplied by young men at any given wage rate is a leftward shift in the market labor supply curve. The result is a movement from the initial equilibrium point E_1 to the new equilibrium point E_2. The market clearing wage rate increases, and the equilibrium quantity of labor decreases.

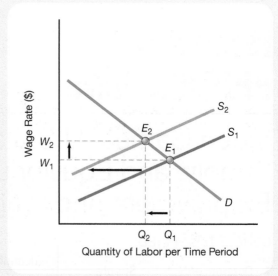

What You Should Know

LEARNING OBJECTIVES	KEY TERMS

28.1 **Understand why a firm's marginal revenue product curve is its labor demand curve** *The marginal revenue product of labor equals marginal revenue times the marginal product of labor. Because of the law of diminishing marginal product, the marginal revenue product curve slopes downward. To maximize profits, a firm hires labor to the point at which the marginal factor cost of labor—the addition to total input costs resulting from employing an additional unit of labor—equals the marginal revenue product. Marginal revenue product curves shift when product prices change. Hence, the demand for labor is derived from the demand for final products.*

marginal product (MP) of labor, 606
marginal revenue product (MRP), 608
marginal factor cost (MFC), 608
derived demand, 609
Key Figures
Figure 28-1, 607
Figure 28-2, 609
Figure 28-3, 611

28.2 **Describe how equilibrium wage rates are determined for perfectly competitive firms** *In a competitive labor market, at the equilibrium wage rate, the quantity of labor demanded by all firms is equal to the quantity of labor supplied by all workers. At this wage rate, each firm looks to its own labor demand curve to determine how much labor to employ.*

Key Figure
Figure 28-4, 612

28.3 **Contrast wage determination under monopoly and perfect competition** *If a product market monopolist competes for labor in a competitive labor market, it takes the market wage rate as given. Its labor demand curve, however, lies to the left of the labor demand curve that would have arisen in a competitive industry. Thus, at the competitively determined wage rate, a monopolized industry employs fewer workers than the industry otherwise would if it were perfectly competitive.*

Key Figure
Figure 28-5, 615

28.4 **Explain how a monopsonist determines how much labor to employ and what wage rate to pay** *For a monopsonist, which is the only buyer of an input such as labor, paying a higher wage to attract an additional unit of labor increases total factor costs for all other labor employed. The monopsonist employs labor to the point at which the marginal factor cost of labor equals the marginal revenue product of labor. It then pays workers the wage at which they are willing to work, as determined by the labor supply curve, which is less than marginal factor cost and marginal revenue product.*

monopsonist, 618
monopsonistic exploitation, 620
bilateral monopoly, 621
Key Figures
Figure 28-6, 619
Figure 28-7, 620
Figure 28-8, 621

28.5 **Discuss the goals, strategies, and current status of labor unions** *A key goal of most unions is to achieve higher wages. Often this entails bargaining for wages above competitive levels, which produces surplus labor. Thus, a major task of many unions is to ration available jobs. Unions can address this trade-off between wages and the number of jobs by seeking to employ all members, maximizing the total income of all members, or maximizing wages of a subset of members. A decline in manufacturing employment lies behind a decrease in overall union membership and the relative growth in unionization among service workers and government employees.*

labor unions, 622
collective bargaining, 622
right-to-work laws, 623
closed shop, 623
union shop, 623
Key Figures
Figure 28-9, 622
Figure 28-10, 624

PROBLEMS

28-1. The first table depicts the output of a firm that manufactures wireless earbuds. The earbuds sell for $3 each.

Labor Input (workers per hour)	Total Output (earbuds per hour)
10	200
11	218
12	234
13	248
14	260
15	270
16	278

Calculate the marginal product and marginal revenue product at each input level above 10 units. What is the maximum wage the firm will be willing to pay if it hires 15 workers?

28-2. Explain how the following events would affect the demand for labor.

  a. A new education program administered by the company increases labor's marginal product.

  b. The firm completes a new plant with a larger workspace and new machinery that workers can utilize and that does not substitute for the functions provided by workers' labor.

28-3. The second table depicts the product market and labor market a digital device manufacturer faces.

Labor Input (workers per hour)	Total Product	Product Price ($)
10	100	53
11	109	52
12	116	51
13	121	50
14	124	49
15	125	48

  a. Calculate the firm's marginal product, total revenue, and marginal revenue product at each input level above 10 units.

  b. The firm competes in a perfectly competitive labor market, and the market wage it faces is $26 per hour. How many workers will the profit-maximizing employer hire?

28-4. Recently, there has been an increase in the market demand for products of firms in manufacturing industries. The production of many of these products requires the skills of welders. Because welding is a dirty and dangerous job compared with other occupations, in recent years fewer people have sought employment as welders. Draw a diagram of the market for the labor of welders. Use this diagram to explain the likely implications of these recent trends for the market clearing wage earned by welders and the equilibrium quantity of welding services hired.

28-5. Since the beginning of this century, there has been a significant increase in the price of corn-based ethanol.

  a. A key input in the production of corn-based ethanol is corn. Use an appropriate diagram to explain what has likely occurred in the market for corn if the supply curve has not shifted.

  b. In light of your answer to part (a), explain why many hog farmers, who in the past used corn as the main feed input in hog production, have switched to cookies, licorice, cheese curls, candy bars, and other human snack foods instead of corn as food for their hogs.

28-6. A firm hires labor in a perfectly competitive labor market. Its current profit-maximizing hourly output is 100 units, which the firm sells at a price of $5 per unit. The marginal product of the last unit of labor employed is 5 units per hour. The firm pays each worker an hourly wage of $15.

  a. What marginal revenue does the firm earn from the sale of the output produced by the last worker employed?

  b. Does this firm sell its output in a perfectly competitive market?

28-7. A profit-maximizing monopolist hires workers in a perfectly competitive labor market. Employing the last worker increased the firm's total weekly output from 110 units to 111 units and caused the firm's weekly revenues to rise from $25,000 to $25,750. What is the current prevailing weekly wage rate in the labor market?

28-8. A monopoly firm hires workers in a perfectly competitive labor market in which the market wage rate is $30 per day. If the firm maximizes profit, and if the marginal revenue from the last unit of output produced by the last worker hired equals $10, what is the marginal product of that worker?

28-9. The current market wage rate is $30, the rental rate of land is $1,000 per unit, and the price per service unit of capital is $500. A firm's managers find that under their current allocation of factors of production, the marginal product of labor is 300, the marginal product of land is 10,000, and the marginal product of capital is 4,000. Is the firm minimizing costs? Why or why not?

28-10. The current wage rate is $30, and the price per service unit of capital is $500. A firm's marginal product of labor is 600, and its marginal product of capital is 20,000. Is the firm maximizing profits for the given cost outlay? Why or why not?

28-11. Consider Figure 28-1, and suppose that the firm is contemplating 14 units of labor, and it knows that doing so would cause its total product to increase to 4,075 units. What would be the resulting marginal product of the 14th unit of labor employed? What would be the resulting marginal revenue product of the 14th unit of labor hired?

28-12. Suppose that the MRP_1 curve in Figure 28-2 is drawn under the assumption the product price is $5 per unit. Which alternative MRP curve—MRP_2 or MRP_3—applies if the market clearing product price drops to $3 per unit? Why?

28-13. Suppose that we were to observe unemployment in the labor market depicted in Figure 28-4. Would this imply that the current wage rate is above or below the $1,000 equilibrium weekly wage rate in the figure? Explain briefly.

28-14. Consider Figure 28-5. Suppose that the monopolist is contemplating hiring 14 units of labor, which it knows would cause the marginal product to decline to 150 units of output per unit of labor. The product price also decreases to $4.50 per unit, and the firm's marginal revenue declines to $3.20 per unit. What would be the firm's marginal revenue product if it hires a 14th unit of labor?

28-15. In the short run, a manufacturer has a fixed amount of capital. Labor is a variable input. The cost and output structure that the firm faces is depicted in the third table:

Labor Supplied	Total Product per Hour	Hourly Wage Rate ($)
10	100	25
11	109	26
12	116	27
13	121	28
14	124	29
15	125	30

Derive the firm's marginal product, marginal revenue product, total wage costs, and marginal factor cost at each level of labor supplied. If the firm sells its output in a perfectly competitive market at which the equilibrium price is $8 per unit, how many workers will it hire, and what hourly wage rate will it pay?

28-16. A single firm is the only employer in a labor market. The marginal revenue product, labor supply, and marginal factor cost curves that it faces are displayed in the diagram.

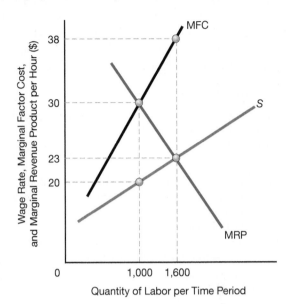

Use this information to answer the following questions.

a. How many units of labor will this firm employ in order to maximize its economic profits?

b. What hourly wage rate will this firm pay its workers?

c. What is the total amount of wage payments that this firm will make to its workers each hour?

28-17. In Figure 28-9, suppose that W_e is a wage rate of $30 per hour, and W_U is a wage rate of $40 per hour. In addition, Q_D is 12,000 workers per hour, Q_e is 15,000 workers per hour, and Q_S is 18,000 workers per hour. If each worker hired corresponds to a job available within the unionized industry, how many jobs must the union ration at the wage rate W_U? What is the shortage of jobs?

28-18. Given the information in Problem 28-17, how much more or less do the firms in this industry spend, in total, on the labor employed each hour as a consequence of establishment of the union wage $W_U = $40 per hour above the equilibrium wage $W_e = $30 per hour?

28-19. Suppose that the objective of a union is to maximize the total dues paid to the union by its membership. Explain the union's strategy, in terms of the wage level and employment level, under the following two scenarios.

a. Union dues are a percentage of total earnings of the union membership.

b. Union dues are paid as a flat amount per union member employed.

REFERENCES

INTERNATIONAL EXAMPLE: A Newly Derived Demand for German Coal Mines Relates to Energy but Not to Coal

L. Michael Buchsbaum, "Will Germany Transform Its Coal Fields into Renewable Energy Sites?" *Energy Transition*, February 15, 2019.

Cristina Belda Font, "New Life for Germany's Coal Mines," *The World Today*, Chatham House Royal Institute of International Affairs, 2018.

"Toxic Coal Mines Transformed into Beautiful Mountain Lakes," *New York Post*, June 14, 2018.

EXAMPLE: Someday, You May Purchase a Largely Robot-Constructed House

Liz Stinson, "Bricklaying Robotic Arm Aims to Build 10 Houses This Year," Curbed.com (https://www.curbed.com/2019/1/24/18195262/hadrian-x-robot-arm-build-homes-fbr), January 24, 2019.

Leanna Garfield, "A Robot Can Build This $10,000 House within 12 Hours," *Business Insider*, March 19, 2018.

Michele Lerner, "Why Aren't More Houses Built by Robots?" *The Independent*, June 28, 2018.

AI—DECISION MAKING THROUGH DATA: Machine Learning as a Threat to Human Service Jobs

Richard Baldwin, "White-Collar Robots Are Coming for Jobs," *Wall Street Journal*, January 31, 2019.

Luke Dormehl, "Replaced by Robots: 10 Jobs That Could Be Hit Hard by the A.I. Revolution," *Digital Trends* (https://www.digitaltrends.com/cool-tech/8-example-of-jobs-automated/), August 11, 2018.

Daniel West, "Will Robots and AI Take Your Job? The Economic and Political Consequences of Automation," *Brookings*, April 18, 2018.

AI—DECISION MAKING THROUGH DATA: Monopsonistic Decisions for Hiring Service Providers

Sidney Fussell, "The Quiet Ways Automation Is Remaking Service Work," *Atlantic*, January 11, 2019.

Arindrajit Dube, Jeff Jacobs, Suresh Naidu, and Siddharth Suri, "Monopsony in Online Labor Markets," *Vox*, May 21, 2018.

Henry Farrell, "Online Labor Markets May Look Competitive. They Aren't," *Washington Post*, August 2, 2018.

POLICY EXAMPLE: In Twenty-Eight U.S. States, "Right to Work" Means No Mandatory Union "Dues" and Shrinking Union Memberships

"Right to Work," AFL-CIO (https://aflcio.org/issues/right-work), 2019.

"Right to Work States," National Right to Work Legal Defense Foundation (www.nrtw.org/right-to-work-states/), 2019.

Sean Redmond, "Right-to-Work Laws: The Economic Evidence," U.S. Chamber of Congress, 2018.

ECONOMICS IN YOUR LIFE: Why Tennis Clubs Are Replacing Human Line Judges with Robots

"In/Out: The Portable Ready-to-Use Line Call Device," InoutTennis (www.inout.tennis/en/index.htm), 2019.

Cindy Schmerler, "Tennis Moves toward Taking the Human Element out of Line Calls," *New York Times*, March 1, 2018.

"Innovation Challenge Winner In/Out Brings Order on the Court," TennisIndustry.org (www.tennisindustry.org/cms/index.cfm/news/innovation-challenge-winner-inout-brings-order-on-the-court/), 2018.

ISSUES & APPLICATIONS: Video Games, U.S. Labor Supply, and Equilibrium Employment and Wages

"Video Game Addiction: Signs, Problems, Risks, and Treatment," TechAddiction.ca (www.techaddiction.ca/video-game-addiction.html), 2019.

Mark Aguiar, Mark Bils, Kerwin Charles, and Erik Hurst, "Leisure Luxuries and the Labor Supply of Young Men," University of Chicago, 2018.

Didem Tüzemen, "Why Are Prime-Age Men Vanishing from the Labor Force?" *Economic Review*, Federal Reserve Bank of Kansas City, First Quarter, 2018.

29 Income, Poverty, and Health Care

Jonathan Weiss/Shutterstock

LEARNING OBJECTIVES

After reading this chapter, you should be able to:

29.1 Describe how to use a Lorenz curve to represent a nation's income distribution

29.2 Identify the key determinants of income differences across individuals and discuss theories of desired income distribution

29.3 Distinguish among alternative approaches to measuring and addressing poverty

29.4 Recognize the role played by third-party payments in rising health care costs

Like everyone else, lower-income individuals must pay their income taxes at a specific marginal tax rate. This marginal rate is a percentage of additional taxable income earned from gainful employment. At the same time, lower-income individuals receive dollar-value benefits from one or more government programs. If such individuals choose to earn income, though, they often have to give up some or all of the benefits they were receiving from the government. The value of the benefits that they sacrifice per dollar of income that they earn by working changes their effective marginal tax rate. In this chapter, you will learn about effective tax rates incurred when lower-income people choose to work for additional earned income and thereby must forgo some government benefits.

Distribution of income
The way income is allocated among the population based on groupings of residents.

a 40-year-old individual whose annual earnings are among the top 1 percent of U.S. income recipients can anticipate living at least 14 years longer than a 40-year-old person whose income is among the bottom 1 percent? Likewise, a typical college-educated 25-year-old can expect to live a decade longer than the average 25-year-old high school dropout who earns a lower income. These facts indicate that the **distribution of income**—the way that income is allocated among the population—influences the distribution of life expectancies across the population. Economists have devised various theories to explain income distribution. We will present some of these theories in this chapter. We will also cover some of the more obvious institutional reasons why income is not distributed equally in the United States. In addition, we will examine the health care problems confronting individuals in all income groups and how the federal government's health care program proposes to solve these problems.

29.1 Describe how to use a Lorenz curve to represent a nation's income distribution

The Distribution of Income

Income provides each of us with the means of consuming and saving. Income can be the result of a payment for labor services or a payment for ownership of one of the other factors of production besides labor—land, physical capital, or entrepreneurship. In addition, individuals obtain spendable income from gifts and government transfers. (Some individuals also obtain income by stealing, but we will not treat this matter here.) Right now, let's examine how money income is distributed across classes of income earners within the United States.

Measuring Income Distribution: The Lorenz Curve

Lorenz curve
A geometric representation of the distribution of income. A Lorenz curve that is perfectly straight represents complete income equality. The more bowed a Lorenz curve, the more unequally income is distributed.

We can represent the distribution of money income graphically with what is known as the **Lorenz curve**, named after a U.S.-born statistician, Max Otto Lorenz, who proposed it in 1905. The Lorenz curve shows what share of total money income is accounted for by different proportions of the nation's households.

Look at Figure 29-1. On the horizontal axis, we measure the *cumulative* percentage of households, lowest-income households first. Starting at the left corner, there are zero households. At the right corner, we have 100 percent of households. In the middle, we have 50 percent of households. The vertical axis represents the cumulative percentage of money income. The 45-degree line represents complete equality: 50 percent of households obtain 50 percent of total income, 60 percent of households obtain 60 percent of total income, and so on.

Of course, in no real-world situation is there such complete equality of income. No actual Lorenz curve would be a straight line. Rather, it would be some curved line, like the one labeled "Actual money income distribution" in Figure 29-1. For example, the bottom 50 percent of households in the United States receive about 22 percent of total money income.

Gini coefficient
On a graph with the cumulative percentage of money income measured along the vertical axis and the cumulative percentage of households measured along the horizontal axis, if A is the area between the line of perfect income equality and the Lorenz curve and B is the area beneath the Lorenz curve, the Gini coefficient equals $A/(A + B)$.

A Numerical Income-Distribution Measure: The Gini Coefficient The Lorenz curve provides a visual depiction of the income distribution. To try to gauge the income distribution with a single number, economists utilize the **Gini coefficient**. The Gini coefficient is the ratio of the area between the line of perfect income equality and the Lorenz curve—area A in Figure 29-1—to the total area beneath the line of perfect income equality—the sum of areas A and B. That is, the Gini coefficient equals the numerical value of the fraction $A/(A + B)$.

The lowest feasible value of the Gini coefficient would arise if a nation exhibited full equality. In this case, the Lorenz curve would correspond to the line of income equality, and there would be no area A. Hence, the value of the Gini coefficient in a nation with complete equality of incomes is equal to 0. As a country's Lorenz curve becomes more bowed, the value of area A increases relative to area B, and the

FIGURE 29-1

The Lorenz Curve

The horizontal axis measures the cumulative percentage of households, with lowest-income households first, from 0 to 100 percent. The vertical axis measures the cumulative percentage of money income, from 0 to 100. A straight line at a 45-degree angle cuts the box in half and represents a line of complete income equality, along which 25 percent of the families get 25 percent of the money income, 50 percent get 50 percent, and so on. The observed Lorenz curve, showing the actual U.S. money income distribution, is not a straight line but rather a curved line, as shown. The difference between complete money income equality and the Lorenz curve is the inequality gap.

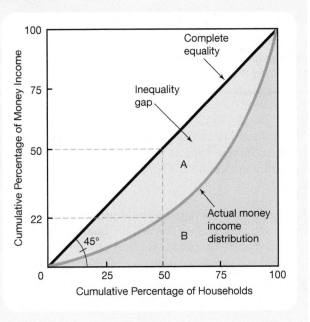

Gini coefficient increases in value. Consequently, a larger value for the Gini coefficient indicates a more bowed Lorenz curve and greater income inequality.

In Figure 29-2, we again show the actual money income distribution Lorenz curve for the United States, and we also compare it to the distribution of money income in 1929. Since that year, the Lorenz curve has generally become less bowed. That is, it has moved closer to the line of complete equality. Accompanying this change in the shape of the U.S. Lorenz curve has been a slight decrease in the value of the nation's Gini coefficient.

FIGURE 29-2

Lorenz Curves of Income Distribution, 1929 and 2020

Since 1929, the Lorenz curve has moved inward toward the straight line of perfect income equality.

Source: U.S. Department of Commerce.

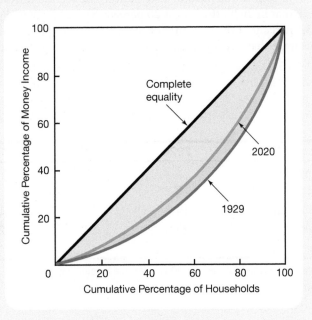

WHAT HAPPENS WHEN...

a nation's Lorenz curve becomes less bowed away from the 45-degree line?

When a country's Lorenz curve takes on a less outward-bowed shape, the distribution of income across the country's population becomes more nearly equal. In addition, the area labeled A in Figure 29-1 becomes smaller, so that the Gini coefficient, which equals A divided by the sum of the areas A and B, also decreases in value.

Criticisms of the Lorenz Curve In recent years, economists have placed less and less emphasis on the shape of the Lorenz curve as an indication of the degree of income inequality in a country. There are five basic reasons why the Lorenz curve has been criticized:

Income in kind

Income received in the form of goods and services, such as housing or medical care. Income in kind differs from money income, which is simply income in dollars, or general purchasing power, that can be used to buy *any* goods and services.

1. The Lorenz curve is typically presented in terms of the distribution of *money* income only. It does not include **income in kind**, such as government-provided food stamps, education, medical care, or housing aid, and goods or services produced and consumed in the home or on the farm.

2. The Lorenz curve does not account for differences in the size of households or the number of wage earners they contain.

3. It does not account for age differences. Even if all families in the United States had exactly the same *lifetime* incomes, chances are that young families would have modest incomes, middle-aged families would have relatively high incomes, and retired families would have lower incomes. Because the Lorenz curve is drawn at a moment in time, it can never tell us anything about the inequality of *lifetime* income.

4. The Lorenz curve ordinarily reflects money income *before* taxes.

5. It does not measure unreported income from the underground economy, a substantial source of income for some individuals.

Income Distribution in the United States

In Table 29-1, we see the percentage share of income for households before direct taxes. The table groups households according to whether they are in the lowest 20 percent of the income distribution, the second lowest 20 percent, and so on. We see that in 2020, the lowest 20 percent had an estimated combined money income of 3.1 percent of the total money income of the entire population. This is a smaller percentage than the lowest 20 percent were receiving at the end of World War II.

TABLE 29-1

Percentage Share of Money Income for Households before Direct Taxes

Income Group	2020	1975	1960	1947
Lowest fifth	3.1	4.4	4.8	5.1
Second fifth	8.2	10.5	12.2	11.8
Third fifth	14.3	17.1	17.8	16.7
Fourth fifth	23.0	24.8	24.0	23.2
Highest fifth	51.4	43.2	41.3	43.3

Note: Figures may not sum to 100 percent due to rounding.
Sources: U.S. Bureau of the Census; author's estimates.

Accordingly, some have concluded that the distribution of money income has become slightly more unequal. *Money* income, however, understates *total* income for individuals who receive in-kind transfers from the government in the form of food stamps, public housing, education, and the like. In particular, since World War II, the share of *total* income—money income plus in-kind benefits—going to the bottom 20 percent of households has more than doubled.

Research by Alan Auerbach of the University of California, Berkeley, Darryl Koehler of Economic Security Planning, and Laurence Kotlikoff of Boston University has sought to restate U.S. income data to take into account income in kind and taxes and to estimate the lifetime spending power of U.S. residents' incomes. After making these adjustments, they find that lifetime after-tax incomes and spending capabilities are less unequal than indicated by pre-tax incomes in a single year. For instance, households ranked in the top 1 percent have a percentage of lifetime after-tax incomes that is several percentage points lower than indicated solely by their pre-tax incomes during a single year. In contrast, households among the lowest 20 percent of income earners receive lifetime after-tax incomes that yield percentages nearly twice as large as implied by a given year's pre-tax incomes.

The Distribution of Wealth

When referring to the distribution of income, we must realize that income—a flow—can be viewed as a return on wealth (both human and nonhuman)—a stock. A discussion of the distribution of income is not necessarily the same thing as a discussion of the distribution of wealth, however. A complete concept of wealth would include not only tangible objects, such as buildings, machinery, land, cars, and houses—nonhuman wealth—but also people who have skills, knowledge, initiative, talents, and the like—human wealth. The total of human and nonhuman wealth in the United States makes up our nation's capital stock.

Figure 29-3 shows that the richest 10 percent of U.S. households hold more than two-thirds of all *measured* wealth. The problem with those data gathered by the Federal Reserve System, however, is that they do not include many important assets. One of these assets is workers' claims on private pension plans, which equal at least $30 trillion. If you add the value of these pensions, household wealth increases by almost 25 percent and reveals that many more U.S. households are middle-wealth households (popularly known as the *middle class*). Another asset excluded from the data is anticipated claims on the Social Security system, which tend to constitute a larger share of the wealth of lower-income individuals.

How has the progressive aging of the baby boom generation affected the current U.S. wealth distribution?

FIGURE 29-3 **Measured Total Wealth Distribution**

The top 10 percent of households have 69 percent of all *measured* wealth, not including other nonmeasured components of wealth, such as claims on private pension plans and on government-guaranteed Social Security commitments.

Source: Board of Governors of the Federal Reserve.

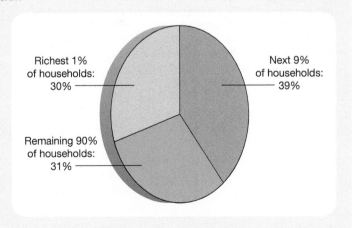

Richest 1% of households: 30%

Next 9% of households: 39%

Remaining 90% of households: 31%

EXAMPLE

Why a Rise in U.S. Wealth Inequality Can Be Blamed in Part on Aging "Baby Boomers"

Many observers have expressed concerns about a gradual increase in the degree of U.S. wealth inequality over recent decades. Often absent from such discussions, however, is the contribution of the shift in the U.S. age distribution to the observed increase in wealth inequality.

It should not be a surprise that the average measured wealth of U.S. residents aged 75 and older is 14 times greater than the average measured wealth of residents younger than 35 and 3½ times greater than that of residents aged 35 to 44. After all, older people simply have been able to accumulate savings from incomes earned over more years than have the younger individuals. Among those who currently are aging and accumulating savings are members of the baby boom generation born between 1944 and 1964. Their share of the U.S. population has been rising. It is expected to increase from about 15 percent today to more than 20 percent by 2030. Thus, a larger percentage of wealth has been shifting to this proportionately older and larger generation. This wealth shift to older "baby boomers" has been contributing to the increase in measured U.S. wealth inequality.

FOR CRITICAL THINKING

Why might we anticipate, other things being equal, that measured wealth inequality eventually will decrease as the baby boom generation gradually passes away?

Sources are listed at the end of this chapter.

29.2 Identify the key determinants of income differences across individuals and discuss theories of desired income distribution

Determinants of Income Differences

We know that there are income differences—that is not in dispute. A more important question is why these differences in income occur. We will look at four determinants of income differences: age, productivity, inheritance, and discrimination.

Age

Age turns out to be a determinant of income because with age come, usually, more education, more training, and more experience. It is not surprising that within every class of income earners, there seem to be regular cycles of earning behavior. Most individuals earn more when they are middle-aged than when they are younger or older. We call this the **age-earnings cycle**.

Age-earnings cycle
The regular earnings profile of an individual throughout his or her lifetime. The age-earnings cycle usually starts with a low income, builds gradually to a peak at around age 50, and then gradually curves down until it approaches zero at retirement.

The Age-Earnings Cycle Every occupation has its own age-earnings cycle, and every individual will probably experience some variation from the average. Nonetheless, we can characterize the typical age-earnings cycle graphically in Figure 29-4. Here we see that at age 18, earnings from wages are relatively low. As a person's productivity increases through more training and experience, earnings gradually rise until they

---

FIGURE 29-4

Typical Age-Earnings Profile

Within every class of income earners, there is usually an age-earnings profile. Earnings from wages are lowest when starting work at age 18, reach their peak at around age 50, and then taper off until retirement around age 65, when they become zero for most people. The rise in earnings up to age 50 is usually due to increased experience, longer working hours, and better training and schooling. (We abstract from economywide productivity changes that would shift the entire curve upward.)

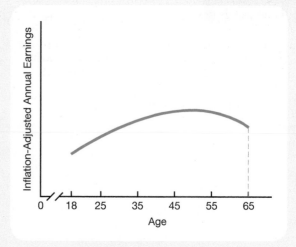

peak at about age 50. Then earnings fall until retirement, when they become zero (that is, currently earned wages become zero, although retirement payments may then commence).

Note that general increases in overall productivity for the entire workforce will result in an upward shift in the typical age-earnings profile depicted in Figure 29-4. Thus, even at the end of the age-earnings cycle, when just about to retire, the worker would receive a relatively high wage compared with the starting wage 45 years earlier. The wage would be higher due to factors that contribute to rising real wages for everyone, regardless of the stage in the age-earnings cycle.

Now we have some idea why specific individuals earn different incomes at different times in their lives, but we have yet to explain why different people are paid different amounts for their labor. One way to explain this is to recall marginal productivity theory.

Marginal Productivity

When trying to determine how many workers a firm would hire, we had to construct a marginal revenue product curve. We found that as more workers were hired, the marginal revenue product fell due to diminishing marginal product. If the forces of demand and supply established a certain wage rate, workers would be hired until their marginal product times marginal revenue (which equals the market price under perfect competition) was equal to the going wage rate. Then the hiring would stop. This analysis suggests what workers can expect to be paid in the labor market: As long as there are low-cost information flows and the labor and product markets are competitive, each worker can expect to be paid his or her marginal revenue product.

Determinants of Marginal Productivity
According to marginal revenue product theory, if people can increase their marginal product, they can expect to earn higher incomes. Key determinants of marginal product are talent, experience, and training.

Talent Talent is the easiest factor to explain, but it is difficult to acquire if you don't have it. Innate abilities and attributes can be very strong, if not overwhelming, determinants of a person's potential productivity. Strength, coordination, and mental alertness are facets of nonacquired human capital and thus have some bearing on the ability to earn income. Someone who is tall and agile has a better chance of being a basketball player than someone who is short and unathletic. A person born with a superior talent for abstract thinking has a better chance of earning a relatively high income as a mathematician or a physicist than someone who is not born with that capability.

Experience Additional experience at particular tasks is another way to increase productivity. Experience can be linked to the well-known *learning curve* that applies when the same task is done over and over. The worker repeating a task becomes more efficient: The worker can do the same task in less time or in the same amount of time but better. Take an example of a person starting to work on developing a new digital device. At first she is able to contribute in a small way to the design of an additional feature after several weeks of work. Then the worker becomes more adept and can provide a significant contribution to the next developmental stage. After a few more weeks, another task can be added. Experience allows this individual to improve her productivity. The more effectively people learn to do something, the more productive they are.

Training Training is similar to experience but is more formal. Many companies have training programs for new workers.

Why Investment in Human Capital Is Important for You
Investment in human capital is just like investment in anything else. Suppose that you invest in yourself by going to college, rather than going to work after high school and earning more current income.

If so, you will likely be rewarded in the future with a higher income or a more interesting job (or both). This is exactly the motivation that underlies the decision of many college-bound students to obtain formal higher education.

As with other investments, we can determine the rate of return on an investment in a college education. To do so, we first have to figure out the cost of going to school. The cost is not simply what you have to pay for books, fees, and tuition but also includes the income you forgo. *A key cost of education is the income forgone—the opportunity cost of not working*. In addition, the direct expenses of college must be paid for. Certainly, not all students forgo all income during their college years. Many work part-time. Taking account of those who work part-time and those who are supported by tuition grants and other scholarships, the average annual rate of return from a college degree exceeds 6 percent per year. For people with degrees in certain fields, such as engineering, computer sciences, and business, the average annual rate of return can be more than double that percentage. The gain in lifetime income has a present value ranging from $200,000 to more than $500,000.

Why is greater access to books when a person is young associated with higher lifetime earnings?

BEHAVIORAL EXAMPLE

The Lasting Positive Effect on Lifetime Earnings of Childhood Access to Books and Parental Readings

Behavioral economists and other social scientists have documented that a greater degree of literacy among children is associated with higher measured earnings gains from education and training attained by the adults whom those children ultimately become. Research indicates that children's access to books and parental readings are associated with future acquisitions of education and skills that ultimately yield higher future earnings. Thus, providing books to a child and reading aloud to the child both help to contribute to the child's lifetime earnings prospects.

FOR CRITICAL THINKING

Why do you suppose that behavioral researchers typically find evidence that people who had access to fewer books or heard fewer book readings when young tend to fall within the group of lower-income earners?

Sources are listed at the end of this chapter.

Inheritance

It is not unusual to inherit cash, jewelry, stocks, bonds, homes, or other real estate. Yet only about 10 percent of income inequality in the United States can be traced to differences in inherited wealth. If for some reason the government confiscated all property that had been inherited, the immediate result would be only a modest change in the distribution of income in the United States. In any event, at both federal and state levels substantial inheritance taxes generally are levied on the estates of relatively wealthy deceased Americans (although there are some legally valid ways to avoid certain estate taxes).

Discrimination

Economic discrimination occurs whenever workers with the same marginal revenue product receive unequal pay due to some noneconomic factor such as their race, gender, or age. It is possible—and indeed quite obvious—that discrimination affects the distribution of income. Certain groups in our society are not paid wages at rates comparable to those received by other groups, even when we correct for productivity. Differences in income remain between whites and nonwhites and between men and women. For example, the median income of black families is about 66 percent that of white families. The average wage rate of women is about 83 percent that of men. Some people argue that all of these differences are due to discrimination against nonwhites and against women.

We cannot simply assume that *any* differences in income are due to discrimination, though. What we need to do is discover why differences in income between groups exist and then determine if factors other than discrimination in the labor market can explain them. The unexplained part of income differences can rightfully be considered the result of discrimination.

Theories of Desired Income Distribution

We have talked about the factors affecting the distribution of income, but we have not yet mentioned the normative issue of how income *ought* to be distributed. This, of course, requires a value judgment. We are talking about the problem of economic justice. We can never completely resolve this problem because there are always going to be conflicting values. It is impossible to give all people what each thinks is just. Nonetheless, two particular normative standards for the distribution of income have been popular with economists. These are income distribution based on productivity and income distribution based on equality.

Productivity
The *productivity standard* for the distribution of income can be stated simply as "To each according to what he or she produces." This is also called the *contributive standard* because it is based on the principle of rewarding according to the contribution to society's total output. It is also sometimes referred to as the *merit standard* and is one of the oldest concepts of justice. People are rewarded according to merit, and merit is judged by one's ability to produce what is considered useful by society.

We measure a person's productive contribution in a capitalist system by the market value of that person's output. We have already referred to this as the marginal revenue product theory of wage determination.

Equality
The *egalitarian principle* of income distribution is simply "To each exactly the same." Everyone would have exactly the same amount of income. This criterion of income distribution has been debated as far back as biblical times. This system of income distribution has been considered equitable, meaning that presumably everybody is dealt with fairly and equally. There are problems, however, with an income distribution that is completely equal.

Differences in Job Characteristics Some jobs are more unpleasant or more dangerous than others. Should the people undertaking these jobs be paid exactly the same as everyone else? Indeed, under an equal distribution of income, what incentive would there be for individuals to take risky, hazardous, or unpleasant jobs at all? What about overtime? Who would be willing to work overtime without additional pay? There is yet another problem: If everyone earned the same income, what incentive would there be for individuals to invest in their own human capital—a costly and time-consuming process?

Just consider the incentive structure within a corporation. Within corporations, much of the differential between, say, the pay of the CEO and the pay of all of the vice presidents is meant to create competition among the vice presidents for the CEO's job. The result is higher productivity. If all incomes were the same, much of this competition would disappear, and productivity would fall.

Income Differences and Economic Growth There is some evidence that differences in income lead to higher rates of economic growth. Future generations are therefore made better off. Elimination of income differences may reduce investments in physical and human capital and decrease the rate of economic growth. Erasing differences in income therefore may cause future generations to be poorer than they otherwise might have been.

29.3 Distinguish among alternative approaches to measuring and addressing poverty

Poverty and Attempts to Eliminate It

Throughout the history of the world, mass poverty has been accepted as inevitable. This nation and others, particularly in the Western world, however, have sustained enough economic growth in the past several hundred years so that *mass* poverty can no longer be said to be a problem for these fortunate countries. As a matter of fact, the residual of poverty in the United States strikes us as bizarre, an anomaly. How can there still be so much poverty in a nation of such abundance? Having talked about the determinants of the distribution of income, we now have at least some idea of why some people are destined to remain low-income earners throughout their lives.

Income can be transferred from the relatively well-to-do to the relatively poor by various methods, and as a nation we have been using them for a long time. Today, we have a vast array of welfare programs set up for the purpose of redistributing income. As we know, however, these programs have not been entirely successful. Are there alternatives to our current welfare system? Is there a better method of helping the poor? Before we answer these questions, take a look at Figure 29-5, which displays the percentage of the U.S. population estimated to be in a state of poverty by the U.S. government. This percentage, called the *poverty rate*, has varied between roughly 11 percent and 16 percent since 1965.

Defining Poverty

The threshold income level, which is used to determine who falls into the poverty category, was originally based on the cost of a nutritionally adequate food plan designed by the U.S. Department of Agriculture. The threshold was determined by multiplying the food plan cost by 3 on the assumption that food expenses account for approximately one-third of a poor family's income. Annual revisions of the threshold level were based only on price changes in the food budget.

In 1969, a federal interagency committee looked at the calculations of the threshold and decided to set new standards, with adjustments made on the basis of changes in the Consumer Price Index. For example, in 2020, the official poverty level for an urban family of four was around $26,000. It typically goes up each year to reflect whatever inflation has occurred.

Absolute Poverty

Because the low-income threshold is an absolute measure, we know that if it never changes in real terms, we will reduce poverty even if we do nothing. How can that be?

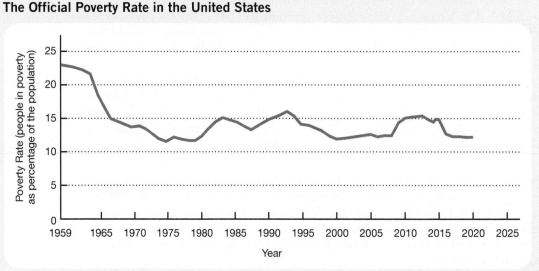

FIGURE 29-5

The official poverty rate, or the number of people in poverty as a percentage of the U.S. population, has remained in a range of roughly 11 to 16 percent since 1965.

Source: U.S. Department of Labor.

The Official Poverty Rate in the United States

The reasoning is straightforward. Real incomes in the United States have been growing at a compounded annual rate of almost 2 percent per capita for at least the past century and at about 2.5 percent since World War II. If we define the poverty line at a specific real income level, more and more individuals will make incomes that exceed that poverty line. Thus, in absolute terms, we will eliminate poverty (assuming continued per capita growth and no change in income distribution).

Relative Poverty

Be careful with this analysis, however. Poverty can also be defined in relative terms, that is, in terms of the income levels of individuals or families relative to the rest of the population. As long as the distribution of income is not perfectly equal, there will always be some people who make less income than others, even if their relatively low income is high by historical standards. Thus, in a relative sense, the problem of poverty will always exist.

Attacks on Poverty: Major Income Maintenance Programs

There are a variety of income maintenance programs designed to help the poor. We examine a few of them here.

Social Security For the retired and the disabled, social insurance programs provide income payments in prescribed situations. The best known is Social Security, which includes what has been called old-age, survivors', and disability insurance (OASDI). Recall that Social Security was originally supposed to be a program of compulsory saving financed from payroll taxes levied on both employers and employees. Workers pay for Social Security while working and receive the benefits after retirement. The benefit payments are usually made to people who have reached retirement age. When the insured worker dies, benefits accrue to the survivors, including widows and children. Special benefits provide for disabled workers.

More than 90 percent of all employed persons in the United States are covered by OASDI. Today, Social Security is an intergenerational income transfer that is only vaguely related to past earnings. It transfers income from U.S. residents who work (the young through the middle-aged) to those who do not work—older retired persons.

In 2020, more than 63 million people were receiving OASDI checks averaging about $1,400 per month. Benefit payments from OASDI redistribute income to some degree. Benefit payments, however, are not based on recipient need. Participants' contributions give them the right to benefits even if they would be financially secure without the benefits. Social Security is not really an insurance program because people are not guaranteed that the benefits they receive will be in line with the "contributions" they have made. It is not a personal savings account. The benefits are legislated by Congress. In the future, Congress may not be as sympathetic toward older people as it is today. It could (and probably will have to) legislate for lower real levels of benefits instead of higher ones.

Why does Social Security face bleak long-term funding prospects?

POLICY EXAMPLE

The Unavoidable Implications of Some Basic Social Security Arithmetic

In 1980, the ratio of people working and contributing to Social Security per individual receiving benefits was equal to about 3.5. Today, the ratio is about 2.6, and it is projected to drop to about 2.0 by 2040.

These figures indicate that about forty years ago, taxes on the earnings of more than three employed people provided each Social Security recipient's benefits. In contrast, two decades from now, taxes on the earnings of only about two employed people will have to provide the benefits of each recipient. This explains why most economists conclude that

Social Security taxes paid by employed people eventually will have to increase and that benefits to recipients will have to decrease.

REAL APPLICATION

Given the rather grim statistics on the future of Social Security, what should you be doing as a consequence?

Sources are listed at the end of this chapter.

Supplemental Security Income and Temporary Assistance to Needy Families Many people who are poor but do not qualify for Social Security benefits are assisted through other programs. The federally financed and administered Supplemental Security Income (SSI) program was instituted in 1974. The purpose of SSI is to establish a nationwide minimum income for the aged, the blind, and the disabled. SSI has become one of the fastest-growing transfer programs in the United States. Whereas in 1974 less than $8 billion was spent, the estimate for 2021 is in excess of $65 billion. U.S. residents currently eligible for SSI include children and individuals with mental disabilities, including drug addicts and alcoholics.

Temporary Assistance to Needy Families (TANF) is a state-administered program, financed in part by federal grants. The program provides aid to families in need. TANF payments are intended to be temporary. Estimated expenditures for TANF in 2021 are in excess of $25 billion.

Supplemental Nutrition Assistance Program The Supplemental Nutrition Assistance Program (SNAP, commonly known as "food stamps") provides government-issued, electronic debit cards that can be used to purchase food. In 1964, some 367,000 U.S. residents were receiving SNAP benefits. For 2021, the estimate is about 40 million recipients. The annual cost has jumped from $860,000 to more than $70 billion. In 2020, about one in every eight citizens (including children) was receiving SNAP benefits.

The Earned Income Tax Credit Program In 1975, the Earned Income Tax Credit (EITC) Program was created to provide rebates of Social Security taxes to low-income workers. More than one-fifth of all tax returns claim an earned income tax credit. Each year the federal government grants about $70 billion in these credits. In some states, such as Mississippi, nearly half of all families are eligible for an EITC. The program works as follows: Single-income households with two children who report income up to almost $54,000 (exclusive of welfare payments) receive EITC benefits up to about $6,500.

There is a catch, though. Those with earnings up to a threshold of about $25,000 receive higher benefits as their incomes rise. Families earning more than this threshold income, however, are penalized about 18 cents for every dollar they earn above the income threshold. Thus, on net the EITC discourages work by low- or moderate-income earners more than it rewards work. In particular, it discourages low-income earners from taking on second jobs. The Government Accountability Office estimates that hours worked by working wives in EITC-beneficiary households have consequently decreased by 15 percent. The average EITC recipient works 1,500 hours a year compared to a normal work year of about 1,800 hours.

No Apparent Reduction in Poverty Rates

In spite of the numerous programs in existence and the trillions of dollars transferred to the poor, the *officially* defined rate of poverty in the United States has shown no long-run tendency to decline. From 1945 until the 1970s, the percentage of U.S. residents in poverty fell steadily every year. As Figure 29-5 shows, it reached a low of around 11 percent in 1974, shot back up beyond 15 percent in 1983, fell to nearly 12 percent by 2007, rose close to 15 percent until 2016, and then declined back toward 12 percent. Why this pattern has emerged is a puzzle. Since the War on Poverty was launched under President Lyndon B. Johnson in 1965, more than $15 trillion has been transferred to the poor, and yet more U.S. residents are poor today than ever before. This fact created the political will to pass the Welfare Reform Act of 1996, putting limits on people's use of welfare. The law's goal was to get people off public assistance and into jobs.

29.4 Recognize the role played by third-party payments in rising health care costs

Health Care

It may seem strange to be reading about health care in a chapter on the distribution of income and poverty. Yet health care is intimately related to those two topics. For example, sometimes people become poor because they do not have adequate health insurance (or have none at all), fall ill, and deplete all of their wealth in obtaining

FIGURE 29-6

Percentage of Total National Income Spent on Health Care in the United States

The portion of total national income spent on health care has risen steadily since 1965.

Sources: U.S. Department of Health and Human Services; Centers for Medicare and Medicaid Services.

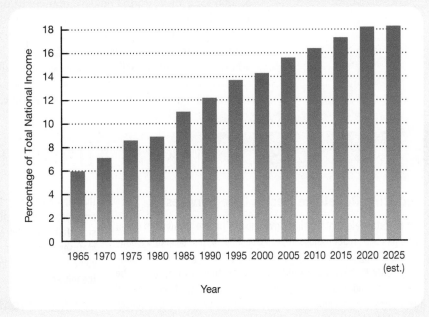

medical care. Moreover, some individuals remain in certain jobs simply because their employer's health care package seems so good that they are afraid to change jobs and risk not being covered by health insurance in the process.

As you will see, much of the cause of the increased health care spending in the United States can be attributed to a change in the incentives that U.S. residents face. Finally, we will examine the economic impact of the 2010 national health care program.

The U.S. Health Care Situation

Spending for health care is estimated to account for more than 18 percent of U.S. real GDP. You can see from Figure 29-6 that in 1965, about 6 percent of annual income was spent on health care, but that percentage has been increasing ever since.

Why Have Health Care Costs Risen So Much? There are numerous explanations for why health care costs have risen so much. At least one has to do with changing demographics: The U.S. population is getting older.

The Age–Health Care Expenditure Equation The top 5 percent of health care users incur more than 50 percent of all health costs. The bottom 70 percent of health care users account for only 10 percent of health care expenditures. Not surprisingly, the elderly make up most of the top users of health care services. Nursing home expenditures are made primarily by people older than 70. The use of hospitals is also dominated by the aged.

The U.S. population is aging steadily. More than 15 percent of the 327 million U.S. residents are over 65. It is estimated that by the year 2035, senior citizens will constitute about 22 percent of our population. This aging population increases the demand for health care. The elderly consume more than four times as much per capita health care services as the rest of the population. In short, whatever the demand for health care services is today, it is likely to be considerably higher in the future as the U.S. population ages.

New Technologies Another reason that health care costs have risen so dramatically is advancing technology. Each new CT (computerized tomography) scanner costs at least $90,000. An MRI (magnetic resonance imaging) scanner usually sells at a higher price, as does a PET (positron emission tomography) scanner. All of these machines have become increasingly available in recent decades and are desired throughout the country. Typical fees for procedures using them range from $300 to $400 for a CT scan to as high as $2,000 for a PET scan. The development of new technologies that help physicians and hospitals prolong human life is an ongoing process in an ever-advancing industry. New procedures at even higher prices can be expected in the future, although some economists note that if these new procedures also boost the quality of health care, quality-adjusted prices likely will not rise as substantially as estimated.

How does the application of machine learning promise to help offset cost increases associated with utilization of new technologies in health care?

AI | DECISION MAKING THROUGH DATA

Reducing Repetitive Health Care Services

One important element that has driven up health care spending in recent years has been readmissions of people sent home from hospitals following initial diagnoses and treatments. Many patients go home from hospitals only to have flare-ups that require them to return and be reevaluated and treated again. The same resources effectively are used the second time around, which thereby doubles the overall expenses incurred in addressing their health problems.

Hospitals now are using machine learning and diverse and plentiful sources of data regarding past experiences of many patients around the country. The hospitals have begun to screen admitted patients more carefully in an effort to ensure utilization of the most appropriate and thorough diagnostic and treatment procedures. AI techniques also are employed to make certain that evaluations prior to hospital release consider fully every bit of available information about how the patients' statuses compare with those of past patients who have experienced the same health issues. In this way, hospitals are seeking to guarantee that the initial hospital entry is not followed by expensive readmissions.

FOR CRITICAL THINKING

How might an incorrect diagnosis or incomplete treatment lead to readmission that could considerably raise the expenses associated with treating a patient's underlying health care problem?

Sources are listed at the end of this chapter.

Third-Party Financing Currently, government spending on health care constitutes more than 60 percent of total health care spending (of which *federal* taxpayers fund about 70 percent). Private insurance funded by consumers' premium payments accounts for about 30 percent of payments for health care. The remainder—about 10 percent—is paid out of pocket by individuals. Figure 29-7 shows the change in the payment scheme for medical care in the United States since 1930. Medicare and Medicaid (including the Children's Health Insurance Program) are the main sources

FIGURE 29-7

Third-Party versus Out-of-Pocket Health Care Payments

Out-of-pocket payments for health care services have been falling steadily since the 1930s. In contrast, third-party payments for health care have risen to the point that they account for about 90 percent of all such outlays today.

Sources: U.S. Department of Health and Human Services; Centers for Medicare and Medicaid Services.

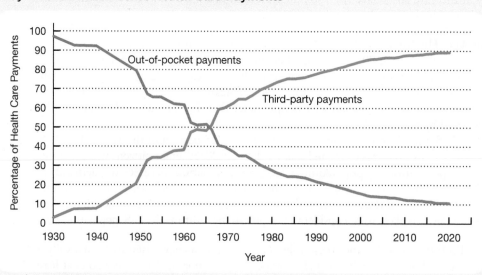

of hospital and other medical benefits for about 120 million U.S. residents. Most of the approximately 60 million Medicare recipients are over age 65. Medicaid—the joint state-federal program—provides long-term health care for more than 75 million additional individuals, particularly for people living in nursing homes. More than 10 million Medicare recipients also receive some Medicaid benefits as well.

Overall, Medicaid enrollments have expanded considerably. Between 1995 and 2010, gradual loosening of eligibility requirements for Medicaid benefits expanded the number of Medicaid recipients from 33 million to about 55 million. The Affordable Care Act of 2010 reduced requirements further, and today in excess of 75 million people—more than 20 percent of the U.S. population—are enrolled in the Medicaid program.

Medicare, Medicaid, and private insurance companies are considered **third parties** in the medical care equation. Health care providers and patients are the two primary parties. When third parties step in to pay for medical care, the quantity demanded of those services increases. For example, within four years after Medicare went into effect in 1966, the volume of federal government–reimbursed medical services increased to a level 65 percent higher than predicted when the program was enacted.

Price, Quantity Demanded, and the Question of Moral Hazard Although some people may think that the demand for health care is insensitive to price changes, significant increases in quantities of medical services demanded follow reductions in people's out-of-pocket costs. Look at Figure 29-8. There you see a hypothetical demand curve for health care services. To the extent that third parties—whether government or private insurance—pay for health care, the out-of-pocket cost, or net price, to the individual decreases. If all medical expenses were paid for by third parties, dropping the price to zero in Figure 29-8, the quantity demanded would increase.

One of the issues here has to do with the problem of *moral hazard*. Consider two individuals with two different health insurance policies. The first policy pays for all medical expenses, but under the second, the individual has to pay the first $1,000 a year (this amount is known as the *deductible*). Will the behavior of the two individuals be different? Generally, the answer is yes.

The individual with no deductible is more likely to seek treatment for health problems after they develop rather than try to avoid them and will generally seek medical attention on a more regular basis. In contrast, the individual who faces the first $1,000 of medical expenses each year will tend to engage in more wellness activities and will be less inclined to seek medical care for minor problems. The moral hazard here is that the individual with the zero deductible for medical care expenses will tend to engage in a less healthful lifestyle than will the individual with the $1,000 deductible.

Moral Hazard as It Affects Physicians and Hospitals The issue of moral hazard also has a direct effect on the behavior of physicians and hospital administrators. Due to

ECONOMICS IN YOUR LIFE

To consider the types of in-kind, government-provided health care services that provide greatest measurable benefits to recipients, read **Targeting In-Kind Care in Government Health Programs** on page 646.

Third parties
Parties who are not directly involved in a given activity or transaction. For example, in the relationship between health care providers and patients, fees may be paid by third parties (insurance companies, government).

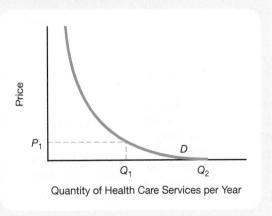

FIGURE 29-8

The Demand for Health Care Services

At price P_1, the quantity of health care services demanded per year would hypothetically be Q_1. If the price fell to zero (third-party payment with zero deductible), the quantity demanded would expand to Q_2.

FIGURE 29-9

Federal Medicare Spending

Federal spending on Medicare has increased about 10 percent per year, *after adjusting for inflation*, since its inception in 1966. (All figures are expressed in constant 2012 dollars per year.)

Sources: Economic Report of the President; U.S. Bureau of Labor Statistics.

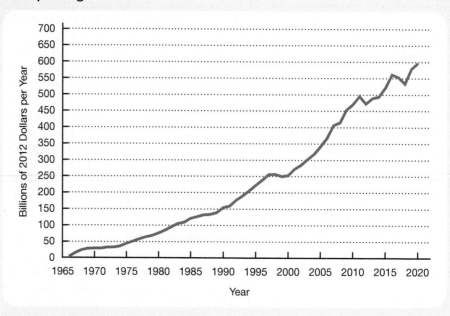

third-party payments, patients rarely have to worry about the expense of operations and other medical procedures. As a consequence, both physicians and hospitals order more procedures. Physicians are typically reimbursed on the basis of medical procedures. Thus, they have no financial interest in trying to keep hospital costs down. Indeed, many have an incentive to increase costs.

Rising Medicare expenditures are one of the most serious problems facing the federal government today. Figure 29-9 shows that as the number of beneficiaries increased from 19.1 million in 1966 (first year of operation) to more than 60 million in 2020, federal inflation-adjusted spending on Medicare has grown at an average of about 10 percent per year. The rate of growth in Medicare spending increased further following adoption of the Medicare prescription drug benefit in 2006.

ECONOMICS IN YOUR LIFE

Targeting In-Kind Care in Government Health Programs

Ethan Lieber of the University of Notre Dame and Lee Lockwood of Northwestern University have been trying to evaluate the most beneficial forms of governmental in-kind transfer programs. Lieber and Lockwood have zeroed in on studying health care programs that receive substantial taxpayer funding.

The government provides many health care services as direct in-kind transfers. Consequently, Lieber and Lockwood have focused on determining which forms of in-kind health care services come closer to maximizing the benefits perceived by recipients. The two researchers have identified services that the Medicare and Medicaid programs provide to people directly in their homes. Many recipients of such services suffer from conditions that limit their ability to travel comfortably outside their homes at low expense. A consequence is that, as compared with all other governmental health care services, home-directed services such as home nursing provide the greatest measurable benefits per dollar spent by the government.

Lieber and Lockwood have concluded, therefore, that the government's efforts should be targeted on delivering more services to recipients in their own homes.

FOR CRITICAL THINKING

How might the fact that many in-kind health care services that the government can deliver to people in their homes can be provided by nurses instead of physicians also help to reduce expenses of providing the services?

REAL APPLICATION

At some point in your life, you may be mobility restricted such that it is not easy for you to travel to see a physician. To obtain health care services, what might be your options?

Sources are listed at the end of this chapter.

ISSUES & APPLICATIONS

The Effective Marginal Tax Rate Faced by Beneficiaries of Anti-Poverty Programs Who Wish to Work

Jonathan Weiss/Shutterstock

CONCEPTS APPLIED

➤ Anti-Poverty Programs

➤ Earned Income Tax Credit (EITC)

➤ Supplemental Nutrition Assistance Program

When a low- or moderate-income individual contemplates earning additional income in the labor market, the *explicit* marginal income tax rate is an obvious disincentive. Many low- and moderate-income U.S. individuals, however, also qualify for federal anti-poverty programs. Whenever these people opt to earn income by working, they typically lose eligibility for some benefits provided by these programs. Because they sacrifice some government benefits for each additional dollar of income that they earn, they effectively incur additional implicit taxes equal to the dollar value of sacrificed benefits.

Marginal Benefits Tax Rates on Earned Income

When people lose dollar values of benefits from a government program by choosing to earn an additional dollar by working, they confront an effective *marginal benefits tax rate*. For each type of government program, this tax rate equals the dollar value of sacrificed benefits

expressed as a percentage of an additional dollar in earnings from work.

Figure 29-10 shows marginal benefits tax rates that the Congressional Budget Office (CBO) estimates a typical low- to moderate-income individual faces for selected programs, such as the Earned Income Tax Credit and the Supplemental Nutritional Assistance Program (food stamps). The CBO estimates that the average low- to moderate-income

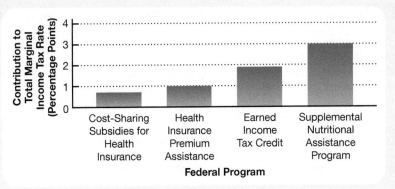

FIGURE 29-10

Marginal Benefits Tax Rates for Selected Government Programs

Displayed are lost dollar values of federal program benefits, expressed as percentages of an additional dollar of earned income, resulting from a decision by a typical low- to moderate-income individual to hold an income-earning job.

Source: Congressional Budget Office

individual confronts a combined effective marginal benefits tax rate across all programs of about 15 percent.

The Total Marginal Tax Rate Faced by Low- to Moderate-Income Individuals

Of course, the *total* marginal tax rate faced by a typical low- to moderate-income individual equals the sum of the explicit marginal income tax rate and the combined effective marginal benefits tax rate. The U.S. Congressional Budget Office (CBO) has estimated that the marginal income tax rate faced by an average low- to moderate-income individual is 25 percent. Low- to moderate-income people thereby confront a *total* marginal tax rate on earned income equal to this marginal income tax rate plus the combined effective marginal benefits tax rate of about

15 percent. Thus, a low- to moderate-income person considering earning additional income faces a *total* marginal tax rate equal to approximately 40 percent.

FOR CRITICAL THINKING

What is the *net* additional income actually received by an average low- to moderate-income person who chooses to earn an additional pre-income-tax, pre-lost-benefits dollar by working? Explain briefly.

REAL APPLICATION

Imagine that you are living in poverty and therefore benefit from numerous anti-poverty programs. You are offered a relatively good job. Are there any reasons you might turn it down?

Sources are listed at the end of this chapter.

What You Should Know

Here is what you should know after reading this chapter.

LEARNING OBJECTIVES

29.1 **Describe how to use a Lorenz curve to represent a nation's income distribution** *A Lorenz curve depicts the distribution of income geometrically by measuring the percentage of households in relation to the cumulative percentage of income earnings. A perfectly straight Lorenz curve depicts perfect income equality because at each percentage of households measured along a straight-line Lorenz curve, those households earn exactly the same percentage of income. The resulting value of the Gini coefficient is zero. The more bowed a Lorenz curve is, the more unequally income is distributed and the larger is the value of the Gini coefficient.*

29.2 **Identify the key determinants of income differences across individuals and discuss theories of desired income distribution** *Because of the age-earnings cycle, in which people typically earn relatively low incomes when young, age is an important factor influencing income differences. So are marginal productivity differences, which arise from variations in talent, experience, and training due to different investments in human capital. One theory of desired income distribution is the productivity standard, according to which each person receives income based on the value of what he or she produces. The other is the egalitarian principle of income distribution, which proposes that each person should receive exactly the same income.*

29.3 **Distinguish among alternative approaches to measuring and addressing poverty** *One approach to measuring poverty is to define an absolute poverty standard. Another approach defines poverty in terms of income levels relative to the rest of the population. Currently, the U.S. government seeks to address poverty via income maintenance programs such as Social Security, Supplemental Security Income, Temporary Assistance to Needy Families, Supplemental Nutrition Assistance Program benefits, and the Earned Income Tax Credit Program.*

29.4 **Recognize the role played by third-party payments in rising health care costs** *Third-party financing of health care expenditures by private and government insurance programs provides an incentive to buy more health care than if all expenses were paid out of pocket.*

KEY TERMS

distribution of income, 632
Lorenz curve, 632
Gini coefficient, 632
income in kind, 634
Key Figures
Figure 29-1, 633
Figure 29-2, 633

age-earnings cycle, 636
Key Figure
Figure 29-4, 636

Key Figure
Figure 29-5, 640

Third parties, 645
Key Figures
Figure 29-6, 643
Figure 29-7, 644
Figure 29-8, 645

PROBLEMS

29-1. Consider the graph nearby, which depicts Lorenz curves for countries X, Y, and Z.

    a. Which country has the least income inequality?

    b. Which country has the most income inequality?

    c. Countries Y and Z are identical in all but one respect: population distribution. The share of the population made up of children below working age is much higher in country Z. Recently, however, birthrates have declined in country Z and risen in country Y. Assuming that the countries remain identical in all other respects, would you expect that in 20 years the Lorenz curves for the two countries will be closer together or farther apart? (*Hint:* According to the age-earnings cycle, what typically happens to income as an individual begins working and ages?)

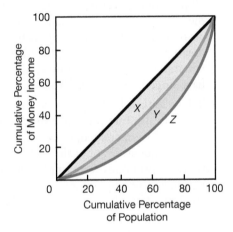

29-2. Consider the following estimates from the early 2020s of shares of income to each group. Use graph paper or a hand-drawn diagram to draw rough Lorenz curves for each country. Which has the most nearly equal distribution, based on your diagram?

Country	Poorest 40%	Next 30%	Next 20%	Richest 10%
Bolivia	13	21	26	40
Chile	13	20	26	41
Uruguay	22	26	26	26

29-3. Consider Figure 29-1 to answer the questions that follow.

    a. What is the value of the Gini coefficient if area *B* is twice as large as area *A*?

    b. Suppose that the Lorenz curve becomes more bowed, with the result that area *B* becomes exactly the same size as area *A*. What will be the new value of the Gini coefficient?

29-4. Suppose that a nation has implemented a system for applying a tax rate of 2 percent to the incomes earned by the 10 percent of its residents with the highest incomes. All funds collected are then transferred directly to the 10 percent of the nation's residents with the lowest incomes. What is the general effect on the shape of a Lorenz curve based on incomes after collection and redistribution of the tax?

29-5. Estimates indicate that in recent years, the poorest 40 percent of the population earned about 15 percent of total income in Argentina. In Brazil, the poorest 40 percent earned about 10 percent of total income. The next-highest 30 percent of income earners in Argentina received roughly 25 percent of total income. In Brazil, the next-highest 30 percent of income earners received approximately 20 percent of total income. Can you determine, without drawing a diagram (though you can if you wish), which country's Lorenz curve was bowed out farther to the right?

29-6. Explain why the productivity standard for the distribution of income entails rewarding people based on their contribution to society's total output. Why does the productivity standard typically fail to yield an equal distribution of income?

29-7. Identify whether each of the following proposed poverty measures is an absolute or relative measure of poverty, and discuss whether poverty could ever be eliminated if that measure were utilized.

    a. An inflation-adjusted annual income of $25,000 for an urban family of four

    b. Individuals with annual incomes among the lowest 15 percent

    c. An inflation-adjusted annual income of $10,000 per person

29-8. Some economists have argued that if the government wishes to subsidize health care, it should do so by providing predetermined amounts of payments (based on the type of health care problems experienced) directly to patients, who then would be free to choose their health care providers. Whether or not you agree, can you give an economic rationale for this approach to governmental health care funding?

29-9. Suppose that a government agency guarantees to pay all of an individual's future health care expenses after the end of this year, so that the effective price of health care for the individual will be zero from that date onward. In what ways might this policy induce the individual to consume "excessive" health care services in future years?

29-10. Suppose that a group of physicians establishes a joint practice in a remote area. This group provides the only health care available to people in the local community, and its objective is to maximize total economic profits for the group's members. Explain how the price and quantity of health care will be determined in this community. (*Hint:* How does a single producer of any service determine its output and price?)

29-11. A government agency determines that the entire community discussed in Problem 29-10 qualifies for a special program in which the government will pay for a number of health care services that most residents previously had not consumed. Many residents immediately make appointments with the community physicians' group. Given the information in Problem 29-10, what is the likely effect on the profit-maximizing price and the equilibrium quantity of health care services provided by the physicians' group in this community?

29-12. A government agency notifies the physicians' group in Problem 29-10 that to continue providing services in the community, the group must document its activities. The resulting paperwork expenses raise the cost of each unit of health care services that the group provides. What is the likely effect on the profit-maximizing price and the equilibrium quantity of health care services provided by the physicians' group in this community?

29-13. Suppose that in Figure 29-1 the area labeled A is one-fourth of the area denoted B. What is the value of the Gini coefficient?

29-14. Now suppose that in the situation described in Problem 29-13, the distribution of income changes in such a way that A increases to one-third of the area denoted B. What is the new value of the Gini coefficient?

29-15. Based on your answers to Problems 29-13 and 29-14, when A increased, did the degree of income inequality increase or decrease? Explain why your answer makes sense by referring to the implied change in the shape of the Lorenz curve.

29-16. Take a look at Figure 29-4. During the past decade, many members of the baby boom generation have passed through ages ranging from the middle 40s to the late 50s. Do you suppose that the fact that there have been more members of this generation than other generations in the population during this past decade tends to imply that there was higher or lower measured inequality over the period? Why?

29-17. Consider Figure 29-5, in which the poverty rate has risen in some years and fallen in others but since 1985 has tended to lie in a range between 10 percent and just over 15 percent. If the government's official poverty rate had been based on an absolute measure of poverty instead of a relative measure, would the data plot likely have tended generally to have sloped upward over time or to have sloped downward? Explain.

29-18. Take a look at both Figure 29-7 and Figure 29-8. When health care programs such as Medicare and Medicaid were created, Congress based projected costs on quantities of health care consumed at the time the programs were implemented. Was this a reasonable assumption given that the programs all cut out-of-pocket payments for beneficiaries? Explain.

REFERENCES

EXAMPLE: Why a Rise in U.S. Wealth Inequality Can Be Blamed in Part on Aging "Baby Boomers"

"Wealth Inequality in the United States," Inequality.org (https://inequality.org/facts/wealth-inequality/), 2019.

Patricia Buckley, "Are We Headed for a Poorer United States? Growing Wealth Inequality by Age Puts Young Households Behind," *Deloitte Issues by the Numbers*, March 2018.

Dayana Yochim, "How Your Net Worth Compares—and What Matters More," NerdWallet.com (https://www.nerdwallet.com/article/how-your-net-worth-compares-and-what-matters-more), September 6, 2018.

BEHAVIORAL EXAMPLE: The Lasting Positive Effect on Lifetime Earnings of Childhood Access to Books and Parental Readings

"Why Books?" BookHarvestNC.org (https://bookharvestnc.org/why-books/statistics/), 2019.

Tony Hockley, "Behavioral Insights and Parenting," *Behavioural Public Policy Blog* (https://bppblog.com/2018/04/19/behavioral-insights-and-parenting/), April 19, 2018.

John List, Anya Samek, and Dana Suskind, "Combining Behavioral Economics and Field Experiments to Reimagine Early Childhood Education," *Behavioural Public Policy*, 2018.

POLICY EXAMPLE: The Unavoidable Implications of Some Basic Social Security Arithmetic

Mark Hulbert, "How Likely Is It That Social Security Will Go Broke?" MarketWatch, February 3, 2019.

Janet Adamy and Paul Overberg, "Growth in Retiring Baby Boomers Strains U.S. Welfare Programs," *Wall Street Journal*, June 21, 2018.

Peter G. Peterson Foundation, "Worker-to-Beneficiary Ratio in the Social Security Program" (https://www.pgpf.org/chart-archive/0004_worker-benefit-ratio), June 25, 2018.

AI—DECISION MAKING THROUGH DATA: Reducing Repetitive Health Care Services

Suryatapa Bhattacharya, "In Fast-Aging Japan, Elder Care Is a High-Tech Pursuit," *Wall Street Journal*, January 12, 2019.

Paul Black, "Changing the Game: Machine Learning in Healthcare," *Healthcare IT News*, April 20, 2018.

Daniel Faggella, "Seven Applications of Machine Learning in Pharma and Medicine," TechEmergence (https://www.techemergence.com/machine-learning-in-pharma-medicine/), July 19, 2018.

ECONOMICS IN YOUR LIFE: Targeting In-Kind Care in Government Health Programs

"Home Health Care," Center for Medicare Advocacy (http://www.medicareadvocacy.org/medicare-info/home-health-care/), 2019.

Dhruv Khullar and Austin Frakt, "Can Low-Intensity Care Solve High Health Care Costs?" *New York Times*, June 11, 2018.

Ethan Lieber and Lee Lockwood, "Targeting with In-Kind Transfers: Evidence from Medicaid Home Care," National Bureau of Economic Research Working Paper No. 24267, March 2018.

ISSUES & APPLICATIONS: A Marginal Tax Rate Faced by Beneficiaries of Anti-Poverty Programs Who Wish to Work

"How Work Affects Your Benefits," Social Security Administration (https://www.ssa.gov/pubs/EN-05-10069.pdf), 2019.

Gopi Shah Goda, John Shoven, and Sita Nataraj Slavov, "Disincentives in the Social Security Disability Benefit Formula," *Journal of Pension Economics and Finance*, 2018.

"Welfare Reform: Some Poor Face 80 Percent Marginal Tax Rates," *Investor Business Daily*, June 29, 2018.

30 Environmental Economics

tomas1111/123RF GB Limited

LEARNING OBJECTIVES

After reading this chapter, you should be able to:

30.1 Distinguish between private costs and social costs and understand market externalities and possible ways to correct them

30.2 Explain how economists can conceptually determine the optimal quantity of pollution

30.3 Describe how governments are trying to cap the use of pollution-generating resources

30.4 Contrast the roles of private and common property rights in problems such as the fates of endangered species

European environmental regulators call it the Market Stability Reserve. When these authorities conclude that emissions of carbon and other elements deemed to be harmful pollutants are "too high," they add to this reserve. If the authorities conclude that emissions are "too low," they reduce it. What do European environmental regulators place in their Market Stability Reserve, and how do they add to it or reduce it? How do these authorities decide when flows of emissions of carbon dioxide are "too high" or "too low"? After you have finished reading this chapter, you will be able to answer these questions, because at that point you will understand the concept of an *optimal quantity of pollution*.

DID YOU KNOW THAT...

melting and purifying the silicon incorporated into all of the solar panels manufactured since 1975 has released more carbon gases into the atmosphere than have been saved by using the solar panels to generate energy? Most people who thought that using solar panels to cool or heat buildings would prevent injecting the air with additional carbon gases probably did not realize that solar-panel production processes generated such gases. Seeking to protect the environment using new technologies such as solar panels sometimes creates harder-to-discern economic costs alongside more obvious economic benefits. The economic way of thinking about personal choices or regulatory policies intended to reduce pollution emissions and wildlife threats requires that *all* the costs of such choices and policies be considered. How much of your weekly wages are you willing to sacrifice in efforts to reduce aggregate emissions from gasoline-burning vehicles? To some people, framing questions in terms of the dollars-and-cents costs of environmental improvement sounds anti-ecological. This is not so, however. Economists want to help citizens and policymakers select informed policies that have the maximum possible *net* benefits (benefits minus costs). As you will see, every decision made in favor of "the environment" involves a trade-off.

Private versus Social Costs

Human actions often give rise to unwanted side effects—the destruction of our environment is one. Human actions generate pollutants that go into the air and the water. The question often asked is, Why do individuals, businesses, and governments continue to create pollution without paying directly for the negative consequences?

Private Costs

Until now, we've been dealing with settings in which the costs of an individual's actions are borne directly by the individual. When a business has to pay wages to workers, it knows exactly what its labor costs are. When it has to buy materials or build a plant, it knows quite well what these will cost. An individual who has to pay for car repairs or a movie ticket knows exactly what the cost will be. These costs are what we term *private costs*. **Private costs** are borne solely by the individuals who incur them. They are *internal* in the sense that the firm or household must explicitly take account of them.

Social Costs

Now consider the actions of a business that dumps the waste products from its production process into a nearby river or an individual who litters a public park or beach. Obviously, these actions involve a cost. When the firm pollutes the water, people downstream suffer the consequences. They may not want to swim in or drink the polluted water. They may catch fewer fish than before because of the pollution. In the case of littering, the people who come along after the litterer has cluttered the park or the beach are the ones who bear the costs.

The cost of these actions is borne by people other than those who commit the actions. The creator of the cost is not the sole bearer. The costs are not internalized by the individual, firm, or government agency—they are external.

When we add *external* costs to *internal*, or private, costs, we obtain **social costs**. Pollution problems—indeed, all problems pertaining to the environment—may be viewed as situations in which social costs exceed private costs. Because some economic participants pay only the smaller private costs of their actions, not the full social costs, their actions ultimately contribute to higher external costs on the rest of society. Therefore, in such situations in which social and private costs diverge, we see "too much" steel production, automobile driving, or beach littering, to name only a few of the many possible examples.

30.1 Distinguish between private costs and social costs and understand market externalities and possible ways to correct them

Private costs
Costs borne solely by the individuals who incur them. Also called *internal costs*.

Social costs
The full costs borne by society whenever a resource use occurs. Social costs can be measured by adding external costs to private, or internal, costs.

The Costs of Polluted Air

Why is the air in much of China so polluted that more than 90 percent of the nation's population breathes in very unhealthful concentrations of pollution for at least two weeks each year? The answer is that when drivers step into their cars and businesses manufacture products in China, they bear only the private costs of driving and producing commodities. These individuals and businesses generate an additional cost, though—air pollution—which they are not forced to take into account when they make decisions to drive or to produce commodities.

Air pollution is a cost because it causes harm to individuals—burning eyes, respiratory ailments, and dirtier clothes, cars, and buildings. Air pollution also adds to accumulations of various gases that may contribute to climate change. The air pollution created by automobile exhausts is a cost that individual operators of automobiles do not yet bear directly. The social cost of driving includes all the private costs plus at least the cost of air pollution, which many other individuals bear. Decisions made only on the basis of private costs lead to too much automobile driving. Clean air is a scarce resource used by automobile drivers free of charge. They use more of it than they would if they had to pay the full social costs.

Externalities

Externality

A consequence of a diversion of a private cost (or benefit) from a social cost (or benefit). A situation in which the costs (or benefits) of an action are not fully borne (or gained) by the decision makers engaged in an activity that uses scarce resources.

When a private cost differs from a social cost, we say that there is an **externality** because individual decision makers are not paying (internalizing) all the costs. Some of these costs remain external to the decision-making process. Remember that the full cost of using a scarce resource is borne one way or another by all who live in the society. That is, members of society must pay the full opportunity cost of any activity that uses scarce resources. The individual decision maker is the firm, consumer, or government, and external costs and benefits will not enter into that entity's decision-making processes.

We might want to view the problem as it is presented in Figure 30-1. Here we have the market demand curve, D, for product X and the supply curve, S_1, for product X. The supply curve, S_1, includes only internal, or private, costs. The intersection of the demand and supply curves as drawn will be at price P_1 and quantity Q_1 (at E_1). We now

---

FIGURE 30-1

Reckoning with Full Social Costs

The supply curve, S_1, is equal to the horizontal summation (represented by the capital Greek letter sigma, Σ) of the individual marginal cost curves above the respective minimum average variable costs of all the firms producing good X. These individual marginal cost curves include only internal, or private, costs.

If the external costs were included and added to the private costs, we would have social costs. The supply curve would shift upward to S_2. When social costs are not taken into account, the equilibrium price is P_1, and the equilibrium quantity is Q_1.

In the situation in which social costs are taken into account, the equilibrium price would rise to P_2, and the equilibrium quantity would fall to Q_2.

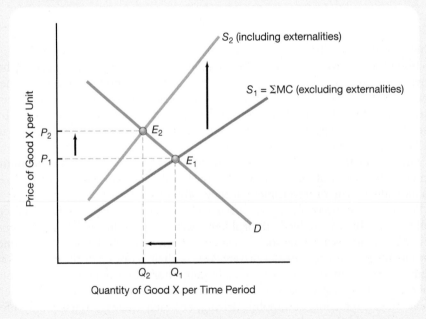

assume that the production of good X involves externalities that the private firms did not take into account. Those externalities could be air pollution, water pollution, scenery destruction, or anything of that nature.

We know that the social costs of producing product X exceed the private costs. We show this by drawing curve S_2. It is above the original supply curve S_1 because it includes the full social costs of producing the product. If firms could be made to bear these costs, their willingness to supply the good would be reduced, so the price would be P_2 and the quantity Q_2 (at E_2). The inclusion of external costs in the decision-making process would lead to a higher-priced product and a decline in quantity produced. Thus, we see that when social costs are not fully borne by the creators of those costs, the quantity produced is "excessive" because the price to consumers is too low.

Correcting for Externalities We can see here a method for reducing pollution and environmental degradation. Somehow the signals in the economy must be changed so that decision makers will take into account *all* the costs of their actions. If such signals can be found, then decision makers will take into account the correct (social) costs of their actions, rather than merely the private costs.

In the case of automobile pollution, we might want to devise some method of taxing motorists according to the amount of pollution they cause. In the case of a firm, we might want to devise a system of taxing businesses according to the amount of pollution for which they are responsible. They might then have an incentive to install pollution abatement equipment.

The Choices That Polluters Confront Facing an additional private cost for polluting, firms will be induced to (1) install pollution abatement equipment or otherwise change production techniques so as to reduce the amount of pollution, (2) reduce pollution-causing activity, or (3) simply pay a government-mandated cost for the right to pollute. The relative costs and benefits of each option for each polluter will determine which one or combination will be chosen.

Allowing the choice is the efficient way to decide who pollutes and who doesn't. In principle, just as with the use of all other scarce resources, each polluter faces the full social cost of its actions and makes a production decision accordingly. No matter what each firm decides, the firm is forced to take into account the additional cost. Hence, the cost of pollution-causing activity is now higher, so pollution will be reduced.

Is a Uniform Tax Appropriate? It may not be appropriate to levy a *uniform* tax according to physical quantities of pollution. After all, we're talking about external costs. Such costs are not necessarily the same everywhere in the United States for the same action.

Determining the Economic Damages from Pollution Essentially, we must establish the amount of *economic damages* rather than the amount of physical pollution. A polluting electrical plant in New York City will cause much more damage than the same plant in Montana. There are already innumerable demands on the air in New York City, so the pollution from smokestacks will not be cleansed away naturally. Millions of people will breathe the polluted air and thereby incur the costs of sore throats, sickness, emphysema, and even early death. Buildings will become dirtier faster because of the pollution, as will cars and clothes. A given quantity of pollution will cause more harm in concentrated urban environments than it will in less dense rural environments.

Focusing on the Economic Costs of Pollution If we were to establish some form of taxation to align private costs with social costs and to force people to internalize externalities, we would somehow have to come up with a measure of *economic* costs instead of *physical* quantities. The tax, in any event, however, would fall on the private sector and modify individuals' and firms' behavior.

Therefore, because the economic cost for the same physical quantity of pollution would be different in different locations, depending on population density, natural formations of mountains and rivers, and the like, so-called optimal taxes on pollution would vary from location to location. (Nonetheless, a uniform tax might make sense when administrative costs, particularly the cost of ascertaining the actual economic costs, are relatively high.)

WHAT HAPPENS WHEN...

a nation's government imposes a uniform pollution tax even though the economic cost for the same quantity of pollution differs across locations?

A uniform tax causes the supply curve to shift upward by the same amount in each of the nation's product-market locations. In a market for a product for which per-unit economic costs of pollution are higher than the uniform tax, the supply curve will not shift upward by an amount sufficient to induce firms to account for all economic costs. The equilibrium quantity will decline, but not to the optimal level. In a market for a product in which per-unit economic costs of pollution are lower than the uniform tax, the supply curve will shift upward in excess of the required amount. The equilibrium quantity will decrease to a level below the optimal quantity. Thus, in some industries, pollution-creating production will still be too high in relation to the social costs caused by pollution, whereas in other industries the quantity of output of the item produced will be lower than is optimal.

30.2 Explain how economists can conceptually determine the optimal quantity of pollution

Pollution

The term *pollution* is used quite loosely and can refer to a variety of by-products of any activity. Industrial pollution involves mainly air and water but can also include noise and even aesthetic pollution, as when a landscape is altered in a negative way. For the most part, we will be analyzing the most common forms—air and water pollution.

Assessing the Appropriate Amount of Pollution

When asked how much pollution there should be in the economy, many people will respond, "None." If, however, we ask those same people how much starvation or deprivation of consumer products should exist in the economy, many will again say, "None." On the one hand, because such questions do not make the nature of the inherent trade-off obvious, many of these people ignore the problem of scarcity when offering these answers. On the other hand, there is no unambiguously "correct" answer to how much pollution should be in an economy because when we ask how much pollution there *should* be, we are entering the realm of normative economics. When we ask people to express values, it is not possible to disprove somebody's value system scientifically.

An economic approach to a discussion of the "correct" amount of pollution is to set up the same type of marginal analysis we used in our discussion of a firm's employment and output decisions. That is, we can consider pursuing measures to reduce pollution only up to the point at which the marginal benefit from pollution reduction equals the marginal cost of pollution reduction.

The Marginal Benefit of a Less Polluted Environment Look at Figure 30-2. On the horizontal axis, we show the degree of air cleanliness. A vertical line is drawn at 100 percent cleanliness—the air cannot become any cleaner. Consider the benefits of obtaining a greater degree of air cleanliness. The benefits of obtaining cleaner air are represented by the marginal benefit curve, which slopes downward.

When the air is very dirty, the marginal benefit from air that is a little cleaner appears to be relatively high, as shown on the vertical axis. As the air becomes cleaner, however, the marginal benefit of a little bit more air cleanliness falls.

The Marginal Cost of Pollution Abatement Consider the marginal cost of pollution abatement—that is, the marginal cost of obtaining cleaner air. In the 1960s, automobiles had no pollution abatement devices. Eliminating only 20 percent of the pollutants emitted by internal-combustion engines entailed a relatively small cost per unit of

FIGURE 30-2

The Optimal Quantity of Air Pollution

As we attempt to achieve a greater degree of air cleanliness, the marginal cost rises until trying to increase air cleanliness even slightly leads to a very high marginal cost, as can be seen at the upper right of the graph. Conversely, the marginal benefit curve slopes downward: The more pure air we have, the less we value an additional unit of pure air. Marginal cost and marginal benefit intersect at point E. The optimal degree of air cleanliness is something less than 100 percent at Q_0. The price that we pay for the last unit of air cleanup is no greater than P_0, for that is where marginal cost equals marginal benefit.

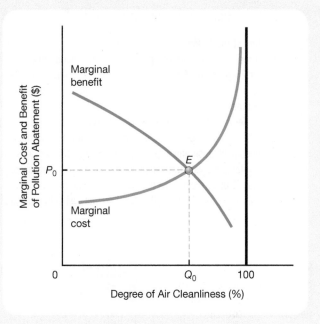

pollution removed. The per-unit cost of eliminating the next 20 percent increased, though. Finally, as we now get to the upper limits of removal of pollutants from the emissions of internal-combustion engines, we find that the elimination of one more percentage point of the amount of pollutants becomes astronomically expensive.

In the short run, moving from 97 percent cleanliness to 98 percent cleanliness involves a marginal cost that is many times greater than the marginal cost of going from 10 percent cleanliness to 11 percent cleanliness.

It is realistic, therefore, to draw the marginal cost of pollution abatement as an upward-sloping curve, as shown in Figure 30-2. (The marginal cost curve slopes up because of the law of diminishing marginal product.)

The Optimal Quantity of Pollution

In Figure 30-2, the point at which the increasing marginal cost of pollution abatement equals the decreasing marginal benefit of pollution abatement defines the **optimal quantity of pollution**. This is point E, at the intersection of the marginal cost and marginal benefit curves. Analytically, this solution is exactly the same as for every other economic activity. If we increased pollution control by one unit beyond Q_0, the marginal cost of that small increase in the degree of air cleanliness would be greater than the marginal benefit to society. In contrast, if we reduced pollution abatement activities by one unit below Q_0, the marginal benefit of the resulting small decrease in the degree of air cleanliness would be greater than the marginal cost. In each case, society's total benefits net of the costs of pollution abatement are maximized by returning to Q_0, at which the optimal quantity of pollution is attained.

Recognizing that the optimal quantity of pollution is not zero becomes easier when we realize that it takes scarce resources to reduce pollution. A trade-off exists between producing a cleaner environment and producing other goods and services. In that sense, environmental cleanliness is a good that can be analyzed like any other good, and a cleaner environment must take its place with other human wants.

Why might a recent effort by Kenya's government to clean up plastics pollution have a high marginal cost of pollution abatement?

Optimal quantity of pollution
The level of pollution for which the marginal benefit of one additional unit of pollution abatement just equals the marginal cost of that additional unit of pollution abatement.

INTERNATIONAL POLICY EXAMPLE

A Potentially High Marginal Cost of Plastic-Pollution Abatement in Kenya

The population of the African nation of Kenya is 14 percent of the U.S. level. The nation's people, however, generate plastics pollution equivalent to about 25 percent of the U.S. level. This fact has motivated Kenya's government to try to achieve a considerably higher degree of plastics cleanliness.

To prevent Kenya's residents from using and discarding its past norm of 100 million plastic bags per year, the government plans to implement a complete ban on production and sale of all plastic bags. The Kenya Association of Manufacturers estimates that 170 Kenyan firms previously had employed about 60,000 people in the production and distribution of plastic bags. Thus, this organization argues that the marginal cost of this specific method of pollution abatement, in the form of decreased profits of plastic-bag-producing firms and reduced labor incomes of their workers, will be substantial.

FOR CRITICAL THINKING

Why do you suppose that some critics of the plastic-bag ban argue that the adverse effects of deforestation caused by increased production of paper bags also should be added to the marginal cost of plastic-pollution abatement?

Sources are listed at the end of this chapter.

30.3 Describe how governments are trying to cap the use of pollution-generating resources

Reducing Humanity's Carbon Footprint: Restraining Spillovers

In light of the costs arising from spillovers that polluting activities create, one apparent solution might be for governments to try putting a stop to them. Why don't more governments simply *require* businesses and households to cut back on pollution-causing activities?

Mixing Government Controls and Market Processes: Cap and Trade

In fact, many governments are implementing schemes aimed at capping and controlling the use of pollution-generating resources. In recent years, certain scientific research has suggested that emissions of carbon dioxide and various other so-called *greenhouse gases* are contributing to atmospheric warming. The result, some scientists fear, might be global climate changes harmful to people inhabiting various regions of the planet.

In response, the governments of 196 nations agreed in 2015 to participate in the *Paris Agreement on Climate Change*. Under this agreement, the governments of participating nations have agreed to reduce their overall emissions of greenhouse gases with an aim to yield by 2050 a net increase in the overall average global temperature of no more than 2.7 degrees Fahrenheit (1.5 degrees Celsius). Although the Paris Agreement specifies no explicit enforcement mechanism to ensure that nations adhere to its terms, it provides a framework through which individual nations announce "nationally determined contributions" of actions intended to help achieve the agreement's goals.

Emissions Caps and Permits Trading Nations of the European Union (EU) have been trying to reduce greenhouse gas emissions via an overall emissions cap and system of permits trading for more than a decade. In January 2005, the EU established a set of rules called the *Emissions Trading System*. Under this so-called cap-and-trade program, each EU nation seeks to cap its total greenhouse gas emissions. After setting its cap, each EU nation established an *allowance* of metric tons of gas, such as carbon dioxide, that each firm legally can release. If the firm's emissions exceed its allowance—that is, if its "carbon footprint" is too large—then the firm must buy more allowances through a trading system. These allowances can be obtained, at the market clearing price, from companies that are releasing fewer emissions than their permitted amounts and therefore have unused allowances.

The United States so far has not implemented an EU-style emissions trading system. Nevertheless, in 2013 California began implementing its own cap-and-trade program. That state also placed a limit on emissions of greenhouse gases within its borders. Under the California program, the overall limitation on emissions will tighten over seven years. Electrical power companies, oil refiners, and other firms—more than 600 companies in all—that generate greenhouse gases will have to reduce their emissions or buy allowances to continue releasing the emissions. Ultimately, California's stated objective is to push the state's total carbon emissions 40 percent below 1990 levels by 2030.

In Europe, Theory Confronts Policy and Market Realities The European cap-and-trade program has yielded mixed results to date. In theory, if EU governments had set the national emissions caps low enough to force companies to reduce greenhouse gases, the market clearing price of emissions allowances should have reflected this constraint. In addition, as governments voluntarily continued to tighten the caps to meet EU limits that require greenhouse gas emissions to be reduced, the governments anticipated that more firms would respond by purchasing allowances.

Then the market clearing price of allowances would rise. Rather than paying a higher price for emissions allowances, many firms would instead opt to develop methods of reducing their emissions. In this way, this market-based mechanism established by the Emissions Trading System would induce firms to reduce their emissions, and the EU nations would achieve the emissions targets.

The Theory of Capping Emissions Meets the Reality of Too Many Allowances
In fact, in the spring of 2006, the market clearing price of EU emissions allowances dropped by more than 60 percent. The reason that prices dropped, many economists agree, is that most EU governments issued more allowances than were consistent with capping emissions. Indeed, the price drop was consistent with an initial surplus of more than 200 million allowances, which amounted to about 10 percent of the total allowances outstanding.

The Problem of Inflated Emissions Estimates by National Governments Most observers suspect that the Emissions Trading System's fundamental weakness was that each nation's government was permitted to establish the emissions target and allowances for its own country. Each government feared making its own nation's firms less cost-competitive than those in other nations, so every government inflated its estimate of its mid-2000s emissions of greenhouse gases. Doing so allowed each government to set its overall emissions cap at a level that actually failed to constrain emissions.

One result of this policy was the significant drop in prices of emissions allowances. Another outcome was that instead of declining, greenhouse gas emissions by companies based in the EU actually *rose* during the following decade. Only recently have the prices of European pollution allowances increased sufficiently to generate incentives for companies to cut back somewhat on their emissions.

Why are a number of European company managers utilizing AI systems to manage decisions about carbon emissions within the European Emissions Trading System?

 AI | DECISION MAKING THROUGH DATA

Managing Decisions Within the European Emissions Trading System

The Emissions Trading System's market for carbon emissions was created by and remains subject to policy changes on the part of European policymakers. As a consequence, equilibrium prices of emissions allowances are strongly influenced by policymakers' actions. Such actions often are brought about by unexpected changes in public opinion that alter policymakers' preferences. These political uncertainties complicate firms' decisions about future emissions using existing carbon-emitting equipment and possible investments in new equipment that emit less carbon.

Indeed, the complex task of predicting future prices of emissions allowances in light of political uncertainties has induced a number of European firms to utilize AI systems to assist them in managing carbon-emissions planning. Such AI systems enable managers to conduct simulations of profit outcomes over different ranges of possible future policy actions. The firms' managers use the results to identify carbon-emissions choices that maximize expected future profits given the political uncertainties confronted within the Emissions Trading System.

FOR CRITICAL THINKING

Why do you suppose that in light of the fact that European firms are increasing the use of AI systems in their emissions planning, some European policymakers also have begun to employ those same AI systems to guide their own policy actions?

Sources are listed at the end of this chapter.

Are There Alternatives to Pollution-Causing Resource Use?

Some people cannot understand why, if pollution is bad, we still use pollution-causing resources such as coal and oil to generate electricity. Why don't we forgo using resources that generate emissions in favor of an alternative, such as solar energy? The plain fact is that the cost of generating solar power in many circumstances is much higher than generating that same power through conventional means. We do not yet have the technology that allows us the luxury of driving solar-powered cars. Moreover, with current technology, the solar panels necessary to generate the electricity for the average town would cover massive sections of the countryside, and the manufacturing of those solar panels would itself generate pollution.

30.4 Contrast the roles of private and common property rights in problems such as the fates of endangered species

Private property rights
Exclusive rights of ownership that allow the use, transfer, and exchange of property.

Common property
Property that is owned by everyone and therefore by no one. Air and water are examples of common property resources.

ECONOMICS IN YOUR LIFE

To consider common property issues associated with maintaining public forests, read **Removing Individual Trees from View to Ensure Seeing the Forest** on page 663.

Common Property and Wild Species

In most cases, you do not have **private property rights**, or exclusive ownership rights, to the air surrounding you, nor does anyone else. Air is a **common property**, or a nonexclusive resource. Therein lies the crux of the problem. When no one owns a particular resource, no one has any incentive (conscience aside) to consider externality spillovers associated with that resource. If one person decides not to add to externality spillovers and avoids polluting the air, normally there will not be any significant effect on the total level of pollution. If one person decides not to pollute the ocean, there will still be approximately the same amount of ocean pollution—provided, of course, that the individual was previously responsible for only a small part of the total amount of ocean pollution.

Property Rights and Spillovers

Basically, pollution and other activities that create spillovers occur when we have open access to a nonexclusive resource and poorly defined private property rights, as in air and common bodies of water. We do not, for example, have a visual pollution problem in people's attics. That is their own property, which they keep as clean as they want, depending on their preferences for cleanliness weighed against the costs of keeping the attic neat and tidy.

When private property rights exist, individuals have legal recourse for any damages sustained through the use of their property. When private property rights are well defined, the use of property—that is, the use of resources—will generally involve contracts between the owners of those resources. If you own land, you might contract with another person who wants to access your land for raising cattle. The contract would most likely take the form of a written lease agreement.

Voluntary Agreements and Transaction Costs

Is it possible for externalities to be internalized via voluntary agreement? Suppose that you live in a house with a nice view of a lake. The family living between you and the lake plants a tree. The tree grows so tall that it eventually starts to cut off your view. In most cities, no one has property rights to views, so you usually cannot go to court to obtain relief. You do have the option of contracting with your neighbors, however.

Voluntary Agreements: Contracting You have the option of paying your neighbors (contracting) to trim the tree. You could start out by offering a small amount and keep going up until your neighbors agree or until you reach your limit. Your limit will equal the value you place on having an unobstructed view of the lake. Your neighbors will be willing if the payment is at least equal to the reduction in their intrinsic property value due to a stunted tree. Your offer of the payment makes your neighbors aware of the social cost of their actions. The social cost here is equal to the care of the tree plus the cost suffered by you from an impeded view of the lake.

In essence, then, your offer of money income to your neighbors indicates to them that there is an opportunity cost to their actions. If they don't agree, they forfeit the payments that you are offering them. The point here is that *opportunity cost always exists, no matter who has property rights.* Therefore, we would expect that under some circumstances voluntary contracting will occur to internalize externalities. The question is, When will voluntary agreements occur?

Transaction Costs One major condition for the outcome just outlined is that the **transaction costs**—all costs associated with making and enforcing agreements—must be low relative to the expected benefits of reaching an agreement. If we expand our example to a much larger one such as air pollution, the transaction costs of numerous homeowners trying to reach agreements with the individuals and companies that create the pollution are relatively high. Consequently, people may not always engage in voluntary contracting, even though it can be an effective way to internalize the externality of air pollution.

Transaction costs
All costs associated with making, reaching, and enforcing agreements.

Changing Property Rights

We can approach the issue of property rights by assuming that initially in a society, many property rights to resources are not defined. This situation does not cause a problem so long as no one wants to use the resources for which there are no property rights or resources are available in desired quantities at a zero price.

The Problem of a Zero Price Only if and when a use is found for a resource with an explicit zero price might a problem develop. Unless some decision then is made about property rights, the resource may be wasted and possibly even destroyed.

Another way of viewing the problem of pollution spillovers is to argue that it will not continue if a way can be found to assign and enforce private property rights for all resources. We can then say that no individual has the right to act on anything that is not his or her property. Hence, no individual has the right to create pollution spillovers on property that the individual does not specifically own.

Aligning Private and Social Costs If costs are not prohibitive, how might we consider filling the gap between private costs and social costs in situations in which property rights are not well defined or assigned? There are three ways to fill this gap: taxation, subsidization, and regulation.

Unfortunately, government does not have perfect information and may not pick the appropriate tax, subsidy, or type of regulation. Furthermore, in some situations, it may be difficult to enforce taxes or direct subsidies to "worthy" recipients. In some cases, such as when monitoring pollution levels is difficult or even release of small amounts of pollution can cause severe damage, outright prohibition of the polluting activity may be the optimal solution.

Why do nations with abundant natural resources managed by government officials often deplete those resources at a faster pace than countries with fewer resources managed by firms possessing private property rights?

BEHAVIORAL EXAMPLE

Common Property, the "Paradox of Plenty," and Gains from Assigning Resource Property Rights

Social scientists call it the "paradox of plenty." On the one hand, they have observed that when natural resources are abundant within a nation and held as common property, governmental institutions typically manage resource utilization. One consequence is prevention of competition that otherwise might have taken place among private resource developers for the most productive, least-cost means of using the resources. Another result commonly observed is that governments seek to exploit resources as rapidly as possible and quickly use them up.

On the other hand, more resource-constrained countries whose governments assign resource private property rights tend to obtain higher productive yields using fewer resources. In these countries, therefore, natural resources tend to be extracted at a slower pace.

(*Continued*)

Behavioral economists have found experimental evidence that a group entity, such as a government, that manages small amounts of resources held as common property tends to limit resource exploitation. When resources are abundant, however, such an entity tends to use up the resources more rapidly. Assigning private property rights to individuals subject to regulated access to abundant resources provides a mechanism for limiting resource use. The consequence is more restrained, sustainable resource utilization.

Wild Species, Common Property, and Trade-Offs

One common property problem that receives considerable media attention involves endangered species, usually in the wild. Few are concerned about not having enough dogs, cats, cattle, sheep, and horses. The reason is that those species are almost always private property. People have economic incentives—satisfaction from pet ownership or desire for food products—to protect members of these species. In contrast, spotted owls, bighorn mountain sheep, condors, and the like are typically openly accessible common property. Therefore, no one has a vested interest in making sure that they perpetuate in good health.

In 1973, the federal government passed the Endangered Species Act in an attempt to prevent species from dying out. Initially, few individuals were affected by the rulings of the Interior Department regarding which species were listed as endangered. Eventually, however, as more and more species were put on the endangered list, a trade-off became apparent. Nationwide, the trade-off was brought to the public's attention when the snail darter was declared an endangered species in the Tennessee Valley. Ultimately, thousands of construction jobs were lost when the courts halted construction of a dam in the snail darter's habitat. Then two endangered small birds, the spotted owl and marbled murrelet, were found in the Pacific Northwest, and the government required lumber companies to cut back their logging practices. In 1995, the U.S. Supreme Court ruled that the federal government has the right to regulate activities on private land in order to save endangered species.

The issues are not straightforward. Today, the earth has only 0.02 percent of all of the species that have ever lived, and nearly all the 99.98 percent of extinct species became extinct before humans appeared. Every year 1,000 to 3,000 new species are discovered and classified. Estimates of how many species are actually dying out range from a high of 50,000 a year (based on the assumption that undiscovered insect species are dying off before being discovered) to a low of one every four years.

Why might legalizing the exchange of rhino horns help to save more rhinos?

INTERNATIONAL POLICY EXAMPLE

Could South African Rhino Poaching Be Stopped by Legalizing Trade in Rhino Horns?

Estimates indicate that illegal poaching is accounting for the deaths of several hundred African rhinos per year. This is a dramatic increase from about a decade ago, when losses to poaching were fewer than 20 per year. The sharp rise in rhino losses from poaching is more than offsetting a recent recovery in the rhino fertility rate. As a consequence, the rhino population, most of which is restricted to grazing solely on government-owned lands, continues to dwindle.

Poachers kill rhinos to obtain material from their horns that some people in Southeast Asia regard as sources of powerful medicines. In recent years, black market prices of material from rhino horns have risen to levels exceeding $25,000 per pound. Some researchers argue that the solution is improved enforcement of anti-poaching laws. Others, however, contend that a more effective approach might be to permit private African ranchers to raise rhinos partly for the purpose of harvesting material from

their horns. Allowing rhino ranching and legal trade in rhino horns, these researchers contend, would generate an increase in the supply of material from rhino horns that would greatly reduce the price of that material. The likely result, they conclude, would be a dramatic reduction in poaching and, ultimately, a substantial increase in the rhino population.

FOR CRITICAL THINKING

Critics of the idea of legalizing private rhino ranching and trade in rhino horns worry that it could generate an additional increase in demand for the horns. Is it possible that the overall population of rhinos still might increase even if a further rise in demand for legally traded rhino horns were to occur? Explain your reasoning.

Sources are listed at the end of this chapter.

ECONOMICS IN YOUR LIFE

Removing Individual Trees from View to Ensure Seeing the Forest

Brian Chamberlain has decided that it is time for a break. "They work me like a rented mule," he says, as he wipes perspiration from his forehead and sets to one side his "masticator," a machine that chops small trees into tiny bits of wood. He and other workers have spent much of the day cutting down trees in a dense California forest. Now they have completed the day's efforts to saw up the trees, stack large pieces of trunks and limbs in neat piles to cart away later, and use masticators to grind up smaller limbs.

Chamberlain and the others are participating in an effort to save California's forests. By clearing the forests of dead and dying trees and various small, dry trees, they are seeking to address a common property problem associated with forests that grow on public lands. Because no specific people own these forests, no one person individually has an incentive to consider an external spillover. This spillover is the potential for wildfires to create air pollution that affects everyone and fire damages that harm owners of private properties. During previous years, California officials had taken a hands-off approach to forests. After years of experience with massive, ravaging wildfires, however, the officials have changed course. The best way to maintain the forests, they have decided, is to thin the forests of many individual trees that expose the forests to the greatest wildfire risks.

FOR CRITICAL THINKING

Can you think of any transaction costs that would hinder efforts to address common property problems associated with a forest by assigning property rights to plots of lands containing trees that make up the forest?

REAL APPLICATION

If your house is located in a forested area, what is the optimal amount of forest maintenance that you should undertake?

Sources are listed at the end of this chapter.

ISSUES & APPLICATIONS

tomas1111/123RF GB Limited

European Authorities Restrain the Supply of Emissions Allowances to Push Up Their Price

CONCEPTS APPLIED

➤ Private Costs

➤ Social Costs

➤ Optimal Quantity of Pollution

When Europe's Emissions Trading System was created in 2005, the underlying rationale was that market forces would induce firms to reduce their pollution to amounts close to the optimal levels. The prevailing view was that such market forces would quickly equalize the quantity of emissions allowances demanded with the quantity of allowances supplied. This outcome would occur at a price that would reflect external social costs as well as private costs. Firms would respond by reducing the amount of emissions-generating production to the optimal level from the perspective of society. The result would be the optimal quantity of pollution. In fact, however, only very recently have the market clearing prices of emissions allowances increased sufficiently to bring about such responses by firms.

How European Environmental Authorities Learned about the Forces of *Both* Supply *and* Demand

When European environmental regulators set up the Emissions Trading System, they focused on the demand side of the market for emissions allowances. Projections by government planners indicated that as economic activity increased, firms would boost output rates of goods and services produced using technologies that generated emissions of carbon and other undesired elements. Thus, authorities anticipated that the demand for emissions allowances would persistently and speedily increase.

To prevent prices of emissions allowances from increasing so fast that companies' profits might plummet dramatically, the regulators supplied a large number of permits at any given price. A European recession occurred between 2008 and 2010, however. Economic activity was subdued, so pollution-emitting companies' demand for emissions allowances ended up being much lower than expected. Market clearing prices of emissions allowances fell by more than 50 percent after 2008 and remained at these low levels until 2017.

Taking Action to Adjust the Supply of Emissions Allowances

Between 2010 and 2016, European environmental regulators designed and implemented a mechanism aimed at preventing such a price collapse from occurring again. The centerpiece of this mechanism is the *Market Stability Reserve*, which is a large quantity of emissions allowances owned by European governments.

European companies' demand for allowances increased in recent years as European economic activity picked up. Environmental regulators simultaneously purchased allowances and placed them unused in the Market Stability Reserve. These actions reduced the quantity of allowances supplied in the market at each possible price, so the market supply curve shifted leftward. As a result of the simultaneous increase in demand and decrease in supply, the equilibrium price of allowances more than tripled after 2017. This significant increase in the price of pollution allowances gave European firms whose production processes create emissions a greater incentive to switch to new technologies that generate fewer emissions. Hence, more than a decade after it was created, the Emissions Trading System finally is showing signs of accomplishing its original purpose.

FOR CRITICAL THINKING

If carbon-dioxide-emission restrictions are working, what would you expect to see happen to our climate?

REAL APPLICATION

You have just been elected governor of a mountain state with a small population and relatively little industry. Would you ask your state legislature to implement the equivalent of the European Emissions Trading System? Why or why not?

Sources are listed at the end of this chapter.

What You Should Know

Here is what you should know after reading this chapter.

LEARNING OBJECTIVES

30.1 Distinguish between private costs and social costs and understand market externalities and possible ways to correct them *Private, or internal, costs are borne solely by individuals who use resources. Social costs are the full costs that society bears whenever resources are used. A market externality arises if a private cost (or benefit) differs from the social cost (or benefit) associated with a market transaction between two parties or from the use of a scarce resource. An externality can be corrected by requiring individuals to account for all the social costs (or benefits).*

30.2 Explain how economists can conceptually determine the optimal quantity of pollution *The marginal benefit of pollution abatement declines and the marginal cost of pollution abatement increases as more and more resources are devoted to achieving an improved environment. The optimal quantity of pollution is the amount of pollution for which the marginal benefit of pollution abatement just equals the marginal cost of pollution abatement.*

KEY TERMS

private costs, 653
social costs, 653
externality, 654
Key Figure
Figure 30-1, 654

optimal quantity
  of pollution, 657
Key Figure
Figure 30-2, 657

30.3 Describe how governments are trying to cap the use of pollution-generating resources
Under the European Union's (EU's) Emissions Trading System, each EU government established an overall target for greenhouse gas emissions and distributed allowances, or permits, granting firms the right to emit a certain amount of gases. If a firm's emissions exceed its allowances, it must purchase sufficient allowances from firms emitting less than the allowances they possess. In theory, the market clearing price of allowances will increase, giving firms incentives to restrain their emissions of greenhouse gases.

30.4 Contrast the roles of private and common property rights in problems such as the fates of endangered species *Private property rights permit the use and exchange of a resource. Common property is owned by everyone and hence by no single person. A pollution problem often arises because air and many water resources are common property and private property rights are not well defined. Issues related to wild species, such as spotted owls or tigers, likewise arise because they are common property. No specific individuals have incentives to keep these species in good health.*

private property rights, 660
common property, 660
transaction costs, 661

PROBLEMS

30-1. The market price of insecticide is initially $10 per unit. To address a negative externality in this market, the government decides to charge producers of insecticide for the privilege of polluting during the production process. A fee that fully takes into account the social costs of pollution is determined, and once it is put into effect, the market supply curve for insecticide shifts upward by $4 per unit. The market price of insecticide also increases, to $12 per unit. What fee is the government charging insecticide manufacturers?

30-2. One possible method for reducing emissions of greenhouse gases such as carbon dioxide is to inject the gases into deep saltwater-laden rock formations, where they would be trapped for thousands of years. Suppose that the federal government provides a fixed per-unit subsidy to firms that utilize this technology in West Virginia and other locales where such rock formations are known to exist.

  a. Consider the effects of the government subsidy on the production and sale of equipment that injects greenhouse gases into underground rock formations. What happens to the market clearing price of such pollution abatement equipment?

  b. Who pays to achieve the results discussed in part (a)?

30-3. Examine the following marginal costs and marginal benefits associated with water cleanliness in a given locale:

Quantity of Clean Water (%)	Marginal Cost ($)	Marginal Benefit ($)
0	3,000	200,000
20	15,000	120,000
40	50,000	90,000
60	85,000	85,000
80	100,000	40,000
100	Infinite	0

  a. What is the optimal degree of water cleanliness?

  b. What is the optimal degree of water pollution?

  c. Suppose that a company creates a food additive that offsets most of the harmful effects of drinking polluted water. As a result, the marginal benefit of water cleanliness declines by $40,000 at each degree of water cleanliness at or less than 80 percent. What is the optimal degree of water cleanliness after this change?

30-4. Consider the following diagram, which displays the marginal cost and marginal benefit of water pollution abatement in a particular city, and answer the following questions.

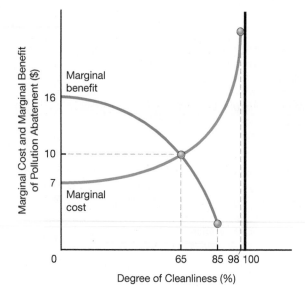

a. What is the optimal percentage degree of water cleanliness?

b. When the optimal percentage degree of water cleanliness has been attained, what cost will be incurred for the last unit of water cleanup?

30-5. Consider the diagram in Problem 30-4, and answer the following questions.

    a. Suppose that a new technology for reducing water pollution generates a reduction in the marginal cost of pollution abatement at every degree of water cleanliness. After this event occurs, will the optimal percentage degree of water cleanliness rise or fall? Will the cost incurred for the last unit of water cleanup increase or decrease? Provide a diagram to assist in your explanation.

    b. Suppose that the event discussed in part (a) occurs and that, in addition, medical studies determine that the marginal benefit from water pollution abatement is higher at every degree of water cleanliness. Following *both* events, will the optimal percentage degree of water cleanliness increase or decrease? In comparison with the *initial* optimum, can you determine whether the cost incurred for the last unit of water cleanup will increase or decrease? Use a new diagram to assist in explaining your answers.

30-6. Under an agreement with U.S. regulators, American Electric Power Company of Columbus, Ohio, has agreed to offset part of its 145 million metric tons of carbon dioxide emissions by paying another company to lay plastic tarps. These tarps cover farm lagoons holding rotting livestock wastes that emit methane gas 21 times more damaging to the atmosphere than carbon dioxide. The annual methane produced by a typical 1,330-pound head of cattle translates into about 5 metric tons of carbon dioxide emissions per year.

    a. How many cattle's worth of manure would have to be covered to offset the carbon dioxide emissions of this single electric utility?

    b. Given that there are about 90 million head of cattle in the United States in a typical year, what percentage of its carbon dioxide emissions could this firm offset if it paid for all cattle manure in the entire nation to be covered with tarps?

30-7. A government agency caps aggregate emissions of an air pollutant within its borders, establishes initial pollution allowances across all firms, and grants the firms the right to trade these allowances among themselves. The demand and supply curves for these pollution allowances have normal shapes and intersect at a positive price. Explain in your own words the government's likely goal in establishing this private market for pollution allowances.

30-8. Suppose that a new chief of the government agency discussed in Problem 30-7 decides to reduce the supply of pollution allowances. Evaluate the effects this policy change will have on the market price of pollution allowances, and discuss whether the policy appears to be fully consistent with the original intent of creating the market for these allowances.

30-9. The following table displays hypothetical annual total costs and total benefits of conserving wild tigers at several possible worldwide tiger population levels.

Population of Wild Tigers	Total Cost ($ millions)	Total Benefit ($ millions)
0	0	40
2,000	25	90
4,000	35	130
6,000	50	160
8,000	75	185
10,000	110	205
12,000	165	215

    a. Calculate the marginal costs and benefits.

    b. Given the data, what is the socially optimal world population of wild tigers?

    c. Suppose that tiger farming is legalized and that this has the effect of reducing the marginal cost of tiger conservation by $15 million for each 2,000-tiger population increment in the table. What is the new socially optimal population of wild tigers?

30-10. The following table gives hypothetical annual total costs and total benefits of maintaining alternative populations of Asian elephants.

Population of Asian Elephants	Total Cost ($ millions)	Total Benefit ($ millions)
0	0	0
7,500	20	100
15,000	45	185
22,500	90	260
30,000	155	325
37,500	235	375
45,000	330	410

a. Calculate the marginal costs and benefits, and draw marginal benefit and cost schedules.

b. Given the data, what is the socially optimal world population of Asian elephants?

c. Suppose that two events occur simultaneously. Technological development allows machines to do more efficiently much of the work that elephants once did, which reduces by $10 million the marginal benefit of maintaining the elephant population for each 7,500 increment in the elephant population. In addition, new techniques for breeding, feeding, and protecting elephants reduce the marginal cost by $40 million for each

7,500 increment in the elephant population. What is the new socially optimal population of Asian elephants?

30-11. Take a look at Figure 30-1. Why does "including externalities" cause the supply curve S_2 to lie above the supply curve S_1 that has been drawn "excluding externalities"?

30-12. Consider Figure 30-1. What is the specific reason that accounting for externalities and thereby shifting the market supply curve causes the equilibrium quantity of Good X to decline from Q_1 to Q_2?

30-13. Take a look at Figure 30-2. Suppose that initially society experiences a degree of air cleanliness that is lower than Q_0. What would be true of the marginal benefit in relation to the marginal cost, and why would this fact induce society to increase the degree of air cleanliness toward Q_0?

30-14. Consider Figure 30-2. Suppose that initially society experiences a degree of air cleanliness that is higher than Q_0. What would be true of the marginal cost in relation to the marginal benefit, and why would this fact induce society to reduce the degree of air cleanliness toward Q_0?

30-15. Take a look at Figure 30-2. Explain why 100 percent air cleanliness is not optimal.

30-16. Consider Figure 30-2. Explain why a society usually would not determine that a degree of 0 percent air cleanliness is optimal.

REFERENCES

INTERNATIONAL POLICY EXAMPLE: A Potentially High Marginal Cost of Plastic-Pollution Abatement in Kenya

Edith Mutethya, "Kenya Steps Up Bans on Plastic Bags," *China Daily*, February 13, 2019.

Daily Nation, "Kenya Court Upholds Plastic Bag Ban," *East African*, June 27, 2018.

Jonathan Watts, "Eight Months On, Is the World's Most Drastic Plastic Bag Ban Working?" *Guardian*, April 25, 2018.

AI—DECISION MAKING THROUGH DATA: Managing Decisions within the European Emissions Trading System

"CarbonSim: EDF's Carbon Market Simulation Tool," Environmental Defense Fund (https://www.edf.org/climate/carbonsim-edfs-carbon-market-simulation-tool), 2019.

Peter Deeney, Mark Cummins, Michael Dowling, and Alan Smeaton, "Negativity Bias in the European Emissions Market: Evidence from High-Frequency Twitter Sentiment," Working Paper, Dublin City University, 2018.

Jianfeng Guo, Bin Su, Guang Yang, Lianyong Feng, Yinpeng Liu, and Fu Gu, "How Do Verified Emissions Announcements Affect the Co-Movements between Trading Behaviors and Carbon Prices? Evidence from the EU ETS," *Sustainability*, 2018.

BEHAVIORAL EXAMPLE: Common Property, the "Paradox of Plenty," and Gains from Assigning Resource Property Rights

Grace Avila Casanova, "The Paradox of Plenty and Natural-Resource-Driven Conflict," London International Development Center (https://lidc.ac.uk/the-paradox-of-plenty-and-natural-resource-driven-conflict/), 2019.

Andreas Leibbrandt and John Lynham, "Does the Paradox of Plenty Exist? Experimental Evidence on the Curse of Resource Abundance," *Experimental Economics*, 2018.

S. Mansoob Murshed, *The Resource Curse*, New York, Columbia University Press, 2018.

INTERNATIONAL POLICY EXAMPLE: Could South African Rhino Poaching Be Stopped by Legalizing Trade in Rhino Horns?

Mark Carwardine, "An Introduction to Trophy Hunting," Discover Wildlife.com (https://www.discoverwildlife.com/animal-facts/an-introduction-to-trophy-hunting/), 2019.

John Herskovitz, "Permit to Hunt Endangered Rhino Sells for $350,000 Despite Protests," *Scientific American* (https://www.scientificamerican.com/article/permit-to-hunt-endangered-rhino-sel/), 2018.

Jason Morris, "Big Game Hunters: We're the Answer to Preventing Extinction," CNN (https://www.cnn.com/2018/01/12/us/trophy-film-big-game-hunting-convention/index.html), January 12, 2018.

ECONOMICS IN YOUR LIFE: Removing Individual Trees from View to Ensure Seeing the Forest

Umair Irfan, "California Has 149 Million Dead Trees Ready to Ignite Like a Matchbook," Vox.com (https://www.vox.com/2019/2/13/18221822/california-149-million-dead-trees-wildfire), February 15, 2019.

Jim Carlton, "Facing Deadlier Fires, California Tries Something New: More Logging," *Wall Street Journal*, November 17, 2018.

Jeff Daniels, "California Timber Industry May Be a 'Piece of the Puzzle' to Help Reduce State's Raging Wildfires," CNBC, August 3, 2018.

ISSUES & APPLICATIONS: European Authorities Restrain the Supply of Emissions Allowances to Push Up Their Price

European Commission, "Market Stability Reserve" (https://ec.europa.eu/clima/policies/ets/reform_en), 2019.

Mark Lewis, "EU Carbon Allowance Market to Shake Its Over-Supply Problem," *Financial Times*, April 26, 2018.

Mike Scott, "Europe's Carbon Market Starts Doing Its Job of Cutting Emissions—A Decade Late," September 3, 2018.

31

Comparative Advantage and the Open Economy

Travel mania/Shutterstock

LEARNING OBJECTIVES

After reading this chapter, you should be able to:

31.1 Explain why nations can gain from specializing in production and engaging in international trade

31.2 Understand common arguments against free trade

31.3 Describe ways that nations restrict foreign trade

31.4 Identify key international agreements and organizations that adjudicate trade disputes among nations

Britain opted to exit the European Union (EU), and the United States chose not to join the Trans-Pacific Partnership (TPP). The EU and TPP are *regional trade blocs*, or groups of countries that agree to establish common rules under which goods and services may be internationally traded among the blocs' member nations. British and U.S. residents and political leaders chose to decline membership in these regional trade blocs because in their judgment the overall costs of membership to their nations exceeded potential benefits. Many economists nonetheless perceive substantial *economic* benefits of membership in regional trade blocs. When you have completed this chapter, you will understand the economic gains that joining a regional trade bloc can offer a nation contemplating agreement with the bloc's common rules for international trade. Your first step, however, is to develop an understanding of essential gains from specialization and trade.

about 34 billion cubic feet of physical items in shipping containers are carried in holds of cargo ships that pass through the Panama Canal each year? Although a portion of this volume of goods transported through the canal traverse between U.S. coasts as interstate trade, the large majority of these items passing through the Panama Canal are in transit between nations other than the United States or between United States and foreign ports. A recent widening of the Panama Canal to permit the transit of more massive ships is expected to allow at least 20 percent of the growing volume of U.S. exports of liquefied natural gas to more speedily make their way to Asian countries such as China and Japan.

31.1 Explain why nations can gain from specializing in production and engaging in international trade

Why We Trade: Comparative Advantage and Mutual Gains from Exchange

You have already been introduced to the concepts of specialization and mutual gains from trade in a previous chapter. These concepts are worth repeating because they are essential to understanding why the world is better off on net because of more international trade. First, however, let's take a look at the growing volumes of international trade undertaken by the world's peoples in recent years.

The Worldwide Importance of International Trade

Look at panel (a) of Figure 31-1. Since 1960, world output of goods and services (world real gross domestic product, or world real GDP) has increased almost every year. It is now about 8 times what it was then. Look at the top line in panel (a) of Figure 31-1. Even taking into account its recent dip, world trade has increased to more than 24 times its level in 1960.

The United States has figured prominently in this expansion of world trade relative to GDP. In panel (b) of Figure 31-1, you see annual U.S. imports and exports expressed as a percentage of the nation's total annual yearly income (GDP). Whereas imports amounted to barely 4 percent of annual U.S. GDP in 1950, today they account for more than 16 percent. International trade has become more important to the U.S. economy, and it may become even more so as other countries loosen their trade restrictions.

The Output Gains from Specialization

The best way to understand the gains from trade among nations is first to understand the output gains from specialization between individuals. Suppose that during any given month, a traditional aerospace engineer who specializes in developing designs for various passenger-aircraft components can, via the aid of basic apps, digital devices, and other tools and equipment, create one virtual, three-dimensional layout viewable on a digital device. Alternatively, during a month the same engineer can create two physical, nuts-and-bolts prototypes for aircraft components. At the same time, an aircraft-component designer who utilizes AI-assisted technology to formulate designs for aircraft components can within a month's time either create one virtual design or one physical prototype. Here the traditional aerospace engineer who uses basic apps, digital devices, and other equipment can come up with more physical prototypes than the aircraft-component designer who utilizes AI-assisted technology and seemingly is just as good as the AI expert at creating virtual designs. Is there any reason for the traditional aerospace engineer and the AI-assisted designer to "trade"? The answer is yes because such trading will lead to higher output.

The Situation with No Trade Consider the scenario of no trading. Assume that during the coming year, the traditional aerospace engineer and the AI-assisted

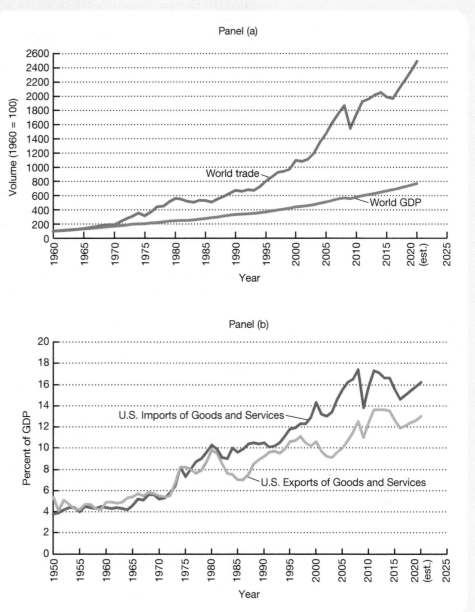

FIGURE 31-1

The Growth of World Trade

In panel (a), you can see the growth since 1960 in the world's international trade and in the world's GDP. Even though world GDP has risen strongly since 1960, international trade has grown even faster. In the United States, both imports and exports, expressed as a percentage of annual national income (GDP) in panel (b), generally rose after 1950 and generally recovered following the 2008–2009 recession.

Sources: World Trade Organization; Bureau of Economic Analysis; author's estimates.

aircraft-component designer devote half of their time to creating physical prototypes and half to developing virtual designs. The traditional engineer would create 12 component-part prototypes (6 months × 2 per month) and 6 virtual designs (6 × 1 per month).

During that same year, the AI-assisted aircraft-component designer would create 6 physical prototypes (6 months × 1 per month) and 6 virtual designs (6 × 1 per month). Each year, the combined output for the traditional engineer and the AI-assisted designer would be 18 physical prototypes and 12 virtual designs.

Specialization If the traditional aerospace engineer specialized only in developing physical prototypes and the AI-assisted component designer specialized only in creating designs, their combined output would rise to 24 physical prototypes (12 months × 2 per month) and 12 virtual designs (12 × 1 per month).

Overall, production would increase by 6 physical prototypes per year with no decline in virtual designs.

Note that this example implies that to create one additional virtual design during a month, the traditional aerospace engineer has to sacrifice the creation of two physical prototypes. The AI-assisted component designer, in contrast, has to give up the creation of only one physical prototype to generate one more virtual design. Thus, the traditional engineer has a comparative advantage in creating physical prototypes, and the AI-assisted designer has a comparative advantage in developing virtual designs. **Comparative advantage** is simply the ability to produce something at a lower *opportunity cost* than other producers, as we pointed out in an earlier chapter.

Comparative advantage
The ability to produce a good or service at a lower opportunity cost than other producers.

Specialization among Nations

To demonstrate the concept of comparative advantage for nations, let's consider a simple two-country, two-good world in which opportunity costs of producing goods are constant. As a hypothetical example, let's suppose that the nations in this world are India and the United States. Initially we assume that international trade between these two nations is not feasible.

Production and Consumption Capabilities in a Two-Country, Two-Good World In Table 31-1, we show maximum feasible quantities of high-performance commercial digital apps (apps) and tablet devices (tablets) that can be produced during an hour using all resources—labor, capital, land, and entrepreneurship—available in the United States and in India. As you can see from the table, U.S. residents can utilize all their resources to produce either 90 apps per hour or 225 tablets per hour. If residents of India utilize all their resources, they can produce either 100 apps per hour or 50 tablets per hour.

Comparative Advantage Suppose that in each country, there are constant opportunity costs of producing apps and tablets. Table 31-1 implies that to allocate all available resources to production of 50 tablets, residents of India would have to sacrifice the production of 100 apps. Thus, the opportunity cost in India of producing 1 tablet is equal to 2 apps. At the same time, the opportunity cost of producing 1 app in India is 0.5 tablet.

In the United States, to allocate all available resources to production of 225 tablets, U.S. residents would have to give up producing 90 apps. This means that the opportunity cost in the United States of producing 1 tablet is equal to 0.4 app. Alternatively, we can say that the opportunity cost to U.S. residents of producing 1 app is 2.5 tablets ($225 \div 90 = 2.5$).

TABLE 31-1

Maximum Feasible Hourly Production Rates of Either Digital Apps or Tablet Devices Using All Available Resources

This table indicates maximum feasible rates of production of digital apps and tablet devices if all available resources are allocated to producing either one item or the other. If U.S. residents allocate all resources to producing a single good, they can produce either 90 digital apps per hour or 225 tablets per hour. If residents of India allocate all resources to manufacturing one good, they can produce either 100 apps per hour or 50 tablets per hour.

Product	United States	India
Digital apps	90	100
Tablet devices	225	50

TABLE 31-2

U.S. and Indian Production and Consumption without Trade

This table indicates two possible hourly combinations of production and consumption of digital apps and tablet devices in the absence of trade in a "world" encompassing the United States and India. U.S. residents produce 30 apps, and residents of India produce 25 apps, so the total apps that can be consumed worldwide is 55. In addition, U.S. residents produce 150 tablets, and Indian residents produce 37.5 tablets, so worldwide production and consumption of tablets amount to 187.5 tablets per hour.

Product	United States	India	Actual World Output
Digital apps (per hour)	30	25	55
Tablet devices (per hour)	150	37.5	187.5

The opportunity cost of producing a tablet is lower in the United States than in India. At the same time, the opportunity cost of producing apps is lower in India than in the United States. Consequently, the United States has a comparative advantage in manufacturing tablets, and India has a comparative advantage in producing apps.

Production without Trade Table 31-2 displays possible sets of production choices in which it is infeasible for U.S. and Indian residents to engage in international trade. Let's suppose that in the United States, residents choose to produce and consume 30 digital apps per hour. To produce this number of apps requires that 75 fewer tablets (30 apps times 2.5 tablets per app) be produced than the maximum feasible tablet production of 225 tablets, or 150 tablets. Thus, in the absence of trade, 30 apps and 150 tablets are produced and consumed per hour in the United States.

Table 31-2 indicates that during an hour's time in India, residents choose to produce and consume 37.5 tablets. Obtaining this number of tablets entails the production of 75 fewer apps (37.5 tablets times 2 apps per tablet) than the maximum of 100 apps, or 25 apps. Hence, in the absence of trade, 37.5 tablets and 25 apps are produced and consumed in India.

Finally, Table 31-2 displays production of apps and tablets for this two-country world, given the nations' production (and, implicitly, consumption) choices in the absence of trade. In an hour's time, U.S. app production is 30 units, and Indian app production is 25 units, so the total apps produced and available for consumption worldwide is 55. Hourly U.S. tablet production is 150 tablets, and Indian tablet production is 37.5 tablets, so a total of 187.5 tablets per hour is produced and available for consumption in this two-country world.

Specialization in Production Let's suppose that international trade between residents of the United States and India becomes feasible. Residents of the United States now will choose to specialize in the activity for which they experience a lower opportunity cost. In other words, U.S. residents will specialize in the activity in which they have a comparative advantage—the production of tablet devices, which they can offer in trade to residents of India. Likewise, Indian residents will specialize in the manufacturing industry in which they have a comparative advantage—the production of digital apps, which they can offer in trade to U.S. residents.

By specializing, the two countries can gain from engaging in international trade. To see why, suppose that U.S. residents allocate all available resources to producing 225 tablets, the good in which they have a comparative advantage. In addition, residents of India utilize all resources they have on hand to produce 100 apps, the good in which they have a comparative advantage.

Consumption with Specialization and Trade U.S. residents will be willing to buy an Indian digital app as long as they must provide in exchange no more than 2.5 tablet devices, which is the opportunity cost of producing 1 app at home. At the same time,

ECONOMICS IN YOUR LIFE

To learn about how U.S. producers are utilizing high-tech harvesting and production methods to strive for a comparative advantage in olive oil trade, read **A Potential Shift of Comparative Advantage in Olive Oil Production toward the United States** on page 685.

TABLE 31-3

U.S. and Indian Production and Consumption with Specialization and Trade

According to this table, U.S. residents produce 225 tablet devices and no digital apps, and Indian residents produce 100 digital apps and no tablets. Residents of the two nations then agree to a rate of exchange of 1 tablet for 1 app and proceed to trade 75 U.S. tablets for 75 Indian apps. Specialization and trade allow U.S. residents to consume 75 apps imported from India and to consume 150 tablets produced at home. By specializing and engaging in trade, Indian residents consume 25 apps produced at home and import 75 tablets from the United States.

Product	U.S. Production and Consumption with Trade		Indian Production and Consumption with Trade	
Digital apps (per hour)	U.S. production	0	Indian production	100
	+ Imports from India	75	− Exports to U.S.	75
	Total U.S. consumption	75	Total Indian consumption	25
Tablet devices (per hour)	U.S. production	225	Indian production	0
	− Exports to India	75	+ Imports from U.S.	75
	Total U.S. consumption	150	Total Indian consumption	75

residents of India will be willing to buy a U.S. tablet as long as they must provide in exchange no more than 2 apps, which is their opportunity cost of producing a tablet.

Suppose that residents of both countries agree to trade at a rate of exchange of 1 tablet for 1 app and that they agree to trade 75 U.S. tablets for 75 Indian apps. Table 31-3 displays the outcomes that result in both countries. By specializing in tablet production and engaging in trade, U.S. residents can continue to consume 150 tablets. In addition, U.S. residents are also able to import and consume 75 apps produced in India. At the same time, specialization and exchange allow residents of India to continue to consume 25 apps. Producing 75 more apps for export to the United States allows India to import 75 tablets.

Gains from Trade Table 31-4 summarizes the rates of consumption of U.S. and Indian residents with and without trade. Column 1 displays U.S. and Indian app and tablet consumption rates with specialization and trade from Table 31-3, and it sums these to determine total consumption rates in this two-country world. Column 2 shows U.S., Indian, and worldwide consumption rates without international trade from Table 31-2. Column 3 gives the differences between the two columns.

Table 31-4 indicates that by producing 75 additional tablets for export to India in exchange for 75 apps, U.S. residents are able to expand their app consumption from 30 to 75. Thus, the U.S. gain from specialization and trade is 45 apps. This is a net gain in app consumption for the two-country world as a whole, because neither country had to give up consuming any tablets for U.S. residents to realize this gain from trade.

In addition, without trade, residents of India could have used all resources to produce and consume only 37.5 tablets and 25 apps. By using all resources to specialize in producing 100 apps and engaging in trade, residents of India can consume 37.5 *more* tablets than they could have produced and consumed alone without reducing their app consumption. Thus, the Indian gain from trade is 37.5 tablets. This represents a worldwide gain in tablet consumption, because neither country had to give up consuming any tablets for Indian residents to realize this gain from trade.

Why are on-going efforts to utilize machine-learning and automated data-analytics techniques likely to affect nations' comparative advantages in international trade?

TABLE 31-4

National and Worldwide Gains from Specialization and Trade

This table summarizes the consumption gains experienced by the United States, India, and the two-country world. U.S. and Indian app and tablet consumption rates with specialization and trade from Table 31-3 are listed in column 1, which sums the national consumption rates to determine total worldwide consumption with trade. Column 2 shows U.S., Indian, and worldwide consumption rates without international trade, as reported in Table 31-2. Column 3 gives the differences between the two columns, which are the resulting national and worldwide gains from international trade.

Product	(1) National and World Consumption with Trade		(2) National and World Consumption without Trade		(3) Worldwide Consumption Gains from Trade	
Digital apps (per hour)	U.S. consumption	75	U.S. consumption	30	Change in U.S. consumption	+45
	+ Indian consumption	25	+ Indian consumption	25	Change in Indian consumption	0
	World consumption	100	World consumption	55	**Change in world consumption**	**+45**
Tablet devices (per hour)	U.S. consumption	150	U.S. consumption	150	Change in U.S. consumption	+ 0
	+ Indian consumption	75	+ Indian consumption	37.5	Change in Indian consumption	+37.5
	World consumption	225	World consumption	187.5	**Change in world consumption**	**+37.5**

AI | DECISION MAKING THROUGH DATA

Reshaping International Trade Flows

Considerable media coverage of the international trade implications of AI technologies has focused on the potential trade gains from developing comparative advantages specifically involving these technologies. Those nations whose firms are able to provide AI technologies at the lowest opportunity costs in relation to production of other goods and services likely will specialize and trade these technologies internationally. These nations thereby will experience gains from trade.

More broadly, however, accumulation of data, automated analysis of these data, and implementation of machine-learning techniques promise to alter the opportunity costs of producing a vast array of goods and services already traded across national borders. Thus, not just comparative advantages in the direct provision and trade of AI technologies will be at stake in the coming years. The implementation of such techniques in production processes within a wide range of industries could alter comparative advantages for many goods and services. The results likely will be changes in national specializations, redirection of large volumes of international trade, and altered gains from trade across the world's nations.

FOR CRITICAL THINKING

Suppose that the application of AI technologies to production of a large array of goods and services causes some items that currently are not traded internationally to become exported and imported for the first time. Do you think that total global gains from international trade would increase or decrease as a result? Explain your reasoning.

Sources are listed at the end of this chapter.

Specialization Is the Key The example of U.S.-Indian trade shows that when nations specialize in producing goods for which they have a comparative advantage and engage in international trade, considerable consumption gains are possible for those nations and hence for the world. Why is this so?

Why Specialization Yields Gains from Trade The answer is that specialization and trade enable Indian residents to obtain each tablet device at an opportunity cost of 1 digital app instead of 2 apps and permit U.S. residents to obtain each app at an opportunity cost of 1 tablet instead of 2.5 tablets.

Indian residents effectively experience a gain from trade of 1 app for each tablet purchased from the United States, and U.S. residents experience a gain from trade of 1.5 tablets for each app purchased from India. Thus, specializing in producing goods for which the two nations have a comparative advantage allows both nations to produce more of each item. As a consequence, worldwide production capabilities increase. This makes greater worldwide consumption possible through international trade.

FIGURE 31-2

World Trade Flows

International trade in goods and services amounts to about $40 trillion worldwide. The percentage figures show the proportion of world trade flowing in the various directions among the nations that engage in the most trade.

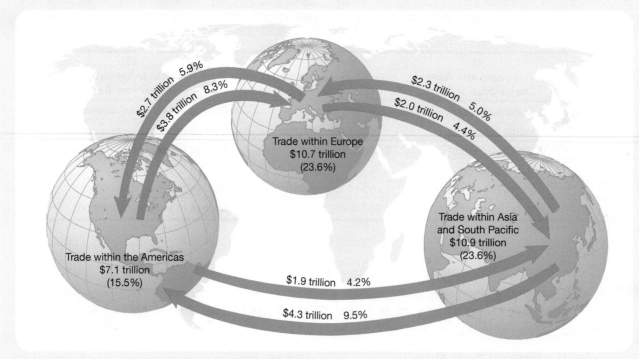

Sources: International Monetary Fund and author's estimates (data are estimated for 2020).

The Losers from Trade Of course, not everybody in our example is better off when free trade occurs. In our example, the U.S. app industry and Indian tablet industry have disappeared. Thus, U.S. app makers and Indian tablet manufacturers are worse off.

Some people worry that the United States (or any country, for that matter) might someday "run out of exports" because of overaggressive foreign competition. The analysis of comparative advantage tells us the contrary. No matter how much other countries compete for our business, the United States (or any other country) will always have a comparative advantage in something that it can export. In 10 or 20 years, that something may not be what we export today, but it will be exportable nonetheless because we will have a comparative advantage in producing it. Thus, the significant flows of world trade of exports and imports of both goods and services shown in Figure 31-2 will continue because the United States and other nations will retain comparative advantages in producing various goods and services.

Why do inland farmers located at some distance from their nation's borders often incur substantial expenses to export their products abroad?

INTERNATIONAL EXAMPLE

Gains from Agricultural Specialization and Trade Conquer Distance

Many farmers whose agricultural products are traded internationally are located far inland in relation to their nation's borders. Most of the grains grown on the world's farms that are shipped abroad are harvested from fields many hundreds of miles from the nearest seaports. In Uganda, for

example, considerable expenses must be incurred to transport cotton grown by that nation's farms to seaports hundreds of miles distant over rough, rutted roads and via checkpoints at which corrupt officials often demand bribes. These costs reduce the net export price received by

Uganda's farmers to less than 70 percent of the net export price received by U.S. cotton farmers, who are also located far from seaports. Nevertheless, Uganda's farmers continue to export about 80 percent of their annual cotton crops. Farmers located far inland within Uganda, within the United States, and within other nations clearly experience sufficient gains from specialization in agricultural production and trade to compensate them for the costs required to cover moving their products from their farms to consumers located abroad.

FOR CRITICAL THINKING

Why do you suppose that a number of Midwesterners in the United States experience gains from trade by growing and exporting corn to such far-distant nations as Egypt, Japan, and South Korea?

Sources are listed at the end of this chapter.

Other Benefits from International Trade: The Transmission of Ideas

Beyond the fact that comparative advantage results in an overall increase in the output of goods produced and consumed, there is another benefit to international trade. International trade also aids in the transmission of ideas.

According to economic historians, international trade has been the principal means by which new goods, services, and processes have spread around the world. For example, coffee was initially grown in Arabia near the Red Sea. Around 675 A.D., it began to be roasted and consumed as a beverage. Eventually, it was exported to other parts of the world, and the Dutch started cultivating it in their colonies during the seventeenth century and the French in the eighteenth century. The lowly potato is native to the Peruvian Andes. In the sixteenth century, it was brought to Europe by Spanish explorers. Thereafter, its cultivation and consumption spread rapidly. Finally, it became part of the North American agricultural scene in the early eighteenth century.

New processes have also been transmitted through international trade. An example is the Japanese manufacturing innovation that emphasized redesigning the system rather than running the existing system in the best possible way. Inventories were reduced to just-in-time levels by reengineering machine setup methods.

In addition, international trade has enabled *intellectual property* to spread throughout the world. New music, such as rock and roll in the 1950s and 1960s and hip-hop in the 1990s and 2000s, has been transmitted in this way, as have the digital-devices applications and application tools that are common for online and wireless users everywhere.

What idea to reduce the costs of shipping physical goods has considerably boosted trade in merchandise transported by oceangoing freight ships?

EXAMPLE

Shipping Containers and International Trade

Prior to the 1960s, the time that a freight ship normally languished in ports being loaded and unloaded was nearly as long as was required to sail the ship from one nation to another. Dozens of workers in the port of embarkation spent several days loading into a typical freight ship tens of thousands of individual items of varying shapes and sizes. The workers used lumber and ropes to secure items to the floors, bulkheads, and ceilings of the ship's storage compartments. Often, the workers would have to respond to late-arriving bulky or oddly shaped items by rearranging and repacking compartments just before sailing—which sometimes delayed ships' departures and pushed up the owners' expenses.

The widespread adoption of standard-sized shipping containers—metal boxes that are 8 feet wide, 8½ feet tall, and either 20 feet or 40 feet in length—fundamentally altered the economics of shipping. Using the containers has allowed ship owners to standardize the dimensions of ships' freight compartments, to utilize more deck space to carry freight, and to substitute capital equipment in place of labor for loading and unloading.

The results have been substantial reductions in required loading and unloading times and decreases in labor expenses. A. Kerem Coşar of the University of Virginia and Banu Demir of Bilkent University analyzed data involving 5,000 items that 27,000 exporters shipped during a recent year from Turkey to 139 nations. These researchers estimate that the use of standardized shipping containers reduces the costs of merchandise trade transported via ships by as much as 22 percent. They conclude that today's flow of about 700 million shipping-container transports per year has raised the volume of merchandise trade carried by freight ships by 25 percent.

FOR CRITICAL THINKING

Why do you suppose that the standardization of the dimensions of shipping containers particularly played a crucial role in enabling shippers to reduce their expenses?

Sources are listed at the end of this chapter.

The Relationship between Imports and Exports

The basic proposition in understanding all of international trade is this:

> *In the long run, imports are paid for by exports.*

The reason that imports are ultimately paid for by exports is that foreign residents want something in exchange for the goods that are shipped to the United States. For the most part, they want U.S.-made goods and services. From this truism comes a remarkable corollary:

> *Any restriction of imports ultimately reduces exports.*

This is a shocking revelation to many people who want to restrict foreign competition to protect domestic jobs. Although it is possible to "protect" certain U.S. jobs by restricting foreign competition, it is impossible to make *everyone* in a nation better off by imposing import restrictions. Why? The reason is that ultimately such restrictions lead to a reduction in employment and output—and hence incomes—in the export industries of the nation.

International Competitiveness

"The United States is falling behind." "We need to stay competitive internationally." Statements such as these are often heard when the subject of international trade comes up. There are two problems with such talk. The first has to do with a simple definition. What does "global competitiveness" really mean? When one company competes against another, it is in competition. Is the United States like one big corporation, in competition with other countries? Certainly not. The standard of living in each country is almost solely a function of how well the economy functions *within that country*, not relative to other countries.

Another point relates to real-world observations. According to the Institute for Management Development in Lausanne, Switzerland, the United States is among the top ten nations in overall productive efficiency. According to the report, the relatively high ranking of the United States over the years has been due to widespread entrepreneurship, economic restructuring, and information-technology investments. Other factors include the open U.S. financial system and large investments in scientific research.

31.2 Understand common arguments against free trade

Arguments against Free Trade

Numerous arguments are raised against free trade. These arguments focus mainly on the costs of trade. These arguments do not consider the benefits of trade. Nor do the arguments typically contemplate possible alternatives for reducing the costs of free trade so that benefits of trade can be retained.

The Infant Industry Argument

A nation may feel that if a particular industry is allowed to develop domestically, it will eventually become efficient enough to compete effectively in the world market. Therefore, the nation may impose some restrictions on imports to give domestic producers time to reach the point at which they can compete in the domestic market without any restrictions on imports.

The Basis of the Argument In graphic terminology, we would expect that if the protected industry truly does experience improvements in production techniques or technological breakthroughs toward greater efficiency in the future, the supply curve will shift outward to the right so that the domestic industry can produce larger quantities at each and every price.

National policymakers often assert that this **infant industry argument** has some merit in the short run. They have used it to protect a number of industries in their infancy around the world.

Problems with Infant Industry Protection Such a policy can be abused, however. Often the protective import-restricting arrangements remain even after the infant has matured. If other countries can still produce more cheaply, the people who benefit from this type of situation are obviously the owners of the protected firms. In addition, owners of specialized factors of production will earn higher-than-normal rates of return in the industry that is still being protected from world competition.

The people who lose out are the consumers, who must pay a price higher than the world price for the product in question. In any event, because it is very difficult to know beforehand which industries will eventually survive, it is possible, perhaps even likely, that policymakers will choose to protect industries that have no reasonable chance of competing on their own in world markets. Note that when we speculate about which industries "should" be protected, we are in the realm of *normative economics*. We are making a value judgment, a subjective statement of what *ought to be*.

Countering Foreign Subsidies and Dumping

Another common argument against unrestricted foreign trade is that a nation might wish to counter other nations' subsidies to their own producers. When a foreign government subsidizes its producers, our producers claim that they cannot compete fairly with these subsidized foreign producers. To the extent that such subsidies fluctuate, it can be argued that unrestricted free trade will seriously disrupt domestic producers. They will not know when foreign governments are going to subsidize their producers and when they are not. Our competing industries will be expanding and contracting frequently.

At the same time, however, per-unit subsidies provided by foreign governments to foreign firms raise total domestic market supply, which depresses the domestic price of the subsidized foreign product. In this sense, foreign subsidies effectively are gifts to our domestic consumers on the part of foreign taxpayers.

The phenomenon called *dumping* is also used as an argument against unrestricted trade. **Dumping** is said to occur when a producer sells its products abroad below the price that is charged in the home market or at a price below its cost of production. Often, when a foreign producer is accused of dumping, further investigation reveals that the foreign nation is in the throes of a recession. The foreign producer does not want to slow down its production at home. Because it anticipates an end to the recession and doesn't want to hold large inventories, it dumps its products abroad at prices below home prices. U.S. competitors may also allege that the foreign producer sells its output at prices below its full costs to be assured of covering variable costs of production.

Protecting Domestic Jobs

Perhaps the argument used most often against free trade is that unrestrained competition from other countries will eliminate jobs in the United States because other countries have lower-cost labor than we do. Less restrictive environmental standards in other countries might also lower their private costs relative to ours.

Proposed Benefits of Domestic Jobs Protection For many people, and particularly for politicians from areas that might be threatened by foreign competition, the jobs-protection argument is compelling. For example, a congressional representative from an area with shoe factories would certainly be upset about the possibility of lower employment of their U.S. constituents because of competition from lower-priced shoe manufacturers in Brazil and Italy. Of course, this argument against free trade is equally applicable to trade between the states within the United States.

Infant industry argument
The contention that tariffs should be imposed to protect from import competition an industry that is trying to get started. Presumably, after the industry becomes technologically efficient, the tariff can be lifted.

Dumping
Selling a good or a service abroad below the price charged in the home market or at a price below its cost of production.

Economists David Gould, G. L. Woodbridge, and Roy Ruffin examined the data on the relationship between increases in imports and the unemployment rate. They concluded that there is no causal link between the two. Indeed, in half the cases they studied, when imports increased, the unemployment rate fell.

Costs of Protecting Domestic Jobs Another issue involves the cost of protecting U.S. jobs by restricting international trade. The Institute for International Economics examined the restrictions on foreign textiles and apparel goods. The study found that U.S. consumers pay $9 billion a year more than they would otherwise pay for those goods to protect jobs in those industries. That comes out to $50,000 *a year* for each job saved in an industry in which the average job pays only $30,000 a year.

Similar studies have yielded similar results: Restrictions on imports of Japanese cars have cost $160,000 *per year* for every job saved in the auto industry. Every job preserved in the glass industry has cost $200,000 each and every year. Every job preserved in the U.S. steel industry has cost an astounding $750,000 per year.

Emerging Arguments against Free Trade

In recent years, two new antitrade arguments have been advanced. One of these focuses on environmental and safety concerns. For instance, many critics of free trade have suggested that genetic engineering of plants and animals could lead to accidental production of new diseases. These critics also contend that people, livestock, and pets could be harmed by tainted foods imported for human and animal consumption. These worries have induced the European Union to restrain trade in such products.

Another argument against free trade arises from national defense concerns. Major espionage successes by China in the late 1990s and 2000s led some U.S. strategic experts to propose sweeping restrictions on exports of new technology.

Free trade proponents counter that at best these are arguments for the judicious regulation of trade. They continue to argue that, by and large, broad trade restrictions mainly harm the interests of the nations that impose them.

31.3 Describe ways that nations restrict foreign trade

Ways to Restrict Foreign Trade

International trade can be stopped or at least stifled in many ways. These include quotas and taxes (the latter are usually called *tariffs* when applied to internationally traded items). Let's talk first about quotas.

Quotas

Quota system

A government-imposed restriction on the quantity of a specific good that another country is allowed to sell in the United States. In other words, quotas are restrictions on imports. These restrictions are usually applied to one or several specific countries.

Under a **quota system**, individual countries or groups of foreign producers are restricted to a certain amount of trade. An import quota specifies the maximum amount of a commodity that may be imported during a specified period of time. For example, in a typical year, the U.S. government limits imports of beef from New Zealand to no more than about 500,000 pounds.

Consider the example of quotas on textiles. Figure 31-3 presents the demand and supply curves for imported textiles. In an unrestricted import market, the equilibrium quantity imported is 900 million yards at a price of $1 per yard (expressed in constant-quality units). When an import quota is imposed, the supply curve is no longer S. Instead, the supply curve becomes vertical at some amount less than the equilibrium quantity—here, 800 million yards per year. The price to the U.S. consumer increases from $1.00 to $1.50.

Clearly, the output restriction generated by a quota on foreign imports of a particular item has the effect of raising the domestic price of the imported item. Two groups benefit. One group is importers that are able to obtain the rights to sell imported

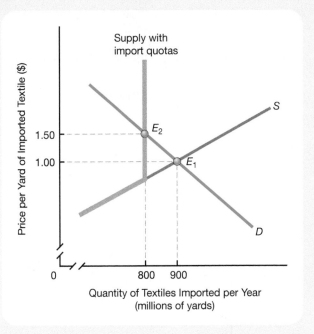

FIGURE 31-3

The Effect of Quotas on Textile Imports

Without restrictions, at point E_1, 900 million yards of textiles would be imported each year into the United States at the world price of $1.00 per yard. If the federal government imposes a quota of only 800 million yards, the effective supply curve becomes vertical at that quantity. It intersects the demand curve at point E_2, so the new equilibrium price is $1.50 per yard.

items domestically at the higher price, which raises their revenues and boosts their profits. The other group is domestic producers. Naturally, a rise in the price of an imported item induces an increase in the demand for domestic substitutes. Thus, the domestic prices of close substitutes for the item subject to the import restriction also increase, which generates higher revenues and profits for domestic producers.

WHAT HAPPENS WHEN...

a nation's government reduces an existing quota limit on foreign imports of a specific item?

A reduction in a quota further tightens a quantity restriction on an imported good or service. The consequence is that the vertical supply curve already in place below the equilibrium quantity shifts farther to the left along the demand curve for the imported item. The price of the imported good or service rises even more. The demand for domestic substitutes for the imported item increases in response, so prices of these domestic substitutes also rise. Revenues and profits received by domestic firms that produce these substitute items increase.

Voluntary Quotas Quotas do not have to be explicit and defined by law. They can be "voluntary." Such a quota is called a **voluntary restraint agreement (VRA)**. In the early 1980s, Japanese automakers voluntarily restrained exports to the United States. These restraints stayed in place into the 1990s. Today, there are VRAs on machine tools and textiles.

The opposite of a VRA is a **voluntary import expansion (VIE)**. Under a VIE, a foreign government agrees to have its companies import more foreign goods from another country. The United States almost started a major international trade war with Japan in 1995 over just such an issue. The U.S. government wanted Japanese automobile manufacturers to voluntarily increase their imports of U.S.-made automobile parts. Ultimately, Japanese companies did make a token increase in their imports of U.S. auto parts.

Voluntary restraint agreement (VRA)
An official agreement with another country that "voluntarily" restricts the quantity of its exports to the United States.

Voluntary import expansion (VIE)
An official agreement with another country in which it agrees to import more from the United States.

Tariffs

We can analyze tariffs by using standard supply and demand diagrams. Let's use as our commodity tablet devices, some of which are made in China and some of which are

FIGURE 31-4

The Effect of a Tariff on Chinese-Made Tablet Devices

Without a tariff, the United States buys 10 million tablet devices per year imported from China at an average price of $200, at point E_1 in panel (a). U.S. producers sell 5 million domestically made tablets, also at $200 each, at point E_1 in panel (b). A $50 tariff per tablet will shift the Chinese import supply curve to S_2 in panel (a), so that the new equilibrium is at E_2 with price increased to $225 and quantity sold reduced to 8 million per year. The demand curve for U.S.-made tablets (for which there is no tariff) shifts to D_2, in panel (b). Domestic sales increase to 6.5 million per year, at point E_2.

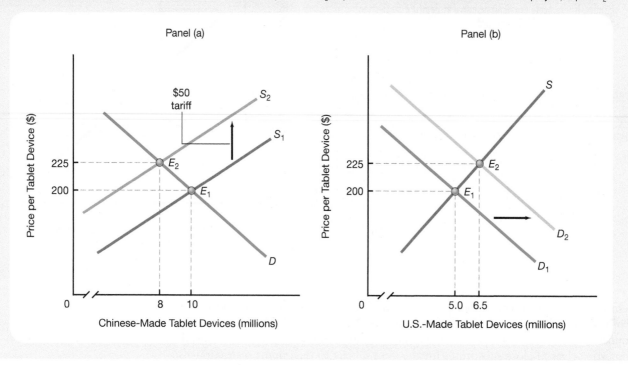

made domestically. In panel (a) of Figure 31-4, you see the demand for and supply of Chinese tablets. The equilibrium price is $200 per constant-quality unit, and the equilibrium quantity is 10 million per year. In panel (b), you see the same equilibrium price of $200, and the *domestic* equilibrium quantity is 5 million units per year.

Now a tariff of $50 is imposed on all tablet devices imported from China. The supply curve shifts vertically upward by $50 to S_2. For purchasers of Chinese tablets, the price increases to $225. The quantity demanded falls to 8 million per year. In panel (b), you see that at the higher price of tablets imported from China, the demand curve for U.S.-made tablets shifts outward to the right to D_2. The equilibrium price increases to $225, and the equilibrium quantity increases to 6.5 million units per year. The tariff benefits domestic tablet producers, then, because it increases the demand for their products due to the higher price of a close substitute, Chinese tablets. This causes a redistribution of income from Chinese producers and U.S. consumers of tablets to U.S. producers of tablets.

Tariffs in the United States In Figure 31-5, we see that tariffs on all imported goods have varied widely. The highest rates in the twentieth century occurred with the passage of the Smoot-Hawley Tariff in 1930.

Current Tariff Laws The Trade Expansion Act of 1962 gave the president the authority to reduce tariffs by up to 50 percent. Subsequently, tariffs were reduced by about 35 percent. In 1974, the Trade Reform Act allowed the president to reduce tariffs further. In 1984, the Trade and Tariff Act resulted in the lowest tariff rates ever. All such trade agreement obligations of the United States were carried out under the auspices of the **General Agreement on Tariffs and Trade (GATT)**, which was signed in 1947. Member nations of the GATT accounted for more than 85 percent of world

General Agreement on Tariffs and Trade (GATT)
An international agreement established in 1947 to further world trade by reducing barriers and tariffs. The GATT was replaced by the World Trade Organization in 1995.

FIGURE 31-5

Tariff Rates in the United States since 1820

Tariff rates in the United States have bounced around like a football. Indeed, in Congress, tariffs are a political football. Import-competing industries prefer high tariffs. In the twentieth century, the highest tariff was the Smoot-Hawley Tariff of 1930, which was about as high as the "tariff of abominations" in 1828.

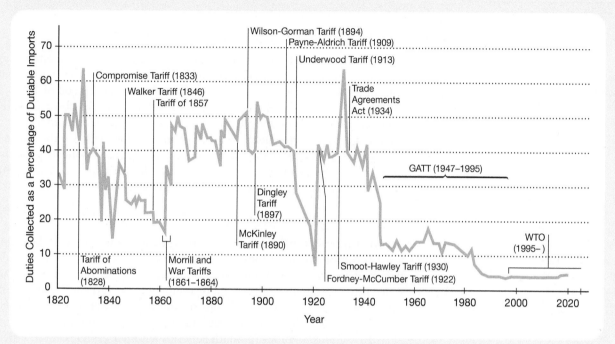

Source: U.S. Department of Commerce.

trade. As you can see in Figure 31-5, U.S. tariff rates generally declined between the early 1960s and the late 2010s when several rounds of negotiations under the WTO were initiated. The U.S. government increased tariff rates on several products, including, in particular, items imported from China, such as imported machinery, electrical and office equipment, machine tools, and medical and optical devices. The altered tariff rates applied to a relatively small portion of U.S. trade, however, so average U.S. tariff rates only increased very slightly as a result.

When a government imposes a protective tariff on food items, who incurs the greatest increase in the percentage of family income spent on such items?

INTERNATIONAL POLICY EXAMPLE

Identifying Who Loses Out as a Consequence of Asian Tariffs on Rice Imports

The governments of Japan and South Korea take very seriously the task of protecting domestic rice producers from competition. Japan's government assesses an import tariff on rice in excess of 300 percent, and South Korea's government imposes a tariff of just over 200 percent.

The governments of Indonesia, the Philippines, and most other Asian countries with lower per capita incomes have responded by putting into place their own protective rice tariffs. Imposition of these tariffs across much of Asia has caused prices of rice in these countries to rise well above the levels that otherwise would have prevailed. For millions of poor residents of less advanced nations of Asia, paying these higher prices for the rice that provides up to 50 percent of their calorie intake increases the already large percentages of their incomes allocated to buying rice.

FOR CRITICAL THINKING

Who do you suppose arguably stands to lose the most when governments of American and European nations impose tariffs on imports of key dietary foodstuffs such as wheat and corn?

Sources are listed at the end of this chapter.

31.4 Identify key international agreements and organizations that adjudicate trade disputes among nations

International Trade Organizations

The widespread effort to reduce tariffs around the world has generated interest among nations in joining various international trade organizations. These organizations promote trade by granting preferences in the form of reduced or eliminated tariffs, duties, or quotas.

The World Trade Organization (WTO)

World Trade Organization (WTO)
The successor organization to the GATT that handles trade disputes among its member nations.

The most important international trade organization with the largest membership is the **World Trade Organization (WTO)**, which was ratified by the final round of negotiations of the General Agreement on Tariffs and Trade at the end of 1993. The WTO, which as of 2020 had 164 member nations and included 22 observer governments, began operations on January 1, 1995. The WTO has fostered important and far-reaching global trade agreements. There is considerable evidence that since the WTO was formed, many of its member nations have adopted policies promoting international trade. The WTO also adjudicates trade disputes between nations in an effort to reduce the scope of trade protection around the globe.

Regional Trade Agreements

Regional trade bloc
A group of nations that grants members special trade privileges.

Numerous other international trade organizations exist alongside the WTO. Sometimes known as **regional trade blocs**, these organizations are created by special deals among groups of countries that grant trade preferences only to countries within their groups. Currently, more than 475 bilateral or regional trade agreements are in effect around the globe. Examples include groups of industrial powerhouses, such as the European Union, the North American Free Trade Agreement, and the Association of Southeast Asian Nations. Nations in South America with per capita real GDP nearer the world average have also formed regional trade blocs called Mercosur and the Andean Community. In addition, less developed nations have formed regional trade blocs, such as the Economic Community of West African States and the Community of East and Southern Africa.

Do Regional Trade Blocs Simply Divert Trade? Figure 31-6 shows that the formation of regional trade blocs, in which the European Union and the United States are often

FIGURE 31-6

The Percentage of World Trade within Regional Trade Blocs

As the number of regional trade agreements has increased since 1990, the share of world trade undertaken among nations that are members of regional trade blocs—involving the European Union (EU), the United States, and developing nations—has also increased.

Sources: World Bank and author's estimates.

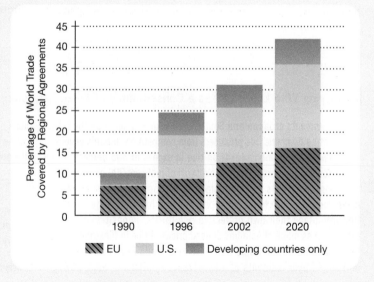

key participants, is on an upswing. An average African nation participates in four separate regional trading agreements. A typical Latin American country belongs to eight different regional trade blocs.

In the past, economists worried that the formation of regional trade blocs could mainly result in **trade diversion**, or the shifting of trade from countries outside a regional trade bloc to nations within a bloc. Indeed, a study by Jeffrey Frankel of Harvard University found evidence that some trade diversion does take place. Nevertheless, Frankel and other economists have concluded that the net effect of regional trade agreements has been to boost overall international trade, in some cases considerably.

The Trade Deflection Issue Today, the primary issue associated with regional trade blocs is **trade deflection**. This occurs when a company located in a nation outside a regional trade bloc moves goods that are not quite fully assembled into a member country, completes assembly of the goods there, and then exports them to other nations in the bloc. To try to reduce incentives for trade deflection, regional trade agreements often include **rules of origin**, which are regulations carefully defining categories of products that are eligible for trading preferences under the agreements. Some rules of origin, for instance, require any products trading freely among members of a bloc to be composed mainly of materials produced within a member nation.

Proponents of free trade worry, however, about the potential for parties to regional trade agreements to use rules of origin to create barriers to trade. Sufficiently complex rules of origin, they suggest, can provide disincentives for countries to utilize the trade-promoting preferences that regional trade agreements ought to provide. Indeed, some free trade proponents applaud successful trade deflection. They contend that it helps to circumvent trade restrictions and thus allows nations within regional trade blocs to experience additional gains from trade.

Trade diversion
Shifting existing international trade from countries outside a regional trade bloc to nations within the bloc.

Trade deflection
Moving partially assembled products into a member nation of a regional trade bloc, completing assembly, and then exporting them to other nations within the bloc, so as to benefit from preferences granted by the trade bloc.

Rules of origin
Regulations that nations in regional trade blocs establish to delineate product categories eligible for trading preferences.

ECONOMICS IN YOUR LIFE

A Potential Shift of Comparative Advantage in Olive Oil Production toward the United States

Gregg Kelley, chief executive officer of California Olive Ranch, a top U.S. producer of olive oil, has sought over the past several years to apply the latest technologies to the production of this product. The company grows more than 1.5 million trees in densely planted rows. After the trees' olives ripen, two-stories-tall harvesting machines strip away tons of olives within 30 minutes, which 15 human workers would have required a full day's work to pick by hand. Automatic conveyers move the olives from the harvesting machines to trucks, which transport the olives to mills located on the company's own grounds. These mills produce more than 3,000 gallons of olive oil per hour.

Kelley likes to point out that the speedy harvesting and production of oil from ripened olives permits the company's olive oil to be produced at the time judged most opportune for the highest-quality product. Another advantage of the high-tech production methods utilized by the firm is that they dramatically reduce labor and transportation expenses below those of producers in other parts the world. Other U.S. olive oil manufacturers have sought to replicate California Olive Ranch's techniques. As a consequence, the U.S. opportunity cost of producing olive oil has decreased, and a comparative advantage

previously held by producers in nations such as Cyprus and Egypt has begun shifting toward the United States.

FOR CRITICAL THINKING

Although California Olive Ranch's methods for producing olive oil heavily utilize machinery, why might being able to specialize and export olive oil induce U.S. firms using those methods to hire more workers overall?

REAL APPLICATION

Assume that your family owns and operates a small olive oil production enterprise in a western state. Assume further that you have just been named manager. Your family-run enterprise employs farm workers to pick your olives. Under what circumstances would you recommend to the family that your harvesting and production techniques should be modernized?

Sources are listed at the end of this chapter.

ISSUES & APPLICATIONS

What Do Countries Gain from Involvement in Regional Trade Agreements?

Travel mania/Shutterstock

CONCEPTS APPLIED

➤ Regional Trade Blocs

➤ Trade Diversion

➤ Rules of Origin

Highly visible recent withdrawals of Britain from the European Union and of the United States from the initial formation of a Trans-Pacific Partnership agreement have publicized drawbacks from participation in regional trade blocs. Among the highlighted drawbacks are possible employment losses to other nations and potential inabilities of domestic industries to compete effectively with industries of these nations. Nevertheless, economists have identified a number of key economic benefits that a nation derives from a regional trade agreement.

Protecting against Trade Diversion Caused by Other Nations Joining a Trade Bloc

When nations establish a regional trade agreement, they typically agree to reduce tariffs and other barriers to trade among themselves. If a key trading partner of a country initially outside a regional trade bloc joins the bloc, then the trading partner might divert trade away from that country to other members of the bloc. To defend against this possibility, that country outside the bloc has an incentive to join the bloc, too.

Simplification of Cross Border Trade of Key Inputs in Firms' "Supply Chains"

Regional trade agreements often establish rules of origin governing international exchange among participating nations. Knowledge of such rules and confidence that they will be enforced assist firms in coordinating movements across national borders of inputs at various intermediate stages of their firms' production processes, which firm managers call "supply chains." Membership in trade blocs helps nations' firms maintain these "chains."

Productive Efficiency Gains That Contribute to Higher and More Stable Economic Growth

Because joining a trade bloc can enable firms to more effectively manage their production processes, production efficiencies can result, with the same quantities of inputs

yielding greater output of goods and services. Indeed, estimates indicate that the worldwide formation of regional trade blocs has raised global per capita real GDP by at least 0.1 percentage point per year. In addition, members of regional trade blocs tend to develop more diversity in the types of goods and services that their firms produce, which has the effect of making per capita real GDP growth more stable. Thus, participating in regional trade agreements tends both to increase and to stabilize economic growth.

Consequently, participating in regional trade blocs offers several potential benefits. Naturally, nations' residents and leaders must weigh these benefits against the perceived drawbacks of membership in such blocs when deciding whether to participate in regional trade agreements.

FOR CRITICAL THINKING

How might making rules of origin overly detailed and complex have a trade-reducing effect?

REAL APPLICATION

Under what personal circumstances would you support and vote for senators and representatives who are in favor of increasing the number of regional trade agreements?

Sources are listed at the end of this chapter.

What You Should Know

LEARNING OBJECTIVES

31.1 **Explain why nations can gain from specializing in production and engaging in international trade** *A country has a comparative advantage in producing a good if it can produce that good at a lower opportunity cost, in terms of forgone production of a second good, than another nation. Both nations can gain by specializing in producing the goods in which they have a comparative advantage and engaging in trade. Together, they can consume more than they would have in the absence of specialization and trade.*

31.2 **Understand common arguments against free trade** *One argument against free trade is that temporary import restrictions might permit an "infant industry" to develop. Another argument concerns dumping, in which foreign firms allegedly sell some of their output in U.S. markets at prices below the prices in their own markets or even below their costs of production. In addition, some environmentalists support restrictions on foreign trade to protect their nations from exposure to environmental hazards. Finally, some contend that countries should limit exports of technologies that could pose a threat to their national defense.*

31.3 **Describe ways that nations restrict foreign trade** *One way to restrain trade is to impose a quota, or a limit on imports of a good. This action restricts the supply of the good in the domestic market, thereby pushing up the equilibrium price of the good. Another way to reduce trade is to place a tariff on imported goods. This reduces the supply of foreign-made goods and increases the demand for domestically produced goods, thereby bringing about a rise in the price of the good.*

31.4 **Identify key international agreements and organizations that adjudicate trade disputes among nations** *From 1947 to 1995, nations agreed to abide by the General Agreement on Tariffs and Trade (GATT), which laid an international legal foundation for relaxing quotas and reducing tariffs. Since 1995, the World Trade Organization (WTO) has adjudicated trade disputes that arise between or among nations. Now there are also more than 475 bilateral and regional trade blocs, including the North American Free Trade Agreement and the European Union, that provide special trade preferences to member nations.*

KEY TERMS

comparative advantage, 672
Key Figures
Figure 31-1, 671
Figure 31-2, 676

infant industry argument, 679
dumping, 679

quota system, 680
voluntary restraint agreement (VRA), 681
voluntary import expansion (VIE), 681
General Agreement on Tariffs and Trade (GATT), 682
Key Figures
Figure 31-3, 681
Figure 31-4, 682
Figure 31-5, 683

World Trade Organization, 684
regional trade bloc, 684
trade diversion, 685
trade deflection, 685
rules of origin, 685

PROBLEMS

31-1. To answer the questions below, consider the following table for the neighboring nations of Northland and West Coast. The table lists maximum feasible hourly rates of production of pastries if no sandwiches are produced and maximum feasible hourly rates of production of sandwiches if no pastries are produced. Assume that the opportunity costs of producing these goods are constant in both nations.

Product	Northland	West Coast
Pastries (per hour)	50,000	100,000
Sandwiches (per hour)	25,000	200,000

    a. What is the opportunity cost of producing pastries in Northland? Of producing sandwiches in Northland?

    b. What is the opportunity cost of producing pastries in West Coast? Of producing sandwiches in West Coast?

31-2. Based on your answers to Problem 31-1, which nation has a comparative advantage in producing pastries? Which nation has a comparative advantage in producing sandwiches?

31-3. Suppose that the two nations in Problems 31-1 and 31-2 choose to specialize in producing the goods for which they have a comparative advantage. They agree to trade at a rate of exchange of 1 pastry for 1 sandwich. At this rate of exchange, what are the maximum possible numbers of pastries and sandwiches that they could agree to trade?

31-4. Residents of the nation of Border Kingdom can forgo production of 8K televisions and utilize all available resources to produce 300 bottles of high-quality wine per hour. Alternatively, they can forgo producing wine and instead produce 60 8K TVs per hour. In the neighboring country of Coastal Realm, residents can forgo production of 8K TVs and use all resources to produce 150 bottles of high-quality wine per hour, or they can forgo wine production and produce 50 8K TVs per hour. In both nations, the opportunity costs of producing the two goods are constant.

    a. What is the opportunity cost of producing 8K TVs in Border Kingdom? Of producing bottles of wine in Border Kingdom?

    b. What is the opportunity cost of producing 8K TVs in Coastal Realm? Of producing bottles of wine in Coastal Realm?

31-5. Based on your answers to Problem 31-4, which nation has a comparative advantage in producing 8K TVs? Which nation has a comparative advantage in producing bottles of wine?

31-6. Suppose that the two nations in Problem 31-4 decide to specialize in producing the good for which they have a comparative advantage and to engage in trade. Would residents of both nations find a rate of exchange of 4 bottles of wine for 1 8K TV potentially agreeable? Why or why not?

To answer Problems 31-7 and 31-8, refer to the following table, which shows possible combinations of hourly outputs of portable power banks and flash memory drives in South Shore and neighboring East Isle, in which opportunity costs of producing both products are constant.

South Shore		East Isle	
Portable Power Banks	Flash Drives	Portable Power Banks	Flash Drives
75	0	100	0
60	30	80	10
45	60	60	20
30	90	40	30
15	120	20	40
0	150	0	50

31-7. Consider the table and answer the questions that follow.

    a. What is the opportunity cost of producing portable power banks in South Shore? Of producing flash memory drives in South Shore?

    b. What is the opportunity cost of producing portable power banks in East Isle? Of producing flash memory drives in East Isle?

    c. Which nation has a comparative advantage in producing portable power banks? Which nation has a comparative advantage in producing flash memory drives?

31-8. Refer to your answers to Problem 31-7 when answering the following questions.

    a. Which *one* of the following rates of exchange of portable power banks for flash memory drives will be acceptable to *both* nations: (i) 3 portable power banks for 1 flash drive; (ii) 1 portable power bank for 1 flash drive; or (iii) 1 flash drive for 2.5 portable power banks? Explain.

    b. Suppose that each nation produces only the good for which it has a comparative advantage and agrees to the rate of exchange identified in part (a). Prior to trade, South Shore residents produced and consumed 30 portable power banks and 90 flash drives per hour, and East Isle residents produced and consumed 40 portable power banks and 30 flash drives per hour. Now, South Shore residents export the same quantity of their specialty good to East Isle that East Isle residents consumed prior to engaging in international trade. How many units of East Isle's specialty good does South Shore import from East Isle?

    c. What is South Shore's hourly consumption of portable power banks and flash drives after the nation specializes and trades with East Isle? What is East Isle's hourly consumption of portable power banks and flash drives after the nation specializes and trades with South Shore?

    d. What consumption gains from trade are experienced by South Shore and East Isle?

31-9. Critics of the North American Free Trade Agreement (NAFTA) suggest that much of the increase in exports from Mexico to the United States now involves goods that Mexico otherwise would have exported to other nations. Mexican firms choose to export the goods to the United States, the critics argue, solely because the items receive preferential treatment under NAFTA tariff rules. What term describes what these critics are claiming is occurring with regard to U.S.-Mexican trade as a result of NAFTA? Explain your reasoning.

31-10. Some critics of the North American Free Trade Agreement (NAFTA) suggest that firms outside NAFTA nations sometimes shift unassembled inputs to Mexico, assemble the inputs into final goods there, and then export the final product to the United States in order to take advantage of Mexican trade preferences. What term describes what these critics are claiming is occurring with regard to U.S.-Mexican trade as a result of NAFTA? Explain your reasoning.

31-11. How could multilateral trade agreements established for all nations through the World Trade Organization help to prevent both trade diversion and trade deflection that can occur under regional trade agreements, thereby promoting more overall international trade?

31-12. Consider the data in Table 31-1. Would U.S. residents gain from trade of U.S. tablets for Indian apps if the rate of exchange of tablet devices for digital apps happened to be 3 tablets per app?

31-13. Take a look at the data in Table 31-1. Would Indian residents gain from trade of Indian apps for U.S. tablets if the rate of exchange of tablet devices for digital apps happened to be 0.75 tablet per app?

31-14. Take a look at Figure 31-3. What is the effect on foreign textile importers' total revenues of the imposition of the quota that generates a movement from point E_1 to point E_2?

31-15. Consider Figure 31-3. What is the effect on U.S. textile consumers' total expenditures of the imposition of the quota that generates a movement from point E_1 to point E_2?

31-16. Take a look at panel (a) of Figure 31-4. On a per-unit basis, how much of the $50-per-unit tariff on imported tablet devices is paid by U.S. consumers? On a per-unit basis, how much of the $50-per-unit tariff is paid by Chinese tablet-producing firms?

31-17. Based on your answer to Problem 31-16, what are the total tariff revenues of the U.S. government? What percentage do U.S. consumers ultimately pay because of a higher price generated by the tariff?

REFERENCES

AI—DECISION MAKING THROUGH DATA: Reshaping International Trade Flows

Anand Rao, "Is AI the Next Frontier for National Competitive Advantage?" Strategy-Business.com (https://www.strategy-business.com/blog/Is-AI-the-Next-Frontier-for-National-Competitive-Advantage?gko=9bfef), January 22, 2019.

Avi Goldfarb and Daniel Trefler, "AI and International Trade," National Bureau of Economic Research Working Paper No. 24254, 2018.

Daniel West and John Allen, "How Artificial Intelligence Is Transforming the World," *Brookings*, April 24, 2018.

INTERNATIONAL EXAMPLE: Gains from Agricultural Specialization and Trade Conquer Distance

"Uganda Exports," TradingEconomics.com (https://tradingeconomics.com/uganda/exports), 2019.

Fred Ojambo, "Ugandan Cotton Crop Climbs 34 Percent as Higher Prices Attract Farmers," *Bloomberg*, May 17, 2018.

U.S. Department of Agriculture, "Grain: World Markets and Trade" (https://www.fas.usda.gov/data/grain-world-markets-and-trade), 2018.

EXAMPLE: Shipping Containers and International Trade

World Bank, "Container Port Traffic" (http://data.worldbank.org/indicator/IS.SHP.GOOD.TU), 2019.

A. Kerem Coşar and Banu Demir, "Shipping Inside the Box: Containerization and Trade," *Journal of International Economics*, 2018.

"Slow and Steady Recovering for Container Shipping," *Global Trade*, April 24, 2018.

INTERNATIONAL POLICY EXAMPLE: Identifying Who Loses Out as a Consequence of Asian Tariffs on Rice Imports

"Italy Wins Three-Year EU Tariffs on Rice from Cambodia, Myanmar," *Bloomberg*, January 16, 2019.

Ben de Vera, "Tariff on Rice to Curb Inflation by 0.4 Percentage Point," *Philippine Daily Inquirer*, August 29, 2018.

Pearly Neo, "Philippine Rice Crisis Escalates as Shortages Push Prices to a Three-Year High," FoodNavigator-Asia (https://www.foodnavigator-asia.com/Article/2018/08/30/Philippine-rice-crisis-escalates-as-shortages-push-prices-to-a-three-year-high#), August 30, 2018.

ECONOMICS IN YOUR LIFE: A Potential Shift of Comparative Advantage in Olive Oil Production toward the United States

California Olive Ranch, "Harvesting Methods" (https://californiaoliveranch.com/olive-oil-101/harvesting-methods/), 2019.

Daniel Dawson, "California Olive Ranch Announces Expansion," *Olive Oil Times*, August 27, 2018.

Elaine Watson, "California Olive Ranch: 'The Global Olive Oil Industry Is Going through a Fundamental Transition," FoodNavigator-USA.com (https://www.foodnavigator-usa.com/Article/2018/10/22/California-Olive-Ranch-The-global-olive-oil-industry-is-going-through-a-fundamental-transition#), October 22, 2018.

ISSUES & APPLICATIONS: What Do Countries Gain from Involvement in Regional Trade Agreements?

Kimberly Amadeo, "Free Trade Agreements with Their Pros and Cons," TheBalance.com (https://www.thebalance.com/free-trade-agreement-pros-and-cons-3305845), February 14, 2019.

"Free Trade Area," Corporate Finance Institute (https://corporatefinanceinstitute.com/resources/knowledge/economics/free-trade-area/), 2019.

Brock R. Williams, "Bilateral and Regional Trade Agreements: Issues for Congress," Congressional Research Service Report, May 17, 2018.

32

Exchange Rates and the Balance of Payments

sunsinger/Fotolia

LEARNING OBJECTIVES

After reading this chapter, you should be able to:

32.1 Distinguish between the balance of trade and the balance of payments and identify the key accounts within the balance of payments

32.2 Explain the demand for and supply of foreign exchange

32.3 Outline how exchange rates are determined in the markets for foreign exchange and discuss factors that can induce changes in equilibrium exchange rates

32.4 Understand how policymakers can go about attempting to fix exchange rates

Venezuela's government has for many years established the official value of its currency, the *bolivar*, in relation to the U.S. dollar. The government's main rationale for doing so has been to protect the nation's residents from rapid unexpected changes in the number of dollars they would be able to obtain with the bolivars they owned. Nevertheless, Venezuela's government has many times announced the *new* official value for the bolivar in terms of the U.S. dollar. The government's justification for these numerous changes was to enable variations in the bolivar's value relative to the dollar to help prevent undesired shocks to Venezuelan economic activity. One announced change in the official value of the bolivar, however, turned out to be one of the largest adjustments in a currency's official valuation in world history. This adjustment was felt as a major shock to conditions in the Venezuela's *foreign exchange market*, which is a concept that is among the key topics you will encounter in this chapter.

people working in foreign nations send back to family members and friends in their home countries about $700 billion annually in *remittances*—the formal term for such international funds transfers? The annual flow of remittances is almost large as the current-dollar GDP of the nation of Turkey. As a consequence, this total flow of remittance payments across countries' borders ranks within the world's top twenty national GDP flows. Let's consider now how we keep track of the flows of payments across a country's borders.

32.1 Distinguish between the balance of trade and the balance of payments and identify the key accounts within the balance of payments

Balance of trade
The difference between exports and imports of physical goods.

Balance of payments
A system of accounts that measures transactions of goods, services, income, and financial assets between domestic households, businesses, and governments and residents of the rest of the world during a specific time period.

Accounting identities
Values that are equivalent by definition.

The Balance of Payments and International Financial Flows

Governments typically keep track of each year's economic activities by calculating the gross domestic product—the total of expenditures on all newly domestically produced final goods and services—and its components. A summary information system has also been developed for international trade. It covers the balance of trade and the balance of payments. The **balance of trade** refers specifically to exports and imports of physical goods, or merchandise, as discussed previously. When international trade is in balance, the value of exports equals the value of imports. When the value of imports exceeds the value of exports, we are running a deficit in the balance of trade. When the value of exports exceeds the value of imports, we are running a surplus.

The Balance of Payments

The **balance of payments** is a more general concept that expresses the total of all economic transactions between a nation and the rest of the world, usually for a period of one year. Each country's balance of payments summarizes information about that country's exports and imports of services as well as physical goods, earnings by domestic residents on assets located abroad, earnings on domestic assets owned by residents of foreign nations, international financial flows, and official transactions by central banks and governments.

In essence, then, the balance of payments is a record of all the transactions between households, firms, and the government of one country and the rest of the world. Any transaction that leads to a *payment* by a country's residents (or government) is a deficit item, identified by a negative sign (−) when the actual numbers are given for the items listed in the second column of Table 32-1. Any transaction that leads to a *receipt* by a country's residents (or government) is a surplus item and is identified by a plus sign (+) when actual numbers are considered. Table 32-1 provides a list of the surplus and deficit items on international accounts.

Accounting Identities

Accounting identities—definitions of equivalent values—exist for financial institutions and other businesses. We begin with simple accounting identities that must hold for families and then go on to describe international accounting identities.

If a family unit is spending more than its current income, the family unit must necessarily be doing one of the following:

1. Reducing its money holdings or selling stocks, bonds, or other assets

2. Borrowing

3. Receiving gifts from friends or relatives

4. Receiving public transfers from a government, which obtained the funds by taxing others (a transfer is a payment, in money or in goods or services, made without receiving goods or services in return)

TABLE 32-1

Surplus (+) and Deficit (−) Items on the International Accounts

Surplus Items (+)	Deficit Items (−)
Exports of merchandise	Imports of merchandise
Private and governmental gifts from foreign residents	Private and governmental gifts to foreign residents
Foreign use of domestically operated travel and transportation services	Use of foreign-operated travel and transportation services
Foreign tourists' expenditures in this country	U.S. tourists' expenditures abroad
Foreign military spending in this country	Military spending abroad
Interest and dividend receipts from foreign entities	Interest and dividends paid to foreign individuals and businesses
Sales of domestic assets to foreign residents	Purchases of foreign assets
Funds deposited in this country by foreign residents	Funds placed in foreign depository institutions
Sales of gold to foreign residents	Purchases of gold from foreign residents
Sales of domestic currency to foreign residents	Purchases of foreign currency

We can use this information to derive an identity: If a family unit is currently spending more than it is earning, it must draw on previously acquired wealth, borrow, or receive either private or public aid. Similarly, an identity exists for a family unit that is currently spending less than it is earning: It must be increasing its money holdings or be lending and acquiring other financial assets, or it must pay taxes or bestow gifts on others. When we consider businesses and governments, each unit in each group faces its own accounting identities or constraints. Ultimately, *net* lending by households must equal *net* borrowing by businesses and governments.

Disequilibrium Even though our individual family unit's accounts must balance, in the sense that the identity discussed previously must hold, sometimes the item that brings about the balance cannot continue indefinitely. *If family expenditures exceed family income and this situation is financed by borrowing, the household may be considered to be in disequilibrium because such a situation cannot continue indefinitely.* If such a deficit is financed by drawing on previously accumulated assets, the family may also be in disequilibrium because it cannot continue indefinitely to draw on its wealth.

Eventually, the family will find it impossible to continue that lifestyle. (Of course, if the family members are retired, they may well be in equilibrium by drawing on previously acquired assets to finance current deficits. This example illustrates that it is necessary to understand all circumstances fully before pronouncing an economic unit in disequilibrium.)

Equilibrium Individual households, businesses, and governments, as well as the entire group of all households, businesses, and governments, must eventually reach equilibrium. Certain economic adjustment mechanisms have evolved to ensure equilibrium. Deficit households must eventually increase their income or decrease their expenditures. They will find that they have to pay higher interest rates if they wish to borrow to finance their deficits. Eventually, their credit sources will dry up, and they will be forced into equilibrium. Businesses, on occasion, must lower costs or prices—or go bankrupt—to reach equilibrium.

An Accounting Identity among Nations When people from different nations trade or interact, certain identities or constraints must also hold. People buy goods from

TABLE 32-2

U.S. Balance of Payments Account, Estimated for 2020 (in billions of dollars)

Current Account		
(1) Exports of merchandise goods	+1,816.1	
(2) Imports of merchandise goods	−2,738.8	
(3) Balance of merchandise trade		−922.7
(4) Exports of services	+910.2	
(5) Imports of services	−591.6	
(6) Balance of services		+318.6
(7) Balance on goods and services [(3) + (6)]		−604.1
(8) Net unilateral transfers	−136.3	
(9) Balance on current account		−740.4
Financial Account		
(10) Net acquisitions of financial assets by U.S. residents and government entities	+301.6	
(11) Net incurrences of financial liabilities by U.S. residents and government entities	+438.8*	
(12) Balance on financial account [(10) + (11)]		+740.4
(13) Total (balance)		0

Sources: U.S. Department of Commerce, Bureau of Economic Analysis; author's estimates.

*Includes an approximately $17 billion statistical discrepancy, probably uncounted financial transactions, many of which relate to the illegal drug trade.

people in other nations. They also lend to and present gifts to people in other nations. If residents of a nation interact with residents of other nations, an accounting identity ensures a balance (but not necessarily an equilibrium, as will soon become clear). Let's look at the two categories of balance of payments transactions: current account transactions and financial account transactions.

Current Account Transactions

Current account
A category of balance of payments transactions that measures the exchange of merchandise, the exchange of services, and unilateral transfers.

During any designated period, all payments and gifts that are related to the purchase or sale of both goods and services constitute the **current account** in international trade. Major types of current account transactions include the exchange of merchandise, the exchange of services, and unilateral transfers.

Merchandise Trade Exports and Imports The largest portion of any nation's balance of payments current account is typically the importing and exporting of merchandise. During 2020, for example, as shown in lines 1 and 2 of Table 32-2, the United States exported an estimated $1,816.1 billion of merchandise and imported $2,738.8 billion. The balance of merchandise trade is defined as the difference between the value of merchandise exports and the value of merchandise imports. For 2020, the United States had a balance of merchandise trade deficit because the value of its merchandise imports exceeded the value of its merchandise exports. This deficit was about $922.7 billion (line 3).

Service Exports and Imports The balance of (merchandise) trade involves tangible items—things you can feel, touch, and see. Service exports and imports involve invisible or intangible items that are bought and sold, such as shipping, insurance, tourist expenditures, and banking services. Also, income earned by foreign residents on U.S. investments and income earned by U.S. residents on foreign investments are part of service imports and exports. As shown in lines 4 and 5 of Table 32-2, in 2020, estimated service exports were $910.2 billion, and service imports were $591.6 billion. Thus, the balance of services was about $318.6 billion in 2020 (line 6). Exports constitute receipts or inflows into the United States and are positive. Imports constitute payments abroad or outflows of money and are negative.

When we combine the balance of merchandise trade with the balance of services, we obtain a balance on goods and services equal to –$604.1 billion in 2020 (line 7).

Unilateral Transfers U.S. residents give gifts to relatives and others abroad, the federal government makes grants to foreign nations, foreign residents give gifts to U.S. residents, and in the past some foreign governments have granted funds to the U.S. government. In the current account, we see that net unilateral transfers—the total amount of gifts given by U.S. residents and the government minus the total amount received from abroad by U.S. residents and the government—came to an estimated –$136.3 billion in 2020 (line 8). The minus sign before the number for unilateral transfers means that U.S. residents and the U.S. government gave more to foreign residents than foreign residents gave to U.S. residents.

Balancing the Current Account The balance on current account tracks the value of a country's exports of goods and services (including income on investments abroad) and transfer payments (private and government) relative to the value of that country's imports of goods and services and transfer payments (private and government). In 2020, it was estimated to be –$740.4 billion (line 9).

> *If the sum of net exports of goods and services plus net unilateral transfers plus net investment income exceeds zero, a current account surplus is said to exist. If this sum is negative, a current account deficit is said to exist. A current account deficit means that we are importing more goods and services than we are exporting. Such a deficit must be paid for by the export of financial assets.*

Financial Account Transactions

In world markets, it is possible to buy and sell not only goods and services but also financial assets. These international transactions are measured in the **financial account**.

Financial account
A category of balance of payments transactions that measures flows of financial assets.

Types of Financial Account Transactions Financial account transactions occur because of changes in total foreign investments. Such changes occur either when foreign residents alter the amounts of their investments in the United States or when U.S. residents change the amounts of their investments in other countries. In the latter case, U.S. residents make changes in their holdings of foreign assets. The purchase of shares of stock in British firms on the London stock market by a U.S. resident is a U.S. asset acquisition that causes an outflow of funds from the United States to Britain. A U.S. resident's sale of British stock shares to someone in the United Kindom, in contrast, generates an inflow of funds from Britain to the United States.

Foreign residents also may alter their holdings of financial liabilities incurred by U.S. residents and government entities. Any time foreign residents buy U.S. government securities, there is an inflow of funds from other countries to the United States. For instance, U.S. government borrowing from a Japanese company that purchases U.S. Treasury bills entails the incurrence of a liability and generates an accompanying inflow of funds from Japan to the United States. Conversely, any time U.S. residents buy foreign government securities, there is an outflow of funds from the United States to other countries. If the Japanese company just discussed decides to sell some existing holdings of U.S. Treasury bills to a U.S. financial institution, then that transaction brings about an outflow of funds from the United States to Japan.

Loans to and from foreign residents likewise cause both outflows and inflows.

The U.S. Financial Account Line 10 of Table 32-2 indicates that in 2020, the value of net acquisitions of financial assets by U.S. residents and government entities was an estimated +$301.6 billion, and line 11 shows that what the government calls "net incurrences of liabilities"—that is, net additions to U.S. debts held abroad—by U.S. residents and government entities (including a statistical discrepancy) was +$438.8 billion. On both lines, the net cross-border exchanges of assets and liabilities involving U.S. and foreign residents and government entities resulted in positive balances. Thus, there was a positive net financial inflow of +$740.4 billion into the United States (line 12). This net financial inflow is also called the *balance on financial account*.

There is a relationship between the current account balance and the financial account balance.

> ***In the absence of interventions by finance ministries or central banks, the current account balance and the financial account balance must sum to zero. Stated differently, any nation experiencing a current account deficit, such as the United States, must also be running a financial account surplus.***

This basic relationship is apparent in the United States, as you can see in Figure 32-1. As the figure shows, U.S. current account deficits experienced since the early 1980s have been balanced by financial inflows.

The overall balance (line 13) in Table 32-2 is zero, as it must be with double-entry bookkeeping. Hence, as shown in Figure 32-1, the current account balance is a mirror image of the financial account balance.

What Affects the Distribution of Account Balances within the Balance of Payments?

A major factor affecting the distribution of account balances within any nation's balance of payments is its rate of inflation relative to that of its trading partners. Assume

---

FIGURE 32-1

The Relationship between the Current Account and the Financial Account

The current account balance is the mirror image of the financial account balance. We can see this in years since 1970. When the current account balance was in surplus, the financial account balance was negative. When the current account balance was in deficit, the financial account balance was positive.

Sources: International Monetary Fund; *Economic Indicators.*

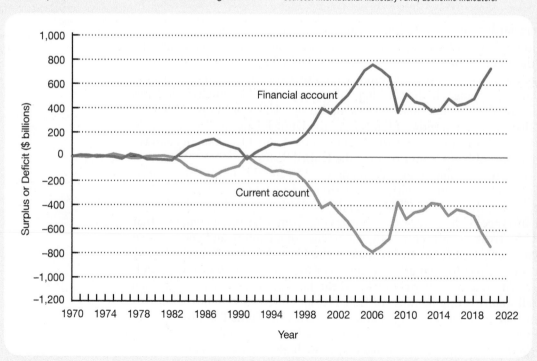

that the rates of inflation in the United States and Britain are equal. Now suppose that all of a sudden, the U.S. inflation rate increases. British residents will find that U.S. products are becoming more expensive, so U.S. firms will export fewer of them to Britain. At the current dollar–pound exchange rate, U.S. residents will find British products relatively cheaper, so they will import more.

Other things being equal, the reverse will occur if the U.S. inflation rate suddenly falls relative to that of Britain. All other things held constant, whenever the U.S. rate of inflation exceeds that of its trading partners, we expect to see a larger deficit in the U.S. balance of merchandise trade and in the U.S. current account balance. Conversely, when the U.S. rate of inflation is less than that of its trading partners, other things being constant, we expect to see a smaller deficit in the U.S. balance of merchandise trade and in the U.S. current account balance.

Another important factor that sometimes influences account balances within a nation's balance of payments is its relative political stability. Political instability causes *capital flight*. Owners of financial assets that are titles of ownership to capital in countries anticipating or experiencing political instability will often move assets to countries that are politically stable, such as the United States. Hence, the U.S. financial account balance is likely to increase whenever political instability looms in other nations in the world.

WHAT HAPPENS WHEN...

. . . U.S. spending on merchandise imports increases during the same year that foreign expenditures on U.S. merchandise exports decrease, other things being equal?

The immediate effect of a rise in U.S. residents' spending on imported goods and services simultaneous with a decrease in foreign spending on U.S. exports would be a larger merchandise trade deficit. In addition, the deficit in the balance on goods and services would widen, as would the negative U.S. balance on the current account. The total across all accounts within the overall balance of payments would remain equal to zero. Hence, the positive financial account balance would have to increase in value.

Deriving the Demand for and Supply of Foreign Exchange

32.2 Explain the demand for and supply of foreign exchange

When you buy foreign products, such as pharmaceuticals made in Britain, you have dollars with which to pay the British manufacturer. The British manufacturer, however, cannot pay workers in dollars. The workers are British; they live in Britain, where the pound is the nation's currency. People employed by British pharmaceutical firms must have pounds to buy goods and services in Britain. There has to be a way to exchange dollars for pounds that the pharmaceutical manufacturer will accept. That exchange occurs in a **foreign exchange market**, which in this case involves the exchange of pounds and dollars.

The particular **exchange rate** between pounds and dollars that prevails—the dollar price of the pound—depends on the current demand for and supply of pounds and dollars. In a sense, then, our analysis of the exchange rate between dollars and pounds will be familiar, for we have used supply and demand throughout this book. If it costs you $1.50 to buy 1 pound, that is the foreign exchange rate determined by the current demand for and supply of pounds in the foreign exchange market. The British person going to the foreign exchange market would need about 0.67 pound to buy 1 dollar.

Now let's consider what determines the demand for and supply of foreign currency in the foreign exchange market. We will continue to assume that the only two regions in the world are Britain and the United States.

Foreign exchange market
A market in which households, firms, and governments buy and sell national currencies.

Exchange rate
The price of one nation's currency in terms of the currency of another country.

Demand for and Supply of Foreign Currency

You wish to purchase British-produced pharmaceuticals directly from a manufacturer located in Britain. To do so, you must have pounds. You go to the foreign exchange market (or your U.S. bank). Your desire to buy the pharmaceuticals causes you to offer (supply) dollars to the foreign exchange market. Your demand for pounds is equivalent to your supply of dollars to the foreign exchange market.

> *Every U.S. transaction involving the importation of foreign goods constitutes a supply of dollars and a demand for some foreign currency, and the opposite is true for export transactions.*

In this case, the import transaction constitutes a demand for pounds.

In our example, we will assume that only two goods are being traded, British pharmaceuticals and U.S. tablet devices. The U.S. demand for British pharmaceuticals creates a supply of dollars and a demand for pounds in the foreign exchange market. Similarly, the British demand for U.S. tablet devices creates a supply of pounds and a demand for dollars in the foreign exchange market. Under a system of **flexible exchange rates**, the supply of and demand for dollars and pounds in the foreign exchange market will determine the equilibrium foreign exchange rate. The equilibrium exchange rate will tell us how many pounds a dollar can be exchanged for—that is, the pound price of dollars—or how many dollars a pound can be exchanged for—the dollar price of pounds.

Appreciation, Depreciation, and Demand for and Supply of Foreign Exchange

To determine the equilibrium foreign exchange rate, we have to find out what determines the demand for and supply of foreign exchange. We will ignore for the moment any speculative aspect of buying foreign exchange. That is, we assume that there are no individuals who wish to buy pounds simply because they think their price will go up in the future.

The idea of an exchange rate is no different from the idea of paying a certain price for an item you want to buy. Suppose that you have to pay about $2.00 for a cup of coffee. If the price goes up to $2.50, you will probably buy fewer cups. If the price goes down to $1.00, you will likely buy more. In other words, the demand curve for cups of coffee, expressed in terms of dollars, slopes downward following the law of demand. The demand curve for pounds slopes downward also, and we will see why.

Let's think more closely about the demand schedule for pounds. If it costs you $1.50 to purchase 1 pound, that is the exchange rate between dollars and pounds. If tomorrow you have to pay $1.60 for the same pound, the exchange rate would have changed. Looking at such a change, we would say that there has been an **appreciation** in the value of the pound in the foreign exchange market. Another way to view this increase in the value of the pound is to say that there has been a **depreciation** in the value of the dollar in the foreign exchange market. The dollar used to buy 0.67 pound, but tomorrow the dollar will be able to buy only about 0.63 pound at a price of $1.60 per pound.

If the dollar price of pounds rises, you will probably demand fewer pounds. Why? The answer lies in the reason you and others demand pounds in the first place.

Appreciation and Depreciation of Pounds Recall that in our example, you and others demand pounds to buy British pharmaceuticals. The demand curve for British pharmaceuticals follows the law of demand and therefore slopes downward. If it costs more U.S. dollars to buy the same quantity of British pharmaceuticals, presumably you and other U.S. residents will not buy the same quantity. Your quantity demanded will be less. We say that your demand for pounds is *derived from* your demand for British pharmaceuticals.

In panel (a) of Figure 32-2, we present the hypothetical demand schedule for packages of British pharmaceuticals by a representative set of U.S. consumers, other things being equal, during a typical week. In panel (b) of Figure 32-2, we show graphically the U.S. demand curve for British pharmaceuticals in terms of U.S. dollars taken from panel (a).

Panel (a)
Demand Schedule for Packages of British Pharmaceuticals in the United States per Week

Price per Package	Quantity Demanded
$200	100
175	300
150	500
125	700

Panel (b)
U.S. Demand Curve for British Pharmaceuticals

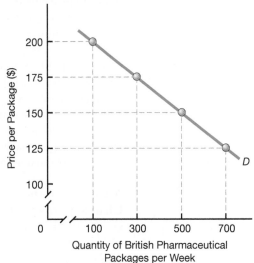

Panel (c)
Pounds Required to Purchase Quantity Demanded (at P = 100 Pounds per package of pharmaceuticals)

Quantity Demanded	Pounds Required
100	10,000
300	30,000
500	50,000
700	70,000

Panel (d)
Derived Demand Schedule for Pounds in the United States with Which to Pay for Imports of Pharmaceuticals

Dollar Price of One Pound	Dollar Price of Pharmaceuticals	Quantity of Pharmaceuticals Demanded	Quantity of Pounds Demanded per Week
$2.00	$200	100	10,000
1.75	175	300	30,000
1.50	150	500	50,000
1.25	125	700	70,000

Panel (e)
U.S. Derived Demand for Pounds

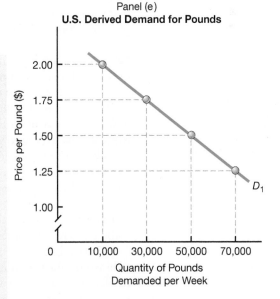

FIGURE 32-2

Deriving the Demand for British Pounds

In panel (a), we show the demand schedule for British pharmaceuticals in the United States, expressed in terms of dollars per package of pharmaceuticals. In panel (b), we show the demand curve, D, which slopes downward. In panel (c), we show the number of pounds required to purchase up to 700 packages of pharmaceuticals. If the price per package of pharmaceuticals is 100 pounds, we can now find the quantity of pounds needed to pay for the various quantities demanded. In panel (d), we see the derived demand for pounds in the United States in order to purchase the various quantities of pharmaceuticals given in panel (a). The resultant demand curve, D_1, is shown in panel (e). This is the U.S. derived demand for pounds.

An Example of Derived Demand Let us assume that the price of a package of British pharmaceuticals in Britain is 100 pounds. Given that price, we can find the number of pounds required to purchase, say, 500 packages of British pharmaceuticals.

The Quantity of Foreign Exchange Demanded at a Given Exchange Rate That information is given in panel (c) of Figure 32-2. If purchasing one package of British pharmaceuticals requires 100 pounds, 500 packages require 50,000 pounds. Now we have enough information to determine the derived demand curve for pounds. If 1 pound costs $1.50, a package of pharmaceuticals would cost $150 (100 pounds per package × $1.50 per pound = $150 per package). At $150 per package, the representative group of U.S. consumers would, we see from panel (a) of Figure 32-2, demand 500 packages of pharmaceuticals.

From panel (c), we see that 50,000 pounds would be demanded to buy the 500 packages of pharmaceuticals. We show this quantity demanded in panel (d). In panel (e), we draw the derived demand curve for pounds.

A Change in the Quantity of Foreign Exchange Demanded in Response to a Change in the Exchange Rate Now consider what happens if the price of pounds goes up to $1.75. A package of British pharmaceuticals priced at 100 pounds in Britain would now cost $175. From panel (a), we see that at $175 per package, 300 packages of pharmaceuticals will be imported from Britain into the United States by our representative group of U.S. consumers. From panel (c), we see that 300 packages of pharmaceuticals would require 30,000 pounds to be purchased. Thus, in panels (d) and (e), we see that at a price of $1.75 per pound, the quantity demanded will be 30,000 pounds.

We continue similar calculations all the way up to a price of $2.00 per pound. At that price, a package of British pharmaceuticals with a price of 100 pounds in Britain would have a U.S. dollar price of $200 and our representative U.S. consumers would import only 100 packages of pharmaceuticals.

Downward-Sloping Derived Demand As can be expected, as the price of the pound rises, the quantity of pounds demanded will fall. The only difference here from the standard demand analysis developed in an earlier chapter and used throughout this text is that the demand for pounds is derived from the demand for a final product—British pharmaceuticals in our example.

Supply of Pounds Assume that British pharmaceutical manufacturers buy U.S. tablet devices. The supply of pounds is a derived supply in that it is derived from the British demand for U.S. tablet devices. We could go through an example similar to the one for pharmaceuticals to come up with a supply schedule of pounds in Britain. It slopes upward. Obviously, British residents want dollars to purchase U.S. goods. British residents will be willing to supply more pounds when the dollar price of pounds goes up, because they can then buy more U.S. goods with the same quantity of pounds. That is, the pound would be worth more in exchange for U.S. goods than was the situation when the dollar price for pounds was lower.

An Example Let's take an example. Suppose a U.S.-produced tablet device costs $200. If the exchange rate is $1.50 per pound, a British resident will have to come up with 133.33 pounds ($200 ÷ $1.50 per pound, which is approximately equal to 133.33 pounds) to buy one tablet. If, however, the exchange rate goes up to $1.75 per pound, a British resident must come up with only 114.29 pounds ($200 ÷ $1.75 per pound is approximately equal to 114.29 pounds) to buy a U.S. tablet. At this lower price (in pounds) of U.S. tablets, British residents will demand a larger quantity.

In other words, as the price of pounds goes up in terms of dollars, the quantity of U.S. tablets demanded will go up, and hence the quantity of pounds supplied will go up. Therefore, the supply schedule of pounds, which is derived from the British demand for U.S. goods, will slope upward, as seen in Figure 32-3.

FIGURE 32-3

FIGURE 32-3

The Supply of Pounds

If the market price of a U.S.-produced tablet device is $200, then at an exchange rate of $1.50 per pound, the price of the tablet to a British consumer is approximately 133.33 pounds. If the exchange rate rises to $1.75 per pound, the price of the tablet in Britain falls to 114.29 pounds. This induces an increase in the quantity of tablets demanded by British consumers and consequently an increase in the quantity of pounds supplied in exchange for dollars in the foreign exchange market. In contrast, if the exchange rate falls to $1.25 per pound, the British price of the tablet rises to 160 pounds. This causes a decrease in the quantity of tablets demanded by British consumers. As a result, there is a decline in the quantity of pounds supplied in exchange for dollars in the foreign exchange market. Hence, the pound supply curve slopes up.

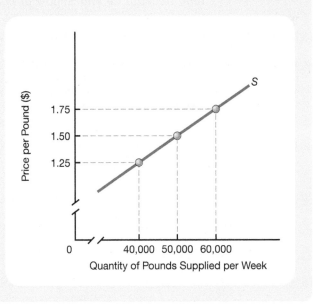

Why are portions of the global demand for and supply of U.S. dollars derived from *foreign* expenditures on goods and services produced in nations *other* than the United States and unrelated to actions of U.S. residents?

INTERNATIONAL EXAMPLE

The Non-U.S. Derived Demand for and Supply of U.S. Dollars

Residents of many nations around the world prefer to pay for imported goods and services using U.S. dollars, and many exporters located in other countries prefer to receive U.S. dollars in payment for their goods and services. Indeed, recent estimates indicate that about 40 percent of international trade not involving U.S.-based exporters or importers is financed using dollars. Thus, significant portions of the global demand for and supply of U.S. dollars are derived from international trade transactions that take place entirely outside the United States.

FOR CRITICAL THINKING

How might the fact that 30 to 60 percent of other nations' holdings of various bonds and other financial assets are denominated in dollars also contribute to non-U.S. derived demand for and supply of U.S. dollars? (Hint: *Another source of the derived demand for and supply of U.S. dollars involves dollar-denominated assets outside the United States.*)

Sources are listed at the end of this chapter.

Determining Foreign Exchange Rates

Now that you understand the derived demand for and supply of foreign exchange, we can contemplate the determination of exchange rates. The values of exchange rates are determined by the interacting forces of demand and supply in foreign exchange markets.

> **32.3** Outline how exchange rates are determined in the markets for foreign exchange and discuss factors that can induce changes in equilibrium exchange rates

Total Demand for and Supply of Foreign Exchange

Let us now look at the total demand for and supply of the foreign currency we are considering, the British pound. We take all U.S. consumers of British pharmaceuticals and all British consumers of U.S. tablet devices and put their demands for and supplies of pounds together into one diagram. Thus, we are showing the total demand for and

FIGURE 32-4

Total Demand for and Supply of Pounds

The market supply curve for pounds results from the total British demand for U.S. tablet devices. The demand curve, *D*, slopes downward like most demand curves, and the supply curve, *S*, slopes upward. The foreign exchange price, or the U.S. dollar price of pounds, is given on the vertical axis. The number of pounds is represented on the horizontal axis. If the foreign exchange rate is $1.75—that is, if it takes $1.75 to buy 1 pound—U.S. residents will demand 20 billion pounds.

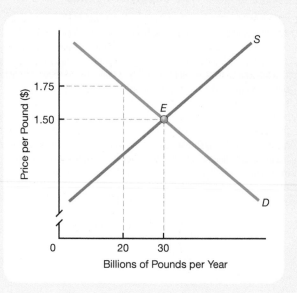

total supply of pounds. The horizontal axis in Figure 32-4 represents the quantity of foreign exchange—the number of pounds per year. The vertical axis represents the exchange rate—the price of foreign currency (pounds) expressed in dollars (per pound). The foreign currency price of $1.75 per pound means it will cost you $1.75 to buy 1 pound. At the foreign currency price of $1.50 per pound, you know that it will cost you $1.50 to buy 1 pound. The equilibrium, *E*, is again established at $1.50 for 1 pound.

The equilibrium exchange rate is at the intersection of *D* and *S*, or point *E*. The equilibrium exchange rate is $1.50 per pound. At this point, 30 billion pounds are both demanded and supplied each year.

In our hypothetical example, assuming that there are only representative groups of pharmaceutical consumers in the United States and tablet consumers in Britain, the equilibrium exchange rate will be set at $1.50 per pound.

This equilibrium is not established because U.S. residents like to buy pounds or because British residents like to buy dollars. Rather, the equilibrium exchange rate depends on how many tablet devices British residents want and how many British pharmaceuticals U.S. residents want (given their respective incomes, their tastes, and, in our example, the relative prices of pharmaceuticals and tablet devices).

Changes in the Equilibrium Exchange Rate

By definition, currency appreciations and depreciations correspond to variations in exchange rates. Let's consider how changes in the demand for or supply of foreign exchange can alter equilibrium exchange rates.

A Shift in Demand Assume that a successful advertising campaign by U.S. pharmaceutical importers causes U.S. demand for British pharmaceuticals to rise. U.S. residents demand more pharmaceuticals at all prices. Their demand curve for British pharmaceuticals shifts outward to the right.

The increased demand for British pharmaceuticals can be translated into an increased demand for pounds. All U.S. residents clamoring for British pharmaceuticals will supply more dollars to the foreign exchange market while demanding more pounds to pay for the pharmaceuticals. Figure 32-5 presents a new demand schedule, D_2, for pounds. This demand schedule is to the right of the original demand schedule.

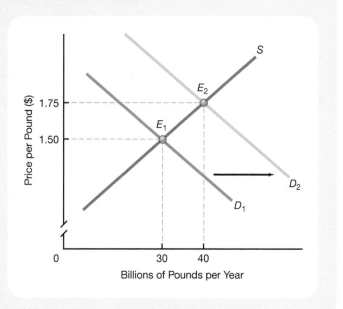

FIGURE 32-5

A Shift in the Demand Schedule

The demand schedule for British pharmaceuticals shifts to the right, causing the derived demand schedule for pounds to shift to the right also. We have shown this as a shift from D_1 to D_2. We have assumed that the supply schedule for pounds has remained stable—that is, British demand for U.S. tablet devices has remained constant. The old equilibrium foreign exchange rate was $1.50 per pound.

If British residents do not change their desire for U.S. tablet devices, the supply schedule for pounds will remain stable.

A new equilibrium will be established at a higher exchange rate. In our particular example, the new equilibrium is established at an exchange rate of $1.75 per pound. It now takes $1.75 to buy 1 pound, whereas formerly it took $1.50. This will be translated into an increase in the price of British pharmaceuticals to U.S. residents and into a decrease in the price of U.S. tablet devices to British residents. For example, a package of British pharmaceuticals priced at 100 pounds that sold for $150 in the United States will now be priced at $175. Conversely, a U.S. tablet priced at $200 that previously sold for 133.33 pounds will now sell for 114.29 pounds.

The new equilibrium exchange rate will be E_2. It will now cost $1.75 to buy 1 pound. The higher price of pounds will be translated into a higher U.S. dollar price for British pharmaceuticals and a lower pound price for U.S. tablet devices.

A Shift in Supply We just assumed that the U.S. demand for British pharmaceuticals shifted due to a successful ad campaign. The demand for pounds is derived from the demand by U.S. residents for pharmaceuticals. This change in pharmaceuticals demand is translated into a shift in the demand curve for pounds. As an alternative exercise, we might assume that the supply curve of pounds shifts outward to the right. Such a supply shift could occur for many reasons, one of which is a relative rise in the price level in Britain. For example, if the prices of all British-manufactured tablets went up 20 percent in pounds, U.S. tablets would now be relatively cheaper. This would mean that British residents would want to buy more U.S. tablets. Remember, though, that when they want to buy more U.S. tablets, they supply more pounds to the foreign exchange market.

Thus, we see in Figure 32-6 that the supply curve of pounds moves from S to S_1. In the absence of restrictions—that is, in a system of flexible exchange rates—the new equilibrium exchange rate will be $1.25 equals 1 pound. The quantity of pounds demanded and supplied will increase from 30 billion per year to 60 billion per year.

We say, then, that in a flexible international exchange rate system, shifts in the demand for and supply of foreign currencies will cause changes in the equilibrium foreign exchange rates. Those rates will remain in effect until world supply or demand shifts.

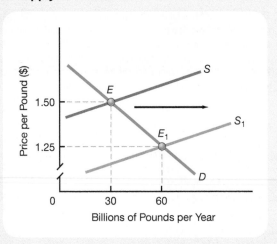

FIGURE 32-6

A Shift in the Supply of Pounds

There has been a shift in the supply curve for pounds. The new equilibrium will occur at E_1, meaning that $1.25, rather than $1.50, will now buy 1 pound. After the exchange rate adjustment, the annual amount of pounds demanded and supplied will increase from 30 billion to 60 billion.

Market Determinants of Exchange Rates

The foreign exchange market is affected by many other variables in addition to changes in relative price levels, including the following:

- *Changes in real interest rates.* Suppose that the U.S. interest rate, corrected for people's expectations of inflation, increases relative to the rest of the world. Then international investors elsewhere seeking the higher returns now available in the United States will increase their demand for dollar-denominated assets. As a consequence, the demand for dollars rises in foreign exchange markets. An increased demand for dollars in foreign exchange markets, other things held constant, will cause the dollar to appreciate and other currencies to depreciate.

- *Changes in consumer preferences.* If British citizens, for example, suddenly develop a heightened taste for U.S.-made digital tablets, this will increase the derived demand for U.S. dollars in foreign exchange markets.

- *Perceptions of economic stability.* Suppose that perceptions change and the United States looks economically and politically more stable relative to other countries. Foreign residents thereby will want to put their savings into U.S. assets rather than in their own domestic assets. This will increase the demand for dollars.

32.4 Understand how policymakers can go about attempting to fix exchange rates

Fixed Versus Floating Exchange Rates

The current U.S. system of more or less freely floating exchange rates is a relatively recent development. In the past, we have had periods of a gold standard, fixed exchange rates under the International Monetary Fund, and variants of the two. A number of nations continue to maintain fixed exchange rates for their currencies, so it is important to understand how a fixed-exchange-rate system functions.

The Gold Standard

Until the 1930s, many nations were on a gold standard. The value of their domestic currency was fixed, or *pegged*, in units of gold. Nations operating under this gold standard agreed to redeem their currencies for a fixed amount of gold at the request of any holder of that currency. Although gold was not necessarily the means of exchange for world trade, it was the unit to which all currencies under the gold standard were pegged. Because all currencies in the system were pegged to gold, exchange rates between those currencies were fixed.

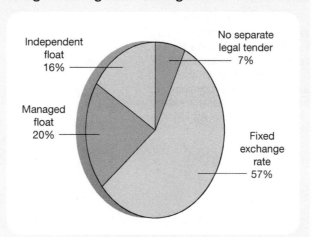

FIGURE 32-7

Current Foreign Exchange Rate Arrangements

Today, 16 percent of the member nations of the International Monetary Fund have an independent float, and 20 percent have a managed float exchange rate arrangement under which central banks sometimes seek to influence the exchange rate. Another 7 percent of all nations use the currencies of other nations instead of issuing their own currencies. The remaining 57 percent of countries have fixed exchange rates.

Source: International Monetary Fund.

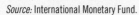

Two problems plagued the gold standard, however. One was that by fixing the value of its currency in relation to the amount of gold, a nation gave up control of its domestic monetary policy. Another was that the world's commerce was at the mercy of gold discoveries. Throughout history, each time new veins of gold were found, desired domestic expenditures on goods and services increased. If production of goods and services failed to increase proportionately, inflation resulted.

Bretton Woods and the International Monetary Fund

On December 27, 1945, the world's capitalist countries, which in 1944 had sent representatives to meetings in Bretton Woods, New Hampshire, created a new permanent institution, the International Monetary Fund (IMF).

The Purpose of the IMF in the Bretton Woods System The IMF's task was to lend to member countries for which the sum of private components of the current account balance and the financial account balance was negative. Hence, the IMF helped these nations maintain an offsetting surplus in their financial accounts.

Governments that joined the Bretton Woods system agreed to keep the values of their currencies close to the declared **par value**—the officially determined value. For most nations, this entailed maintaining the value of their currencies within 1 percent of the par value.

Par value
The officially determined value of a currency.

The Dollar's Role under Bretton Woods The United States, which owned most of the world's gold stock, was similarly obligated to maintain gold prices within a 1 percent margin of the official rate of $35 an ounce. Except for a transitional arrangement permitting a one-time adjustment of up to 10 percent in par value, members could alter exchange rates thereafter only with the approval of the IMF.

The United States went off the Bretton Woods system of fixed exchange rates in 1973. As Figure 32-7 indicates, many other nations of the world have been less willing to permit the values of their currencies to vary in the foreign exchange markets.

Fixing the Exchange Rate

How did nations fix their exchange rates in years past? How do many countries accomplish this today? Let's now consider the answers to these questions.

Confronting Pressures for the Exchange Rate to Change Figure 32-8 shows the market for *dinars*, the currency of Bahrain. At the initial equilibrium point E_1, U.S. residents had to give up $2.66 to obtain 1 dinar.

FIGURE 32-8

A Fixed Exchange Rate

This figure illustrates how the Central Bank of Bahrain could fix the dollar–dinar exchange rate in the face of an increase in the supply of dinars, from S to S_1, caused by a rise in the demand for U.S. goods by Bahraini residents. In the absence of any action by the Central Bank of Bahrain, the result would be a movement from point E_1 to point E_2. The dollar value of the dinar would fall from $2.66 to $2.00. The Central Bank of Bahrain can prevent this exchange rate change by purchasing dinars with dollars in the foreign exchange market, thereby increasing the demand for dinars, from D to D_2. At the new equilibrium point, E_3, the dinar's value remains at $2.66.

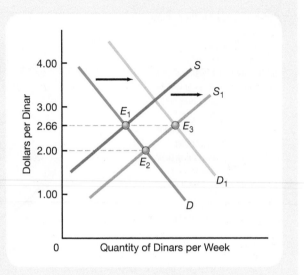

Suppose now that there is an increase in the supply of dinars for dollars, perhaps because Bahraini residents wish to buy more U.S. goods. Other things being equal, the result would be a movement to point E_2 in Figure 32-8. The dollar value of the dinar would fall to $2.00.

Maintaining a Fixed Exchange Rate To prevent a dinar depreciation from occurring, however, the Central Bank of Bahrain could increase the demand for dinars in the foreign exchange market by purchasing dinars with dollars. The Central Bank of Bahrain can do this using dollars that it has on hand as part of its *foreign exchange reserves*. All central banks hold reserves of foreign currencies. Because the U.S. dollar is a key international currency, the Central Bank of Bahrain and other central banks typically hold billions of dollars in reserve so that they can make transactions such as the one in this example.

Note that a sufficiently large purchase of dinars could, as shown in Figure 32-8, cause the demand curve to shift rightward to achieve the new equilibrium point E_3, at which the dinar's value remains at $2.66. Provided that it has enough dollar reserves on hand, the Central Bank of Bahrain could maintain—effectively fix—the exchange rate in the face of the rise in the supply of dinars.

The Central Bank of Bahrain has since 2001 maintained the dollar–dinar exchange rate by varying the amount of its national currency demanded at any given exchange rate in the foreign exchange rate. This basic approach is the way that *any* central bank seeks to keep its nation's currency value unchanged in light of changing market forces.

> *Central banks can keep exchange rates fixed as long as they have enough foreign exchange reserves to deal with potentially long-lasting changes in the demand for or supply of their nation's currency.*

Pros and Cons of a Fixed Exchange Rate

Why might a nation such as Bahrain wish to keep the value of its currency from fluctuating? One reason is that changes in the exchange rate can affect the market values of assets that are denominated in foreign currencies. This variation in asset values can increase the financial risks that a nation's residents face, thereby forcing them to incur costs to avoid these risks.

Foreign Exchange Risk The possibility that variations in the market value of assets can take place due to changes in the value of a nation's currency is the **foreign exchange risk** that residents of a country face because their nation's currency value

---

ECONOMICS IN YOUR LIFE

To consider recent actions taken to prevent the Hong Kong currency's exchange rate from changing, take a look at **The Hong Kong Monetary Authority Acts to Keep Its Currency's Exchange Rate Fixed** on page 708.

Foreign exchange risk
The possibility that changes in the value of a nation's currency will result in variations in the market value of assets.

can vary. Suppose that companies in Bahrain have many loans denominated in dollars but earn nearly all their revenues in dinars from sales within Bahrain. A decline in the dollar value of the dinar would mean that Bahraini companies would have to allocate a larger portion of their earnings to make the same *dollar* loan repayments as before. Thus, a fall in the dinar's value would increase the operating costs of these companies, thereby reducing their profitability and raising the likelihood of eventual bankruptcy.

How have decisions about currency denominations of public debts exposed several African governments to considerable foreign exchange risk?

INTERNATIONAL POLICY EXAMPLE

African Governments with Dollar-Denominated Debts Confront Foreign Exchange Depreciations

In the past, governments of more than a dozen African governments, including those of Angola, Cameroon, South Africa, and Zambia, experienced difficulties inducing foreign investors to hold their nations' public debts because of concerns about foreign exchange risks. These governments decided to issue more than $20 billion in debts denominated in U.S. dollars. These choices assured foreign investors that their dollar-denominated returns from holding those debts would not be affected by domestic currency depreciations in the borrowing nations' currencies in relation to the dollar. When significant depreciations did occur in recent years, the African governments discovered that they had to pay out many more units of their own nations' currencies to obtain the dollars they owed foreign investors. Thus, the African governments absorbed all of the foreign exchange risk associated with their dollar-denominated debts.

FOR CRITICAL THINKING

Who ultimately has to finance the higher payments that the African governments must make to obtain dollars to pay foreign holders of their public debts? (Hint: *Who always provides the funds that governments spend?*)

Sources are listed at the end of this chapter.

Limiting foreign exchange risk is a classic rationale for adopting a fixed exchange rate. Nevertheless, a country's residents are not defenseless against foreign exchange risk. In what is known as a **hedge**, they can adopt strategies intended to offset the risk arising from exchange rate variations.

Hedge
A financial strategy that reduces the chance of suffering losses arising from foreign exchange risk.

For example, a company in Bahrain that has significant euro earnings from sales in Germany but sizable loans from U.S. investors could arrange to convert its euro earnings into dollars via special types of foreign exchange contracts called *currency swaps*. The Bahraini company could likewise avoid holdings of dinars and shield itself—*hedge*—against variations in the dinar's value.

Just how "big" are the data associated with trading in foreign exchange markets and the related risks?

 # AI | DECISION MAKING THROUGH DATA

Foreign Exchange Markets Involving *Really* Big Data

Total annual trading of foreign currencies is "only" about $6 trillion per year, or roughly one-third of the value of the total flow of U.S. annual income. Total global exposures to foreign exchange risks at any given time, in contrast, are estimated to exceed $250 trillion. These aggregate exposures to foreign exchange risks thereby amount to more than a dozen times the magnitude of annual U.S. real GDP.

Hence, analysis of even a small fraction of activity in global foreign exchange markets typically entails examining details from hundreds of thousands of transactions involving the values of traded currencies. Such analysis also must take into account foreign-currency-denominated financial assets totaling many trillions of dollars. Data flows in foreign exchange markets truly are *big*. In light of human limitations, institutions that trade currencies and seek to assess their risks are utilizing AI technologies capable of tracking and evaluating these massive flows of data.

FOR CRITICAL THINKING

How can individuals or firms holding large quantities of multiple currencies be exposed to foreign exchange risks even if they are not actively trading currencies in foreign exchange markets from day to day?

Sources are listed at the end of this chapter.

The Exchange Rate as a Shock Absorber If fixing the exchange rate limits foreign exchange risk, why do so many nations allow the exchange rates to float? The answer must be that there are potential drawbacks associated with fixing exchange rates.

A Nation with Immobile Residents and a Fixed Exchange Rate One key drawback is that exchange rate variations can actually perform a valuable service for a nation's economy. Consider a situation in which residents of a nation speak only their own nation's language. As a result, the country's residents are very *immobile*: They cannot trade their labor skills outside their own nation's borders.

Now think about what happens if this nation chooses to fix its exchange rate. Imagine a situation in which other countries begin to sell products that are close substitutes for the products its people specialize in producing, causing a sizable drop in demand for that nation's goods. If wages and prices do not instantly and completely adjust downward, the result will be a sharp decline in production of goods and services, a falloff in national income, and higher unemployment.

A Nation with Immobile Residents and a Floating Exchange Rate Contrast the situation described above with an alternative situation in which the exchange rate floats. In this case, a sizable decline in outside demand for the nation's products will cause it to experience a trade deficit, which will lead to a significant drop in the demand for that nation's currency. As a result, the nation's currency will experience a sizable depreciation, making the goods that the nation offers to sell abroad much less expensive in other countries. People abroad who continue to consume the nation's products will increase their purchases, and the nation's exports will increase. Its production will begin to recover somewhat, as will its residents' incomes. Unemployment will begin to fall.

This example illustrates how exchange rate variations can be beneficial, especially if a nation's residents are relatively immobile. It can be difficult, for example, for a Polish resident who has never studied Portuguese to move to Lisbon, even if she is highly qualified for available jobs there. If many residents of Poland face similar linguistic or cultural barriers, Poland could be better off with a floating exchange rate even if its residents must incur significant costs hedging against foreign exchange risk as a result.

ECONOMICS IN YOUR LIFE

The Hong Kong Monetary Authority Acts to Keep Its Currency's Exchange Rate Fixed

Since 1983, the Hong Kong Monetary Authority (HKMA) has fixed the exchange rate for its currency, the *Hong Kong dollar*, exactly at 12.8 U.S. cents per Hong Kong dollar. Now, for the first time in a number of years, the nation's fixed exchange rate is under pressure. A reduction in the demand for Hong Kong dollars has caused the actual rate at which U.S. dollars trade for Hong Kong dollars to drop close to 12.7 cents per Hong Kong dollar.

HKMA's chief executive, Norman Chan, authorizes actions to push the exchange rate back up to the official target of 12.8 cents per Hong Kong dollar. Acting on Chan's orders, the HKMA buys Hong Kong dollars with U.S. dollar reserves. This action has the effect of increasing the amount of Hong Kong dollars demanded in the foreign exchange market at any given exchange rate. The resulting reduction in the supply of Hong Kong dollars pushes the exchange rate back up to 12.8 cents per Hong Kong dollar.

Chan issues a formal statement to the news media. "The HKMA is fully capable of maintaining the stability of the Hong Kong dollar," says Chan. "There is no need to be concerned."

FOR CRITICAL THINKING

Why does the HKMA's capability of keeping the exchange rate fixed as the demand for Hong Kong dollars drops depend on having a sufficient number of U.S. dollars in reserves to continue buying Hong Kong dollars?

REAL APPLICATION

Let's say that you are going to take a month's trip to a Latin American country that has a relatively stable economy. Are you better off exchanging your dollars for that nation's currency as soon as you know that you are going to make the trip, or should you wait to buy that foreign currency just before you leave the United States?

Sources are listed at the end of this chapter.

ISSUES & APPLICATIONS

How Changing a Fixed Exchange Rate to Try to *Absorb* Shocks Eventually Can *Cause* Shocks

sunsinger/Fotolia

CONCEPTS APPLIED

➤ Fixed Exchange Rate

➤ Foreign Exchange Risk

➤ Exchange Rate as a Shock Absorber

A classic rationale for fixing a nation's exchange rate is to limit foreign exchange risks of the country's residents. For a number of years, Venezuela's government sought to keep the value of its currency, the *bolivar*, fixed relative to the U.S. dollar for this reason. Nevertheless, a specific action undertaken by the Venezuelan government ultimately caused one of the largest realized foreign exchange risks in world history.

Trying to Limit Foreign Exchange Risks Yet Allow the Exchange Rate to Function as a Shock Absorber

Two decades ago, the Venezuelan government sought to sell sufficient bolivars for U.S. dollars (or buy enough dollars with bolivars) to maintain a fixed exchange rate close to 2 bolivars per dollar. Over time, however, the government decided to alter the official exchange rate for its currency via actions known as *devaluations*, which entailed raising the fixed bolivar-per-dollar exchange rate.

As the end of the 2010s approached, the government had implemented so many devaluations that its official exchange rate had increased to about 285,000 bolivars per dollar. Between these official devaluations, the government sought to keep its exchange rate fixed for intervals of sufficient length to derive some benefit in the form of reduced exchange rate risk. Nevertheless, by devaluing often in large increments, the government simultaneously tried to allow the exchange rate to function as a shock absorber.

Devaluation *Becomes* an Economic Shock

Then, during a single weekend, the government made a decision to engage in one of the largest currency devaluations in global history. The government raised its official

exchange rate from 285,000 bolivars per dollar to about *6 million* bolivars per dollar. Over the course of a single weekend, Venezuelan residents experienced a nearly 95 percent reduction in the dollar value of the bolivars that they held.

Following this bolivar devaluation, the bolivar's value also declined dramatically relative to all other currencies in the world. Consequently, bolivar prices of imported goods and services skyrocketed. Overall Venezuelan economic activity quickly plummeted. Instead of helping to reduce foreign exchange risks while absorbing economic shocks, the government's devaluation policy itself created a massive economic shock.

FOR CRITICAL THINKING

What do you suppose happened to Venezuelan import spending following the massive bolivar devaluation? Explain your reasoning.

REAL APPLICATION

Assume that you have been hired as an economist for the Venezuelan government. What recommendations might you make to improve that country's situation?

Sources are listed at the end of this chapter.

What You Should Know

Here is what you should know after reading this chapter.

LEARNING OBJECTIVES

32.1 Distinguish between the balance of trade and the balance of payments and identify the key accounts within the balance of payments *The balance of payments is a system of accounts for all transactions between a nation's residents and the residents of other countries of the world. There are two accounts within the balance of payments. The current account measures net exchanges of goods and services, transfers, and income flows across a nation's borders. The financial account measures net flows of financial assets. Because each international exchange generates both an inflow and an outflow, the sum of the balances on the two accounts must equal zero.*

32.2 Explain the demand for and supply of foreign exchange *From the perspective of the United States, the demand for another nation's currency by U.S. residents is derived largely from the demand for imports from that nation. Likewise, the supply of another nation's currency is derived mainly from the supply of U.S. exports to that country.*

32.3 Outline how exchange rates are determined in the markets for foreign exchange and discuss factors that can induce changes in equilibrium exchange rates *The equilibrium exchange rate is the rate of exchange between the dollar and the other nation's currency at which the quantity of the currency demanded is equal to the quantity supplied. The equilibrium exchange rate changes in response to changes in the demand for or supply of another nation's currency. Changes in desired flows of exports or imports, real interest rates, tastes and preferences of consumers, and perceptions of economic stability affect the positions of the demand and supply curves in foreign exchange markets and induce variations in equilibrium exchange rates.*

32.4 Understand how policymakers can go about attempting to fix exchange rates *If the current price of the home currency in terms of another nation's currency starts to fall below the level at which the home country wants it to remain, the home country's central bank can use its reserves of the other nation's currency to purchase the home currency in foreign exchange markets. This raises the demand for the home currency and thereby pushes up the currency's value in terms of the other nation's currency.*

KEY TERMS

balance of trade, 692
balance of payments, 692
accounting identities, 692
current account, 694
financial account, 695
Key Figure
Figure 32-1, 696

foreign exchange market, 697
exchange rate, 697
flexible exchange rates, 698
appreciation, 698
depreciation, 698
Key Figures
Figure 32-2, 699
Figure 32-3, 701

Key Figures
Figure 32-4, 702
Figure 32-5, 703
Figure 32-6, 704

par value, 705
foreign exchange risk, 706
hedge, 707
Key Figure
Figure 32-8, 706

PROBLEMS

32-1. Suppose that during a recent year for the United States, merchandise imports were $2 trillion, unilateral transfers were a net outflow of $0.2 trillion, service exports were $0.2 trillion, service imports were $0.1 trillion, and merchandise exports were $1.4 trillion.

   a. What was the merchandise trade deficit?

   b. What was the balance on goods and services?

   c. What was the current account balance?

32-2. Suppose that during a recent year for the United States, the current account balance was −$0.5 trillion, and the net acquisitions of financial assets by U.S. residents and government entities was +$0.1 trillion.

   a. What was the balance on the financial account during the year?

   b. What was the net incurrence of financial liabilities by U.S. residents and government entities during the year?

32-3. Over the course of a year, a nation tracked its foreign transactions and arrived at the following amounts:

Merchandise exports	500
Service exports	75
Net unilateral transfers	10
Net change in domestic liabilities abroad (financial outflows)	−215
Net change in foreign assets at home (financial inflows)	300
Merchandise imports	600
Service imports	50

What are this nation's balance of trade, current account balance, and financial account balance?

32-4. Identify whether each of the following items creates a surplus item or a deficit item in the current account of the U.S. balance of payments.

a. A Central European company sells products to a U.S. hobby-store chain.

b. Japanese residents pay a U.S. travel company to arrange hotel stays, ground transportation, and tours of various U.S. cities, including New York, Chicago, and Orlando.

c. A Mexican company pays a U.S. accounting firm to audit its income statements.

d. U.S. churches and mosques send relief aid to Pakistan following a major earthquake in that nation.

e. A U.S. microprocessor manufacturer purchases raw materials from a Canadian firm.

32-5. Explain how the following events would affect the market for the Mexican peso, assuming a floating exchange rate.

a. Improvements in Mexican production technology yield superior guitars, and many musicians around the world buy these guitars.

b. Perceptions of political instability surrounding regular elections in Mexico make international investors nervous about future business prospects in Mexico.

32-6. Explain how the following events would affect the market for South Africa's currency, the *rand*, assuming a floating exchange rate.

a. A rise in U.S. inflation causes many U.S. residents to seek to buy gold, which is a major South African export good, as a hedge against inflation.

b. Major discoveries of the highest-quality diamonds ever found occur in Russia and Central Asia, causing a significant decline in purchases of South African diamonds.

32-7. Suppose that the following two events take place in the market for China's currency, the *yuan*: U.S. parents are more willing than before to buy action figures and other Chinese toy exports, and China's government tightens restrictions on the amount of U.S. dollar-denominated financial assets that Chinese residents may legally purchase. What happens to the dollar price of the yuan? Does the yuan appreciate or depreciate relative to the dollar?

32-8. On Wednesday, the exchange rate between the Japanese yen and the U.S. dollar was $0.010 per yen. On Thursday, it was $0.009. Did the dollar appreciate or depreciate against the yen? By how much, expressed as a percentage change?

32-9. On Wednesday, the exchange rate between the euro and the U.S. dollar was $1.12 per euro, and the exchange rate between the Canadian dollar and the U.S. dollar was U.S. $0.76 per Canadian dollar. What is the exchange rate between the Canadian dollar and the euro?

32-10. Suppose that signs of an improvement in the Japanese economy lead international investors to resume lending to the Japanese government and businesses. How would this event affect the market for the yen? How should the central bank, the Bank of Japan, respond to this event if it wants to keep the value of the yen unchanged?

32-11. Briefly explain the differences between a flexible exchange rate system and a fixed exchange rate system.

32-12. Suppose that under a gold standard, the U.S. dollar is pegged to gold at a rate of $35 per ounce and the pound sterling is pegged to gold at a rate of £17.50 per ounce. Explain how the gold standard constitutes an exchange rate arrangement between the dollar and the pound. What is the exchange rate between the U.S. dollar and the pound sterling?

32-13. Suppose that under the Bretton Woods system, the dollar is pegged to gold at a rate of $35 per ounce and the pound sterling is pegged to the dollar at a rate of $2 = £1. If the dollar is devalued against gold and the pegged rate is changed to $40 per ounce, what does this imply for the exchange value of the pound in terms of dollars?

32-14. Suppose that the People's Bank of China wishes to peg the rate of exchange of its currency, the yuan, in terms of the U.S. dollar. In each of the following situations, should it add to or subtract from its dollar foreign exchange reserves? Why?

a. U.S. parents worrying about safety begin buying fewer Chinese-made toys for their children.

b. U.S. interest rates rise relative to interest rates in China, so Chinese residents seek to purchase additional U.S. financial assets.

c. Chinese furniture manufacturers produce high-quality early American furniture and successfully export large quantities of the furniture to the United States.

32-15. At the point *E* in Figure 32-4, how many dollars per year are traded for the equilibrium quantity of pounds?

32-16. Take a look at Figure 32-5. Suppose that in response to a significant rise in interest in Jane Austen's works and life, millions of U.S. residents suddenly purchase British-published books by and about the famous author and travel to Britain to visit Jane Austen's former home. What will happen to the equilibrium dollar price of the pound, and why? Does the dollar appreciate or depreciate in relation to the pound?

32-17. Consider Figure 32-5. Suppose that the real interest rate in Britain increases relative to the U.S. real interest rate. What will happen to the equilibrium dollar price of the pound, and why? Does the dollar appreciate or depreciate in relation to the pound?

32-18. Take a look at Figure 32-6. Suppose that the preferences of most British residents alter toward purchasing more downloaded online streaming videos of Hollywood movies distributed by U.S. firms. What will happen to the equilibrium dollar price of the pound, and why? Does the dollar appreciate or depreciate in relation to the pound?

32-19. Consider Figure 32-6. A sudden increase in economic and political instability throughout Europe and Asia has caused the United States to appear to British residents to be economically and politically relatively more stable than was previously the case. What will happen to the equilibrium dollar price of the pound, and why? Does the dollar appreciate or depreciate in relation to the pound?

32-20. Suppose that initially in Figure 32-8, the market for Bahrain's currency, the dinar, is in equilibrium at point E_1. Now, however, an increase in the U.S. real interest rate has occurred even as real interest rates in Bahrain and elsewhere in the world either have declined or have remained unchanged. What must Bahrain's central bank do, and why, if it wishes to maintain a fixed exchange rate?

REFERENCES

INTERNATIONAL EXAMPLE: The Non-U.S. Derived Demand for and Supply of U.S. Dollars

Kimberly Amadeo, "Why the U.S. Dollar Is the Global Currency," The Balance (https://www.thebalance.com/world-currency-3305931), January 28, 2019.

Linda Goldberg and Robert Lerman, "The U.S. Dollar's Global Roles: Where Do Things Stand?" *Liberty Street Economics*, Federal Reserve Bank of New York, February 11, 2019.

Daniel Moss, "Currency That Matters Most Is Still the Dollar," *Bloomberg*, August 23, 2018.

INTERNATIONAL POLICY EXAMPLE: African Governments with Dollar-Denominated Debts Confront Foreign Exchange Depreciations

James Anyanzwa, "Loan Repayments Could Cripple African Countries' Growth Prospects," *East African*, January 21, 2019.

"Increasing Debt in Many African Countries Is a Cause for Worry," *Economist*, March 8, 2018.

Rafiq Raji, "Africa's New Debt Binge: What Are the Risks?" *African Business*, April 16, 2018.

AI—DECISION MAKING THROUGH DATA: Foreign Exchange Markets Involving Really Big Data

Warren Venketas, "Forex Market Size: A Trader's Advantage," DailyFX.com (https://www.dailyfx.com/forex/education/trading_tips/daily_trading_lesson/2019/01/15/forex-market-size-.html), January 15, 2019.

Ryan Daws, "AI Defeats Humans in Predicting ForEx," *Artificial Intelligence News*, February 1, 2018.

Jackie Edwards, "How Machine Learning Can Help Reduce Foreign Exchange Risk," *Inside Big Data*, March 18, 2018.

ECONOMICS IN YOUR LIFE: The Hong Kong Monetary Authority Acts to Keep Its Currency's Exchange Rate Fixed

Kimberly Amadeo, "The Dollar Peg, How It Works and Why It's Done," The Balance (https://www.thebalance.com/what-is-a-peg-to-the-dollar-3305925), January 7, 2019.

Saumya Vaishampayan, "The Weakest Link: Hong Kong Dollar Hits Trading-Band Floor," *Wall Street Journal*, April 12, 2018.

Karen Yeung, "Hong Kong Monetary Authority Intervenes in Currency Market for First Time since May," *South China Morning Post*, August 15, 2018.

ISSUES & APPLICATIONS: How Changing a Fixed Exchange Rate to Try to *Absorb* Shocks Eventually Can *Cause* Shocks

Mayela Armas and Corina Pons, "Venezuela Approves Parallel Currency Exchange System Amid Political Crisis," Reuters (https://www.reuters.com/article/us-venezuela-economy/venezuela-approves-parallel-currency-exchange-system-amid-political-crisis-idUSKCN1PM2AA), January 28, 2019.

Rachelle Krygier and Anthony Faiola, "Venezuela Is Swept by Economic Chaos as Currency Plan Takes Effect," *Washington Post*, August 21, 2018.

Eduardo Thomson and Fabiola Zerpa, "Venezuela Adds to Chaos with One of the Biggest Currency Devaluations Ever," *Bloomberg*, August 19, 2018.

National Income Accounts and Real GDP Since 1929*

In this table, in which all amounts are in billions of dollars, we see historical data for the various components of nominal GDP. These are given in the first four columns. We then show the rest of the national income accounts going from GDP to NDP to NI to PI to DPI. The last column gives real GDP.

	The Sum of Expenditures				Equals	Less	Equals	Plus	Less	Equals	Less			Plus	Equals	Less	Equals	
Year	Personal Consumption Expenditures	Gross Private Domestic Investment	Government Purchases of Goods and Services	Net Exports	Gross Domestic Product	Depreciation	Net Domestic Product	Net U.S. Income Earned Abroad	Statistical Discrepancy	National Income	Corporate Profits	Social Security Taxes	Taxes on Production and Imports Net of Subsidies	Net Transfers and Interest Earnings	Personal Income	Personal Income Taxes and Nontax Payments	Disposable Personal Income	Real GDP (2012 Dollars)
1929	77.4	17.2	9.6	0.4	104.6	10.4	94.2	0.7	−0.7	94.2	10.5	0.1	12.6	14.3	85.3	1.7	83.6	1109.4
1933	45.9	2.3	8.9	0.1	57.2	8.0	49.2	0.3	−0.6	48.9	−1.2	0.1	15.9	13.1	47.2	0.8	46.4	817.3
1940	71.3	14.6	15.6	1.4	102.9	10.6	92.3	0.3	−1.1	91.5	2.0	1.9	26.2	18.0	79.4	1.7	77.7	1330.2
1944	108.6	9.2	108.6	−2.0	224.4	21.3	203.1	0.4	−2.6	200.9	23.8	4.3	33.7	30.6	169.7	17.6	152.1	2351.6
1950	192.1	56.5	50.5	0.7	299.8	33.4	266.4	1.5	−1.3	266.6	37.7	5.3	42.0	52.1	233.7	18.9	214.8	2289.5
1955	258.3	73.8	93.0	0.4	425.5	48.9	376.6	2.6	−2.3	376.9	46.9	8.8	55.1	58.1	324.2	32.9	291.3	2871.2
1960	331.2	86.5	120.5	4.2	542.4	67.9	474.5	3.1	1.3	478.9	49.9	16.0	54.1	63.2	422.1	46.0	376.1	3260.0
1965	443.8	129.6	164.1	4.8	742.3	88.0	654.3	5.3	−0.8	658.8	76.1	22.7	64.7	75.4	570.7	57.7	513.0	4170.8
1970	646.7	170.1	252.6	3.9	1073.3	136.8	936.5	6.4	−5.4	937.5	86.2	45.5	86.6	145.8	865.0	103.0	762.0	4951.3
1976	1147.7	323.2	404.2	−1.6	1873.4	260.3	1613.1	16.8	−20.6	1609.4	174.3	99.8	141.3	308.7	1502.6	172.7	1330.0	5949.0
1977	1274.0	396.6	434.3	−23.1	2081.8	289.8	1792.0	20.3	−19.5	1792.8	205.8	111.1	152.6	335.9	1659.2	197.9	1461.4	6224.1
1978	1422.3	478.4	476.3	−25.4	2351.6	327.1	2024.5	21.6	−23.4	2022.7	238.6	128.7	162.0	370.4	1863.7	229.6	1634.1	6568.6
1979	1585.4	539.7	524.8	−22.5	2627.3	373.8	2253.5	31.9	−45.1	2240.3	249.0	149.8	171.6	412.7	2082.7	268.9	1813.8	6776.6
1980	1750.7	530.1	589.6	−13.1	2857.3	428.4	2428.9	34.2	−44.5	2418.6	223.6	163.6	190.5	482.8	2323.6	299.5	2024.1	6759.2
1981	1934.0	631.2	654.4	−12.5	3207.0	487.2	2719.8	32.9	−38.1	2714.7	247.5	193.0	224.2	555.2	2605.1	345.8	2259.3	6930.7
1982	2071.3	581.0	711.5	−20.0	3343.8	537.0	2806.8	36.5	−8.8	2834.5	229.9	206.0	225.9	619.0	2791.6	354.7	2436.9	6805.8
1983	2281.6	637.5	766.6	−51.6	3634.0	563.1	3070.9	37.1	−56.5	3051.5	279.8	223.1	242.0	674.4	2981.1	352.9	2628.2	7117.7
1984	2492.3	820.1	827.9	−102.7	4037.6	598.7	3438.9	36.3	−41.3	3433.9	337.9	254.1	268.7	719.5	3292.7	377.9	2914.8	7632.8
1985	2712.8	829.7	910.5	−114.0	4339.0	640.3	3698.7	25.4	−54.1	3669.9	354.5	277.9	286.9	774.3	3524.9	417.8	3107.1	7951.1
1986	2886.3	849.1	976.1	−131.9	4579.6	685.1	3894.5	17.0	−80.2	3812.2	324.4	298.9	298.5	823.7	3733.1	437.8	3295.3	8226.4
1987	3076.3	892.2	1031.5	−144.8	4855.2	730.1	4125.1	17.5	−44.1	4098.5	366.0	317.4	317.3	863.8	3961.6	489.6	3472.0	8511.0
1988	3330.0	937.0	1078.9	−109.4	5236.4	784.4	4452.0	22.7	−3.1	4471.6	414.9	354.8	345.0	926.5	4283.4	505.9	3777.5	8866.5
1989	3576.8	999.7	1151.9	−86.7	5641.6	838.3	4803.3	24.8	−67.9	4760.1	414.2	378.0	371.4	1029.0	4625.6	567.7	4057.9	9192.1
1990	3809.0	993.4	1238.6	−77.9	5963.1	888.6	5074.5	34.7	−95.5	5013.8	417.2	402.0	398.0	1117.3	4913.8	594.7	4319.1	9365.5

Note: Some rows may not add up due to rounding.

	The Sum of Expenditures				Equals	Less	Equals	Plus	Less	Equals	Less			Plus	Equals	Less	Equals	
Year	Personal Consumption Expenditures	Gross Private Domestic Investment	Government Purchases of Goods and Services	Net Exports	Gross Domestic Product	Depreciation	Net Domestic Product	Net U.S. Income Earned Abroad	Statistical Discrepancy	National Income	Corporate Profits	Social Security Taxes	Taxes on Production and Imports Net of Subsidies	Net Transfers and Interest Earnings	Personal Income	Personal Income Taxes and Nontax Payments	Disposable Personal Income	Real GDP (2012 Dollars)
1991	3943.4	944.3	1299.0	−28.6	6158.1	932.4	5225.7	31.6	−93.0	5164.4	451.3	420.6	429.6	1222.1	5084.9	588.9	4496.0	9355.4
1992	4197.6	1013.0	1344.5	−34.7	6520.3	960.3	5560.0	31.1	−115.9	5475.2	475.3	444.0	453.3	1318.2	5420.9	612.8	4808.1	9684.9
1993	4452.0	1106.8	1364.9	−65.2	6858.6	1003.3	5855.3	31.2	−156.1	5730.3	522.0	465.5	466.4	1381.6	5657.9	648.8	5009.2	9951.5
1994	4721.0	1256.5	1402.3	−92.5	7287.2	1055.6	6231.6	23.0	−140.0	6114.6	621.9	496.2	512.7	1463.2	5947.1	693.1	5254.0	10352.4
1995	4962.6	1317.5	1449.4	−89.8	7639.7	1122.4	6517.3	28.0	−93.0	6452.3	703.0	521.9	523.1	1587.1	6291.4	748.4	5543.0	10630.3
1996	5244.6	1432.1	1492.8	−96.4	8073.1	1175.3	6897.8	30.9	−58.1	6870.6	786.1	545.4	545.5	1684.9	6678.5	837.1	5841.4	11031.4
1997	5536.8	1595.6	1547.1	−102.0	8577.6	1239.1	7338.5	23.3	−11.8	7349.9	865.8	579.4	577.8	1765.6	7092.5	931.8	6160.7	11521.9
1998	5877.2	1736.7	1611.6	−162.7	9062.8	1309.7	7753.1	17.4	55.2	7825.7	804.1	617.4	603.1	1805.5	7606.7	1032.4	6574.2	12038.3
1999	6279.1	1887.1	1720.4	−255.8	9630.7	1399.0	8231.7	25.5	33.2	8290.4	830.2	654.8	628.4	1824.9	8001.9	1111.9	6890.0	12610.5
2000	6761.1	2038.4	1826.8	−375.1	10252.3	1511.0	8741.3	35.0	96.3	8872.6	781.2	698.6	662.7	1922.4	8652.6	1236.3	7416.3	13131.0
2001	7065.6	1934.8	1949.3	−367.9	10581.8	1599.9	8981.9	48.8	113.5	9144.2	754.0	723.3	669.0	2007.7	9005.6	1239.0	7766.6	13262.1
2002	7342.7	1930.4	2088.7	−425.4	10936.4	1658.0	9278.4	45.2	72.7	9396.4	907.2	739.4	721.2	2130.4	9159.0	1052.2	8106.8	13493.1
2003	7723.1	2027.1	2211.2	−503.1	11458.2	1719.2	9739.0	58.4	13.8	9811.2	1056.4	763.3	758.9	2254.9	9487.5	1003.5	8484.0	13879.1
2004	8212.7	2281.3	2338.9	−619.1	12213.7	1821.6	10392.1	78.2	21.8	10492.2	1283.3	809.0	817.6	2452.8	10035.1	1048.7	8986.4	14406.4
2005	8747.1	2534.7	2476.0	−721.2	13036.6	1970.9	11065.7	78.0	55.0	11198.7	1477.7	853.4	873.6	2604.3	10598.2	1212.4	9385.8	14912.5
2006	9260.3	2701.0	2624.2	−770.9	13814.6	2124.0	11690.6	50.4	207.8	11948.8	1646.5	905.7	940.5	2925.5	11381.7	1356.8	10024.9	15338.3
2007	9706.4	2673.0	2790.8	−718.4	14451.9	2252.0	12199.9	109.0	−18.5	12290.4	1529.0	947.3	980.0	3173.7	12007.8	1492.2	10515.6	15626.0
2008	9976.3	2477.6	2982.0	−723.1	14712.8	2358.8	12354.0	154.6	−182.9	12325.8	1285.1	974.5	989.4	3365.4	12442.2	1107.6	10935.0	15604.7
2009	9842.2	1929.7	3073.5	−396.5	14448.9	2371.5	12077.4	141.9	−192.1	12027.2	1386.8	950.7	968.5	3337.8	12059.1	1152.0	10907.1	15208.8
2010	10185.8	2165.5	3154.6	−513.9	14992.1	2390.9	12601.2	195.7	−61.1	12735.8	1728.7	970.9	1007.3	3522.7	12551.6	1237.3	11314.3	15598.8
2011	10641.1	2332.6	3148.4	−579.5	15542.6	2474.4	13068.2	236.4	53.2	13357.7	1809.8	903.2	1043.7	3725.7	13326.8	1453.2	11873.6	15840.7
2012	11006.8	2621.8	3137.0	−568.6	16197.0	2575.9	13621.1	232.3	241.2	14094.7	1997.4	938.0	1078.1	3928.9	14010.1	1508.9	12501.2	16197.0
2013	11317.2	2826.0	3132.4	−490.8	16784.9	2681.2	14103.7	230.7	160.3	14494.7	2010.7	1091.8	1129.0	3917.9	14181.1	1675.8	12505.3	16495.4
2014	11824.0	3038.9	3167.0	−508.3	17521.7	2816.9	14704.8	241.7	298.9	15245.5	2118.8	1140.3	1182.8	4188.3	14991.8	1785.4	13206.4	16899.8
2015	12294.5	3212.0	3234.2	−521.4	18219.3	2917.4	15301.9	226.2	254.9	15783.0	2057.3	1191.4	1212.6	4397.8	15719.5	1935.2	13784.3	17386.7
2016	12766.9	3169.9	3291.0	−520.6	18707.2	2990.5	15716.7	215.3	126.9	16058.9	2035.0	1225.0	1241.9	4568.1	16125.1	1954.3	14170.9	17659.2
2017	13321.4	3368.0	3374.4	−578.4	19485.4	3116.2	16369.2	243.7	143.2	16756.1	2099.3	1283.2	1285.9	4743.3	16830.9	2034.6	14796.3	18050.7
2018	13948.5	3650.1	3520.8	−618.8	20500.6	3280.1	17220.5	254.8	68.6	17544.0	2260.7	1344.8	1362.2	5006.0	17582.4	2050.3	15532.1	18571.3
2019a	14506.5	3796.1	3661.7	−643.5	21320.7	3411.3	17909.4	265.0	71.4	18245.8	2351.1	1398.6	1416.7	5206.3	18285.7	2132.3	16153.4	18942.7
2020a	15086.7	3947.9	3808.1	−669.2	22173.5	3547.8	18625.7	275.6	74.2	18975.6	2445.2	1454.5	1473.4	5414.5	19017.1	2217.6	16799.5	19321.7

a = Author's estimates

GLOSSARY

A

Absolute advantage The ability to produce more units of a good or service using a given quantity of labor or resource inputs. Equivalently, the ability to produce the same quantity of a good or service using fewer units of labor or resource inputs.

Accounting identities Values that are equivalent by definition.

Accounting profit Total revenues minus total explicit costs.

Action time lag The time between recognizing an economic problem and implementing policy to solve it. The action time lag is quite long for fiscal policy, which requires congressional approval.

Active (discretionary) policymaking All actions on the part of monetary and fiscal policymakers that are undertaken in response to or in anticipation of some change in the overall economy.

Ad valorem **taxation** Assessing taxes by charging a tax rate equal to a fraction of the market price of each unit purchased.

Adverse selection The tendency for high-risk projects and clients to be overrepresented among borrowers.

Age-earnings cycle The regular earnings profile of an individual throughout his or her lifetime. The age-earnings cycle usually starts with a low income, builds gradually to a peak at around age 50, and then gradually curves down until it approaches zero at retirement.

Aggregate demand The total of all planned expenditures in the entire economy.

Aggregate demand curve A curve showing planned purchase rates for all final goods and services in the economy at various price levels, all other things held constant.

Aggregate demand shock Any event that causes the aggregate demand curve to shift inward or outward.

Aggregate supply The total of all planned production for the economy.

Aggregate supply shock Any event that causes the aggregate supply curve to shift inward or outward.

Aggregates Total amounts or quantities. Aggregate demand, for example, is total planned expenditures throughout a nation.

Anticipated inflation The inflation rate that we believe will occur. When it does occur, we are in a situation of fully anticipated inflation.

Antitrust legislation Laws that restrict the formation of monopolies and regulate certain anticompetitive business practices.

Appreciation An increase in the exchange value of one nation's currency in terms of the currency of another nation.

Artificial intelligence (AI) technologies The development and implementation of methods of utilizing automated data-analytics techniques, machine learning, or virtual- or augmented-reality techniques to examine and evaluate information in an effort to help consumers, businesses, and governments to make decisions.

Asset demand Holding money as a store of value instead of other assets such as corporate bonds and stocks.

Assets Amounts owned; all items to which a business or household holds legal claim.

Asymmetric information Information possessed by one party in a financial transaction but not by the other party.

Automatic, or built-in, stabilizers Special provisions of certain federal programs that cause changes in desired aggregate expenditures without the action of Congress and the president. Examples are the federal progressive tax system and unemployment compensation.

Autonomous consumption The part of consumption that is independent of (does not depend on) the level of disposable income. Changes in autonomous consumption shift the consumption function.

Average fixed costs Total fixed costs divided by the number of units produced.

Average product Total product divided by the variable input.

Average propensity to consume (APC) Real consumption divided by real disposable income. For any given level of real income, the proportion of total real disposable income that is consumed.

Average propensity to save (APS) Real saving divided by real disposable income. For any given level of real income, the proportion of total real disposable income that is saved.

Average tax rate The total tax payment divided by total income. It is the proportion of total income paid in taxes.

Average total costs Total costs divided by the number of units produced.

Average variable costs Total variable costs divided by the number of units produced.

B

Balance of payments A system of accounts that measures transactions of goods, services, income, and financial assets between domestic households, businesses, and governments and residents of the rest of the world during a specific time period.

Balance of trade The difference between exports and imports of physical goods.

Balance sheet A statement of the assets and liabilities of any business entity, including financial institutions and the Federal Reserve System. Assets are what is owned; liabilities are what is owed.

Balanced budget A situation in which the government's spending is exactly equal to the total taxes and other revenues it collects during a given period of time.

Bank run Attempt by many of a bank's depositors to convert transactions and time deposits into currency out of fear that the bank's liabilities may exceed its assets.

Barter The direct exchange of goods and services for other goods and services without the use of money.

Base year The year that is chosen as the point of reference for comparison of prices in other years.

Base-year dollars The value of a current sum expressed in terms of prices in a base year.

Behavioral economics An approach to the study of consumer behavior that emphasizes psychological limitations and complications that potentially interfere with rational decision making.

Bilateral monopoly A market structure consisting of a monopolist and a monopsonist.

Black market A market in which goods are traded at prices above their legal maximum prices or in which illegal goods are sold.

Bond A legal claim against a firm, usually entitling the owner of the bond to receive a fixed annual coupon payment, plus a lump-sum payment at the bond's maturity date. Bonds are issued in return for funds lent to the firm.

Bounded rationality The hypothesis that people are *nearly*, but not fully, rational, so that they cannot examine every possible choice available to them but instead use simple rules of thumb to sort among the alternatives that happen to occur to them.

Budget constraint All of the possible combinations of goods that can be purchased (at fixed prices) with a specific budget.

Bundling Offering two or more products for sale as a set.

Business fluctuations The ups and downs in business activity throughout the economy.

C

Capital consumption allowance Another name for depreciation, the amount that businesses would have to put aside in order to take care of deteriorating machines and other equipment.

Capital gain A positive difference between the purchase price and the sale price of an asset. If a share of stock is bought for $5 and then sold for $15, the capital gain is $10.

Capital goods Producer durables; non-consumable goods that firms use to make other goods.

Capital loss A negative difference between the purchase price and the sale price of an asset.

Capture hypothesis A theory of regulatory behavior that predicts that regulators will eventually be captured by special interests of the industry being regulated.

Cartel An association of producers in an industry that agree to set common prices and output quotas to prevent competition.

Central bank A banker's bank, usually an official institution that also serves as a bank for a nation's government treasury. Central banks normally regulate commercial banks.

Ceteris paribus [KAY-ter-us PEAR-uh-bus] **assumption** The assumption that nothing changes except the factor or factors being studied.

Ceteris paribus **conditions** Determinants of the relationship between price and quantity that are unchanged along a curve. Changes in these factors cause the curve to shift.

Closed shop A business enterprise in which employees must belong to the union before they can be hired and must remain in the union after they are hired.

Collective bargaining Negotiation between the management of a company and the management of a union for the purpose of reaching a mutually agreeable contract that sets wages, fringe benefits, and working conditions for all employees in all the unions involved.

Collective decision making How voters, politicians, and other interested parties act and how these actions influence nonmarket decisions.

Common property Property that is owned by everyone and therefore by no one.

Air and water are examples of common property resources.

Comparative advantage The ability to produce a good or service at a lower opportunity cost than other producers.

Complements Two goods are complements when a change in the price of one causes an opposite shift in the demand for the other.

Concentration ratio The percentage of all sales contributed by the leading four or leading eight firms in an industry; sometimes called the *industry concentration ratio*.

Constant dollars Dollars expressed in terms of real purchasing power, using a particular year as the base or standard of comparison, in contrast to current dollars.

Constant returns to scale No change in long-run average costs when output increases.

Constant-cost industry An industry whose total output can be increased in the long run without an increase in input prices. Its long-run supply curve is horizontal.

Consumer optimum A choice of a set of goods and services that maximizes the level of satisfaction for each consumer, subject to limited income.

Consumer Price Index (CPI) A statistical measure of a weighted average of prices of a specified set of goods and services purchased by typical consumers in urban areas.

Consumer surplus The difference between the total amount that consumers would have been willing to pay for an item and the total amount that they actually pay.

Consumption Spending on new goods and services to be used up out of a household's current income. Whatever is not consumed is saved. Consumption includes such things as buying food and going to a concert. *Also*, the use of goods and services for personal satisfaction.

Consumption function The relationship between amount consumed and disposable income. A consumption function tells us how much people plan to consume at various levels of disposable income.

Consumption goods Goods bought by households to use up, such as food and movies.

Contraction A business fluctuation during which the pace of national economic activity is slowing down.

Cooperative game A game in which the players explicitly cooperate to make themselves jointly better off. As applied to firms, it involves companies colluding in order to make higher than perfectly competitive rates of return.

Corporation A legal entity that may conduct business in its own name just as an individual does. The owners of a corporation, called shareholders, own shares of the firm's profits and have the protection of limited liability.

Cost-of-living adjustments (COLAs) Clauses in contracts that allow for increases in specified nominal values to take account of changes in the cost of living.

Cost-of-service regulation Regulation that allows prices to reflect only the actual average cost of production and no monopoly profits.

Cost-push inflation Inflation caused by decreases in short-run aggregate supply.

Creative response Behavior on the part of a firm that allows it to comply with the letter of the law but violate the spirit, significantly lessening the law's effects.

Credence good A product with qualities that consumers lack the expertise to assess without assistance.

Credit policy Federal Reserve policymaking involving direct lending to financial and nonfinancial firms.

Cross price elasticity of demand (E_{xy}) The percentage change in the amount of an item demanded (holding its price constant) divided by the percentage change in the price of a related good.

Crowding-out effect The tendency of expansionary fiscal policy to cause a decrease in planned investment or planned consumption in the private sector. This decrease normally results from the rise in interest rates.

Cumulative fiscal multiplier The multiplier effect of a fiscal policy action that applies to a long-run period after all influences on equilibrium real GDP have been taken into account.

Current account A category of balance of payments transactions that measures the exchange of merchandise, the exchange of services, and unilateral transfers.

Cyclical unemployment Unemployment resulting from business recessions that occur when aggregate (total) demand is insufficient to create full employment.

D

Dead capital Any capital resource that lacks clear title of ownership.

Deadweight loss The portion of consumer surplus that no one in society is able to obtain in a situation of monopoly.

Decreasing-cost industry An industry in which an increase in output in the long run leads to a reduction in input prices, such that the long-run industry supply curve slopes downward.

Deflation A sustained decrease in the average of all prices of goods and services in an economy.

Demand A schedule showing how much of a good or service people will purchase at any price during a specified time period, other things being constant.

Demand curve A graphical representation of the demand schedule. It is a negatively sloped line showing the inverse relationship between the price and the quantity demanded (other things being equal).

Demand-pull inflation Inflation caused by increases in aggregate demand not matched by increases in aggregate supply.

Dependent variable A variable whose value changes according to changes in the value of one or more independent variables.

Depository institutions Financial institutions that accept deposits from savers and lend funds from those deposits out at interest.

Depreciation A decrease in the exchange value of one nation's currency in terms of the currency of another nation. *Also,* a reduction in the value of capital goods over a one-year period due to physical wear and tear and obsolescence; also called *capital consumption allowance.*

Depression An extremely severe recession.

Derived demand Input factor demand derived from demand for the final product being produced.

Development economics The study of factors that contribute to the economic growth of a country.

Diminishing marginal utility The principle that as more of any good or service is consumed, its *extra* benefit declines. Otherwise stated, increases in total utility from the consumption of a good or service become smaller and smaller as more is consumed during a given time period.

Direct expenditure offsets Actions on the part of the private sector in spending income that offset government fiscal policy actions. Any increase in government spending in an area that competes with the private sector will have some direct expenditure offset.

Direct marketing Advertising targeted at specific consumers, typically in the form of postal mailings, telephone calls, or e-mail messages.

Direct relationship A relationship between two variables that is positive, meaning that an increase in one variable is associated with an increase in the other and a decrease in one variable is associated with a decrease in the other.

Discount rate The interest rate that the Federal Reserve charges for reserves that it lends to depository institutions. It is

sometimes referred to as the *rediscount rate* or, in Canada and England, as the *bank rate.*

Discounting The method by which the present value of a future sum or a future stream of sums is obtained.

Discouraged workers Individuals who have stopped looking for a job because they are convinced that they will not find a suitable one.

Diseconomies of scale Increases in long-run average costs that occur as output increases.

Disposable personal income (DPI) Personal income after personal income taxes have been paid.

Dissaving Negative saving; a situation in which spending exceeds income. Dissaving can occur when a household is able to borrow or use up existing assets.

Distribution of income The way income is allocated among the population based on groupings of residents.

Dividends Portion of a corporation's profits paid to its owners (shareholders).

Division of labor The segregation of resources into different specific tasks. For instance, one digital-device assembler inserts touchscreen connectors, another attaches the screen, and so on.

Dominant strategies Strategies that always yield the highest benefit. Regardless of what other players do, a dominant strategy will yield the most benefit for the player using it.

Dumping Selling a good or a service abroad below the price charged in the home market or at a price below its cost of production.

Durable consumer goods Consumer goods that have a life span of more than three years.

Dynamic tax analysis Economic evaluation of tax rate changes that recognizes that the tax base declines with ever-higher tax rates, so that tax revenues may eventually decline if the tax rate is raised sufficiently.

E

Economic freedom The rights to own private property and to exchange goods, services, and financial assets with minimal government interference.

Economic goods Goods that are scarce, for which the quantity demanded exceeds the quantity supplied at a zero price.

Economic growth Increases in per capita real GDP measured by its rate of change per year.

Economic profits Total revenues minus total opportunity costs of all inputs used, or the total of all implicit and explicit costs.

Economic rent A payment for the use of any resource over and above its opportunity cost.

Economic system A society's institutional mechanism for determining the way scarce resources are used to satisfy human desires.

Economics The study of how people allocate their limited resources to satisfy their unlimited wants.

Economies of scale Decreases in long-run average costs resulting from increases in output.

Effect time lag The time that elapses between the implementation of a policy and the results of that policy.

Efficiency The case in which a given level of inputs is used to produce the maximum output possible. Alternatively, the situation in which a given output is produced at minimum cost.

Effluent fee A charge to a polluter that gives the right to discharge into the air or water a certain amount of pollution; also called a *pollution tax.*

Elastic demand A demand relationship in which a given percentage change in price will result in a larger percentage change in quantity demanded.

Emerging nations Developing countries that have adopted policy changes that have generated sufficiently increased economic growth to move the nations closer to advanced-nation status.

Empirical Relying on real-world data in evaluating the usefulness of a model.

Endowments The various resources in an economy, including both physical resources and such human resources as ingenuity and management skills.

Entitlements Guaranteed benefits under a government program such as Social Security, Medicare, or Medicaid.

Entrepreneurship The component of human resources that performs the functions of raising capital; organizing, managing, and assembling other factors of production; making basic business policy decisions; and taking risks.

Equation of exchange The formula indicating that the number of monetary units (M_s) times the number of times each unit is spent on final goods and services (V) is identical to the price level (P) times real GDP (Y).

Equilibrium The situation in which quantity supplied equals quantity demanded at a particular price.

Exchange rate The price of one nation's currency in terms of the currency of another country.

Excise tax A tax levied on purchases of a particular good or service.

Expansion A business fluctuation in which the pace of national economic activity is speeding up.

Expenditure approach Computing GDP by adding up the dollar value at current market prices of all final goods and services.

Experience good A product that an individual must consume before the product's quality can be established.

Explicit costs Costs that business managers must take account of because they must be paid. Examples are wages, taxes, and rent.

Externality A consequence of a diversion of a private cost (or benefit) from a social cost (or benefit). A situation in which the costs (or benefits) of an action are not fully borne (or gained) by the decision makers engaged in an activity that uses scarce resources. *Also,* a consequence of an economic activity that spills over to affect third parties. Pollution is an externality.

F

Federal Deposit Insurance Corporation (FDIC) A government agency that insures the deposits held in banks and most other depository institutions. All U.S. banks are insured this way.

Federal funds market A private market (made up mostly of banks) in which banks can borrow reserves from other banks that want to lend them. Federal funds are usually lent for overnight use.

Federal funds rate The interest rate that depository institutions pay to borrow reserves in the interbank federal funds market.

Fiduciary monetary system A system in which money is issued by the government and its value is based uniquely on the public's faith that the currency represents command over goods and services and will be accepted in payment for debts.

Final goods and services Goods and services that are at their final stage of production and will not be transformed into yet other goods or services. For example, wheat ordinarily is not considered a final good because it is usually used to make a final good, bread.

Financial account A category of balance of payments transactions that measures flows of financial assets.

Financial capital Funds used to purchase physical capital goods, such as buildings and equipment, and patents and trademarks.

Financial intermediaries Institutions that transfer funds between ultimate lenders (savers) and ultimate borrowers.

Financial intermediation The process by which financial institutions accept savings from businesses, households, and governments and lend the savings to other businesses, households, and governments.

Firm A business organization that employs resources to produce goods or services for profit. A firm normally owns and operates at least one "plant" or facility in order to produce.

Fiscal policy The discretionary changing of government expenditures or taxes to achieve national economic goals, such as high employment with price stability.

Fixed costs Costs that do not vary with output. Fixed costs typically include such expenses as rent on a building. These costs are fixed for a certain period of time (in the long run, though, they are variable).

Fixed investment Purchases by businesses of newly produced producer durables, or capital goods, such as production machinery and office equipment.

Flexible exchange rates Exchange rates that are allowed to fluctuate in the open market in response to changes in supply and demand. Sometimes called *floating exchange rates.*

Flow A quantity measured per unit of time; something that occurs over time, such as the income you make per week or per year or the number of individuals who are fired every month.

FOMC Directive A document that summarizes the Federal Open Market Committee's general policy strategy, establishes near-term objectives for the federal funds rate, and specifies target ranges for money supply growth.

Foreign direct investment The acquisition of more than 10 percent of the shares of ownership in a company in another nation.

Foreign exchange market A market in which households, firms, and governments buy and sell national currencies.

Foreign exchange rate The price of one currency in terms of another.

Foreign exchange risk The possibility that changes in the value of a nation's currency will result in variations in the market value of assets.

45-degree reference line The line along which planned real spending equals real GDP per year.

Fractional reserve banking A system in which depository institutions hold reserves that are less than the amount of total deposits.

Free-rider problem A problem that arises when individuals presume that others will pay for public goods so that, individually, they can escape paying for their portion without causing a reduction in production.

Frictional unemployment Unemployment due to the fact that workers must search for appropriate job offers. This activity takes time, and so they remain temporarily unemployed.

Full employment An arbitrary level of unemployment that corresponds to "normal" friction in the labor market.

G

Gains from trade The sum of consumer surplus and producer surplus.

Game theory A way of describing the various possible outcomes in any situation involving two or more interacting individuals when those individuals are aware of the interactive nature of their situation and plan accordingly. The plans made by these individuals are known as *game strategies.*

GDP deflator A price index measuring the changes in prices of all new goods and services produced in the economy.

General Agreement on Tariffs and Trade (GATT) An international agreement established in 1947 to further world trade by reducing barriers and tariffs. The GATT was replaced by the World Trade Organization in 1995.

Gini coefficient On a graph with the cumulative percentage of money income measured along the vertical axis and the cumulative percentage of households measured along the horizontal axis, if A is the area between the line of perfect income equality and the Lorenz curve and B is the area beneath the Lorenz curve, the Gini coefficient equals $A/(A + B)$.

Goods All things from which individuals derive satisfaction or happiness.

Government budget constraint The limit on government spending and transfers imposed by the fact that every dollar the government spends, transfers, or uses to repay borrowed funds must ultimately be provided by the user charges and taxes it collects.

Government budget deficit An excess of government spending over government revenues during a given period of time.

Government budget surplus An excess of government revenues over government spending during a given period of time.

Government, or political, goods Goods (and services) provided by the public sector; they can be either private or public goods.

Government-inhibited good A good that has been deemed socially undesirable through the political process. Heroin is an example.

Government-sponsored good A good that has been deemed socially desirable through the political process. Museums are an example.

Gross domestic income (GDI) The sum of all income—wages, interest, rent, and profits—paid to the four factors of production.

Gross domestic product (GDP) The total market value of all final goods and services produced during a year by factors of production located within a nation's borders.

Gross output The total market value of all goods and services produced during a year by factors of production located within a nation's borders, including all forms of business-to-business expenditures and thereby double counting business spending across all stages of production.

Gross private domestic investment The creation of capital goods, such as factories and machines, that can yield production and hence consumption in the future. Also included in this definition are changes in business inventories and repairs made to machines or buildings.

Gross public debt All federal government debt irrespective of who owns it.

H

Habit formation An inclination for household choices, such as decisions to purchase goods and services, to become automatic, or habitual, through frequent repetition.

Hedge A financial strategy that reduces the chance of suffering losses arising from foreign exchange risk.

Herfindahl-Hirschman Index (HHI) The sum of the squared percentage sales shares of all firms in an industry.

Horizontal merger The joining of firms that are producing or selling a similar product.

Human capital The accumulated training and education of workers.

I

Impact fiscal multiplier The actual immediate multiplier effect of a fiscal policy action after taking into consideration direct fiscal offsets and other short-term crowding out of private spending.

Implicit costs Expenses that managers do not have to pay out of pocket and hence normally do not explicitly calculate, such as the opportunity cost of factors of production that are owned. Examples are owner-provided capital and owner-provided labor.

Import quota A physical supply restriction on imports of a particular good, such as sugar. Foreign exporters are unable to sell in the United States more than the quantity specified in the import quota.

Incentive structure The system of rewards and punishments individuals face with respect to their own actions.

Incentives Rewards or penalties for engaging in a particular activity.

Income approach Measuring GDP by adding up all components of national income, including wages, interest, rent, and profits.

Income elasticity of demand (E_i) The percentage change in the amount of a good demanded, holding its price constant, divided by the percentage change in income. The responsiveness of the amount of a good demanded to a change in income, holding the good's relative price constant.

Income in kind Income received in the form of goods and services, such as housing or medical care. Income in kind differs from money income, which is simply income in dollars, or general purchasing power, that can be used to buy *any* goods and services.

Income velocity of money (V) The number of times per year a dollar is spent on final goods and services; identically equal to nominal GDP divided by the money supply.

Increasing-cost industry An industry in which a long-run increase in industry output is accompanied by an increase in input prices, such that the long-run industry supply curve slopes upward.

Independent variable A variable whose value is determined independently of, or outside, the equation under study.

Indifference curve A curve composed of a set of consumption alternatives, each of which yields the same total amount of satisfaction.

Industry supply curve The set of points showing the minimum prices at which given quantities will be forthcoming; also called the *market supply curve.*

Inefficient point Any point below the production possibilities curve, at which the use of resources is not generating the maximum possible output.

Inelastic demand A demand relationship in which a given percentage change in price will result in a less-than-proportionate percentage change in the quantity demanded.

Infant industry argument The contention that tariffs should be imposed to protect from import competition an industry that is trying to get started. Presumably, after the industry becomes technologically efficient, the tariff can be lifted.

Inferior goods Goods for which demand falls as income rises.

Inflation A sustained increase in the average of all prices of goods and services in an economy.

Inflationary gap The gap that exists whenever equilibrium real GDP per year is greater than full-employment real GDP, as shown by the position of the long-run aggregate supply curve.

Information product An item that is produced using information-intensive inputs at a relatively high fixed cost but distributed for sale at a relatively low marginal cost.

Informational advertising Advertising that emphasizes transmitting knowledge about the features of a product.

Innovation Transforming an invention into something that is useful to humans.

Inside information Information that is not available to the general public about what is happening in a corporation.

Interactive marketing Advertising that permits a consumer to follow up directly by searching for more information and placing direct product orders.

Interest The payment for current rather than future command over resources; the cost of obtaining credit.

Interest rate effect One of the reasons that the aggregate demand curve slopes downward: Higher price levels increase the interest rate, which in turn causes businesses and consumers to reduce desired spending due to the higher cost of borrowing.

Intermediate goods Goods used up entirely in the production of final goods.

International financial crisis The rapid withdrawal of foreign investments and loans from a nation.

International Monetary Fund (IMF) A multinational organization that aims to promote world economic growth through more financial stability.

Inventory investment Changes in the stocks of finished goods and goods in process, as well as changes in the raw materials that businesses keep on hand. Whenever inventories are decreasing, inventory investment is negative. Whenever they are increasing, inventory investment is positive.

Inverse relationship A relationship between two variables that is negative, meaning that an increase in one variable is associated with a decrease in the other and a decrease in one variable is associated with an increase in the other.

Investment Spending on items such as machines and buildings, which can be used to produce goods and services in the future. (It also includes changes in business inventories.) The investment part of real GDP is the portion that will be used in the process of producing goods *in the future.* *Also,* any use of today's resources to expand tomorrow's production or consumption.

J

Job leaver An individual in the labor force who quits voluntarily.

Job loser An individual in the labor force whose employment was involuntarily terminated.

K

Keynesian short-run aggregate supply curve The horizontal portion of the aggregate supply curve in which there is excessive unemployment and unused capacity in the economy.

L

Labor Productive contributions of humans who work.

Labor force Individuals aged 16 years or older who either have jobs or are looking and available for jobs; the number of employed plus the number of unemployed.

Labor force participation rate The percentage of noninstitutionalized working-age individuals who are employed or seeking employment.

Labor productivity Total real domestic output (real GDP) divided by the number of workers (output per worker).

Labor unions Worker organizations that seek to secure economic improvements for their members. They also seek to improve the safety, health, and other benefits (such as job security) of their members.

Land The natural resources that are available from nature. Land as a resource includes location, original fertility and mineral deposits, topography, climate, water, and vegetation.

Law of demand The observation that there is a negative, or inverse, relationship between the price of any good or service and the quantity demanded, holding other factors constant.

Law of diminishing marginal product The observation that after some point, successive equal-sized increases in a variable factor of production, such as labor, added to fixed factors of production will result in smaller increases in output.

Law of increasing additional cost The fact that the opportunity cost of additional units of a good generally increases as people attempt to produce more of that good. This accounts for the bowed-out shape of the production possibilities curve.

Law of supply The observation that the higher the price of a good, the more of that good sellers will make available over a specified time period, other things being equal.

Leading indicators Events that have been found to occur before changes in business activity.

Lemons problem The potential for asymmetric information to bring about a general decline in product quality in an industry.

Lender of last resort The Federal Reserve's role as an institution that is willing and able to lend to a temporarily illiquid bank that is otherwise in good financial condition to prevent the bank's illiquid position from leading to a general loss of confidence in that bank or in others.

Liabilities Amounts owed; the legal claims against a business or household by nonowners.

Life-cycle theory of consumption A theory in which a person bases decisions about current consumption and saving on both current income and anticipated future income.

Limited liability A legal concept in which the responsibility, or liability, of the owners of a corporation is limited to the value of the shares in the firm that they own.

Limited liability company (LLC) A hybrid form of business enterprise that offers the limited liability of a corporation and the tax advantages of a partnership.

Liquidity The degree to which an asset can be acquired or disposed of without much danger of any intervening loss in *nominal* value and with small transaction costs. Money is the most liquid asset.

Liquidity approach A method of measuring the money supply by looking at money as a temporary store of value.

Long run The time period during which all factors of production can be varied.

Long-run aggregate supply (*LRAS*) curve A vertical line representing the real output of goods and services after full adjustment has occurred. It can also be viewed as representing the real GDP of the economy under conditions of full employment—the full-employment level of real GDP.

Long-run average cost curve The locus of points representing the minimum unit cost of producing any given rate of output, given current technology and resource prices.

Long-run industry supply curve A market supply curve showing the relationship between prices and quantities after firms have been allowed the time to enter into or exit from an industry, depending on whether there have been positive or negative economic profits.

Lorenz curve A geometric representation of the distribution of income. A Lorenz curve that is perfectly straight represents complete income equality. The more bowed a Lorenz curve, the more unequally income is distributed.

Lump-sum tax A tax that does not depend on income. An example is a $1,000 tax that every household must pay, irrespective of its economic situation.

M

M1 The money supply, measured as the total value of currency plus transactions deposits plus traveler's checks not issued by banks.

M2 M1 plus (1) savings deposits at all depository institutions, (2) small-denomination time deposits, and (3) balances in retail money market mutual funds.

Macroeconomics The study of the behavior of the economy as a whole, including such economywide phenomena as changes in unemployment, the general price level, and national income.

Majority rule A collective decision-making system in which group decisions are made on the basis of more than 50 percent of the vote. In other words, whatever more than half of the electorate votes for, the entire electorate has to accept.

Marginal cost pricing A system of pricing in which the price charged is equal to the opportunity cost to society of producing one more unit of the good or service in question. The opportunity cost is the marginal cost to society.

Marginal costs The change in total costs due to a one-unit change in production rate.

Marginal factor cost (MFC) The cost of using an additional unit of an input. For example, if a firm can hire all the workers it wants at the going wage rate, the marginal factor cost of labor is that wage rate.

Marginal product The output that is due to the addition of one more unit of a variable factor of production. The change in total product occurring when a variable input is increased and all other inputs are held constant.

Marginal product (MP) of labor The change in output resulting from the addition of one more worker. The MP of the worker equals the change in total output accounted for by hiring the worker, holding all other factors of production constant.

Marginal propensity to consume (MPC) The ratio of the change in consumption to the change in disposable income. A marginal propensity to consume of 0.8 tells us that an additional $100 in take-home pay will lead to an additional $80 consumed.

Marginal propensity to save (MPS) The ratio of the change in saving to the change in disposable income. A marginal propensity to save of 0.2 indicates that out of an additional $100 in take-home pay, $20 will be saved. Whatever is not saved is consumed. The marginal propensity to save plus the marginal propensity to consume must always equal 1, by definition.

Marginal revenue The change in total revenues resulting from a one-unit change in output (and sale) of the product in question.

Marginal revenue product (MRP) The marginal product (MP) times marginal revenue (MR). The MRP gives the additional revenue obtained from a one-unit change in labor input.

Marginal tax rate The change in the tax payment divided by the change in income, or the percentage of *additional* dollars that must be paid in taxes. The marginal tax rate is applied to taxable income in the highest tax bracket reached.

Marginal utility The change in total utility due to a one-unit change in the quantity of a good or service consumed.

Market All of the arrangements that individuals have for exchanging with one another. Thus, for example, we can speak of the labor market, the automobile market, and the credit market.

Market clearing, or equilibrium, price The price that clears the market, at which quantity demanded equals quantity supplied; the price where the demand curve intersects the supply curve.

Market demand The demand of all consumers in the marketplace for a particular good or service. The summation at each price of the quantity demanded by each individual.

Market failure A situation in which an unrestrained market operation leads to either too few or too many resources going to a specific economic activity.

Mass marketing Advertising intended to reach as many consumers as possible, typically through television, newspaper, radio, or magazine ads.

Medium of exchange Any item that sellers will accept as payment.

Microeconomics The study of decision making undertaken by individuals (or households) and by firms.

Minimum efficient scale (MES) The lowest rate of output per unit time at which long-run average costs for a particular firm are at a minimum.

Minimum wage A wage floor, legislated by government, setting the lowest hourly rate that firms may legally pay workers.

Models, or theories Simplified representations of the real world used as the basis for predictions or explanations.

Money Any medium that is universally accepted in an economy both by sellers of goods and services as payment for those goods and services and by creditors as payment for debts.

Money balances Synonymous with money, money stock, money holdings.

Money illusion Reacting to changes in money prices rather than relative prices. If a worker whose wages double when the price level also doubles thinks he or she is better off, that worker is suffering from money illusion.

Money multiplier A number that, when multiplied by a change in reserves in the banking system, yields the resulting change in the money supply.

Money price The price expressed in today's dollars; also called the *absolute*, *nominal*, or *money price*.

Money supply The amount of money in circulation.

Monopolist The single supplier of a good or service for which there is no close substitute. The monopolist therefore constitutes its entire industry.

Monopolistic competition A market situation in which a large number of firms produce similar but not identical products. Entry into the industry is relatively easy.

Monopolization The possession of monopoly power in the relevant market and the willful acquisition or maintenance of that power, as distinguished from growth or development as a consequence of a superior product, business acumen, or historical accident.

Monopoly A firm that can determine the market price of a good. In the extreme case, a monopoly is the only seller of a good or service.

Monopsonist The only buyer in a market.

Monopsonistic exploitation Paying a price for the variable input that is less than its marginal revenue product; the difference between marginal revenue product and the wage rate.

Moral hazard The possibility that a borrower might engage in riskier behavior after a loan has been obtained.

Multiplier The ratio of the change in the equilibrium level of real GDP to the change in autonomous real expenditures. The number by which a change in autonomous real investment or autonomous real consumption, for example, is multiplied to get the change in equilibrium real GDP.

N

National income (NI) The total of all factor payments to resource owners. It can be obtained from net domestic product (NDP) by adding net U.S. income earned abroad and adjusting for statistical discrepancies.

National income accounting A measurement system used to estimate national income and its components. One approach to measuring an economy's aggregate performance.

Natural monopoly A monopoly that arises from the peculiar production characteristics in an industry. It usually arises when there are large economies of scale relative to the industry's demand such that one firm can produce at a lower average cost than can be achieved by multiple firms.

Natural rate of unemployment The rate of unemployment that is estimated to prevail in long-run macroeconomic equilibrium, when all workers and employers have fully adjusted to any changes in the economy.

Negative market feedback A tendency for a good or service to fall out of favor with more consumers because other consumers have stopped purchasing the item.

Negative-sum game A game in which players as a group lose during the process of the game.

Net domestic product (NDP) GDP minus depreciation.

Net investment Gross private domestic investment minus an estimate of the wear and tear on the existing capital stock. Net investment therefore measures the change in the capital stock over a one-year period.

Net public debt Gross public debt minus all government interagency borrowing.

Net wealth The stock of assets owned by a person, household, firm, or nation (net of any debts owed). For a household, net wealth can consist of a house, cars, personal belongings, stocks, bonds, bank accounts, and cash (minus any debts owed).

Network effect A situation in which a consumer's willingness to purchase a good or service is influenced by how many others also buy or have bought the item.

New entrant An individual who has never held a full-time job lasting two weeks or longer but is now seeking employment.

New growth theory A theory of economic growth that examines the factors that determine why technology, research, innovation, and the like are undertaken and how they interact.

New Keynesian inflation dynamics In new Keynesian theory, the pattern of inflation exhibited by an economy with growing aggregate demand—initial sluggish adjustment of the price level in response to increased aggregate demand followed by higher inflation later.

Nominal rate of interest The market rate of interest observed in contracts expressed in today's dollars. *Also*, the market rate of interest expressed in today's dollars.

Nominal values The values of variables such as GDP and investment expressed in current dollars, also called *money values*; measurement in terms of the actual market prices at which goods and services are sold.

Noncontrollable expenditures Government spending that changes automatically without action by Congress.

Noncooperative game A game in which the players neither negotiate nor cooperate in any way. As applied to firms in an industry, this is the common situation in which there are relatively few firms and each has some ability to change price.

Nondurable consumer goods Consumer goods that are used up within three years.

Nonprice rationing devices All methods used to ration scarce goods that are price-controlled. Whenever the price system is not allowed to work, nonprice rationing devices will evolve to ration the affected goods and services.

Normal goods Goods for which demand rises as income rises. Most goods are normal goods.

Normal rate of return The amount that must be paid to an investor to induce investment in a business. Also known as the *opportunity cost of capital*.

Normative economics Analysis involving value judgments about economic policies; relates to whether outcomes are good or bad. A statement of *what ought to be*.

Number line A line that can be divided into segments of equal length, each associated with a number.

O

Oligopoly A market structure in which there are very few sellers. Each seller knows that the other sellers will react to its changes in prices, quantities, and qualities.

Open economy effect One of the reasons that the aggregate demand curve slopes downward: A higher price level induces foreign residents to buy fewer U.S.-made goods and U.S. residents to buy more foreign-made goods, thereby reducing net exports and decreasing the amount of real goods and services purchased in the United States.

Open market operations The purchase and sale of existing U.S. government securities (such as bonds) in the open private market by the Federal Reserve System.

Opportunistic behavior Actions that focus solely on short-run gains because long-run benefits of cooperation are perceived to be smaller.

Opportunity cost The highest-valued, next-best alternative that must be sacrificed to obtain something or to satisfy a want.

Opportunity cost of capital The normal rate of return, or the available return on the next-best alternative investment. Economists consider this a cost of production, and it is included in our cost examples.

Optimal quantity of pollution The level of pollution for which the marginal benefit of one additional unit of pollution abatement just equals the marginal cost of that additional unit of pollution abatement.

Origin The intersection of the *y* axis and the *x* axis in a graph.

P

Par value The officially determined value of a currency.

Partnership A business owned by two or more joint owners, or partners, who share the responsibilities and the profits of the firm and are individually liable for all the debts of the partnership.

Passive (nondiscretionary) policymaking Policymaking that is carried out in response to a rule. It is therefore not in response to an actual or potential change in overall economic activity.

Patent A government protection that gives an inventor the exclusive right to make, use, or sell an invention for a limited period of time (currently, 20 years).

Payoff matrix A matrix of outcomes, or consequences, of the strategies available to the players in a game.

Perfect competition A market structure in which the decisions of *individual* buyers and sellers have no effect on market price.

Perfectly competitive firm A firm that is such a small part of the total *industry* that it cannot affect the price of the product it sells.

Perfectly elastic demand A demand that has the characteristic that even the slightest increase in price will lead to zero quantity demanded.

Perfectly elastic supply A supply characterized by a reduction in quantity supplied to zero when there is the slightest decrease in price.

Perfectly inelastic demand A demand that exhibits zero responsiveness to price changes. No matter what the price is, the quantity demanded remains the same.

Perfectly inelastic supply A supply for which quantity supplied remains constant, no matter what happens to price.

Permanent income hypothesis A theory of consumption in which an individual determines current consumption based on anticipated average lifetime income.

Personal Consumption Expenditure (PCE) Index A statistical measure of average prices that uses annually updated weights based on surveys of consumer spending.

Personal income (PI) The amount of income that households actually receive before they pay personal income taxes.

Persuasive advertising Advertising that is intended to induce a consumer to purchase a particular product and discover a previously unknown taste for the item.

Phillips curve A curve showing the relationship between unemployment and changes in wages or prices. It was long thought to reflect a trade-off between unemployment and inflation.

Physical capital All manufactured resources, including buildings, equipment, machines, and improvements to land that are used for production.

Planning curve The long-run average cost curve.

Planning horizon The long run, during which all inputs are variable.

Plant size The size of the facilities that a firm owns and operates to produce its output. Plant size can be defined by square footage, maximum capacity, and other measures of the scale of production of goods or services.

Platform firms Companies whose services link people to other individuals who share their interests or who seek to buy firms' products, often via networks that the companies operate.

Policy irrelevance proposition The conclusion that policy actions have no real effects in the short run if the policy actions are anticipated and none in the long run even if the policy actions are unanticipated.

Portfolio investment The purchase of less than 10 percent of the shares of ownership in a company in another nation.

Positive economics Analysis that is *strictly* limited to making either purely descriptive statements or scientific predictions. For example, "If A, then B." A statement of *what is*.

Positive market feedback A tendency for a good or service to come into favor with additional consumers because other consumers have chosen to buy the item.

Positive-sum game A game in which players as a group are better off at the end of the game.

Potential money multiplier The reciprocal of the reserve ratio, assuming no leakages into currency. It is equal to 1 divided by the reserve ratio.

Precautionary demand Holding money to meet unplanned expenditures and emergencies.

Present value (PV) The value of a future amount expressed in today's dollars; the most that someone would pay today to receive a certain sum at some point in the future.

Price ceiling A legal maximum price that may be charged for a particular good or service.

Price controls Government-mandated minimum or maximum prices that may be charged for goods and services.

Price differentiation Establishing different prices for similar products to reflect differences in marginal cost in providing those commodities to different groups of buyers.

Price discrimination Selling a given product at more than one price, with the price difference being unrelated to differences in marginal cost.

Price elasticity of demand (E_p) The responsiveness of the quantity demanded of a commodity to changes in its price; defined as the percentage change in quantity demanded divided by the percentage change in price.

Price elasticity of supply (E_s) The responsiveness of the quantity supplied of a commodity to a change in its price—the percentage change in quantity supplied divided by the percentage change in price.

Price floor A legal minimum price below which a good or service may not be sold. Legal minimum wages are an example.

Price index The cost of today's market basket of goods expressed as a percentage of the cost of the same market basket during a base year.

Price searcher A firm that must determine the price-output combination that maximizes profit because it faces a downward-sloping demand curve.

Price system An economic system in which relative prices are constantly changing to reflect changes in supply and demand for different commodities. The prices of those commodities are signals to everyone within the system as to what is relatively scarce and what is relatively abundant.

Price taker A perfectly competitive firm that must take the price of its product as given because the firm cannot influence its price.

Principle of rival consumption The recognition that individuals are rivals in consuming private goods because one person's consumption reduces the amount available for others to consume.

Principle of substitution The principle that consumers shift away from goods and services that become priced relatively higher in favor of goods and services that are now priced relatively lower.

Prisoner's dilemma A famous strategic game in which two prisoners have a choice between confessing and not confessing to a crime. If neither confesses, they serve a minimum sentence. If both confess, they serve a longer sentence. If one confesses and the other doesn't, the one who confesses goes free. The dominant strategy is always to confess.

Private costs Costs borne solely by the individuals who incur them. Also called *internal costs*.

Private goods Goods that can be consumed by only one individual at a time. Private goods are subject to the principle of rival consumption.

Private property rights Exclusive rights of ownership that allow the use, transfer, and exchange of property.

Producer durables, or capital goods Durable goods having an expected service life of more than three years that are used by businesses to produce other goods and services.

Producer Price Index (PPI) A statistical measure of a weighted average of prices of goods and services that firms produce and sell.

Producer surplus The difference between the total amount that producers actually receive for an item and the total amount that they would have been willing to accept for supplying that item.

Product differentiation The distinguishing of products by brand name, color, and other minor attributes. Product differentiation occurs in other than perfectly competitive markets in which products are, in theory, homogeneous, such as wheat or corn.

Production Any activity that results in the conversion of resources into products that can be used in consumption.

Production function The relationship between inputs and maximum output. A production function is a technological, not an economic, relationship.

Production possibilities curve (PPC) A curve representing all possible combinations of maximum outputs that could be produced, assuming a fixed amount of productive resources of a given quality.

Profit-maximizing rate of production The rate of production that maximizes total profits, or the difference between total revenues and total costs. Also, it is the rate of production at which marginal revenue equals marginal cost.

Progressive taxation A tax system in which, as income increases, a higher percentage of the additional income is paid as taxes. The marginal tax rate exceeds the average tax rate as income rises.

Property rights The rights of an owner to use and to exchange property.

Proportional rule A decision-making system in which actions are based on the proportion of the "votes" cast and are in proportion to them. In a market system, if 10 percent of the "dollar votes" are cast for blue cars, 10 percent of automobile output will be blue cars.

Proportional taxation A tax system in which, regardless of an individual's income, the tax bill comprises exactly the same proportion.

Proprietorship A business owned by one individual who makes the business decisions, receives all the profits, and is legally responsible for the debts of the firm.

Public debt The total value of all outstanding federal government securities.

Public goods Goods for which the principle of rival consumption does not apply and for which exclusion of nonpaying consumers is too costly to be feasible. They can be jointly consumed by many individuals at no additional cost and with no drop in quality or quantity. Furthermore, no one who fails to help pay for the good can be denied benefits.

Purchasing power The value of money for buying goods and services. If your money income stays the same but the price of one good that you are buying goes up, your effective purchasing power falls, and vice versa.

Purchasing power parity Adjustment in exchange rate conversions that takes into account differences in the true cost of living across countries.

Q

Quantitative easing Federal Reserve open market purchases intended to generate an increase in bank reserves at a zero interest rate.

Quantity theory of money and prices The hypothesis that changes in the money supply lead to equiproportional changes in the price level.

Quota subscription A nation's account with the International Monetary Fund, denominated in special drawing rights.

Quota system A government-imposed restriction on the quantity of a specific good that another country is allowed to sell in the United States. In other words, quotas are restrictions on imports. These restrictions are usually applied to one or several specific countries.

R

Random walk theory The theory that there are no predictable changes in securities prices that can be used to "get rich quick."

Rate of discount The rate of interest used to discount future sums back to present value.

Rate-of-return regulation Regulation that seeks to keep the rate of return in an industry at a competitive level by not allowing prices that would produce economic profits.

Rational expectations hypothesis A theory stating that people combine the effects of past policy changes on important economic variables with their own judgment about the future effects of current and future policy changes.

Rational inattention Choosing to acquire information infrequently and to make decisions based on incomplete knowledge of the state of the economy during the intervals between updates.

Rationality assumption The assumption that people do not intentionally make decisions that would leave them worse off.

Reaction function The manner in which one oligopolist reacts to a change in price, output, or quality made by another oligopolist in the industry.

Real disposable income Real GDP minus net taxes, or after-tax real income.

Real rate of interest The nominal rate of interest minus the anticipated rate of inflation.

Real values Measurement of economic values after adjustments have been made for changes in the average of prices between years.

Real-balance effect The change in expenditures resulting from a change in the real value of money balances when the price level changes, all other things held constant; also called the *wealth effect*.

Real-income effect The change in people's purchasing power that occurs when, other things being constant, the price of one good that they purchase changes. When that price goes up, real income, or purchasing power, falls, and when that price goes down, real income increases.

Recession A period of time during which the rate of growth of business activity is consistently less than its long-term trend or is negative.

Recessionary gap The gap that exists whenever equilibrium real GDP per year is less than full-employment real GDP as shown by the position of the long-run aggregate supply curve.

Recognition time lag The time required to gather information about the current state of the economy.

Reentrant An individual who used to work full-time but left the labor force and has now reentered it looking for a job.

Regional trade bloc A group of nations that grants members special trade privileges.

Regressive taxation A tax system in which as more dollars are earned, the percentage of tax paid on them falls. The marginal tax rate is less than the average tax rate as income rises.

Reinvestment Profits (or depreciation reserves) used to purchase new capital equipment.

Relative price The money price of one commodity divided by the money price of another commodity; the number of units of one commodity that must be sacrificed to purchase one unit of another commodity.

Relevant market A group of firms' products that are closely substitutable and available to consumers within a particular geographic area.

Rent control Price ceilings on rents.

Repricing, or menu, cost of inflation The cost associated with recalculating prices and printing new price lists when there is inflation.

Reserve ratio The fraction of transactions deposits that banks hold as reserves.

Reserves In the U.S. Federal Reserve System, deposits held by Federal Reserve district banks for depository institutions, plus depository institutions' vault cash.

Resources Things used to produce goods and services to satisfy people's wants.

Retained earnings Earnings that a corporation saves, or retains, for investment in other productive activities; earnings that are not distributed to stockholders.

Ricardian equivalence theorem The proposition that an increase in the government budget deficit has no effect on aggregate demand.

Right-to-work laws Laws that make it illegal to require union membership as a condition of continuing employment in a particular firm.

Rule of 70 A rule stating that the approximate number of years required for per capita real GDP to double is equal to 70 divided by the average rate of economic growth.

Rules of origin Regulations that nations in regional trade blocs establish to delineate product categories eligible for trading preferences.

S

Sales taxes Taxes assessed on the prices paid on most goods and services.

Saving The act of not consuming all of one's current income. Whatever is not consumed out of spendable income is, by definition, saved. *Saving* is an action measured over time (a flow), whereas *savings* are a stock, an accumulation resulting from the act of saving in the past.

Say's law A dictum of economist J. B. Say that supply creates its own demand. Producing goods and services generates the means and the willingness to purchase other goods and services.

Scarcity A situation in which the ingredients for producing the things that people desire are insufficient to satisfy all wants at a zero price.

Search good A product with characteristics that enable an individual to evaluate the product's quality in advance of a purchase.

Secular deflation A persistent decline in prices resulting from economic growth in the presence of stable aggregate demand.

Securities Stocks and bonds.

Services Mental or physical labor or assistance purchased by consumers. Examples are the assistance of physicians, lawyers, dentists, repair personnel, housecleaners, educators, retailers, and wholesalers; items purchased or used by consumers that do not have physical characteristics.

Share of stock A legal claim to a share of a corporation's future profits. If it is *common stock*, it incorporates certain voting rights regarding major policy decisions of the corporation. If it is *preferred stock*, its

owners are accorded preferential treatment in the payment of dividends but do not have any voting rights.

Share-the-gains, share-the-pains theory A theory of regulatory behavior that holds that regulators must take account of the demands of three groups: legislators, who established and oversee the regulatory agency; firms in the regulated industry; and consumers of the regulated industry's products.

Short run The time period during which at least one input, such as plant size, cannot be changed.

Short-run aggregate supply curve (SRAS) The relationship between total planned economywide production and the price level in the short run, all other things held constant. If prices adjust incompletely in the short run, the curve is positively sloped.

Short-run break-even price The price at which a firm's total revenues equal its total costs. At the break-even price, the firm is just making a normal rate of return on its capital investment. (It is covering its explicit and implicit costs.)

Short-run economies of operation A distinguishing characteristic of an information product arising from declining short-run average total cost as more units of the product are sold.

Short-run shutdown price The price that covers average variable costs. It occurs just below the intersection of the marginal cost curve and the average variable cost curve.

Shortage A situation in which quantity demanded is greater than quantity supplied at a price below the market clearing price.

Signals Compact ways of conveying to economic decision makers information needed to make decisions. An effective signal not only conveys information but also provides the incentive to react appropriately. Economic profits and economic losses are such signals.

Slope The change in the y value divided by the corresponding change in the x value of a curve; the "incline" of the curve.

Small menu costs Costs that deter firms from changing prices in response to demand changes—for example, the costs of renegotiating contracts or printing new price lists.

Social costs The full costs borne by society whenever a resource use occurs. Social costs can be measured by adding external costs to private, or internal, costs.

Specialization The organization of economic activity so that what each person (or region) consumes is not identical to what that person (or region) produces. An individual may specialize, for example, in law or medicine. A nation may specialize in the production of coffee, e-book readers, or digital cameras.

Stagflation A situation characterized by lower real GDP, lower employment, and a higher unemployment rate during the same period that the rate of inflation increases.

Standard of deferred payment A property of an item that makes it desirable for use as a means of settling debts maturing in the future; an essential property of money.

Static tax analysis Economic evaluation of the effects of tax rate changes under the assumption that there is no effect on the tax base, meaning that there is an unambiguous positive relationship between tax rates and tax revenues.

Stock The quantity of something, measured at a given point in time—for example, an inventory of goods or a bank account. Stocks are defined independently of time, although they are assessed at a point in time.

Store of value The ability to hold value over time; a necessary property of money.

Strategic dependence A situation in which one firm's actions with respect to price, quality, advertising, and related changes may be strategically countered by the reactions of one or more other firms in the industry. Such dependence can exist only when there is a small number of major firms in an industry.

Strategy Any rule that is used to make a choice, such as "Always pick heads."

Structural unemployment Unemployment of workers over lengthy intervals resulting from skill mismatches with position requirements of employers and from fewer jobs being offered by employers constrained by governmental business regulations and labor market policies.

Subsidy A negative tax; a payment to a producer from the government, usually in the form of a cash grant per unit.

Substitutes Two goods are substitutes when a change in the price of one causes a shift in demand for the other in the same direction as the price change.

Substitution effect The tendency of people to substitute cheaper commodities for more expensive commodities.

Supply A schedule showing the relationship between price and quantity supplied for a specified period of time, other things being equal.

Supply curve The graphical representation of the supply schedule; a line (curve) showing the supply schedule, which generally slopes upward (has a positive slope), other things being equal.

Supply-side economics The theory that creating incentives for individuals and firms to increase productivity will cause the aggregate supply curve to shift outward.

Surplus A situation in which quantity supplied is greater than quantity demanded at a price above the market clearing price.

T

Tariffs Taxes on imported goods.

Tax base The value of goods, services, wealth, or incomes subject to taxation.

Tax bracket A specified interval of income to which a specific and unique marginal tax rate is applied.

Tax incidence The distribution of tax burdens among various groups in society.

Tax rate The proportion of a tax base that must be paid to a government as taxes.

Taylor rule An equation that specifies a federal funds rate target based on an estimated long-run real interest rate, the current deviation of the actual inflation rate from the Federal Reserve's inflation objective, and the gap between actual real GDP per year and a measure of potential real GDP per year.

Technology The total pool of applied knowledge concerning how goods and services can be produced.

The Fed The Federal Reserve System; the central bank of the United States.

Theory of public choice The study of collective decision making.

Third parties Parties who are not directly involved in a given activity or transaction. For example, in the relationship between health care providers and patients, fees may be paid by third parties (insurance companies, government).

Thrift institutions Financial institutions that receive most of their funds from the savings of the public. They include savings banks, savings and loan associations, and credit unions.

Tie-in sales Purchases of one product that are permitted by the seller only if the consumer buys another good or service from the same firm.

Tit-for-tat strategic behavior In game theory, cooperation that continues as long as the other players continue to cooperate.

Total costs The sum of total fixed costs and total variable costs.

Total income The yearly amount earned by the nation's resources (factors of production). Total income therefore includes wages, rent, interest payments, and profits that are received by workers, landowners, capital owners, and entrepreneurs, respectively.

Total revenues The price per unit times the total quantity sold.

Trade deflection Moving partially assembled products into a member nation of a regional trade bloc, completing assembly, and then exporting them to other nations within the bloc, so as to benefit from preferences granted by the trade bloc.

Trade diversion Shifting existing international trade from countries outside a regional trade bloc to nations within the bloc.

Trading Desk An office at the Federal Reserve Bank of New York charged with implementing monetary policy strategies developed by the Federal Open Market Committee.

Transaction costs All of the costs associated with exchange, including the informational costs of finding out the price and quality, service record, and durability of a product, plus the cost of contracting and enforcing that contract. *Also,* all costs associated with making, reaching, and enforcing agreements.

Transactions approach A method of measuring the money supply by looking at money as a medium of exchange.

Transactions demand Holding money as a medium of exchange to make payments. The level varies directly with nominal GDP.

Transactions deposits Checkable and debitable account balances in commercial banks and other types of financial institutions, such as credit unions and savings banks. Any accounts in financial institutions from which you can easily transmit debit-card and check payments without significant restrictions.

Transfer payments Money payments made by governments to individuals for which no services or goods are rendered in return. Examples are Social Security old-age and disability benefits and unemployment insurance benefits.

Transfers in kind Payments that are in the form of actual goods and services, such as food stamps, subsidized public housing, and medical care, and for which no goods or services are rendered in return.

Traveler's checks Financial instruments obtained from a bank or a nonbanking organization and signed during purchase that can be used in payment upon a second signature by the purchaser.

Two-sided market A market in which an intermediary firm provides services that link groups of producers and consumers.

U

Unanticipated inflation Inflation at a rate that comes as a surprise, either higher or lower than the rate anticipated.

Unemployment The total number of adults (aged 16 years or older) who are willing and able to work and who are actively looking for work but have not found a job.

Union shop A business enterprise that may hire nonunion members, conditional on their joining the union by some specified date after employment begins.

Unit elasticity of demand A demand relationship in which the quantity demanded changes exactly in proportion to the change in price.

Unit of accounting A measure by which prices are expressed; the common denominator of the price system; a central property of money.

Unit tax A constant tax assessed on each unit of a good that consumers purchase.

Unlimited liability A legal concept whereby the personal assets of the owner of a firm can be seized to pay off the firm's debts.

Util A representative unit by which utility is measured.

Utility The want-satisfying power of a good or service.

Utility analysis The analysis of consumer decision making based on utility maximization.

V

Value added The dollar value of an industry's sales minus the value of intermediate goods (for example, raw materials and parts) used in production.

Variable costs Costs that vary with the rate of production. They include wages paid to workers and purchases of materials.

Variables Choices that people make or other human outcomes that are subject to change.

Versioning Selling a product in slightly altered forms to different groups of consumers.

Vertical merger The joining of a firm with another to which it sells an output or from which it buys an input.

Voluntary exchange An act of trading, done on a mutually agreed basis, in which both parties to the trade expect to be better off after the exchange.

Voluntary import expansion (VIE) An official agreement with another country in which it agrees to import more from the United States.

Voluntary restraint agreement (VRA) An official agreement with another country that "voluntarily" restricts the quantity of its exports to the United States.

W

Wants What people would buy if their incomes were unlimited.

World Bank A multinational agency that specializes in making loans to about 100 developing nations in an effort to promote their long-term development and growth.

World Trade Organization (WTO) The successor organization to the GATT that handles trade disputes among its member nations.

X

x **axis** The horizontal axis in a graph.

Y

y **axis** The vertical axis in a graph.

Z

Zero-sum game A game in which any gains within the group are offset by equal losses by the end of the game.

INDEX